Lewis/Goodman/Fandt   xtra!

CONGRATULATIONS!

Your purchase of this new textbook includes complimentary access to the Lewis Xtra! Web Site (http://lewisxtra.swlearning.com). This site offers a robust set of online multimedia learning tools to help you gain a deeper and richer understanding of management, including:

EXPERIENCING MANAGEMENT

Reinforces key management principles in a dynamic learning environment by exposing you to the central constructs of each topic through text, animated models or graphs, audio narration, and a variety of interactive activities and applications.

VIDEO CASES

The videos that accompany the video cases in the text are available here for viewing, along with the discussion questions to submit for credit.

CNN VIDEOS

CNN video segments and exercises let you see Management in action, in the real world, to help you learn theoretical material by applying it to current events.

XTRA! QUIZZING

You can create and take randomly-generated quizzes on whichever chapter(s) you wish to test yourself, and endlessly practice for exams.

Tear Out Card Missing?

If you did not buy a new textbook, the tear-out portion of this card may be missing, or the Access Code may not be valid. Access Codes can be used only once to register for access to Lewis Xtra!, and are not transferable. You can choose to either buy a new book or purchase access to the Lewis Xtra! site at http://lewisxtra.swlearning.com.

HOW TO REGISTER YOUR SERIAL NUMBER

STEP 1   Launch a Web browser and go to http://lewisxtra.swlearning.com

STEP 2   Click the "Register" button to enter your serial number.

STEP 3   Enter your serial number exactly as it appears here and create a unique User ID, or enter an existing User ID if you have previously registered for a different product via a serial number.

SERIAL NUMBER: SC-00044YD9-LEWX

STEP 4   When prompted, create a password (or enter an existing password, if you have previously registered for a different product via a serial number). Submit the necessary information when prompted. Record your User ID and password in a secure location.

STEP 5   Once registered, follow the link to enter the product, or return to the URL above and select the "Enter" button. Note that the duration of your access to the product begins when registration is complete.

xtra!

THOMSON
SOUTH-WESTERN

For technical support, contact
1-800-423-0563
or email
support@thomsonlearning.com.

EDITION 4

MANAGEMENT

CHALLENGES FOR TOMORROW'S LEADERS

PAMELA S. LEWIS
Queens University of Charlotte

STEPHEN H. GOODMAN
University of Central Florida

PATRICIA M. FANDT
University of Washington, Tacoma

THOMSON

SOUTH-WESTERN

Australia · Canada · Mexico · Singapore · Spain · United Kingdom · United States

THOMSON

SOUTH-WESTERN

Management: Challenges for Tomorrow's Leaders, 4th Edition

Pamela S. Lewis, Stephen H. Goodman, Patricia M. Fandt

VP/Editor Director:
Jack Calhoun

VP/Editor-in-Chief:
Michael Roche

Senior Publisher:
Melissa Acuña

Executive Editor:
John Szilagyi

Developmental Editor:
Monica Ohlinger

Senior Marketing Manager:
Rob Bloom

Production Editor:
Robert Dreas

Manufacturing Coordinator:
Rhonda Utley

Compositor:
GGS Information Services, Inc.

Production House:
Litten Editing and Production, Inc.

Printer:
Transcontinental Printing
Beaucville, Quebec

Design Project Manager and Internal Designer:
Michael H. Stratton

Cover Designer:
Anne Marie Rekow

Photography Manager:
Deanna Ettinger

Photo Researcher:
Terri Miller/E-Visual Communications

Media Development Editor:
Kristen Meere

Media Production Editor:
Karen Schaffer

Library of Congress
Control Number: 2003100006

ISBN: 0-324-15557-3

To my family, for your unwavering support of my efforts.
PSL

To Cynthia and Whitney, for the joy you continue to bring into my life each day.
SHG

A special thank you to my family, JD and SB, and to my colleagues and students.
PMF

ABOUT THE AUTHORS

PAMELA S. LEWIS

Dr. Pamela S. Lewis is President of Queens University of Charlotte. Prior to becoming President, Dr. Lewis served at the Dean of the McColl School of Business at Queens and as Dean of the Lebow College of Business at Drexel University in Philadelphia. Throughout her career, Dr. Lewis has distinguished herself through her commitment to providing innovative and high-quality education. Her particular focus has been on increasing community involvement and forging industry and academic partnerships that enhance the relevance and applicability of academic programs. Dr. Lewis, who holds a Ph.D. in strategic planning and international business from the University of Tennessee, has written numerous articles in the areas of strategic planning, international strategy, and entrepreneurship/new venture strategy. Dr. Lewis also has been active in executive education and consulting, serving as a strategic planning consultant for numerous organizations across a wide variety of industries. Dr. Lewis serves on the Board of Directors for two public companies—C&D Technologies, Inc., a leading manufacturing firm, and Charming Shoppes, a retail apparel firm—as well as on the board of numerous not-for-profits such as Central Carolinas United Way, Presbyterian Hospital, Communities in Schools, the Charlotte Museum of History, the YMCA of Greater Charlotte, and WFAE radio.

STEPHEN H. GOODMAN

Stephen H. Goodman is an Associate Professor of Management Information Systems at the University of Central Florida. He received his Ph.D. in Business Administration from Pennsylvania State University, where he specialized in operations management and operations research. Prior to his doctoral study he received a B.S. in Aeronautical Engineering and an M.B.A., also from Penn State. During his academic career, he has taught, researched, and published primarily in production planning and control. He has also served as a coauthor of a textbook in the field of production/operations management. Currently he has a major teaching and research focus in quality management. He is an active member of the Decision Sciences Institute (DSI) and the American Production and Inventory Control Society (APICS), having held offices in each, has engaged in journal review activities, and has conducted professional training classes. He has achieved the distinction of Certified Fellow in Production and Inventory Management (CFPIM) from APICS.

PATRICIA M. FANDT

Dr. Patricia Fandt is a professor and director of Business Administration at the University of Washington, Tacoma. In addition to administrative and leadership responsibilities, she is a member of the graduate faculty and teaches in the MBA program. Her undergraduate teaching includes courses in team processes, organizational change, and leadership. Dr. Fandt serves as the faculty coordinator for the organizational leadership concentration and adviser to the Business Student Ambassadors.

BRIEF CONTENTS

PART 1 MEETING THE CHALLENGES OF THE 21ST CENTURY 1

CHAPTER 1 Management and Managers: Yesterday, Today, and Tomorrow 2
CHAPTER 2 Evolution of Management Thought 42
CHAPTER 3 Social Responsibility and Ethics 76

PART 2 PLANNING CHALLENGES IN THE 21ST CENTURY 113

CHAPTER 4 Planning in the Contemporary Organization 114
CHAPTER 5 Strategic Planning in a Global Environment 146
CHAPTER 6 Effective Managerial Decision Making 180
CHAPTER 7 Decision-Making Tools and Techniques 208

PART 3 ORGANIZING CHALLENGES IN THE 21ST CENTURY 243

CHAPTER 8 Organizing for Quality, Productivity, and Job Satisfaction 244
CHAPTER 9 Designing the Contemporary Organization 280
CHAPTER 10 Strategic Human Resource Management 314
CHAPTER 11 Organizational Culture, Change, and Development 346

PART 4 LEADERSHIP CHALLENGES IN THE 21ST CENTURY 369

CHAPTER 12 Communicating Effectively Within Diverse Organizations 370
CHAPTER 13 Leading in a Dynamic Environment 400
CHAPTER 14 Exploring Individual Differences and Team Dynamics 424
CHAPTER 15 Motivating Organizational Members 458

PART 5 CONTROL CHALLENGES IN THE 21ST CENTURY 487

CHAPTER 16 Organizational Control in a Complex Business Environment 488
CHAPTER 17 Productivity and Quality in Operations 522
CHAPTER 18 Information Technology and Control 558

GLOSSARY 597
ENDNOTES 607
NAME INDEX NI-1
COMPANY INDEX CI-1
SUBJECT INDEX SI-1

CONTENTS

PART 1 MEETING THE CHALLENGES
OF THE 21ST CENTURY 1

1 Management and Managers: Yesterday,
Today, and Tomorrow 2

  FACING THE CHALLENGE:
  Southwest Airlines: Surviving
  the Turbulence in the Airline
  Industry 4
  INTRODUCTION 4
  MANAGEMENT AND WHY WE STUDY IT 5
    Management Defined 5
    The Organizational Context of
    Management 6
    The Process of Management 6
      Planning 6
      Organizing 6
      Leading 7
      Controlling 7
  WHAT WE KNOW ABOUT MANAGERS 7
    Managerial Roles 8
      Interpersonal Roles 8
      Informational Roles 9
      Decisional Roles 9
    Scope and Levels of Managers 10
      Scope of Responsibility 10
      Levels of Management 10
  LEADERS IN ACTION:
  Flying High at Southwest Airlines 14
  MANAGING IN THE 21ST CENTURY 15
    Environmental Trends 17
      Advances in Information Technology 17
      Globalization of the Marketplace 19
  AT THE FOREFRONT:
  One Sweet World: Wal-Mart's Global
  Strategy for Super Growth 20
      Increasing Predominance of Entrepreneurial
      Firms 20
      The Growing Importance of Intellectual
      Capital 21
    Organizational Changes 23
      A New Model of Leadership 23
      From Hierarchy to Collaborative Work
      Relationships 25
      Increasing Diversity in the Workplace 27
      A New Organizational Model 27
  THE CONTEMPORARY MANAGER 28
    The New Manager Profile 29
    Competencies of Tomorrow's Managers
    and Leaders 29
  IMPLICATIONS FOR LEADERS 31

  NOW APPLY IT:
  Are You Ready to Lead in the 21st
  Century? 32
  MEETING THE CHALLENGE:
  Southwest Airlines: Surviving the
  Turbulence
  in the Airline Industry 32
  SUMMARY 33
  REVIEW QUESTIONS 34
  DISCUSSION QUESTIONS 34
  THINKING CRITICALLY: DEBATE THE
  ISSUE 34
  EXPERIENTIAL EXERCISES 35
  CAPTURING THE POWER OF
  INFORMATION TECHNOLOGY 36
  ETHICS: TAKE A STAND 36
  VIDEO CASE Management and Managers:
  On-Target Supply and Logistics 37
  CASE A Day in the Life of Lindsey Clarke 39

2 Evolution of Management Thought 42

  FACING THE CHALLENGE:
  For UPS the Old Practices Don't Always Fit
  in the New Era 44
  INTRODUCTION 44
  ENVIRONMENTAL FACTORS
  INFLUENCING MANAGEMENT THOUGHT 45
    Economic Influences 45
    Social Influences 45
    Political Influences 46
    Technological Influences 47
    Global Influences 47
  SCHOOLS OF MANAGEMENT THOUGHT 48
    Classical Perspective 48
      Scientific Management 49
      Administrative Management 51
      Bureaucratic Management 53
    Behavioral Perspective 55
  LEADERS IN ACTION:
  Crisis Management at UPS 56
      Mary Parker Follett 56
      Elton Mayo 57
      Douglas McGregor 57
      Chester Barnard 58
  NOW APPLY IT:
  Theory X and Theory Y 59
    Quantitative Perspective 59
    Systems Perspective 60
    Contingency Perspective 62
  INFORMATION TECHNOLOGY AND
  MANAGEMENT STYLE 63

FUTURE ISSUES: DIVERSITY,
GLOBALIZATION, AND QUALITY   65
   AT THE FOREFRONT:
   Changing Style Keeps Harley-Davidson
   Rolling   66
IMPLICATIONS FOR LEADERS   67
   MEETING THE CHALLENGE:
   For UPS the Old Practices Don't Always
   Fit in the New Era   68
SUMMARY   69
REVIEW QUESTIONS   69
DISCUSSION QUESTIONS   70
THINKING CRITICALLY: DEBATE THE
ISSUE   70
EXPERIENTIAL EXERCISES   70
CAPTURING THE POWER OF
INFORMATION TECHNOLOGY   71
ETHICS: TAKE A STAND   71
VIDEO CASE Evolution of Management
Thought: Sunshine Cleaning Systems, JIAN,
and Archway Cookies   72
CASE Growing Green Changes Its
Management Style   74

3   Social Responsibility and Ethics   76
   FACING THE CHALLENGE:
   The Rise and Fall and Rise of Paul
   Wieand: A Leader's Journey   78
INTRODUCTION   78
ORGANIZATIONAL STAKEHOLDERS IN A
GLOBAL ENVIRONMENT   79
SOCIAL RESPONSIBILITY   80
   The Premises of the Social Responsibility
   Debate   80
   The Three Perspectives of Social
   Responsibility   81
      Economic Responsibility   82
      Public Responsibility   82
      Social Responsiveness   83
   The Four Faces of Social Responsibility   84
   Social Responsibility Strategies   85
      Reaction   86
      Defense   86
      Accommodation   87
      Proaction   87
SOCIAL RESPONSIBILITY IN THE NEW
MILLENIUM   88
   AT THE FOREFRONT:
   Social Entrepreneurs   89
ETHICS   91
   Understanding Business Ethics   91
      Foundations of Ethics   92
   LEADERS IN ACTION:
   Honesty Is the Best Policy   93

      Business Ethics   94
      Pressures to Perform   94
   Managerial Guidelines for Ethical
   Dilemmas   96
      Utility Approach   96
      Human Rights Approach   97
      Justice Approach   97
   Fostering Improved Business Ethics   98
      Codes of Ethics   99
      Ethics Training Programs   101
      Whistleblowing   102
IMPLICATIONS FOR LEADERS   104
   NOW APPLY IT:
   Ethics in the Workplace   104
   MEETING THE CHALLENGE:
   The Rise and Fall and Rise of Paul
   Wieand: A Leader's Journey   105
SUMMARY   105
REVIEW QUESTIONS   106
DISCUSSION QUESTIONS   106
THINKING CRITICALLY: DEBATE THE
ISSUE   107
EXPERIENTIAL EXERCISES   107
CAPTURING THE POWER OF
INFORMATION TECHNOLOGY   108
ETHICS: TAKE A STAND   108
VIDEO CASE Social Responsibility and
Ethics: Timberland   109
CASE Ford Motor Company Announces
Major Restructuring   111

PART 2   PLANNING CHALLENGES IN
           THE 21ST CENTURY   113

4   Planning in the Contemporary Organization   114
   FACING THE CHALLENGE:
   Home Depot's "Mr. Fix-It" Focuses on the
   Future   116
INTRODUCTION   116
MANAGERIAL PLANNING   116
   What Is Planning?   117
   Why Should Managers Plan?   117
      Benefits of Planning   118
      Costs of Planning   120
   AT THE FOREFRONT:
   Strategic Human Resource Management:
   Maintaining a Competitive Edge in the
   Global Marketplace   121
   Where Should Planning Begin?   122
STRATEGIC VERSUS OPERATIONAL
PLANNING   124
   Strategic Planning   124
      Levels of Strategic Planning   124

Customizing the Strategic Planning Process   127
Operational Planning   127
Standing Plans   128
Single-Use Plans   130
Individual Plans   131
CONTINGENCY PLANNING FOR CHANGING ENVIRONMENTS   134
LEADERS IN ACTION:
GM's First Ever CIO Is Betting on Technology as a Strategic Advantage   135
THE IMPACT OF INFORMATION TECHNOLOGY ON PLANNING   135
FACILITATING THE PLANNING PROCESS   136
Barriers to Effective Planning   136
Demands on the Manager's Time   136
Ambiguous and Uncertain Operating Environments   136
Resistance to Change   136
Overcoming the Barriers to Planning   137
Involve Employees in Decision Making   137
Tolerate a Diversity of Views   137
Encourage Strategic Thinking   137
IMPLICATIONS FOR LEADERS   138
MEETING THE CHALLENGE:
Home Depot's "Mr. Fix-It" Focuses on the Future   138
SUMMARY   139
REVIEW QUESTIONS   139
DISCUSSION QUESTIONS   140
THINKING CRITICALLY: DEBATE THE ISSUE   140
EXPERIENTIAL EXERCISES   140
CAPTURING THE POWER OF INFORMATION TECHNOLOGY   141
ETHICS: TAKE A STAND   141
VIDEO CASE Planning in the Contemporary Organization: The Vermont Teddy Bear Company, Inc.   142
CASE TIX4U.com   144

5 Strategic Planning in a Global Environment   146

FACING THE CHALLENGE:
FedEx and UPS: A Strategic Alliance for the Future   148
INTRODUCTION   148
THE IMPORTANCE OF STRATEGIC PLANNING   149
The Benefits of Strategic Planning   149
Strategic Planning as a Process   150
STRATEGIC ANALYSIS: ASSESSMENT IN A GLOBAL ENVIRONMENT   151
Assessing the Mission of an Organization   152

Conducting an Internal Analysis   152
Conducting an External Environmental Analysis   153
General Environment   154
Task Environment   157
STRATEGY FORMULATION: ACHIEVING A COMPETITIVE ADVANTAGE   159
Casting the Vision for the Organization   160
Setting Strategic Goals   160
NOW APPLY IT:
Developing a Vision Statement   161
Identifying Strategic Alternatives   162
Grand Strategies   162
Generic Strategy   164
Evaluating and Choosing Strategy   165
STRATEGY IMPLEMENTATION: FOCUSING ON RESULTS   166
Formulating Functional Strategy   166
Institutionalizing Strategy   166
Organizational Structure   167
Organizational Culture   168
Organizational Leadership   169
STRATEGIC CONTROL: ENSURING QUALITY AND EFFECTIVENESS   170
Feedforward Controls   170
Feedback Controls   170
INFORMATION TECHNOLOGY AND STRATEGIC PLANNING   171
LEADERS IN ACTION:
DuPont: Harnessing the Power of Partnerships   171
IMPLICATIONS FOR LEADERS   172
MEETING THE CHALLENGE:
FedEx and UPS: A Strategic Alliance for the Future   173
SUMMARY   173
REVIEW QUESTIONS   174
DISCUSSION QUESTIONS   174
THINKING CRITICALLY: DEBATE THE ISSUE   175
EXPERIENTIAL EXERCISES   175
CAPTURING THE POWER OF INFORMATION TECHNOLOGY   175
ETHICS: TAKE A STAND   176
VIDEO CASE Strategic Planning in a Global Environment: Kropf Fruit Company   176
CASE Developing a Strategic Plan for the Center City Club   178

6 Effective Managerial Decision Making   180

FACING THE CHALLENGE:
Gaylord Entertainment Faces Some Tough Decisions   182
INTRODUCTION   182

STEPS IN THE DECISION-MAKING
PROCESS 182
 NOW APPLY IT:
 Assessing Your Decision-Making Skills 183
 Identifying Opportunities and Diagnosing
 Problems 184
 AT THE FOREFRONT:
 BP Connects with the Future 185
 Identifying Objectives 186
 Generating Alternatives 186
 Evaluating Alternatives 187
 Reaching Decisions 187
 Choosing Implementation Strategies 187
 Monitoring and Evaluating 188
INFORMATION TECHNOLOGY AND THE
DECISION-MAKING PROCESS 189
MODELS OF DECISION MAKING 189
 Rational-Economic Decision Model 189
 Behavioral Decision Model 191
  Bounded Rationality 191
  Intuition 191
 LEADERS IN ACTION:
 Universal Orlando's President Connects
 with Workers 192
  Satisficing 192
  Escalation of Commitment 192
WHAT MAKES A HIGH-QUALITY
DECISION? 193
GROUP CONSIDERATION IN DECISION
MAKING 194
 Participative Decision Making 194
  Participative Models 194
  Group Size 195
 Advantages of Group Decision Making 196
 Disadvantages of Group Decision
 Making 197
 Techniques for Quality in Group Decision
 Making 199
  Brainstorming 199
  Nominal Group Technique 199
  Delphi Technique 200
  Devil's Advocacy Approach 200
  Dialectical Inquiry 200
IMPLICATIONS FOR LEADERS 200
 MEETING THE CHALLENGE:
 Gaylord Entertainment Gets on Course 201
SUMMARY 202
REVIEW QUESTIONS 203
DISCUSSION QUESTIONS 203
THINKING CRITICALLY: DEBATE THE
ISSUE 203
EXPERIENTIAL EXERCISES 203
CAPTURING THE POWER OF
INFORMATION TECHNOLOGY 204
ETHICS: TAKE A STAND 204

VIDEO CASE Effective Managerial Decision
Making: Next Door Food Store 205
CASE Disney Auction Site Arouses Ire 206

7 Decision-Making Tools and Techniques 208
 FACING THE CHALLENGE:
 Tupperware Goes Stale 210
INTRODUCTION 210
MANAGERIAL DECISION SITUATIONS 211
 Sources of Organizational and
 Entrepreneurial Decisions 211
 Classification of Decision Situations 212
 AT THE FOREFRONT:
 Hard Rock Café CEO Goes Back to the
 Roots 213
STRATEGIC DECISION-MAKING TOOLS 214
 Strategy Selection: The Strategic
 Decision-Making Matrix 214
 Evaluation of Portfolios 215
  The Growth-Share Matrix 215
 NOW APPLY IT:
 Developing a BCG Matrix for Your
 College 217
 The Industry Attractiveness/Business
 Strength Matrix 218
OPERATIONAL DECISION MAKING 221
 LEADERS IN ACTION:
 9/11 Stung Entrepreneur Decides to
 Reinvent His Business 222
 Applying Structure to the Decision-Making
 Process 222
  Alternative Courses of Action 222
  States of Nature 222
  Payoffs 223
  Payoff Tables 223
 Techniques that Enhance Quality in
 Decision Making 223
  Decision Making Under Certainty 224
  Decision Making Under Risk 224
  Decision Making Under Uncertainty 226
 Ethical and Social Implications in Decision
 Making 227
 Quantitative Decision-Making Aids 228
  Breakeven Analysis 228
  Linear Programming 230
  PERT 230
INFORMATION TECHNOLOGY AND
DECISION-MAKING TOOLS 233
IMPLICATIONS FOR LEADERS 233
 MEETING THE CHALLENGE:
 Tupperware Decisions Respond to
 Changing Domestic Demographics 234
SUMMARY 235
REVIEW QUESTIONS 235

DISCUSSION QUESTIONS 236
THINKING CRITICALLY: DEBATE THE
ISSUE 236
EXPERIENTIAL EXERCISES 237
CAPTURING THE POWER OF
INFORMATION TECHNOLOGY 237
ETHICS: TAKE A STAND 237
VIDEO CASE Decision-Making Tools and
Techniques: Machado & Silvetti
Associates, Inc. 238
CASE Capacity Decision Making at the North
American Culinary Institute 240

PART 3   ORGANIZING CHALLENGES
          IN THE 21ST CENTURY 243

8   Organizing for Quality, Productivity, and
    Job Satisfaction 244

        FACING THE CHALLENGE:
        St. Luke's: Somewhere Between Fear and
        Safety Lies Creativity 246
INTRODUCTION 246
WHAT IS ORGANIZING? 246
JOB DESIGN 247
    Core Job Dimensions 248
        Skill Variety 248
        Task Identity 249
        Task Significance 249
        Autonomy 249
        Feedback 250
    NOW APPLY IT:
    Job Assessment and Redesign 251
    The Evolution of Job Design Theory 252
        Mechanistic Approaches: Focus on Efficiency 252
        Behavioral Approaches: Focus on
        Motivation, Satisfaction, and Productivity 254
        Participatory Approaches: Focus on Quality 257
    AT THE FOREFRONT:
    Paid-Time-Off (PTO) Programs Really
    Pay Off 260
ORGANIZATIONAL RELATIONSHIPS 262
    Chain of Command 262
    Span of Control 263
    Line and Staff Responsibilities 265
    Delegation 265
        The Process of Delegation 265
        The Benefits of Delegation and
        Empowerment 267
    LEADERS IN ACTION:
    Employee Ownership: Bringing
    Empowerment to the Bottom Line 268
        Reasons for Failing to Delegate 269
        Learning to Delegate Effectively 269

IMPLICATIONS FOR LEADERS 271
    MEETING THE CHALLENGE:
    St. Luke's: Somewhere Between Fear and
    Safety Lies Creativity 271
SUMMARY 272
REVIEW QUESTIONS 273
DISCUSSION QUESTIONS 273
THINKING CRITICALLY: DEBATE THE
ISSUE 273
EXPERIENTIAL EXERCISES 274
CAPTURING THE POWER OF
INFORMATION TECHNOLOGY 274
ETHICS: TAKE A STAND 274
VIDEO CASE Organizing for Quality,
Productivity, and Job Satisfaction: Machado
and Silvetti Associates, Inc. 275
CASE Business Process Reengineering at Star
Electronics 277

9   Designing the Contemporary Organization 280

        FACING THE CHALLENGE:
        How EDS Blew Up Its Structure to Change
        Its Culture 282
INTRODUCTION 282
ORGANIZATIONAL DESIGN FROM A
CONTINGENCY PERSPECTIVE 282
COMPONENTS OF ORGANIZATIONAL
DESIGN 283
    Organization Structure 284
        Functional Structure: Enhancing
        Operational Efficiency 285
        Divisional Structures: Providing Focus 286
        Matrix Structure: Providing a Dual
        Focus 289
        Network Structures: The Key to Flexibility 291
    LEADERS IN ACTION:
    Dell Computer's Flexible Structure Creates
    a Competitive Advantage 293
    Managing Complexity Through
    Integration 294
    NOW APPLY IT:
    Assessing Organizational Structure 294
        Interdependence and Integration Needs 295
        Integrating Mechanisms 296
        Matching Integrating Mechanisms with
        Coordination Needs 300
    Focus of Decision Making 301
        Centralized versus Decentralized Decision
        Making 301
        Mechanistic versus Organic Systems 302
        The Impact of Environmental Stability 303
ORGANIZATIONAL DESIGN FOR A
CHANGING ENVIRONMENT 304
IMPLICATIONS FOR LEADERS 304

AT THE FOREFRONT:
When Chaos Comes: The Dynamic Nature
of Organizational Structure on U.S. Navy's
Aircraft Carriers   305
MEETING THE CHALLENGE:
How EDS Blew Up Its Structure to Change
Its Culture   306
SUMMARY   306
REVIEW QUESTIONS   307
DISCUSSION QUESTIONS   307
THINKING CRITICALLY: DEBATE THE
ISSUE   308
EXPERIENTIAL EXERCISES   308
CAPTURING THE POWER OF
INFORMATION TECHNOLOGY   310
ETHICS: TAKE A STAND   310
VIDEO CASE Designing the Contemporary
Organization: JIAN Corporation   311
CASE Growing Pains at Carolina Carpets   313

10 Strategic Human Resource Management   314

      FACING THE CHALLENGE:
      Finding the Right CEO for JC Penney   316
INTRODUCTION   316
STRATEGIC HUMAN RESOURCE
MANAGEMENT   316
   Job Analysis   316
   Forecasting   318
      LEADERS IN ACTION:
      John Stanton and the Running Room   319
   Recruitment Issues   319
      NOW APPLY IT:
      Search for a Job on the Internet   321
   Selection Methods   321
      Application Forms and Résumés   322
      Tests   322
      Interviews   324
   Physical Exams and Drug Tests   325
   Training   326
      Types of Training   326
   The Role of Performance Appraisal   327
      Rating Performance   328
      Problems with Performance Appraisal   329
   Rewards   329
      Direct Compensation: Base Pay and
      Incentives   330
      Indirect Compensation: Benefits   330
      Designing Equitable Reward Systems   331
LEGAL ENVIRONMENT OF STRATEGIC
HUMAN RESOURCE MANAGEMENT   331
   Important Laws   332
      Affirmative Action   333
      Workforce Diversity   334
      Sexual Harassment   334

LABOR-MANAGEMENT RELATIONS   335
CHALLENGES OF SHRM IN THE
MULTINATIONAL ORGANIZATION   336
IMPLICATIONS FOR LEADERS   337
      MEETING THE CHALLENGE:
      Finding the Right CEO for JC Penney   338
SUMMARY   338
REVIEW QUESTIONS   339
DISCUSSION QUESTIONS   339
THINKING CRITICALLY: DEBATE THE
ISSUE   340
EXPERIENTIAL EXERCISES   340
CAPTURING THE POWER OF
INFORMATION TECHNOLOGY   340
ETHICS: TAKE A STAND   340
      AT THE FOREFRONT:
      "Change Agents" Are Redefining the
      Modern Workplace   341
VIDEO CASE Strategic Human Resource
Management: Fannie Mae   341
CASE Should C.J. Be Hired?   343

11 Organizational Culture, Change, and
    Development   346

      FACING THE CHALLENGE:
      Olive Garden: Changing for the Better   348
INTRODUCTION   348
FOUNDATIONS OF ORGANIZATIONAL
CULTURE   349
      AT THE FOREFRONT:
      Hire for Attitude; Train for Skill   349
COMPONENTS OF AN ORGANIZATION'S
CULTURE   350
   Examining Culture Through
   Organizational Artifacts   350
      Rites, Rituals, and Ceremonies   350
      Language, Metaphors, and Symbols   351
      Stories and Sagas   352
THE IMPACT OF CULTURE ON THE
ORGANIZATION   352
      LEADERS IN ACTION:
      Leader of the "Best Corporate Culture"   353
   Aligning Culture to Maximize Technology   354
CHANGING ORGANIZATIONAL CULTURE   355
THE CHALLENGE OF ORGANIZATIONAL
CHANGE   356
   Targets for Change   356
MANAGING ORGANIZATIONAL CHANGE   357
A FRAMEWORK FOR CHANGE   357
   Steps for Planned Change   357
      Creating a Vision   358
      Communicating and Sharing Information   360
EMPOWERING OTHERS TO ACT ON THE
VISION   360

Institutionalizing or Refreezing the New
Approaches   361
Evaluation   361
IMPLICATIONS FOR LEADERS   361
  NOW APPLY IT:
  Needed: A Culture to Support the
  Mission   362
  MEETING THE CHALLENGE:
  Olive Garden: Changing for the Better   363
SUMMARY   363
REVIEW QUESTIONS   364
DISCUSSION QUESTIONS   364
THINKING CRITICALLY: DEBATE THE
ISSUE   365
EXPERIENTIAL EXERCISES   365
CAPTURING THE POWER OF
INFORMATION TECHNOLOGY   365
ETHICS: TAKE A STAND   365
VIDEO CASE Organizational Culture,
Change, and Development: Peter Pan Bus
Lines   366
CASE Is the Culture Right?   368

PART 4 LEADERSHIP CHALLENGES IN THE 21ST CENTURY

PART 4   LEADERSHIP CHALLENGES IN
            THE 21ST CENTURY   369

12 Communicating Effectively Within Diverse
Organizations   370

      FACING THE CHALLENGE:
      Communicating at Hanes: One Voice or
      Three?   372
INTRODUCTION   372
COMMUNICATION COMPLEXITY   372
DEFINING COMMUNICATION AND
ACHIEVING QUALITY   373
COMPONENTS OF THE
COMMUNICATION PROCESS   374
      Social Context: Global, Diversity, and
      Technology Impact   374
      Sender   375
      Message   375
      Channel   375
      Receiver   376
      Feedback   376
      Noise   376
CATEGORIES OF INTERPERSONAL
COMMUNICATION   376
      Oral Communication   376
      Written Communication   377
      Nonverbal Communication   377
      NOW APPLY IT:
      Test Your Awareness of Nonverbal
      Communication   378
      Technological Communication   379

      AT THE FOREFRONT:
      To do, or not to do…instant messaging…   381
WHY MANAGERS COMMUNICATE   381
BARRIERS TO EFFECTIVE
COMMUNICATION   382
      Cross-Cultural Diversity   382
      Trust and Credibility   383
      Information Overload   383
      Language Characteristics   384
      Gender Differences   384
      Other Factors   385
COMMUNICATION CHANNELS   385
      Formal Communication Channels   385
        Vertical Communication   386
        Horizontal Communication   388
      Spontaneous Communication Channels   388
COMMUNICATION COMPETENCY
CHALLENGES   389
      Develop Feedback Skills   390
      Advanced Listening Skills   390
IMPLICATIONS FOR LEADERS   391
      LEADERS IN ACTION:
      Mitch Meyers of Zipatoni   392
      MEETING THE CHALLENGE:
      Communicating at Hanes: One Voice or
      Three?   393
SUMMARY   393
REVIEW QUESTIONS   394
DISCUSSION QUESTIONS   394
THINKING CRITICALLY: DEBATE THE
ISSUE   395
EXPERIENTIAL EXERCISES   395
CAPTURING THE POWER OF
INFORMATION TECHNOLOGY   395
ETHICS: TAKE A STAND   396
VIDEO CASE Communicating Effectively
within Diverse Organizations: Le Meridien
Hotels and Resorts Ltd.   396
CASE A Performance Review   398

13 Leading in a Dynamic Environment   400

      FACING THE CHALLENGE:
      The Globetrotters Are Back!   402
INTRODUCTION   402
LEADERSHIP SIGNIFICANCE   402
LEADER-CENTERED APPROACHES   403
      Trait Focus   403
      Behavior Focus   404
      AT THE FOREFRONT:
      Can Only CEOs Be Leaders?   405
      Power Focus   406
        Position Power   406
        Personal Power   407
FOLLOWER-CENTERED APPROACHES   408

Self-Leadership Focus 408
LEADERS IN ACTION:
New Leader at Alberto-Culver North
America 409
Leadership Substitutes 410
INTERACTIVE APPROACHES 411
Situational Leadership Model 411
Empowerment 412
Transformational Leadership 413
A NEW MODEL OF LEADERSHIP 414
WOMEN AS LEADERS 414
LEADERS OF THE FUTURE 415
NOW APPLY IT:
Finding a Good Leader 416
IMPLICATIONS FOR LEADERS 416
MEETING THE CHALLENGE:
The Globetrotters Are Back! 417
SUMMARY 418
REVIEW QUESTIONS 418
DISCUSSION QUESTIONS 418
THINKING CRITICALLY: DEBATE THE
ISSUE 419
EXPERIENTIAL EXERCISES 419
CAPTURING THE POWER OF
INFORMATION TECHNOLOGY 420
ETHICS: TAKE A STAND 420
VIDEO CASE Leading in a Dynamic
Environment: The Buffalo Zoo 420
CASE Steve Ballmer at Microsoft 422

14 Exploring Individual Differences and Team
Dynamics 424

FACING THE CHALLENGE:
Teamwork at United Technologies 426
INTRODUCTION 426
APPRECIATING INDIVIDUAL
DIFFERENCES 427
Personality Characteristics 427
Self-Esteem 427
Locus of Control 427
NOW APPLY IT:
Measuring Your Locus of Control 428
Type A and B Personalities 429
Resilience 430
Self-Monitoring 430
Authoritarianism 430
MYERS-BRIGGS TYPE INDICATOR 431
THE "BIG FIVE" PERSONALITY TRAITS 433
MATCHING PERSONALITIES WITH
JOBS 433
Perception 434
Perceptual Process 435
Stereotyping 435
Halo-and-Horn Effect 435

Selective Perception 436
Reducing Perceptual Errors 436
Attitudes 436
Relationship between Satisfaction and
Performance 437
Ability 438
KEY INPUTS FOR DESIGNING EFFECTIVE
TEAMS 438
LEADERS IN ACTION:
Keith Alper: Leader of Team Leaders 439
Group Categories 440
Formal Groups 440
Informal Groups 440
Membership Composition 441
Roles 441
Member Characteristics 442
Diversity 443
Size 443
Team Goals 444
AT THE FOREFRONT:
Best Practice: Creating Learning Teams 444
PROCESSES FOR TEAM EFFECTIVENESS 445
Team Development 446
Forming 446
Storming 446
Norming 446
Performing 448
Adjourning 448
IMPLICATIONS FOR LEADERS 448
MEETING THE CHALLENGE:
Teamwork at United Technologies 449
SUMMARY 449
REVIEW QUESTIONS 450
DISCUSSION QUESTIONS 450
THINKING CRITICALLY: DEBATE THE
ISSUE 451
EXPERIENTIAL EXERCISES 451
CAPTURING THE POWER OF
INFORMATION TECHNOLOGY 452
ETHICS: TAKE A STAND 453
VIDEO CASE Exploring Individual
Differences and Team Dynamics:
Cannondale I: Teamwork 453
CASE Building a Team at Altrec 455

15 Motivating Organizational Members 458

FACING THE CHALLENGE:
Nucor Steel Corporation 460
INTRODUCTION 460
BASIC MOTIVATION PROCESS 460
MOTIVATIONAL APPROACHES 461
NEEDS-BASED APPROACHES OF
EMPLOYEE MOTIVATION 462
Maslow's Hierarchy of Needs 462

Physiological Needs   462
Security Needs   463
Affiliation Needs   463
Esteem Needs   463
Self-Actualization Needs   463
Two-Factor Model   463
Motivator Factors   464
Hygiene Factors   464
Acquired-Needs Model   465
Need for Achievement   465
Need for Power   465
Need for Affiliation   465
PROCESS APPROACHES TO EMPLOYEE
MOTIVATION   466
Expectancy Model   466
Expectancy   466
Instrumentality   466
Valence   466
Equity Model   467
Goal Setting   469
Reinforcement Theory   470
Positive Reinforcement   470
Negative Reinforcement   470
Extinction   470
Punishment   471
Schedules of Reinforcement   472
Using Behavior Modification   473
LEADERS IN ACTION:
Sallie Krawcheck Rewards, and Gets,
Accurate Analysis   474
Criticisms of Behavior Modification   474
CONTEMPORARY MOTIVATIONAL
APPROACHES   474
Money as a Motivator   475
Employee Ownership as a Motivator   476
Rewarding Team Performance   476
AT THE FOREFRONT:
Successful Senior Executives Under 40   477
INTERNATIONAL PERSPECTIVES   477
IMPLICATIONS FOR LEADERS   478
NOW APPLY IT:
What Is Your Motivation Related to
Goals?   479
MEETING THE CHALLENGE:
Nucor Steel Corporation   480
SUMMARY   480
REVIEW QUESTIONS   481
DISCUSSION QUESTIONS   482
THINKING CRITICALLY: DEBATE THE
ISSUE   482
EXPERIENTIAL EXERCISES   482
CAPTURING THE POWER OF
INFORMATION TECHNOLOGY   482
ETHICS: TAKE A STAND   483

VIDEO CASE Motivating Organizational
Members: Buffalo Zoological Gardens   483
CASE How's My [Teenage] Driving?   485

**PART 5   CONTROL CHALLENGES IN
             THE 21ST CENTURY   487**

16 Organizational Control in a Complex
Business Environment   488
FACING THE CHALLENGE:
KARLEE Company's Quest to Break Away
from the Pack   490
INTRODUCTION   490
A PROCESS OF CONTROL FOR DIVERSE
AND MULTINATIONAL ORGANIZATIONS   491
Setting Standards of Performance   491
LEADERS IN ACTION:
Culinary Concepts/Chef Creations   492
Measuring Actual Performance   493
Comparing Actual Performance with
Standards   494
Responding to Deviation   494
AT THE FOREFRONT:
Federal Aviation Administration Updates
Its Control Systems   495
DESIGNING QUALITY AND
EFFECTIVENESS INTO THE CONTROL
SYSTEM   496
Design Factors Affecting Control System
Quality   496
Amount of Variety in the Control System   496
Ability to Anticipate Problems   498
Sensitivity of the Measuring Device   499
Composition of Feedback Reports   499
Criteria for Effective Control   499
Is Related to Organizational Strategy   500
Utilizes All Steps in the Control Process   500
*Is Composed of Objective and Subjective
Measures*   500
*Incorporates Timeliness in Feedback
Reporting*   500
Is Acceptable to a Diverse Work Force   501
Selecting the Proper Amount of Control   501
NOW APPLY IT:
Checklist for Designing Effective Control
Systems   502
Costs in Control Systems   502
Reliability of the System   503
Importance of the Process Being Controlled 504
Selecting the Focal Point for Control   504
Preventive Control   504
Concurrent Control   506
Corrective Control   506
Multiple Focal Points   506

CONTROL PHILOSOPHIES FOR LEADERS   507
Bureaucratic Control   507
Organic Control   507
Selecting a Control Style in Today's
Diverse and Multinational Organizations   508
IMPACT OF INFORMATION
TECHNOLOGY ON ORGANIZATIONAL
CONTROL   509
MECHANISMS FOR FINANCIAL
CONTROL   510
Financial Statements   510
Balance Sheet   510
Income Statement   510
Financial Ratios   511
Liquidity Ratios   512
Profitability Ratios   512
Debt Ratios   512
Activity Ratios   512
ETHICAL ISSUES IN THE CONTROL OF A
DIVERSE WORK FORCE   512
Drug Testing   513
Undercover Surveillance   513
Computer Monitoring   514
IMPLICATIONS FOR LEADERS   514
MEETING THE CHALLENGE:
KARLEE Company Breaks from the Pack   515
SUMMARY   516
REVIEW QUESTIONS   516
DISCUSSION QUESTIONS   517
THINKING CRITICALLY: DEBATE THE
ISSUE   517
EXPERIENTIAL EXERCISES   517
CAPTURING THE POWER OF
INFORMATION TECHNOLOGY   518
ETHICS: TAKE A STAND   518
VIDEO CASE Organizational Control in a
Complex Business Environment: Cannondale   518
CASE Motorola's Control of Quality   520

17 Productivity and Quality in Operations   522

FACING THE CHALLENGE:
Operational Changes Needed at Clarke
American Checks, Inc.   524
INTRODUCTION   524
WHAT IS OPERATIONS MANAGEMENT?   525
Manufacturing versus Service Operating
Systems   525
NOW APPLY IT:
Checklist for Manufacturing/Service
Classification   527
Structural Differences Among Operating
Systems   527
Types of Manufacturing Systems   527
Types of Service Systems   529

Operations Management Decision Areas   529
Long-Term System Design Decisions   529
Short-Term Operating and Control
Decisions   533
AT THE FOREFRONT:
From Just-in-Case to Just-in-Time at State
Industries   536
THE ROLE OF PRODUCTIVITY AND
QUALITY IN OPERATIONS   537
Fundamentals of Productivity   538
Improving Productivity   539
Fundamentals of Quality   540
LEADERS IN ACTION:
Conway's BBQ Launches New Venture   541
Factors for Assessing Quality   542
Cost of Quality   542
Total Quality Management as a Tool for
Global Competitiveness   544
Customer-Driven Standards   544
Management and Labor Commitment   545
Organization and Coordination of Efforts   545
Employee Participation   545
Prominent Quality Management
Philosophers   546
IMPACT OF INFORMATION
TECHNOLOGY ON PRODUCTIVITY AND
QUALITY   548
IMPLICATIONS FOR LEADERS   549
MEETING THE CHALLENGE:
Clarke American Responds with
Operational Changes   550
SUMMARY   551
REVIEW QUESTIONS   551
DISCUSSION QUESTIONS   552
THINKING CRITICALLY: DEBATE THE
ISSUE   552
EXPERIENTIAL EXERCISES   553
CAPTURING THE POWER OF
INFORMATION TECHNOLOGY   553
ETHICS: TAKE A STAND   553
VIDEO CASE Productivity and Quality in
Operations: PING Golf Clubs   554
CASE Inventory Decision Making at
ArtSource   555

18 Information Technology and Control   558

FACING THE CHALLENGE:
What Kind of Information Systems Are
Needed to Run the Olympic Winter
Games?   560
INTRODUCTION   560
ORGANIZATIONAL FOUNDATIONS OF
INFORMATION SYSTEMS   561

The Changing Business Environment 561
   Increasing Globalization 562
   Shifting Economies 562
   Flattening of Organizations 562
   Emerging Technology-Driven Innovations 563
   Types of Information Systems 563
   Operational-Level Information Systems 565
   Knowledge-Level Information Systems 565
   Management-Level Information Systems 566
   Strategic-Level Information Systems 567
Integration of Systems 567
LEADERS IN ACTION:
Hughes Supply Streamlines Operations 568
TECHNICAL FOUNDATIONS OF
INFORMATION SYSTEMS 569
   Information System Components 569
   Input 570
   Processing 570
   Output 570
   Hardware 570
   Software 570
   Database 571
Information versus Data 571
Characteristics of Useful Information 572
   Quality 572
   Timeliness 573
   Completeness 573
Steps in the Development of High-Quality
Information Systems 574
   Investigation 574
   Systems Analysis 574
   Systems Design 575
   Systems Implementation 575
   Systems Maintenance 576
Attributes of Successful Information
Systems 577
   Feasibility 577
   Ability to Meet Needs of Diverse Users 577

NOW APPLY IT:
Checklist for Successful Information
System Design 578
THE NEW TECHNOLOGIES 578
   Telecommunications and Networking 579
AT THE FOREFRONT:
IT Prevents Pfizer and the FDA from
Drowning in a Sea of Paper 581
   Electronic Commerce 582
   Artificial Intelligence 584
   Expert Systems 584
   Robotics 584
IMPACT OF INFORMATION
TECHNOLOGY ON DYNAMIC
ORGANIZATIONS 585
LIMITATIONS OF COMPUTER-BASED
INFORMATION SYSTEMS 586
IMPLICATIONS FOR LEADERS 587
MEETING THE CHALLENGE:
Building the Information Systems Needed
to Run the Olympic Winter Games 588
SUMMARY 589
REVIEW QUESTIONS 590
DISCUSSION QUESTIONS 590
THINKING CRITICALLY: DEBATE THE
ISSUE 591
EXPERIENTIAL EXERCISES 591
CAPTURING THE POWER OF
INFORMATION TECHNOLOGY 592
ETHICS: TAKE A STAND 592
VIDEO CASE Cannondale III: IT 593
CASE Safe Haven House 595

GLOSSARY 597
ENDNOTES 607
NAME INDEX NI-1
COMPANY INDEX CI-1
SUBJECT INDEX SI-1

PREFACE

When the journey of this book began in the mid 1990s, we wanted to fill the students with enthusiasm and excitement for the course of study they were about to undertake. The field of management was then, and continues to be now, one of the most important and interesting disciplines of business. We recognized that times were changing, as were the functions and roles of managers. As the 21st century approached, we saw a frenzy of activity as the business community prepared itself for the dreaded Y2K, whose predictions of doom and gloom barely caused a blip on the radar screen. The economy continued to soar. But recently we have seen some dramatic changes that have altered the face of business and, to some extent, have altered our way of life. The dot.coms were flying high and e-business was supposed to take over. However, we are all aware of the shakeout that has occurred in this area. We are also painfully aware of the pernicious worldwide events of September 11, 2001, and beyond. Early in the new millennium, we find ourselves facing an economy that is not riding the crest of the wave that it once surfed.

Businesses have had to tighten belts, and business leaders are finding it necessary to turn their full attention to meeting the challenges of a highly dynamic and rapidly changing business environment. As students of management and future business leaders, you must also prepare to face these challenges, for the business environment is destined to remain on this volatile course. As the times continue to change, so, too, do the functions and roles of managers. Change is coming from many directions: the global marketplace has redefined the competitive structure of many industries; the increasing predominance of entrepreneurial and service-based organizations has altered the structure of our economy; quality management has radically changed the way many organizations do business, and extremist militant groups are doing all in their power to disrupt the world's free market economy. Organizations are being restructured and redesigned to be lean, flexible, and adaptable to change; leaders in all areas and at all levels of the organization are expected to be proactive, team-oriented, and focused on results; and diversity in the workforce has become the rule rather than the exception. Succeeding as a leader in the organization of today and tomorrow requires a special set of management skills and competencies.

It has never been more true that this is an exciting time to begin studying one of the most important and interesting disciplines of business: the field of management. *Management: Challenges for Tomorrow's Leaders* will pique your excitement about this discipline. As you progress through the chapters you will be exposed to the new challenges and contemporary issues that the leaders of today and tomorrow will continually face. Global competition; organizational restructuring; entrepreneurial, service-based, and quality initiatives; and emphasis on gender, ethnic, and racial diversity in the workforce are just a few of the issues that you and other contemporary managers will confront. Our overriding objective in developing this book was to capture the excitement and challenges that business leaders will face in the environment of the 21st century.

In the few short years since the prior edition of this book was prepared, much has happened in the business environment that needed to be captured in this new edition. As authors, we also have had to adapt to change.

While significant changes have been made in each chapter, the theoretical content of the chapters remains true to the earlier editions and the pedagogical objective has not wavered. *Management: Challenges for Tomorrow's Leaders* still provides comprehensive coverage of traditional and emerging management theory, and has a special focus on honing the leadership skills that will be necessary for survival in the dynamic, global environment of business. More specifically, in this edition of the book we address what we consider to be the three essential components for

Successful organizations need leaders at all levels who are responsive to new opportunities and can help the organization execute key strategic imperatives. Are you an effective leader? That is a refrain we want you to come back to again and again as you work your way through Management.

We focus our attention on three leadership fundamentals—competence, character, and community.

effective leadership: (1) competence—an effective leader must be knowledgeable and skilled in his or her area of expertise, (2) character—an effective leader must be of strong character, acting with integrity and honesty; and (3) community—an effective leader must understand what is required for healthy and vibrant communities and be willing to accept responsibility for contributing to those communities.

The application orientation of the book has also remained strong. There are a number of features that provide you with an opportunity to implement the material you learn and to understand a wide variety of real-world management situations. In short, the book is designed to help you develop an understanding of the field of management and to develop the competencies and skills that will enable you to succeed in the business environment of the future.

CHANGES IN THIS EDITION

Southwest Airlines continues to defy the odds, showing increases in passenger travel in a year of unprecedented industry losses. How do they do it? Breaking away from the pack, it is commonly acknowledged, takes leadership. We're inclined to agree.

- In the prior editions of this book, each chapter opened with an incident that details a real-life organizational problem or situation that is related to the content of the chapter. This pedagogy was very well received and continues in this edition. However, each chapter opener, now called "Facing The Challenge," has been changed to provide fresh illustrations of situations or problems and how they were dealt with within the realm of the content and theory of the chapter. The challenge is referred to often as the chapter unfolds. At the close of the chapter, "Meeting The Challenge" describes how the problem was solved or the situation was addressed.
- The boxed material (highlighted examples) in each chapter has been replaced with updated or new illustrations and applications of contemporary management practice. These highlighted examples fall into the categories of Leaders In Action, At The Forefront, Now Apply It, and of course, the Facing The Challenge and Meeting The Challenge so prominent in each chapter.
- Every chapter has been updated to reflect many of the changes that have occurred in the business world during the past few years. Along with the major features noted above, many new illustrative examples have been woven into the fabric of each of the chapters.
- To keep students on the cutting edge of technology, a feature called Capturing the Power of Information Technology continues to be included at the end of each chapter. This feature gives students the opportunity to gain experience in using the Internet to search for information in some area related to the materials in the chapter, and to use the latest technology in spreadsheet, word processing, and presentation software to present the information to the class.

In all, more than 70 new company situations and scenarios have been developed to accompany the theoretical content of the chapters, as well as numerous additional company examples interspersed throughout the text.

TEXT HIGHLIGHTS

Our global knowledge-based economy, driven by technology, access, information, and speed, accelerates the demand for upgradeable skills. Want to make sure you possess the right skill sets? Use our Information Technology exercises to acquire them.

This book includes a number of features designed to prepare students to be leaders in this new millennium. These features focus on (1) meeting the challenges inherent in a dynamic, rapidly changing business environment, (2) developing the competencies and skills that leaders will need in the future, and (3) responding to the contemporary management trends that will affect both organizations and managers in the 21st century.

- *Challenges for Tomorrow's Leaders.* The underlying, integrating theme that forms the foundation of this book is meeting the leadership challenge as we begin the new millennium. As tomorrow's leaders, you will be challenged continually to respond to opportunities and threats that arise in the dynamic, global environment of business. You will need to be creative in the way you think about and respond to these challenges. As competitive pressures continue to escalate and consumers around the globe demand increasing levels of quality, you will find it necessary to strive for excellence in all facets of your organizations. Our focus in this book is to prepare you to meet these challenges as they affect the activities in which you will engage and the roles you will play.

- *Competencies and Skills.* Beyond our theme of meeting the challenge, we have developed this book with an emphasis on the competencies and skills needed by contemporary leaders. As students of management, you must be prepared to translate theory into practice as you move into the workplace. To do so, you will need to develop fully your skills in such important areas as teamwork, critical thinking, problem solving, communication, and adapting to change.

- *Theory and Practice.* This book bridges the gap between management theory and practice by using an interdisciplinary, applied approach to the material in the text. Because leaders come from all areas of an organization (e.g., production departments, finance and accounting departments, sales and marketing departments), it is important to understand how the concepts of management are applied in the various functional areas of organizations of all sizes. Further, an interdisciplinary approach to the study of management is essential given the blurring of the lines separating the traditional functions of business (e.g., management, marketing, finance, etc.) and the increasing predominance of cross-functional work teams within contemporary organizations.

- *Contemporary Management Trends.* Finally, we have identified and highlighted several contemporary management trends that present challenges for organizations and leaders today. They include global management, entrepreneurship, service management, quality, team-based management, ethics, and cultural diversity. Rather than adding a separate chapter on each of these trends, we introduce them very early in the text and then integrate the topics into each and every chapter of the book.

Michael Dell's now-familiar story of assembling and selling computers from his dormitory room at the University of Texas in the 1980s continues to astonish 20 years after the fact. How can this be in an industry where obsolescence is an everyday occurrence? Management: Challenges for Tomorrow's Leaders will help you unravel the "Dell system."

ORGANIZATION

Part 1 of the text addresses the basic concepts of management, the roles of the manager, and the changing nature of both the contemporary organization and the contemporary manager. The contemporary management trends discussed above are introduced, and a foundation is laid for examining how these trends affect management theory and practice. In addition, the history of management thought is reviewed, and the topics of social responsibility and ethics are addressed in light of their increasing importance in modern organizations.

Part 2 explores the managerial function of planning. This section examines the basic principles of the planning process, as well as planning from a strategic perspective. Strategy is examined as a tool for responding to challenges in today's highly competitive, global business environment and for achieving quality in every aspect of an organization's operations. Further, decision making is addressed as a key managerial responsibility, and a number of tools and techniques for decision making are presented.

Part 3 of the text focuses on the organizing function of management. More specifically, this section addresses the fundamental principles of organizing, as well as the models of organizational design that are appropriate for contemporary, team-oriented organizations. Issues of organizational culture, change, and human resource management are also addressed in this section. Particular emphasis is placed upon organizing to improve flexibility, facilitate change, utilize team management, and respond to the challenges of a diverse and heterogeneous work environment.

Part 4 explores the managerial function of leadership. This section focuses on factors that influence the behavior of people. Separate chapters examine individual and group behavior, what motivates members of the workforce, the nature of leadership, and communicating with others. Special attention is given to developing a leadership style that empowers the members of diverse organizations to excel in everything they do and to work as a team to achieve the goals and objectives of the organization.

Part 5 examines the management function of control. The foundational principles of control are addressed, and specific attention is given to productivity, quality control, and information systems control. Control is presented as a principal tool for achieving quality in the products, services, and processes of the organization, as well as a tool for developing a competitive advantage based on enhanced productivity, increased efficiency, and superior quality.

APPLICATIONS-ORIENTED APPROACH

Consistent with our application-oriented approach to the presentation of contemporary management trends, we have included the following elements, which are designed to help you become a more effective manager:

- *Chapter Overview.* Every chapter opens with a summary that describes the general content of the chapter. This opening summary highlights the primary topics and concepts to be covered in the chapter and explains why the information is important to the manager of the future.
- *Learning Objectives.* Each chapter contains a well-defined set of learning objectives. These objectives focus on the specific topics covered in the chapter and provide a checklist of important points discussed in the chapter. Each learning objective is keyed to the appropriate section of the chapter text, the chapter summary, and the chapter review questions.
- *Facing The Challenge/Meeting The Challenge.* There is an opening Facing The Challenge in each chapter that details a real-life organizational problem or situation that is related to the content of the chapter. This incident is referred to often as the chapter unfolds. At the close of the chapter, a Meeting The Challenge describes how the problem was solved or the situation was addressed using the management concepts discussed in the chapter. This allows the student to see how the concepts and theories presented in each chapter are applied to business situations in actual companies.
- *Capturing the Power of Information Technology.* A set of information technology exercises is presented at the end of each chapter. These exercises give students the opportunity to use technology to search for information in an area related to the materials in the chapter. Much of the information can be gathered via the Internet or by phone or fax from the appropriate company sources. Each of these exercises typically has some classroom presentation aspect associated with it, requiring the use of spreadsheet, word processing, or presentation software to arrange and present the information.
- *Ethics: Take a Stand.* An ethical dilemma related to the material presented in the chapter appears at the end of each chapter. Students evaluate various alternative courses of action in terms of their ethical implications and select one that is both ethical and meets the objectives of the organization. The Ethics: Take a Stand feature highlights the increasing importance of leaders making decisions that are founded on strong individual and organizational ethics.
- *Thinking Critically: Debate the Issue.* Each chapter contains a debate topic related to the content of the chapter. Students are asked to work in teams to develop arguments to support a particular position. The instructor selects two teams to present their findings to the class in a debate format. This exercise helps stu-

Some brands are positioned at the very top of their product category. How BMW achieves a distinctive competitive position based on engineering excellence, pricing, distribution, manufacturing design, and advertising are questions every future manager should find as exhilarating as driving the new Z4 Roadster.

Enron, only one in a series of recent corporate meltdowns, provides an especially compelling commentary on the shortcomings of corporate governance. We look at the ethical and financial consequences surrounding how this large, seemingly invincible corporate giant fell so far and so fast.

dents to develop critical thinking skills, teamwork skills, and oral communication skills.

- *Chapter Video Cases.* At the end of every chapter there is a video case that presents a real organization that uses contemporary management practices. Fourteen of the cases are new to this edition.
- *End-of-Chapter Cases.* In addition to the video case at the close of each chapter, a second case details a situation that provides an opportunity for students to apply the concepts and tools presented in the chapter. These cases are designed to help students develop their analytical thinking skills and to apply the knowledge they gained from the chapter to resolve problems or address situations that often occur in contemporary organizations.
- *Chapter Summary.* Each chapter closes with a summary of the major points presented in the chapter. This overview of the chapter contents provides students with an overall perspective of the topics covered. Each chapter's summary is tied directly to that chapter's learning objectives.
- *Review/Discussion Questions.* A set of review and discussion questions is provided at the end of each chapter. The review questions relate directly to the content of the chapter and are keyed to the learning objectives. The discussion questions are application-oriented in that they require students to respond to real-world situations or issues using the knowledge gained from the chapter.
- *Experiential Exercises.* Structured experiential exercises are provided at the close of each chapter. These exercises can be used in either large or small class environments and are designed get students directly involved in the learning process by requiring them to apply management theory to real-world situations. Many of these exercises involve "self-assessment" and will help students gain a greater understanding of their own management competencies and skills.
- *Now Apply It.* In each chapter, Now Apply It provides an opportunity for students to practice the management principles they have studied. For example, students are given the opportunity to use self-assessment instruments to describe their own personal management or leadership styles, and organizational assessment skills to evaluate organizations.
- *Key Terms.* Key terms are highlighted throughout the chapter and are defined in the margins. A comprehensive glossary is provided at the back of the text.
- *Highlighted Examples.* Throughout the book, organizations that provide examples of contemporary management practices are highlighted. These examples are designed to profile real companies that are confronting management challenges and responding in proactive and innovative ways. Each of the chapters contains the following highlighted examples:
  - *Leaders In Action.* Business leaders who have achieved excellence through their management practices and leadership skills are featured in Leaders In Action.
  - *At The Forefront.* Companies that have achieved excellence through their management practices are featured in At the Forefront. Of particular interest are those organizations that have adopted a quality orientation in everything they do.

SUPPLEMENT PACKAGE

A professor's job is demanding. Because of this, we expect professors to demand a lot in return from the publisher and the authors of *Management*. Both the textbook and the accompanying ancillary materials have been developed to help instructors excel when performing their vital teaching function. We also include a number of supplements to aid students in their study of the material.

FOR STUDENTS

STUDENT STUDY GUIDE (ISBN 0-324-27405-X)　The extended study guide for *Management* was updated by Craig V. Van Sandt, Augustana College. For each chapter, this comprehensive guide includes learning objectives with detailed descriptions; a chapter outline; multiple-choice and agree-or-disagree questions with answers; exercises; and a chapter summary.

INFOTRAC COLLEGE EDITION　InfoTrac College Edition is a fully searchable **online database** of full-text articles, with anytime, anywhere access, fast and easy search tools, and daily updates. Hundreds of periodicals, both scholarly and popular—*Fortune, Newsweek, Sloan Management Review, Entrepreneur,* to name a few—are available all at a single site. For more information or to log on, please visit **http://www.infotrac-college.com**. Just enter your passcode as provided on the subscription card packaged free with every new copy of *Management: Challenges for Tomorrow's Leaders.*

LEWIS XTRA! (HTTP://LEWISXTRA.SWLEARNING.COM)　Free access to the Lewis Xtra! Web site (a $25 value) is packaged with every new copy of *Management: Challenges for Tomorrow's Leaders.* Students purchasing a used book can buy access to Lewis Xtra! online at **http://lewisxtra.swlearning.com**. Lewis Xtra! offers a variety of online learning enhancements, including Xtra! Quizzing; *Experiencing Management,* an award-winning collection of Web-based concept-reinforcement modules; streaming video of each chapter's video case; and additional video from CNN.

FOR INSTRUCTORS

INSTRUCTOR'S MANUAL WITH VIDEO GUIDE (ISBN 0-324-16899-3)
The instructor's manual for *Management* was prepared by Joseph F. Michlitsch, Southern Illinois University, and provides important information for each chapter. Each chapter of the manual includes the following information:

- Learning Objectives for each chapter.
- Chapter Overviews.
- Pedagogy Grids in every chapter to highlight the main points covered in the feature boxes.
- Lecture Notes with narratives under each major point to flesh out the discussion and show alternative examples and issues to bring forward.
- Detailed Responses to the review questions, discussion questions, Ethics: Take a Stand exercises, cases, and experiential exercises.
- A Video Guide describing the video cases that accompany each chapter, including questions for discussion and detailed responses. The video guide was prepared by Cynthia L. Sutton of Metropolitan State College of Denver.
- Additional Cases with suggested answers for those instructors who wish to supplement the case material included in the text.

TEST BANK (ISBN 0-324-16950-7)　Special attention was given to the preparation of the test bank because it is one of the most important ancillary materials. Joseph F. Michlitsch, Southern Illinois University, has updated the third edition test bank. The test bank contains over 3,500 multiple-choice, true/false, matching, case, and essay questions.

EXAMVIEW® TESTING SOFTWARE　ExamView, a computerized testing program, contains all of the questions in the printed Test Bank. This easy-to-use test-creation program is compatible with Microsoft Windows and Macintosh and enables instructors to create printed tests, Internet tests, and LAN-based tests quickly. The QuickTest Wizard lets test generators assemble a test in minutes, using a step-by-step selection process. Blackboard- and WebCT-ready versions of the Lewis Test Bank are also available to qualified instructors. Please contact your South-Western/Thomson Learning sales representative for more information.

POWERPOINT™ PRESENTATION SLIDES Developed by Zulema Seguel in close coordination with the text authors, over 600 slides are available to supplement course content, providing a comprehensive review of each chapter in the book. Available online at **http://lewis.swlearning.com**.

MANAGEMENT POWER! POWERPOINT™ PRESENTATION SLIDES (ISBN 0-324-13253-0) Management Power! Is a CD-ROM of PowerPoint slides covering 14 major management and organizational behavior topics, such as leadership, communication, control, decision making, designing organizations, ethics, and innovation and change. These multimedia-rich slides can be easily customized to suit individual preferences.

VIDEO PACKAGE: 18 CHAPTER VIDEO CASES (ISBN 0-324-27406-8) In this edition we have incorporated 14 new and 4 revised video segments that highlight all aspects of today's management. One video segment ranging from 5 to 30 minutes accompanies each of the chapters and helps to explain the concepts of that chapter. The videos are supported by cases, which are included in the text, and a video guide, which is included in the Instructor's Manual. The cases and video guide were prepared by Cynthia L. Sutton of Metropolitan State College of Denver.

New videos in this edition highlight management issues at organizations such as Ping Golf Clubs, Cannondale, Fannie Mae, The Buffalo Zoo, and Timberland. The video to accompany Chapter 1 profiles a small business (On-Target Supply and Logistics) that is owned and operated by a man who has built his success based on the 3Cs of leadership: Competence, Character, and Community.

LEWIS WEB SITE (HTTP://LEWIS.SWLEARNING.COM) Broad instructional and student support is provided online at **http://lewis.swlearning.com**, including downloadable ancillaries, interactive quizzes, news summaries, and more.

INSTRUCTOR'S RESOURCE CD-ROM (ISBN 0-324-16952-3) This CD-ROM provides instructors with "one-stop shopping" for various teaching resources, including the chapter PowerPoint slides, the Instructor's Manual, and the Test Bank.

TEXTCHOICE: MANAGEMENT EXERCISES AND CASES TextChoice is the home of Thomson Learning's online digital content. TextChoice provides the fastest, easiest way for you to create your own learning materials. South-Western's Management Exercises and Cases database includes a variety of experiential exercises, classroom activities, management in film exercises, and cases to enhance any management course. Choose as many exercises as you like and even add your own material to create a supplement tailor-fitted to your course. Contact your South-Western/Thomson Learning sales representative for more information.

ACKNOWLEDGMENTS

A book such as this does not come to fruition solely by the hands of the authors. Many individuals have had significant involvement with this project, and their contributions must not go unrecognized. First, we would like to thank our colleague Joseph F. Michlitsch for stepping in to revise Chapters 10–15. He made a valuable contribution to this edition. In addition, many reviewers made insightful comments and valuable suggestions on the preliminary drafts of this book. Although criticism is sometimes a bitter pill to swallow, we can now look back and agree that the reviewer comments led to modifications that greatly strengthened the final product. We would like to express our gratitude to each of the following reviewers:

Fourth Edition Reviewers:
    Maha W. Alul, Maryville University
    Bruce Barringer, University of Central Florida
    Jerry Biberman, University of Scranton
    Donna Cooke, Florida Atlantic University
    Max E. Douglas, Indiana State University
    Lorena B. Edwards, Belmont University
    Kathleen Jones, University of North Dakota
    Thomas R. Mahaffey, Siena College
    John Mastriani, El Paso Community College
    Susan S. Nash, University of Oklahoma
    Charles Stubbart, Southern Illinois University
    Cynthia L. Sutton, Metropolitan State College of Denver
    Andrew Ward, Emory University

Third Edition Reviewers:
    Cheryl Adkins, Louisiana State University
    Mitchell Adrian, Longwood College
    Jim Bell, Southwest Texas State University
    Glenn M. Blair, Jr., Baldwin-Wallace College
    George Carnahan, Northern Michigan University
    Sally Dresdow, University of Wisconsin, Green Bay
    Lorena Edwards, Belmont University
    Jud Faurer, Metro State College of Denver
    Ronald M. Faust, University of Evansville
    Andre L. Honoree, Spring Hill College
    Velma Jesser, Lane Community College
    Edward Joyce, University of Nevada, Las Vegas
    Joan R. Keely, Washington State University
    Cynthia Krom, Mount St. Mary College
    John P. McGovern, Nassau Community College
    Dan McNamara, University of St. Thomas
    Bonnie L. McNeely, Murray State University
    Arlyn J. Melcher, Southern Illinois University
    W.T. O'Donnell, University of Phoenix
    Phillip Patton, Northwestern College
    Glenn Perser, Houston Community College System
    Preston D. Probasco, San Jose State University
    Linda Beats Putchinski, University of Central Florida
    Gayla R. Sherry, University of Phoenix, Oklahoma City
    Linda Shonesy, Athens State University
    William L. Smith, Emporia State University
    Paul L. Starkey, Delta State University
    Chuck Stubbart, Southern Illinois University
    Merry Peterson Stubblefield, University of New Mexico
    John Sullivan, Montreat College
    Vicki L. West, Southwest Texas State University

Second Edition Reviewers:
    Royce L. Abrahamson, Southwest Texas State University
    Lynn Bowes-Sperry, James Madison University

Janice M. Feldbauer, Austin Community College
Robert A. Figler, University of Akron
Edwin L. Hoying, Jr., University of Phoenix
Natalie J. Hunter, Portland State University
Gerald H. Kramer, Northwestern Missouri State University
Thomas R. Mahaffey, Siena College
Sandra M. Martinez, New Mexico State University
Daniel W. McAllister, University of Nevada, Las Vegas
Joseph F. Michlitsch, Southern Illinois University
James D. Oldson, The George Washington University
Robert J. Paul, Kansas State University
Khush K. Pittenger, Ashland University
John Wallace, Marshall University
John Washburn, University of Wisconsin, Whitewater
Terrence E. Williamson, South Dakota School of Mines and Technology

First Edition Reviewers:
Royce Abrahamson, Southwest Texas State University
Jeffrey Bailey, University of Idaho
Edward Bewayo, Montclair State University
Allen Bluedorn, University of Missouri
Peggy Brewer, Eastern Kentucky University
Deborah Brown, Santa Fe Community College
George Carnahan, Northern Michigan University
James F. Cashman, University of Alabama
Daniel S. Cochran, Mississippi State University
Roy Cook, Fort Lewis College
John Cotton, Marquette University
Marian Crawford, University of Arkansas, Little Rock
Carol Danehower, Memphis State University
Arthur Darrow, Bowling Green State University
Richard V. Dick, Missouri Western State University
Kenneth K. Eastman, Oklahoma State University
Stanley W. Elsea, Kansas State University
Roy Farris, Southeast Missouri State University
Jan Feldbauer, Austin Community College
Diane Ferry, University of Delaware
Robert A. Figler, University of Akron
George Foegen, Metro State College
Sonia Goltz, University of Notre Dame
Richard Grover, University of Southern Maine
Ted Halatin, Southwest Texas State University
John Hall, University of Florida
Dorothy Heide, California State University, Fullerton
Marvin Hill, Northern Illinois University
Phyllis Holland, Valdosta State College
John Jackson, University of Wyoming
Dewey Johnson, California State University, Fresno
Forest Jourden, University of Illinois, Champaign
Marvin Karlins, University of South Florida
Robert E. Kemper, Northern Arizona University
Russell Kent, Georgia Southern University
David G. Kuhn, Florida State University
James M. Lahiff, University of Georgia
Lars Erik Larson, University of Wisconsin, Whitewater
Esther Long, University of West Florida

Barbara Marting, University of Southern Indiana
Dan McAllister, University of Nevada, Las Vegas
James McElroy, Iowa State University
Joseph Michlitsch, Southern Illinois University
Edward J. Morrison, University of Colorado, Boulder
Diana Page, University of West Florida
Robert J. Paul, Kansas State University
Allayne Pizzolatto, Nicholls State University
Paul Preston, University of Texas, San Antonio
Richard Randall, Nassau Community College
Bill Ryan, Florida Atlantic University
Jerry D. Scott, Southeastern Oklahoma State University
Dawn Sheffler, Central Michigan University
Jane Siebler, Oregon State University
Mary Thibodeaux, University of North Texas
Ronald Vickroy, University of Pittsburgh at Johnstown
John Villareal, California State University
John Wallace, Marshall University
Deborah Wells, Creighton University
Carolyn Wiley, University of Tennessee, Chattanooga
Mimi Will, Foothill College
Jack Wimer, Baylor University
Lou J. Workman, Utah State University

In addition to these manuscript reviewers, other colleagues have contributed greatly by developing several of the high-quality, comprehensive supplements that support this book. These individuals, and their contributions for which we are so grateful, include:

Instructor's Manual	Joseph F. Michlitsch, Southern Illinois University
Study Guide	Craig V. Van Sandt, Augustana College
Test Bank	Joseph F. Michlitsch Southern Illinois University
Video Cases	Cynthia Sutton, Metropolitan State College of Denver
PowerPoint Slides	Zulema Seguel

Our Acquisitions Editor, John Szilagyi, and other individuals at South-Western made valuable contributions to this project. They include Monica Ohlinger, our developmental editor, who played a critical role in linking the huge network of contributors to this project. We also acknowledge the stamina of Bob Dreas, our production editor, who not only tolerated our continual changes to the manuscript as it moved through production but actually encouraged us to change whatever was necessary to make this product the very best possible. Our thanks also go to Rob Bloom, Marketing Manager, for coordinating the outstanding sales and marketing efforts awarded this text.

Finally, we'd like to thank our families for their support throughout this project. Their tolerance of our absence from many family activities, their understanding of the time commitment a project like this requires, and their continual encouragement to push on enabled us to endure the long nights and lost weekends that made it possible for us to complete this book. For that support and commitment, we will always be grateful.

Pamela S. Lewis
Stephen H. Goodman
Patricia M. Fandt

PART 1

MEETING THE CHALLENGES OF THE 21ST CENTURY

CHAPTER 1

MANAGEMENT AND MANAGERS:
YESTERDAY, TODAY, AND TOMORROW

CHAPTER 2

EVOLUTION OF MANAGEMENT THOUGHT

CHAPTER 3

SOCIAL RESPONSIBILITY AND ETHICS

CHAP

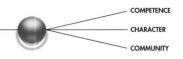

LEADERSHIP

- COMPETENCE
- CHARACTER
- COMMUNITY

TER 1

CHAPTER OVERVIEW

The world of business has undergone radical and dramatic changes in the last decade—changes that present significant challenges for the contemporary manager. These changes include advances in information technology that have reshaped the ways organizations function and people work, escalating global competition, and an unprecedented demand for speed and flexibility on the part of virtually all organizations. Perhaps more importantly, tomorrow's managers will face an even more demanding business environment. To meet the challenges of the business environment of today and tomorrow, managers must be flexible, proactive, and focused on quality in everything they do.

In this chapter, we examine the manager of yesterday, today, and tomorrow. Our primary focus is on the manager's job and how it has and will change as a result of changes in the business environment. We pay particular attention to the need for today's managers to serve as leaders within their organizations. As the business environment becomes increasingly complex and competitive, managers at all levels must be prepared to provide leadership for those around them. The competencies associated with being both a successful manager and effective leader are explored.

LEARNING OBJECTIVES

When you have finished studying this chapter, you should be able to:

1. Describe the terms *management* and *leadership*, as well as the relationship between the two concepts.
2. Define the concept of management within an organizational context and as a process.
3. Identify the roles managers play.
4. Discuss the scope of responsibilities of functional and general managers.
5. Describe the three levels of managers in terms of the skills they need and the activities in which they are involved.
6. Discuss the underlying forces of the new economy.
7. Describe the environmental trends that are affecting the way organizations operate and the way managers do their jobs.
8. Identify and discuss the organizational changes that are affecting managers' jobs.
9. Describe the manager of tomorrow in terms of the managerial style, leadership capabilities, and skill sets that will be necessary for success.

Facing The Challenge

Southwest Airlines: Surviving the Turbulence in the Airline Industry

Nothing could have prepared the leaders of the U.S. airline industry for the downturn experienced in 2001. The year was marked with unexpected increases in fuel costs, which led to less passenger travel and lower earnings. Rumors swirled about possible mergers between major carriers that were thought necessary in order for some of the airlines to stay in business. And all of this occurred before September 11, 2001, the day of attacks on the World Trade Center in New York and the Pentagon in Washington, D.C. Airlines suffered enormous losses and dramatic drops in stock prices during the industry's worst year ever, resulting in thousands of workers being laid off. Major carriers saw their stock prices tumble as much as 80 percent. Congress quickly enacted legislation to provide billions of dollars in financial assistance. While every airline was affected, one carrier seemed to have weathered the storm practically unscathed—Southwest Airlines.

Southwest Airlines managed to not only survive during this tumultuous period, but actually reported increased passenger travel. Southwest was the only airline to report a profit for the third quarter in 2001, and no employees were laid off as a result of September 11th.

Herb Kelleher, cofounder of Southwest, along with Rollin King, started Southwest Airlines 30 years ago in Dallas, Texas. They had a simple idea: Get people where they want to go safely, on time, and at discounted fares. And perhaps most importantly, have fun while you're doing it! This simple formula has paid tremendous dividends over the years as this once little-known airline is now the nation's fifth largest carrier. The corporate culture of Southwest Airlines is routinely described as fun and upbeat, where employees are committed to the company's vision and motivated to provide excellent customer service.

Despite its past successes, however, Southwest Airlines faces a number of challenges going forward. The future for the airline industry in general is highly uncertain. Overall, airline passenger travel is lower and not expected to increase significantly in the near term. Many of the major carriers plan additional cuts, some as much as 20 percent. Compared to these carriers, Southwest has smaller fleets, fewer employees, and less access to some of the major markets along the East Coast. Maintaining its unique corporate culture, while attempting to capture the emerging markets created by the cuts of the major carriers, is a major challenge Southwest faces as it heads into the future.

INTRODUCTION

The situation facing Southwest Airlines was a challenging one—one that would require strong leadership throughout the organization. Could the company expand its service to capture emerging markets in an industry that was suffering a downturn? Dramatic and unforeseen environmental changes, along with escalating demands for quality and value, had created a business environment characterized by risk and uncertainty. Southwest's future would depend upon the abilities of Herb Kelleher and the employees of Southwest to identify and respond to the opportunities that would emerge as the company moved into the future.

Although the specific issues facing the airline industry are unique, the risk and uncertainty facing Southwest are common for managers across all industries. Today, organizations of all sizes and types are operating in a business environment that is more competitive and complex than ever before. As a result, contemporary managers face significant challenges and must often rethink the way they manage their operations. Yesterday's management styles, practices, and processes may simply be ineffective given the very different challenges today's managers face.

The purpose of this chapter is to introduce students to the field of management. Management, as a discipline, has been greatly affected by the significant environmental and organizational changes that have occurred in recent years. We will explore the effect of these changes on the contemporary manager and learn how managers can achieve success in the dynamic business environment of the 21st century. More specifically, we will explore the role of managers as leaders within their organizations.

Because people sometimes find the terms *management* and *leadership* to be confusing, let's take a moment to explore these concepts. Management, as you will learn in one of the following sections, involves four primary functions: planning, organizing, leading, and controlling. Leading has always been an important component of management, and historically, the most effective managers have often been those with strong leadership skills. Today, however, managers *must* be effective leaders if they are to be successful. Why?

This question may be best answered by examining the work of John Kotter, one of the world's most respected management scholars. According to Kotter, while management is, in general, about coping with complexity, leadership is, more specifically, about coping with change.[1] Leaders must be able to foresee, assess, and effect change in their organizations and their work groups. Because the business environment is dynamic and rapidly changing, leadership skills have become increasingly important for managers at all levels of the organization. As a consequence, we believe that the managers of the future must develop their leadership skills more than ever before. Therefore, because we believe that managers today must also be leaders, we will use these terms interchangeably throughout the text.

MANAGEMENT AND WHY WE STUDY IT

Everything that we will address in the subsequent chapters of this book relates to managing organizations and the job of the manager. Consequently, it is important to develop a clear understanding of the concept of management at the outset. Let's look at a definition of management, the organizational context in which management occurs, and the process of management from a functional perspective.

MANAGEMENT DEFINED

Management has been defined in many ways. Mary Parker Follett, an early management scholar, offered what has come to be known as the classic definition when she described management as "the art of getting things done through people."[2] Although this definition captures the human dimension of management, a more comprehensive definition is needed.

For the purposes of this book, **management** is defined as the process of administering and coordinating resources effectively, efficiently, and in an effort to achieve the goals of the organization. **Effectiveness** is achieved when the organization pursues appropriate goals. **Efficiency** is achieved by using the fewest inputs (such as people and money) to generate a given output. In other words, effectiveness means "doing the right things" and efficiency means "doing things right."[3] The end result of effective and efficient management will be organizational success.

Today, managing for success requires a comprehensive set of managerial skills. While many of the traditional managerial skills that we will discuss throughout this book are still essential for effective management, the fast pace of change in today's business world has created a need for new kinds of managerial skills. For example, as mentioned earlier, managers today must possess strong leadership capabilities. Leading people during changing environmental and organizational conditions is a critical function for most managers today. Consider, also, the impact of information technology on the job of today's managers. Modern business technologies have created a new work environment in virtually all organizations, impacting nearly every aspect of the way organizations function. Technology affects how organizations formulate and implement strategy and how they structure their operations, motivate and reward their people, and measure and control their performance. Therefore, contemporary managers must understand how technology is affecting their industries and organizations, as well as know how to utilize technology to ensure the success of their organizations.

LEARNING OBJECTIVE 1

Describe the terms *management* and *leadership*, as well as the relationship between the two concepts.

Management
The process of administering and coordinating resources effectively and efficiently in an effort to achieve the goals of the organization.

Effectiveness
Pursuing the appropriate goals—doing the right things.

Efficiency
Using the fewest inputs to generate a given output—doing things right.

THE ORGANIZATIONAL CONTEXT OF MANAGEMENT

Management, as we have defined it, occurs within an organizational context. The management processes, tools, and techniques that we will examine and discuss in this book are those appropriate for managers who work in organizations. But what is an organization?

An **organization** is a group of individuals who work together toward common goals. Organizations can be for profit, such as the business organizations with which we are all familiar (for example, Microsoft, Pizza Hut, Wal-Mart), or not for profit, such as churches, fraternities, and public universities. Whether they are for profit or not for profit, organizations have one characteristic in common: they are made up of people. The efforts of these people must be coordinated if the organization is to accomplish its goals.

THE PROCESS OF MANAGEMENT

As mentioned previously, four major functions are associated with the process of management: (1) planning, (2) organizing, (3) leading, and (4) controlling. Figure 1.1 illustrates these functions and shows how they relate to the goals of the organization. These four functions form the foundation of this book, and each is examined in detail in a separate part of the text (planning in Part 2, organizing in Part 3, leading in Part 4, and controlling in Part 5). Also keep in mind that, given the importance of leading to the success of managers today, we will address issues of leadership throughout the text. A brief introduction of the four functions of management follows.

PLANNING   Managers at all levels of the organizational hierarchy must engage in **planning**. Planning involves setting goals and defining the actions necessary to achieve those goals. While top-level managers establish overall goals and strategy, managers throughout the hierarchy must develop operational plans for their work groups that contribute to the efforts of the organization as a whole. All managers must develop goals that are in alignment with and supportive of the overall strategy of the organization. In addition, they must develop a plan for administering and coordinating the resources for which they are responsible so that the goals of their work groups can be achieved.

ORGANIZING   The managerial function of **organizing** involves determining the tasks to be done, who will do them, and how those tasks will be managed and co-

Organization
A group of individuals who work together toward common goals.

Planning
Setting goals and defining the actions necessary to achieve those goals.

Organizing
The process of determining the tasks to be done, who will do them, and how those tasks will be managed and coordinated.

Figure 1.1 | The Process of Management

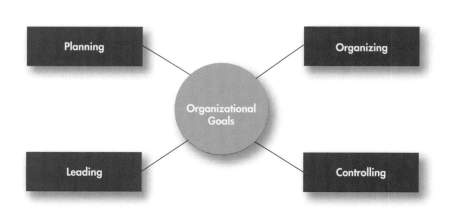

ordinated. Managers must organize the members of their work groups and organization so that information, resources, and tasks flow logically and efficiently through the organization. Issues of organizational culture and human resource management are also key to this function. Most important, the organization must be structured in light of its strategic and operational goals so that it can be responsive to changes in the business environment.

LEADING   Managers must also be capable of **leading** the members of their work groups toward the accomplishment of the organization's goals. To be effective leaders, managers must understand the dynamics of individual and group behavior, be able to motivate their employees, and be effective communicators. In today's business environment, effective leaders must also be visionary—capable of envisioning the future, sharing that vision, and empowering their employees to make the vision a reality. Only through effective leadership can the goals of the organization be achieved.

> **Leading**
> Motivating and directing the members of the organization so that they contribute to the achievement of the goals of the organization.

Later in the chapter, we will explore a model of leadership that we believe to be very appropriate for today's managers. That model, called the 3Cs of Leadership, suggests that effective managers/leaders must: (1) be highly **competent**, that is possess the necessary business acumen and skills to make good business decisions; (2) be of strong **character**, that is have integrity, behave ethically, and demonstrate qualities such as courage and persistence; and (3) have a commitment to their **community**, that is be concerned about people and issues beyond themselves. While this model of leadership acknowledges the need for leaders to possess the knowledge, skills, and tools to make good management decisions, it suggests that leaders be more than simply competent in business terms. It calls for leaders who understand the importance of character in leadership and who have a genuine concern for others. You will learn more about this model of leadership in a subsequent section of this chapter.

CONTROLLING   Managers must monitor the performance of the organization, as well as their progress in implementing strategic and operational plans. **Controlling** requires identifying deviations between planned and actual results. When an organization is not performing as planned, managers must take corrective action. Such actions may involve pursuing the original plan more aggressively or adjusting the plan to the existing situation. Control is an important function in the managerial process because it provides a method for ensuring that the organization is moving toward the achievement of its goals.

> **Controlling**
> Monitoring the performance of the organization, identifying deviations between planned and actual results, and taking corrective action when necessary.

With the four functions of management in mind, let's move on to examine the manager. **Managers** are the people who plan, organize, lead, and control the activities of the organization so that its goals can be achieved. Over the years, researchers have examined managers in detail to find out who they are and what they do. These studies can help us develop a general understanding of managers.

> **Managers**
> Organizational members who are responsible for planning, organizing, leading, and controlling the activities of the organization so that its goals can be achieved.

WHAT WE KNOW ABOUT MANAGERS

Regardless of your particular career interest, you may someday become a manager. Accountants become managers, salespeople become managers, and so do computer scientists and engineers. Some musicians are managers, as are some actors. In fact, even professors become managers. If you are successful in your chosen career and have administrative and leadership skills, you may be called upon to manage others.

Much of the research on management has focused on who managers are and what they do.[4] More specifically, many studies have examined the roles managers play, the skills they need, and how they spend their time.[5] Other studies have examined how roles, skills, and time allocation vary according to managerial level and scope of responsibility.[6] Let's examine some of the more enlightening research on the subject of managers.

MANAGERIAL ROLES

LEARNING OBJECTIVE 2
Define the concept of management within an organizational context and as a process.

According to a widely referenced study by Henry Mintzberg, managers serve three primary roles: interpersonal, informational, and decision making.[7] Figure 1.2 illustrates Mintzberg's theory of managerial roles, and the following discussion describes each role in greater detail.[8]

INTERPERSONAL ROLES   The first set of roles identified by Mintzberg are **interpersonal roles**. These roles, which arise directly from the manager's formal authority base, involve relationships with organizational members and other constituents. The three interpersonal roles played by the manager are those of figurehead, leader, and liaison.

Interpersonal roles
The manager's responsibility for managing relationships with organizational members and other constituents.

As the heads of organizational units, managers must perform certain duties that are primarily ceremonial in nature. For example, managers may have to appear at community functions, attend social events, or host luncheons for important customers. In doing so, managers fulfill their role as figureheads.

Because managers are largely responsible for the success or failure of their organizational units, they must also play the role of leaders within their work groups. In this capacity, managers work with and through their employees to ensure that the organization's goals are met.

Finally, managers must serve as organizational liaisons. They act as liaisons both in working with individuals and work groups within the organization and in developing favorable relationships with outside constituents. Managers must be politically sensitive to important organizational issues so that they can develop relationships and networks both within and beyond their organizations.

Figure 1.2 | Mintzberg's Managerial Roles

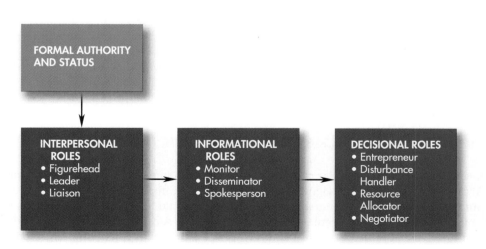

INFORMATIONAL ROLES The second set of managerial roles identified by Mintzberg are informational roles. In their **informational roles**, managers are responsible for ensuring that the people with whom they work have sufficient information to do their jobs effectively. By the very nature of managerial responsibilities, managers become the communication centers of their units and are a communication source for other work groups within the organization. People throughout the organization depend upon the management structure and the managers themselves to disseminate or provide access to the information they need to do their jobs.

One of the informational roles a manager must assume is that of monitor. As monitors, managers continually scan the internal and external environments of their organizations for useful information. Managers seek out information from their subordinates and liaison contacts and may receive unsolicited information from their networks of personal contacts. From this information, managers identify potential opportunities and threats for their work groups and organizations.

© AP/WIDE WORLD PHOTOS

Manager's often act as liasons between individuals and work groups as well as outside constituents.

Informational roles
The manager's responsibility for gathering and disseminating information to the stakeholders of the organization.

In their role as disseminators, managers share and distribute much of the information they receive as information monitors. As disseminators, managers pass on important information to the members of their work groups. Depending on the nature of the information, managers may also withhold information from work group members. Most important, managers must ensure that their employees have the information necessary to perform their duties efficiently and effectively.

The final informational role played by managers is that of spokesperson. Managers must often communicate information to individuals outside their units and their organizations. For example, directors and shareholders must be advised about the financial performance and strategic direction of the organization; consumer groups must be assured that the organization is fulfilling its social obligations; and government officials must be satisfied that the organization is abiding by the law.[9]

DECISIONAL ROLES Finally, managers play the role of decision maker. In their **decisional roles**, managers process information and reach conclusions. Information in and of itself is nearly meaningless if it is not used to make organizational decisions. Managers make those decisions. They commit their work groups to courses of action and allocate resources so that the groups' plans can be implemented.

Decisional roles
The manager's responsibility for processing information and reaching conclusions.

One of the decisional roles played by managers is that of entrepreneur. Recall that in the monitor role, managers scan the internal and external environments of the organization for changes that may present opportunities. As an entrepreneur, the manager initiates projects that capitalize on opportunities that have been identified. This may involve developing new products, services, or processes.

A second decisional role that managers play is that of disturbance handler. Regardless of how well an organization is managed, things do not always run smoothly. Managers must cope with conflict and resolve problems as they arise. This may involve dealing with an irate customer, negotiating with an uncooperative supplier, or intervening in a dispute between employees.

As a resource allocator, the manager determines which projects will receive organizational resources. Although we tend to think primarily in terms of financial or equipment resources, other types of important resources are allocated to projects as well. Consider, for example, the manager's time. When managers choose to spend their time on a particular project, they are allocating a resource. Information is also an important resource. By providing access to certain information, managers can influence the success of a project.

The final decisional role played by the manager is that of negotiator. Studies of managerial work at all levels have found that managers spend a good portion of their time negotiating. Managers may negotiate with employees, suppliers, customers, or other work groups. Regardless of the work group, the manager is responsible for all negotiations necessary to ensure that the group is making progress toward achieving the goals of the organization.

SCOPE AND LEVELS OF MANAGERS

LEARNING OBJECTIVE 3

Identify the roles managers play.

We have looked at the various roles that managers play within the organization. To this point, however, we have not distinguished among types of managers. Is it true that all managers are alike? No, it is not. Managers often differ with regard to both the scope of their responsibilities and their level within the vertical structure of the organization.

SCOPE OF RESPONSIBILITY   The nature of the manager's job will depend on the scope of his or her responsibilities. Some managers have functional responsibilities, whereas others have general management responsibilities.

Functional managers

Managers who are responsible for managing a work unit that is grouped based on the function served.

Functional managers are responsible for work groups that are segmented according to function. For example, a manager of an accounting department is a functional manager. So are the managers of a production department, a research and development department, and a marketing department. Work groups segmented by function tend to be relatively homogeneous. Members of the group often have similar backgrounds and training and perform similar tasks. Functional managers often have backgrounds similar to those of the people they manage. Their technical skills are usually quite strong, as they are typically promoted from within the ranks of their work groups. The greatest challenge for these managers lies in developing an understanding of the relationship between their work groups and the other work units within the organization. Equally important, functional managers must convey information back to their work groups and ensure that the members of their units understand their roles within the organization as a whole.

General managers

Managers who are responsible for managing several different departments that are responsible for different tasks.

In contrast to functional managers, **general managers** manage several different departments that are responsible for different tasks. For example, the manager of a supermarket is responsible for managing all the departments within the store. The produce manager, grocery manager, bakery manager, and floral manager all report to the general manager. Because general managers manage diverse departments, their technical skills may not be as strong as the skills of the people they manage. The manager of the supermarket, for example, may not know the difference between a chrysanthemum and a violet or have the faintest idea how croissants are made. Whatever general managers lack in technical skills, however, they make up for in communication skills. General managers must coordinate and integrate the work of diverse groups of people. They are responsible for ensuring that all the discrete parts of their organizations function together effectively so that the overall goals of the organization can be achieved.

LEARNING OBJECTIVE 4

Discuss the scope of responsibilities of functional and general managers.

LEVELS OF MANAGEMENT   Managers exist at various levels in the organizational hierarchy. A small organization may have only one layer of management, whereas a large organization may have several. Consider, for example, the number of levels of management in a single-unit family restaurant versus a large restaurant chain such as Chili's. While the small family restaurant may have only one level of management (the owner), Chili's has several layers, such as general store managers, area directors, and regional directors.

In general, relatively large organizations have three levels of managers: first-line managers, middle managers, and top-level managers. Figure 1.3 illustrates these managerial levels, as well as the "operatives," or the individuals who are not in the managerial ranks, but who actually deliver the product or service of the organization. The pyramid shape of the figure reflects the number of managers at each level. Most organizations have more first-line managers than middle managers, and more middle managers than top-level managers. As we will see later in this chapter, however, the trend of the 1990s was to reduce the number of employees in organizations in an effort to improve efficiency. The net effect of such downsizing was a significant reduction in the number of middle managers within many corporate structures.

The skills required of managers at different levels of the organizational hierarchy vary just as their job responsibilities vary. In other words, managers at different levels have different job responsibilities and therefore require different skills. The skills necessary for first-line managers to be effective are not the same as the skills needed by middle or top-level managers, just as the skills needed by middle managers differ from those needed by top-level managers.

While managers at each level must generally possess planning, organizing, leading, and controlling skills, certain job-specific skills are more important at one level than at another. Figure 1.4 illustrates three broad types of managerial skills that vary in importance according to the level of management. As we will discuss, technical skills are likely to be most important for first-line managers, human skills for middle managers, and conceptual skills for top-level managers. Nevertheless, it is important to note that managers at all levels use these skills to some degree, and human skills, in particular, are important at all three levels of the management hierarchy.[10]

Just as skills vary across levels of management, so do the activities in which managers are involved. A study of over 1,000 managers examined the extent to which managers at each level engaged in certain basic activities such as managing individual performance, instructing subordinates, planning and allocating resources, coordinating interdependent groups, managing group performance, monitoring

Figure 1.3 | Managerial Levels

Figure 1.4 | Skills Needed at Different Levels of Management

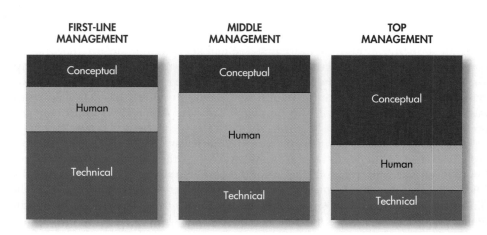

the business environment, and representing one's staff. The results of the study suggest that managers at different levels of the organizational hierarchy are involved in these activities to varying degrees.

As we examine the levels of management in more detail, we will look at the skills that are required of managers at each level, as well as the activities in which they are involved. By doing so, we can gain a better understanding of how managers' jobs vary according to their positions within the organization.

First-Line Managers: One-to-One with Subordinates   First-line managers supervise the individuals who are directly responsible for producing the organization's product or delivering its service. They carry titles such as production supervisor, line manager, section chief, or account manager. First-line managers are often promoted from the ranks based on their ability to deliver the product or service of the organization, as well as their ability to manage others who do the same. The primary objective of first-line managers is to ensure that the products or services of their organization are delivered to customers on a day-to-day basis.

Technical skills are most important for first-line managers. **Technical skills** enable managers to use their knowledge of the tools, techniques, and procedures that are specific to their particular field. These skills are usually teachable; they can be taught to other members of the work group where necessary. Surgeons, secretaries, computer programmers, and autoworkers use technical skills every day.

First-line managers are most involved in two of the basic activities listed earlier—managing individual performance and instructing subordinates. Managing individual performance involves motivating and disciplining subordinates, monitoring performance, providing feedback, and improving communications. Instructing subordinates includes training, coaching, and instructing employees on how to do their jobs. Both of these activities become less important as managers rise in the managerial ranks.

Middle Managers: Linking Groups   Middle managers supervise first-line managers or staff departments. They carry titles such as department head, product manager, or marketing manager. Middle managers may come from the ranks of first-line managers in a particular department or from other areas of the organization. These managers are typically selected because they have a strong understanding of the overall strategy of the organization and a commitment to ensuring that it is implemented well. The primary objective of most middle managers is to allocate re-

Technical skills
The ability to utilize tools, techniques, and procedures that are specific to a particular field.

sources effectively and manage the work group so that the overall goals of the organization can be achieved.

Middle managers must possess strong human skills, commonly known as interpersonal or people skills. **Human skills** involve the ability to work effectively with members of one's work group, as well as with other work groups within the organization. Within the work group, middle managers must manage group dynamics, encourage cooperation, and resolve conflicts. They must listen to the opinions of others and be tolerant of differing beliefs and viewpoints. Furthermore, they should create a work environment wherein members of the work group can express themselves freely, offer ideas, and participate in the planning activities of the unit. When interacting with outside work groups, middle managers serve as liaisons, communicating the needs and issues of their teams to other members of the organization and conveying information from other work groups back to their units. Fulfilling these responsibilities requires the constant use of human skills.[11] Managers who do not possess these skills are unlikely to be effective middle managers.

Consistent with their linking function, middle managers are most involved in three basic activities—planning and allocating resources, coordinating interdependent groups, and managing group performance. The importance of these three activities rises sharply as one moves from first-line to middle management, but interestingly, as we will see later, it declines slightly for the top-level management group.

Planning and allocating resources involves setting target dates for project completion, estimating resource requirements, determining where resources should be spent, interpreting the implications of overall organizational strategy for the activities of the work group, and developing evaluation criteria to measure the group's performance. Coordinating interdependent work groups includes reviewing the work and plans of the manager's unit, as well as those of other work groups, and setting priorities for activities. This may also require persuading others to provide the information or resources needed by the manager's group. Finally, in managing group performance, managers must define areas of responsibility for managerial personnel, monitor the performance of group members, and provide feedback on their performance.

Top-Level Managers: An Eye on the Outside   Top-level managers provide the strategic direction for the organization. They carry titles such as chief executive officer (CEO), president, chief operations officer, chief financial officer, chief information officer, and executive vice president.

Occasionally, top-level managers work their way up the organizational hierarchy from the first-line management level. More often, however, CEOs of large organizations come with management experience gained from other organizations. For example, ADC Telecommunications recently hired Richard Roscitt as CEO, who came from AT&T with over 28 years of experience. Turner Broadcasting System (TBS) announced that Jamie Kellner had been recruited from the WB Network to be its new CEO. Lucent Technologies hired Patricia Russo from Eastman Kodak to be CEO. Interestingly, she had only been with Eastman Kodak for nine months. Prior to this, she had held senior-level positions at Lucent.

Regardless of their background, top-level managers should be selected because they have a vision for the organization and the leadership skills necessary to guide the organization toward reaching that vision. Top-level managers must set the strategic direction of the organization in light of organizational resources, assets, and skills and the opportunities and threats that exist in the external environment. This was the primary challenge facing Herb Kelleher when he started Southwest Airlines. Southwest's long-term success has been largely a function of Kelleher's ability to communicate his unique and innovative vision for the company to employees and potential customers alike.

Human skills
The ability to work effectively with others.

Leaders In Action

Flying High at Southwest Airlines

Herb Kelleher, cofounder of Southwest Airlines, was never interested in flying in formation. His zany antics and offbeat attitude helped propel Southwest from a small regional carrier to the nation's fifth largest airline. Case in point—Herb Kelleher engaged in one of the most unusual conflict resolution tactics in business history. Both Southwest and Stevens Aviation, a South Carolina Charter company, used the slogan "Plane Smart" in their advertising. Rather than file legal action against Stevens, Kelleher suggested they settle the dispute with a CEO-versus-CEO arm wrestling match. Kelleher lost the match but as a result of the publicity and goodwill created by the event, he retained the rights to the slogan.

Herb Kelleher is one of the most celebrated and unconventional business leaders of the 20th century. His innovative policies and rock-bottom fares have created a company

where employees are appreciated and customers are valued. Southwest was conceived by Rollin King, a Texas businessman, and Kelleher on a cocktail napkin. Their venture began in 1971 with only four planes and 70 employees. When Southwest ran into financial trouble early on, it faced a dilemma that would forever set its course—either lay off some employees or sell one of its planes. Southwest opted to sell the plane and asked employees in return to cut gate turnaround time to 15 minutes. The employees obliged, and one of the friendliest management-labor relationships in the airline industry was born.

The corporate culture of Southwest Airlines has been studied and emulated by many of the major carriers. Flight attendants regularly sing the safety instructions, contests to see how many passengers can fit into a bathroom are not uncommon, and dressing up for Halloween is

practically a national holiday at Southwest.

Beneath the fun and laid-back attitude of Southwest lie simple yet powerful leadership principles and business policies. First and foremost, Kelleher focuses on employees. Employees feel appreciated, and they are dedicated to the airline's mission of providing safe, low-fare service while meeting the needs of their customers. In fact, Kelleher credits all of Southwest's success to its employees. His simple philosophy of hiring the best people, treating them with respect, and allowing them to make decisions while having fun along the way has propelled Southwest to great heights.

SOURCES: K.T. Beddingfield and M. Loftus, "American's Funniest Flyboy," *U.S. News and World Report*, December 21, 1998, 65; "Chief Executive of the Year: Herb Kelleher," *Chief Executive*, September 1999, 24–34.

Conceptual skills
The ability to analyze complex situations and respond effectively to the challenges faced by the organization.

Top-level managers need to have strong conceptual skills if they are to be effective. **Conceptual skills** enable managers to process a tremendous amount of information about both the internal and the external environment of the organization and to determine the implications of that information. Conceptual skills also enable top-level managers to look at their organization as a whole and understand how separate work groups and departments relate to and affect each other. Finally, strong conceptual skills enable top-level managers to develop a distinctive personality or culture for their organizations.

Research indicates that top-level managers are much more heavily involved in one particular management activity than are their first-line and middle manager counterparts: monitoring the business environment. Although this activity ranks lowest in importance for both first-line and middle managers, it is extremely important at the executive level. Monitoring the business environment involves scanning the external environment for sales, business, economic, and social trends that might affect the organization. In addition, it involves developing and maintaining relationships with outside constituents of the organization. It is important to note that while historical research suggests that this activity is important only at the top level of the organization, that may change in the future. Later in the chapter, we will examine some changes in the business arena that suggest that monitoring the environment will become an important activity at all levels of the organization.

It is interesting to note that one managerial activity was considered equally important by all three levels of managers: representing staff. From the lower to the upper ranks of management, managers felt that this was an important responsibility. Representing staff is consistent with the spokesperson role outlined by Mintzberg, for it involves communicating on behalf of one's work group with other work groups and helping subordinates to interact with other groups. In essence, this activity requires managers to be ambassadors for their units.

All managers must have technical, human, and conceptual skills if they are to be successful. Most managers are responsible, to some degree, for all of the managerial activities discussed here. However, as we have seen, and as is illustrated in Table 1.1, each level of management requires a slightly different mix of skills and involves a somewhat different set of activities. Furthermore, since managers will be involved in different activities at various levels of the organization, they need to develop new skills as they move up the corporate ladder.

We have examined a number of research studies that have focused on managers—who they are, what they do, and how they spend their time. At this point, it is important to examine some environmental and organizational trends that are influencing the job of the manager. Contemporary management theory recognizes the accelerating rate of change in today's business environment and the significant impact of such change on the manager's job. Accordingly, we turn our attention to a review of the changes that are occurring and their effect on the job of the manager of today and tomorrow.

MANAGING IN THE 21ST CENTURY

Virtually everyone would agree that we live in a dynamic and rapidly changing world. While some might argue that change is nothing new, others would suggest that we are now experiencing hyperchange. **Hyperchange** involves changes that come more quickly; are more dramatic, complex, and unpredictable; and have a more significant impact on the way organizations are managed than did the changes of the past.[12] Most important, the success both of an organization and of individual managers is often dependent upon their ability to lead others within an environment of hyperchange.

Today we hear a great deal about the "new economy." While the term is used frequently, many people still lack a clear understanding of what the new economy is really all about. In order to understand the new economy better, let's start with what it is not. It is not about a single sector of our economy, such as the telecom industry, or a specific geographic region, like Silicon Valley. It is not just about dotcoms, venture capitalists, IPOs, and irrational exuberance in the stock market. While the get-big-fast, get-rich-quick schemes seemed to dominate the new economy landscape at the outset, more rational approaches to organizational success have prevailed.

So what is the new economy all about? According to *Fast Company* magazine, the new economy is about three things:[13]

Hyperchange
A condition of rapid, dramatic, complex, and unpredictable changes that has a significant effect on the ways in which organizations are managed.

Table 1.1 | Technical, Human, and Conceptual Skills/Managerial Activities

First-line	Technical	Managing individual performance Instructing subordinates Representing staff
Middle	Human	Planning and allocating resources Coordinating interdependent groups Managing group performance Representing staff
Top/executive	Conceptual	Monitoring the business environment Representing staff

1. *The expansion of individual opportunity.* One person with one great idea can make a difference in the new economy. That person may be an evangelist for change within a large corporate structure, the leader of a rapidly growing start-up, or the sole creator of a Web site that serves thousands of people. The new economy recognizes and supports the individual contributor in a way that the old economy system simply did not.

2. *The disruptive energy that comes from ceaseless innovation.* While old economy companies often took an incremental approach to effecting change in their products, services, and processes, new economy companies look for more innovative approaches to change. The era of stable, predictable competition is over; new economy companies must constantly seek new ideas, practices, and opportunities that can radically improve the ways in which they operate.

3. *The transformative power of information and communication technologies.* Advances in networked digital technologies have provided, and will continue to provide, an enabling platform for improving the ways work can be structured, companies can be operated, and the future can be created. Never before have organizations had the capability of altering every aspect of their operations with a single, integrated technology solution.

Individual opportunity. Disruptive innovation. Information and communication technologies. The new economy is a product of the convergence of these forces—forces that challenge conventional wisdom and test traditional ways of managing organizations. The new economy has unleashed entirely new methods of crafting strategy, launching products, serving customers, and organizing to support creativity and productivity. The managers of today and tomorrow must be willing to harness the forces that comprise the new economy and embrace the changes that undoubtedly lie ahead.

So the question becomes, "What about all the companies that were part of the old economy?" Many old economy companies have responded extremely well to the challenges of the new economy.[14] Consider, for example, Wal-Mart's pioneering efforts to transform how products are acquired and distributed through retail outlets. Their success has forced other retailers to look for more innovative approaches to processes and technology. Charles Schwab, the discount investment brokerage that pioneered online retail security trading, provides another good example of an old economy company that flourished in the new economy environment. By 1999, 40 percent of retail securities were traded online, forcing more conventional retail brokers to rethink their business models as well. Both of these companies have achieved great success by proactively addressing changing market conditions that were inherent in the new economy business environment.

As technology has become more prevalent, it has also become more mobile. Today, we can access information in a variety of ways, no matter where we are.

© JONNIE MILES/GETTYIMAGES/PHOTODISC

Change in the business world will continue at a rapid rate.[15] While the 1980s were called the "White Knuckle Decade" and the 1990s were characterized by dramatic changes across virtually all industries, most analysts believe that the changes experienced in those periods will pale in comparison to what will happen in the future. Competition is intense and is coming from sources unimaginable 20 years ago. Advances in transportation, communication, and information technology have made it possible to do business across the globe with a level of efficiency that has redefined the competitive structure of many industries. Furthermore, companies cannot win with just the lowest price or the highest quality anymore—they have to have both. We are living in a radically different world that calls for radically different methods of management. Achieving organizational success will be extremely challenging in the business environment of the future.

Tomorrow's managers must be prepared to cope with change if they are to be effective. Some changes are the result of internal forces such as advances in technology or diversity management initiatives. In the case of Southwest and the airline industry, some changes are unforeseen and come from external forces in the organization's environment. Let's take a look at some of the changes, both environmental and organizational, that will influence the job of the manager and how organizations will function in the future.

ENVIRONMENTAL TRENDS

Many changes have affected and will continue to affect the modern business environment.[16] The next paragraphs describe four of the most significant developments. These four deserve special emphasis because of the far-reaching and profound effect they will have on managers and organizations. Because each of these trends will be addressed in greater detail throughout the book, here we will only briefly consider how they will affect the ways in which organizations are managed.

LEARNING OBJECTIVE 5

Describe the three levels of managers in terms of the skills they need and the activities in which they are involved.

ADVANCES IN INFORMATION TECHNOLOGY   As discussed previously, one of the most significant trends affecting organizations today is the increasing availability of sophisticated information technology.[17] In the 1960s, individual organizations maintained big, cumbersome mainframe computers to support specific business functions. In the 1980s, the development of the personal computer brought the power of information technology to the individual user. Today, the Internet provides access to an expansive network of information that goes far beyond the individual organization or individual user. Rather, it provides connectivity between users and organizations across the globe and, in doing so, has transformed the ways in which firms are organized and operated.[18]

Information technology has become an integral part of both our personal and professional lives. As Joel Birnbaum, senior vice president of research and development at Hewlett-Packard, stated:

> Information technology is becoming pervasive in our society, and that means it will be more noticeable by its absence than its presence. Electricity is an example of a pervasive technology. One assumes its availability (in the developed world), and only its absence is notable. Although information technology is commonplace today, it is not yet integrated into our environment the way telephones, televisions, and automobiles are. Alan Kay, the great visionary who dreamed of a portable, hand-held computer 20 years ago while he was at Xerox, once said that technology is only technology for people who were born before it was invented. From that viewpoint, it's too late for us to become the great application pioneers of the information highway. However, just as our children don't think of TVs as technology, children born today are not going to think of computers as technology.[19]

Indeed, the growth rate for personal computers grew at a robust 52 percent per year from 1990 to 2000, with 58 percent of all U.S. homes having at least one computer by the year 2000.[20] Similarly, in 1990, U.S. companies were spending 16 percent of their capital budgets on information technology; by the year 2000, information technology accounted for 59 percent of all capital spending.[21] Although the recession of 2001 reduced capital expenditures on information technology, the general consensus has been that information technology will continue to be a critical and growing sector of the U.S. economy.[22] From corporations to not-for-profits, to government and education,[23] organizations are embracing the power of information technology and using it to improve the efficiency and effectiveness of what they do. Increasingly, information technology is affecting virtually all aspects of our lives as both workers and consumers.

Today, three central themes of change in the area of information technology are affecting business:

1. *The Internet and other forms of globally connected networks.* This infrastructure provides the ability to share information on a worldwide basis. It creates the need to think beyond our individual jobs or organizations and toward the capabilities of operating on a global basis. As will be discussed in the next section, globally connected networks have enabled the globalization of countless organizations within numerous industries.

2. *Electronic commerce.* Increasingly, the complete operating process, from manufacturing to distribution to human resource management, will be automated using electronic data interchange (EDI) systems. This technology will enable managers to reshape their business processes to improve response time and efficiency and reduce costs both within and beyond their organizations. General Electric, for example, has used the Internet and its e-business capabilities to add $1.6 billion to its bottom line. The benefits to the company came from cost savings associated with purchasing goods through an online auction and from improved operational efficiencies made possible by electronic commerce.[24]

3. *Mobile computing.* Individuals can now have access to information technology irrespective of their physical location. The increasing availability of portable computing devices will enable individuals to access information and communicate with others from remote sites across the globe.[25] This will have a tremendous impact on both where and how people do their work. Pepsi Cola, for example has transformed its order entry and fulfillment processes through the use of a wireless mobile computing system.

All of these trends are reshaping traditional thinking about the ways in which business is conducted. For example, in 1999, virtually every major business publication (e.g., *Business Week, Fortune, Forbes*) ran cover stories on the impact of e-commerce on the world of business. The transition to electronic forms of commerce has caused companies to rethink, among other things, how they structure their organizations, sell their products, and provide customer service. Table 1.2 provides an illustration of seven different companies that are using e-commerce to improve their effectiveness and efficiency. These companies demonstrate the potential impact of e-commerce on various aspects of an organization's operations. Not only will you find some of the hot new e-businesses that have made the headlines in recent years, like Yahoo! and Amazon.com, but you will also find traditional bricks-and-mortar manufacturing companies like Ford Motor and Pitney Bowes. Clearly, the Internet provides connectivity that can benefit virtually every kind of organization.[26]

One could hardly discuss information technology and the Internet without acknowledging the "dot-com debacle" of the year 2000.[27] In the late 1990s, with e-commerce being touted as the next industrial revolution, hundreds of entrepreneurial organizations emerged, poised to capitalize on the opportunities presented by the connectivity of the Internet. The exuberance over the potential of e-commerce and its transforming effect on the world of business led to inflated valuations for countless dot-com companies. As it became apparent that many of these overvalued dot-coms were created based on flawed business models and unrealistic assumptions about the marketplace, the technology sector of the economy headed into a serious decline. The "tech wreck," as it eventually came to be known, contributed greatly to the economic recession of 2001.

Despite the fact that the dot-com bubble has burst, most experts agree that advances in information technology will continue to shape the business environment of the future. An understanding of emerging trends in today's technological environment is critical to making informed business decisions and developing business

Table 1.2 | Companies That Are Capitalizing on the Web

Dell Computer **(http://www.dell.com)**	Utilizes the Web to provide excellent product support to its corporate customers.
Ford Motor Company **(http://www.ford.com)**	Uses a sophisticated intranet (internal to the company) to communicate a massive amount of information to its more than 100,000 employees.
Pitney Bowes **(http://www.pitneybowes.com)**	Uses the Internet to link its vendors, providing for just-in-time deliveries of inventory, streamlining its supply chain, and improving its efficiency dramatically.
Sun Microsystems **(http://www.sun.com)**	Developed a sophisticated online recruiting program that enables the company to hire 6,000 people annually in an intensely competitive employment market.
Yahoo! **(http://www.yahoo.com)**	Provides creative services to entice users to register with the portal and keep coming back time and time again.
NextCard **(http://nextcard-visa-credit-card.com)**	Utilizes the Web for both direct marketing of its credit card and to advertise the kinds of products its credit card customers are most likely to buy.
Cisco Systems **(http://www.cisco.com)**	Uses the Web to coordinate its highly sophisticated financial management systems.

SOURCE: E. Brown, "9 Ways to Win on the Web," *Fortune*, 139, 10, May 24, 1999, Time Inc. All rights reserved.

strategy. As Paul Turner, executive director of the PricewaterhouseCoopers World Technology Centre, observed, "For anyone intending to stay on the leading edge there are two important questions: What are the new key technologies? What are the current trends that should direct my planning for the future of my business?" Aligning the information technology infrastructure of a company with its business strategy has become a key challenge for contemporary organizations, and today's managers must be prepared to respond to that challenge if they are to achieve long-term organizational success.[28] Therefore, we will address issues of technology throughout the book.

GLOBALIZATION OF THE MARKETPLACE One need only glance at the trends in international trade and foreign direct investment to recognize that the global marketplace continues to grow in size and economic importance. Most organizations today are involved, in some way, in the international business environment. Consider Wal-Mart, for example. With over 3,200 stores in the United States, one might think that they had little room to expand. But with 1,100 units operating outside the United States and aggressive plans to double their revenue in five years, we can readily see the impact of their global strategy on organizational performance. And while globalization used to be associated only with large, mature organizations such as Wal-Mart, General Motors, and Procter & Gamble, with the availability of the Internet and the trend toward e-commerce, even the smallest business can reach a global marketplace with relative ease.[29]

Organizations that are involved in the international business arena often face unique managerial challenges. The global business environment is more complex than the domestic environment, and organizations operating in the international marketplace face a much broader set of environmental forces. Capitalizing on today's global opportunities demands global leadership skills that were not required of managers in years gone by.[30] For example, decisions about where to locate a plant to minimize labor and transportation costs, how to coordinate production schedules across national borders, and how to disseminate new technology on a global basis are far more common today than in the past. Furthermore, many or-

At The Forefront

One Sweet World: Wal-Mart's Global Strategy for Super Growth

Wal-Mart is the world's leading retailer with annual company revenue approaching $200 billion. Most companies would be content with this level of phenomenal success and develop a strategy for maintaining their market, but not Wal-Mart. Wal-Mart plans to double its revenue to $400 billion over the next five years.

Wal-Mart offers everyday low prices to its customers and as it looks to the future, its management team has developed an aggressive plan for growth based on dramatically increasing its global presence. In addition to the 3,200 stores in the United States, Wal-Mart operates over 1,200 stores in nine countries. Wal-Mart plans to expand into several more countries, including Germany, China, Korea, Brazil, and Argentina. Wal-Mart's corporate culture of rigid cost control and employee responsibility has resulted in record-setting results, and this formula has translated very well to markets outside the United States.

In addition to Wal-Mart's strong corporate culture, long-term strategy has been aligned with the technology available to facilitate its continued growth. Advances in technology, such as barcode scanning and inventory management, have been a cornerstone in Wal-Mart's strategy development. A dedicated international management team recognizes that while there may be no such thing as a global consumer, products and merchandise can be adapted to regional or national tastes and needs. It seems that low prices and value translate well, regardless of the culture.

If the prospect of a company that already has annual revenues in the $200 billion range doubling its revenue sounds overly optimistic, consider this—

In 1996 with annual revenue at just under $100 billion, Wal-Mart's management team announced an almost unbelievable

goal. They revealed a strategic initiative to double Wal-Mart's annual revenue to $200 billion in five years. Five years later, Wal-Mart has done the unthinkable and doubled in size. These staggering numbers are hard to grasp because they reflect so much more than any other company has accomplished before. Thanks to a well-defined strategy, aggressive measures to contain costs, and a global perspective, Wal-Mart seems positioned to repeat history. Its past track record and current momentum go a long way in the retail world, and today, it seems, the world is Wal-Mart's oyster.

SOURCES: F. Crawford, "Business Without Borders," *Chain Store Age*, December 2001, 86–96; M. Troy, "The Super Growth Leaders: Wal-Mart: Global Dominance Puts Half Trillion in Sight," *DSN Retailing Today*, December 2001, 17–20.

ganizations are finding that they must form partnerships with other firms to maintain their competitiveness worldwide. The recognition of the need to "cooperate to compete" has led to many global partnerships that require very special international management skills.[31] Ethical challenges may exist as organizations across the globe attempt to understand the cultures and expectations of other nations.[32]

Not only has the evolution of the world marketplace forced many organizations to radically change the way they operate, but it will continue to influence the way industries will be structured and the way organizations will function for many years to come. Cross-national managers who can respond to the globalization of the marketplace will be increasingly in demand.[33] Consequently, in order to help students understand the managerial challenges associated with international business, we have focused on issues of global management throughout this book.

INCREASING PREDOMINANCE OF ENTREPRENEURIAL FIRMS

Despite the importance of large organizations to the U.S. economy, few would dispute the tremendous contribution of entrepreneurs and entrepreneurial firms. Although estimates vary widely, entrepreneurship is believed to be responsible for the creation of over 50 percent of all new jobs in the United States. In fact, millions of new jobs are created annually from business start-ups alone.

The spirit of the entrepreneur has flourished in the mainstream of American management philosophy throughout the past century. From oil baron John D. Rockefeller to modern-day entrepreneur Bill Gates (Microsoft), entrepreneurial success has come to those who have the ability to recognize new opportunities that arise out of changing business conditions and develop strategies for capitalizing on those opportunities. Entrepreneurs and entrepreneurial companies will continue to influence the business environment in the years ahead. Consider the following:

- Entrepreneurial firms are responsible for a disproportionate number of new products, services, and processes. Those new products, services, and processes are coming faster than ever before. For example, gunpowder took 200 years to move from the laboratory to artillery. Today, the equivalent innovation would travel the same path in only a few months.

- Entrepreneurial activities place pressure on large, bureaucratic firms to be more innovative and proactive. In fact, some would suggest that entrepreneurship represented a key solution to problems in product and service quality, poor productivity, and the declining competitiveness of American industry during the 1980s.

- Entrepreneurship provides opportunities for minorities and others who may face barriers in traditional corporate environments.[34] For example, both immigrants and women have benefited greatly from entrepreneurial activities. Increasingly, young people are also choosing a path of entrepreneurship.[35] In fact, more and more colleges and universities are now offering curricula in entrepreneurship and even hosting competitions to identify the highest-potential entrepreneurial ideas.[36] And interestingly, some predict that we will see a "gray wave" of entrepreneurs. With the first of 76 million baby boomers turning 55 in 2001, many have or will take early retirement packages and start their own businesses. This is the healthiest and best-educated generation in history, and these individuals have years of experience and an extensive network of business contacts that will help them to develop new businesses.[37] Clearly, entrepreneurship provides opportunities for a wide variety of individuals.

The trends just discussed—advances in information technologies and globalization of markets—have significant implications for potential entrepreneurs. The Internet makes possible the access to geographic markets that would have previously been out of reach for most small organizations. Suddenly, entrepreneurs have the world at their fingertips, and they are developing products and services that are attractive to global consumers. Electronic commerce has also made it possible to compete in industries that once required significant capital investments. Consider the health care industry for example. The growth in the number of Internet-focused health care organizations has been explosive in recent years as entrepreneurs seek out opportunities to use the World Wide Web to provide connectivity services within the $1 trillion health care industry.[38] Table 1.3 describes three entrepreneurial health care-related businesses that are capitalizing on the Internet.

The entrepreneurial phenomenon in the United States is also being duplicated across the globe. From South America to Europe to Asia, there is worldwide recognition of the power of entrepreneurship to stimulate and strengthen economies. Kyoto, Japan, for example, is awash in a new spirit of entrepreneurship as dozens of high-tech start-ups have emerged in recent years. According to some, Kyoto is more aggressive and entrepreneurial than any other city in the country. While it does not rival Silicon Valley quite yet, if it keeps up the stellar performance, Kyoto may well redefine excellence for all of Japan and Asia.[39]

Entrepreneurs and entrepreneurially spirited companies will continue to influence the world of business in significant ways. In fact, innovation, proactiveness, and flexibility have become prerequisites for success in most industries. Managers must be prepared to respond quickly to changing customer demands and to be proactive with regard to product, service, or process innovation. For that reason, we have highlighted entrepreneurial management practices throughout this book.

THE GROWING IMPORTANCE OF INTELLECTUAL CAPITAL For most of the 20th century, the critical factors of production were considered to be land, labor, and raw materials. The charge to managers was to use these production factors to create products that were more valuable than the sum of their parts. Today, however, the key factors of production have changed: intellectual capital has become the critical resource for the 21st-century organization.

Table 1.3 | Internet Health Care Companies

drkoop.com Inc. (**http://www.drkoop.com**)
Founded by former U.S. Surgeon General C. Everett Koop, M.D., the company helps integrated delivery systems build online information and provider referral services for patients and consumers. Also offers an Internet-based patient record for consumers.

WebMD (**http://www.my.webmd.com**)
Provides credible health-related information, a supportive community, and educational services. Also provides a method for individuals to maintain health care records online.

Physicians' Online Inc. (**http://www.po.com**)
Operates a private online network for physicians featuring medical databases, news, private e-mail accounts, continuing medical education, Internet access, and other services.

Intellectual capital
The sum and synergy of an organization's knowledge, experience, relationships, processes, discoveries, innovations, market presence, and community influence.

Structural capital
The accumulated knowledge and know-how of the organization represented by its patents, trademarks and copyrights, proprietary databases, and systems.

Customer capital
The value of established relationships with customers and suppliers.

Human capital
The cumulative skills and knowledge of the organization.

In this new millennium, fewer and fewer people will do physical work and more and more people will do knowledge-based work. In fact, most employees in the United States will work in knowledge companies, and the value of their knowledge, as both an input and output, will determine their value to the organization.[40] They will be rewarded not for what they achieve by muscle, but for how they use their know-how to enhance the worth of the organization.

What is intellectual capital? In general, **intellectual capital** encompasses the sum and synergy of an organization's knowledge, experience, relationships, processes, discoveries, innovations, market presence, and community influence.[41] Thomas Stewart, the well-known popularist of the notion of knowledge management and the author of *Intellectual Capital: The Wealth of New Organizations*,[42] provides a classification for knowledge assets. The three major categories of intellectual capital are:

- **Structural capital:** The accumulated knowledge and know-how of the organization represented by its patents, trademarks and copyrights, proprietary databases, and systems.
- **Customer capital:** The value of established relationships with customers and suppliers.
- **Human capital:** The cumulative skills and knowledge of the organization.

Stewart and others contend that contemporary organizations must develop, measure, and manage these intellectual assets if they are to be successful. There are many examples of organizations that do this well, as well as those that don't. For example, Wal-Mart, Microsoft, and Toyota fall into the victors' category, whereas Sears, IBM, and General Motors have been less successful in this area. Some companies are developing proactive programs for managing their intellectual capital. Hewlett-Packard has instituted a Knowledge Management Initiative designed to capture, store, and leverage the decentralized knowledge of the company's consultants to enhance the performance of the organization as a whole.[43] Similarly, Toshiba utilizes an innovative knowledge management system called "Knowledge Works" to achieve a competitive advantage in some of its factories.[44] Even small companies can leverage their intellectual capital if they put their mind to it. For example, Virtual Loom, a small textile design company, used technology to capture the design knowledge of its entrepreneur and founder. The company now makes that knowledge more accessible to its customers.[45]

Southwest Airlines is an excellent example of how intellectual capital makes an important difference in the success of the organization. Employees at Southwest are dedicated to the company's mission of providing safe, low-cost travel to their customers. The fun and sometimes zany way they provide service to their customers is part of the intellectual capital element that makes Southwest unique. The synergy created by Southwest's knowledge and innovative spirit provides a unique competitive advantage over other airlines.

Despite its obvious importance to organizations, intellectual capital isn't easily accounted for on a company's financial statements. In fact, some experts estimate that in knowledge-intensive companies, over half their organizational assets are not included on the balance sheet.[46] Consider Microsoft, a company that is often used to illustrate this point. In 2002, Microsoft's physical assets were about $10 billion, but its total market value was $341.6 billion. Intellectual capital represents the gap between the company's physical asset value and its value as assessed by investors. Leif Edvinsson, corporate director of intellectual capital for Skandia, Sweden's biggest financial services company, made history when he devised a model for accounting for the company's intellectual capital in financial reports. While some may quibble about the details of Edvinsson's model, his actions have attracted some much-needed attention to the importance of valuing the intellectual capital assets of an organization.[47]

Knowledge and intellectual capital have become a critical strategic resource for contemporary organizations. Managing this resource effectively will require special management skills. Therefore, we will address these issues throughout the book.

The four environmental trends outlined here have had a significant impact on today's business environment and will continue to influence the business environment of the future. Related to these environmental changes are a number of fundamental changes that are occurring within organizations. The nature of the workplace is changing dramatically, and these changes will also have significant implications for the manager of the future.

ORGANIZATIONAL CHANGES

Contemporary organizations are experiencing a number of important changes that revolve around achieving excellence.[48] The inflexible, authoritarian rulers of the past have been replaced by more participatory, visionary leaders. Similarly, you'll find fewer middle managers among the organizational hierarchies of today. Rather, you'll find collaborative work teams with a focus on bottom-line results. The relative homogeneity that once characterized the management teams of most U.S. organizations has vanished as the U.S. workforce has become more heterogeneous and culturally diverse. Finally, the rigid, hierarchial corporate structures that were predominant in American corporations over the last several decades are being abandoned for streamlined, flexible structures that permit greater adaptability to change. While these topics will be discussed in detail elsewhere in the book, let's examine each briefly here.

LEARNING OBJECTIVE 6
Discuss the underlying forces of the new economy.

A NEW MODEL OF LEADERSHIP   Over the last several decades, most public organizations have grown significantly. With that growth came a larger and more fragmented shareholder base. As the relative power of individual shareholders began to decline, the model for chief executive officers and other organizational leaders became that of "professional managers"—in theory accountable to everyone, but in actuality accountable to no one. Such managers built self-sufficient hierarchies with explicit chains of command. The command-control military model of management was often characteristic of these World War II-generation managers.[49] But today things have changed dramatically.

Leaders in today's business environment cannot be afraid of change; they have to love it and be eager to influence its course. They often have to shake things up and make what some might see as radical decisions to ensure the competitive strength of their organizations. They must be willing to abandon rigid hierarchies in favor of flatter, more flexible, participatory designs; encourage dialogue and tolerate dissenting opinions and views; and instill a team-oriented culture that makes quality the first priority. And perhaps most important, today's leaders must be able to build management teams that know how to execute their organizations' strategies. Execution translates to decisiveness, follow-through, and delivering on commitments.[50]

In short, the 21st-century leader must have a broad-based perspective in leading their work groups and organizations. The 3Cs leadership model, as illustrated in Figure 1.5, provides a framework that is applicable to leaders at all levels of the 21st-century organization.[51] This leadership model suggests that in order to be effective as a leader, one must be competent, be of strong character, and have a commitment to their communities. More specifically, *competence* refers to having the requisite business acumen and skills to be effective as a leader. In other words, today's leaders must know how to analyze financial statements, develop marketing plans, and be able to think strategically. They must also understand the economic environment, accounting methods, and production systems. In addition to having a strong knowledge of the functions of business, they must be competent in their interpersonal capabilities. That is, they must have the ability to manage individuals, teams, and relationships to accomplish organizational goals.

Followers demand competence from their leaders, and business schools are designed to develop competence in their graduates. Yet, while competence is a necessary condition for effective leadership, competence is, in and of itself, insufficient. Leaders must possess other important attributes as well.

Character is the second important "C" in the 3Cs leadership model. Character refers to the leadership values and behaviors that elicit trust, commitment, and followership. In its simplest form, character is about integrity, honesty, truthfulness, ethics, and reliability. But character is also about attributes such as courage, discipline, and persistence. Being a successful leader demands the courage to assume risks and take bold actions that will improve the performance of the team and the organization. It requires having the discipline and persistence to move forward, making progress despite any barriers and impediments that may exist within and beyond the organization. The importance of strong character to effective leadership cannot be overstated. Leaders who demonstrate strong character traits will be able to build loyal, reliable, and stable teams that can contribute to the success of their organizations.

The business world is replete with examples of leaders who have behaved with strong character and those who have not. Consider, for instance, the classic Tylenol product tampering case of the early 1980s. When eight Chicago residents died as a result of taking cyanide-laced Tylenol capsules purchased in local stores, the leaders of Johnson & Johnson, the manufacturer of Tylenol, acted quickly to address the situation. In an effort to protect consumers, the company immediately recalled and destroyed all Tylenol products worldwide—despite evidence that would suggest the poisoning incident was restricted to the Chicago area. In addition, and at significant costs to the company, Johnson & Johnson immediately added seals to all products in

Figure 1.5 | 3Cs Leadership Model

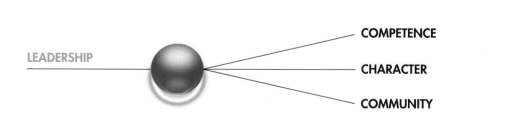

LEADERSHIP

COMPETENCE

CHARACTER

COMMUNITY

an effort to prevent future product tampering. Because of the strong character demonstrated by leadership team at Johnson & Johnson, the public's trust in the company and their products was restored. Contrast the actions of the Johnson & Johnson leadership team with the behaviors of the leaders of Enron. Did the top management of Enron demonstrate strong character in their business decisions and actions? Will the management of Enron ever regain the trust of the American public?

Community, the third "C" in the 3Cs leadership model, refers to the need to be aware of things beyond oneself and even beyond one's team and organization. Good leaders have a commitment to supporting the communities around them. This requires that they understand what it takes to have healthy and vibrant communities, both within and beyond their organizations, and they are willing to embrace their responsibility for contributing to those communities. When leaders demonstrate a sincere concern for others, it instills followership in those around them and builds strong communities in which people work and live.

A leader's responsibility to the community beyond his or her organization is reflected in the concept of corporate citizenship. Corporate citizenship, which is discussed in Chapter 3, requires that organizations be good citizens within their communities. Hugh McColl, the recently retired CEO of Bank of America, provides an excellent example of a leader who understands the importance of building communities and being a good corporate citizen. Not only did he build a strong and supportive community within the bank by pursuing aggressive diversity initiatives, taking proactive steps to provide a family-friendly environment for his employees, and providing ample professional development opportunities for all staff members, he also worked hard to build the communities in which his banks were located. From investments in education, human social services, and the arts, Hugh McColl demonstrated a sincere concern for the men, women, and children who lived and worked in the communities he served. As a result, McColl is often acknowledged as one of America's most prominent and successful leaders.

The 3Cs model of leadership is applicable to managers at all levels of the organization. As you continue this course and your education, you should explore opportunities to develop your competence, to strengthen your character, and to contribute to your community. Those experiences will help to make you a better leader in the years to come.

Effective leadership will be critical for organizations that must operate in the highly volatile business environment of the future. Therefore, we will focus on this aspect of management throughout the book.

FROM HIERARCHY TO COLLABORATIVE WORK RELATIONSHIPS

In an effort to be more responsive to the challenges of the 21st century, many organizations have moved away from traditional hierarchical organizational structures. During the 1990s, we saw the de-layering of management, the "right-sizing" of the corporate workforce, and the rapid disappearance of the middle manager who brought little added value to the company. Simultaneously, we have seen new forms of collaborative work relationships emerge.

Some collaborative relationships take the form of cross-functional teams—that is, teams comprised of individuals from different functional areas of the organization. For example, a product development team may be cross-functional in that it is comprised of a product engineer, marketing professional, financial analyst, and operations specialist. These individual specialists work through a comprehensive product development process that encompasses tasks from product design to production to distribution.

At Roche, a leading pharmaceutical company, cross-functional teams have revolutionized the company's approach to developing new medicines. One of those teams, for example, was charged with finding new cancer cures by using emerging knowledge about genetics. A cross-functional team was formed comprised of researchers from immunology to statistics, who were born in countries as far apart as Germany and China. Despite their diversity, these team members had a common purpose—to identify new cancer drugs using genetic tools. While the collaboration was not without its challenges, the scientists gradually learned to leverage their relative strengths. In the end, the research team isolated new drug targets that would have been overlooked by specialists working alone. In this case, the power of the cross-functional team led to important new medical discoveries that may save lives.

Self-managed teams (SMTs)
Groups of employees who design their jobs and work responsibilities to achieve the self-determined goals and objectives of the team.

Another form of collaborative work relationships that is common in organizations today is the self-managed team.[52] **Self-managed teams** (SMTs) are groups of employees who work together toward the development of strategy for their work unit and the achievement of established goals and objectives, without being directed by a formal supervisor.[53] While an SMT might be cross-functional in nature, its distinguishing feature is that the team is self-directed. Many companies today use SMTs to reduce middle-management costs and foster teamwork throughout the organization. In most cases, the team-oriented culture that results leads to better organizational performance.[54] From Rolls Royce to 3M to Intel, organizations have found self-managed teams to be an effective empowerment strategy that improves productivity, quality, and employee commitment.[55]

The trend toward globalization has created new complexities for international companies that are committed to collaborative approaches to work design.[56] Managing teams across national borders involves many challenges, including time and space logistics, language barriers, and cultural differences, that impede communication. Despite these challenges, many international organizations understand that their long-term success depends on their ability to create and manage high-performance global teams.[57] Companies such as ExxonMobil, Compaq, Motorola, and Ford Motor Company have recognized the need for global teams and have taken proactive steps to ensure that critical work teams include representation from all over the world.

The availability of more sophisticated information technology has enhanced communication among collaborative work groups, whether they are based in the same location or scattered across the globe.[58] "Virtual teams," or teams that are connected by technology, can overcome the challenges of time, space, and organizational or national boundaries. These networked teams can accomplish their common purpose without having to meet face-to-face for every decision. For example, when NCR was spun off by AT&T, the company used a virtual team to implement a turnaround strategy. Despite the fact that team members were located on different continents, they worked together on a daily basis. Together, they developed NCR's next-generation computer system in just 11 months, proving that dispersed, global teams can be highly effective.[59]

Self-managed teams work together to develop a strategy for their work unit without being directed by a formal supervisor. Team-oriented culture leads to better organizational performance.

In the future, the middle-management function will be performed by managers who are prepared to be team leaders for collaborative work groups. Their primary responsibility will be to empower others to do whatever is needed to achieve the goals of the team. This new breed of middle manager may carry the title of coach, facilitator, sponsor, or team leader rather than manager.

Although the implementation of a collaborative work environment has not been problem-free for all organizations,[60] today's competitive business arena encourages many organizations to consider its use. Consequently, we will focus on this team-oriented approach to management as we work our way through this book.

© GETTYIMAGES/DIGITAL VISION

INCREASING DIVERSITY IN THE WORKPLACE Closely connected to the globalization of business has been the globalization of the labor market. Just as goods and services flow relatively freely across national boundaries, so do human resources. The result has been increased diversity of the population base in the United States as well as other countries and increased diversity in the workplace.[61] **Diversity** refers to the heterogeneity of the population and workforce. No longer does the workplace include only individuals who are very similar to one another (that is, white men); it now includes individuals of both sexes,[62] as well as people of various races, nationalities, and ethnic backgrounds.

Diversity presents new challenges for businesses and managers. As we will see in subsequent chapters, organizational success requires a strong organizational culture and group cohesiveness. Achieving this may be more difficult when the workplace includes people with different backgrounds, from different nations, or with different cultural frames of reference. Men, women, Caucasians, Hispanics, African Americans, and others with diverse racial, national, and ethnic backgrounds often have very different perceptions about the same situations. As a consequence, it may be more difficult for diverse groups to reach a consensus on common goals and on the methods for achieving those goals.[63]

Many organizations today have established training programs to help employees develop an appreciation for diversity and to foster cooperation among culturally diverse groups. Most of these programs focus on valuing, even celebrating, diversity and the breadth of thought and experience that results from diverse work groups. Some organizations have implemented such programs because they feel it is "politically correct" to do so. Many other organizations, however, have implemented aggressive diversity training programs because they believe that a diverse workforce provides a significant competitive advantage. Allstate Insurance, for example, views diversity as a key strategic tool for ensuring its success in the highly competitive insurance market.[64] US West is another organization that has a long history of taking proactive measures to manage the changing workforce effectively. According to management, their efforts have paid off in terms of greater productivity and employee satisfaction.

The heightened awareness of diversity issues in corporate America has created some difficulties as well. In fact, some people feel as though it has resulted in reverse discrimination in some cases. White males, in particular, may view aggressive efforts to create a diverse workforce to be disadvantageous to them.[65] Reverse discrimination has been a controversial issue in recent years; thus, we have included it as a topic in the end-of-chapter feature "Thinking Critically: Debate The Issue" on page 34.

The globalization of business will undoubtedly continue to escalate, and therefore issues of diversity will continue to influence the thinking and behaviors of managers.[66] Consequently, this topic is discussed in much greater detail throughout the book.

A NEW ORGANIZATIONAL MODEL For decades, organizations have aspired to be large. Growth was considered to be synonymous with success, and the "bigger is better" syndrome governed the strategic decision making of most firms. Some of the largest and most successful companies of the past (for example, IBM and General Motors) have embraced this philosophy for decades. Today, however, this model presents problems for many companies. Maintaining flexibility and responding quickly to change are often impossible in large, complex organizations.[67] Being lean and flexible has now become preferable to being big for many organizations.[68] This is particularly true for organizations that operate within rapidly changing markets.

In addition, while an organization may be able to develop superior skills in certain core areas of its business, maximizing effectiveness over a broad range of business activities is becoming increasingly difficult. As a result, a number of successful

Diversity
The heterogeneity of the workforce in terms of gender, race, nationality, and ethnicity.

organizations today have adopted an alternative organizational model that offers advantages over the traditional model.[69] While this new model goes by a number of names—the modular corporation, the virtual corporation, and the network corporation, to name a few—the concept is similar.[70] The strategy is to focus on core business activities and outsource other business functions to organizations that can perform those functions more effectively and efficiently. For example, an organization may outsource the production function, the marketing function, the distribution function, or all three. The central organization simply coordinates the activities of others so that the product reaches the ultimate consumer in the most efficient manner possible.

Success with this model requires an ability to develop and manage a set of relationships with organizations that can fulfill business functions that are best outsourced. Consider, for example, the strategy of Sun Microsystems, a company that considers itself an intellectual holding company with the singular purpose of designing computers. All other business functions such as manufacturing, marketing, and customer service are managed through relationships with partner companies located throughout the world.

Toys "R" Us has also benefited from adopting a more flexible organizational structure. The company and its Toysrus.com division was once the laughingstock of the online industry, suffering from excessive customer complaints and significant losses from its Internet operations. That all changed, however, when Toysrus.com forged a strategic partnership with Amazon.com. Amazon provides Toysrus.com with the well-oiled fulfillment services and personalization technology that made Amazon famous. Since forming the partnership, Toysrus.com has realized a 300 percent increase in revenues and a 40 percent reduction in operating costs. Its conversion rate—the percentage of site visitors who make purchases—has doubled since the alliance was forged. During the 2000 holiday season, Toysrus.com boasted a 99 percent on-time delivery, well above industry standards at that time. Because Toysrus.com was willing to outsource fulfillment to Amazon, it was able to achieve a level of success that was previously thought unachievable.[71]

Examples of other companies who have adopted, at least in part, a virtual organizational model include Nike, Reebok, Wal-Mart, Boeing, and Motorola.[72] Partnerships provide these companies with an important competitive advantage—flexibility and efficiency.

The virtual corporation is not a fad; rather, it is a streamlined organizational model that fits the rapidly changing environment of today and tomorrow.[73] It provides maximum flexibility and efficiency because partnerships and relationships with other firms can be created and disbanded as needed. In addition, this model allows companies to direct their capital and other critical resources toward developing a core competency that provides a competitive advantage. Focusing on a core competency and outsourcing the rest is a trend that will most likely continue in the years to come.[74] Therefore, we will address challenges associated with managing such organizations throughout the book.

The environmental and organizational changes we have described will have a far-reaching impact on tomorrow's business leaders and managers. Table 1.4 provides a list of urgent questions that arise given the rapidly changing business conditions of the new millennium. These questions are difficult to answer, but doing so will be critical to the success of all organizations.[75]

THE CONTEMPORARY MANAGER

LEARNING OBJECTIVE 7

Describe the environmental trends that are affecting the way organizations operate and the way managers do their jobs.

What effect will changes in the business environment have on the managers and leaders of tomorrow? Will they require the same set of skills and competencies as managers of the past, or will there be new demands for managerial success? As we begin our study of management, it is helpful to identify the characteristics and competencies of managers who will be successful in the future.[76]

Table 1.4 | Urgent Questions

The unprecedented complexity and uncertainty that characterize today's business environment, coupled with the rapid-fire developments in information technology and organizational dynamics, pose a host of urgent questions for today's business leaders.

- *Learning to adapt.* How can an organization effectively deal with constant and multidimensional change? How can it boost its capacity for learning and adaptability?

- *Structure.* How should a company be organized for maximum responsiveness to continuous and often unpredictable changes in the marketplace? How should it relate to its network of customers and suppliers?

- *Skills.* What leadership qualities are needed to guide tomorrow's organizations? What skills will be crucial to success at all levels of an organization operating in such a dynamic environment?

- *Management styles.* What happens when command-and-control styles of management collide with ongoing efforts to empower workers? When more workers have greater access to more information, how should business decisions be made?

- *Impact of information technology.* What will happen to industry structures when electronic markets and information highways make it possible for buyers and sellers of any size to find each other easily anywhere in the world without human intermediaries?

- *New ways of working.* With greatly increased capabilities for communication and coordination, how will individuals work together? How will their work be evaluated? Will there be less need for large offices and factories? Will more people become telecommuters?

- *Innovation.* In such a competitive world where the winners are likely to be companies that are the first to recognize new ideas and implement them, how can an organization create the environment needed to spur continuous innovation?

- *Measures of success.* As intellectual capital and other intangibles play a larger role in a firm's success, can we adapt traditional accounting measures to more accurately portray the true assets, liabilities, and long-term prospects of a company?

THE NEW MANAGER PROFILE

Successful managers will have a different managerial style in the future.[77] Managers will no longer think of themselves as "the boss," but will view themselves as sponsors, team leaders, or internal consultants. The chain of command will be less relevant as managers seek out whomever they need to get the job done. They will work within a fluid organizational structure, involve others in decision making, and share information freely. They will develop their cross-functional skills so they can be more flexible. And, importantly, these new managers will demand results, not just long hours, from their work teams.[78] The leaders of the 21st century will not wield control from the top of a pyramid nor will they control the action from the sidelines. Rather, they will empower individual employees of the organization to do whatever is necessary to achieve its goals and work with them to ensure that they have the resources to get the job done.

LEARNING OBJECTIVE 8

Identify and discuss the organizational changes that are affecting managers' jobs.

COMPETENCIES OF TOMORROW'S MANAGERS AND LEADERS

This profile implies that new managers will require certain competencies to be successful.[79] As you study about management and business, you must try to develop these competencies.[80] In effect, the manager of tomorrow must be all of the following:

- *The great communicator.* Communication skills can make or break a career as well as an organization. A good leader spends more time informing, persuading, and inspiring than doing anything else. Although speaking is essential, active

LEARNING OBJECTIVE 9

Describe the manager of tomorrow in terms of the managerial style, leadership capabilities, and skill sets that will be necessary for success.

listening is a critical managerial talent for the future. Your ability to understand and apply the techniques of business does not exist in a vacuum. Solutions are hardly ever simple. It is imperative that you learn to read with comprehension, listen intently, question effectively, and write persuasively.

- *The individual coach.* Helping others achieve their highest potential is one of the most important activities for leaders. Leaders today recognize that organizational effectiveness requires the very best effort of everyone. Your ability to provide guidance, motivation, and feedback to others is a crucial part of the process of developing those around you and helping them to succeed. Coaches must be aware of the barriers that impede individual excellence and remove these obstacles to facilitate performance.

- *The team player.* Today, managers spend most of their time working with others, and they must be capable of functioning effectively both as team members and as team leaders. Whether these are work teams within the organization or partnerships and team efforts between organizations, managers will require strong team-management skills. Productivity and effectiveness can be greatly enhanced when people work together toward common goals. Team leaders are responsible for ensuring that individual team members are selected appropriately, trained well, encouraged to contribute in meaningful ways to the group effort, and rewarded equitably for their contributions.

- *The technology master.* The information age is now! As Tom Peters notes in his book *Thriving on Chaos,* "Technology is . . . a wild card affecting every aspect of doing business."[81] Almost every business, large and small, has come to view technology as a critical strategic resource. Certainly, managers of the future must be proficient in utilizing information technology. Business has transformed from manufacturing products to managing information, and managers must be capable of making this transition as well. Organizations will continue to have high expectations of their desktop computers—and the people who use them.

- *The problem solver.* The ability to solve problems is essential for the contemporary manager. The problem solver does not confuse opinions with arguments or association with causality. He or she can both evaluate arguments and construct them. The ability to think incisively, evaluate evidence judiciously, recognize hidden assumptions, and follow lines of reasoning to the sometimes tortuous end are essential competencies for successful managers.

- *The foreign ambassador.* The global marketplace has become an economic reality. Although the United States continues to be a dominant player in the world economy, maintaining this leadership position depends on having well-managed U.S. corporations. Success in the international marketplace requires managers who are prepared to function effectively in a global environment. These managers must appreciate cultural diversity, understand the complexities of the global environment, and be willing to adapt their skills and strategies to cope with international business challenges.

- *The change agent.* Managers of the future must be capable of both facilitating and adapting to change. Effective managers cannot be threatened by changing environmental and organizational conditions, but rather they must embrace such change and desire to influence its course.[82] In fact, tomorrow's managers will be the architects of change to the extent that they respond proactively to environmental trends, look for new ways to meet the needs of their customers, and explore methods of increasing the efficiency and effectiveness of their organizations.

- *The lifelong learner.* Tomorrow's managers will not have the luxury of using only one tactic or technique to be effective. Managers must view the process of learning as a day-to-day activity necessary for both personal performance and organizational effectiveness. This perspective will require managers to seek relevant

Table 1.5 | Evolving Managerial Skills

TRADITIONAL MANAGERIAL SKILL SETS	EMERGING MANAGERIAL SKILL SETS
Planning	Adapting
Leading	Coaching
Organizing	Facilitating
Controlling	Learning

information from different sources, be willing to take risks and make mistakes, and embrace the changes that result from their continued growth.

Table 1.5 illustrates some of these emerging managerial skill sets compared to the traditional managerial profile. The "Now Apply It" feature on page 32 provides a questionnaire that will help assess your readiness to be a leader in the 21st century. It evaluates your leadership orientation with regard to some of the skill sets for tomorrow's leaders. If you find that your scores are lower in some areas than you would like, you may want to focus on building your teamwork skills as you continue your education.

Students of management who have already begun their careers may want to look at Experiential Exercise 1.2 on page 35. This "Test for Success" will give you a sense of whether a promotion is likely or you need to be looking for a new organization to join.

IMPLICATIONS FOR LEADERS

The leaders of the future must be better and brighter and have more energy, enthusiasm, and insight than the leaders of the past. The flatter, leaner structures that characterize today's organizations leave fewer avenues for promotion.[83] As a result, only the very best will make their way up the corporate ladder. The jobs of tomorrow's managers will be increasingly demanding and challenging, but they will be rewarding for those who rise to the challenge of leadership. That is, those who demonstrate competence, character, and a commitment to their community, will emerge as the leaders of the future. To be a leader, you must remember to:

- Keep abreast of changing conditions that affect the organization.
- Develop an understanding of the major environmental trends that are affecting organizations across the globe.
- Be flexible and adaptable to organizational changes, as well as proactive in initiating change when appropriate.
- Understand the changing role of the manager within the corporate structure.
- Make the most of your education and develop the skills and competencies necessary for managerial success.
- Focus on excellence and quality in everything you do.
- Take every opportunity to enhance your leadership skills.

As you read this book and study the field of management, concentrate on learning how to be an effective manager. Only through a conscious effort to develop your managerial talent can you hope to prosper as a leader in the business environment of tomorrow.

Are You Ready to Lead in the 21st Century?

Use the following scale to rate the frequency with which you perform the behaviors described below. Place the number (1–7) in the blank preceding the statement.

Almost Never	Irregularly	Occasionally	Sometimes	Usually	Frequently	Almost Always
1	2	3	4	5	6	7

____ **1.** I thrive in uncertain situations where the outcome is unknown.
____ **2.** I provide guidance to others.
____ **3.** I am willing to make mistakes when learning a new process.
____ **4.** I recognize the contributions and performance of others.
____ **5.** I see change as an opportunity, not a threat.
____ **6.** I challenge others to consistently do a better job.
____ **7.** I seek new ways to do things better and faster.
____ **8.** I motivate others to reach their highest potential.

Transfer your scores to the columns below. Circle your highest score.

COLUMN A	COLUMN B	COLUMN C	COLUMN D
Question 1 ____	Question 2 ____	Question 3 ____	Question 4 ____
Question 5 ____	Question 6 ____	Question 7 ____	Question 8 ____
Total ____	Total ____	Total ____	Total ____

If your highest score was for column A, you demonstrate *Adapting* leadership skills. You recognize that change is a natural part of growth and are comfortable in dealing with ambiguity. If your highest score was for column B, you demonstrate *Coaching* leadership skills. You see the importance of motivating people around you and are willing to help others when necessary. If your highest score was column C, you recognize the role of *Learning* in being an effective leader. You consistently look for new ways to work more effectively and realize that making mistakes is a part of the learning process. If your highest score was for column D, you demonstrate *Empowering* leadership skills. You know the importance of developing others and encourage the people around you to reach their potential. Of course, you may show a mixed pattern of leadership skill sets. In any case, examine your answers to these questions carefully—they may reveal important information about your leadership orientation. Effective leaders in the future will excel in both traditional and emerging leadership activities.

Meeting The Challenge

Southwest Airlines: Surviving the Turbulence in the Airline Industry

Despite the downturn experienced across the entire airline industry, the original vision of Southwest's founders has enabled the company to be poised for record growth in both the short and long term. In addition to experiencing a full recovery from the events of September 11, Southwest has resumed an aggressive expansion strategy that will place 20 new aircraft into service. Management took some very specific steps, such as drastically cutting fares, to get customers back in the air, but that's only part of the reason for Southwest's remarkable re-

bound. Southwest's corporate culture is unique, considered by many to be the industry standard. Some of the reasons for its ability to adapt to the unprecedented changes it faced include:

- Principles Guide Business Practices—Long-term success must be built slowly and strategically. Southwest's strategic principles guide their business decisions and determine what actions are taken. This approach helps ensure that changes made are consistent with the frame-

work of Southwest's overall vision.

- Employees Work for a Worthy Cause—The cornerstone of Southwest's strategy is to provide low-cost service for its customers. Employees have internalized this vision as more than just a credo. It is a cause worthy of their time and energy. Associates continually look for ways to cut costs while maintaining safety, value, and service.
- Employees Listen to Their Customers—Employees of Southwest engage in "dynamic listening"

with their customers, proactively seeking ways to improve service. Customers are frequently asked how a job could be performed better. Managers listen to their employees, and it is not uncommon for managers to take unscheduled flights with their customers for the sole purpose of listening to their suggestions for making improvements.

- Managers Focus on Participation, Not Control—Southwest's corporate culture encourages employees to participate because they are devoted to the company's vision. Leaders are there to serve their associates, not control them.

Time will tell what the future holds for Southwest. Southwest is the only airline to earn a profit every year for the past 30 years. After surviving the recent events in the airline industry, it seems poised to grow and flourish. Visionary leadership and a committed workforce have Southwest situated to revolutionize an industry that has experienced a great deal of turbulence.

SOURCES: M. Trottman, "Southwest Air to Resume Fleet Growth, Take Delivery of 2 Jets to Boost Service," *The Wall Street Journal,* December 18, 2001, B14; W.C. Taylor, "The Leader of the Future," *Fast Company,* June 1999, 130–136.

SUMMARY

1. While the concepts of management and leadership are sometimes confused, they are distinct concepts. Leading has always been one of the important functions of management. However, given the rapidly changing and dynamic business environment of th 21st century, leadership has become increasingly important in recent years. This is because leadership is about coping with change. Effective leaders must be able to foresee, assess, and effect change in the organizations and their work groups. Because today's managers confront change regularly, they must have the leadership skills to cope with that change effectively. As a consequence, we have used the terms *manager* and *leader* interchangeably throughout the text.

2. Management is defined as the process of administering and coordinating resources effectively, efficiently, and in an effort to achieve the goals of the organization. Management typically occurs in an organizational setting. Organizations comprise a group of individuals who work together toward common goals. The process of management involves four primary functions: planning, organizing, leading, and controlling.

3. Henry Mintzberg identified three primary roles played by managers—interpersonal roles, informational roles, and decisional roles. In their interpersonal roles, managers act as figureheads, leaders, and liaisons. In their informational roles, managers serve as monitors, disseminators, and spokespeople. Finally, managers in their decisional roles function as entrepreneurs, disturbance handlers, resource allocators, and negotiators.

4. Managers' scope of responsibility varies depending on whether they are functional or general managers. Functional managers are responsible for work groups that are segmented according to function. General managers oversee several different departments that are responsible for different tasks. Functional managers typically have strong technical skills, whereas general managers require strong human skills.

5. Most large organizations have three levels of managers: first-line, middle, and top-level managers. These managers differ in terms of both the skills they require and the way they spend their time.

6. The new economy that has emerged in recent years is largely a function of three trends: (1) an expansion of individual opportunity, (2) a growing commitment to continuous innovation on the part of new economy companies, and (3) a continuing evolution of information and communication technologies. The convergence of these forces—forces that challenge conventional wisdom and test traditional ways of managing organizations—has created a "new economy" that embraces new methods of crafting strategy, launching products, serving customers, and organizing to support creativity and productivity.

7. Four environmental trends will continue to have a significant effect on the way organizations operate and the way managers do their jobs. These trends are (1) advances in information technology, (2) the globalization of business, (3) the increasing predominance of entrepreneurial firms, and (4) the growth of knowledge companies and the importance of intellectual capital.

8. Additionally, a number of important organizational changes are occurring today. A new model of leadership is prevalent in successful organizations today. Effective leaders must be competent, in that they possess the requisite business acumen and skills; they must be of strong character, possessing attributes such as integrity, courage, and persistence; and they must be willing to contribute to their communities in meaningful ways. Collaborative work relationships, such as cross-functional teams and self-managed teams, are pervasive in contemporary organizations. Culturally diverse work groups have become the norm rather than the exception. Finally, the large, complex corporate structures of the past are being replaced by streamlined, flexible structures that depend on outsourcing to achieve efficiency.

9. The managers of tomorrow will be quite different from the managers of yesterday. They will be more team-oriented, participatory, flexible, and focused on results. They must be strong communicators, team players, masters of technology, problem solvers, foreign ambassadors, change makers, and leaders.

REVIEW QUESTIONS

1. *(Learning Objective 1)* Distinguish between the concepts of management and leadership. Why has leadership become increasingly important in recent years?

2. *(Learning Objective 2)* Define the concept of management within an organizational context. Describe the major functions of the management process, and why they are important.

3. *(Learning Objective 3)* Describe the roles of the manager as outlined by Mintzberg.

4. *(Learning Objective 4)* Describe the responsibilities of the functional manager. Describe the responsibilities of the general manager. How do the skills needed by each type of manager differ?

5. *(Learning Objective 5)* Distinguish among the three levels of managers in terms of the skills they need and the activities in which they are involved.

6. *(Learning Objective 6)* What are the underlying forces of the new economy?

7. *(Learning Objective 7)* What are the four environmental trends affecting organizations today? Explain how each of these trends may affect the job of the contemporary manager.

8. *(Learning Objective 8)* Identify and discuss the organizational changes that are occurring today. What is the anticipated impact of these changes on the job of the contemporary manager?

9. *(Learning Objective 9)* Describe the manager of tomorrow in terms of both managerial style and the skill sets that will be necessary for success.

DISCUSSION QUESTIONS

Improving Critical Thinking

1. How is the increasing diversity of this nation influencing the student body at your university? Is the university administration taking proactive steps to ensure diversity on your campus? Does it maintain programs to ensure that diversity is celebrated rather than simply tolerated? Brainstorm on additional ways in which your university could encourage and support diversity on your campus.

2. Review the business curriculum at your university. In what ways is it designed to support the development of the managerial and leadership style that will be needed by the manager of the future? What could you do outside the classroom to develop this profile further?

Enhancing Communication Skills

3. How will the forces of the new economy affect the attributes of an effective leader. Write a one-page summary of your conclusions.

4. Identify a company that you feel has a strong global presence and one that you feel does not. Compare and contrast these organizations. Present your assessment to the class orally.

Building Teamwork

5. We have concluded that the contemporary manager is somewhat different from the manager of the past. If Mintzberg were to conduct his research on managerial roles today, how would you expect his results to differ? With a small group of your fellow students, formulate a response that can be presented to the class.

6. As organizations change in response to changing environmental conditions, how might the responsibilities of first-line managers, middle managers, and top-level managers change? How might technology be used to facilitate these changes? Form a student team to respond to these questions.

THINKING CRITICALLY: DEBATE THE ISSUE

Diversity and Reverse Discrimination

As this chapter explained, the workplace is becoming increasingly diverse. Many organizations have responded to this trend by developing aggressive recruitment plans to attract women and minority candidates, providing special programs to support and develop women and minority employees, and implementing training programs that encourage awareness and appreciation of diversity among the entire workforce. While such efforts are generally perceived in a positive light, some people believe that one segment of our population has been the victim of reverse discrimination—white males. In other words, they believe that efforts to provide women and minorities greater opportunities may result in fewer opportunities for equally qualified white men.

Form teams with four to five students on each team. Half of the teams should prepare to argue the benefits of aggressive efforts to develop a diverse workforce, while the other teams should present the negative consequences of such efforts from the white male perspective. Your instructor will select two teams to present their findings to the class in a debate format. (*Hint:* Search the Internet for male support groups such as National Organization for Men, National Coalition of Free Men, and National Organization for Men Against Sexism, all of which address workplace negativism toward men.)

EXPERIENTIAL EXERCISE 1.1

The Emerging Leadership Profile

Purpose: To identify the skills and competencies that are associated with effective leadership and to determine if these skill sets are associated primarily with the traditional or emerging profile of leadership.

Step 1. Ask class members to consider examples of effective leadership. These examples may be drawn from their personal or work experiences. Have each class member list three specific characteristics of an effective leader.

Step 2. Divide the class into groups of four or five people. One person from each group should act as a reporter to record the group's output and report to the class. Each group member takes a turn discussing one characteristic until all of the skills have been listed.

Step 3. The class reassembles and the reporter from each group writes the group's leadership profile on a chalkboard or flip chart for the rest of the class to discuss.

For Discussion

1. How different were the original individual lists from the group's final leadership profile?

2. How similar are the group's profiles to each other? Are any of the skills or characteristics listed in every group's profile?

3. Does a consensus exist among the entire class for a general profile of leadership? Are the skill sets more closely associated with the traditional or emerging profile of leadership?

EXPERIENTIAL EXERCISE 1.2

Test for Success

To stay or not to stay—that is the question. Use the first part of this quiz to figure out whether you are in line for a promotion. If not, the second part will help you determine when the right time is to make a move.

Part I: Will I be promoted soon?

If your answer is YES, add:

1. Is your company doing well? Is it posting good financial results, drumming up new business, hiring, and promoting others?

    10 points _____

2. Do you get choice assignments? Are you put on projects that showcase your talents? Are you pushed to learn new things and increase your skills?

    10 points _____

3. Are you popular? Does your boss like you? Do you like your boss? Are you getting along well with your peers?

    10 points _____

4. Is your input solicited? Are you included in key meetings? Do people come to you with questions about matters outside your usual domain?

    5 points _____

5. Do you have the skills? Can you take the next logical step in your company right now without further training or experience?

    5 points _____

6. Are you golden with the grapevine? Do others drop hints that you are in good standing? Have you heard any rumors that your boss likes your work?

    5 points _____

7. Have you groomed a successor? Were you to be promoted, is there someone who could step into your job right away?

    5 points _____
    Total points: _____

If you scored higher than 40, start thinking about how to decorate that corner office. You are primed for a promotion.

If you scored 25 to 40, stay tuned.

If you scored less than 25, move to the second part of this quiz.

Part II: Is it time to move on?

1. Have you stopped learning? Are you getting stale? Do you no longer get the chance to increase your skills and broaden your experience?

    10 points _____

2. Has your status slipped? Are exchanges with your boss becoming increasingly one-sided? Do you feel as if you have less freedom to act than in the past?

    10 points _____

3. Is your company faltering? Has it lost market share or taken a major hit on its stock price? Has it been sharply criticized by Wall Street, the press, or its own employees?

    10 points _____

4. Are big changes on the horizon? Has your company merged with another recently? Is any kind of major organizational restructuring underway? Have new high-level executives come in from the outside?

5 points _____

5. Are you out of the loop? Have you stopped hearing gossip? Do you feel you are the last to know about key decisions?

5 points _____

6. Do you dread going to work? Are you anxious on Sunday nights? Have your eating and sleeping habits changed? Do friends and family comment that you look tired or seem unhappy?

5 points _____

7. Is your salary stagnating? Are your raises on a downward trend in terms of percentage?

5 points _____

Total points: _____

If you scored higher than 40, close this book, take a deep breath, then start your search immediately!

If you scored 25 to 40, put out feelers.

If you scored less than 25, your situation may improve, but remain open to outside opportunities.

CAPTURING THE POWER OF INFORMATION TECHNOLOGY

1. Many firms today are using Internet services to identify qualified employees. Identify three companies that have a high demand for knowledge workers, and research how they utilize the Web to recruit employees. Compare and contrast the three companies on the effectiveness of their Web-based recruiting strategies.

2. A number of universities (for example, Michigan State University, University of South Carolina, and UCLA) maintain centers for international business education and research (CIBERs). Locate and visit one of these sites. What kinds of information does this center provide for practicing managers? Suggest some ways in which the center could improve its services for today's global managers.

3. Identify two retail competitors (for example, Zany Brainy, Toys "R" Us) who are using e-commerce to sell their products. Evaluate the Web site of each competitor, comparing and contrasting the effectiveness of the site for consumers. Make recommendations on how each company could improve its e-commerce strategy to reach and serve consumers.

ETHICS: TAKE A STAND

Chuck Bolin was recently promoted to vice president of Human Resources for ScentSational Corporation (SSC), a national supplier of room and car deodorizers. Chuck has been with SSC for 14 years and was both respected as a manager and liked by his employees. He was looking forward to an uneventful first day when he received word that the president had called an unexpected meeting with him.

The president was worried that employees were using too much company time for personal affairs. The former VP for Human Resources had started an investigation into computer use among employees. It turned out that employees were using their computers to access the Internet for personal use. Although employees were using the Internet for fairly harmless activities, such as checking stock prices and shopping, the president wanted Chuck to pick up the investigation where his predecessor left off and put an immediate end to the unauthorized use of company computers. The president believed if they "made an example" of one employee, the other employees would know that he meant business. Chuck agreed to make this concern his number one priority and promised the president an update the next morning.

As Chuck contemplated his situation, he became uncomfortable at the prospect of firing someone for using the Internet during work hours. Even though it was clearly unauthorized and against company policy, he suspected that just about everyone had accessed the Internet during work hours at one time or another. He himself was guilty of doing some last-minute shopping and checking sports scores on the Internet in the past.

Two alternative courses of action came to Chuck's mind. He could follow the president's order at face value, track the use of computer applications among employees, and fire the first one guilty of accessing the Internet. This alternative would please the president, be cost effective and timely, and might bolster his reputation as a no-nonsense manager to the other vice presidents.

A second alternative he considered was to develop a plan of employee education and awareness. Such a plan would convey the president's strong desire for Internet access among employees to stop and would let each employee know that a policy enforcement change was being put into effect. He then reasoned he would not feel guilty about taking the appropriate action if an employee violated this policy.

Although the second approach made more sense to Chuck, he had some serious reservations. First, he wanted to make a good impression to the president in his new role and did not want anyone to think he was afraid to make the tough decisions required by upper-level management. Moreover, the second alternative would take time and cost money, neither of which the president would be interested in spending.

As Chuck ate lunch at his new desk, he thought of another possible course of action. He reasoned that he could begin telling co-workers informally about the new enforcement policy. He knew if he could tap into SSC's "grapevine," most employees would get the message. Would this course of action be fair to all employees? Would it be fair to the president?

For Discussion

1. Is it ethical to "spy" on an employee's computer use at work? Why or why not?

2. Is it fair for a company to begin enforcing a formal policy that has been in place but rarely or never enforced without advanced notice to employees? Why or why not?

3. What are the advantages and disadvantages of each of the alternatives identified by Chuck? Which course of action would you choose if you were Chuck? Why?

VIDEO CASE

Management and Managers: On-Target Supply and Logistics

After college graduation, Albert C. Black, Jr., started On-Target Supplies and Logistics as a two-person, part-time janitorial service and supply company with annual revenues of $10,000. Albert and his wife, Gwyneith had to work second jobs to support their new business. Albert had two main goals for his second job: earn an income and learn management skills he could use to make On-Target successful. To further On-Target's chances for success, Albert established a board of advisers made up of customers and a board of directors that included successful businesspeople.

To better position his company, Albert phased out janitorial services in 1987, added warehousing services in 1990, and added venture management in 1998. Albert reorganized On-Target into four strategic business units adding a business services staff to manage the firm's growth. He also recently opened a state-of-the-art Conference Center to address local businesses' needs. On-Target has grown to 117 employees (mostly inner-city) with revenues of $27.3 million. It currently provides logistics and supply-chain management services to global corporations including Raytheon, Ericsson, Texas Instruments, American Airlines, and Wyndham Hotels and Resorts. Albert estimates that On-Target's inner-city locations create at least a 30 percent efficiency advantage over most of his competitors. Their offices and warehouses are located in Dallas, San Antonio, Glen Rose, and Houston, Texas.

A major part of On-Target's mission is community awareness and enrichment. Albert has done a great job of promoting On-Target by positioning himself as a community leader. For example, he served as chair of the Greater Dallas Chamber of Commerce's Board of Directors and as a board member for the Dallas Black Chamber of Commerce. Volunteering for not-for-profit organizations has given On-Target exposure to major corporations. Collectively, On-Target employees have followed Albert's example, contributing almost 100 hours each month to community service-related activities.

Albert has established values based on commitment to quality, professionalism, and community support. On-Target is ISO 9002 certified and is working toward other quality awards (e.g., Malcolm Baldrige National Quality Award). Albert frequently has been recognized for his business achievements and community support. He was the first recipient of the Award for Outstanding Contribution to the Logistics Community and received a Congressional District Award for Outstanding achievement in business. He also received the Ernst & Young Southwest Region Entrepreneur of the Year. This award recognizes outstanding entrepreneurs who have achieved in areas including quality, innovation, pace of organizational growth, personal commitment, and future potential.

Albert believes On-Target's success is contingent upon his putting together a team of well-trained, highly motivated, customer service-oriented professionals. In addition to paying for and strongly encouraging his employees to obtain college degrees, Albert provides training for his employees and those of select customers. He promises his employees that they will know how to run a business after several years and encourages them to start their own businesses. More than ten former employees have done just that. Albert also believes small business owners should have college degrees. Albert sees the future as being developed by service providers thinking with customers, defining the future, and building that future.

On-Target's success is due to the efforts and guidance of Albert, its president and chief executive officer (CEO). His values were learned from his family while living in government-subsidized (inner-city) housing. As a hotel doorman, Albert's father interacted daily with Dallas's business leaders and he passed that wisdom to his son. Although they lived in poverty, Albert's mother expected all seven of her children to earn high grades in school and to see themselves as champions. Albert also credits his grandmother with instilling the values of treating people with compassion, doing what you say you're going to do, taking care of others before yourself, and being honest. Because of his successes in business and the community, Albert believes that he has dispelled several myths: (1) small businesses cannot fund growth, (2) minority businesses can't put together successful management teams, (3) Blacks (African-Americans) do not have the right stuff to take full advantage of the American free-enterprise system.

Albert remembers the poverty of his youth and the positive influence of his family, and he strives to have a positive impact on the community and businesses. His reasons for going into business in 1982 are the same reasons he's in business today: create jobs, hire people, improve the infrastructure of inner cities, pay taxes, provide leadership, and get rich along the way. He has been successful on all fronts. His new 6,000-square-foot home is built across the street from where he polished wood floors to earn extra cash.

For Discussion

1. In what ways does Albert Black illustrate the 3Cs of leadership? Can a business leader be successful if he or she does not have the 3Cs? Explain.

2. What environmental trends do Albert Black and his management team at On-Target Supplies and Logistics need to consider when making decisions about the future?

3. What organizational changes should Albert Black and his management team consider when making decisions about the future?

4. What competencies of tomorrow's managers and leaders does Albert Black appear to possess? Support your answers with examples from the case and video.

www.otsl.com/web/default.htm

CASE

A Day in the Life of Lindsey Clarke

Lindsey Clarke is a project manager with Resource Solutions, Inc. (RSI), an information technology and computer systems consulting firm with offices in Virginia, Maryland, and Washington, D.C.

She arrives at her office in suburban D.C. every day at 7:30 A.M. Today begins with her usual morning ritual—cup of coffee, quick check of voice and e-mail messages, and a careful review of her electronic planner for today's activities. She has a busy but fairly typical day planned, beginning with her team's meeting at 8:30 A.M.

At 7:45 A.M. she reviews the output from her team's meeting last week and begins developing today's meeting agenda. The telephone rings at 8:10 A.M. Her manager is concerned about the latest contract their company was awarded. Her manager confesses to having some serious reservations about RSI's ability to complete the work on time. Lindsey tries to reassure her manager that they will meet the deadlines, but as she's talking, she feels her mind wandering to the team meeting that is set to begin in less than 15 minutes. She promises her manager that she will put together a short report on the technical progress with regards to the contract and hangs up. With less than 10 minutes to the meeting she stares at the blank sheet of paper entitled "Meeting Agenda." She quickly types out what she can remember from the last meeting and walks briskly to the meeting room.

At 8:30 A.M., she stares at the mostly tired and yawning faces and begins by thanking everyone for coming. Before she can start the meeting, Greg, the team member with the most skill but least formal education, tells her that they can never meet the new deadline. An argument follows with some group members saying the work can be done and the others disagreeing. After an hour and a half debate, Lindsey ends the meeting and agrees to meet with Greg later in the week to discuss his reservations.

She gets back to her office at 10:10 A.M. to discover a voice mail message inviting her to attend her manager's meeting with one of the company's partners during lunch. She had planned to run some errands over lunch but agrees it would be a good idea for her to attend.

At 10:45 A.M., Greg stops by her office to schedule their meeting for later in the week. She tells Greg that she trusts his computer savvy and will defer to his judgment if he does not think the deadline can be met. He admits that he may have overreacted a bit during the meeting and promises to reassess their proposed scope of work. She spends the next 45 minutes returning phone messages and replying to e-mail messages. She leaves her office at 11:30 A.M. to meet her manager for the 30-minute drive to downtown D.C. for lunch.

Lindsey and her manager arrive at the restaurant at 12 noon and are greeted by the partner. They enjoy a friendly exchange and settle into their booth. Lindsey immediately senses the concern in the partner's tone about the newly awarded contract and begins a two-hour discussion of the project's merits and feasibility. With both her manager and partner satisfied, she returns to her office at 2:45 P.M. and begins returning phone messages. She has a conference call at 3:30 P.M. to discuss the project with the client's management team and it lasts for 45 minutes.

As she walks down the hall to the break room for a soda after the conference call, she bumps into Greg who is talking with another team member. Greg is happy to tell Lindsey that he believes with a little overtime and extra effort on the team's part, the project should be completed on time and on budget. Lindsey sincerely thanks Greg for his input and hard work, and they agree to meet later in the week to discuss the project.

Lindsey returns to her office and calls her manager to relay the good news. She then answers her waiting voice and e-mail messages and begins outlining her schedule for tomorrow in her daily planner. Finally, at 5:30 P.M. she goes home exhausted.

For Discussion

1. At what points during the day did Lindsey engage in traditional leadership roles, and when did she use skills from the emerging leadership profile?

2. When did Lindsey act in (1) interpersonal roles, (2) informational roles, and (3) decisional roles?

3. Did Lindsey practice time management? Could she have managed her time more efficiently? If so, in what ways?

CHAP

EVOLUTION OF MANAGEMENT THOUGHT

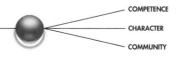

LEADERSHIP ——————— COMPETENCE

——————— CHARACTER

——————— COMMUNITY

TER 2

CHAPTER OVERVIEW

The concept of management and the basic management functions of planning, organizing, leading, and controlling are not new phenomena. Throughout recorded history, activities have been conducted that most certainly would have required careful attention to these management functions. The Great Wall of China, the Pyramids of Egypt, and many other wonders of the ancient world would not have been possible without management of the activities required to complete them. Endeavors such as these certainly would have required planning, organizing, leading, and controlling. Not only was management important in the past, but it continues to be important in the present as governments construct massive public works projects, private enterprise engages in the delivery of large-scale projects, and business leaders engage in commerce and industry around the globe. Management will continue to be important as long as humans survive on earth.

Despite management's lengthy tenure, formal theories on management began to emerge only during the past 100 years or so. In this chapter, we will examine the historical evolution of management theories and philosophies and the factors that helped influence their development. This historical tour will explore the five major schools of management thought that have emerged over the years. Our trip through time will reveal that the degree of support for and use of these different perspectives have shifted as times, conditions, and situations have changed. Despite this shifting support and use, components of each of these schools of thought still exist in current management thinking. Furthermore, they are likely to continue influencing management thought in the future. If we understand the managerial philosophies of the past and present, we will be better equipped to be successful leaders in the future.

LEARNING OBJECTIVES

When you have finished studying this chapter, you should be able to:

1. Describe the major influences on the development of management thought.
2. Identify the five major perspectives of management thought that have evolved over the years.
3. Describe the different subfields that exist in the classical perspective of management and discuss the central focus of each.
4. Describe the theories of the major contributors to the behavioral perspective of management.
5. Describe the characteristics of the quantitative perspective of management.
6. Describe the systems perspective building blocks and their interactions.
7. Discuss the nature of the contingency perspective of management.
8. Discuss the future issues that will affect the further development of management thought.

Facing The Challenge

For UPS the Old Practices Don't Always Fit in the New Era

United Parcel Service (UPS) has come a long way since that time 90+ years ago when 19-year-old Jim Casey borrowed $100 to open the American Messenger Company. Casey began delivering everything from handwritten notes and telegrams to bail money and assorted small parcels around his hometown of Seattle, Washington. Soon, he expanded into home delivery for local retail outlets. The company's initial fleet of delivery vehicles consisted of a single Model T Ford. Within 10 years, the company extended its delivery service to reach several other major West Coast cities. By 1929, the company, now renamed United Parcel Service, had begun using aircraft to carry packages to all the major West Coast cities and as far inland as Texas. It was in those early days that UPS adopted its familiar corporate color for its delivery vehicles, purely for practical reasons. Research had shown that the dirt and dust accumulated from hundreds of daily road miles showed up least on brown vehicles!

My how UPS has grown! Today it is the largest transportation company in the United States. With a fleet of 88,000 ground vehicles and 253 company-owned aircraft (and another 346 chartered aircraft), UPS delivers more than 13.6 million packages and documents daily and

provides service to more than 200 countries and territories. This volume is nearly four times the volume of its nearest private competitor. Annual revenue exceeds $30 billion. On any given day, the company carries about 7 percent of the U.S. gross domestic product. UPS has long been renowned for its ability to provide dependable, low-cost delivery of small parcels, competing with the United States Postal Service for most of its life.

Over the years, the company has built a reputation for efficient and reliable deliveries, thanks to the work of company engineers who conducted time-and-motion studies to analyze every step of a package's journey from pickup to delivery. Drivers were instructed on the best way for workers to perform each task, having been given 340 precise company-directed movements to follow in order to save precious seconds. Rules, regulations, policies, and procedures at UPS maintain a well-defined hierarchy of workers and division of labor. In addition to job performance guidelines, explicit policies exist for hiring and promotion. Throughout the years, most UPS workers seemed willing to accept this highly regimented system.

However, in recent years, many UPS workers began to feel stress brought on by competition-induced changes, like the expansion into

global delivery in the mid-1970s. UPS drivers had to learn how to deliver new services, some of which require speedier deliveries, more lifting, and heavier loads. In addition, rapidly advancing technological innovations have brought new demands on UPS personnel. Drivers have had to learn how to use several generations of UPS's sophisticated and technical package-tracing systems. As UPS Vice President Ted Gradolf recently noted, "We have to strike a balance between activity and results. In years past we may have focused too much on activity—make X number of calls a day, Y number of these kinds of visits, etc. The pendulum swung a little bit too far." He went on to say, "We're trying to bring the pendulum back to find that ideal balance between activities that we want salespeople performing as part of a routine and an increased focus on bottom-line results."

SOURCES: "New Supply Chain Solutions Links Logistics, Freight and Financial Services," *UPS Press Release*, February 20, 2002; "UPS Once Again 'America's Most Admired,' " *UPS Press Release*, February 19, 2002; M. Fleschner, "Worldwide Winner: The UPS Success Story," *SellingPower.Com*, November 8, 2001; "UPS Begins Direct Service to China," *UPS Press Release*, March 30, 2001; and F. Robert, "As UPS Tries to Deliver More to Its Customers, Labor Problem Grows," *The Wall Street Journal*, May 23, 1994, A1ff.

INTRODUCTION

Leadership at United Parcel Service (UPS) was beginning to realize that the management style and practices that had worked well in the past might need some fine tuning as the company embarked on a new millennium with new services, new markets, new technologies, and new expectations among its workforce. Despite the company's tradition of well-paid employees with meaningful opportunities for advancement and job security, the ripple of discontent would have to be dealt with before it became a disruptive wave. The dilemma UPS leadership faced was whether they should deal with this situation by continuing the practices that had proven so successful in the past, or should they consider making some changes? As we saw in Chapter 1, changes are occurring that are causing business leaders to revise their managerial styles and become more creative in their thinking. But change is nothing new—all that is new are the types of change and the speed of change. Management thinking has evolved throughout the centuries to deal with the ever-changing environment. Today, management thinking continues to evolve to meet the challenges raised by rapid and dramatic societal changes. These factors will undoubtedly continue to influence future management developments. Before examining the historical developments in management thinking, let's first identify those factors that have influenced the evolution of modern management thought.

ENVIRONMENTAL FACTORS INFLUENCING MANAGEMENT THOUGHT

Through the years, many environmental factors have caused management theorists and management practitioners to alter their views on what constitutes a good approach to management. These environmental factors can be conveniently categorized as economic, social, political, technological, and global influences. We will examine each of these influences and the effects they have had on the evolution of management thought in turn.

LEARNING OBJECTIVE 1

Describe the major influences on the development of management thought.

ECONOMIC INFLUENCES

Economic influences relate to the availability, production, and distribution of resources within a society. With the advent of industrialization, the goal of most manufacturing organizations was to find the most profitable way to provide products for newly emerging markets. They needed a variety of resources to achieve this objective. Some resources were material and some were human, but in each case, they tended to become scarcer over time.

When there was a seemingly endless expanse of virgin forests, loggers didn't think twice about clear-cutting a mountainside. Coal reserves were once stripped away with no thought of depletion. Flaring off surplus natural gas, the practice of burning it in the atmosphere, was once common. But as resources became scarce, it became increasingly important that they be managed effectively. Time and circumstances dictate that supplies will not always be available when needed. Through gradual depletion over time, resources can simply run out.

Disruptions of supplies can also occur because of temporary but immediate circumstances. Early in 1999, a fire at a major California oil refinery caused an immediate upward spiral in gasoline prices that had been experiencing a steady decline. Hurricane Floyd, one of the largest Atlantic hurricanes of the 20th century, had a sudden and dramatic impact on the management of resources as it skirted the southeast coast of the United States before moving inland through North Carolina and then proceeding into the mid-Atlantic and northeast states in late 1999. This storm led to the largest evacuation in U.S. history, and it caused manufacturers and distributors of construction materials to quickly rethink their manufacturing and distribution strategies so they could act in a socially responsible manner. The leaders of businesses that engaged in the retail sale of these commodities also found it necessary to manage their resources differently. For example, Home Depot closely monitored the track of the storm and moved such items as emergency generators, plywood, and building materials to areas in the ever-changing projected path.[1] In short, scarcity makes it necessary for resources to be allocated among competing users.

SOCIAL INFLUENCES

Social influences relate to the aspects of a culture that influence interpersonal relationships. The needs, values, and standards of behavior among people help to form the social contract of the culture. The social contract embodies unwritten rules and perceptions that govern interpersonal relationships, as well as the relationships between people and organizations. Business leaders need to be familiar with these perceptions if they are to act effectively. The ethnic, racial, and gender composition of today's workforce is becoming increasingly diverse. Recognizing and satisfying the varying needs and values of this diverse workforce present a challenge to business leaders.

Throughout modern business history, management thinking and practice have been shaped, in part, by work stoppages, labor insurrections, and strikes by mineworkers, autoworkers, teamsters, and many others. Most of these incidents were precipitated not just by demands for more pay, but by safety concerns, welfare issues, and other social considerations. Just recently, the General Motors Corporation was pressured into expanding existing job-security protections to effectively give many of its United Auto Workers employees lifetime protection against losing their jobs to subcontracting or efficiency gains.[2]

Although some of these examples of social influence have a negative flavor, this need not always be the case. In recent years, the social contract of our culture has been changing. Workers have become more vocal in their desire to be treated as more than just muscle to do the job. They are insisting on using their mental abilities as well as their physical skills. As we will see throughout this book, these changes have led to some of the contemporary approaches that empower workers, giving them decision-making authority and responsibility for their activities. This approach has had a positive impact on organizations that have tried it.[3] Empowered workers often exhibit pride of ownership for their work and a dedication to quality and excellence in all that they do. Changing its view of the workforce in this manner was one of the key factors contributing to the dramatic resurgence of the Harley-Davidson Motor Company, as described in "At the Forefront" later in this chapter on page 66.[4]

POLITICAL INFLUENCES

Political influences relate to the impact of political institutions on individuals and organizations. At a basic level are the various civil and criminal laws that influence individual and organizational behavior. In addition, the political system has bestowed various rights upon individuals and organizations that also impact behavior. Among these rights are the right to life and liberty, contract rights, and property rights. Finally, government regulations are yet another source of political influence. The laws, rules, and regulations that form the political influences on management in many instances have been the outgrowth of economic and social influences. Environmental regulations have often been precipitated by reckless disregard for the preservation of our natural resources. Child labor laws and OSHA (Occupational Safety and Health Administration) regulations trace their origin to social outcries over exploitative and dangerous working conditions.

Political forces have influenced management thinking in a variety of ways. For example, over the years increasing concern for individual rights has forced management to adapt to a shorter work week for employees, provide a safe work environment, and make increasing contributions to employees' welfare. Such political influences can extend across international boundaries in today's global economy. Nike, Inc. found it necessary to increase wages for its workers in Indonesia in the face of that government's plan to raise the minimum wage.[5] Pressures from the court of public opinion have also prompted Nike and other companies such as Kmart and Wal-Mart to eliminate child labor practices in foreign countries producing their merchandise. Regulations against monopolies have caused some businesses to restructure and some industries to reorganize. Increased environmental regulation has caused changes in many organizations. Deregulation of banking and trucking has had a dramatic in-

Child labor laws, OSHA, and political forces have compelled management to provide a safe work environment and eliminate child labor practices in foreign countries.

© MICHAEL S. YAMASHITA/CORBIS

fluence on organizations in these industries. In short, evolving laws, rules, and regulations have tended to transform the way many organizations conduct business, necessitating changes in their management philosophies and styles over the years.

TECHNOLOGICAL INFLUENCES

Technological influences relate to advances and refinements in any of the devices used in conjunction with conducting business. As was noted in Chapter 1, advances in transportation, communication, and information technology have made it possible to conduct business on a global basis. Business leaders in the global economy must be alert to all opportunities for improvement. They must stay abreast of the new technology so they can make intelligent, informed decisions. The stakes are high because these decisions affect both the human and the technical aspects of operations. Whether or not an organization adopts the new technology may determine whether it retains its competitive edge.[6] This is evident in the UPS situation described in the opening "Facing The Challenge" on page 44. During the decade of the 1990s, UPS developed three generations of its computer-based parcel tracking system, Delivery Information Acquisition Device (DIAD). In 1990, DIAD I was developed, followed by DIAD II in 1993, and DIAD III in 1999. This latest generation was the first device in the industry to both capture and transmit real-time delivery information. UPS spends more than $1 billion a year on information technology, which is more than it spends for its ground vehicles and nearly as much as it spends on its airplanes.[7]

As we will see in more detail in Chapter 18, electronic commerce (e-commerce), and its associated product sales via the Internet, is becoming increasingly critical to the competitiveness of many organizations. As the 20th century wound to a close, Compaq, then the world's largest personal-computer manufacturer, replaced its CEO and CFO because they failed to adapt quickly enough to this new technology. Compaq's profits were starting to be squeezed as upstart competitor Dell Computer Corporation dramatically outperformed Compaq by embracing e-commerce more quickly than Compaq.[8]

Business leaders are seeing constant innovations in communications and information exchange capabilities, including voice mail, electronic mail, fax transmission of documents, electronic data interchange, and the growth of the Internet. Cellular telephones and portable computers provide two familiar examples of dramatic technological advances that have occurred in the past few years. Early cellular telephones were not very portable and required separate battery packs carried over the shoulder in briefcase-sized satchels. Now Motorola, Nokia, and a host of other manufacturers offer battery-powered units that can fit into a shirt pocket or be concealed in the palm of one's hand. These will no doubt shrink even more as technological innovations continue. Notebook-style computers that weigh a few pounds now allow managers to exchange information with their company computers while flying virtually anywhere in the world. Using these same devices, information can be quickly retrieved from almost any source in the world by means of the Internet. Factories of the future will incorporate such technologies as computer-aided design (CAD), computer-aided manufacturing (CAM), computer-integrated manufacturing (CIM), computerized numerically controlled machines (CNCM), automated storage and retrieval systems (AS/RS), and flexible manufacturing systems (FMS). Innovations such as these are transforming workers' job responsibilities and, consequently, the way in which they should be managed.[9]

GLOBAL INFLUENCES

Global influences relate to the pressures to improve quality, productivity, and costs as organizations attempt to compete in the worldwide marketplace. The international, or global, dimension of an organization's environment has had the most profound impact on management thinking in recent years. In the world of business, national boundaries are quickly disappearing. Global competition has begun to affect all businesses. For example, U.S. automakers can no longer claim this country as their exclusive domain. Foreign competitors continually penetrate the U.S. market with high-quality, low-priced cars. To survive, U.S. automakers have found it necessary to compete on the same quality and price dimensions as their foreign competitors and to seek foreign markets of their own.[10]

As time progresses, even the lines between domestic and foreign automobiles continue to become more blurred. U.S. automobiles continue to incorporate more and more imported components, while "foreign" automobiles are increasingly being manufactured in the United States with U.S.-made parts and U.S. labor. For example, Marysville, Ohio, boasts a Honda manufacturing plant and Georgetown, Kentucky, can claim a Toyota manufacturing plant.

Similar situations in electronics and other industries could be cited. In all cases, increasing global competition has caused organizations to focus on using all the skills and capabilities of their workers in an effort to improve quality, productivity, and costs. This increased globalization, coupled with the immediate access organizations have to one another through the Internet, has led to many global partnerships. Small companies that are seemingly isolated in small-town America can easily become suppliers to foreign companies and vice versa. Contemporary and future perspectives on management have been and will continue to be influenced most heavily by the global dimension of the environment.[11]

SCHOOLS OF MANAGEMENT THOUGHT

LEARNING OBJECTIVE 2

Identify the five major perspectives of management thought that have evolved over the years.

Beginning in the late 19th century and continuing through the 20th century, managers and scholars developed theoretical frameworks to describe what they believed to be good management practice. Their efforts have led to five different perspectives on management: the classical perspective, the behavioral perspective, the quantitative perspective, the systems perspective, and the contingency perspective. Each perspective is based on different assumptions about organizational objectives and human behavior. To help place these perspectives in their proper chronological sequence, Figure 2.1 displays them along a historical time line.

You might wonder why it is important to study the historical development of management thought. We've probably all heard it before in our secondary education: Studying history allows us to learn about mistakes made in the past so that they can be avoided in the future. Furthermore, it allows us to learn of past successes so that they can be repeated in the appropriate future situations. This certainly applies to the study of management history.

As Figure 2.1 shows, all these perspectives continue to influence the thinking of business leaders, although opinions differ as to how influential each is. Consequently, it is important that future leaders become familiar with the basic concepts of each school of thought. The following sections examine these major perspectives on management thought in more detail.

CLASSICAL PERSPECTIVE

LEARNING OBJECTIVE 3

Describe the different subfields that exist in the classical perspective of management and discuss the central focus of each.

The oldest of the "formal" viewpoints of management emerged during the late 19th and early 20th centuries and has come to be known as the classical perspective. The classical perspective had its roots in the management experiences that were occurring in the rapidly expanding manufacturing organizations that typified U.S. and European industrialization. Early contributions came from management practitioners and theorists in several corners of the world.

Figure 2.1 | Chronological Development of Management Perspectives

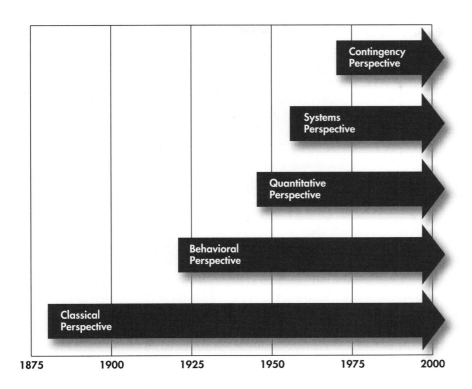

The classical perspective consists of three main subfields: scientific management, administrative management, and bureaucratic management.[12] We will see shortly that scientific management tends to focus on the productivity of the individual worker, administrative management tends to focus on the functions of management, and bureaucratic management tends to focus on the overall organizational system. Keep in mind, though, that things are not as sharply defined as this synopsis might suggest. As Figure 2.2 illustrates, these three subfields also contain some overlapping elements and components.

SCIENTIFIC MANAGEMENT **Scientific management** focuses on the productivity of the individual worker. As 19th-century society became more industrialized, businesses had difficulty improving productivity. Frederick Winslow Taylor (1856–1915), an American mechanical engineer, suggested that the primary problem lay in poor management practices. While employed at the Midvale Steel Company in Philadelphia, Pennsylvania, Taylor began experimenting with management procedures, practices, and methods that focused on worker/machine relationships in manufacturing plants. He contended that management would have to change, and that the manner of change should be determined by scientific study. Taylor's observations led him to formulate opinions in the areas of task performance, supervision, and motivation.[13]

Task Performance Taylor was convinced that there was an ideal way to perform each separate work task, and he attempted to define those optimal procedures through systematic study. His celebrated "science of shoveling" refers to his observations and experiments on the best way for workers to perform this manual task during the manufacture of pig iron. Taylor experimented with different shovel sizes and designs to find the one that was most comfortable. He varied the size of

Scientific management
Perspective on management that focuses on the productivity of the individual worker.

Figure 2.2 | Subfields of the Classical Perspective on Management

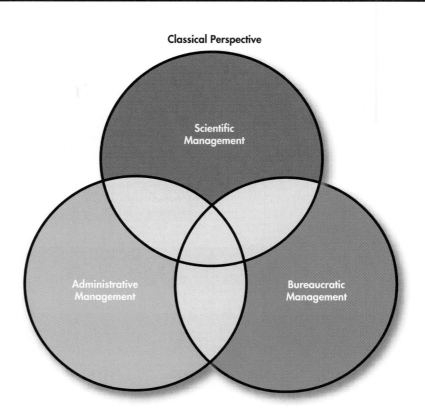

the load scooped up onto the shovel to find the least fatiguing amount. He experimented with different combinations of work time and rest intervals in an attempt to improve the worker recovery rate. Ranges of physical motion on the part of the workers were also examined. Based upon Taylor's suggestions, Midvale was able to reduce the number of shovel handlers needed from 600 to 140, while at the same time more than tripling the average daily worker output.[14]

These types of observations and measurements are examples of time-and-motion studies. Time-and-motion studies identify and measure a worker's physical movements while the worker performs a task and then analyze the results to determine the best way of performing that task. In the attempt to find the best way of performing each task, scientific management incorporates several basic expectations of management, which include the following:

- *Development of work standards.* Standard methods should be developed for performing each job within the organization.
- *Selection of workers.* Workers with the appropriate abilities should be selected for each job.
- *Training of workers.* Workers should be trained in the standard methods.
- *Support of workers.* Workers should be supported by having their work planned for them.

While Taylor is most remembered for his contributions in the area of task performance, his scientific management contributions went well beyond determining the one best way of performing a task. He also maintained strong convictions about supervision and motivation.[15]

Supervision   In the area of supervision, Taylor felt that a single supervisor could not be an expert at all tasks. This was because most supervisors were promoted to their positions after demonstrating high levels of skill in performing a particular function within the organization. Consequently, each first-level supervisor should be responsible only for workers who perform a common function familiar to the supervisor, such as machine operator, material handler, or inspector. Each supervisor's area of expertise would become an area of authority. Since in Taylor's era these supervisors were referred to as foremen, Taylor called this concept functional foremanship. Several foremen would be assigned to each work area, with each having a separate responsibility for such duties as planning, production scheduling, time-and-motion studies, material handling, and so forth.

Motivation   In the area of motivation, Taylor felt that money was the way to motivate workers to their fullest capabilities. He advocated a piecework system, in which workers' pay was tied to their output. Workers who met a standard level of production were paid at a standard wage rate. Workers whose production exceeded the standard were paid at a higher rate for all of their production output. Taylor felt that such financial incentives would induce workers to produce more so that they might earn more money. He also felt that management should use financial incentives judiciously. If the increased employee earnings were not accompanied by higher profits generated by the productivity increases, then the incentives should not be used. While Taylor's views on the power of money as a motivator may have been well suited to the conditions that prevailed in the early part of the 20th century, there is ample evidence to suggest that, with a few exceptions, now it is not usually the most important motivator of workers. In some instances today, it can be something as simple as allowing casual dress that is a prime motivator of workers.[16]

While Frederick Taylor is generally acknowledged to be the father of scientific management, the husband-and-wife team of Frank and Lillian Gilbreth also made substantial pioneering contributions to the field.[17] Frank Gilbreth specialized in time-and-motion studies to determine the most efficient way to perform tasks.[18] He identified 17 work elements (such as lifting, grasping, and positioning) and called them therbligs (roughly the reverse spelling of his last name).[19] In one of his more notable studies, Gilbreth used the new medium of motion pictures to examine the work of bricklayers. He was able to change that task's structure in a way that reduced the number of motions from 18 to 5, resulting in a productivity increase of more than 200 percent. Contemporary industrial engineers still use Frank Gilbreth's methods to design jobs for the greatest efficiency.

Lillian Gilbreth concentrated her efforts on the human aspects of industrial engineering. She was a strong proponent of better working conditions as a means of improving efficiency and productivity. She favored standard days with scheduled lunch breaks and rest periods for workers. She also strived for the removal of unsafe working conditions and the abolition of child labor. The Gilbreths' time-and-motion experiments attracted quite a bit of notoriety. In fact, their application of time-and-motion studies and efficiency practices to their personal lives and the raising of their 12 children was eventually chronicled in the long-running Broadway play and subsequent motion picture *Cheaper by the Dozen.*

While Taylor and the Gilbreths dominated the scientific management subfield of the classical perspective with their focus on the productivity of the individual worker, their views were not embraced by all classical thinkers. Others focused on the functions of management or the overall organizational structure, as will be seen in the next two sections.

ADMINISTRATIVE MANAGEMENT   **Administrative management** focuses on managers and the functions they perform. This approach to management is most closely identified with Henri Fayol (1841–1925), a French mining engineer whose

Administrative management
Perspective on management that focuses on managers and the functions they perform.

major views emerged in the early 20th century.[20] Fayol made his mark when he revitalized a floundering mining company and turned it into a financial success. He later attributed his success as a manager to the methods he employed rather than to his personal attributes. Fayol was the first to recognize that successful managers had to understand the basic managerial functions. He identified these functions as planning, organizing, commanding (leading), coordinating, and controlling. He also contended that successful managers needed to apply certain principles of management to these functions. Fayol developed a set of 14 general principles of management, which are listed in Table 2.1.[21]

Many of Fayol's principles are quite compatible with the views of scientific management. For example, the objective of Fayol's principle on the division of work is to produce more and better work with the same amount of effort. Taylor was attempting the same thing with his shoveling experiments. Fayol's order principle, stating that everything and everyone should be in their proper place, is consistent with the orderly objective of time-and-motion studies.

Some of Fayol's classical theories and principles may not seem compatible with contemporary management as described in Chapter 1. For example, his principle of centralization of power and authority at upper levels of the organization is contrary to the contemporary management view of allowing frontline workers more

---

Table 2.1 | Fayol's General Principles of Management

1. *Division of work.* By dividing the work into smaller elements and assigning specific elements to specific workers, the work can be performed more efficiently and more productively.
2. *Authority and responsibility.* Authority is necessary to carry out managerial responsibilities. Managers have the authority to give orders so that work will be accomplished.
3. *Discipline.* To ensure the smooth operation of the business, it is essential that members of the organization respect the rules that govern it.
4. *Unity of command.* To avoid conflicting instructions and confusion, each employee should receive orders from only one superior.
5. *Unity of direction.* Similar activities within an organization should be coordinated under and directed by only one manager.
6. *Subordination of individual interest to the common good.* The goals of the overall organization should take precedence over the interests of individual employees.
7. *Remuneration of personnel.* Financial compensation for work done should be fair both to the employees and to the organization.
8. *Centralization.* Power and authority should be concentrated at upper levels of the organization with managers maintaining final responsibility. However, managers should give their subordinates enough authority to perform their jobs properly.
9. *Scalar chain.* A single, uninterrupted chain of authority should extend from the top level to the lowest position in the organization.
10. *Order.* Materials should be in the right place at the right time, and workers should be assigned to the jobs best suited to them.
11. *Equity.* Managers should display friendliness and fairness toward their subordinates.
12. *Stability of personnel tenure.* High rates of employee turnover are inefficient and should be avoided.
13. *Initiative.* Subordinates should be given the freedom to take initiative in carrying out their work.
14. *Esprit de corps.* Team spirit and harmony should be promoted among workers to create a sense of organizational unity.

SOURCE: Based on Henri Fayol, *General and Industrial Management*, trans. by Constana Storrs. (London: Pittman & Sons, 1949).

autonomy and authority for making and carrying out decisions. Furthermore, contemporary managers rarely demand that the goals of the overall organization take precedence over the interests of individual employees. Contemporary management thinking views employees as a valuable resource whose interests must be considered. Therefore, considerable importance is placed on satisfying the wants, needs, and desires of individual workers.

Despite the apparent incompatibility between some of Fayol's principles and the philosophies of contemporary management, several of his principles continue to be embraced by today's managers. His managerial functions of planning, organizing, leading, and controlling are routinely used in modern organizations. In fact, these functions form the framework for the organization of the material in this textbook. In addition, Fayol's principles on subordinate initiative, harmony, and team spirit are particularly applicable to the modern trend toward encouraging creativity and teamwork in the workplace.

Whereas scientific management focuses on the productivity of the individual worker and administrative management focuses on the functions of the manager, bureaucratic management, the final subfield of classical management, shifts its focus to the overall organizational system.[22]

BUREAUCRATIC MANAGEMENT **Bureaucratic management** focuses on the overall organizational system and is based upon firm rules, policies, and procedures; a fixed hierarchy; and a clear division of labor. Max Weber (1864–1920), a German sociologist and historian, is most closely associated with bureaucratic management.[23] Weber had observed that many 19th-century European organizations were managed on a very personal basis. Employees often displayed more loyalty to individuals than to the mission of the organization. As a consequence, resources were often used to satisfy individual desires rather than the organization's goals.

To counter this dysfunctional consequence, Weber envisioned a system of management that would be based upon impersonal and rational behavior.[24] Management of this sort is called a bureaucracy, and it has the following characteristics:

- *Division of labor.* All duties are divided into simpler, more specialized tasks so that the organization can use personnel and resources more efficiently
- *Hierarchy of authority.* The organization has a pyramid-shaped hierarchical structure that ranks job positions according to the amount of power and authority each possesses. Power and authority increase at each higher level, and each lower-level position is under the direct control of one higher-level position, as in Figure 2.3.
- *Rules and procedures.* A comprehensive set of rules and procedures that provides the guidelines for performing all organizational duties is clearly stated. Employees must strictly adhere to these formal rules.
- *Impersonality.* Personal favoritism is avoided in the operation of the organization. The specified duties of an employee dictate behavior. The rules and procedures are applied to all employees impersonally and uniformly.
- *Employee selection and promotion.* All employees are selected on the basis of technical competence and are promoted based upon their job-related performance.[25]

Weber felt that an organization exhibiting these characteristics would be more efficient and adaptable to change, for such a system would be able to maintain continuity. Regardless of the individual personalities who might enter or leave the system over the years, the formal rules, structure, and written records would allow the organization to continue to operate as it had in the past.

Weber believed there were three different types of authority: traditional, charismatic, and rational-legal.[26] **Traditional authority** is based upon custom or tradition.

Bureaucratic management
Perspective on management that focuses on the overall organizational system.

Traditional authority
Subordinates comply with a leader because of custom or tradition.

Figure 2.3 | Bureaucratic Hierarchical Power Structure

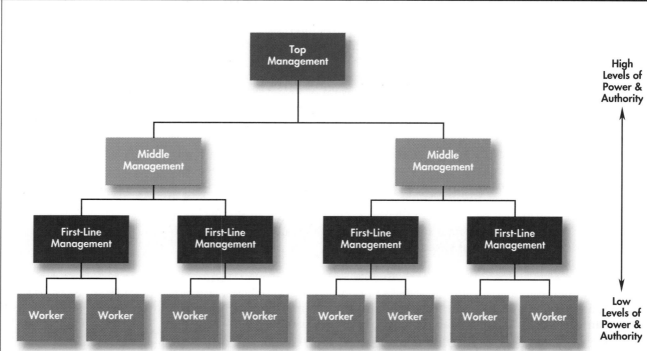

Charismatic authority
Subordinates voluntarily comply
with a leader because of his or
her special personal qualities or
abilities.

Rational-legal authority
Subordinates comply with a
leader because of a set of impersonal rules and regulations that
apply to all employees.

Charismatic authority occurs when subordinates voluntarily comply with a leader because of his or her special personal qualities or abilities. **Rational-legal authority** is based upon a set of impersonal rules and regulations that apply to all employees. Superiors are obeyed because of the positions they hold within the organization. Table 2.2 briefly describes these three types of authority and provides examples of each.

The term *bureaucracy* has taken on a negative connotation today. In many cases negative opinions about a bureaucracy are fully justified, especially when its rules and regulations are imposed in an inflexible and unyielding manner. Who among us has not been frustrated by an encounter with the bureaucratic "red tape" of some government agency or university office? At a recent Compaq shareholders meeting, frustration over not getting anyone in the company to listen to them was summed up by one angry shareholder who fumed, "Try getting a human being on the phone at Compaq." These complaints prompted Compaq's chairman to admit that the company had become too "bureaucratic."[27] An inflexible and unyielding imposition of the rules and regulations is in direct conflict with the changing face of contemporary organizations as described in Chapter 1. There we noted that future leaders must typically display a greater reliance on work teams that are empowered to use their creativity, self-motivation, and initiative to make decisions and solve problems as they work toward achieving the organization's goals.

Even though the trend is toward less bureaucracy, we should not be too quick to bury its basic tenets. Despite its associated rules and red tape, it can still provide some effective control devices in organizations where many routine tasks must be performed. Low-level employees should be able to accomplish such work by simply following the rules. Consider for the moment the situation described for United Parcel Service in the opening "Facing The Challenge" on page 44. UPS has become quite successful and efficient in its package delivery service. In fact, UPS can

Table 2.2 | Weber's Three Authority Types Authority

TYPE	DESCRIPTION	EXAMPLES
Traditional	Subordinate obedience based upon custom or tradition	Indian tribal chiefs, royalty (kings, queens, etc.)
Charismatic	Subordinate obedience based upon special personal qualities associated with certain social reformers, political leaders, religious leaders, or organizational leaders	Martin Luther King, Jr., Cesar Chavez, Mahatma Gandhi, Billy Graham, Bill Gates (Microsoft), Mary Kay Ash (Mary Kay Cosmetics), Dave Thomas (Wendy's)
Rational-legal	Subordinate obedience based upon the position held by superiors within the organization	Police officers, organizational executives, managers, and supervisors

deliver packages more efficiently and cheaply than the U.S. Postal Service. The early success of UPS was due in part to its bureaucratic structure. Rules, regulations, policies, and procedures at UPS maintained a well-defined hierarchy of workers and a well-defined division of labor. In recent years UPS management has recognized the need to soften its staunch, bureaucratic stance. In fact, it was a shifting corporate culture which empowers local managers to make decisions that enabled UPS to respond quickly to the 9/11 crisis, as described in "Leaders In Action" on page 56. Not all bureaucratic organizations can claim the success and efficiency of UPS, however. Sometimes, the rules and red tape can be carried to an unhealthy extreme. When General Motors wanted to construct a truck assembly plant in Egypt, the proposal had to pass through many ministries and required a multitude of signatures to gain approval. As a result of this sea of red tape, more than three years elapsed before final approval was granted.[28]

The classical thinkers of the late 19th and early 20th centuries made many valuable contributions to the theory and practice of management. However, their theories did not always achieve desirable results in the situations that were developing in the early 20th century. Changes were occurring in the workplace that gave rise to new perspectives on management. As a result, the behavioral perspective of management, which represents a significant departure from classical thinking, emerged.

BEHAVIORAL PERSPECTIVE

During the first few decades of the 20th century, the industrialized nations of the world were experiencing many social and cultural changes. Standards of living were rising, working conditions were improving, and the length of the average workweek was declining. Although these improvements temporarily stopped during the Great Depression and World War II, they did continue during the remainder of the century. One of the most profound changes was the newfound ability of workers to influence managerial decisions through the formation of powerful labor unions. Amid these changes, managers were increasingly finding that workers did not always exhibit behaviors that were consistent with what classical theorists had called rational behavior. Furthermore, effective managers were not always being true to the principles laid down by these traditionalists. Managers were being presented with more and more evidence that human behavior has a significant impact

LEARNING OBJECTIVE 4

Describe the theories of the major contributors to the behavioral perspective of management.

Leaders In Action

Crisis Management at UPS

September 11, 2001, dawned inauspiciously for Joe Liana, UPS district manager for Manhattan. A rare day off had given him the opportunity to play a round of golf. Liana became suspicious early in his game when several cell phone calls to his office and home were met with busy signals. On the third hole, he heard the news—the World Trade Center had been attacked. Liana, who had 27 people working there, raced off the course and caught one of the last trains to Manhattan that day. He then flagged down a UPS truck driver, and together they headed to the UPS complex on 43rd Street near the Hudson River. From the UPS complex, he had wireless messages sent to the computerized clipboards of each of his drivers, instructing them to call in. By early afternoon, he had learned that his only casualties were four trucks that were crushed in the collapse of the

buildings. By now, all air traffic had been halted, and many Manhattan streets were closed or impassable. Liana issued a call for all 4,000 of his employees to assemble at the 43rd Street complex. There, they sorted through tens of thousands of packages, searching for medical supplies. Drivers then made 200 deliveries to hospitals, doctors, and pharmacies.

On an even larger scale was the issue of air deliveries. Since most UPS air deliveries are made at night, the bulk of UPS's 620 planes were on the ground when air traffic was halted. The 56 planes that were in the air had to divert to the nearest airport—few landed at their intended destinations. Vice Chairman Michael Eskew and other senior officials quickly decided that, if all air deliveries were transferred to trucks, the UPS ground fleet would choke on the extra volume. They de-

cided to transfer to trucks only those deliveries that could reach their destinations within three days. Their guess was that UPS would be able to resume air deliveries by then. That hunch proved to be correct, and with the exception of two ZIP codes that were obliterated in lower Manhattan and five that could not be reached by UPS trucks, UPS was able to bring operations back to normal rather quickly. UPS has long been cited as an organization with a strong bureaucratic structure. Despite this tradition, its corporate culture that empowers district managers to make key decisions enabled the company to avoid bureaucratic red tape and quickly react to this crisis situation.

SOURCE: Charles Haddad, "How UPS Delivered Through the Disaster," *Business Week online*, October 1, 2001.

on the actions of workers. Observations and evidence such as this gave rise to the behavioral perspective of management, which recognizes the importance of human behavior patterns in shaping managerial style. The next sections describe the observations and research findings of several of the major contributors to this behavioral perspective.

MARY PARKER FOLLETT In the first decades of the 20th century, Mary Parker Follett, an early management scholar, made several significant contributions to the behavioral perspective of management. Follett's contributions were based upon her observations of managers as they performed their jobs. She concluded that a key to effective management was coordination. It was Follett's contention that managers needed to coordinate and harmonize group efforts rather than force and coerce people. She developed the following four principles of coordination to promote effective work groups:[29]

1. Coordination requires that people be in direct contact with one another.
2. Coordination is essential during the initial stages of any endeavor.
3. Coordination must address all factors and phases of any endeavor.
4. Coordination is a continuous, ongoing process.

Follett believed that management is a continuous, dynamic process in which new situations and problems are likely to arise as the process is applied to solve a problem. She felt that the best decisions would be made by people who were closest to the decision situation. Consequently, she thought that it was inappropriate for managers to insist that workers perform a task only in a specifically prescribed way. She argued that subordinates should be involved in the decision-making process whenever they are likely to be affected by the decision. Follett's beliefs that workers must be involved in solving problems and that management is a dynamic process rather than a static principle are certainly in contrast to the earlier views of Taylor, Fayol, and Weber, but they are more consistent with contemporary management philosophy.

Follett also made early contributions in the area of conflict management. She felt that managers could help to resolve interdepartmental conflict by communicating with one another and with the affected workers. She recognized that conflict could actually be a positive force in an organization, for, if managed properly, it could serve as an integrating factor that stimulates production efforts.[30]

ELTON MAYO Beginning in 1924, studies of several situational factors were being performed at the Western Electric Company's plant in Hawthorne, Illinois. One of these experiments was designed to demonstrate that increased levels of lighting could improve productivity.[31] Test groups and control groups were formed. The test group was subjected to a variety of lighting conditions, while the control group operated under constant lighting conditions. The results demonstrated that when illumination levels were increased, the productivity of the test group improved, as was expected. The experimenters were surprised, however, to find a similar increase in productivity when the test group's level of illumination was dramatically decreased. Equally puzzling was the fact that the control group's productivity also increased, even though its lighting conditions remained constant.

Elton Mayo, a Harvard professor and management consultant, was brought in to investigate these puzzling results. After reviewing the results of these and other newly designed experiments, Mayo and his colleagues explained the results by what has come to be known as the **Hawthorne effect**. Productivity increases were being caused not by a physical event but by a human behavior phenomenon. Workers in both groups perceived that special attention was being paid to them, causing them to develop a group pride, which in turn motivated them to improve their performance. The Hawthorne studies revealed that factors not specified by management may directly influence productivity and worker satisfaction. It was found, for example, that an informal group leader in a task group may have more power among group members than the formal supervisor. Although the Hawthorne studies were conducted between 1924 and 1933, they did not have much impact until the 1950s because of world events (the Great Depression and World War II).[32]

It has been said that the Hawthorne studies "represent the transition from scientific management to the early human relations movement" and that they "brought to the forefront the concept of the organization as a social system, encompassing individuals, informal groups, and intergroup relationships, as well as formal structure."[33] In short, the Hawthorne studies added the human element to management thinking, an element that had been missing in the classical approaches to managerial thought.

DOUGLAS MCGREGOR Douglas McGregor, whose background and training were in psychology, had a variety of experiences as a manager, consultant, and college president. McGregor was not totally satisfied with the assumptions about human behavior that were to be found in the classical perspective and the early contributions to the behavioral perspective. His experiences and background helped McGregor formulate his Theory X and Theory Y, which pose two contrasting sets of assumptions with which managers might view their subordinates. Table 2.3 provides a summary of the assumptions inherent in these contrasting views.[34]

McGregor proposed that **Theory X** managers perceive that their subordinates have an inherent dislike of work and that they will avoid it if at all possible. This theory further suggests that subordinates need to be coerced, directed, or threatened in order to get them to work toward the achievement of organizational goals. Finally, Theory X assumes that subordinates have little ambition, wish to avoid re-

Hawthorne effect
Phenomenon whereby individual or group performance is influenced by human behavior factors.

Theory X
Managers perceive that subordinates have an inherent dislike of work and will avoid it if possible.

Table 2.3 | Comparison of Theory X and Theory Y Assumptions

FACTOR	THEORY X ASSUMPTIONS	THEORY Y ASSUMPTIONS
Employee attitude toward work	Employees dislike work and will avoid it if at all possible.	Employees enjoy work and will actively seek it.
Management view of direction	Employees must be directed, coerced, controlled, or threatened to get them to put forth adequate effort.	Employees are self-motivated and self-directed toward achieving organizational goals.
Employee view of direction	Employees wish to avoid responsibility; they prefer to be directed and told what to do and how to do it.	Employees seek responsibility; they wish to use their creativity, imagination, and ingenuity in performing their jobs.
Management style	Authoritarian style of management.	Participatory style of management.

Theory Y
Managers perceive that subordinates enjoy work and will gain satisfaction from their jobs.

Douglas McGregor formulated Theory X and Theory Y, contrasting two sets of assumptions which managers might use to view their subordinates.

© BETTMANN/CORBIS

sponsibility, and prefer to be directed. Managers who subscribe to this theory are likely to exercise an authoritarian style, telling people what to do and how to do it.

In contrast, **Theory Y** managers perceive that their subordinates enjoy work and that they will gain satisfaction from performing their jobs. Furthermore, this theory assumes that subordinates are self-motivated and self-directed toward achieving the organization's goals. Commitment to the organization's goals is a direct result of the personal satisfaction that they feel from a job well done. Finally, Theory Y assumes that subordinates will seek responsibility; display ambition; and use their imagination, creativity, and ingenuity when working toward the fulfillment of organizational goals. Managers who subscribe to Theory Y are likely to exercise a participatory style, consulting with subordinates, soliciting their opinions, and encouraging them to take part in decision making.[35] In Chapter 1, we looked at the ways management and managers are changing. The greater reliance on employees as decision makers, problem solvers, and team players is a strong endorsement for McGregor's Theory Y assumptions. "Now Apply It" on page 59 provides a self-assessment exercise that allows you to assess your own tendency toward Theory X or Theory Y assumptions. This exercise can be used to apply the theory to yourself and others with whom you work to assess your management styles.[36]

CHESTER BARNARD Chester Barnard studied economics at Harvard, and although he never completed the requirements for his degree, he had a very successful management career. He started in the statistical department of AT&T, and by 1927 he had become the president of New Jersey Bell. Barnard made two major contributions to management thought: One dealt with the functions of executives, and the other was his theory of authority. He felt that executives serve two primary functions. First, executives must establish and maintain a communications system among employees. Barnard regarded organizations as social systems that require employee cooperation and continuous communication to remain effective. Second, executives are responsible for clearly formulating the purposes and ob-

Now Apply It

Theory X and Theory Y

Complete the following questionnaire. Indicate your agreement or disagreement with each of the statements by placing the appropriate number next to the statement. This is not a test, and there are no right or wrong answers. Use the following scale: Strongly Agree—5; Agree—4; Undecided—3; Disagree—2; Strongly Disagree—1.

___ **1.** Most people prefer to be directed and want to avoid responsibility.

___ **2.** Most people can learn leadership skills regardless of their particular inborn traits and abilities.

___ **3.** The best way to encourage high performance is by using rewards and punishment.

___ **4.** A leader will lose influence over subordinates if he or she allows them to make decisions without direction and strict rules.

___ **5.** A good leader gives detailed and complete instructions to subordinates, rather than depending on their initiative to work out the details.

___ **6.** Because groups do not set high goals, individual goal setting offers advantages over group goal setting.

___ **7.** A leader should give subordinates only the information necessary for them to do their immediate tasks.

___ **8.** People are bright, but under most organizational conditions, their potentials are underutilized.

___ **9.** Most people dislike work and, when possible, avoid it.

___ **10.** Leaders have to control, direct, and threaten employees to get them to work toward organizational goals.

___ **11.** Most people will exercise self-direction and self-control if they are committed to the objectives.

___ **12.** People do not naturally dislike work; it is a natural part of their lives.

___ **13.** Most people are internally motivated to reach objectives to which they are committed.

___ **14.** People are capable of innovation in solving organizational problems.

___ **15.** Most people place security above all other work factors and will display little ambition.

Scoring Key: Reverse score items 2, 11, 12, 13 (1 = 5, 2 = 4, 3 = 3, 4 = 2, 5 = 1). Sum all 15 items. A score of more than 55 indicates a tendency to manage others according to the principles in Theory X. A score of less than 35 indicates a tendency to manage others according to the principles in Theory Y. Scores between 35 and 55 indicate flexibility in the management of others.

jectives of the organization and for motivating employees to direct all their efforts toward attaining these objectives.

Barnard's other major contribution was his theory on authority. According to Barnard, authority flows from the ability of subordinates to accept or reject an order. His acceptance theory of authority suggests that employees will accept a superior's orders if they comprehend what is required, feel that the orders are consistent with organizational goals, and perceive a positive, personal benefit.[37] Many management scholars consider Barnard the father of the behavioral approach to management. In fact, many believe that his work laid the foundation for several contemporary approaches to management.

As the mid-20th century was approached on the timeline shown in Figure 2.1, new problem-solving and decision-making tools were developed, giving rise to a quantitative perspective on management. As you will see, the quantitative school provided managers with sophisticated new analytical tools and problem-solving techniques.

QUANTITATIVE PERSPECTIVE

The quantitative perspective had its roots in the scientific management approaches and is characterized by its use of mathematics, statistics, and other quantitative techniques for management decision making and problem solving. The most significant developments in this school of thought occurred during World War II, when military strategists had to contend with many monumentally complex problems, such as determining convoy routes, predicting enemy locations, planning invasion

LEARNING OBJECTIVE 5

Describe the characteristics of the quantitative perspective of management.

strategies, and providing troop logistical support.[38] Such massive and complicated problems required more sophisticated decision-making tools than were available at that time. To remedy this situation, the British and the Americans assembled groups of mathematicians, physicists, and other scientists to develop techniques to solve these military problems. Because the problems often involved the movement of large amounts of materials and the efficient use of large numbers of people, the techniques they devised could be readily transferred from the military arena to the business arena.

The use of mathematical models and quantitative techniques to solve managerial problems is often referred to as *operations research.* This term comes from the names applied to the groups of scientists during World War II (operational research teams in Great Britain and operations research teams in the United States).[39] This approach is also referred to as *management science* in some circles. Regardless of the name, the quantitative perspective has four basic characteristics:

1. *Decision-making focus.* The primary focus of the quantitative approach is on problems or situations that require some direct action, or decision, on the part of management.
2. *Measurable criteria.* The decision-making process requires that the decision maker select some alternative course of action. To make a rational selection, the alternatives must be compared on the basis of some measurable criterion, or objective, such as profit, cost, return on investment, output rate, to name a few.
3. *Quantitative model.* To assess the likely impact of each alternative on the stated criteria, a quantitative model of the decision situation must be formulated. Quantitative models make use of mathematical symbols, equations, and formulas to represent properties and relationships of the decision situation.
4. *Computers.* Although many quantitative models can be solved manually, such a process is often time-consuming and costly. Consequently, computers are quite useful in the problem-solving process (and often necessary for extremely complex quantitative formulations).[40]

In the past few decades, giant strides in microchip capability have enabled computer sophistication to advance tremendously. Computer hardware that fits in the palm of one's hand can outperform hardware that filled rooms a few decades ago. It has been said that today's average consumers have more computing power in their wristwatches than existed in the entire world before 1961. Similarly, a host of quantitative decision-making tools evolved in this century, including such tools as linear programming, network models, queuing (waiting line) models, game theory, inventory models, and statistical decision theory. Several of these are described in more detail in Chapter 7.

SYSTEMS PERSPECTIVE

LEARNING OBJECTIVE 6

Describe the systems perspective building blocks and their interactions.

Systems analysis
An approach to problem solving that attacks complex systems by breaking them down into their constituent elements.

An approach to problem solving that is closely aligned with the quantitative perspective is **systems analysis**. Because many of the wartime problems reflected exceedingly complex systems, the operations research teams often found it necessary to analyze them by breaking them into their constituent elements. Since any system is merely a collection of interrelated parts, identifying each of these parts and the nature of their interrelationships should simplify the model-building process. Systems can be viewed as a combination of three building blocks: inputs, outputs, and transformation processes. These blocks are connected by material and information flows.[41] Figure 2.4 illustrates the interaction of these blocks and flows.

Although a more thorough discussion of inputs, outputs, and transformation processes can be found in Chapters 16 and 17, the basic components of the sys-

Figure 2.4 | Basic Structure of Systems

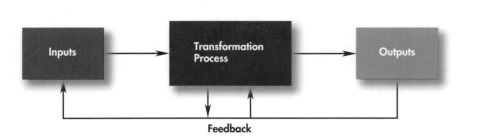

tems model can be briefly introduced here. **Inputs** can vary greatly depending upon the nature of the system. Such diverse items as materials, workers, capital, land, equipment, customers, and information are potential inputs. **Outputs** typically consist of some physical commodity or some intangible service or information that is desired by the customers or users of the system. The **transformation process** is the mechanism by which inputs are converted to outputs. We usually think in terms of a physical transformation process, in which material inputs are reconfigured into some desired output. This scenario would be typical of a manufacturing system. Several other types of transformation processes are found in nonmanufacturing types of systems, however.[42] For example, in a transportation or distribution system such as Delta Air Lines or United Parcel Service, the transformation process merely alters the location of the inputs, not their form. In storage systems such as a U-Haul storage facility or a Bank of America safety deposit box, the inputs change in the time dimension, but not in form or location. **Feedback** represents information about the status and performance of the system.

Systems are often further distinguished by whether or not they interact with the external environment. **Open systems** must interact with the external environment to survive. The interactions can be reflected in the exchange of material, energy, information, and so forth. **Closed systems** do not interact with the environment. In both the classical and early behavioral perspectives, systems were often thought of as closed. In fact, the quantitative perspective often uses a closed-system assumption to simplify problem structures. Nevertheless, the difficulty of totally eliminating environmental interactions makes it hard to defend the concepts of open and closed systems in the absolute. Perhaps more appropriately, we might view systems as relatively open or relatively closed.[43] Thus, we might think of the production department of an organization as a relatively closed system. It can manufacture products in a continuous fashion while maintaining little interaction with the external environment. Meanwhile, the marketing department would be more appropriately viewed as an open system, for it must constantly interact with external customers to assess their wishes and desires. Long-run organizational survival requires that all organizations have some interaction with the external environment; therefore, it is appropriate to think of contemporary business organizations as open systems.

Most complex systems are often viewed as a collection of interrelated subsystems. Because changes in any subsystem can affect other parts of the organization, it is crucial that the organization be managed as a coordinated entity. If decisions are made independently at the subsystem level, the organization as a whole will often achieve less-than-optimal performance. But when all organizational subsystems work together, the organization can accomplish more than when the subsystems are working alone. This property, in which the whole is greater than the sum of its parts, is referred to as **synergy**.

Inputs
Such diverse items as materials, workers, capital, land, equipment, customers, and information used in creating products and services.

Outputs
The physical commodity, or intangible service or information, that is desired by the customers or users of the system.

Transformation process
The mechanism by which inputs are converted to outputs.

Feedback
Information about the status and performance of a given effort or system.

Open systems
Systems that must interact with the external environment to survive.

Closed systems
Systems that do not interact with the environment.

Synergy
A phenomenon whereby an organization can accomplish more when its subsystems work together than it can accomplish when they work independently.

Entropy
The tendency for systems to de-cay over time.

Another important property of systems is **entropy**, which refers to their ten-dency to decay over time. As is the case with living systems, organizations must con-tinuously monitor their environments and adjust to economic, social, political, technological, and global changes. Survival and prosperity often require that new inputs be sought. A system that does not continually receive inputs from its envi-ronment will eventually die.

CONTINGENCY PERSPECTIVE

LEARNING OBJECTIVE 7

Discuss the nature of the contin-gency perspective of manage-ment.

Contingency perspective
Perspective on management which proposed that the best managerial approach is contin-gent on key variables in a given organizational situation.

In the 1960s, managers were becoming increasingly aware that the effectiveness of different management styles varied according to the situation. With this awareness came the emergence of the **contingency perspective**, which proposes that there is no one best approach to management. This perspective recognizes that any of the four previously discussed management perspectives might be used alone or in com-bination for different situations.[44] In the contingency perspective, managers are faced with the task of determining which managerial approach is likely to be most effective in a given situation. This requires managers to first identify the key con-tingencies, or variables, in the given organizational situation. For example, the ap-proach used to manage a group of teenagers working in a fast-food restaurant would be quite different from the approach used to manage a medical research team try-ing to discover a cure for AIDS.

The young fast-food worker might best be managed in a classical, authoritative style. Bureaucratic rules and regulations might be put in place to guide all worker actions and behaviors. Scientific management principles would probably be used to define the best way to perform each work task. Variation from the prescribed method would not and probably should not be tolerated in this situation. This is not the time or place to experiment with different ways to fry the burgers or mix the shakes!

It is doubtful that the medical research team would succeed under this ap-proach to management. The team is faced with a very complex, unstructured en-deavor that will require the team members to bring together all of their unique problem-solving skills. Such a situation requires that the team be given the auton-omy to try out different solutions, pursue different avenues, and take risks that would simply be out of the question for the teenaged burger flippers.

Because the contingency perspective proposes that managerial style is situa-tion-specific, it has not yet developed to the point where it can dictate the pre-ferred way to manage in all situations. A particularly important factor to consider in the contingency approach is the type of technology being used by the organi-zation. In pioneering contingency studies conducted in the 1960s, Joan Woodward discovered that a particular managerial style was affected by the organization's tech-nology. Woodward identified and described three different types of technology:

1. *Small-batch technology.* Organizations of this type exhibit job-shop characteristics in which workers produce custom-made products in relatively small quantities.
2. *Mass-production technology.* Organizations of this type exhibit assembly-line char-acteristics in which standardized parts and components are used to produce large volumes of standardized products.
3. *Continuous-process technology.* Organizations of this type have a process in which the product flows continuously through the various stages of conversion.

The level of human interaction varies with each of these technology types. Small-batch technology tends to have the most human involvement (that is, it is the most labor intensive) due to the customized outputs. Mass-production tech-nology tends to have less human involvement due to the automated and robotic equipment that typifies assembly-line operations. Continuous-process technology has the lowest level of human involvement as the product flows through the stages of conversion. Consider, for example, how little "hands-on" human involvement is needed in an ExxonMobil oil refinery as crude oil flows through the various processing stages on its way to becoming gasoline. Examples of each of these production technologies appear in Table 2.4, and all three are discussed more thoroughly in Chapter 17.[45]

Some of Woodward's findings showed that bureaucratic management methods were most effective in organizations using mass-production technology. Conversely, organizations using small-batch and continuous-process technologies had little need for the formalized rules and communication systems of the bureaucratic style.[46] Continued studies of this type will fill in all the gaps and eventually provide more definitive guidelines as to which managerial style is desirable for a particular situation.

Other important factors to consider in defining the contingencies for each situation include environment, organizational size, and organizational culture.[47] For example, large organizations may find it necessary to use more structured and rigid rules, regulations, and policies to control organizational activities. On the other hand, smaller organizations may find that they can rely less on the formal structure and allow workers the autonomy to make decisions for the situations and problems they encounter. In this example, the larger organization would undoubtedly tend toward a more bureaucratic management style, while the smaller organization would display a more behavioral orientation. As Figure 2.5 shows, parts of all of the management perspectives we have examined might be combined to form a contingency approach.

INFORMATION TECHNOLOGY AND MANAGEMENT STYLE

In recent years, we have all been witness to the tremendous advances that have occurred in the systems and devices that can process, disseminate, and transfer information. Each of our lives has been affected by cellular telephones, microcomputers, fax machines, specialty software packages, and access to information on the Internet. These same devices and systems can have a profound effect on the choice of a management style. In many instances they can facilitate the adoption of a particular style.

The most obvious areas in which technological advances in information processing facilitate the use of a particular style are the quantitative and systems perspectives. The geometric increase in microchip processing capability makes it easier

Table 2.4 | Production Technology Examples

PRODUCTION TECHNOLOGY	EXAMPLES
Small-batch technology	Custom fabrication machine shop, manufacturer of neon advertising signs, print shop specializing in personal business cards, trophy-engraving shop
Mass-production technology	Manufacturer of automobiles, manufacturer of refrigerators, manufacturer of hair dryers, manufacturer of pencils
Continuous-process technology	Oil refinery, flour mill, soft drink bottler, chemical processor

Figure 2.5 | Blending Components into a Contingency Perspective

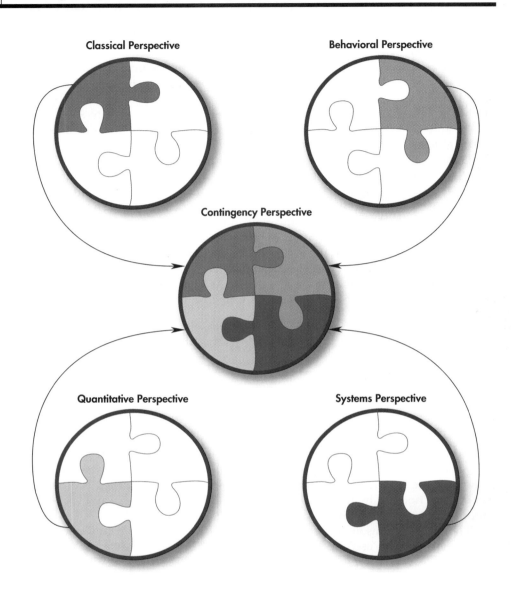

to develop ultrasophisticated quantitative models of complex management systems. Rapid processing and feedback of information in these system models allow the organization to be managed as a coordinated entity. Perhaps less obvious is the impact that information-processing technology has on the subfields of the classical perspective on management. For example, classical theories might suggest how many workers should report to a single superior (span of control) and how many hierarchical levels of authority are needed in a particular organization. But these can be altered when each employee has at his or her disposal devices that relay critical decision-making information. In addition, the centralization principle of Fayol may not be desirable in these new situations. When low-level workers are empowered to make decisions and have the needed information readily available, it is not necessary for all decisions to be made at upper levels of management.

But technological advances can be a two-edged sword. In addition to facilitating the adoption of a particular management style, they may, at times, force a change. This is evident for UPS, as described in the opening "Facing The Challenge" on page 44. The additional workload and stress to drivers brought on by a new, computerized package-tracing system has forced UPS to ease up on its traditional bureaucratic management style.[48]

FUTURE ISSUES: DIVERSITY, GLOBALIZATION, AND QUALITY

As you might expect, the theories and ideas that have emerged thus far do not represent the end of the road in the evolution of management thought. The economic, social, political, technological, and global forces that influence management thinking continue to change. A major trend in recent years has been heightened concern for diversity within the workplace. The workforce has become increasingly more varied, and the number of minority-owned businesses has continued to increase. Census Bureau data indicate that the recent growth rate of Hispanic-owned businesses in the United States is triple that of general business growth. In the words of one Commerce Department official, "Entrepreneurship is the flame that heats the American melting pot; it is the vehicle through which racial and ethnic minorities can enter the American mainstream, and it is visibly their most productive method for doing so."[49] The ranks of management need to exhibit a level of diversity that is similar to these levels of workforce and entrepreneurial diversity. Diversity within an organization can have an added side benefit. When government contracts stipulate that minority suppliers must be used, businesses displaying cultural, ethnic, and gender diversity stand a better chance of winning government business.

In recent years, Japanese management styles have received considerable scrutiny due to the tremendous successes achieved by Japanese industries. Most readers are surely aware of the degree to which the Japanese have taken control of the global automobile and electronics markets. This success has been achieved in part because of a managerial philosophy that is committed to quality and a just-in-time operating philosophy (a concept that is treated in more detail in Chapter 17).[50] This is a concept that has been adopted by virtually all of the world's other automobile manufacturers. Its benefits are not limited to automakers, however. Many other industries have successfully adopted its principles. Earlier in this chapter, we noted one of the factors that was important in the dramatic turnaround of The Harley-Davidson Motor Company. "At The Forefront" on page 66 provides a more detailed look at this company and the way in which it was able to reverse its fortunes by adopting new management philosophies. Harley-Davidson, which was nearly bankrupt, emerged as a giant in the global motorcycle market. It is ironic that Harley-Davidson's reemergence as a very desirable motorcycle has also resulted in its being the number one target for motorcycle theft.[51]

The successes of the Japanese management style are not due entirely to the technical operating system, however. Many aspects of the Japanese management style follow the prescriptions for successful management in the 21st century that were discussed in Chapter 1. A focus on quality is certainly central to the Japanese style. It is somewhat ironic that the Japanese emphasis on quality was a result of the teachings of the noted American quality philosophers W. Edwards Deming and Joseph Juran. Another noted American, Armand Feigenbaum, originated the concept of total quality control, which was quickly

LEARNING OBJECTIVE 8
Discuss the future issues that will affect the further development of management thought.

The emphasis of Japanese managers on quality is a result of the teachings of noted Americans W. Edwards Deming and Joseph Juran.

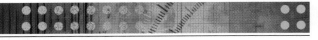

At The Forefront

Changing Style Keeps Harley-Davidson Rolling

As the year 2002 began, things could not have been rosier for Harley-Davidson Motor Company, the only major U.S.-based motorcycle manufacturer. Sales had been rising dramatically over the past several years, averaging a better than 15 percent increase per year. Even during the trying economic times of the post 9/11 fourth quarter of 2001, Harley-Davidson saw a 17.4 percent increase over the same period in the prior year. In the past decade, the number of women motorcyclists had more than doubled, the median age of motorcyclists had risen by almost 10 years, and rider median income had risen by more than $30,000 per year. Clearly, the demographics of motorcycle riders were changing, and leadership at Harley was responding to those changes. Jeffrey Bleustein, chairman and CEO of Harley-Davidson, had just announced plans for major expansions at Harley production facilities. The icing on the cake came in early 2002 when *Forbes* named Harley-Davidson the "Company of the Year." This recognition was due in part to the company's record sales growth and earnings, the company's long and storied history, the devotion of its enthusiasts, and the passion Harley-Davidson stirs in its riders, dealers, and employees. Now the company was about to embark on a 14-month odyssey that would usher in its second 100 years. That extravaganza would kick off on July 1, 2002, with a round-the-globe traveling festival of musical entertainment, activities, and exhibits of Harley history. The celebration would culminate with "one of the largest birthday parties the world has ever seen" in Milwaukee's Veteran's Park on August 31, 2003.

The atmosphere wasn't always this bright for Harley-Davidson. The company had seen as many twists and turns and ups and downs as its motorcycle riders encounter on the winding backroads of America. Although Harley once held a dominant position in the U.S. motorcycle market, its market share slipped to less than 4 percent in the late 1970s. Quality problems were rampant within the company. Dealers often resorted to placing pieces of cardboard under display models to prevent leaking oil from staining showroom floors. Honda, Kawasaki, and Yamaha motorcycles had come roaring in from Japan, offering not only lower prices but also higher-quality, state-of-the-art machines. Unable to compete with the Japanese imports on quality and price, Harley tried to prove in court that the Japanese were dumping their cycles in the United States at prices below cost to gain market share. However, it was revealed in court that the Japanese manufacturers' operating costs were 30 percent lower than Harley's. These revelations forced Harley's leadership to realize that the company would have to turn its attention inward to reverse its downslide. Company officials soon determined that the company's problems were many and varied. The company had been laboring under an outmoded production technology and a rather cumbersome organizational hierarchy. Performance was suboptimal due to lack of coordination between subsystems. Employees' opinions were seldom solicited—they were simply viewed as the muscle needed to carry out prescribed job duties. These technological, organizational, and personnel problems all contributed to production inefficiencies and motorcycles that were inferior in quality and price.

Many significant changes and improvements were, and continue to be, made at Harley-Davidson. Its tall vertical hierarchy was replaced with a flatter structure. Management revised its view of the workforce; it stopped assigning workers to narrowly defined jobs and no longer disregarded their opinions and expertise. This Theory X–like practice was replaced with a Theory Y–type attitude in which job descriptions were enlarged and workers were cross-trained to provide them with more flexibility, variety, and job security. Perhaps even more importantly, workers were brought into the decision-making and problem-solving processes. Several philosophies of the highly successful Japanese automobile manufacturers were also adopted. The result has been a complete reversal of fortunes. Both employee productivity and product quality have increased. At the same time, significant reductions in material costs, production costs, and inventory levels have been achieved. The company has been continuously profitable since these changes were implemented. Harley-Davidson has shown a commitment to continue adapting its management style with the most recent labor agreements ratified by union workers in 2001 and 2002. These agreements assure that decisions to run the business will be made by consensus of both labor and management. Such commitments should ensure that Harley-Davidson will continue to be a key player in the global motorcycle market for years to come.

SOURCES: "Get Ready to Rock, Roll and Rumble As Harley-Davidson Hits the Road to Celebrate the Next 100 Years," *Harley-Davidson Press Release*, February 4, 2002; "Harley-Davidson's Kansas City Unions Ratify Labor Agreement," *Harley-Davidson Press Release*, February 1, 2002; J. Fahey, "Love into Money," *Forbes*, January 7, 2002; "Harley-Davidson Announces Plans to Expand York, Pennsylvania Manufacturing Operation," *Harley-Davidson Press Release*, July 11, 2001; "Harley-Davidson Wisconsin Unions Ratify Seven-Year Labor Agreement," *Harley-Davidson Press Release*, April 1, 2001; J. Van, "Message to American Companies: Rebuild from Scratch," *The Orlando Sentinel*, December 8, 1991, F1; and J. A. Conway, "Harley Back in Gear," *Forbes*, April 20, 1987, 8.

adopted by the Japanese. Many American firms have now embraced the concept of quality and have been successful enough to win the coveted Malcolm Baldrige National Quality Award. Some of the more recognizable recent winners of this award include AT&T, Cadillac, Corning, Eastman Kodak, Federal Express, GTE, IBM, Motorola, Ritz-Carlton Hotels, Texas Instruments, Westinghouse, and Xerox.[52]

It would be difficult to dispute that the Japanese maintain a global focus. Although not as apparent to observers from abroad, their management style also incorporates the concept of workers as decision makers, problem solvers, and team players. These were all identified in Chapter 1 as keys to operating successfully in the 21st century. It should also be noted that the Japanese management style embraces aspects from several of the historically evolving management perspectives discussed in this chapter. The Japanese philosophy includes a strong behavioral component, for it recognizes the importance of workers as decision makers and problem solvers. There is also a hint of bureaucratic management in the Japanese philosophy with its tradition of lifelong career commitment to employees. But even that is in a state of evolution. The mounting pressure to streamline in the increasingly competitive global business environment is causing many Japanese organizations to abandon the lifetime employment concept.[53]

The Japanese management style spawned the development of **Theory Z** by William Ouchi, a contemporary management scholar.[54] Theory Z is a management approach that advocates trusting employees and making them feel like an integral part of the organization. According to the theory, once a trusting relationship is established with workers, production will increase.

Theory Z
Advocates that managers place trust in the employees and make them feel like an integral part of the organization.

Many question whether the Japanese management style has developed and evolved to the point where it can be considered a major school of management thought. Perhaps the bigger question is whether we should be calling this style "Japanese management" or something else. Much of what we call the Japanese management philosophy originated in the Japanese automobile industry. However, these manufacturers readily admit that most of their technical innovations and ideas were borrowed from the methods used by U.S. automobile manufacturers in the heyday of Henry Ford. The Japanese simply refined these technical practices and principles, as they did the behavioral and classical components that form the total package. With this awareness, perhaps a name other than "Japanese management" would be more appropriate. Whatever the name, we must still ask whether this management style has evolved to the point where it can be considered a major school of management thought. Probably not yet, for it still must stand the test of time. Nevertheless, in time this philosophy or another might be more thoroughly developed and added to the list of major management schools of thought. Any new philosophy that emerges will undoubtedly contain bits and pieces from prior theories, but these will most assuredly be combined with new elements that have evolved in response to political, economic, social, technological, and global influences. Each era presents new problems and challenges, and new management styles arise to deal with them.

IMPLICATIONS FOR LEADERS

Over the years, management theorists have developed several views on the best way to manage an organization. Each of these views is based on differing assumptions about organizational objectives and human behavior. To demonstrate quality in the management of an organization, it is important that leaders use the appropriate management approach. The 3Cs leadership model provides a prescription for success in the search for the appropriate approach. Leaders must be competent in their understanding of the evolution of management thought, and the factors that have affected and will continue to affect management thinking. In addition, their character traits must be strong, honest, and sincere if they are to build loyal followers who will contribute to the success of their organizations. Finally, a commitment to community will ensure that their actions will promote not only healthy organizations, but also healthy and vibrant communities in which their organizations operate. Therefore, tomorrow's leaders must be:

- Thoroughly schooled in the different management perspectives that have evolved over the years.
- Able to understand the various economic, political, social, technological, and global influences that have affected management thinking over the years and will continue to shape future evolutionary changes in management thought.
- Capable of identifying and understanding such key variables as environment, production technology, organization culture, organization size, and international culture as they relate to the organization.
- Prepared to select elements from the various management perspectives that are appropriate for the situation.
- Adaptable to change, because future conditions and developments can quickly render the chosen approaches obsolete.

In this chapter, we toured the major historical developments in the evolution of management thought. We saw the emergence of five major perspectives on management and many subfields within those major classifications. This march through time has revealed that certain aspects of every one of these evolutionary views are still appropriate for use in both today's and tomorrow's organizations. The successful leaders of tomorrow will be the ones who can blend together the appropriate components from the wide body of management theory.

Meeting The Challenge

For UPS the Old Practices Don't Always Fit in the New Era

When signs of worker discontent began to surface at UPS near the close of the 20th century, UPS leadership began reacting positively to head off any problems. Management acknowledged that the degree of difficulty has increased for many jobs. The UPS guarantee of 10:30 A.M. delivery for overnight letters often requires drivers to make duplicate runs during the same day. A morning run is made to deliver the overnight letters, while a later run is made to deliver the remaining parcels. Heavier parcels add a level of difficulty, as does the requirement to log in information for the parcel-tracing system. UPS Vice President Ted Gradolf's observation that "the pendulum has swung a little bit too far" has been taken to heart. Changes are being made that reflect less regimentation and greater attention to behavioral issues.

Added to these demands and those associated with learning new technologies is the fact that UPS is expanding its emphasis on developing new lines of business that com-plement the company's core package operations. UPS recently entered the logistics arena to fulfill a vision of operating across the entire stream of commerce, from goods to information to funds. It is now venturing into supply chain services to capitalize on its expertise in building and operating global information technology and physical infrastructures and managing complex networks. Historically, UPS hires had been predominantly high school graduates. However, UPS has begun to hire more skilled and college-educated workers to deal with these new job demands and has implemented programs whereby current employees can further their education. UPS is proud of its diversity initiative. Minorities make up one-third of its 320,500 U.S. employees and more than one-half of its new hires for 2001. *Fortune* ranks UPS as one of the "50 Best Companies for Minorities." However, as the diversity of the UPS workforce has increased, management has encountered an increasing number of workers who are less tolerant of rigid work rules. UPS has included language in its new contract with employees stating that management will not coerce, harass, intimidate, or overly supervise any employee and that no one will be discriminated against because of race, sex, national origin, disability, sexual orientation, age, or religion. These measures have helped placate matters for now, but as change continues to be a part of this work environment, UPS management must remain receptive to further modifications to its management policies.

SOURCES: "New Supply Chain Solutions Links Logistics, Freight and Financial Services," *UPS Press Release*, February 20, 2002; "UPS Once Again 'America's Most Admired'," *UPS Press Release*, February 19, 2002; M. Fleschner, "Worldwide Winner: The UPS Success Story," *SellingPower.Com*, November 8, 2001; "UPS Begins Direct Service to China," *UPS Press Release*, March 30, 2001; and F. Robert, "As UPS Tries to Deliver More to Its Customers, Labor Problem Grows," *The Wall Street Journal*, May 23, 1994, A1ff.

SUMMARY

1. As agricultural societies were transformed into industrial societies as a result of the Industrial Revolution, managerial thinking was shaped by a variety of economic, political, social, technological, and global influences. Such influences continue to affect the way in which leaders function.

2. In the past century, five major perspectives of management thought have evolved: the classical, behavioral, quantitative, systems, and contingency perspectives. The classical perspective developed in the later part of the 19th century and the first part of the 20th century. The behavioral perspective began to evolve in the first third of the 20th century. Development of the quantitative perspective began in earnest during World War II. The systems perspective began to evolve in the 1950s, while the contingency perspective is the most recent, having begun in the 1960s.

3. The classical perspective includes scientific management, administrative management, and bureaucratic management subfields, each of which has a different focus. Scientific management focuses on the improvement of individual worker productivity. Time-and-motion studies observe and measure a worker's physical movements in order to determine the best way of performing a task. The expectation in scientific management is that managers will develop standard methods for performing each job, select workers with the appropriate abilities for each job, train workers in standard methods, and support workers by planning their work. Scientific management proponents believe that financial incentives are the major motivating factor that will induce workers to produce more. Administrative management focuses on the managerial process and the functions of the manager. Fayol identified planning, organizing, leading, coordinating, and controlling as the basic managerial functions. Bureaucratic management has as its primary focus the overall structure of the organization. This subfield emphasizes the division of labor into specialized tasks, a hierarchy of authority in which power and authority increase at higher levels of the organization, a comprehensive set of rules and procedures for performing all organizational duties, a climate of impersonality in which personal favoritism is to be avoided, and an employee selection and promotion process that is based on technical competence and performance.

4. The behavioral perspective of management had several major contributors. Mary Parker Follett emphasized the importance of coordination and harmony in group efforts. Elton Mayo recognized that the human element could play a significant role in determining worker behavior and output. Douglas McGregor proposed Theory X and Theory Y to explain employee attitudes and behavior. Chester Barnard examined the functions of executives. He contended that executives are responsible both for establishing and maintaining a communications system among employees and for clearly formulating the purposes and objectives of the organization and motivating employees toward attaining those objectives. Barnard also contributed an acceptance theory on authority, which was a new way of describing how subordinates accept or reject orders from their superiors.

5. The major impetus for the emergence of the quantitative perspective of management was World War II and the many monumentally complex problems associated with the war effort. The quantitative perspective has a decision-making focus in which an alternative course of action must be selected as a solution to some problem. It requires the establishment of some measurable criteria so that alternatives can be compared prior to selection. Quantitative models are used to assess the impact of each alternative on the stated criteria, and computers are often helpful in the problem-solving process.

6. The systems perspective takes a set of inputs and subjects them to some transformation process, thereby generating some type of output. Inputs, transformation processes, and outputs can be quite varied, but the basic structure remains the same. Throughout this process, feedback loops constantly filter information about the status and performance of the system.

7. The contingency perspective of management suggests that there is no one best approach to management. It is a situational approach, for the proper managerial style is dependent upon the key variables, or contingencies, within the given situation.

8. In the future, cultural, racial, and gender diversity will have a huge influence on management thinking. In addition, quality and globalization will have an enormous impact on how businesses and industries are managed.

REVIEW QUESTIONS

1. *(Learning Objective 1)* Describe the major factors that have influenced the evolution of management thought.

2. *(Learning Objective 2)* Identify the five major perspectives of management thought.

3. *(Learning Objective 3)* Describe the central focus of the scientific management, administrative management, and bureaucratic management subfields of the classical perspective on management.

4. *(Learning Objective 4)* Describe the major behavioral perspective contributions of Follett, Mayo, McGregor, and Barnard.

5. *(Learning Objective 5)* Discuss the four basic characteristics of the quantitative perspective of management.

6. *(Learning Objective 6)* Describe the various building blocks of a systems perspective and indicate how they interconnect and interact.

7. *(Learning Objective 7)* What is the main contention of the contingency perspective of management?

8. *(Learning Objective 8)* What future issues are likely to affect further development of management thought?

DISCUSSION QUESTIONS

Improving Critical Thinking

1. Reexamine Weber's characteristics of a bureaucracy and Taylor's opinions in the areas of task performance, supervision, and motivation. Discuss aspects of their views that are similar in nature.

2. Some suggest that Japanese management is just the same old stuff in a new package, while others suggest that this style is a new and different departure. Provide arguments in support of both of these views.

Enhancing Communication Skills

3. In your own life experiences, you probably have had some occasion to use aspects of the scientific management approach. Try to recall some physical task that you analyzed to determine the best or most efficient way to perform it. To enhance your oral communication skills, prepare a short (10–15 minute) presentation for the class in which you describe that task and the results of your analysis.

4. Based upon your personal observations of well-known authority figures, identify at least two authority figures in each of Weber's authority types (traditional, charismatic, and rational-legal). To enhance your written communication skills, write a short essay describing these authority figures and why you classified each of them as you did.

Building Teamwork

5. Have you ever been influenced by the Hawthorne effect? Try to recall some incident in which your performance was affected because you knew you were being watched. To refine your teamwork skills, meet with a small group of students who have been given this same assignment. Compare and discuss your experiences and then reach a consensus on the group's two most interesting experiences with the Hawthorne effect. The group members whose experiences were judged the most interesting will act as spokespersons to describe these experiences to the rest of the class.

6. Try to recall an encounter that you have had with a bureaucratic organization. Think about both the positive and negative aspects of that experience. To refine your teamwork skills, meet with a small group of students who have been given this same assignment. Compare and discuss your experiences, and then reach a consensus on which two experiences represented the most rigid and unwavering bureaucratic response from the organizations. The group members whose experiences were judged to have the most rigid bureaucratic response will act as spokespersons to describe these experiences to the rest of the class.

THINKING CRITICALLY: DEBATE THE ISSUE

Bureaucratic Management—Good or Bad?

Form teams of four or five students as directed by your instructor. Research the topic of bureaucratic management, identifying both its positive and its negative aspects. Look for situations in which it works effectively and others in which it seems to be ineffective. Prepare to debate either the pros or cons of this approach. When it is time to debate this issue in front of the class, your instructor will tell you which position you will take.

EXPERIENTIAL EXERCISE 2.1

Theory X and Theory Y

Purpose: To give class members an opportunity to reflect on McGregor's Theory X and Theory Y concepts.

Procedure: Perform the following five steps.

Step 1. Divide the class into small teams of approximately three to five students per group.

Step 2. Based on team members' personal observations of businesses with which they have interacted, have each team identify a business where employees seem to fall into McGregor's Theory X category and one where employees seem to fall into his Theory Y category.

Step 3. Have each team present its observations to the entire class.

Step 4. Identify all examples that exhibited overlap among teams.

Step 5. Identify whether the overlapping businesses were categorized the same or differently. When differences occurred, try to have the selecting teams explain those differences.

Fayol's Principles Versus Woodward's Technology Types: How Do They Fit?

Purpose: To assess how well each of Fayol's 14 principles fits with Woodward's three technology types.

Procedure: Perform the following three steps.

Step 1. Construct a matrix containing 14 rows and 3 columns. Label each of the rows with one of Fayol's principles and each of the columns with one of Woodward's technology types.

Step 2. Place a rating between 1 and 10 in each of the cells of the matrix. The rating in a cell is to be your subjective assessment of how well the principle identified by the row fits or applies to the technology type identified by the column. A rating of 1 indicates the least applicable (or worst fit), and a rating of 10 indicates the most applicable (or best fit). Since your ratings for a principle might vary for different companies in the same technology type, try to make each rating an average of your observations, experiences, or knowledge of different companies in each technology type.

Step 3. With the aid of your instructor, assemble the ratings from your classmates who have had this same assignment. Compute a class mean rating for each cell of the matrix.

1. Using whatever search vehicle you prefer (Internet, fax, telephone, etc.), develop a list of all services provided and fees charged by United Parcel Service and Federal Express. Then, using any presentation software package, prepare a slide show presentation for your classmates that compares the services of these two companies.

2. Use the Internet to search for information on foreign automobile companies that have manufacturing plants in the United States. Then put this information into an electronic spreadsheet that can be sorted by manufacturer, state, or model name of automobile. Compare your lists with the lists of classmates to discover who performed the most thorough search.

3. Use the Internet to search for the names of all Malcolm Baldrige National Quality Award winners since its inception. Then arrange this information into an electronic spreadsheet that will allow you to provide three lists. The first list will use the year of the award as the primary sort and category of award as the secondary sort. The second list will use category as the primary sort and year as the secondary sort. The third list will use company name as the primary sort.

In the continuing evolution of management thinking, much attention is currently being paid to what is called the "Japanese style of management," which is often associated with a just-in-time (JIT) operating philosophy. In a manufacturing environment, JIT proposes many departures from the traditional Western way of operating. In a high-volume, repetitive manufacturing environment, one of the traditional Western ways of thinking advocates a division of labor coupled with a highly specialized workforce. Worker responsibilities are often very narrowly defined, and each worker's skill expectations are quite specific. In fact, over the years union contracts have often evolved that specify precisely what a worker can and cannot be expected to do.

The emerging JIT philosophy holds that there is no room in such an environment for highly specialized workers. Instead, multiskilled, cross-trained workers are essential to make the system operate effectively. Often, long-time, specialized workers find that they are out of their element in such situations and are in danger of being phased out.

For Discussion

1. Discuss the ethical issues and dilemmas when workers no longer fit the mold.

2. Discuss potential remedies for this problem.

VIDEO CASE

Evolution of Management Thought: Sunshine Cleaning Systems, JIAN, and Archway Cookies

During this century, business leaders and management theorists have continually asked the question, "What is the best way to manage?" A search for the answer to this question has revealed that there is no one best way to manage. Instead, a variety of management techniques and viewpoints have proven effective. Through experience, business leaders have learned that three of the most effective viewpoints are found in the behavioral perspective, the contingency perspective, and the quality focus. The success of an individual firm often hinges on its business leaders' abilities to match its unique circumstances to an appropriate overall management viewpoint. Sunshine Cleaning Systems, JIAN, and Archway Cookies are organizations that are leaders in their respective industries. Each of these companies effectively has applied a different overall management viewpoint to create a successful organization.

Sunshine Cleaning Systems, which emphasizes the behavioral perspective, is a privately held company with annual revenues of $10 million. The company, founded in 1976 by former major league baseball player Larry Calufetti, employs approximately 1,000 people and offers janitorial services, pressure cleaning, and window cleaning. The company sees itself as a "people business" because cleaning is a labor-intensive business requiring a highly dedicated workforce for the company to succeed. To nurture and motivate its employees, Sunshine employs a supportive management style dedicated to helping employees become proficient at and feel good about their jobs. They respect their employees, train them, and establish a mutual trust with them. As a result, Sunshine maximizes its abilities and provides clients an exemplary level of customer service. Sunshine believes its focus on and support of its employees has enabled the company to achieve these impressive results in a highly competitive industry.

JIAN Corporation is an innovative software company located in the Silicon Valley of northern California. The company, created in 1988 by Burke Franklin, is a leader in producing software products for emerging and established businesses. JIAN's first product, BizPlan Builder, has sold more than 300,000 copies. JIAN is in a highly competitive industry that requires the firm to respond quickly to changing market demands. As a result, the firm has adopted the contingency approach to management, taking into account changes in important environmental variables: external environment and entrepreneurial employees. To build on JIAN's strengths, Burke created a virtual corporation by establishing close partnerships with Bindco and ExecuStaff. Bindco manufactures and distributes JIAN products worldwide, while ExecuStaff provides human resource functions such as recruiting and hiring JIAN employees. Thus, JIAN is able to maintain a small headquarters staff who concentrate on developing and marketing new software products. JIAN has established a culture of collaboration, teamwork, and open communications enabling it to respond quickly to frequent market changes.

Archway Cookies, the third largest cookie manufacturer in the United States, has built its success by emphasizing quality. The company manufactures and markets high-quality, homestyle-baked products sold fresh by baking, packaging, and distributing the cookies within 48 hours. This gives Archway a quality advantage over competitors who store their cookies in warehouses before distributing them. Archway's philosophy on quality is a key part of its mission and culture. Archway managers assert that their employees are an integral part of Archway's success. The employees are dedicated to producing high-quality, good-tasting cookies; many employees have worked for Archway all of their working lives. Archway carefully monitors quality in all areas of their operations. For example, they carefully train their employees, monitor the quality of their suppliers' operations and ingredients, and test the moisture content, color, size, and texture of the cookies. They keep a sample of each batch of cookies to test for shelf-life and to make sure they don't run into any unforeseen problems. Archway asserts that the ultimate test of quality is how the cookies taste.

Sunshine Cleaning Systems, JIAN, and Archway Cookies emphasize various management practices. Their successes have depended largely on their business leaders' abilities to match their unique characteristics to appropriate management viewpoints.

For Discussion

1. Do you believe that the leaders of Sunshine Cleaning Systems, JIAN, and Archway Cookies have selected appropriate management viewpoints for their respective firms? Why or why not? How would a firm know if it has selected the wrong approach?

2. How do environmental factors of management thought appear to impact Sunshine, JIAN, and Archway's managerial approaches?

3. Will a firm's management viewpoint remain stable over the life of the firm or should a firm be continually reviewing its approach to management? Explain your answer.

4. Do you see evidence of management viewpoints other than the dominant ones noted in the case or video? Provide examples of other viewpoints illustrated for the three companies.

www.sunshinecleaning.com
www.jian.com
www.archwaycookies.com

CASE

Growing Green Changes Its Management Style

Growing Green, Inc. of St. Louis, founded in 1973 by entrepreneur Teri Pesapane and her husband, Joel, was formed to operate as a plantscaping and plant care business and small gift shop. Their venture was capitalized with $3,200 from their savings. In the early years of operation, Teri and Joel were able to handle all aspects of the business. Generally, Teri negotiated the deals, and Joel handled the deliveries. By 1988, the Pesapanes had seen their business grow to the point where their revenues were $700,000 and their staff consisted of 16 employees. It seemed that this two-person operation had come a long way. Unfortunately, all was not as rosy as this picture might seem. The Pesapanes had a real crisis on their hands. Employee morale was low, turnover was high, and employees either couldn't or wouldn't make decisions. They felt compelled to check with Joel on everything, even for such routine decisions as what sprays or fertilizers needed to be applied to certain plants and when they should be applied. Teri and Joel felt that they were prisoners of the business; they couldn't even go away for a weekend without fear that their business might fall apart.

Realizing that they had to relinquish some control, the Pesapanes attended a seminar on work team management. Armed with the insights gained from the seminar, they divided the staff of Growing Green into small action teams, each with decision-making authority. A sales team was formed to bring in new business, an operations team was designated to handle plant installations, a service team was assigned the responsibility of maintaining plants at customer sites, and an administrative team took care of billing and other financial matters. The senior-level employees from each of these teams compose a management team. Teri and Joel no longer get involved in the daily decision making; this responsibility has been taken over by various work teams. In fact, the two have been able to be away from the business for extended periods of time without the previously feared catastrophic results. With this new structure, Growing Green has seen its client base more than double and its revenues grow to well beyond $1 million.

For Discussion

1. Describe how the managing and leadership philosophy changed at Growing Green after the Pesapanes attended the team management seminar.

2. Even after the changes, some might see elements of scientific management thinking in the organization. Try to relate Frederick Taylor's concept of functional foremanship to the restructuring into a sales team, an operations team, and a service team.

CHAP

SOCIAL RESPONSIBILITY AND ETHICS

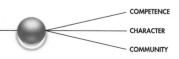

LEADERSHIP

COMPETENCE

CHARACTER

COMMUNITY

TER ³

Corporate social responsibility and business ethics have been the focus of a great deal of attention in recent years. Organizations are increasingly being held accountable for the contributions they make to society, as well as for the degree to which their individual members adhere to an appropriate code of ethical conduct. Furthermore, managers of the future will be expected to address important social issues proactively and to maintain a high standard of ethical behavior if they are to succeed within the corporate environment.

This chapter begins with a discussion of the stakeholder view of the firm. With that view in mind, we will explore the concept of social responsibility, examine three perspectives of social responsibility, and consider several strategies for approaching social issues. In addition, recommendations for developing a socially responsive position are offered. With regard to business ethics, we will consider values and the role they play in shaping one's ethical behavior. Approaches for addressing ethical dilemmas are discussed as well. Our examination of ethics concludes with a discussion of ways to encourage and support ethical behavior in a corporate environment. Implications for tomorrow's managers are also discussed.

LEARNING OBJECTIVES

When you have finished studying this chapter, you should be able to:

1. Discuss the stakeholder view of the firm and the impact of the globalization of business on social responsibility and ethics.
2. Describe the concept of corporate social responsibility and the primary premises upon which it is based.
3. Distinguish among the three perspectives of corporate social responsibility.
4. Identify and evaluate different strategies for responding to social issues.
5. Discuss the 10 commandments of social responsibility.
6. Explain what values are, how they form the basis of an individual's ethical behavior, and how they may vary in a global business environment.
7. Describe how advances in information technology have created new ethical challenges.
8. Identify and discuss the differences in the utility, human rights, and justice approaches to ethical dilemmas.
9. Explain the methods used by an organization to encourage ethical business behavior.
10. Describe the different approaches used in ethics training programs.
11. Discuss what is meant by whistleblowing in monitoring ethical behavior.

Facing The Challenge

The Rise and Fall and Rise of Paul Wieand: A Leader's Journey

Paul Wieand's rocket ride to success in the banking industry had all the makings of a Hollywood movie. In the early 1980s, at the age of 33, he was president of Independence Bancorp, a $2 billion, 1,000-employee bank in suburban Philadelphia. He had it all—money, power, and a celebrity lifestyle. By age 37, he was positioned to become the country's youngest CEO of a major corporation.

Growing up with an undiagnosed learning disability, Wieand's life had not always been so glamorous. He barely graduated from high school and spent his early years only dreaming of being rich. In part to avoid the draft during the Vietnam War, he entered a two-year business school and then later enrolled at Dyke College in Cleveland, Ohio. When he began dating a student whose father had a Harvard Ph.D., he decided to take academics more seriously. He was

drawn to a field where he had always shown a natural aptitude: finance and economics. After graduating from college, Wieand took an entry-level position with Bucks County Bank, a small but prestigious bank. He worked tirelessly to move up the corporate ladder—from credit analyst to president in less than 10 years. During this time, he also earned an MBA and began teaching Executive MBA college courses.

As his career progressed, Wieand orchestrated a number of megamergers that more than tripled the size of the bank. He renamed his holding company Independence Bancorp and modeled it after the U.S. federal banking system. But even at the pinnacle of his business success, small cracks were beginning to surface in his personal life. He began to lose touch with his coworkers and himself. He became "intoxicated" with his own success,

seeing himself only as a "bank president" and no longer as a person.

When Wieand became involved in a bitter battle for Independence Bancorp's CEO position, he began lobbying, and alienating, Bancorp's board of directors. After Wieand convinced his rival to give up his bid for CEO and concede the position to Wieand, a celebration was in order. Wieand and his wife left for a vacation in Paris to celebrate his imminent appointment as Bancorp's CEO. When he returned from his vacation, however, his victory began to unravel. The bank's retiring CEO and legal counsel were waiting for him in his office with a letter of resignation for him to sign. Stunned and disappointed, Wieand signed the letter and plummeted into a deep depression. His dream had turned into a nightmare and his world began to collapse.

INTRODUCTION

The circumstances surrounding Paul Wieand's rise and fall are tragic and, unfortunately, not uncommon. Wieand's career progression led to greater success for him and the bank, but it also insulated him from critical feedback and honest introspection. As he climbed the corporate ladder, he lost touch with his own identity. This led to alienation from his peers and coworkers, and more importantly, Bancorp's board of directors.

The situation facing Bancorp and Paul Wieand are relevant to all of us because they can teach us valuable lessons about personal ethics and leadership. When the leader of an organization loses touch with his employees or customers, the negative consequences are often felt by many both inside and outside the organization. As such, leaders must take care to act responsibly and ethically with regard to the issues that affect those around them.

As we examine corporate social responsibility and ethics, you will see examples that illustrate the benefits of responsible and ethical behavior, as well as others that illustrate the negative consequences of irresponsible or unethical behavior. First, however, we must answer a very important question: To whom is business responsible? Is it the stockholders of the company? The customers? The employees? Answering this question requires an understanding of the stakeholder view of the firm.

ORGANIZATIONAL STAKEHOLDERS IN A GLOBAL ENVIRONMENT

Central to the issues of corporate social responsibility and ethics is the concept of stakeholders.[1] **Stakeholders** are all those who are affected by or can affect the activities of the organization.[2] While it has long been accepted that a corporation must be responsible to its stockholders, contemporary social responsibility theory maintains that a corporation has obligations to all of its stakeholders. This perspective broadens the scope of the business's obligations beyond a relatively narrow group of shareholders to a much broader set of constituents that includes such groups as government, consumers, owners, employees, and communities throughout the globe.[3]

Figure 3.1 illustrates the many and varied constituent groups that can be stakeholders in a given organization. The primary stakeholders of a firm are those who have a formal, official, or contractual relationship with the organization. They include owners (stockholders), employees, customers, and suppliers. Peripheral to this group are the secondary stakeholders, who include other societal groups that are affected by the activities of the firm. Consider, for example, who might represent primary and secondary stakeholders for your college or university. As a student, are you a primary or secondary stakeholder? What about the employers in your community? Are they primary or secondary stakeholders? What about Bancorp's stakeholders? Which stakeholders were affected by Paul Wieand's actions?

LEARNING OBJECTIVE 1

Discuss the stakeholder view of the firm and the impact of the globalization of business on social responsibility and ethics.

Stakeholders
People who are affected by or can affect the activities of the firm.

Figure 3.1 | The Stakeholder View of the Firm

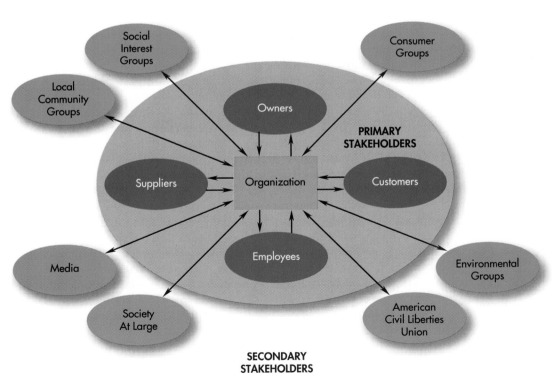

SOURCE: *From Business & Society: Ethics and Stakeholder Management*, 3rd edition, by A.B. Carroll. © 1996. Reprinted with permission of South-Western, a division of Thomson Learning. Fax 800-730-2215.

As organizations become involved in the international business arena, they often find that their stakeholder base becomes wider and more diverse. Organizations that must cope with stakeholders from across the globe face special challenges that require a heightened sensitivity to and awareness of economic, political, and social differences among groups. For example, international firms must be responsive to customers with very different needs, owners with varied expectations, and employees with distinct, and perhaps dissimilar, motivations.[4] Dealing effectively with such groups requires a focus on understanding the global nature of stakeholders and developing strategies that recognize and respond to such differences. As an example of the challenges that come from managing within an international environment, consider the controversy over purchasing products from economically depressed nations. Many people believe that big U.S. corporations take advantage of poorer nations and exploit their labor by purchasing goods at an unreasonably low price.

With the stakeholder view of the organization in mind, let's move on to examine the concepts of social responsibility and ethics. Although these two topics are integrally related, they can and should be addressed independently. Corporate social responsibility is an organizational issue that relates to the obligation of business to society. In contrast, ethical issues are most relevant at an individual level, for ethics are maintained by people, not organizations. Nevertheless, both are important topics that have significant implications for the long-term success of any organization.

SOCIAL RESPONSIBILITY

LEARNING OBJECTIVE 2

Describe the concept of corporate social responsibility and the primary premises upon which it is based.

Few issues have been the subject of more heated debate than corporate social responsibility. For decades, practitioners and academics have argued over the nature and extent of the obligations business has to society. Perspectives on the issue of corporate social responsibility have varied dramatically over the years, and even today achieving consensus on the subject is difficult.[5]

In the wake of the collapse of Enron, questions surrounding corporate social responsibility are being asked more intently than ever before. Issues such as hiding debt from investors, losing the retirement pensions of loyal employees, and senior executives cashing out their stock before the value declines are very serious matters that are more relevant today than ever before.

Corporate social responsibility
The interaction between business and the social environment in which it exists.

What is corporate social responsibility? It is a complex concept that resists precise definition. In a very general sense, **corporate social responsibility** can be thought of as the interaction between business and the social environment in which it exists. Most would agree that being socially responsible means acting in a way that is acceptable to society and that all organizations should act in a socially responsible manner.

The debate over corporate social responsibility focuses on the nature of socially responsible behavior. Does being socially responsible mean that the corporation's actions must not harm society, or does it mean that the corporation's actions should benefit society? How does one distinguish between harm and benefit? These issues are at the heart of the controversy over corporate social responsibility.

To gain a better understanding of corporate social responsibility, we will first examine the two basic premises of the concept. Then, with these premises in mind, we will explore three perspectives of corporate social responsibility that exist today, as well as a model for evaluating corporate social behavior.

THE PREMISES OF THE SOCIAL RESPONSIBILITY DEBATE

Many would argue that the controversy over the responsibility of business is inevitable, given the moral and ethical challenges that corporate America has faced over the last several decades. You don't need to look far to find examples of organizations that have acted "irresponsibly" in the eyes of some segment of society. Whether it involved a violation of worker safety regulations, insufficient attention to product safety for consumers, or the relocation of a plant (and numerous jobs) to a foreign country with lower labor costs, corporate America has been besieged with accusations of social irresponsibility in recent years.[6]

The discussion of social responsibility began over 35 years ago when H.R. Bowen proposed that businesses and managers have an obligation to "pursue those policies, to make those decisions, or to follow those lines of action that are desirable in terms of the objectives and values of our society."[7] This simple proposition inspired the modern debate about social responsibility.

Bowen's assertions rest on two fundamental premises, social contract and moral agent, which can be summarized as follows:

- **Social contract.** Business exists at the pleasure of society, and as a result, it must comply with the guidelines established by society. An implied set of rights and obligations is inherent in social policy and assumed by business. This set of rights and obligations can be thought of as a social contract between business and society.
- **Moral agent.** Business must act in a way that is perceived as moral. In other words, business has an obligation to act honorably and to reflect and enforce values that are consistent with those of society. Furthermore, business can be held accountable as a moral agency.

These two premises have provided the foundation for the concept of social responsibility, but they have also served as targets for critics of the concept. In fact, there are several perspectives on social responsibility that differ mainly in their view of these two premises. Let's examine these perspectives in greater detail.

Social contract
An implied set of rights and obligations that are inherent in social policy and assumed by business.

Moral agent
A business's obligation to act honorably and to reflect and enforce values that are consistent with those of society.

THE THREE PERSPECTIVES OF SOCIAL RESPONSIBILITY

Three primary perspectives of corporate social responsibility have emerged over the years: economic responsibility, public responsibility, and social responsiveness.[8] Table 3.1 outlines the primary tenets of these perspectives. Each perspective views

LEARNING OBJECTIVE 3

Distinguish among the three perspectives of corporate social responsibility.

Table 3.1 | Three Perspectives of Social Responsibility

PERSPECTIVE	BASIC TENETS
Economic responsibility	• The responsibility of business is to make a profit within the "rules of the game." • Organizations cannot be moral agents. Only individuals can serve as moral agents.
Public responsibility	• Business should act in a way that is consistent with society's view of responsible behavior, as well as with established laws and policy.
Social responsiveness	• Business should proactively seek to contribute to society in a positive way. • Organizations should develop an internal environment that encourages and supports ethical behavior at an individual level.

SOURCE: S.L. Wartick and P.L. Cochran, "The Evolution of the Corporate Social Performance Model," *Academy of Management Review*, 10, 1985, 764.

Bowen's two premises somewhat differently and, consequently, offers a different view of the concept of corporate social responsibility.[9]

ECONOMIC RESPONSIBILITY   Although many hold the economic responsibility perspective, one of its most outspoken proponents is Milton Friedman. Friedman maintains that the only social responsibility of business is to maximize profits within the "rules of the game." In his opinion, the only constituents to which business is responsible are the stockholders, and it is the firm's responsibility to maximize the wealth of this constituent group. This is the only social contract to which business should be committed. If socially responsible behavior on the part of the corporation serves to reduce the financial return to the stockholders, the managers of the business have undermined the market mechanism for allocating resources and have violated the social contract of business as it should be in a free market society. In fact, some business leaders, such as Harold Geneen, the long-time leader of ITT, suggest that the clearest expression of social responsibility is to provide steady, well-paying jobs.[10]

Proponents of the economic responsibility perspective also argue that corporations cannot be moral agents. Only individuals can serve as moral agents. When individuals choose to direct their own assets or resources toward the public good, that behavior is appropriate and to the benefit of society. However, when they begin to direct corporate resources toward that end, they have violated their commitment to the owners (that is, the stockholders) of those assets or resources.

Critics of the economic responsibility perspective argue that many of today's business organizations are not merely economic institutions and to view them as such is both unrealistic and naïve. Many large corporations wield significant political power and have tremendous influence on a wide variety of public policies and regulations across the globe. Moreover, the activities of many corporations are essential to realizing important social goals such as equal opportunity, environmental protection, and increased global competitiveness in critical industries. Viewing the modern corporation as simply an economic institution is myopic and ignores the reality of the worldwide evolution of business.[11] Figure 3.2 illustrates, in a somewhat humorous way, how decisions that are economically desirable can be very negative from a social welfare perspective, reinforcing the view that business has a significant impact on society.[12]

PUBLIC RESPONSIBILITY   The public responsibility perspective represents an alternative view of social responsibility. Focusing almost exclusively on the social contract premise, proponents of public responsibility argue that business should act in ways that are consistent with public policy. Rather than viewing public policy as simply the laws and regulations with which business must comply, supporters of this philosophy define public policy as "the broad pattern of social direction reflected in public opinion, emerging issues, formal legal requirements, and enforcement or implementation practices."[13] In other words, public policy refers to the overall perceptions and expectations of the public with regard to the interaction between business and society.

Critics of the public responsibility position argue that it lacks clarity. If public responsibility means adhering to existing public policy, which is traditionally considered to be the laws and regulations of the legal system, then this perspective differs little from the economic perspective. Like the economic perspective, this view would imply only that business should comply with the "rules of the game." If, however, a broader view of public policy is assumed, the public responsibility perspective differs little from the traditional view of social responsibility and Bowen's concept of social contract. Consequently, critics of the public responsibility position argue that it does not reflect a unique philosophy and that, unless it is defined more clearly, it is redundant to other perspectives.

Figure 3.2 | Economic Consequences Versus Social Consequences

SOURCE: © 1992 Jimmy Margulies, *The Record*, New Jersey.

SOCIAL RESPONSIVENESS The third perspective of social responsibility is that of social responsiveness. Proponents of this perspective argue that corporate social responsibility should not be simply an obligation on the part of business to meet the minimum expectations of society. Viewing social responsibility in this way suggests that it is a burden. Rather, modern corporations should proactively seek to act in ways that improve the welfare of society. Social responsiveness implies a proactive and tangible effort to contribute to the well-being of society.

The social responsiveness perspective also recognizes the moral agency aspect of corporate social responsibility. While proponents of this perspective agree with the economic responsibility proponents that morality is an individual rather than an organizational obligation, they maintain that the organization is responsible for creating and maintaining an environment in which moral behavior on the part of individual organizational members is encouraged and supported.

Many have endorsed the social responsiveness perspective, arguing that profitability and social responsibility are not antagonistic concepts, but rather are interdependent. In fact, some argue that there are several trends that are converging to shape a new social imperative in the 21st century. These trends include a deepening consumer conscience, an increase in socially conscious investing, and the growing impact of global media.[14] Despite the growing acceptance of this perspective, however, this philosophy sparks some interesting and legitimate questions. One of the most pervasive has been the question of how much social responsiveness is enough. The perspective fails to define the extent to which an organization should proactively attempt to benefit society. At what point do the efforts of the organization come at the expense of profitability?

Critics of this perspective also argue that it ignores issues of social irresponsibility. Acting irresponsibly is often of greater consequence than failing to act responsively. Consider, for example, how Exxon's irresponsible behavior during the Valdez oil spill affected the environment. Table 3.2 provides some examples of socially irresponsible behavior that have occurred in the last two decades. As is clear

Table 3.2 | Socially Irresponsible Behaviors

Unfortunately, you need not look far to find examples of socially irresponsible corporate behaviors. Consider the following incidents:

- Swiss conglomerate Nestlé marketed infant formula in developing countries by encouraging new mothers to give up breast-feeding and switch to formula. The company used so-called "milk nurses" to promote their products in maternity wards. These women, who were actually sales representatives for the company, dressed as nurses, increasing their credibility with new mothers. As a result, many new mothers made the switch. But there were problems: (1) The formula had to be mixed with water, which was contaminated in many countries, causing health problems for many infants; (2) the mothers could not easily afford the product so they would overdilute it, causing malnutrition problems for their babies; and (3) once these mothers had given up breast-feeding, they were completely dependent on this product to feed their babies. Eventually bowing to organized protests and boycotts from numerous activist groups, the company finally agreed to alter its marketing practices. Did Nestlé have an obligation to fully educate mothers in these Third World countries about product usage and safety issues?

- A chemical leak at a Union Carbide plant in Bhopal, India, killed 2,500 people and injured 200,000 more. Investigations revealed that appropriate safety precautions had not been taken and that the deficiencies were made possible because of lax regulation and enforcement practices in India. (For example, while the Environmental Protection Agency in the United States has a staff of over 4,000, the counterpart organization in India has a staff of about 150.) Did Union Carbide have an obligation to pursue the same safety measures in India as it did in the United States, irrespective of the government's ability to monitor and enforce such standards?

- When the dangers of silicone breast implants became apparent in the United States, the Food and Drug Administration asked all domestic manufacturers to adopt a voluntary moratorium on exports. Dow Corning ceased all sales in the international marketplace, citing the need to apply the same standards internationally as it follows domestically. Three other manufacturers continued to export their silicone breast implants. Should multinational companies apply the same product standards internationally as they do domestically?

And what about the more recent activities of some American companies?

- An American manufacturer of textiles and sporting gear subcontracts with producers in Latin America and Southeast Asia, whose employees, including some 13-year-olds, work 12-hour days and are paid a small fraction of U.S. wages. Is this appropriate labor policy?

- A large corporation announces that it will be laying off a significant portion of its workforce, and then announces a pay increase for its top executives. Does this represent a fair allocation of limited resources?

- A major corporation announces that it's considering relocating a facility where it now employs several thousand people to any state in the region that will give it the largest tax break. As a result, it receives a package of tax abatements worth several million dollars—a sum that otherwise would have been spent improving the local schools. Is it appropriate to divert tax dollars in this way?

SOURCE: R. Reich, "The New Meaning of Corporate Social Responsibility," *California Management Review*, 20, 2, Winter 1998, 8–17. Copyright © 1988, by The Regents of the University of California. Reprinted from the California Management Review, Volume 40, No. 2. By permission of the Regents.

from these incidents, irresponsible behavior by organizations can have far-reaching and long-term effects.

Evaluating the social behavior of organizations can be quite difficult given the diversity of perspectives regarding social responsibility. The following section describes one framework for evaluating the extent to which organizations demonstrate socially responsible behavior.

THE FOUR FACES OF SOCIAL RESPONSIBILITY

In a very general sense, an organization's social behavior can be categorized according to two dimensions: legality and responsibility. As illustrated in Figure 3.3, four combinations of legal and responsible behaviors are possible: (1) legal/responsible, (2) legal/irresponsible, (3) illegal/responsible, and (4) illegal/irresponsible.[15]

Although one would hope that all organizations would operate in a legal and responsible manner, the evidence suggests otherwise. In fact, there are far too many

Figure 3.3 | The Four Faces of Social Responsibility

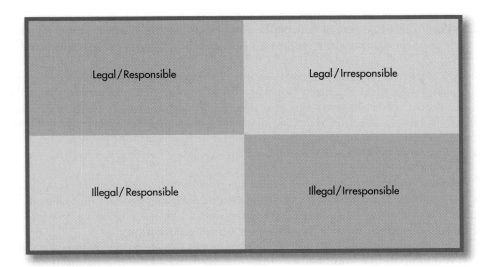

SOURCE: D.R. Dalton and R.A. Cosier, "The Four Faces of Social Responsibility." Reprinted with permission from *Business Horizons*, May/June 1982, 19–27. Copyright © 1982 by the Trustees at Indiana University, Kelley School of Business.

examples of firms that have behaved in an illegal or irresponsible way. Why would a company choose to behave illegally or irresponsibly? Let's consider a situation where that might happen.

Suppose a manufacturing company has been notified of a new pollution regulation that will affect one of its plants. The cost of complying with the regulation is $1.2 million, while the fine for failing to comply is $25,000. The likelihood of being caught in noncompliance is 10 percent, and even if the organization is caught, there will be little publicity. Although noncompliance would be both illegal and irresponsible, a cost-benefit analysis might suggest that the organization not comply with the regulation. Is this an appropriate decision? Absolutely not. Yet some companies facing such a situation might make that choice. When the penalty associated with breaking the law is less costly than complying with the law, an organization may make an inappropriate decision.

Consider the other two quadrants in the model. Can you think of examples of organizations that have acted legally but irresponsibly? Illegally but responsibly? Under what conditions might an organization choose to act in such ways? Consider both the classic and more contemporary incidents profiled in Table 3.2. In which quadrant would each of these incidents fall? Clearly, at least some of the examples were legal. In fact, the organizations involved might argue that they took those actions to maximize shareholder wealth.[16] But were their actions socially responsible?

Organizations typically will behave in ways that are consistent with their overall strategy for responding to social issues. Social responsibility strategies may range from doing nothing to making an attempt to benefit society in tangible ways. The following section identifies four different strategies for social responsibility and examines reasons why an organization might choose a particular strategy.

SOCIAL RESPONSIBILITY STRATEGIES

As we know, organizations take very different approaches to corporate social responsibility. Some organizations do little more than operate to ensure profitability

LEARNING OBJECTIVE 4

Identify and evaluate different strategies for responding to social issues.

for their stockholders, while others maintain aggressive and proactive social responsiveness agendas.

Figure 3.4 illustrates a continuum of social responsibility strategies that range from "do nothing" to "do much." Four distinct strategies can be identified along this continuum: reaction, defense, accommodation, and proaction. They vary according to the organization's tendency to be socially responsible or responsive.[17]

REACTION   An organization that assumes a reaction stance simply fails to act in a socially responsible manner. Consider, for example, the classic case of Manville Corporation.[18] Over 40 years ago, the medical department of Manville Corporation (then known as Johns Manville) discovered evidence to suggest that asbestos inhalation causes a debilitating and often fatal lung disease. Rather than looking for ways to provide safer work conditions for company employees, the firm chose to conceal the evidence.

Why? That's hard to say, but evidence suggests that the company was more concerned about profitability than about the health and safety of its employees. Presumably, top executives at Manville thought it would be less costly to pay workers' compensation claims than to develop safer working conditions.

Manville's irresponsibility did not go without notice, however. Eventually, as a result of litigation, the company was forced to pay a $2.6 billion settlement, which forced a reorganization that left the company on very shaky ground. Was shareholder wealth maximized by the irresponsibility of Manville's leaders? Obviously not. The stockholders of the firm lost a substantial amount of money as a result of the company's reactive social responsibility strategy.

DEFENSE   Organizations that pursue a defense strategy respond to social challenges only when it is necessary to defend their current position. Consider, for example, the three major automobile manufacturers in this country. How did they react to the social issues of air pollution, vehicle safety, and gas shortages in the 1970s?

When Dr. Haagan-Smit, the prophet of smog, proclaimed that automobiles were the major contributor to U.S. smog, domestic car manufacturers argued that the problem was really a function of poorly maintained vehicles. When Ralph Nader brought the issue of vehicle safety to the foreground of social consciousness, the automakers argued that bad drivers were the problem, not unsafe cars. And when the oil crisis struck and consumers demanded more fuel-efficient automobiles, car manufacturers continued to give them new models of the same gas hogs of the past.[19]

Can we call this social responsiveness? Hardly. The U.S. car manufacturer's strategy was one of defense. Not until Japanese automakers proposed solutions to these social issues and U.S. automakers began to see the effect of their complacency on the bottom line did they begin to act in a socially responsible manner.

Figure 3.4 | Social Responsibility Strategies

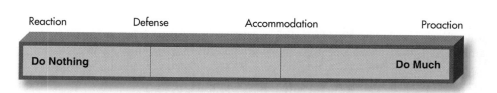

SOURCE: A. Carroll, "A Three-Dimensional Conceptual Model of Corporate Performance," *Academy of Management Review*, 4, 1979, 497–505.

They were forced to respond to the needs of society (and their customers) as a result of pressures from foreign competitors.

ACCOMMODATION   Corporations with an accommodation strategy of corporate social responsibility readily adapt their behaviors to comply with public policy and regulation where necessary and, more important, attempt to be responsive to public expectations.[20]

Consider, for example, financial services companies that are required by regulation to disclose certain information. While virtually every financial services company meets the minimum requirements of disclosure regulation, some companies maintain a more proactive code for voluntary, on-demand disclosure of bank information requested by its customers or by any other member of the public. This policy of "ask and you shall receive" is an example of an accommodation strategy of social responsibility.[21]

PROACTION   Organizations that assume a proaction strategy with regard to corporate social responsibility subscribe to the notion of social responsiveness. They do not operate solely in terms of profit; nor do they consider compliance with public policy, regardless of how it is defined, to be sufficient. These organizations proactively seek to improve the welfare of society.

As we move into the 21st century, most of the world's role-model companies acknowledge that they have a broader role in society than simply making profits for investors. These companies understand that they must invest in their local, regional, national, and international communities. Consider, for example, Becton Dickinson & Co., a medical-supply firm that has targeted its charitable contributions to projects it believes "will help eliminate unnecessary suffering and death from disease around the world." In one new program, the company partnered with the United Nations Children's Fund in a five-year effort to conquer neonatal tetanus, a disease that is unfamiliar to Americans but kills more than 1,000 newborns daily in 58 developing countries. Table 3.3 describes other organizations, like Becton Dickinson & Co., that go above and beyond the call of duty to address important social issues.

But don't be mistaken. These companies may not be purely altruistic in their giving. Recent studies seem to suggest that consumers respond well to companies with established social responsibility agendas.[22] Thus, corporate giving programs may simply make good business sense. As a result, numerous companies have begun to integrate "cause-related marketing" into their overall marketing mix. Cause-related marketing takes place when a company links itself to a charitable cause through an ongoing program. Companies that select causes that complement their mission and enhance their image tend to be the most successful. For example, Norwich Union, a comprehensive insurance company in Ireland, chose to build on its slogan "No one protects more" by linking with St. John Ambulance of the United Kingdom to provide free first-aid courses to the public. The company advertised its strategy on national TV, and after 15 months, 13,000 people had been trained in its program. Of those 13,000 people, 60 percent said they felt more positive about Norwich Union as a result of the campaign.[23] Other companies have used cause-related marketing as well. For example, food companies such as General Mills, Kraft, and Sara Lee support antihunger organizations such as food banks and soup kitchens; McDonald's helps ill children and their families through their Ronald McDonald Houses; and Mary Kay Cosmetics focuses on women's health issues such as breast cancer.[24] Key to the success of any such strategy, however, is convincing the public that the company is sincere about its efforts and that the initiative is fully integrated into its business plan.

Which strategy is the best? Should all organizations assume a proaction strategy with respect to corporate social responsibility? Not neces-

McDonald's helps ill children and their families by offering a place to stay at its Ronald McDonald houses.

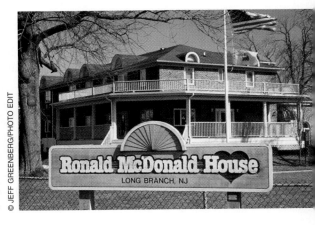

© JEFF GREENBERG/PHOTO EDIT

Table 3.3 | Examples of Proactive Social Responsiveness

- *Honda.* Voted #1 by *Consumer Reports* for its safety-oriented self-propelled lawn mowers. It beat its competitors to the market with the mower even before safety legislation was passed. (**http://www.honda.com**)
- *Pennsylvania Power & Light Company.* Set up a citizen advisory board to discuss company issues that affect the general public. (**http://www.ppl-inc.com**)
- *Xerox Corporation.* Allows employees with at least three years of company service to take a one-year leave of absence to participate in a community service project. Employees receive normal pay and raises from Xerox and are promised a comparable job when they return. (**http://www.xerox.com**)
- *3M Company.* Initiated an environmental protection program called "Pollution Prevention Pays." As part of the program, 3M set a goal of reducing its air, land, and water releases 90 percent by the year 2000. So far it has been successful in cutting pollutants by more than 500,000 tons since 1975. The National Wildlife Federation's Corporate Conservation Council gave 3M an Environmental Achievement Award in recognition of its progress to date. (**http://www.mmm.com**)
- *Kaiser Aluminum.* Agreed to an affirmative-action plan that would place more racial minorities in craftwork positions. (**http://www.kaiseral.com**)
- *GE Plastics.* At GE company conferences, employees teamed up to discuss ways of renovating old community buildings in San Diego. (**http://www.ge.com/plastics**)
- *Merck & Company.* Spent millions of dollars to develop Mectizan, a drug that prevents river blindness, a disease found mostly in West Africa. The company also distributed the drug free of charge in all countries where river blindness is found. (**http://www.merck.com**)
- *Gulf Power Company.* Pensacola, Florida-based Gulf Power Company helped find and fund a new home for wildlife when the original site of a wildlife sanctuary was sold. The company helped recruit its employees to volunteer and also donated money to the effort. (**http://www.gulfpower.com**)
- *Kraft General Foods.* Now uses recycled plastic for its salad dressing bottles, making it the first company to use recycled plastics in food containers other than soft-drink bottles. (**http://www.kraftfoods.com**)
- *Rubbermaid.* Came out with a litterless lunch box called the "Sidekick." It features plastic sandwich, drink, and snack containers and means that plastic wrap, cans, and milk cartons will no longer be necessary to pack a lunch. The box has developed a strong market share and has become the rage among grade-schoolers. (**http://www.rubbermaid.com**)
- *Monsanto.* Chairman and CEO Richard J. Mahoney pledged that the company would be environmentally responsible by reducing emissions, eliminating waste, working for sustainable agriculture, and managing corporate land to benefit nature. (**http://www.monsanto.com**)
- *Eastman Kodak.* Encourages its 100,000 employees to volunteer in local community programs by allowing them to take time off from work with pay (up to 40 hours a year) to volunteer for public service. The time does not offset vacation or sick leave and is typically used for volunteering at churches, schools, shelters, and environmental organizations. (**http://www.kodak.com**)

SOURCES: "Corporations Going Green," *Business Ethics*, March/April 1992, 10; D. Bihler, "The Final Frontier," *Business Ethics*, March/April 1992, 31; and "On Company Time: The New Volunteerism," *Business Ethics*, March/April 1992, 33. Reprinted with permission from *Business Ethics Magazine*, 612/962–4701, 52 South 10th St., Ste. 110, Minneapolis, MN 55403.

sarily. There are, however, some basic social responsibility principles to which all organizations should subscribe.

SOCIAL RESPONSIBILITY IN THE NEW MILLENNIUM

LEARNING OBJECTIVE 5

Discuss the 10 commandments of social responsibility.

All evidence points to a growing emphasis on social responsibility in the future.[25] The fallout from the collapse of Enron will only intensify this emphasis as employees, customers, and investors demand accountability from the actions of cor-

At The Forefront

Social Entrepreneurs

The term "social entrepreneur" sounds like an oxymoron to most of us. "Social" is often associated with social services provided by government agencies, while "entrepreneur" calls to mind big money and big business. According to Michael Young, founder of the School for Social Entrepreneurs in London, a social entrepreneur is someone with the heart of a do-gooder and the mind of a businessperson. They are true business entrepreneurs who are seeking innovative solutions for social problems that government agencies have been unable to solve.

Even with this definition, the line between lending a helping hand and making a healthy profit is often blurred. Perhaps the most well-known social entrepreneur is Anita Roddick, founder of The Body Shop. Roddick was a tireless activist for social causes when she founded The Body Shop, but she readily concedes that at the end of the day, a business enterprise has to make money first.

If one hopes to become a social entrepreneur, several things should be considered:

- Accept that financial rewards will not be huge—social entrepreneurs are committed to positive social change, not get-rich-quick schemes.
- Tackle a problem of which you have firsthand knowledge and start in your own community.
- Have a serious business plan with concrete financial goals.
- Don't try to cure all of society's ills with one project.
- Refine your idea to a specific need.

- Remember that the more seriously you take your business, the more seriously others in the community will take you.

Social entrepreneurship is founded on the view that many of the conventional structures and attitudes in the social sector simply do not work. Individuals with a cause, not committees, are agents for positive change. And while social entrepreneurs may not command the celebrity status of their business counterparts, they are gaining recognition and endorsement as their good works in the social sector cause ripple effects throughout their communities at large.

SOURCE: A. Garrett, "Dynamic Leaders with a Social Conscience," *Management Today*, November 2000, 138–143.

porate leaders. Organizations that wish to attract socially conscious consumers know they must be socially conscious themselves if they are to meet the needs of those consumers. Similarly, organizations that have invested in their communities and have demonstrated socially responsive behaviors often find it easier to attract high-quality workers.[26] This is particularly true for organizations that are dependent upon the knowledge workers we described in Chapter 1. Organizations that strive to respond effectively to the expectations and needs of all of their stakeholders, including customers and employees, may have a competitive edge over others in their industry.

But in the new millennium, organizations may have to go beyond social responsiveness to what some are calling **social innovation**.[27] Social innovation involves a partnership between private enterprise and public interest that produces profitable and enduring change for both parties. It requires businesses to think beyond traditional charitable contributions to address social problems and toward innovative strategies that bring about real and sustainable solutions. While this model represents a new way of thinking about social responsibility, some of the premier companies in the United States are already paving the way. For example, companies such as Bell Atlantic, Marriott International, and IBM have pursued a strategy of social innovation to create win-win solutions to some of this country's most significant social challenges.

As corporations and managers look for ways to fulfill their obligations to society in the highly dynamic business environment of the future, they can benefit by keeping the following 10 commandments in mind:[28] In "At The Forefront: Social Entrepreneurs" above, you are introduced to the entrepreneurial opportunities offered in social innovation. The "Thinking Critically: Debate the Issue" feature on page 107 asks you to consider how companies strike a balance between community investment and the need to make a profit.

- *Commandment I:* Thou shall take corrective action before it is required. Compliance with self-imposed standards is almost always preferable to compliance with standards that are imposed by outside constituencies. Organizations should continually look for ways to improve product safety and reliability before they are forced to do so by lawsuits, regulatory bodies, or competition. (See Table 3.3 for an example of how Honda demonstrated this commandment.)

- *Commandment II:* Thou shall work with affected constituents to resolve mutual problems. Organizations should not make decisions that have significant social implications in isolation. Instead, they should work with those involved to try to find mutually acceptable solutions. For example, many organizations that have considered closing plants have found that discussing the issues with plant employees has led to alternative solutions (cost-cutting measures, employee stock-option plans, and the like) that have been preferable for all parties involved.

- *Commandment III:* Thou shall work to establish industrywide standards and self-regulation. Companies and industries can preserve their freedom to conduct business as they see fit by behaving responsibly before a regulatory body forces them to do so. Although developing industrywide standards requires cooperation and coordination among the players in the industry, the effort is well worth the price if it can avert ill-conceived regulations.[29] Always remember that regulations developed by those outside the industry are likely to be less effective than self-developed policy.

- *Commandment IV:* Thou shall publicly admit your mistakes. Few things are worse for a company's image than being caught trying to cover up socially irresponsible behavior. It is far better to admit mistakes as soon as they are discovered, make restitution as expediently as possible, and establish control systems to ensure that such mistakes never happen again.

- *Commandment V:* Thou shall get involved in appropriate social programs. Most organizations that are truly concerned about their responsibility to society become involved in one or more social programs. Where possible, organizations should look for programs that have a need for some special talent or skill that they possess so that the benefits of their contribution are magnified.[30]

- *Commandment VI:* Thou shall help correct environmental problems. Regardless of the industry in which a firm operates, there are always opportunities to address environmental issues in a proactive manner.[31] At a minimum, doing so can help a company build a favorable image in its community, and in many cases, it can even lead to significant cost savings.

- *Commandment VII:* Thou shall monitor the changing social environment. Like other components of the external environment, the social environment is ever changing. Socially responsible organizations should monitor these changes and act proactively to address social trends as they occur. For example, the increasing diversity of the workforce requires organizations to make an aggressive effort to ensure that people of different racial, ethnic, and cultural backgrounds are given equal opportunities for advancement. Being on the "cutting edge" of social responsiveness will enhance the image of the organization and provide greater benefits for those affected by such trends.

- *Commandment VIII:* Thou shall establish and enforce a corporate code of conduct. Every business organization should establish a code of conduct that governs the actions of the organization as well as the behavior of its individual members. This code of conduct should be distributed throughout the organization and should be used as a guide for decision making and action by all individuals and groups in the organization.

- *Commandment IX:* Thou shall take needed public stands on social issues. Organizations should never ignore social issues or refrain from taking a position.

Clearly, many organizations would prefer to avoid controversial issues, but it is important that they stand up for what is right, whether the issue is discrimination, unsafe products, or disregard for the environment. It is important to take a stand.

- *Commandment X:* Thou shall strive to make profits on an ongoing basis. Ignoring the need to make profits is one of the most severe acts of irresponsibility. An organization cannot provide jobs and employ workers if it is not in a position to make consistent profits. To fail to recognize the importance of profitability is to threaten the livelihood of the employees of the organization.

Managers today must act in a socially responsible fashion. Their actions will be in vain, however, if the individual members of the organization do not have strong ethical values. In the next section of the chapter, we will examine more closely how ethics influence the behavior of individuals in the organization.

ETHICS

Ethics is everyone's business, from top-level managers to employees at the lowest levels of the organization. One of management's most important challenges is to conduct business ethically while achieving high levels of economic performance. Why ethical problems arise in business and what can be done about them are some of the issues that will be addressed in this section.

UNDERSTANDING BUSINESS ETHICS

Should you pay a bribe to obtain a business contract in a foreign country? Is it acceptable to allow your company to dispose of hazardous waste in an unsafe fashion? Can you withhold information that might discourage a job candidate from joining your organization? Is it appropriate to conduct personal business on company time? These are just a few examples of ethical and moral dilemmas you may face as a manager.

In recent years, increasing attention has been focused on ethics in business, due in large part to media coverage of a number of unethical actions.[32] Embezzlement, Defense Department favoritism to suppliers, fraudulent billing practices, immoral politicians—these are just a few of the issues recently raised by the news media and stockholders. Consider, for example, how insider trading and other improprieties on Wall Street captured the attention of many people. Books such as *Liar's Poker* and *Nightmare on Wall Street* provide an all-too-vivid depiction of the corruption and unethical behavior that characterized the "jungle" of trading stocks and bonds.[33] In fact, as described in one book, the hapless trainee who was new to the jungle "didn't worry much about ethics—he was just trying to stay alive." More recently, worries have begun to emerge regarding day trading in the stock industry. Some fear that there may be a dark and seedy side of day trading that will create some new ethical challenges in the investments industry.[34]

But the investments business is not the only industry to attract attention for ethical violations. Consider, for example, the scandals profiled in Table 3.4, all of which involved charitable institutions.[35]

Ethics reflect established customs and morals and fundamental human relationships that may vary throughout the world. Often ethical issues are controversial because they raise emotional questions of right and wrong behaviors. For our purposes, we will define **ethical behavior** as behavior that is morally accepted as "good" and "right" as opposed to "bad" or "wrong" in a particular setting. Right behavior is considered ethical behavior, while wrong behavior is considered un-

Ethics
The established customs, morals, and fundamental human relationships that exist throughout the world.

Ethical behavior
Behavior that is morally accepted as good or right as opposed to bad or wrong.

Table 3.4 | Examples of Ethical Problems in Charitable Organizations

- *UNICEF.* Staff personnel in Kenya were charged with fraud when they stole $10 million by mismanaging funds, padding expense accounts, double-billing for services, and channeling money to phony organizations.
- *United Way.* President William Aramony and two associates defrauded the national charity of $1 million, partly to fund Aramony's high living.
- *American Parkinson Disease Association.* Executive director Frank Williams embezzled about $80,000 a year for 10 years, in part because he felt undercompensated by the association.
- *Foundation for New Era Philanthropy.* Founder John G. Bennett, Jr. was charged with fraud when he bilked $100 million from other charities by way of a pyramid scheme.

SOURCE: D. Stipp, "I Stole to Get Even: Yet Another Charity Scam," *Fortune,* October 30, 1995, 24. © 1995 Time Inc. All rights reserved.

ethical. Corporate executives are concerned with business ethics because they want their companies to be perceived as "good" and "right" in their interactions with stakeholders. In many cases, the goal is to avoid illegal or unethical corporate behavior leading to adverse governmental or societal reactions such as warnings, recalls, injunctions, monetary or criminal penalties, adverse public opinion, or loss of contracts.[36]

In the business world, however, the difference between right and wrong behavior is not always clear—particularly when organizations are operating in an international, multicultural environment.[37] Although many unethical behaviors are illegal in the United States, some may be within the limits of the law in other countries. The three international ethical issues that have been subject to the greatest scrutiny by the media, government, and other social agencies are corruption (for example, bribery and improper payments), inadequate labor conditions, and environmental responsibility.[38] For many years, international social activists have been calling for U.S. corporations to develop global codes of ethics that would be applied in all international markets.[39] Recent surveys suggest that U.S. companies have moved boldly in that direction, developing global ethical principles to guide their overseas organizations.[40] In fact, as you will read later in this chapter, many of the premier U.S. companies have developed global codes of ethics that are disseminated across the world.

LEARNING OBJECTIVE 6

Explain what values are, how they form the basis of an individual's ethical behavior, and how they may vary in a global business environment.

Values

Relatively permanent and deeply held preferences upon which individuals form attitudes and personal choices.

FOUNDATIONS OF ETHICS Although ethical behavior in business does reflect social and cultural factors, it is also highly personal and is shaped by an individual's own values and experiences. In your daily life, you face situations in which you can make ethical or unethical decisions. You make your choices based on what you have learned from parents, family, teachers, peers, friends, and so forth. Your ethics are also determined by your values.

Values are the relatively permanent and deeply held preferences of individuals or groups; they are the basis upon which attitudes and personal choices are formed. Values are among the most stable and enduring characteristics of individuals. Much of what we are is a product of the basic values we have developed throughout our lives. An organization, too, has a value system, usually referred to as its organizational culture. We will discuss organizational culture in more detail in Chapter 11.

To better understand the role of values as the foundation for ethical behavior, let's look at a basic values framework. Rokeach developed a values framework and identified two general types of values: instrumental values and terminal values.[41]

Instrumental values, also called means-oriented values, prescribe desirable standards of conduct or methods for attaining an end. Examples of instrumental values include ambition, courage, honesty, and imagination. **Terminal values**, also called ends-oriented values, prescribe desirable ends or goals for the individual and reflect what a person is ultimately striving to achieve. Terminal values are either personal (such as peace of mind) or social (such as world peace). Examples of terminal values are a comfortable life, family security, self-respect, and a sense of accomplishment.

Different groups of people tend to hold different values. For example, business school students and professors tend to rate ambition, capability, responsibility, and freedom higher than people in general do. They tend to place less importance than the general public on concern for others, helpfulness, aesthetics, cultural values, and overcoming social injustice.[42] In most cases, the ethical standards and social responsibility of an organization or business reflect the personal values and ideals of the organization's founders or dominant managers.[43] Over the years, those values and ideals become institutionalized and become integral to the organization's culture.[44] For example, Thomas Watson's personal values and ethics formed the basis of IBM's culture. At Johnson & Johnson, the culture is based on the ideals of General Robert Wood Johnson. At Hewlett-Packard, the values reflect the personalities and beliefs of Bill Hewlett and David Packard. At General Motors, Alfred Sloan was credited with being the moral voice of the culture. In each case, these individuals were the source of their organizations' experiences, values, and principles. They were the behavioral role models for the organizations' ethical behavior and commitment to social responsibility.

Instrumental values
Standards of conduct or methods for attaining an end.

Terminal values
Goals an individual will ultimately strive to achieve.

Leaders In Action

Honesty Is the Best Policy

The excitement and entrepreneurial spirit that permeate the hallways of small start-up companies can be overwhelming. Employees are anxious to share their personal stories about their company. This spirit is perhaps most apparent in the computer and information technology industries; Silicon Valley in California is at the center of this excitement.

If you were to ask employees what makes their company special, most would discuss their inspirational founder, their tireless efforts to succeed, or their laidback culture. A few, however, would emphasize a quality that rarely takes center stage in Silicon Valley, or anywhere else for that matter—integrity.

Employees of CenterBeam Inc., an information technology solutions company based in Santa Clara, California, relate story after story of how their chairman and CEO, Sheldon Laube, espouses and acts on in-

tegrity. Many times, he has kept his word to customers and suppliers, even when canceling an order or asking for an extension would have saved the company money. Laube reminds his employees that if Center-Beam is going to be a company people can trust, it must keep its promises—even when it hurts.

Building a reputation of honesty and integrity is critical to both capital funding and long-term success. As the dot-com industry suffered a recent downturn, venture capital for these start-up businesses dried up. Darlene Mann, a partner with the venture capital firm Onset Ventures, states that honesty and integrity are important core values that she considers when making investment decisions. According to Mann, if integrity is going to be a cornerstone in a company's mission, leaders need to think hard about three issues: the growth goals that they promise to customers and investors,

the career opportunities that they promise to employees, and the tone that they strike in day-to-day negotiations with business partners. In some cases, Mann acknowledges, keeping one's word carries extra short-term costs. But wiggling away from the truth can be disastrously expensive in the long run.

In the fast-paced Internet economy, it's easy to think there isn't time to worry over the finer points of honesty and integrity. But without attending to these critical issues, things actually become more complicated and in the long term, business suffers. In a world that has been forever changed by the Internet, it's nice to know that some of the most astute business leaders believe that honesty is still the best policy.

SOURCE: G. Anders, "Honesty Is the Best Policy—Trust Us," *Fast Company*, 37, August 2000, 262–264.

An organization's culture and the practices of its senior managers can influence the ethical behavior, not only of its employees, but also of other individuals and entities associated with the organization. Therefore, the challenge facing an organization is how to successfully develop, sustain, review, and adapt its ethical standards and its commitment to socially responsible behavior.[45]

BUSINESS ETHICS   Business ethics is not a special set of ethical rules that differ from ethics in general. **Business ethics** is the application of the general ethical rules to business behavior. If a society deems dishonesty to be unethical and immoral, then anyone in business who is dishonest with employees, customers, creditors, stockholders, or competition is acting unethically and immorally.

Businesses pay attention to ethics because the public expects a business to exhibit high levels of ethical performance and social responsibility. Many ethical rules operate to protect society against various types of harm, and business is expected to observe these ethical principles. High ethical standards also protect the individuals who work in an organization. Employees resent invasions of privacy, being ordered to do something against their personal convictions, or working under hazardous conditions. Businesses that treat their employees with dignity and integrity reap many rewards in the form of high morale and improved productivity. People feel good about working for an ethical company because they know they are protected along with the general public. In contrast, most employees do not feel good about working for companies that demonstrate unethical behaviors.

Recent improvements in information technology have raised new issues with regard to business ethics.[46] From an employee perspective, concerns about information privacy have escalated in recent years, as business organizations and government agencies have gained greater access to private information about individuals.[47] From an organizational perspective, unethical acts by employees are increasing as a result of access to information technology in the workplace. In fact, according to a recent study conducted by International Communication Research, nearly half of American workers engaged in unethical behavior as a result of technology. Such behaviors include accessing personal files, sabotaging data, and using the computer for personal reasons.[48] Another area of concern raised by sophisticated information technology relates to businesses providing customer information to other organizations. Such concerns have led some companies to publicly express their promise to protect their customers' privacy. For example, see Hewlett-Packard's core values statement in Table 3.5.

An emerging ethical issue related to information technology relates to its use as a persuasive technology. In other words, computers can be used to persuade users—that is, intentionally alter their attitudes or behavior—through a variety of means. But some people are concerned that it may go beyond persuasion to manipulation in some cases.

The debate on how to deal with the ethical challenges presented by advancing information technologies continues today. Perhaps the greatest consensus lies in developing ethical codes related specifically to the appropriate use of computer technology in the workplace.[49] However, as advances in information technologies continue, concerns regarding the ethical use of such technologies are certain to increase.

PRESSURES TO PERFORM   In the past few years, the negative and questionable ethical practices of many public figures and corporations have attracted considerable media attention. White-collar crimes such as insider trading and money laundering drain billions of dollars a year from corporations and governments. This cost is ultimately borne by consumers and taxpayers. Unethical behavior is often blamed on the emphasis on materialism, as well as on economic and competitive pressures to perform.[50] In today's environment of intense com-

Table 3.5 | The Core Values of HP

HP receives very high marks as a socially responsible company for its support of educational programs and community development. Its core values are as follows:

- Customers
- Management
- Profit
- Our People
- Growth
- Fields of Interest
- Citizenship

HP's corporate statement regarding citizenship follows:

Citizenship

To honor our obligations to society by being an economic, intellectual and social asset to each nation and each community in which we operate.

All of us should strive to improve the world in which we live. As a corporation operating in many different communities throughout the world, we must make sure that each of these communities is better for our presence. This means identifying our interests with those of the community; it means applying the highest standards of honesty and integrity to all our relationships with individuals and groups; it means creating desirable jobs and generating exports and tax revenues; it means building attractive plants and offices of which the community can be proud; it means designing and providing products and services that are safe to use and can be manufactured, operated and disposed of in an environmentally responsible manner; it means contributing talent, time and financial support to worthwhile community projects.

Each community has its particular set of social problems. As citizens of the community, HP people can and should do whatever they reasonably can to improve it—either working as individuals or through such groups as charitable, educational, civic or religious institutions. In a broader sense, HP's "community" also includes a number of business and professional organizations whose interests are closely identified with those of the company and its individual employees. These, too, are deserving of our support and participation. In all cases, managers should encourage HP people to fulfill their personal goals and aspirations in the community as well as attain their individual objectives within HP.

At a national and international level, it is essential that the company be a good corporate citizen of each country in which it operates. This means looking for creative ways to apply technology to societal problems and contributing HP products and support to philanthropic programs that address immediate or long-term societal needs. Moreover, our employees, as individuals, should be encouraged to help find solutions to national or international problems by contributing their knowledge and talents. The betterment of our society is not a job to be left to a few; it is a responsibility to be shared by all.

SOURCE: **http://www.hp.com**

petition, some have even questioned whether or not ethics is a liability that limits an organization's ability to succeed.[51] Yet, most would agree that good ethics makes good business sense. In fact, there are long-term costs to unethical behavior that can have very negative consequences for any organization.[52]

The pressures to perform are nowhere more evident than in the sports industry. Coaches often feel pressure from demanding fans and/or owners—so much so that they are tempted to "bend the rules" to ensure a winning season. But according to Penn State University head football coach Joe Paterno, that's just not necessary. Paterno, who is world renowned for winning football games, is also well-known for maintaining a highly principled football program. He is up front with all players about his personal commitment to do the right thing, in each and every circumstance. This commitment is well evidenced by the following quote:

> I wish I had known in those early days what I think I know today about coaching. I don't mean about techniques and play selection and strategies. I mean about coaching in its first and highest sense. A coach, above all other duties, is a teacher. Coaches have the same obligation as all teachers, except we may have more moral and life-shaping influence over our players than anyone else outside of their families. I think you have to demand ethical conduct. Number one, you don't say, "Well we're gonna try." You go in with the idea that you have certain convictions, certain beliefs, morals, and that they make good sense over the long run. Ethics and honesty are investments.

Coach Paterno's "investments" in a solid ethical environment in his football program have earned his teams tremendous respect from fans and others.

Managers must continually choose between maximizing the economic performance of the organization (as indicated by revenues, costs, profits, and so forth) and improving its social performance (as indicated by obligations to customers, employees, suppliers, and others). Many ethical trade-offs are conflicts between these two desirable ends—economic versus social performance.[53] Making decisions in such situations is not merely a matter of choosing between right and wrong or between good and bad. Most of the alternatives are not so clear cut. Individuals who effectively manage these ethical trade-offs have a clear sense of their own values and the values of their organization. They have developed their own internal set of universal, comprehensive, and consistent principles upon which to base their decisions.

MANAGERIAL GUIDELINES FOR ETHICAL DILEMMAS

LEARNING OBJECTIVE 8

Identify and discuss the differences in the utility, human rights, and justice approaches to ethical dilemmas.

Ethical dilemma

A situation in which a person must decide whether or not to do something that, although benefiting oneself or the organization, may be considered unethical and perhaps illegal.

Utility approach

A situation in which decisions are based on an evaluation of the overall amount of good that will result.

An **ethical dilemma** is a situation in which a person must decide whether or not to do something that, although beneficial to oneself or the organization or both, may be considered unethical. Ethical dilemmas are common in the workplace. In fact, research suggests that managers encounter such dilemmas in their working relationships with superiors, subordinates, customers, competitors, suppliers, and regulators. Common issues underlying the dilemmas include honesty in communications and contracts, gifts and entertainment, kickbacks, pricing practices, and employee terminations.

Organizations need a set of guidelines for thinking about ethical dilemmas. These guidelines can help managers and employees identify the nature of the ethical problem and decide which course of action is the most likely to produce the most ethical results. The following three approaches—utility, human rights, and justice—provide managerial guidelines for handling ethical dilemmas.

UTILITY APPROACH   The **utility approach** emphasizes the overall amount of good that can be produced by an action or a decision. It judges actions, plans, and policies by their consequences. The primary objective of this approach is to provide the greatest good for the greatest number of people. It is often referred to as a cost-benefit analysis because it compares the costs and benefits of a decision, a policy, or an action. These costs and benefits can be economic (expressed in dollars), social (the effect on society at large), or human (usually a psychological or emotional impact). This type of results-oriented ethical reasoning tries to determine whether the overall outcome produces more good than harm—in other words, more utility or usefulness than negative results. The utility approach supports the ethical issues of profit maximization, self-interest, rewards based on abilities and achievements, sacrifice and hard work, and competition.[54]

The main drawback to the utility approach is the difficulty of accurately measuring both costs and benefits. For example, some things, such as goods produced, sales, payrolls, and profits, can be measured in monetary terms. Other items, such as employee morale, psychological satisfactions, and the worth of human life, do not easily lend themselves to monetary measurement. Another limitation of the utility approach is that those in the majority may override the rights of those in the minority.

Despite these limitations, cost-benefit analysis is widely used in business. If benefits (earnings) exceed costs, the organization makes a profit and is considered to be an economic success. Because this method uses economic and financial outcomes, managers sometimes rely on it to decide important ethical questions without being fully aware of its limitations or the availability of other approaches that may improve the ethical quality of decisions. One of these alternative approaches is the impact of the decisions on human rights.

HUMAN RIGHTS APPROACH   Human rights is a second method for handling ethical dilemmas. The **human rights approach** to ethics holds that human beings have certain moral entitlements that should be respected in all decisions. These entitlements guarantee an individual's most fundamental personal rights (life, freedom, health, privacy, and property, for example). These have been spelled out in such documents as the U.S. Bill of Rights and the United Nations Declaration of Human Rights.[55] A right means that a person or group is entitled to something or is entitled to be treated in a certain way. The most basic human rights are those claims or entitlements that enable a person to survive, make free choices, and realize his or her potential as a human being. Denying those rights to other persons and groups or failing to protect their rights is considered to be unethical. Respecting others, even those with whom we disagree or whom we dislike, is the essence of human rights, provided that others do the same for us.

The human rights approach to ethical dilemmas holds that individuals are to be treated as valuable ends in themselves simply because they are human beings. Using others for your own purposes is unethical if, at the same time, you deny them their rights to their own goals and purposes. For example, an organization that denies women employees an opportunity to bid for all jobs for which they are qualified is depriving them of some of their rights.

The main limitation on using the human rights approach as a basis for ethical decisions is the difficulty of balancing conflicting rights. For example, using a polygraph test to evaluate an employee's honesty to protect the organization's financial responsibilities may be at odds with the employee's right to privacy. Many difficult decisions have involved minorities and women who are competing with white men for the right to hold jobs in business and government. Rights also clash when U.S. multinational corporations move production to a foreign nation, causing job losses at home while creating new jobs abroad. In such cases, whose job rights should be protected?

The degree to which human rights are protected and promoted is an important ethical benchmark for judging the behavior of individuals and organizations. Most people would agree that the denial of a person's fundamental rights to life, freedom, privacy, growth, and human dignity is generally unethical. Thus, the protection of such rights becomes a common denominator for making ethical decisions.

JUSTICE APPROACH   A third method of ethical decision making concerns justice. Under the **justice approach**, decisions are based on an equitable, fair, and impartial distribution of benefits (rewards) and costs among individuals and groups. Justice is essentially a condition characterized by an equitable distribution of the benefits and burdens of working together, according to some accepted rule. For

Guidelines for ethical dilemmas can help managers and employees identify the nature of a problem and decide which course of action will produce the most ethical results.

Human rights approach
A situation in which decisions are made in light of the moral entitlements of human beings.

Justice approach
A situation in which decisions are based on an equitable, fair, and impartial distribution of benefits and costs among individuals and groups.

society as a whole, social justice means that a society's income and wealth are distributed among the people in fair proportions.

A common question is, "Is it fair or just?" For example, employees want to know whether pay scales are fair; consumers are interested in fair prices when they shop. When new tax laws are proposed, there is much debate about their fairness: Where will the burden fall, and will all taxpayers pay their fair share? Using the justice approach, the organization considers who pays the costs and who gets the benefits. If the shares seem fair, then the action is probably just.

Determining what is just and what is unjust can be an explosive issue if the stakes are high. Since distributive rules usually grant privileges to some groups based on tradition and custom, sharp inequalities between groups can generate social tensions and clamorous demands for a change to a fairer system.

As with the utilitarian approach, a major limitation of the justice approach is the difficulty of measuring benefits and costs precisely. Another limitation is that many of society's benefits and burdens are intangible, emotional, and psychological. People unfairly deprived of life's opportunities may not willingly accept their condition. Few people, even those who are relatively well off, are ever entirely satisfied with their share of society's wealth. For these reasons, the use of the justice approach can be tricky. Although everyone is intensely interested in being treated fairly, many are skeptical that justice will ever be fully realized. In spite of these drawbacks, the justice approach to ethical dilemmas can still be applied in many business situations. How would you respond to these situations?

FOSTERING IMPROVED BUSINESS ETHICS

LEARNING OBJECTIVE 9

Explain the methods used by an organization to encourage ethical business behavior.

Many well-publicized and questionable business practices have brought business ethics to the forefront of concerns in the business community. Until the late 1980s, business ethics was little more than an obscure debate among some scholars. However, in the wake of many questionable events in recent years, businesses, business leaders, and academic institutions have placed greater emphasis on developing ethical standards and fostering an appreciation for adherence to ethical business behavior.[56] Initially, many of these efforts seemed to be more image than substance. But today, more and more companies are beginning to see their efforts affecting the core culture of their organizations. In fact, recent studies have shown that many companies are demonstrating a real commitment to improving their ethical environment.[57]

To foster improved business ethics in an organization, action must be directed at five levels: the international, societal, association, organizational, and individual levels. The most fundamental effort is directed at the individual.

Agreements among nations help to foster ethical behavior at the international level. Laws established by international governing bodies such the World Trade Organization and the United Nations help shape ethical behavior across nations. Nongovernmental organizations (NGOs) also play an important role in promoting ethical behavior on a global basis. NGOs are nonprofit, voluntary citizens' groups that are organized on a local, national, or international level to address international issues. You can learn more about NGOs and their activities by visiting http://www.ngo.org.

Societal ethics are fostered to the extent that laws and regulations discourage unethical behavior, and systems exist for recognizing and rewarding behaviors that epitomize strong ethical values. For example, the Foreign Corrupt Practices Act governs the actions of U.S. firms engaged in international business activities. Award programs, such as the Business Ethics Award given annually by the Center for Business Ethics at Bentley College, help to reinforce the value of ethical behavior within our society.

At the association level, groups can join together and establish codes of ethics for their industry or profession and provide mechanisms for monitoring and disciplining members who violate the code. For example, the Society of Professional Journalists, an organization of 13,500 people involved in journalism, has developed a code of ethics that provides guidance for journalists across the globe. Not only has the association established such a code, but it invites on-line debate about proposed changes to the code. This debate has evolved to include discussions of both real and hypothetical ethical issues in the journalism profession.

At the organizational level, improving business ethics requires leaders who can model the expected ethical behavior, set realistic goals for workers, and encourage ethical behavior by providing an organizational environment that rewards such behavior and punishes violators. Leadership is perhaps the most important ingredient in developing an ethical organizational culture. According to Shirley Peterson, vice president of ethics and business conduct at Northrop Grumman Corporation, Northrop's value statement was drafted by the top 12 people in the organization. Why? Because at Northrop, management believes that ethics starts at the top of the organization and filters through the organization from there.[58]

At the individual level, the challenge for organizations is to develop employees' awareness of business ethics (see Table 3.6) as well as to help them confront complex ethical issues. Employees find it helpful when their organization publicly announces what it believes in and expects in terms of employee behavior.[59] Ultimately, though, ethical business behavior comes from the individual, not the organization.[60]

In the next section, we examine two of the most common ways in which organizations foster ethical behavior: (1) creating codes of conduct and (2) developing ethics training programs. In general, such activities must reflect relevant employee concerns and must be tailored to specific needs and value statements.

CODES OF ETHICS   A **code of ethics** describes the general value system, ethical principles, and specific ethical rules that a company tries to apply. It can be an effective way to encourage ethical business behavior and raise an organization's standards of ethical performance. Such a document may be called a code of ethics, credo, declaration of business principles, statement of core values, or something similar.

In response to the ethical problems that have been arising in the United States, many companies and professional societies are now publishing codes of conduct. In fact, about 90 percent of Fortune 500 firms and almost half of all other firms

Code of ethics
The general value system, principles, and specific rules that a company follows.

Table 3.6 | Developing Employee Awareness of Ethics

1. Enabling the ethical component of a decision to be recognized.
2. Legitimizing the consideration of ethics as part of decision making.
3. Avoiding variability in decision making caused by lack of awareness of rules or norms.
4. Avoiding ambivalence in decision making caused by an organizational reward system that psychologically pulls a person in opposite directions.
5. Avoiding ambivalence in decision making caused by confusion as to who is responsible for misdeeds, particularly when the employee has received an order from a superior.
6. Providing decision-making frameworks for analyzing ethical choices and helping employees to apply such frameworks.

SOURCE: S.J. Harrington, "What Corporate America Is Teaching about Ethics," *Academy of Management Executives,* 5, 1991, 21–29.

have ethics codes.[61] These organizations have likely determined that maintaining an ethical organization can be a strategic advantage.

Typically, a code of ethics covers a wide range of issues and potential problem areas that an organization and its members may encounter. It is a set of carefully articulated statements of ethical principles rooted in the organization's goals, objectives, organizational history, and traditions. A code contains explicit statements and precepts intended to guide both the organization and its employees in their professional behavior. A code helps employees know what is expected when they face uncertain ethical situations. It becomes the basis for establishing continuity and uniformity in managerial action and can be a unifying force that holds the organization together so that its employees can act in a cohesive and socially responsible manner.

An organization's code of ethics can serve several purposes. First, it creates employee awareness that ethical issues need to be considered in making business decisions. Second, it demonstrates that the organization is fully committed to stating its standards and incorporating them into daily activities. Third, a code can contribute to transforming an "us-them" relationship between the organization and its employees into an "us-us" relationship.[62] A code's impact on employee behavior is weakened if the code's purpose is primarily to make the company look good or if it is intended to give the company's top executives a legal defense when illegal or unethical acts are committed by lower-ranking employees.

A code of ethics can resemble a set of regulations ("Our employees will not . . ."), aspirations ("Our employees should . . ."), or factual statements ("Our organization is committed to . . ."), but all effective codes appear to share at least three characteristics:

1. They generally govern activities that cannot be supervised closely enough to ensure compliance.
2. They ask more of employees than would otherwise be expected.
3. They can serve the long-term interest of the organization.

In today's global business environment, a growing number of organizations are establishing global ethics codes. Companies such as Shell, Hewlett-Packard, Sara Lee Corporation, and Baxter International, Inc., have led the way in developing comprehensive codes of ethics that are disseminated on a worldwide basis. Table 3.7 outlines the major issues addressed by a majority of global codes of ethics.

Merck & Company has been particularly aggressive with regard to developing a comprehensive and relevant code of ethics. The company has long subscribed to a belief that core values and an adherence to the highest standards of ethical behavior are key to global success, and Merck is committed to ensuring that the company culture reflects this philosophy. How did the company achieve this? First, the company conducted an organizational analysis that involved participation of over 10,000 employees in 21 countries. Based on the feedback from the interviews and surveys of these employees, an ethics code was drafted. The final document, which was translated into 22 languages, was tested with focus groups in each major geographic region of the company. Ultimately, the company's code was distributed to employees across the globe, who simultaneously participated in ethics training. Key to Merck's success was ensuring that the code was embraced by the leadership of the company. By selecting leaders throughout the organization and across the globe who subscribe to and support fully the Merck core values and code of ethics, Merck has created an organizational culture that is based on the highest ethical standards.[63]

Ethics statements and social responsibility policies are not sufficient by themselves to cause people to behave in a socially responsible manner. A 20-page policy statement by General Dynamics failed to prevent a widespread lapse in ethical conduct involving government contracts. The real challenge for top-level manage-

Table 3.7 | Subjects Addressed by Most Codes of Ethics

- Bribery/improper payments
- Conflict of interest
- Security of proprietary information
- Receiving gifts
- Discrimination/equal opportunity
- Giving gifts
- Environment
- Sexual harassment
- Antitrust
- Workplace safety

- Political activities
- Community relations
- Confidentiality of personal information
- Human rights
- Employee privacy
- Whistleblowing
- Substance abuse
- Nepotism
- Child labor

SOURCE: R. Berenbeim, "Global Corporate Ethics Practices," *The Conference Board Research Report*, 121243-99-RR, 1999.

ment is to create an environment that sustains, promotes, and develops ethical behavior and a commitment to social responsibility. The effort must begin at the highest levels of the organization. Unless top-level management, beginning with the CEO, provides leadership, commitment, and role modeling, no organization can hope to attain high ethical standards or consistently behave in a socially responsible manner. Top-level management must also ensure that the organization's expectations of ethical behavior and social responsibility are clearly conveyed to its employees and to all parties involved with the organization—that is, the stakeholders. This requires extensive communication among all parties and the establishment of systems within the organization to reinforce ethical behavior.[64]

ETHICS TRAINING PROGRAMS Many organizations and associations provide ethics training for employees. In fact, a recent Conference Board report suggests that 78 percent of companies that have an ethics code reinforce it with ethics training.[65] The combination of a widely distributed code of ethics and comprehensive ethics training for all employees can greatly enhance the ethical environment within an organization.

The reasons for ethics training vary widely from organization to organization. Some of the most prominent reasons include avoiding adverse publicity, potential lawsuits, illegal behavior, and monetary and criminal penalties. Many organizations also use ethics training to gain a strategic advantage, increase employee awareness of ethics in business decision making, and help employees become more attentive to ethical issues to which they may be exposed.[66]

Ethics training programs have been shown to help employees avoid rationalizations often used to legitimize unethical behavior. Among the rationalizations often advanced to justify organizational misconduct are believing that (1) the activity is not really illegal or immoral, (2) it is in the individual's or the corporation's best interest, (3) it will never be found out, or (4) the company will condone it because it helps the company.

Ethics training programs can help managers clarify their ethical framework and practice self-discipline when making decisions in difficult circumstances. Lockheed-Martin, Hershey Foods, Pitney Bowes, and General Dynamics are among the prominent companies with training programs for managers, supervisors, and anyone else likely to encounter an ethical question at work.[67] Motorola's ethics training program, for example, suggests using philosophical methods of analysis and resolution and includes commentaries by business ethicists on 24 individual cases.

LEARNING OBJECTIVE 10

Describe the different approaches used in ethics training programs.

The content and approach of ethics training programs may differ depending on the organization's goals. Case studies, often specific to the business functions of the organization's audience, are the most widely used approach. Other popular approaches include presenting rules or guidelines for deciding ethical issues (such as the Golden Rule or the utilitarian approach), developing a checklist to aid managers in making ethical decisions, or using cognitive approaches that attempt to develop higher levels of ethical understanding such as the one shown in Table 3.8.[68]

The training approach at Boeing Corporation, where more than 145,000 employees have been exposed to the ethics value program, is a customized in-house program tailored to meet the organization's ethics goals. First, a division general manager delivers a message emphasizing ethical business practices. Next, employees receive a company-created pamphlet titled "Business Conduct Guidelines," which stresses policies on ethics and standards of conduct and compliance. Hypothetical situations are presented, and a business ethics advisor in each division leads discussions. The training also stresses the procedures for discussing or reporting unethical behavior or infractions.

LEARNING OBJECTIVE 11

Discuss what is meant by whistleblowing in monitoring ethical behavior.

Whistleblower

Someone who exposes organizational misconduct or wrongdoing to the public.

WHISTLEBLOWING   One method of evaluating the ethical conviction of the organization is to observe its approach to professional dissent or, as it is more commonly called, whistleblowing. Whistleblowing occurs when an insider reports alleged organizational misconduct to the public. A **whistleblower** is someone who exposes organizational wrongdoing in order to preserve ethical standards and protect against wasteful, harmful, or illegal acts.

Whistleblowing has become a staple on the front pages of newspapers and an all-too-frequent segment on *60 Minutes* and other such "news magazine" programs.[69] An employee—or, more often, a former employee—of a big corporation or government agency goes public with charges that the organization has been playing dirty. The next step is a lawsuit that sets out the details of the misconduct and charges that the whistleblower was at best ignored and at worst harassed, demoted, or fired.

Doubtless, some whistleblower suits are brought by employees with an ax to grind. Others may be in search of a big payoff. For example, under the False Claims Act, whistleblowers can receive up to 25 percent of any money recovered by the government. A classic case that illustrates the magnitude of potential payoffs for whistleblowers was that of Christopher M. Urda. Urda was awarded $7.5 million in July 1992 for providing evidence that his employer, then a unit of Singer Corporation, bilked the Pentagon out of $77 million in the 1980s.[70]

Generally, employees are not free to speak out publicly against their employers because there is an expectation that organizational problems are handled in-

Table 3.8 | A Leader's Guide for Developing a Strong Ethics Policy

1. Develop a written policy on ethics and communicate it regularly to your employees.
2. Make sure that all employees understand the policies and procedures in place for determining ethical behavior.
3. Establish fair and consistent rules for disciplining violators.
4. Develop and continually monitor audit systems to prevent and detect violations of the law or corporate policy.
5. Create a safe environment where employees can report suspected violations anonymously without fear of retribution.
6. Allow those accused of violating ethics policies the opportunity to explain or defend their behavior.

ternally. Organizations face countless ethical issues and internal conflicts in their daily operations. Choices must be made where there are many opinions. Mistakes are made, and waste does occur, but usually corrective action is taken.

Although whistleblowing typically exposes unethical practices, how it is done and how it is handled may also be ethically questionable. The costs of whistleblowing are high for both the company and the whistleblower. The company's reputation is damaged whether it wins or loses, which can create considerable internal conflict. The company spends much time and money defending itself and may damage general employee morale by seeming to be unsympathetic to legitimate concerns expressed by employees. The whistleblower also suffers. Many times whistleblowers are subject to retaliatory action by disgruntled employers, and they often are blackballed for not being team players. Even if the whistleblower wins, the costs can be high: legal expenses, mental anguish, ostracism by former coworkers, or a damaged career.

To avoid the costs for both the company and the employee, many companies have become more receptive to employee complaints. Some organizations have established regular procedures for professional dissent, such as hotlines that employees can use to report dangerous or questionable company practices or the use of ombudsmen who can act as neutral judges and negotiators when supervisors and employees disagree over a policy or practice.[71] Tenet Healthcare, for example, maintains an Ethics Action Line for all employees. Confidential questionnaires are another device to encourage potential whistleblowers to report their concerns before they become a big issue. In these ways, progressive companies attempt to lessen the tensions between the company and its employees and maintain the confidence and trust between them.

Whistleblowers may be subject to retaliatory actions by disgruntled employers and ostracism by former coworkers.

Table 3.9 shows a model whistleblower policy developed by The Conference Board.[72] The policy can work in the real world if managers emphasize that ethics is more than fancy policy. Managers should ask employees whether they have confidence in the company's ethics system and make them believe that exposing internal wrongdoing is part of their job. Whistleblowers who raise real issues should be rewarded.[73] Whatever technique is used, it should permit individuals to expose

Table 3.9   A Model Whistleblower Policy

- *Shout it from the rooftops.* Aggressively publicize a reporting policy that encourages employees to bring forward valid complaints of wrongdoing.
- *Face the fear factor.* Defuse fear by directing complaints to someone outside the whistleblower's chain of command.
- *Get right on it.* An independent group, either inside or outside the company, should investigate the company immediately.
- *Go public.* Show employees that complaints are taken seriously by publicizing the outcome of investigations whenever possible.

SOURCE: L. Driscoll, "A Better Way to Handle Whistle-Blowers: Let Them Speak," 36. Reprinted from July 27, 1992, issue of *Business Week* by special permission, copyright © 1992 by McGraw-Hill Companies, Inc.

unethical practices or lapses in socially responsible behavior without disrupting the organization.

IMPLICATIONS FOR LEADERS

We have explored two important concepts in this chapter: social responsibility and ethics. Achieving social responsibility and business ethics at an organizational level is a challenge that tomorrow's managers will face.[74] Tomorrow's leaders must be highly cognizant of the importance of strong character for leadership effectiveness. Character can be best demonstrated by acting ethically and fully considering the impact of decisions on the community at large. Toward that end, keep the following tips in mind as a leader:

- Explore ways in which the organization can be more socially responsive.
- Recognize the effect of the organization's actions on its stakeholders.
- Make sure that a code of ethics is put in place and followed.
- Ensure that whistleblowing and ethical concerns procedures are established for internal problem solving.
- Involve line and staff employees in the identification of ethical issues to help them gain understanding and resolve issues.
- Determine the link between departments and issues affecting the company and make them known to employees in the departments.
- Integrate ethical decision making into the performance appraisal process.
- Publicize, in employee communications and elsewhere, executive priorities and efforts related to ethical issues.

By following these guidelines, managers will be taking a major step toward achieving a high level of social responsibility in the organization and increasing employee awareness of ethical issues. Managers of the future will be expected to address important social issues proactively and to maintain a high standard of ethical behavior.

Now Apply It

Ethics in the Workplace

Ethics in the workplace is a critical issue that affects all employees. The following three scenarios highlight specific potential ethical issues. As you read these scenarios, consider how you might react.

Scenario 1: John is a production manager at a toy manufacturing plant. In his role, he selects vendors for a number of the materials used in the production process. You know that John usually picks suppliers with whom he has a good relationship, even when they are not the lowest bidder. Most recently, you have noticed that a very large purchase was made from a vendor that regularly hosts John at the local pro basketball games. You know another vendor has a significantly lower price

and you wonder whether John's decisions are biased. When you ask him about it, he explains that having a good relationship with your supplier ensures good-quality service, which is more important than price.

Scenario 2: Janice travels frequently for her company, and, since she is a bit disorganized, maintaining accurate expense records has never been her strength. She tends to tuck receipts in her suit pockets, briefcase, bag, or even books she may be carrying. Many of the receipts (for example, taxi receipts and restaurant receipts) are blank because Janice has failed to note the amount of her expenditure at the time she made it. Janice turns in her

receipts sporadically, guessing at the expenditures she has made. You, as her office mate, note the sloppy fashion in which Janice reports her expenses and bring it to her attention. Janice responds by saying that she is sure that it all balances out in the end.

Scenario 3: Robert is the equivalent of a "class clown" in the office. He is always telling jokes, playing silly pranks, and otherwise entertaining the office staff. While most of Robert's antics are harmless, he occasionally tells ethnic jokes that could be offensive to others. When you mention this to Robert, he tells you to "lighten up." No one else in the office seems to be offended.

Meeting The Challenge

The Rise and Fall and Rise of Paul Wieand: A Leader's Journey

Paul Wieand's rise and fall at Independence Bancorp seemed sudden and unexpected to him, but in fact, the leadership of the bank had been struggling with Wieand for some time. Six months after his departure, he accepted a position with the federal government to turn around a failing savings and loan. Wieand took the bank public, renamed it Sovereign, and successfully turned it around. Although he was now making more money than ever before, he was no longer passionate about his work. His ousting at Independence Bancorp still stung, and he began to focus his interest on why it had happened. Now financially independent, he retired at age 41 and began pursuing a Ph.D. in psychology at Temple University.

It was during Wieand's doctoral study that he reclaimed a passion for living. He began researching the psychological aspects of leadership, focusing on the role that emotions play in making decisions and taking actions. It was during this time that Wieand defined two paradoxical

laws of leadership that led to his own downfall: (1) Successful leaders often think they know more than anyone else and (2) When leaders become intoxicated with their personal success, they start to define themselves only in terms of their job title and lose touch with who they really are inside.

After completing his Ph.D., Wieand founded the Center for Advanced Emotional Intelligence (AEI). AEI offers intensive leadership development programs for executives and entrepreneurs that focus on personal introspection. AEI's goal is to turn super-achievers into learning leaders by demonstrating the impact that their emotions, not their intelligence, have on decision making and communicating with others. AEI's program includes several points:

- Leaders often resist soul-searching and introspection when they reach their pinnacle, which is precisely when they need it most.
- In order to distract themselves from clarifying their true values

and understanding their emotions, leaders tend to narrowly define themselves by their work and job title.
- Leaders should surround themselves with people who are as talented as or more talented than themselves and then listen to them intensely when they voice disagreement or concern.
- When communicating to others, either one on one or in a group setting, effective leaders should appeal to both logic and emotion.
- In order to establish and maintain trust, leaders must take care to ensure that their private conversations mirror their public ones.

Wieand's message has resonated with many top executives. AEI has enjoyed great success in helping people become more authentic and more effective leaders.

SOURCE: P. Kruger, "A Leader's Journey," *Fast Company*, 25, June 1999, 116–122.

SUMMARY

1. The concepts of social responsibility and ethics require an understanding of the stakeholder view of the organization. Whereas the traditional view of socially responsible behavior considers only the stockholders, contemporary theory recognizes a much broader group of constituents—stakeholders. Stakeholders include any individual or group that is affected by or can affect the organization. As the business environment has globalized, the stakeholders of many organizations have become more diverse. As a company's operations become more international, it will be required to understand and respond to a broader group of stakeholders.

2. Corporate social responsibility has been the subject of much controversy and debate over the last several decades. Although the concept defies precise definition, in a very general sense social responsibility refers to the interaction between business and the social environment in which it exists. The concept of social responsibility rests on two premises: social contract and moral agent.

3. Three perspectives of corporate social responsibility have significant support from both practitioners and academics. The economic responsibility perspective suggests that the

only social responsibility of business is to maximize profits within the "rules of the game." The public responsibility perspective argues that business has an obligation to act in a way that is consistent with society's overall expectations of business. Supporters of the social responsiveness perspective suggest that it is the responsibility of business to act proactively to improve the welfare of society.

4. There are four distinct strategies for responding to social issues. These strategies, which span a continuum ranging from "do nothing" to "do much," are (1) reaction, (2) defense, (3) accommodation, and (4) proaction. Although none of these strategies is appropriate for all organizations, the accommodation and proaction approaches to social responsibility are appropriate in most cases.

5. As organizations consider a strategy for social responsibility, a number of "commandments" should be considered. In general, these commandments suggest that organizations should be observant of social issues, honest with their constituents, cooperative with stakeholders with regard to social concerns, and proactive in their efforts to fulfill their obligations to society.

6. Values are the relatively permanent and deeply held desires of individuals or groups. They are the bases upon which attitudes and personal preferences are patterned. Values are among the most stable and enduring characteristics of individuals; they form the foundation of an individual's ethical behavior. Instrumental, or means-oriented, values describe desirable standards of conduct or methods for attaining an end. Terminal, or ends-oriented, values describe desirable ends or goals for the individual and reflect what a person is ultimately striving to achieve. People from different international and cultural environments may hold very different values and thus have different perspectives on ethical issues.

7. As information technology has become more sophisticated, new ethical issues have emerged. Issues regarding privacy of individual information and the personal use of computers in the workplace are just two of the technology-related ethical concerns in today's business environment. Additional ethical issues may arise as technology improvements continue.

8. Three primary approaches can be taken in dealing with ethical dilemmas. The utility approach emphasizes the overall amount of good that can be produced by an action or a decision. The human rights approach holds that decisions should be consistent with fundamental rights and privileges such as those of life, freedom, health, privacy, and property. Under the justice approach, decisions are based on an equitable, fair, and impartial distribution of benefits (rewards) and costs among individuals and groups.

9. Organizations often develop codes of ethics along with training programs to encourage and reinforce ethical business behavior. A code of ethics describes the organization's general value system, its ethical principles, and the specific ethical rules that it tries to apply.

10. Several different approaches can be used in ethics training programs. These approaches include case studies, the presentation of rules or guidelines for deciding ethical issues, and cognitive approaches that attempt to develop higher levels of ethical understanding.

11. A whistleblower is someone who exposes organizational wrongdoing in order to preserve ethical standards and protect against wasteful, harmful, or illegal acts. Organizations should develop and maintain policies and procedures that encourage reports of wrongful doing yet discourage employees from making frivolous or unjustified allegations against others.

REVIEW QUESTIONS

1. *(Learning Objective 1)* Describe the stakeholder view of the organization. How does the stakeholder view differ from the stockholder view, and what are the implications of these differences for the concept of corporate social responsibility? How has the globalization of the business environment impacted issues of social responsibility and ethics?

2. *(Learning Objective 2)* Define the concept of corporate social responsibility. What are the two premises advanced by Bowen in his original definition of social responsibility?

3. *(Learning Objective 3)* Compare and contrast the three perspectives of corporate social responsibility.

4. *(Learning Objective 4)* Evaluate the four different strategies for social responsibility. Describe how these strategies differ, and give an example of a company that has pursued each strategy.

5. *(Learning Objective 5)* What are the 10 commandments of social responsibility? Which perspective of social responsibility (see question 2) is most consistent with these commandments?

6. *(Learning Objective 6)* What are values? Why are they the basis of an individual's ethical behavior? How might values vary across multinational, multicultural environments?

7. *(Learning Objective 7)* Describe how advances in information technology have created new ethical challenges.

8. *(Learning Objective 8)* Describe the utility, human rights, and justice approaches to ethical dilemmas, and explain how they differ.

9. *(Learning Objective 9)* What is a code of ethics? Describe the different goals an organization can have for developing a code of ethics.

10. *(Learning Objective 10)* What are the common approaches used in ethics training programs?

11. *(Learning Objective 11)* Explain what is meant by whistleblowing. What are the benefits that come from whistleblowing? What are some of the problems it might cause?

DISCUSSION QUESTIONS

Improving Critical Thinking

1. Consider the implications of self-regulation versus government-imposed regulation (refer to Commandments I and III). Why is it preferable for an industry to be self-regulated?

2. Describe an ethical dilemma you have experienced at work or as part of a business or social organization. What was your response? If you faced a similar dilemma now, would your response differ?

Enhancing Communication Skills

3. Select an organization with which you are familiar or that you are interested in researching. Evaluate the social responsibility strategy of that company with regard to the following social issues: (1) environmental protection, (2) worker health and safety, and (3) product safety. Has this company been in a reaction, defensive, accommodation, or proaction mode with regard to these social issues? Make an oral presentation of your findings to the class.

4. Using current business periodicals or newspapers, find an example of an organization that has faced an ethical problem. How did it solve the problem? Did the organization have a code of ethics? Write a summary of your findings as a way to demonstrate your understanding of the issue and practice your written communication skills.

5. Examine the policy your college or university has for handling academic dishonesty. How appropriate is the policy? Would you suggest any changes? Write up your suggestions and discuss them with a small group or your class.

Building Teamwork

6. As part of a small group, consider the following argument: If one looks far enough into the future, the interests of all stakeholders converge. That is, all stakeholders ultimately benefit from a strong economy, well-paid employees, and a healthy and clean environment. Thus organizations should not find a conflict between their primary stakeholders (stockholders) and their secondary stakeholders (the community at large). Is this statement true? Why or why not? Provide an example of an organizational situation that supports your position.

7. In small groups or as directed by your instructor, select a company that is considering relocating its major manufacturing plant from a domestic site to a country with lower labor costs. What are the social considerations that are most relevant for this company? Evaluate how this decision would be viewed by proponents of each of the three perspectives of social responsibility (economic responsibility, public responsibility, and social responsiveness).

8. As part of a small group, develop a code of ethics for an organization to which one or more of you belong, such as a fraternity, a sorority, a business association, or your college. What are the key issues that need to be addressed? Share your code with the class and the organization.

THINKING CRITICALLY: DEBATE THE ISSUE

Social Innovation: Community Investment or Corporate Greed?

Form teams with four to five students on each team. Each team should evaluate the following statement and prepare to argue either for social innovation as a form of community investment, or against it as an example of corporate greed. Your instructor will select the two teams to present their arguments in a debate format.

Traditionally, companies view the social sector as a dumping ground for their spare cash, obsolete equipment, and tired executives. This activity is sometimes referred to as "corporate social responsibility." Some companies are moving beyond social responsibility to an emerging paradigm called social innovation. Social innovation views the community needs of the social sector as business opportunities that have both community and business payoffs. The new approach is not charity, rather, it is a strategic business investment meant to produce profitable and lasting change for both sides.

SOURCE: Adapted from R.M. Kanter, "From Spare Change to Real Change," *Harvard Business Review*, 77, pp. 122–133, May–June, 1999.

EXPERIENTIAL EXERCISE 3.1

Observing and Reporting Unethical Behavior

For each of the following statements place an O on the line if you have observed someone doing this behavior. Place an R on the line if you reported this behavior within the organization.

O = Observed; R = Reported

_____ **1.** Coming to work late and getting paid for it.

_____ **2.** Leaving work early and getting paid for it.

_____ **3.** Taking long breaks or lunches and getting paid for them.

_____ **4.** Calling in sick when one is not ill.

_____ **5.** Using the company copier or fax for personal use.

_____ **6.** Using company postage for personal correspondence.

_____ **7.** Taking company supplies or merchandise for personal use at home.

_____ **8.** Accepting gifts, meals, or trips from customers or suppliers in exchange for giving them business.

_____ **9.** Filing for reimbursements or for other expenses that were not actually incurred.

_____ **10.** Using the company car for personal business.

_____ **11.** A student copying a friend's homework assignments.

_____ **12.** A student cheating on an exam.

_____ **13.** A student falsely passing off a term paper as his or her own work.

Complete the following questions either individually or in small groups as directed by your instructor.

1. From items 1 through 10, select the three behaviors that you consider the most unethical. Who is harmed by and who benefits from these unethical behaviors?

2. Who is harmed by and who benefits from the unethical behaviors in items 11 through 13? Who is responsible for changing these behaviors? Develop a realistic plan to accomplish this goal.

3. If you observed unethical behavior but didn't report it, why didn't you? If you did report the behavior, why did you? What was the result?

4. What other behaviors that you consider unethical have you observed or reported?

EXPERIENTIAL EXERCISE 3.2

What Good Is an Honor System?

Working in a small group of three to five individuals, read the following scenario and then answer the questions that follow. Try to come to a consensus with your group members about your responses. Report your answers to your instructor or to the whole class.

I went to a small liberal arts college where they had a very strict honor system. For example, if you saw another student cheating, you were supposed to turn that student in to the authorities. In reality, some students did cheat, but only rarely did other students report the problem. There seemed to be several reasons for this: (1) it was a hassle to get involved because you had to go to meetings, fill out forms, and answer numerous questions; (2) nobody wanted to be considered a "tattletale"; and (3) even if you were sure the person had cheated, you had to have very specific evidence to support the charge.

Ten years later, I am out of college and law school and practice law with a large firm. We have an honor system here, too, but bringing a complaint against another professional is difficult: (1) it takes time and energy to get involved; (2) no one trusts or likes a person who turns in a peer; and (3) evidence to support a complaint is often poor or difficult to obtain.

For Discussion

1. What are the ethical dilemmas students face while going to college? What examples can you provide from your own or others' experience to support this?

2. Discuss the ethical dilemmas lawyers face in performing their jobs. Give some specific examples (consider recent news reports or stories from current television shows).

3. Discuss ethical dilemmas faced by other professional groups such as accountants, professors, engineers, and psychologists.

4. Discuss the pros and cons of an honor system.

CAPTURING THE POWER OF INFORMATION TECHNOLOGY

1. A recent study suggests that 82 percent of the Fortune 500 companies with Web sites used them to address at least one corporate social responsibility issue.[75] Examine the Web sites of at least three Fortune 500 companies and compare and contrast their use of the Web to present themselves as socially responsible corporate citizens.

2. Visit the Web site of the Institute for Business and Professional Ethics (**http://www.depaul.edu/ethics/**). How could managers use the information provided on the Web site to enhance the ethical culture in their organizations?

3. Using the Internet, locate information on the Society for Professional Journalists. Access the association's code of ethics. Review and analyze the code in a small group of students. Provide input on your assessment (good or bad) to the association using the society's on-line mechanism for discussing ethical issues in the journalism profession.

ETHICS: TAKE A STAND

Clay Martin graduated from college with honors and started his professional career with a large consulting firm. His hard work and dedication to the company paid off in advancement and increased responsibility. After only a few short years, he was promoted to project manager where he was responsible for developing a proposal for a major, multiyear government contract.

As Clay worked on the project it became apparent that his primary competition for the contract would be another large consulting firm. In fact, he had interviewed with this firm after graduation but was not offered a job. Now, he thought, he would be able to show them the mistake they had made by not hiring him.

As soon as the project was underway, problems began. Clay was out sick with the flu for a week and fell behind. Without his leadership, many in his staff "slacked off" while they waited for his return. Once the project did get underway, there was an unusual amount of arguing and disagreement among his team as to which approach to take. One side argued that they could provide superior technological and change management skills to the government agency and should sell the proposal on the basis of their expertise. Others in the team argued that they should focus on cost, emphasizing that many government contracts are usually awarded on price, not quality.

As Clay wrestled with these issues, the deadline for the proposal quickly approached. He decided to focus the proposal on his firm's expertise and hoped that his budget would be comparable to what his competitor would be offering.

One week before the proposal was due, Clay received an anonymous e-mail from a disgruntled associate with the other consulting firm. The e-mail contained their entire proposal and budget. Clay was convinced the information contained in the e-mail message was correct. He had to decide what, if anything, he would do with it. If he used the information in the e-mail he could fine-tune his proposal to look more favorable than his competition, as well as propose a lower budget. Using this information would almost guarantee that his firm would be awarded the contract. Clay would be touted as a "hero" and further career advancement and pay raises would surely follow. If he doesn't use this information, he may not win the contract and could be cast as the "scapegoat" for the team's failure. If he decides to use the information, it is very unlikely that anyone would ever find out.

For Discussion

1. What are the ethical issues facing Clay?

2. What is motivating Clay to win this proposal?

3. If you were Clay, what would you do and why?

VIDEO CASE

Social Responsibility and Ethics: Timberland

The Timberland Company designs, engineers, markets, distributes, and sells premium-quality footwear, apparel, and accessories for men, women, and children. Timberland employs 5,400 people worldwide with revenues of about $1.2 billion. Timberland products are sold worldwide through independent retailers, better-grade department stores, athletic specialty stores, and Timberland retail stores.

The Timberland Company was founded by Nathan Swartz, whose legacy of craftsmanship, integrity, and quality is carried on today through the active involvement of his son, Sidney Swartz (Chair), and his grandson, Jeffrey Swartz (President and CEO). Their guiding purpose is to create outstanding products, create value for shareholders, employees, and consumers around the world, and to try to make a difference in their communities.

Timberland also places importance on protecting the rights of their vendors' workers worldwide. For example, Timberland has compliance monitors in Asia that visit factories every 8–12 weeks. Timberland believes these auditing efforts have helped improve worker conditions. Employee compensation, overtime payments, discrimination, break times, along with health and safety issues, have shown improvement.

Jeff Swartz, President and CEO, states that doing well and doing "good" are inextricably linked. In the 21st century, the standards for business have changed for the better. No longer is it enough to measure business by profit, efficiency, and market share. Citizens also must ask how the private sector contributes to standards of social justice, environmental sustainability, the health and strength of community, and the values by which we choose to live.

Timberland demonstrates its commitment to doing well and doing "good" through its unique worldwide Path of Service program. Through this program, Timberland employees are given up to 40 hours of paid time off for community service or they may apply for up to six months' paid time off to make long-term improvements in their communities. Since 1992, Timberland has partnered with over 200 not-for-profit organizations to invest over 200,000 hours of service in 13 countries. One such not-for-profit organization is City Year, a national youth service corps that unites over 1,000 diverse 17–24-year-olds for a year of leadership development, civic engagement, and full-time service. Timberland is a National Leadership Sponsor of City Year, and Jeff Swartz is Chair of City Year's National Board of Trustees. One service activity in which Timberland employees participate is City Year's Serv-A-Palooza.

Serv-A-Palooza is an annual, companywide celebration of community and service uniting over 1,400 Timberland employees, vendors, community partners, and youth in a day of community service in countries around the world. To participate in City Year's Serv-A-Palooza, all of Timberland's international offices close their offices for a day.

During a recent Serv-A-Palooza, over 900 people worked at 20 different sites in 13 communities in New Hampshire and the sea coast area building playgrounds, opening summer camps, and refurbishing schools. That year, their focus was on schools and agencies that serve the youth. Several of these projects were prospected by Timberland people, many of whom served on a committee Timberland knows as PIES (Partners in Education & Service). The success of the projects depends on the project coordinators who serve as on-site experts.

"Participating in our communities is at the core of how we do business at Timberland," said Jeffrey Swartz, President and CEO. "Corporate America can and must acknowledge its responsibility to help in the building and rebuilding of our nation, one community at a time. Timberland does it through service, but everyone has their own strength to share. Serv-A-Palooza is the annual manifestation of our ethic of service and an opportunity to come together, find common ground, share common purpose, and achieve positive, impactful change."

For six years, Timberland has been recognized as one of *Fortune* magazine's "100 Best Places to Work" and *Business New Hampshire* magazine's "Best Places to Work." Other awards include Business Ethics Corporate Social Responsibility Report's 100 Best Corporate Citizens and Kennedy Center Community IMPACT! Corporate Leadership Award. The Timberland Company continues to grow through innovation, global awareness, and a strong sense of community.

For Discussion

1. Who are the major stakeholders of the Timberland Company? Does any one stakeholder appear to have more influence on Timberland's decisions than another? Explain.

2. How has globalization influenced issues of social responsibility and ethics? Has Timberland addressed these issues? Explain.

3. Which social responsibility strategy does Timberland appear to have adopted? Explain.

4. Which of the "10 Commandments" appear to be addressed by Timberland? Explain.

www.timberland.com

CASE

Ford Motor Company Announces Major Restructuring

Like most companies in today's global marketplace, Ford Motor Company faces intense pressure from its competition. As the No. 2 automaker in the world, Ford must continually revamp and redesign its product lines to keep pace with its competitors, all the while maintaining quality and value in its cars, trucks, and SUVs.

In addition to the Ford Motor Company producing the Lincoln-Mercury line of cars, Ford has developed strategic relationships with a number of foreign automobile companies including Mazda, Jaguar, and Land Rover. While these strategic partnerships have proven profitable, Ford has seen its overall earnings steadily decline over the last couple of years with many of its signature models.

Trouble with Ford started when the company was accused of having a poor design with some of its SUVs that led to tires coming apart, resulting in highway fatalities. Other critics charged that the Firestone tires found on Ford's SUVs were to blame. As a result of the inquiry that followed, the relationship between Ford and Bridgestone/Firestone, which was established between the companies' respective founders, Henry Ford and Harvey Firestone, ended.

In early 2002, Ford announced a massive restructuring effort. This announcement followed other money-saving efforts on the part of the company. Some of these efforts included ending Ford's 401(k) employee retirement matching plan, freezing salaries for many executives, and increasing health insurance premiums. Over the next several years, Ford will cease producing several models, including the Mercury Villager, the Lincoln Continental, and the Ford Escort. Several U.S. plants will be closed due to the termination of these production lines, including plants in Edison, New Jersey, St. Louis, Missouri, and Dearborn, Michigan. Because Ford has contracts with the United Auto Workers (UAW) Union, these plants cannot be closed until late 2003. Most importantly, Ford will be eliminating more than 35,000 jobs over the next several years. The positions to be cut include both salaried and hourly employees. Although Ford will try to reduce its workforce through attrition and early retirement, many employees will have to be fired to reach the target number of 35,000.

For Discussion

1. Based on Ford's current condition, do you think it is ethical to reduce the number of employees? Why or why not?

2. What responsibility does Ford have toward its employees? Does Ford have the same responsibility to the employees of its suppliers?

3. Should Ford have taken any additional steps to save money before announcing the restructuring plans?

4. In light of these actions, can Ford still be a socially responsible company? If so, how?

SOURCE: C. Isidore, "Ford Cutting 35,000 Jobs," taken from the Web site **http://money.cnn.com/2002/01/11/companies/ford** on February 25, 2002.

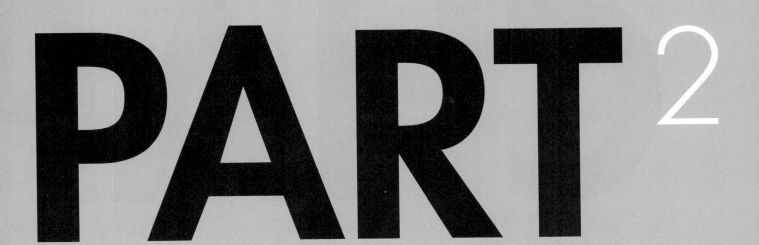

PART 2

PLANNING CHALLENGES IN THE 21ST CENTURY

CHAPTER 4

PLANNING IN THE CONTEMPORARY
ORGANIZATION

CHAPTER 5

STRATEGIC PLANNING IN A GLOBAL
ENVIRONMENT

CHAPTER 6

EFFECTIVE MANAGERIAL DECISION MAKING

CHAPTER 7

DECISION-MAKING TOOLS AND
TECHNIQUES

CHAP

PLANNING IN THE CONTEMPORARY ORGANIZATION

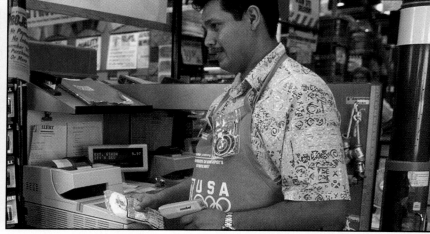

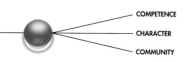

LEADERSHIP

COMPETENCE

CHARACTER

COMMUNITY

TER 4

CHAPTER OVERVIEW

Planning is one of the most important responsibilities of organizational leaders today. Plans provide a foundation for coordinating and directing the activities of the organization so that goals can be achieved. Through planning, managers prepare their organizations to achieve success in both the long term and the short term. Given the highly competitive nature of the business environment today, effective planning has never been more important.

In this chapter, we focus on planning in the contemporary organization. We explore the planning function and give special attention to understanding the planning process at both the strategic and the operational levels. We also examine methods for encouraging, supporting, and rewarding effective planning.

When you have finished studying this chapter, you should be able to:

1. Describe the managerial function of planning and explain why planning is critical for effective leadership.
2. Discuss approaches for initiating the planning process.
3. Define strategic planning and describe the three levels of strategic planning.
4. Define operational planning and distinguish between standing and single-use plans.
5. Describe individual planning systems such as management by objectives programs and the Balanced Scorecard.
6. Define contingency planning and identify the circumstances under which contingency planning would be appropriate.
7. Discuss how advances in information technology have affected operational planning.
8. Describe the common barriers to effective planning and explain ways to reduce these barriers.
9. Discuss how tomorrow's leaders can achieve success through planning.

Facing The Challenge

Home Depot's "Mr. Fix-It" Focuses on the Future

Home Depot's CEO and President Bob Nardelli's do-it-yourself career was not always as high profile as it is today. His early escapades in home improvement on a personal level were a mixed bag of successes and failures. Cofounders of Home Depot, Bernard Marcus and Arthur M. Blank, were not attracted to Nardelli for his do-it-yourself flair; it was his impressive track record at General Electric that caught their attention. Many thought Nardelli was a shoe-in to replace retiring CEO Jack Welch at GE. When Nardelli was not chosen as Welch's successor, Marcus and Blank were waiting nervously on the sidelines. They presented him with their signature orange Home Depot apron and an offer to take over the leadership reins at Home Depot. The founders had reasons to be concerned. Soaring operating expenses, a slowing economy, and an inefficient organizational structure were creating serious problems for Home Depot. The company needed a new strategic direc-

tion, and Marcus and Blank believed that Nardelli was the man to set it.

Home Depot was started in Atlanta with four stores in 1979. The original strategic vision was to sell a wide assortment of products with well-trained associates who provided exemplary customer service. This formula brought immediate success. Within the first five years of the company's founding, stores were opened in Alabama, Florida, Louisiana, and Texas. Today, Home Depot is the world's largest home improvement retailer with over 1,300 stores worldwide. This expansion was fueled by the economic boom of the early and mid-1990s, producing years of record sales and phenomenal growth.

By the late 1990s, however, problems at Home Depot were beginning to surface. The organization's structure, which was highly decentralized and entrepreneurial, was not ideally suited for the expanding organization. This meant that Home Depot would need to

consider reorganizing to a more centralized organization. Nardelli would have to develop a structure that would provide for the implementation of a common vision and strategy, yet still enable each individual store to meet the unique needs of its customers. The slowdown in the economy meant that operating expenses, which had largely gone unchecked, would now have to be closely watched. Competition in the home improvement market also increased the pressure on Home Depot. In late 2000, Home Depot's declining profits resulted in an almost 50 percent loss in its stock price.

Nardelli, who did accept the top post at Home Depot, faced serious challenges when he stepped in. He would need to develop a new strategic vision if the company was to continue its rapid growth and success.

SOURCE: J. Pellet, "Mr. Fix-it Steps In," *Chief Executive*, 171, October 2001, 44–48.

INTRODUCTION

Bob Nardelli and his leadership team were facing exciting challenges as Home Depot moved into the 21st century. Meeting these challenges successfully would require Home Depot to rethink its strategic vision and develop new plans for the future. Nardelli knew that effectively communicating his vision for Home Depot would be crucial if his strategic plans were to be embraced and acted on by Home Depot's employees.

Planning provides a foundation for all organizational activities. Through planning, managers coordinate organizational activities so that the goals of the organization can be achieved. Organizational success is dependent upon the ability of managers to develop a plan that brings together, in a logical way, the diverse set of tasks that occur within the organization. In its simplest form, planning involves understanding the current situation of the organization, knowing what results the organization desires to achieve, and devising the means to achieve those results. Organizational leaders must understand the importance of planning and be prepared to provide guidance to other organizational members in devising and implementing plans.

LEARNING OBJECTIVE 1

Describe the managerial function of planning and explain why planning is critical for effective leadership.

MANAGERIAL PLANNING

Planning is an essential, but potentially complex, managerial function. To gain a better understanding of the planning function, let's start by answering a few key questions: What is planning, why should managers plan, and where should the planning process begin?

WHAT IS PLANNING?

Planning is the process of outlining the activities that are necessary to achieve the goals of the organization. Through planning, managers determine how organizational resources are to be allocated and how the activities of the organization will be assigned to individuals and work groups. The output of the planning process is the plan. A **plan** is a blueprint for action; it prescribes the activities necessary for the organization to realize its goals.[1]

The purpose of planning is simple—to ensure that the organization is both effective and efficient in its activities. In a broad sense, an organization must develop a plan that ensures that the appropriate products and services are offered to its customers. More specifically, planning gives guidance and direction to the members of the organization as to their role in delivering those products and services.[2]

Critical to understanding the planning process is an understanding of the relationships between goals, plans, and controls (see Figure 4.1). In general, **goals** provide a clear, engaging sense of direction and specify what is to be accomplished. From the highest-level goal of maximizing shareholder wealth down to the goals of first-line operating managers, these targets for achievement are important determinants of the plans that an organization will develop. Plans, as we know, establish the means for achieving the organization's goals. Through planning, managers outline the activities necessary to ensure that the organization's goals are achieved. **Controls** monitor the extent to which goals have been achieved and ensure that the organization is moving in the direction suggested by its plans. Goals, plans, and controls are inextricably intertwined and must be well integrated if the planning process is to be successful.[3] "Now Apply It" provides an opportunity for you to develop a plan for professional development that both delineates your goals and establishes control mechanisms to ensure your plan is being implemented.

WHY SHOULD MANAGERS PLAN?

Planning is a critical managerial function for any organization that strives for success. In fact, it has often been said that "failing to plan is planning to fail." Just ask the leadership at General Mills about that old adage. With its recent acquisition of Pillsbury, General Mills was poised to be the darling of the food industry. General Mills CEO, Stephen Sanger, promised investors stellar returns as the merged company broke into fast-growing food categories with new products to augment its tried and true, yet quite mature, cereal product lines (for example, Cheerios, Wheaties and Chex). But those stellar returns failed to materialize, largely because of a

Planning
Setting goals and defining the actions necessary to achieve those goals.

Plan
A blueprint for action that prescribes the activities necessary for the organization to realize its goals.

Goals
Specific statements that provide a clear, engaging sense of direction and specify what is going to be accomplished.

Controls
The mechanisms used to monitor the organization's performance relative to its goals and plans.

Figure 4.1 | Planning as a Linking Mechanism

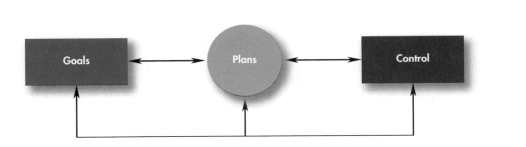

failure to plan effectively. Integrating Pillsbury into the General Mills organization proved to be more challenging than expected, so much so that new product development efforts had to be delayed. Competitors, sensing the turmoil at General Mills, took advantage of the company's lack of focus, launching a slew of new products that cut into General Mills' market share. By the time the merger was complete, General Mills' profits had declined significantly, the stock price had fallen, and the company had lost its market leadership position in the cereal business to Kellogg. With the integration of Pillsbury now finished, the leadership at General Mills is promising that they are back in the saddle and ready to restore the profitability and market position of the company. In fact, they plan to launch 80 new products in the latter half of 2002. Investors are hoping that the plans for 2002 are better thought out than the plans for the previous year.[4]

While most experienced managers recognize that planning is critical, they also realize that there are both benefits and costs to planning.

BENEFITS OF PLANNING   Theoretically, planning leads to superior performance for the organization. From a very general perspective, the planning process offers four primary benefits: (1) better coordination, (2) a focus on forward thinking, (3) a participatory work environment, and (4) more effective control systems.

Better Coordination   Planning provides a much-needed foundation for the coordination of a broad range of organizational activities. Most organizations comprise multiple work groups, each of which is responsible for contributing to the accomplishment of the goals of the organization. A plan helps both to define the responsibilities of these work groups and to coordinate their activities. Without such a mechanism for coordination, directing the efforts of organizational members and groups toward common organizational goals would be difficult.

Consider, for example, the problem facing Home Depot with regard to its decentralized structure. Should Nordelli move to centralize the organization's opera-

Now Apply It

Developing a Professional Development Plan

Developing a professional development plan helps you focus on your primary career objectives. The planning process includes three major activities: goal setting, developing a plan of action, and monitoring your progress. Start by identifying a professional goal. This goal can be either short term (such as making the Dean's List) or long term (such as owning your own business). With that goal in mind, develop a list of three things you can do to achieve it. Finally, develop a method to control your progress. How can you make sure that your plan is being implemented properly?

Goal: Establish a professional goal.

_____

Plan: Delineate activities that will help you attain your professional goal.

1. _____
2. _____
3. _____

Control: Identify ways to monitor the implementation of your plan.

1. _____
2. _____
3. _____

tions, it would require closer coordination of many activities. Functions from a wide variety of departments would be affected, including information technology, human resources, marketing, and others. Planning provides a mechanism for coordinating the activities of these diverse groups so that their efforts are consistent and synergistic, and ultimately lead to the achievement of the company's strategic vision.

At an even higher level of complexity, consider the coordination needed to establish global brand recognition for a particular product. Global brand recognition requires that the product's market position, advertising strategy, personality, look, and feel must be essentially the same from one country to another. Many companies, such as IBM, Visa, Mobil Oil, and Volkswagen, seek to achieve a consistent brand image across the dozens of international markets they serve. These companies, like many other global organizations, use the planning process to help build consistency in their brands across international markets. Using the same planning template, terminology, and process helps managers coordinate their efforts to achieve the same brand attributes and identity throughout the global marketplace.[5]

Global brand recognition requires that the product's market position, advertising strategy, personality, look, and feel must be essentially the same from one country to another.

Focus on Forward Thinking   The planning function forces managers to think ahead and consider resource needs and potential opportunities or threats that the organization may face in the future. While the identification of organizational problems and solutions is an important by-product of the planning process, its overriding focus should be on preparing the organization to perform more effectively and efficiently in the future than in the past.

While today's highly competitive and dynamic business environment demands that managers be forward thinking, many companies find it challenging to anticipate the changes that will affect their businesses. Consider, for example, the music industry. It wasn't so long ago that the distribution channels for music were pretty easy to understand and to control. But with the arrival of digital mediums for distributing music, some feel that the entire industry has been turned upside down. Some companies have focused on battling the Napsters of the world; others have looked for innovative ways to utilize digital technologies to enhance their business. AOL, for example[6]—a company with both tremendous online capabilities and major recording labels through its Warner Music Group subsidiary, the Number 2 record company in terms of market share in the United States—has developed an aggressive plan to capitalize on the potential future changes in the industry. That plan leverages digital technology to stimulate demand for new product launches. For example, when it was time to launch newcomer Michelle Branch, AOL offered free downloads of one of her songs, "All You Wanted," four weeks before it played on radio stations. This fueled significant interest in the artist well before the official release of her music. For bigger-name artists, the strategy is somewhat different. Prior to the release of Jewel's new CD, AOL plastered its Web site with her picture and sound clips and even hosted virtual listening parties, all of which provided tremendous exposure to her newest music. AOL estimates that first-week sales of Jewel's CD were 30 percent greater because of the online exposure. These kinds of forward-thinking plans can make the difference between success and failure for organizations that operate in rapidly changing environments.

Participatory Work Environment   The successful development and implementation of organizational plans require the participation of a wide range of organizational members. As a consequence, a more participatory work environment typically evolves. Participatory work environments provide two important benefits to an organization.

First, the organization benefits from having access to a broad base of expertise and knowledge in developing its plans. This is particularly true in organizations with diverse groups of employees. Participatory planning usually leads to a more fully developed plan that reflects the multiple, diverse, and sometimes contradictory issues faced by the organization. Volvo, for example, found that involving employees in its plans to improve manufacturing quality contributed greatly to the success of that initiative.[7]

Second, organizational members are more likely to "buy in" to a plan that they have helped to develop. Employees who have participated in the planning process will typically be more committed to and supportive of their organization and its goals than those who have not been involved. This kind of commitment and buy-in may be particularly important for companies that are experiencing financial difficulties and need a plan to address their business problems. For example, when the CEO of Lincoln Electric, a global manufacturer of machinery, realized that the company's financial position was deteriorating, he knew the company needed a plan to solve its problems and restore its profitability. Through involving the employees in developing solutions to the company's difficulties, the CEO was able to formulate a plan to turn the company around. The participatory work environment that resulted from the planning process was key to the implementation of the plan and, ultimately, to Lincoln Electric's success.[8]

More Effective Control Systems   An organization's plan provides a foundation for control of the processes and progress of the company. The implementation of the activities prescribed by the plan can be evaluated, and progress toward the achievement of performance objectives can be monitored. Controls provide mechanisms for ensuring that the organization is moving in the right direction and making progress toward achieving its goals.[9] For example, General Mills could have likely benefited from a well-developed control system to ensure that its efforts to integrate Pillsbury into its operations were proceeding as planned. Such a control system may have alerted management to some of the integration problems in time to make some adjustments to their plan.

COSTS OF PLANNING   Despite these benefits, planning also entails costs. These costs can be significant and may discourage managers from planning.

Management Time   Done properly, the planning process requires a substantial amount of managerial time and energy. Managers must work with their employees to evaluate existing resources, identify opportunities to improve the operations of the work group, and establish organizational goals. Some work groups may find that planning requires an assessment of external information related to the products, prices, and strategies of competing firms. The collection, analysis, and interpretation of such information can be time consuming and costly.[10]

Organizations that participate in the global business environment often find that planning is more complex and time consuming than it is for purely domestic firms. International firms must analyze multiple economies, market forces, customer profiles, and other such variables. Yet taking the time to plan carefully may be the key to the success of an international initiative. As a case in point, consider the experience of General Motors (GM) when it attempted to make the role of human resources strategic instead of operational. "At The Forefront" describes how GM realized that proactive planning on the part of human resources would be necessary to provide innovative compensation packages to diverse groups of employees across the globe.

Delay in Decision Making   Another potential cost of planning is that it may delay decision making. This is particularly true when planning processes require time-consuming acquisition of information and data.[11] Further, some managers argue

At The Forefront

Strategic Human Resource Management:
Maintaining a Competitive Edge in the Global Marketplace

In the past, human resource (HR) functions were often thought of as tactical and reactive. Today, companies are changing their perspective about HR. Many now see the role of HR as strategic. Proactive planning and innovative compensation packages can provide a critical competitive advantage in an increasingly competitive global environment.

General Motors (GM), for example, has come to believe that in order to truly compete and succeed in the global market, HR must take an active role in strategy formulation. To this end, GM's HR strategy now espouses the 3Ts: Technology, Talent, and Transformation. Technology has driven GM to completely revamp its HR processes. It now has an "HR Portal" via the company intranet site that allows employees to access most HR services and forms online. Recognizing and developing GM's talent is vital to its ongoing success. In 1997, the company founded GM University (GMU), which is one of the largest corporate educational programs in the

world. GMU facilitates a wealth of professional development opportunities for GM's employees, which will better prepare them for leadership positions with increased responsibilities. Transformation refers to the overall impact that HR's strategic role has had for GM. The focus of many jobs has changed from a narrow perspective to a much broader appreciation for GM as an organizational system and for the global environment in which it operates. This change has led to increased communication from corporate headquarters in Detroit and across the many divisions and plants spanning the globe.

The diversity of the global market makes defining "innovative" and "competitive compensation" quite difficult. A creative and competitive compensation package in one market or company may not be effective in another. When companies expand overseas, strategic HR planning involves three distinct phases, which are as follows:

1. Philosophy—Understand the regional needs and address compensation plans to meet these needs.
2. Design—Determine the laws and local customs that govern labor and consider economic trends in preparing a payroll and compensation strategy.
3. Implementation—Establish operations and put into practice compensation and benefits packages that offer a competitive advantage.

Although operating in the global market adds an element of complexity and uncertainty to a company's operation, focusing on HR as a strategic function illustrates to employees and applicants that they are a priority to the organization.

SOURCES: N.B. Krupp, "Global Compensation Planning: Establishing and Maintaining a Competitive Edge in the International Marketplace," *Compensation & Benefits Management*, 18, Spring 2002, 54–56; and B. Leonard, "GM Drives HR to the Next Level," *HRMagazine*, 47, March 2002, 46–50.

that planning directs the focus toward evaluating rather than doing. This can delay the organization's response to changes in the industry, marketplace, or internal operations. The delay can be particularly detrimental when an organization's success is dependent upon its ability to respond to change quickly. Nevertheless, taking the time to plan effectively may be more important to the success of the initiative than the loss of time it takes to do so.

In the business environment of the 21st century, speed in response time is critical for success in most industries. Nimble competitors will seize opportunities that are missed by those who are too slow at the planning process. According to Barbara Kux, once vice president of Switzerland's Nestlé S.A., global managers have to be able to analyze, plan, and execute quickly to stay on top in the international marketplace. As she explained, "The first trait of a global manager is to be nimble. Move fast, but don't hipshoot. Do some analysis, but not too much analysis, and then act . . . it's better to be 70 percent right and move fast than to be perfect and wait. Speed is a plus in a global business."[12] When you weigh the potential benefits of planning against the potential costs, it is clear that planning pays.

Firms on the brink of failure have recovered through effective planning; highly successful firms have stayed that way through effective planning; and some organizations have had both experiences. Many people are familiar with the challenges Harley-Davidson faced in the mid-1990s. The company came dangerously close to bankruptcy before working its way back to stability through effective planning. The company now has even higher aspirations. Harley-Davidson developed Plan 2003—

an ambitious vision to more than double its production of motorcycles. Plan 2003 is a comprehensive plan that calls for the reorganization of the company around highly interdependent work groups, the development of an aggressive training program, and the creation of a highly participatory work environment. Company leaders are counting on Plan 2003 to ensure Harley-Davidson's success for many years to come.[13]

In the final analysis, managers plan because planning leads to better performance. In today's highly competitive business environment, planning can help managers cope with the challenges they face and ensure the long-term success of their companies.

WHERE SHOULD PLANNING BEGIN?

Assuming that organizations should plan, the question then becomes, "Who should initiate the planning process?" Planning is carried out at various levels of the organization and for various departments, work groups, and individuals at each level. Although a broad range of organizational members should be involved in the planning process, the process must be initiated and coordinated at some specific point in the organizational hierarchy. At what organizational level should planning begin?

Traditionally, two basic approaches have been taken to planning, depending on where in the organizational hierarchy the planning function is initiated—the top-down approach and the bottom-up approach. Table 4.1 illustrates some of the differences between these two approaches. Today, however, many organizations take a more integrated approach that combines aspects of both top-down and bottom-up planning.

With a top-down approach, planning efforts begin with the board of directors and the top-level executives of the organization. They determine the general direction of the organization and establish a master plan to achieve its overall goals.

Table 4.1 | Top-Down versus Bottom-Up Planning

	TOP-DOWN	BOTTOM-UP
Level at which planning is initiated	Board of directors, top-level managers	Individuals closest to products, services, or customers
Role of organizational units	As the plan moves down the hierarchy, units determine actions that willsupport the plan	Units develop their own goals and plans. As these plans move up the hierarchy, they are evaluated and adjusted for accuracy and feasibility
Specificity of plan	Begins broad, becomes more specific as it moves down the hierarchy	Begins very fragmented and specific, becomes cohesive and integrated as it moves up the hierarchy
Advantages	Plans are driven by top-level managers who are most knowledgeable about all factors affecting the organization	Those closest to customers, suppliers, and operating systems provide focus of plans
Disadvantages	Top-level managers are often far removed from the front line	Lower-level managers may lack understanding of all factors affecting the organization
Appropriateness	When the organization's success is dependent on quick response to external pressure and threats	When an organization's success is dependent on its ability to respond quickly to changes in operational systems

The master plan establishes the parameters within which the organization's work groups develop their plans. Managers develop plans for their work groups based on what their units must accomplish to support the master plan.

In contrast, bottom-up planning is initiated at the lowest levels of the organizational hierarchy—with the individuals who are most directly involved in the delivery of the organization's products and services and who are closest to the organization's customers or suppliers. The managers and employees at the operational level begin the planning process by estimating sales potential, describing needed product and service modifications or new product and service developments, and identifying potential problems or opportunities in the supply of input resources. As these plans move up through the organization, they are developed further, refined, and evaluated for accurateness and feasibility. Finally, the board of directors and top-level executives bring together all the plans of the organization's work groups to develop a cohesive and well-integrated master plan that establishes the overall direction of the organization.[14]

Both the top-down and bottom-up approaches to planning have advantages and disadvantages. The primary advantage of top-down planning is that the top-level managers, who presumably are most knowledgeable about the organization as a whole, drive the development of the plan. Although one might argue that the people at the lowest level of the organization know the most about how the organization actually operates, top-level management has a more comprehensive understanding of the wide variety of internal and external factors that affect the overall success of the organization.

Having those closest to the operating system, customers, and suppliers provide the focus for the planning process does have advantages. These individuals may have a better understanding of the competitive and operational challenges faced by the organization than the board of directors and top-level executives, who are far removed from the front line.

Which approach is better? The answer to that question depends on the specific circumstances facing the organization. When success is largely a function of the organization's ability to respond quickly and effectively to changes in its operating system, customer focus, or supplier relationships, bottom-up planning may be more appropriate. When success is dependent upon the ability to make high-level organizational changes in response to more general external threats and pressures (such as industry consolidation via mergers and acquisitions, changes in the regulatory environment, or demographic trends), a top-down planning approach may be more appropriate. For example, computer firms such as Hewlett-Packard may find that a bottom-up planning approach supports efforts to be sensitive to the technological needs of customers in designing new products. In contrast, a pharmaceutical company such as Eli Lilly, which must respond to Food and Drug Administration (FDA) directives and other regulatory issues, might benefit from a top-down approach.

Perhaps most important, these planning modes are not mutually exclusive. Many organizations use a bottom-up approach to formulate plans in one area (such as marketing) but develop plans in other areas (such as finance) from a top-down perspective. Still others, like Charming Shoppes, Inc., a speciality retailer of women's apparel, uses both approaches simultaneously. While the board of directors and the top-level management team are focused on growing the company through acquisition strategies, such as the recent acquisitions of Catherines and Lane Bryant, the managers and employees of the functional areas of the business are developing plans for integrating the operations and systems of the merged companies.

Now that we have sketched out the managerial function of planning in general, let's examine the two primary types of planning that occur in most organizations: strategic and operational planning.

STRATEGIC VERSUS OPERATIONAL PLANNING

In general, most organizations engage in both strategic and operational planning. Although strategic and operational planning differ in a number of ways, they are also interrelated. Let's explore both of these important planning processes.

STRATEGIC PLANNING

LEARNING OBJECTIVE 3

Define strategic planning and describe the three levels of strategic planning.

Strategic planning
The process by which an organization makes decisions and takes actions to enhance its long-term performance.

Strategic plan
A plan that identifies the markets in which an organization competes, as well as the ways in which it competes in those markets.

Competitive advantage
Any aspect of an organization that distinguishes it from its competitors strategically.

Each level of strategic planning can be determined by the focus of the strategic planning process and the participants involved in the process.

Planning that is strategic in nature focuses on enhancing the competitive position and overall performance of the organization in the long term.[15] In other words, **strategic planning** is the process by which an organization makes decisions and takes actions that affect its long-run performance. A **strategic plan** is the output of the strategic planning process. Strategic plans define both the markets in which the organization competes and the way in which it competes in those markets.[16]

The purpose of strategic planning is to move the organization from where it is to where it wants to be and, in the process, to develop and maintain a competitive advantage within the industries in which it competes.[17] A **competitive advantage** is any aspect of an organization's operations that distinguishes it from its competitors strategically.[18] For example, most would point to Compaq's reputation for quality and service as being a key competitive advantage, while Apple Computer has distinguished itself through its innovative and user-friendly system designs. Dell, of course, nearly redefined the entire computer industry by providing computers that are customized to meet individual needs, delivered quickly, and priced very reasonably. Although Hewlett-Packard's competitive edge has traditionally come from its reputation for technologically advanced scientific computing equipment, a newly announced strategy will position the company as an e-services provider in addition to a hardware provider.[19] Through their strategies, each of these firms has developed a distinct competitive advantage and leadership position in the computer industry.[20] Yet the market for computers is highly dynamic, and these companies must continually reassess their strategies to ensure their continued leadership.[21]

You don't have to look far to find an organization that attributes its success to its strategy.[22] Similarly, numerous examples of organizations would attribute their failure or the failure of a given product, service, or project to the absence of an effective strategic plan.[23] For example, one-time industry giant CBS Entertainment evolved from a company with a strong strategic direction to a company suffering from the lack of a strategic plan and declining performance in the mid-1990s.[24] Ultimately, the floundering company was acquired by Viacom and began to develop a new strategy for competing with some very powerful competitors, including Disney-ABC and Fox.[25] By 2001, the "Tiffany Network," as the New York City-based network has been called, had regained its shine, winning the Number 1 spot in the ratings war for the year.[26] The recent success of CBS can be attributed, in large part, to its very effective strategic plan.

LEVELS OF STRATEGIC PLANNING   Strategic planning occurs at three primary levels within the organization: the corporate, business, and functional levels.[27] Each level can be distinguished by the focus of the strategic planning process, the participants in the process, the specificity of the strategy, and the time horizon of the plan. Table 4.2 summarizes the key differences in these three levels of strategic planning; the discussion that follows elaborates on each.

Corporate Strategic Planning   Strategic planning that occurs at the corporate level of the organization focuses on developing corporate strategy. **Corporate strategy**

Table 4.2 | Levels of Strategic Planning

	FOCUS	SPECIFICITY	PARTICIPANTS	TIME HORIZON
Corporate strategy	To develop a mix of business units that meets the company's long-term growth and profitability goals	Broad	Board of directors Top-level executives	5–10 years
Business strategy	To develop and maintain a distinctive competitive advantage that will ensure long-term profitability	More specific than the corporate strategy	Top-level executives Managers within the business unit	1–5 years
Functional strategy	To develop action plans that ensure that corporate and business strategies are implemented	Very specific	Middle-level managers Lower-level managers	1–2 years

addresses the question "What business should we be in?" and is relevant for organizations that operate in single or multiple lines of business. Corporate strategic planning involves assessing the organization's portfolio of businesses to determine whether an appropriate mix exists.[28] The objective is to develop a mix of business units that meets the long-term growth and profitability goals of the organization.

Diversification is often at the core of corporate strategy.[29] Diversification occurs when an organization chooses to add a new business unit to its portfolio of businesses. A company may pursue a strategy of diversification if it wishes to reduce its dependence on its existing business units or to capitalize on its core competencies by expanding into another business. Philip Morris (soon to be know as the Altria Group, Inc.)[30] for example, embarked on a fairly aggressive strategy of diversification to lessen its dependence on the slow-growing and highly threatened tobacco industry. The acquisitions of Miller Brewing, General Foods, and Kraft, Inc. were intended to diversify Philip Morris's revenue base.[31] In contrast, Xerox, which originally sold only copy machines, acquired numerous firms in the office products industry, such as makers of printers, fax machines, and scanners, in an effort to expand its product lines and capitalize on its name recognition in the copier business. Diversifying was a desirable option for both firms, although for very different reasons.

Because corporate strategy defines the very nature of the organization, it is formulated by the organization's board of directors and top-level executives. In developing their strategic plans, however, these individuals rely to a great extent on information provided by middle- and lower-level managers.

Corporate strategy is relatively broad and general in nature and may extend as far as 5 to 10 years into the future. While many would argue that it is impossible to formulate strategy 10 years into the future in today's rapidly changing business environment,[32] it is important for corporate leaders to have a strategy for the long-term future of the organization—even if that strategy has to be adapted and adjusted in light of environmental and competitive changes that occur over the years.

Business Strategic Planning The product of the strategic planning process at the business level is business strategy. **Business strategy** defines how each business unit in the organization's corporate portfolio will operate in its market arena. Strategy formulated at this level addresses the question "How do we compete in our existing lines of business?" The primary focus of strategic planning at the business level is to develop and maintain a distinct competitive advantage that will lead to organizational success.

Corporate strategy
Decisions and actions that define the portfolio of business units that an organization maintains.

Business strategy
Focused plans that define how each business unit in the firm's corporate portfolio will operate in its market arena.

Consider the various business strategies that must be developed for Philip Morris's portfolio of businesses. The tobacco segment of the business must have a strategy for dealing with the proposed increases in regulation and competing with the other tobacco companies both at home and abroad; Miller must have a strategy that focuses on competing with the United States' leading brewer, Anheuser-Busch, as well as with the many other brewers that compete for market share in this "dog-eat-dog" industry; and Kraft Foods, (the company that resulted from the eventual merger of two Philip Morris companies—General Foods and Kraft, Inc.) must have a strategy for adding new food products. For example, Kraft Foods is pursuing a business strategy designed to penetrate the high-growth market for energy and nutrition foods. Toward that end, the company has acquired Boca Burger, Inc., a marketer of soy-based meat alternatives, and Balance Bar, a product line of energy/nutrition snacks and beverages. These acquisitions will help Kraft Foods to become a market leader in the energy/nutrition food category, which doubled in size from 1997–2000.

Business strategy should be formulated by the individuals who are most familiar with the operations of the business unit. Consequently, the board of directors and corporate executives are typically not involved with strategy formulation at the business level. Instead, this responsibility lies with the top-level executives and managers within the specific business units.[33] For example, the CEO and top-level management teams at Philip Morris's tobacco company, Miller Brewing, and Kraft Foods will be most instrumental in formulating business strategy for their respective units.

Functional Strategic Planning   Functional strategic planning leads to the development of functional strategy. **Functional strategy** specifies the production, research and development, financial, human resource management, and marketing activities necessary to implement the organization's corporate and business strategies. Table 4.3 lists some of the areas in which functional planning occurs and gives examples of functional strategies in each area.

Strategy formulation at the functional level addresses the question "How do we implement our corporate and business strategies?" While an organization's corporate and business strategies address what should be done, functional strategy focuses on how things will get done. In other words, corporate and business strategies deal with "doing the right thing," while functional strategy deals with "doing things right."

Consider, for example, the functional strategies necessary to implement Kraft's business-level strategy to penetrate the energy/nutrition food segment. The addition of newly acquired or developed products in this category will affect multiple

Functional strategy
Specifies the production, research and development, financial, human resource management, and marketing activities necessary to implement the organization's corporate and business strategies.

Table 4.3 | Examples of Functional Strategies

Human Resource Strategies:	*Finance Strategies:*
• Recruit for management positions.	• Secure debt financing.
• Design commission structure.	• Evaluate capital structure.
• Develop training program.	• Initiate and manage budget process.
• Design benefit package.	• Review and revise credit policies.
Marketing Strategies:	*Production Strategies:*
• Develop market research study.	• Evaluate robotics system.
• Identify additional distribution channels.	• Redesign quality control processes.
• Create promotional program.	• Locate alternative sources of supply.
• Evaluate pricing structure.	• Develop inventory management system.

departments within the company. The production department will have to prepare to manufacture the new products; the marketing department must develop appropriate pricing, promotion, and advertising plans; and the sales department must devise a strategy for educating its sales force on the attributes of the new products. Each of these activities represents functional strategy.

Functional strategic planning is carried out by middle- and lower-level managers, who develop functional strategies to ensure that their units are supporting the corporate and business strategies of the organization. Strategic planning at the functional level is more specific than corporate and business strategic planning, and functional strategies typically span a shorter time frame, usually one or two years at most.

CUSTOMIZING THE STRATEGIC PLANNING PROCESS In today's competitive business environment, virtually every company engages in some kind of strategic planning process. Yet, no one model of planning fits all organizations. Some organizations that use similar models experience quite different results, just as many successful organizations employ contrasting planning processes. In general, a successful planning process must fit the organization's focus on creating value for its customers and its shareholders. In other words, it must be customized for the organization based on its specific and unique needs.

Consider, for example, the planning processes at three companies with very different needs: Granada, a British conglomerate that operates businesses in television programming and broadcasting, hotels, catering, and appliance rentals; Dow Chemical Company, a leading plastics and chemicals manufacturer; and Emerson Electric, a manufacturer of electronic products. While each of these companies can boast of highly effective planning processes, they each take a very different approach to planning. At Granada, where the ultimate objective is growth, the planning process is focused on setting "stretch" goals that encourage managers to raise their ambitions and take on highly challenging endeavors. In contrast, Dow Chemical's planning process is focused on efficiency and cost control. Given the highly cyclical nature of its business, Dow's planning priority is to be prepared for the "bottom of the cycle" in the demand for its products. Finally, Emerson Electric has designed its planning process to achieve the "steady rhythm" that wins over time in the industries in which it operates. The focus of Emerson's planning process is on consistent incremental improvements in sales of and profits from its products. Table 4.4 illustrates the fundamental differences in the planning processes of these organizations. Despite their differences, these companies share a common result—strong performance in their industries.[34] General Motors is another company that illustrates how important it is to customize the strategic planning process to meet the needs of the organization. As described in "Leaders In Action" on page 135, Ralph Szygenda, GM's first chief information officer (CIO), had to demonstrate to GM's top leadership why it was crucial for GM to consider technology as a competitive advantage.

At this point, you should have a broad understanding of strategic planning. We will explore the process of strategic planning much more fully in Chapter 5. For now, let's turn our attention to the second type of planning—operational planning.

OPERATIONAL PLANNING

Operational planning focuses on determining the day-to-day activities that are necessary to achieve the long-term goals of the organization. **Operational plans** outline the tactical activities that must occur to support the ongoing operations of the organization. Operational plans are more specific than strategic plans, address shorter-term issues, and are formulated by the middle- and lower-level managers who are responsible for the work groups in the organization.

LEARNING OBJECTIVE 4

Define operational planning and distinguish between standing and single-use plans.

Operational planning
The process of determining the day-to-day activities that are necessary to achieve the long-term goals of the organization.

Operational plans
An outline of the tactical activities necessary to support and implement the strategic plans of the organization.

Table 4.4 | Three Successful Planning Processes

	GRANADA	DOW	EMERSON
Design Drivers			
Value-creation focus	Make dramatic increases in profits	Help units focus on reducing costs	Help units find incremental performance gain
Skills of the CEO	Charles Allen's frontline knowledge and ability to build consensus	Arnold Allemang's manufacturing experience in highly cyclical industries	Chuck Knight's operations experience and comfort with confrontation
Design Features			
Performance measure	Profit	Economic profit	Growth in return on sales
Planning techniques	Price-value-cost analysis Contingency analysis	Bottom-of-the-cycle forecasts Competitive cost analysis	Profitability analysis by segment Competitive cost analysis
Organizational process	Series of meetings starting with planning	Part of larger planning process	Planning conference
Attendance at planning review meetings	Key unit managers only	Unit chief chooses people	Full unit management team and representatives of corporate function
Role of functions	Finance function helps bridge gaps between business units and CEO	Manufacturing function builds buy-in	Managers from corporate functions sit in as observers to provide operating support when asked
Meeting length and tone	Four hours per unit	Part of broader process	One day per unit Confrontational
Follow up	Direct link with monthly budget	Corporate manufacturing function monitors process	Letter from Knight Operational plan

SOURCE: Reprinted by permission of Harvard Business Review. From "Tailored, Not Benchmarked: A Fresh Look at Corporate Planning," A. Campbell, *Harvard Business Review*, 77, 2, March/April 1999, 41–50. Copyright © by the Harvard Business School Publishing Corporation; all rights reserved.

In general, plans can be categorized as standing or single-use plans, depending on whether they address recurring issues or are specific to a given set of circumstances. Most organizations maintain both standing and single-use plans, as both are applicable to a broad range of organizational situations. While standing and single-use plans are usually developed for work groups within the organization, operational planning can also occur for individual organizational members. Individualized approaches to planning include both management by objectives (MBO) programs and the Balanced Scorecard.

Standing plans
Plans that deal with organizational issues and problems that recur frequently.

STANDING PLANS **Standing plans** are designed to deal with organizational issues or problems that recur frequently. By using standing plans, management avoids the need to "reinvent the wheel" every time a particular situation arises. In addition, such plans ensure that recurring situations are handled consistently over time. This may be particularly important for an organization with a highly diverse workforce. Individuals from different cultural and social backgrounds may react to certain situations differently. Standing plans ensure that such situations will be handled in prescribed ways.

Standing plans can, however, limit employees' flexibility and make it more difficult to respond to the needs of the customer. Given the customer focus of most successful businesses today, rigid constraints on employee behavior could have a negative effect on the performance of the organization. Therefore, managers should carefully consider how standing plans can be used most effectively before they design and implement such plans. Standing plans include policies, procedures, and rules. Each provides guidance in a different way.

Policies   **Policies** are general guidelines that govern how certain organizational situations will be addressed. Policies provide guidance to managers who must make decisions about circumstances that occur frequently within the organization. Most organizational units establish policies to provide direction for decision making.

For example, human resource management departments maintain policies that govern sick leave, vacation leave, and benefit options. Production departments establish policies for procurement, inventory management, and quality control. A university's administration maintains policies about admittance to certain academic programs, grade appeals, and permissible course waivers or substitutions. These policies provide a framework for decision making that eliminates the need to evaluate the specific circumstances surrounding each individual case.

Procedures   **Procedures** are a second type of standing plan. Procedures are more specific and action-oriented than policies and are designed to give explicit instructions on how to complete a recurring task. Most companies maintain some sort of procedures manual to provide guidance for certain recurring activities. Many use a standard operating procedures (SOPs) manual to outline the basic operating methods of the organization.

Most units of an organization have procedures as well as policies. For example, human resource management departments develop procedures for filing benefit claims, documenting the reasons for sick leave, and requesting vacation time. Production departments establish procedures for identifying and evaluating suppliers and ordering supplies, operating the inventory management system, and identifying and implementing specific quality-control criteria. Universities maintain specific procedures for applying for admittance to certain programs, appealing grades, and requesting course waivers and/or substitutions.

Rules   **Rules** are the strictest type of standing plan found in organizations. Rules are not intended to serve as guidelines for making organizational decisions; instead, they provide detailed and specific regulations for action.

For example, a human resource management department may have rules governing the number of sick days an employee may take with pay, the months in which vacation time can be scheduled, and the length of time an organizational member must be employed before qualifying for benefits. The production department may have rules governing the percentage of supplies that can be purchased from a single supplier, the method in which inventory must be accounted for, and the way in which products of substandard quality are handled. A university may have rules to govern the minimum grade point average necessary for admission to a given academic program, the period in which a grade can be appealed after a course is completed, and the specific courses that may be substituted for one another.

Consider once again, the speciality women's apparel retailer, Charming Shoppes. When Charming Shoppes acquired Lane Bryant, organizational leaders had to develop an integration plan to merge the operating systems of the two companies and to address the policies, procedures, and rules of both organizations. Undoubtedly, Charming Shoppes and Lane Bryant had different standing plans in place. For example, vacation, sick leave, and other benefits differed. As the companies merged, these differences had to be resolved, and a consistent set of standing plans had to be developed for the organization as a whole.

Consider how GM's human resource management policies should address sick pay, vacation, compensation, and other benefits among the different divisions and

Policies
General guidelines for decision making within the organization.

Procedures
Instructions on how to complete recurring tasks.

Rules
Detailed and specific regulations for action.

plants across the globe. It is important that GM's strategic human resource management plan integrate these various benefits in order to be consistent and fair.

Experiential Exercise 4.1 on page 140 provides an opportunity for you to evaluate and adapt standing plans for an organization with which you are familiar. Based on this exercise, you should see the potential value of establishing standing plans to cope with recurring organizational situations.

Single-use plans

Plans that address specific organizational situations that typically do not recur.

SINGLE-USE PLANS   **Single-use plans** are developed to address a specific organizational situation. Such plans are typically used only once because the specific situation to which they apply does not recur. Consider, for example, the plan of SAP Americas, a leading provider of enterprise resource planning (ERP) and e-commerce solutions, to build a new corporate headquarters. A sophisticated plan was necessary to finance, construct, and move into the new building. This was a single-use plan because SAP would not need to build such a building or relocate its employees again for a very long time.

Three primary types of single-use plans are possible: programs, projects, and budgets. Each offers a different degree of comprehensiveness and detail. Programs are the most comprehensive plans; projects have a narrower scope and, in fact, are often undertaken as a part of a program; and budgets are developed to support programs or projects.

Programs

Single-use plans that govern a comprehensive set of activities designed to accomplish a particular set of goals.

Programs   **Programs** are single-use plans that govern a relatively comprehensive set of activities designed to accomplish a particular set of goals. Such plans outline the major steps and specific actions necessary to implement the activities prescribed by the program. The timing and sequencing of the efforts of individuals and units are also articulated in the plan.

Many organizations today have implemented diversity programs. Such programs are designed to recruit and hire a more diverse workforce, as well as to educate employees on issues related to diverse work environments. As you may recall from Chapter 3, for example, Allstate Corporation took proactive steps to recruit minority candidates and to provide diversity training for managers and employees at all levels of the organization. This program was developed to meet Allstate's goal of having a productive and diverse workforce that reflects the organization's customer base.[35]

Implementing a company-wide career development plan can help a company recruit and hire a more diverse workforce.

Projects

Single-use plans that direct the efforts of individuals or work groups toward the achievements of a specific goal.

Projects   **Projects** direct the efforts of individuals or work groups toward the achievement of specific, well-defined objectives. Projects are typically less comprehensive and narrower in focus than programs and usually have predetermined target dates for completion. Many projects are designed to collect and analyze information for decision-making purposes or to support more comprehensive planning efforts, such as programs. For example, the marketing department at Allstate might be asked to undertake a project to heighten awareness of Allstate among minority populations. This project would have a narrower scope than the overall diversity program, but it would be undertaken to support Allstate's overall efforts to create a more diverse employee base. Similarly, the food services group might take on a project to create a diversity week, featuring different cultural foods, entertainment, and artwork in the company lounge. Again, the project would be of narrower scope than the diversity program as a whole, but it would contribute to the overall diversity goals of the company.

Budgets

Single-use plans that specify how financial resources should be allocated.

Budgets   **Budgets** are the final form of single-use plans. Budgets often are undertaken as a part of other planning efforts because they specify the financial resource requirements associated with other plans, such as programs and projects. In addition, budgets serve as a mechanism for controlling the financial aspects of implementing the plan.[36]

Allstate would undoubtedly establish a budget to support the implementation of the overall diversity program and to ensure that it is carried out in an effective and efficient manner. In fact, the size of that budget might provide some insight as to the importance of the project to the organization.

Although all the types of standing and single-use plans discussed here can be used for specialized planning purposes, they are often interrelated. For example, projects are often subcomponents of more comprehensive programs or are undertaken in an effort to develop or implement policies, procedures, and rules. In fact, most organizations engage in all of these forms of planning over time.

INDIVIDUAL PLANS Increasingly, organizations are looking for ways to translate broader organizational plans to the level of individual employees. Two approaches for doing so are management by objectives (MBO) and the Balanced Scorecard.

Management by Objectives A special planning technique, **management by objectives (MBO)**, provides a method for developing personalized plans that guide the activities of individual members of the organization. The MBO approach to planning helps managers balance conflicting demands by focusing the attention of the manager and the employee on the tasks to be completed and the performance to be achieved at an individual level.[37]

Figure 4.2 outlines the primary steps in an MBO program. As the figure illustrates, MBO programs are circular and self-renewing in nature. The process begins when employees, in conjunction with their managers, establish a set of goals that serve as the foundation for the development of their work plans. Once a set of mu-

LEARNING OBJECTIVE 5

Describe individual planning systems such as management by objectives programs and the Balanced Scorecard.

Management by objectives (MBO)
A method for developing individualized plans that guide the activities of individual members of an organization.

Figure 4.2 | Management by Objectives: The Cycle

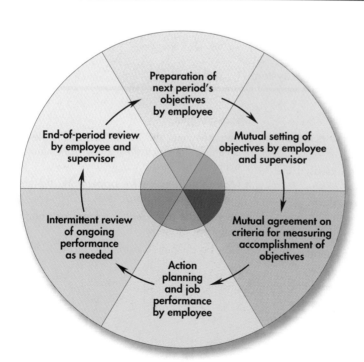

SOURCE: K. Davis and J. Newstrom. *Human Behavior at Work: Organizational Behavior* (New York: McGraw-Hill, 1989), 209. Reproduced with permission of The McGraw-Hill Companies.

tually agreeable goals has been determined, criteria for assessing work performance are identified. Next, employees formulate and implement the action plans necessary to achieve their goals and review their progress with their managers on an intermittent basis. At the end of the MBO period, the performance of the employees is compared to the goals established at the beginning of the period. Performance rewards should be based on the extent to which the goals have been achieved. Once the MBO cycle is complete, employees begin formulating goals to drive the next MBO planning period.[38]

As originally conceived, MBO programs provide three primary benefits:

1. MBO programs provide a foundation for a more integrated and system-oriented approach to planning. Establishing goals and action plans for individual employees forces managers to examine how the activities of each individual in the work group contribute to the achievement of the overall goals of the group. As an MBO system works its way up the hierarchy of the organization, it provides a mechanism for ensuring system-wide coordination of work efforts.

2. The MBO approach to planning requires communication between employees and their managers, since they must agree on the performance goals outlined in the plan. This increased communication often serves to build stronger relationships between managers and their employees.

3. MBO systems lead to more participatory work environments in which employees feel they have a voice and can have input into how their jobs should be designed and what their performance targets should be. Furthermore, employees gain a greater understanding of the organization when they are forced to plan their activities in line with the organization's overall goals.[39]

In addition to these general benefits, MBO systems offer the more specific advantages listed in Table 4.5.[40] These benefits include such things as higher overall performance levels, prioritized goals, and greater opportunities for career development for both managers and employees.[41]

At the same time, however, a number of disadvantages are associated with the use of MBO systems (see Table 4.5). These systems require a significant commit-

Table 4.5 | Advantages and Disadvantages of an MBO System

Advantages
- Results in better overall management and the achievement of higher performance levels.
- Forces managers to establish priorities and measurable targets or standards of performance.
- Encourages the participation of individual employees and managers in establishing objectives.
- Facilitates the process of control.
- Provides a golden opportunity for career development for managers and employees.
- Lets individuals know what is expected of them.
- Provides a more objective and tangible basis for performance appraisal and salary decisions.
- Improves communications within the organization.
- Helps identify promotable managers and employees.
- Facilitates the organization's ability to change.
- Increases motivation and commitment of employees.

Disadvantages
- Requires time and commitment of top-level managers, diverting their activities away from other important activities.
- May require excessive paperwork, thereby complicating administrative processes.
- May create a tendency to focus on short-term versus long-term planning.
- Can be difficult to establish and put into operation.

SOURCE: Adapted from J. Gordon, Et Al., *Management and Organizational Behavior*, published by Allyn and Bacon, Boston MA. Copyright © 1990 by Pearson Education. Adapted by permission of the publisher. 129–132.

ment on the part of management and, as a result, may divert attention away from other important activities. Many systems require excessive paperwork that complicates the administrative processes within the organization. Furthermore, some argue that MBO programs focus attention on short-run problems rather than on issues that are relevant to the long-term success of the organization. Finally, goals may be difficult to establish and put into operation in some cases. As a consequence, MBO systems may not be suitable for all job designs.[42]

The increasing diversity of the workforce has created new challenges for those involved in MBO programs. While MBO systems work well for many employees from the United States, people from other cultures may not adapt well to this type of planning. The MBO concept is predicated on an employee's desire to be reasonably independent and willingness to work toward predetermined goals—both of which are relatively common characteristics of workers in the United States. In many other cultures, however, such attitudes toward work are not common. MBO programs may be far less effective when used with individuals from such cultures.[43] Consequently, managers must be sensitive to the diversity of their work teams and may need to modify the MBO concept to suit different individuals.

In general, MBO systems are considered an effective tool. Although they can be cumbersome if implemented throughout every unit of an organization, these programs can be beneficial to the planning process when used selectively. Monsanto is an example of a firm that has embraced the MBO approach to planning. Corporate executives credit this system for the high level of commitment of Monsanto employees to the overall plans and strategy of the firm.[44]

Balanced Scorecard More recently, organizations have developed system-wide performance measurement processes that align individual goals with the strategic goals of the organization. One widely popular process, the **Balanced Scorecard** (BSC), has been used in a variety of organizations across both the private and public sectors.[45]

Balanced Scorecard
A planning system that aligns the goals of individual employees with the strategic goals of the organization.

The BSC process allows an organization to translate its strategy into operational actions at every level. Thus, employees can ensure that their individual action plans and goals are consistent with the overall strategic direction of the organization. Many organizations, including AT&T, UPS, CIGNA, and the Department of Defense have successfully developed and implemented BSCs to help measure progress toward their strategic objectives. Table 4.6 provides an overview of the BSC system.

Table 4.6 | Measuring Performance with the Balanced Scorecard (BSC)

KEY PRINCIPLES	MEASUREMENT CRITERIA	IMPLICATIONS FOR LEADERS
Align organization to the strategy	Customers	Understand the "big picture"
Translate the strategy to operational terms	Internal processes	BSC measures performance at all levels
View strategy as a continual process	Innovation	Execute strategy into action
Make strategy everyone's job	Growth	Empower frontline employees

SOURCE: J. Steele, "Transforming the Balanced Scorecard into Your Strategy Execution System," *Manage*, 53, September/October 2001, 22–23.

CONTINGENCY PLANNING FOR CHANGING ENVIRONMENTS

Contingency planning is a popular approach in today's rapidly changing business environment. Virtually all organizations face strategic and operating conditions that are subject to change and could, therefore, benefit from a contingency approach to planning. This approach is especially useful when an organization's effectiveness is highly dependent on a set of business conditions that are particularly volatile.

Contingency planning requires the development of two or more plans, each of which is based on a different set of strategic or operating conditions that could occur. Which plan is implemented is determined by the specific circumstances that come to pass.[46] For example, while an organization may plan to begin production at a new plant facility in June 2002, managers should develop a contingency plan that ensures uninterrupted production in the event that the plant opening is delayed for some reason. As another example, consider the airline industry. Herb Kelleher, CEO of Southwest Airlines, says that it is virtually impossible to employ traditional long-range planning in the airline industry. Things change too much and too quickly—schedules, routes, competitors, and fares change continually.[47] Therefore, contingency planning is particularly important in that industry. Nevertheless, it is important to note that effective contingency planning requires that potential changes in strategic and operating conditions are somewhat predictable. Do you think that Southwest had a contingency plan to deal with the chaos that hit the airline industry in the wake of 9/11? Should they have had such a plan?

Many organizations worldwide engaged in contingency planning to cope with the much-publicized Y2K issue.[48] These organizations formulated contingency plans that would be implemented in the event that unanticipated Y2K problems emerged. From utilities to manufacturers, universities, financial services institutions, and government agencies, organizations across the globe developed contingency plans to ensure a smooth transition to the new millennium. The government of Hong Kong, for example, spent $58 million to develop four levels of "mission critical" contingency plans to avert a Y2K meltdown.[49] Mexico, too, was proactive with regard to Y2K readiness, presenting the results of elaborate testing and contingency plans to international panels.[50] President Clinton appointed a U.S. Y2K czar, John Koskinen, who was charged with ensuring the readiness of the United States for Y2K. But now that the clock has rolled over and the bulk of the impact of Y2K has been realized, some fear that one of the most important lessons of Y2K was missed by many organizations. According to Koskinen, that lesson relates to the high dependence most organizations have on sophisticated information technology to operate their systems and thus the need to continue to have contingency plans in place.

Today, there is a great deal of contingency planning related to possible terrorism in the United States. From universities, to hospitals, to corporations, managers are developing contingency plans to cope with disasters that could result from acts of terrorism. Advanced information technology is particularly useful in these kinds of contingency plans. For example, ESRI, a leading supplier of Global Information Systems (GIS) software, has developed "what-if" scenarios in its software regarding a wide variety of terrorist activities. This software can help organizations pinpoint the nature of the problem and quickly assess alternative responses in the event of a terrorist attack.[51]

Royal Dutch/Shell, an early pioneer in the area of contingency planning, has developed a sophisticated system of scenario planning to support the creation of its contingency plans.[52] The company creates a set of scenarios that reflect potential changes in the world that would affect its operations. Contingency plans can be developed based on the conditions in each scenario. If you would like to read

Leaders In Action

GM's First Ever CIO Is Betting on Technology as a Strategic Advantage

GM, the world's largest automaker, recently announced that Ralph Szygenda would become the company's first-ever chief information officer (CIO). Szygenda was charged with what some analysts saw as an almost impossible task: transform GM into a digital enterprise. As recently as the late 1990s, GM was described as "The company that information technology (IT) forgot!"

Szygenda views this challenge as an opportunity to transform GM while broadening the company's long-term strategy. He emphasizes the emerging role of IT to create better value for GM's customers and increased profits for the company. Szygenda's success in this endeavor will depend not only on advances in technology but also on his ability to meld IT with GM's current business design and, most importantly, to convince GM's top decision makers that IT will be crucial in shaping the company's strategic direction.

By the mid-1990s, IT systems had become prolific at GM, but they were almost always isolated from other IT endeavors. Not having a fully integrated IT strategy led to significant barriers in sharing information and aligning strategic initiatives. Even worse, top management did not fully appreciate the application and implication potential of IT. Szygenda started the IT revolution at GM with a very simple approach—one executive at a time. He spent a lot of time working to educate senior leadership about the strategic role of IT for the company. This effort led to the realization that IT's function at GM had to be more strategically relevant.

After his appointment as GM's CIO, Szygenda began a series of changes to improve efficiency and reduce some of the clutter, all the while raising the profile of IT's strategic role. GM's worldwide telecommunications structure was completely overhauled to improve bandwidth for Internet access. Computer systems have been standardized. For example, GM now has only one computer-aided automobile design system, instead of the more than 20 systems that were in place when Szygenda arrived. These highly visible improvements at GM now have top management supporting the strategic view of IT.

Szygenda has moved on to more complex tasks as he continues to make the case for the role of IT in GM's long-term strategic planning. Due in part to recent advances in IT, over 40 call centers have been consolidated into three and 19 information warehouses into three. GM recently launched GMBuyPower.com in the United States and over 40 other countries. This Internet site allows customers to configure vehicles with different options, search dealer inventories, and investigate financing opportunities.

All of these changes have put IT at the forefront in GM's strategic initiatives. Szygenda believes that IT has helped transform GM from being big, slow, and clumsy to being big, fast, and nimble.

SOURCE: J. Teresko, "Transforming GM," *Industry Week*, 250, 15, January 2002, 34–42.

more about Royal Dutch/Shell's scenarios, visit their Web site at http://www.shell.com/scenarios.

THE IMPACT OF INFORMATION TECHNOLOGY ON PLANNING

While global information systems software is clearly important information technology for disaster planning, there are multiple other ways that information technology can be used to facilitate the planning process. From the establishment of corporate- and business-level goals and strategies to the development of functional strategies and operational plans, information technology can be used to improve the effectiveness and efficiency of the planning process. Since strategic planning is the focus of the next chapter, let's focus our attention here on how information technology can be used to support operational planning.

As we have learned, operational plans include standing plans such as policies, procedures, and rules. Advances in information technology in recent years have supported the more efficient development of such plans, as well as more effective implementation. Consider, for example, how a university might use information systems to communicate policies, streamline procedures, and monitor compliance with rules. Policies related to such things as admission to certain programs, grade

LEARNING OBJECTIVE 7

Discuss how advances in information technology have affected operational planning.

appeals, permissible course waivers, and substitutions can be communicated to students via the Internet or a campus local area network. This enables students to have online, real-time access to important information rather than having to wait for the next year's catalog to be distributed. Class registration procedures have also been improved through the use of information technology. At many universities, students can register via the Internet without ever coming to campus. This is a dramatic improvement over the long registration lines of days gone by. Monitoring compliance with rules such as minimum grade point average, prerequisite completion, and course substitution is also more efficient with the use of information technology. Database systems that maintain individual student records allow university administrators to readily identify students who are in violation of university rules.

The development and implementation of single-use plans can also be improved through the use of information technology. For example, project management software systems allow managers to track their progress on completing specific projects, and spreadsheet software allows the monitoring of the budgets for a wide variety of programs and projects.

FACILITATING THE PLANNING PROCESS

Presuming that one accepts the proposition that planning is a critical organizational activity, it is important to examine ways to facilitate the planning process. While most managers would admit that they need to plan, many would also admit that they do much less planning than they should. This situation is a result of a number of barriers to planning.

BARRIERS TO EFFECTIVE PLANNING

LEARNING OBJECTIVE 8

Describe the common barriers to effective planning and explain ways to reduce these barriers.

Why do some managers fail to plan effectively? They do so for a number of reasons, all of which may be overcome by developing an organizational culture that encourages and supports the planning process. However, this requires a clear understanding of the main reasons why managers fail to plan effectively.

DEMANDS ON THE MANAGER'S TIME   Some managers may simply be too busy "putting out fires" to take the time to plan properly. Managers often feel as though they face a continuous stream of problems from the time they arrive at work until they leave. Although this constant troubleshooting may seem to leave few opportunities for planning, the hectic nature of the manager's day in itself suggests that planning is very much needed. Through better planning, such as policies, rules, and the like, managers can develop operational systems that are more effective and less problematic and demanding of their time.

AMBIGUOUS AND UNCERTAIN OPERATING ENVIRONMENTS   Environmental complexity and volatility are other commonly cited reasons for not planning. Managers who are uncomfortable with ambiguity may find it difficult and frustrating to plan under conditions of uncertainty. Yet, while it may be difficult to develop plans under such circumstances, effective managers make an effort to do so. Organizations that operate in rapidly changing and complex environments often find that planning provides a mechanism for coping with such conditions.

RESISTANCE TO CHANGE   Finally, managers may hesitate to plan because they are resistant to change. Organizational members may associate planning with a need to change the way they do their jobs. Their hesitancy to change may discourage them from initiating the planning process.[53] Given the current focus on quality and continuous improvement, resistance to change can have very detrimental results for the organization in the long term.

OVERCOMING THE BARRIERS TO PLANNING

As discussed previously, achieving success through planning requires the participation of a broad range of organizational members. Consequently, organizations must develop and maintain a culture that encourages planning and rewards those who plan effectively. To do so, managers must involve employees in decision-making processes, tolerate a diversity of views, and encourage strategic thinking.

INVOLVE EMPLOYEES IN DECISION MAKING   Employee involvement in the planning process is essential for its success.[54] Regardless of whether a top-down or bottom-up approach is used, input from all levels of the organization is essential to the success of the organization's planning system. Managers should solicit the opinions and views of their employees when formulating plans, and they should maintain an open-door policy that encourages individual members of the organization to communicate about the planning efforts of the unit and the firm. Discouraging employees from sharing information that might be important to the planning process (see Figure 4.3) will result in less effective organizational plans.[55]

TOLERATE A DIVERSITY OF VIEWS   Managers who are intolerant of a diversity of views within their unit eliminate one of the primary benefits associated with a participatory planning system. Diverse views and perspectives lead to a broader assessment and evaluation of organizational problems and opportunities. In fact, this is one of the primary benefits of maintaining a diverse workforce.[56] Organizations that encourage a wide range of different ideas and views are more likely to produce plans that are comprehensive and fully developed.

ENCOURAGE STRATEGIC THINKING   Developing an organizational culture that encourages strategic and results-oriented thinking will lead to more effective planning. Thinking is a skill and, as is the case with most skills, it can be developed through training and practice.[57] Employees should be provided with the training necessary to develop strategic thinking skills and given the opportunity to practice those skills in their work environment. Furthermore, individuals should be rewarded for thinking strategically when developing their plans.[58]

Figure 4.3

Frank & Ernest reprinted by permission of Newspaper Enterprise Assocation, Inc.

LEARNING OBJECTIVE 9

Discuss how tomorrow's leaders can achieve success through planning.

IMPLICATIONS FOR LEADERS

Tomorrow's manager will face many challenges in developing effective strategic and operational plans. Planning has become increasingly difficult as the pace of change in the business environment has accelerated. While change makes the planning process more difficult, it also makes planning more critical. Managers of the future must be forward thinking and focused on achieving the goals of their work groups and their organizations through effective planning. Leaders of the future must be able to demonstrate effective planning skills, which are among the key competencies that ensure a leader's success. An effective leader will approach the planning process in a way that demonstrates strong character, as well as a concern for both the organizational community and relevant external communities.

The ultimate objective of the planning process is the development of good plans. Plans are good if they can be implemented successfully and result in the accomplishment of the goals for which they were designed. Managers are more likely to develop good plans when they:

- Recognize and communicate the importance of planning in achieving organizational success.
- Understand the difference between and the relationships among strategic and operational planning initiatives.
- Involve those responsible for implementing the plan in the planning process.
- Look to contingency planning as a means of maintaining flexibility in rapidly changing business environments.
- Utilize technology to enhance the effectiveness and efficiency of the planning process.
- Remove the barriers to planning at the work group and individual levels.
- Reward those who think strategically and follow through with operational planning.

In this chapter, we have examined the managerial function of planning. Our focus, at both the strategic and operational levels, has been on achieving organiza-

Meeting The Challenge

Home Depot's "Mr. Fix-It" Focuses on the Future

When Bob Nardelli took over as CEO and president of Home Depot in 2000, the company was facing serious problems. Current strategic initiatives called for very aggressive store openings in both large and small markets. Nardelli shifted the strategic focus from square footage to revenue. Rather than focus simply on the number of new stores opened, Nardelli's new strategy for Home Depot was to focus on increasing the top-line revenue in the largest U.S. metro areas.

Nardelli also addressed the organizational structure of Home Depot. The entrepreneurial culture of Home Depot was very effective when the company was smaller. A decentral-ized structure allowed store managers greater autonomy in choosing supplies, products, and specialty items. As Home Depot continued to grow, this structure became less and less efficient. Nardelli felt that efficiency could be greatly improved by buying larger quantities of items and shipping them to a centralized location. The centralized distributor would then take responsibility for ordering supplies and products.

Additionally, Nardelli focused on the layers of management that had developed over the years. Seeing inefficiencies and redundancies in management, he streamlined Home Depot's structure and top leadership so that divisional vice presidents would report directly to him.

Only time will tell what the future holds for Home Depot and its new strategic initiatives. The company has announced that it expects to continue to grow double-digit revenues through 2004 and has projected to double its size to $100 billion in revenue by 2005. Nardelli will have to balance the need for efficiency with the entrepreneurial spirit and superior customer satisfaction that made Home Depot's orange aprons synonymous with home improvement.

SOURCE: J. Pellet, "Mr. Fix-it Steps In," *Chief Executive*, 171, October 2001, 44–48.

tional success through planning. The process of strategic planning is examined in much greater detail in the next chapter, where we discuss strategy as a tool for achieving competitive success in the 21st century.

SUMMARY

1. Planning is an important managerial function through which managers outline the activities necessary to achieve the goals of the organization. The purpose of planning is to ensure organizational effectiveness and efficiency in both the short term and the long term.

2. Traditionally, organizations used either a top-down or a bottom-up approach to planning. Most organizations today plan from an integrative perspective, using a top-down approach in some areas of the organization and a bottom-up approach in others.

3. Strategic planning is the process by which an organization makes decisions and takes actions that affect its long-run performance. Strategy is the output of the strategic planning process. Corporate, business, and functional strategies vary with respect to focus, specificity, time horizon, and the participants in the planning process.

4. Operational planning determines the day-to-day activities that are necessary to achieve the long-term goals of the organization. Standing plans, which include policies, procedures, and rules, are developed to address issues that recur frequently in the organization. Single-use plans address a specific issue or problem that the organization experiences only once. Single-use plans include programs, projects, and budgets.

5. Individual planning systems guide the behaviors and actions of individual organizational members. Management by objectives (MBO) and the Balanced Scorecard focus the attention of the manager and the employee on the tasks to be completed and the performance to be achieved at an individual level. While individual planning systems can be time-consuming and complex, employing this approach to plan the work activities of employees is often highly beneficial.

6. Contingency planning involves the development of a set of plans that are designed for the varied strategic or operating conditions the firm might face. Contingency planning is most appropriate for organizations operating in environments that are subject to frequent or significant change.

7. Advances in information technology have improved both the effectiveness and efficiency of the planning function. Information technology can be used to establish and implement the strategic and operational plans of an organization.

8. The three common barriers to planning are demands on the manager's time, ambiguous and uncertain environmental conditions, and resistance to change. Overcoming the barriers to planning requires the development of an organizational culture that supports and encourages planning.

9. The highly competitive, rapidly changing nature of the business environment will create many planning challenges for tomorrow's managers. Managers of the future must not only develop their own planning skills but must also create a work environment in which effective planning is encouraged and rewarded.

REVIEW QUESTIONS

1. *(Learning Objective 1)* Describe the managerial function of planning, explaining what it is and why managers should plan.

2. *(Learning Objective 2)* At what levels of the organization can planning start? What are the advantages and disadvantages associated with the various approaches to planning?

3. *(Learning Objective 3)* Define strategic planning. What are the three levels at which strategy is formulated, and how do they differ in terms of (a) focus, (b) participants, (c) specificity, and (d) time horizon?

4. *(Learning Objective 4)* What is operational planning, and how does it differ from strategic planning? Describe standing and single-use plans, and identify the various types of plans that fall into these two categories.

5. *(Learning Objective 5)* Describe the two types of individualized planning systems outlined in the chapters. What are some advantages and disadvantages of these types of planning?

6. *(Learning Objective 6)* What is contingency planning? Under what circumstances would it be most appropriate to use a contingency approach to planning?

7. *(Learning Objective 7)* How have advances in information technology affected operational planning?

8. *(Learning Objective 8)* What are the common barriers to planning? What might a manager do to reduce the barriers to planning?

9. *(Learning Objective 9)* How can tomorrow's manager achieve excellence through planning?

DISCUSSION QUESTIONS

Improving Critical Thinking

1. Evaluate the benefits of MBO as an employer and as an employee. Would you want to participate in an MBO program? Why or why not?

2. Planning can begin at the top of the organization and flow downward or start at the bottom of the organization and move upward. As an employee of an organization, would you prefer a top-down or bottom-up approach to planning? What would you consider to be the advantages and disadvantages of each from an employee's perspective? From an employer's perspective?

Enhancing Communication Skills

3. Consider an organization with which you have been fairly closely affiliated as an employee or a member, such as a business, church, sorority, and the like. Describe the planning system of this organization. Was it effective? If not, why? What might the managers of the organization have done to ensure better planning? To improve your oral communication skills, present your analysis of this situation to the class.

4. How might the planning process for a new business venture differ from the process in an established business? How would it differ for small versus large businesses? To practice your written communication skills, prepare a one-page written summary of your response.

Building Teamwork

5. We know that planning occurs at the strategic and operational levels. Is it more important to plan at one level than at the other? Why or why not? Discuss this question in teams of four to five students and develop a position that you can present to the class.

6. Evaluate some of the standing plans at your university or college that directly affect you as a student. Are the policies, procedures, or rules that you identified meant to benefit or hinder the students? Why do you think the administration at your school feels that it is necessary to have well-defined standing plans? What would happen if none of the plans that you identified existed? Form teams of four to five students, answer the preceding questions, and present your responses to the class.

THINKING CRITICALLY: DEBATE THE ISSUE

Strategic Planning or Corporate Rain Dancing: Can We Plan for the Unknown?

Developing an effective strategy involves carefully assessing both internal organizational processes and external changes in the environment. A careful assessment of the environment allows leaders to predict where future business opportunities will exist. Some have argued that in light of the dramatic changes in global markets, advances in technology, and the political unrest in much of the world, prediction is not possible. Therefore, strategic planning should be approached as more of an art than a science.

Form teams of four to five students as directed by your instructor. Half of the teams should prepare to argue that strategic planning is more of a science and should be approached methodically, while the other teams should prepare to argue that strategic planning is more of an art form and should be approached less formally. It would be helpful for teams to draw from personal experiences or current events to illustrate their positions. Your instructor will choose two teams to present their findings to the class in a debate format.

EXPERIENTIAL EXERCISE 4.1

Evaluating Standing Plans

Choose an organization with which you are familiar. This can be a company for whom you work or have worked, a social organization with which you are associated, such as a church, sorority, or fraternity, or even your university. Identify three policies, procedures, and rules that exist within that organization. Evaluate the purpose and effect of each.

    Would you change the plan in some way? If so, indicate your proposed change and explain the effect that you feel it would have on the functioning of the organization. A format similar to the following can be used to summarize your assessment.

Policy	Purpose	Effect	Proposed Change	Effect
1.				
2.				
3.				
Procedure	Purpose	Effect	Proposed Change	Effect
1.				
2.				
3.				
Rule	Purpose	Effect	Proposed Change	Effect
1.				
2.				
3.				

CAPTURING THE POWER OF INFORMATION TECHNOLOGY

1. To learn more about how technology is being utilized to improve the efficiency and effectiveness of the U.S. government, visit **http://www.govexec.com**. From what you can learn from this site, do you think the government is leading the way in utilizing technology effectively, or do you think the government is learning from business and industry practices? How do you think information technology will impact the planning process within government agencies in the future?

2. Healthcare informatics is a critical area of study that focuses on how information technology can be used in the field of healthcare. Visit **http://www.RX2000.org** to learn more

about information technology and its use in healthcare. How do you think advancements in technology will affect the plans of healthcare organizations in the future?

3. Carnegie Mellon University maintains a federally funded research and development center that studies Internet security vulnerabilities. This center, the Computer Emergency Response Team (CERT) provides valuable information regarding the security of information systems. Visit the site at **http://www.cert.org**. How can managers use this site or similar sites to plan for the security of their information systems?

ETHICS: TAKE A STAND

The board of directors of EZSystems has just met to approve the company's new strategic plan. Based on what they learned in the presentation of the strategic plan, the board is extremely enthusiastic about the future of the company. More important, they know that when news of the company's new strategy hits Wall Street, the company's stock will undoubtedly begin to rise.

Central to EZSystems' new strategic plan is the development of an innovative, Internet-based inventory management software application called EZ-IM. EZ-IM promises to revolutionize the way companies acquire, store, and distribute their inventories. Initially the product will be targeted to retailers, but eventually it can be adapted and customized to fit any industry for which inventory management is relevant. EZSystems has developed an aggressive marketing, public relations, and sales campaign to launch EZ-IM and will be issuing a press release announcing its introduction within the next month. EZ-IM promises to take the company to new levels of sales and profitability over the next year.

Patricia Wilson, the technology manager of EZ-IM, has just learned that the product is at the core of the company's new strategic plan. Patricia is literally dumbstruck when she hears that the plan calls for the launch of the product within one month. She immediately contacts her boss, John Fulbright, the chief technology officer of EZSystems. "Mr. Fulbright," Patricia starts, "I have just learned of the company's plans to launch EZ-IM within a month's time. I believe you know that this is impossible.

The product is still in the early stages of development and will not be ready for distribution for at least six months. Furthermore, as you are aware, we have encountered some very challenging technical problems that may make it impossible to develop the product as originally conceived. In my opinion, it is premature to even discuss this product with the board of directors, much less issue a press release announcing its introduction."

"Calm down, Patricia," John says, patting her arm lightly. "This is the way things are done at the top. It's important to keep the board happy, and the best way to do that is to make sure they believe that the company is making progress in developing new products. You just keep working along . . . let me worry about what the board and the public at large believe about EZ-IM. Trust me—all of our jobs depend on it."

For Discussion

1. Did Patricia do the right thing in contacting her boss about the announcement of EZ-IM?

2. What do you think about John Fulbright's response to Patricia? Were there any "hidden" messages in his reaction to her query?

3. What are Patricia's alternative courses of action at this point, and what are the implications of each? If you were Patricia, what would you do?

VIDEO CASE

Planning in the Contemporary Organization: The Vermont Teddy Bear Company, Inc.

The first Vermont Teddy Bears were made in 1981 by the wife of founder and former CEO John Sortino and sold mostly to friends. Two years later, Sortino sold his teddy bears from a pushcart at a downtown pedestrian mall in Burlington, Vermont. It took four days to sell his first bear and a year to sell 200 bears. Today, the Vermont Teddy Bear Company is the leading manufacturer of hand-crafted, U.S.-made teddy bears. Each year more than 150,000 people visit the Vermont Teddy Bear Company to see how teddy bears are made, make their own teddy bears, or purchase a premade and dressed bear. Annually, the company sells more than 450,000 bears for its Bear-Gram gift delivery service and employs over 274 full-time employees. Bear-Gram gifts are a creative alternative to sending flowers.

Vermont Teddy Bear has been named "Best Small Company in U.S.A." by Dun & Bradstreet and listed as one of *Inc.* magazine's "100 Fastest Growing Privately Owned U.S. Companies." It has a Five-Star Merchant with a 98 percent "Top Service" rating from Yahoo! customers and is named as one of the "best of the best" online stores by BizRate.com. The company has been growing at an annual rate of around 50 percent with about $39 million in revenues. Corporate sales comprises the company's fastest growing segment.

The company's increasing skill in demand forecasting has played a role in its recent success. Forecasting consumer demand for over 140 different teddy bears is complicated. Nevertheless, forecasting is the first important step in the production planning process, influencing how much raw materials to order, how to schedule production, and whether to outsource the work and how much of it.

Product demand is influenced by factors internal and external to the firm. Internal factors include their decision-making processes, variety of products, services provided, and how much to spend on advertising to see profitable returns. External factors include popular cultural trends, region, holiday seasons, and special occasions. Snowboarding was identified through regular brainstorming meetings as a popular trend, so it added the Snowboarding Bear to the line. Seasonal trends are related to gift-giving holidays such as Valentine's Day. The company recently introduced *The Elvis Bear* in honor of the 100th birthday of the teddy bear. Licensed by Elvis Presley Enterprises, Inc., this teddy bear is dressed in a white polyester jumpsuit with tassels and a pair of silver metallic sunglasses.

After determining forecast objectives, Vermont Teddy Bear uses a multistep forecasting process. It focuses on forecasting revenues by analyzing many different markets, numbers, and sales methods. This provides a quarterly forecast for each product of its dynamic product mix that changes weekly. Generally, Vermont Teddy Bear forecasts six months out, allowing time for purchasing, substitutions, receipt of raw materials, production, and distribution of the bears. The company uses detailed information from the same quarter of each of three years to identify trends.

It also takes qualitative factors into account such as which bear is featured on its catalog cover, where each bear is located in the catalog, whether a bear may appeal to collectors, and changes in pricing. Finally, the company monitors and compares actual performance to forecasted performance for each product, sales method, and other relevant factors. Forecast information is used by all its departments.

Demand forecasting at Vermont Teddy Bear Company is an evolving process that changes as the company continues to grow. Now that it has transitioned from entrepreneurial to be more managerial, Vermont Teddy Bear plans to expand forecasting to track different operational costs associated with the Bear-gram vs. retail vs. wholesale lines of business.

The Vermont Teddy Bear Company uses a comprehensive demand forecasting process to aid in decision making. Forecasting will continue to be an important factor in the company's success. According to Vermont Teddy Bear's CEO, Elisabeth Robert, "We've grown . . . and maintained our profitability as we've invested in two new gift delivery services offering our customers gift products in addition to teddy bears. Looking ahead to continued growth in the core Bear-Gram® business as well as new opportunities with our PajamaGram℠ and TastyGram℠ gift services, we are excited about our evolution as a gift company and our prospects for the future."

For Discussion

1. How has the Vermont Teddy Bear Company benefited from demand forecasting? What are the costs?

2. What levels of strategic planning are involved in forecasting product demand for Vermont Teddy Bears? Explain.

3. Do you think the Vermont Teddy Bear Company needs to prepare contingency plans? Explain.

4. What barriers to effective planning might Vermont Teddy Bear experience? Explain how the company overcomes or lessens these barriers.

www.vermontteddybear.com

CASE

TIX4U.com

Growing up in the Southeast, Randy Lee had two passions—music and sports. Some of his best memories were traveling with his dad to a large city in a neighboring state to watch major league baseball and football games. Inevitably, Randy and his dad would arrive at the stadium in plenty of time to negotiate with others to trade tickets for better seats. They would always have a couple of extra tickets to sell in case they needed more money to pay for their upgraded seats.

When Randy attended college in the same city, he found himself again negotiating ticket sales and trades for music concerts. He became so well-known that many students, and even some professors, approached him for tickets to sold-out shows and sporting events. Randy majored in computer science, and after graduation, he moved back home to work in a small IT department with a manufacturing company.

Although working full time, Randy never lost his passion for sporting events and concerts. After a couple of months, Randy developed a Web site, TIX4U.com, for customers who wanted to trade concert tickets over the Internet. His business strategy was fairly simple. He developed a message board for users who were interested in buying, selling, or trading tickets to contact each other. For this service, he would charge a yearly membership fee.

What started out as a part-time endeavor quickly grew. Randy resigned from his IT position after only six months to devote his energy to running the business full time. Customers from several surrounding states had bought memberships, and he eventually began hiring employees to help with the growing workload.

Seven years after he started TIX4U.com, his hometown had turned into a city. Corporate sponsors lobbied for, and were awarded, expansion franchises in two major league sports. This was on top of two minor league teams that were already there. The minor league teams generated a lot of excitement and fan support, and he had already expanded his company's services to provide a bulletin board for these sports fans. Now, with the major league teams on their way, Randy was both excited and overwhelmed.

TIX4.com's staff had grown from one to 17 full-time employees over the last seven years. Randy estimated that his company's size would need to double, if not triple, to handle the increased demand for tickets with year-round sports games and concerts. While exciting, these changes created a unique set of challenges for Randy. He realized that he needed a comprehensive plan that would provide strategic guidance for him and his growing number of employees. The company had started out small, but dramatic changes in the environment meant that he would need to make significant investments in computer hardware and personnel to meet this growing demand. These challenges and opportunities now surpassed Randy's ability to effectively manage them alone. If he was going to remain successful and capitalize on the growing market, he would need a business strategy to provide operational plans for both the short and long term. Randy was overwhelmed and not sure where to begin. How could he develop a strategic plan that would give TIX4U.com a competitive advantage and better ensure its future viability?

For Discussion

1. How has the changing business environment created problems for TIX4U.com? What opportunities have been created?

2. Based on this scenario, what specific planning challenges do you see for TIX4U.com? What impact should the fact that his business will soon double have on his operational planning?

3. How would you advise Randy to begin developing a comprehensive system for planning?

CHAP

STRATEGIC PLANNING IN A GLOBAL ENVIRONMENT

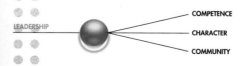

LEADERSHIP — COMPETENCE
— CHARACTER
— COMMUNITY

TER⁵

CHAPTER OVERVIEW

The development of effective strategy is essential for survival in today's business world. Organizations don't just happen to be successful; rather, they develop and implement strategies that are designed to ensure their long-term success. Through strategic planning, managers initiate the actions necessary to get the organization from where it is to where it wants to be. Developing a competitive advantage that leads to organizational success is the primary purpose of the strategic planning process.

This chapter examines strategic planning as a managerial process. This process involves four primary activities: (1) strategic analysis, (2) strategy formulation, (3) strategy implementation, and (4) strategic control. Special emphasis is given to strategic planning and strategy as a tool for competitive success.

LEARNING OBJECTIVES

When you have finished studying this chapter, you should be able to:

1. Define strategic planning and describe its purpose and benefits.
2. Explain the four stages of the strategic planning process.
3. Discuss how a strategic analysis is conducted, as well as the value of the analysis to the strategic planning process.
4. Explain the purpose of strategy formulation and describe the two types of strategic alternatives.
5. Explain the role of strategy implementation in the strategic planning process and ways to enhance the likelihood of implementation success.
6. Describe strategic control systems.
7. Explain how advances in information technology have affected strategic planning.
8. Discuss how tomorrow's leaders can achieve success through strategic planning.

Facing The Challenge

FedEx and USPS: A Strategic Alliance for the Future

Fred Smith, founder and CEO of FedEx and the creator of overnight delivery, helped revolutionize the business world. FedEx's now famous slogan, "When it absolutely, positively has to be there overnight," represents the speed of business for many companies across the globe. As a result of the reliable and efficient service FedEx provides, the company has enjoyed remarkable success in a market niche Smith created—overnight delivery.

What started out as an idea for a college paper in the early 1970s turned into a major global corporation with yearly sales exceeding $20 billion. Based in Memphis, Tennessee, FedEx employs over 215,000 couriers, pilots, customer service representatives, and sorters. The company currently delivers packages overnight to 210 countries with over 650 planes. FedEx is one of the largest airlines in the world. The company has built its reputation on efficient operations, exceptional customer relations, and reliable service.

Looking into the future, Smith realized that FedEx would need to develop a relationship with a major mail carrier if it was to continue to grow and prosper while maintaining its standard of excellence for on-time delivery. Although FedEx enjoys a major share of package shipping by air, it does not dominate package delivery via ground transportation. Shipping parcels by truck is the fastest growing segment of the industry, and that was precisely where Smith wanted to focus FedEx's plans for strategic growth.

The United States Postal Service (USPS) was the natural candidate for forming a strategic alliance. The USPS is omnipresent in the United States, with carriers, mailboxes, and retail offices located in virtually every town across the country. Yet, developing a relationship with USPS would not be easy. For years, Smith had been an outspoken critic of the USPS. He had often made references to an oversized, overpriced bureaucracy that lacked attention to detail and an orientation toward customer service.

The USPS was also struggling at the dawn of the 21st century. After years of operating in the black, Postmaster General William Henderson was looking at the prospect of major losses. Alternative communications, such as e-mail and electronic banking, coupled with rising fuel costs, led to a daunting $350 million loss for the pseudo-federal agency at the end of 2000. As both Smith and Henderson looked toward the future, they realized that they might just need each other.

SOURCES: T. Roche, "Who's Got Mail?" *Time*, October 16, 2000, 86–88; and M. Tatge, "Going Postal," *Forbes*, February 5, 2001, 56.

INTRODUCTION

Fred Smith had a vision for Federal Express (FedEx), as did Postmaster General William Henderson for the United States Postal Service (USPS). Once fierce competitors, a merger between these two large and very different organizations would provide them both with strategic positioning. Making the strategic alliance work, however, would require a comprehensive strategic plan for both organizations.

Organizational strategy has been a topic of great interest for academics and practitioners for the last several decades.[1] In fact, few managerial topics have received more attention in recent years than strategic planning. Effective strategic planning was once touted as a key solution to the reactive behavior that characterized many U.S. corporations during the 1970s and 1980s. As we look ahead, strategic planning will be critical for organizations to compete successfully in the rapidly evolving business economy of tomorrow. CEOs and managers who confront this new business environment—one that is enabled by information technology and characterized by increasingly open global markets—will realize the increasing importance of strategic planning.[2]

Many experts predict that successful organizations in the future will be those that challenge the status quo, bringing an entrepreneurial focus to the strategic planning process.[3] One need only look at the creators of today's new wealth to understand this phenomenon. For example, Cisco Systems, Amazon.com, Starbucks, Charles Schwab, Dell, Southwest Airlines, and SAP didn't even exist a generation ago. But these companies challenged the incumbent leaders in their industries with innovative new strategies and eventually became the industry leaders.[4] Will they maintain that leadership position? Maybe, maybe not. But one thing is certain—

achieving a competitive advantage and remaining an industry leader in the business environment of the 21st century will continue to require innovative and proactive strategies.[5] Again, consider the potential alliance between FedEx and the USPS—this would undoubtedly be an innovative strategy of collaboration that might result in industry leadership if it works.

THE IMPORTANCE OF STRATEGIC PLANNING

As you may recall from Chapter 4, **strategic planning** is the process by which an organization makes decisions and takes actions that affect its long-run performance. A **strategic plan** is the output of the strategic planning process.[6] An organization's strategic plan provides direction by defining its strategic approach to business.[7]

Central to the concept of strategic planning is the notion of competitive advantage. As we noted in Chapter 4, the fundamental purpose of strategic planning is to move the organization from where it is to where it wants to be and, in the process, to develop a competitive advantage in its industry. A competitive advantage can only be sustained, however, if the organization continues to out-innovate their competitors.[8] Products and services are only temporary solutions to customers' problems; eventually someone always comes up with a better solution. Organizations that continuously focus on finding the better solution will be the ones that maintain their competitive advantage. Doing so requires effective strategic planning throughout the ranks of the organization.

THE BENEFITS OF STRATEGIC PLANNING

Strategic planning requires a great deal of managerial time, energy, and commitment. To justify the associated costs, strategic planning must also produce tangible benefits.[9] Research suggests that the benefits of strategic planning are both economic and behavioral.[10]

From an economic perspective, a number of studies suggest that organizations that plan strategically outperform those that do not. Researchers have examined organizations in such industries as petroleum, food, drugs, steel, chemicals, and machinery, focusing on a variety of financial measures including return on investment, return on equity, and earnings per share. Their findings suggest that there are financial benefits associated with strategic planning.

The process of strategic planning can also produce behavioral benefits. Since effective planning requires the involvement of a broad base of organizational members, the benefits associated with participatory management are typically associated with strategic planning. These include:

- An increased likelihood of identifying organizational and environmental conditions that may create problems in the long term.
- Better decisions as a result of the group decision-making process.
- More successful implementation of the organization's strategy because organizational members who participated in the planning process understand the plan and are more willing to change.[11]

Given the potential benefits of strategic planning and the potential costs of the failure to plan, most organizations recognize that strategic planning is essential. In fact, many organizations stress that being a strategist is an important part of being a leader.[12]

Strategic planning
The process by which an organization makes decisions and takes actions to enhance its long-term performance.

Strategic plan
A plan that identifies the markets in which an organization competes, as well as the ways in which it competes in those markets.

LEARNING OBJECTIVE 1

Define strategic planning and describe its purpose and benefits.

STRATEGIC PLANNING AS A PROCESS

LEARNING OBJECTIVE 2

Explain the four stages of the strategic planning process.

Strategic planning can be thought of as a process.[13] Figure 5.1 illustrates a process-driven strategic planning model that is simple, straightforward, and applicable to a wide variety of organizational situations. While the level of sophistication and formality of the strategic planning process will differ among organizations, the process itself should be similar across all organizations.[14]

As Figure 5.1 indicates, the strategic planning process is carried out in four stages, each of which raises an important question that must be addressed when developing a strategic plan.[15] Furthermore, the feedback lines in the model suggest that the strategic planning process is interactive and self-renewing, continually evolving as changes in the business environment create a need for revised strategic plans.[16]

Strategic analysis

An assessment of the internal and external conditions of the firm.

The **strategic analysis** phase of the strategic planning process addresses the question, "What is the current position of the organization?" Accordingly, the mission and internal and external environmental conditions faced by the organization are evaluated during this phase of the process. The information gathered during the strategic analysis serves as a foundation for the formulation of the organization's strategic plan.

Strategy formulation

The establishment of an organizational vision, goals, and corporate- and business-level strategies.

Strategy formulation answers the question, "Where does the organization want to be?" The intent of strategy formulation is to establish a vision, goals, and overall strategic direction for the organization. Strategies are developed with the intention of bridging the gap between the current and desired position of the organization.

Strategy implementation

The actions required to ensure that the corporate- and business-level strategy of the organization is put into place.

Strategy implementation answers the question, "How can the organization get to where it wants to be?" This phase of the process involves doing whatever is necessary to ensure that the strategy of the organization is executed effectively. Functional strategies are developed during the strategy implementation stage, and organizational systems are adapted and modified to support the implementation of the organization's strategy.

Strategic control

The methods by which the performance of the organization is monitored.

The final stage of the strategic planning process, **strategic control**, answers the question, "How will the organization know when it has arrived?" This phase of strategic planning is designed to monitor the organization's progress toward implementing its plans and achieving its goals. Strategic control mechanisms identify deviations between actual and planned results so that managers can make the adjustments necessary to ensure that organizational goals can be achieved in the long term.[17]

Figure 5.1 | The Process of Strategic Planning

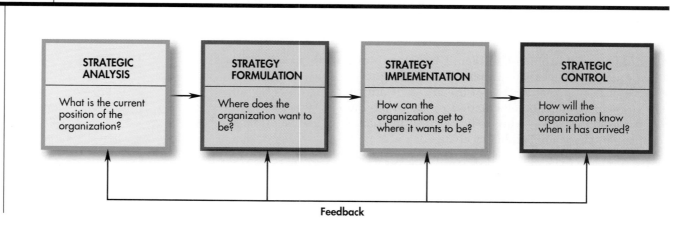

The strategic planning process is the focus of the remainder of this chapter. While the strategic planning process can and should be applied at both the corporate and business levels (see Chapter 4), this chapter will focus on developing strategies at the business level only. In other words, this chapter highlights the process of strategic planning as it relates to determining how to operate a specific business (business-level strategy), rather than addressing how to determine what business(es) to be in (corporate-level strategy). The specific activities associated with each stage of the strategic planning process are discussed in the following sections.

STRATEGIC ANALYSIS: ASSESSMENT IN A GLOBAL ENVIRONMENT

The first stage of the strategic planning process is strategic analysis. The purpose of a strategic analysis is to assess the current condition of the organization.[18] Until you understand where an organization is in its development, it is impossible to determine where it could and should be. Strategic analysis requires three primary activities: (1) assessing the mission of the organization, (2) conducting an internal environmental analysis, and (3) conducting an external environmental analysis.[19] Figure 5.2 illustrates these three components of a strategic analysis.

As you will learn in the following section, an organization's mission expresses its fundamental purpose for existence by describing its products, services, target markets, and strategies for growth. An assessment of an organization's internal and external environments involves the identification of its primary strengths, weaknesses, opportunities, and threats. Such an assessment is often referred to as a SWOT analysis—S (strengths), W (weaknesses), O (opportunities), and T (threats). By understanding the mission of the organization, as well as its current SWOTs, managers are prepared to identify and assess the strategic alternatives that are appropriate for the organization. Let's examine the components of a strategic analysis more closely.

LEARNING OBJECTIVE 3

Discuss how a strategic analysis is conducted, as well as the value of the analysis to the strategic planning process.

Figure 5.2 | The Components of Strategic Analysis

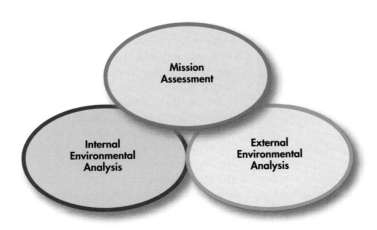

ASSESSING THE MISSION OF AN ORGANIZATION

Organizational mission
The reasons for which the organization exists; it provides strategic direction for the members of the organization.

The mission of an organization reflects its fundamental reasons for existence.[20] An **organizational mission** is a statement of the overall purpose of the organization that provides strategic direction to the members of an organization and keeps them focused on common goals.[21] A mission statement should be more than words on a piece of paper. It should be a living, breathing document that provides critical information for the members of the organization.[22]

Although mission statements vary greatly among organizations, every mission statement should describe three primary aspects of the organization: (1) its primary products or services, (2) its primary target markets, and (3) its overall strategy for ensuring long-term success. This information serves as the foundation upon which strategies are built. For example, if the mission of your university is to meet the educational needs of individuals in your state by offering innovative programs in the arts, science, business, engineering, and health care, the strategy of the university should be developed to fulfill that mission.

While a few management experts have questioned the real value of mission statements,[23] most believe missions to be of critical importance in setting the strategic direction of an organization and for providing a foundation for the development of business strategy.[24] In fact, one study indicated that mission-driven companies outperformed their rivals by an average of 30 percent in key financial measures.[25] Further, the success of some of America's most highly revered corporate leaders can be attributed to their commitment to providing a compelling mission for their organizations. From Andrew Carnegie to Henry Ford to Sam Walton, these legendary CEOs shaped their vision of a particular market environment into a mission that could be understood and acted upon by all of the members of their organizations. Their commitment to developing and communicating the mission of the organization contributed greatly to the success of their companies.[26]

CONDUCTING AN INTERNAL ANALYSIS

Strategic analysis also requires a thorough evaluation of the internal environment of the organization. The purpose of an internal analysis is to identify assets, resources, skills, and processes that represent either strengths or weaknesses of the organization. *Strengths* are aspects of the organization's operations that represent potential competitive advantages or distinctive competencies,[27] while *weaknesses* are areas that are in need of improvement.

Several areas of the organization's operations should be examined in an internal analysis. Key areas to be assessed include the company's products and services, as well as its marketing expertise, operations, human resources, and financial performance. These areas are typically evaluated in terms of the extent to which they support the competitive advantage sought by the organization. Table 5.1 lists a number of variables in each key area that should be evaluated when conducting an internal analysis.[28]

An organization's operation includes evaluation of its competitive advantages.

© PHOTOLINK/GETTYIMAGES/PHOTODISC

Human resources are one of the most important aspects of an organization's internal environment. In fact, some management scholars suggest that the only thing that truly distinguishes one organization from another is its people. The human resources of the organization, from top-level management down to frontline

Table 5.1 | Internal Factors

PRODUCT/ SERVICES	MARKETING	OPERATIONS	HUMAN RESOURCES	FINANCE
Breadth and mix	Market research	Productivity	Recruitment processes	Profitability
Quality	Distribution channels	Quality control	Training & development	Revenue growth
Reliability	Brand equity	Plant facilities	Compensation systems	Asset utilization
Image	Sales force	Supply chain management	Organizational culture	Debt/Leverage position
R&D commitment	Customer service	Technology	Leadership	Liquidity
	Market share	Information systems		Equity position

workers, are what determine the ability of the organization to achieve a competitive advantage in its industry.[29] Southwest Airlines, Gillette, and Tyson Foods are examples of organizations that view their human resources as their most significant competitive strength. These companies compete, in part, by recruiting the best talent and by utilizing the power of their workforce more effectively than their competitors.[30] Today, more than ever, companies compete aggressively to attract and retain the best human resources talent available.[31] Having insufficient or mediocre human resources is a weakness that would likely create a competitive disadvantage.

An important human resource issue relates to the increasing diversity of the U.S. workforce. Capitalizing on workplace diversity presents a potential strategic advantage for many organizations.[32] Developing a diverse employee base is not about abiding by regulations or meeting organizational quotas. Diversity is not a problem to be solved, but an opportunity to be embraced.[33] To the extent that managers are prepared to capitalize on the breadth of thought and experience that is inherent in a diverse workforce, they can formulate more creative strategies and plans and be more responsive to a diverse customer base. Conducting an internal analysis of the organization and assessing its relative strengths and weaknesses is a critical part of the strategic planning process. Managers will use this information to formulate strategies that capitalize on the organization's strengths and remediate its weaknesses.

Think back to the "Facing the Challenge" scenario on page 148. FedEx and the USPS were considering a strategic alliance. The alliance would overcome some weaknesses for the organizations and leverage some of their strengths. What were the strengths and weaknesses that were most relevant for these two companies as they crafted their strategic plans?

CONDUCTING AN EXTERNAL ENVIRONMENTAL ANALYSIS

The second area to be assessed in a strategic analysis is the external environment of the organization. The purpose of an external analysis is to identify those aspects of the environment that represent either an opportunity or a threat to the organization. *Opportunities* are those environmental trends on which the organization can capitalize and improve its competitive position. External *threats* are conditions that jeopardize the organization's ability to prosper in the long term.

Figure 5.3 illustrates the primary dimensions of a global external environment. The external environment is divided into two major components—the general environment and the task environment. The **general environment** includes environ-

General environment
Those environmental forces that are beyond a firm's influence and over which it has no control.

Figure 5.3 | Dimensions of the Global External Environment

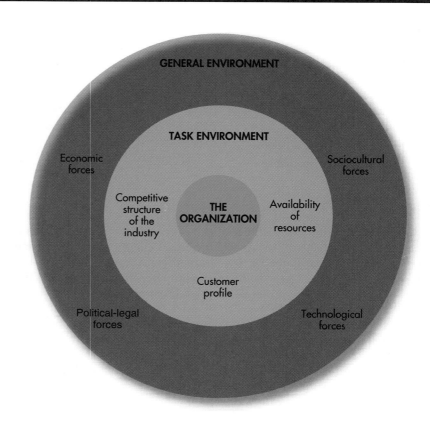

Task environment

Those environmental forces that are within the firm's operating environment and over which the firm has some degree of control.

mental forces that are beyond the influence of the organization and over which it has no control. Forces in the **task environment** are within the organization's operating environment and may be influenced to some degree.

GENERAL ENVIRONMENT   An organization's general environment includes economic, sociocultural, technological, and political-legal factors. A strategic analysis must consider the global dimensions of all of these factors as well as their domestic effects. Table 5.2 lists examples of trends in each of these areas that might represent an opportunity and/or a threat that would influence an organization's strategic plan.[34]

Economic Environment   The economic component of the general environment is represented by the general state of both the domestic and the world economy. The health of the domestic economy is reflected by variables such as total gross domestic product (GDP), growth in the GDP, interest rates, the inflation rate, the consumer price index, and unemployment rates. Similar measures can be used to evaluate the world economy. World trade and foreign direct investment trends are also useful for such an analysis.

A favorable economic climate represents opportunities for growth for most businesses. For example, in times of economic prosperity people typically spend more money on consumer goods. They tend to eat out more frequently, travel more often, and purchase more products and services. So hotels, restaurants, and retailers are just some of the organizations that would typically find growth opportunities when economic conditions are positive. However, the demand for some products and services grows during times of economic decline. For example, mo-

Table 5.2 | Sample Issues in the General Environment

SOCIOCULTURAL	ECONOMIC	TECHNOLOGICAL	POLITICAL-LEGAL
Demographic trends	Interest rates	Availability of information technology	Anti-trust regulation
The graying of America	Inflation rates		Intellectual property and patent laws
Consumerism	Unemployment rates	Sophistication of information technology	
Regional shifts in population	Minimum wage	Federal and industry spending on R&D	Affirmative action
Changes in work attitudes	Currency fluctuations		Tax laws
Trend toward health consciousness	Stock market trends	Production technology trends	Environmental protection policy
			International trade regulation

bile homes, bologna, and car repair services are examples of products and services that tend to be in greater demand during poor economic times. Other products and services are essentially recession proof and remain in relatively constant demand irrespective of the economic conditions. Consider Denstply, for example, the world's largest manufacturer of products used by dentists. Even during the dramatic economic downturn that began in the summer of 2000, Dentsply experienced steady sales and profitability. According to CEO John Miles, the demand for dentistry service remains relatively steady irrespective of economic conditions. This means that the demand for his products tends to be very stable which has implications for his company's strategic plan.[35]

The economy is a strong determinant of the demand for most goods and services. Consequently, forecasts of economic activity will influence the strategic plans of most organizations.

Sociocultural Environment The sociocultural component of the general environment is represented by the attitudes, behavior patterns, and lifestyles of the individuals who ultimately purchase the products or services of the organization. In addition, the analysis must consider demographic conditions and trends. As these aspects of the sociocultural environment change, so must the strategy of organizations that are affected by such changes.

Although some sociocultural trends cross national boundaries (such as the popularity of jeans among young people), not all developments occur on a global basis. In fact, many aspects of the sociocultural environment are specific to certain nations or groups of nations. Consequently, organizations that operate internationally often must cope with multiple heterogeneous sociocultural environments and, therefore, must develop strategies to deal with different environmental conditions.

One of the most important sociocultural trends in the United States in the last decade has been the increasing number of senior citizens. The "graying of America" is a demographic trend that will have significant impact for organizations with products that appeal to an older target market.[36] As more and more baby boomers move into their 50s, opportunities will emerge for companies that can meet the needs of this large and aging segment of the population. Campbell Soup, for example, recognizes that older consumers eat more soup than their younger counterparts, and it is prepared to take advantage of this demographic trend.[37] CBS, once plagued by declining ratings, refocused on its traditional market of older viewers,[38] a timely strategy, given the maturing of the baby boomers, and a successful one that resulted in a CBS victory in the 2000 season's rating wars.[39] Home improvement centers, such as Home Depot and Lowes, are also developing strategies to serve the aging and more affluent baby boomers who have transitioned from "do-it-yourself" consumers to "do-it-for-me" consumers.[40] Yet other companies, Levi's, for example, find the aging baby boomer market to represent a strategic threat. Since older people do not wear jeans as much as younger people, Levi's is trying to shed its image of serving the aging baby boomers and associate its products with the very different emerging youth market.[41]

Technological Environment Technological forces are the third component of the general environment. They include changes in technology that affect the way organizations operate or the products and services they provide. To keep abreast of technological trends, many organizations engage in *technology forecasting*. Such forecasts identify trends in technology that require adaptation on the part of the organization.

Clearly, the most significant technological advances of the recent past have been related to information technology. Not only have new software applications, such as enterprise resource planning (ERP) systems, revolutionized many organizational processes, but the advent of the Internet has changed the way industries function, organizations operate, and consumers purchase goods and services. Business-to-business e-commerce has enabled more efficient supply chain management strategies for virtually all organizations, while business-to-consumer e-commerce has radically changed the retail industry, from books to music to apparel. More important, even greater changes will be likely in the years to come.

The success of virtually all organizations today is dependent, at least in part, upon their ability to identify and respond to technological changes. IBM, General Motors, and UPS are just a few firms that must keep abreast of technological changes to ensure their long-term success. UPS, for example, has made tremendous inroads in its industry by investing heavily in technology and utilizing the Internet as a sales channel. It was the first among the competition to offer customers a wide array of services made possible by advanced information technology. The result—UPS handles 55 percent of all Net purchases versus 32 percent for the U.S. Postal Service and 10 percent for FedEx. That is quite an accomplishment in the dog-eat-dog parcel delivery business.[42]

Technology improvements have also affected the health care industry dramatically.[43] For example, given the aging population in the United States, medical services related to cardiovascular disease have become a very lucrative business, with expenditures totaling approximately $286 billion in 1999. Internet-based technologies will make possible innovative new monitoring products that will enable clinicians to better track daily patient measurements, store and retrieve historical data, and generate patient reports. No longer will health care professionals have to be at each patient's bedside, since they will be able to monitor patients from remote sites. Manufacturers that develop innovative products that capitalize on these new technologies will emerge as market leaders.[44]

From a more creative perspective, consider how improvements in technology have affected the entertainment industry. A "digital convergence" of Hollywood and Silicon Valley has made possible the production of films like *Toy Story*, *Contact*, and *The Matrix*, taking the movie industry to a new level of creativity and innovation. The music industry has been heavily impacted as well. The availability of music in a digital format has created new challenges and opportunities for artists, as well as music producers.[45] Clearly, technology is impacting all kinds of industries, organizations, products, and services.

Political-Legal Environment The final component of an organization's general environment is its political-legal environment. The political-legal environment includes the regulatory parameters within which the organization must operate. Tax policy, trade regulations, minimum-wage legislation, and pollution standards are just a few kinds of political-legal issues that can affect the strategic plans of an organization. Consider, for example, the Bush-Gore presidential campaign and the positions taken by the various candidates on the minimum-wage issue. The Democratic candidates, Senator Bill Bradley and Vice President Al Gore, indicated that they would raise the minimum wage if elected to office.[46] How do you think McDonald's and other fast-food restaurants would be affected by such an increase? How about retail apparel stores like Gap and American Eagle? Given an increase in the minimum wage, these companies would likely look for new ways to maximize the efficiency of their human resources. In addition, new pricing strategies might be necessary in light of increased labor costs.

Today, President Bush's administration is setting policies that have a significant impact on organizations and their strategic plans. Consider the issues that President Bush faced in the first year of his presidency: terrorism, corporate corruption, and economic turmoil. The Bush administration has established numerous policies and regulations to address these critical matters. For example, the acts of terrorism on September 11, 2001, resulted in many changes in airline regulations. These changes impact the airlines and the travel and tourism industry, as well as countless organization that rely on air travel to conduct important business. Corporate corruption, which first came to light with the Enron scandal and escalated quickly with the Arthur Andersen, Worldcom, and Adelphia debacles, was addressed with new SEC regulations to protect investors from fraudulent corporate activity.[47] As a result, thousands of publicly traded companies had to adjust the way they conducted business to meet those regulations. And in an effort to abate the economic decline that began in 2000, the Federal Reserve established fiscal policies meant to stimulate economic activity.[48] All of these policy and regulatory changes had implications for the strategic plans of many organizations.

Like the sociocultural environment, the political-legal environment of an organization often varies dramatically from nation to nation. As a consequence, organizations that operate internationally must develop a strategy for dealing with multiple political-legal systems.

TASK ENVIRONMENT In addition to general environmental issues, organizations must be aware of trends in the task environment. Recall that these forces are within the organization's operating arena and may be influenced to some degree by the organization. Critical task environmental variables include the competition in an industry, the profiles of the targeted customer base, and the availability of resources.

Competition Over the last decade, competition has been heating up across the board. In fact, some have gone so far as to use the term *hypercompetition* to describe the competitive environment of the 1990s,[49] and the new millennium promises to be even more competitive. In such an environment, success goes to organizations that have a clear understanding of the mission, strategies, and competitive advantages of their competitors.[50] This is why competitive analysis is so important in today's business environment.

Consider, for example, the degree of competitive analysis that takes place between Coca-Cola and Pepsi, Sears and JCPenney, or Nike and Reebok. These companies make it their business to know as much about their competitors as they know about themselves. In doing so, they are better able to anticipate what their competitors might do and how these actions might influence the marketplace.

In assessing the competition in a given industry, it is important to evaluate both individual competitors and the way they interact. When possible, and especially when the competitive field is relatively broad, each competitor should be evaluated using a common set of characteristics that can be compared across all competitors. For ex-

Competition analysis includes evaluating individual competitors and the way they interact with each other.

© TERRI MILLER/E-VISUAL COMMUNICATIONS, INC.

ample, each competitor might be assessed in light of its market share, marketing strategy, product mix, product quality, and financial strength. Such information provides managers with a better understanding of how their organization compares to its competitors, as well as with a general sense of the roles that each plays within the industry. For example, you can be sure that IBM, Apple, Dell, and Hewlett-Packard maintain sophisticated systems for tracking and evaluating the strategic moves of all the competitors in the computer industry.

Competitive analysis has become increasingly complex as more and more industries have globalized. Some organizations simply overlook important international competitors because they are "hard to see."[51] Even if such competitors are easily identified, it is often difficult to obtain information about them, since few international organizations are subject to the same disclosure regulations as U.S. organizations. Nevertheless, competitive analysis is an essential aspect of the strategic planning process, and managers must commit the time and energy necessary to gain a clear understanding of their competitors both domestically and globally.

Customer Profiles   Customer profiles must also be assessed as part of the strategic analysis. At a time when "the customer is king" philosophy has been embraced by organizations across the globe, it is imperative to have an in-depth understanding of the characteristics, needs, and expectations of the organization's customers.

An organization's customer may be another company in the production chain, or it may be the ultimate consumer. When an organization's customers are mainly industrial or wholesale clients, it needs information about the types of organizations that are using its products and services, their specific needs and expectations, their financial health, and the extent to which they are dependent upon the organization's products and services.

When an organization's customers are consumers, their demographic and psychographic characteristics, as well as their specific needs and expectations, are the most relevant dimensions for analysis. Relevant demographic characteristics include average age, income level, gender, and marital status. Psychographic characteristics related to the consumer's lifestyle and personality may also be critical determinants of buying behavior.

Historically, a number of prominent companies like American Express, Sears, and IBM have learned the hard way that understanding your customer is essential for success in fast-changing, highly competitive markets. American Express, for example, at one time, seemed to turn a deaf ear to consumers who wanted more innovative product features and retailers who wanted better rates. As a result, American Express lost market share to its two largest competitors, MasterCard and Visa.[52] Today, however, American Express is back with an aggressive Internet strategy that could make it a powerful player in online banking and smart cards.[53] This is one company that learned the hard way to pay attention to its customers and the competition. Other companies, Amazon.com for example, have always prioritized the customer. Jeff Bezos, founder and CEO of Amazon.com, describes his company as having a culture of "customer obsession." That customer obsession has earned Amazon.com its place as the Internet's most powerful merchant.[54]

Again, as with competitive analysis, the globalization of the marketplace has complicated the process of customer analysis. With customers spread across the globe, the relevant dimensions for analysis are more difficult to identify, evaluate, and predict. Therefore, managers in international organizations must take special care to ensure that they have a clear understanding of their customers in each national market served.

Resource Availability   Resource availability is the final component of the organization's task environment. The term *resource* can be applied to a broad range of inputs and may refer to raw materials, personnel or labor, and capital. To the extent that high-quality, low-cost resources are available to the organization, opportunities exist to create marketable products or services. When any resource is constrained, the organization faces a threat to its operations. Thus, strategic plans will be affected by the availability of the resources needed, both domestically and globally, to produce goods and services.

Consider, for example, the labor shortage experienced in the United States as it entered the new millennium. While the labor supply was inadequate in nearly every category of worker, the scarce supply of professional and technical personnel was particularly problematic. Employers, desperate to attract qualified workers, turned to more creative methods of compensation in an effort to address the problem.[55] Nonmonetary forms of compensation, such as flexible work arrangements, were often more effective in attracting workers than enhanced salary packages. For organizations that had the flexibility to design creative compensation programs, the labor shortage might have actually provided an opportunity to "out-hire" their more traditional competitors.

Yet, how quickly times can change. With the recession of 2001–2002, labor shortages abated as corporation after corporation announced layoffs in response to weakening demand for their products and services. As staffs were reduced, those who remained in their jobs were expected to do more and more to make up for the loss of their coworkers. In fact, the most recent recession was the first since World War II in which the productivity of the labor force rose rather than fell. According to a study by the Bureau of Labor Statistics, this rise in productivity was due, in part, to the fact that nearly 20 percent of the workforce reported spending more than 49 hours a week at work.[56] Clearly, labor is a critical organizational resource. Both labor shortages, as we saw in the late 1990s and labor excesses, which we saw in 2001 and 2002, will have a significant impact on the strategic plans of virtually all organizations. As is clear from the discussion above, strategic analysis provides important information about the organization's existing situation. Recall that the purpose of this stage of the strategic planning process is to answer the question, "What is the current position of the organization?" By examining its internal and external environment, an organization can answer this important question and lay the foundation for defining and developing its competitive advantage.

Remember, however, that in rapidly changing business environments, the results of a strategic analysis can change quickly. For example, as we noted earlier, internal strengths form the basis of competitive advantage for most organizations. But changes in external environmental conditions can affect the value of any particular organizational strength. Consider some historical examples of this phenomenon: General Electric's capabilities in transistor technology were devalued with the introduction of semiconductors; American Airlines' strong relationship with the Civil Aeronautics Board became far less valuable when the airline industry was deregulated; and the advent and growth of the personal computer devalued IBM's capability in the mainframe computer business. Most recently, consider how advances in e-commerce have affected the competitive advantages of traditional bricks-and-mortar bookstores such as Borders and Barnes & Noble.[57] While internal strengths are clearly an important source of competitive advantage, organizations must be sensitive to the ways in which changing external environmental and competitive conditions might affect the relative value of any particular strength.[58]

STRATEGY FORMULATION: ACHIEVING A COMPETITIVE ADVANTAGE

LEARNING OBJECTIVE 4

Explain the purpose of strategy formulation and describe the two types of strategic alternatives.

Once the strategic analysis is completed and the current position of the organization has been assessed, corporate and business strategy can be formulated. Recall that strategy formulation addresses the question, "Where does the organization want to be?" Answering that question requires (1) casting the vision for the organization, (2) setting strategic goals, (3) identifying strategic alternatives, and (4) evaluating and choosing the strategy that provides a competitive advantage and optimizes the performance of the organization in the long term.

CASTING THE VISION FOR THE ORGANIZATION

Central to any strategic plan is the development of a vision for the organization. A vision statement, although sometimes confused with a mission statement, has a distinctive and specific purpose. While a mission statement describes the products and services, target markets, and strategies for growth for an organization, a **vision statement** describes what the organization aspires to be in the long term. It is a description of the way in which the organization wants to be perceived by others at some future date.

Once again, consider the mission statement of your university. The mission statement most likely describes the educational programs offered by the institution and the kinds of students it serves. In contrast, the vision statement for your university probably speaks to a much bigger desire. For example, perhaps your university has a strong technology focus, and thus its vision is to be "a global leader in advancing knowledge related to information technology and e-commerce." Or maybe your university is highly focused on preparing students for career success, and its vision is to be "internationally recognized as a premier university, differentiated by its commitment to career-focused education." Each of these statements describes a way in which the university wants to be perceived by its stakeholders.

Top-level managers are responsible for casting a vision for their organizations. In fact, visionary leaders must see their organizations not just as they exist, but as how they can become. But envisioning the future is not enough; leaders must be able to communicate that vision and empower their followers to achieve it. According to Stephen Covey, a prominent management expert, vision plays a critical role in providing strategic direction for the members of an organization. In fact, Covey likens vision to the true north (N) on a compass—it enables employees to align their decisions, behaviors, and actions to the strategic direction of the organization.

When a new CEO takes the helm of an organization, everyone awaits the day when that person shares his or her vision for the company. Think back to when Lou Gerstner first took over troubled IBM. Stockholders, employees, customers, and competitors all anxiously awaited the announcement of his vision for the company.[59] While Gerstner surprised everyone with his delay in making such a pronouncement, eventually he communicated his vision for a less monolithic, more nimble organization focused on providing customers with total solutions. Less than a decade later, Gerstner was espousing a vision for IBM that put e-business solutions at the core of the company. Sam Palmisano, a long-time IBM'er, took the helm of the company in 2002 and is still formulating his vision for IBM. His first few months in office were plagued by declining sales as the American economy continued to struggle. At the time, Palmisano was hunkered down and doing what he could to adjust to the difficult economic times. But when the recession begins to subside, Palmisano is sure to emerge with a vision for a growth-oriented IBM that will lead to a brighter future for the company.[60] Now that you understand how important it is for an organization to have a vision statement, you can try your hand at developing one. The "Now Apply It" feature provides a format for you to develop a vision statement for an organization with which you are familiar.

SETTING STRATEGIC GOALS

Once the vision of the organization has been established, strategic goals can be determined. **Strategic goals** are very broad statements of the results that an organi-

Vision statement
Description of what the organization aspires to be in the long term.

It is the responsibility of new CEOs to develop and share their vision for the organization with their followers.

© AP/WIDE WORLD PHOTOS

Strategic goals
The results that an organization seeks to achieve in the long term.

Now Apply It

Developing a Vision Statement

Vision statements are powerful tools for providing strategic direction for an organization. Yet, developing a vision statement can be difficult. Several easy steps for developing a vision statement are outlined here. Choose an organization with which you are familiar (for example, your place of work, fraternity, sorority, church, or university), and follow the given steps to develop a vision statement for that organization. Remember: A vision statement should describe the organization as it desires to be perceived in the long term (10–20 years in the future), not as it is right now. Share your vision statement with the management of the organization you selected.

Step 1: Form a group of five to seven who can help you develop the vision statement. Visioning is best done with a group of people who can brainstorm the most relevant issues.

Step 2: Begin by having the group brainstorm a list of stakehold-

ers for the organization. For example, if the organization you chose is your university, stakeholders would include students, faculty, administrators, parents, alumni, employers, and so on.

Step 3: Assign each stakeholder group to two-person teams in your work group. These teams should brainstorm about the adjectives that their assigned stakeholders would want to use when describing the organization. Using your university as an example once again, parents might like to use adjectives such as *safe, affordable,* and *academically challenging.* Students might have a different set of adjectives, as would faculty, administrators, alumni, and employers. If the teams do not feel that they have a good understanding of the stakeholder group they have been assigned, they may wish to interview members of that group to learn more about their views.

Step 4: Once each team has completed the adjective list for the

stakeholder group(s) it was assigned, the adjectives lists for all stakeholders should be shared with the work group as a whole. The work group should look for common adjectives across stakeholder groups. Certain adjectives will be repetitive across stakeholder groups, and these adjectives should form the basis for your vision statement.

Step 5: Using the most important adjectives identified in the stakeholder assessment exercise, construct a vision statement that describes the ideal future organization. You may wish to begin your vision statement with "Our vision is to be . . . a place where . . . or a community that . . . or a leader in . . ." You can start your vision statement in numerous ways. The most important thing is that it describes some desirable future state for the organization you selected.

zation wishes to achieve in the long term. Such goals relate to the mission and vision of the organization and specify the level of performance that it desires to achieve.

Most organizations establish their goals to reflect their perception of success. In many organizations, managers look to profit as an indicator of success, and maximizing profit becomes their primary strategic goal. However, Peter Drucker, a prominent management theorist, warns against focusing solely on profit as a measure of success. He suggests that a preoccupation with profits alone can lead to short-term thinking and reactive management behavior. Rather, success should be operationalized more broadly and should include such things as market standing, innovation, productivity, physical and financial resources, profitability, managerial performance and development, worker performance and attitudes, and public responsibility.[61]

It is important to recognize that strategic success can vary greatly across organizations and between industries. Two organizations may measure and evaluate success in dramatically different ways. For example, a growth-oriented company may stress market share gains, whereas an organization that operates in a mature, slow-growth industry may place its emphasis on maximizing bottom-line profitability.

Several characteristics are associated with effective strategic goals. Because the goals established during the planning process serve as a benchmark by which the organization eventually will evaluate its performance, it is important that they be (1) specific, (2) measurable, (3) time linked, and (4) realistic but challenging. Table 5.3 provides some guidance on how to develop goals that meet these criteria.

Table 5.3 | Criteria for Effective Goals

Effective goals should meet the following criteria:

- *Specific goals* relate to a particular and easily defined performance area. For example, setting a goal of increasing productivity by 40 percent is not meaningful if "productivity" is not defined. Will productivity be measured by sales per employee? Sales per square foot? Cost per unit? Effective goals must be specific as to what will be evaluated.

- *Measurable goals* are usually expressed in quantitative terms. For example, increasing sales by 20 percent and reducing costs by 15 percent are examples of quantitative goals. Sometimes, however, it is necessary to express goals in qualitative terms. For example, an organization might establish a goal of being more socially responsive. While this goal cannot be expressed quantitatively, it is an important qualitative goal against which the organization will eventually evaluate its performance. When possible, however, goals should be established in clearly measurable, quantitative terms.

- *Time-linked goals* are to be achieved within a specified time period. For example, an organization might establish a goal of increasing market share by 3 percent by 2002. Because the goal is time linked, it provides the organization with a deadline for achieving its target performance.

- *Realistic but challenging goals* provide a challenge for those who must meet them, but the challenge should not be so great that the goal cannot be achieved. People don't strive to achieve goals that are set unrealistically high. On the other hand, a goal that is set too low is not motivating. Finding the balance between challenge and realism is important in setting goals.

IDENTIFYING STRATEGIC ALTERNATIVES

The third stage of the strategy formulation process involves identifying strategic alternatives. These alternatives should be developed in light of the organization's mission; its strengths, weaknesses, opportunities, and threats; and its vision and strategic goals. Strategic alternatives should focus on optimizing organizational performance in the long term.[62]

Strategy can be defined in a variety of ways. The following sections describe two ways to define strategic alternatives—grand strategies and generic strategies.

Grand strategy
A comprehensive, general approach for achieving the strategic goals of an organization.

GRAND STRATEGIES   Many organizations define their strategic alternatives in terms of grand strategies. A **grand strategy** is a comprehensive, general approach for achieving the strategic goals of an organization.[63] Grand strategies, fall into three broad categories: stability, growth, and retrenchment strategies.

Stability Strategies   Stability strategies are intended to ensure continuity in the operations and performance of the organization. At the business level, stability strategies require very little, if any, change in the organization's product, service, or market focus. Organizations that pursue a stability strategy continue to offer the same products and services to the same target markets as in the past. They may, however, attempt to capture a larger share of their existing market through market penetration or improve bottom-line profits through greater operational efficiency.

Market penetration is the initial strategy of most start-up organizations. At the outset, organizations enter a specific geographic market with a particular set of products and services. Stability is the primary goal of organizations at this stage of development as they are focused on generating the sales and revenues to succeed in their businesses. Once the market they serve has been fully penetrated, the organization may move on to pursue the next category strategies—growth.

Growth Strategies   Growth strategies are designed to increase the sales and profits of the organization. At the business level, growth strategies involve the development of new products for new or existing markets or the entry into new markets with existing products. The purpose of growth strategies is to increase the sales and profits of the organization in the long term and to position the organization as a market leader within its industry.

In many cases, growth strategies focus on being innovative, seeking out new opportunities, and taking risks. Such strategies are suitable for organizations that operate in dynamic, growing environments in which creativity, innovation, and organizational responsiveness are often more important than efficiency. Sony is an example of a company that pursues a growth strategy by offering a steady stream of new, innovative product. Some new product innovations even displace existing products (for example, the digital camcorder is replacing VHS recorders), but they all contribute to the organization's long-term growth in sales and profits.

Over the last several decades, many organizations have pursued a growth strategy by entering the international marketplace. When an organization has fully penetrated the domestic marketplace, international markets provide an opportunity to grow sales further. Consider, for example, the growth strategy of Martha Stewart Omnimedia Inc. Having fully penetrated the market in the United States, the company began to look toward the international marketplace for growth. In 2001, Martha Stewart opened its first retail boutique in a Tokyo department store. Less than six months later, the company announced its plans to accelerate its rollout of retail locations, spurn the sale of its popular Martha Stewart magazine in Japan, and promote heavily Martha's television program in that market. If the company continues to do well in Japan, it will launch a similar strategy in parts of Asia and Europe. The Yankee icon who made the glue gun a "must have" home improvement tool in the United States is about to work her magic in the international markets as well.[64]

Retrenchment Strategies   The purpose of a retrenchment strategy is to reverse negative sales and profitability trends. At the business level, retrenchment strategy focuses on streamlining the operations of the organization by reducing costs and assets. Such reductions may require plant closings, the sale of plants and equipment, spending cuts, or a reduction in the workforce of the organization. Furthermore, new systems, processes, and procedures must be designed to support the new, leaner organization. If the retrenchment strategy is successful, stability or growth strategies may be considered in the long term.

During the economic woes of 2001–2002, many of the United States' most prominent organizations pursued retrenchment strategies. Consider the travel industry, for example. By mid-2001, airline executives knew they were in trouble. The slowing economy was having a very negative impact on their revenues, with losses projected to be as much as $2.5 billion. And as if that wasn't bad enough—then came September 11. The terrorist attacks sent the airline industry into a freefall, necessitating aggressive and proactive cutbacks to survive. Airlines grounded roughly 20 percent of their fleets and began the painful process of layoffs and restructuring.[65] Aerospace companies, who served the airline industry, also had to retrench their operations. Boeing laid off 30,000 workers, approximately one-third of its workforce, and cut production by nearly half. Suppliers of tires, engines, and other parts of aircrafts, such as Goodrich and General Electric, also shaved thousands of jobs.[66] But it was not just the airlines and aircraft manufacturers who were hurt. The hotel business was negatively affected, as were car rental companies. In fact, ANC Rental, the parent company of Alamo Rent A Car and National Car Rental, was forced into bankruptcy following the September 11 tragedy. With 90 percent of its business serving airline passengers, the company had to implement a retrenchment strategy to survive. It cut its fleet by 35 percent, brought in a chief

Generic strategies
The fundamental way in which an organization competes in the marketplace.

Cost leadership strategy
A strategy for competing on the basis of price.

restructuring officer, and renegotiated its loan repayment agreements with some lenders. But even that was insufficient to stop the bleeding. Only time will tell how ANC Rental will fare from its retrenchment strategy.

GENERIC STRATEGY   While no two strategies are exactly alike, the strategies of some organizations do have common characteristics. Michael Porter, a well-known Harvard professor of industrial economics, has identified three **generic strategies** that can be used to describe the strategy of most organizations.[67] Generic strategies reflect the primary way in which an organization competes in its market. These strategies are commonly referred to as (1) cost leadership, (2) differentiation, and (3) focus.

Porter defines the generic strategies along two primary dimensions—the competitive advantage provided by the strategy and the competitive scope of the strategy. *Competitive advantage* is achieved by offering customers superior value, either through a lower price or through a differentiated product or service that justifies a higher price. *Competitive scope* refers to the breadth of the market targeted by the organization. Some organizations target their products and services to very broad markets, while others identify a relatively narrow segment of the market.

The matrix in Figure 5.4 identifies the three generic strategies based on competitive advantage and competitive scope.[68] The focus strategy has been broken into two separate strategies, depending on whether the competitive advantage sought is cost leadership or differentiation.

Cost Leadership   Organizations that pursue a **cost leadership strategy** compete on the basis of price. To do so, the organization must be highly efficient so that it can achieve a low-cost position in the industry. Costs may be minimized by maximizing capacity utilization, achieving size advantages (economies of scale), capitalizing on technology improvements, or employing a more experienced workforce.

Numerous organizations and products have succeeded based on cost leadership. Examples include Bic pens, Timex watches, Hampton Inns, and Food Lion

Figure 5.4 | Generic Strategies Matrix

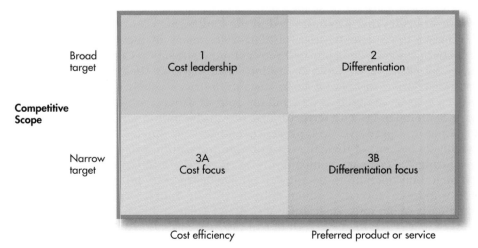

SOURCE: Adapted with the permission of The Free Press, a Division of Simon & Schuster Adult Publishing Group, from *Competitive Advantage: Creating and Sustaining Superior Performance* by Michael E. Porter. Copyright © 1985, 1998 by Michael E. Porter.

supermarkets. Each has concentrated on maximizing the efficiency of its production and delivery systems, achieving a lower cost structure than its competitors, and passing the benefit of lower costs on to the consumer in the form of lower prices.

Differentiation   Organizations that pursue a **differentiation strategy** compete by offering products or services that are differentiated from those of their competitors in some way. They charge a higher price based on the differentiated product or service feature. Distinctive characteristics may include exceptional customer service, quality, dependability, availability, innovation, or image.

Many organizations pursue a differentiation strategy. Examples of products that have succeeded through such a strategy include Cross pens, Seiko watches, and Maytag appliances. Consider Volvo cars for a moment. What is the differentiating characteristic of these vehicles? Has this differentiation strategy been successful for Volvo?

Focus   The final generic strategy identified by Porter is a **focus strategy**. A focus strategy occurs when an organization targets a specific, narrow segment of the market and thereby avoids competing with other competitors that target a broader segment of the market. Companies that pursue a focus strategy may compete in their niche market with either a cost leadership or a differentiation strategy. Therefore, the focus strategy appears in two boxes of the matrix shown in Figure 5.4. If the market segment is very narrow and competition is extremely limited, however, neither competitive advantage may be necessary.

Examples of products that have succeeded based on a focus strategy include BMW motorcycles, A&W root beer, and White Castle hamburgers. Prime examples of organizations that have used such a strategy within the grocery store industry are Fiesta Mart, a Texas-based grocery store chain that caters to Hispanic consumers, and Fresh Fields, a store that meets the needs of the health-conscious consumer.

EVALUATING AND CHOOSING STRATEGY

Designing strategy can be a challenging task. When determining an optimal strategy for the organization, managers can draw upon a variety of tools and techniques to generate, evaluate, and choose among strategic alternatives. Among the most popular evaluation and decision-making techniques are portfolio assessment models and decision matrices.

Portfolio assessment models provide a mechanism for evaluating an organization's portfolio of businesses, products, or services. These models classify the organization's portfolio of holdings into categories based on certain important criteria, such as growth rate or competitive position. Based on that classification, the organization's portfolio is assessed as to the appropriateness of the mix of business units, products, or services. The optimal strategy for each business unit, product, or service may vary according to its position in the portfolio. Popular portfolio assessment models include the Boston Consulting Group (BCG) growth-share matrix and the General Electric industry attractiveness/business strength matrix. Both of these portfolio assessment models will be discussed in Chapter 7.

Decision matrices help managers choose among strategic alternatives. A decision matrix provides a method for evaluating alternative strategies according to the criteria that the organization's managers consider most important, such as contribution toward sales growth, market share growth, profitability, and the like. Managers rate strategic alternatives according to the established criteria and select the alternative that has the best overall rating. Chapter 7 also provides a detailed discussion of decision matrices that can be used to make strategic choices.

Once the strategy formulation stage of the strategic planning process is complete, it is time to begin implementing the strategy. Strategy implementation is a critical and complex component of the strategic planning process.

Differentiation strategy
A strategy for competing by offering products or services that are differentiated from those of competitors.

Focus strategy
A strategy for competing by targeting a specific and narrow segment of the market.

STRATEGY IMPLEMENTATION: FOCUSING ON RESULTS

LEARNING OBJECTIVE 5

Explain the role of strategy implementation in the strategic planning process and ways to enhance the likelihood of implementation success.

The importance of strategy implementation should never be underestimated, for the best-formulated strategy is virtually worthless if it cannot be implemented effectively. If an organization is to achieve the best results from its strategic planning efforts, it must ensure that its strategy is put into action.

While managers may find it relatively easy to formulate competitive strategy, they may find execution of that strategy to be more difficult. Why is that so? Often, managers simply underestimate and undermanage the strategy implementation process.[69] Organizations that achieve strategic success commit a tremendous amount of time, energy, and effort to making sure that the strategy is implemented effectively.[70]

Recall that strategy implementation addresses the question, "How can the organization get to where it wants to be?" Answering that question requires two primary activities. First, functional strategy must be developed. Second, various aspects of the organizational system must be designed to ensure that the selected strategy can be institutionalized.[71]

FORMULATING FUNCTIONAL STRATEGY

Recall from Chapter 4 that functional strategy provides an action plan for strategy implementation at the level of the work group and individual. It puts the selected strategy into operation by defining the activities needed for implementation.

Depending on the specific strategy to be implemented, functional strategy may need to be formulated by a variety of work groups within the organization. Consider, for example, the functional strategies that would be necessary if Coca-Cola decided to develop a new line of fruit juices. The research and development department would have to develop a formula; the marketing department would have to conduct taste tests, develop promotional campaigns, and identify the appropriate distribution channels; and the production department would have to purchase new equipment and perhaps build new facilities to produce the fruit juice line. Table 5.4 outlines just a few of the functional strategies necessary to introduce a new line of fruit juices.

The most significant challenge lies in coordinating the activities of the various work groups that must work together to implement the strategy. The strategies must be consistent both within each functional area of the business (such as the marketing department) and between functional areas (such as the marketing department and the production department).[72] For example, if Coca-Cola's new fruit juice line is to be priced at a premium level, it must be promoted to buyers who desire a premium product and distributed through channels that reach those buyers. These marketing decisions must be consistent. Furthermore, the production department must purchase high-quality raw materials and produce a product that is worthy of a premium price. Without consistency within and between the work groups of the organization, the implementation process is sure to fail.

INSTITUTIONALIZING STRATEGY

While functional strategies are essential to the strategy implementation process, it is also important that the strategy be institutionalized within the organization. Institutionalizing a strategy means that every member, work group, department, and division of the organization subscribes to and supports the organization's strategy with its plans and actions. Theory suggests that a fit must exist between the strategy of the organization and its structure, culture, and leadership if the strategy is

| **Table 5.4** | Examples of Functional Strategies Needed to Implement a New Product Development Strategy |

Marketing:
- Coordinate with R&D for formula development.
- Conduct market research with consumers.
- Develop a pricing strategy.
- Design promotional materials.
- Identify and negotiate with potential distributors.
- Coordinate with Production as to product specifications.
- Coordinate with Human Resources regarding personnel needs.

Production:
- Identify suppliers of input materials.
- Negotiate purchasing agreements.
- Arrange for storage facilities for both raw materials and finished goods.
- Design and/or purchase new production equipment.
- Coordinate with Human Resources regarding personnel needs.

Human Resources:
- Work with Production to assess human resource needs.
- Work with Marketing to assess human resource needs.
- Identify potential candidates for new positions.
- Develop compensation and benefits packages for new employees.
- Design and provide training for new employees.

to be institutionalized. Each of these topics will be examined in much greater detail in a subsequent chapter (organizational structure in Chapter 9, culture in Chapter 11, and leadership in Chapter 13), but here we will briefly discuss their relationship to strategy.

ORGANIZATIONAL STRUCTURE **Organizational structure**, most commonly associated with the organization chart, defines the primary reporting relationships that exist within an organization.[73] The structure of an organization establishes its chain of command and its hierarchy of responsibility, authority, and accountability.[74]

Departmentalization of organizational activities is the focus of the structuring process. Organizing work responsibilities into departments requires grouping individuals on the basis of the tasks they perform. For example, if work units are structured so that all production tasks are grouped together, all marketing tasks are grouped together, and all finance tasks are grouped together, then the departments are organized on the basis of function. Similarly, if work units are structured so that all tasks related to serving the U.S. market are grouped together, all tasks for the European market are grouped together, and all tasks for the Asian market are grouped together, then organizational members are grouped according to the geographic market served.

Alfred Chandler, one of the earliest researchers in the area of strategy, originally advanced the idea that "structure follows strategy."[75] In essence, Chandler's findings indicate that an organization's strategy should influence its choice of organizational structure. For example, organizations that pursue growth through product development may benefit from a structure that is departmentalized by

Organizational structure
The primary reporting relationships that exist within an organization.

products. In contrast, those that pursue a geographic market development strategy may find an area-based structure to be most suitable. Furthermore, when an organization fails to change its structure in response to changes in its strategy, it will most likely experience operational problems that will eventually result in declining performance.[76] Since Chandler's classic research, a significant body of research has developed that suggests that organizations should develop structures that are appropriate for and supportive of their strategies. Several studies have successfully linked a strategy-structure fit to superior financial performance.[77]

In Chapter 9, a number of organizational structures will be identified and discussed. In addition, we will examine the advantages and disadvantages of the different structures as well as their suitability for varying strategic conditions.

ORGANIZATIONAL CULTURE   The second organizational component that should be aligned with an organization's strategy is organizational culture. **Organizational culture** refers to the shared, emotionally charged beliefs, values, and norms that bind people together and help them make sense of the systems within an organization. It guides the behavior of and gives meaning to the members of the organization.[78]

Peters and Waterman's classic survey of America's best-managed companies has drawn attention to the contribution of organizational culture to strategic success. Peters and Waterman attributed the success of such firms as Procter & Gamble, General Electric, and 3M in large part to an organizational culture that supports their strategic initiatives.[79] Many organizations that wished to emulate the success of these companies began to look to changes in organizational culture as a means of doing so.

In an organization with an effective culture, employees are convinced that top-level management is committed to the implementation of its strategy. Furthermore, employees believe that they will receive the support necessary to implement the organization's plans. For example, 3M, which maintains a culture that values innovation, supports its "champions" of new product designs by removing bureaucratic impediments, giving them access to whatever resources they need, and providing executive support for their efforts. Individuals who champion new product concepts are confident that they will get the support necessary to bring their ideas to fruition.[80]

Developing a strong, pervasive organizational culture has become more challenging as the workforce in the United States has become more culturally diverse. As we mentioned in Chapter 1, people with different backgrounds, from different nations, or with different cultural frames of reference often have very diverse views about organizations and how they should function.[81] Reaching agreement can be more difficult in such groups, both in establishing common goals and in determining methods for achieving those goals. Managers must be prepared to work harder and more creatively to ensure that a strong organizational culture exists within culturally diverse organizations.

Organizational culture is also critically important when two organizations are brought together through a strategic alliance. Strategic alliances take many shapes and forms, from formal partnerships to informal gatherings. Regardless of the form, most strategic alliances bring together two different organizational cultures. Consider, for example, how the cultures of FedEx and the USPS might vary. Would the differences in their organizational cultures have an impact on the implementation of a strategic alliance between these two companies? Undoubtedly. If FedEx and the USPS are to implement their strategies successfully, the management teams must be attentive to issues of organizational culture.

"At The Forefront" on page 169 provides some ideas for facilitating the strategic alliance process by focusing on managing the cultures of the organizations. Would this information be helpful for the executives at FedEx and the USPS?

Organizational culture
The shared, emotionally charged beliefs, values, and norms that bind people together and help them make sense of the systems within an organization.

At The Forefront

Making Strategic Alliances Stick

Global competition, rapid advances in technology, and customers who demand better service around the clock have created the need for many organizations to develop strategic partnerships. Strategic alliances allow organizations to better meet customer needs through partnering with other companies. These changes have led some to wonder if the days of stand-alone organizations are numbered.

Strategic alliances take many forms. Some are very formal relationships such as legally constituted joint ventures, while others are less formal such as communities of practice outings. In many ways, the new coalition government of Afghanistan represents a strategic alliance. Former competitors now see that it is in everyone's best interest to work together for a common goal. The eventual leadership ensemble of Afghanistan will, in many ways, resemble the corporate boardroom when one company sits down with another to discuss their ongoing strategic relationship. Regardless of the form, two universal truths seem

to apply to strategic alliances: partnering with another company is hard work, and many alliances fail after only a short period of time.

Although it is imperative for partners in a strategic alliance to have a common goal, it isn't enough to only share a mutual purpose. Leaders must also be prepared to manage the relationships that will emerge between the newly formed alliances. Communicating effectively across these often fragile and volatile networks is part of making the alliance work. The following Top 10 List outlines the most important aspects of strategic alliances:

1. Assess the impact of the alliance on people and their current relationships.
2. Commit to the alliance on the basis of mutual value and service.
3. Develop clear lines of communication and responsibilities.
4. Establish ground rules to govern the new alliance.
5. Support an open style of leadership.

6. Foster relationship building across the organizations.
7. Help people learn new skills and approaches.
8. Model the effective alliance behaviors.
9. Provide a vehicle for people to share learning.
10. Communicate effectively and honestly across the organizations.

As organizations compete on a global playing field, developing strategic relationships will become increasingly important. Organizations across all business sectors will need to compensate for deficiencies in skills, resources, or technology. Rather than trying to acquire or develop these missing attributes, organizations will need to rely on long-term strategic partnerships for sustaining a competitive advantage.

SOURCES: L. Holbeche, "Making Strategic Alliances Work," *Training Journal*, January 2002, 14–18; and L. Tischler, "Seven Strategies for Successful Alliances," *Fast Company*, December 2001.

ORGANIZATIONAL LEADERSHIP Leadership is the third organizational component that should be aligned with the strategy of the organization. If an organization is to implement its strategy effectively, it must have the appropriate leadership.[82] Without effective leadership, it is unlikely that the organization will realize the benefits of its selected strategy.[83]

At the top of the organization must be the visionary leader. As we discussed earlier, visionary leaders can envision the future, communicate their vision to those around them, empower the people of the organization to make the vision happen, and reward them when it becomes a reality.[84] Bill Gates of Microsoft has often been described as a visionary leader. Gates saw an opportunity to redefine the market for personal computer operating systems and made that vision a reality. The effective implementation of that strategy has made Microsoft one of the most successful organizations in the United States. Even in the government sector, NASA chief, Daniel Goldin, adopted a big vision of transforming the lumbering behemoth into a more agile, lean government agency. His leadership was key to making that transformation successful.[85]

Equally important to strategy implementation is effective leadership in the ranks of managers. In today's organizations, they may be team leaders, coaches, or champions rather than traditional middle-level managers, but the idea is the same. These individuals must do whatever is necessary to ensure that their work groups are making a contribution toward fulfilling the mission of the organization, achieving its goals, and implementing its strategy. For example, Canon, the $19 billion maker of cameras, copiers, printers, and fax machines, has attributed its success to strong leadership throughout the organization. Leadership is discussed in Chapter 13, where we examine the relationship between leadership and strategy in greater detail.

It is essential for an organization to develop the systems necessary to support its strategy. Structure, culture, and leadership are particularly relevant for effective strategy implementation. When a strategy is being implemented, it is also important to monitor both the success of the implementation process and the effectiveness of the strategy. Strategic control provides the mechanism for doing that.

STRATEGIC CONTROL: ENSURING QUALITY AND EFFECTIVENESS

LEARNING OBJECTIVE 6

Describe strategic control systems.

The last stage of the strategic planning process is strategic control. Strategic control involves monitoring the implementation of the strategic plan and ensuring quality and effectiveness in terms of organizational performance. An effective control system identifies problems and signals the organization that a change may be needed.

Achieving strategic control in organizations that are heavily involved in the international marketplace can be particularly difficult. When operating units are in geographically dispersed locations, differences in time, language, and culture complicate the control process. Acquiring information is more difficult when the scope of the organization's operations is broad, and processing and interpreting information from such diverse sources can be challenging. Consequently, organizations that pursue international strategies must often maintain very sophisticated control systems.

In general, control mechanisms can be either feedforward or feedback controls. Let's examine what each involves.

FEEDFORWARD CONTROLS

Feedforward controls

Controls designed to identify changes in the external environment or the internal operations of the organization that may affect its ability to fulfill its mission and achieve its strategic goals.

Feedforward controls are designed to identify changes in the external environment or the internal operations of the organization that may affect its ability to fulfill its mission and meet its strategic goals. Premise controls are one of the most common feedforward controls. Premise controls are designed to identify changes in any condition, internal or external, upon which the strategy of the organization was based.

Consider, for example, a large construction company that plans to develop 500,000 acres of residential property over the next three years. By the end of the first year of the company's plan, the economy begins to deteriorate, and interest rates, inflation, and unemployment begin to rise. If premise controls are in place and are designed to detect changes in the economic conditions upon which the construction company's plan is based, the company will know to adapt its strategy to the changing economic conditions.

FEEDBACK CONTROLS

Feedback controls

Controls that compare the actual performance of the organization to its planned performance.

Feedback controls compare the actual performance of the organization to its planned performance. These controls usually target the goals established in the organization's strategic and operational plans. One of the primary benefits of feedback control is that it focuses the attention of managers on the results for which they are responsible in the organization's plan. This may discourage managers from spending too much time on situations and issues that are unrelated to the overall goals of the organization. Often, feedback controls evaluate financial results, such as revenues, profitability, stock price, and budget variances. Other feedback controls monitor nonfinancial results, such as customer relations, product and service quality, productivity, and employee turnover.

Organizations should maintain both feedforward and feedback controls. Relying on only one type of control could be a mistake because these controls focus on different issues that could affect the organization's plans. Just as organizations establish different goals and pursue different strategies, they should develop control systems to meet their specific strategic needs. An organization's control system must be in alignment with its strategic initiatives.[86] For example, an organization pursuing a growth strategy is unlikely to develop the same control system as one that is pursuing a retrenchment strategy. The growth-oriented firm would monitor such variables as forecasts for demand, sales levels, sales growth, increases in market share, and brand awareness. In contrast, the organization pursuing retrenchment would monitor such variables as supply costs, productivity, sales per employee, sales-to-assets ratios, gross and net margins, and other indicators of efficiency and bottom-line profitability.

INFORMATION TECHNOLOGY AND STRATEGIC PLANNING

The increasing availability and sophistication of information technology have had a tremendous impact on the ability of organizations to develop effective strategic plans. Such technology has made both internal and external sources of information more readily available to managers who are responsible for strategic planning. For example, tracking the sales of individual products in specific regions and at various price levels is much simpler given the information technology available to-

LEARNING OBJECTIVE 7

Explain how advances in information technology have affected strategic planning.

Leaders In Action

DuPont: Harnessing the Power of Partnerships

DuPont's chairman and CEO Charles Holliday, Jr., believes in the power of global partnerships. In fact, much of his management experience comes from overseas. Before taking over as chairman and CEO, Holliday was the head of DuPont's Asia Pacific Operations in Tokyo, Japan. Today, DuPont has partnered with numerous organizations across the globe to provide cutting-edge technology and environmentally sound products to a diverse customer population.

A major part of DuPont's global strategy has been to develop and nourish alliances related to information technology. DuPont formed a strategic relationship with ICG, an Internet venture capital firm, to facilitate DuPont's entry into e-commerce. This partnership has allowed DuPont to extend existing business lines and to identify emerging business opportunities.

More recently, DuPont launched aggressive strategic initiatives involv-

ing its global information systems and technology infrastructure. DuPont partnered with Accenture to design, build, and run an enterprise resource planning (ERP) solution. Computer Sciences Corporation (CSC) has also formed a strategic relationship with DuPont to operate its global IT systems and infrastructure and to provide software and applications support. In both instances, DuPont sees value in working with these organizations by developing long-term relationships.

DuPont's strategic alliances are not limited to the IT field. As a company that once fell short of environmental standards, DuPont now recognizes that it can gain a sustainable competitive advantage by exceeding minimum EPA regulations. Today, Holliday ensures that environmental and social policies are an integral part of DuPont's corporate strategy. To this end, DuPont recently announced a strategic alliance with EarthShell to provide

biodegradable packaging for disposable food service packaging materials. This strategic partnership will help ensure that DuPont continues to exceed safety and environmental standards in its diverse business lines.

Whether leading organizational efforts to improve IT operations or packaging product supplies, DuPont is demonstrating that developing strategic relationships with different organizations helps to improve its overall commitment to quality and customer service. In a setting where DuPont's range of assorted product lines may be matched only by the diversity of the global market in which it operates, strategic partnerships are paying off.

SOURCES: B. Glasgow, "Information Technology Insights: DuPont's Mighty Global IT Alliance Keeps Rolling and Evolving," *Chemical Market Reporter*, March 25, 2002, 13–14; and C. Murphy, "Revenge of the Giants," *Informationweek*, May 1, 2000, RB4–RB12.

day. Similarly, information regarding such things as market share fluctuations, profitability, and productivity measures is more readily available, and operational activities such as purchasing, inventory management, and human resource management are more easily monitored. Competitive intelligence, a method by which companies track the strategies and actions of their competitors, has been enhanced greatly through the use of comprehensive databases and analytical tools. New approaches to meeting the needs of customers have emerged as companies use information technology to better understand their customers' profiles and track their preferences.[87] Clearly, a well-designed management information system can provide accurate, timely information to managers throughout the organization.

Unfortunately, many organizations fail to use the information made available by management information systems to ensure effective strategic planning.[88] Given the increasing competitiveness in most industries, however, many organizations are searching for ways to improve their strategic planning processes. More effective use of information technology will provide a solution for many such organizations. The "Leaders In Action" section describes how DuPont CEO Charles Holliday, Jr., uses IT as a global strategy for developing strategic alliances.

Strategic planning is a critical organizational activity that will affect the long-term performance of most organizations. We conclude by exploring the implications of strategic planning for the manager and leader of tomorrow.

LEARNING OBJECTIVE 8

Discuss how tomorrow's manager can achieve success through strategic planning.

IMPLICATIONS FOR LEADERS

At several points so far in this book, we have suggested that the business environment is in a state of constant change. These changes will present special challenges for those who must plan strategically.

While the future of the business environment remains uncertain, it is important for you, as a leader of the future, to recognize the changing nature of the environment and the implications of those changes for strategic planning. Always remember that leaders must be highly competent, and being competent requires excellent strategic thinking and planning skills. Employees will follow those who they believe have a clear understanding of the present and a vision for the future. As you engage in strategic planning, you may want to keep the following tips in mind:

- Use a participatory approach to planning whenever possible.
- Recognize the importance of a thorough and accurate assessment of the current situation of the organization. A plan will be only as good as the analysis on which it is based.
- Make sure your mission statement is a working document that provides direction for the members of the organization.
- Understand the realities of the environment in which you operate—both internally and externally.
- Strategic vision is critical for ensuring a common strategic direction for the organization.
- Strategic goals serve as targets for achievement. Make sure they are measurable, specific, and realistic.
- Strategy should be designed to provide the organization with a distinctive competitive advantage in the long term. Never lose sight of that imperative.
- Strategy is meaningless if it is not implemented well. Ensure that you plan for successful implementation all along the way.
- Never underestimate the importance of strategic control. It is the only means of ensuring that the company is on track.

Meeting The Challenge

FedEx and USPS: A Strategic Alliance for the Future

FedEx founder and CEO Fred Smith and USPS Postmaster General William Henderson were about as an unlikely a pair of strategic collaborators as could be imagined. Smith had been an outspoken critic of the USPS for years, and Henderson and the USPS enjoyed a retail presence that other companies could only dream of. What brought these two former competitors together was the realization that in today's global environment, FedEx and the USPS needed each other.

In early 2001, FedEx and the USPS announced a major strategic alliance. Each organization had something to offer the other. The USPS bought space on FedEx air-planes to transport Express, Priority, and First-Class mail. In return, FedEx placed their package collection boxes at thousands of USPS offices across the country, giving FedEx a coast-to-coast retail presence.

Many agree that this strategic alliance will benefit both organizations. In a digital world where success will be determined by optimizing networks and managing information as opposed to delivering envelopes, the USPS stands to gain a great deal. Likewise, FedEx gains from the new stream of revenue through leasing its unused aircraft cargo space. Perhaps more importantly, FedEx now has a presence at post office locations, which greatly increases both its visibility and convenience to customers.

Only time will tell how well this strategic partnership performs. Both organizations are working in a market that has weathered dramatic changes as a result of e-mail and the Internet. As the global marketplace continues to drive business, the strategic alliance between FedEx and the USPS seems poised to capitalize on the synergy created by their unlikely partnership.

SOURCES: T. Roche, "Who's Got Mail?" *Time*, October 16, 2000, 86–88; and M. Tatge, "Going Postal," *Forbes*, February 5, 2001, 56.

In this chapter, you have learned about the process of strategic planning. This process provides a strong foundation for the development and implementation of effective strategy. Although strategic planning creates many challenges for managers, it is essential for those organizations that strive to achieve excellence in the highly competitive business environment of today and tomorrow.

SUMMARY

1. Strategic planning is the process by which an organization makes decisions and takes actions that affect its long-term performance. The purpose of strategic planning is to move the organization from where it is to where it wants to be. Both economic and behavioral benefits are associated with strategic planning.

2. The strategic planning process consists of four primary stages: (1) strategic analysis, which answers the question "What is the current position of the organization?" (2) strategy formulation, which answers the question "Where does the firm want to be?" (3) strategy implementation, which answers the question "How can the organization get to where it wants to be?" and (4) strategic control, which answers the question "How will the organization know when it has arrived?"

3. The first stage of the strategic planning process is strategic analysis. The purpose of strategic analysis is to assess the current condition of the organization. Strategic analysis requires three primary activities: (1) assessing the mission of the organization, (2) conducting an internal environmental analysis to identify the strengths and weaknesses of the organization, and (3) conducting an external environmen-tal analysis to identify the opportunities and threats facing the organization. The results of the strategic analysis are critical to determining the future direction of the organization.

4. Strategy formulation follows strategic analysis and results in the development of business strategy. Strategy formulation requires the development of an organizational vision, the determination of strategic goals, the identification of strategic alternatives, and the evaluation and selection of a strategy that distinguishes the organization from its competitors. Strategy can be described as grand strategies or generic strategies. Grand strategies include stability, growth, and retrenchment. Generic strategies include cost leadership, differentiation, and focus.

5. The most effective strategy formulation process is virtually worthless if the strategy formulated is not implemented effectively. Strategy implementation is the action phase of the strategic planning process as it puts the strategy of the organization into effect. Strategy implementation requires two primary activities: (1) functional strategy must be developed, and (2) the organizational system must be designed to ensure institutionalization of the strategy.

6. Strategic control involves monitoring the organization's progress toward implementing its plans and achieving its goals. Strategic control mechanisms identify deviations between actual and planned results so that managers can make the adjustments necessary to ensure that organizational goals can be achieved in the long term. In general, control mechanisms can be either feedforward or feedback controls.

7. Information technology can be used to improve the strategic planning efforts of most organizations. From data collection to support strategic analysis to the monitoring of performance indicators, management information systems provide managers with data that can enhance the effectiveness of the strategic planning process.

8. The rapidly changing business environment creates many challenges for managers who must plan strategically. Managers of the future must remember the basic principles of strategic planning as they attempt to ensure the competitiveness of their organizations through the development of effective strategy.

REVIEW QUESTIONS

1. (*Learning Objective 1*) Why is it important for organizations to engage in strategic planning? What are the benefits of the strategic planning process?

2. (*Learning Objective 2*) Describe the process of strategic planning. How are the four stages of the process interrelated?

3. (*Learning Objective 3*) What is involved in conducting a strategic analysis? More specifically, how does one (a) develop or assess an organizational mission, (b) identify the strengths and weaknesses of an organization, and (c) identify the opportunities and threats facing the organization?

4. (*Learning Objective 4*) What is the purpose of strategy formulation? What roles do vision and goals play in formulating strategy? Describe the three grand strategies discussed, as well as the generic strategies. Give examples of organizations that have pursued each of these strategic alternatives.

5. (*Learning Objective 5*) What role does strategy implementation play in the strategic planning process? What are functional strategies? What aspects of a firm's organizational system need to be in alignment with its strategy?

6. (*Learning Objective 6*) Describe the elements of strategic control.

7. (*Learning Objective 7*) How has information technology affected the strategic planning process in contemporary organizations?

8. (*Learning Objective 8*) How can the managers of the future enhance their effectiveness through strategic planning?

DISCUSSION QUESTIONS

Improving Critical Thinking

1. What are some of the changes in the business environment in the last 20 years that have increased the need for strategic planning for many organizations?

2. How has the emergence of a global marketplace complicated the process of strategic analysis for organizations that pursue international strategies?

Enhancing Communication Skills

3. Consider an organization that you have worked for at some time or that you currently work for. Would you classify that organization as having a stability, growth, or retrenchment strategy? Do the organization's culture, leadership, and control systems match its strategy? To improve your oral communication skills, prepare a brief presentation for the class.

4. Under what conditions might an organization choose to shift from a cost leadership strategy to a product differentiation strategy? Would this be a difficult adjustment for most organizations? To practice your written communication skills, write a one-page summary of your response.

Building Teamwork

5. Describe the effect each of the following would have on an organization:

    a. Ineffective implementation of a good strategy.
    b. Effective implementation of a poor strategy.
    c. Ineffective implementation of a poor strategy.

    Discuss this with a group of four or five students.

6. Form teams of four or five students. For each of the following strategies, identify an organization (beyond those cited in the text) that can be characterized as pursuing each strategy: (a) cost leadership, (b) differentiation, and (c) focus. Why did you choose these particular organizations? Be prepared to discuss your selections with the class.

THINKING CRITICALLY: DEBATE THE ISSUE

Strategic Planning: Form or Function

The process of strategic planning often leads to changes in an organization's mission and business operation. Two critical aspects of organizational life, organizational structure and organizational culture, must be transformed if a new strategy is to be institutionalized. Some argue that an organization's structure, which represents the formal lines of authority and accountability, is the most important element to implementing strategy. Others believe that organizational culture, which contains the informal lines of communication and unwritten rules of an organization, is more important in institutionalizing a new strategy.

Form teams of four to five students. Half the teams should prepare to argue that an organization's structure is the most critical aspect of implementing a new strategy. The other half should prepare to argue that organizational culture is more important for having the new strategy accepted and endorsed by members of an organization. Your instructor will select two teams to present their arguments to the class in a debate format.

EXPERIENTIAL EXERCISE 5.1

Developing a Conceptual Image Document

Developing a conceptual image document is similar to creating a personal strategic plan. It helps you identify your personal goals while considering your strengths and weaknesses. When completed thoughtfully, this document can help you make decisions that are crucial for achieving your career goals. Answer the following questions based on your current situation. For example, for "Who am I?" you might list that you are a son or daughter, brother or sister, student, employee, and the like. After you have answered all of the questions, form teams of four to five to discuss your answers.

1. Who am I?
2. What do I do?
3. How do I do it?
4. Who do I do it to?
5. What are my strengths?
6. What are my weaknesses?
7. What do I want to be doing three years from now?
8. When I retire, what accomplishment will be most important to me?

EXPERIENTIAL EXERCISE 5.2

Developing a Strategic Analysis

Form a team with at least four other people. As a group, assume that you are the executive committee for the college of business administration at your university. Develop a strategic analysis for your college. In doing so, address the following:

1. Assess the mission statement for the college.
2. Identify the strengths and weaknesses of the college.
3. Identify the opportunities and threats facing the college.

Make a presentation to the class of your analysis. How does your analysis compare to the analyses of other groups in your class? Did you have to make assumptions about the internal and external environment of the college? How might those assumptions affect the strategic plan of the college?

CAPTURING THE POWER OF INFORMATION TECHNOLOGY

1. Select an industry in which you have a particular interest (such as banking, restaurant, or sporting goods). Using the Internet, identify the three or four top competitors in that industry. Also using the Internet, research the strategy of each of these firms and categorize them according to the generic strategies advanced by Michael Porter.

2. As mentioned earlier, the U.S. International Competition Policy Review Committee was formed to facilitate global merger activity across national borders. Go to the home page of this group (**http://www.usdoj.gov/**) and research what the committee has been doing to encourage global mergers. Has the committee been effective?

3. In 1999, in the early days of e-commerce activity, *Fortune* magazine named ten companies as those who "get it" when it comes to e-commerce.[89] These companies were (1) Petco, (2) Southwest Airlines, (3) Lands' End, (4) Charles Schwab,

(5) Bertelsman, (6) W. W. Grainger, (7) Ticketmaster, (8) Office Depot, (9) Fingerhut, and (10) the U.S. Postal Service. Select three of these companies that have a business-to-consumer focus and visit their Web sites to compare and contrast their e-commerce strategies from a consumer per-spective. What features do you find most appealing about their Web sites? What would you change about their Web sites? Do you think that these companies are still leaders in e-commerce today?

ETHICS: TAKE A STAND

Mitch Akers, senior vice president for research and development with Well Path Pharmaceuticals (WPP), had finally reached his career goal of becoming head of R&D. Following the completion of his Ph.D. in biology and a short stint as a college professor, Akers transitioned his career into the corporate world. After managing several successful projects for WPP that were brought in on time and under budget, Akers quickly climbed the corporate ladder. Although he enjoyed the new administrative challenges of being the youngest executive at WPP, his true passion was being actively involved in the science and technology aspects of biomedical research.

Mitch Akers's most exciting project involved an experimental drug for the treatment of nicotine addiction. Although the drug testing process was still in its infancy, preliminary results were very positive. His budget request for managing this project had been quickly approved and he was assured that he had top management's total support.

When Akers received a call from WPP's president Frank Carlson to discuss the progress of the drug's testing, he didn't think too much about it. When Carlson stopped by Akers' office, he gladly shared the results of the latest round of laboratory tests. Akers estimated that the drug would be ready for human testing, and eventual FDA approval, in 18 months. "Not soon enough," replied Carlson. WPP's president explained to Akers that a private drug company located in Europe had approached their company. The foreign company had heard of the experi-mental drug and was interested in forming a strategic alliance with WPP. Essentially, the company wanted to buy WPP's product as-is with no further testing. Then, they would market, distribute, and sell it as a "wonder cure to stop smoking." The proposed alliance would mean much-needed revenue for WPP, and the prospect of a long-term relationship would give WPP leverage in the global market. Carlson told Akers to think it over and let him know his reaction in a day or two. "I won't push this if you think it's a bad idea," Carlson said on his way out, "but I think this is the right direction for us to take. Chances are that if anyone ever should find out, we would already have FDA approval."

Akers sighed as he fell back into his leather chair and stared out of his corner window. He was feeling some pretty intense pressure to go along, but he his gut instinct told him that it was wrong.

For Discussion

1. What are the ethical issues facing Mitch Akers? Which of these issues apply to Frank Carlson?

2. Is it ethical to follow one standard in one country and a different standard in another country?

3. If you were Mitch Akers, how would you handle the situation?

VIDEO CASE

Strategic Planning in a Global Environment: Kropf Fruit Company

Kropf Fruit Company is a family-owned business consisting of orchards, storage, and packing facilities. In the early 1990s, the owners of Kropf faced a critical decision. Increasingly dynamic market conditions favored large fruit processors over medium-sized processors such as Kropf. This trend resulted from a consolidation in the grocery store industry resulting in fewer retailers purchasing fruit.

In order to identify a new strategy, Kropf analyzed its SWOT based on its mission. Kropf's strengths included being a family business, being a good market fit, the willingness to adapt to changing markets, grower support, and good relationships with growers. Its weaknesses included low-yielding trees producing less popular fruit, inability to supply the demand, no equipment to sort a wide variety of sizes and grades of fruit, no temperature-controlled storage so fruit could be made available year-round, and no funding for expansion. Opportunities (stated as alternative solutions that may benefit Kropf) included building a packing facility, obtaining expanded storage, and exporting fruit (due to worldwide demand). Kropf's threats included a limited number of grocery stores, larger fruit packers (e.g., Dole), and imported fruit (e.g., the mango).

As a result of analyzing its mission and SWOT, the owners of Kropf were left with two strategic options: (1) remain a medium-sized processor or (2) expand and become a major player. Both options involved risk. Remaining a medium-sized processor meant the company would continue to face unfavorable market conditions and younger family members might not have a future in the business. Becoming a major player would allow the company to compete with other large growers and processors for major grocery store accounts.

During the planning process, the owners remained open to suggestions from their stakeholders such as their growers, customers, and employees. The owners of Kropf decided to expand operations and double in size over the next ten years. They developed their storage and packing facilities by updating to the newest technologies. This allowed them to lower their overhead so fruit could be packed and stored at the lowest possible cost. In addition, Kropf needed to increase its acreage and all varieties of fruit by at least 50 percent, which also served to attract new growers. Although the owners of Kropf have worked long and hard and the firm has suffered some growing pains, the expansion has been successful in many ways. It has provided an example for neighbor growers who are growing with Kropf. The expansion allows them to talk with some of the largest U.S. retailers who now treat Kropf similarly to Chiquita or Dole. In the two years since its initial expansion, Kropf's domestic and export sales have grown 30 percent and 300 percent, respectively.

Two constant challenges to its growth have been implementing short-term operating plans such as tailoring the varieties of the crops to meet the various demands of each customer and creating new markets for its fruit. Moreover, Kropf recognizes that its success depends on its relationship with growers and packers throughout the state. Therefore, it continues to support growers by providing chemicals and fertilizer, half of the boxes, trucks, and advice the growers might need. Of course, Kropf also stores, packs, and markets the growers' fruit. Other important aspects of its strategic and operational plans include forecasting worldwide demand for its fruit and guarding against adverse weather conditions. Finally, Kropf's leaders have found that they must carefully coordinate their activities to successfully manage their day-to-day activities as well as their phenomenal growth.

At this point, the owners of Kropf are satisfied with their expansion efforts accomplished through careful planning and implementation. Kropf's ten-year growth package includes major steps scheduled to be implemented every two years. They've already talked to their lending association about their plans for future expansion of their facilities.

For Discussion

1. Describe how Kropf progressed through the four stages of the strategic planning process.

2. Identify any aspects of the four stages of the strategic planning process that are *not* addressed in the case or video. Do you believe these aspects also needed to be addressed? Explain.

3. Who and what alerted them to the potential dangers of remaining a medium-sized fruit processor? Do you believe Kropf's future success might be different if no one had alerted them? Explain.

4. Describe whether Kropf's strategic and operational plans support each other in achieving business success. Based on the information provided, would you have proposed similar goals? Explain.

CASE

Developing a Strategic Plan for the Center City Club

Carolyn Richards smiled as she placed the telephone receiver back into its cradle. She had dreamt of a career in business consulting while completing her MBA. Now, after deciding to strike out on her own, the telephone was finally starting to ring. Her first client, the Center City Club, was a nonprofit wellness center with seven locations throughout the city. The city had experienced explosive growth over the last five years and as a result, the Center City Club had grown from one downtown location to a total of seven branches. Center City Club's expansion was not planned. Rather, it was a reaction to the increased demand for customer membership and convenience as the city grew larger and more diverse. Now, the organization needed a vision for the future. Center City Club's executive director, Marc Wyatt, was hoping that Richards could provide a road map to accomplish this vision.

Richards replayed her conversation with Wyatt back in her mind. She reviewed the hastily scribbled notes that she had taken. After some initial pleasantries, Wyatt got right to the point. He explained that Center City Club, while performing well during the past few years, ". . . desperately needed to develop a strategic plan for the future. We have seven branches scattered throughout the city, each providing different services to their unique customer bases." Richards asked Wyatt about Center City Club's greatest strengths. "That's an easy one," Wyatt said. "We own prime real estate throughout the city and have some of the best locations in town. We also have a committed workforce who is, for the most part, dedicated and hard working. The city is growing so fast that we are having trouble keeping up with the demand." "That's a good problem to have," remarked Richards, "tell me about your organization's weaknesses. What concerns you the most about the future?" There was a long pause and a deep sigh on the other end of the line. "Well," Wyatt said, "we have probably grown too fast too soon. I used to know every employee's first name. I don't anymore. And we used to really know our customers. It seems we have lost our personal touch for reaching out to our members." When Richards asked Wyatt about competition, he stated that there had been increased competition from some of the larger companies who offered wellness programs onsite for their employees. In addition, gyms offering extended operating hours and a greater variety of fitness programs, including training in the martial arts and yoga, seemed to be popping up every day.

Richards had a few days to put together a one-day strategic planning session for Wyatt and the senior leaders of the organization, including members of the board of directors. She felt she had a lot of information to make a good start but wanted to organize the meeting so that the group could make the most of their strategic planning time.

For Discussion

1. How might Wyatt and the members of Center City Club have avoided their current situation?

2. What information do you think is critical in developing an outline for the strategic planning session?

3. Using the terms introduced in the chapter, develop an agenda for the strategic planning meeting. Where do you think Center City Club's management team should start? Why?

CHAP

EFFECTIVE MANAGERIAL DECISION MAKING

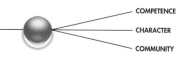

LEADERSHIP

COMPETENCE

CHARACTER

COMMUNITY

CHAPTER OVERVIEW

Consider all the decisions necessary to carry out any major effort—from launching a space satellite to marketing and producing a new line of automobiles. The leaders responsible for these decisions rely on good decision-making skills. A manager's responsibility as a decision maker is very important. While all managers are called upon to make decisions, the kinds of decisions that are required will vary with their level of authority and type of assignment. Poor decisions can be disastrous to a department and an organization. Good decisions facilitate the smooth flow of work and enable the organization to achieve its goals.

This chapter introduces concepts and models that focus on the demands of managerial decision making. Managers and leaders may not always make the right decision, but they can use their knowledge of appropriate decision-making processes to increase the odds of success. Skill as a decision maker is a distinguishing characteristic of most successful managers.[1] We will explore how leaders in organizations make decisions by discussing the seven steps in the decision-making process and examining two commonly used models of decision behavior. Since leaders are frequently involved with groups and teams, we focus on the participative model of group decision making by looking at techniques that leaders can use to improve this process.

LEARNING OBJECTIVES

When you have finished studying this chapter, you should be able to:

1. Describe the nature of the decision-making process and explain each of its seven steps.
2. Describe the rational-economic model of decision making.
3. Discuss the behavioral decision model and its related concepts of bounded rationality, intuition, satisficing, and escalation of commitment.
4. Describe the participative approach to decision making.
5. Discuss the advantages and disadvantages of group decision making.
6. List the various techniques used to improve group decision making.

Facing The Challenge

Gaylord Entertainment Faces Some Tough Decisions

Gaylord Entertainment Company, owner of the Grand Ole Opry and other Nashville, Tennessee, attractions, was a conglomerate in need of some focused decisions and new direction as the 20th century wound down. The company was reeling from a rash of business failures. Originally a broadcasting company, Gaylord bought the Grand Ole Opry and a few related businesses in 1983. In recent years, it seemed as if everything it touched turned sour. In 1998, Gaylord had opened an Orlando branch of its Wild Horse Saloon, a country music nightclub complete with big-screen televisions and balconies overlooking the dance floor. In a stroke of bad timing, that opening coincided with a decline in the popularity of country music, which saw a 26 percent drop in its share of music sales in 2000.

Beginning in 1999, the company spent $29.9 million to acquire a pair of Christian music Web sites, Musicforce.com and Lightsource.com. These acquisitions formed the foundation of the company's online division, Gaylord Digital. Unfortunately, like countless other online start-ups, Gaylord Digital lost far more money than it took in. In addition, its two flagship television stations, The Nashville Network (TNN) and Country Music Television (CMT), were not doing as well as had been expected. Even the crown jewel in the company's assets, its WSM-AM radio station in Nashville, was seeing declining revenues. This is the station that, since the 1920s, has carried the longest-running live program in radio history, The Grand Ole Opry. These and other underperforming ventures

caused the company to suffer losses in 2000 and 2001 that totaled approximately $400 million. Then, there was the matter of The Opryland Hotel of Florida, which was under construction near Orlando. With tourism travel in a slump, was this going to be another case of a good idea with bad timing? Gaylord Entertainment was forced to find out how to get itself back on the road to profitability. In the words of one New York investment analyst, the company "certainly did screw up. They wasted a lot of money down various black holes."

SOURCES: T. Pack, "Gaylord's Story Sounds Like a Country Song," *Central Florida Business*, January 7, 2002, 14–16; and A. Hunt, "Resort Books 1 Million," *The Orlando Sentinel*, January 5, 2002, B1ff.

INTRODUCTION

As the 21st century began, the leaders of Gaylord Entertainment Company were facing some critical decisions. What should they do with their money-losing nightclub, music company, and online services? What did the future hold for its underperforming television stations and radio station? What would their future direction be to get them back on the road to profitability?

Some decisions, like those faced by Gaylord Entertainment, are critical and can have a major impact on personal and organizational lives. Other decisions are more routine but still require that we select an appropriate course of action. This chapter introduces concepts and models that focus on the demands of managerial decision making.

STEPS IN THE DECISION-MAKING PROCESS

LEARNING OBJECTIVE 1

Describe the nature of the decision-making process and explain each of its seven steps.

Decision making

The process through which managers identify and resolve problems and capitalize on opportunities.

Decision making is the process through which managers and leaders identify and resolve problems and capitalize on opportunities. Good decision making is important at all levels in the organization. It begins with recognition or awareness of problems and opportunities and concludes with an assessment of the results of actions taken to solve those problems. Before we begin to examine these steps in greater detail, think about how you make decisions. How skilled a decision maker are you?

Take a few minutes to complete the decision-making process questionnaire (DMPQ) in "Now Apply It." The DMPQ evaluates your current level of decision-making ability.[2] As we progress through the chapter, you will learn more about sharpening these skills, which are an important part of most managerial experiences.

Now Apply It

Assessing Your Decision-Making Skills

This decision-making process questionnaire (DMPQ) evaluates your current decision-making skills. These behaviors are part of most managerial experiences, but you will find that the questions are applicable to your own experience even if you are not yet a manager. If you do not have experience in a management-level position, consider a group you have worked with either in the classroom or in an organization such as a fraternity, sorority, club, church, or service group. Use the following scale to rate the frequency with which you perform the behaviors described in each statement. Place the appropriate number (1–7) in the blank preceding the statement.

RARELY	IRREGULARLY	OCCASIONALLY	USUALLY	FREQUENTLY	ALMOST ALWAYS	CONSISTENTLY/ ALWAYS
1	2	3	4	5	6	7

_____ **1.** I review data about the performance of my work and/or my group's work.
_____ **2.** I seek outside information, such as articles in business magazines and newspapers, to help me evaluate my performance.
_____ **3.** When examining data, I allow for sufficient time to identify problems.
_____ **4.** Based on the data, I identify problem areas needing action.
_____ **5.** To generate alternative solutions, I review problems from different perspectives.
_____ **6.** I list many possible ways of reaching a solution for an identified problem.
_____ **7.** I research methods that have been used to solve similar problems.
_____ **8.** When generating alternative courses of action, I seek the opinions of others.
_____ **9.** I explicitly state the criteria I will use for judging alternative courses of action.
_____ **10.** I list both positive and negative aspects of alternative decisions.
_____ **11.** I consider how possible decisions could affect others.
_____ **12.** I estimate the probabilities of the possible outcomes of each alternative.
_____ **13.** I study information about problems that require my decisions.
_____ **14.** I determine if I need additional data in light of my objectives and the urgency of the situation.
_____ **15.** To reach a decision, I rely on my judgment and experience as well as on the available data.
_____ **16.** I support my choices with facts.
_____ **17.** Before finally accepting a decision, I evaluate possible ways to implement it.
_____ **18.** I choose the simplest and least costly methods of putting my decisions into effect.
_____ **19.** I select resources and establish time frames as part of my implementation strategy.
_____ **20.** I choose implementation strategies that help achieve my objectives.

Enter your score for each category in the following table, and sum the five category scores to obtain your total score. Enter that total score in the space indicated. Scores can range from a low of 4 to a high of 28 in each skill category. Total scores can range from a low of 20 to a high of 140. The higher the score in a particular category, the more refined your skill in that aspect of the decision-making process.

SKILL AREA	STATEMENTS	SCORE
Diagnosing the problem	1, 2, 3, 4	_____
Generating alternatives	5, 6, 7, 8	_____
Evaluating alternatives	9, 10, 11, 12	_____
Reaching decisions	13, 14, 15, 16	_____
Choosing implementation strategies	17, 18, 19, 20	_____
Total Score		_____

SOURCE: P. Fandt, *Management Skills: Practice and Experiences* (St. Paul, Minn.: West Publishing, 1994).

An effective decision-making process generally includes the seven steps shown in Figure 6.1. Although the figure shows the steps proceeding in a logical, sequential order, managerial decision making often unfolds in a quite disorderly and complex manner. Keep in mind that managers are influenced at each step in the decision-making process by their individual personalities, attitudes, and behaviors (as we will discuss in Chapter 14), ethics and values (as discussed in Chapter 3), and culture, as we will discuss later in this chapter. First, though, we will briefly examine each of the seven steps in managerial decision making.

Figure 6.1 | Seven Steps in the Decision-Making Process

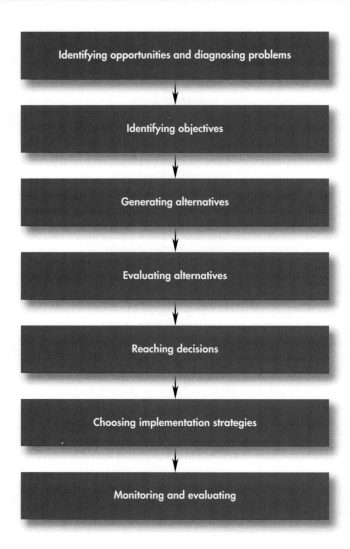

IDENTIFYING OPPORTUNITIES AND DIAGNOSING PROBLEMS

Decision makers must know where action is required. Consequently, the first step in the decision-making process is the clear identification of opportunities or the diagnosis of problems that require a decision. Managers regularly review data related to their areas of responsibility, including both outside information and reports and information from within the organization. The BP Company, described in "At The Forefront," studied consumer and lifestyle trends before making the decision to develop its upscale convenience stores, called BP Connect.[3] Discrepancies between actual and desired conditions alert a manager to a potential opportunity or problem. Identifying opportunities and problems is not always easy, considering human behavior in organizations. Sometimes, the origins of a problem may be deeply rooted in an individual's past experience, the complex structure of the organization, or some combination of individual and organizational factors. Therefore, a manager must pay particular attention to ensure that problems and op-

At The Forefront

BP Connects with the Future

BP Products North America (formerly known as British Petroleum) is redefining the concept of convenience in the gas station/food mart service sector. Historically, a store was branded "convenient" based on its location and hours of operation. But now the gas-and-convenience store industry is wrestling with a new wave of competition. Many grocery store chains have entered the fuel business just as many drug store chains have entered the food business. While some convenience chains struggle to compete on price and promotions, BP has decided to compete by investing in innovation.

Convenience means a lot more than location and hours of operation to today's consumers. People live much busier lives, so BP is trying to add convenience at all levels by combining different products and services under one roof in its BP Connect stores, which it views as the convenience store of the new century. These upscale convenience stores feature a gourmet coffee, pastry, and sandwich shop called The Wild Bean Café. While sipping their cappuccino, travelers can access weather information, travel data, and road maps through an online information kiosk. BP has seen its position in the convenience sector rise in each market where these new stores have been introduced.

In spite of the fact that they are in the oil and gas business, London-based BP executives have been outspoken advocates of developing renewable energy sources. As such, BP has a solar energy division that is considered one of the world's largest manufacturers of photovoltaic systems, which convert sunlight into electricity. Next time you pass by a BP Connect store, take a close look at the top of that high arching canopy above the gasoline pumps. What you are looking at is an array of those same photovoltaic cells, generating much of the electricity needed to pump BP's low pollution blend gasoline and power the BP Connect store.

SOURCE: R. Burnett, "BP Connects With the Future," *The Orlando Sentinel*, January 19, 2002, B1ff.

portunities are assessed as accurately as possible. Other times the problem may be so obvious that it is easily recognized, even by the casual observer.

An assessment of opportunities and problems will be only as accurate as the information on which it is based. Therefore, managers put a premium on obtaining accurate, reliable information. Poor-quality or inaccurate information can waste time and lead a manager to overlook the underlying causes of a situation.[4] This basic principle is well understood by U.S. business leaders, who spend millions of dollars each year on market research to identify trends in consumer preferences and buying decisions. For example, it was Mattel's monitoring the trends and shifting tastes of young girls that prompted the company to update its aging Barbie doll. The year 2002 would see the introduction of an array of new Barbies, including a soft-body version with glow-in-the-dark hair and pajamas—the perfect combination for little girls to bring to bed. Mattel's plan called for establishing Barbie as a ubiquitous "lifestyle brand," with a product for a girl's every fashion need.[5] Nevertheless, crucial information is sometimes overlooked. In a classic blunder several years ago, the Coca-Cola Company developed the infamous "New Coke" after exhaustive taste tests were conducted. However, the company failed to assess one crucial factor: brand loyalty. The unveiling of the New Coke was one of the most spectacular marketing flops of all time.[6]

Even when high-quality information is collected, it may be misinterpreted. Sometimes, misinterpretations accumulate over time as information is consistently misunderstood or problematic events are unrecognized.[7] Most major disasters or accidents turn out to have had long incubation periods in which warning signs were misunderstood or overlooked. Consider the following regarding some recent news-headline-grabbing events. Months before ValuJet Flight 592 crashed into the Florida Everglades, killing all 110 people on board, the Federal Aviation Administration had the safety data it later used to ground the airline. Unfortunately, this information was stored in warehouses out of sight of the FAA's key decision makers. In Saudi Arabia, U.S. authorities wanted to widen the security zone that surrounded the complex that housed U.S. troops, but the Saudis denied the request.

It wasn't until four days after a terrorist bomb killed 19 Americans that Defense Secretary William Perry learned about the denial.[8] And none of us is likely to soon forget how misinterpreted information regarding O-ring safety led to the space shuttle Challenger disaster, in which all seven crew members perished.[9]

To complicate matters further, even when managers have accurate information and interpret it correctly, factors beyond their control may affect the identification of opportunities and problems. Nevertheless, by insisting on high-quality information and interpreting it carefully, managers will improve their chances of making good decisions.

IDENTIFYING OBJECTIVES

Objectives
The desired results to be attained when making decisions.

Objectives reflect the results the organization wants to attain. Both the quantity and quality of the desired results should be specified, for these aspects of the objectives will ultimately guide the decision maker in selecting the appropriate course of action. In the opening "Facing the Challenge," the objective of Gaylord Entertainment was to reduce its mounting debt and return to profitability.

As you will recall from Chapters 4 and 5, objectives are often referred to as targets, standards, and ends. They may be measured along a variety of dimensions. For example, profit or cost objectives are measured in monetary units, productivity objectives may be measured in units of output per labor hour, and quality objectives may be measured in defects per million units produced.

Objectives can be expressed for long spans of time (years or decades) or for short spans of time (hours, days, or months). Long-range objectives usually direct much of the strategic decision making of the organization, while short-range objectives usually guide operational decision making. Regardless of the time frame, the objectives guide the ensuing decision-making process.

GENERATING ALTERNATIVES

Once an opportunity has been identified or a problem diagnosed correctly, a manager develops various ways to solve the problem and achieve objectives. This step requires creativity and imagination. In generating alternatives, the manager must keep in mind the goals and objectives that he or she is trying to achieve. Ideally, several different alternatives will emerge. In this way, the manager increases the likelihood that many good alternative courses of action will be considered and evaluated. In the never-ending burger wars, Burger King recently considered many alternative additions to its menu to combat rival McDonald's menu changes. In an effort to provide more choices, Burger King evaluated such additions as a veggie burger, eggwich, Chicken Whopper, King Supreme, onion rings with zesty sauce, and an old-fashioned, ice cream-based milk shake.[10]

Managers may rely on their training, personal experience, education, and knowledge of the situation to generate alternatives. Viewing the problem from varying perspectives often requires input from other people, such as peers, employees, supervisors, and groups within the organization. For example, consumer product companies such as Procter & Gamble often use customer focus groups to supply information that can be used in this stage of decision making.

The alternatives can be standard and obvious as well as innovative and unique. Standard solutions often include options that the organization has used in the past. Innovative approaches may be developed through such strategies as brainstorming, nominal group technique, and the Delphi technique. These strategies, which encourage consideration of multiple alternatives, will be discussed in more detail later in the chapter as methods for enhancing group decision making.

EVALUATING ALTERNATIVES

The fourth step in the decision-making process involves determining the value or adequacy of the alternatives generated. Which solution is the best? Fundamental to this step is the ability to assess the value or relative advantages and disadvantages of each alternative under consideration. Predetermined decision criteria, such as the quality desired, anticipated costs, benefits, uncertainties, and risks of each alternative, may be used in the evaluation process. The result should be a ranking of the alternatives. For example, the manager might ask, "Will this alternative help achieve our quality objective? What is the anticipated cost of this alternative? What are the uncertainties and risks associated with this alternative?" In Chapter 7, we will examine more thoroughly the tools used by managers to evaluate alternatives.

REACHING DECISIONS

Decision making is commonly associated with making a final choice. Reaching the decision is really only one step in the process, however. Although choosing an alternative would seem to be a straightforward proposition (that is, simply consider all the alternatives and select the one that best solves the problem), in reality, the choice is rarely clear-cut. Because the best decisions are often based on careful judgments, making a good decision involves carefully examining all the facts, determining whether sufficient information is available, and finally selecting the best alternative.[11]

In a classic example of cautious restraint, when Lou Gerstner took over as CEO of IBM Corporation, Wall Street expected him to take quick and bold action since IBM was losing its strong hold in the computer industry. When he took no action that Wall Street could see in his first year, he came under fire for being indecisive. But Gerstner was doing his homework, reviewing every IBM planning document that had been written since the late 1970s. Then, during 1994 and early 1995, Gerstner removed many ingrained operating procedures as he began reshaping IBM's organizational culture. Six billion dollars in expenses were cut, and stock prices doubled as IBM had its first profitable year since 1990.[12]

CHOOSING IMPLEMENTATION STRATEGIES

The bridge between reaching a decision and evaluating the results is the implementation phase of the decision-making process. When decisions involve taking action or making changes, choosing ways to put these actions or changes into effect becomes an essential managerial task. The keys to effective implementation are (1) sensitivity to those who will be affected by the decision and (2) proper planning and consideration of the resources necessary to carry out the decision.

Those who will be affected by the decision must understand the choice and why it was made; that is, the decision must be accepted and supported by the people who are responsible for its implementation. These needs can be met by involving employees in the early stages of the decision process so that they will be motivated and committed to its successful implementation. This is advice that a top-level MCI executive would have been wise to heed a few years ago when he decided to relocate MCI's 4,000-employee systems division from Washington, D.C., to Colorado Springs. This decision was made with the thought that the spectacular setting in this new location would inspire workers. Instead,

© GETTYIMAGES/DIGITAL VISION

Involving employees in the early stages of the decision-making process helps these employees become motivated and committed to its successful implementation.

numerous executives and engineers, as well as hundreds of the division's minority population, refused to relocate or left MCI shortly after relocating. These workers had been accustomed to living in larger, ethnically diverse urban areas and found Colorado Springs to be too isolated and politically conservative, with little diversity and fewer cultural activities.[13]

According to recent research, senior executives frequently complain that middle and operating managers fail to take actions necessary to implement decisions. Implementation problems often occur as a result of poor understanding and lack of commitment to decisions on the part of middle management.[14] Poor understanding and lack of commitment tend to be less prevalent at upper levels of management. This is certainly evident in the case of a recent major automobile recall by the Saturn Motor Company. Executives at Saturn operated swiftly and decisively when it was learned that there was a small chance of engine fires due to an alternator wiring problem. While only 34 fires had been reported, company officials initiated a media blitz of information detailing the recall of over 380,000 automobiles to make the necessary repairs.[15]

The planning process is a key to effective implementation. Without proper planning, the decision may not be accepted by others in the organization, cost overruns may occur, needed resources may not be available, and the objectives may not be accomplished on schedule. To plan properly for implementation, managers need to perform the following activities:

* Determine how things will look when the decision is fully operational.
* Draw up a chronological schedule of the activities and tasks that must be carried out to make the decision fully operational.
* List the resources and activities required to implement each activity or task.
* Estimate the time needed for each activity or task.
* Assign responsibility for each activity or task to specific individuals.

MONITORING AND EVALUATING

No decision-making process is complete until the impact of the decision has been evaluated. Managers must observe the impact of the decision as objectively as possible and take further corrective action if it becomes necessary. Quantifiable objectives can be established even before the solution to the problem is put into effect. For example, when 3M began a five-year program dubbed "Challenge '95" to increase quality control and reduce manufacturing costs by 35 percent, the company constantly monitored its efforts to determine whether it was making progress toward those goals.

Monitoring the decision is useful whether the feedback is positive or negative. Positive feedback indicates that the decision is working and that it should be continued and perhaps applied elsewhere in the organization. Negative feedback indicates either that the implementation requires more time, resources, effort, or planning than originally thought or that the decision was a poor one and needs to be reexamined.

The importance of assessing the success or failure of a decision cannot be overstated. Evaluation of past decisions as well as other information should drive future decision making as part of an ongoing decision-making feedback loop.

Thus far, we have explored how managers in organizations make decisions by examining the seven steps in the decision-making process. The process starts when the organization recognizes a problem or becomes aware that an opportunity exists. It concludes with an assessment of the results. As we have stressed, the ability to make effective decisions is a distinguishing characteristic of most successful managers.[16] After reviewing the importance of information technology on the decision-making process, we will discuss two models of decision behavior.

INFORMATION TECHNOLOGY AND THE DECISION-MAKING PROCESS

While timely and accurate information is useful in virtually every stage of the decision-making process, it is especially critical at the first and last steps. Problems are identified when information reveals that some aspect of performance is less than desirable. The sooner accurate performance information can be placed in the hands of the decision makers, the sooner problems can be corrected, lessening the potentially undesirable or costly consequences to the organization. When a decision is finally made and implemented, the follow-up monitoring and evaluating process is performed to ensure that desirable results are again being achieved. Once again, timeliness and accuracy in performance feedback are critical, for if the selected decision alternative was not a good one, undesirable consequences will continue to be suffered. The quantum leaps that are being made in the processing and distribution of information are providing managers with greatly improved capabilities for problem recognition and successful solution as they engage in the decision-making process. Even on a personal level, advances in information technology can facilitate the decision-making process. For example, through its specially designed Web site, General Motors provides consumers with access to a variety of pieces of critical information that will aid in their automobile purchase decisions.[17]

MODELS OF DECISION MAKING

Many models of the decision-making process can be found in the management literature. Although these models vary in scope, assumptions, and applicability, they are similar in that each focuses on the complexity of decision-making processes. In this section, we examine two decision-making models: the rational-economic model and the behavioral model. Our goal is to demonstrate the variations in how decision making is perceived and interpreted.[18]

RATIONAL-ECONOMIC DECISION MODEL

The rational-economic decision model is prescriptive rather than descriptive; that is, it concentrates on how decisions should be made, not on how they actually are made. This model, which focuses on how a decision maker should behave, is said to be normative. The model makes several important assumptions about the manager and the decision-making process:

LEARNING OBJECTIVE 2
Describe the rational-economic model of decision making.

- The manager is assumed to have "perfect" (that is, completely accurate) information and to have all the information that is relevant to the situation.
- The model assumes that the decision maker operates to accomplish objectives that are known and agreed upon and has an extensive list of alternatives from which to choose.
- As the model's name implies, it assumes that the manager will be rational, systematic, and logical in assessing each alternative and its associated probabilities.
- The model assumes that the manager will work in the best interests of the organization.

Also implicit in the model is the assumption that ethical dilemmas do not arise in the decision-making process.

As these assumptions suggest, the rational-economic decision model does not address the influences that affect the decision environment or describe how managers actually make decisions; instead, it provides guidelines to help the organization or group reach an ideal outcome. As a consequence, in practice, the model may not always be a realistic depiction of managerial behavior. For example, the model portrays decision making as a straightforward process. In reality, making a decision is rarely that simple. First, people hardly ever have access to complete and perfect information. Second, even if information about all possible alternatives were available, individuals are limited in their ability to comprehend and process vast amounts of information. Third, decision makers seldom have adequate knowledge about the future consequences of alternatives. Furthermore, in most decision-making situations, personal factors (such as fatigue, emotions, attitudes, motives, or behaviors) are likely to intervene to prevent a manager from always acting in a completely rational manner. In addition, an individual's culture and ethical values will influence the decision process.

From a global perspective, it is especially important to be sensitive to how culture influences decision making. Individuals from different backgrounds and cultures have different experiences, values, and behaviors, which in turn influence the way they process information and make decisions. It is particularly important for managers to recognize and appreciate this as modern organizations become increasingly global in their operations. We will discover in Chapter 18 the full extent to which organizations, large and small, are forming global alliances through e-commerce and Internet linkages. For example, Japanese managers follow a unique consensual decision-making process in which subordinates are involved in considering the future direction of their companies. Individuals and groups who have ideas for improvement or change discuss them extensively with a large number of peers and managers. During this lengthy information communication process, some agreements are hammered out. At this point, a formal document is drafted and circulated for the signature or personalized stamp of every manager who is considered relevant to the decision. Only after all the relevant managers have put their seals on the proposal is the idea or suggestion implemented.[19]

Managerial decision making is also influenced by the individual's ethics and values. As we discussed in Chapter 3, managers have power by virtue of their positions to make decisions that affect people's lives and well-being; consequently the potential for ethical dilemmas is always present.[20] In an **ethical dilemma**, managers must decide whether or not to do something that will benefit themselves or the organization but may be considered unethical and perhaps illegal.

Ethical dilemmas are going to occur more and more frequently in the future as a result of the dramatic changes the business environment is undergoing. For example, managers may have to answer questions such as the following: What do companies owe employees who are let go after 30 years of service? Is it right to cancel a contract with a loyal distributor when a cheaper supplier becomes available? Is it proper to develop condominiums on land that is an unofficial wildlife refuge?

The following questions may help you when you face a situation that has ethical implications:[21]

- Have you accurately assessed the problem?
- Do you have all the necessary information?
- Where are your loyalties?
- Have you generated a list of possible alternatives and considered how each will affect the other parties involved?
- Have you tested each alternative by asking whether it is legal, fair, and just to all parties involved?
- Would your decision change if you were to disclose it to your family, your boss, or society as a whole?
- Does your decision have any symbolic potential? Could it be misunderstood?

Managers should encourage ethical decision making throughout the organization by providing subordinates with clear guidelines for making decisions and es-

Ethical dilemma
A situation in which a person must decide whether or not to do something that, although benefiting oneself or the organization, may be considered unethical and perhaps illegal.

tablishing rules for enforcing the guidelines. Both the guidelines and the rules should be communicated to subordinates on a regular basis.

BEHAVIORAL DECISION MODEL

Unlike the rational-economic model, the **behavioral decision model** acknowledges human limitations that make rational decisions difficult to achieve. The behavioral decision model is descriptive and provides a framework for understanding the process that managers actually use when selecting from among alternatives.

The behavioral decision model suggests that a person's cognitive ability to process information is limited. In other words, a human being can handle only so much information before overload occurs. Even if complete information were available to decision makers, these cognitive limitations would impede them from making completely rational decisions.

Applying this assumption to managerial decision making, the model suggests that managers usually attempt to behave rationally within their limited perception of a situation. But most organizational situations are so complex that managers are forced to view problems within sharply restricted bounds. They frequently try to compensate for their limited ability to cope with the information demands of complex problems by developing simple models. Thus, managers' behaviors can be considered rational, but only in terms of their simplified view of the problem.

The behavioral decision model introduces several concepts that are important to understanding how we make decisions. These concepts include bounded rationality, intuition, satisficing, and escalation of commitment.

BOUNDED RATIONALITY The notion of **bounded rationality** recognizes that people cannot know everything; they are limited by such organizational constraints as time, information, resources, and their own mental capacities.[22] Bounded rationality is a useful concept because it explains why different individuals with exactly the same information may make different decisions.

Bounded rationality affects several key aspects of the decision-making process. First, decision makers do not search out all possible alternatives and then select the best. Rather, they identify and evaluate alternatives only until an acceptable solution is found. Having found a satisfactory alternative, the decision maker stops searching for additional solutions. Other, and potentially better, alternatives may exist, but they will not be identified or considered because the first workable solution has been accepted. Therefore, only a fraction of the available alternatives may be considered due to the decision maker's information-processing limitations.

INTUITION Intuition has been described as everything from an unconscious analysis based on past experience to a paranormal ability called a "sixth sense."[23] Several theories have attempted to explain intuition, but none has been proved. We do know that intuition is based on the individual's years of practice and experience. For example, a decision maker who detects similarities between the current situation and one encountered previously will select or modify actions that proved effective in that situation in the past.[24] Managers use intuition to obtain a quick understanding of a situation and to identify solutions without going through extensive analysis. With four decades of experience in the theme park industry, Bob Gault, described in "Leaders In Action," relies heavily on intuition as he interacts with workers and surveys guests' opinions while walking around Universal Orlando's two

Good decision makers search out all possible alternatives and then select the best.

LEARNING OBJECTIVE 3

Discuss the behavioral decision model and its related concepts of bounded rationality, intuition, satisficing, and escalation of commitment.

Behavioral decision model
A descriptive framework for understanding that a person's cognitive ability to process information is limited.

Bounded rationality
Recognizes that people are limited by such organizational constraints as time, information, resources, and their own mental capacities.

Intuition
An unconscious analysis based on past experience.

Leaders In Action

Universal Orlando's President Connects with Workers

While studying as a pre-dental student in 1964, Bob Gault's career path took an abrupt turn. As he swept streets at Sea World San Diego on a summer job, Gault was captivated by the atmosphere of fun in the park. He realized then and there that his life wasn't going to be spent looking into people's mouths. Fast forward almost 40 years and we find Gault being installed as the president and chief operating officer of Universal Orlando's two theme parks—Universal Studios Orlando and Islands of Adventure. In those intervening years, Gault had been a 29-year veteran of three Sea World parks. He left Sea World Orlando in 1993 to assume the presidency of Universal Studios Hollywood and later oversaw the immensely successful opening of Universal Studios Japan in 2001. Now, he was back on home soil, and the challenges he faced were significant.

Attendance at the two Universal Orlando parks had fallen about 9 percent in 2001, largely due to the post 9/11 downturn in the tourism market. Morale among the 12,000 hourly workers was low due to staff cutbacks and reductions in work schedules. Upon arrival, Gault decided that he had to "gain their confidence and get them pumped up." Gault immediately made decisions that quickly won over the workers. Pay raises were given to hourly workers. Work schedules that had been cut back after September 11 were restored. A new generation of high-voltage, song-and-dance street performers was introduced. New live-action stage shows and roving impromptu music, dancing, comedy, magic, and action performances were added to the two parks. Plans were made for three new major rides or shows to debut in 2003.

Gault is a hands-on manager with a fun-loving nature. Colleagues say that this gives him an edge when it comes to figuring out what vacationers want. He is always out in the park listening to guests and employees for one purpose: to make improvements. In the words of a senior vice president for one of Gault's Orlando competitors, "I call his style Management by Walking Around." So far Gault is getting a thumbs up from workers. His decisions to give raises and restore hourly workers' schedules have won him plenty of early warmth from the ranks.

Despite a strong year-end in 2001 and an even stronger beginning to 2002, Gault understands that the fight for tourists' attention and repeat business will be tougher than when he ran Orlando's Sea World in the 1980s (before Universal Orlando was even built and when Disney World had only half of the four theme parks it has today). Gault says, "Now Orlando is the Super Bowl of tourism. We're in a big, tough game here every day." Any future decisions Gault makes will undoubtedly fit his philosophy of future theme park entertainment: creating a mood that combines fantasy and ideals such as heroism and friendship. "People want to come and hold hands with each other. The human spirit needs bonding and connecting, especially now. We all need to escape sometimes—together."

SOURCES: Robert Johnson, "Universal Orlando's New Thrill Seeker," *Central Florida Business*, April 15, 2002, 14–15; Robert Johnson, "Universal Orlando Thinks Big," *The Orlando Sentinel*, March 16, 2002, A1ff; and R. Johnson, "It's Official: Gault Is in Charge of Recharging Universal Orlando," *The Orlando Sentinel*, February 26, 2002, C1ff.

parks.[25] Some experts on corporate decision making feel that it would be a good thing if there was more behavior like this. They feel that many U.S. corporations place too much emphasis on decision analysis and suggest that managers should trust their feelings and experience more often.[26]

Satisficing
The search for and acceptance of something that is satisfactory rather than perfect or optimal.

SATISFICING   Satisficing means searching for and accepting something that is satisfactory rather than insisting on the perfect or optimal. Satisficers do not try to find optimal solutions to problems, but search until they find an acceptable or satisfactory solution and then adopt it. In short, managers tend to satisfice rather than optimize in considering and selecting alternatives. Some satisficing behavior is unavoidable, because managers do not have access to all possible contingencies in making decisions. When the Hewlett-Packard Corporation decided it was going to enter the home personal computer business, it established a goal of simply becoming one of the top three competitors in this market. This could be viewed as a satisficing decision, for Hewlett-Packard management had identified a level of performance that would be satisfactory, but certainly not perfect.[27]

ESCALATION OF COMMITMENT   When managers face evidence that an initial decision is not working, they frequently react by committing more resources, even when feedback indicates the action is wrong.[28] This **escalation of commitment** phenomenon is the tendency to commit more to a previously selected course of action than would be expected if the manager followed an effective decision-making process.[29] One reason for escalation of commitment is that individuals feel responsible for negative consequences and try to justify their previous decisions. Managers may also stay with a course of action simply because they believe consistency is a desirable behavior. In addition, managers may worry that if they change course, others may regard the original decision as a mistake or a failure. For example, Honda continued to invest in and produce electric-powered cars for two years after their introduction despite their low popularity and the industry trends away from pure electrics and toward developing low-emission hybrids. Eventually, in early 1999, Honda decided to stop building pure electric cars, and wrote them off as expensive, inconvenient, and unpopular flops.[30]

In contrast, consider how Fred Smith, CEO of FedEx, changed course and cut the company's losses on ZapMail. ZapMail was a satellite-based network that was to provide two-hour document delivery service. Believing FedEx's hard-copy delivery services would be severely eroded by the burgeoning electronic mail market, Smith decided to invest heavily in ZapMail. Unfortunately, he failed to anticipate the impact of low-cost fax machines, and FedEx lost over $300 million in the first year alone. Smith admits that making the decision to disband ZapMail was difficult after the organization had committed so many resources to the concept and the technology.

Escalation of commitment
The tendency to increase commitment to a previously selected course of action beyond the level that would be expected if the manager followed an effective decision-making process.

WHAT MAKES A HIGH-QUALITY DECISION?

How can managers tell whether they have made the best possible decision? One way is to wait until the results are in, but that can take a long time. In the meantime, managers can focus on the decision-making process. Although nothing can guarantee a perfect decision, using vigilance can make a good decision more likely. **Vigilance** means being concerned for and attentive to the correct decision-making procedures. Vigilant decision makers use the following procedures:[31]

Vigilance
The concern for and attention to the process of making a decision that occurs when the decision maker considers seven critical procedures.

- Survey the full range of objectives to be fulfilled and identify the values and qualities implicated by the choices.
- Thoroughly canvass a wide range of alternative courses of action. This is the idea-gathering process, which should be separate from idea evaluation.
- Carefully weigh whatever they know about the costs and risks of both the negative and positive consequences that could flow from each alternative.
- Intensively search for new high-quality information relevant to further evaluation of the alternatives.
- Assimilate and take into account any new advice or information to which they are exposed, even when the information or advice does not support the course of action initially preferred.
- Reexamine all the possible consequences of all known alternatives before making a final choice, including those originally regarded as unacceptable.
- Make detailed provisions for implementing or executing the chosen course of action and give special attention to contingency plans that might be required if various known risks materialize.

While vigilance will not guarantee perfect decisions every time, this approach can help managers be confident they have followed procedures that will yield the best possible decision under the circumstances. Spending more time at this stage can save time later in the decision process.

GROUP CONSIDERATIONS IN DECISION MAKING

So far in this chapter, we have been examining how managers make decisions individually. In practice, managers often work with their employees and peers in the company and may need to solicit input from them. Decision making is frequently entrusted to a group—a board, standing committee, ad hoc committee, or task force. Group decision making is becoming more common as organizations focus on improving customer service through quality management and push decision making to lower levels.[32] Accordingly, this section examines some of the issues related to using groups to make decisions.

PARTICIPATIVE DECISION MAKING

LEARNING OBJECTIVE 4

Describe the participative approach to decision making.

Participative decision making is not a single technique that can be applied to all situations. As we will see, managers can use a variety of techniques to involve the members of the organization in decision making. The appropriate level of subordinate participation in decision making depends on the manager, the employees, the organization, and the nature of the decision itself.

PARTICIPATIVE MODELS Vroom and Yetton developed a model for participation in decision making that helps managers determine when group decision making is appropriate.[33] According to this participative model, the effectiveness of a group decision is governed by both its quality and its acceptance (the degree to which group members are committed to the decision they have made). Updated by Vroom and Jago to reflect the decision-making environment of managers more adequately, this model expands the three basic decision-making methods (individual, consultative, and group) into five styles of possible decision participation.[34] To arrive at the best decision, a manager needs to analyze the situation and then choose one of the five decision-making styles.

As Table 6.1 shows, the five styles can be arranged along a continuum. The decision methods become progressively more participative as one moves from the highly autocratic style (AI), in which the manager decides alone, to the consultative style (CI), in which the manager consults with the group before deciding, to the group style (GII), in which the manager allows the group to decide.[35]

According to Vroom and Jago, the nature of the decision itself determines the appropriate degree of participation, and they provide diagnostic questions to help managers select the appropriate level. Figure 6.2 shows how these questions can be used in a decision tree format to arrive at the appropriate decision style. (The structure and use of decision trees will be discussed in more detail in Chapter 7.) For the sake of simplicity, the decision tree in Figure 6.2 treats each question as having only two answers. By starting at the left and answering the questions, managers can follow the tree to arrive at one of the decision styles described in Table 6.1.

In general, a participative decision style is desirable when subordinates have useful information and share the organization's goals, when subordinates' commitment to the decision is essential, when timeliness is not crucial, and when conflict is unlikely. At the same time, group decision making is more complex than decision making by individuals, but good communication and conflict-management skills can overcome this difficulty.[36]

It is important to note that inappropriate use of either group or individual decision making can be costly. Ineffective use of groups wastes organizational resources because the participants' time could have been spent on other tasks; it can also lead to boredom and reduce motivation when participants feel that their time has been wasted. Making decisions individually that would have been better made

Table 6.1 | Decision Styles

	DECISION STYLE	DESCRIPTION
Highly autocratic	AI	The manager solves the decision problem alone using information available at the time.
	AII	The manager solves the decision problem alone after obtaining necessary information from subordinates.
	CI	The manager solves the decision problem after obtaining ideas and suggestions from subordinates individually. The decision may or may not reflect their counsel.
	CII	The manager solves the decision problem after obtaining ideas and suggestions from subordinates as a group. The decision may or may not reflect their counsel.
	GII	The group analyzes the problem, identifies and evaluates alternatives, and makes a decision. The manager acts as coordinator of the group of subordinates and accepts and implements any solution that has the support of the group.
Highly democratic		

NOTE: A = autocratic; C = consultative; G = group.

SOURCE: Adapted and reprinted from LEADERSHIP AND DECISION-MAKING, by Victor H. Vroom and Philip W. Yetton, by permission of the University of Pittsburgh Press. © 1973 by University of Pittsburgh Press.

by groups can lead to poor coordination among organization members, less commitment to quality, and little emphasis on creativity, as well as poor decisions.[37]

GROUP SIZE In deciding whether a participative model of decision making is appropriate, a manager must also consider the size of the group. In general, as group size increases, the following changes in the decision-making process are likely to be observed:[38]

- The demands on the leader's time and attention are greater, and the leader is more psychologically distant from the other members. This becomes much more of a problem in self-managed teams, in which several individuals can take on leadership roles.
- The group's tolerance of direction from the leader is greater, and the team's decision making becomes more centralized.
- The atmosphere is less friendly, actions are less personal, more subgroups form, and in general, members are less satisfied.
- Rules and procedures become more formalized.

As our discussion thus far suggests, both group and individual decision making offer potential advantages and disadvantages. These are examined in the next sections. Then, we turn our attention to structured techniques managers can use to improve group decision making.

Figure 6.2 | Vroom and Jago Decision Tree

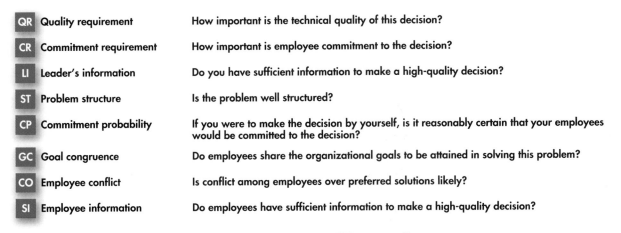

QR	Quality requirement	How important is the technical quality of this decision?
CR	Commitment requirement	How important is employee commitment to the decision?
LI	Leader's information	Do you have sufficient information to make a high-quality decision?
ST	Problem structure	Is the problem well structured?
CP	Commitment probability	If you were to make the decision by yourself, is it reasonably certain that your employees would be committed to the decision?
GC	Goal congruence	Do employees share the organizational goals to be attained in solving this problem?
CO	Employee conflict	Is conflict among employees over preferred solutions likely?
SI	Employee information	Do employees have sufficient information to make a high-quality decision?

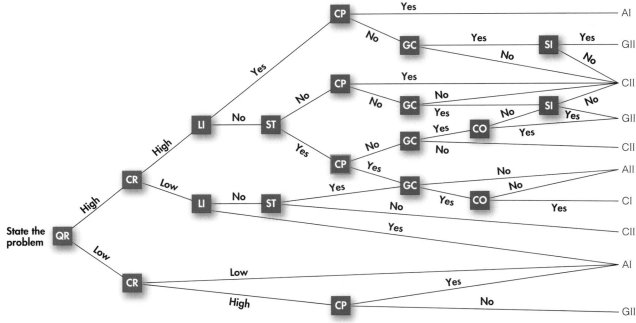

SOURCE: Reprinted from V.H. Vroom and A.G. Jago, *The New Leadership: Managing Participation in Organizations* 1988. Upper Saddle River, NJ: Prentice Hall. Copyright 1988 by V.H. Vroom and A.G. Jago. Used with permission of the authors.

ADVANTAGES OF GROUP DECISION MAKING

LEARNING OBJECTIVE 5

Discuss the advantages and disadvantages of group decision making.

Committees, task forces, and ad hoc groups are frequently assigned to identify and recommend decision alternatives or, in some cases, to actually make important decisions. In essence, a group is a tool that can focus the experience and expertise of several people on a particular problem or situation. Thus, a group offers the advantage of greater total knowledge. Groups accumulate more information, knowledge, and facts than individuals and often consider more alternatives. Each person in the group is able to draw on his or her unique education, experience, insights, and other resources and contribute those to the group. The varied backgrounds, training levels, and expertise of group members also help overcome tunnel vision by enabling the group to view the problem in more than one way.

Participation in group decision making usually leads to higher member satisfaction. People tend to accept a decision more readily and to be better satisfied with it when they have participated in making that decision. In addition, people will better understand and be more committed to a decision in which they have had a say than to a decision made for them. As a result, such a decision is more likely to be implemented successfully. A summary of the advantages of group decision making appears in Table 6.2.

DISADVANTAGES OF GROUP DECISION MAKING

While groups have many potential benefits, we all know that they can also be frustrating. In fact, the traditional interacting group is prone to a variety of difficulties. One obvious disadvantage of group decision making is the time required to make a decision (see Table 6.2). The time needed for group discussion and the associated compromising and selecting of a decision alternative can be considerable. Time costs money, so a waste of time becomes a disadvantage if a decision made by a group could have been made just as effectively by an individual working alone. Consequently, group decisions should be avoided when speed and efficiency are the primary considerations.

A second disadvantage is that the group discussion may be dominated by an individual or subgroup. Effectiveness can be reduced if one individual, such as the group leader, dominates the discussion by talking too much or being closed to other points of view. Some group leaders try to control the group and provide the major input. Such dominance can stifle other group members' willingness to participate and could cause decision alternatives to be ignored or overlooked. All group members need to be encouraged and permitted to contribute.

Another disadvantage of group decision making is that members may be less concerned with the group's goals than with their own personal goals. They may become so sidetracked in trying to win an argument that they forget about group performance. On the other hand, a group may try too hard to compromise and consequently may not make optimal decisions. Sometimes this stems from the desire to maintain friendships and avoid disagreements. Often groups exert tremendous social pressure on individuals to conform to established or expected patterns of behavior. Especially when they are dealing with important and controversial issues, interacting groups may be prone to a phenomenon called groupthink.[39]

Groupthink is an agreement-at-any-cost mentality that results in ineffective group decision making. It occurs when groups are highly cohesive, have highly

The varied backgrounds, training levels, and expertise of group members enable the group to view a problem in more than one way.

Groupthink
An agreement-at-any-cost mentality that results in ineffective group decision making.

Table 6.2 | Advantages and Disadvantages of Group Decision Making

ADVANTAGES	DISADVANTAGES
• Experience and expertise of several individuals available	• Greater time requirement
• More information, data, and facts accumulated	• Minority domination
• Problems viewed from several perspectives	• Compromise
• Higher member satisfaction	• Concern for individual rather than group goals
• Greater acceptance and commitment to decisions	• Social pressure to conform
	• Groupthink

directive leaders, are insulated so they have no clear ways to get objective information, and—because they lack outside information—have little hope that a better solution might be found than the one proposed by the leader or other influential group members.[40] These conditions foster the illusion that the group is invulnerable, right, and more moral than outsiders. They also encourage the development of self-appointed "mind guards" who bring pressure on dissenters. In such situations, decisions—often important decisions—are made without consideration of alternative frames or alternative options. It is difficult to imagine conditions more conducive to poor decision making and wrong decisions.

Recent research indicates that groupthink may also result when group members have preconceived ideas about how a problem should be solved.[41] Under these conditions, the team may not examine a full range of decision alternatives, or it may discount or avoid information that threatens its preconceived choice.

Irving Janis, who coined the term *groupthink,* focused his research on high-level governmental policy groups faced with difficult problems in complex and dynamic environments. The groupthink phenomenon has been used to explain numerous group decisions that have resulted in serious fiascoes. Classic examples of such decisions include the Bay of Pigs invasion, the Watergate coverup, and NASA's decision to launch the space shuttle *Challenger.*[42] Of course, group decision making is common in all types of organizations, so it is possible that groupthink exists in private-sector organizations as well as in those in the public sector. Table 6.3 summarizes the characteristics of groupthink and the types of defective decision making that will likely result.

Groupthink is common in tightly knit groups that believe in what they are doing, such as citizen groups who censor book acquisitions for the local library, environmental groups who will save us from ourselves at any price, business leaders who presume that they control other people's economic destinies, or government functionaries who think they know better than the voters what is in the national interest. None of the decisions made by these groups is necessarily wrong, but that is not the point. Rather, it is the single-mindedness of the decision process, the narrow framing, and limited deliberation that are of concern.[43]

Table 6.3	Characteristics of Groupthink and the Types of Defective Decisions That May Result

Characteristics of Groupthink
- Illusion of invulnerability
- Collective rationalization
- Belief in the morality of group decisions
- Self-censorship
- Illusion of unanimity in decision making
- Pressure on members who express arguments

Types of Defective Decisions
- Incomplete survey of alternatives
- Incomplete survey of goals
- Failure to examine risks of preferred decisions
- Poor information search
- Failure to reappraise alternatives
- Failure to develop contingency plans

TECHNIQUES FOR QUALITY IN GROUP DECISION MAKING

Managers can use several structured techniques to foster quality in group decision making.[44] Here, we will briefly explore brainstorming, the nominal group technique, the Delphi technique, devil's advocacy, and dialectical inquiry.

BRAINSTORMING **Brainstorming** is a technique that encourages group members to generate as many novel ideas as possible on a given topic without evaluating them. As a group process, brainstorming can enhance creativity by overcoming pressures for conformity that can retard the development of creative decision making. Brainstorming primarily focuses on generating ideas rather than on choosing an alternative. The members of the group, usually 5 to 12 people, are encouraged to generate ideas during a specific time period while withholding criticism and focusing on nonevaluative presentation.[45] In this way, individuals who may be concerned about being ridiculed or criticized feel more free to offer truly novel ideas.

The following rules should guide the brainstorming process:[46]

- Freewheeling is encouraged. Group members are free to offer any suggestions to the facilitator, who lists ideas as people speak.
- Group members will not criticize ideas as they are being generated. Consider any and all ideas. No idea can be rejected initially.
- Quantity is encouraged. Write down all the ideas.
- The wilder the ideas the better.
- Piggyback on or combine previously stated ideas.
- No ideas are evaluated until after all alternatives are generated.

Brainstorming enhances creativity and reduces the tendency of groups to satisfice in considering alternatives. One advocate of brainstorming is Bill Gates, CEO of Microsoft. He often joins programmers in the brainstorming sessions that give birth to new products. According to Gates, it is very important to him and to those who work with him at Microsoft to encourage creative group decision making.[47]

NOMINAL GROUP TECHNIQUE The **nominal group technique (NGT)** is a structured process designed to stimulate creative group decision making where agreement is lacking or the members have incomplete knowledge of the nature of the problem.[48] It is a means of enhancing creativity and decision making that integrates both individual work and group interaction with certain basic guidelines. NGT was developed to foster individual as well as group creativity and further overcome the tendency of group members to criticize ideas when they are offered.

NGT is used in situations in which group members must pool their judgments to solve the problem and determine a satisfactory course of action. First, individual members independently list their ideas on the specific problem. Next, each member presents his or her ideas one at a time, without discussion. As with brainstorming, members are asked to generate ideas without direct comment, but the idea-generation phase of NGT is more confined than it is with brainstorming because group members present ideas in a round-robin manner rather than through freewheeling. Members' ideas are recorded so everyone can see them. After all the members' ideas are presented, the group discusses the ideas to clarify and evaluate them. Finally, members vote on the ideas independently, using a rank-ordering or rating procedure. The final outcome is determined by the pooled individual votes and is thus mathematically derived.

NGT may be most effective when decisions are complex or when the group is experiencing blockages or problems, such as a few dominating members. NGT is generally effective in generating large numbers of creative alternatives while maintaining group satisfaction.[49]

LEARNING OBJECTIVE 6
List the various techniques used to improve group decision making.

Brainstorming
A technique used to enhance creativity that encourages group members to generate as many novel ideas as possible on a given topic without evaluating them.

Nominal group technique (NGT)
A structured process designed to stimulate creative group decision making where agreement is lacking or where the members have incomplete knowledge concerning the nature of the problem.

Delphi technique
Uses experts to make predictions and forecasts about future events without meeting face to face.

DELPHI TECHNIQUE   The **Delphi technique** was originally developed by Rand Corporation to enable groups to consult experts and use their predictions and forecasts about future events.[50] Using survey instruments or questionnaires, a group leader solicits and collects written expert opinions on a topic. The leader collates and summarizes the information before distributing it to the participants. This process continues until the experts' predictions are systematically refined through feedback and a consensus emerges.

Like NGT, the Delphi technique can be used to define problems and to consider and select alternatives. The Delphi technique is also best used under special circumstances. The primary difference between NGT and the Delphi technique is that with the Delphi technique participants do not meet face to face.

A significant advantage of the Delphi technique is that it completely avoids group interaction effects. Even NGT is not completely immune to social facilitating pressure that results from having an important person in the same room. With Delphi, participant experts can be thousands of miles apart.

Devil's advocacy
An individual or subgroup is appointed to critique a proposed course of action and identify problems to consider before the decision is final.

DEVIL'S ADVOCACY APPROACH   The last two techniques to enhance group decision making, devil's advocacy and dialectical inquiry, were developed to deal with complex, strategic decisions. Both techniques encourage intense, heated debate among group members. A recent study found that disagreement in structured settings like meetings can lead to better decision making.[51] Disagreement is particularly useful for organizations operating in uncertain environments.

The **devil's advocacy** approach appoints an individual or subgroup to critique a proposed course of action. One or more individuals are assigned the role of devil's advocate to make sure that the negative aspects of any attractive decision alternatives are considered.[52] The usefulness of the devil's advocacy technique was demonstrated several years ago by Irving Janis in his discussion of famous fiascoes attributed to groupthink. Janis recommends that everyone in the group assume the role of devil's advocate and question the assumptions underlying the popular choice. An individual or subgroup can be formally designated as the devil's advocate to present critiques of the proposed decision. Since groups often exhibit a desire to agree, using this technique avoids the problem of having this tendency interfere with the decision-making process. Potential pitfalls are identified and considered before the decision is final.

Dialectical inquiry
Approaches a decision from two opposite points and structures a debate between conflicting views.

DIALECTICAL INQUIRY   With **dialectical inquiry**, a decision situation is approached from two opposite points, and advocates of the conflicting views conduct a debate, presenting arguments in support of their positions. Each decision possibility is developed, and assumptions are identified. The technique forces the group to confront the implications of their assumptions in the decision process.[53] Bausch and Lomb successfully uses this technique by establishing "Tiger teams" composed of scientists from different disciplines. Team members are encouraged to bring up divergent ideas and offer different points of view. Xerox uses round-table discussions composed of various functional experts to encourage divergent and innovative decision making.

IMPLICATIONS FOR LEADERS

The most important characteristic of successful decision makers is that they do not approach decisions unprepared. Responsibility for decision making comes only to those who have earned it. Responsibility is earned by decision makers who demonstrate both a record of success and an understanding of their organization. This is most easily achieved by leaders who exhibit the traits captured in the 3Cs leadership model. They must be competent in their understanding of the decision-making process, their character must be infused with integrity, honesty, and ethical behavior, and their commitment must extend beyond the boundaries of the organization. This commitment to community will ensure that there will be a societal as well as an organizational benefit to the decision made. As a leader, you need to realize that successful decision making means understanding the organization's basic beliefs and culture, its goals and vision, and its activities and the plans that guide them.[54]

How will changes in the managerial role in this new millennium affect the decision making of tomorrow's leaders? The following guidelines, developed by Robert Denhardt in his recent book *The Pursuit of Significance*, reflect current thinking about leadership techniques that foster quality decision making:[55]

- Be committed to the decision-making process; use it, and let data, not emotions, drive decisions.
- Seek employees' input before you make key decisions.
- Believe in, foster, and support group decision making in the organization.
- Believe that the best way to improve the quality of decisions is to ask and listen to employees who are doing the work.
- Seek and use high-quality information.
- Avoid "top-down" power-oriented decision making wherever possible.
- Encourage decision-making creativity through risk taking, and be tolerant of honest mistakes.
- Develop an open atmosphere that encourages organization members to offer and accept feedback.

In this chapter, we have set forth some fundamentals of how managers and leaders in organizations make decisions. We examined the steps in the decision-making process, issues related to ethical decision dilemmas, and two models of decision behavior. Since leaders are often involved with groups, we discussed group decision-making concerns and techniques that leaders can use to improve the group decision process. In Chapter 7, we will build on these fundamentals by presenting quantitative tools for making better decisions.

Meeting The Challenge

Gaylord Entertainment Gets on Course

In response to the recent flow of red ink, Gaylord Entertainment began making moves to stem the tide. In 2000, Gaylord recorded a $59 million loss when the company decided to pull the plug on Gaylord Digital, its online Christian Music Division. Gaylord closed the Orlando Wild Horse Saloon in 2001, recording another $16 million loss. Most recently, Gaylord sold its underperforming Christian music company, World Entertainment, to AOL Time Warner, Inc. In addition, Gaylord

parted with The Nashville Network (TNN) and Country Music Television (CMT). These moves were made to pay off mounting debt. During 2001, the company also sold or shuttered many of its assets, including a pair of film production companies, a sports management firm, and a campground. The unthinkable even happened to long-time radio station WSM, which proved to be not only venerable, but also vulnerable. Plans were being hatched to syndicate the Saturday night Grand

Ole Opry broadcasts, and convert WSM's format from country music to sports/talk radio.

In early 2001, Gaylord Entertainment handed over its future to a pair of executives from Harrah's Entertainment Inc. (known primarily as a casino operator). Colin Reed was installed as president and CEO, and Michael Rose was named chairman. One of Reed's first decisions was to recruit several executives from the gaming industry to help lead Gaylord to profitability. Despite his gaming ties, Reed is quick to point out that he has no plans to turn Gaylord into a casino company. Reed decided that "the core strategy for the company going forward is going to be in the convention and meeting hospitality niche." He hired people who have expertise in running and marketing large hotels. In Reed's words, "There aren't many 1,500–2,000-room hotels outside the casino business." Gaylord's Opryland Hotel in Nashville could boast of almost 3,000 rooms and over 600,000 square feet of meeting space. Gaylord executives were aware that it sometimes had trouble retaining large groups. People often tire of visiting the same hotel in the same place year after year. This prompted Gaylord's decision to open hotels in other states. This would allow the company to retain customers by steering them to the company's other hotels. One often overlooked advantage of the convention and business meeting strategy is that it reduces the risk of operating a multi-million dollar hotel during a slump in leisure travel. Un-

like family trips, which may be planned only a few weeks or days in advance, conventions and business meetings typically are booked several years in advance.

That thinking reshaped the direction of The Opryland Hotel of Florida, which was under construction near Orlando. After re-christening the hotel as "The Gaylord Palms," the company quietly began its push for advanced bookings and convention business. With its planned 1,400+ rooms, 380,000 square feet of meeting space and huge ballroom, this property was a prime candidate for convention business. And let's face it—with its proximity to Walt Disney World, Gaylord clearly expected business travelers to bring their families, as evidenced by the decision to include an octopus-shaped pool slide and La Petite Academy children's day camp on the property. Other decisions were made to appeal to business travelers who often complain of lack of places to network at night. The Orlando hotel would include three sit-down restaurants, a coffee shop, and several

bars. Throughout construction, the advanced booking effort continued. By the beginning of 2002, the hotel had booked 1 million room nights, and it still had not yet opened its doors to guests. At 2:02 P.M. on February 2, 2002 (which would be 02/02/02), with much fanfare, The Gaylord Palms finally opened its doors. Gaylord's commitment to this decision to focus on conventions and business meetings will continue with the opening of a similar hotel near Dallas, Texas, in 2004. Reed expressed hope that the company could build another three to five hotels of this type during the next 10 years. The investment analyst who declared that Gaylord had once "screwed up" could now claim that "it's probably more focused. It made a mess of things, but they've been cleaning up everything."

SOURCES: T. Pack, "Gaylord's Story Sounds Like a Country Song," *Central Florida Business*, January 7, 2002, 14–16; and A. Hunt, "Resort Books 1 Million," *The Orlando Sentinel*, January 5, 2002, B1ff.

SUMMARY

1. Decision making is the process through which managers and leaders identify and resolve problems or capitalize on opportunities. The decision-making process includes seven steps: (1) identifying and diagnosing the problem; (2) identifying objectives; (3) generating alternatives; (4) evaluating alternatives; (5) reaching decisions; (6) choosing implementation strategies; and (7) monitoring and evaluating.

2. The rational-economic decision model assumes that the decision maker has completely accurate information and an extensive list of alternatives from which to choose. It also assumes that he or she will be rational and systematic in assessing each alternative and will work in the best interests of the organization.

3. The behavioral decision model acknowledges human limitations to decision making and addresses the issues of bounded rationality, intuition, satisficing, and escalation of commitment. Bounded rationality recognizes that people cannot know everything and are limited by such organizational constraints as time, information, resources, and their own mental capacities. Intuition has been described as everything from an unconscious analysis based on past experience to a paranormal ability called a "sixth sense." Satisficing means searching for and accepting something that is satis-

factory rather than optimal. Escalation of commitment is the tendency to commit more resources to a previously selected course of action than would be expected if the manager followed an effective decision-making process.

4. The increased involvement of groups and teams in management actions requires that leaders understand group considerations in decision making. The participative model of group decision making provides guidelines for the appropriate level of subordinate participation in decision making.

5. A leader must consider both the advantages and disadvantages of group decision making. The advantages include greater experience and expertise, more information, higher satisfaction, and greater acceptance of and commitment to the decisions. The disadvantages are that group decisions take more time; one member or subgroup may dominate; individual goals may supplant group goals; social pressure to conform may be brought to bear on members; and groupthink may develop.

6. Leaders can use several structured techniques to aid in group decision making. These include brainstorming, the nominal group technique, the Delphi technique, devil's advocacy, and dialectical inquiry.

REVIEW QUESTIONS

1. *(Learning Objective 1)* Describe each of the seven steps in the decision-making process.

2. *(Learning Objective 2)* Describe the rational-economic model for decision making.

3. *(Learning Objective 3)* Describe the behavioral model for decision making and indicate how it differs from the rational-economic model.

4. *(Learning Objective 4)* Describe the five decision-making styles on the Vroom-Jago continuum of decision making.

5. *(Learning Objective 5)* Describe the advantages and disadvantages of group decision making when compared to individual decision making.

6. *(Learning Objective 6)* Describe the devil's advocacy approach and dialectical inquiry, and indicate how they can help deal with complex, strategic decisions.

DISCUSSION QUESTIONS

Improving Critical Thinking

1. How big a part do you feel culture plays in the decision-making process? Consider both the culture of the decision maker and the culture of those affected by the decision.

2. Recall a situation in which you made a decision for which the outcome was satisfactory, but not optimal. Describe the reasons you accepted this satisficing decision rather than pushing on to make an optimal decision.

Enhancing Communication Skills

3. What types of ethical dilemmas do you think future managers will face? How can you prepare yourself to handle ethical dilemmas? To develop your written communication skills, find some recent examples in business publications and/or the news media and write a short paper on this subject.

4. Consider an important decision that you recently made, such as choosing a major or buying a car. How much vigi-

lance did you exercise to ensure making a quality decision? To practice your oral communication skills, be prepared to present your decision process to the class or a small group as directed by your instructor.

Building Teamwork

5. Interview one of your college professors. Ask the professor to describe a decision that was made regarding one of the policies on the course syllabus and to explain the process that led to that decision. Analyze the professor's decision with regard to the two models of decision making described in the chapter. Form small groups and share the results of your interview with the team. Did the team members find any issues in common among all the professors interviewed?

6. Reflect on recent decisions made by groups with which you were involved in various college courses. Try to recall an experience that showed signs of groupthink. Be prepared to report this experience to the class and describe what might have been done to prevent this phenomenon.

THINKING CRITICALLY: DEBATE THE ISSUE

Who Should Make the Decision?

Form teams as directed by your instructor. Half of the teams should take the position that group decision making leads to high-quality decisions and high organizational performance. The other teams should take the position that group decision mak-

ing impedes organizational performance and that decisions should not be made by groups. Research the topic using current business publications to provide support for your team's position. Your instructor will select two teams to present your arguments in a debate format.

EXPERIENTIAL EXERCISE 6.1

Brainstorming: Creative Group Decision Making

Step 1. Form small groups as directed by your instructor. Each group will have an opportunity to develop some creative

solutions to problems that typically arise on a college campus. Before beginning the exercise, review the rules for brainstorming discussed in the chapter.

Step 2. From a current campus newspaper, select a problem or issue that needs to be solved on your campus. Possible issues might include student apathy about elections, the need for recycling programs, or the lack of funding for student programs.

Step 3. You have 10 minutes after the words "begin brainstorming" to generate ideas. Have one person write down all the alternatives. Remember, do not evaluate ideas.

Step 4. You have 10 to 15 minutes to discuss and evaluate the ideas that were generated in Step 3.

Step 5. You have 5 minutes to decide on the final solution that you will present to the class.

Step 6. Discuss as a class what happened in your group. How did your ideas emerge? Did you experience frustrations? What did you find most difficult about trying to use the brainstorming process?

EXPERIENTIAL EXERCISE 6.2

Examining Decision-Making Ethics

Examine recent issues of business periodicals, news magazines, and newspapers. Identify a significant decision made by a major company that has some ethical implications associated with it. Then write a short (one- to two-page) report that addresses the following questions:

1. In the decision you identified, did the manager or managers appear to use good decision-making skills?

2. Did they follow the decision-making steps?

3. Was the decision made by a group or an individual?

4. What are the ethical implications of this decision, and who is likely to be impacted?

CAPTURING THE POWER OF INFORMATION TECHNOLOGY

1. Use the Internet to gather information on the games available for the latest game consoles of Sony, Nintendo, and Sega. Using presentation software, develop a slide show that will illustrate to your classmates the extent of each company's offerings, and highlight any overlaps or duplications among these companies.

2. Use the Internet to locate information on manufacturers of infant and baby products that have made the decision to recall any of their products during the last 12 months. Then arrange this information in an electronic spreadsheet that will allow you to sort the information by manufacturer, product category, specific product, and child age group.

3. Using database software, store your infant and baby product recall data in a fashion that would allow you to add more information as additional recalls occur. The structure of your database should also allow you to retrieve information on manufacturers issuing recalls, month and year of recalls, and the categories of products recalled.

ETHICS: TAKE A STAND

Many of the plastic toys that babies and toddlers love to gnaw on are made with chemicals (phthalates) that are used to soften the plastic. Teething rings, squeeze toys, bathtub toys, and many other playthings have concentrations of the chemical exceeding 50 percent. Recent studies have suggested that phthalates may be linked to liver and kidney damage if ingested. While no government edict has been issued banning the use of these chemicals in children's toys, the Consumer Products Safety Council has recommended that manufacturers stop using them until more research is done. While several manufacturers have discontinued using these chemicals in teething rings, they continue to be used in a variety of infants' and children's toys. Their use will probably continue until scientists can find a biodegradable, non-petroleum replacement for phthalates.[56]

For Discussion

1. What stand do you feel the U.S. government should take on this issue?

2. What role should the U.S. Food and Drug Administration play in this issue, given that studies have not yet shown conclusively that ingesting phthalates can lead to liver and kidney damage?

3. What do you feel the toy manufacturers should do while they wait for the discovery of a safer softening agent?

VIDEO CASE

Effective Managerial Decision Making: Next Door Food Store

Next Door Food Store is a chain of over 30 small convenience stores and gas stations located throughout Michigan and northern Indiana. Similar to other convenience stores, the overall purpose of Next Door Food Store (NDFS) is to provide gasoline and convenience products 24 hours a day to people who are in a hurry. Since many people are in a hurry and willing to pay more for convenience, the convenience store industry is very competitive. Leaders at NDFS's corporate headquarters and their stores are continually challenged to respond to routine problems and emerging industry trends. Two of their most fundamental decisions are (1) how to manage their channels of distribution and (2) what and how many products should be stocked in each store.

NDFS's main objectives are to maintain a variety of products, manage their cost of distribution, keep inventory levels low, and use just-in-time inventory. Their major constraints include a lower volume than supermarkets, less shelf and storage space than supermarkets, a limited number of stores, and difficulty in serving their geographically dispersed stores from a central warehouse because they currently do not have a trucking system to ship goods.

As for its their first fundamental decision, NDFS has to decide whether to manage its channels of distribution by building and operating its own warehouse or hiring wholesale distributors (such as Fabiano Foods) to stock each store on a just-in-time basis. Hiring Fabiano Foods appears preferable over the advantages (and disadvantages) associated with a new warehouse. Since making the decision, NDFS has found Fabiano Foods to be a valuable business partner in providing important marketing, inventory, and product-mix information. This is especially important because product demand varies for NDFS's geographically dispersed stores.

Another ongoing challenge is deciding which products to sell in the stores. There are literally hundreds of products to choose from, and some suppliers are very aggressive. On one occasion, NDFS accepted a cash payment from Coca-Cola in exchange for a commitment to discontinue selling Pepsi products and sell only Coca-Cola soft drink products. This decision resulted in NDFS losing several loyal Pepsi drinkers as customers. However, it took the NDFS leaders only a few weeks to respond to customer complaints and cancel their agreement with Coca-Cola.

Another aspect of determining what products to stock is identifying emerging market trends and deciding whether such trends represent profitable opportunities or just a passing fad. An example of such an emerging trend is bottled waters, teas, and sport drinks for the health-conscious. Early on, the leaders of NDFS identified the potential of this emerging trend through articles they read and seeing how much cooler space convenience stores in other states had allocated to these products. The decision to dedicate a generous amount of cooler space to bottled waters, teas, and sport drinks was risky at the time and was questioned by many local people. Nevertheless, the decision has proven to be very profitable. James Salisbury, vice president of NDFS Operations, asserts they added bottled waters, teas, etc., to their product mix and have never looked back. He also notes they need to consider where this trend might be headed and whether they want to stay ahead of their competition in this trend.

Next Door Food Store is constantly looking for new ideas so it can continue to lead the convenience store industry. It frames decisions in terms of the company's overall mission: To operate the best and most profitable convenience stores in Michigan and Indiana with the best trained people providing the best customer service through high-quality products, a clean environment, and well-stocked stores. The decisions made regarding distribution channels, product mix, and other critical areas play an important role in determining the company's present and future success.

For Discussion

1. What are Next Door Food Store's mission and objectives? Do you believe that the company's mission and objectives help guide its decision-making process? Explain.

2. Select one decision made by NDFS. Briefly explain how it applied (or did not apply) each of the seven steps in the decision-making process in making this decision. Do any steps appear to be particularly critical in the convenience store industry?

3. Do you think NDSF has "never looked back" or re-evaluated its decision regarding allocating generous cooler space to bottled waters, teas, and sport drinks? Explain.

4. Are the leaders of NDFS affected by bounded rationality? If so, provide an example from the case that illustrates this concept.

http://www.nextdoor1.com

CASE

Disney Auction Site Arouses Ire

When The Walt Disney Company launched its official auction site on eBay in October 2000, George Grobar, vice president of the new business, said, "We don't want negative feedback, and we don't expect that to happen." Such optimism was certainly warranted; who could find fault with the concept. Here was an auction site that was offering thousands of pieces of Disney memorabilia, selling such items as costumes and props from movies, collectibles, and artwork.

Unfortunately, negative feedback did come. The Disney auction site experienced a small, but growing number of customer complaints about service and quality. For example, a Florida resident purchased a set of collectible Disney character pins in October 2001, planning to surprise his wife for Christmas. However, after purchasing the pins, he was told that the merchandise probably wouldn't arrive until after the holidays. This came as quite a surprise, knowing that eBay expects its sellers to make a good faith effort to ship within 30 days. Said one Disney spokesperson, "Our general policy is to have the merchandise we advertise on hand. But, we don't always." Other complaints centered on costumes and movie memorabilia items that did not appear to be authentic or were not of the condition depicted in auction site photos. At least one dissatisfied customer went so far as to file a lawsuit.

In one seven-day period in late 2001, the company received 99 negative customer ratings. While eBay has suspended some auction sites from doing business for as few as five complaints, Disney's complaint rate was still relatively low, with roughly 400 negative responses to 17,000 favorable ones in its first 13 months in business, so eBay imposed no sanctions on Disney. Despite the auction site's 98 percent approval rate, Disney Internet Group spokeswoman Kim Kerscher noted that "one unhappy customer is too many."

Auction customers can register positive or negative responses about their buying experiences on the 37 million sellers' Web sites that appear on eBay, information that is invaluable for potential auction customers. However, Disney is among a small minority of regular auctioneers who elect to keep the identities and specific comments of dissatisfied customers secret. In the words of one of Disney's disgruntled customers, "Disney Internet customer service is essentially nonexistent."

For Discussion

1. Where did Disney fail in its implementation strategy when the company decided to get into the online auction business?

2. What might the company have done differently to make this decision more successful?

3. What might Disney have done to be more sensitive to customer satisfaction and avoid negative feedback?

SOURCE: R. Johnson, "Angry Customers Train Their Ire on Disney Auction Site," *The Orlando Sentinel*, December 8, 2001, C1ff.

CHAP

DECISION-MAKING TOOLS AND TECHNIQUES

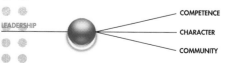

LEADERSHIP

COMPETENCE

CHARACTER

COMMUNITY

TER 7

CHAPTER OVERVIEW

As we saw in Chapter 6, every day leaders face situations in which they must make a decision. Many times a decision is needed because a problem has arisen. Other times a decision is needed because an opportunity has presented itself. Regardless of the reason, when a decision is needed, successful leaders will be ready to leap into action and make the decision to avoid losing ground in the increasingly competitive marketplace. We also learned from Chapter 6 that decision making is a multistep process and that tomorrow's leaders must possess decision-making skills.

Merely understanding the steps in the decision-making process is not enough, however. Many quantitative tools and techniques can be used to evaluate alternative courses of action prior to making a decision. Tomorrow's leaders must be equipped with these analytical tools, for their proper use will help them improve the quality of their decision making.

Organizational decisions are often categorized as either long-range strategic decisions or short-range operational decisions. Analytical tools and techniques have evolved to help business leaders make better choices in both of these areas. This chapter focuses on the methodologies, procedures, and applications for some of the more prominent decision-making aids.

LEARNING OBJECTIVES

When you have finished studying this chapter, you should be able to:

1. Describe the situations in which managerial decisions are called for.
2. Discuss the basic classifications for managerial decisions.
3. Describe the nature of strategic decision making as well as the strategic decision-making matrix approach for strategy selection.
4. Identify the differences between the growth-share matrix and the industry attractiveness/business strength matrix approaches for evaluating business portfolios.
5. Describe the nature of operational decision making.
6. Discuss the basic elements that add structure to the decision-making process.
7. Discuss the differences between decision making under certainty, risk, and uncertainty.
8. Describe the solution approaches that would be taken for risk and uncertainty situations.
9. Discuss the basics of breakeven analysis, linear programming, and PERT analysis.

Facing The Challenge

Tupperware Goes Stale

Tupperware, that venerable mainstay of plastic food storage containers, was born shortly after World War II when Earl Tupper saw the possibilities for an airtight container coupled with that modern marvel, the refrigerator. Having had experience manufacturing plastic gas masks during the war, Tupper knew that a plastic food storage container could seal in flavor and moisture. Refrigerators and Tupper-produced bowls would be a perfect pair, and the inventor wasted no time putting his idea into production. In 1946 he rolled out his first sealable container called the Wonder-Bowl. However, Tupper was clueless about marketing. He tried selling his containers in hardware and department stores, but they failed to attract much attention.

Fortunately, these products did catch the eye of Ann Damigella who, with her husband, sold assorted products via direct selling with "sales parties" in their home. The Damigellas saw this marketing strategy as the perfect vehicle for selling Earl Tupper's products. Fast forward a few years to 1951 when the success of the Damigellas was so great that Tupper completely removed his products from America's department stores. From that point forward, direct selling through Tupperware Home Parties would be the company's sales strategy. An annual Jubilee sales rally, still the high point of the Tupperware calendar, would be held to build esprit de corps, confidence, and enthusiasm among the sales force. Hostesses would be encouraged to become dealers, dealers to become managers, and managers to become distributors. At

each level prizes and rewards would become more plentiful.

In 1960 the company began expanding beyond the U.S. borders, first into Canada, and soon thereafter into the United Kingdom, Western Europe, Latin America, and Asia. Tupperware had become a corporate alchemist, turning plastic into gold. There was a sense of invincibility. Tupperware's direct sales culture flourished domestically and in the expanding markets of the free world. In 1975 CBS News' *60 Minutes* profiled the company, focusing on its off-beat rituals and game-laden sales parties. "It may be the most brilliant marketing scheme ever devised," said reporter Morley Safer, "for it is based less on sales pitch than on friendship."

But, dramatic changes were beginning to reshape Tupperware's core domestic market. More women were entering the workforce, and families began eating on the run. If Americans were eating at McDonald's, would they need as many plastic bowls? As women went to work and scurried to taxi their kids to various activities, where would they find the time for Tupperware Parties? The brilliant marketing scheme was beginning to lose its luster. Tupperware began to see a steady decline in U.S. sales, sales force, and profits. In 1989 the United States and Europe were running neck and neck as the company's most lucrative markets. By the close of the century U.S. sales were about one third of Europe's, and last among Tupperware's four divisions. The United States was the only division that made less now than it did 10 years ago. In addi-

tion to these disturbing financial figures, Tupperware's new products operation had grown stale when new products started becoming mostly old items in new colors. Then, a highly publicized new product failed to perform as advertised, leading to a write off of about $140 million. Other attempts to reinvigorate the company proved less than successful. In 1989 the company launched Tupperware Express, a parcel post system designed to get orders to customers more quickly. This system proved to be more costly than doing things the old way. It also drove off many distributors, so it was eventually abandoned. A 1991 plan to use direct mail to customer lists upset distributors, who suspected a plot to steal their business. At the close of the 20th century, Tupperware seemed jinxed. Bad decisions seemed to be the rule rather than the exception. The challenge to Tupperware was to make some good decisions that would help to reinvigorate the U.S. domestic market.

SOURCES: R. Burnett, "Tupperware to Sell Its Products in Kroger-Owned Stores in 3 States," *The Orlando Sentinel*, October 17, 2001, B1ff; C. Boyd, "Comeback Plan: Sell Where People Shop," *The Orlando Sentinel*, February 22, 2000, A1ff; C. Boyd, "As Problems Piled Up, Tupperware Partied On," *The Orlando Sentinel*, February 21, 2000, A1ff; C. Boyd, "The Plastic Empire: How Tupperware Went Stale," *The Orlando Sentinel*, February 20, 2000, A1ff; "Tupperware and Kroger Announce Marketing Agreement," *Tupperware Press Release*, October 16, 2001; "Tupperware Launches New Web Site With E-Commerce Feature," *Tupperware Press Release*, August 10, 1999; "Tupperware Announces Agreement with Home Shopping Network," *Tupperware Press Release*, May 19, 1999.

INTRODUCTION

In "Facing The Challenge," we saw that Tupperware officials had made some less than stellar decisions as they tried to reverse declining sales in the U.S. domestic market. They would have to improve their decision-making track record in order to improve their profitability in the United States. We will see as this chapter unfolds that Tupperware's decisions would be strategic in nature and would be made under conditions of extreme uncertainty.

In Chapter 6 we saw that any person or organization faced with a decision has a rather straightforward task at hand. By following a systematic set of steps, the decision maker can select a course of action (the decision) from a set of many potential alternatives. After the decision is implemented, follow-up monitoring will enable the decision maker to assess whether the chosen alternative has been producing desirable results. As routine as the decision-making process may seem, it does require considerable preparation to assemble and analyze all available information.

We begin this chapter with a discussion of the different categories of decision-making situations and then distinguish between strategic decision making and operational decision making. Several analytical tools and techniques have been developed to aid in making both strategic decisions and operational decisions, and we will examine them here. Much of the material you will encounter in this chapter is a direct outgrowth of the quantitative perspective on management described in Chapter 2.

MANAGERIAL DECISION SITUATIONS

Before examining specific tools and techniques for decision making, let's review the conditions under which a decision situation might arise and the different ways of classifying those situations.

LEARNING OBJECTIVE 1
Describe the situations in which managerial decisions are called for.

SOURCES OF ORGANIZATIONAL AND ENTREPRENEURIAL DECISIONS

Managers are faced with decisions when a problem occurs or when an opportunity arises. A **problem** occurs when some aspect of organizational performance is less than desirable. This definition is purposely broad so that it will cover any aspect of organizational performance, such as overall bottom-line profits, market share, output productivity, quality of output, or worker satisfaction and harmony, to name just a few of the countless possibilities. When such unsatisfactory results have occurred, the successful manager will both recognize the problem and find a solution for it.[1] The decisions Tupperware officials would eventually make were in response to profit declines in the U.S. domestic market caused by the demographics of a changing workforce and changing lifestyles. Think back to Chapter 6 where we spoke of the decision by Saturn to recall almost 400,000 cars in a single recall program. That decision was also made in response to a problem—the wiring problem and its potential to cause engine fires.

Problem
A situation in which some aspect of organizational performance is less than desirable.

Managers do not always make decisions in response to problem situations. Often decisions are made because an opportunity arises. An **opportunity** is any situation that has the potential to provide additional beneficial outcomes. When an opportunity presents itself, success will be achieved by those who recognize the potential benefits and then embark upon a course of action to achieve them. For example, consider Pepsi-Cola's decision to add a freshness date on its beverage containers.[2] This decision was precipitated by a perceived opportunity to capture additional market share by offering something that Pepsi's competitors were not offering. Not to be outdone in the never-ending cola wars, Coca-Cola soon followed with freshness dates on its own products. Eventually, this service was to become standard practice in the beverage industry. Later colas with the added flavor of lemon or cherry were lining up for shelf space. The latest salvo in the flavored cola wars is the introduction of Vanilla Coke.[3] The cola wars have soared to dizzying heights, both figuratively and literally. In trying to capitalize on an opportunity to have its products prominently displayed, Pepsi sponsored the Russian space station

Opportunity
A situation that has the potential to provide additional beneficial outcomes.

Mir, while Coke was flying a spaceship version of a soda fountain as an experiment aboard the space shuttle *Endeavour*.[4]

Much like the freshness dating situation in soft drinks, there are numerous other illustrations of companies following the lead of their competitors to cash in on an opportunity. Duracell first introduced the concept of a battery tester contained in its packaging. However, the Energizer Bunny topped that by introducing batteries with the test mechanism designed as an integral part of the battery. One needed only to squeeze the buttons on the battery and its LCD display would indicate the strength of its charge. Duracell soon followed suit with a version of that innovation. And let's not forget about the breakfast cereal wars. When Post cut its prices, the remaining members of the "Big Four" began to lose market share. In rapid order, Kellogg, General Mills, and finally Quaker Oats reduced the prices of their breakfast cereals.[5] The post 9/11 era presented many opportunities that companies seized upon. When the United States Postal Service had an episode of anthrax tainted letters, the Bayer Corporation more than tripled its production of the anthrax antibiotic Cipro.[6] In early 2002 heavyweights Boeing, Northrup Grumman, TRW, Raytheon, and eventual winner Lockheed Martin all began preparing bids, seeking to win a federal airport security contract for a system to screen passengers and baggage in the post 9/11 era.[7]

From an entrepreneurial perspective, it is hard to top the serendipitous opportunity that presented itself to firefighter John Bartlett, founder of Barricade International. While rummaging through the charred trash from a house fire, he noticed that the only thing that hadn't burned in a huge pile of garbage was a disposable diaper. After considerable experimentation, he developed a gel made from the same superabsorbent polymers found in baby diapers. When sprayed on structures or foliage with a garden hose or a "Ghostbuster" style backpack, the gel can hold off the flames of an advancing fire for up to 30 hours. When no longer needed, the gel can be hosed off with plain water. So effective is the product that it has received rave reviews from fire departments, and it was instrumental in saving many homes during a recent rash of Florida wild fires.[8]

Recognizing the importance of finding new opportunities, the 3M Corporation spends nearly twice the industry average on research and development. In fact, researchers spend about 15 percent of their time brainstorming and working on projects of their own choosing. This initiative is in support of the company's objective to maintain an innovative spirit, and its goal to generate 30 percent of annual revenue from products that are less than four years old.[9]

In "At The Forefront" on page 213 we can see the decision strategy employed by the CEO of Hard Rock Cafés as he pursued new market opportunities. There we can also see how the mad cow disease problem in Europe resulted in menu change decisions.[10] Regardless of whether a decision is precipitated by a problem, an opportunity, or both, it is important to understand the nature of the decision situation. Accordingly, we turn our attention to methods of classifying decision situations.

CLASSIFICATION OF DECISION SITUATIONS

LEARNING OBJECTIVE 2

Discuss the basic classifications for managerial decisions.

Programmed decision
Decisions made in response to situations that are routine or recurring.

On a very basic level, Herbert Simon, a management scholar and prolific researcher in the area of decision making, proposed that decisions can be classified as either programmed or nonprogrammed.[11] When the decision situation is one that has occurred in the past and the response is routine, the decision is referred to as a **programmed decision**. Identifying alternative courses of action in such situations is usually routine, for the alternatives are quite familiar to the decision maker. As an example of a programmed decision, consider the customer assistance operator for the Charleswood Company, a manufacturer of kits of unassembled furniture. If a customer discovers that a component or hardware item is missing from her kit,

At The Forefront

Hard Rock Café CEO Goes Back to the Roots

Hard Rock Café—there is a very good chance that you've seen someone wearing the T-shirt, and if you've done a little traveling, you've probably even had a meal there. After all, there are 111 Hard Rock Cafés scattered in 41 countries around the world, each filled with rock and roll memorabilia, and each pulsating with the chain's trademark rock music. Although Hard Rock Café International opened its first outlet in 1971 in London during the British explosion into the rock music world, the United States, with more than 40 locations, became the chain's primary market. Europe chips in with about a dozen, and the rest are scattered around the world, mostly in tourist destinations. Curiously, until late in the 1990s the United Kingdom—the birthplace of the concept—could claim only one.

There is a drawback associated with locating one's business in a tourist destination and then relying on tourist traffic. Such businesses could be susceptible to sudden drops in revenue when travel is down. This danger was apparent to Hard Rock CEO Peter Beaudrault, and it had an impact on strategic decisions for expansion. His marketing analysis revealed that the United Kingdom and Europe provided a huge market potential. So, it was back to the motherland (the U.K.) for the opening of a Hard Rock in Edinburgh, Scotland, in 1998, units in Birmingham and Manchester, England, in 2001, and a fifth U.K. Hard Rock in Nottingham, England, in 2002. Munich, Germany, would also see the opening of a café in 2002. That European push doesn't mean that Hard Rock isn't going to continue expanding in the United States. The year 2002 also saw the opening of Hard Rocks in Phoenix, Arizona, and Austin, Texas. In keeping with the strategic expansion decision, none of these new locations is in a city that would be classified as "hot tourist destinations." By venturing into regional communities such as Nottingham and industrial towns such as Birmingham, Manchester, and Edinburgh, Beardrault has signaled that the company is targeting locals more than tourists.

The U.K. and European expansion has presented an interesting challenge. Circumstances in Europe and the U.K. have dictated that new menu decisions be made along with the expansions in those areas. The Hard Rock Café menu has traditionally been heavy on U.S.-style hamburgers and beef dishes. However, mad cow disease and mad cow scares in countries such as England and Germany have caused Hard Rock to tweak its menu there to focus less on the beef and more on upscale dishes. Analysts in the industry predict that Hard Rock's expansion strategy will help insulate the company from volatile swings in tourist travel.

SOURCE: J. Jackson, "Rockin' Back to Its Roots," *The Orlando Sentinel*, February 21, 2002, C1ff.

she can call an 800 number for assistance. The operator routinely obtains the missing part number from the customer and then authorizes immediate UPS shipping of that part.

When a decision is made in response to a situation that is unique, unstructured, or poorly defined, it is called a **nonprogrammed decision**. These decisions often require considerable creativity, cleverness, and innovation to elicit a list of reasonable alternative courses of action. When an investment group took control of the Schwinn Bicycle Company and tried to reverse the slide that Schwinn had been in for years, many nonprogrammed decisions were made as they restructured the company, shifted to a customer focus, and developed some hot new models. These decisions helped Schwinn roll back to its former prominence in the industry.[12]

The changing nature of today's business environment presents an interesting dilemma for decision makers. On one hand, the rapidly changing, global business environment creates a need for more nonprogrammed decisions than ever before. With quality and continuous improvement as major strategic initiatives, organizations are constantly being challenged to find creative and innovative solutions to unique new problems and opportunities. On the other hand, the changing composition of the workforce suggests that more programmed decisions might be beneficial. Today's workforce continues to become more diverse in racial, ethnic, and gender composition. Workers with diverse backgrounds and cultural values often have different perceptions of appropriate organizational goals and objectives and, therefore, respond differently to the same decision situation. In such circumstances, the more programmed the decision responses can be, the more likely that workers will make consistent, high-quality decisions.

Nonprogrammed decision
Decisions made in response to situations that are unique, unstructured, or poorly defined.

Whatever the type of decision situation, managers can use certain tools and techniques to achieve excellence in the decision-making process. We will first examine tools that aid in making long-range strategic decisions and then shift our attention to tools and techniques that are useful for making shorter-range operational decisions.

STRATEGIC DECISION-MAKING TOOLS

LEARNING OBJECTIVE 3
Describe the nature of strategic decision making as well as the strategic decision-making matrix approach for strategy selection.

Strategic decision making occurs at the highest levels in organizations. As we saw in Chapter 5, this type of decision making involves the selection of a strategy that will define the long-term direction of the firm. Two important areas for strategic decision making are in strategy selection and evaluation of portfolios.

STRATEGY SELECTION: THE STRATEGIC DECISION-MAKING MATRIX

Strategic decision-making matrix
A two-dimensional grid used to select the best strategic alternative in light of multiple organizational objectives.

Many times, organizations find that there is not one clear-cut, obvious strategy that should be pursued. Instead, several potentially attractive alternatives may exist. The task for management is to select the strategy that will best facilitate the achievement of the multiple objectives of the organization. A tool that can be helpful in such cases is the **strategic decision-making matrix**.[13]

When management faces several strategic alternatives and multiple objectives, it is helpful to organize these factors into a two-dimensional decision-making matrix.[14] To illustrate, let's consider the case of an organization that has established a goal of strong growth and has implemented that goal by specifying three objectives: increased profit, increased market share, and increased production output. Suppose management has determined that three alternative growth strategies are reasonable options for the organization—product development, horizontal integration, and a joint venture. To form the strategic decision-making matrix, the alternative strategies are listed along the side of the matrix, while the objectives are listed along the top, as in Table 7.1.[15]

Since the objectives of the organization won't always be equally important, different weights can be assigned to them. Management usually assigns the weights based upon its subjective assessment of the importance of each objective. The weights are shown directly below the objectives in Table 7.1. In this example, increased profit is the most important objective; therefore, it has received the highest weight. Note that the sum of the weights must equal 1.0.

To use the matrix, management must first rate each alternative strategy on its potential to contribute to the achievement of each objective. A 1-to-5 rating scale is used, with 1 indicating little or no potential for achieving an objective and 5 indicating max-

Table 7.1 | Strategic Decision-Making Matrix

	OBJECTIVES			
	INCREASED PROFIT	INCREASED MARKET SHARE	INCREASED PRODUCTION OUTPUT	TOTAL WEIGHTED SCORE
ALTERNATIVE STRATEGIES/WEIGHT	0.5	0.3	0.2	
Product Development	2	2	3	$0.5(2) + 0.3(2) + 0.2(3) = 2.2$
Horizontal Integration	4	2	2	$0.5(4) + 0.3(2) + 0.2(2) = 3.0$
Joint Venture	5	3	3	$0.5(5) + 0.3(3) + 0.2(3) = 4.0$

imum potential. Once an alternative strategy has been rated for each objective, the strategy's total weighted score can be computed by multiplying its rating for each objective by the corresponding weight of the objective and then summing across all objectives, as shown in the last column in Table 7.1. The decision maker can then select the strategy with the highest weighted score. In this example, the joint venture strategy is the most desirable alternative, because it will allow the organization to achieve the best combination of profitability, market share, and production output.

EVALUATION OF PORTFOLIOS

Whenever an organization becomes involved in several businesses and industries or with several products and services, it becomes necessary to make decisions about the role each business line will play in the organization and the manner in which resources will be allocated among the business lines. Although this discussion of the portfolio approach focuses on the evaluation of multiple business lines, these approaches can also be used at the product or service level. This is done by replacing business lines on the matrix with products or services. The most popular technique for assessing the balance of the mix of business lines in an organization is portfolio matrix analysis. A **business portfolio matrix** is a two-dimensional grid that compares the strategic positions of each of the organization's businesses.

A portfolio matrix can be constructed using any reasonable pair of indicators of a firm's strategic position. As we will see, usually one dimension of the matrix relates to the attractiveness of the industry environment and the other to the strength of a business within its industry.[16] The two most frequently used portfolio matrices are the growth-share matrix and the industry attractiveness/business strength matrix.

THE GROWTH-SHARE MATRIX   The earliest business portfolio approach to be widely used for corporate strategy formulation is the growth-share matrix. This technique was developed by the Boston Consulting Group (BCG), a leading management consulting firm. Figure 7.1 illustrates a BCG matrix.[17]

The **BCG matrix** is constructed using market growth rate and relative market share as the indicators of the firm's strategic position. Each of these indicators is divided into two levels (high and low), so that the matrix contains four cells. The rows of the matrix show the market growth rate, while the columns show the relative market share. Market growth rate is the percentage at which the market in which the business operates is growing annually. In the BCG matrix, 10 percent is generally considered the dividing line between a low rate and a high rate of market growth. Relative market share is computed by dividing the firm's market share by the market share of its largest competitor. For example, a relative market share of 0.4 means that the sales volume of the business is only 40 percent of the largest competitor's sales volume. In the BCG matrix, a relative market share of 1.0 is usually set as the dividing line between high and low relative market share.

To use the BCG matrix, each of the organization's businesses is plotted in the matrix according to its market growth rate and relative market share. Figure 7.1 illustrates a BCG matrix for an organization with six businesses. Each circle represents a business unit. The size of a circle reflects the proportion of corporate revenue generated by that business, and the pie slice indicates the proportion of corporate profits generated by that business.[18] Note that each cell in the BCG matrix has a descriptive label; these labels reflect the roles that the businesses in the cells play in the overall strategy of the firm.

LEARNING OBJECTIVE 4
Identify the differences between the growth-share matrix and the industry attractiveness/business strength matrix approaches for evaluating business portfolios.

Business portfolio matrix
A two-dimensional grid that compares the strategic positions of each of the organization's businesses.

BCG matrix
Business portfolio matrix that uses market growth rate and relative market share as the indicators of the firm's strategic position.

Organizations involved in several businesses and industries or with several products and services must make decisions about the role of each business line and the manner in which resources will be allocated among the business lines.

Figure 7.1 | The BCG Growth-Share Matrix

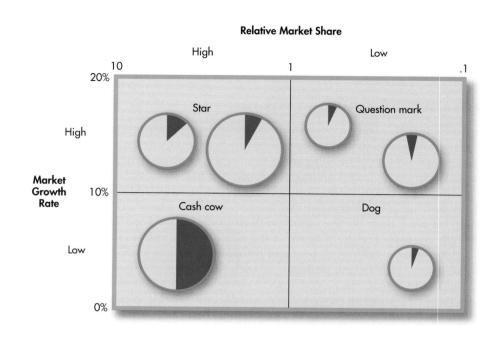

Stars
Businesses that fall into the high market growth/high market share cell of a BCG matrix.

Cash cows
Businesses that fall into the low market growth/high market share cell of a BCG matrix.

Dogs
Businesses that fall into the low market growth/low market share cell of a BCG matrix.

Question marks
Businesses that fall into the high market growth/low market share cell of a BCG matrix.

Stars   Businesses that fall into the high market growth/high market share cell are referred to as **stars**. These businesses offer attractive profit and growth opportunities. However, they also require a great deal of money to keep up with the market's rate of growth. Consequently, in the short term they are often cash-using rather than cash-generating units, but usually this situation reverses in time. BCG analysis advocates retaining stars in the corporate portfolio.

Cash Cows   Businesses that fall into the low market growth/high market share cell are referred to as **cash cows**. These businesses generate substantial cash surpluses over what they need for reinvestment and growth. Cash cows are generally yesterday's stars whose industries have matured. Although not attractive from a growth standpoint, they are quite valuable, for the cash surpluses they generate can be used to pay bills, cover dividends, provide funds for investment, or support struggling businesses, such as the question marks described in a following section. BCG analysis also views cash cows favorably and advocates keeping them in the corporate portfolio.

Dogs   Businesses that fall into the low market growth/low market share cell are known as **dogs**. These businesses typically generate low profits, and in some cases they may even lose money. They also frequently consume more management time than they are worth. Unless there is some compelling reason to hold onto a dog, such as an expected turnaround in market growth rate, BCG analysis suggests that such businesses be removed from the portfolio.

Question Marks   Businesses that fall into the high market growth/low market share cell are referred to as **question marks**. The rapid market growth makes these businesses look attractive from an industry standpoint. Unfortunately, their low market share makes their profit potential uncertain. Question-mark businesses are often called cash hogs because they require large infusions of resources to keep up with the rapid growth and product development of the market. BCG analysis suggests that the organization must consider very carefully whether continued funding for

Developing a BCG Matrix for Your College

To get experience in developing a BCG matrix, examine the various academic departments of your business school. Consider that the total market consists of your university's school of business and its three geographically closest competing business schools. The academic departments in your school will be the "business units" being analyzed. Construct a BCG matrix using the following guidelines:

- Allow the market growth rate axis to reflect a unit's average annual growth.
- Allow the relative market share axis to reflect the ratio of a particular department's student enrollment to the enrollment of that department's largest competitor (from among the four schools being studied).
- Use a circle to plot each department on the BCG matrix. The size of the circle can represent the proportion of the total business school enrollment generated by students majoring in that department's curriculum. The circle's pie slice can reflect the percentage of the total business school faculty assigned to that department.

Even though this is a not-for-profit organization, the location of the circles on the matrix will be some indication of the stature of the different departments. Some departments may have large student enrollments with low faculty staffing levels, while others may have relatively small student enrollments but high faculty staffing levels. This analysis can then be used in allocating resources to individual departments or in making expansion and contraction decisions about individual departments.

SOURCE: Adapted from *Strategic Management*, 6th ed., by David, Fred. R., © 1996. Reprinted by permission of Prentice-Hall, Inc., Upper Saddle River, N.J.

a question mark is worthwhile. Management must consider the question mark's potential to gain market share and move into the star category.

BCG portfolio analysis can be used in both for-profit and not-for-profit organizations and in manufacturing and service organizations. Turn your attention, for the moment, to "Now Apply It."[19] Here is an opportunity for you to gain hands-on experience in developing a BCG matrix using your own business school as the industry and the various academic departments as the business units.

The BCG business portfolio matrix makes valuable contributions in the area of strategic decision making. It enables a corporation to highlight the flow of cash resources among the units in its portfolio, and it provides a sound rationalization for resource allocation, investment, expansion, and contraction decisions. It also enables management to assess the balance among the units within its portfolio. A balanced portfolio should contain units in several cells. The status of individual business units can shift over time. For example, question marks can move into the star category, and stars will eventually evolve into cash cows. For these reasons, it is important to have question marks "waiting in the wings" to replace stars and stars waiting to replace any cash cows that might slip into the dog category.

Darden Restaurants (parent company to Red Lobster and Olive Garden Restaurants) is a classic example of a service organization that tries to balance its portfolio to ensure its long-term success. In addition to the seafood and Italian segments of casual dining, Darden has recently ventured into the Caribbean and barbeque segments with its Bahama Breeze Restaurants and Smokey Bones BBQ Sports Bars. Each restaurant chain is in a different stage of development and occupies a different position on the BCG matrix. With 631 restaurants, Red Lobster is a mature chain in a mature segment of the restaurant industry. Although Red Lobster still has opportunities for expansion, its growth rate has subsided since the early 1980s, when units were popping up everywhere. When Olive Garden was started in 1982, the intention was to build this chain into a leader in its segment by penetrating the domestic market. While Olive Garden, with its 482 restaurants, has already achieved this leadership position and is moving beyond the middle growth stage, it should continue

Although Red Lobster, a mature chain in a mature segment of the restaurant industry, has seen its growth rate subside since the early 1980s, it is still a cash cow.

to enjoy significant growth for several years to come. Placing these restaurant chains on a BCG matrix, we find that Red Lobster is a cash cow and Olive Garden is a star that is approaching the cash cow category.

In the early 1990s Darden moved into the Chinese segment with its China Coast Restaurants. As the China Coast venture was beginning its growth, it fell into the question mark category. With only 51 restaurants and a short track record, its future was uncertain. The questions about China Coast were certainly answered when Darden abruptly closed all China Coast restaurants in August 1995. Darden replaced China Coast in its portfolio with the Bahama Breeze Restaurants. This segment has been setting and resetting records for Darden at each of its restaurants since opening. With 26 restaurants thus far, it is quickly moving from the question mark category toward the star category. Darden's newest concept restaurant, Smokey Bones BBQ Sports Bar currently falls into the question mark category with its 16 prototype outlets. The BCG matrix will continue to be an important tool for Darden as long as it continues to experiment with new dining concepts.

The BCG business portfolio matrix approach is not without its shortcomings. Some critics have argued that the four-cell classification scheme is overly simplistic. Others contend that accurately measuring market share and growth rate can be difficult. Furthermore, when the analysis is based on just these two factors, other important variables may be overlooked.[20] In an attempt to overcome some of the limitations of the BCG approach, more refined models have been proposed. One of the early refinements of the BCG approach is the General Electric model, which attempts to overcome some of the BCG shortcomings.

THE INDUSTRY ATTRACTIVENESS/BUSINESS STRENGTH MATRIX

GE matrix

A business portfolio matrix that uses industry attractiveness and business strength as the indicators of the firm's strategic position.

General Electric (GE) developed a nine-cell business portfolio matrix that overcomes some of the limitations of the BCG matrix. The **GE matrix** uses several factors (listed in Table 7.2) to assess industry attractiveness and business strength.[21] The GE approach also allows for three levels of industry attractiveness and business strength, resulting in its nine-cell structure.

To use the GE matrix, each of the organization's businesses is rated as to industry attractiveness and business strength. To measure the attractiveness of an industry, the decision maker first selects from Table 7.2 those factors that are likely to contribute to the attractiveness of the industry in question. Each factor is assigned a weight based upon its perceived importance. These weights must sum to 1.0. The industry is then assigned a rating for each of these factors using some uniform scale (for example, a 1-to-5 rating scale). Finally, a weighted score is obtained by multiplying weights by factor scores, and then adding to obtain a total weighted value. To arrive at a measure of business strength, each business is rated using the same procedure as for industry attractiveness. Table 7.3 illustrates these calculations for a hypothetical business in a corporation's portfolio.[22]

The total weighted scores for industry attractiveness and business strength are used to locate the business on the nine-cell matrix. Figure 7.2 illustrates a GE business portfolio matrix that contains eight businesses, with each circle reflecting one business.[23] The area of a circle is proportional to the size of the entire industry, while the pie slice within the circle represents the business's share of that market.

The GE matrix provides the decision maker with rationalization for resource allocation, investment, expansion, and contraction decisions within different cells, in much the same way as the BCG matrix. Businesses that fall into the three green cells at the upper left of the GE matrix are given top investment priority. These are the combinations of industry attractiveness and business strength that are most favorable. The strategic prescription for businesses located in these three cells is

Table 7.2 | Factors Contributing to Industry Attractiveness and Business Strength

INDUSTRY ATTRACTIVENESS	BUSINESS STRENGTH
MARKET FORCES	
Size (dollars, units, or both)	Your share (in equivalent terms)
Size of key segments	Your share of key segments
Growth rate per year:	Your annual growth rate:
Total	Total
Segments	Segments
Diversity of market	Diversity of your participation
Sensitivity to price, service, features, and external factors	Your influence on the market
Cyclicality	Lags or leads in your sales
Seasonality	
Bargaining power of upstream suppliers	Bargaining power of your suppliers
Bargaining power of downstream suppliers	Bargaining power of your customers
COMPETITION	
Types of competitors	Where you fit, how you compare in terms of products, marketing capability, service, production strength, financial strength, and management
Degree of concentration	
Changes in type and mix	
Entries and exits	Segments you have entered or left
Changes in share	Your relative share change
Substitution by new technology	Your vulnerability to new technology
Degrees and types of integration	Your own level of integration
FINANCIAL AND ECONOMIC FACTORS	
Contribution margins	Your margins
Leveraging factors, such as economies of scale and experience	Your scale and experience
Barriers to entry or exit (both financial and nonfinancial)	Barriers to your entry or exit (both financial and nonfinancial)
Capacity utilization	Your capacity utilization
TECHNOLOGICAL FACTORS	
Maturity and volatility	Your ability to cope with change
Complexity	Depths of your skills
Differentiation	Types of your technological skills
Patents and copyrights	Your patent protection
Manufacturing process technology required	Your manufacturing technology
SOCIOPOLITICAL FACTORS IN YOUR ENVIRONMENT	
Social attitudes and trends	Your company's responsiveness and flexibility
Laws and government agency regulations	Your company's ability to cope
Influence with pressure groups and government representatives	Your company's aggressiveness
Human factors, such as unionization and community acceptance	Your company's relationships

SOURCE: *Strategic Market Planning* by Abell/Hammond, © 1979. Reprinted by permission of Prentice-Hall, Inc., Upper Saddle River, NJ.

Table 7.3 | Illustration of Industry Attractiveness and Business Strength Computations

INDUSTRY ATTRACTIVENESS	WEIGHT	RATING (1–5)	VALUE
Overall market size	0.20	4.00	0.80
Annual market growth rate	0.20	5.00	1.00
Historical profit margin	0.15	4.00	0.60
Competitive intensity	0.15	2.00	0.30
Technological requirements	0.15	3.00	0.45
Inflationary vulnerability	0.05	3.00	0.15
Energy requirements	0.05	2.00	0.10
Environmental impact	0.05	1.00	0.05
Social/political/legal	Must be acceptable		
	1.00		3.45

BUSINESS STRENGTH	WEIGHT	RATING (1–5)	VALUE
Market share	0.10	4.00	0.40
Share growth	0.15	4.00	0.60
Product quality	0.10	4.00	0.40
Brand reputation	0.10	5.00	0.50
Distribution network	0.05	4.00	0.20
Promotional effectiveness	0.05	5.00	0.25
Productive capacity	0.05	3.00	0.15
Productive efficiency	0.05	2.00	0.10
Unit costs	0.15	3.00	0.45
Material supplies	0.05	5.00	0.25
R&D performance	0.10	4.00	0.40
Managerial personnel	0.05	4.00	0.20
	1.00		3.90

SOURCE: Adapted from *Strategic Management: Text and Cases on Business Policy* by Hosmer, © 1984. Reprinted by permission of Prentice-Hall, Upper Saddle River, NJ.

to invest and grow. Businesses positioned in the three gold cells are next in priority. These businesses deserve selective reinvestment to maintain and protect their industry positions. Finally, businesses positioned in the three orange cells at the lower right of the matrix are serious candidates for divestiture due to their low overall strength.[24]

Although similar to the BCG approach, the GE matrix offers several improvements. For one thing, it allows for intermediate rankings between high and low and between weak and strong, yielding nine rather than four cells. A second improvement is that it incorporates a much wider variety of strategically relevant variables. Whereas the BCG matrix considers only two factors (industry growth rate and relative market share), the GE matrix takes many factors into consideration (see again Table 7.2) to determine industry attractiveness and business strength. Finally, and perhaps most important, the GE approach emphasizes allocating corporate resources to businesses with the greatest chance of achieving competitive advantage and superior performance.[25]

Despite these improvements, the GE matrix does have its critics. Like the BCG matrix, it prescribes only a general strategic posture and provides no real guidance on the specifics of the business strategy. Another criticism of the GE approach (and the BCG approach, for that matter) is that they are static. They portray businesses as they are at one point in time and do not take into account that businesses evolve

Figure 7.2 | The GE Industry Attractiveness/Business Strength Matrix

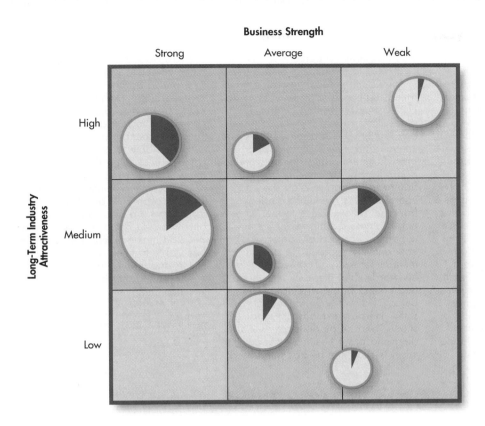

over time. Consequently, these approaches do not detect businesses that are about to become winners because their industries are entering the takeoff stage or businesses that are about to become losers as their industries enter the decline stage.[26] This was certainly the case as Darden was expanding the China Coast restaurant chain. The BCG matrix was not capable of helping management foresee this chain's sudden demise.

OPERATIONAL DECISION MAKING

The strategic decision making just examined is typically conducted at high levels within the organization and covers long time horizons. Operational decision making, on the other hand, relates to decision situations that cover much shorter spans of time. In "Leaders In Action" on page 222 we see how limousine service owner John Lenhard had to make some operational level decisions related to his marketing efforts if he was going to survive the post 9/11 downturn in his industry.[27] While operational decisions are typically made at lower levels within the organization, this need not always be the case. In Chapter 6 and earlier in this chapter, we spoke of Saturn's decision to recall almost 400,000 automobiles due to faulty wiring. Whether or not to recall is by no means a long-term strategic decision. This decision applied to the immediate short-term future. Nevertheless, you can be sure that it received the full attention of top-level management. In the next sections, we will introduce structure to the operational decision-making process. Once that structure is in place, a variety of computational decision-making techniques can be applied.

LEARNING OBJECTIVE 5

Describe the nature of operational decision making.

9/11 Stung Entrepreneur Decides to Reinvent His Business

The events of 9/11 had a dramatic impact on contemporary society around the world. The effects were felt in large corporations and small businesses alike. One such small business was John Lenhard's Sterling Services, a Miami limousine service that catered to telecom and software executives, celebrities, corporate clients, and other well-heeled travelers. Business had been quite good at Sterling. Word-of-mouth brought a steady stream of top paying clients; Lenhard barely needed to advertise his shiny stretched limousines. Then came 9/11 and the party ended. Many executives, celebrities, and tourists abruptly quit flying to South Florida, and many corporate clients cut back on unnecessary expenses. Revenues, which had been rising at least 20 percent annually before these tragic events, tumbled. During some post 9/11 weeks, revenue

was less than 10 percent of what it was prior to the attacks on America.

While many local limousine firms failed, Lenhard made a series of decisions that reinvented his business. Not willing to rely on word-of-mouth any longer, Lenhard joined the Convention and Visitors Bureau and other business groups for networking and referrals. He hired a marketing firm to redesign his Web site and coordinate his marketing strategy from the Yellow Pages to the Internet. Business that he might have turned his nose up at earlier was now actively courted. He became a member of every chamber, and in his words, "I'm there shaking hands and kissing babies. I enjoy it. But before, I didn't have to do that stuff." He now exhibits at wedding shows, and he gladly accepts wedding and prom business. His optimism is such that he has purchased

a $250,000 luxury recreational vehicle, complete with leather couches, TVs, and a barbecue. "It's perfect for tailgating," Lenhard says. He is marketing it as a display vehicle for companies to rent at outdoor events. To some extent, Lenhard has actually been able to capitalize on that same fear of flying that has afflicted many travelers and affected his business. Recently a family rented his stretch Yukon SUV and two drivers for a road trip to Upstate New York and Niagara Falls. Through creative decision making, John Lenhard has been able to keep his business surviving and thriving while many others in the industry have failed.

SOURCE: M. Adams, "Limo Company Reinvents Itself to Survive, Thrive," *USA Today,* April 9, 2002, 2E.

APPLYING STRUCTURE TO THE DECISION-MAKING PROCESS

LEARNING OBJECTIVE 6

Discuss the basic elements that add structure to the decision-making process.

Several basic elements of decision making can be identified in the decision-making steps described in Chapter 6. They are referred to as alternative courses of action, states of nature, and payoffs. These elements can often be conveniently arranged into a structured array to aid in the decision analysis. Such an array is called a payoff table.

Alternative courses of action
Strategies that might be implemented in a decision-making situation.

ALTERNATIVE COURSES OF ACTION   The **alternative courses of action** in a decision-making situation are the strategies that the decision maker might implement to solve the problem or respond to the opportunity. To make high-quality decisions, the decision maker must first identify viable and potentially attractive alternative courses of action.

States of nature
Conditions over which the decision maker has little or no control.

STATES OF NATURE   **States of nature** are conditions that can occur in the future. They will affect the outcome of the decision, yet the decision maker has little or no control over them.[28] For example, corporate financial officers must often decide how to invest surplus funds. Future interest rates are a state of nature that will affect the outcome of their decisions. States of nature can reflect any type of future event that is likely to affect the outcome of a decision, including such events as weather, competitor behavior, economic conditions, political events, new laws, and consumer behavior. The more certain the decision maker is about the likelihood of various states of nature, the easier the decision making will be. Unfortunately, as we will see later, decision makers are rarely able to foresee future events with complete certainty. The degree of certainty that the decision maker possesses will affect the decision-making process.

PAYOFFS The interaction of each alternative course of action with each state of nature will result in a decision outcome. Each combination of alternative and state of nature will produce a separate outcome. Suppose that a company can choose to invest surplus funds in fixed-rate certificates of deposit (CDs) or in a money market account. If the company invests in CDs and interest rates rise, the yield will not be as great as it would have been if the money had been invested in a money market account. Outcomes of decision situations are often referred to as **payoffs**, since the objective in many business decisions can be measured in units of monetary value.

PAYOFF TABLES By properly organizing these elements, a systematic decision analysis can be undertaken. In decision theory, payoffs are called conditional values, because each payoff is conditional upon a particular alternative course of action's having first been selected and a particular state of nature's having subsequently occurred. Whenever a decision situation is to be analyzed, the basic elements of the situation can be arranged in a matrix called a **payoff table**, or a conditional value matrix, due to the conditional nature of the payoffs.[29] The alternative courses of action form the rows of the table, and the states of nature form the columns, as in Table 7.4.[30] Then each cell in the table contains the outcome, or payoff, for a particular combination of an alternative course of action and state of nature. Organizing the decision-making elements in this structured format allows for the systematic analysis of the decision problem and the eventual selection of an appropriate course of action.

If you compare the payoff table for operational decision making with the strategic decision-making matrix discussed earlier, you will see some similarity. Both use a two-dimensional matrix with decision alternatives arranged along the left side. But here the similarity ends. The strategic decision-making matrix employs multiple objectives and arranges them across the top of the matrix. The payoff table uses a single objective whose measurements appear within the cells of the matrix. External factors (that is, states of nature) affecting the outcomes of the decisions are arranged across the top of the payoff table.

Payoffs
The outcomes of decision situations.

Payoff table
A matrix that organizes the alternative courses of action, states of nature, and payoffs for a decision situation.

TECHNIQUES THAT ENHANCE QUALITY IN DECISION MAKING

The manner in which the information in the payoff table is analyzed is a function of the decision-making environment. At a basic level of analysis, three different decision-making environments are generally identified, depending on the amount

LEARNING OBJECTIVE 7

Discuss the differences between decision making under certainty, risk, and uncertainty.

Table 7.4 | Structure of a Payoff Table

ALTERNATIVE COURSES OF ACTION	STATES OF NATURE		
	S_1	S_2	S_3
A_1	O_{11}	O_{12}	O_{13}
A_2	O_{21}	O_{22}	O_{23}
A_3	O_{31}	O_{32}	O_{33}
A_4	O_{41}	O_{42}	O_{43}

NOTE: A_i = alternative courses of action; S_j = states of nature; O_{ij} = outcome associated with alternative i and state of nature j.

of knowledge that exists about future conditions that might occur: (1) decision making under certainty, (2) decision making under risk, and (3) decision making under uncertainty.[31] The more information the decision maker has about future conditions, the easier the selection of an alternative course of action will be. As the future becomes more clouded, it becomes more difficult to identify one best tool for analyzing the decision. As a result, in such cases, decision makers tend to have less confidence in the alternative they select for implementation.

DECISION MAKING UNDER CERTAINTY   In decision making under certainty, the decision maker knows with certainty what conditions will subsequently occur and affect the decision outcomes. Hence, the decision maker knows what the outcome will be for each alternative course of action. In such a situation, a rational decision maker will logically select the alternative with the most desirable outcome. For example, suppose you have $1,000 that you would like to place in your neighborhood bank for one year. Suppose further that your alternatives are limited to depositing the money in a savings account that yields 5 percent annual interest or a CD that yields 6 percent annual interest. If both investments are equally secure, you will not need access to this money during the year, and your objective is to maximize your monetary payoff, then you would choose the CD.

LEARNING OBJECTIVE 8

Describe the solution approaches that would be taken for risk and uncertainty situations.

DECISION MAKING UNDER RISK   Decision makers seldom encounter conditions of certainty. In most instances decision makers do not know with certainty which future state of nature will occur and subsequently influence the decision outcome. In many cases, however, the decision maker may have a reasonable idea of the chance, or probability, that each state of nature will occur. Consider the financial officer's decision on investing surplus funds. Examination of economic forecasts might provide the officer with the likelihood, or probability, that future interest rates will reach certain levels. When such probabilities are present, the process is referred to as decision making under risk. In decision making under risk, the probabilities are used to obtain expected values of outcomes for each decision alternative. The decision maker then selects the alternative that maximizes the expected outcome, assuming that the outcomes in the payoff table are attractive (for example, profits). If the outcomes in the payoff table represent an undesirable parameter (such as cost), then the decision maker should, of course, select the alternative that minimizes the expected outcome.

Table 7.5 shows the structure of a decision situation that has been scaled down for ease of illustration.[32] In this situation, an organization has a surplus of $100,000 available for short-term (one-year) investment. The financial officer is considering three simple investment alternatives: the stock market, bonds, or a money market account. In this example, the gain to be realized after one year will depend upon the economic conditions that prevail during that year. For simplicity, assume that the economy might rise, remain stationary, or fall. The conditional payoffs for each combination of alternative and state of nature are displayed in the payoff table shown in Table 7.5. Notice that in one cell the return is a negative number, indi-

Table 7.5   Payoff Table for Sample Illustration: Conditional Value Matrix

	STATES OF NATURE		
ALTERNATIVES	**RISING ECONOMY**	**STATIONARY ECONOMY**	**FALLING ECONOMY**
Stock Market	$20,000	$5,000	−$8,000
Bonds	5,000	5,000	5,000
Money Market	10,000	7,000	4,000

cating a loss if the money is invested in the stock market and the economy subsequently falls.

Expected Monetary Value   An **expected value** is the product of a conditional value and the probability of its occurrence. In a decision-making matrix, each alternative strategy has a total **expected monetary value (EMV)**, which is the sum of each expected value for that alternative.[33] In Table 7.6, probabilities have been assigned to each state of nature.[34] The decision maker would have estimated these probabilities after careful analysis of various economic indicators.

The matrix shown in Table 7.6 illustrates the calculation of the EMVs for each alternative course of action. This is referred to as an expected value matrix. The expected values within Table 7.6 are obtained by multiplying the conditional values in Table 7.5 by their probabilities of occurrence. The figures indicate that the most desirable alternative is the money market option, which yields $7,300, the highest expected monetary value. This highest EMV of $7,300 is an interesting figure. You might mistakenly conclude that the money market will generate a return of $7,300, but in fact this can never happen. If the money market account is the selected alternative, the conditional values, as shown in Table 7.5, indicate that the only possible returns are $10,000, $7,000, or $4,000. Then what does the $7,300 figure reflect? The $7,300 value is the long-run average return that would occur if the decision maker faced this situation repeatedly and selected the money market alternative each time. On some occasions the return would be $10,000 (30 percent of the time, assuming that the probabilities reflect long-run frequencies for different economic conditions). Furthermore, 50 percent of the time, the return would be $7,000, and 20 percent of the time, a return of $4,000 would be realized. Averaging the returns from repeated decisions over a long period of time gives the $7,300 figure.

Decision Trees   As we have just seen, the payoff matrix is a convenient way to analyze alternatives in decision making under risk situations. Our investment example might also have been structured in a **decision tree** format, with various tree branches and junctions (or nodes) depicting the same decision scenario.[35] Figure 7.3 displays this problem in a decision tree format.

In this tree diagram, the box represents a decision point, with alternatives emanating from it. Circles represent points in time after the potential decision has been made when states of nature (future events) are about to occur. Each circle in this diagram has the three states of nature emanating from it. Each state of nature is accompanied by its probability of occurrence. Finally, payoffs are shown at the termination of each state-of-nature branch. Each payoff is still a conditional value. The events the payoffs are conditional upon can be found by tracing from the decision point to the payoff. For example, if the money market alternative is selected and the economy remains stationary (with a 0.5 probability), the payoff

Expected value
The product of a payoff and its probability of occurrence.

Expected monetary value (EMV)
The sum of each expected value for an alternative.

Decision tree
A branching diagram that illustrates the alternatives and states of nature for a decision situation.

Table 7.6 | Calculation of Expected Monetary Values: Expected Value Matrix

	STATES OF NATURE			
Probability	0.3	0.5	0.2	
ALTERNATIVES	**RISING ECONOMY**	**STATIONARY ECONOMY**	**FALLING ECONOMY**	**EXPECTED MONETARY VALUE**
Stock Market	$6,000	$2,500	−$1,600	$6,900
Bonds	1,500	2,500	1,000	5,000
Money Market	3,000	3,500	800	7,300

Maximum expected monetary value = $7,300, associated with the money market alternative.

Figure 7.3 | Decision Tree

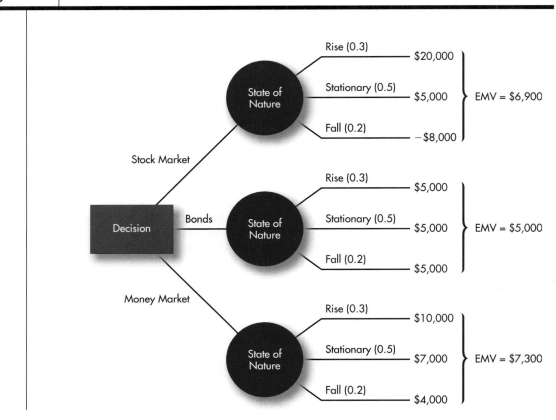

will be $7,000. The tree can be used to compute expected monetary values and will give the same results as the payoff table, as Figure 7.3 shows. Although a decision tree can be used for simple problems such as this, this approach is most useful for situations in which sequential decisions must be made over time. In such cases an alternative-choice branch will be followed by a state-of-nature branch, which may be followed by another decision point with more branches emanating from it. With such a complex series of interrelated decisions, decision trees are the only recourse for obtaining a solution.

A decision tree approach proved to be quite helpful to the United States Postal Service (USPS) in the early 1980s, when it began to explore the possibility of expanding the five-digit ZIP code. The USPS viewed the developmental study as a two-phase decision process. Phase I focused on information dissemination and the acquisition of automated equipment for pilot testing. Phase II dealt with the continuation of the postal automation strategy. Six alternatives were included in this phase (one of which was to cancel Phase II and terminate the expanded ZIP code concept). We all know through our daily dealings with the USPS that the expanded ZIP code concept (called ZIP+4) was adopted. What we probably don't know is that this decision was prompted by an extensive decision tree analysis of the alternatives based on internal rate of return and net present value of cash flows.[36]

DECISION MAKING UNDER UNCERTAINTY   In some cases a decision maker cannot assess the probability of occurrence for the various states of nature. When no probabilities are available, the situation is referred to as decision making under uncertainty. In such situations the decision maker can choose among several possible approaches for making the decision. Each approach takes a different view of the likelihood of future events.[37] To illustrate two extremes, consider an optimistic approach and a pessimistic approach to decision making under uncertainty. The optimistic approach assumes that the best payoff will occur regardless of the alternative selected by the decision maker. If you were an optimistic decision maker facing the investment decision described earlier, you would choose the stock market alternative, because it has the highest of the optimistic payoffs ($20,000). On the other extreme, a pessimistic approach assumes that the worst payoff will occur regardless of the alternative selected by the decision maker. If you were a pessimistic decision maker facing the same investment decision, you would choose the bond alternative, because it has the highest of the pessimistic payoffs ($5,000).

Different decision makers will have different perceptions about which future events are likely to occur and different levels of aversion to risky ventures; both will influence their decision making. To accommodate these differences, several uncertainty approaches have been developed. Although the details will not be covered here, we can note that these approaches generally fall between the optimistic and pessimistic extremes described earlier. None of these approaches can be described as the "best" approach, for there is no one best uncertainty approach. Each has utility for different decision makers, since different people often have different ways of looking at a problem.[38]

ETHICAL AND SOCIAL IMPLICATIONS IN DECISION MAKING

The treatment of decision making presented thus far may leave the impression that all managers need to do is plug in the numbers to generate the best choice of an alternative. However, managers must also be careful to consider more than just the numbers. Often they will have to look beyond the numbers and consider the ethical and social implications of their decisions. We saw in "Facing the Challenge" on page 210 that Tupperware officials wrestled with the decisions they could make to improve U.S. profitability. Negative repercussions from past failed decisions made them realize that they needed to be sensitive to the concerns of their dealers, managers, and distributors in any future decisions.

Many examples can be cited for decisions that went beyond bottom-line profitability and included a component of ethical behavior and social responsibility. At considerable expense The Walt Disney Company is refurbishing many of its resort swimming pools into "zero entry" pools. Also called "zero grade" or "zero barrier" pools, these pools lack a traditional elevated ledge, instead offering a gradual "shore-like" entrance and exit. Handicapped bathers can simply roll into the pool in special water-resistant wheelchairs.[39] Burger King has decided to double the number of welfare recipients hired.[40] In response to tragic incidents of children dying after becoming trapped in car trunks, General Motors announced its decision to equip its family cars with an infrared sensing device that automatically unlocks the trunk if anyone is trapped inside.[41] Partly due to the rising number of fatal handgun incidents (and partly due to corresponding liability issues), the Colt Manufacturing Company, Inc., has decided to remove itself from the consumer handgun business.[42] In an effort to help the homeless break out of the endless cycle of poverty, the Orlando/Orange County Expressway Authority made hiring the homeless a condition for contractors bidding on a highway project.[43] And how about Bob Thompson? When he sold his road-building firm, one of the conditions of the sale was that his employees would not lose their jobs. Then, as a reward for their loyalty and hard work, he decided to split $128 million from the sale among his 550 flabbergasted workers. More than 80 of them became instant millionaires![44]

LEARNING OBJECTIVE 9

Discuss the basics of breakeven analysis, linear programming, and PERT analysis.

Breakeven analysis
A graphic display of the relationship between volume of output, revenue, and costs.

QUANTITATIVE DECISION-MAKING AIDS

Many quantitative models, tools, and techniques are available that can aid in various types of decision-making situations. Although a detailed presentation of these models is beyond the scope of this book, it is important to have some awareness of these tools and techniques. The next sections provide a brief overview of some of the more important models.

BREAKEVEN ANALYSIS   **Breakeven analysis** is a quantitative technique that allows managers to examine the relationships between output levels, revenues, and costs. By analyzing these factors, managers can determine the level of output at which the firm will break even (that is, where total revenue equals total cost; at this point, the firm makes no profit but incurs no loss). Furthermore, managers can project the profit or loss associated with any level of output. For a familiar example, consider the situation faced by the promoter of a rock concert. Revenue generated by the concert will be determined largely by the price charged per ticket and the number of tickets sold. (In some cases concession and souvenir sales might add to this revenue.) Expenses, for the most part, will consist of the contracted fee negotiated with the rock act, concert hall rental charges, and other personnel services, such as ticket takers and security guards. The promoter can use breakeven analysis to help determine ticket prices and the number of tickets that must be sold to break even or, more important to the promoter, to generate varying levels of profit.

Breakeven analysis depicts the output, revenue, and cost relationships in a graphical format, as illustrated in Figure 7.4.[45] In this format, output volume (in units of product) is represented on the horizontal axis of the graph, while the vertical axis indicates the levels of costs and revenues (in dollars).

Seven elements can be defined and illustrated on the breakeven graph.[46]

© LYNN GOLDSMITH/CORBIS

A promoter of a rock concert can use breakeven analysis to determine ticket prices and number of tickets sold to provide enough revenue to break even.

1. *Fixed cost.* Fixed cost includes those costs that remain constant regardless of the volume of output. Fixed cost comprises such items as overhead, administrative salaries, rent, and mortgage payments. It is shown by a horizontal line on the graph.

2. *Total variable cost.* This reflects the costs that increase as the volume of output rises. Variable costs include such items as raw material cost, direct labor cost, and the cost of energy consumed in the manufacture of the product. Total variable cost is obtained by multiplying the output level by the variable cost per unit (that is, the material, labor, and energy costs consumed per unit of output). On the graph, the total variable cost is zero when there is no output, but increases as the output level rises.

3. *Total cost.* The sum of fixed cost and total variable cost is the total cost. It is represented by a line that is parallel to the total variable cost line, but shifted upward due to the addition of the fixed cost.

4. *Total revenue.* This is the total dollars received from the sale of the output. Total revenue is obtained by multiplying the per-unit selling price by the output level. On the graph, revenue is zero when there is no output, but increases as the output level rises.

5. *Breakeven point.* On the graph, there is one level of output where total cost equals total revenue. This is defined as the breakeven point, for it is here that the organization will realize no profit, but incur no loss.

Figure 7.4 | Breakeven Analysis

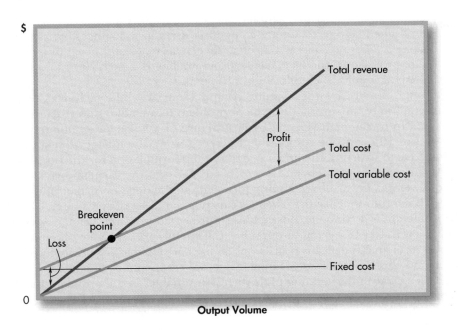

6. *Profit.* Profit is the amount by which total revenue exceeds total cost on the graph. Profit will be realized at all output levels to the right of the breakeven point.
7. *Loss.* Loss is the amount by which total cost exceeds total revenue. On the graph, a loss will be incurred at all output levels to the left of the breakeven point.

Breakeven analysis is a useful tool for analyzing the costs, revenues, profits, and losses at various levels of output. The simple linear structure displayed here does have its limitations, though. Often fixed cost does not remain constant through all levels of output. For example, to exceed some critical volume of output, it may be necessary for the organization to expand its plant, thereby incurring a sudden increase in its overhead, administrative expenses, and other contributors to fixed cost. A situation like this would be reflected as a step increase in the fixed cost line.

Similarly, price and unit variable cost may change as output volume changes. Higher levels of output may result in quantity discounts in the purchase of raw materials. Lower raw material costs would lead to a decrease in the slope of the variable cost line. Higher levels of output may also require more overtime from workers. The higher cost of labor would lead to an increase in the slope of the variable cost line. If higher levels of output occur, management must often reduce the selling price to encourage consumption of this additional output. Lowering the selling price would lead to a decrease in the slope of the revenue line. When situations such as these occur, the breakeven graph will not display the crisp, uniform, linear relationships shown in Figure 7.4. Instead, the lines may contain bends, curves, breaks, and kinks. Furthermore, these lines generally represent estimates of costs and revenues that will occur in the future. Since estimates are rarely exact, the lines will not be precise and sharp. Instead, the actual values might be above or below those lines. Consequently, the breakeven point should be regarded not as a single, indisputable value, but as an indication of an approximate range of output levels where breakeven is most likely to occur. Regardless of the amount of irregularity in these graphs, however, the fundamental relationships will remain intact. Profit will occur when total revenue exceeds total cost, losses will occur when total cost exceeds total revenue, and breakeven will occur when total cost equals total revenue.

LINEAR PROGRAMMING   Often managers are faced with the decision of how to allocate limited resources among competing users in a manner that optimizes some objective. These resources can be as diverse as materials, machines, money, energy, employees, and the like. **Linear programming** is a powerful tool that can help the manager solve such allocation problems.

Although the linear programming computations are quite technical, desktop computer software for solving this type of problem is available. Nevertheless, managers need to be familiar with the basic structure of a linear programming problem. After all, they will be responsible for recognizing these allocation situations and will have to structure the linear programming formulation for the decision situation before the computer can take over and perform the calculations.

To develop a linear programming formulation, the decision maker must structure two basic components: the objective function and a set of constraints.[47] An **objective function** is a symbolic, quantitative representation of the primary goal that the decision maker is seeking to optimize. **Constraints** are algebraic statements, in equation form, that reflect any restrictions on the decision maker's flexibility in making-decision choices. Before developing these two components, the decision maker must have a clear understanding of the decision variables in the problem. **Decision variables** represent the factors that the decision maker can manipulate, that is, the decisions that must be made. Table 7.7 illustrates a simple production decision where two products (bookcases and compact disc racks) are to be manufactured from three raw materials (wood, plastic laminate, and glue) whose supplies are limited. The data in the table indicate the amount of each raw material used in making each product, the amount of each raw material available, and the profit contribution for each product. The decision maker must decide how much of each product to manufacture to maximize profit, while at the same time being careful not to exceed the available supplies of each raw material. Steps 1 to 4 at the bottom of Table 7.7 show how the decision maker would define algebraic symbols to represent the number of units of each product to make (the decision variables) and the subsequent objective function and constraints that would have been formulated. This linear programming model is now ready for desktop computer solution.

The linear programming situation illustrated in Table 7.7 was kept exceedingly simple for illustration purposes. In reality, managers often face resource allocation problems consisting of hundreds or even thousands of decision variables and similar numbers of constraint equations. Linear programming has seen some very diverse applications over the years. For example, Owens Corning Fiberglas uses it to develop multiproduct production schedules, American Airlines uses it for scheduling flight crews and aircraft, and Major League Baseball uses it to assign umpires to baseball games.[48]

PERT   Organizations must often undertake large, unique projects that involve many highly interrelated work activities. In such cases, managers must be prepared to schedule all of those activities and the resources they consume so that the project can be completed in a timely fashion.

PERT (Program Evaluation and Review Technique) is a technique designed to aid in scheduling project activities. The PERT approach uses a network diagram to arrange and visually display project activities. Such a diagram can help managers to plan far in advance, pinpoint potential bottlenecks and trouble spots, and determine whether resources should be reallocated among activities.

In the PERT approach, four preliminary steps must be performed before the project analysis can begin: (1) activity identification, (2) precedence identification, (3) activity time estimation, and (4) network construction.[49] Activity identification

---

Linear Programming
A powerful quantitative tool that can help managers solve resource allocations problems.

Objective function
A symbolic, quantitative representation of the primary goal that the decision maker is seeking to optimize.

Constraints
Algebraic statements, in equation form, that reflect any restrictions on the decision maker's flexibility in making decision choices.

Decision variables
The factors that the decision maker can manipulate.

PERT (Program Evaluation and Review Technique)
A network approach for scheduling project activities.

Table 7.7 | Linear Programming

PRODUCT INFORMATION

Raw Material	BOOKCASES	COMPACT DISC RACKS	Raw Material Available
Lumber	8	5	400
Plastic laminate	4	2	120
Glue	1	2	60
Profit per unit	$15	$10	

Step 1. Definition of decision variables:
Let X_1 = the number of book cases manufactured.
Let X_2 = the number of CD racks manufactured.

Step 2. Establish objective function:
Maximize profit, or MAX $15X_1 + 10X_2$.

Step 3. Establish constraints:
Resource constraints: Amount of each raw material used must be less than or equal to the amount available.
Lumber constraint: $8X_1 + 5X_2 \leq 400$.
Plastic laminate constraint: $4X_1 + 2X_2 \leq 120$.
Glue constraint: $1X_1 + 2X_2 \leq 60$.
Nonnegativity constraints: You cannot make a negative number of bookcases or CD racks.

$$X_1 \geq 0$$
$$X_2 \geq 0$$

Step 4. Summarize problem:
MAX $15X_1 + 10X_2$
subject to: $8X_1 + 5X_2 \leq 400$
$\qquad 4X_1 + 2X_2 \leq 120$
$\qquad 1X_1 + 2X_2 \leq 60$
$\qquad X_1 \geq 0$
$\qquad X_2 \geq 0$
(Solution: $X_1 = 20$; $X_2 = 20$; profit = $500)

requires that managers determine all of the elements of work (activities) that must be performed for the project to be completed. To establish the activity precedence relationships, managers must determine which activities can be conducted simultaneously and which must be performed sequentially. It is also necessary to estimate the amount of time each activity will consume so that a time schedule eventually can be developed for the project activities. Finally, all of this information must be assembled into a network model to facilitate the analysis.

Figure 7.5 shows a network model for a simple project consisting of only five activities. In this project, a team of fraternity brothers will build a bicycle shed for the fraternity house. The arrows in the PERT diagram represent the activities, while the circles (nodes) represent events. The amount of time each activity will take is indicated on the appropriate arrow. The nodes (events) represent points in time. For example, at node 2, activity A (design the dimensions of the shed) has been completed, and activities B and C (set the forms for the concrete slab and cut the lumber for the shed) are ready to be started. Furthermore, precedence relation-

Figure 7.5 | PERT Analysis

Data generated in preliminary analysis of project:

Activity	Description	Immediate Predecessors	Activity Time (Days)
A	Design dimensions of shed	—	2
B	Set forms for concrete slab	A	1
C	Cut lumber for shed to proper dimensions	A	2
D	Pour concrete slab and allow to cure	B	4
E	Assemble shed	C, D	3

Resulting project network generated:

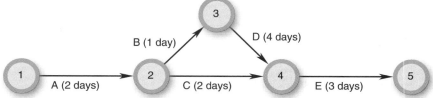

Identification of critical path:

Path	Time	
ABDE	10 days	(critical path)
ACE	7 days	

Earliest start (ES), earliest finish (EF), latest start (LS), and latest finish (LF) time estimates:

Activity	ES	EF	LS	LF	
A	0	2	4	6	ES for first activity = 0, or today's calendar date.
B	2	3	6	7	ES for other activities = largest EF of activity's immediate predecessors.
C	2	4	9	11	EF for activity = its ES + its activity time.
D	3	7	7	11	LF for last activity = some target completion time (14 days here).
E	7	10	11	14	LF for other activities = smallest LS of activity's immediate successors.
					LS for activity = its LF – its activity time.

ships can be recognized immediately from the diagram. For example, setting the forms for the concrete slab (activity B) and cutting the lumber for the shed (activity C) cannot begin until after the shed has been designed and its dimensions are known (activity A). Also, activities B and C (setting forms and cutting lumber) can be conducted simultaneously, since no precedence relationship exists between them.

Once the preliminary PERT steps have been performed, the network can be analyzed to determine reasonable start and finish times for each activity and a likely project duration. Project duration is determined from the network's critical path. A path is any sequence of activities that extends from the beginning to the end of the project. In our simple illustration, two paths extend from the beginning to the end of the project (path A-B-D-E and path A-C-E). The most time-consuming path in the network is the critical path. The critical path dictates the minimum amount of time in which the project can be completed and also indicates which activities are most critical to getting the project completed on time. In this example, the critical path is path A-B-D-E (10 days). Any delays on these activities will lengthen the duration of the project. We have assumed in this example that the fraternity brothers' main concern is finishing the project in 14 days, so that it will be completed when the other brothers return for the fall semester. Figure 7.5 summarizes the results from all the calculations of start and finish times for each of the project's activities.

This overview of PERT has described the technique in its most basic form. By expanding this form, managers can deal with situations in which the time required for activities is uncertain or those in which resources can be reallocated among activities to alter a project's completion time and cost. British Airways successfully used PERT to analyze the necessary activities in a program to create a new image for the corporation.[50]

INFORMATION TECHNOLOGY AND DECISION-MAKING TOOLS

We were introduced in Chapter 6 to a seven-step decision-making process and focused on how timely and accurate information is extremely beneficial in the first step (problem identification) and the last step (monitoring and evaluating). The tools and techniques introduced in this chapter are quantitative models that enable us to assess the promise of various alternative courses of action. Consequently, these tools and techniques have their biggest impact on the midsection of the decision-making process, where alternatives are evaluated and decisions reached. When we use quantitative models of this type, the old axiom rings true: Garbage in, garbage out. Regardless of how sophisticated these analytical tools are, their output (decision recommendations) will be worthless if the information being processed is suspect. Once again, the huge advances in information-gathering, -processing, and -dissemination technology serve to make this aspect of the decision-making process more reliable. The confidence we can place in our decisions will only increase as the technological advances in information handling continue.

IMPLICATIONS FOR LEADERS

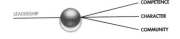

Decision making has always been one of the primary activities of business leaders. As the global business economy continues to expand and change dramatically, the level of managerial decision making can only be expected to increase in the future. If leaders are to make high-quality decisions, they will have to become thoroughly familiar with the structure of decision making and at the same time must equip themselves with the tools and techniques that can aid in the decision-making process. This embodies the competence component of the 3Cs leadership model. However, good decision making requires more than just competence; it also encompasses the remaining elements of the 3Cs leadership model. Good decision making requires that the decision maker possess strong character, infused with honesty, integrity, and driven by ethical behavior. It also requires a recognition that the impact of the decisions made may extend to the community and not be confined to the boundaries of the organization. To be effective decision makers, tomorrow's leaders should:

- Be able to recognize quickly problems and opportunities that call for a decision.
- Be able to recognize the different time frames and scopes of strategic decisions versus operational decisions.
- Be equipped with all the tools and techniques that can aid in making strategic decisions.
- Be familiar with the framework for operational decision making as well as the structural components for displaying operational decisions.
- Be able to recognize the different decision-making environments in which their operational decisions will be made.
- Have an awareness and understanding of the various quantitative tools that can aid in making operational decisions.

This chapter has presented several quantitative tools and techniques that can aid in making both strategic and operational decisions. These tools and techniques are quite analytical, suggesting that we need only "plug in the numbers" to select the best alternative. As we saw several times in our discussions, however, decision making cannot always go entirely by the numbers. Many times, experience, good judgment, and even intuition are valuable commodities when making decisions about future courses of action, especially since we can never be entirely certain about what the future holds in store.

Meeting The Challenge

Tupperware Decisions Respond to Changing Domestic Demographics

In mid-1970 Tupperware inspired legions of American women to take their first step into the work world. At the height of its success, tens of thousands of women were selling its storage containers through home parties attended by millions of their friends, relatives, and neighbors. But Tupperware would soon encounter a changing world in which women held full-time jobs and had little free time to attend Tupperware parties. Also, since so many sales people had quit and were not replaced, consumers who wanted Tupperware products often had no connection to a party hostess and had no easy way to obtain the products.

After years of not paying attention to the changing U.S. demographics, Tupperware finally stood up and took notice at the close of the 20th century. Decisions were made that were aimed at reinvigorating the United States market. Tupperware made a monumental departure from its direct selling tradition during the 1998 Christmas season. Temporary kiosks were set up in shopping malls. Eight percent of the company's fourth quarter business that year came from those kiosks, despite the fact that they were only open for six weeks. This

success prompted Tupperware Chairman E. V. "Rick" Goings to announce, "I want these in every mall where we can make money and have them open 12 months a year." Distributor-owned kiosks (called Tupperware Mall Showcases) have subsequently opened in many more malls, and many have been made permanent. In 1999 a decision was made to offer Tupperware products on television's Home Shopping Network. In that same year Tupperware introduced a Web site that features direct sales to consumers. Goings sees the Internet as a vehicle to reach what he calls the "'A' customer"—a working-woman with plenty of money but little time or inclination to attend a Tupperware party. In mid-2001 Tupperware selected the Target discount chain as an outlet for its products, and later that year unveiled a deal to sell its kitchenware through The Kroger Company—the nation's largest grocery chain. The decisions to sell online, on television, in malls, and in stores were critical. Goings noted that, "Our biggest new market is the United States. We need to reopen that market." Goings realizes that demographics will no longer allow the U.S. market to rely solely on

direct-sales parties. Some business will come from direct sales, but some will come from malls and stores, and some from the Internet. "I really can't say what the mix will be," says Goings, "but the future is no longer a mass market. It's stitching together niches." Goings predicts that these changes will bring the U.S. operation out of its slump and grow at 6 percent to 8 percent per year. If successful, similar changes may soon be in the works for Western Europe, which is seeing the beginnings of the demographic changes that hurt the company in the United States.

SOURCES: R. Burnett, "Tupperware to Sell Its Products in Kroger-Owned Stores in 3 States," *The Orlando Sentinel*, October 17, 2001, B1ff; C. Boyd, "Comeback Plan: Sell Where People Shop," *The Orlando Sentinel*, February 22, 2000, A1ff; C. Boyd, "As Problems Piled Up, Tupperware Partied On," *The Orlando Sentinel*, February 21, 2000, A1ff; C. Boyd, "The Plastic Empire: How Tupperware Went Stale," *The Orlando Sentinel*, February 20, 2000, A1ff; "Tupperware and Kroger Announce Marketing Agreement," *Tupperware Press Release*, October 16, 2001; "Tupperware Launches New Web Site With E-Commerce Feature," *Tupperware Press Release*, August 10, 1999; "Tupperware Announces Agreement With Home Shopping Network," *Tupperware Press Release*, May 19, 1999.

SUMMARY

1. Managerial decisions are called for when a problem occurs or an opportunity presents itself. A problem occurs when some aspect of organizational performance is less than desirable, while an opportunity occurs whenever there is a situation that has the potential to provide additional beneficial outcomes to the organization.

2. On a basic level, decisions can be classified as either programmed or nonprogrammed. Programmed decisions are routine responses to decision situations that may have occurred in the past or with which the decision maker is familiar. Nonprogrammed decisions are responses to situations that are unique, unstructured, or poorly defined.

3. Strategic decision making occurs from a broad perspective and is performed at the highest levels within organizations. It involves the selection of a corporate-level strategy and the choice of competitive strategies to be pursued by the various business units of the organization. Strategic decision making is most often nonroutine by nature. Selection of a business strategy can be facilitated by means of the strategic decision-making matrix approach. This tool allows the decision maker to evaluate a variety of potential strategies in conjunction with several objectives. Objectives are ranked by their importance, and strategies are rated by their likelihood of achieving those objectives. This method ultimately allows for the ranking of alternative strategies.

4. Two popular matrix approaches for evaluating a business portfolio are the BCG growth-share matrix and the GE industry attractiveness/business strength matrix. Although both have two dimensions, they measure different factors and include a different number of levels for each factor. The two factors in the BCG matrix are market growth rate and relative market share. With two levels for each factor, a four-cell matrix results. The GE matrix uses industry attractiveness and business strength as its factors. Three levels for each factor are defined, resulting in a nine-cell matrix. In both approaches, an organization's business units are placed in the appropriate cell; then prescriptions for strategic decision making are made relative to the cell occupied by the business unit.

5. Operational decision making pervades all levels in the organization and is usually concerned with routine day-to-day decisions.

6. Alternative courses of action, states of nature, and payoffs are the basic elements that add structure to decision situations. Alternative courses of action are the decision options available to the decision maker. States of nature are future conditions that will affect the outcome of the decision options. Payoffs represent the interaction of each alternative course of action with each state of nature. Each payoff represents the outcome or consequence associated with a particular alternative course of action having been selected and a particular state of nature eventually occurring.

7. In decision making under certainty, the decision maker knows exactly which future state of nature will occur. In decision making under risk, the decision maker is not sure which state of nature will occur, but can assess the probability, or likelihood, of each occurring. In decision making under uncertainty, the decision maker is not sure which of the states of nature will occur and can make no reasonable estimates of the probabilities of their occurrence.

8. Various computational criteria exist for analyzing decision making under conditions of certainty, risk, and uncertainty. When risk conditions prevail, payoff tables can be used in conjunction with state-of-nature probabilities to arrive at expected payoffs for each alternative. The alternative with the best expected payoff will then be selected. Decision trees provide another format for assessing decision making under risk situations. Alternative courses of action and states of nature are laid out in a tree diagram rather than in a matrix. Decision trees are particularly useful when the decision maker faces a sequence of interrelated decisions that occur over time. When uncertainty conditions prevail, decision makers must assess their degree of optimism about the likely occurrence of future events in order to make a choice.

9. Breakeven analysis is a quantitative technique that allows managers to graphically examine the relationships between output levels, revenue, and costs. Linear programming is a technique that allows managers to determine how to best allocate limited resources among competing users in a manner that optimizes some objective. PERT is a network technique that allows managers to schedule a complex set of interrelated activities that must be performed to complete large, unique projects.

REVIEW QUESTIONS

1. *(Learning Objective 1)* Identify the two situations that are likely to result in a business decision being made.

2. *(Learning Objective 2)* Identify and describe the two basic classifications for managerial decisions.

3. *(Learning Objective 3)* Describe the strategic decision-making matrix technique for selecting from among strategy alternatives.

4. *(Learning Objective 4)* Describe the structure, purpose, and approach of the four-cell BCG matrix and the nine-cell GE matrix.

5. *(Learning Objective 5)* How does operational decision making differ from strategic decision making?

6. *(Learning Objective 6)* Describe the components of a payoff matrix and explain how it adds structure to the decision-making process.

7. *(Learning Objective 7)* Describe how decision making under certainty, risk, and uncertainty differ.

8. *(Learning Objective 8)* Describe how decision trees can aid with decision making under conditions of risk.

9. *(Learning Objective 9)* Briefly describe the difference in the situations for which breakeven analysis, linear programming, and PERT analysis are applicable.

DISCUSSION QUESTIONS

Improving Critical Thinking

1. Discuss the pros and cons associated with the two business portfolio matrix techniques described in this chapter. Which, if either, do you find more appealing? Why?

2. Assume that you are about to prepare for an examination in one of your business courses and have several alternatives as to the amount of studying that you can do. The exam can have several possible degrees of difficulty (depending upon how tough your professor decides to make it). Discuss how this situation could be cast into a decision-making matrix format. What would you use as a measure of payoffs for this situation?

3. Refer back to Question 2. Think for a moment about your own personal feelings and premonitions as to how difficult the exam might be. Using these premonitions on exam difficulty and the payoffs you described in Question 2, which alternative would you select and why?

Enhancing Communication Skills

4. Assume that you are employed as a counter attendant in a fast-food restaurant. What are two requests that a customer might make that would require a routine decision? Two requests that would require a nonroutine decision? To enhance your oral communication skills, prepare a short (10–15 minute) presentation for the class in which you describe these requests and explain why you classified them in this way.

5. Think of some task, project, or endeavor that you have recently faced that required you to make a series of interre-

lated decisions. Thoroughly describe that situation and the decisions you made. Then convert this verbal description into a decision tree diagram that displays these interrelationships. To enhance your written communication skills, write a one to two page essay describing this endeavor, the decisions you faced, and the tree diagram displaying these interrelationships.

Building Teamwork

6. Put yourself in the position of a student member of your campus homecoming committee. One of your committee's duties is to book a successful comedian (fee $10,000) for one of your homecoming events and develop a plan to conduct that event. To refine your teamwork skills, meet with a small group of students who have been given this same assignment. Assign each team member some aspect of this endeavor to research in order to determine the costs you are likely to incur, potential sources of revenue, available concert halls or auditoriums, and any other pertinent information. Then, use breakeven analysis to develop a thorough plan for staging this entertainment event. Finally, select a spokesperson to present the details of your plan to the rest of the class.

7. List several objectives with different units of payoff measure that might be encountered in various business decisions. To refine your teamwork skills, meet with a small group of students who have been given the same assignment. Compare your lists for common items, then consolidate your ideas into a single list. Select a spokesperson to present to the rest of the class your list of payoff measures and where they might be encountered.

THINKING CRITICALLY: DEBATE THE ISSUE

BCG Analysis—Good or Bad?

Form teams of four or five students as directed by your instructor. Research the use of the BCG growth-share matrix for business portfolio analysis. In particular, try to ascertain and understand both the positive and negative aspects of this approach. Prepare to debate either the positive or the negative aspects of the BCG approach. When it is time to debate this issue in front of the class, your instructor will tell you which position you will take.

EXPERIENTIAL EXERCISE 7.1

Decision Making Under Risk

Purpose: To gain experience in the analysis of a risk decision situation through the use of payoff tables.

Procedure: Review the conditional values of profit provided in the accompanying payoff table. Then, assuming that the probabilities for the states of nature are 0.2, 0.2, and 0.6 for S1, S2, and S3, respectively, perform the analysis requested.

Step 1. Use the conditional values and the probabilities to derive an expected value matrix.

Step 2. Calculate the total expected value for each alternative.

Step 3. Select the best alternative and provide an interpretation for its total expected value.

STATES OF NATURE

Alternatives	S1	S2	S3
A1	32	25	19
A2	21	28	29
A3	18	20	26

EXPERIENTIAL EXERCISE 7.2

Using Decision Trees in Everyday Life

Purpose: To gain a better appreciation for the fact that many everyday decision situations are composed of a sequence of interrelated decisions that could be displayed as a decision tree.

Procedure: Think about the decisions you make each semester before registering for your college courses. Your course selections are no doubt driven to a large extent by the requirements for your program of study. Your selection of specific class sections, however, is probably influenced by such factors as the instructor, the time of day and days of the week the class meets, conflicts with other classes, conflicts with work schedules, and conflicts with sleep schedules. Your decision process probably has some sequential elements to it, for example, "If I schedule this class at this time, then these classes cannot be scheduled because. . . ." Develop a tree diagram to illustrate the sequential decision aspects of the class scheduling process that you went through in a recent semester.

CAPTURING THE POWER OF INFORMATION TECHNOLOGY

1. Use the Internet to locate information on Tupperware's line of kitchenware. Generate a list of all sealable food storage containers. Information should include colors, sizes, special features, and prices. Arrange this information into an electronic spreadsheet that can be sorted by any of these aspects of the refrigerators.

2. Use the Internet to locate information and generate a list of all products introduced by 3M during the most recent calendar year. Place these products into appropriate categories (such as office supplies, household items, and so on), and store the information in an electronic spreadsheet that can be sorted by category.

3. Use the Internet to locate information on the Coca-Cola Company and the Pepsi-Cola Company. Use a word-processing package to prepare a brief synopsis of what's new in the cola wars for your classmates.

ETHICS: TAKE A STAND

The Florida citrus industry has traditionally relied on a large contingent of laborers (about 40,000) to harvest its crop, and these laborers have relied on the citrus industry to provide a large proportion of their livelihood. In recent years machines have begun making headway in the race to replace human labor. Currently only about 6,000 acres of oranges (about 1 percent of the crop destined for the juice market) are harvested by tree-shaking devices, but many grove owners are wrestling with the decision to adopt such mechanical harvesters. Of course, as more citrus is harvested mechanically, fewer jobs will be available for these unskilled farm workers.

For Discussion

1. Discuss the social and ethical implications associated with conversion to mechanical harvesting devices.

2. Discuss the likely economic implications of mechanical harvesting to you personally, the citrus growers, and the human citrus harvesters.

SOURCE: J. Jackson, "Harvesting Machines Shake Up Citrus Labor," *The Orlando Sentinel*, March 12, 1999, B1.

VIDEO CASE

Decision-Making Tools and Techniques: Machado & Silvetti Associates, Inc.

Machado and Silvetti Associates, an architectural firm based in Boston, has been successfully making decisions on high-stakes, high-profile projects since 1974. Such diverse projects include private residences; museums; parks; buildings for Harvard, Princeton, and Rice Universities; and the Allston Branch of the Boston Public Library. To date, its largest project is the master plan to renovate and expand the Getty Villa and Museum in Malibu, California. The firm has accepted design awards worldwide including the First Award in Architecture for 20 years of boldly conceived and brilliantly executed urban projects. Also, the firm's principals, Rodolfo Machado and Jorge Silvetti, are architecture professors at Harvard University.

On a recent project for a large dormitory at a Boston university, every architectural and construction decision was carefully considered. For this project, Mike Yusem was named project manager overseeing all aspects of the project and acting as the liaison between the principals and client. In addition, architect David Martin was assigned to the project to monitor the technical aspects. The firm and its client also brought a construction manager on board to oversee certain crucial, high-risk decisions. The construction manager helped the project manager and architect deal with the unpredictable economy, strict budget, and labor shortage.

Although decision making on the project was very democratic, the project manager, principals, or client made the final decisions. The designer prepared several options regarding design features such as window sizes or masonry patterns. Then the project architect, project manager, client, and designer discussed each option in light of the project goals and the different needs of the building, client, and architectural firm.

Nevertheless, democracy can prove impractical on a project this large and managers sometimes have to take risks. The hardest decision for Mike Yusem was choosing materials for the project and all the details associated with those choices. Because the principals are attentive to the use of materials and patterns, Yusem must make optimal decisions. Both the project manager and architect operate under constant pressure to make effective decisions because every decision is scrutinized by both the client and the principals. In construction, it is typically too late to correct a decision after it is implemented.

This project is on what is called a fast-track process; the construction started before all of the construction documents were completed. A lot of decisions had to be made immediately without the benefit of complete written plans. Of course, this involves risk because once the steel is in place, the building cannot be changed. The project's very strict budget created some tough challenges in integrating the mechanical systems, plumbing, and electrical layout in a smaller space than is typical. As the project progressed, they had to be certain there would be enough money to complete the 365-bed dormitory in the manner originally planned. They had to be prepared for unanticipated things that come up on every project that can further tax an already tight budget. The hardest part about the project manager's and architect's jobs is being comfortable in their abilities to respond to those situations. Dealing with crisis situations is the nature of such projects; only through experience can one become calmer when faced with such crises.

Adding a high-profile contemporary building to a historical campus setting raised concerns. Managers tried to address these concerns when deciding how to effectively incorporate some of those historical details into the new building. The project manager did a lot of coalition building to get community members to work with the university, architect, state historical organizations, and environmental organizations.

The university dormitory project in Boston shows how good decision-making skills are critical for a business to succeed. In today's fast-changing world, decisions must be made quickly. Managers must stay open to creativity and innovation. Machado and Silvetti Associates shows how a firm can remain true to its creative vision by making timely, well-thought-out, and cost-effective decisions.

For Discussion

1. In the video case, is the majority of decision making treated as programmed or nonprogrammed decisions? Explain. Is this an appropriate way to address these types of decisions?

2. Explain how project managers could use a payoff table or other technique to structure their operational decision making.

3. Is the majority of the decision making made under certainty, risk, or uncertainty? Explain. What techniques might be useful to Machado & Silvetti Associates when making decisions under these conditions?

4. In your opinion, why might Machado and Silvetti feel confident that appropriate decisions are being made during a fast-track process even though they are not present on the work site?

http://www.machado-silvetti.com

Capacity Decision Making at the North American Culinary Institute

As the prestigious North American Culinary Institute (NACI) began planning for its expansion into Florida, decisions in the area of capacity planning were set into motion. NACI had leased 100,000 square feet of space in a vacant building in a Central Florida office-industrial park. Now the company had to decide how to carve that space into kitchen classrooms, traditional classrooms, and dining areas. The kitchens would be equipped with state-of-the-art restaurant equipment, and the school would be staffed with the finest teaching chefs at NACI. However, before the institute could announce its plans, begin accepting applicants to the 18-month program, and begin collecting the $32,000 tuition, NACI needed to get a better sense of the demand for the school and the capacity it should provide. Rene LeBlanc, recently named NACI Director of New Programs and Expansion, was given the task of overseeing this new venture. LeBlanc had been with NACI for 20 years, having begun as a teaching apprentice, and then gradually working his way up through the ranks to this new position. This was to be the first program expansion that he would direct.

Being familiar with the design of teaching kitchens, LeBlanc knew that capacity would come in discrete increments. A standard teaching kitchen and accompanying classrooms and dining rooms could accommodate about 40 students and would require about 50,000 square feet of space. LeBlanc could see that this Central Florida space could be used to set up a "large" school, accommodating about 80 students. Such a setup would fully utilize the available space. Alternatively, a "small" school could be set up, accommodating about 40 students. In this configuration only half of the available space would be used. Regardless of the capacity selected, subsequent demand could end up being less than capacity, about equal to capacity, or greater than capacity. LeBlanc was beginning to grasp the notion that, after the initial capacity decision was made, external conditions (such as the demand for the school) would trigger subsequent decisions. For example, a small school with demand less than or equal to capacity might require NACI to consider subleasing its surplus space. On the other hand, a small school with demand greater than capacity might prompt NACI to consider using the surplus space for an expansion into an 80 student capacity school. If a large school had initially been set up, demand less than capacity might trigger a decision to contract the size of the school and a subsequent decision about what to do with the surplus space. Demand greater than the capacity of the school might cause NACI to seek additional space and explore opportunities for further expansion. As all of these thoughts (and others like them) began spinning around in LeBlanc's head, he started to become overwhelmed. He muttered to himself, "I wish I could get all this organized. I don't want to blow this first assignment."

For Discussion

1. Develop a decision tree diagram that traces out the sequence of decisions and alternative courses of action and states of nature that might occur in the decision problem being faced by Rene LeBlanc.

2. Discuss the additional information that LeBlanc will have to obtain or estimate if he is to use this diagram to systematically analyze the sequence of decisions that he faces.

PART ³

ORGANIZING CHALLENGES IN THE 21ST CENTURY

CHAPTER 8

ORGANIZING FOR QUALITY, PRODUCTIVITY, AND JOB SATISFACTION

CHAPTER 9

DESIGNING THE CONTEMPORARY ORGANIZATION

CHAPTER 10

STRATEGIC HUMAN RESOURCE MANAGEMENT

CHAPTER 11

ORGANIZATIONAL CULTURE, CHANGE, AND DEVELOPMENT

CHAP

ORGANIZING FOR QUALITY, PRODUCTIVITY, AND JOB SATISFACTION

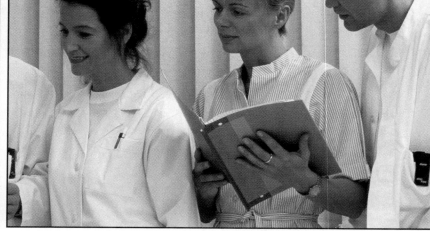

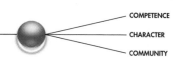

LEADERSHIP

COMPETENCE

CHARACTER

COMMUNITY

TER 8

CHAPTER OVERVIEW

This chapter and the three that follow focus on the managerial function of organizing. Increasingly, organizations are finding that their long-term success is dependent upon their ability to organize activities effectively, efficiently, and with a priority on quality. Management theory clearly recognizes the importance of organizing to support the strategic and operational needs of the contemporary organization.

This chapter describes organizing as a process and focuses on the first stage of that process. Special attention is given to contemporary approaches to organizing that support delegation and employee empowerment and on improving the organization's ability to respond to environmental change.

LEARNING OBJECTIVES

When you have finished studying this chapter, you should be able to:

1. Explain why organizing is an important managerial function, describe the process of organizing, and outline the primary stages of the process.
2. Discuss the concept of job design and identify the core job dimensions that define a job.
3. Explain how and why job design theory has evolved.
4. Describe the mechanistic, behavioral, and participatory approaches to job design.
5. Understand both the vertical and horizontal associations that exist between individuals and work groups within the organization.
6. Define delegation and discuss why it is important for managers to delegate.
7. Explain why managers often fail to delegate and suggest methods for improving delegation skills.

Facing The Challenge

St. Luke's: Somewhere Between Fear and Safety Lies Creativity

Andy Law, the co-founder and chairman of London-based St. Luke's Communications, takes a long time when making hiring decisions. Applicants to one of the world's leading advertising firms can expect an average of seven intense, often grueling, interviews before being offered a job. A job offer is contingent upon the applicant having the internal fortitude to work at what has been described as the ". . . scariest place on the planet." Applicants to St. Luke's need more than original ideas and creative slogans, they need courage.

When Law co-founded St. Luke's in 1995, he decided to break the traditional advertising agency mold. He brought together a small group of talented, creative people who loved to work but hated the workplace. The problem with the workplace, according to Law's colleagues, was that traditional hierarchy instilled complacency and stifled creativity. As such, Law decided to organize St. Luke's as a business without organization. The result: An extremely profitable, creative place to work with a very unique structure—none. There are no bosses, no organizational charts, and no hierarchy. The agency is owned entirely by the employees.

At the heart of St. Luke's phenomenal growth and success lies a paradox. Employees are encouraged to take enormous risks for the sake of creativity, yet St. Luke's is a "safe" place to work. For example, once a month associates come together to publicly evaluate and critique each other's work. Since there is no pecking order, seasoned veterans often find advertising rookies criticizing their latest effort. St. Luke's, however, is also considered a safe place to work because people are rarely fired. Moreover, a supportive climate exists where employees can relate their personal stories of victory and defeat.

In order to facilitate creativity, associates are constantly challenging each other's assumptions. Law purposely created an organization without structure, offices, or nameplates. The physical layout of the organization is one, large open space. No one has his or her own office, desk, or corner, and employees have no idea where they will be working when they arrive each morning. Law believes that creativity emerges from overcoming habit, and destabilizing the workplace imposes change and facilitates originality and creativity. Was he truly innovative?

INTRODUCTION

St. Luke's Communications achieved phenomenal success in a highly competitive industry by developing a corporate culture that, at first glance, seems paradoxical. Andy Law, the co-founder and chairman of St. Luke's Communications, wanted to create a work environment where people felt empowered to be creative, secure to take risks, and committed to customer service, all the while touting St. Luke's as the most frightening place to work on the planet. The success of the company would depend on Law's ability to find the right balance between fear and safety, and creativity and commitment.

As you will recall, all organizations exist to fulfill a specific mission and achieve a specific set of goals. If an organization is to fulfill its mission and achieve its goals, certain activities must occur. When an organization is small and relatively simple, those activities may be defined and coordinated fairly easily. As organizations become larger and more complex, however, organizational activities may be more difficult to define and coordinate. In general, the challenges associated with organizing activities and allocating resources become greater as the size and complexity of the organization increase. Nevertheless, organizing is an important managerial function in organizations of all sizes and types.

LEARNING OBJECTIVE 1

Explain why organizing is an important managerial function, describe the process of organizing, and outline the primary stages of the process.

Organizing

The process of determining the tasks to be done, who will do them, and how those tasks will be managed and coordinated.

WHAT IS ORGANIZING?

Organizing refers to the process of determining the tasks to be done, who will do them, and how those tasks will be managed and coordinated. It is an interactive and ongoing process that occurs throughout the life of the organization. As an organization develops and matures, so must its organizational system. Many times companies must adapt their organizational systems to cope with changes that oc-

Figure 8.1 | The Process of Organizing

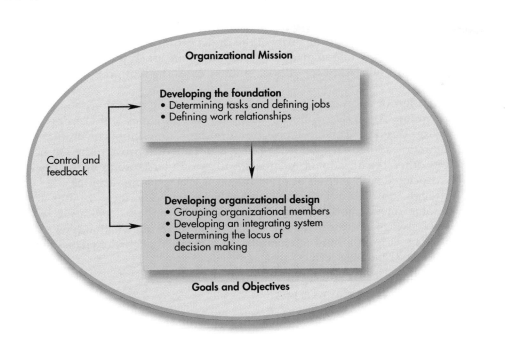

cur in their competitive environment. For example, Andy Law of St. Luke's knew that if his communications company was going to be successful, an innovative approach to organizational design would be needed.

As Figure 8.1 shows, the process of organizing can be divided into two primary stages. In the first stage, the foundation of the organizational system is developed. Work activities are determined and assigned to specific job positions, and working relationships between individuals and work groups are defined. This chapter will focus specifically on these aspects of the organizing process. The second stage of the organizing process involves developing an organizational design that supports the strategic and operational plans of the organization. This requires grouping organizational members into work units, developing integrating mechanisms to coordinate the efforts of diverse work groups, and determining the extent to which decision making in the organization is centralized or decentralized. These aspects of organizing will be addressed in Chapter 9.

JOB DESIGN

As we noted, the first stage of the organizing process involves outlining the tasks and activities to be completed and assigning them to individuals and groups within the organization. Before managers can design specific jobs, they need to identify the work that must be done to achieve the organization's strategic and operational goals.

Consider, for example, an organization that manufactures and distributes small appliances. To fulfill its mission and achieve its goals, the organization must complete a number of tasks and activities. Raw materials must be acquired and inventoried; people must be hired, trained, and compensated; the plant must be managed and maintained; and the product must be delivered to customers. These are just a few of the activities that must occur.

LEARNING OBJECTIVE 2

Discuss the concept of job design and identify the core job dimensions that define a job.

Job design
The set of tasks and activities that are grouped together to define a particular job.

Once the tasks and activities that must be completed have been identified, jobs must be designed and assigned to employees within the organization. **Job design** refers to the set of tasks and activities that are grouped together to constitute a particular job position. The importance of effective job design should not be underestimated, as the overall productivity of the organization will be affected by the way jobs are structured. While managers commonly blame an employee's poor performance on his or her lackluster efforts, in many cases the real problem is poor job design.

The design of a job can be assessed, to a degree, by reviewing the associated **job description**. A job description details the responsibilities and tasks associated with a given position. Table 8.1 provides a position description for a director of Web communications. This job description is intended to provide the job holder, as well as other organizational members, with an understanding of the responsibilities associated with the job of the director of Web communications.

Job description
Details of the responsibilities and tasks associated with a given position.

Although job descriptions are commonly used to describe how jobs are designed, some relevant job characteristics may not be evident from a job description. Before we go on to discuss the various job design models that have evolved over the years, it is important to examine the fundamental characteristics that can be used to describe most jobs.

CORE JOB DIMENSIONS

A number of core job dimensions can be used to characterize any job: (1) skill variety, (2) task identity, (3) task significance, (4) autonomy, and (5) feedback.[1] Each of these core job dimensions can significantly affect the satisfaction and performance of the individual who occupies the job. As Table 8.2 illustrates, these dimensions affect the degree to which employees find their work meaningful, feel responsibility for the outcomes of their job, and understand the results of their work activities. More specifically, skill variety, task identity, and task significance can affect the degree to which employees find their work meaningful; autonomy can affect the extent to which employees feel responsible for the outcomes of their jobs; and feedback can affect the degree to which employees understand the results of their work activities.[2] Let's explore these core job dimensions and relationships in more detail.

Skill variety
The degree to which a job challenges the job holder to use various skills and abilities.

SKILL VARIETY   The first of the job dimensions, **skill variety**, refers to the degree to which a job challenges the job holder to use his or her skills and abilities. When a variety of skills are necessary to complete a task and those skills are perceived to be of value to the organization, employees find their work to be more meaningful.

Consider, for example, how a production manager and a mailroom clerk might feel about the meaningfulness of their work. The production manager's job re-

Table 8.1 | Job Description of a Director of Web Communications

- Develop and implement communication projects, content through completion.
- Develop editorial and graphical guidelines for communication projects.
- Monitor compliance with/adherence to communication guidelines.
- Ensure that all communications are consistent in message and tone.
- Direct technical staff in other departments.
- Monitor developments in technology/communication media.
- Perform related duties as assigned.

Table 8.2 | The Core Dimensions of a Job

CORE JOB DIMENSION	EFFECT OF DIMENSION
• Skill variety	
• Task identity →	Meaningfulness of the work
• Task significance	
• Autonomy →	Responsibility for outcomes of the work
• Feedback →	Knowledge of results of the work activities

SOURCE: Adapted from J. R. Hackman, G. Oldham, R. Janson, and K. Purdy, "A New Strategy for Job Enrichment." Copyright © 1975 by The Regents of the University of California. Reprinted from *California Management Review, 17,* 4. By permission of The Regents.

quires the use of a relatively diverse and highly valued set of skills and abilities, and he or she may therefore perceive the job to be quite meaningful. The job of the mailroom clerk, in contrast, is more narrow in terms of skill variety and of less perceived value to the organization than the production manager's job. As a result, the mailroom clerk is likely to feel that his or her job is less meaningful.

TASK IDENTITY **Task identity**, the second dimension, refers to the degree to which the job requires the completion of an identifiable piece of work—a tangible outcome that can be attributed to the employee's efforts. For example, individuals who design computers will likely find their jobs to have higher task identity and to be more meaningful than employees who simply slide a chip into place on the circuit board of the computer, and thus have low task identity.

Task identity
The degree to which a job requires the completion of an identifiable piece of work.

TASK SIGNIFICANCE The third job dimension, **task significance**, relates to the degree to which the job contributes to the overall efforts of the organization or to the world at large. Where task significance is high, the work will be more meaningful. For example, civil engineers who design an entire highway system will likely find their jobs to be more meaningful than assembly-line workers who are responsible for producing a component that goes into other products. This is particularly true when the employees don't know what the end product is, what it does, or who uses it.

Task significance
The degree to which a job contributes to the overall efforts of the organization.

AUTONOMY The fourth job dimension, **autonomy**, reflects the degree to which job holders have freedom, independence, and decision-making authority in their jobs. When employees are highly autonomous in their work roles, their success is dependent upon their own capabilities and their desire to complete the task. Therefore, they tend to feel greater responsibility for the success or failure of their efforts and, in general, greater job satisfaction.[3] When there is low autonomy, employees are less likely to feel accountable for the outcomes of their work.

Autonomy
The degree to which job holders have freedom, independence, and decision-making authority.

Consider, for example, organizational trainers who teach a seminar that prepares participants to pass a national certification exam. These trainers may have little latitude in selecting the material to be covered in the course and often must employ a course design that is prescribed by the testing agency. They have little autonomy in conducting their jobs. In contrast, consider trainers who teach a management development seminar that is intended to help participants learn more about their own management style. These trainers are free to determine both the material to be covered and the methods by which it should be delivered. They are likely to feel more personal responsibility for their work than the trainers who deliver a prepackaged training seminar.

At The Limited, Beth Thomas, director of The Limited training, can testify to the benefits of autonomy in developing training programs. Thomas and her team were given complete autonomy to redesign the training programs at The Limited. Through highly creative approaches to learning, the team revitalized the company's training function. Training programs now take a game show approach wherein employees play "Let's Make a Deal" to learn more about The Limited's products, participate in a session inspired by "Jeopardy!" to demonstrate their knowledge of critical financial metrics, and compete with one another in "Lingo Bingo," which helps them develop a mastery of retail buzzwords. The Training Group has experienced tremendous success with their new training programs, largely because they were given the autonomy to be creative in their work.[4]

In Nashville, Tennessee, Hatch Show Print produces CD covers and posters for some of the hottest musicians around, including the Beastie Boys, Pearl Jam, and Bruce Springsteen. According to employees at Hatch, the best part of working at the company is the autonomy of the job. Once someone is assigned a CD cover or poster, they make all the decisions about the project from concept to production. The autonomy associated with the job makes Hatch highly appealing to the "artistic types" the company must attract to be successful.[5]

Feedback

Information about the status and performance of a given effort or system.

FEEDBACK   The final dimension of job design is **feedback**, or the extent to which job holders are provided information about the effectiveness of their efforts. When feedback is frequent and constructive, employees develop a better understanding of the relationship between their efforts and the outcomes of their work. When feedback is insufficient, employees have little understanding of the value of their efforts.[6]

© PAUL BARTON/CORBIS

The final dimension of job design is feedback, or the extent to which job holders are provided information about the effectiveness of their efforts.

In recent years, there has been a movement to provide employees at the middle to upper levels of management with feedback from all the individuals with whom they work, including their supervisor, employees, and peer managers. Such evaluation mechanisms, often referred to as 360-degree feedback systems, are used in organizations such as AT&T, Bank of America, Exxon, General Electric, Caterpillar, and DaimlerChrysler.[7] An interesting new developmental approach at the McColl School of Business at Queens University of Charlotte requires all MBA students to participate in a 360-degree assessment of their leadership capabilities. Feedback is solicited from individuals who know that students via e-mail and the surveys are completed online. The efficiency of the process has contributed to a high response rate from those asked to participate in the assessment and thus better feedback for the MBA students as they work to improve their leadership capabilities.

Some organizations even provide customer feedback to their employees. Such feedback encourages employees to be more customer oriented in their work. Caterpillar, Monsanto, and Chaparral Steel are examples of companies that have provided regular customer feedback to employees to focus their attention on the need for quality in all aspects of the business. Solectron, the world's largest contract equipment manufacturer, attributes much of its success to its system of providing comprehensive customer satisfaction feedback to its employees on a weekly basis.[8]

Because the core dimensions of job design affect the extent to which job holders find their work meaningful, feel responsibility for their efforts, and understand the relationship between their activities and the results of those activities, they have a significant effect on the attitudes of the job holders.[9] Motivation, quality of work performance, job satisfaction, absenteeism, and turnover will all be a function of the core job dimensions to some degree. Consequently, managers should consider the effect of various job designs on each core dimension as they assign tasks and work activities to individuals within the organization.

The increasing diversity of the workforce has made the assessment of job design more complicated. Individuals from diverse cultural backgrounds may view certain job characteristics differently. For example, while many people from an American culture may perceive a job with low autonomy negatively, people from other cultures may perceive low autonomy favorably. Managers who work in the international environment must also consider how perceptions of job design may differ among diverse cultures. As a general rule of thumb, managers should avoid making broad generalizations about employees' perceptions of specific job characteristics. Rather, where possible, managers should assess their employees' suitability for a particular job on an individual basis.[10]

How does your job stack up with regard to these job characteristics? "Now Apply It" provides an opportunity for you to assess a past or present position you've held in an organization (such as a business, church, social club, or student organization) in terms of skill variety, task identity, task significance, autonomy, and feedback. At this point, you are prepared to complete the assessment aspect (Part A) of the exercise. After reading the next section, you'll be prepared to suggest ways in which the job could be redesigned to improve job satisfaction (Part B).

It is interesting to examine how the principles of job design have evolved over time and, more specifically, how changes in design theory have affected the five core job dimensions. Table 8.3 outlines how job theory has evolved, the major job design approaches that have resulted from each school of thought, and how each approach affects core job dimensions. The discussion that follows provides a rationale for the evolution of job design theory.

Now Apply It

Job Assessment and Redesign

This exercise enables you to assess a job that you currently hold or have held in the past in terms of the five core job dimensions and to make recommendations for improving its design.

Part A: Using the following scales, rate the job you are assessing in terms of its skill variety, task identity, task significance, autonomy, and feedback.

To the extent that your responses fall toward the left end of the scales, you probably find the job to be meaningful and challenging. To the extent that your responses fall toward the right end of the scales, the job probably could be redesigned to improve job satisfaction and enhance productivity.

Part B: Based on your responses to Part A, how might you redesign your job to improve each of the five core job dimensions? Would any of the participatory approaches to job redesign be appropriate? If so, which one(s)? Why do you feel it (they) would be appropriate?

|____|____|____|____|____|____|____|____|____|____|
High   Skill variety   Low
|____|____|____|____|____|____|____|____|____|____|
High   Task identity   Low
|____|____|____|____|____|____|____|____|____|____|
High   Task significance   Low
|____|____|____|____|____|____|____|____|____|____|
High   Autonomy   Low
|____|____|____|____|____|____|____|____|____|____|
High   Feedback   Low

Table 8.3 | Job Design Theory Evolution

THEORY	CORE JOB DIMENSION	EFFECT*
Classical theory/scientific management (mechanistic approaches)	Skill variety	Negative
	Task identity	Negative
	Task significance	Negative
	Autonomy	Negative
	Feedback	Negative
Human relations (behavioral approaches)	Skill variety	Positive
	Task identity	Positive
	Task significance	Positive
	Autonomy	Positive
	Feedback	None
Contemporary management (participatory approaches)	Skill variety	None
	Task identity	Positive
	Task significance	Positive
	Autonomy	Positive
	Feedback	Positive

*None = no appreciable effect.

THE EVOLUTION OF JOB DESIGN THEORY

LEARNING OBJECTIVE 3

Explain how and why job design theory has evolved.

As management theory has evolved, so have many of the basic principles of job design. As we discussed in Chapter 2, classical management theory and scientific management theory supported the concepts of division of labor and specialization. These early theories of management gave rise to a mechanistic approach to job design in which jobs are highly structured and rigidly defined. The movement toward the human relations school of thought introduced other job design variables, most of which dealt with human behavior. As a result, more behavioral approaches to job design gained acceptance. Today, as we consider issues of job design in the organizations of the 21st century, we must continue to explore what work means in the postindustrial era. Clearly, in industrial economies, machinery, metal, and muscle define how work is done. But in postindustrial societies, the raw material is information and the production worker is the knowledge worker. Thus, in many ways, contemporary management thought has focused on a different type of work, and participatory approaches to job design have emerged. Let's examine how each of these approaches has affected the concept of job design, as well as the core job dimensions.

LEARNING OBJECTIVE 4

Describe the mechanistic, behavioral, and participatory approaches to job design.

MECHANISTIC APPROACHES: FOCUS ON EFFICIENCY   Recall from Chapter 2 that scientific management theorists emphasized the benefits of division of work and specialization. Productivity and efficiency were the driving forces for job design. Repetition, skill simplification, and time-and-motion efficiency were the primary focus of job design efforts. The result was highly specialized jobs that were routine, repetitive, and highly efficient.

One need only think of the classic example of a pinmaking operation in Adam Smith's *Wealth of Nations* to understand the potential efficiencies of division of labor and highly specialized work roles. Smith suggested that the productivity of 10 pinmakers could be greatly improved by applying these concepts. One pinmaker performing all the tasks necessary to make a pin could make only 10 pins per day. The total productivity of 10 pinmakers making pins in this fashion would be 100 pins per day. But if the 10 pinmakers organized the activities of the group so that one pinmaker drew the wire, another straightened it, a third cut it, and a fourth sharpened it to a point, while others were performing the operations necessary to complete the head of the pin and prepare the final product, the group could produce 48,000 pins per day—an average of 4,800 pins per pinmaker per day. Obviously, the productivity of the group improved dramatically when jobs were redesigned to be highly specialized.

The benefits of specialization are easy to identify (see Table 8.4). Specialized tasks are considered to be more efficient because work activities are broken down into routine, repetitive actions. Furthermore, such actions can be mastered readily by individual workers and require less training than more complex tasks. Additionally, when tasks are highly specialized, workers may be selected based on specific characteristics that make them uniquely qualified to perform the task effectively and efficiently.

Specialization also has disadvantages, however (see Table 8.4). Often, the skill variety, task identity, and task significance associated with such tasks are low. Moreover, job holders typically have less autonomy and may receive no feedback or feedback that is inconsequential. To the extent that these conditions exist, job holders will find little challenge in their work and may lose interest in their jobs.

In cases where excessive specialization has created jobs that are perceived to be unrewarding and uninteresting, it is difficult to motivate workers to perform well. Absenteeism and turnover are often greater, and even when employees are on the job, they may take frequent and lengthy breaks or socialize with other employees excessively. In some cases, the benefits of specialization may be offset by the loss of productivity associated with job dissatisfaction and nonproductive work time.

Historically, many manufacturing firms have sought the benefits of specialization in designing jobs. The assembly-line production scheme is founded on the concept of highly routine and specialized tasks. Consider, for example, the traditional automobile manufacturing plant. As the chassis of the car flows through the assembly line, workers perform a series of highly specialized tasks that contribute in some way to the production of the final product. While any given worker may do little more than attach a specific component or insert and tighten several screws, the result of the combined efforts of all the participants in the assembly process is a complete and fully functioning vehicle. Nevertheless, the individual jobs associated with producing the vehicle would typically rate poorly on all five core job dimensions.

Today, there are fewer highly specialized jobs in the United States than in the past. Robotics technology has replaced many specialized jobs, particularly in the manufacturing environment. In addition, many organizations that require low-skilled labor have moved their operations overseas, where there is access to less-

Table 8.4 | Potential Advantages and Disadvantages of Job Specialization

ADVANTAGES	DISADVANTAGES
• Greater efficiency due to repetition	• Low skill variety, task identity, and task significance
• Tasks are easier to master and require little training	• Little autonomy and feedback, resulting in low interest and motivation
• May select workers based on specific qualifications	• Lower productivity due to high absenteeism and frequent breaks

expensive labor. Finally, other organizations, have developed innovative approaches to improving job satisfaction for their assembly-line workers. General Electric and Consolidated Diesel, for example, have developed new management approaches that help workers with highly specialized jobs feel more ownership of the final product. By creating a work environment that values employee involvement and participation, both companies have improved satisfaction among their employees.[11]

Over time, concerns about the net benefits of specialization continued to grow. In fact, a new group of management thought leaders emerged, the human relations theorists, who believed that highly specialized jobs could be redesigned in ways that would improve both productivity and employee satisfaction. Their emphasis moved from division of labor and specialization toward job designs that had greater breadth, depth, and challenge.

BEHAVIORAL APPROACHES: FOCUS ON MOTIVATION, SATISFACTION, AND PRODUCTIVITY   Behavioral approaches to job design became popular during the movement toward the human relations school of thought. Managers began to explore methods for enhancing the ways jobs were structured. Such efforts led to the development of more innovative approaches to job design, including job enlargement, job enrichment, and job rotation programs.

Job Enlargement   To understand job enlargement programs, one must understand the concept of job scope. **Job scope** refers to the number of different activities that a specific job requires and the frequency with which each activity is performed. Jobs that involve many different activities have broader scope than jobs that are limited to a few activities. Jobs with broad scope typically rate more favorably in terms of skill variety, task identity, and task significance than do jobs with a narrower scope. As a consequence, jobs with broad scope often are more meaningful for job holders than jobs with narrow scope.

Consider, for example, how the job scope of an office manager and a data-entry clerk might differ. The office manager's job will involve a relatively broad set of tasks and thus will have relatively wide scope. In any given day, the office manager may prepare a letter; complete and sign time cards; make travel arrangements; schedule appointments; order supplies; and interview, hire, or fire office staff. The data-entry clerk's job, in contrast, is much narrower in that it involves only entering data into a database file.

Job enlargement programs are designed to broaden the scope of a specific job. The intent of job enlargement is to increase the horizontal tasks and responsibilities associated with a given work position to reduce the monotony of the job and provide greater challenge for the employee. For example, a data-entry clerk's job could be enlarged by assigning additional job responsibilities such as answering the phones, processing payroll forms, and providing copying services. The data-entry clerk would be responsible for a greater variety of tasks and might be less bored and more highly satisfied with the job.

While many companies have implemented job enlargement programs in an effort to redesign highly specialized and routine jobs, many other firms have done so out of necessity. As industries consolidate, companies merge, and organizations downsize and streamline to remain competitive, it often requires changes in the way jobs are designed. Employees are frequently called upon to assume responsibility for a broader range of tasks than in the past.

It must also be noted, however, that while job enlargement programs have typically been considered as a means of enriching jobs, sometimes *reducing* job scope has a positive impact on productivity and job satisfaction. Consider, for example, the situation at UPS. UPS was experiencing high turnover among its drivers. Management was very concerned about this issue as the drivers at UPS are critical employees for the company. Not only did it take several months to train every new

Job scope
The number of different activities required in a job and the frequency with which each activity is performed.

Job enlargement
Programs designed to broaden job scope.

driver on a particular route, but, over time, these drivers tended to develop strong relationships with the customers on their route. So, when UPS lost a driver, they incurred significant training costs and put customer satisfaction at risk. As the company explored the cause of the driver turnover, it discovered that it was the front-end of the work—loading the packages on to the truck—that was causing the turnover. Management restructured the job to provide loaders for the drivers, reducing their job scope. This action improved job satisfaction greatly and reduced turnover among drivers. The relatively simple change in the job design had big benefits for UPS and its customers.[12]

Job Depth and Job Enrichment   Central to the concept of job enrichment is the notion of **job depth**, which refers to the degree of control that individuals have over the jobs they perform. Job depth is high when the planning, doing, and controlling aspects of the job are the responsibility of the job holder. When one or more of these aspects is the responsibility of some other organization member, job depth is lower. Jobs that have high job depth typically rate more favorably on the core job dimensions of skill variety, task identity, and autonomy than jobs with low job depth. Just as specialization has led to jobs with a narrow job scope, highly specialized jobs often lack depth. In such cases, the planning, doing, and controlling aspects of a job may be separate.

For example, consider a computer services center within an organization and how the tasks might be divided to provide high or low job depth. Assume that this computer services center has three employees. If all three employees are responsible for receiving work orders, clarifying instructions with the originator of the work, setting priorities for scheduling the work orders they receive, providing the technical services required by the work order, and confirming the acceptability of the work with the originator, their jobs are of significant depth as they plan, do, and control their work. In contrast, if the tasks of the computer services center were divided among the three employees such that one person received work orders, clarified instructions, and scheduled the work, while another performed the services required, and yet another followed up with the originator of the work to ensure that the services were performed satisfactorily, the tasks performed would be more highly specialized and the three members of the group would have lower job depth.

Job enrichment programs are designed to increase the depth of individual jobs and to close the gap between planning, doing, and controlling a particular set of activities.[13] Through vertical loading, the job holder may be given greater discretion in setting schedules and planning work activities, determining appropriate methods for completing the task, and monitoring the quality of the output from the work process. Job enrichment can be an effective means of motivating employees and improving job satisfaction.[14]

Just as downsizing has led to enlarged jobs, such efforts have also led to enriched jobs. When a layer of management is eliminated, the group of employees above and below that management level must assume greater responsibility. This creates a situation of vertical loading of job responsibilities and leads to jobs with greater job depth.

In addition, quality management programs have also created greater job depth in some organizations. Individual accountability for contributing to the goals of the organization increases in quality-oriented companies, and with that accountability often comes greater job depth. Key to greater accountability, however, is the availability of information. Employees must have the information they need to make the decisions necessary to plan, do, and control their work. Toward that end, some organizations have developed innovative methods of sharing performance and customer-critical information with their employees. For example, Chevron maintains "visualization centers" throughout its headquarters where people can gather around enormous screens that project data and graphics (for example, subsurface seismic

Job depth
The degree of control given to a job holder to perform the job.

Job enrichment
Programs designed to increase job depth.

surveys), enabling them to do their jobs better. At one of Micron Electronics' computer manufacturing plants, a sophisticated information scoreboard tracks defects, breakdowns along the assembly lines, daily and weekly goals, and the company's stock price for all employees to see.

But US West has developed perhaps the most innovative approach to sharing information with its employees through its network-reliability operations center in Littleton, Colorado. At this center, the company uses cutting-edge information technology to track the company's most basic offering: the telephone dial tone. Simply by looking at the names and numbers on the big screens around the room, the 700 US West people who work in the center can instantly see how the company is performing—where customers in 14 states are having problems with their phones and how many people are affected by the problems. The most serious problems (those affecting the largest number of customers) are shaded in red; less-severe outages are shaded in yellow and in green. Managers have the real-time information they need to control the outcomes of their work.[15]

Job rotation

Assigning individuals to a variety of job positions.

Job Rotation   Job rotation is a third method of reducing the level of specialization associated with a given job. **Job rotation** involves shifting individuals from one position to another once they have mastered their original job. Employees rotate through a number of job positions that are at approximately the same level and have similar skill requirements. While job rotation has proven particularly beneficial in manufacturing settings,[16] it can also be used effectively in service organizations. For example, an individual who works in a bank might rotate between being a teller, a customer service representative, a loan processor, a proof operator, and a safe deposit box attendant. At a higher organizational level, a financial manager who works for a multinational firm might rotate among positions at various foreign subsidiaries to gain international business experience.

Job rotation offers several advantages. Organizations that use job rotation typically have more flexibility in developing work schedules, making work assignments, and filling vacancies within the company quickly. In addition, employees are often more challenged and less bored with their jobs and usually have a better understanding of the organization as a whole. At the level of the individual employee, job rotation has been found to have a positive effect on both promotion rates and salary growth.[17] In fact, in many companies job rotation is considered essential for grooming managers for executive-level positions as it provides the breadth of experience necessary for top-level management roles.[18]

A new form of job rotation emerged in response to the downsizing activities of the 1990s. As organizations reduced their workforce, their employees had far fewer internal career opportunities available. With fewer promotions to hand out, some companies tried to motivate employees by shifting them sideways instead of up. American Greetings, for example, found lateral moves to be very effective in rejuvenating employees who had become bored in their present positions. Nabisco Foods, Corning, Inc., and Eastman Kodak are other companies that have looked to lateral job moves as a method of motivating employees whose career progression has been stymied by the restructuring efforts of the organization. Sony and Canon even attribute much of the success at product innovation to the job rotation of their engineers.[19] Ultimately, employees often find that lateral career moves enhance their long-term job satisfaction and career advancement.[20]

Job enlargement, enrichment, and rotation programs represent methods of redesigning specialized jobs to increase the motivation, job satisfaction, and, in some cases, productivity of employees. Such efforts often have a very positive effect on overcoming the disadvantages of more mechanistic approaches to job design. Many managers who are concerned with maintaining a quality orientation in their work units have embraced these programs as one way to do so. In addition, some managers have turned toward more participatory approaches to job design.

PARTICIPATORY APPROACHES: FOCUS ON QUALITY In recent years, both management theorists and practitioners have been rethinking the traditional approaches to job design.[21] Efforts to develop more innovative and effective approaches to job design have been inspired by increasing competitive pressures in many industries. From airlines to banks to manufacturing companies, organizations have had to rethink job design to ensure high product and service quality at the lowest possible cost.

Several participatory approaches to designing jobs have emerged in recent years and have gained widespread acceptance. The benefits of such approaches are similar to the benefits associated with participatory decision making discussed in Chapter 6. Jobs that are designed with the involvement of the affected individuals often lead to greater productivity, higher satisfaction for the job holder, and better organizational results. In a business environment where organizations vie for the very best talent, job design can play a big role in attracting and retaining a high-quality workforce.[22]

Participatory approaches to job design are not intended to replace previous methods of job design, but rather to supplement both the mechanistic and the behavioral theories of job design. The most popular participatory approaches, and the ones that will be discussed here, include business process reengineering, employee-centered work redesign programs, and self-managed teams.

Business Process Reengineering **Business process reengineering** emerged early in the 1990s as a method of enhancing competitiveness through improved product and service quality and operational efficiency. Through reengineering, organizations rethink all aspects of job design in light of the critical processes they use to produce and deliver their products and services. Every manager and employee becomes involved in the process of assessing every aspect of the company's operations and rebuilding the organizational system with a focus on improving efficiency by identifying redundancies, eliminating non-value-added activities, and reducing waste in all possible ways.[23]

Reengineering efforts significantly affect the way jobs are designed.[24] Any reengineering project will raise critical questions about how work and work processes can be optimally configured. Answering such questions requires managers to look for creative approaches to job design that improve the effectiveness and efficiency of the organization. Table 8.5 outlines one method for reengineering that will help develop appropriate job design.[25]

Reengineering was never touted as being easy or cheap, since it can literally turn an organization upside down in the short term. Yet, the results have been impressive for some companies. Union Carbide, GTE, and AlliedSignal were all early adopters of reengineering that reported positive results from their efforts. Among the benefits reported were improvements in product and service quality, cost reductions, and improved customer and employee satisfaction. At Fleet Financial Services, reengineering was undertaken for the specific purpose of improving the quality of life and reducing stress for employees while maintaining productivity. Fleet reported a successful outcome and even claims that the new work design provided a competitive advantage, since it enables the company to attract a better-quality workforce.[26]

Despite the notable success of these organizations, numerous other companies failed miserably in their reengineering efforts.[27] As the reports of failure continued to come in, many managers came to think of reengineering as simply a method of job consolidation and downsizing, and enthusiasm for the management tool began to wane.

For many, however, the jury is still out on reengineering.[28] Although it is clearly a method of job design that has the potential to improve organizational efficiency and effectiveness, execution has proven difficult for many companies. Michael Ham-

Business process reengineering
Radically changing the organizational processes for delivering products and services.

Table 8.5 | Steps in Business Process Reengineering

1. *Seize control of the process.* Many processes vitally important to a firm's success "just happen." The sequence of activities that count the most usually require interventions from many organization units. Good ideas for new products dissipate in the path from one unit to another. Seizing control of a process means giving it an owner who has authority to break through the departmental walls.

2. *Map it out.* Most companies are organized in ways that make it difficult to identify key processes. Reengineering can only be accomplished if the organization is mapped out, usually graphically, so as to provide a step-by-step description of how the process works. Then, by carefully identifying and eliminating problem areas, a more streamlined operation can be reengineered.

3. *Eliminate sources of friction.* One method of eliminating organizational friction is to devise an alternative to the traditional passing of work down the established hierarchy. Many companies have set up coordinating "brand management" or "czar" positions to keep things moving along. Other methods include streamlining administrative processes (purchasing, billing, etc.), minimizing handoffs by having as few units processing transactions as possible, creating new, higher-paying positions with greater authority, and time compression through responsibility expansion.

4. *Close the loop.* Becoming a fast-cycle company involves mind-set change as well as technique adoption. In reengineered businesses, the most common phrase you hear is "Life is short." This is not so much a philosophical justification as a plea to get on with it. Reengineering studies can create volumes of paperwork and creative and colorful flowcharts. But the only studies worth doing are those that make change happen.

5. *Don't drop the ball.* The only studies whose changes will stick are those done with eyes wide open about the transitory nature of improvement programs. Few improvements last indefinitely. Technologies will change, allowing for further enhancements in speed. Also, superior approaches will be developed for common problems. Knowing that the results of this year's reengineering will need reengineering at some point is essential to making any effort successful.

SOURCE: R. M. Tomasko, "Intelligent Resizing: View from the Bottom Up (Part II)," 18–23. Reprinted by permission of publisher, from *Management Review*, June 1993. © 1993, American Management Association, New York. All rights reserved.

mer, one of the originators of the concept, claims that to achieve the full benefit from reengineering, companies cannot simply redesign their critical processes but must go to the next step and restructure their organizations around those processes. He cites the positive experiences of Texas Instruments, IBM, and Duke Power as evidence of the potential benefits of going that next step.[29]

Employee-centered work redesign
An approach whereby employees design their work roles to benefit the organization and satisfy their individual goals.

Employee-Centered Work Redesign **Employee-centered work redesign** is an innovative approach to job design that presents a practical solution to one of the most significant challenges of job design—bridging the gap between the individual and the organization. This method of job design links the mission of the organization with the needs of the individual by allowing employees to design their work roles to benefit the organization as well as themselves. The unique aspect of this job design approach is that employees are accountable for justifying how their job will support the mission of the organization as well as improving their productivity and job satisfaction.[30]

A number of benefits are associated with employee-centered work redesign programs. Because jobs are designed by the job holder, these programs tend to favorably affect the core job dimensions that are most relevant to the individual employee. Studies suggest that tangible improvements in both productivity and job satisfaction result from employee-centered work redesign efforts. Furthermore, such programs foster an organizational climate that supports cooperative efforts between individuals and work groups. Finally, employee-centered work redesign programs are consistent with the quality improvement efforts of many companies. Because the employees of an organization are in the best position to know where quality improvements can be achieved, jobs can be designed so quality problems can be identified and resolved more quickly.[31]

St. Luke's is an excellent example of a company that uses the employee-centered approach to work design. Employees are asked to choose roles and projects that fit their unique talents and abilities. This approach helps ensure that workers are playing to their strengths and are committed to the vision of the organization.

Today, many companies are looking to work redesign programs to address a critical work problem that can result in significant losses in productivity—stress.[32] Based on a survey by International Survey Research in Chicago, about 40 percent of U.S. workers say workloads are excessive, and about the same percentage indicate that they are bothered by too much pressure on the job. A few companies, such as Bank of America, Hewlett-Packard, Merck, and Deloitte Touche, have looked at innovative ways to redesign jobs to reduce stress and provide a better work/life balance. Bank of America's efforts began with 1,100 employees at two customer-service call centers. The employees were asked to report on those aspects of their work that were frustrating and an impediment to balancing work and family life. A tidal wave of suggestions poured in through focus groups and an 800-number hotline. When all was said and done, 60 percent of the employees at the two call centers had offered suggestions on how to change their work. Bank of America moved quickly to implement many of the changes. Not only were the employees delighted, but the customers benefited as well. The proportion of customers reporting satisfaction with the service they received rose from 80 percent to 85 percent at one call center and from 79 percent to 82 percent at the other. Bank of America's experience in this case clearly demonstrates that employees and customers can both benefit from employee-centered work redesign, which ultimately benefits the business as a whole.[33]

While some companies are now rethinking how jobs can be designed to eliminate stress, other companies have long recognized the importance of achieving a balance between work and personal lives. Paid-time-off (PTO) programs have emerged as innovative benefit packages to allow for greater flexibility in helping employees achieve work/life balance. PTO programs usually combine sick leave, vacation time, and short-term disability leave. Employees can take time off for any reason under PTOs as long as the leave is scheduled and approved by management. "At the Forefront" on page 260 describes the benefits of PTOs for both the organization and the employee.

Self-Managed Teams   All of the approaches to job design discussed so far have focused on designing the jobs of individual organizational members. The **self-managed team (SMT)** approach to job design shifts the focus from the individual to a work group. Instead of managers dictating a set of narrowly defined tasks to each employee, responsibility for a substantial portion of the organization's activities is assigned to a team of individuals who must determine the best way to fulfill those responsibilities. Today, self-managed teams exist in organizations of all sizes and types and in and across departments within those organizations.[34] When self-managed teams exist across departments and include representatives from the different functional areas of the organization (for example, engineering, marketing, finance), they are considered cross-functional teams.[35]

The distinguishing feature of the self-managed team approach to job design is that the group is largely independent. The team must justify its choice of work

Both customers and employees benefited when Bank of America implemented employee suggestions in redesigning their call centers.

© MATTHEW BORKOSKI/INDEX STOCK

Self-managed teams (SMTs)
Groups of employees who design their jobs and work responsibilities to achieve the self-determined goals and objectives of the team.

Paid-Time-Off (PTO) Programs Really Pay Off

Competition for talent in the business world has created the need for organizations to offer increasingly creative benefit packages for enticing new hires and retaining current employees. Managers are responding to employees' needs for a work/life balance, empowerment, and greater flexibility. A result of these trends has been the introduction of Paid-Time-Off, or PTOs.

PTO programs typically combine sick leave, vacation time, floating holidays, bereavement, and short-term disability leave. With PTOs, employees can take time off for any reason as long as it is scheduled and approved by the employee's manager. Although PTOs can be used for unplanned reasons, such as illness or emergencies, they are designed to encourage scheduled time off for personal or professional development. Time off can typically be taken in hourly, daily, or weekly in-crements, allowing maximum flexibility for the employee.

From the employer's perspective, PTOs really pay off. Although some productivity issues are out of management's control, employee morale and motivation can be boosted through the use of PTOs. Unplanned absenteeism can have a detrimental effect on a department's productivity, impacting the organization's overall performance. PTOs allow employees greater flexibility and facilitate scheduling time off in advance, allowing managers the opportunity to plan accordingly.

From the employee's perspective, PTOs are an enticing benefit that helps them achieve a great balance between work/life issues. PTOs allow employees to choose time off that is important to them, regardless of the reason. As our workforce becomes increasingly diverse, common holidays are shared by fewer work-ers, and outside responsibilities become more important. PTOs let employees tailor their vacation schedule to suit their individual needs. Additionally, PTOs have an inherent element of privacy to them because employees do not have to explain their absences.

PTOs are gaining in popularity. Today, twice as many companies offer PTOs compared to 1997, and this trend shows no sign of slowing. PTOs offer a much needed benefit to busy professionals at minimal cost to the employer. They allow employees greater flexibility to meet their developmental needs, while providing organizations with an innovative tool for better managing productivity.

SOURCE: J. Reinberg, "It's About Time PTOs Gain Popularity," *Workspan*, 45 (2), 53–55.

methods only in terms of strong productivity and contribution to the overall effort of the organization. As with employee-centered work redesign programs, jobs that are designed by SMTs tend to reflect the core job dimensions that are most relevant to the individual employees of the work group.

While research has suggested that self-managed teams can achieve higher productivity and deliver better-quality products and services with lower relative costs,[36] a number of situational factors appear to influence the effectiveness of such groups. These factors include the personalities of the group members[37] as well as the nature of the job responsibilities. In addition, it is important for managers to remember that SMTs are very different from single-leader work groups.[38] The advantages of job redesign work most effectively with true SMTs. Table 8.6 describes the difference between these two groups.

Organizations that have designed narrow, highly specialized jobs in an effort to maximize efficiency may find self-managed teams to be advantageous. The team approach has been credited with improving overall organizational effectiveness in ways such as avoiding redundant efforts, increasing cooperation between organizational members, spawning new ideas, generating solutions to problems, maintaining motivation, improving product quality, and increasing profits.[39] From the classic example of teamwork success at NUMMI (New United Motors Manufacturing, Inc.), the joint venture between General Motors and Toyota, to more recent examples of success at Levi Strauss, 3M, and BP Amoco Norge, organizations across the globe have improved their quality and productivity through the use of self-managed teams.[40] Other companies have used the SMT approach to develop new products and processes. For example, companies as diverse as Chrysler, Medtronic, IBM, and Eli Lilly have used SMTs to create new processes so that they could develop new and better products.[41]

Table 8.6 | Teams and Work Groups: It Pays to Know the Difference

Managers tend to label every working group in an organization a "team," whether it's a roomful of customer service operators or a string of assemblers on a manufacturing line. But employees quickly lose motivation and commitment when they're assigned to a team that turns out to be a single-leader work group. If executives want to spark energy and commitment on the front lines, they must know how a team differs from a single-leader work group and when to create one or the other.

	TEAM	SINGLE-LEADER WORK GROUP
Run by:	the members of the team best suited to lead the tasks at hand; the leadership role shifts among the members	one person, usually the senior member, who is formally designated to lead
Goals and agenda set by:	the group, based on dialogue about purpose; constructive conflict and integration predominate	the formal leader, often in consultation with a sponsoring executive; conflict with group members is avoided, and the leader integrates
Performance evaluated by:	the members of the group, as well as the leader and sponsor	the leader and the sponsor
Work style determined by:	the members	the leader's preference
Success defined by:	the members' aspirations	the leader's aspirations
Most appropriate business context:	a complex challenge that requires people with various skill sets working together much of the time	a challenge in which time is of the essence and the leader already knows best how to proceed; the leader is the primary integrator
Speed and efficiency:	low until the group has learned to function as a team; afterward, however, the team is as fast as a single-leader group	higher than that of a team initially, as the members need no time to develop commitment or learn to work as a team
Primary end-products:	largely collective, requiring several team members to work together to produce results	largely individual and can be accomplished best by each person working on his or her own
Accountability characterized by:	"We hold one another mutually accountable for achieving the goals and performance of the team."	"The leader holds us individually accountable for our output."

SOURCE: Reprinted by permission of *Harvard Business Review*. From "Firing Up the Front Line," by J. Katzenbach and J. Santamaria. May/June 1999, 107–17. Copyright © 1999 by the Harvard Business School Publishing Corporation; all rights reserved.

In recent years, organizations have begun to encourage their self-managed teams to engage in what has come to be known as "action learning." Simply stated, action learning involves learning by doing. SMTs assume responsibility for solving real problems and, in the process, they develop new individual and team skills that help them to do their jobs more effectively.[42] While the solution to the problem is important, the process of finding the solution is equally important from an individual and team development perspective. Companies who have used action learning include General Mills, Amoco, Aramark, Deloitte Touche, and Mercedes-Benz Credit Corp. General Mills, for example, used action learning in designing new greenfield manufacturing plants and transforming many of its existing plants to high-performance work systems.[43] Amoco Corporation used action learning to revise its performance-management system. Through action learning, Aramark developed two important new programs—SelectService, which redesigns a medical facility's food-service operation around the patient and saves money at the same time, and School Support Services, a program designed to convince students to eat greater amounts of nutritious food.[44] All of these companies used SMTs coupled with action learning to develop innovative systems, processes, or products.

As businesses have globalized, the need to develop global work teams has increased. Yet, many challenges exist in developing highly effective work teams that cross national borders. Cultural and communication differences among team members, as well as the barriers that arise from time-and-distance differences, all complicate the development of effective global teams. Nevertheless, some organizations, such as Mobil Oil, Digital Equipment, and 3Com have developed innovative ways to make global teams work effectively.[45] In recent years, improvements in technology have enabled many global teams to overcome the barriers of time and distance. In fact, through the use of advanced information technology, so-called virtual teams have emerged.[46] These teams can work together from all over the world, as long as they share a common purpose and a means of communicating. The existence of virtual teams will likely change the way many people work in the years to come.

Now that we have concluded our discussion of job design, take a moment to go back to Part B of "Meeting The Challenge." How might you redesign the position you evaluated to improve job satisfaction? productivity? quality? Would a participatory approach to job design be appropriate?

Thus far, we have explored how managers determine the work to be done and assign that work to individual employees or work groups. Equally important, however, is the process of defining the working relationships, both vertical and horizontal, that exist within the organization. The next section examines how working relationships can be established to ensure that the organization fulfills its mission and achieves its goals.

ORGANIZATIONAL RELATIONSHIPS

LEARNING OBJECTIVE 5
Understand both the vertical and horizontal associations that exist between individuals and work groups within the organization.

The working relationships that exist within an organization will affect how its activities are accomplished and coordinated. Consequently, it is essential to understand both the vertical and horizontal associations that exist between individuals and work groups within the organization. Organizational relationships are defined by (1) chain of command, (2) span of control, and (3) line and staff responsibilities. Delegation is also an important concept that will have an impact on the relationships that exist within the organization.

CHAIN OF COMMAND

Chain of command
The line of authority and responsibility that flows throughout the organization.

Unity of command
A principle that each employee in the organization is accountable to one, and only one, supervisor.

The vertical relationships that exist within an organization are defined by its chain of command. The **chain of command** delineates the line of authority and responsibility that flows throughout the organization and identifies the supervisor and subordinate relationships that govern decision making.

One of the most basic principles of organizing, unity of command, is used in defining vertical relationships. The **unity of command** principle suggests that each employee in the organization should be accountable to one, and only one, superior. When individual employees must report to more than one superior, they may be forced to prioritize their work assignments and resolve conflicting demands on their time. This can be a difficult situation, even for the most savvy employees.

As you will recall from Chapter 2, the concept of a well-defined chain of command was originally advanced by the classical management theorists. In its purest form, the concept is consistent with the bureaucratic organizational system. Although contemporary managers still embrace the idea of a chain of command, the flexibility of the organization to respond to change quickly and proactively may be severely limited when decision making is rigidly tied to the official hierarchy. For that reason, organizations that operate in very dynamic environments may prefer to maintain flexibility in their chain of command so that they can respond to change more effectively.

As an example of contrasting views on the value of the chain of command, consider the perspectives of Herb Baum, president and chief executive officer of toy company Hasbro, versus those of Roger Sant and Dennis Bakke, cochairs of power company AES. When Herb Baum joined Hasbro, one of the first things he did was establish a clear chain of command with division chiefs reporting directly to him. This represented a major change for Hasbro, a company that had traditionally operated with many autonomous units. Baum felt that the change would bring the management focus where it should be—on bottom-line profitability in each division.[47] In contrast, AES' co-chairs, Sant and Bakke, have gone on record as saying they "abhor layers" and avoid traditional hierachial chains of command at all costs. They have developed AES as a system of empowered teams who take responsibility for their work. They believe that this type of management system enables the company to be more flexible and responsive to changing competitive conditions.[48]

SPAN OF CONTROL

A second important aspect of working relationships is **span of control**, which refers to the number of employees who report to a single manager. At one time it was thought that there was a universally appropriate span of control (for example, six employees should report to each manager), but managers now recognize that span of control will vary in accordance with a number of variables. Organizational characteristics such as task complexity, the volatility of the competitive environment, and the capabilities of both the employees and the manager will influence the appropriate span of control.

As an example of how certain conditions might affect span of control, consider the job characteristic of task complexity. In theory, when tasks are very complex, span of control should be relatively narrow. This allows the manager to spend more time with each subordinate to help him or her deal with the complexity of the job. In contrast, where jobs are highly standardized and routine (low complexity), a manager will not need to spend as much time supporting individual subordinates, and the span of control may be larger.

Which comes first—job design or span of control? That depends. Although one typically thinks of jobs being designed first and span of control being determined by the nature of the job, the reverse can happen. Jobs may be designed to support a company's needed span of control. For example, in an effort to cut costs, many health care organizations have reduced management levels and increased the average span of control. To ensure continued effectiveness, these organizations must often rethink the ways in which jobs are designed.[49]

Span of control is a critical organizational variable for a number of reasons. It defines the layers of management that exist within the company. An organization that maintains a relatively narrow span of control will have more hierarchical levels than an organization with the same number of employees but a wider span of control. As Figure 8.2 illustrates, the span of control and the resulting layers of management determine whether the organization maintains a tall or a flat structure.[50]

In general, tall structures are associated with a long chain of command and bureaucratic controls. Consequently, they are often thought to be ineffective in rapidly changing environments. On the other hand, managers in tall structures have fewer subordinates to supervise and are less likely to be overcommitted and overburdened. Free from the burden of excessive numbers of subordinates, such managers may have more time to analyze situations, make effective decisions, and

Span of control
The number of employees reporting to a particular manager.

Figure 8.2 | Tall versus Flat Structure

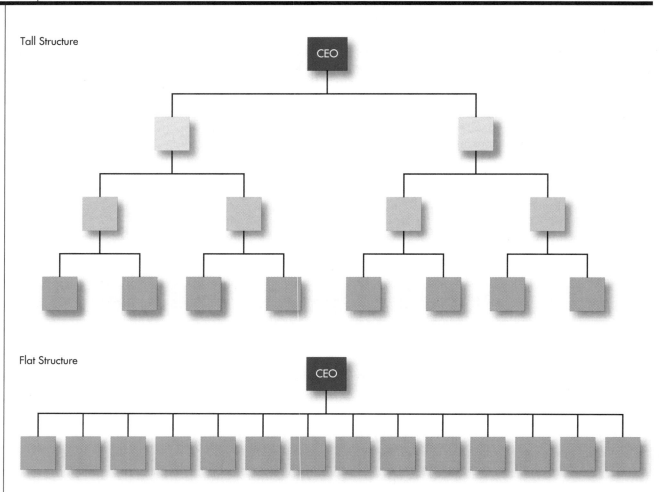

Tall Structure

Flat Structure

SOURCE: Adapted from *The Structuring of Organizations* by Mintzberg, © 1991. Reprinted by permission of Prentice-Hall, Inc., Upper Saddle River, NJ.

execute the actions associated with their decisions. Consequently, they may be more effective than managers in flat organizations.

Managers in flat organizations, by contrast, have greater demands in terms of direct supervision because they have wider spans of control. They may feel hassled, frustrated, and incapable of coping effectively with the nonsupervisory demands of their job. Yet flat structures are often thought to facilitate decentralized decision making, participatory management, and responsiveness to the challenges inherent in highly competitive environments. Wide spans of control suggest a need for greater self-direction and initiative on the part of individual employees and may result in more effective employee development.

Clearly, advantages and disadvantages are associated with both tall and flat structures. Therefore, organizations must choose a span of control that supports their particular strategic and operational goals. For example, global firms may find they need a relatively small span of control at the upper levels of the organization. The challenges of managing geographically dispersed and culturally diverse operating units may require a narrower span of control. Yet, as technology improvements continue and more information is available to employees throughout these organizations, spans of control may be broadened.

LINE AND STAFF RESPONSIBILITIES

The third aspect of organizational relationships is that of line and staff responsibilities. Line and staff positions exist within virtually all organizations, but the individuals who occupy these positions play very different roles.

Line personnel are directly involved in delivering the product or service of the organization. The individuals and work groups that have formal authority for decisions affecting the core production efforts of the firm are the line personnel. **Staff personnel**, in contrast, are not part of the product or service delivery system chain of command but, rather, provide support to line personnel. Line personnel or work groups may call upon staff personnel to provide expert advice or perform specific support services. Staff personnel do not have authority or responsibility for decisions that relate to the core delivery system of the organization.

As organizations experiment with less rigid hierarchical structures and team-oriented approaches, the distinction between line and staff responsibilities is blurring. U.S. West, for example, has moved away from making distinctions between line and staff, preferring to call employees either supervising managers or individual contributors. This is consistent with the quality-management movement, which suggests that all members of the organization must contribute to fulfilling the mission and achieving the goals of the organization. The differences in the way employees contribute is far less important than the commonality inherent in working to achieve the same organizational goals. As a consequence, the distinction between line and staff has become less important.

In addition, line and staff personnel now frequently coexist within work teams that collectively pursue a specific set of tasks. Consider once again the power company AES. The leaders of AES, Sant and Bakke, have done everything they can to eliminate the staff function at the corporate level by moving all staff personnel onto the teams around which the organization is structured. The finance, marketing, and environmental compliance departments have all been disaggregated and their staff personnel reassigned to teams that are responsible for delivering core products and services. AES believes this system enables all team members to understand all aspects of the business.[51]

DELEGATION

Another important aspect of organizational relationships involves delegation. One of the most challenging skills that successful managers must master is the ability to delegate effectively.[52] **Delegation** refers to the process of transferring the responsibility for a specific activity or task to another member of the organization and empowering that individual to accomplish the task effectively. Traditionally, supervisors delegate tasks to employees in their work group. The **scalar principle** of management suggests that a clear line of authority should run through the organization (chain of command) so that all persons in the organization understand to whom they can delegate and from whom they should accept delegated tasks.[53]

THE PROCESS OF DELEGATION   To delegate effectively, managers must understand that delegation involves three distinct but highly related activities: (1) assigning responsibility, (2) granting authority, and (3) establishing accountability. All are essential to the success of the delegation process.

Assigning Responsibility   The delegation process begins when a manager assigns a subordinate the responsibility for a specific task or set of tasks. **Responsibility** refers to the employee's obligation to complete the activities that he or she has been assigned. Clear communication of the specific activities for which the employee is responsible is essential if the task is to be delegated successfully.

Line personnel
Those organizational members who are directly involved in delivering the products and services of the organization.

Staff personnel
Those organizational members who are not directly involved in delivering the products and services of the organization, but provide support for line personnel.

LEARNING OBJECTIVE 6
Define delegation and discuss why it is important for managers to delegate.

Delegation
The process of transferring the responsibility for a specific activity or task to another member of the organization and empowering that individual to accomplish the task effectively.

Scalar principle
A clear line of authority must run throughout the organization.

Responsibility
An obligation on the part of an employee to complete assigned activities.

Authority
The formal right of an employee to marshal resources and make decisions necessary to fulfill work responsibilities.

In today's age of greater access to information, employees may feel frustrated by the fact they know about a problem, but do not have the authority to address that problem.

© FREDDE LIEBERMAN/INDEX STOCK

Granting Authority   Managers must give their employees the authority to accomplish their work successfully.[54] **Authority** is the formal right of an employee to marshal the resources and make the decisions necessary to fulfill her or his work responsibilities. Without sufficient authority, it is unlikely that employees will complete delegated tasks successfully.

Consider, for example, a restaurant manager who has to leave early one evening and says to one of the waiters: "Make sure all the employees complete their closing duties." Assuming that the statement is made only to the waiter and not to the other employees, the manager has put the waiter in a difficult position. She has just delegated the responsibility for ensuring that closing activities are completed properly without giving the waiter the authority he needs to succeed at that task. The other employees are unlikely to feel compelled to cooperate with the waiter so that he can fulfill his responsibility to the restaurant manager. To complete any task successfully, one must be given the authority necessary to carry out that task.

In today's age of greater access to information, employees may feel frustrated by the fact they know about a problem, but do not have the authority to address that problem. Consider, for example, the warehouse worker who can see that an order will be late, but has no authority to expedite it. Or the airline reservationists who know that there are many seats available on certain flights but cannot book a standby passenger on those flights because they do not have the authority to override the policy requiring standby passengers to register at the gate. In both cases, the employees have the knowledge to do their jobs better and create greater customer satisfaction, but they do not have the authority to act on that knowledge. As information becomes increasingly available to frontline workers, organizations must consider how to provide the authority for those workers to act appropriately in light of that information.[55]

Accountability
Employees' justification for their decisions and actions with regard to the task they have been assigned.

Establishing Accountability   Managers must hold their employees accountable for completing the tasks for which they assume responsibility and are given the necessary authority. When there is **accountability** for performance, employees understand that they must justify their decisions and actions with regard to the tasks for which they have assumed responsibility. Delegating decision-making responsibility without the associated accountability will compromise the overall benefits of the delegation process. In fact, as Christopher Galvin, CEO of Motorola, says, "Sometimes delegation does work and sometimes it does not." While he believes strongly in the power of delegation, he also knows that when it doesn't work, managers have to become more involved in managing the delegated tasks.[56]

As Figure 8.3 illustrates, delegation can be thought of as a triangle, with each of these elements representing a point. Should one element be missing, the delegation process will be ineffective. To delegate successfully, managers must clearly communicate the responsibilities they are delegating, provide their employees with the formal authority necessary to fulfill those responsibilities, and develop the necessary control and feedback mechanisms to ensure that the employees are held accountable for successfully completing the delegated tasks.[57]

Scientific Applications International Corporation (SAIC) is a leading provider of scientific and information technology solutions to customers in both the public and private sectors. When Dr. Robert Beyster founded SAIC over thirty years ago, he wanted employees to be vested in the company and accountable for their decisions. To help facilitate employee accountability, he designed an innovative stock option process for employees. Today, SAIC is the world's largest employee-owned

Figure 8.3 | The Delegation Triangle

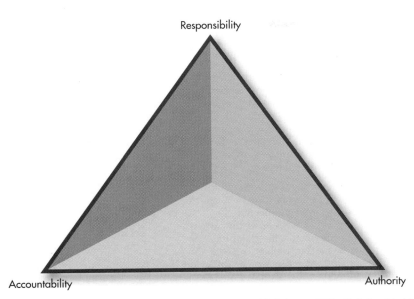

Responsibility

Accountability

Authority

SOURCE: C. O. Longnecker, "The Delegation Dilemma," *Supervision*, 52, February 1991, 3–5. Reprinted by permission of © National Research Bureau, P.O. Box 1, Burlington, Iowa 52601-0001.

research and engineering firm, and Dr. Beyster's innovative model of creating accountability through employee-ownership is highlighted in "Leaders In Action" on page 268.

THE BENEFITS OF DELEGATION AND EMPOWERMENT Delegation offers a number of advantages. When used properly, delegation can lead to a more involved and empowered workforce.[58] As we discussed in Chapter 1, empowerment can lead to heightened productivity and quality, reduced costs, more innovation, improved customer service, and greater commitment from employees.[59] Delegation involves empowering employees at all levels to make decisions, determine priorities, and improve the way work is done. The end result is a more effective organization.[60]

Delegating decisions and activities to individuals lower in the organizational hierarchy often leads to better decision making. Those who are closest to the actual problem to be solved or the customer to be served may be in the best position to make the most effective decisions. In addition, response time may be improved, since information and decisions need not be passed up and down the hierarchy. This is particularly critical in organizations where delays in decision making can make the difference between success and failure.

Delegation is also beneficial from an employee development perspective.[61] By delegating tasks and decision-making responsibility to their employees, managers provide an opportunity for the development of analytical and problem-solving skills. The employees are forced to accept responsibility, exercise judgment, and be accountable for their actions. The development of such skills will benefit the organization in the long term.[62]

Finally, through delegation and empowerment, managers magnify their accomplishments. By delegating tasks that their employees have the ability to complete, managers can use their time to accomplish more complicated, difficult, or important tasks. This can lead to a more creative and productive work group as a whole.[63]

Leaders In Action

Employee Ownership: Bringing Empowerment to the Bottom Line

When Dr. Robert Beyster founded Science Applications International Corporation (SAIC) over 33 years ago, he wanted every employee to own a stake in the company. The financial interests of outside stakeholders often drove his previous employer, a large defense contractor. Dr. Beyster wanted to work in an environment where the people most invested in the organization—the employees—drove business decisions.

SAIC is a leading provider of scientific and information technology solutions to a variety of customers in the public and private sectors. Business diversity is the main reason for SAIC's continued growth and success, even during economic downturns. When the dot-com industry went into a tailspin and some of their IT business dried up, investments SAIC had made in the public sector, including the development of its own Center for Counterterrorism

Technology and Analysis, helped the company maintain its growth.

In addition to business diversification, SAIC is the largest employee-owned research and engineering firm in the world. In fact, Dr. Beyster credits SAIC's success to employee ownership of the company. SAIC's rationale for employee ownership rests on three principles:

1. It is fair for those who contribute to the company to own it and benefit from its success.
2. Employees who have an ownership interest in the company are motivated to deliver a better product to the customer and work together as teammates.
3. Employee-owned companies are driven by the broad perspectives of employees, managers, and shareholders, rather than the narrow interests of a few outside owners.

Dr. Beyster is considered by many to be the premier "spread the wealth" manager. He encourages employees to invest in the company. Employees contribute their creativity and energy to make the corporation survive and flourish, and they should be rewarded financially for the company's success. Dr. Beyster has found that almost anyone can lead during good times, but during a downturn in the economy, leading becomes more difficult. This is especially true when a leader feels pulled between loyalty to employees and the interests of stockholders. SAIC has the benefit of an entire workforce owning a stake in the company. As Dr. Beyster states, " . . . when the going gets tough, employee owners get tougher."

SOURCE: D. Lindquist, "There Is No 'I' in This Team," *Chief Executive*, March 2002, 56–60.

Many organizations have benefited from empowering employees through delegation. Xerox, the American Society for Quality Control, and FedEx are a few examples of organizations that have claimed significant success from employee empowerment. Anthony Balsamo, CEO of TAC Worldwide, provides a great example of how empowerment can spread through an organization. TAC Worldwide is a provider of contract and temporary personnel. Balsamo initially brought his top-level management team together to solicit their help in solving a particularly difficult business problem he was facing. He thought he had the solution, but he put aside his plan and empowered the team to develop their own solution. Much to his surprise, they came up with a much better plan than his, having anticipated and planned for every possible barrier and roadblock. Balsamo, who was extremely pleased with the outcome, was even more pleased with what happened next. His management team began to empower their employees, much like they had been empowered themselves. So what began as a collaborative effort to address a particularly difficult business decision rapidly became a way of life throughout all levels of TAC Worldwide. Today, Balsamo speaks with pride about his organization that is founded on collaborative problem solving.[64]

Managers should be cautioned, however, about the potentially negative perceptions that ineffective delegation can create. Delegation must never be used to avoid work responsibilities that should legitimately be assumed by the manager. Delegation is not a way to "pass the buck" but, rather, a method for enhancing the overall productivity of the work group. If employees perceive the delegation as a way to reduce the manager's responsibilities and increase their own, their respect for the manager will deteriorate. This may be particularly problematic in diverse work groups, where perceptions of delegation may vary. In such situations, it may be appropriate for managers to explain to their employees how delegation benefits the entire work group.

In general, effective delegation is a vital skill for successful managers. Yet it is a skill that many managers lack. Why? There are a number of reasons why managers fail to delegate.[65]

REASONS FOR FAILING TO DELEGATE Delegation requires planning—and planning takes time. How often have you heard someone say, "By the time I get done explaining this task to someone, I could have done it myself"? This is a common excuse for maintaining responsibility for tasks rather than delegating them.[66] In some cases, such a decision may make sense. However, when tasks are recurring and would warrant the time to train someone who could assume responsibility for the work, such a decision would not be appropriate. "Experiential Exercise 8.1" at the end of this chapter provides a tool for managers to use in determining whether a task is appropriate for delegation.

LEARNING OBJECTIVE 7

Explain why managers often fail to delegate and suggest methods for improving delegation skills.

Another reason for failure to delegate is that managers may simply lack confidence in the abilities of their subordinates. Such a situation fosters the attitude "If you want it done well, do it yourself." This problem is particularly difficult to overcome when the manager feels pressure for high-level performance in a relatively short time frame. The manager simply refuses to delegate, preferring to retain responsibility for tasks to ensure that they are completed properly.

As a further complication, managers experience dual accountability. Managers are accountable for their own actions and the actions of their subordinates. If a subordinate fails to perform a certain task or performs it poorly, it is the manager who is ultimately responsible for the subordinate's failure. Therefore, when the stakes are high, managers may prefer to perform certain tasks themselves.[67]

Finally, managers may refrain from delegating because they are insecure about their value to the organization. Such managers may refuse to share the information necessary to complete a given task or set of tasks because they fear they will be considered expendable.

LEARNING TO DELEGATE EFFECTIVELY Despite the perceived disadvantages of delegation, the reality is that managers can improve the performance of their work groups and their organizations by empowering their employees. So how do managers learn to delegate effectively? They apply the basic principles of delegation.

Principle 1: Match the Employee to the Task Managers should carefully consider the employees to whom they delegate. The individual selected should possess the skills and capabilities needed to complete the task and, where possible, should stand to benefit from the experience. Furthermore, managers should delegate duties that challenge employees somewhat, but which they can complete successfully. There is no substitute for success when it comes to getting an employee to assume responsibility for more challenging assignments in the future.

Implicit in this principle is an acceptance of an incremental learning philosophy. This philosophy suggests that as employees prove their ability to perform effectively in a given job, they should be given tasks that are more complex and challenging. In addition to employee development benefits, such a strategy will be beneficial for the overall performance of the work group.[68]

Principle 2: Be Organized and Communicate Clearly Most cases of failed delegation can be attributed to either poor organization or poor communication. When managers or employees do not clearly understand what is expected, the delegation process is sure to fail. Both the manager and the employee must have a clear understanding of what needs to be done, what deadlines exist, and what special skills will be required.[69] Delegation is a consultative process whereby managers and employees gain a clear understanding of the scope of their responsibilities and how their efforts relate to the overall efforts of the group or organization.[70]

Furthermore, managers must be capable of communicating their instructions effectively if their subordinates are to perform up to the managers' expectations.[71] Effective communication about delegated tasks is particularly important in diverse work groups. People from different cultures may have different frames of reference and may interpret messages differently. Consequently, managers should be sure to clarify their instructions very carefully if they have any reason to believe that they may not be understood.

Principle 3: Transfer Authority and Accountability with the Task   The delegation process is doomed to failure if the individual to whom the task is delegated is not given the authority to succeed at accomplishing the task and is not held accountable for the results. The manager must expect employees to carry the ball and let them do so.[72] This means providing employees with the necessary resources and power to succeed, giving them timely feedback on their progress, and holding them fully accountable for the results of their efforts.

Principle 4: Choose the Level of Delegation Carefully   Delegation does not mean that the manager can walk away from the task or the person to whom the task is delegated. The manager may maintain some control of both the process and the results of the delegated activities. Depending upon the confidence the manager has in the subordinate and the importance of the task, the manager can choose to delegate at several levels (see Figure 8.4).[73]

Figure 8.4   Degree of Delegation

Managers can delegate in degrees. Consider the following alternative levels of delegation.

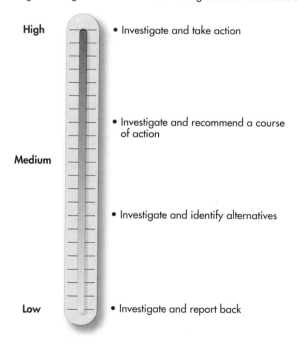

High   • Investigate and take action

• Investigate and recommend a course of action

Medium

• Investigate and identify alternatives

Low   • Investigate and report back

Many good managers find it difficult to delegate. Yet few managers have been successful in the long term without learning to delegate effectively.[74] As a future manager, you must develop effective delegation skills.

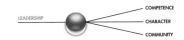

IMPLICATIONS FOR LEADERS

In this chapter, we have learned how jobs are designed and organizational relationships are determined. Effective leaders must demonstrate competence by designing jobs and working relationships in such a way that achieves the goals of the organization. As a future manager, you should keep the following organizing tips in mind:

- Identify the tasks and activities that must be completed in order for the goals of the organization to be achieved.
- Design jobs so that job holders will find their jobs interesting and challenging.
- Look for ways to use participatory approaches to job design as a means of improving quality.
- Consider reengineering business processes as a means of improving organizational performance.
- Don't be trapped by traditional hierarchical organizational relationships. More flexible and adaptable organizational designs are appropriate in many situations.
- Remember: All successful managers delegate. Develop a system of delegation that works for you and your work group.

This chapter has focused on some of the foundation principles of organization theory and, more specifically, on the first stage of the organizing process. The next chapter will address the second stage of the process and the concept of organizational design. The design of an organization defines the way organizational members are configured or grouped together; the types of mechanisms used to integrate and coordinate the flow of information, resources, or tasks between organizational members; and the degree of centralization or decentralization of decision making within the organization. An understanding of these organizing concepts, along with those discussed in this chapter, is essential for understanding the managerial function of organizing.

Meeting The Challenge

St. Luke's: Somewhere Between Fear and Safety Lies Creativity

Building an organization on the radical seesaw between fear and safety has proven to be enormously successful from both a bottom-line and a human growth perspective. St. Luke's profits have increased eightfold in three years, and the number of employee-owners has almost doubled. In addition, the lives of St. Luke's associates have been enhanced. Employees are loyal, and St. Luke's enjoys a turnover rate less than one-half the industry average.

According to Law, the changes that have occurred at St. Luke's resemble a fundamental shift occurring within our larger society, namely, a quest for meaning and dignity where change is embraced. Law is convinced that co-ownership, a creative work environment, and the opportunity to collaborate with peers are the fundamental reasons for St. Luke's ongoing success.

Hiring the right person for this radical way of organizing is ab-

solutely critical. People must be willing to embrace change. They must be capable of dealing effectively with ambiguity and they must discard their egos and be willing to ask for help. Law has some tips for anyone considering adopting a similar organizing approach:

1. Try mentoring instead of traditional managing. People want to grow and develop, and mentoring is a process that encourages

individual development through risk taking instead of dependency on the "boss."

2. Encourage individual accountability through ownership instead of empowerment. Empowerment assumes that someone has to empower someone else, which reinforces traditional ideas about hierarchy and sustains dependency. Employee ownership, on the other hand, ensures that the employee is motivated to act responsibly because he or she has a stake in the business.

3. Hire a counselor/trainer to assist employees with problems as they emerge. Organizing without hierarchy and without the traditional manager/subordinate relationship forces employees to grow and develop in ways that may be difficult. Problems associated with growth and change can and do emerge. Having an expert on staff to help diagnose individual or group issues and recommend training or counseling helps to ensure that people develop at their own, healthy pace.

According to Law, the real secret of St. Luke's success is its people. Law sees his role as inspiring others to change and to remind everyone to forget about yesterday or tomorrow, and live only in the moment.

SOURCE: D. L. Coutu, "Creating the Most Frightening Company on Earth," *Harvard Business Review*, 78 (5), September/October 2000, 142–49.

SUMMARY

1. The managerial function of organizing is critical for all managers and all organizations. In order for an organization to fulfill its mission and achieve its goals, the employees of the organization must complete many tasks and activities. These varied tasks and activities must be organized and coordinated to ensure the effectiveness and efficiency of the organization. Organizing is a two-stage process. The first stage involves delineating the work that needs to be done, assigning that work to specific job holders, and creating the work relationships necessary to support the organization's product and service delivery system. The second stage involves assigning organizational members to work groups, developing an integrating system to coordinate the work of those groups, and defining the locus of decision making in the organization.

2. Job design issues relate to the first stage of the organizing process. Job design refers to the way tasks and activities are grouped to constitute a particular job. Core job dimensions that can be used to describe a job include (1) skill variety, (2) task identity, (3) task significance, (4) autonomy, and (5) feedback. The first three dimensions determine the meaningfulness of jobs; the fourth dimension, autonomy, determines the degree to which individuals feel responsible for their work; and the final dimension, feedback, relates to the extent to which job holders understand the outcomes of their jobs.

3. As management theory has evolved, so have the basic principles of job design. Classical management theory and scientific management supported the concepts of division of labor and specialization. These early theories of management gave rise to a mechanistic approach to job design in which jobs are highly structured and rigidly defined. However, as researchers and managers became more concerned with the human dimension of the production process, the human relations school of thought emerged, spawning more behavioral approaches to job design. In today's postindustrial society, the raw material of the production process is information and the production worker is the knowledge

worker. In light of these changes, contemporary management thought has focused on participatory approaches to job design

4. Mechanistic approaches to job design focus on efficiency. Specialization and division of labor are key features of mechanistic approaches to job design. Behavioral approaches to job design focus on the human aspect of work and seek to enhance the motivation, satisfaction, and productivity of employees. Job enlargement, job enrichment, and job rotation are considered behavioral approaches to job design. Participatory approaches to job design focus largely on improving the quality of the products, services, and processes of the organization. Business process reengineering, employee-centered work redesign programs, and self-managed teams are three examples of job design programs that are participatory in nature.

5. Organizational work relationships are defined by the concepts of (1) chain of command, (2) span of control, and (3) line versus staff personnel. The chain of command defines the vertical relationships that exist within the organization. Span of control refers to the number of subordinates who report to any supervisor. Line personnel are individuals or work groups that have direct responsibility for the delivery of the organization's product or service, while staff personnel provide an advisory or support function to the line personnel.

6. Delegation involves the assignment of responsibility for a task, the granting of the authority necessary to complete the task, and the transfer of accountability to the individual to whom the task has been delegated. Successful managers must be able to delegate effectively, because delegation makes better decisions possible, provides development opportunities for employees, and magnifies the accomplishments of the manager.

7. Managers often fail to delegate because of a failure to plan, a lack of confidence in their subordinates, hesitancy to assume dual accountability for their own actions as well as the

actions of those to whom they delegate, or insecurity about their own value to the organization. Effective delegation requires matching the employee to the task, clearly communicating task responsibilities, giving authority to and imposing accountability on the person to whom the task is delegated, and choosing the appropriate level of delegation.

REVIEW QUESTIONS

1. *(Learning Objective 1)* Why is organizing an important managerial function? Describe the process of organizing. What does each stage in the process entail?

2. *(Learning Objective 2)* Define job design. What are the core job dimensions that define a specific job?

3. *(Learning Objective 3)* How and why has job design theory evolved over the last century?

4. *(Learning Objective 4)* What are the various mechanistic, behavioral, and participatory approaches to job design?

5. *(Learning Objective 5)* Discuss the following concepts: (1) chain of command, (2) span of control, and (3) line versus staff personnel.

6. *(Learning Objective 6)* What is delegation, and why is it important to delegate?

7. *(Learning Objective 7)* Why might managers find it difficult to delegate? How might they improve their delegation skills?

DISCUSSION QUESTIONS

Improving Critical Thinking

1. Consider an organization that you have either worked for or have been affiliated with in some way. How might you redesign the jobs that must be done in that organization to achieve (a) increased efficiency, (b) improved employee satisfaction, and (c) enhanced quality of the products or services? Are these objectives mutually exclusive? Could you design the jobs so that all of these objectives could be achieved?

2. The concept of self-managed teams has gained popularity in recent years. Consider moving toward that type of job design in a job you have held or hold currently. What would be the advantages and disadvantages of this approach?

Enhancing Communication Skills

3. Certain advantages and disadvantages are associated with having a fairly rigid chain of command. What are they? Can you identify certain business conditions and/or organizations in which a rigid chain of command would be appropriate? What conditions and/or organizations would benefit from the use of a more flexible chain of command? Present your conclusions to the class orally.

4. Consider the job design of the following grocery store positions: (a) cashier, (b) produce manager, and (c) general

manager. How would these jobs differ with regard to the core job dimensions discussed in this chapter? How would these jobs rate in terms of meaningfulness, the responsibility the job holder feels for outcomes, and the job holder's understanding of the results of work activities? To practice writing, develop a written summary of your response.

Building Teamwork

5. The competitive pressures of today's business climate (such as stronger global competition, advancing technology, greater demands from consumers) have forced many firms to reconsider how they might operate more efficiently and effectively. Form a team with four or five fellow students. As a group, identify and research at least three firms that have responded to such pressures by reassessing and adjusting their organizational system. Have their efforts been effective?

6. Your boss is a terrible delegator. She rarely delegates tasks, preferring to retain the responsibility for the efforts of your entire work unit rather than take a risk by assigning the task to a member of the group. Even when she does delegate a meaningful task, she rarely gives the authority necessary to complete the task successfully. Form a team of four to five fellow students and discuss ways to encourage your boss to delegate more.

THINKING CRITICALLY: DEBATE THE ISSUE

Innovative Design or Organizational Malfunction?

Think back to the opening scenario described in "Facing The Challenge." St. Luke's operates as an organization without an organizational chart. Employees are constantly challenging each other to

be more creative. Offices are nonexistent and there are no bosses. Most organizations, however, have some degree of structure. Employees are assigned specific duties and responsibilities, and a clear line of authority exists between managers and subordinates.

Form teams of four to five students. Half the teams should prepare to argue the benefits of adopting the organizing philosophy of St. Luke's that encourages individual accountability, innovative thinking, and constant change. The other half should prepare to argue the benefits of maintaining a more traditional organizational structure where explicit expectations exist for employee performance and some degree of hierarchy is maintained. Your instructor will select two teams to present their arguments to the class in a debate format.

EXPERIENTIAL EXERCISE 8.1

Assuring Positive Delegation

Using either your present job or a past job as an example, think about a task that you would like to delegate. Answer the following questions about the task and the existing situation. Based on your answers, decide whether the task should have been delegated.

1. *Precise task.* Could I specify in writing the precise task I'm going to delegate? In other words, could I specify what it is, how much of it needs to be done, and within what time frame?

2. *Benefits.* Could I specify in writing why delegating this particular task to this particular individual is good for him or her, good for the organization, and good for me?

3. *Measure of results.* Could I specify in writing how I will know (a) whether the task has been done and (b) how well it has been done?

4. *Competence.* Is the person to whom I intend to delegate this task (a) competent to do it or (b) in need of step-by-step instructions or supervision?

5. *Motivation.* Is there any evidence in my past relationship with this person that he or she wants, needs, or is motivated to do work outside the customary job?

6. *Measure of cost.* If the person makes an error, specifically what would be the dollar costs? The human costs?

7. *Check of performance.* Is it possible for me to oversee or measure the employee's performance on the task without interfering with the work?

8. *Correction of mistakes.* If problems arise, can we correct mistakes quickly without great cost or difficulty?

9. *Clearance.* Do I need to check with my boss to delegate this task?

10. *Rewards.* What are the rewards, both formal and informal, that I can give this person if the delegated task is done well? Do I need to tell the person what these rewards are?

11. *Next tasks.* If the person masters the task that has been delegated, what are the specific subsequent tasks that should be delegated to him or her?

12. *Responsibility and authority.* Can I, in delegating this task, delegate both the responsibility and the authority to this person?[75]

CAPTURING THE POWER OF TECHNOLOGY

1. International Survey Research (ISR) is an organization that specializes in the design and implementation of customized employee and management opinion and attitude surveys for national and multinational companies. ISR also regularly tracks trends regarding employee satisfaction in the United States and globally. Visit the ISR Web site and review their latest research on employee satisfaction. Does any of the information you have found have implications for job design?

2. Use the Internet to conduct research on virtual teams. What kinds of technology are available today to support virtual teams? Identify at least one organization that is using virtual teams, and interview someone on a virtual team to determine the type of technology support they use and to assess how effectively the team is operating.

3. A number of universities across the country maintain centers for international business education and research. Visit the Web sites of some of these centers and look for resources to support the development of global teams. What kinds of research and training programs are available for companies that wish to develop global teams?

ETHICS: TAKE A STAND

NewSounds, Inc., is one of the fastest-growing recording companies in the music business. Having signed some of the most popular up-and-coming bands in the past couple of years, NewSounds is enjoying success in a traditionally competitive, almost impenetrable market.

The company's president is not content to sit back and relax. She is convinced that creating an open, innovative environment will be crucial to motivate the employees of NewSounds to greater heights. To this end, she changed the physical layout of the organization. Gone are the corner offices and cubbyholes.

Now the company is structured in an open-space environment. Employees can work at whatever stations are available when they arrive in the morning. Some stations are closer to windows than others, but none have any walls for privacy. The only encased room is the "war room," a room enclosed with glass walls in the center of the office. With a long conference table, flip charts, and white boards, this room is used primarily for brainstorming sessions and weekly team meetings.

Ted Jenkins, a vice president who has been with the company since its founding, has the difficult task of reprimanding employees who are performing below expectations. Although this is a part of his job that he never really enjoyed, he did have the luxury of his own office and a closed door to ensure privacy. This changed when the office was redesigned. He is still a vice president, but he hunts for a workstation in the morning just like everyone else.

He has talked to the president about his wish to have his own office, or at the very least, the need to conduct performance appraisals in private. The president has flatly refused Jenkin's request,

telling him that everyone has to "walk the talk." She has acknowledged that her intended culture change for NewSounds may result in a few minor inconveniences but states these problems are worth enduring to create the open organization she envisions.

Jenkins takes a deep breath as he opens the front door this particular morning. The employee he is to appraise is already there and at a workstation in the middle of the office. The "war room" is currently occupied with the marketing team's weekly brainstorming session. Jenkins decides to go ahead and get the performance appraisal behind him. As he sits down somewhat awkwardly at the employee's desk, he can't help but feel like he is being watched under a microscope.

For Discussion

1. What are the ethical issues facing Jenkins?

2. Should the employee's right to privacy take precedent over the new office design and organizational culture?

3. If you were Jenkins, what would you do and why?

VIDEO CASE

Organizing for Quality, Productivity, and Job Satisfaction: Machado and Silvetti Associates, Inc.

Machado and Silvetti Associates is a highly successful Boston-based firm of about 50 people specializing in architectural and urban design. The firm's projects include the Utah Museum of Fine Arts; buildings for Harvard, Princeton, Rice, Notre Dame, and other universities; a New York City park; a development master plan for the five-block Con Edison site in Manhattan; and the Allston Branch of the Boston Public Library, which has been highly praised by community leaders and architectural critics. The firm has received numerous prestigious awards for its designs in the United States and around the world. To date, its largest project is the master plan to renovate and expand the J. Paul Getty Villa and Museum in Malibu, California, over an 11-year time period. Although the firm wasn't incorporated until 1985, the principals (Rodolfo Machado and Jorge Silvetti) have worked together since 1974.

At Machado and Silvetti Associates, two vice presidents report to the principals and nine associates report to the vice presidents. Typically, various teams work on six or seven long-term projects simultaneously. The principals provide the teams with their vision of the design projects. Then, team members work through the details of their respective design projects.

One team has been working on the large dormitory for a Boston university for about three years. Sixteen team members worked together during the design phase of this project. Now in the construction phase, about six team members concentrate on various aspects of the dormitory. The team's project manager is Associate Mike Yusem. This structure is typical of Machado and Silvetti Associates' projects.

The principals created the team structure because they believe several people can come up with better ideas than a single person can. The firm also employs young and inexperienced team members. The team structure allows them to contribute to the team discussions and gain the confidence that comes from experience. At the beginning of the dormitory project, team members got together to talk, sketch, and work through ideas. During the construction phase, they meet weekly or more often if necessary.

Although each team member has a role in the project, the roles overlap, requiring careful coordination among team members. The senior designer's primary responsibilities on the dormitory project involve the building's interiors such as walls, doors, etc. These responsibilities overlap with the designers who coordinate the dormitory's mechanical systems, shafts, and stairs, etc. It's critical for these team members to talk. They then involve the project manager and architect to discuss and resolve potential problems.

As project manager, Mike's main functions are to encourage the team to produce and serve as liaison between the client and his bosses who aren't available every day. He makes sure the client's needs are met and the project is adhering to the principals' original design. His secondary goals include keeping a young team focused, motivated, and productive. The project manager serves as coach, liaison, and "camp counselor."

To keep the process moving on such a large project, Mike knows he needs to delegate effectively. However, he finds it difficult to delegate to team members partly because of their youth and inexperience. He also considers them his friends and they all have a lot of fun. At times, he has to separate himself so he can delegate to them, possibly overload them, and trust them to do the tasks well. Though sometimes his team members look at him angrily, his job is to delegate and make sure the job gets done. Like a camp counselor, Mike works with his team, empowers them, and keeps everything moving toward completion. Although he delegates tasks, he still shares the work and responsibility. David, the project architect, praises Mike's skills as project manager because Mike takes the time to ask the right questions of the right people.

Their design team structure is based on the experience of their principals who have spent most of their lives as architecture professors in a college environment. The principals created the design team structure as an experiment. Since it worked, they've kept it. The team-oriented structure has stabilized the small firm of about 50 people and is crucial to its success. At Machado and Silvetti Associates, everyone is involved, contributing, doing his or her own thing, and coordinating with one another.

For Discussion

1. Explain how the structure Machado and Silvetti adopted illustrates the stages associated with the process of organizing.

2. Provide examples of the core job dimensions that appear to be part of Mike's job as project manager.

3. Explain the vertical and horizontal associations that appear to exist at Machado and Silvetti Associates.

4. Why does Mike seem to have difficulties delegating to team members? Suggest how he could improve his delegation skills.

http://www.machado-silvetti.com

CASE

Business Process Reengineering at Star Electronics

Star Electronics, a medium-sized firm located in the northwestern United States, was undergoing what the CEO referred to as "growing pains." One year ago the company was awarded a substantial government contract to provide electronic parts for the military. Part of Star Electronics' strategic plan, which was made explicit in their proposal to the government, was to reengineer their organizational design in order to improve quality. After being awarded the contract, the organization hired some very well-known and high-priced consultants to assist in their process improvement efforts.

Chuck Hartley, CEO of Star, told his employees that the process improvements would not result in anyone being downsized. In fact, Star had been looking to hire and train additional employees to help meet the demands of the new contract. But, Hartley was very clear that the changes that lie ahead for Star would disrupt normal routines and that the organization would look very different in the future. Departments would be merged, some teams would be disbanded, and employees would be expected to share their knowledge and expertise with everyone in the organization. These changes were needed in order to identify and eliminate redundant activities, and most importantly, to empower employees on the front lines to make recommendations for improvements.

Almost one year from the time these changes were first introduced, the results have been a mixed bag. On the positive side, quality has improved as the number of defects has drastically been reduced. Many of the line employees seem to be happier because their suggestions for improvement were acted on and they feel like a more important part of Star. Unfortunately, not everyone is happy with the changes. The staff personnel, which include Human Resources (HR), Accounting, and Marketing, are having difficulty adjusting to the new organizational design. This seems especially true in the HR Department, which has six employees. Before the changes were introduced, the HR Department was generally seen as a close-knit group who shared duties. Meg Cosinni, the vice president of HR, allowed her direct reports to work on a variety of tasks. She encouraged members of her department to avoid specializing in one area, such as compensation. Instead, she allowed her staff to operate as HR generalists, where each member was given the opportunity to perform tasks related to hiring, appraising performance, salary and benefits, and compensation.

Based on the recommendations of the consultants, this has all changed. Employees in the HR Department were asked to focus on the one part of their job they like best and to focus, or specialize, in that area. At first, Cosinni thought this approach might actually help her department's productivity and cause fewer headaches. Unfortunately, it has had the opposite effect. Morale in the department is down, many associates are calling in sick, and their productivity has declined.

For Discussion

1. What was Star Electronics trying to accomplish with the restructuring effort? Overall, were they successful? Why or why not?

2. Using the terms introduced in the chapter, describe what happened to the HR Department employees' jobs. How were their five core job dimensions affected by the changes in the department?

3. Were the reactions of the HR staff to the redesign effort what you would have expected? Why or why not?

4. How could the problems in the HR Department been avoided?

ability of its managers to develop an organizational design that supports its strategic and operational goals.

Design provides a mechanism for coping with the complexity that results from managing multiple tasks, functions, products, markets, or technologies. Although organizational design issues are important to all organizations, the more complex an organization's operations, the more sophisticated its design must be. For example, a small organization that produces a single product with a small workforce will likely find it easier to organize and coordinate its organizational members than will a multinational organization with multiple product lines, operating facilities spread across the globe, and a highly diverse workforce. Furthermore, growth-oriented organizations will find that effective design is a key to managing the complexity that results from developing new products, entering new geographic markets, or pursuing new customer groups. In sum, all organizations—small, large, and growing—must maintain an organizational design that is appropriate for the level of complexity they face.

No universal design is appropriate for all organizations. In fact, the contingency approach to organizing suggests that organizational design must be consistent with a fairly broad range of variables that are largely a function of the organization's strategy, such as size, level of development, product diversity, geographic coverage, customer base, and information processing needs.[2] Consequently, just as strategy varies among organizations, so will organizational design.

The 1990s and early 2000s have been characterized by a need for corporate redesign as organizations struggled to find an alignment between their strategy and structure. The highly volatile and competitive business environment forced many companies to reconsider their strategic focus and, consequently, the way in which their organizations were designed.[3] Pressures for efficiency led some companies into reengineering efforts. Yet efficiency alone was not enough. Simultaneously, competitive pressures to have the highest-quality products and services forced companies to look at designs that fostered employee creativity and commitment.[4] Some companies, such as Rubbermaid, DaimlerChrysler, and Harley-Davidson, have responded to this challenge effectively, reformulating their strategies in light of the competitive challenges they face and redesigning their organizations to support those strategies. Other companies, such as Sears and Kodak, have not responded to the challenge effectively and struggle to define an effective strategy and organizational design to this day.[5]

Most experts agree that developing an effective organizational design will continue to be a challenge for most companies. As competition in the business environment continues to intensify, organizations will be forced to explore new strategies, and with them, new organizational designs. Information technology will be the critical organizational design element in the years ahead.[6] Advances in technology will provide information-processing capacity that will support new, nontraditional forms of organizational design.[7] Success will go to those who innovate and experiment with ways to design their organizations, utilizing information technology to enhance their competitiveness.[8] Some organizations that have achieved early success include Microsoft, Cisco Systems, Intel, and Starbucks.[9]

COMPONENTS OF ORGANIZATIONAL DESIGN

As noted earlier and illustrated in Figure 9.1, an organization's overall design is defined by three primary components: (1) organization structure, (2) integrating mechanisms, and (3) locus of decision making. As a system, these components enable the members of the organization to fulfill their mission and work toward the

LEARNING OBJECTIVE 2

Identify the three major components of organizational design.

Figure 9.1 | Dimensions of Organizational Design

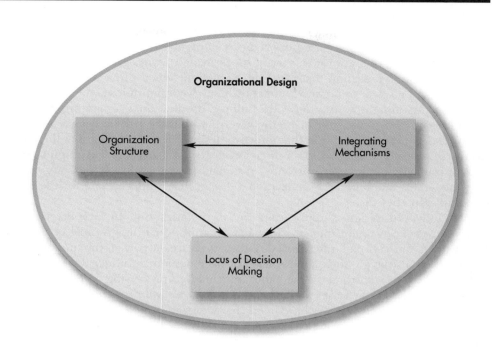

achievement of their goals. Each of these components will vary with the overall strategy of the organization.

ORGANIZATION STRUCTURE

LEARNING OBJECTIVE 3

Discuss the four types of organizational structure and the strategic conditions under which each might be appropriate.

Organization structure
The primary reporting relationships that exist within an organization.

Organization structure is the first component of organizational design. **Organization structure** refers to the primary reporting relationships that exist within an organization. The chain of command and hierarchy of responsibility, authority, and accountability are established through organizational structure. These relationships are often illustrated in an organization chart.

The structuring process involves creating departments by grouping tasks on the basis of some common characteristic such as function, product, or geographic market. If, for example, work units are created by grouping all production tasks together, all marketing tasks together, and all finance tasks together, then the units are organized by function. In contrast, if work units are formed by grouping together all tasks related to serving a specific region of the U.S. market (such as northeast, southeast, central, or west), then the geographic market served is the basis for departmentalization.

An organization's strategy has significant implications for its structure.[10] Organizations group their members along the aspect of their operations that is most complex. For example, an organization with significant product diversity will likely find a structure departmentalized by product to be most suitable for managing its broad range of products. If, in contrast, a firm has a relatively narrow product line but serves a wide geographic market, it might find a geographically based structure to be most appropriate.

In general, four types of organization structure are predominant in organizations today. Three of these—the functional, divisional, and matrix structures—are traditional organizational forms that have been used by U.S. corporations for decades. The fourth, the network structure, has emerged more recently as an ap-

proach to meeting the challenges of today's business environment. In the next several sections, we will describe each structural alternative, suggest some strategic conditions for which each might be appropriate, and outline some of the major advantages and disadvantages associated with each structure.

FUNCTIONAL STRUCTURE: ENHANCING OPERATIONAL EFFICIENCY Functional structures are the most commonly used organizational form. The **functional structure** groups organizational members according to the particular function they perform within the organization and the set of resources they draw upon to perform their tasks.

When an organization's greatest source of complexity comes from the diverse tasks and responsibilities that must be performed, rather than from its products, geographic markets, or customer groups, a functional structure may be appropriate. Entrepreneurial organizations or organizations that are in the early stages of the organizational life cycle often have limited product diversity and geographic scope. Task diversity may represent the organization's greatest source of complexity, and as a consequence, a functional structure may be most suitable.

Figure 9.2 illustrates a functional organization chart for a fictional company—PGP, Inc. PGP distributes hair care products in the southeastern United States. Given the narrow scope of the company's products and markets, its greatest source of complexity arises out of the nature of the tasks to be done. Therefore, the company has organized its workers by function—marketing, production, sales, human resources, and finance. The vice presidents of the company oversee these functional departments and report directly to PGP's chief executive officer.

Table 9.1 outlines the major advantages and disadvantages associated with the functional structure. On the positive side, functional structures support task specialization and may help employees develop better job-related skills. In addition, work groups may be more cohesive, because employees work with individuals with similar skills and interests and the group's leader has a common functional orientation with the group members. Finally, this structure supports tight, centralized control and may result in greater operational efficiency.

But this structure has disadvantages as well. Most of these disadvantages stem from the problems associated with coordinating diverse work groups. Work groups organized along functional lines are often insulated from the activities of other departments and may not truly understand the priorities and initiatives of other work groups. This has become particularly problematic for organizations attempting to implement enterprise resource planning (ERP) systems that utilize information technology to coordinate information across organizational departments.[11] Another disadvantage of the functional structure is that it leads to the development

Functional structure
Members of the organization are grouped according to the function they perform within the organization.

Figure 9.2 | Functional Structure: PGP, Inc.

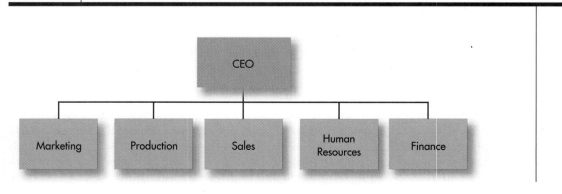

Table 9.1 | Advantages and Disadvantages of Traditional Organizational Structures

	ADVANTAGES	DISADVANTAGES
Functional	• Facilitates specialization • Cohesive work groups • Improved operational efficiency	• Focus on departmental versus organizational issues • Difficult to develop generalists needed for top-level management • Only top-level management held accountable for profitability
Divisional	• Allows focus on specific products, geographic markets, or customers • Adaptable to specific growth strategies of the organization	• Duplication of resources across divisions • Coordination and integration of activities among divisions may be difficult
Matrix	• Can achieve simultaneous objectives • Managers focus on two organizational dimensions, resulting in more specific job skills	• Complex, leading to difficulties in implementation • Behavioral difficulties from "two bosses" • Time-consuming from a planning/coordination perspective
Network	• Maximizes the effectiveness of the core unit • Can do more with fewer resources • Flexibility	• Fragmentation makes it difficult to develop control systems • Success is dependent on ability to locate sources • Difficult to develop employee loyalty

Divisional structure

Members of the organization are grouped on the basis of common products, geographic markets, or customers served.

Product divisional structure

A structure in which the activities of the organization are grouped according to specific products or product lines.

of specialized managers, rather than generalists who may be more appropriate for top-level management positions. Finally, profit centers usually do not exist in a functionally structured organization. Therefore, only top-level corporate executives can be held clearly accountable for bottom-line profitability.

DIVISIONAL STRUCTURES: PROVIDING FOCUS A second common form of organizational structure is the divisional structure. In most cases, a **divisional structure** is designed so that members of the organization are grouped on the basis of common products or services, geographic markets, or customers served. The primary advantage of a divisional structure is that it focuses the company's attention on the aspects of its operations that are of greatest importance from a strategic perspective. The primary disadvantage is that resources and efforts may be duplicated across divisions (see Table 9.1).

Product Divisions In a **product divisional structure**, product managers assume responsibility for the production and distribution of a specific product or product line to all the geographic and customer markets served by the organization. These managers coordinate all functional tasks (finance, marketing, production, and so on) related to their product line. Product divisional structures can be based on services as well as products.

Product divisional structures are considered most appropriate for organizations with relatively diverse product lines that require specialized efforts to achieve high product quality. When products are targeted to different, distinct groups; require varied technologies for production; or are delivered through diverse distribution systems, a product-based structure may be suitable. For example, consider IBM's move to create autonomous operating divisions based on the firm's distinct product lines. Recognizing the importance of a product orientation to IBM's overall success, top-level management believed that a product divisional structure would provide the product focus necessary to regain their competitive edge. Royal Dutch Shell is another company that has found that a product divisional structure provides an appropriate focus on distinct and diverse product lines.[12] Figure 9.3 illus-

Figure 9.3 | Product Divisional Structure: Clariant

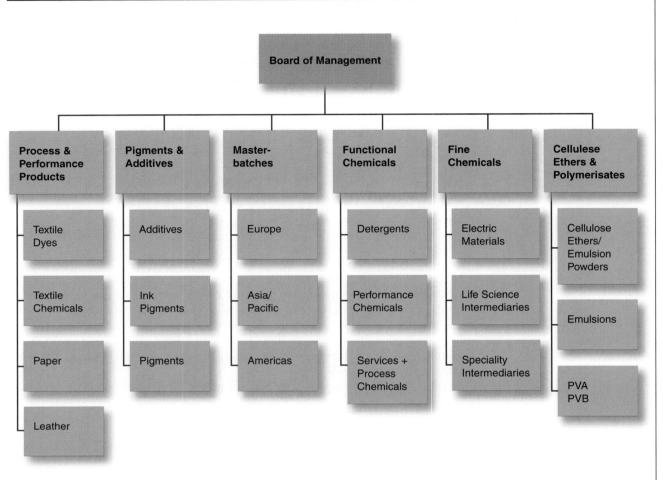

trates the product divisional structure of Clariant, a specialty chemicals company headquartered in Switzerland. Clariant's six divisions, which operate as profit centers and bear worldwide responsibilities for their operations, enable the company to focus on its distinct products and the market needs they serve.[13]

Many large organizations not only have diverse product lines, but actually operate several diverse and distinct businesses. In such cases, the product divisional structure actually takes the form of an SBU (strategic business unit) divisional structure, in which each business unit is maintained as a separate and autonomous operating division. PepsiCo, Inc., provides an excellent example of a company organized around its primary businesses—Pepsi Cola Company (soft drinks), Frito-Lay Company (snack foods), and Tropicana Products (juices).[14]

Geographic Divisions The **geographic divisional structure** groups the activities of the organization along geographic lines. Each geographic division is responsible for distributing products or services within a specific geographic region. Canadian National Railway Company, for example, organizes its operations into five geographic divisions that cover the regions it serves. The geographic divisional structure, which was precipitated by the merger of Canadian National with Illinois Central, focuses managers on serving the needs of the particular market they serve.[15] Figure 9.4 illustrates the structure of Canadian National Railway Company.

Geographic divisional structure
A structure in which the activities of the organization are grouped according to the geographic markets served.

Figure 9.4 | Geographic Divisional Structure: Canadian National Railway Company

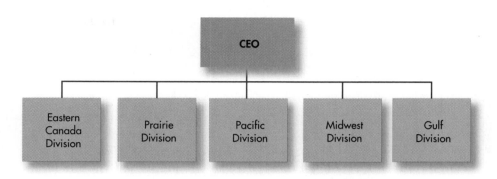

SOURCE: "Illinois Central Deal Spurs Reorganization by Canadian National," *The Wall Street Journal*, April 15, 1999, A4.

A geographic divisional structure is appropriate for organizations of varying strategic conditions. In general, this structure is most appropriate for organizations with limited product lines that either have wide geographic coverage or desire to grow through geographic expansion. This structure permits organizations to concentrate their efforts and allocate their resources toward penetrating multiple regional markets with products and services that are, when necessary, adapted to meet local needs and preferences.[16]

Organizations pursuing international strategies often choose a geographically based structure.[17] Companies with relatively narrow, mature product lines may find that their primary growth opportunities are in the international marketplace. Entering those markets effectively often requires a strong understanding of local market conditions and customer preferences. A geographic divisional structure provides a mechanism for learning more about local markets and making the necessary adaptations to the company's products and services. Multinational organizations in the food, beverage, and cosmetics industries have found that this organizational structure supports their efforts to respond to local market demands.

Kellogg provides an excellent example of a firm that maintains a geographic divisional structure. As the world's leading ready-to-eat cereal producer, Kellogg produces a variety of cereals and convenience foods such as cookies, crackers, and frozen waffles. These products are manufactured in 19 countries and marketed in more than 160 countries around the world. Because of its relatively narrow product focus, Kellogg's primary source of complexity comes from the broad geographic markets it serves. Thus, a geographic divisional structure is ideal for this company. Kellogg's operations are structured around six main geographic regions—the United States, Europe, Latin America, Canada, Australia, and Asia.[18]

While Kellogg enjoys a strong international presence that justifies separate divisions based on geographic area, organizations that are just venturing into the international marketplace often begin by adding an international division to support their international sales efforts. For example, Houghton Mifflin, a publisher of educational materials, added an international division in an effort to stimulate sales of its products overseas.[19]

To effectively enter the international marketplace, companies must have a strong understanding of local market conditions and customer preferences.

© AP/WIDE WORLD PHOTOS

Customer Divisions   A **customer divisional structure** groups tasks according to different customers. Each customer-based unit focuses on meeting the needs of a specific group of the organization's customers. A customer-based structure is appropriate for organizations that have separate customer groups with specific and distinct needs. With the intense competitive environment in most industries and the emphasis on meeting the needs of the customer first and foremost, this structure is highly appropriate for organizations that must adapt their products and services for different customer groups. It may also be suitable for organizations that wish to grow by targeting new and distinct customer groups. Resources can be allocated to support the customer groups with the greatest growth potential.

Interest in customer-based structures has increased in recent years. For example, while Microsoft is organized into five semiautonomous product divisions, those divisions focus on very different customer segments. Microsoft touts the structure as one that enables the company to focus on customer needs and supports the company's strategy for growth in its customer base.[20] Cisco Systems actually abandoned a product divisional structure to move to a structure that is focused on its primary customer segments. John Chambers, Cisco's president and CEO, said, "This alignment will enable us to bring increased focus to our customers and provide them with complete end-to-end solutions. . . ." Like Microsoft, Cisco feels that the move from a product-focused structure to a customer-oriented, solutions-based structure will support its future growth plans.[21]

Think back to the scenario facing EDS in "Facing the Challenge" on page 282. EDS had become complacent and lost touch with customer needs. Additionally, the 48 different units made it very difficult to coordinate activities and align procedures, much less provide superior customer service. Getting EDS employees to refocus on the customer was the driving force for redesigning the organization's structure.

MATRIX STRUCTURE: PROVIDING A DUAL FOCUS   The organizational structures discussed so far have grouped activities along a specific, single dimension of the organization's operations (function, product, geographic region, or customer base). Rather than focusing on a single dimension of the organization's operations, a **matrix structure** defines work groups on the basis of two dimensions simultaneously (such as product/function, product/geographic region, and so on). Davis and Lawrence defined a matrix structure as one that "employs a multiple command system that includes not only a multiple command structure but also related support mechanisms and an associated organizational culture and behavior patterns."[22] In other words, the distinguishing characteristic of the matrix structure is its dual chain of command.[23]

For illustrative purposes, let's once again consider PGP, Inc., the fictitious company introduced earlier in the chapter. When PGP was founded, it offered hair care products within the southeastern United States. As discussed previously, a functional organizational structure was appropriate for the company when it offered a limited product line to a limited geographic market. However, as the company grew and evolved, it expanded the scope of both its products and the geographic markets it serves. Today, PGP is a multinational company that distributes a relatively broad range of health and beauty products to worldwide markets. The organizational structure that is appropriate for PGP today is far different from the structure that was appropriate during the early years of the company's existence. In fact, PGP benefits greatly from a matrix structure that combines the product and geographic dimensions of its operations.

As illustrated in Figure 9.5, PGP maintains both product and geographic divisions. The vice presidents of the product and geographic divisions report directly to PGP's CEO and assume full responsibility for the operations of their respective divisions. For example, the vice president for South America is ultimately respon-

Customer divisional structure
A structure in which the tasks of the organization are grouped according to customer segments.

Matrix structure
A structure in which the tasks of the organization are grouped along two organizing dimensions simultaneously (such as product/geographic market, product/function).

Figure 9.5 | A Multinational Matrix Structure: PGP, Inc.

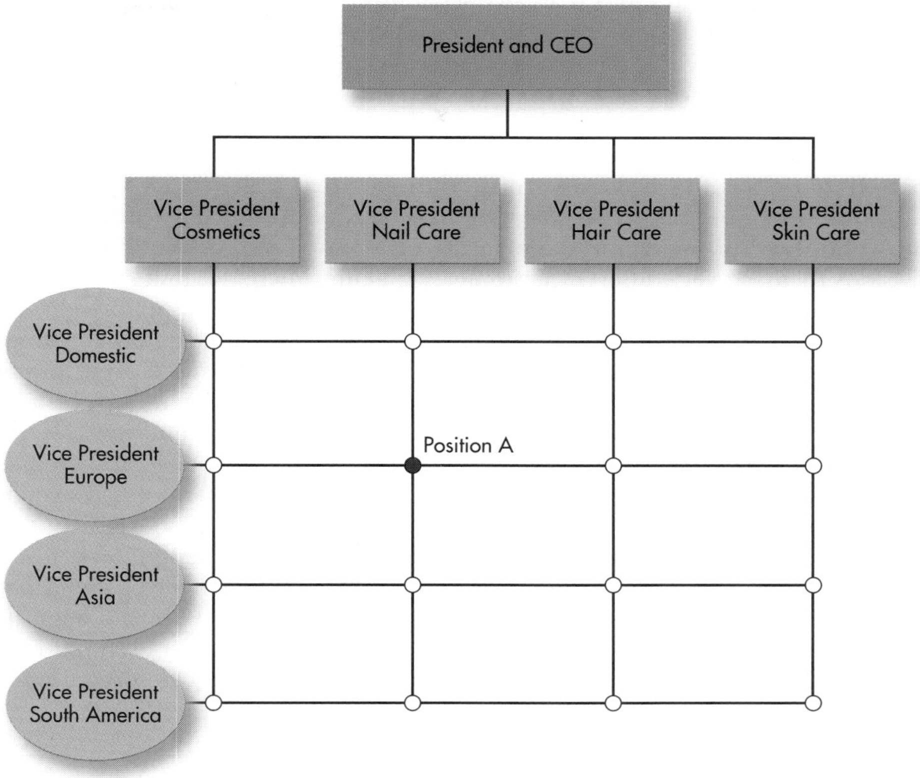

sible for the distribution of all products (hair care, nail care, cosmetics, skin care) to the South American market. In contrast, the vice president of the nail care division assumes responsibility for the distribution of nail care products worldwide. Theoretically, these vice presidents have equal organizational power.

The dual chain of command is illustrated at the next level of the hierarchy. Consider the manager occupying position A. What are this person's job responsibilities? Who is her boss? Is it the vice president of nail care products or the vice president for Europe? The person who occupies position A on PGP's organization chart is responsible for distributing nail care products in Europe. Therefore, this manager has both a product and area focus to her job, and as a result, she can develop more specific job skills. In addition, this manager has two bosses to whom she is equally accountable—the vice president of nail care products and the vice president for Europe.

The matrix structure provides PGP with a viable way to focus on both specific products and geographic markets, thereby enabling the company to achieve simultaneous objectives. If forced to organize around only one organizational dimension, PGP would forgo the benefits associated with the other dimension. The matrix structure enables many global organizations to focus both on enhancing the quality of their products through the product dimension and on achieving greater penetration of discrete national or regional markets through the geographic dimension of the structure.

Despite the obvious advantages of the matrix structure, it also has a number of disadvantages (see Table 9.1). Most notable is the complexity inherent in a dual

chain of command. Managing within this structure requires extraordinary planning and coordination between work groups.[24]

A number of prominent companies have found the matrix structure to be highly effective. For example, Asea Brown Boveri became the world's leading technology and engineering company through its penetration of worldwide markets, facilitated by its sophisticated global matrix structure. Texas Instruments credits a functional/product matrix with its ability to bring products to market more quickly.[25] And, Unisys recently adopted a matrix structure in an attempt to bring a stronger customer focus to the company. The new matrix structure is organized around global industries (such as financial services, transportation, communications) and worldwide product and services groups (such as Systems and Technology, Global Network Services, Global Outsourcing, and E-Business Solutions). However, before Digital Equipment Company (DEC) was acquired by other companies, it reported a very different experience with the functional/product matrix structure. DEC found that the matrix structure led to "people spending endless hours in meetings trying to build consensus between the two factions in the matrix: the functional bosses and the team bosses."[26] The delays associated with the structure left DEC behind in the fast-paced technology race in the computer industry. DEC's experience provides an important reminder that while the matrix structure can be effective, the benefits of the design will come only with successful implementation.

NETWORK STRUCTURES: THE KEY TO FLEXIBILITY For decades, organizations aspired to be large. Growth was considered to be synonymous with success, and the "bigger is better" syndrome governed the strategic decision making of most companies. But today, an alternative view has emerged. Organizations are finding that being lean and flexible is often preferable to being big. This may be particularly true for companies that operate within rapidly changing industries or face intense global competition.[27]

In response to these changes, a number of successful organizations have abandoned the traditional organizational structures of the past and have moved toward a more contemporary form of organizational structure—the network structure.[28] The **network structure** is a sophisticated product delivery system that is built around alliances between organizations within the network. Each member of the network performs some portion of the activities necessary to deliver the products and services of the network as a whole.[29] At the core of each network is an organization that performs some key functions for the network and coordinates the activities of other network members. For example, the central organization may coordinate the production, marketing, financing, and distribution activities necessary to market a particular product without owning a single manufacturing plant, creating a single line of advertising copy, or even taking possession of the product. The central organization simply coordinates the activities of others so that the product reaches the ultimate consumer in the most efficient method possible.[30] Figure 9.6 illustrates the network organizational structure.[31]

Consider Benetton, the clothing company that is known throughout the world. Benetton is the central organization in a complex network of companies that contribute to its overall mission. Benetton handles the design decisions for the network and coordinates the manufacturing, advertising, marketing, and distribution aspects of the network. Around Benetton is an array of manufacturing companies, advertisers, distributors, and retailers who actually perform the activities necessary to move the product from the factory to the consumer. Benetton supports its network of companies by providing access to state-of-the-art information systems, financial support, and specialized knowledge. This system provides the smaller companies in the network with some of the advantages of a larger organization (for example, access to resources).[32]

Network structure
A contemporary organizational structure that is founded on a set of alliances with other organizations that serve a wide variety of functions.

Figure 9.6 | Network Structure

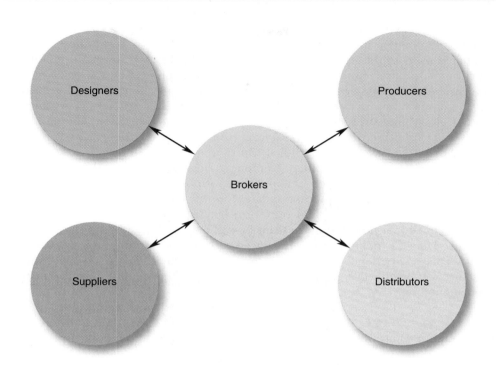

SOURCE: R. E. Miles and C. C. Snow, "Organizations: New Concepts for New Forms," 62–73. Copyright © 1986 by The Regents of the University of California. Reprinted from *California Management Review*, Vol. 28, No. 3. By permission of The Regents.

Michael Dell, founder and CEO of Dell Computers, has created an innovative network structure that is considered by many to be the standard in the computer industry. "Leaders In Action" on page 293 describes Dell's approach to organizational structure, which focuses on the core relationships between manufacturing, distribution, and sales.

Three primary types of network structures are found in organizations today—internal, stable, and dynamic networks.[33] These structures vary in the extent to which the central organization relies on outsourcing. (Recall from Chapter 1 on page 28 that outsourcing occurs when one organization contracts with a separate organization to perform some aspect of its operations.)

An **internal network** exists in organizations that choose to avoid outsourcing, but wish to develop internal entrepreneurial ventures that are driven by market forces and thus are competitive with alternative sources of supply. These internal units operate independently and negotiate with the central unit like any outside vendor. Each unit functions as a profit center that specializes in a particular aspect of the organization's product delivery system.

The component business of General Motors (GM) serves as an excellent example of an internal network structure. GM's component business maintains eight independent divisions that specialize in the production of some aspect of the automotive system, such as AC spark plugs. These divisions are encouraged to conduct business on the open market, yet they cooperate with the central unit of GM's component business whenever appropriate. The net result is greater effectiveness for the corporation as a whole.[34]

Organizations that maintain a **stable network** rely to some degree on outsourcing to add flexibility to their product delivery system. The central organiza-

Internal network

A network structure that relies on internally developed units to provide services to a core organizational unit.

Stable network

A network structure that utilizes external alliances selectively as a mechanism for gaining strategic flexibility.

Leaders In Action

Dell Computer's Flexible Structure Creates a Competitive Advantage

As business organizations move into the 21st century, what constitutes the actual "organization" is changing dramatically. Traditional organizations with layers of hierarchy are often inflexible and unable to respond to the rapid changes in the global environment. As a result, these structures are disappearing from the corporate landscape. The structures that are replacing them are very different from what most of us are accustomed. Michael Dell, founder and CEO of Dell Computers, is leading this charge by creating a more flexible and adaptable structure at Dell.

Dell Computers was founded in 1984 as the first computer company to sell custom-built systems. Since then, Dell has grown to be the preferred computer systems company with yearly revenues in excess of $31 billion. At the heart of Dell's incredible success has been the willingness of leadership to adopt unconventional organizing policies to improve efficiency and customer service.

Dell has a simple structure that allows associates to focus on core competencies, such as PCs and customer service. What sets Dell apart from its competitors is its model of direct customer relationship. Dell is lauded for building individual systems to meet unique customer needs, and it is routinely rated as the number one provider of customer service in the PC industry.

Most recently, Dell has been an industry leader in redefining the relational structure it has with suppliers. The supply chain is typically thought of as the organizations involved between the supplier of a product and the customer. Various links in the traditional supply chain include distributors and retailers. Dell has succeeded in changing the traditional model of the supply chain in a number of ways, and the results have been very successful.

When Dell receives a customer order, it immediately sends the customer's request to its production facility. There the computer is assembled and shipped within a week. Using this innovative approach, no computer is assembled unless a specific customer request has been made. This structure prevents Dell from having the burden of carrying an expensive inventory. The company is able to operate effectively with half the number of employees and one-tenth the inventory of its traditional computer competitor.

Dell also has the unique advantage of selling directly to the customer. In essence, Dell eliminated the "retail" link in the supply chain because is builds, sells, and ships its product directly to the customer and corporate clients. Dell has demonstrated that eliminating ineffective structures and unnecessary links in the supply chain leads to better customer service and a distinct competitive advantage.

SOURCE: T. C. Lawton, "Advancing to the Virtual Value Chain: Learning from the Dell Model," *Irish Journal of Management*, 22, 1, 2001, 91–112.

---

tion contracts with outside vendors to provide certain products and services that are essential to its product delivery system. Although these vendors are independent of the central organization, they typically are highly committed to the core firm.

BMW is an example of a company that has adopted a stable network structure. Somewhere between 55 and 75 percent of BMW's production comes from outsourcing. Partnerships with vendors serve a critical function in the company's product delivery system. Although BMW does not own its vendor firms outright, as GM does, it does maintain stable relationships with them and may even make a financial investment in these organizations where appropriate.[35]

A **dynamic network** differs from internal and stable networks in that organizations with this structure make extensive use of outsourcing to support their operations. Partnerships with vendors are less frequent, and less emphasis is placed on finding organizations to service the central organization only. Typically, the central organization focuses on some core skill and contracts for most other functions. For example, Motorola capitalizes on its manufacturing strengths, Reebok on its design strengths, and Dell Computer on its design and assembly strengths; in each case, the company prefers to outsource most other aspects of its product delivery system.[36] Benetton is a dynamic network, as is Nike.[37]

A number of advantages and disadvantages are associated with the network structure (see Table 9.1). The effectiveness and efficiency of the core unit are max-

BMW maintains stable relationships with its vendor firms and may invest in them financially where appropriate.

© TERRI MILLER/E-VISUAL COMMUNICATIONS, INC.

Dynamic network
A network structure that makes extensive use of outsourcing through alliances with outside organizations.

imized by the use of a network structure, particularly if the network is characterized by enduring, mutually beneficial business relationships.[38] The organization can do more with less because it is using others' resources. Flexibility is an inherent benefit of this organizational form, because the core unit can change vendors quickly should product changes be necessary. Many international firms have found that the network structure provides them with the speed and flexibility necessary to compete effectively in highly competitive global markets. In fact, some multinationals have abandoned the matrix structure in favor of the more adaptable network form.[39]

The primary disadvantage of a network structure is that because operations are fragmented, it may be difficult to develop a control system that effectively monitors all aspects of the product delivery system.[40] However, advanced information technology can be utilized to better monitor the activities of networked companies. In fact, specialized systems have been developed that address the unique needs of the network organization.[41] Companies such as Benetton and Nike are utilizing such systems to effectively coordinate the activities of their diverse networks. As business-to-business e-commerce solutions continue to evolve, more organizations may find the network structure feasible and appealing.[42] In fact, some experts believe that the flexibility inherent in strategic network structures will be critical for competitive success in the 21st century.[43]

Organizations commonly use some type of network structure to get into a specific market very quickly and then adopt a more traditional structure later. IBM, for example, utilized a dynamic network structure to enter the personal computer market. Lagging the competition in this market, IBM assembled a network of suppliers, designers, and marketers to bring its product to market very quickly. Once the company had established itself in the personal computer arena, it reintegrated many of these functions into its central operations.[44]

We have examined the four basic types of structures that are commonly used in organizations today. These structures define how the employees of the organization are grouped and specify reporting relationships within the organizational hierarchy. "Now Apply It" on this page gives you an opportunity to assess the organizational structure of an organization with which you are familiar. Take some time to work through the exercise before moving on to learn about the second component of organizational design—integrating mechanisms.

LEARNING OBJECTIVE 4

Describe the factors that affect an organization's need for coordination and explain how integrating mechanisms can be used to coordinate organizational activities.

MANAGING COMPLEXITY THROUGH INTEGRATION

Integrating the activities of an organization involves controlling and coordinating the flow of information, resources, and tasks among organizational members and work groups. Whereas structure serves to segregate organizational members into different work units, the goal of the integration component of organizational de-

---

Now Apply It

Assessing Organizational Structure

Select an organization for which you can develop an organization chart (such as a business, university, church, social organization, or student organization). Develop an organization chart that shows how the organization is departmentalized.

Then answer the following questions about its structure:

1. Is the structure consistent with the strategy of the organization?
2. Are the work units grouped according to the aspect of the organization that presents the greatest complexity (such as task/function, products, geographic market)?
3. Would another organizational structure make more sense than the existing structure? If so, why?

sign is to coordinate the work of these distinct groups. An organization's many and diverse work groups are linked together through integrating mechanisms. As we will soon learn, integrating mechanisms include such things as management information systems, liaison personnel, and cross-functional work teams.

The complexity of an organization's operations will affect its need for integration. For example, a purely domestic firm with a narrow product line and a single manufacturing facility will find the integration of its work groups to be more manageable than will a multinational corporation with broad product lines and manufacturing facilities spread across the globe. In general, the more complex an organization's operations, the more sophisticated its coordinating mechanisms must be.

In general, an organization's integration needs will vary with the level of interdependence that exists among work groups.[45] In organizations where work groups must closely coordinate their activities to achieve organizational goals, integration needs will be high. In contrast, where work groups exist relatively independently and without significant interaction, integration needs are low. Before we discuss specific integrating mechanisms that might be used to coordinate the activities of an organization, let's examine the various levels of interdependence that may exist in an organization and how that interdependence affects its integration needs.

INTERDEPENDENCE AND INTEGRATION NEEDS Central to the discussion of integration is the concept of interdependence. **Interdependence** refers to the degree to which work groups are interrelated and the extent to which they depend upon one another to complete their work. The level of interdependence between work groups will affect the need for integrating mechanisms.[46] Figure 9.7 illustrates the three primary levels of work group interdependence, and the following discussion describes each in greater detail.

Pooled Interdependence **Pooled interdependence** occurs when organizational units have a common source of resources but have no interrelationship with one another. Consider, for example, a local bank with branch offices spread around the

Interdependence
The degree to which work groups are interrelated.

Pooled interdependence
Occurs when organizational units have a common resource but no interrelationship with one another.

Figure 9.7 | Levels of Work Group Interdependence

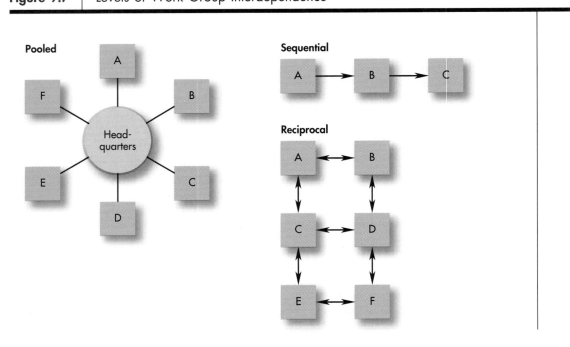

city. Although all branches must coordinate their efforts with the central office, they have limited interaction with one another. They have little need to cooperate and coordinate with one another to achieve their goals. Managers work independently to achieve the goals of their own work groups, which, in turn, contribute to the overall performance of the organization.

Sequential interdependence
Occurs when organizational units must coordinate the flow of information, resources, and tasks from one unit to another.

Sequential Interdependence **Sequential interdependence** exists when work groups must coordinate the flow of information, resources, or tasks from one unit to another. Sequential interdependence is associated with a typical manufacturing assembly line. The output of one unit becomes the input for another unit. Organizations with sequentially interdependent units have greater coordination needs than organizations with units that have pooled interdependence.

Reciprocal interdependence
Occurs when information, resources, and tasks must be passed back and forth between work groups.

Reciprocal Interdependence **Reciprocal interdependence** represents the greatest level of interrelatedness between work groups, in that work is passed back and forth between work units. The final product requires the input of a number of different departments at varying times during the production process. Consider a university system, in which students' registration materials must be shuffled from one administrative unit to another and back. These work groups are interrelated, and the effective functioning of the system requires a high level of integration among the groups.

The higher the level of interdependence of an organization's work groups, the greater its needs for coordination. The sophistication of an integrating system should be in alignment with its specific coordination needs. For example, an organization with pooled interdependence between its work groups may be able to function effectively with a few relatively simple integrating mechanisms. In contrast, an organization with reciprocal interdependence between work groups will require more sophisticated integrating mechanisms.

Integrating mechanisms are not without costs. As we will discuss, many of the tools for coordinating the activities of the organization have human or financial costs that are tangible and measurable. Therefore, organizations must carefully evaluate their coordination needs so that they can develop integrating mechanisms that are cost-effective and in line with those needs.

Integrating mechanisms
Methods for managing the flow of information, resources, and tasks within the organization.

INTEGRATING MECHANISMS   At the foundation of an organization's ability to coordinate the activities of its subunits is its information-processing capacity. Effective coordination is dependent upon the flow of information between the individual units of the organization so that work can be scheduled, resources shared and transferred, and conflicting objectives resolved. Toward this end, organizations develop integrating mechanisms that enhance their information-processing capacity and support their need for coordination. **Integrating mechanisms** are methods for managing the flow of information, resources, and tasks throughout the organization.

Many different mechanisms can be used to process information and coordinate the activities of interdependent work units. Some of these mechanisms are characteristic of general management systems. Others are developed specifically to increase the coordination potential of the organization. Still others are designed to reduce the organization's need for coordination. Figure 9.8 illustrates the three major categories of integrating mechanisms, each of which is discussed next.[47]

General Management Systems   Some coordination of work units may be achieved through the development of general management systems such as the managerial hierarchy, basic rules and procedures, and plans and goals. Such mechanisms form the foundation of an organization's integration system.

As we have discussed, an organization's managerial hierarchy is established by its organizational structure. Recall that organizational structure defines work groups

Figure 9.8 | Integrating Mechanisms

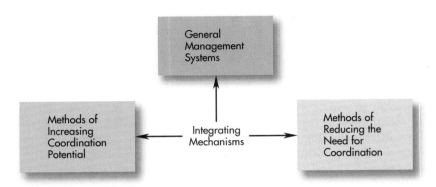

SOURCE: Adapted by permission, J. R. Galbraith. "Organizational Design: An Information Processing View," *Interfaces*, 4, May 1974, 3. Copyright 1974, The Institute of Management Sciences and the Operations Research Society of America (currently INFORMS), 2 Charles Street, Suite 300, Providence, RI 02904 USA.

on the basis of the task characteristic that presents the greatest source of diversity (that is, function, product, geographic, market, or customer). By grouping organizational members in this fashion, coordination within the groups is enhanced. Consider the structures of Hewlett-Packard, Eaton, and Dana for example. These companies have designed their structures in such a way that separate business units serve different customer segments or provide different products. Thus, they have grouped employees based on their need to coordinate with one another.[48]

Similarly, most organizations develop basic rules and procedures that govern the behavior of their members. Organizations that make extensive use of rules and procedures often are thought to be bureaucratic, highly formalized, and closely governed. In contrast, organizations that use fewer rules and procedures are considered to be more flexible, less formal, and participatory in nature. Yet too few rules can result in significant problems, particularly when coordination between organizational members is required.

Most universities make extensive use of rules and procedures to coordinate the activities of their colleges and departments. Student records must be processed according to specific guidelines; overrides into classes must be handled systematically; and parking tickets and overdue library books must be dealt with before the registration process can be completed. These rules and procedures are mechanisms that ensure that the activities of the various units of the university are well coordinated.

The development of plans and goals can also serve as a means of integrating the operations of an organization. Plans that require implementation by multiple work groups provide a foundation for action by those units. A well-developed business plan will detail the activities of specific departments within an organization, thereby providing guidance about how those activities are to be coordinated. Similarly, certain behaviors are implied by specific achievement-based goals. Quality management programs serve as an excellent integrating mechanism for many companies. The plans that result from such programs provide a foundation for integrating and coordinating the activities of diverse groups toward common quality-oriented goals.

Increasing Coordination Potential For most organizations, general management systems do not provide sufficient coordination potential. Additional integrating mechanisms are needed to coordinate the organization's activities effectively. In-

formation systems and lateral relationships are two of the most common mechanisms for increasing coordination potential both vertically and horizontally within the organization.

Information systems facilitate the flow of information up and down the traditional chain of command and across organizational units. Management information systems have become increasingly important mechanisms for implementing strategy[49] and increasing coordination potential in recent years.[50] The computerized transfer of important information and data provides a powerful tool for coordinating diverse departments or operating units.[51] Additionally, information technology can provide control mechanisms that ensure that coordination problems are identified and resolved in a timely fashion.[52] In fact, some have argued that information technology has advanced organizational coordination to the same magnitude that mass-production technologies advanced manufacturing in the Industrial Revolution.[53] Today, advanced enterprise resource planning (ERP) systems provide the information capacity to coordinate the activities of the entire organization with a single software application.[54]

Many multinational corporations have developed sophisticated management information systems to support their global operations. With the advent of more sophisticated and affordable computer technology, decision-making data can be transmitted almost simultaneously from division to division around the globe. Computer and telecommunication networks provide the infrastructure for coordinating operations on a worldwide scale. Electronic mail, teleconferencing, and high-speed data systems are a few of the mechanisms used by multinational organizations. The second important method for increasing coordination potential is to establish lateral relationships. Such relationships exist across horizontal work units and serve as mechanisms for exchanging decision-making information. In general, lateral relationships can be thought of as **boundary-spanning roles**. The primary purpose of the boundary-spanning function is to develop an understanding of the activities of units outside the boundaries of one's own work group. Such knowledge helps employees and work groups understand how their actions and performance affect others within the organization, as well as the organization as a whole. The effectiveness of the networks that exist between people within different units of the organization will often determine the success of the individual units and the organization as a whole.[55]

The boundary-spanning function can be served through a number of different relationships that vary in formality and level of commitment to the coordinating function. Integrating relationships include liaisons, committees and task forces, and cross-functional work teams.

When two or more work units have a recurring need to communicate with each other, it may be beneficial to establish a liaison position to support their communication needs. People who occupy such positions retain their association with their primary unit, but they also assume responsibility for interacting with other work groups. For example, the marketing department of an organization might identify an individual to act as a formal liaison with the company's engineering department. Although this individual remains in his marketing role, he also serves as the primary contact point for the interaction between the marketing department and the engineering department.

When the effective management of multiple interdependent units is critical to the success of the organization, it may be appropriate to establish a committee (a permanent group) or a task force (a temporary group) to facilitate communication between the groups. The committee or task force would be made up of representatives from each of the work groups involved. As was the case with the formal liaison position, the committee or task force assignment is only a part of each representative's job; the representatives' primary job responsibilities remain with the units they represent.[56] Multinational corporations, for example, often use committees or councils

Boundary-spanning roles
Lateral relationships that help to integrate and coordinate the activities of the organization (that is, liaisons, committees, task forces, integrating positions, and cross-functional work teams).

composed of corporate executives and representatives from both domestic and foreign subsidiaries. These councils assume responsibility for both assimilating and disseminating critical information needed by the operating units of the organizations.

When an organization has very high integration needs, it may be appropriate to establish cross-functional work teams. Cross-functional work teams represent a more aggressive approach to integration, in that members from various functional groups are permanently assigned to a team that is given responsibility for completing a particular set of tasks (see the discussions of self-managed teams in Chapters 1 and 8). Cross-functional teams are often used to support the product development function in organizations. Toyota, for example, utilizes a cross-functional team approach to support its vehicle development process. These teams enable the company to achieve cross-functional integration while still capturing functional expertise from the team members. The cross-functional team provides a balanced approach that overcomes many of the disadvantages associated with a pure functional structure (chimney extreme) or a formalized committee structure (committee extreme). Table 9.2 illustrates Toyota's balanced approach to integration and coordination.[57]

Table 9.2 | How Toyota Avoids Extremes

CHIMNEY EXTREME	TOYOTA BALANCE	COMMITTEE EXTREME
Mutual Adjustment		
Little face-to-face contact.	Succinct written reports for most communication.	Reliance on meetings to accomplish tasks.
Predominantly written communication.	Meetings for intensive problem solving.	Predominantly oral communication.
Direct Supervision		
Close supervision of engineers by managers.	Technically astute functional supervisors who mentor, train, and develop their engineers.	Little supervision of engineers.
Large barriers between functions.	Strong functions that are evaluated based on overall system performance.	Weak functional expertise.
Integrative Leadership		
No system design leader.	Project leader as system designer, with limitations on authority.	System design dispersed among team members.
Standard Skills		
No rotation of engineers.	Rotation on intervals that are longer than the typical product cycle, and only to positions that complement the engineers' expertise.	Rotation at rapid and broad intervals.
Standard Work Processes		
New development process with every vehicle.	Standard milestones—project leader decides timing, functions fill in details.	Lengthy, detailed, rigid development schedules.
Complex forms and bureaucratic procedures.	Standard forms and procedures that are simple, devised by the people who use them, and updated as needed.	Making up procedures on each project.
Design Standards		
Obsolete, rigid design standards.	Standards that are maintained by the people doing the work and that keep pace with current company capabilities.	No design standards.

Today, information technology has enabled the development of a new kind of cross-functional team—the virtual team. A group of technologies including desktop video conferencing, collaborative software, and Internet/Intranet systems is converging to support a revolution in the work environment. This new work environment will be unrestrained by geography, time, and organizational boundaries; it will be a virtual workplace that will permit organizations to achieve unprecedented levels of productivity, flexibility, and collaboration. Virtual teams may be geographically dispersed coworkers within the same organization, or they may exist across organizations as in a network organization structure. What virtual teams have in common is that they are in separate physical locations, yet they are brought together by advanced telecommunications and information technologies to achieve a specific task.[58] Today, many organizations such as Microsoft, Intel, and Xerox are utilizing virtual teams to achieve important organizational objectives. British Petroleum (BP) has developed a virtual team network that has made it possible to flatten and decentralize its organizational design. By capitalizing on advances in information systems and digital communications, BP virtual team members are able to share knowledge and information with each other without concern for boundaries created by most organizational structures.[59] Although integrating mechanisms designed to increase coordination potential can be quite costly, they may be warranted when strategic effectiveness requires close coordination and cooperation between organizational subunits. Most organizations today acknowledge that facilitating communication, integration, and coordination among work groups is critical to organizational success.[60]

Virtual teams may be in separate geographical locations, yet they can work together on a task using advanced telecommunications and information technologies.

© GETTY/IMAGES/EYE WIRE

Reducing the Need for Coordination   The third and final method of integration is to reduce or eliminate the need for coordination between work groups. In essence, the organization creates "slack resources" that reduce the interdependence of the work groups and, as a result, the need for integrating mechanisms. For example, an organization might establish longer lead times for sequentially interdependent work to be completed or maintain larger inventories of work in progress. Both measures would reduce the need for tight coordination between units. Although this is an effective way to reduce the need for coordination, it is not necessarily the most efficient. Creating slack resources in this way is inconsistent with the need for improved productivity and efficiency. As a result, such a practice may lead to suboptimal organizational performance.

Another way organizations can reduce the need for coordination is to create work units that have only pooled interdependence. By doing so, they minimize the need for integration. One benefit of cross-functional work teams is that work groups are relatively independent, thereby reducing the need for integration between diverse functional units. However, forming cross-functional teams simply to reduce integration needs may not be appropriate if it results in redundant resource utilization. In general, independent units should be formed only when there are other strategic reasons to do so.

MATCHING INTEGRATING MECHANISMS WITH COORDINATION NEEDS   The hardware and software support for management information systems have very tangible costs. So do the personnel who must manage the information systems. Integrating positions have clearly identifiable costs as well. While not as easily measured, the management time and energy that go into developing effective management systems (managerial hierarchy, rules and procedures, plans and goals) and acting in lateral relationship roles (liaisons, committees and task forces, integrating positions) also have costs. Therefore, it is important for an or-

ganization to develop a cost-effective integration system that satisfies its coordination needs while minimizing the financial and managerial resources required to maintain the system.

LOCUS OF DECISION MAKING

The third component of organizational design involves the locus of decision making within the organization. Essentially, **locus of decision making** refers to whether the organization's decision making is centralized or decentralized. This may be determined by examining how decision-making authority is divided between corporate headquarters and the operating units or between the top-level management of an operating unit and the departmental work groups.[61]

If an organization's decision-making authority rests with corporate headquarters or the top levels of management of an operating facility, its organizational design is centralized. An organization that maintains its locus of decision making at lower levels, such as at the department or employee level, is decentralized. IBM's reorganization into autonomous operating units, for example, was an attempt to decentralize by pushing decision-making authority down to the lower levels of the organizational hierarchy.

It is helpful to think of centralized and decentralized decision making as two ends of a continuum. Most organizations' locus of decision making will fall somewhere between those two extremes. Moreover, the locus of decision making in most organizations is mixed, with decisions in some areas (such as finance) being relatively centralized, while decisions in other areas (such as marketing) being relatively decentralized.

CENTRALIZED VERSUS DECENTRALIZED DECISION MAKING
Certain advantages and disadvantages are associated with both centralized and decentralized decision making. Their respective advantages and disadvantages are nearly mirror images of each other, relating primarily to a trade-off between control and flexibility.

In general, centralized decision making gives top-level management more control than does decentralized decision making. This may be appropriate when work groups are highly interdependent or when maximizing the efficient use of resources is essential to the success of the organization. The primary disadvantage of centralized decision making is that it may limit the organization's ability to respond quickly and effectively to changes in its environment.

In contrast, the primary advantage of decentralized decision making is that organizations can respond to environmental changes more rapidly and effectively when decisions are being made by the people closest to the situation.[62] In addition, many experts would argue that the individuals who are closest to the customers and suppliers are best prepared to make most decisions. Coordination between units may be hindered by decentralized decision making, however, and achieving efficiency through standardization may be more difficult to accomplish. Furthermore, the growing diversity of the workforce has increased the variability in decision-making styles.

Organizations must determine their locus of decision making in light of the advantages they seek, as well as the specific strategic and operational conditions they face. Today, many organization leaders are attempting to decentralize decision making in an effort to enhance the speed, flexibility, and responsiveness of their organizations. Hitachi, for example, redesigned its structure around 10 autonomous units that maintain nearly all decision-making power. Hitachi president Etushiko Shoyama implemented the new organizational design in an effort to speed up decision making within the company and be more responsive to customer needs.[63]

LEARNING OBJECTIVE 5

Explain the concept of locus of decision making and the advantages and disadvantages of centralized and decentralized decision making.

Locus of decision making
The degree to which decision making is centralized versus decentralized.

There are also examples of firms that have used both forms of decision making at different times in their history. Apple Computer, for example, has vacillated between a decentralized and centralized design several times over the last three decades, depending on the organizational and competitive pressures at the time.[64] United Way had long been a very decentralized organization when their new president, Betty Beene, made moves to centralize some key decision-making processes. The local United Way agencies, however, did not agree with Beenes' centralization strategy and worked aggressively to stop the move. In the end, the local organizations prevailed, and Beene was forced to resign. United Way's new president, Brian Gallagher, now faces the same challenge of defining the appropriate level of centralization/decentralization within the organization as a whole. Only time will tell how the decision will unfold.[65]

Further, a blended style of decision making may make sense for some companies. John Brown, CEO of Stryker Corporation, believes that the locus of decision making should be flexible according to the circumstances. He has achieved remarkable success at Stryker, an orthopedic implant and medical equipment company, by both decentralizing decision making with some managers and retaining decision-making authority centrally when it comes to other managers. Brown drives decision making down to managers who are performing well and hitting targets. Those who are faltering, however, hear from Brown a lot more often. As said by Edward Lipes who runs Stryker's implant business, "John gives you a lot more help than you want when you're having trouble. When things are going well, you're the captain of your ship." Brown's management style must be working—Stryker has achieved a 20 percent growth in annual earning for the 25 years that Brown has been in charge.[66]

Historically, the decision to be centralized or decentralized involved a trade-off between control (characterized by centralized systems) and flexibility and responsiveness (characterized by decentralized systems). Today, however, advanced information technology can be used to resolve such trade-offs, allowing organizations to retain reasonable central control while decentralizing the decisions that are most critical to meeting the needs of customers.[67] Given the environmental volatility and increased competition experienced in most industries, achieving such a balance will likely be critical to organizational success.

LEARNING OBJECTIVE 6

Describe organic and mechanistic organizational systems and discuss the relationships between these systems and environmental stability.

Mechanistic systems

Highly centralized organizations in which decision-making authority rests with top-level management.

Organic systems

Decentralized organizations that push decision making to the lowest levels of the organization in an effort to respond more effectively to environmental change.

MECHANISTIC VERSUS ORGANIC SYSTEMS An organization's locus of decision making will determine the extent to which it is mechanistic or organic. This typology, originally advanced by Tom Burns and Gene Stalker, describes organizations according to the level of centralization or decentralization in their decision-making process.[68]

Mechanistic systems are associated with highly centralized organizations where decision-making authority rests with the top levels of management. Tasks are highly specialized, and work procedures are governed by detailed rules and guidelines. Interorganizational communication flows primarily from superior to subordinate, and hierarchical relationships serve as the foundation for authority, responsibility, and control. Mechanistic systems are usually designed to maximize specialization and improve efficiency. However, organizations with this design may find it difficult to respond quickly and effectively to changes that affect their operations.

Organic systems, in contrast, are designed to enhance an organization's ability to respond to environmental change by decentralizing decision making to those in the organization who are closer to customers, suppliers, and other external constituents. Organizational members are not only permitted to participate in decision making, but are encouraged to do so. Tasks are often broader and more interdependent than in mechanistic systems. Rules and guidelines are far less prevalent and may exist only to provide the parameters within which organizational members can make decisions. The patterns of communication are far more intricate,

and horizontal communication is common. While a vertical hierarchy typically exists, extensive use of teams and other lateral relationships facilitates communication and decision making across vertical lines. An organic system may be less efficient than a mechanistic system, however.

The need for organic systems has escalated in recent years with the increasing predominance of knowledge companies and knowledge workers. By their very nature, organic systems are more appropriate for such organizations and employees. Knowledge workers tend to enjoy higher levels of freedom in how and when they perform their work responsibilities, and thus experience more discretion and autonomy in their jobs. Thus, day-to-day task controls that are typically imposed on administrative or operational workers cannot be imposed on knowledge workers. Rather, their activities must be monitored on a much broader level, with a focus on ensuring that they are contributing to the strategic goals of the organization. This management system is consistent with that of an organic organizational design.

You may want to stop at this point and take a look at "Experiential Exercise 9.2" on page 309. This exercise provides an assessment instrument that can be used to evaluate the degree to which an organization demonstrates mechanistic versus organic characteristics. Think of an organization with which you have been associated. How does it rate according to this assessment instrument? If appropriate, what could you do from your level to change the organization?

THE IMPACT OF ENVIRONMENTAL STABILITY Which system is better—a mechanistic system that enhances efficiency or an organic system that enhances responsiveness? There is no simple answer to that question. The most effective system for any organization will vary as a function of the specific circumstances the organization faces. More specifically, the stability of the environment in which the organization operates will have a significant impact on the effectiveness of either system.

The external environment for any organization can be characterized along a continuum ranging from stable to turbulent. In general, **stable environments** experience relatively little change, or the change is of low impact to the organization. Product life cycles are long and enduring; marketing strategies remain relatively constant; and economic and political factors have little influence on the strategic or operational aspects of the firm. Competitive pressures are manageable, and changes in buyers' needs are minimal. Although few industries would fit this description, some organizations do operate in relatively stable environments. For example, manufacturers of staple items such as detergents, cleaning supplies, and paper products enjoy relatively stable environmental conditions.[69]

Turbulent environments, in contrast, are characterized by rapid and significant change. An organization that faces turbulent environmental conditions must cope with shorter decision windows, changing buyer patterns, fragmented markets, greater risk of resource and product obsolescence, and a general lack of long-term control. Such conditions intensify the pressure for organizations to respond effectively to change. For example, most computer-related companies, like IBM, Cisco, Unisys, Microsoft, and Dell, face a relatively turbulent environment in which technological change creates competitive pressures for all industry players. The key to success in such an environment lies in developing an organizational design that allows managers to identify and respond quickly to the opportunities and threats facing the organization. In general, organizations that operate in stable external environments find the mechanistic system to be advantageous. This system provides a level of efficiency that enhances the long-term performance of these organizations. In contrast, organizations that operate in volatile and frequently changing environments are more likely to find that an organic system provides the greatest benefits. This system allows the organization to respond to environmental change more proactively.

Stable environments
Environments that experience little change.

Turbulent environments
Environments that are characterized by rapid and significant change.

ORGANIZATIONAL DESIGN FOR A CHANGING ENVIRONMENT

LEARNING OBJECTIVE 7

Describe how organizational design will likely change in the future.

While many organizations have been coping with changing environmental conditions and intense competition for decades, others have begun to feel the effects of escalating rates of technological change and an increasingly competitive global marketplace more recently. Such business conditions will continue to affect a wide variety of organizations and industries in the future. As this occurs, organizations will continue to seek innovative organizational designs to cope with the challenges of the business environment.

Although most organizations will maintain traditional hierarchical structures to some degree, many will increasingly make use of alliances among people and organizations. Surrounding the conventional chain of command will be a complex network of committees, task forces, cross-functional teams, partnerships, and other informal relationships that will provide a forum for creativity and innovation. This new model of organizational design goes by a number of names; some of the most common are the **adaptive organization**, the flexible organization, the lateral organization, the horizontal corporation, and the centerless corporation.[70] While these organizational models may vary slightly, the fundamental purpose of such designs is to reduce the bureaucracy that stifles employee creativity and puts an unacceptable distance between the customer and the decision makers in the organization. Such organizations pull out all the stops to capitalize on their human resources, develop partnerships with other organizations with common objectives, and let the needs of the customer drive the actions of the organization. As Raymond Gilmartin, CEO of the high-tech medical equipment manufacturer Becton Dickinson, said, "Forget structures invented by the guys at the top. You've got to let the task form the organization." Becton Dickinson has done just that, enabling the company to move from a controlled hierarchy to a decentralized, swift, and adaptive organization. The results have been improved performance for the company as a whole.[71]

"At The Forefront" on page 305 describes the dynamic nature of organizational structure of a U.S. Navy aircraft carrier. During normal times, a functional structure with layers of hierarchy promotes efficiency and accountability. During a crisis, however, a very different structure emerges that facilitates cooperation, communication, and adaptation. This looser structure allows personnel to operate effectively in stressful situations, and then dissolves as the traditional structure reemerges during times of normality.

Moving from a traditional organizational design to an adaptive or flexible organizational design may be the key to success for organizations in the future. Table 9.3, which describes the characteristics of the traditional versus flexible (or adaptive) organizational design, provides some guidance on how to move toward a flexible organizational design.

Adaptive organization

An organization that eliminates bureaucracy that limits employee creativity, and brings the decision makers of the organization closer to the customer.

IMPLICATIONS FOR LEADERS

The manager of tomorrow must be aware of the importance of organizational design to the long-term performance of his or her company. The increasing availability and sophistication of technology will change the way organizations are designed and coordinated. The ever-increasing demands for quality will create additional pressures for achieving maximum efficiency and effectiveness in every aspect of an organization's operations. As more and more industries globalize, organizations will be faced with the challenge of coordinating their efforts across different nations and among diverse people. Effective leadership demands that one possess the competence to design organizations so they are prepared to cope with

At The Forefront

When Chaos Comes: The Dynamic Nature of Organizational Structure on U.S. Navy's Aircraft Carriers

Some organizations have the luxury of not worrying too much about bad luck. Unforeseen events that have a negative impact on the bottom line are often balanced out by "lucky" events for the company. Luck is not an option for some organizations because bad luck can lead to devastating, irreversible events. Such a climate exists for U.S. Navy's aircraft carriers. Carriers are responsible for launching aircraft that must accelerate to 180 miles per hour in two seconds. In this stressful environment, there is no room for luck.

Traditional organizational theory would predict that any organizational system as complex and interconnected as that of an aircraft carrier would be highly vulnerable to seemingly minor events. Just the slightest, rarest degree of bad luck would be expected to have enormous detrimental consequences. Since disastrous accidents do not occur at the degree they should, University of California political scientist Todd La Porte examined the hierarchy and structure of the personnel on aircraft carriers.

Dr. La Porte's findings are amazing. On the surface, aircraft carriers are organized around a very rigid command and control hierarchy. During normal conditions, orders are given and followed down the line, from the ship's captain down to the lowest-ranking sailor. This structure increases efficiency and promotes accountability among the crew. However, during times of high demand and extreme tension, such as launching an aircraft or recovering a plane, the rigid hierarchy dissolves and the ship's personnel collaborate as colleagues. According to La Porte, constant communication and the flow of information are crucial for promoting flexibility and adaptability. The alternate structure that occurs seems to evolve naturally, as no officer is consciously trying to create a more fluid climate. Whether conscious or not, the structure that emerges turns out to be well-suited for adapting to unforeseen, often chaotic, circumstances facing U.S. Navy personnel.

SOURCE: R. Pool, "In the Zero Luck Zone," *Forbes*, 166, 14, November 27, 2000, 85–90.

and capitalize on a changing business environment. In preparing to meet such challenges, managers must:

- Remember that organizational design provides an important mechanism for achieving the strategic and operational goals of the organization.
- Structure their organizations to cope with their source of greatest complexity.
- Consider ways that partnerships between members of the organization, as well as alliances with other organizations, can create synergy and improve organizational performance.

Table 9.3 | Comparison of Organizational Design Approaches

	TRADITIONAL	FLEXIBLE
Executive Focus	Usually little or no attention paid to design issues, reliance on the design that the executives are familiar with our design	Which organizational design best fits at this point in time, how do we gain competitive advantage with our design
Design Preference	Faddish, depends on what seems to be working for the most publicized corporations	Varies to fit market needs, host culture, industry type, and core competencies
Change Strategy	Usually focused on choosing a methodology, tactically oriented, concern about involving too many people	What do we need to change to be aligned and congruent, how to build in flexibility
Change Process	Destination-oriented, stages of individual change, leading to clear endpoint	Journey of continual adaptation, based on a model of cyclical continuous renewal, endpoint always changes

SOURCE: Reprinted with permission from *Human Resources Planning*, Vol. 20, No. 1 (1997). Copyright 1997 by the Human Resource Planning Society, 317 Madison Avenue, Suite 1509, New York, NY 10017, Phone: (212) 490-6387, Fax: (212) 682-6851.

- Utilize advanced information technology to support dispersed operations, people, and partners.
- Look for ways to increase the integration potential of the organization or to reduce the need for integration.
- Evaluate the advantages and disadvantages associated with centralized versus decentralized decision making, given the specific circumstances of the organization.
- Strive to develop an adaptive and flexible organization that is effective in a dynamic business environment.

Managers must recognize the importance of organizational design to the long-term success of their companies. They must create organizational designs that support the strategies of their companies and enable them to meet the challenges of the 21st century.

Meeting The Challenge

How EDS Blew Up Its Structure to Change Its Culture

When Dick Brown took over as CEO of EDS, he knew the company was facing serious problems. People talked about collaboration and teamwork, but few employees acted on it. EDS lacked an overarching vision, and the company often rolled out duplicate services and offerings. Worse still, different units often had diametrically opposed strategies. Brown's first initiative, dubbed "Project Breakaway," was focused on changing the organizational structure at EDS. This effort consisted of top leaders within EDS who had different areas of expertise and unique perspectives. Their mandate was to redesign EDS with one goal: focus on the client.

The strategic planning sessions led to the formulation a new structure. The 48 units were slashed to four business lines. Each client now had a "client executive" who is responsible for solving problems and maintaining customer relationships. The new structure promotes accountability and productivity in a number of ways. Employees who meet their goals are rewarded, and those who don't are given the opportunity to improve. EDS developed the "Service Excellence Dashboard," a color-coded system for measuring customer satisfaction. Results of customer feedback are shared throughout the organization. This system not only measures customer service, it promotes collaboration. The color-rating system allows peers to know the status of each other's customer service levels, and to offer advice and assistance when needed.

The results of the changes in EDS's organizational structure have been impressive. Streamlining the structure helped create a culture that facilitates open communication and attention to customer service. EDS recently announced dramatic increases in profit, growth in revenue, and an $80 billion backlog of signed contracts. And as for their e-mail system, Brown sends a message to every employee once a week about the challenges and opportunities facing EDS. The message is also meant to convey an explicit request for dialogue and feedback, as employees are encouraged to reply back. Or if they choose, they may call Dick Brown on his office phone. The line has been restored.

SOURCE: B. Breen, "How EDS Got Its Groove Back," *Fast Company*, 51, October 2001, 106–112.

SUMMARY

1. Organizing is an important managerial function that leads to the development of organizational design. An organization's design serves as a mechanism for managing its tasks, functions, products, markets, and technologies effectively.

2. Organizational design determines the configuration of organizational members (structure); the flow of information, resources, and tasks throughout the organizational system (integration); and the centralization or decentralization of decision-making authority (locus of decision making).

3. Organizations structure their activities by grouping certain tasks and responsibilities into work units. The four primary forms found in organizations today are functional, divisional, matrix, and network structures. Certain strategic conditions imply certain organizational structures. In general,

organizations should employ a structure that enables them to cope with their greatest source of complexity (such as function, product diversity, geographic market diversity, or customer diversity).

4. An organization's need for coordination will be determined, to a large degree, by the level of interdependence among its subunits. Integrating mechanisms help to coordinate the flow of information, resources, and tasks between work groups. Integrating mechanisms include general management systems (managerial hierarchy, rules and procedures, plans and goals), methods for increasing coordination potential (information systems and lateral relationships), and methods for reducing the need for coordination (creation of slack resources and independent work units).

5. The extent to which an organization centralizes or decentralizes decision-making authority will determine its locus of decision making. While centralized decision making gives top-level management more control, decentralized decision

making provides for faster and more effective responses to change.

6. An organization can be described as mechanistic or organic depending on its locus of decision making. Mechanistic systems maintain a centralized locus of decision making and are most suitable for organizations that operate in mature, stable environments. Organic systems maintain a decentralized locus of decision making and are most appropriate for organizations operating in dynamic, rapidly changing environments.

7. Many organizations will implement an adaptive or flexible organizational design in the future. Adaptive and flexible organizations rely on teams, lateral relationships, and alliances to supplement the traditional hierarchy. This network of relationships is designed to foster creativity and support proactive responses to environmental changes that affect the organization.

REVIEW QUESTIONS

1. (*Learning Objective 1*) What is organizational design? Why is it important for an organization to develop an effective design?

2. (*Learning Objective 2*) What are the three primary components of organizational design?

3. (*Learning Objective 3*) Identify and describe each of the four types of organizational structure discussed in the chapter.

4. (*Learning Objective 4*) How does interdependence affect the need for coordination and integration? Outline the three major categories of integrating mechanisms.

5. (*Learning Objective 5*) Explain the concept of locus of decision making. What are the advantages and disadvantages of centralized decision making? What are the advantages and disadvantages of decentralized decision making?

6. (*Learning Objective 6*) What are the differences between mechanistic and organic organizational systems? What effect would the environment have on an organization's choice of a mechanistic versus an organic system?

7. (*Learning Objective 7*) How is organizational design likely to change in the future?

DISCUSSION QUESTIONS

Improving Critical Thinking

1. How might the organizational design of a research and development firm in the pharmaceutical industry differ from the organizational design of a consumer food products manufacturer?

2. Consider the organization you currently work for or one that you worked for in the past. Would you characterize that organization as having a centralized or decentralized locus of decision making? What are the advantages and disadvantages associated with the locus of decision making in that organization? If you had the power to change the locus of decision making, what would you do?

Enhancing Communication Skills

3. Suppose the dean of the College of Business hired you to coordinate the efforts of five different student organizations,

each of which was affiliated with a different functional department within the college. What integrating mechanisms might you use to coordinate the activities of the groups? To practice your oral communication skills, make a brief presentation of your ideas to the class.

4. Identify a company that you feel has a very traditional organizational design and one that you think has a flexible design. Compare and contrast the companies based on the four areas described in Table 9.3. Develop a written draft of your analysis for your instructor to review.

Building Teamwork

5. Think of several different businesses that might be started on your campus to serve the needs of students. Select one of those business concepts and, with a team of students, discuss how that business might be developed using a dynamic network system.

6. With a group of fellow students, identify a set of organizations that maintain relatively mechanistic organizational systems. Also develop a list of organizations that are more organic. Share your lists with the class, as well as your rationale for classifying these organizations as you did.

THINKING CRITICALLY: DEBATE THE ISSUE

Empty on the Inside? The Pros and Cons of the Hollow Organization

Rapid changes in global markets, advances in information technology, and increased competition have led many organizations to adopt innovative structures. Virtual organizations allow employees to work together remotely without having to come together in a central location. Taking this concept one step further, the hollow organization model outsources many core functions that have traditionally been performed in organizational departments. For example, Amazon.com is a bookstore without the books or the physical store. There is no need to pay for inventory, retail space, or staff salaries because orders are taken over the Internet, fulfilled, and shipped by suppliers who contract with Amazon.com.

Form teams of four to five students. Half the teams should prepare to argue the benefits of adopting the hollow organization structure and outsourcing many traditional functions. The other half should prepare to argue the benefits of maintaining a more traditional organizational structure where departments are maintained and employees work and communicate face-to-face. Your instructor will select two teams to present their arguments to the class in a debate format.

EXPERIENTIAL EXERCISE 9.1

Organizational Characteristics Questionnaire

This brief assessment instrument measures the degree to which five characteristics are present in a particular organization's structure. It can be used to examine any real organization.
Instructions: The 10 questions that follow ask about certain organizational conditions. You must refer to a specific organization in order to respond to these questions. Give your best overall judgment about how well each statement actually describes conditions in the organization that you have in mind. Since the purpose of the exercise is simply to describe an existing organization's conditions and characteristics, there are no right or wrong answers.

	Completely	Mostly	Partly	Slightly	Not at All
1. Work roles in this organization are highly specialized; each person has clear-cut authority and responsibility.	____	____	____	____	____
2. The hierarchy in this organization is formal to the point of being rigid and inflexible.	____	____	____	____	____
3. In this organization people are selected and promoted on the basis of their demonstrated technical competence.	____	____	____	____	____
4. People in this organization often seem so concerned with conforming to rules and procedures that it interferes with their mental health.	____	____	____	____	____
5. Everyone in this organization expects to be subject to the same set of rules and controls; there are no favorites.	____	____	____	____	____
6. People in this organization are often so wrapped up in their own narrow specialties that they can't see that we all have common interests; this causes unnecessary conflicts.	____	____	____	____	____
7. The offices and positions in this organization are arranged in a clear and logical hierarchy.	____	____	____	____	____
8. Overall, this organization is a political bureaucracy, with a "managerial elite" who got where they are through political savvy.	____	____	____	____	____

	Completely	Mostly	Partly	Slightly	Not at All
9. Managers in this organization see themselves as being on a clear "career ladder" and expect to make regular progress in their career paths.	——	——	——	——	——
10. Many of the rules in this organization either have become ends in themselves, with no logical function, or have come to specify the minimum tolerable performance levels.	——	——	——	——	——

Scoring: To score your answers, use the following key. Add up the points for all 10 questions to get your score. A high score indicates a "good" bureaucracy, while the lower the score, the less the organization is a good bureaucracy; it either lacks the right bureaucratic characteristics or goes far overboard on some. A score between 25 and 35 is about average; scores above 35 are suggestive of a "good" bureaucratic structure. Scores from 18 to 24 are a cause for concern, and scores below 18 indicate serious problems: either overbureaucratic rigidity or underbureaucratic chaos.

RESPONSE

QUESTION NUMBERS	Completely	Mostly	Partly	Slightly	Not at All
1, 3, 5, 7, 9	5 points	4 points	3 points	2 points	1 point
2, 4, 6, 8, 10	1 point	2 points	3 points	4 points	5 points

EXPERIENTIAL EXERCISE 9.2

ORGMECH Survey

This assessment instrument places an organization along the organic-mechanistic dimension first defined by Tom Burns and Gene Stalker. The mechanistic end of the dimension approximates the classic highly formalized bureaucracy, while the organic end can be used to describe a more participatory type of organization.

Instructions: Consider an organization with which you are familiar. Indicate the extent to which each of the following 10 statements is true of or accurately characterizes the organization in question.

	To a Very Great Extent	To a Considerable Extent	To a Moderate Extent	To a Slight Extent	To Almost No Extent
1. This organization has clear rules and regulations that everyone is expected to follow closely.	——	——	——	——	——
2. Policies in this organization are reviewed by the people they affect before being implemented.	——	——	——	——	——
3. In this organization a major concern is that all employees be allowed to develop their talents and abilities.	——	——	——	——	——
4. Everyone in this organization knows who his or her immediate supervisor is; reporting relationships are clearly defined.	——	——	——	——	——
5. Jobs in this organization are clearly defined; everyone knows exactly what is expected in any specific job position.	——	——	——	——	——
6. Work groups are typically temporary and change often in this organization.	——	——	——	——	——

	To a Very Great Extent	To a Considerable Extent	To a Moderate Extent	To a Slight Extent	To Almost No Extent
7. All decisions in this organization must be reviewed and approved by upper-level management.	____	____	____	____	____
8. In this organization the emphasis is on adapting effectively to constant environmental change.	____	____	____	____	____
9. Jobs in this organization are usually broken down into highly specialized, smaller tasks.	____	____	____	____	____
10. Standard activities in this organization are always covered by clearly outlined procedures that everyone is expected to follow.	____	____	____	____	____

Scoring: On the scoring grid, note the number that corresponds to your response to each of the 10 questions. Enter the numbers in the boxes, then add up all the numbers in the boxes. This is the organization's ORGMECH score.

	1	2	3	4	5	6	7	8	9	10
Great	5	5	1	5	5	1	5	1	5	5
Considerable	4	4	2	4	4	2	4	2	4	4
Moderate	3	3	3	3	3	3	3	3	3	3
Slight	2	2	4	2	2	4	2	4	2	2
No	1	1	5	1	1	5	1	5	1	1

Total score ☐

Interpretation: High scores indicate high degrees of mechanistic/bureaucratic organizational characteristics. Low scores are associated with adaptive/organic organizational characteristics.

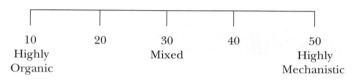

10 — Highly Organic   20   30 — Mixed   40   50 — Highly Mechanistic

For Discussion

1. How would you feel (or how do you feel) about working in a mechanistic organization?

2. How would you feel (or how do you feel) about working in an organic organization?

3. Is it desirable to have as low a score as possible? Why or why not?

4. Are certain characteristics of the organization you describe inconsistent with one another? What effects does this have?

CAPTURING THE POWER OF INFORMATION TECHNOLOGY

1. Using the Internet, research the concept of virtual teams. Identify and describe at least three technology-based tools that can be used to support virtual teams.

2. Identify an international organization in which you have an interest. Research the ways in which the organization uses technology to support its international operations. Report your findings to the class.

3. Identify three leading companies that provide enterprise resource planning (ERP) systems. Go to the Web sites of these three companies. What can you learn about the organizational design of these companies from their Web sites? Compare and contrast the three organizations.

ETHICS: TAKE A STAND

DV8, a medium-sized firm specializing in computer animation software, has distinguished itself in the field as a leader in inno-vation and creativity. Candice Clarke, the founder and president, has gone out of her way to hire, train, and reward the best and

the brightest artists and software engineers. As DV8 has grown, their client base has expanded from the West Coast to cities all across the United States. Clarke considered relocating DV8's headquarters to a more central location, but after soliciting feedback from her associates, she decided to employ a "virtual organization" structure.

The virtual organization model is founded on the notion that physical proximity between managers and employees is not needed to be effective. Associates work from remote locations, usually a home office, and communicate via telephone, e-mail, and teleconferencing. There are several advantages with this structural approach. Virtual organizations reduce office lease expenses, allow for greater flexibility among employees, and often lead to increased productivity. In DV8's case, it seemed especially appropriate to allow the artists and software engineers the freedom to work and be creative at home anytime during the day or night, rather than confined to a typical workday schedule.

While the benefits of adopting a virtual structure are numerous, concerns exist among DV8's top management. Many managers are worried that this new structure will lead to drastic declines in productivity. Several managers have commented that people need a certain degree of structure and routine in order to perform at optimal levels. They fear that going virtual will undermine quality and service. Moreover, it will be more difficult for managers to accurately appraise performance of associates they are not able to observe and monitor.

For Discussion

1. What are the ethical issues facing DV8?

2. Are management's concerns legitimate?

3. If you were Candice Clarke, how would you handle the situation?

VIDEO CASE

Designing the Contemporary Organization: JIAN Corporation

JIAN Corporation is a successful U.S.-based software company located in the Silicon Valley area of California. JIAN was created in 1988 by Burke Franklin, an entrepreneur who recognized the need for effective time-saving software that could be used to start, build, and manage businesses better. Today, JIAN is recognized as a leader in providing software products to emerging and established organizations. Some of its top sellers are BizPlan Builder, Marketing Builder, Agreement Builder, SafetyPlan Builder, Business Black Belt, and Employee Manual Maker.

Started as a home business, JIAN quickly outgrew Burke Franklin's apartment. He had to decide how best to attain and manage his company's growth. Most business start-ups in this position would purchase equipment and hire people to manufacture, market, and distribute the products and services. Burke rejected this method because it was expensive and took him away from his areas of expertise: software development and advertising. To increase its productivity and flexibility, JIAN developed into a virtual corporation highly dependent upon business partners.

Initially, Burke outsourced the manufacturing and distribution of JIAN's products to various vendors. He became frustrated with this approach. When things went wrong, Burke found that vendors tended to focus on placing blame rather than working together to solve the problems. To avoid this problem, Burke outsourced all production and distribution of his products to Bindco Corporation and his human resource functions to ExecuStaff (http://www.execustaff.net). This approach to organizing allows JIAN to focus on its core activities: software dvelopment and marketing. In turn, Bindco and ExecuStaff focus on their core competencies.

Also located near Silicon Valley in California, Bindco is a leading manufacturing and fulfillment center for software companies including Apple, Hewlett-Packard, Netscape, Sun, and (of course) JIAN. Thus, Bindco itself is a virtual corporation. For JIAN, Bindco provides all necessary manufacturing services (e.g., duplicate disks, make boxes, print books, and labels) and distribution services (e.g., customer service, taking customer orders). ExecuStaff considers itself to be a "high-tech co-employer" specializing in providing human resource services to high-tech companies like JIAN. ExecuStaff provides JIAN a complete "bolt-on" human resource management department providing such services as payroll, benefits, and recruiting, hiring, and firing JIAN employees.

JIAN and its partners have made their relationships work by establishing excellent communications and carefully defining their roles and responsibilities. Each organization works closely with the other and relies upon open communications and trust to make the relationship work. For instance, Bindco and JIAN have designated key contact persons who coordinate their joint projects. As time goes on, the organizations become more knowledgeable about each other's operations, expectations, etc., thus leading to smoother operations.

JIAN's manner of organizing has served it well in the highly competitive and rapidly changing computer software industry. Its "virtual" approach has enabled it to grow and remain flexible, giving the company a competitive advantage in the global marketplace.

For Discussion

1. Which of the four types of organizational structure mentioned in the chapter is closest to JIAN's concept of a "virtual" corporation? Explain your answer. What are some of the advantages and disadvantages of JIAN's choice of organizational structure?

2. Would you characterize JIAN as mechanistic or organic? Explain your answer.

3. In what ways do JIAN, Bindco, and ExecuStaff manage the complexities of their operations through integration? Provide specific case examples and explain how each example addresses the various aspects of integration.

4. If JIAN were to reorganize using one of the organizational structures not currently utilized, which structure would you suggest as optimal? Prepare a diagram illustrating the new organizational structure incorporating the major functional areas noted in the case and video. Briefly explain why this structure would be viable.

http://www.jian.com

CHAP

DESIGNING THE CONTEMPORARY ORGANIZATION

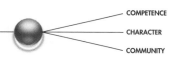

LEADERSHIP

COMPETENCE

CHARACTER

COMMUNITY

CASE

Growing Pains at Carolina Carpets

Jay McBride was smiling. Reading letters from satisfied customers always put him in a good mood. His smile faded, though, as he put the letter down and returned to the task at hand. His young company was facing its biggest challenge in its eight-year history. Markets were changing, competition was becoming more intense, and the need for developing strategic alliances was becoming more apparent every day. Jay had grown Carolina Carpets from a part-time hobby conducted out of his garage to a multimillion-dollar textile company. He employed over 100 people in three plants across North and South Carolina. The structure of Carolina Carpets was organized around the functional model with Jay serving as CEO and president. He had four vice presidents responsible for finance, human resources, manufacturing, and marketing. While this structure had been highly efficient during the company's early years of operation, changes in market were pressing this structure's utility to the limit.

When Carolina Carpets was first founded, Jay was able to tap several close friends and business associates to work for him. They were all well known and respected in their local communities and brought a wealth of business experience and expertise to his operation. For several years, Jay equated business success with physical growth. He and his senior leaders believed "bigger was better." Recent changes in the market and advances in information technology, however, had led Jay to believe that being bigger may not necessarily be better. In fact, he was starting to believe that bigger meant slower, and slower meant eventual extinction.

In an effort to remedy the situation, Jay began reading business articles on the topic of organizational structure. He talked to friends and associates at other companies in a variety of industries to ascertain what organizational structure seemed most efficient. Jay rubbed his eyes and thought about what the future held. One thing was certain—the functional structure of Carolina Carpets was no longer a viable option. He knew that if his company was going to survive and continue to flourish, he would need a new organizational blueprint.

For Discussion

1. Do you think the functional structure was appropriate for Carolina Carpets in their early days? Why or why not?

2. What do you think are the forces driving the need to change the company's design?

3. If you were a consultant working for Jay, what organizational structure would you recommend that he adopt? Why?

4. Is there any structure that you would not recommend for Carolina Carpets? Why?

CHAP

STRATEGIC HUMAN RESOURCE MANAGEMENT

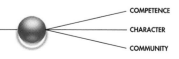

LEADERSHIP

COMPETENCE

CHARACTER

COMMUNITY

CHAPTER OVERVIEW

"The old adage 'People are your most important asset' is wrong. The *right* people are your most important asset." So says Jim Collins, a highly respected management consultant and author.[1] This statement sounds quite logical. If an organization does not have people with the knowledge, skills, abilities, and attitudes that are needed to achieve its overall strategy, it won't be successful. It won't be able to satisfy its customers. Coordinating and managing all of the things that are necessary to find the right people and guide them toward achieving the overall strategy is called **strategic human resource management (SHRM)**. Is the CEO of JC Penney doing all of this right? (See Facing The Challenge on page 316.)

SHRM involves many other parts of overall management, such as motivation, leadership, and communication that are discussed in other chapters of this book. While managers need to understand the relatedness of these things in order to be successful managers, in this chapter, we will focus on the things that are normally managed or coordinated by managers who are specialists in human resource issues. We explore the major SHRM activities that help the organization attract, retain, and develop the quality and quantity of employees needed to meet organizational goals. More specifically, we examine job analysis, staffing, training, performance appraisal, rewards, the legal environment, labor relations, and multinational issues.

While specialists in the discipline of SHRM might coordinate these things and actually carry out many of the related details, every manager in an organization is directly or indirectly involved in all aspects of SHRM. Therefore, managers should be aware that their behavior and attitudes can, and probably will, influence many aspects of guiding people in their pursuit of the organization's overall strategy and goals. Managers can take a leadership role in these areas and set a good example of competence, character, and community, as discussed in Chapters 1 and 13.

Strategic human resource management (SHRM)
Managing in such a way as to coordinate all human resource components and focus them on achieving organizational goals and overall strategy.

LEARNING OBJECTIVES

When you have finished studying this chapter, you should be able to:

1. Identify and explain the components of the strategic human resource management process.
2. Define job analysis and explain its importance.
3. Explain the role of forecasting in human resource planning.
4. Summarize the different recruiting techniques used by organizations.
5. Clarify the major employee selection methods.
6. Explain the different types of employee training.
7. Describe the role of performance appraisals in the organization.
8. Explain how compensation and benefits are used in organizations.
9. Describe the key factors of the legal environment in which human resource management functions.
10. Explain the importance of labor-management relations.
11. Clarify the primary challenges of SHRM in the multinational organization.

Facing The Challenge

Finding the Right CEO for JC Penney

By the 1990s, department store JC Penney was in trouble. Once a very successful store, it now was widely believed to have no clear image, no clear differentiation in customers' eyes. Penney was being squeezed out between the more upscale stores such as May, Federated, and Dillards and the more mass-market stores on the other side, such as Kohl's, Target, and even Wal-Mart.

The main problems at JC Penney included losing touch with what consumers wanted, thereby not having the right assortment of products in the stores. Part of this probably was caused by decentralized buying which tended to blur the Penney image. In addition, many believed that JC Penney was not very customer-friendly anymore. Topping it all off, the corporate culture was widely believed to be very unresponsive and stodgy, and no one from outside of the company had been the CEO in its 99-year history.

While JC Penney is not in danger of going out of business yet, the price of its stock had fallen 80 percent over the past two years. The competition from other stores continues to intensify and the economy is weak. JC Penney has some serious challenges.

SOURCES: "Allen Questrom to Take Helm at JC Penney," *The Los Angeles Times*, July 28, 2000, C1; D. Stankevich, "Questrom's Quest," *Retail Merchandiser*, May 2001, 22; "J.C. Penney's Questrom Stresses Fundamentals," *Home Textiles Today*, June 11, 2001; "Merchant of Panache," *Chain Store Age Executive*, September 2000, 61–64; S. Forest, "Can an Outsider Fix JC Penney?" *BusinessWeek*, February 12, 2001, 57–58.

INTRODUCTION

In part two of this book, we discussed the importance of an organization establishing and understanding its mission or purpose and the strategic and operational goals that support the mission. Then, in Chapters 8 and 9, we discussed establishing an organizational design, including the design of jobs, that will support and guide actions and jobs in such a way that the mission and the overall strategy will be achieved.

In order to achieve the strategy of an organization, a certain set of actions, behaviors, and attitudes from the employees is necessary. In order to ensure the right behaviors and attitudes, an organization must have the "right" people who are guided by proper human resource policies and operations.[2] If this is done well, an organization will have people with the right skills and motivation to make the organization successful. The customers of the organization will be satisfied,[3] and the organization will have a combination of people with the right skills and motivation and practices that would be impossible to imitate by another organization. The organization would have a sustainable competitive advantage.

STRATEGIC HUMAN RESOURCE MANAGEMENT (SHRM)

LEARNING OBJECTIVE 1

Identify and explain the components of the strategic human resource management process.

Tying all of this together and focusing it on the overall strategy of an organization is called strategic human resource management (SHRM). This is all based on strategic planning and is guided by organizing, leading, and controlling. Of course, main elements of these things are discussed in other chapters of this book. Here, we focus on the concepts and tools that are needed to guide the overall management of human resources (see Figure 10.1).

To begin with, we need to have some way to determine who the "right people" are, so we need to understand what knowledge, skills, and abilities are needed in each job.

JOB ANALYSIS

LEARNING OBJECTIVE 2

Define job analysis and explain its importance.

Job analysis
Studying a job to understand what knowledge, skills, abilities, and attitudes are required for successful performance.

Job analysis refers to studying a job in order to understand what knowledge, skills, abilities, and attitudes are needed as a foundation for the behaviors that would help the job holder perform that job successfully.

Figure 10.1 | Strategic Human Resource Management Process

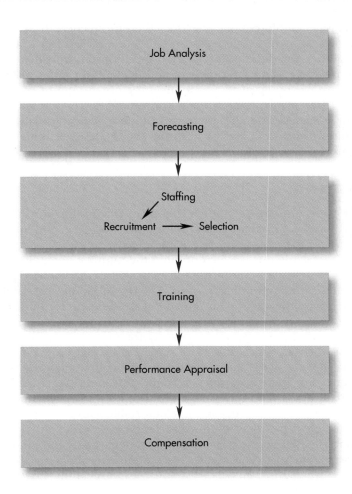

One must be very objective and careful when analyzing jobs in order to understand what behaviors are really required by the job, rather than what one might assume to be required. A somewhat controversial example is the job of a firefighter. Estimates of the percent of time that a firefighter spends actually fighting fires are as low as 2 percent! That is especially true if the firefighter teaches and practices fire prevention, as is true in the Lisle-Woodridge Fire District, near Chicago.[4] So, a firefighter may well need the knowledge, skills, abilities, and attitude to teach people in the community, including grade-school children, to practice fire prevention. Similarly, a job as salesperson in a retail store might require sincerely listening to customers and being able to interact with them well, especially if the company's strategy includes developing loyal long-term customers. A job in a factory might require skills needed to successfully engage in groups and group decision making, in addition to being able to operate certain equipment. As discussed earlier in this chapter related to "high performance" human resources practices and later in the "tests" section, a person's attitude and other personality characteristics may become a more important component of a job. The reason for this is that a person can be more successful if he or she fits into the culture of the organization, into the "way things are done." If a person really does not like working in groups or with very flexible work rules, then a culture that thrives on group work and flexible rules might not work well for the person.

Job description
Details of the responsibilities and tasks required by a job.

Job specification
A list of the knowledge, skills, abilities, and other employee characteristics needed to perform the job.

From the job analysis, a **job description** is established. The job description lists the tasks, behaviors, responsibilities, and other information that help explain the job. Related to this is the **job specification** that lists the specific knowledge, skills, abilities, and other employee characteristics that are needed to perform the job successfully.

Taken together, job descriptions and job specifications provide managers with a foundation for forecasting the supply of and demand for labor within the organization and for developing programs to meet the organization's human resource requirements. These activities are usually coordinated by or actually done by the human resource manager. Job descriptions and job specifications also help the organization comply with EEO laws by ensuring that SHRM decisions are based on job-related information.

FORECASTING

LEARNING OBJECTIVE 3

Explain the role of forecasting in human resource planning.

Demand forecasting
Determining the number of employees that the organization will need in the future as well as the knowledge, skills, and abilities these employees must possess.

An important aspect of strategic human resource planning is forecasting the demand for and supply of human resources for both short-term and long-term planning. Both types of forecasts require looking into the future.

Demand forecasting involves determining the number of employees the organization will need at some point in the future as well as the knowledge, skills, and abilities that these employees must possess. The organization's external and internal environments are the major determinants of the demand for human resources. For example, the link between rapid technological change and the emergence of the global economy has created the necessity for profound change and the demand for a product or service, therefore requiring changes in a company's strategy and operations. Despite the downturn for dot-com companies during 2001, many companies are increasing sales over the Internet. One reason for this is that the companies are developing the systems to do this. Another reason is that more and more customers are becoming comfortable with buying things over the Internet. Ultimately this affects the need for employees with special skills.[5] In addition, demand is based on the organization's strategic goals and internal changes in the workforce, such as retirements, resignations, terminations, and leaves of absence.

Supply forecasting
Determining what human resources will be available both inside and outside the organization.

Supply forecasting involves determining what human resources will be available both inside and outside the organization. Internal practices that affect promotions, transfers, training, and pay incentives are designed to meet demand with existing employees. Internal supply forecasts estimate the effect that these practices will have on turnover, termination, retirement, promotion, and transfer rates.[6]

To meet human resource demand, most organizations must rely to some extent on bringing in employees from the outside. Human resource professionals use labor market analysis to forecast external labor supply. Together, internal and external supply forecasts allow the organization to estimate the number of people who will enter and leave various organizational jobs, as well as the effects of SHRM programs on employee skills and productivity.[7]

After estimating the demand and supply of human resources, the human resource manager must reconcile the two forecasts. If a shortage is forecast, emphasis must be put on employee hiring, promotions, transfers, and training. If an excess is predicted, workforce reduction must be implemented. While workforce reduction is a very serious issue, it tends to be one-time, or short-term. Plus, if downsizing is done properly, it must include using the SHRM concepts and tools to identify those jobs that are no longer needed and the "right" people and jobs to remove from the organization. In the longer run though, even those companies that downsize certainly have to continue to manage the remaining employees and probably have to add and replace people. Therefore, we turn our attention to recruitment.

John Stanton and the Running Room

"We hire our customers." So says John Stanton, president and founder of the Running Room, a business with 42 stores across Canada and the United States. Mr. Stanton started the Running Room in 1984 in Edmonton, Canada, when he couldn't find a place to buy quality running shoes from someone who was knowledgeable about running.

All of the Team Members (All employees are Team Members—both words capitalized. We'll get back to that later.) are runners, foremost Stanton. Runners can relate to the customers, who are runners, and understand why they would come to the store and what they want. At the base of all of this is a buy-in to a healthy, active lifestyle.

Team Members not only buy into the lifestyle, but also the culture of the company. That culture is based on a three-way win: Team Members win because they are interested in a fulfilling career that can be achieved when they share the values of the company. The buy-in to the active lifestyle and the values of the company create an enjoyable job that increases performance. Stanton and the managers "nurture these Team Members into responsibilities."

There is the second win. The company is profitable because the Team Members learn to truly operate like a team. Teams make 99 percent of the decisions and take responsibility as a team. They learn to want to make decisions.

The third win comes from "community." Team Members must care about the community. They are expected to help at various community events. The events are directly (various runs, marathons, running clinics, among others) or indirectly related to running. This brings us full circle back to the customers. The events not only help the community at large, but they assist runners, the customers of the Running Room.

Stanton is an accomplished runner and the lead Team Member, that is, President of the Company. He combines these two roles into one—successful leader.

Stanton runs at least five days a week, many times at various stores across Canada and the United States or at various running events, marathons, and other running-related activities. While running, Stanton speaks to customers. Sometimes, especially during the winter when everyone is all bundled up, he

is running with people who do not recognize him. What better way to get real customer feedback when he asks a runner what he or she thinks about certain running equipment and expertise and the runner does not know that the questioner is Stanton?

In addition to running with customers, Stanton runs with Team Members at the stores and actually sells shoes every Saturday at one of the stores. This is his way of providing encouragement to, and getting direct feedback from, Team Members. It also sets a very good example of desired behavior for all Team Members.

Stanton and the Team Members are truly a team in buying into a healthy, active lifestyle that, in turn, is the base for delivering products and expertise and services to the customers of the Running Room, who also buy into the healthy, active lifestyle. Throughout, Stanton exhibits the competence, character, and community associated with a successful leader.

SOURCES: John Stanton, Interview, April 1, 2002; **http://www.Runningroom.com**, Web site, March 27, 2002.

RECRUITMENT ISSUES

Recruitment is the process of finding and attracting job candidates who are qualified to fill job vacancies. The qualifications are listed and explained in the job descriptions and job specifications, as we discussed earlier.

Recruitment can occur in a variety of settings, both inside and outside the organization. Both approaches have certain advantages and disadvantages.[8] These are summarized in Table 10.1 and discussed in more detail below.

Internal recruitment involves identifying internal candidates and encouraging them to apply for and be willing to accept organizational jobs that are vacant. Methods of internal recruitment include job banks, employee referral systems, job postings, and advertisements in company newsletters. Every organization represents an internal labor market to some degree. Many employees, both entry level and upper level, aspire to move up the ranks through promotion. Promotion from within becomes more feasible when companies invest in training and development activities. At higher levels, transfers can be an important development tool for acquiring additional job knowledge, as well as a means of creating new job ladders for upward mobility. Both promotion and transfer policies can create a favorable climate for attracting qualified employees and retaining valued ones. According to the director of staffing at Advanced Micro Devices in Silicon Valley, it is more ef-

LEARNING OBJECTIVE 4

Summarize the different recruiting techniques used by organizations.

Recruitment
Finding and attracting qualified job candidates.

Table 10.1 | Internal versus External Recruitment

	ADVANTAGES	DISADVANTAGES
Internal Recruitment	• Motivator for good performance • Causes succession of promotions • Better assessment of abilities • Increased commitment, morale • Lower cost for some jobs • Have to hire only at entry level	• Strong personnel development, training needed • Possible morale problems of those not promoted • Political infighting for promotions • Inbreeding
External Recruitment	• New ideas, insights • Possibly cheaper than training a professional • No group of political supporters in the organization already	• Selected person may not fit job or organization • Possible morale problems for internal candidates not promoted • Long adjustment time may be needed

ficient to move workers within the organization than to start from scratch with new employees. Allowing workers to change jobs with the organization, rather than recruiting only from outside, saves time and money and boosts morale.[9]

External recruitment involves advertising for and soliciting applicants from outside the company. If internal sources do not produce an acceptable candidate, or if it is decided that the best candidate would come from the outside, a wide variety of external sources are available. These sources differ in terms of ease of use, cost, and the quality of applicants obtained.

External sources include walk-ins, public employment agencies, temporary-help agencies, labor unions, educational institutions, referrals from current and past employees, recruiting employees from competitors, newspaper and trade publications, and of course, a growing use of the Internet. The source used will depend upon the job skills required and the current availability of those skills in the labor market. For example, organizations frequently use external placement firms and private employment agencies to find applicants for upper-level managerial positions, but they look to educational institutions for candidates for entry-level managerial positions. As technology develops, human resource managers are increasingly using computerized databases as well as the Internet. Bristol Technology (http://www.bristol.com) recruits 80 percent of new hires through the company's Web page and gives anyone who successfully recommends a hire a Cannondale mountain bike. AccuData America awards $2,000 to any employee whose referral results in a new hire. The amount is paid out in $500 increments for every three months the new hire stays. AccuData's recruiting page is http://www.funwork.com! See the "Now Apply It" box on page 321 for more information about how companies recruit and related job-search information.

Now Apply It

Search for a Job on the Internet

Most organizations have Web sites. In addition to providing information about products and services and actually selling products, many organizations also use their Web sites for recruiting. Given this trend, it is good to get some experience in using the Internet to search for a job.

First, identify what kind of job you want. If you want to work for a certain company or in a certain type of culture, then clarify these things. You could proceed several ways: One is to go to a Web site such as

monster.com and begin the search by types of jobs.

If you would like to work for a certain organization, go to that organization's Web site and look for information there. This should include information about jobs available and information about the company.

Another way to search is to do a broad search on the Internet. Search by job type, organization type, geographical area, or whatever else if available on the search site and that might be of interest to you.

Get enough information about a job and the organization so that you could be ready to apply for a job or decide that a certain job or organization is not for you. If you decide that the job is what you would like, then get enough information to prepare for a successful interview with the organization. This includes not only being prepared to impress the interviewer(s) but also to ask the right questions so that you get further information about the job and organization so that you can make an informed decision.

The search for high-tech workers has become increasingly difficult and controversial with the explosive growth of positions in technology. Many U.S. companies have developed a strategy of recruiting skilled workers from other countries, claiming that the labor pool of workers in the United States is not adequate. Opposing this strategy, many employee organizations claim that increasing the number of temporary visas issued to workers from other countries is a form of digital age discrimination. They argue that the high-tech industries can pay lower salaries to temporary workers from other countries than they can to older and more experienced U.S. workers.[10]

A great company can't be built without great people, and that requires attention and commitment to the process.[11] According to a foremost authority on hiring, the best way to select people who will thrive in the company is to identify the personal characteristics of people who are already thriving and hire people just like them. To do this, it is necessary to understand star performers, identify their target behaviors and attitudes, and then use methods to find people with those attributes.[12]

© ANTARCTIC/INDEX STOCK

As positions in technology grow, many U.S. companies now recruit skilled high-tech workers from other countries.

LEARNING OBJECTIVE **5**

Clarify the major employee selection methods.

SELECTION METHODS

Selection is the process of evaluating and choosing the best-qualified candidate from the pool of applicants available for the position. It entails the exchange of accurate information between employers and job candidates to optimize the person-job match. Although organizations usually make these decisions, applicants also self-select into organizations that meet their requirements or choose to not join or to leave organizations that they think don't meet their needs.

At the heart of the selection process is the prediction of whether or not a particular applicant is capable of performing the job tasks associated with the position for which he or she is being considered. A wrong decision in either choosing a candidate who is not suited for the position or not choosing a candidate who would be very successful is costly. A "wrong candidate" is not productive and might have to be replaced. A "missed opportunity," not selecting a candidate who would have been very good, is a costly missed opportunity. Also, if a person is not selected for "non-valid" reasons, illegal discrimination might be an issue. This could cause negative consequences in how the organization operates and could lead to a lawsuit. (See legal issues on page 331.)

Validity

An employment tool must show that it predicts actual job performance.

Reliability

An employment tool measures the same thing each time it is used.

In order to select the right person for a job, any method used to make an employment decision, for example, original selection, promotion, demotion, or selection for personal development, must demonstrate **validity**. That means the method must accurately measure or predict what it is intended to measure or predict. There must be a strong relationship between the selection method and some criterion. For example, if scores on a test are used to select a person for a job, then those scores must be associated with or predict performance on the job. An interview must be conducted in such a way that the person selected for the job as a result of the interview must be able to perform better than the person not selected. The same is true for all other employment or selection methods.

In addition to being valid, a selection method must also demonstrate **reliability**. That means, it must measure or predict the same thing each time it is used. If it is not, then it can't be valid. For example, if a thermometer is very inaccurate, sometimes being 10 degrees too high, sometimes 5 degrees too low, it cannot measure the actual temperature. A selection method that is erratic cannot consistently choose the best candidate.

Does that mean that if a selection method is reliable, it automatically is valid also? No. Instead of being unreliable, as above, the thermometer now is exactly 12 degrees too high all the time. It is quite reliable; always 12 degrees too high. However, it is never valid; it never measures the temperature accurately. A selection method might be quite reliable, always choosing the candidate who is "mediocre" rather than the one who would perform much higher.

Now we turn our attention to the more commonly used selection methods. Usually, some combination of the following methods is used. In any case, the methods must be used in such a way so that they are valid and reliable.

Application form

A form used to gather information about a job applicant.

Résumé

Information prepared by a job applicant usually stating career goal, qualifications, and some related information.

APPLICATION FORMS AND RÉSUMÉS   The **application form** and a **résumé** are usually the first sources of information about a potential employee. Both ususaly record the applicant's desired position, job-related qualifications and experience, such as the applicant's educational background, previous job experience, and other information that may be useful in assessing the individual's ability to perform a job. Both the application form and résumé tend to serve as prescreening devices to help determine whether an applicant meets the minimum requirements of a position and allow preliminary comparisions with the credentials of other candidates.

Employers sometimes conduct background checks to evaluate the accuracy of information on the application form and résumé. Occasionally other things such as credit history and criminal record might be checked. Similarly, employers might contact references listed in a résumé usually to check the accuracy of past employment or to ask for an appraisal of a candidate's past performance.

According to a Society for Human Resource Management survey, 69 percent of companies do some kind of a background check. This probably is wise because about 30 percent of applications contain misstatements of fact, usually claiming longer employment in previous jobs than was the case. Sometimes, the applicant has a criminal record, as was the case when Becton Dickinson, a large medical device company, hired a very competent medical researcher as its medical director. Unfortunately, the newly hired director had been previously convicted of attempted murder.[13]

A background check costs on average $3,000 but can go as high as $10,000 for higher-level jobs. People who make employment decisions, therefore, must judge whether or not it is worth it to conduct background checks or contact references listed on a résumé.[14]

Employment test

Any instrument or device used to assess the qualifications of a job applicant.

TESTS   Any instrument, device, or information used to make an employment decision is considered an **employment test** by the EEOC's Uniform Guidelines on Employee Selection. An employment testing measure is a means of assessing a job applicant's knowledge, skills, and abilities, for example, through written responses (such as a math test), simulated exercises, or performance tests (such as a word-processing test), or verbal responses (such as a test of language skills). Regardless of what test is used, it should help select the best candidate for the position. That is, the test should predict the success of the candidate. We will discuss three categories of tests—written tests, performance tests, and personality or personal characteristics tests. While the personality test can be a written test, personality and personal characteristics can also be assessed through interviews and observations. We will discuss the assessment of personality separately because it is being used with increased frequency and it may be controversial.

Written tests usually are those that test knowledge, ability, skill, intelligence, or interest. They usually are called "paper and pencil" tests, although that title is outdated since many are now computerized. However, the tests still are designed to test one's knowledge about math, knowledge about a certain job or task, intelligence level, interest in certain types of careers, or other factors. If these tests are valid, the results of them predict job performance. A simple example of this type of test is the driver's examination. It is presumed that the higher one's scores, the better driver that he or she is. Hopefully, the driver's exam is valid!

Performance tests require the job candidate to actually perform in the job, usually some small part of the job, or for a short time. Since performance tests are based directly on job analysis, they should accurately predict job performance. Performance tests consist of actual job behaviors. There are two common types of performance tests—work samples and assessment centers.

Work samples are more appropriate for jobs that might be more routine or more specific. For example, to see whether or not a person can weld pieces of steel together properly in making a product, why not have the person actually perform the task—weld steel? To judge whether a person might write creative, and hopefully effective, advertisements, have the person prepare a portfolio (a collection or sample) of his or her work. In its factory in South Carolina, BMW built a simulated assembly line. Job applicants get 90 minutes to perform a variety of work-related tasks. Only those who have the "mental stamina" to meet BMW's "aerobic workplace" requirements are hired.[15]

Work sample
A small part of an actual job completed by an applicant to predict performance on the job.

If work samples are designed or selected well, then a person's performance in the work sample should accurately predict the person's performance on the job. In fact, work samples do show high validity scores, especially when compared to written aptitude, personality, or intelligence tests.[16]

Assessment centers are usually more appropriate to judge a candidate's predicted performance in a more complex job. For example, a candidate's readiness to be selected for a managerial position or to be promoted can be assessed by judging performance on a simulation of a group of tasks that a manager might actually do. The candidate typically is presented with a fairly large number and varying types of tasks to do. The tasks might include meetings to attend, speeches to make, decisions to make, among other tasks. This is sometimes called an "in-basket," referring to the tasks awaiting a manager.

Assessment center
A type of simulation of a more complex or higher-level managerial job used to predict a job applicant's performance.

The intent of the assessment center is to judge how a candidate would behave and perform in the selected tasks to predict performance as a manager. At the same time, the assessment center probably includes more tasks than can reasonably be done. This is usually included to see how the manager selects which tasks to do and which to ignore.

In a typical assessment center, a team of managers, psychologists, and others "trained" in judging performance in such a center observe the candidate's performance and judge it. Assessment centers usually last several days so they can be costly. However, assessment centers, like work samples, show good results in predicting performance in managerial jobs, so they may be worth it, especially for higher-level jobs.[17]

Personality test
Assessment of personality characteristics of a job applicant.

Personality tests are discussed here because increasing numbers and types of organizations are using some form of personality assessment in order to judge whether a person "fits," whether the organization hires the "right" people. Many now believe what Herb Kelleher, the charismatic and very successful chairman and co-founder of Southwest Airlines, has long believed: that is, hire people who already have characteristics and attitudes that are in line with the core values of the organization and with its culture and then teach them the details of the job. It is probably a lot easier to teach a person the details of a job than it is to teach him or her to change deeply held attitudes or change personality characteristics. Chances are high that those who do not fit the culture of the organization will leave anyway—voluntarily because they do not like the culture or involuntarily because they do not perform well in the culture.[18]

Personality tests include any method used to assess personal attributes or characteristics. It might be a written test that measures locus of control or self-esteem, an in-depth evaluation by a trained psychologist, or an assessment by an interviewer or a group of current employees.

Interview
Relatively formal, in-depth conversations used to assess a candidate's readiness for a job, and to provide information to the candidate.

INTERVIEWS **Interviews** are relatively formal, in-depth conversations conducted for the purpose of assessing a candidate's knowledge, skills, and abilities, as well as providing information to the candidate about the organization and potential jobs. They are used for more than 90 percent of all people hired for industrial positions.

Interviews permit a two-way exchange of information. Most interview questions are straightforward inquiries about the candidate's experience or education. At Microsoft, however, prospective employees are asked questions that reveal the candidate's capabilities of (a) grasping new knowledge extremely quickly and generating acute questions on the spot; (b) possessing such familiarity with programming structures that a quick glance is sufficient for him or her to understand a long printout of code; and (c) having photographic recall of code he or she has written. In other words, Microsoft is testing how the applicant thinks.[19]

Related closely to the Microsoft example, many organizations use interviews to assess the job candidate's personal characteristics and attitudes to see whether the candidate will fit into the company culture. Carrying the interview a bit further, some organizations require presentations or performances, usually to a group of current employees, so that they can assess whether or not they want the candidate to be hired.[20]

Interviews, overall, tend to have low validity. One reason for this is that while many people conduct interviews, many are not trained in how to do them well. Another reason is that interviews tend to be fairly informal and no two are alike. This raises serious problems with reliability, even if the interview might otherwise be valid.[21]

In a typical interview, the interviewer draws a conclusion about the candidate within the first two minutes. The rest of the interview is spent looking for reasons to support the quick decision.[22] Therefore, people who conduct interviews must take steps to increase their effectiveness, validity, and reliability. Typically, a structured interview format works best. This includes the interviewer asking the same questions, in the same order, and having the same type of information about each candidate in order to be more objective.

While it is usually important for the interviewer to probe for more information and to follow up, based on what the interviewee said, this must be done carefully. If it is not done carefully, the interview could stray far from job-related issues. Also, the interviewer could easily be influenced by his or her biases, stereotypes, and previous information that the interviewer has about the interviewee.

Interviewers can increase the validity and reliability of the interview by following these guidelines:

- Base the interview questions on a complete and current job analysis.
- Ask precise, specific questions that are job related.
- Avoid biases and making snap judgments, stereotyping, or looking for only negative, or only positive, information.
- Be careful about having a perception or stereotype of what the "good" candidate is.
- Be careful about making up your mind about the applicant in the first several minutes, as is usually the case.
- Avoid questions that can lead to discrimination. (See Table 10.2.)
- Keep written records of the interview. Because there is questionable validity and reliability for interviews, they should never be the sole basis for selecting a candidate. Instead, they should be used along with other selection devices to provide additional information on candidates' strengths and weaknesses.

An interview can also include a **realistic job preview**. That is, the interviewer can explain to the job applicant what the job really requires rather than give just the positive points of a job or company and avoid the negative. Some people think that if the negative aspects of a job or company are mentioned, perhaps night hours or a large amount of travel, the applicant won't want the job. Therefore, they suggest that these negatives should not be mentioned. On the other hand, if the negatives are not mentioned, the applicant will find them out anyway after he or she takes the job. If this happens, the person hired may well leave once these negatives are known. Of course, it is not wise to focus mainly on the negatives, but it might be best to give the job applicant an accurate picture of the job and company.[23]

> **Realistic job preview**
> An accurate description of a job and/or company.

PHYSICAL EXAMS AND DRUG TESTS

Physical exams and drug tests are required by many organizations. The physical exam is intended to be sure that a person is physically able to carry out certain job

Table 10.2 | Interview Questions That Can Lead to Discrimination

DON'T ASK	ASK THIS INSTEAD
Are you married? Do you have children? Do you have child-care arrangements? What is your spouse's name?	Do you have any responsibilities that might conflict with job attendance or your availability for shift work?
What is your race?	No acceptable question.
What is your religion? Which church do you attend? What are your religious holidays?	Are you available for weekend work?
Are you male or female?	No acceptable question.
How old are you? What is your birth date?	If hired, can you prove that you are at least 18?
Have you ever been arrested?	Have you ever been convicted of a crime?
Are you a U.S. citizen? Where were you born?	Can you show proof that you are eligible to work in the United States?
Are you disabled? In your condition, do you think you can do the job?	Are you able to perform the essential functions of this job with or without reasonable accommodation?

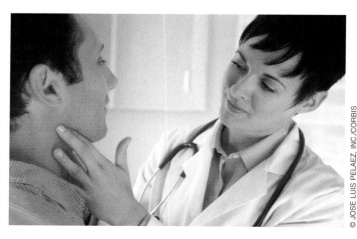

© JOSE LUIS PELAEZ, INC./CORBIS

Many companies require physical exams and drug tests to be sure that a person is physically able to meet the job requirements.

Training

A planned effort to assist employees in learning job-related behaviors that will improve their performance.

requirements. It also can be used to enroll employees in fringe benefits such as health, life, and disability insurance.

Drug tests are also used by some organizations, both for hiring and for continued employment. These tests tend to be very controversial. Occasionally, physical exams can be controversial also, depending upon how the information is used. The main thing to keep in mind with both physical exams and drug tests is that they must be important to the job.

TRAINING

Of course, all employees must know what to do in their jobs in order to perform well. Some, or most, of what they need to know may have been learned in some form of education or training before they got to the job. They might have a high school education, a college degree, a license, or experience in a similar job in the same or another organization. Or, the job might require things that are quite new to them. In the later case, **training** is obviously required. However, even with previous learning, there will be things that a person will need to learn as circumstances change in the industry. Also, new learning will probably be needed in order to move to a new job in the current organization or to move to a different organization. Some training will be necessary in almost every case.

Training is vital to the success of modern organizations, both large and small. This is evidenced by the fact that organizations spend $50 billion every year on formal training. The figure is much higher when all types of training are included.[24] Rapidly changing technology requires that employees possess the knowledge, skills, and abilities needed to cope with new processes and production techniques. Changes in management philosophy create a need for management development as well. For example, when faced with a tough global challenge, Xerox and Motorola increased their investment in employee training.[25] Training helped Xerox regain market share from Japanese companies. At Motorola, training gave the company the edge to grow in the face of strong Japanese competition in cellular phones and semiconductors.

Co-founders of Kate Spade, an accessory design company, begin training all new people they hire with a copy of Emily Post's *Etiquette* and remind salespeople that, when customers are spending their money with the company, it is critical to show appreciation. Since 1993, when the company was founded, intensive individual training for each new hire has focused on how customers are to be treated with respect, dignity, and a sense of grace.

An organization's training needs can be identified through three types of needs assessment: organizational, task, and individual.[26] Organizational assessment determines where in the organization the training is needed; task assessment is what is to be trained; and individual assessment determines who needs to be trained based on actual versus desired skills.

LEARNING OBJECTIVE 6

Explain the different types of employee training.

TYPES OF TRAINING Once the training needs of the organization have been assessed, training must be designed and developed. The first step in the training process is to get new employees off to a good start. This is generally accomplished through orientation. Orientation is the formal process of familiarizing new employees with the organization, their job, and their work unit. Orientation procedures vary widely from organization to organization. Generally, their purpose is to enable new employees to fit in so that they become productive members of the organization. A newcomer may need several hours, several weeks, or several months of work with other employees to become completely familiar with the organization.

In recent years, many organizations have realized that the socialization process begins in orientation and can make a significant difference to new employees. For example, one division of Intel revised its orientation program and experienced significant decreases in turnover and increases in employees mastering their jobs.[27]

Technical training programs are designed to provide non-managerial employees with specialized skills and knowledge in the methods, processes, and techniques associated with their jobs or trade. In union settings, apprenticeship training programs are common for skilled occupations. With advances in training technology, many organizations are using computer-assisted instruction and interactive video training for their non-managerial employees. However, approximately 90 percent of technical training programs still use on-the-job training methods.[28] On-the-job training is conducted while employees perform job-related tasks. This type of training is the most direct approach and offers employers the quickest return in terms of improved performance.[29]

Management development programs are designed to improve the technical, interpersonal, and conceptual skills of supervisors, managers, and executives. On-the-job training for managers might include rotating through a variety of positions, regular coaching and mentoring by a supervisor, committee assignments to involve individuals in decision-making activities, and staff meetings to help managers become acquainted with the thinking of other managers and with activities outside their immediate area. Most of these on-the-job training methods are used to help managers broaden their organizational knowledge and experience. Some popular off-the-job training techniques include classroom training, simulations, roleplaying, and case discussion groups.

THE ROLE OF PERFORMANCE APPRAISAL

Judging or appraising the performance of everyone in an organization is necessary so that the effort of everyone can be focused on achieving the mission of the organization. **Performance appraisal** is a systematic process of evaluating each employee's job-related achievements, strengths, and weaknesses, as well as determining ways to improve performance.

Performance appraisals are valuable aids in making many SHRM decisions; they are essential for distinguishing between good and poor performers. Managers can use performance appraisal information in four ways:

1. *Motivation.* Organizations try to motivate employees by rewarding them for good performance. This can be done by basing rewards, both financial (pay, bonuses) and non-financial (recognition "pat on the back"), on good performance. Therefore, it is important to evaluate performance so that those rewards can be provided fairly and serve as a motivator for future performance. Merit pay plans, for example, are designed to compensate people according to their job performance.
2. *Personnel movement.* Performance appraisal information helps managers develop an inventory of people appropriate for personnel movement. In other words, performance appraisals can be used to determine who should receive a promotion, transfer, or demotion, and who should be dismissed.
3. *Training.* By identifying areas of poor performance, performance appraisals help the manager suggest training or other programs to improve certain skills or behaviors.
4. *Feedback for improvement and personal development.* Performance appraisals provide a mechanism for giving employees feedback about their work performance. If employees are to do their jobs better in the future, they need to know how well they have done them in the past so that they can adjust their work patterns as necessary for better performance or to get ready for a promotion.

LEARNING OBJECTIVE **7**

Describe the role of performance appraisals in the organization.

Performance appraisal
Any method used to assess a person's performance on the job.

RATING PERFORMANCE   Effective performance appraisals usually consider various dimensions of a job. A variety of methods is available, but the most widely used approaches evaluate either behaviors or performance results.[30] Behavior-oriented approaches focus on assessing employee behavior based on the idea that certain behaviors will lead to successful performance on the job. Two commonly used methods are graphic rating scales and behavioral-anchored rating scales.

Graphic rating scales assess employees on a series of performance dimensions, such as initiative, tardiness, and accuracy of work, using a five- or seven-point scale. For example, a typical rating scale ranges from 1 to 5, with 1 representing poor performance and 5 representing outstanding performance. The rater evaluates the employee on each performance dimension by checking the appropriate place on the scale.

Performance dimensions on a graphic rating scale tend to be fairly general, and as a result, the scales are relatively flexible and can be used to evaluate individuals in a number of different jobs. Because the graphic rating scale is general, considerable interpretation is needed to apply it to specific jobs. As a result, the scale sometimes produces inconsistent and inaccurate ratings of employees. In general, the more clearly and specifically the scales and performance dimensions are defined, the more effective is the evaluation.

To define various aspects of an employee's job more clearly, some organizations use behavioral-anchored rating scales (BARSs). BARSs are similar to graphic rating scales, but they use more detailed examples of job behaviors to represent different levels of performance. The BARS approach relies on job analysis information to describe a range of desirable and undesirable behaviors for each performance dimension. Each of these behavioral descriptors is used as an anchor to distinguish between high, moderate, and low performance. Using BARS reduces subjective interpretation of performance because they are based on clearly stated job-related activities. They are costly to construct, however, and both subordinates and supervisors require training in their use.[31]

Results-oriented methods of performance appraisal are an alternative to the behavior-based ones. Results-based methods require the establishment of goals, targets, or results expected, and then a person's performance is judged against these. Some organizations use **360-degree feedback** for performance appraisal. The approach includes feedback about performance from four sources: the supervisor, the subordinates, coworkers, and self-appraisal. Feedback from all of these sources can give a more complete picture. However, this approach requires trust and communication skills. People need to understand how to give constructive feedback (see the communication chapter starting on page 370) and they must be comfortable with appraising their supervisor.[32]

Lockheed Martin Corporation, one of the world's leading defense and aerospace technology and systems companies, uses a very interesting method. Employees at Lockheed follow three strategic steps to convince their supervisors that they deserve a pay increase. The first step includes courting feedback. Employees are encouraged to ask for feedback from superiors on a regular basis. Once employees have feedback, they can work on strengthening the areas that need improvement. The second step is to demonstrate value. This includes taking on projects or asking to help other teams, and it demonstrates the willingness to learn and add value to the organization. The final step is to get on the fast track. Every organization has a fast track to higher management. To get on the right track, employees are taught to let their managers know they are willing to tackle challenging projects. This demonstrates worth.

Many organizations encourage continuous learning, whether it is formal education at a college or university or training programs within the organization. Lockheed Martin uses training or tuition or even a supplemental bonus as compensation for extra contributions to the firm.[33]

360-degree feedback
Feedback from the supervisor, subordinates, coworkers, and self-appraisal.

PROBLEMS WITH PERFORMANCE APPRAISAL   While we would like to believe that every manager carefully assesses each employee's performance, most people who have given or received a performance appraisal are aware of the subjective nature of the process. This subjectivity can lead to the following common problems.

The Halo Effect   The **halo effect** occurs when a manager rates an employee high or low on all items because of one characteristic. For example, a worker who has few absences might receive high ratings in all other areas of work, including quantity and quality of output. The manager may not really think about the employee's other characteristics separately. While an employee may perform at the same level across all dimensions, most people do some things better than others. Thus, the ratings should differ from one dimension to another.

Rater Patterns   Managers may develop rating patterns. For example, some managers have a problem with **central tendency**. Central tendency occurs when the rater judges all employees as average, even though their performance varies.

Another common rater pattern is the leniency-severity error. A **leniency error** occurs when the rater evaluates some in a group higher than they should be or when the rater is unjustifiably easy in evaluating performance. In contrast, a **severity error** occurs when a rater tends to be unjustifiably harsh in evaluating employee performance.

Contrast Error   A **contrast error** is the tendency to rate employees relative to each other rather than to performance standards. If almost everyone in a group is doing a mediocre job, then a person performing somewhat better may be rated as excellent because of the contrast effect. But, in a higher-performing group, the same person might have received only an average rating. Although it may be appropriate to compare people at times, performance appraisal ratings should evaluate performance against job requirements rather than against other employees.

Recency Error   If a manager bases an evaluation on the employee's most recent performance, it is considered a **recency error**. This is typically a problem when the evaluations are not frequent enough for the rater to recall performances over a long period of time. One way to help remedy this is to make weekly or bi-weekly notations on performance for all employees. When it is time for the performance review, information on the employee can be assembled with accurate documentation.

Eliminating the problems associated with performance appraisal is never simple. However, making raters aware of the potential problems through training programs is beneficial in overcoming the errors and the problems that result.[34]

REWARDS

Organizations must reward employees for doing a good job and for helping to achieve the goals and mission of the organization. Frequently, when the word "reward" is used, we think of money. Certainly money is important, but there are very important nonmonetary rewards also. Many of these nonmonetary rewards will be discussed in other chapters. For example, things like recognition, encouragement from the manager, teaching from the manager, and supportive types of communication will be discussed in the chapters on motivation, leadership, and communication. Notice that many of these types of rewards are part of the manager being a good leader. Since these things will be discussed elsewhere, we turn our attention to money (compensation) and related rewards.

Compensation consists of wages or salary paid directly for time worked, or just for work in the case of salary, and incentives for better performance. Benefits are the things that employees receive as part of their employment relationship with the organization, usually not tied directly to doing the job.

Halo effect
Rating an employee high or low on all items because of one characteristic.

Central tendency
Judging all employees as average, even though their performance varies.

Leniency error
Evaluating someone in a group higher than the person should be rated or when the rater is unjustifiably easy in evaluating performance.

Severity error
Being unjustifiably harsh in evaluating employee performance.

Contrast error
The tendency to rate employees relative to each other rather than to performance standards.

Recency error
Evaluation on the employee's most recent performance rather than all of it.

LEARNING OBJECTIVE 8

Explain how compensation and benefits are used in organizations.

Base pay
Wages and salary received for performing a job

Incentives
Bonuses, commissions, sometimes stock options directly tied to performance or extraordinary performance.

Benefits
Indirect compensation given to employees as a reward for organizational membership.

DIRECT COMPENSATION: BASE PAY AND INCENTIVES **Base pay** refers to wages and salaries employees receive in exchange for performing their jobs. Base pay rates are determined by an assessment of how valuable the job itself is to an organization, by economic forces in the labor market, by wages that competitors pay, and in unionized firms, by negotiation. In most jobs, base pay represents the majority of the compensation an employee receives because there are no provisions for bonuses or other forms of incentives.

To attract, retain, and motivate employees, however, many organizations offer compensation beyond base pay in the form of **incentives** such as bonuses, commissions, profit-sharing plans, and increasingly, some form of stock options. A recent study of 350 large U.S. companies revealed that 39 percent now offer stock options to more than half of their employees, not just the higher-ranking managers. This compares to only 17 percent doing so in 1993.[35] These incentives are designed to encourage employees to produce results beyond expected performance norms. In order to accomplish this, the incentives must be directly tied to performance. (Refer to the topic of motivation in Chapter 15.)

INDIRECT COMPENSATION: BENEFITS **Benefits** are payments beyond wages or salaries that are given to employees as a reward for organizational membership. Benefits can be categorized into several types: required and voluntary security, retirement, time-off, insurance and financial, and social and recreational. Examples of the benefits an organization can provide are listed in Table 10.3.[36]

Table 10.3 | Examples of Benefits

REQUIRED SECURITY	VOLUNTARY SECURITY	RETIREMENT	TIME-OFF	INSURANCE	FINANCIAL	SOCIAL AND RECREATIONAL
Worker's compensation	Severance pay	Social security	Vacation	Medical	Credit union	Recreational facilities
Unemployment compensation	Supplemental unemployment	Pension fund	Company-paid travel	Accident	House or car	Company publications
Old age, survivors', and disability insurance	Leave of absence	Early retirement	Holidays	Group rates	Legal services	Professional memberships
			Sick pay	Disability		
State disability insurance		Pre-retirement counseling	Military reserve pay	Life	Purchase discounts	Counseling
Medicare benefits		Disability retirement benefits	Social-service sabbatical	Auto	Stock plans	Sponsored events
					Financial counseling	Child-care
					Moving expenses	Food services
					Tuition assistance	Wellness and health services
						Service awards

Organizations commonly provide health, dental, disability, and life insurance coverage for employees and sometimes for their families. The costs of these plans may be paid entirely by the company or shared with the employee. Also, employees usually receive some pay for time that they don't work, such as vacations, sick days, and holidays. Retirement programs are also a common benefit.

Some organizations even provide benefits such as counseling, wellness programs, credit unions, legal advice, tuition reimbursement for educational expenses, on-site child care, or emergency child-care arrangements. For example, Chase Bank of Texas has three backup child-care centers for its Texas employees. Employees can also get up to 20 days a year of free child care for times when personal arrangements aren't available.[37]

A benefits package can represent a significant cost to an organization. In a recent survey of major U.S. manufacturing firms, benefits represented an average of 37.7 percent of the organizational payroll.[38] Although benefits represent a major cost to an organization, they are also a key factor in attracting and retaining employees.

DESIGNING EQUITABLE REWARD SYSTEMS Most organizations attempt to develop a compensation system that carefully considers issues of equity or fairness. Compensation is often the prime reason an individual works. However, compensation usually has several meanings to employees. It has economic meaning because it allows people to obtain the necessities and luxuries they need and want; it is symbolic because it is a means of "keeping score" and a measure of achievement; and an increase in compensation indicates growth because it reflects how well employees' performance and capabilities have grown.

In practice, developing an equitable or fair compensation system is quite challenging, primarily because most organizations have very complex compensation systems. Equity theory, discussed in Chapter 15 on page 467, is the basis for designing fair pay plans. Compensation designers are concerned with three sources of fairness expectations: external fairness, internal fairness, and employee fairness.[39]

External fairness refers to expectations that the pay for a job in one organization is fair relative to the pay for the same job in other organizations. Wage surveys are used to compare the organization's pay rates with other organizations in the industry to ensure that the pay remains competitive. **Internal fairness** refers to expectations that the pay for the job the individual is performing within the organization is fair relative to the pay of higher- and lower-level jobs in the same organization. Job evaluation procedures use job specifications to determine the relative worth of jobs in the organization.

Employee fairness refers to expectations that individuals on a given job are paid fairly relative to coworkers on the same job. Differences in pay among coworkers are acceptable if the variations are based on differences in performance or seniority. Because compensation can be so complex, many organizations have compensation specialists in the human resource department who develop, administer, and oversee the compensation system. They ensure that the organization provides compensation that is both competitive and equitable.

Disputes concerning fairness in pay have been one reason for legal issues surrounding human resource decisions. Certainly, pay disputes have not been the only reason, however. We now turn our attention to the legal environment of human resources.

LEGAL ENVIRONMENT OF STRATEGIC HUMAN RESOURCE MANAGEMENT

One factor that has contributed to the increased importance of human resource managers is the number and complexity of legal issues faced by organizations.

External fairness
Pay in one organization is fair relative to the pay for the same job in other organizations.

Internal fairness
Pay for the job within the organization is fair relative to the pay of higher- and lower-level jobs in the same organization.

Employee fairness
Expectations that individuals on a given job are paid fairly relative to coworkers on the same job.

LEARNING OBJECTIVE 9
Describe the key factors of the legal environment in which human resource management functions.

Federal and state laws that specify required, acceptable, and prohibited employment practices place many constraints on recruitment, selection, placement, training, and other human resource activities. For example, Xerox sets recruitment and representation goals in accordance with federal guidelines and reviews them continually to make sure that they reflect workforce demographics. While all companies with federal contracts are required to make this effort, Xerox extends the guidelines by setting diversity goals for its upper-level jobs and holding division and group managers accountable for reaching those goals.[40]

IMPORTANT LAWS

In an effort to reduce employment discrimination based on biases and stereotypes, Congress passed several laws that directly address the problem of employee discrimination.[41] The Civil Rights Act of 1964, the Civil Rights Restoration Act of 1988, and the Civil Rights Act of 1991 are equal employment opportunity (EEO) laws that prohibit the consideration of race, color, religion, national origin, or gender in employment decision making. Other legislation, such as the Americans with Disabilities Act of 1990 and the Age Discrimination in Employment Act of 1967, prohibits employment decisions based on biases against qualified individuals with disabilities and the elderly.[42] In general, the purpose of EEO legislation is to ensure that employment decisions are based on job-related criteria only. Toward that end, a substantial amount of legislation deals with various forms of employee protection. Table 10.4 summarizes the major federal laws and regulations that affect the management of human resources.

Table 10.4 | Major Employment Laws

LAW OR REGULATION	YEAR	DESCRIPTION
Fair Labor Standards Act	1938	Established minimum wage and 40-hour workweek; regulates child labor.
Social Security Act	1935	Established Social Security System.
Equal Pay Act	1963	Requires that men and women receive equal pay for equal work.
Title VII of Civil Rights Act	1964, amended 1972	Makes it illegal to discriminate on basis of race, color, religion, national origin, or gender.
Age Discrimination in Employment Act	1967, amended 1986	Prevents discrimination based on age for persons between 40 and 70.
Occupational Safety and Health Act	1970	Requires organizations to provide safe, nonhazardous working conditions.
Pregnancy Discrimination Act	1978	Broadens discrimination to include pregnancy, childbirth, and related conditions.
Americans with Disabilities Act	1990	Prohibits discrimination against persons with physical or mental disabilities or with chronic illness.
Civil Rights Act	1991	Amends and clarifies Title VII, Americans with Disabilities Act, and other EEO laws.
Family and Medical Leave Act	1993	Provides unpaid leave for care of family member, self, or child.

There are exceptions to discrimination based on the protected areas listed previously. If a requirement of a job is very important in order to perform that job, then if a person in a protected class is not hired or promoted, it is not illegal discrimination. That is, if a **bona fide occupational qualification**, also known as business necessity, inadvertently discriminates, it is not illegal. For example, if a job requires certain physical strength, then it is not discriminatory to not hire someone if he or she does not have the strength, even if the strength level might be associated with gender or race or other biases. Managers have to be very careful here. The bona fide occupational qualification must be based on job analysis, not personal attitude, opinion, bias, or stereotype.

The most current piece of legislation to take effect is the Family and Medical Leave Act of 1993 (FMLA), which allows individuals to take up to 12 weeks of unpaid leave per year for the birth or adoption of a baby or the illness of a family member. Some companies have been slow to inform employees of their rights under this act because of the disruption that they perceive will happen in the workplace.

The Civil Rights Act of 1964 established the Equal Employment Opportunity Commission (EEOC). This organization is responsible for enforcing federal laws related to job discrimination. Although the EEOC can prosecute an organization that violates the law, it usually tries to persuade offending organizations to change their policies and pay damages to anyone who has encountered discrimination. To help organizations comply with federal employment regulations, the EEOC also publishes written guidelines that clarify the law and instruct organizations on their legal obligations and responsibilities. Current federal law prohibits discrimination on the basis of gender, age, physical or mental disability, military experience, religion, race, ethnic origin, color, or national origin. Check all of this out on the EEOC Web site, http://www.eeoc.gov/facts/qanda/html.

AFFIRMATIVE ACTION **Affirmative action** refers to the legal requirement that federal contractors, some public employees, and private organizations under court order for short-term remedies must actively recruit, hire, and promote members of minority groups and other protected classes if such individuals are underrepresented in the organization. Individuals who fall within a group identified for protection under equal employment laws and regulations constitute a protected class. For example, if the qualified labor pool in a community is 20 percent African American and 12 percent Hispanic American, then 20 percent and 12 percent of the labor force of an organization operating in that community should be African American and Hispanic American, respectively, assuming that they are otherwise qualified.[43]

Organizations often have patterns of employment in which protected groups are underrepresented relative to the number of group members who have appropriate credentials in the marketplace. To correct such imbalances, organizations may adopt affirmative action programs. An affirmative action program is a written, systematic plan that specifies goals and a timetable for hiring, training, promoting, and retaining groups protected by EEO laws and regulations. While affirmative action is not synonymous with quotas, under federal regulations, all companies with federal contracts greater than $50,000 and with 50 employees or more are required to establish annual plans in the form of numerical goals or timetables for increasing employment of women and minorities.

During the last several years, there has been vocal opposition to affirmative action plans across the United States. In the November 1996 elections, California voters overwhelmingly supported the dismantling of the state's affirmative action programs by passing Proposition 209. A similar action, Initiative 200, was approved by Washington State voters in November 1998. These initiatives banned race and gender preferences in public hiring, contracting, and education. Supporters said

Bona fide occupational qualification
A qualification of a job that is legal to use even if it tends to rule out members of employee classes protected by Title VII.

Affirmative action
Emphasizing the recruiting, hiring, and promoting of members of minority groups and other protected classes if such individuals are underrepresented in the organization.

the goal was to create a color-blind society and eliminate gender preference in hiring. Opponents branded the initiatives as a negative attack on diversity and the needed affirmative action programs.[44]

Public institutions have created measures to manage the new mandates and have developed innovative programs to create opportunities for diverse populations while staying within the law. Many organizations have found that pursuing diversity for diversity's sake, rather than for the sake of good business, doesn't make sense.

WORKFORCE DIVERSITY   Avon, Chase Manhattan, IBM, Wal-Mart, Lucent Technologies, and Bell Atlantic are just a few of the organizations that have recognized the trend toward a more diverse workforce and have developed plans for managing that diversity effectively. Demographic changes in the workforce have forced organizations to introduce new SHRM programs, beginning with the recruiting and hiring of diverse individuals. The changing demographic profile of the available talent pool, such as the influx of women and minorities, is having a tremendous impact on the workplace. Women accounted for 60 percent of the total growth of the U.S. workforce between 1970 and 1985, and they made up a similar percentage of new entry-level employees between 1991 and 2001. Many of these women have children. In fact, one of the fastest-growing segments of the labor market is mothers with infants.[45] In addition, one-third of the newcomers into the workforce between 1996 and the year 2000 were minority group members.

Diversity can be a competitive advantage if people in an organization are accepting of diverse perspectives and issues and are taught to work well together. Bell Atlantic's CEO Ivan Sendenberg argues that diverse groups make better decisions, and for companies that operate globally, diversity means understanding minority marketing and customer relations in various ways that make big bottom-line differences.[46] But there are some challenges to managing a diverse work group. There is considerable research that shows that diversity in groups tends to reduce cohesion within the group, but innovation and performance tend to be good. The reduced cohesion could be a problem if adjustments are not made to deal with it.[47]

SEXUAL HARASSMENT   A serious legal issue that organizations must be sensitive to is sexual harassment. Sexual harassment refers to actions that are sexually directed, are unwanted, and subject the worker to adverse employment conditions.[48] Sexual harassment complaints increased by 10 percent each year from 1995 until very recently. Two-thirds of these complaints were found to be serious, or "had merit."[49] Part of the reason for the increase in complaints might just be that more people are aware of sexual harassment or that they can file a complaint. On the other hand, it might mean that there really is an increase in this type of harassment.

Sexual harassment or any type of harassment can disrupt performance in an organization and subjects some employees to unfair situations and treatment. These are serious enough reasons to be concerned about harassment and to learn how to get rid of it. In addition, it is illegal. The Supreme Court and the EEOC recognize two major forms of sexual harassment.[50]

"Quid pro quo" harassment
Sexual harassment requiring sexual favors in exchange for positive job treatment.

Hostile environment harassment
Harassment produced by workplace conduct and/or setting that is considered to make an abusive working environment.

The first is **"quid pro quo" harassment**, in which sexual compliance is required for job-related benefits and opportunities such as pay and promotions. Harassment by supervisors and managers who expect sexual favors as a condition for a raise or promotion is inappropriate and unacceptable behavior in the work environment. The second form of sexual harassment has been termed **hostile environment harassment**. In this case, the victim does not suffer any tangible economic injury, but workplace conduct is sufficiently severe to create an abusive working environment. A pattern of lewd jokes and comments in one instance and sexually oriented graffiti and posters in another have been viewed by the courts as sexual harassment.[51]

Table 10.5 | EEOC Guidelines for Preventing Sexual Harassment

- Establish a policy on sexual harassment and distribute a copy to all employees.
- Develop mechanisms for investigating complaints. The organization needs a system for complaints that ensures that they are satisfactorily investigated and acted upon.
- Develop mechanisms for handling accused people so that they are assured of a fair and thorough investigation that protects their individual rights.
- Communicate to all employees, especially to supervisors and managers, concerns and regulations regarding sexual harassment and the importance of creating and maintaining a work environment free of sexual harassment.
- Discipline offenders by using organizational sanctions up to and including firing the offenders.
- Train all employees, especially supervisors and managers, about what constitutes sexual harassment, and alert employees to the issues and behaviors involved.

Sexual harassment can occur between a manager and a subordinate, among coworkers, and among people outside the organization who have business contacts with employees. The vast majority of situations involve harassment of women by men, although recent cases have involved harassment of men by women and harassment by someone of the same gender. More people are becoming increasingly aware of sexual harassment, and more research and writing is concerned with this issue.[52] Consequently, organizations are becoming more conscious of sexual harassment and are doing more to protect the rights of women and others who are victims. Training sessions, booklets, guidelines, and company policies regarding acceptable workplace behavior are some of the proactive methods for discouraging sexual harassment. Some actions suggested by the EEOC guidelines are listed in Table 10.5.

Certainly, the SHRM process is affected by the legal environment. Moreover, due to societal and political forces, the legal landscape of SHRM is constantly changing. Therefore, it is important for managers to keep abreast of which employment practices are permissible and which are prohibited. For example, many organizations have appearance and grooming rules and guidelines for employees, especially those who deal with the public. Although there have been cases of so-called appearance discrimination, businesses generally retain the right to require their employees to meet appearance standards. In contrast, there is growing pressure to prohibit employment decisions based on sexual preference.

LABOR-MANAGEMENT RELATIONS

In many organizations, the strategic human resource process that we have been examining is affected by **labor-management relations**. The term *labor-management relations* refers to the formal process through which labor unions represent employees to negotiate terms and conditions of employment, including pay, hours of work, benefits, and other important aspects of the working environment.

Given the turbulent history of labor-management relations, it should come as no surprise that the process of forming a union is closely regulated by the government. The National Labor Relations Board (NLRB) is the government agency that oversees this process in the private sector. It enforces the provisions of the Wagner Act of 1935 and the Taft-Hartley Act of 1947 (an amendment to the Wagner Act), two major laws governing labor-management relations. When recognized

LEARNING OBJECTIVE 10

Explain the importance of labor-management relations.

Labor-management relations
The formal process through which labor unions represent employees in negotiating with management.

Unions can provide workers with an opportunity to participate in determining the conditions under which they work.

by the NLRB, unions have the legal right to negotiate with private employers over terms and conditions of employment and to help administer the resulting contract.

Unions have political power and use their lobbying efforts to support legislation that is in their own interests and the interests of all employees.[53] They can also provide workers with an opportunity to participate in determining the conditions under which they work. Studies have shown that workers who belong to a union perceive that they are treated with greater dignity and respect on the job than if they didn't belong to a union.

Management can pursue several different strategies in dealing with organized labor/unions. With a conflict orientation, management refuses to give in to labor and recognizes the union only because it is required to do so by law.[54] Managers can also use a more cooperative approach in which each party recognizes that the other party is necessary for attaining their respective goals. Recognition of shared interests has led to labor-management relationships characterized by mutual trust and friendly attitudes.[55] DaimlerChrysler, Ford Motor Company, Cummins Engine Company, and especially Southwest Airlines have established cooperative relations with unions in the hope that teamwork will boost productivity and quality and hold down costs.[56]

Union membership has declined in the United States from a high of 35 percent of the workforce in 1945 to 22 percent in 1980 to less than 11 percent in 2000. There are several reasons for this decline. Effective SHRM practices in organizations have reduced the need for union protection. The very nature of high-tech industries also hampers organizing efforts. Many software designers and biotechnical engineers work for small start-up companies that unions find difficult and expensive to organize. Many young workers are taking jobs in the rapidly growing services sector, including banking, financial services, computer programming, and other types of services, that unions traditionally have not penetrated.

In some larger firms, workers are sometimes part of flexible teams that change tasks and work closely with management. This type of teamwork usually is associated with empowerment and leaves little role for unions to play. Other reasons for the decline in union membership include a decrease in union-organizing attempts, a decline in traditionally unionized industries, and a change in the economic well-being of organizations (making it more difficult for unions to pressure for better wages and benefits).

CHALLENGES OF SHRM IN THE MULTINATIONAL ORGANIZATION

LEARNING OBJECTIVE 11

Clarify the primary challenges of SHRM in the multinational organization.

Effective management of human resources is of critical importance to multinational organizations that compete in the global marketplace. Multinational organizations face greater diversity in their workforce and, as a result, must develop an SHRM system that is flexible and adaptable to a wide variety of cultural situations. Perhaps one of the most significant challenges associated with the SHRM process in multinational organizations lies in managing expatriate personnel. An expatriate is an organizational member who is a citizen of the country in which the multinational organization is headquartered, but is assigned to a position in one of the organization's facilities in another country. An example of this is a French firm sending a French manager to oversee its plant in Australia.

Managing expatriates presents some unique challenges for human resource professionals in terms of selection, training, and compensation.[57] For example, expatriates must be selected based on a broader set of characteristics than domestic personnel. Situational factors such as stage of career development and family commitments become more important, as do personal characteristics such as flexibility, cultural empathy, and maturity. Furthermore, the training process is more complex for expatriate managers. Language and cross-cultural training for both the expatriate and his or her family is essential. An expatriate's compensation package is also more complex than a domestic manager's compensation package. In addition to the traditional base salary, incentives, and benefits, expatriates may receive a cost-of-living adjustment, an overseas premium to compensate for the hardship of living in a foreign environment, and other perquisites, such as membership in social clubs, transportation allowances, and home-leave expenses to make the overseas assignment more attractive.[58]

Historically, many multinational organizations have experienced disappointing results from managers sent on overseas assignments. In general, U.S. multinationals have had much less success with expatriates than have most Japanese and many European firms. The disappointing results for U.S.-based organizations have been attributed, in large part, to ineffective SHRM practices, but all indications are that U.S. organizations are improving their international HRM systems tremendously.[59]

At The Forefront

"Change Agents" Are Redefining the Modern Workplace

Donny Deutch, chairman of Deutch, Inc., and iDeutch, advertising and communications companies, had a shocking encounter with a new attitude in the workplace.

"We have one area of the office which is a kind of pit or open area where there are maybe twenty young people sitting—they all happen to do a job where they are all in their early twenties. A couple of times a year, I will go into this area, so I walk in not long ago, and I say, 'Hey, how's everybody doing?' and, you know, out of the twenty people, maybe fifteen kind of quickly hang up the phone and turn to the big boss, or whatnot. And I happen to see that there is one young woman still on the phone. I come up to her, face her, and I say—kidding around, 'Hey, that must be a really important call— who are you on the phone with?' It was a kind of 'Why don't you hang up—after all, the big boss is here?' Finally she hangs up the phone, and I say, 'That must have been an important client.' And she says, 'Well, no, actually it was a friend of mine.'"

"Now, if you think back twenty years ago, and you are junior person and the head of the company walks in, you would stand up, you'd salute. I am not somebody who is ceremonious, but the fact is that she not only didn't do that, but she was so comfortable saying 'Oh, this is a friend on the phone.' I don't want to say this is a lack of regard for authority. It's not. It's this entitlement thing. This is 'I have a great job here, but I can get another one tomorrow, and I can probably get more money.'"

This entitlement attitude is just one characteristic of a new type of worker referred to by Liz Nickles as a "Change Agent." These young people, ranging from their teens to their thirties, represent a psychographic segment of the workforce that is setting new rules to work and live by. They are highly adapted to the newest technologies and extremely ambitious. They are willing to work exceedingly long hours and expect to be well compensated for their efforts. Most plan to retire young. At the same time, they are demanding more from their employers, especially in terms of benefits that help them simultaneously fulfill the requirements of their work and personal lives. Examples include on-site exercise facilities, full kitchens, concierge services, and the latest technological equipment.

Change agents do not expect to follow a traditional career path, but rather see themselves as immediately capable of handling a high level of responsibility. They are willing to take risks, are confident in their abilities, and do not feel tied to a single employer. They approach their careers as entrepreneurs and are constantly on the lookout for promising opportunities.

Nickles sees these people as "early adopters" of a cultural shift likely to become widespread in the future. The Internet boom of the late 1990s likely initiated this trend, especially when stories quickly spread about young entrepreneurs becoming millionaires almost overnight. However, change agents have continued to be a guiding force in the workplace even after the stock market correction in April 2000, when many Internet companies failed.

SOURCE: L. Nickles, *the Change Agents: Decoding the New Workforce and the New Workplace* (New York: St. Martin's Press, 2001).

IMPLICATIONS FOR LEADERS

In this chapter, you were introduced to the role of strategic human resource management in today's organizations. As a manager, you will be called upon to make many decisions involving people. Therefore, it is important to remember the following points:

- Recognize that strategic human resource management is a critical element of the strategic planning process and is essential for long-term organizational success.
- Keep in mind that job analysis is essential in order to understand what knowledge, skills, abilities, and attitudes each job requires.
- Carefully evaluate both internal and external sources for recruiting people.
- Base all SHRM decisions on job-related criteria and not on racial, gender, or other unjustified biases.
- To keep pace with rapid changes in technology, be sure to upgrade the knowledge and skill base of employees through training programs.
- Develop equitable pay systems, unbiased performance appraisals, and equal access to training opportunities.
- Be innovative in scheduling work, designing jobs, and rewarding employees so that you can respond effectively to the changing composition and needs of the workforce.

By managing human resources well, the organization will have the right people in the right jobs. The right people, guided and motivated to achieve the organization's overall strategy, are the most important assets of the organization. The right people include managers who are successful leaders. A manager who has competence, character, and a sense of community, as discussed in the 3Cs Model of Leadership, has a much higher chance of leading an organization to success. These characteristics will help the manager as leader to not only lead the organization in a successful direction, by establishing a good strategy, but also will help the leader in guiding the people well. In addition, a leader with competence, character, and a sense of community can also set a very positive example for others in the organization to follow.

Meeting The Challenge

Finding the Right CEO for JC Penney

JC Penney hired Allen Questrom to be the new CEO in September 2000. Is he the right person for the job?

On news of Questrom's hiring, the price of JC Penney's stock jumped 16 percent. The financial analysts believe he can make the company much more successful. They apparently are influenced by Questrom's past successes of bringing Federated Department Stores out of bankruptcy and reviv-ing Neiman Marcus and Barneys New York.

Questrom got right to work. He closed underperforming stores and set the tone for a new sense of urgency. He made it clear that things had to change. This may have been one reason why most of the top 20 managers in the company either chose to leave or were fired. They apparently were not able or willing to change to become refo-cused.

Speaking of refocusing, Que-strom and the management team are working on clarifying JC Penney's overall strategy, focusing on certain market segments and understanding what those customers want—to redefine a clear image once again.

Turning to people issues, Questrom hired several new managers with successful retailing experience. But perhaps his most important challenge is giving new purpose, direction, and focus (his favorite word) to the 290,000 people who are employees, or associates as he calls them, of JC Penney. He believes that he must develop a culture of success by focusing the associates on "getting the store right." He believes that one can change people's attitudes, but that has to be done by helping people achieve some successes. He also believes that when a business fails, it is not because of the "bad" people. In fact, he believes that

there are many "very good people" in companies. The challenge is to refocus the people.

Early indications are that Questrom is the "right" person for the job, as indicated by his past successes and early decisions at JC Penney. He has also hired several key top managers. In addition, he now is working on focusing all of the people on an improved overall strategy and is teaching all to gain the right knowledge, skills, abilities,

and attitudes in order to rebuild JC Penney.

SOURCES: "Allen Questrom to Take Helm at JC Penney," *The Los Angeles Times*, July 28, 2000, C1; D. Stankevich, "Questrom's Quest," *Retail Merchandiser*, May 2001, 22; "J.C. Penney's Questrom Stresses Fundamentals," *Home Textiles Today*, June 11, 2001; "Merchant of Panache," *Chain Store Age Executive*, September 2000, 61–64; S. Forest, "Can an Outsider Fix JC Penney?" *BusinessWeek*, February 12, 2001, 57–58.

SUMMARY

1. The components of strategic human resources management include job analysis, forecasting, recruiting, selecting, training, performance appraisal, and compensation. Job analysis is the primary process used for gathering current information about a job in order to understand what knowledge, skills, abilities, and attitudes are needed in order to perform well in the job. It involves assimilating all of the information that is used to develop two important documents: the job description and job specifications.

2. Forecasting is determining the supply of and demand for human resources for both short-term and long-term planning. Two types of forecasting are used: demand forecasting, which involves determining the number of employees the organization will need at some point in the future as well as the knowledge, skills, and abilities that these employees must possess, and supply forecasting, which involves determining what human resources will be available both inside and outside the organization.

3. Recruitment is the process of finding and attracting job candidates who are qualified to fill job vacancies. Both internal and external recruitment have certain advantages and disadvantages. Internal recruitment involves identifying potential internal candidates and encouraging them to apply for and be willing to accept organizational jobs that are vacant. External recruitment involves advertising for and soliciting applicants from outside the company.

4. Selection is the process of evaluating and choosing the best-qualified candidate from the pool of applicants recruited for the position. The major selection methods include application forms, employment testing, personal interviews, and sometimes, physical exams and drug tests.

5. Training is a planned effort to assist employees in learning job-related behaviors that will improve their performance. There is a variety of types of training. Orientation is the for-

mal process of familiarizing new employees with the organization, their job, and their work unit. Technical training is designed to provide employees with specialized skills and knowledge in the methods, processes, and techniques associated with the job. On-the-job training is conducted while employees perform job-related tasks. Management development programs are designed to improve the technical, interpersonal, and conceptual skills of supervisors, managers, and executives.

6. Performance appraisal is a systematic process of evaluating each employee's job-related achievements, strengths, and weaknesses, as well as determining ways to improve performance.

7. Compensation consists of wages paid directly for time worked, incentives for better performance, and indirect benefits that employees receive as part of their employment relationship with the organization.

8. A key factor resulting in the increased importance of human resource managers is the number and complexity of legal issues faced by organizations. Federal and state laws that specify required, acceptable, and prohibited employment practices place many constraints on recruitment, selection, placement, training, and other human resource activities.

9. The increasing number of jobs in services and very flexible high-tech companies plus some improvements in SHRM practices may have caused declines in union membership.

10. One of the primary challenges of SHRM in the multinational organization is to globalize its human resource policies and practices. When entering a new country, U.S. businesses cannot simply export their own employment practices. It is important to have a global strategy while looking at the role of SHRM.

REVIEW QUESTIONS

1. *(Learning Objective 1)* Describe the components of the strategic human resource management process.

2. *(Learning Objective 2)* Explain the importance of job analysis.

3. *(Learning Objective 3)* Specify the different types of forecasting and why each is important.

4. *(Learning Objective 4)* Discuss the role of recruitment in human resource planning.

5. *(Learning Objective 5)* Explain the role that interviews play in the selection process. What format is considered most appropriate?

6. *(Learning Objective 6)* Define what training means and how an organization identifies the need for training of its employees.

7. *(Learning Objective 7)* Why are performance appraisals considered valuable in the organization?

8. *(Learning Objective 8)* Explain the difference between compensation and benefits. What are some of the common types of benefits used in organizations?

9. *(Learning Objective 9)* Explain the primary effects on the hiring process of Title VII.

10. *(Learning Objective 10)* Discuss some of the current trends in labor-management relations.

11. *(Learning Objective 11)* Describe some of the challenges faced by SHRM in multinational organizations.

DISCUSSION QUESTIONS

Improving Critical Thinking

1. Explain why job analysis must be conducted first in order to be sure that the best qualified people can be placed in a job.

2. Look for a current article in a newspaper or magazine that describes sexual harassment. Why is this a problem for managers?

3. Discuss why union membership is declining. Would you be interested in joining a union? Why or why not?

4. Explain why it is important for managers in organizations to set a good example. Will the examples set by the managers be seen as good leadership?

Enhancing Communication Skills

5. Write a report that describes an interview you have had. Was it structured or unstructured? What was your impression of the interviewer? Of the organization? What could have been

done to improve the interview? Present your experiences and suggestions for improvement to the class.

6. Obtain an application form from a local organization. Analyze the form and discuss the impact of any questions that could be discriminatory. Present the form and your analysis to the class.

Building Teamwork

7. Develop a model of a college orientation program that provides all aspects of training that you think are important. Work in a small group as directed by your instructor. Present the group's model program to the class.

8. In a small group, create a detailed list of some of the best and worst questions asked of you in an interview. Are any questions common to several people? Work together to come up with some possible responses to the worst questions. Discuss how interviews can be improved.

THINKING CRITICALLY: DEBATE THE ISSUE

Employee Ownership

As you read in the chapter, more organizations are now including employees other than just managers in stock option, or stock ownership, programs. There is some research that suggests that such ownership helps to increase performance of all employees. Other research has found no such effect.

Form teams of four to five students as directed by your instructor. Search your library and the Internet for articles on the

subject of employee ownership. Be sure to include at least one article that is based on solid research.

Your instructor will assign half of the teams to present the case for giving ownership, in the form of stock, to employees; the other half of the teams to present the case against employee ownership. Your instructor will select two teams to present their findings to the class in a debate format.

EXPERIENTIAL EXERCISE 10.1

Write Your Résumé

As you know, most organizations request a résumé when you apply for a job. You also know that the résumé is frequently used to screen applicants early in the hiring process. Therefore, your résumé has to be good enough to get you past this screening.

If you are now looking for a job, you need a good résumé. If you won't be looking for a while, it is good practice to write one now. So, either re-write or write your résumé.

First, you will need to define what a "good" résumé is. Study some guides to writing résumés, including some Web sites such as **http://www.Microsoft.com**, **http://www.iflyswa.com (Southwest Airlines)**, **http://www.resume.com**, **http://www.reswriter.com**. These sites, and others, include tips on how to write

résumés. Microsoft's site also has a template that you can download. Get some information also from your career center and professors.

Now write your résumé. Will the résumé that you submit to one job and company be different from one that you submit to a different job and company? Ask others to critique your résumé and give you advice.

If you are ready to enter the job market or to seek a new job, try submitting your résumé online. You can do this either directly to a company to which you want to apply, or you can post your résumé on some Web sites, such as **http://www.Monster.com** or **resumezapper.com**.

CAPTURING THE POWER OF INFORMATION TECHNOLOGY

1. Use the Internet to examine how well-known companies are recruiting employees. Select several organizations in the same industry and develop a matrix to compare the different techniques that are being used. What impression do you form about the organization from the way its Web page looks? How much detail is given about positions, such as job descriptions, job specifications, position locations, salary, and benefits?

2. Examine the recruiting strategies used by several colleges or universities as they use their Web sites to attract and interest potential students. Using a similar strategy to the one

you used in item 1, select a general category of college (for example, regional, large state, small private, large private). Compare the different techniques that college recruiting centers are using.

3. Talk to a human resource manager and find out the type of information kept in the organization's Human Resource Information System (HRIS). Was the system written for the organization exclusively, or was it a software program that was purchased? If you were interested in a career in HRM, what type of computer skills would you need?

ETHICS: TAKE A STAND

Organizations are increasingly using some form of personality test or personality assessment in making decisions about which people to hire or promote. The reason given is that if a person fits into the culture of the organization, he or she can be much more productive. If the person does not fit well, he or she will probably not perform well, may leave voluntarily, or may be fired. (See the "At The Forefront" box in Chapter 11 on page 349.)

For Discussion

1. Is it ethical to hire or not hire a person based on his or her personality characteristics?

2. Is it ethical to not hire a person or to fire one if he or she doesn't fit the organization's culture?

3. What are the advantages and disadvantages of all the people in an organization fitting the culture of that organization?

VIDEO CASE

Strategic Human Resource Management: Fannie Mae

In 1938, Congress created Fannie Mae to bolster the housing industry in the aftermath of the Great Depression. At that time, Fannie Mae was part of the Federal Housing Administration (FHA). In 1968, Fannie Mae became a self-sustaining private company. Since then it has coordinated $4 trillion of mortgage financing for more than 45 million families. Today, Fannie Mae operates under a congressional charter directing it to increase availability and affordability of homeownership for low-, moderate-, and middle-income U.S. citizens. Yet it receives no government funding or backing. Fannie Mae is the largest nonbank financial services company in the world and the largest source of financing for home mortgages in the United States.

Fannie Mae's core values permeate how it conducts business, emphasizing honesty, integrity, and respect for others. Its corporate philosophy on diversity is based on respect for one another and recognition that each person brings unique attributes to the corporation. Fannie Mae believes its employees are its most important assets. Its talented and diverse workforce is dedicated to Fannie Mae's common mission and core commitments essential to its success. The employees also want to work at a great place with the best people, make a difference in the world, and have the opportunity to build a solid career. Each Fannie Mae employee is expected to share responsibility in creating and maintaining an environment of mutual respect. Employees are encouraged to use good judgment in what they say and do in the workplace.

Fannie Mae's managers are held responsible for implementing its corporate philosophy on diversity. In addition, the Human Resource Department carefully monitors and facilitates the organization's dedication to have its employee diversity reflect that of its customers. Human resource planning and recruiting trends are among the important elements in monitoring and improving diversity. For technology openings, it found that Hispanic candidates typically were referred by Hispanics already employed by Fannie Mae. Therefore, Fannie Mae decided to ask for further help from its top-performing Hispanic employees. To facilitate recruiting a diverse set of candidates with the required skills, it has also partnered with Howard University, identified job posting Web sites, and identified professional associations and contingent employment firms specializing in key minorities. Fannie Mae also tries to stay aware of trends in its human resource practices.

Fannie Mae's commitment to corporate responsibility helps it maintain, enhance, and expand its diversity, community outreach, work/life balance, employee development, and volunteer programs and initiatives. Its Multicultural Markets team developed a diversity training course to help lenders understand the impact of diversity on each stage of the lending process.

Fannie Mae is committed to retaining and expanding its diverse workforce by offering various opportunities for employees to increase productivity and further their careers. It rewards talent and outstanding effort through competitive salaries and benefits, opportunities for training, new career horizons, and increased responsibility. Fannie Mae's career development opportunities include extensive training programs, job rotations, tuition reimbursement, and mentoring programs. Its family and lifestyle benefits help employees perform their jobs better and balance their career and personal needs. Fannie Mae offers flexible work arrangements, job-sharing, time off for volunteer activities, Phase Back to Work for New Parents program, elder care, Emergency Child Center, and an Employer-Assisted Housing loan program.

Each year, Fannie Mae is repeatedly recognized by numerous organizations for its commitment to diversity and work/life issues, as well as how it does business. In 2002, it was formally recognized for being a "great place to work" more than 22 times including being ranked number one in *Fortune* magazine's "50 Best Companies for Minorities," named "Company of the Year" by *Latina Style* magazine, and listed as one of the 10 Best Companies by *Working Mother* magazine.

Fannie Mae is an equal opportunity employer that develops and promotes a diverse workforce as part of its business plan. Its employees' multicultural backgrounds, unique perspectives, innovation, and commitment to excellence provide its lender customers with products and services that make homeownership more accessible to more people.

For Discussion

1. Illustrate the components of HR Planning utilized at Fanny Mae.

2. What recruiting techniques are being used or considered by Fanny Mae? What other techniques might be appropriate to increase its diversity?

3. How does Fanny Mae use its compensation and benefits to attract and retain a diverse workforce? Explain whether these appear effective.

4. What primary challenges might Fannie Mae face in the future?

http://www.fanniemae.com

CASE

Should C.J. Be Hired?

C.J. Lindstrom was optimistic. He had just applied for a job as a police officer at a university with about 25,000 students. Based on the job specifications, he was confident that he had the right qualifications. In addition to his Bachelor's Degree in Criminal Justice, he had completed the regular training at a local police academy. The three years working in a small police department (2 full-time officers, 1 part-time) had also given him good experience. He earned high performance appraisals and was sure to get a good recommendation from the police chief. Moving to the larger 6-person police department at the university was a nice progression for his career. He thought that he was at the right stage for being 27 years old.

C.J. had sent in his application and résumé, complete with references, and had gone through an interview. He was waiting to hear the results.

A letter arrived in the mail telling him that the university police department would not be hiring him. He contacted the university personnel office to seek information about why he wasn't hired so he could take that into consideration when applying for a job elsewhere. He was told that he was not hired because he had multiple, large, visible tattoos.

C.J. was quite shocked. "What does that have to do with doing a good job as a police officer?" Besides, the tattoos would be mostly covered, especially if he wore a long-sleeved shirt. Yes, they would be visible when he wore short sleeves or shorts. Some were slightly visible above the collar and on one wrist.

The Director of Personnel told him that the tattoos were not professional. C.J. had the opposite view. He thought they might actually help build rapport with some students.

For Discussion

1. Is the university's decision to not hire C.J. appropriate? Is it legal?

2. Discuss this question: "What does appearance have to do with doing a good job?"

3. Expand your discussion to include appearance that is based on someone's race. Is it legal to not hire someone based on his or her appearance then?

CHAP

ORGANIZATIONAL CULTURE, CHANGE, AND DEVELOPMENT

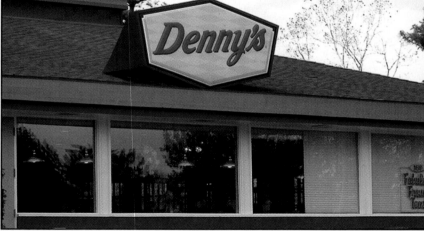

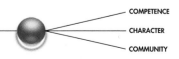

COMPETENCE

LEADERSHIP — CHARACTER

COMMUNITY

TER 11

CHAPTER OVERVIEW

What happened with Enron? Only a short time ago, that company was touted as a company that was doing "everything right." Among many other things, Enron had a culture that strongly encouraged and rewarded creativity and risk taking. Unfortunately, the creativity and risk taking were not guided, nor controlled properly. The company spun out of control. Key people lost sight of the mission and did things that most people consider unethical and perhaps illegal.[1]

Now consider Denny's Restaurants. In the past, some of the company's restaurants were discriminating against African-American people. African-American customers were ignored and treated poorly. Top management at Denny's undertook a comprehensive change effort in order to change the culture of the entire company and its many restaurants because the culture included, or at least allowed, discrimination against African Americans. But it wasn't easy. It took a new CEO, Jim Adamson, who in 1995 implemented a concentrated strategy to change the culture. Adamson first loosened the hierarchical environment, making communication easier. Then, he included progress on diversity when evaluating performance of managers, required attendance at workshops on racial sensitivity, and spoke about diversity repeatedly. He made improving working with diversity a part of everyday life for himself and everyone who was a part of the company. It also took some time. However, by the late 1990s, continuing today, Denny's has a much more positive image related to diversity, both with customers and employees.[2]

Denny's Restaurants was successful in carrying out a major change. Now let's consider change from a broader perspective. It is estimated that the knowledge base, the amount of what we know, triples every eighteen months![3] A personal computer becomes essentially obsolete in the same amount of time. What do you think about this kind of change?

Many people feel very threatened by this change. Others are quite excited. We are entering an age in which both individuals and organizations must learn something new every day, or they will fall behind. At all levels of operations, the focus must be on innovation, value, relationship building, and excellence in management practices. Managers recognize that to build viable organizations, change must be viewed as an integral rather than a peripheral responsibility. After a decade of getting "leaner and meaner," organizations are also becoming "keener." Specifically, they are adopting new structures and practices to take advantage of the unique value-adding capabilities of rapidly maturing information technologies. These organizations are developing their people, and thereby the entire organization, in order to keep up with the changes. Many leading companies, such as

LEARNING OBJECTIVES

When you have finished studying this chapter, you should be able to:

1. Discuss the foundations of organizational culture.
2. List and explain the two components of organizational culture.
3. Clarify the differences between the types of organizational artifacts.
4. Explain the impact of culture on the organization.
5. Explain how organizational culture can be changed.
6. Identify and discuss the targets of planned change.
7. Describe the steps for planned change.
8. Identify ways managers can address employee concerns in the change process.
9. Explain how empowering others to act on a vision affects the change process.

Facing The Challenge

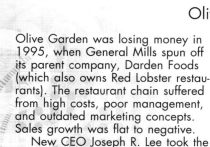

Olive Garden: Changing for the Better

Olive Garden was losing money in 1995, when General Mills spun off its parent company, Darden Foods (which also owns Red Lobster restaurants). The restaurant chain suffered from high costs, poor management, and outdated marketing concepts. Sales growth was flat to negative.

New CEO Joseph R. Lee took the reigns, and overhauled the company. He helped the restaurants lower costs and tightened management. A loss of $91.03 million in 1997 was changed to a profit of $101.71 million in 1998 and $140.54 million by 1999. Sales continued to grow, and Olive Garden claimed a 35 percent share of the Italian casual dining market.

To continue growing, Lee believed the restaurant needed to change and develop a more sophisticated image to gain appeal in the high-end market. Extensive remodeling gave the restaurants a more authentic Italian look, but how could Olive Garden capture the warmth and passion of the Italian dining experience?

SOURCES: J. Cox, "Changes at Olive Garden Have Chain Living La Dolce Vita," *USA Today*, December 18, 2000; N. Kruse, "Focus on Flavor Packs Power Punch with Consumer Bunch," *Nation's Restaurant News*, January 7, 2002, 36, 1, 36–44; J. Ordonez, "Olive Garden Bets on Cachet of Cooking School in Italy," *Wall Street Journal*, October 19, 1999, A1.

GE, Southwest Airlines, Microsoft, Texas Instruments, and IBM, are making or have already made sweeping changes to adjust to 21st century workplace trends. These trends represent truly transformational change in the workplace and offer unparalleled opportunity for organizations and individuals to manage changing cultures, strategies, and practices.[4]

This chapter examines the issues associated with managing change, beginning with the organization's culture. We will explore the components of organizational culture by examining organizational artifacts and then look at how culture affects the organization. Next, we will turn our attention to the responsibility of bringing about change. We will see that this can best be accomplished by analyzing the forces that drive change and those that resist it. Finally, we will examine the processes and interventions that can be used to manage change and thereby develop the organization to be successful in the long run.

INTRODUCTION

This chapter discusses organizational culture, change, and development, that is, successfully dealing with change. An organization's culture guides the behavior and actions of all employees inside the organization. Therefore, the culture needs to be aligned with the mission. If not, the mission will not be achieved.

Change comes into play because it is pervasive in today's global and e-business environment. Organizations that survive accept change as a means of seeking new and better ways of doing business. In major changes, this might include changing the culture. In any case, change must be managed properly in order to train and teach people so they can grow and develop in order to work successfully with the change.

Change comes in many forms. Transition involves a deliberate disturbance of the equilibrium and *status quo* and is a major event in the life of an organization and its employees. Most of the time, such events are drastic and intense, and the changes can be revolutionary and traumatic. Cultural change involves a disruptive break with the past and substantial changes in the way organizational members function.

Contemporary managers face extraordinary challenges.[5] As we have mentioned in previous chapters, today's dynamic, complex, and sometimes unpredictable environment demands that leaders and organizations take a proactive role in keeping up with and responding to change.

Change is a pervasive, persistent, and permanent condition. For many organizations, it is a huge threat and an opportunity for failure. Most change does not come in neatly defined segments; it seems constant and unrelenting. Often that makes change a bigger threat because there is no relief, no easy measure of success, and no sense of closure. Resisting change is natural, but in today's world, failing to change can be deadly. Businesses that do not change and develop disappear.

FOUNDATIONS OF ORGANIZATIONAL CULTURE

Culture guides the behavior of, and gives meaning to, organizational members. Therefore, it has a direct and powerful influence on what the organization does, and on what the people in the organization do. **Organizational culture** is the shared beliefs, values, and norms that bind people together and help them make sense of the systems within an organization. The beliefs, values, and norms tell people "what is to be done," and "how it is to be done." Cultures develop within organizations as their people interact and share ways of managing and coping.

Culture influences how people act in organizations—the ways in which people perform, view their jobs, work with colleagues, and look at the future.[6] In a new book, the son of Thomas Watson, the founder of IBM, says that a strong culture helped IBM rise to its tremendous success. That same belief is echoed today by the incoming CEO, Samuel Palmisano, who says that the success of IBM is a culture focused on the customer.[7] That is why an increasing number of organizations today are doing what Southwest Airlines has done all along: "Hire for attitude; train for skill." That is, hire people who fit into the culture of the organization and train them to acquire the necessary skills. (See the "At The Forefront" below.) It is easier to teach people skills than it is to change their attitudes.

LEARNING OBJECTIVE 1

Discuss the foundations of organizational culture.

Organizational culture
The shared beliefs, values, and norms in an organization.

At The Forefront

Hire for Attitude; Train for Skill

Many organizations are placing primary emphasis on people who fit their cultures when hiring. The reasoning is that if the people have the "right" attitude, they will automatically buy-in to the important things in the organization. The necessary skills can be taught. That is a lot easier than hiring people with the right skills but wrong attitude. A "wrong" attitude probably cannot be changed.

Bristol Technology says on its Web site, "Rather than simply list our open positions, we want to provide you with information on what it's like to work at Bristol" (http://www.Bristol.com/careers/index.html).

Then it says, "The attributes we think are most important are: Intelligence, A sense of urgency, Integrity."

Like Bristol, many other organizations have determined what it takes to succeed in their companies. Then they hire people with these characteristics. Enterprise Rent-A-Car uses a 15-item "enterprise quotient" (EQ) to judge a person's self-awareness, persistence, and empathy. One must thrive on creativity and teamwork in order to be successful at Southwest Airlines. In addition to working well on teams, one must have a high tolerance for ambiguity and change in order to succeed at Dell. Teamwork, loyalty, versatility, good interper-

sonal skills, and a positive work attitude will do it at Toyota in Kentucky. You must be flexible and a risk taker with a social conscience at Athene.

SOURCES: C. Daniels, "Does This Man Need a Shrink?" *Fortune,* February 25, 2001, 205–07; **http://www.Bristol.com,** Web site, March 24, 2002; J. Collins, "Turning Goals Into Results: The Power of Catalytic Mechanisms," *Harvard Business Review,* July/August, 1999, 77; J. Michlitsch, "High-Performing, Loyal Employees: The Real Way to Implement Strategy," *Strategy & Leadership,* November/December, 2000, 28–33; R. Schatz, "Showtime at Athene," *BusinessWeek,* March 5, 2001, E26.

Cultures develop from a variety of factors. When a new organization is formed, the culture reflects the drive and imagination of the founding individual or group. Amazon.com founder and CEO Jeff Bezos prefers customers to visualize the virtual company on the Internet rather than at a physical location. Although customers never see the person they communicate with, a sense of personalization has been built from a culture of trust and comfort within Amazon.com.[8] The culture at Walt Disney Corporation was influenced by its creative founder, Walt Disney, who created entertainment that was focused on family values and traditional beliefs. Southwest Airlines' culture is distinctly Herb Kelleher (see "Leaders In Action" in Chapter 1).

Cultures evolve and change in even the most stable periods. In times of trouble, they may change rapidly because whatever else the culture may value, it prizes survival most of all. Economic crises, changes in laws or regulations, social developments, global competition, demographic trends, explosive technological changes, and other events influence what an organization must do to survive, and its culture tends to evolve accordingly.[9]

Cultures also change when an organization discovers, invents, or develops solutions to problems it faces. Successful approaches to solving problems tend to become part of the culture and are used whenever the organization faces similar conditions. For example, as we mentioned earlier, the culture at Denny's Restaurants was discovered to be one that included racism. CEO Jim Adamson was facing critical issues that he realized needed to be resolved.

COMPONENTS OF AN ORGANIZATION'S CULTURE

LEARNING OBJECTIVE 2

List and explain the two components of organizational culture.

Culture has two components. The first is substance, which consists of shared systems of beliefs, values, expectations, and norms; the second is form, which consists of the observable ways that members of a culture express ideas. These components are shown in Figure 11.1. They are illustrated as an iceberg because the surface elements—the forms—are based on much deeper substance elements.[10] The visible elements are the routines (practices) that constitute the organization's culture. These are sustained by the shared values, beliefs, expectations, and norms that are at the deepest level or core of the organization. Managers must recognize that it may not be possible to change the surface without changing what lies below.[11]

EXAMINING CULTURE THROUGH ORGANIZATIONAL ARTIFACTS

LEARNING OBJECTIVE 3

Clarify the differences between the types of organizational artifacts.

The visible elements in Figure 11.1 consist of a number of artifacts. Artifacts are cultural routines, the rituals, and ceremonies, that we see in public functions and events staged by the organization. Artifacts support and reinforce the organization's shared beliefs, value systems, expectations, and norms. The artifacts level of cultural analysis is tricky, because it is easy to obtain but hard to interpret. While we can often describe the behavior patterns that are evident within organizations, it is hard to explain why these patterns exist.[12]

Rites, rituals, and ceremonies
Relatively dramatic events that have special meaning for organizational members.

RITES, RITUALS, AND CEREMONIES   Some of the most obvious displays of organizational culture are rites, rituals, and ceremonies. **Rites, rituals, and ceremonies** are a relatively dramatic, usually planned, set of recurring activities used at special times to influence the behavior and understanding of organizational members.[13] Evaluation and reward procedures, farewell parties, award banquets, and product promotions are examples. They are carried out through social interaction and usually occur for the benefit of an audience.

Figure 11.1 | Components of Organizational Culture

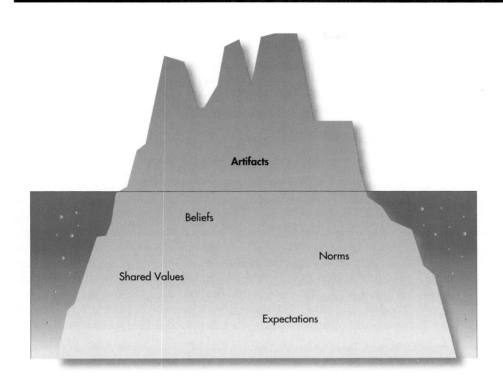

Artifacts

Beliefs

Norms

Shared Values

Expectations

Through rituals and ceremonies, participants gain an understanding of and cement beliefs that are important to the organization's culture. Mary Kay Cosmetics schedules regular ceremonies to spotlight positive work achievements and reinforce high performance expectations. At the company's annual meeting, an affair marked by lavish pomp and intense drama, top salespeople are recognized and rewarded for high sales, usually with pink Cadillacs. Top salespeople praise the opportunities provided to them by Mary Kay, the heroine of the company. Until her death recently, Mary Kay herself was always there. This meeting/party is a major event that gives all Mary Kay employees a sense of purpose—not merely to sell cosmetics, but to reach their full potential. Like Mary Kay, most organizations that make *Fortune* magazine's list of the "100 Best Companies to Work for in America," plus thousands of others, also have a common theme of celebrating success through rites, rituals, and ceremonies.[14]

LANGUAGE, METAPHORS, AND SYMBOLS **Language, metaphors, and symbols** are the ways that organizational members typically express themselves and communicate with each other. Language includes certain words, phrases, and speeches. Metaphors use familiar elements or objects to make behavior or other unfamiliar processes or actions comprehensible.[15] They include special terminology, abbreviations, jargon, slang, and gestures that can be unintelligible to outsiders but are used inside the organization to convey a sense of belonging or community. Symbols can be a picture, a shape, or a particular object.

For example, Levi Strauss management calls its open-door policy the "fifth freedom"; Ruby Tuesday's shareowners (employees) firmly state the company's goal

Companies often use recurring planned activities to influence the behavior and understanding of their organizational members.

© MICHAEL NEWMAN/PHOTO EDIT

Language, metaphors, and symbols
The way that organizational members typically express themselves and communicate with each other.

"to be our guests' first choice, a great place to work, and a great investment"; the people who make the coffee at Starbucks are "baristas;" all of the people at the Running Room are Team Members (see "Leaders In Action" in Chapter 10 on page 319); and Southwest Airlines' official "ticker" symbol, the official name that represents the company's stock in financial trades, is "LUV."

With the increasing use of electronic communication, a new set of words, metaphors, and symbols has arisen. Certain characters on the keyboard are used to denote a smiling face, a sad face, a question mark, for example. Acronyms are becoming ever more popular. For example "ttyl" means "Talk to you later," and rotfl is "Rolling on the floor laughing." If it is really funny, then it is ROTFL, all capitals! There are hundreds, perhaps thousands, more by now.

Stories and sagas

Narratives based on true events, frequently embellished.

STORIES AND SAGAS   As narratives based on true events, but frequently embellished with fictional additions, **stories and sagas** graphically and quickly communicate emotionally charged beliefs to organization members. They are apt to be entertaining and, as a consequence, are sometimes far-fetched. Organizations are rich with stories of winners, losers, successes, and failures. Although these stories have important meaning for all employees, they are especially helpful for new employees for whom the organization is like a foreign culture. These new members have to learn how to fit in and avoid major blunders. Therefore, these organizational stories tell them the real mission of the organization, how it operates, what behavior is acceptable, and how individuals can fit into the organization.[16] For example, the founding of Southwest Airlines is celebrated in the following story:

> Early in 1967, Roland King consulted Herbert Kelleher, a corporate attorney in San Antonio, about legal matters pertaining to the dissolution of a small commuter airline owned by King. King was anxious to start another airline, and he believed that the major cities in Texas needed better air service. When he proposed his idea to Kelleher, the latter responded impulsively, "Roland, you're crazy. Let's do it." They went to dinner together and sketched out on a table napkin a simple triangle of a three-legged air route between Houston, San Antonio, and Dallas that became the original routes of Southwest Airlines. The napkin is now preserved in a wooden plaque hanging in Kelleher's office.[17]

Stories also serve as symbols of the organization's entrepreneurial orientation and promote values that unify employees from diverse organizational units. In many organizations, the members have a collection of stories that they tell repeatedly. Often one of the most important stories concerns the founding of the organization. Such stories may convey the lessons to be learned from the heroic efforts of an entrepreneur whose vision may still guide the organization.

A story may become so embellished that it becomes a saga. Sagas are historical accounts describing the unique accomplishments of a group and its leaders or heroes. Many organizations, especially those with strong cultures, have a large number of sagas that tell about the exploits of the founder or other strong leaders. At Amazon.com, the premier e-commerce bookstore and retailer, sagas told by insiders feature the legendary creative accomplishments of the founder, Jeff Bezos, and the casual, friendly culture. One insider sums up Amazon.com as dynamic, hectic, casual, professional, and everything in between all at once.

THE IMPACT OF CULTURE ON THE ORGANIZATION

LEARNING OBJECTIVE 4

Explain the impact of culture on the organization.

In an organization with a strong culture, shared values and beliefs create a setting in which people are committed to one another and share an overriding sense of mission. This culture can be a source of competitive advantage.[18] Unique, shared

Leader of the "Best Corporate Culture"

The winner for best corporate culture... Rubin, Brown, Gornstein & Co., LLP, (RBG) the largest local accounting and consulting firm in St. Louis, Missouri. This honor was bestowed by the *St. Louis Business Journal* in its selection of the best places to work.

Leading the best corporate culture is James G. Castellano, the Managing Partner of RBG. Just how important is corporate culture? "It makes decision making easy." All team members at RBG are guided by the nine core values in making decisions. The nine core values, posted on a plaque in every room, are:

- Superior quality and service
- Devotion to the people of RBG (Treat each other with dignity and respect.)
- Teamwork (What is in the interest of the entire firm.)
- Objectivity and integrity
- Competence
- Devotion to community and profession
- Innovation and continuous improvement

- Vision (Long-run view.)
- Have fun

These core values "permeate the entire organization." They are seen in the leadership behavior of Castellano and the other managers at RBG, and they are explained and demonstrated to all new employees through extensive orientation and training. They are backed up in performance appraisals.

What if change is needed in the organization's culture or in some other aspect? If it is an incremental change, it can be guided by a knowledgeable leader/manager. If it is a fundamental change, it must be guided by "leaders at all levels." The leaders at all levels are developed at RBG by nurturing and mentoring them into being successful leaders. These leaders then understand and explain the reasons for change and get "buy-in" from all team members.

The timing is perfect for selecting RBG as the best corporate culture because Castellano is also the Chairman of the Board of the Ameri-

can Institute of Certified Public Accountants (AICPA), the main professional association for certified public accountants. As Chairman of AICPA, Castellano has a very important role in guiding the entire accounting profession in setting rules, norms, and values.

So what are the most fundamental, the most crucial things to having a successful career that contributes to a positive organizational culture? Castellano says there are three:

1) Integrity. "There is no excuse for not doing the right thing; there is no excuse for choosing to do the wrong thing."
2) Take control of your own life. Develop competence and do the important but not urgent things (Covey's 7 Habits of Highly Effective People).
3) Have fun! If you're not enjoying what you do, you should do something else.

SOURCES: James G. Castellano, *Interview*, April 26, 2002; **http://www.rgb.com**, Web site, April 25, 2002.

---

values can provide a strong corporate identity, enhance collective commitment, create a stable social system, and reduce the need for formal and bureaucratic controls. A company named Trilogy (http://www.Trilogy.com) believes so strongly in the importance of culture that it puts all new employees through a three-month boot camp, which is part of Trilogy University. The boot camp uses a method called action learning, where new employees work on real business problems under conditions with tight deadlines calling for intense teamwork. It serves as Trilogy's teaching, training, and orientation. While teaching the new employees about many parts of the company, it also teaches teamwork and the basic norms and culture. The intent of all of this is to prepare people to be ready for anything and to know the culture of Trilogy thoroughly. Many other organizations, including General Electric, Ford, Boeing, and General Motors also have forms of boot camps or their own universities to teach many aspects of the organization, including culture.[19] The basic issue is that culture must be aligned with the overall strategy and mission of the organization. If not, truly achieving the mission of the organization is much more difficult, perhaps impossible.

A strong culture can be a double-edged sword, however. A strong culture and value system can reinforce a singular view of the organization and its environment. If dramatic changes are needed, changing the organization may be very difficult. General Motors (GM), which has a strong culture, is experiencing enormous problems in adapting to a dynamic and highly competitive environment. GM's overall market share continues to decline. The Oldsmobile line of cars has been discontinued. It is questionable whether GM can save Cadillac! In the past, "It's the Cadillac of the industry" was applied to anything that was the best product, service, or practice in an industry. Now, Cadillac is struggling to survive. GM's future appears to be brighter recently. But it took a very courageous new CEO bringing in two high-ranking managers from outside of GM to start a major change in the overall culture of the company.[20] Similarly, Campbell's Soup Company seems to have a "culture overcome by inertia," probably at least partly due to its past success. An ex-manager even expressed concerns about whether employees were still breathing! A new CEO is trying to change all that.[21]

Many companies are striving to achieve high levels of performance coupled with high-quality customer service and satisfaction. To compete effectively, companies are increasingly hiring and retaining employees who fit the culture. (See "At The Forefront" on page 349.) Major investments in employee education and extensive training and development are important because they offer valuable benefits to both employer and worker. In addition, a culture of humane treatment and a strong bias against employee layoffs can have dramatic effects on the organization. The culture requiring over 50 hours of work per week was driving away good managers at Marriott, so it had to be changed.[22] Among *Fortune's* 100 Best Companies, more than one-third consider job security as a benefit. Three companies on the list of 100—Southwest Airlines, Harley-Davidson, and FedEx—have adopted official no-layoff policies.[23]

© PATAGONIK WORKS/GETTYIMAGES/PHOTODISC

Two important issues are embedded in an organization's culture—ethics and diversity of employees. The culture strongly influences behavior of employees related to these issues as well as another very important factor—leadership behavior from the managers. How does it all fit together? Managers must use good leadership practices to be sure to introduce, develop, reward, and cement ethical practices and positive ways of working with diversity in the organization culture. One of many examples of this is Carol Lavin Bernick, president of Alberto-Culver North America. Like the CEO of Denny's, she led a major culture change in her organization by implementing deliberate steps to focus upon and to change the culture and make it part of everyday life in the organization. She further insists that the leader has to be passionate about it and must celebrate "what you'd like to see happen again."[24]

Managers recognize that the world is changing at an unprecedented rate and everything is in constant flux, from the economy to markets. Just as cultures evolve, so do business organizations and their management styles. The workplace is beset by changes of all sorts from all sides. All the recent corporate strategies—pursuit of excellence, managing by walking around, reengineering, the learning organization, new organizational paradigms, flattened hierarchies—are indicators of the evolutionary process.[25] Many of these changes are especially evident when we consider the influence of information technology on organizational culture. For an organization to take advantage of the power of technology, it must work to adjust its culture to maximize the impact of technology.

As technology continues to change and evolve, so too must business organizations and their management styles.

ALIGNING CULTURE TO MAXIMIZE TECHNOLOGY

Organizations can benefit from the dramatic changes that are already occurring in technology. The heart of all these new technologies is the same: removing barriers of distance and time, lowering costs, and improving the overall ability of people to communicate their thoughts and needs. Information Age technology won't be effective if it is hobbled by Industrial Age organizational cultures. Technology will accentuate changes that are already under way, and it certainly allows the flattening of organizations. However, it doesn't do it by itself.

An organizational culture aligned to maximize technology will embrace continuous information flows and instantaneous communication within and among businesses. In turn, this pulls together organizational layers, effectively, if not literally, flattening organization charts.[26] Managers can provide data that employees need, and employees can quickly resolve concerns with management. The phenomenon of e-mail alone has changed many organizations; anyone can send e-mail to the CEO. If the culture supports responsiveness, the CEO has to be willing to read and respond to the messages.

People at the bottom of the traditional organization chart were often the ones in contact with customers or involved in the hands-on work of the factory. However, these were the individuals least likely to have any information to assist them in making decisions. Information technology changes that. For example, a FedEx employee who is able to access information on a customer's package can act on it immediately instead of waiting for information from a central office. Neither organizations nor individuals can afford to ignore these new possibilities and cultural influences while all around them both competitors and colleagues build new relationships based on technologies that will soon be as commonplace as the telephone.

Of course, everything has at least two sides. We can "overdo it" with information technology, just as we can overdo anything else. We must be careful not to bury people with e-mail messages, overload everyone with multiple paper copies, or use just e-mails when some things call for face-to-face discussions. Then there are the issues of employees using large amounts of time to do personal business on their computers, for example, sending e-mails and jokes to friends, purchasing various tickets online, or searching for a restaurant to have dinner. Finally, there is the issue of using computers at work to view pornographic sites or to receive unsolicited pornographic e-mails. All of these things need to be managed properly so that they don't interfere with the tremendous contribution that comes from information technology.

Organizational leaders have to work to create a culture of accepting change before technology will be embraced effectively. For an organization to be flexible and responsive to technological innovations, the hierarchical barriers must first be reduced. A better computer network won't buy instant collaboration if there is not a culture of sharing knowledge. Consequently, we now turn our attention to change.

CHANGING ORGANIZATIONAL CULTURE

Changing an organization's culture can be very complicated. Management expert Peter Drucker suggests that managers can modify the visible forms of culture, such as the organization's language, stories, rites, rituals, and sagas. They can change the lessons to be drawn from common stories and even encourage employees to see a different reality. Because of their positions, top-level managers can interpret situations in new ways and adjust the meanings attached to important organizational events. Modifying the culture in these ways takes time and enormous energy, but the long-run benefits can be positive.[27]

Managers who strive for high-quality products and services understand that they must involve the keepers and holders of the culture, build on what all organizational members share, and teach new members how to behave. Sometimes managers attempt to revitalize an organization by dictating minor changes rather than building on shared beliefs and values. While things may change a bit on the surface, a deeper look often finds whole departments and key people resisting

LEARNING OBJECTIVE **5**

Explain how organizational culture can be changed.

change.[28] To be successful, change must be consistent with important values in the culture and emerge from participants within the organization. Anita Roddick, founder and managing director of The Body Shop, has stressed that she wants the organization to preserve its sense of being different while changing to be current. Because success spurs change, a culture is often difficult to maintain. Roddick believes that The Body Shop will never be just like every other company.[29]

THE CHALLENGE OF ORGANIZATIONAL CHANGE

Change is essential to an organization's survival. Change leads to new ideas, technology, innovation, and improvement. Therefore, it is important that organizations recognize the need for change and learn to manage the process effectively.

Organizational change
Any alteration of activities in an organization.

Organizational change is any alteration of activities in an organization. Alterations can involve the structure of the organization; the transfer of work tasks; the introduction of new products, systems, or technologies; or behavior among members.

TARGETS FOR CHANGE

LEARNING OBJECTIVE 6

Identify and discuss the targets of planned change.

A variety of elements in an organization can be changed. Which elements are chosen is partly determined by the leaders' abilities to diagnose the organization's problems or opportunities accurately. There are four primary targets for change: individual, group, organizational, and environmental.

At an individual level, organizations can target several areas. These changes fall under the general category of human resource changes; they include changing the number and skills of the human resource component as well as improving levels of employee motivation and performance. A manager may ask questions such as the following: Who do we reward and how? On what basis will the reward be established—seniority, merit, innovation, bottom-line results, or other considerations?

Changes at the individual level may occur either as a result of new staffing strategies or because the company has embraced the strategic goal of recognizing and valuing diversity in the workforce. Individual targets are accomplished through employee training or development programs.[30] One of the first actions that Denny's took was to establish policies for different hiring and training procedures.

Managers may consider changing the nature of the relationships between managers and subordinates or the relationships within work groups. This might include change or redirection of management leadership styles, group composition, or decision-making procedures. For example, several months after Intel Corporation opened its DuPont, Washington, plant in 1996, the assembly teams proposed a change in production scheduling. Team leaders and the plant manager suggested compressed, alternating shifts so that all workers rotated and the distribution of work days would be more equitable.[31]

At the organizational level, managers can change (1) the basic goals and strategies of the organization; (2) the products, quality, or services offered; (3) the organizational structure; (4) the composition of work units; (5) organizational processes such as reward, communication, or information-processing systems; and (6) the culture. Consider whom the organization has to please. Is it customers, owners, shareholders, regulators, the media, or others? When? Bell Atlantic reduced service time for new connections from 15 days to a few hours. Nordstrom trains all employees to focus on service to the customer above all.[32]

An organization can also work to change sectors of its environment. As we discussed in earlier chapters, sectors in the external environment can be influenced and changed in a number of ways. For example, Weyerhaeuser modified its clear-cutting to meet community concerns before new forestry regulations were mandated.[33]

It is virtually impossible to change one aspect of an organization and not affect other aspects. Changes in products or services offered may require new technology, a new distribution system, new employee skills, or different relationships with consumers.

Adopting new technology, such as utilizing the Internet, has become the next "e-wave," and it has changed the way organizations and customers learn about each other and communicate. It will necessitate hiring different types of employees or revamping the corporate training system, as Sears and Whirlpool have done.[34] Once again, the interconnection of systems and subsystems makes the job of management extremely complex and challenging.

MANAGING ORGANIZATIONAL CHANGE

In recent years, a great deal of research and practical attention have focused on the necessity for change and the change process. If managers could design perfect organizations, and if the scientific, market, and technical environments were stable and predictable, there would be no pressure for change. But such is not the case. We live in the midst of constant change.

Not only is change a constant of the modern business environment, but it is becoming more complex, especially with continuing globalization. Organizations must manage change in order to be responsive to changing environments.[35] Managers must recognize that the forces of change are significant and pervasive. Learning to recognize and manage change is one of the most important skills a manager can develop. Change is natural, and managers must help their organizations work with it, not against it.

The following section examines the numerous issues involved with change. We examine the process as a sequence, although in reality it may not always occur in that way.

A FRAMEWORK FOR CHANGE

One useful tool for understanding change is called **force-field analysis**. That approach is a systematic examination of the pressures that are likely to support or resist a proposed change. It is a framework proposed by organizational researcher Kurt Lewin, whose approach recognizes that merely introducing a change does not guarantee that the change will be successful. Force-field analysis includes the unfreezing process, how change occurs, and the refreezing process of new behaviors.[36] Within the framework for bringing about change, or transformation, in the organization are five steps, as shown in Figure 11.2.

Force-field analysis
A systematic process for examining pressures that support or resist a proposed change.

STEPS FOR PLANNED CHANGE

The change process includes the following steps: (1) creating a vision, (2) communicating and sharing of information, (3) empowering others to act on the vision, (4) institutionalizing or refreezing the new approaches, and (5) evaluation.[37]

LEARNING OBJECTIVE 7

Describe the steps for planned change.

Figure 11.2 | Steps for Planned Change

CREATING A VISION   Establishing a vision or goal is the first step in the process. The vision clarifies and directs the change effort and the strategies for achievement. In setting the vision, a number of critical issues must be considered.

The vision often triggers the beginning of the **unfreezing** process when an initial awareness of the need for change and the forces supporting and resisting change are recognized. Most people and organizations prefer stability and the perpetuation of the *status quo*. In such a state, forces for change, recognized as **driving forces**, are equally offset by forces that want to maintain the status quo, referred to as **restraining forces**. These forces are illustrated in Figure 11.3.

Driving forces for change are either internal or external. While **external forces** are fundamentally beyond the control of management, internal forces generally are within management's control. Changes in one or more of the key environmental sectors discussed in Chapter 5 might be the external forces that provide the impetus for change in an organization. The environment includes many economic, technological, political, and social forces that can trigger the change process. For example, in the economic domain, changes in the inflation rate, interest rates, and the money supply can affect the ability of an organization's managers to get needed resources. New laws and regulations, trade tariffs, and court decisions emanating from the political domain can affect the way an organization conducts its business.[38]

A vision can also be initiated in response to **internal forces** at an organization.[39] For example, in a recent Work USA Survey, workers who were contacted complained that workplace changes had an adverse impact on their workload and morale (44 percent); their relationship with the organization, such as satisfaction or commitment (37 percent); and the quality of the organization's products and services (23 percent).[40] Managers must recognize that external and internal driving forces can be highly interrelated. Because organizations operate as open systems, external and internal driving forces will always be connected. For example, employees' attitudes toward work may change because of a new organizational policy or as a result of new legislation. Additionally, employees must cope with changes in their personal lives as well as changes in the organization.

Unfreezing
Developing an awareness of the need for change and the forces supporting and resisting change.

Driving forces
Things that push for change.

Restraining forces
The forces to keep the *status quo*.

External forces
Forces that are fundamentally beyond the control of management.

Internal forces
Forces that are generally within the control of management.

Figure 11.3 | Driving and Restraining Forces

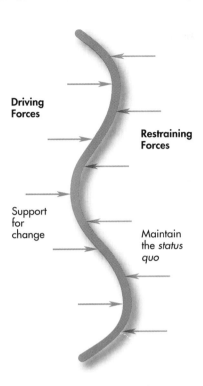

Regardless of the pressure these driving forces exert, the restraining forces are also important. People resist change for several reasons. First, they may genuinely believe that the change is not in their own best interests. They could be right, but often this belief is a result of fear of the unknown, habit, dependence, or the need for security. People may resist change because they lack the abilities or skills to cope with it. If proposed changes are going to require new skills, the organization must include skill training as part of the planned change effort.

Change can be threatening, and some individuals may assess the consequences of the change in a totally different way from those who are initiating the change. It may represent a loss and threaten vested interests such as power, responsibility, authority, control, or prestige.[41] For example, a major obstacle to the introduction of e-commerce for Sears was CEO Martinez's view that e-commerce was a domain of fanatics. Other Sears managers exhibited concerns and fears that they would become expendable. Nevertheless, the Sears.com division was created in late 1999 as a new direction for the company, and the profile of the employees hired constitutes a very diverse workforce.[42]

Finally, organizations have built-in resistance to change. Policies, rules, standard operating procedures, work methods, organization charts, and job descriptions are examples of organizational infrastructures that serve to maintain the *status quo.* An organization's traditions, culture, and top-level management philosophy also resist change because they are developed over a long period of

Communicating with and training employees will help to gain their support and reduce their resistance to change.

time and are not easily cast aside by organizational leaders. Changes that seem to violate the accepted culture will be more difficult to implement successfully than changes that seem to emerge naturally out of the culture.

LEARNING OBJECTIVE 8

Identify ways managers can address employee concerns in the change process.

COMMUNICATING AND SHARING INFORMATION   The second step in the change process is communication and information sharing. Communicating the new vision and the strategies that will be used is a valuable way to help organization members learn to embrace change. New behaviors are learned from verbal, written, and nonverbal messages. Therefore, it is important for everyone to see and hear these messages.[43] For example, if the organization is establishing a work team environment, upper-level managers must act as role models for the new behavior.

The sharing of information and the messages sent to organization members reduce resistance to change. Taking a proactive approach through open communication systems provides opportunities for a manager to listen to and gather feedback.

To gain the support of employees for the change efforts, management should consider their most commonly expressed concerns:[44]

1. *Information.* Employees want the change described with answers to questions such as "What's going to happen? What does the change look like? What does it feel like?"
2. *Personal involvement.* The change is already doomed if the questions "How will I fit in?" and "Will I survive the change?" can't be answered.
3. *Implementation.* If answers to the first two sets of questions are provided, employees will be ready to ask: "How do I get started on the change?"
4. *Impact.* Unless the first three concerns are resolved, employees won't want to hear about the possible benefits of the change. Expect questions such as "How will the change benefit us and the organization?" or "What will be different?"

LEARNING OBJECTIVE 9

Explain how empowering others to act on a vision affects the change process.

EMPOWERING OTHERS TO ACT ON THE VISION   Often considered one of the most important steps in the change process is empowering others to act on the vision. This step, the changing process, focuses on providing training and educational opportunities to help employees learn the new behaviors they need to implement the vision. Many changes that occur in an organization, such as new equipment, policies, or products, are relatively easy to implement in isolation. However, major difficulties can arise when dealing with human reactions to such organizational changes or attempting to change human actions and relationships directly. For example, an organizational change that involves individual employees directly or indirectly can require changes in roles, technical skills, interpersonal skills, or values and attitudes.

Groups must be encouraged to work as teams to solve problems and institutionalize ideas. Risk taking and nontraditional ideas, activities, and actions need to be encouraged and rewarded.

All of these things are components of individual and organizational development. Individual development includes anything that helps an individual learn how to adapt to the change. It includes many forms of training from the organization, training or classes at educational institutions, mentoring from supervisors, and one's own learning from observation. Organizational development refers to teaching people to interact successfully with others in the organization. It includes group and team training, setting goals that coordinate with departmental and organizational goals, and anything else that helps people in the organization contribute in such a way that the organization overall is more successful. The intent of all of this is to improve and develop the people and, thereby, the entire organization.

INSTITUTIONALIZING OR REFREEZING THE NEW APPROACHES

The fourth step is institutionalizing or **refreezing** the new approaches and behaviors. This step centers on reinforcing new behaviors, usually by positive results, feelings of accomplishment, or rewards from others. Once management has implemented changes in organizational goals, products, processes, structures, or people, it cannot sit back and simply expect the change to be maintained over time. Laws of physics dictate that an object moved away from equilibrium will tend to return to the original equilibrium point unless new forces are present to prevent this. Lewin reminds managers that new goals, structures, and behaviors must be solidified, or institutionalized, if that change is to become the new *status quo*.

Behaviors that are positively reinforced tend to be repeated; therefore, new behaviors must be rewarded. In planning for change, attention must be paid to how the new behaviors will be reinforced and rewarded. Reward systems should be considered carefully and redesigned when necessary. If the rewards or reinforcements inherent in the change fall short of employee expectations, the change will likely fail.

In addition, the new way of doing things must be embedded in the culture or in the "new culture," as the case may be. This includes rewards, as discussed previously. However, it also includes changing goals, policies, rules, performance appraisal, and perhaps mostly, the behavior of the manager. Here again, the manager has to be a good leader to establish the tone that sets or influences the culture.

EVALUATION

The fifth step in the change process is an important and often overlooked one—evaluation. Management needs to know whether the change has had the intended effects. Too many managers install changes, undertake training programs, and redesign structures with the mistaken belief that simply because the change was made, it will be successful. In many cases, this assumption proves incorrect. This is particularly true when the change was unilateral or was made without those affected perceiving the need for change. Sabotage of changes imposed by management has been known to occur in such situations.[45]

Evaluation is also beneficial because it forces the manager making the change to establish the criteria for judging its success before the change is instituted. Doing so provides additional guidance when planning the tactics for making the change. It also forces managers to give careful thought to how the results of the change will be measured.

IMPLICATIONS FOR LEADERS

This chapter has focused on the need for managers to understand the culture of their organizations and the role that culture plays in managing change. Culture includes the basic values, beliefs, and norms of the organization. The values, beliefs, and norms essentially dictate what the people in the organization do, how they do it, and what the results are. Therefore, the culture must be aligned with the overall strategy, or mission, of the organization or the mission will not be achieved.

Cultures change through evolution in light of changes in activities, in response to changing internal and external events, or through revolution as the organization deals with major challenges. Change is especially difficult in today's business

Refreezing
The act of applying the new approaches and behaviors.

environment of global competitiveness, diverse workforces, and technological innovations. It is part of the manager's job to help the organization and its members overcome resistance to change. Doing this requires an understanding of both the organization as it currently exists and its vision of what it wants to become. Research suggests a number of activities that will help managers achieve effective organizational culture and change.[46]

1. Solicit input from those who will be affected by organizational change. Involvement is essential to accepting the need for change.
2. Carefully formulate the message regarding the need for and nature of organizational change. The success of the change process will depend on effective communication.
3. Assess the organizational environment and be sure that the tone and the tempo of the change fit the organization. Timing is everything.
4. Serve as a role model, a leader, for the behaviors sought by the organizational change. Actions speak louder than words.

Now let's apply the Three Cs Model of Leadership to the challenges that a manager must deal with concerning culture, change, and development. As the activities listed above suggest, a manager must have the competencies needed in order to help the organization overcome resistance to change and to lead change in such a way as to develop a healthy and successful organization culture. The competencies that the manager needs to lead successful change and development can be enhanced greatly by a character that helps build trust between the manager and employees and between all employees. Finally, a manager's sense of community can help with change and with developing a positive culture because, if all members are treated as important members of the organization, there will be an atmosphere, a culture, that is much more conducive to changing and to developing the organization in a positive direction and in a positive manner.

Now Apply It

Needed: A Culture to Support the Mission

Many organizations have a very good mission and an appropriate overall strategy, including goals, to achieve that mission. They also believe they have the right culture to support activities and behaviors of employees necessary to achieve the mission. However, many times the real attitudes and behaviors of employees do not seem to be in line with achieving the mission, nor even the same as what the culture is believed to be. The real issue is that what the culture is believed to be and what it really is are two different things. Have you seen that in organizations with which you interact?

Select an organization with which you are quite familiar, perhaps one where you have been working for some time. Now try to assess what the "official" culture is—the norms, beliefs, values, and perhaps the activities and behaviors believed to be important. Talk to coworkers, including people working in other areas and levels in the organizations. Ask the CEO if you can. Ask all of these people to list the primary norms, values, beliefs, activities, and behaviors in the organization. Compare this to see whether or not these norms, values, beliefs, behaviors, and actions are supportive of the mission and main goals of the organization.

Now, ask the same people in the organization what they would like the main norms, values, beliefs, behaviors, and actions to be. Compare this list with the first one. Also, compare this new list to see if it would be more, or less, supportive of the mission and main goals of the organization.

Assuming that the preferred norms as well as the other items are supportive of the mission and different from the current norms, what would it take to change to the preferred norms, values, beliefs, and behaviors? Outline a plan to carry out this change. How long would it take?

Meeting The Challenge

Olive Garden: Changing for the Better

Olive Garden decided that the best way to create an authentic Italian dining experience for its guests was to give its staff some real Italian training. In 1999, the company opened a cooking institute about 20 miles outside of Sienna, Italy. The school has trained hundreds of chefs and wait staff in week-long seminars that include lessons on the finer points of winemaking, olive oil production, and the traditions of the Italian kitchen. In particular, students learn to match wine and foods and have an opportunity to dine at some of Tuscany's finest restaurants where they can experience the culture of real Italian dining.

Did the strategy work? The answer appears to be "yes." In June 2000, a new menu was introduced that included seven new dishes inspired by the Italian culinary school. The company's 10 biggest sales weeks followed later that year.

Olive Garden has also successfully added more expensive varieties of wine to its list, including a $110 Amarone. Check sizes and customer satisfaction tend to improve among diners who order wine, so wait staff is trained extensively to help customers pick the proper wine for their meal. It is hard to quantify whether Olive Garden's cooking school has really made the restaurants more au-

thentically Italian, but many indications are positive. Customer satisfaction, average check sizes, and Darden's (the parent of Olive Garden) stock price are all at record highs. Of course, a week in the Tuscan countryside also provides a huge morale boost for Olive Garden staff!

SOURCES: J. Cox, "Changes at Olive Garden Have Chain Living La Dolce Vita," *USA Today*, December 18, 2000; N. Kruse, "Focus on Flavor Packs Power Punch with Consumer Bunch," *Nation's Restaurant News*, January 7, 2002, 36, 1, 36–44; J. Ordonez, "Olive Garden Bets on Cachet of Cooking School in Italy," *Wall Street Journal*, October 19, 1999, A1.

SUMMARY

1. Organizational culture is defined as shared beliefs, values, and norms that bind people together and help them make sense of the systems within an organization. People in organizations develop cultures as they interact and share ways of managing and coping. Culture influences how people act in organizations. The ways in which people perform, view their jobs, work with colleagues, and look at the future are largely determined by cultural norms, values, and beliefs and develop from a variety of factors. When a new organization is formed, the culture reflects the drive and imagination of the founding individual or group, and it evolves and changes over time.

2. Culture has two components. The first is substance, which consists of shared systems of beliefs, expectations, values, and norms; the second is form, which consists of observable ways that members of a culture express ideas.

3. Artifacts are cultural routines that form the substance of public functions and events staged by the organization. Rites, rituals, and ceremonies are the most obvious displays of organizational culture. They are a relatively dramatic, planned set of recurring activities used at special times to influence the behavior and understanding of organizational members. Language, metaphors, and symbols are ways that organizational members typically express themselves and communicate with each other. They include special terminology, abbreviations, jargon, slang, and gestures that are almost unintelligible to outsiders, but are used inside the organization to convey a sense of belonging or community. Stories and sagas are narratives based on true events, but distorted to incorporate fictional embellishment. They

graphically and quickly communicate emotionally charged beliefs to newcomers and are likely to be entertaining and sometimes far-fetched.

4. The culture of an organization can have a significant impact. With a strong culture, shared values and beliefs create a setting in which people are committed to one another and share an overriding sense of mission. This culture can be a source of competitive advantage. However, a strong culture and value system can reinforce a singular view of the organization and its environment. Then, if dramatic changes are needed, it may be very difficult to change the organization.

5. Changing an organization's culture can be very difficult. Managers can modify the visible forms of culture such as the language, stories, rites, rituals, and sagas and the lessons to be drawn from common stories. Managers can interpret situations in new ways and adjust the meanings attached to important organizational events. They must involve the keepers and holders of the culture, build on what all organizational members share, and teach new members how to behave.

6. The targets of change include the individual, group, organizational, and environmental levels. At the individual level, the targets fall under the general category of human resource changes and include changing the number and skills of the human resource component as well as improving levels of employee motivation and performance. At the group level, the targets are the relationships between managers and subordinates or the relationships within work groups. This might include change or redirection of management leadership styles, group composition, or decision-making pro-

cedures. At the organizational level, managers can change (1) the basic goals and strategies of the organization; (2) the products, quality, or services offered; (3) the organizational structure; (4) the composition of work units; (5) organizational processes such as reward, communication, or information-processing systems; and (6) the culture. An organization can also work to change sectors of its environment such as its customers, owners, shareholders, regulators, media, or legal institutions.

7. The five steps for planned change include creating a vision, or the unfreezing process, where clarification and direction toward the change effort start and the strategies for achievement are created. Communication and information sharing involve helping organizational members understand and learn to embrace change. Empowering others to act on the vision includes training and development to implement the vision. Institutionalizing or refreezing the new behaviors includes reinforcing and rewarding the new behaviors. Evaluation establishes the criteria for success and monitors the changes.

8. To gain the support of employees for the change efforts, managers need to consider providing employees with information, involving them in the process of planning and implementation, and sharing the impact of the change.

9. Empowering others to act on the vision is often considered one of the most important steps in the change process. This is the process that focuses on learning new required behaviors. An organizational change that involves individuals directly or indirectly can require changes in roles, technical skills, interpersonal skills, or values and attitudes.

REVIEW QUESTIONS

1. *(Learning Objective 1)* How does an organization's culture evolve?

2. *(Learning Objective 2)* What are the two basic components of organizational culture?

3. *(Learning Objective 3)* Why are rites, rituals, and ceremonies important for organizational members?

4. *(Learning Objective 4)* How can culture influence an organization's competitive advantage?

5. *(Learning Objective 5)* Suggest ways managers can change organizational culture.

6. *(Learning Objective 6)* What are the reasons that organizational change is needed?

7. *(Learning Objective 6)* Identify and describe the targets of planned change.

8. *(Learning Objective 7)* Describe the five steps for planned change, and provide examples. What is the purpose in each step?

9. *(Learning Objective 8)* How can a manager gain the support of employees for a change effort?

10. *(Learning Objective 9)* What is the primary focus of the fourth step of planned change, empowering others to act on the vision?

DISCUSSION QUESTIONS

Improving Critical Thinking

1. Since managers cannot actually see an organizational culture, what aspects of the organization might allow them to make some guesses about the nature of the culture?

2. As a manager, with which of the steps of planned change would you most like to be involved?

3. Provide some examples of situations in which resistance to change ended in a positive alternative.

Enhancing Communication Skills

4. Suggest ways in which a manager can maintain a culture. To practice your oral communication skills, prepare a presentation using some examples from current successful organizations.

5. Why do people resist change? Write a brief paper that gives some examples of this concept.

Building Teamwork

6. Describe the major differences between cultures in
   a. a high school and a college or university.
   b. different college or university classes.
   c. different campus organizations.
   d. a government (public) organization and a private organization.

   In a small group, discuss each of these settings and report your findings to the class.

7. Working in a small group, think of a recent change that has taken place at your college or university. Analyze the driving and restraining forces. Write down the key issues that should be considered and report your findings to the class or instructor.

THINKING CRITICALLY: DEBATE THE ISSUE

Must the Major Parts of Culture Be Formally Written?

Form small teams as directed by your instructor. Half of the teams should prepare to argue that nonverbal aspects of an organization's culture and values are as important, or perhaps more so, than are the written or spoken aspects. The other half should take the perspective that nonverbal aspects are not important because they are not interpreted the same by everyone. Use current organization Web site examples to develop support for your team's arguments. Your instructor will select two teams to present their findings to the class in a debate format.

EXPERIENTIAL EXERCISE 11.1

Examining the Culture of an Organization

Select an organization with which you are familiar. It could be one where you are employed, or a campus organization such as a fraternity, sorority, or a service club. How would you describe the organization's culture to a friend or new employee? Try to be objective in your analysis and identify examples of the artifacts in use. Answer each of the following questions. After you have completed the questions, share the information about the culture of your organization with a small group or the class.

1. What are the main norms (that is, the dos and don'ts)?

2. What are the main ceremonies and rituals, and what purpose do they serve?

3. What dominates everyday conversations?

4. Observe the nonverbal artifacts: For example, what do the work spaces look like? How are employees dressed? Most important, what are they doing—standing around chatting or sitting alone in their offices?

5. What reward systems are in place? What messages do they send in terms of which activities or accomplishments are valued and which are not?

6. What are the dominant stories or sagas that people tell?

7. Think of two influential people in the organization. In what ways do they symbolize the character of the organization?

CAPTURING THE POWER OF INFORMATION TECHNOLOGY

Select several organizations and explore their Web sites. Try to look at the entire Web site for each organization.

- Identify what you believe are the main norms and values in terms of interacting with customers, employees, the community, and owners/stockholders.
- Identify evidence of ceremonies, rites, rituals, and stories.
- Is it obvious that the CEO, or a key manager, plays an important role (such as Herb Kelleher at Southwest Airlines or Howard Schultz at Starbucks)?

- Compare your analysis with that of a classmate.
- Compare your findings from one organization with that of another.
- Do you think that it is possible to get an accurate assessment of an organization's culture from its Web site?

ETHICS: TAKE A STAND

Some retail stores teach their salespeople to hand a product to a potential customer—to get the customer to hold the product. The reason to do this is that once the customer has the product in his or her hands, it increases the chance that the customer will buy it. Several reasons explain this. One is that the customer can feel the product. That might increase the desire to own it. Another is that by holding the product, it might suggest that the product is already owned by the customer. A related issue is that it may take more courage to hand the product back and say no than to say no while the product is still held by the salesperson or is still on the rack or shelf. Also, some retail stores teach the salesperson to refuse to take the product back by not putting out his or her hands to accept it or even to verbally refuse to take it back. This, or course, is intended to encourage or to put pressure on the customer to buy the product.

For Discussion

1. Is the practice described above ethical?

2. Discuss the longer-run effects on customers when businesses teach their salespeople to put pressure on customers to make a purchase.

3. What effects would these practices have on the salespeople? Do you think that the salespeople in these situations would believe that the culture of their company is positive? Would this affect the ethics of employees in their behavior when they interact with coworkers?

VIDEO CASE

Organizational Culture, Change, Development: Peter Pan Bus Lines

The travel industry was changed forever by the terrorist attacks on September 11, 2001. To stay in business, airlines, trains, and bus companies had to scramble to improve their security procedures. Peter Pan Bus Lines was one bus company that had to make major procedural and cultural changes.

Peter Pan Bus Lines operates 150 buses, employs over 850 individuals, and has approximately $60 million in annual gross sales. Its mission is to provide the best transportation service in the United States by adhering to the five cornerstones upon which Peter Pan was founded: safety, quality, dependability, satisfaction, and fairness. Although the necessary changes after the terrorist attacks were consistent with its mission, the bus industry had old-fashioned practices that had been effective for over 40 years. Change is difficult in all situations. However, drastic changes to the strong culture, family-run Peter Pan Bus Lines would prove to be extremely difficult.

For the company to survive, change had to occur quickly. Typically, consultants can help organizations identify needed changes and how to achieve them. This is expensive, and other U.S. bus companies could not help because they were inexperienced in the high levels of security necessary. One of Peter Pan's security directors realized it could adopt practices used by Irish bus companies who have faced terrorist threats for over 30 years. Through Web sites for Ulster Bus and Bus Erin, the security director was able to find appropriate guidelines Peter Pan could adopt at low or no cost. Nevertheless, the Irish bus companies could not guide the cultural shift at Peter Pan, since high-level security procedures had become part of their Irish business mentality. In addition to researching the best security practices, it tried to avoid ineffective but showy policies some U.S. bus companies had adopted. Peter Pan wanted to bring about substantive changes that would take it into the future.

Peter Pan's security directors analyzed their current procedures, solicited employee concerns, and determined how to change procedures. One challenge they faced was how to encourage customers to travel by bus, since people had stopped traveling after the terrorist attacks. Yet an even bigger challenge was how to change the cavalier attitude toward safety that had been a part of its culture. To bring about this change, employees attended security seminars and met with members of the safety department to discuss what changes were necessary and why. The security directors also reeducated their bus drivers on what should and should not be done if anyone threatens the safety of the passengers. In addition, employees and managers had to learn to overcome the tendency to profile passengers. Everyone at Peter Pan had to keep in mind that they are in the business of carrying passengers. If they decided who to allow and not allow on their buses by profiling, Peter Pan could go out of business.

The safety department also prepared and distributed to all employees a comprehensive security manual that addressed fundamental safety concepts, company safety policies, how to recognize warning signs, etc. Employees also know they are to call the safety department immediately if they have questions not addressed in the manual. Finally, they solicited and received the support of Peter Pan's top-level managers. Peter Pan's president informed employees that the new security procedures were part of their new corporate culture and people must adopt them to ensure their safety, their customers' safety, and the survival of the company.

In the beginning, employees resisted the changes mainly because the new procedures and culture were so different and extreme. Now, many Peter Pan employees believe the new safety-focused culture should have been in effect before the terrorist attacks.

The tragic events of September 11, 2001, affected local and global businesses in ways no one could have anticipated. Even a regional firm like Peter Pan Bus Lines had to respond quickly and decisively. The changes had to be soundly structured and well-planned yet quickly implemented. Moreover, every employee and manager had to adopt the new culture. The changes have been very difficult to accomplish in a culture unaccustomed to change. Through education, they are slowly but surely achieving the needed long-term changes.

For Discussion

1. Explain how Peter Pan Bus Lines changed its organizational culture.

2. Identify and discuss the targets of Peter Pan's planned change.

3. Describe the steps for planned change Peter Pan used. How might it have implemented steps not specifically discussed in the video case?

4. Explain how Peter Pan Bus Lines gained support of its employees in the change process. Why was this important?

http://www.peterpanbus.com

CASE

Is the Culture Right?

Snapple was a very successful new juice company in the early 1990s. It was so successful that other very large companies, including the Coca-Cola Company, wanted to buy it to add to their beverage line. The Quaker Oats Company won the bidding for Snapple and purchased it for $1.7 billion dollars in 1993.

Unfortunately, Quaker couldn't get Snapple to "work." Market share decreased, as did profits. In 1997, Quaker sold Snapple to Triarc Beverages for $300 million, $1.4 billion less than its purchase price! Snapple was no longer a valuable company.

Just three years after Triarc purchased Snapple, it has rebuilt Snapple to again be worth about $1.7 billion. What is the reason that Snapple was not successful when Quaker owned it? Quaker's culture was very different from that at Snapple.

For Discussion

1. Read the article cited below and check the Web sites of the companies mentioned above (http://www.quakeroats.com, http://www.snapple.com, http://www.triarc.com). Can you get an idea of the culture at Snapple, just from its Web site? Then discuss the importance of alignment of the mission and strategy of an organization with its culture.

2. Could Quaker Oats Company have managed Snapple without trying to change the culture inside of Snapple? What are the pros and cons of doing this?

3. How important is it for the culture of an organization to also be at least somewhat related to the main characteristics or wants of the customers of the company?

SOURCE: J. Deighton, "How Snapple Got Its Juice Back," *Harvard Business Review*, January 2002, 47–53.

PART 4

LEADERSHIP CHALLENGES IN THE 21ST CENTURY

CHAPTER 12

COMMUNICATING EFFECTIVELY WITHIN
DIVERSE ORGANIZATIONS

CHAPTER 13

LEADING IN A DYNAMIC ENVIRONMENT

CHAPTER 14

EXPLORING INDIVIDUAL DIFFERENCES AND
TEAM DYNAMICS

CHAPTER 15

MOTIVATING ORGANIZATIONAL MEMBERS

CHAP

COMMUNICATING EFFECTIVELY WITHIN DIVERSE ORGANIZATIONS

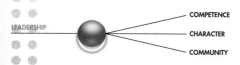

LEADERSHIP

COMPETENCE

CHARACTER

COMMUNITY

TER 12

CHAPTER OVERVIEW

The five most important skills recruiters look for when hiring college and university students include: Number 5, teamwork. Number 4, a tie between critical thinking and leadership. Number 3, interpersonal/social. Number 2, computer literacy. And the number 1 most important skill—communication, both oral and written![1] Of course, this should not be a surprise. Effective communication helps an organization increase profits by helping everyone inside understand the overall strategy and how to coordinate all the parts. It helps customers and other stakeholders understand how they can successfully interact with the organization.[2] The communication skills of the CEO are part of this. His or her communication skills are correlated with the image of the organization and with clarifying the strategy.[3] Frequently, the communication skills of the CEO help to build a more positive communication climate in the organization, which, in turn, is related to a stronger identification of employees with the organization.[4]

So, it is obvious that managers must understand the importance of building and sustaining human relationships through interpersonal communication.[5] Since managers spend the vast majority of their time in the disseminator role—informing, persuading, listening, and inspiring—communication skills are the manager's most important asset or biggest liability. Recent studies show that managers spend from 66 to 80 percent of their time communicating with supervisors, subordinates, peers, and outside constituents. If they do not understand the processes involved in good communication, their best-laid plans can fail. The challenge for effective communication is even greater for managers as organizations become more global, employees become more diverse, and technology becomes more complex.

This chapter focuses on understanding communication in organizations and the task of achieving excellence in interpersonal communication. We start by defining communication and the basic components of the communication process, such as the social context, sender and message encoding, receiver and message decoding, the message, the channel, feedback, and noise. Next, interpersonal communication is addressed, including oral, written, nonverbal, and technological communication. Then we turn our attention to some of the barriers that prevent high-quality communication. Concerns such as cultural factors, trust and credibility issues, information overload, perception, and language characteristics all have the potential to interfere and lead to misunderstandings. We move on to explore ways in which managers handle organizational communication, including formal and spontaneous communication channels. Finally, we conclude by focusing on ways managers can achieve communication competency by improving their feedback and listening skills.

LEARNING OBJECTIVES

When you have finished studying this chapter, you should be able to:

1. Explain the role of communication in the organization and why it is so complex for managers to understand.
2. Define communication and explain how to achieve high-quality communication.
3. Describe the components of the communication process.
4. Identify the primary categories of interpersonal communication.
5. Discuss the role of technological communication and information use in the workplace.
6. Address the primary reasons why managers communicate.
7. Explain the barriers that interfere with effective communication.
8. Discuss the types of formal communication channels.
9. Describe the principles for effective feedback.
10. Specify the guidelines for becoming a good listener.

Facing The Challenge

Communicating at Hanes: One Voice or Three?

Hanes is a big name in several categories of clothes—underwear, sportswear, and casual wear. Each of these areas had its own marketing team. As can be imagined, each marketing team worked independently of the others. While this can be a successful approach, if synergies can be gained by having the teams working in a coordinated manner, then this approach is not ideal because there probably is little or no communication between the teams. When groups do not interact, each will likely develop its own focus, language, and jargon and may see the other group(s) as something to avoid. Customers will probably never know that Hanes sells all three types of clothes. Retailers might not know this either, or they will get different and perhaps contradictory messages from the three marketing teams.

In working separately, some duplication will probably exist. Each team might be doing the same things but will have no opportunities to learn from each other and to cooperate to accomplish something even better. Related, some things could be done better if the teams worked together. For example, buying advertising time or space might result in a lower price for Hanes if the teams purchased in one lump sum, rather than in three separate teams.

Another possibility is that the teams might actually compete against each other in a negative way. Since each team was responsible for its financial results, one team could look better if another did not fare as well. By withholding information or assistance or even making some things more difficult, one team could be successful at the expense of another. In fact, this is fairly likely if the teams develop differing languages, jargon, and beliefs about what is most important.

Hanes decided that there was a better way. Synergies could be developed by coordinating the three clothing areas since many aspects of how the different types of clothes were made and marketed overlapped. Customers could relate better to one Hanes brand with wide variety than to three separate Hanes brands. Many times, customers who purchased one type of Hanes clothes didn't even know that the other existed. Retailers wanted to deal with only one Hanes representative rather than three. They were getting very different messages from the three representatives on what products were "hot" and how to best promote products and almost no information and help on marketing the Hanes products in a related way. Communication was breaking down between Hanes and the customers and between Hanes and the retailers, and essentially no communication existed between the three business units at Hanes. But, how do you get three Hanes marketing groups that are accustomed to working alone cooperating and working together?

SOURCE: L. Williams, "Slow and Easy Will Do Integrated Communication Best," *Communication World*, December 1997/January, 1998, 12.

INTRODUCTION

Excellence in communication can do more to advance an organization or a promising career than almost any other factor. Ask managers, lawyers, systems analysts, healthcare providers, CEOs, and businesspeople to name the most important aspect of their jobs. Is it the technical aspect, or is it interacting with people? Most will agree with what the recruiters said above—it is interacting with and communicating with people.

Every day, you will face communication challenges, such as getting and giving correct information, developing strong working relationships, attracting new customers, working in teams, solving disputes, building consensus, giving feedback, instructing others, and creating communication networks. All of this requires communicating effectively and understanding the complexity of communication.

COMMUNICATION COMPLEXITY

LEARNING OBJECTIVE 1

Explain the role of communication in the organization and why it is so complex for managers to understand.

Communication is the process that managers use to interact with subordinates, peers, supervisors, customers, suppliers, owners, the general public, and others. It is not surprising then that the ability to communicate well is a critical skill in determining managerial success.[6] This ability involves a broad array of activities, including reading, listening, managing and interpreting information, serving clients, writing, speech making, and the use of symbolic gestures.[7] All of these communication activities become more complicated with the integration of technology, increased diversity, and more globalization.

Whether it is a face-to-face meeting or an overseas transmission, communication is a complex process that requires constant attention so that intended messages—that is, intended meanings, understandings, and feelings—are sent and received. Inadequate communication is the source of conflict and misunderstanding. It interferes with productivity and profitability.

Communicating effectively is much more than just saying or writing the correct words. How we communicate is affected by frame of reference, emotional states, the situation, and preferred styles of communication. Consider for example, a time when you experienced frustration because you just couldn't get through to someone. It felt as if you were speaking an unknown language or were on a different wavelength. Communication is essential to management because it encompasses all aspects of an organization and pervades organizational activity; it is the process by which things get done in organizations. Yet communication is a complicated and dynamic process with many factors influencing its effectiveness.[8] First, communication is a process in which the senders, messages, channels, and receivers do not remain constant or static. Second, communication is complex. Even a simple two-person interaction involves multiple variables—such as the individuals, the setting, the experiences each person has had, and the nature of the task—that impact the efficiency and effectiveness of the process. Third, communication is symbolic. We use a variety of arbitrary words and signs to convey meaning to those with whom we are communicating. While there is some agreement about the meanings of most of our words and signs, meanings change over time.

The objective of communicating is to create some degree of accurate understanding among the participants. Clearly then, communication skills are essential for managerial success. This chapter explores the ways managers communicate, both formally and informally. Like the other aspects of the business environment we have examined, communication is affected by the changing environment. In particular, technology, global issues, and diversity in the workforce pose challenges to the way managers communicate, and we will look at these challenges in some detail. Throughout the chapter, emphasis will be placed on ways managers can develop communication competency.

DEFINING COMMUNICATION AND ACHIEVING QUALITY

A division head writes a memo and distributes it electronically. A flag flies at half-mast at the post office. A department chair praises the accomplishments of a faculty member. A pilot signals the ground crew that the flight is ready to depart. A professor writes a grade on a student's term paper. Employees in Seattle and Singapore attend a videoconference meeting. All these incidents involve some form of communication. But what exactly is meant by communication?

Communication is a complex and dynamic process, and like other management terms, it has no universally accepted definition. For our purposes, we will define **communication** as a process in which one person or group evokes an identical meaning in a second person or group. The meaning becomes shared by, or common, to both people or groups.[9] Indeed, the term *communication* stems from the Latin root word "communicare," which means, "to make common." Defining communication is relatively simple, but achieving high-quality communication is complicated and difficult. Successful and high-quality communication results when the receiver of the message understands the exact meaning the sender intended.

LEARNING OBJECTIVE 2

Define communication and explain how to achieve high-quality communication.

Communication

A process in which one person or group evokes an identical or common meaning in another person or group.

COMPONENTS OF THE COMMUNICATION PROCESS

LEARNING OBJECTIVE 3

Describe the components of the communication process.

To improve the quality of communication, managers must understand how the process of communication works. The communication process begins when an individual or group has an idea or concept and wishes to make that information known to someone else. Let's explore the components of the basic communication model in more detail.

The primary components of the communication process are shown in Figure 12.1. They include the sender, the channel, the message, the receiver, feedback, and noise. Since the communication process does not occur in a vacuum, the social context in which the communication takes place is an influential variable that we include in the discussion.

SOCIAL CONTEXT: GLOBAL, DIVERSITY, AND TECHNOLOGY IMPACT

Social context

The setting in which the communication takes place.

The **social context** is the setting in which the communication takes place. The setting has an impact on the other components of the communication process. For example, communication between a manager and a subordinate in the manager's office will be more formal and reserved than it would be if it occurred at the health club. Fewer distractions may occur under these circumstances. However, the subordinate may be less inclined to give the manager candid feedback. The social context is an important consideration in light of the global nature of business and the diversity of employees' and customers' cultural backgrounds. Conducting business in this arena presents many challenges to managers.

Figure 12.1 | Basic Components in the Communication Process

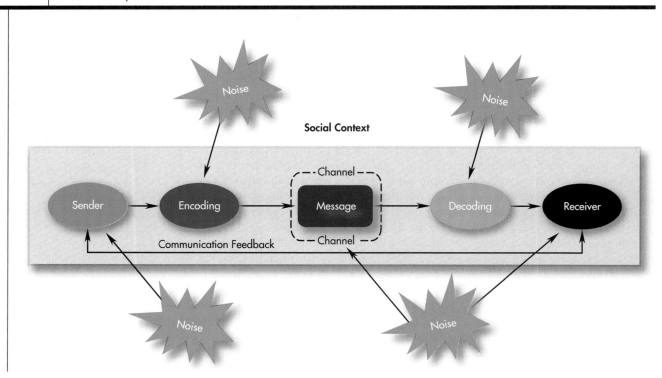

SENDER

The **sender** initiates the communication process by encoding his or her meaning and sending the message through a channel. The **encoding** process translates the sender's ideas into a systematic set of symbols or a language expressing the communicator's purpose. The function of encoding, then, is to provide a form in which ideas and purposes can be expressed as a message. Vocabulary, language, and knowledge play an important role in the sender's ability to encode. But our ability to encode ideas, thoughts, and feelings is far from perfect. A manager has to learn to encode meanings in a form that can be understood by a variety of recipients as well as other professionals in the same field. This, of course, is related to a basic rule for making a speech—analyze your audience. Knowing more about the receiver will help the sender select more effective language and symbols.

MESSAGE

The result of encoding is the **message**. Messages are the tangible forms of coded symbols that are intended to give a particular meaning to the information or data. They are the thoughts and feelings that the communicator is attempting to elicit in the receiver. Words and symbols have no meaning in and of themselves. Their meaning is created by the sender and the receiver and, to a certain extent, by the situation or context. Sometimes messages are conveyed in ways that can be interpreted very differently.[10]

CHANNEL

Once the encoding is accomplished and a message emerges, another issue arises. How can this information be transmitted to the receiver? The answer depends in part on how the message has been encoded. If the message is in the form of a written report, it can be transmitted by mail, messenger, fax machine, or increasingly, by electronic means. If it has been entered into computer storage, it can be sent directly to another computer over phone lines or satellite. If it is expressed orally, it can be presented directly in a face-to-face meeting or over the phone. The overriding consideration in choosing a channel is to ensure that the receiver can comprehend the message.

The **channel** is the carrier of the message or the means by which the message is sent. Organizations provide information to members through a variety of channels, including face-to-face communication, Web sites, telephone conversations, group meetings, fax messages, memos, policy statements, reward systems, behavior of the manager, bulletin boards, and electronic means. One critical impact is the improvement in technology that has made it possible to send and receive messages thousands of times faster than was possible a few years ago. Research has shown that the selection of the appropriate channel for the message and the receivers can have a major impact on communication effectiveness and even managerial performance.[11] Sometimes managers fail to understand or consider how the choice of a channel can affect a communication's impact. Jonathan Katz, CEO of Cinnabar Inc., a special-effects developer, is an example of how channels influence the effect of the message. As electronic communication became more widely available, Katz and client managers began to substitute electronic mail and heavy use of the company's Web site in place of face-to-face and direct meetings. When business dropped off as a result, Katz realized that there was not a good fit between the client, the channel, and the message. He was able to stop the decline and return to the personalized direct contacts that had been a mark of his business success.[12]

Sender
The person who initiates the communication process by encoding his or her meaning and sending the message through a channel.

Encoding
The process that translates the sender's ideas into a systematic set of symbols or a language expressing the communicator's purpose.

Message
The tangible forms of coded symbols that are intended to give a particular meaning to the information or data.

Channel
The carrier of the message or the means by which the message is sent.

Decoding
The translation of received messages into interpreted meanings.

Communication feedback
The process of verifying messages and the receiver's attempts to ensure that the message he or she decoded is what the sender really meant to convey.

Delivering a message orally to the receiver helps to ensure that the message is interpreted correctly.

Noise
Any interference with or distraction from the intended message.

LEARNING OBJECTIVE 4

Identify the primary categories of interpersonal communication.

Oral communication
All forms of spoken information—the type of communication preferred by most managers.

RECEIVER

The receiving person or group must make sense of the information received. **Decoding** involves the translation of received messages into interpreted meanings. Once again, our abilities to accomplish this task are limited. As the workforce becomes more diverse, managers are challenged to decode messages accurately. Since receivers interpret the message based upon previous experience, frames of reference, vocabulary, and culture, this process is not always successful.

FEEDBACK

In our model, **communication feedback** refers to the process of verifying messages and the receiver's attempts to ensure that the message that was decoded is what the sender really meant to convey. Feedback is a way to troubleshoot and avoid communication failure because it provides preliminary information to the sender. Through feedback, communication becomes a dynamic, two-way process. As a sender of information, it is a good idea to see if the receiver understood the meaning that you intended. It is easy to believe that you have conveyed information to someone without being aware that the receiver interpreted you differently than you intended. Unfortunately, if you don't check for shared meaning, you are likely to become aware of this problem after a major problem or issue arises because of the confusion.

Many organizations are beginning to realize the value of feedback from their employees and customers. For example, many give toll-free phone numbers as well as Web site addresses to solicit input. Offering these opportunities provides organizations with valuable feedback that they can use to improve products, strengthen the quality of customer service, and ensure employee involvement.

NOISE

Any internal or external interference with or distraction from the intended message is considered to be **noise**. Noise can cause distortion in the sending and receiving of messages due to physical conditions, as well as emotional states, that make communication more difficult. For example, a radio playing loud music while someone is trying to talk, a fading signal when using a mobile phone, the air conditioner running during a class lecture, and stressful working conditions are examples of noise. Noise can occur during any stage of the communication process, and it reduces the probability of achieving common meaning between sender and receiver. Messages that are encoded poorly (for example, are written in an unclear way), decoded improperly (for example, are not comprehended), or transmitted through inappropriate channels may result in reduced communication quality and effectiveness.

CATEGORIES OF INTERPERSONAL COMMUNICATION

Managers communicate in a variety of ways. We will examine oral, written, nonverbal, and technological communication in this section.

ORAL COMMUNICATION

Oral communication consists of all forms of spoken information and is the type of communication most managers preferred. Research indicates that managers prefer face-to-face and telephone communication to written communication because it permits immediate feedback. For example, individuals can comment or ask questions, and points can be clarified. Managers spend most of their time sharing information orally.[13] Just because it is used so much does not necessarily mean that it is used well. It takes practice and time to develop effective oral communication skills.

Every professional will eventually be called upon to use oral communication, such as in making a formal oral presentation to a large audience, small committee or team, client, customer, or national conference. As we discussed in Chapter 11, professionals are change agents. Changes have to be presented effectively and sold to achieve acceptance and implementation. As a manager, your oral communication skills are vital to your work and your career success.[14] Table 12.1 provides a checklist of key items to keep in mind when you are asked to make an oral presentation, whether to a small group or a large audience.[15]

WRITTEN COMMUNICATION

Written communication includes letters, memos, policy manuals, reports, forms, and other documents used to share information in an organization. Managers use written communication less often than oral communication, but there are many occasions when written documentation is important. Writing down a message and sending it as a letter or memo enables a precise statement to be made, provides a reference for later use, aids in systematic thinking, and provides an official document for the organization. Written messages can also be distributed to many members of the organization at the same time in the form of newsletters or memos.

Written communication
Letters, memos, policy manuals, reports, forms, and other written documents.

NONVERBAL COMMUNICATION

Nonverbal communication involves all messages that are nonlanguage responses. It can be anything that sends a message. Although managers recognize that com-

Nonverbal communication
All messages that are non-language responses.

Table 12.1 | Checklist for Planning More Effective Oral Presentations

1. *Establish your goals.* Have a clear image of your goals or purpose. Ask yourself, "What is it that I want to accomplish?"

2. *Analyze the audience.* Know your audience so you can effectively select the appropriate content, vocabulary, and visual aids. When the members of your audience are from diverse backgrounds or occupations, it is especially important to find a common bond.

3. *Diagnose the environmental conditions.* Be aware of how much time you will have, and use your time effectively. Determine in advance, if possible, the audience size, physical layout of the room and speaking area, and technical equipment.

4. *Organize your material.* Remember that your message can be followed easily if your material is organized. A logical flow of thoughts will help your listeners follow the message. Start with a brief introduction that provides a preview, follow with a body that develops, and finish with a conclusion that reviews.

5. *Design and use visual aids.* Keep in mind that visual aids not only help to clarify material and heighten its impact but also keep an audience alert. Keep the visual aids simple and use them to emphasize, clarify, or pull together important information. Remember, the purpose of visual aids is to support your presentation rather than be the presentation.

SOURCE: Adapted from *Management Skills: Practice and Experience* by P. Fandt. Copyright 1993. By permission of South-Western, a division of Thomson Learning Inc., Mason, Ohio 45040.

munication has a nonverbal component, they often underestimate its importance. Nonverbal communication may contain hidden messages and can influence the process and outcomes of face-to-face communication.[16] Even a person who is silent or inactive in the presence of others may be sending a message that may or may not be what is intended. Before continuing, go to the "Now Apply It" box and test your nonverbal communication skills. How well did you do? Are you comfortable interpreting cues that others send?

Consider how nonverbal communication affects the impressions we make on others.[17] For example, interviewers respond more favorably to job candidates whose nonverbal cues are positive (such as eye contact, appearance, and facial expressions) than to those displaying negative nonverbal cues (such as looking down and slouching).[18]

Individuals can communicate nonverbal messages by how neat they keep their desks and by the artwork and decorations they display in their offices.

© JAVIER PIERINI/GETTYIMAGES/PHOTODISC

The physical arrangement of space, such as that found in various office and work layouts, can also send nonverbal messages. For example, some visitors tend to be uncomfortable in offices where a desk is placed between them and the person to whom they are speaking. This desk might be seen as a separation or a wall that interferes with close communication. Others might see the desk as a symbol of power of the person whose office it is and may be influenced more positively or negatively by it. A desk or table between two people might also be seen as a setting for confrontational, rather than cooperative, communication. Still other things that communicate nonverbal messages about an individual are the artwork and decorations found in an office, as well as its orderliness and neatness.[19] For example, you probably have heard the old saying, "A clean desk is a sign of a sick mind." Hopefully this is said in fun. However, what is your view of someone who has a very clean desk? Do you see that person as having nothing important to do—so he or she has time to clean the desk—or do you see that person as very productive and efficient?

The following are six basic types of nonverbal communication:

1. *Kinesic behavior, or body motion:* gestures, facial expressions, eye behavior, touching, and any other movement of the body.
2. *Physical characteristics:* body shape, physique, posture, height, weight, hair, and skin color.
3. *Paralanguage:* voice quality, volume, speech rate, pitch, and laughing.
4. *Proxemics:* the way people use and perceive space, seating arrangements, and conversational distance.

Now Apply It

Test Your Awareness of Nonverbal Communication

How well can you interpret nonverbal cues in communication? Test your skills by answering "True" or "False" to the following:

1. Women are more sensitive than men to nonverbal cues—especially facial cues—and they transmit more accurate nonverbal cues to others.
2. When contradictory messages are sent through both verbal and nonverbal channels, most adults see the nonverbal message as more accurate.
3. People with low self-esteem use more eye contact when receiving negative messages than when receiving positive ones, while those with high self-esteem do just the opposite.
4. When people are conjuring up a lie, their pupils tend to become smaller. However, when they tell the lie, their pupils tend to dilate (enlarge).
5. The three nonverbal cues an interviewer remembers most about a job applicant are gestures, posture, and handshake.

Score your responses.
1. True, 2. True, 3. True, 4. True,
5. False [Interviewers remember eye contact, appearance, and facial expressions].

5. *Environment:* building and room design, furniture and interior decorating, light, noise, and cleanliness.

6. *Time:* being late or early, keeping others waiting, and other relationships between time and status.

Keep in mind that each of these categories of nonverbal communication becomes additionally complex when we consider diversity and multiple cultural issues in the workplace.

TECHNOLOGICAL COMMUNICATION

Faxes, e-mails, teleconferences, the World Wide Web, and other types of technological communication provide opportunities to communicate with virtually anyone, anywhere, any time of the day or night. **Technological communication** is a broad category of communication that is continuously changing and rapidly influencing how, when, and where managers communicate. For example, videotape recorders, telephone answering devices and services, mobile phones, closed-circuit television systems, fax machines, the Internet, computers, and electronic mail all provide communication flexibility and opportunities. Networked computers create an easy means to store and communicate vast amounts of information. Networking ties computers together, permitting individuals to share information, communicate, and access tremendous amounts of information.

Information technology has led many organizations to spin off their Internet operations into separate companies. Some examples are Bank One with Wingspan, Honeywell with myplant.com, and Sears with Sears.com.[20] It has enabled other organizations to streamline interactions with other businesses, usually almost totally computer-based, now called "business-to-business," or B2B, transactions. Of course, information technology has made it possible for organizations to communicate and interact with customers almost exclusively electronically. Consider Amazon.com and the many e-businesses. While there was a downturn in this type of business in 2001 (the so-called dot-com crash), e-business will continue and will probably grow, now that the managers of e-businesses have learned how to manage those businesses well.[21] **Telecommuting**, or now increasingly called "**telework**," refers to the practice of working at a remote site by using a computer linked to a central office or other employment location. It may also include those who work out of a customer's office or communicate with the office or plant via a laptop computer or mobile phone. The International Telework Association and Council (ITAC) says that 16.5 million people in the U.S. workforce are classified as teleworkers. That is, these people work at least eight hours in every two-week period, the official definition. The number is expected to reach 30 million by 2004.[22]

Teleworkers can essentially create a 24-hour, 7-days a week, or to use the popular phrase, a 24/7 organization. The electronic information and communication links between these workers and the organization creates a virtual organization that can reduce the need for a normal office or work space. The organization can either eliminate the work space or use "hoteling." Hoteling refers to workers who have no permanent space but can schedule the space as they need it. Assuming the wants of the customers are met, a teleworking organization could have employees anywhere in the world working whatever hours they choose. Not only could this be very flexible, it could also cut down on costs associated with a traditional office or work space. Research conducted by Kinetic Workplace, a consulting company working with telework, hoteling, and virtual officing, has found that facilities costs can be reduced by 40 to 60 percent, other costs per worker can be reduced on average $12,000, and absenteeism can be reduced by 25 percent.[23] Ernst & Young's approach is called "office hotel" and saves $40 million per year. Dun & Bradstreet saves $30 million per year with its "telecommuting-and-sharing" version.[24]

LEARNING OBJECTIVE **5**
Discuss the role of technological communication and information use in the workplace.

Technological communication
Any communication that uses an electronic device as the medium.

Telecommuting
The practice of working at a remote site by using a computer linked to a central office or other employment location.

Telework
Another word for telecommuting.

Many organizations on *Fortune's* annual list of the 100 Best Companies to Work For provide the flexibility of telecommuting or teleworking. Many creative freelance workers, contract and temporary workers, and small companies are using this form of communication technology, as are many well-known organizations, including IBM, Xerox, American Express, Du Pont, Apple Computer, and the Environmental Protection Agency.

Electronic mail (e-mail)

A message sent with an electronic device, usually a computer.

Electronic mail (e-mail), sending messages through computerized text-processing and communication networks, provides a fast, inexpensive, and efficient means of communication. Text-based messages can be sent and received by anyone who has access to a computer terminal and has a computer mailbox on the network. Messages can be transmitted almost instantaneously to and from employees in the same building or around the world.

The use of e-mail can enhance vertical and horizontal communication because it can lead to greater information exchanges as well as encourage individuals to learn to manage the information. On the negative side, it is very easy to overload everyone with e-mails that they do not need to do their jobs. In addition, the use of e-mails could result in loss of personal interactions that may be needed for better communication in some situations.[25]

Video conferencing

An umbrella term referring to technologies that use live video to unite widely dispersed company operations or people.

Video conferencing is an umbrella term referring to technologies that use live video to unite widely dispersed organizational operations. This technology offers tremendous savings of time, energy, and money. Business television networks enable organizations to communicate to thousands of employees simultaneously. For example, televised instructions can provide training as well as technical assistance for employees. Video conferencing enables organizations to hold interactive meetings in which groups communicate live with each other via camera and cable transmission of the picture and sound, even though they are hundreds or even thousands of miles apart.[26]

Internet

The vast interconnected electronic equipment that stores massive amounts of data that can be accessed with computers and related electronic equipment.

The meteoric growth of the **Internet** and sophisticated Web sites also impacts communication in organizations. Essentially everything can be done on the Internet. Organizations have Web sites to give information potentially to all of their stakeholders. Customers can get product and service information and can make purchases in many instances. Employees can get a variety of information. Job seekers can get information and can actually apply for a job with many companies. Stockholders can get information about the company, not only from its Web site, but also from many investment-related sites. By using a Web search, anyone can get information about almost any organization.

Organizations too can gather a variety of information with their Web sites or others'. Information about an applicant or a customer is recorded on the Web site. The number of "hits" on the site can be counted, in addition to other information about the person who accessed the site. Opinion surveys, comments, and feedback can be gathered anonymously. Perhaps the greatest impact of the new technology on communication lies in the amount of information it makes available.

While good communication is valuable and an essential part of the manager's job, he or she may drown in an overabundance of information. More information is not necessarily better information or even relevant information. It may encourage managers to make decisions too quickly. Rapid access to data can preclude thoughtful deliberation and make everyone a sender of messages worldwide at low cost. Managers often fail to build face-to-face relationships, so the personal touch in managing is lost. More, faster, and easier communication opens up the possibility for managers to waste a lot of time on "junk" communication.

Used correctly, technology can exert a positive influence on nearly every aspect of productivity and quality. It can be the lifeline of the increasing number of global economic networks and an essential tool for people who want to stay in touch with the rest of the world.[27] However, remember that although technology provides more choices, it does magnify the need to make careful, informed decisions about the appropriateness of the medium.

At The Forefront

To do, or not to do... instant messaging . . .

Instant messaging (IM), that feature in the software of your personal computer or some other electronic devices, lets you know immediately when someone is sending you a message. It's great because you can keep in constant, "real-time" contact and respond to the message immediately. However, is it great for organizations?

The case for IM: IM can keep people informed and coordinated constantly. It provides them the information needed to help them perform their jobs more effectively. IM can get information out immediately.

Essentially, IM could gain some of the benefits of oral, face-to-face, communication because it can enhance feedback. Consequently, communication could be better because the parties could get much closer to true understanding of each other. This would be an improvement over one-way written communication.

IM could improve communication in other ways. Normal e-mails and voice mails can stack-up and not be answered. Once a person gets time to read e-mails and listen to voice mails, so many messages may have accumulated that they are not really taken seriously. They may be erased without the person reading or listening to them. According to a recent study, over 60 percent of phone calls do not get to the intended recipient.

Now consider "remote" workers—those who are either teleworking or are in a location that does not offer contact with other people. IM can at least keep them in contact with other people.

The above things are probably why 42 percent of Internet users now use IM in their jobs.

The case against IM: As with regular e-mails and many phone calls, messages sent with the help of instant messaging may not be work related. In fact, many are personal. Given that, IM may distract the worker even more than regular e-mails and phone calls.

In addition, while improvements are no doubt coming, currently only a few IM programs can talk to one another. This is a problem of software compatibility.

These reasons probably explain why 70 percent of information technology (IT) departments in organizations do not support use of IM. However, with the proper technology and people learning to use IM for work-related communication rather than private, IM could improve communication overall because the "instant" part of it does allow for feedback. The feedback helps clarify messages. Therefore, the two parties come much closer to really understanding each other. And that is the goal of communication.

SOURCE: M. Schwartz, "The Instant Messaging Debate," *Computerworld*, January 7, 2002, 40–41.

WHY MANAGERS COMMUNICATE

Managers communicate for many reasons: to motivate, inform, control, and satisfy social needs. Motivational communication serves the function of influencing the behavior of organizational members. Communication that is intended to motivate must be designed to influence employees to work toward the accomplishment of organizational goals. Communication has an informational purpose when it provides facts and data to be used for decision making. In addition, managers give employees information they need to perform tasks, and employees inform managers of their progress toward meeting their objectives.

Communication also serves a control function. While control is discussed more thoroughly later in the text, it is through communication that work is coordinated and integrated, tasks and responsibilities are clarified, and records are kept to create order. Communication that controls serves the purpose of guiding and coordinating so that multiple goals and tasks can be pursued.

Finally, managers communicate to satisfy social needs. Communication fulfills social needs relating to the emotional and non-task-oriented interactions that occur in every organization. For example, employees need to talk about football games, the weather, politics, the boss's personality, and so forth. While this communication may not directly affect the performance of organizational tasks, it serves important needs and can influence how employees feel about their work conditions and how connected they are with others at work.

Recall that earlier in the chapter we said that successful and high-quality communication results when the message is received and conveys the exact meaning

LEARNING OBJECTIVE 6

Address the primary reasons why managers communicate.

the sender intended. You have probably experienced situations in which this did not happen and the message you sent was not what was intended. Why does this happen? The next section will discuss the main barriers that prevent high-quality communication and actions that managers must take to improve communication.

BARRIERS TO EFFECTIVE COMMUNICATION

LEARNING OBJECTIVE 7

Explain the barriers that interfere with effective communication.

Despite its apparent simplicity, the communication process rarely operates flawlessly. The information transmitted from one party to another may be distorted, and communication problems may result. Communication barriers interfere with organizational excellence. We turn now to common communication barriers that are summarized in Table 12.2.

CROSS-CULTURAL DIVERSITY

Communication, as an exchange of meaning, is bounded by culture.[28] Individuals from different cultures may encode and decode their messages differently; they have different behaviors, styles, and ways of looking at things. All of these can lead to barriers to effective communication. Difficulties may arise between people from different geographical or ethnic groups in the same country, as well as between people from different national cultures.[29]

Ethnocentrism

The tendency to consider one's own culture and its values as being superior to others.

A common problem in cross-cultural communication is **ethnocentrism**, or the tendency to consider one's own culture and its values as being superior to others. Very often such tendencies are accompanied by an unwillingness to try to understand alternative points of view and take seriously the values they represent. This attitude can be highly disadvantageous when trying to conduct business and maintain effective working relationships with people from different cultures.[30]

Studies show that the greater the differences between the sender's and receiver's cultures, the greater the chance for miscommunication.[31] A common criticism of some U.S. business managers is that, although they have the technology and know the business, they are not prepared to deal with cultural differences. Among the cultural elements that affect cross-cultural communication are level of formality, level of directness and explicitness, and perception of time.[32]

Table 12.2 | Sources of Communication Barriers

1. *Cross-cultural diversity.* Cultural differences may arise between people from different geographical or ethnic groups within one country as well as between people from different national cultures.

2. *Trust and credibility.* Without trust, the communicating parties concentrate their energies on defensive tactics, rather than on conveying and understanding meaning.

3. *Information overload.* Individuals can experience information overload when they are asked to handle too much information at one time.

4. *Language characteristics.* Many words or phrases are imprecise. Individuals often use different meanings or interpretations of the same word and do not realize it.

5. *Gender differences.* Since males and females are often treated differently from childhood, they tend to develop different perspectives, attitudes about life, and communication styles.

6. *Other factors.* Time pressures, physical distractions, differing perceptions, and noise can all interfere with good communication.

TRUST AND CREDIBILITY

A very important barrier to effective communication is a lack of trust between the sender and the receiver. This lack of trust can cause the receiver to look for hidden meanings in the sender's message, or it can cause the sender to try to manipulate the message. A trusting relationship is almost a prerequisite for good communication. In the absence of trust and honesty, the communicating parties divert their energies to defensive tactics, rather than trying to convey and understand meaning.[33]

A work environment characterized by trust does not just happen. It takes time and effort to develop. It must be nurtured and reinforced by honesty and accuracy in communication and mutual respect between communicating parties. Managers can develop trust in their working relationships with subordinates by being "trustworthy," as Steven Covey calls it. That is, managers and everyone can be trustworthy by making promises and keeping them—by doing what you say you are going to do and by not telling lies.[34]

Managers can also take advantage of opportunities for face-to-face communication. Management by wandering around (MBWA), first popularized at Hewlett-Packard (HP), is a phrase now popularly acclaimed as one way to do this. It simply means that managers get out of their offices and communicate regularly with employees as they do their jobs. Managers who spend time walking around can greatly reduce the perceived distance between themselves and their subordinates. They can also create an atmosphere of open and free-flowing communication, which makes more and better information available for decision making and makes decisions more relevant to the needs of lower-level personnel. It is no coincidence that trust continues to be an important factor in *Fortune* magazine's annual selection of "The 100 Best Companies to Work For in America."[35]

INFORMATION OVERLOAD

Although information is the lifeblood of the organization, it is possible for managers and organizations to have too much information. The increasing use of technology in organizations often leads to **information overload**, which occurs when the amount of information that one can process is exceeded. Perhaps it would be more appropriate to talk about "data" overload. Essentially, everything is just data, until and unless it has some meaning or is useful. People in organizations must find ways to manage the data so that they do not become overwhelmed. Instead, they need to know how to sort and analyze the data to turn it into useful information.

A somewhat different version of information overload is represented by too much of what might be called "bureaucratic red tape." Until recently, car designers at General Motors (GM) had to read 40 pages—just for rules on designing the crest for one brand of car! Can you imagine how many pages of rules there must have been for designing the entire car? While this probably is only a symptom of more basic problems, it certainly helps explain why GM fell behind competitors in designing cars that consumers wanted. Fortunately, the new high-ranking manager, Robert Lutz whom GM hired, is changing all of that. (You might recall Lutz and his association with a long line of popular Chrysler cars, including the PT Cruiser.)[36]

Information overload can be detrimental to performance, as seen with GM, unless managers develop systems for dealing with it and learn how to implement them. Knowing everything is not as important as knowing how to find the correct answers in a systematic way. Without a system, information overload can lead to:

- Failing to process or ignoring some of the information.
- Processing the information incorrectly.

Information overload
A state that occurs when the amount of information that a person can process is exceeded.

- Delaying the processing of information until the information overload abates.
- Searching for people to help process some of the information.
- Lowering the quality of information processing.
- Withdrawing from the information flow.

LANGUAGE CHARACTERISTICS

The very nature of our language constitutes a source of communication barriers. Many words are imprecise. For example, suppose a manager tells a subordinate to do this task "right away." Does the manager mean for the subordinate to drop what he or she is doing and work on the new task immediately or to finish what he or she is currently working on and then do the new task?

When two individuals are using different meanings or interpretations of the same word and do not realize it, a communication barrier exists. For example, some words sound the same but have multiple meanings. Write (communicate), rite (ceremony), right (not left), and right (privilege) all sound alike, right (correct)? Don't assume that the meaning you give a word will be the one the receiver uses in decoding the message. Language characteristics can lead to encoding and decoding errors and mixed messages that create semantic barriers to communication. For example, a word may be interpreted differently depending on the facial expressions, hand gestures, and voice inflection that accompany it.

The imprecision and multiple meanings of words are one reason why jargon develops. **Jargon** is terminology or language specific to a particular profession or group. One of the best-known uses of jargon is that used at Disney. There, customers are called "guests" and employees are called "cast members." If cast members do a job correctly, it is called a "good Mickey"; if they do a bad job, it is a "bad Mickey."[37]

With more and more organizations becoming involved in electronic commerce, *Fortune* magazine describes some of the Internet jargon created daily. For example, even the U.S. Postal Service is one of the 10 biggest businesses that have become successful e-players or e-tailers. Or, consider "clicks-and-mortar," meaning, an established retail organization with physical outlets that is developing sophisticated Web sites to sell products directly to the public.[38] Although jargon is designed to avoid communication breakdowns, in some cases, it may lead to inefficiency because not everyone will understand what is being communicated, especially new members of the organization or group.

Language characteristics, including imprecision and multiple meanings, are posing an even greater threat to communication as society becomes more interconnected and mobile. The probability of contact with someone from a different background or culture who uses words differently is increasing.

Jargon
Terminology or language specific to a particular profession or group.

GENDER DIFFERENCES

Gender differences can result in barriers and lead to distorted communication and misunderstandings between men and women. Because males and females are often treated differently from childhood, they tend to develop different perspectives, attitudes about life, and communication styles. Historically, stereotypical assumptions about the differing communication styles of males and females have stimulated discrimination against female managers. In recent years, however, more realistic images of how professional men and women behave and communicate have replaced the old stereotypes.[39]

Communication barriers can be explained in part by differences in conversation styles. Research shows that women and men listen differently. Women tend to speak and hear a language of connection and intimacy, while men tend to speak and hear a language of status and independence. Women are more likely to hear emotions and to communicate empathy.[40]

Women's oral communication also differs from men's in significant ways. Women are more likely to use qualifiers, phrases such as "I think" or "It seems to me." Generally, women tend to end statements with an upward inflection that makes statements sound like questions. Female voices are generally higher and softer than male voices. This makes it easy for men to overpower women's voices, and men commonly interrupt women or overlap their speech.

Although a wide range of gender differences can exist in verbal communication, nonverbal differences are even more striking. Men lean back and sit in an open-leg position that takes up considerable space, thereby communicating higher status and a greater sense of control over their environment.[41] Women use much more eye contact than men, yet avert their gaze more often, especially when communicating with a man or someone of higher status. Women smile more frequently and are generally better at conveying and interpreting emotions.

Both men and women can work to change the perception that women are less capable of being competent managers. Women need to monitor their verbal and nonverbal communication and choose behavior that projects professionalism and competence. Men should become more aware of their communication behavior and its impact on female colleagues and choose responses that will facilitate an open exchange of ideas.

OTHER FACTORS

Several other factors are considered barriers to effective communication. Time pressures may cause us to focus on information that helps us make decisions quickly, although the information may not be of high quality. Feedback may be impaired or absent. In one-way communication, such as a written memo, the sender does not receive any direct and immediate feedback from the receiver. Studies show that two-way communication is more accurate and effective than one-way communication, but it is also more costly and time consuming.

Several other factors are related to barriers discussed above. For example, there can be many physical distractions included in nonverbal communications. A manager might not seem open or approachable if he or she sits behind a desk. Someone might be distracted by sounds in the next room or by sounds made by someone "clicking" a pen.

Each person's perception influences what he or she hears and sees. This is closely related to differences in culture and gender discussed previously. Also look at the deeper discussion of perception in Chapter 14.

Of course, noise usually is a large barrier to communication. Noise can include a wide variety of things. It might be actual noise from the surroundings—for example, birds, others speaking, the phone ringing, the sound of equipment. Noise also includes psychological noise—that is, thinking about the death of a loved one, thinking about how hungry you are, or thinking about how silly or how good the speaker's hair looks, while someone is speaking could all be noise. All of these can be large barriers to good communication.

COMMUNICATION CHANNELS

The channel that carries information and the direction of the information can influence effectiveness. The next section focuses on these topics.

FORMAL COMMUNICATION CHANNELS

Formal communication follows the chain of command and is recognized as official. One way to view formal communication within organizations, as shown in

LEARNING OBJECTIVE 8

Discuss the types of formal communication channels.

Figure 12.2 | Formal Communication Flows

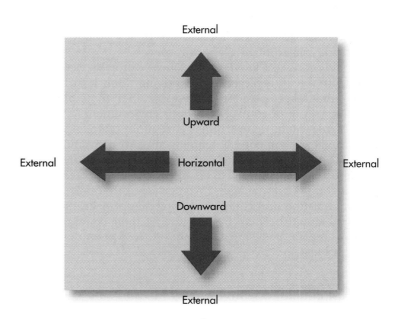

Vertical communication
The flow of information both up and down the chain of command.

Downward communication
Messages sent from individuals at higher levels of the organization to those at lower levels.

Managers sometimes forget that face-to-face communication is best because of its potential for immediate feedback and its encouragement of two-way conversations.

Figure 12.2, is to examine how it flows—vertically and horizontally. Specific types of communication are often associated with directional flow. Briefly examining each type of directional flow will help us appreciate the problems inherent in organizational communication and identify ways to overcome these problems.

VERTICAL COMMUNICATION   **Vertical communication** is the flow of information both up and down the chain of command. It involves an exchange of messages between two or more levels in the organization. When top-level managers make decisions, create strategic plans, convey directions, and so forth, they are often communicating downward. **Downward communication** flows from individuals in higher levels of the organization to those in lower levels. The most common forms of downward communication are meetings, official memos, policy statements, procedures, manuals, information needed to conduct work, and company publications. Information sent downward may include new company goals, job instructions, procedures, and feedback on performance. Studies show that only 20 percent of an intended message sent by top-level management is intact by the time it reaches the entry-level employee.[42] (See Figure 12.3.) This information loss occurs for several reasons. First, managers tend to rely too heavily on written channels; an avalanche of written material may cause the overloaded subordinate to ignore some messages. This is especially true with the glut of information stemming from electronic communications.

Second, the oral face-to-face message, which commands more attention and can provide immediate feedback, is often underutilized. Managers may e-mail the colleague or subordinate down the hall instead of walking over for a chat. They may e-mail a business client across town instead of picking up the phone. Experts agree that managers often forget that the best way to communicate—the richest channel—is face to face, with its potential for abundant feedback.

Figure 12.3 | Information Understanding and Loss

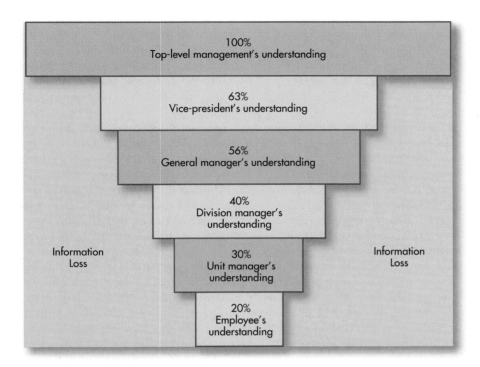

Upward communication consists of messages sent up the line from subordinates to managers. Openness to ideas and input from people in the lower levels of the organization are often the hallmark of a healthy and enjoyable organization. Effective organizations need upward communication as much as downward communication. People at all levels can and will have ideas for organizational improvement. Plus, managers need to have accurate feedback in order to properly guide the entire organization. Upward communication from subordinates to managers usually falls into one of the following categories:

Upward communication
Messages sent up the line from subordinates to supervisors.

- Personal reports of performance, problems, or concerns.
- Reports about others and their performance, problems, or concerns.
- Reactions to organizational policies and practices.
- Suggestions about what tasks need to be done and how they can be accomplished.

This type of communication is frequently sent up only one level in the organization to the person's immediate supervisor. The supervisor may send some of the information to the next higher level, but usually in a modified form. Upward communication is beneficial to both the manager and the subordinate. For the manager, it is often necessary for sound decision making. Upward communication helps managers know employees' accomplishments, problems, and attitudes and allows employees to make suggestions and feel that they are part of the decision-making process. In addition, it provides feedback, encourages ongoing two-way communication, and indicates the subordinates' receptiveness to messages. For the subordinate, upward communication may provide a release of tensions and a sense of personal worth that may lead to a feeling of commitment to the organization.

Jim Lyons, General Manager at Consolidated Diesel, created a two-way communication system for small groups to meet where he could provide and exchange information directly. Employees are kept current on company progress, and management gains valuable information by hearing from employees about their concerns. Lyons also assists upward communication by spending time on the shop floor, listening to employees and responding to questions and concerns through several formal channels.[43]

In addition to all of this, Robert Griggs, owner of Trinity Products, Inc. meets with employees each month and discusses the profit-and-loss statement. This is part of what he calls "open-book management." All information is available to employees, and they are taught to understand it. At the same time, employees can ask any questions.[44]

Achieving effective upward communication—getting open and honest messages from employees to management—is an especially difficult task. While suggestion boxes, employee surveys, and open-door policies are often used to encourage upward communication, upper-level managers are responsible for responding to messages from lower-level employees. If they do not take advantage of this information, the chance to tap into a critical resource is lost. Managers need to act on feedback from subordinates and get back to the individuals who sent it— if only to indicate that the suggestion cannot be carried out or that progress is being made about the problem or suggestion.[45]

The track record on effectively communicating upward is not especially positive. Even for managers, on average, less than 15 percent of their communications is to their supervisors. Also, when managers communicate upward, their conversations tend to be shorter than discussions with peers, and they often highlight their accomplishments and downplay their mistakes if the mistakes will be looked upon unfavorably. In addition, junior managers are not trained in, nor do they see good role models for, how to seek needed information and pass it upward.[46]

As we discussed previously, a trusting relationship is almost a prerequisite for effective communication. Trust cannot be mandated by policy or directives. It must be earned by the manager through credible behavior and communication. Communicating regularly, showing concern for others, and having a willingness to acknowledge mistakes help build trust with colleagues. Here is yet another place where managers can take a crucial leadership role in setting the example of positive behavior. If managers encourage all types of feedback from others in the organization and set good examples of how to do this, then effective upward communication can be developed. More will be said about this later when we discuss developing feedback skills and listening.

Horizontal communication
The flow of information that occurs both within and between departments.

HORIZONTAL COMMUNICATION   **Horizontal communication** is the flow of information that occurs both within and between departments. Effective organizations encourage horizontal communication because it increases coordination, collaboration, and cooperation. As you will recall from the discussion of the coordination function in Chapter 9 (see page 285) communication provides a means for members on the same level of an organization to share information without directly involving their supervisors. Examples include the communication that may occur between members of different departments of an organization and between coworkers in the same department. Self-managed teams create situations in which horizontal communication can flourish. In addition, more formal liaison roles may be created to support information flows. These are important to coordinate activities that support the organizational objectives.

Spontaneous channels of communication
Casual, opportunistic, and informal communication paths that arise from the social relationships that evolve in the organization.

SPONTANEOUS COMMUNICATION CHANNELS

The flows of communication described so far have been part of the formal system used to accomplish the work of the organization. In addition to these formal channels, organizations have spontaneous channels of communication. **Spontaneous**

channels of communication are casual, opportunistic, and informal communication paths arising from the social relationships that evolve in the organization. They are neither required nor controlled by management.

Several organizations have recently experimented with the notion of encouraging employee spontaneous communication to facilitate collaboration and integration of ideas. Among the companies that have found this successful are IDEO Product Development, the Xerox Palo Alto Research Center (PARC), Hewlett-Packard Laboratories, and Home Depot. According to David Kelley, president of IDEO, the spontaneous, "accidental" informal channels are the places where employees can separate themselves from the formal organization and really find out what people are thinking.[47]

A term often associated with spontaneous communication channels is the *grapevine*. The **grapevine** is an informal method of transmitting information, depicted as the wandering of messages throughout the organization. It typically involves small clusters of people who exchange information in all directions through unsanctioned organizational channels and networks. This communication vehicle is a useful and important source of information for managers and employees at all levels, and it should be used as much as the company newsletter or employee meetings.

The grapevine can be quite beneficial. Managers need to at least be aware of the grapevine, since it is probably one of the most prevalent and reliable forms of communication. In fact, one well-known study found that approximately 80 percent of the information transmitted through the grapevine was correct.[48] The remaining 20 percent, though, can often lead to serious trouble. As you probably know from your own experience, a story can be mainly true but still be quite misleading because essential facts are omitted or distorted.

Information in the spontaneous channels is usually unverified and often includes rumors that are exaggerated and frequently wrong. To help prevent incorrect rumors, managers must keep the information that flows through informal channels accurate and rumor-free. To do so, managers should share as much information as possible with employees, tell them of changes far in advance, and encourage employees to ask questions about rumors they hear.

To some extent, the spontaneous channels are always present in any organization and are more than just a means of conveying corporate gossip. The information may be less official, but it is no less important for understanding the organization.

Grapevine
An informal method of transmitting information depicted as the wandering of messages throughout the organization.

COMMUNICATION COMPETENCY CHALLENGES

A key ingredient to developing effective communications in any organization is each person's taking responsibility to assert when he or she doesn't understand a communication or to suggest when and how someone could communicate more effectively. Taking this type of action requires that organizational members develop communication competency. The final section of the chapter provides material about listening and feedback competency.

It is much easier to define what effective communication is than it is to achieve communication competence. Communication is both complicated and difficult, but there is overwhelming agreement that it is very important for personal and organizational success. Les Landes, a well-known consultant even calls it ". . . the central nervous system of your organization."[49] Managers agree that the ability to communicate effectively is crucial to enhancing career success.[50] More than ever before, your ability to communicate well affects your capability to thrive in today's organizations and professions. If you could strive for expertise in but one competence, communication would be the wise choice.

Even a fairly simple and straightforward exchange of factual information is subject to distortion and miscommunication. The three most important points to remember in meeting the challenge of communication competency are to (1) expect to be misunderstood by at least some listeners and readers, (2) expect to misunderstand others, and (3) strive to reduce the degree of such misunderstandings, but never expect total elimination of them or the ability to anticipate all possible outcomes. In this section, we will focus on ways to prevent misunderstandings and improve critical aspects of communication with feedback and listening.

DEVELOP FEEDBACK SKILLS

LEARNING OBJECTIVE 9

Describe the principles for effective feedback.

As we discussed earlier, communication feedback refers to the process of verifying messages from the sender. Through feedback, communication becomes a dynamic, two-way process, rather than just an event. Feedback can include very personal feelings or more abstract thoughts, such as reactions to others' ideas or proposals. The emotional impact of feedback varies according to how personally it is focused.

The first requirement of high-quality feedback is to recognize when it is truly intended to benefit the receiver and when it is purely an attempt to satisfy a personal need. A manager who berates an employee for a software error may actually be angry about personally failing to give clear instructions in the first place. The ability to take an active part in the feedback session can make a person more receptive to what he or she hears.[51]

In addition to giving feedback, being able to receive feedback is also important for effective communication. Learning cannot occur without feedback. Unfortunately, many people and organizations do little to encourage or cultivate useful feedback. Rather, people tend to protect themselves from getting their feelings hurt. Many tune out anything that might undermine their self-confidence. In doing so, they also forfeit an enormous opportunity for growth. You do not have to agree with all feedback. An attitude of feedback receptiveness is vital to the development of your communication skills.[52]

Follow these five principles for giving effective feedback:

1. Give feedback that is specific rather than general. Include clear and preferably recent examples. Saying "You are a poor listener," is not as useful as saying "I watched you interact with the customer, and I believe that you did not listen to what she was saying."
2. Give feedback when the receiver appears ready to accept it. When a person is angry, upset, or defensive, it is probably not the time to bring up new issues.
3. Focus feedback on behavior rather than the person, and focus it on behavior that can be changed.
4. Provide feedback using descriptive information about what the person said or did.
5. Avoid feedback using evaluative inferences about motives, intent, or feelings.

ADVANCED LISTENING SKILLS

LEARNING OBJECTIVE 10

Specify the guidelines for becoming a good listener.

Of the basic communication skills—reading, writing, speaking, and listening—only one is not taught formally in schools. Most of our learning is directed toward reading, speaking, and writing, with little attention given to training in listening.[53]

Since managers spend a large proportion of their time communicating, developing the skill of listening is a distinct asset. In his best-selling book, *The 7 Habits of Highly Effective People*, Stephen Covey suggests that the key to effective listening is to seek first to understand, then to be understood.[54] Communication breakdowns are the result of misleading assumptions, particularly when the listener is in the process of evaluating, approving, or disproving what another person is saying.[55]

How good a listener are you? Before you can begin to improve your listening skills, you need to understand the demands placed on your listening capacities. Most important, listening is an active behavior; it involves careful attention and response to messages. Instead of evaluating the message or preparing a response, an effective listener tries to understand both direct and subtle meanings contained in messages. In other words, be attentive to the feelings of the sender and what he or she is not saying as well as to the verbal content of the message. Observe people while they are speaking. Watch facial expressions, gestures, body movements, and eye contact.

Research indicates that listening skills are related to cultural norms. For example, Native Americans have a reputation for excellent listening skills; they do not feel compelled to fill up silence with idle chatter.[56]

The following guidelines will help you be an effective listener:[57]

- Listen for message content. Try to hear exactly what is being said in the message.
- Listen for feelings. Try to identify how the sender feels about the message content. Is it pleasing or displeasing to the sender?
- Respond to feelings. Let the sender know that you recognize his or her feelings, as well as the message content.
- Be sensitive to both the nonverbal and the verbal content of messages; identify mixed messages that need to be clarified.
- Reflect back to the sender, in your own words, what you think you are hearing. Paraphrase and restate the verbal and nonverbal messages as feedback to which the sender can respond with further information.
- Be attentive and listen to understand, not to reply. Most people are thinking about what they are going to say next or what is going on in the next office. Don't squirm or fidget while someone else is talking. Find a comfortable position and give 100 percent of your attention to the speaker.
- Be patient. Don't interrupt the speaker. Take time to digest what has been said before responding. Don't be afraid to ask questions to clarify and understand every word of what has been said. There is no shame in not knowing, only in not knowing and pretending to know.

Listening is an active process. Effective listening behaviors include maintaining eye contact, rephrasing what has been said, listening for the message beyond the obvious and overt meaning of the words that have been spoken, and observing nonverbal messages. The key to more effective listening is the willingness to listen and respond appropriately to the feelings being expressed, as well as to the content.

IMPLICATIONS FOR LEADERS

Organizational leaders are first and foremost in the communication business. As Mitch Meyers said in the "Leaders In Action" box, "Communication is the most important thing to be good at." This is clearly supported by research and beliefs of essentially all managers. That is, communication is a foundation for success of people in organizations and for success of the organization itself. Whether you are a financial planner, small-business owner, accountant, sales representative, minister, teacher, or any other type of professional, the following issues are key points to consider for managerial effectiveness:[58]

results when the message is received and conveys the exact meaning the sender intended.

chines, and telecommuting.

1. Select any two organizations that offer products or services for sale on their Web sites. It could be Amazon.com, a company that sells tickets for musical concerts, an airline, or similar organization. Go to the Web sites selected to examine and analyze the messages and the way information is presented. Did you encounter any barriers to communication? Compare and contrast the two organizations.

2. What types of information are provided about the companies? How friendly and easy to follow are the Web sites? What makes the sites easy or difficult to use?

3. Recall the topic of organizational culture in the previous chapter. Do you have a perception about what the main culture of the organization might be? Compare your conclusions for all of these questions to those of a classmate. Did you both arrive at the same conclusions? Were there big differences?

Leaders In Action

6. Technological communication is a broad category of communication that is continuously changing and rapidly influencing how, when, and where managers communicate. Examples include videotape recorders, telephone answering devices and services, closed-circuit television systems, fax machines, the Internet, computers, electronic mail, mobile phones, and networked computers.

7. Managers communicate to motivate, inform, control, and satisfy social needs. Motivational communication serves the function of influencing the behavior of organization mem-

language characteristics resulting from the impreciseness of words and meanings and the use of jargon; and gender differences.

9. The organization has two primary formal communication channels, vertical and horizontal. Vertical communication is the flow of information both upward and downward through the chain of command. Horizontal communication is the flow of information that occurs both within and between departments. The primary purpose of horizontal communication is coordination.

ETHICS: TAKE A STAND

It's Just a Small Lie

Scene One: Your job setting.

One of the people whom you supervise is Joe. He has just completed a task in which he has invested a large amount of energy and time. He is quite proud of what he has accomplished. Unfortunately, you don't quite agree. His work is "OK," but it could be better. Because he is so proud of what he has done, you know that if you tell him what you really think, his feelings will be hurt. On the other hand, if you don't say anything, he will sense that "something is wrong," or he might assume that your silence is approval of his work. That could cause a problem in guiding his future work. Do you tell him that you think is work could be improved?

Scene Two: Grandma's house.

Grandma has cooked dinner for you. It is a wonderful gesture and you appreciate it very much. It's not the easiest thing for her

to do since she has some ailments. In spite of that, sometimes what she cooks is quite good; sometimes, not. Tonight, it's "not," even though you know that she has spent at least two hours making this special dinner for you. After a short time, Grandma asks you how you like the food…

For Discussion

1. Is it acceptable to tell a small lie in order to avoid hurting someone's feelings?

2. Is it acceptable to tell Joe that his work is good? Is it acceptable to tell Grandma that you like the dinner?

3. Do the circumstances make it acceptable or not acceptable, depending upon what they are?

4. What might be the long-run ramifications of telling a small lie to someone, especially if the person knows that you are doing it?

VIDEO CASE

Communicating Effectively within Diverse Organizations: Le Meridien Hotels and Resorts Ltd.

Le Meridien is a hotel group with a portfolio of over 140 luxury and upscale hotels in 55 countries worldwide. The majority of its properties are located in the world's largest cities and resorts throughout Europe, the Americas, Asia Pacific, Africa, and the Middle East. Le Meridien also has a strategic alliance with JAL-owned Nikko Hotels providing loyal guests access to an additional 42 properties around the world. Le Meridien promises its customers a hotel experience, delivered through its four core values:

- Sophisticated, elegant European style with a French accent: "La Difference."
- High level of personal service, exciting cuisine, and an extensive range of facilities for business, conferences, meetings, banquets, and leisure.
- Respect for the local culture in which the hotel is located.
- Highly trained and motivated staff committed to providing excellent service and anticipating the needs of every guest.

In Boston, Le Meridien's resident manager, Bob van den Oord, believes that effective communication is critical to maintaining its reputation as one of Boston's premiere hotels. Bob has established many different communications channels such as daily operational meetings with all hotel managers, daily briefing sheets that list hotel activities, meetings with employees of each department, and meetings between departments. In addition, Bob and his hotel staff meet with Le Meridien's general manager each year. During these annual meetings, they discuss the year's results, plans for the next year, and do some team building with all hotel staff and employees. Even with all of this communication, Bob thinks his staff would consider lack of communication to be their one main concern. Perhaps this is due to the large number of departments in the hotel that rely on each other. If one department doesn't perform or communicate well, then everybody at the hotel struggles.

Though Bob also has an e-mail system, he prefers not to use it. He knows of managers who send e-mails when they have difficulty confronting certain issues. While e-mail may facilitate the communication process when it is the appropriate channel, it does not solve all problems. Rather than relying on e-mail to communicate to his people, Bob finds it more effective to go to the person with whom he has an issue. This way, they can discuss the problem and find a solution relatively quickly.

To better establish and facilitate communications, Bob also interacts with his employees through what he calls "management by walk-about" (also known as "MBWA" or management by walking around). Through MBWA, Bob believes that his employees are more willing to come to him when problems arise. He attributes some of his hotel's success to his being visible and talking to his employees during his daily walks around the hotel. During his daily tours around the hotel property, he also can monitor hotel operations and attend to any necessary details.

Of course, managers can walk around not doing anything in particular, yet their mere presence is important. Managers need to realize their staff rely on their guidance. They need to provide frequent and easy opportunity for each staff member to talk with them. In addition, Bob believes that his employees appreciate his walking around versus just his sitting in his office. In this way, he is out there on the floor helping the guests, interacting with the staff, and leading by example. Bob's philosophy is if they have happy staff, they'll have happy guests. If they have happy guests, they'll come back again and the hotel will meet its business objectives. Moreover, the owners of Le Meridien in Hong Kong will be happy the hotel is profitable.

Bob has found that it's important to remember communication is a two-way process. It's not just providing information—the other party has to listen. At Le Meridien, one of management's biggest obstacles is they give a lot of information to their employees, staff, and managers. For the information to be useful, it has to be passed on to the relevant parties and they have to understand what is communicated to act on it. Communication is absolutely key in the hotel industry. Everyone has to stay informed and keep each other informed for hotel operations to run smoothly.

For Discussion

1. Explain the role of communications at Le Meridien and why it is so complex to manage.

2. Discuss when technological communication (such as e-mail) may be appropriate and when it would not. How can managers improve the effectiveness of e-mail and other technological communications?

3. Illustrate the primary reasons why Le Meridien's resident manager (Bob van den Oord) communicates. How does Bob reduce barriers that could interfere with effective communication?

4. Discuss how Le Meridien's resident manager (Bob) communicates via formal and informal communication channels. Do these techniques appear effective? Explain.

http://www.lemeridien.com

CASE

A Performance Review

Jerry Mac was scheduled to receive his first performance review at 10:00 A.M. In his office, he prepared the packet of information required for the review session and left for the conference room with five minutes to spare. He was extremely nervous.

Jerry enjoyed working as an associate sports agent in such a prestigious firm. His company was representing five of the top NFL quarterbacks, numerous all-star baseball players, and almost 8 percent of the NBA players. Jerry expected his first review to be "above average" or possibly "excellent." Although he was still learning his job, Jerry felt positive about his work, the number of hours he put in weekly, client comments, and the fact that he was generating revenues by signing hockey players, an area that no one else in the firm had been able to accomplish. If all went well, he thought he could make partner in a few years.

Five minutes before the meeting was to begin, Jerry entered the conference room for his meeting with his immediate supervisor, Marge Scott. He made himself comfortable, selected the chair at the head of the table, and began to prepare. At 10:15, Jerry began to worry. He called the secretary to confirm his appointment with Marge, or Ms. Scott, as she preferred to be called. Ms. Scott was running a little late, again, and Jerry had no choice but to wait for her.

Meanwhile, Marge Scott had had a very hectic morning. She was behind schedule and had an important client coming in at 11:00 A.M., so she only had 15 minutes to spend on Jerry's review. As she approached the conference room, she recalled that she had rated Jerry's job performance as "average." Jerry had the least seniority of any employee in the company, and she wanted to leave room for improvement. He was consistently bringing in more clients and revenue than his peers, but telling Jerry he was average would get him to work even harder.

As Marge entered the conference room, she saw that Jerry had taken her chair at the head of the table. She decided to stand since this would not take long. "Jerry, in our firm 'performance reviews' means the systematic and regular evaluation of an individual's job performance and potential for development." Jerry nodded in agreement. From a large stack of papers, Marge handed Jerry his performance review and asked him to sign. Jerry replied, "If you don't mind, I would rather sign after I have read the review and we have discussed it."

"I really do not have a lot of time for this right now," said Marge. "You'll notice that your overall rating is 'average.' That is good for a new employee and that is how the numbers worked out." Jerry was shocked. "Average," he said. "How can you rate me that low? My work has been very good. I have worked long hours to make sure that I do a quality job, and you rate that average?" Raising her voice, Marge said defensively, "Are you questioning my evaluation of your work? You are not getting paid to be the judge here!"

Realizing that things were getting a little too heated, Jerry tried to explain, "I'm saying I don't understand your low rating of my job performance." Marge shuffled through her stack of files and pulled one out. She responded, "Well, for one thing, you haven't signed one basketball player for the upcoming draft." Surprised and a bit defensive, Jerry protested, "I did everything you asked me to do, Ms. Scott, and I did it well. I even asked you about several basketball players, but you told me to concentrate on my specialty, hockey. Please give me a valid reason for my low performance rating."

Marge decided to be more firm and said sternly, "I am your supervisor. You work for me, and I evaluate your progress. I complete the performance reviews for all of the new associates. Nobody else has complained. What is your problem, Jerry?"

Angry and frustrated, Jerry replied, "This is just not fair. I know my work is better than half of the others." Marge looked at her watch and asserted emphatically, "It isn't your job to rate the performance of your peers. That's my job. We don't seem to be getting anywhere. If you'll sign and date this to indicate that we have had the required performance review interview, we'll be through here. I have an important appointment at 11:00."

Jerry exclaimed, "I'm not signing anything." Marge gathered her papers and looked at her watch. "Well, it's plain to me that you resent being rated as average. You don't respect my judgment, and you won't follow my instructions. Time to get back to work." She left Jerry sitting in the conference room astonished.

For Discussion

1. Identify and explain the positive and the negative aspects of communication that are represented in the situation above.

2. What factors contributed to the escalation of this situation?

3. What should Marge have done differently? How about Jerry?

4. Based on what you have read above, what type of work environment does the company promote?

CHAP

LEADING IN A DYNAMIC ENVIRONMENT

Hauptversammlung
Annual Meeting
10. April 2002 • April 10, 2002

DAIMLERCHRYSLE

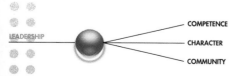

LEADERSHIP

COMPETENCE

CHARACTER

COMMUNITY

TER 13

CHAPTER OVERVIEW

Societies, the broad environments of organizations, keep changing. Of course, this means that the people in the societies and the organizations change as well. The workforce is increasingly diverse in nature, has less loyalty to its employer, and has been slashed because of downsizing or other attempts to cut costs. Often these attempts are misguided because they focus on the short run. Further, organizations are becoming more borderless because of the necessary interactions between organizations (suppliers with manufacturers with retailers) and the continuing globalization of essentially all industries. To manage this successfully requires leaders who are capable of motivating and bringing together people and organizations that comprise a different kind of workforce. Further, what is needed are people who can unite a workforce at a time when confidence in leaders and institutions is at an all-time low.[1]

Leaders face an abundance of challenging opportunities but have no clear blueprint for being a successful leader. The demand for good leaders has fascinated people throughout the ages. In fact, thousands of articles and books have been published on the subject, with many different approaches to looking at leadership. What is a leader? How do we judge a good leader? Are the methods we used to measure effectiveness a few years ago still appropriate in a changing world? Are leaders even necessary? These are the issues we examine in this chapter.

We begin by examining the significance of leadership. Next, we explore the three categories of leadership approaches: leader-centered, follower-centered, and interactive. The chapter continues with a discussion of women as leaders and concludes by examining leadership of the future.

LEARNING OBJECTIVES

When you have finished studying this chapter, you should be able to:

1. Define leadership and explain its significance to an organization.
2. Differentiate among the different leader-centered approaches to leadership.
3. Describe the various types of power leaders use.
4. Explain what is meant by self-leadership and why it is important to organizations.
5. Characterize how leadership substitutes work.
6. Identify and define the variables in the situational leadership model.
7. Clarify how empowerment can increase the power and autonomy of organizational members.
8. Explain transformational leadership.
9. Discuss the changing role of women as leaders.

Facing The Challenge

The Globetrotters Are Back!

In 1992, Mannie Jackson, a former basketball player with the Harlem Globetrotters, bought the team with the idea of disbanding the actual team and work on earning profits from licensing the name. Jackson would rely on his vast and in-depth business knowledge and connections that were built during his 25 years as a successful high-level manager at Honeywell.

The Harlem Globetrotters was a basketball team started in 1926 by Abe Saperstein who selected eight African-American players who excelled at basketball and at entertaining an audience with basketball showmanship/tricks and comedy. Because of segregation in those days, African-American athletes were not hired by professional basketball organizations. They had no place to make good use of their skills. Within a very short time, the Harlem Globetrotters were literally known around the world for entertaining very large audiences, for playing very good basketball, and for contributing to the community by helping young children, especially those disadvantaged, to gain self-esteem, skills, and opportunities to be successful. It was an enormously successful organization.

By the 1980s, African-American ball players were being hired by professional basketball teams, and entertainment choices were wider for people, especially in the United States. In addition, the Harlem Globetrotters was poorly managed.

Jackson had developed a business plan. He would disband the team and work on earning profits by licensing the Globetrotter name and symbols. All he had to do was to announce it to the players on the team. He called them together and began speaking. As he began, he looked at the players. Then he abandoned his prepared speech and told them that he was going to rebuild the team!

SOURCES: **http://www.harlemglobetrotters. com,** Web site, July 12, 2002; Mannie Jackson, "Bringing a Dying Brand Back to Life," *Harvard Business Review,* May 2001, 53–61; "Learning from a Globetrotter," *St. Louis Post-Dispatch,* July 13, 2002, L13.

INTRODUCTION

This chapter is devoted to exploring what leadership is and how managers can develop leadership skills. Our examination of leadership provides a knowledge foundation for developing leader effectiveness in a global and diverse organizational environment. Our emphasis is on leadership in formal organizations such as business corporations, government agencies, hospitals, and universities. We examine leadership principles that can be practiced and applied and conclude with some guiding principles to get you started toward leadership effectiveness.

Throughout the chapter, we focus on individuals who demonstrate successful leadership in various ways. We also offer opportunities for you to apply leadership ideas to practice and enhance your leadership competency.

LEADERSHIP SIGNIFICANCE

LEARNING OBJECTIVE 1

Define leadership and explain its significance to an organization.

Leadership

An influence process; normally to influence people to achieve a common goal.

We broadly define **leadership** as a social influence process. Leadership is not a position, title, or privilege; it is a responsibility and a process—an observable, understandable, learnable set of skills and practices available to everyone, anywhere in the organization.[2] Leadership is the indirect ability to influence people by setting an inspiring example—not just any sort of example, but one that inspires people to pursue goals that benefit the organization. It is indirect because true leaders don't have to try to influence intentionally. Typically, leadership involves creating a vision of the future, devising a strategy for achieving that vision, and communicating the vision so that everyone understands and believes in it. Leadership also entails providing an environment that will inspire and motivate people to overcome obstacles. In this way leadership brings about change.[3]

A debate in the popular management literature concerns whether leading and managing are different behaviors. One view is that managers carry out responsibilities, exercise authority, and worry about how to get things done, whereas leaders are concerned with understanding people's beliefs and gaining their commitment.

Figure 13.1 | Three Categories of Leader Approaches

Leader Centered
Trait focus
Behavior focus
Power focus

Follower Centered
Self-leadership
Leadership substitutes

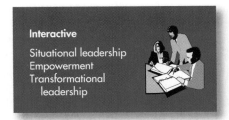

Interactive
Situational leadership
Empowerment
Transformational
  leadership

In other words, managers and leaders differ in what they attend to and in how they think, work, and interact. A related argument contends that leadership is about coping with change, whereas management is about coping with complexity.[4]

Although the leader-manager debate has generated tremendous controversy in the literature, little research exists to support the notion that certain people can be classified as leaders rather than managers, or that managers cannot adopt visionary behaviors when they are required for success. We maintain that it is important for all managers to think of themselves as leaders, and consequently, we use the term *leadership* to encompass both leadership and management functions.[5]

For the purposes of our discussion of leadership, we have grouped leadership approaches into the three categories shown in Figure 13.1: leader-centered approaches, follower-centered approaches, and interactive approaches. We will start with leader-centered approaches.

LEADER-CENTERED APPROACHES

Leader-centered approaches focus on traits, leader behaviors, and power. One of the earliest approaches to studying leadership was the trait focus.

TRAIT FOCUS

Underlying the **trait focus** is the assumption that some people are endowed with certain physical characteristics (such as height and appearance), aspects of personality (such as self-esteem, dominance, and emotional stability), and aptitudes (such as general intelligence, verbal fluency, and creativity). This research com-

LEARNING OBJECTIVE 2

Differentiate among the different leader-centered approaches to leadership.

Trait focus
The assumption that some people are born with certain physical characteristics, aspects of personality, and aptitudes that make them successful leaders.

pared successful and unsuccessful leaders to see how they differed in physical characteristics, personality, ability, and certain skills.[6] The common outcome was that successful leaders possess greater (1) drive, that is, achievement, sense of responsibility, ambition, energy, tenacity, and initiative, (2) motivation, especially power, (3) honesty and integrity, (4) self-confidence, that is, they are persuasive, diplomatic, and socially skilled, (5) conceptual ability, and (6) business knowledge. This does not mean, however, that just because a person has these characteristics that he or she will be a successful leader, or even be a leader.

The evidence just shows that leaders tend to differ from non-leaders with respect to the traits listed. Also, the evidence does not show that leaders are born. They are much more than a combination of traits. To succeed, leaders do not have to be intellectual geniuses or all-wise prophets, but they do have to have certain capabilities and the capacity to use their skills. For example, in Chapter 1, we identified three types of skills that are relevant to managerial effectiveness. Technical skills, including knowledge about methods, processes, procedures, and techniques, are learned through formal education in specialized subjects such as accounting and computer engineering. Interpersonal skills include knowledge about human behavior and group processes; the ability to understand the feelings, attitudes, and motives of others; and the ability to communicate clearly and persuasively. Skills such as analytical ability, logical thinking, and inductive and deductive reasoning are considered conceptual skills.

A certain set of traits and skills, however, does not guarantee successful leadership. Each situation may have particular requirements that make one trait or skill more important in one situation than in another. A different trait or skill, or set of them, may be more important in another situation.[7] For example, many people are influenced by the physical height of a person; normally the taller the person is, especially for a man, the more influential the person seems to be. A study of CEOs of *Fortune* 500 companies showed that over half were six feet or taller. Only three percent were shorter than five feet, seven inches. In the past 25 elections for President of the United States, the taller man won in 21 of them. Does that mean that short people are doomed? Robert Reich has been the Secretary of Labor in a previous presidential administration, has written eight books, is now Professor of Social and Economic Policy at Brandeis University, and is running to be the governor of Massachusetts. He is four feet, ten and a half inches tall![8] And, or course, there are many examples like him.

Possession of the qualities listed above does not guarantee that you will become a leader, nor does the absence of any one of them rule out the possibility of becoming an excellent leader. Since it takes more than certain traits to be successful, researchers began examining behavior of leaders as an influence on leadership.

BEHAVIOR FOCUS

A second major leader-centered approach is the **behavior focus**, which examines what effective leaders do rather than what effective leaders are. We will first examine two primary behaviors leaders use and then consider a leader's power.

Researchers examined two independent patterns of behaviors or styles that are used by effective leaders. The behavior focus assumed that what the leader does is the primary variable that determines effectiveness. Behavioral models defined a leader's effectiveness based on two orientations. The first is **task orientation**, such as setting performance goals, planning and scheduling the work, coordinating activities, giving directions, setting standards, providing resources, and supervising worker performance. The second is **relations orientation**, such as showing empathy for concerns and feelings, being supportive of needs, showing trust, demonstrating appreciation, establishing trusting relationships, and allowing subordinates to participate in decision making.

Behavior focus
The study of the behaviors that make leaders successful.

Task orientation
Leadership behavior that includes setting performance goals, planning and scheduling work, coordinating activities, giving directions, setting standards, providing resources, and supervising worker performance.

Relations orientation
A behavior that shows empathy for concerns and feelings, being supportive of needs, showing trust, demonstrating appreciation, establishing trusting relationships, and allowing subordinates to participate in decision making.

At The Forefront

Can Only CEOs Be Leaders?

Almost always when the topic is leadership, we visualize a person who holds a high-level position, for example, the CEO of a business, the president of the United States, the governor of your state, leaders in the U.S. Congress. Can't a mid-level manager, night shift supervisor at the convenience store, or you, as a member of a student group, be a leader?

A series of articles in *Harvard Business Review* from the fall of 2001 through the spring of 2002 focused upon the leadership of mid-level and lower-level managers. After all, these are the managers who interact with and guide the vast majority of employees in organizations either directly or indirectly. Most or all of these managers are truly engaging in leadership activities and behaviors. For most people in organizations, their direct supervisor frequently is the most influential leader. The focus of the recent articles is on recognizing that many managers at all levels of an organization are excellent leaders.

At a somewhat different but related level, there is the issue of ". . . Real Leaders Pump Gas." That is, in order to really get something accomplished, leaders must give something much more than lip service. They have to truly get engaged and lead. For example, John Stanton—the manager highlighted in the "Leaders In Action" box in Chapter 10, actually runs with employees and customers and sells shoes on the floor every Saturday. Kevin Jenkins, president of Canadian Airlines International Ltd., regularly speaks with pilots, mechanics, flight crews, and others. All kinds of stories are told about Herb Kelleher, now chairman of Southwest Airlines, bringing pizzas at 2 A.M. for the mechanics working on jet engines or getting into coveralls to help the janitors clean the building. Jim Ryan, president of Canadian Tire Corporation, actually pumps gas periodically at the company's gas stations. What is the link between this and the mid- and lower-level managers mentioned above? These

leaders are "engaged" in their organizations. They interact with the employees and influence the employees by their interactions. Many opportunities exist for mid- and lower-level managers to do the same and exercise their leadership.

What is the moral to the story? Many very good leaders are at all levels in organizations. Sometimes we forget about trying to understand and develop leadership skills among many people in organizations because we are overly focused on the top-level managers. We are looking for the superstar CEO or public leader and assume that only they are true leaders. Why not focus on yourself and see where, when, and how you can develop your leadership skills and use them in a successful way?

SOURCES: J. Clemmer, "Why Real Leaders Pump Gas," *Canadian Manager*, Summer 2001, 25–26; "Enter the Everyday Leader—At Last," *Harvard Business Review*, March 2002, 80, 60–61.

Take, for example, Jack Welch, the retired CEO of General Electric. He is still hailed today as one of America's most successful CEOs. In his earlier years, he was nicknamed "Neutron Jack," and in 1984, he was labeled as "the undisputed premier" among America's toughest bosses. He demonstrated all the task-oriented behaviors—demanding high performance standards, establishing rigid rules and procedures, autocratic decision making, and high levels of control and use of power. He is not particularly known for his use of relations-oriented behaviors.[9] However, one relations-oriented behavior does stand out. When he wanted to recognize someone for good performance, he would send the person a hand-written thank-you note. Can you imagine how valuable a hand-written note from Jack Welch would be?[10]

Numerous studies have examined task and relations behaviors, often with differing terms attached to the concepts of task orientation and relations orientation.[11] The general consensus is that one behavior does not occur at the expense of others. Taken together, we can conclude from the research on behaviors that (1) effective leaders use a range of behaviors, (2) these behaviors can be learned, and (3) an important characteristic of effective leaders is their ability to change and adapt to the organizational settings in which they manage.[12] However, it is still not obvious which behaviors are most effective because numerous other factors can influence performance and success. One of the most important results of the behavioral focus studies was that they directed our attention to the value of leadership training.

We tend to associate leaders with power. In fact, power is central to successful leadership. In the next section, we examine the power focus and how a leader can use power.

POWER FOCUS

LEARNING OBJECTIVE 3

Describe the various types of power leaders use.

Power
The ability to get something accomplished.

Power is defined as the ability to use human, informational, or material resources to get something done. Let's distinguish power from authority. Authority is the right to get something done and is officially sanctioned; power is the ability to get results.

Power is important for leaders not only for influencing subordinates, but also for influencing peers, supervisors, and people outside the organization, such as clients and suppliers. To understand the power process better, we will look at the various types of power. In addition, we will consider whether the power is prescribed by the leader's position or is a result of personal attributes and to what degree the leader has a need for power.

Position power
The power attributed to one's position in an organization.

POSITION POWER   Power is derived, in part, from the opportunities inherent in a position in an organization. **Position power** includes legitimate power, coercive power, reward power, and information power.

Legitimate power
The power based on one's formal position.

Legitimate power stems from formal authority.[13] This authority is based on perceptions about the obligations and responsibilities associated with particular positions in an organization or social system. For example, Carly Fiorina has legitimate power as CEO of Hewlett-Packard simply because of the formal position she holds and because others believe she has the legitimate right to influence them. Other people accept this power, as long as it is not abused, because they attribute legitimacy to the formal position and to the person who holds that position.

Coercive power
The power to discipline, punish, or withhold rewards.

Coercive power is the power to discipline, punish, and withhold rewards. Coercive power is important largely as a potential, rather than an actual, type of influence. For example, the threat of being disciplined for not arriving at work on time is effective in influencing many employees to be punctual. Similarly, the possibility that we might get a speeding ticket is enough to cause many of us to drive within acceptable speed limits.

Reward power
Power based on control of resources and rewards.

Another source of power that stems from a leader's position in the organization is influence over resources and rewards. **Reward power** is derived from control over tangible benefits such as a promotion, a better job, a better work schedule, a larger operating budget, an increased expense account, and formal recognition of accomplishments. Reward power is also derived from status symbols, such as a larger office, an invitation to sit at the head table for visibility, or a reserved parking space. In addition to tangible benefits, leaders can also use rewards such the ones Carly Fiorina uses to influence behavior. She is known as being courteous and considerate; she learns and uses employees' names and strives to be in touch with them; she knows how to use "thank you." All of these are simple yet powerful tools.[14]

Information power
Power based on control of information.

Information power is control over information. It involves the leader's power to access and distribute information that is either desired by, or vital to, others. Managerial positions often provide opportunities to obtain information that is not directly available to subordinates or peers. However, some people acquire information power through their unique skill of being able to know all the latest news that others want and often need to know.

Consider, for example, renowned explorer Robert Swan, who was the first person to lead a team to both the North and South Poles. His belief about information was crucial in those endeavors. Swan believes that leaders are responsible for seeing that all team members have all the information needed to make wise decisions. He reasons, for example, that if only one person knows how to navigate, and he or she gets sick, the whole team is going to get lost.[15] After his successful exploration trips, he has taught businesspeople about leadership and sharing information as widely as possible at such companies as Merrill Lynch, Frito-Lay, and IBM. With access to information only a keystroke away, power has shifted from those with titles to those with technology and the skills to use it. Considering the vast changes in the use of information technology in most organizations, you can see how information power has become a centralized focal point.[16]

Consider a very practical aspect of information power. In the past, when buying a car, the customer usually knew little about how much the dealer really paid for the car and how much markup there was. Now with information readily available on many Web sites, a customer can know almost exactly all the costs and markups associated with a certain car. That frequently puts the buyer in a better position to bargain when buying the car. That, of course, assumes that the buyer wants to use the power and otherwise is skilled in negotiating.

Explorer Robert Swan believes that leaders are responsible for providing all team members with the information to make wise decisions.

PERSONAL POWER   Leaders cannot rely solely on power that is derived from their position in the organization. Other sources of power must be cultivated. **Personal power** is derived from the interpersonal relationship between leaders and followers. It includes both expert and referent power.

A major source of personal power in organizations stems from expertise in solving problems and performing important tasks. **Expert power** is the power to influence another person because of expert knowledge and competence. Computer specialists often have substantial expert power in organizations because they have technical knowledge that others need. As we mentioned previously, not only is information technology influential in organizations, but the computer systems and the individuals with the knowledge to operate them provide expertise to everyone in the organization. A technician who knows how to operate and repair the office computer equipment may lack position power within the organization, but has expert power.

Referent power is the ability to influence others based on personal liking, charisma, and reputation. It is manifested through imitation or emulation. Numerous reasons explain why we might attribute referent power to others. We may like their personalities, admire their accomplishments, believe in their causes, or see them as role models. Much of the power wielded by strong political leaders and professional athletes, musicians, and artists is referent power. People who feel a deep friendship or loyalty toward someone usually are willing to do special favors for that person. Mentors are usually individuals that are selected because of their referent power.

Generally people tend to imitate the behavior of someone whom they greatly admire, and they tend to develop attitudes similar to those expressed by a person with whom they identify. Britney Spears, Venus and Serina Williams, and Tiger Woods are just a few of the many individuals who influence behavior with their referent power.

Have you ever considered whether power is good or bad, positive or negative? How do you make a judgment? To answer those questions, you need to understand how and why power is being used.

Most leadership role requirements involve the use of power and influence. In large organizations, leaders must exercise power to influence others. For example, before joining HP, Fiorina used her leadership power at Lucent Technology to control revenues and profits. With her marketing expertise, she influenced division heads to build a brand image while she cultivated relationships with customers.[17]

Leaders need to understand and use power. However, how effective they are depends on how this need finds expression and whether it is a personalized or socialized power orientation.

Personal power
Power based on personal attributes.

Expert power
The power to influence another person because of expert knowledge and competence.

Referent power
The ability to influence others based on personal liking, charisma, and reputation.

Personalized power orientation
Associated with a strong need for esteem and status; power is often used impulsively.

Socialized power orientation
The use of power for the benefit of others to make subordinates feel strong and responsible.

A **personalized power orientation** is associated with a strong need for esteem and status; power is often used impulsively. For example, this orientation is found with centralized and controlled decision making. Information is likely to be restricted, and rewards and punishments are used to manipulate and control subordinates.

The opposite is true of leaders with a socialized power orientation. A **socialized power orientation** is represented by leaders who are mature, exercise power more for the benefit of others than for themselves, are less egoistic and defensive, and are willing to take advice from others in the organization. Such leaders help make subordinates feel strong and responsible.

FOLLOWER-CENTERED APPROACHES

The theme in the section on leader-centered approaches was to identify traits or behaviors leaders use to be effective. The leader-centered approaches focus on a narrow perspective: the leader in isolation. In reality, we know that leadership is affected by many factors. The second leadership category is follower-centered approaches. Let's turn our attention to self-leadership and leadership substitutes.

SELF-LEADERSHIP FOCUS

LEARNING OBJECTIVE 4

Explain what is meant by self-leadership and why it is important to organizations.

While organizations spend millions annually to train potential leaders, not everyone will be a formal leader in all situations. Therefore, a high value has been placed on training potential self-leaders. Self-leadership, sometimes referred to as followership, is a paradigm founded on creating an organization of leaders who are ready to lead themselves.[18]

Teaching employees how to be effective self-leaders may be a wise decision. In many respects, an effective self-leader resembles an effective leader, with many of the skills that every leader must master.[19] Large organizations, discovering that an abundance of baby-boom managers in their 40s and 50s are concerned about career plateauing, have begun to adopt leader partnerships and self-leadership training programs to assure employees that they are contributing even when they are not moving up the corporate ladder. For example, Figure 13.2 offers a personalized strategy plan that lists the essential elements for self-leadership.[20]

Figure 13.2 | Essential Strategies for Self-Leadership

- Come to a realization about self-leadership and dispel the myths about leaders.
- Understand that leadership is not an external event.
- Take a personal inventory.
- Write a personal vision statement.
- Find a purpose or cause.
- Develop a plan.
- Establish a personal monitor, feedback, and correction system.
- Celebrate short-term wins.
- Initiate a personal reward and incentive system.
- Practice continuous learning and improvement.

Leaders In Action

New Leader at Alberto-Culver North America

Carol Lavin Bernick and her husband took over top management of Alberto-Culver in 1994, a business established by her father and mother. She became president, Alberto-Culver North America. While the company had been successful in the past, by 1994 employee turnover was twice the industry average, sales were flat, and profit margins were slipping. The problem? Yes, competition was getting tougher, but Bernick concluded that the real problem was inside the company.

The base of the problem was the culture of the organization. Employees were conditioned to focus on the needs of their supervisors rather than the needs of customers. They were not given information about the business and really didn't understand how it worked or what went into success.

Bernick set out to change all that, guided by four major steps—make culture an issue, focus on fixing the culture, measure success toward changing the culture, and celebrate wins. Then she got to work establishing the "right" culture and leading it.

She wanted everyone focused on the same overall goals. In doing this, she presented a good vision and mission as an overall guide for the company. Then she changed the old culture of keeping information from employees. She began to hold annual "state of the company" meetings in which everyone was told the financial results and other information about the business and the industry. She wanted to turn the employees into businesspeople and help them see where their jobs fit into achieving the mission.

Growth Development Leaders (GDLs) were also established. A GDL is a mentor to about a dozen employees. In addition to helping people in understanding all aspects of the business, he or she also helps the people with work and personal/family balance. After all, Bernick says, the ultimate goal is a personal one. Hers is to raise her three children well. At a broader level, this includes helping the community to be healthy by contributing to charitable organizations, especially those that help with education of employees' children. Overall, she says that finding the right balance and understanding the business, and how one's job fits into it, would result in more committed team players.

Now, Bernick and Alberto-Culver North America measure success and celebrate it. She says that the things that you measure and celebrate are the things that you will get. A few of the rewards for contributions to success include stock awards to outstanding GDLs, the Business Builders Award, and the People's Choice Award. These, plus others, celebrate success. The success? Sales and, more importantly, profits have been on an almost continual upward trend since 1994. The upward rise has increased in the last few years.

SOURCES: **http://www.alberto-culver.com**, Web site, July 12, 2002; Carol Lavin Bernick, "When Your Culture Needs a Makeover," *Harvard Business Review*, June 2001, 53–60.

Lincoln Electric, a Cleveland-based manufacturer of welding machines and electric motors, provides an example of the value of fostering organizational followership. The structure of the organization requires each employee to be accountable for his or her own behavior. Even in recessionary times, employees are loyal to the company and show their cooperation by performing duties not required by their contracts. Employees are asked to serve on an advisory board that meets weekly to assess how the company is doing in a variety of areas. The employees understand the organization and their contributions to it. They are adaptable and take responsibility for their own actions. In essence, the employees of Lincoln Electric are good followers.[21] There are numerous other successful companies that have cultures that encourage self-leadership, including Agilent, a spin-off from Hewlett-Packard,[22] Medtronic, a "best company" selection of *Fortune* magazine,[23] and W. L. Gore & Associates, Goretex fabrics.[24]

Studies show that effective self-leaders have most of the following characteristics:[25]

1. The capacity to motivate themselves and stay focused on tasks.
2. Integrity that demands both loyalty to the organization and the willingness to act according to beliefs.
3. Understanding of the organization and their contributions to it.
4. Willingness to take the initiative to deal with problems.
5. Versatility, skillfulness, and flexibility to adapt to a changing environment.
6. Responsibility for their own careers, actions, and development.

Figure 13.4 | The Leadership Grid® Figure

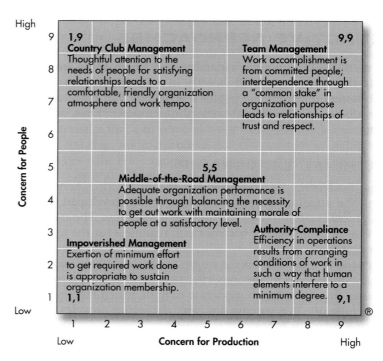

SOURCE: The Leadership Grid® figure, Paternalism figure and Opportunism from *Leadership Dilemmas—Grid Solutions*, by Robert R. Blake and Anne Adams McCanse (formerly the Managerial Grid by Robert R. Blake and Jane S. Mouton). Austin: Grid International, Inc. (Grid figure: p. 29, Paternalism figure: p. 30, Opportunism figure: p. 31). Copyright ©1998, by Grid International, Inc. Reproduced by permission of the owners.

Delegating style

The leader provides the subordinates with few task or relations behaviors. Authority and responsibility rest with the follower.

When leaders use a **delegating style** they provide the subordinates with few task or relations behaviors. When subordinates have reached a readiness level at which they decide how and when to do things and are able and willing to take responsibility for what needs to be done, it is appropriate for the leader to use a delegating style.

Another behavior focused theory is the leadership grid, which uses two leadership behaviors—concern for people and concern for production—to categorize five different leadership styles. Figure 13.4 shows the two-dimensional model of this theory.

LEARNING OBJECTIVE 7

Clarify how empowerment can increase the power and autonomy of organizational members.

Empowerment

Delegating authority to the follower and holding him or her accountable. It includes making sure the follower understands the task, has proper information, training, motivation, guidance, and skills to be successful.

EMPOWERMENT

One of the major forces for cultural and structural changes in organizations has been the empowerment movement. **Empowerment** is designed to increase the power and autonomy of all employees in an organization. It has its roots in the perceptions of Japanese management—the quality-circle efforts of the 1970s and the quality-of-work-life (QWL) approach—and the psychological concept of self-efficacy.[30]

The underlying theme of empowerment is the interaction of the leader who is giving up or sharing power with those who use it to become involved and committed to independent, high-quality performance. Such power sharing provides people with a belief in their ability and their sense of effectiveness.

Empowerment is often described as delegation or devolution of power, authority, or responsibility by those higher in the organizational structure to those at lower levels of the organization.[31] Successful empowerment means that everyone truly understands his or her role in achieving the mission of the organization; has the skills, information, and motivation to make good decisions; is held accountable; and receives appropriate rewards for successful performance. Empowered individuals feel that what they do has meaning and significance; that they have discretion as well as obligations; and that they live in a culture of respect in which they are encouraged to act on their own. Empowered organizations generate and sustain trust as well as communicate constantly.[32]

Research and observations of many leaders strongly suggest that power sharing contributes to an organization's effectiveness if empowerment is developed effectively. Empowerment of employees can also be a powerful motivational tool, as we will discuss in Chapter 15, by providing them with both control and a sense of accomplishment.[33]

TRANSFORMATIONAL LEADERSHIP

Transformational leadership refers to the leader's ability to influence employees to achieve more than was originally expected or thought possible. This is most successful when the leader understands the vision of the organization and is able to articulate it to the employees.[34] In addition, transformational leaders are able to generate feelings of trust, admiration, loyalty, and respect from the followers. Consequently, followers are motivated to achieve more than was originally expected. This motivation is created when the leader makes subordinates more aware of the importance and values of task outcomes, helps them think beyond their own self-interest to the needs of the work teams and the organization,[35] and activates higher-order needs such as creative expression and self-actualization.[36]

Transformational leaders do not accept the *status quo*. They recognize the need to revitalize their organizations and challenge standard operating procedures; they institutionalize change by replacing old technical and political networks with new ones. In other words, transformational leaders transform things from what could be to what is by generating excitement.

Four primary dimensions of transformational leadership include: idealized influence, inspirational motivation, intellectual stimulation, and individualized consideration.[37] As shown in Table 13.1, each dimension involves specific behaviors by the leader that, in turn, inspire follower behavior.

LEARNING OBJECTIVE 8
Explain transformational leadership.

Transformational leadership
Leadership where the leader has the ability to influence subordinates to achieve more than was originally expected.

Table 13.1 | Primary Dimensions of Transformational Leadership

DIMENSION	LEADER'S SPECIFIC BEHAVIOR	FOLLOWER'S BEHAVIOR
Individualized Consideration	Acts as mentor; is attentive to achievement and growth needs.	Is motivated; feels valued.
Intellectual Stimulation	Promotes innovation and creativity; reframes problems.	Is encouraged to be novel and try new approaches.
Inspirational Motivation	Provides meaning and challenge through prosocial, collective action.	Is motivated by team spirit; enthusiastic; optimistic.
Idealized Influence	Shares risks; is considerate of others over own needs; is ethical and moral.	Shows admiration; respect; trust.

Though the literature on transformational leadership focuses on CEOs and top-level managers, transformational leadership involves the actions of individuals at all levels, not just those at the top. Transformational leadership increases follower motivation by activating the higher needs of followers, appealing to their moral ideas, and empowering them.

A NEW MODEL OF LEADERSHIP

All of the models and approaches that we discussed in this chapter offer important knowledge about leadership. The new model that was introduced in Chapter 1 can be used to provide a framework for what we have learned from the other models, and it can offer some new insights into successful leadership. That model is based on three Cs—competence, character, and community.

Competence   Leaders need to have knowledge about how organizations work. They need to know how to develop a vision and mission that are not only correct for the industry, but are also inspiring to the people in the organization. They need to know how to analyze financial statements and how to make sure the organization does achieve its strategy.

Of course, leaders need to know how to interact with people. They need to know how to truly communicate well and understand what influences people. That is the base of leadership.

Character   Character refers to the leadership values and behaviors that elicit trust, commitment, and followership—the things that are essential for an organization to achieve its mission.[38] What does it take to elicit these things? Characteristics such as integrity, honesty, high ethical standards, courage, discipline, and persistence are the foundation. If a leader has these characteristics combined with competence, he or she probably will earn trust from others and will set a good example[39] of the behaviors that are needed for the organization to be successful.

Community   The result of the competency and character will be a vibrant, healthy community within the organization. The healthy atmosphere or culture in the organization will instill followership—organizational members working together to achieve the organization's mission.

The concept of community applied outside of the organization will build strong, positive ties between the organization and its external community, upon which it depends for customers, employees, and overall healthy economic conditions.

The topics in this book and course, plus all of the other topics and courses in your educational career, can help you build a competency base and understand your own character—and how to develop it. Supplemented by experience and mistakes (but you must truly learn from mistakes and not just repeat them), you can build a foundation that is necessary to establish a healthy organizational community. Look at the boxes "Facing The Challenge" and "Meeting The Challenge." Do you think that Mannie Jackson demonstrates the three Cs?

WOMEN AS LEADERS

LEARNING OBJECTIVE 9

Discuss the changing role of women as leaders.

The number of women in leadership positions has increased steadily since 1970. Women occupy slightly over 25 percent of the supervisory positions in U.S. industry and just 11 percent of senior executive positions in *Fortune* 500 companies, although they represented 51 percent of the population.[40] The number of women enrolled in business schools is increasing, and the entrepreneurial spirit of women is also becoming apparent.

More and more organizations are being led by women. Francis Hesselbein is the Director of the Peter Drucker Foundation. Her leadership competence and accomplishments are studied and incorporated into programs at institutes such as Harvard and IBM.[41] Mary Kay, the founder of Mary Kay Cosmetics was well known for her very influential, high-charisma style. Other women leaders include Carly Fiorina, the CEO of Hewlett-Packard; Andrea Jung, CEO of Avon; Mitch Meyers, CEO of Zipatoni, the leader featured in Chapter 12; Sallie Krawcheck, the CEO of Sanford C. Bernstein, the leader featured in Chapter 15; Margaret Whitman, CEO of eBay; Louise Wilmot, until her retirement, the highest ranking woman (Rear Admiral) in the U.S. Navy; and many others.[42]

How well do men accept women as leaders? Research indicates that men's attitudes toward women in the workplace are gradually changing as more women enter the workforce and assume leadership positions. Studies show, however, that both men and women executives believe women have to be exceptional to succeed in the business world. Women leaders still face disadvantages in business and feel they must struggle harder than men to succeed.[43]

© REUTERS NEW MEDIA INC./CORBIS

Do men and women differ in terms of leadership ability? Research shows that men and women perform equally on IQ tests; women are better at expressing feelings and accessing their emotions; and women have an easier time switching from the verbal left brain to the emotional right brain than men do. Men show pain and distress differently than women— they tend to externalize them, while women tend to internalize them.

Experienced female leaders such as Carly Fiorina, CEO of HP, show no difference in leadership ability from their male counterparts.

In the past, successful leaders have been associated with stereotypical masculine attributes such as competitiveness, task orientation, and willingness to take risks. Recent studies, however, show that female middle- and top-level executives no longer equate successful leadership with these masculine attributes. Experienced female managers show no differences in leadership ability from their experienced male counterparts. Both groups possess a high need for achievement and power, and both demonstrate assertiveness, self-reliance, risk taking, and other traits and behaviors associated with leadership. Once men and women have established themselves as leaders in their organizations, women do not behave differently than men.[44] However, a trend exists of more women making their way to the top who are not only adopting styles and habits that have proved successful for men, but are also drawing on the skills and attitudes they have developed from their experiences as women. Generally, women are more likely to use behaviors that are associated with transformational leadership, such as reliance on expertise, charisma, and interpersonal skills. Men are more likely to be directive.[45]

LEADERS OF THE FUTURE

With ever-increasing globalization and change, leaders will be challenged to manage relationships more than in the past. This will include the ability to interact effectively with a diversity of partners and other businesses and within the larger context of differing cultures. Predictions are that the total trade between countries will exceed the total value of trade within countries by the year 2015. This will require truly "global" leaders.[46]

As we have been discussing throughout the book, the changing global environment is likely to continue to stimulate the transformation and revitalization of public and private institutions. Small as well as large U.S. companies such as IBM,

Now Apply It

Finding a Good Leader

Identify someone whom you think is a successful leader in the organization in which you work, for example, a student organization on campus, a fraternity or sorority, or a religious organization. Write down the criteria or things that you used to measure this person's success.

Now identify this leader's main characteristics and behaviors. Explain how and why his or her characteristics and behaviors lead to success. How do the characteristics and behaviors fit with the leadership approaches discussed in this chapter. Could this leader be more suc-

cessful if some things were improved, or the leader developed in some areas? What are they? How could development in these areas help?

Hewlett-Packard, Amazon.com, and Microsoft recognize that they will have to change in order to survive. They have embarked on programs of extensive change that must be accomplished in short periods of time. Such transformations require a new set of leadership guidelines.

It is clear that the successful leader of the 21st century will be one who promotes leadership development and encourages workers to assume his or her role as leader. Individuals working in 21st century organizations must be innovative and creative, practice continuous learning, have values (especially integrity), have a personal vision, be in charge of their own careers, motivate from within, plan, communicate, and seek harmonious relationships with stakeholders.

IMPLICATIONS FOR LEADERS

We conclude this chapter on leadership with a list of guiding principles to start you toward leadership effectiveness. These 10 items get to the core of what leadership is all about.[47] Following these principles will help you develop effective leadership skills. Notice that these 10 principles fit very well in the 3Cs Model of Leadership: competence, character, and community.

1. *Know yourself.* You cannot be an effective leader without knowing your own strengths and weaknesses. Knowing your capabilities will allow you to improve on your weaknesses and trade on your strengths.
2. *Be a role model.* Expect no more than what you yourself are willing to give.
3. *Learn to communicate with your ears open and your mouth shut.* Most problems that leaders are asked to solve are "people" problems created because of a failure in communication. Communication failures are the result of people's hearing but not listening to and understanding one another.
4. *Know your team and be a team player.* As a leader, make the effort to know what other members of the team are doing, not necessarily to monitor their progress but to seek ways and means of providing assistance.
5. *Be honest with yourself as well as with others.* All good leaders make mistakes. Rarely do they make the same mistake more than once. Openly admit a mistake, learn from it, and forget it. Generally, others will forget it too.
6. *Do not avoid risks.* If you are to become an effective leader, you will need to become an effective risk taker. Take "calculated" risks and, if you make a mistake, learn from it. See problems as challenges, challenges as catalysts for change, and changes as opportunities.

7. *Believe in yourself.* All effective leaders share the characteristic of confidence in their own ability to get the job done. This personal confidence is often contagious and quick to permeate an entire organization, boosting confidence levels of all team members.

8. *Take the offense rather than the defense.* The most effective leaders are quicker to act than they are to react. Their best solution to any problem is to solve it before it becomes a problem. If they see something that needs fixing, they will do what they can to repair it before being told to do so by someone else.

9. *Know the ways of disagreement and the means of compromise.* While people may disagree with one another, remember that who wins or loses is not important. The real winner is the leader who can facilitate the opposing side's goals while achieving his or her own.

10. *Be a good follower.* Effective leaders lead as they would like to be led.

This chapter has explored many facets of leadership effectiveness for the dynamic environment in which you are or soon will be working. As we noted earlier, a considerable amount of research has been done on leadership, and many books and articles have been published on the topic. Although leadership means different things to different people, it is critical to understand that leadership is not equivalent to a rank or title, nor are leaders born. Leadership is a process, and it can be learned.

Meeting The Challenge

The Globetrotters Are Back!

Toward the end of the speech to the Harlem Globetrotter basketball players, Mannie Jackson concluded that he would save the team and that he would lead them to success. He also told them that if they didn't want to be part of it, they should leave now. No one left. They believed that he could do it.

Jackson constructed a new business plan. The focus was to recreate a great basketball and entertainment organization. He worked with the players, the media, sponsors, and two levels of what he calls customers—the people who own the arenas and promote the events and the people who actually buy the tickets to see the team perform. All of these people had been basically ignored or treated poorly by the previous managers. Plus, the team wasn't making a profit for its owners. Jackson's past business success and current business plan convinced everyone that he could make it work. He could rebuild the organization.

Jackson managed the team like a business. There was a mission. There were goals. Markets were analyzed. Financial analysis was completed. And, there were building blocks or guiding principles for working with and developing people inside the organizaton:

- Build a culture of accountability. When targets are achieved or exceeded, the entire company takes a three-day trip to celebrate and to learn from the success.
- Seek to improve upon last year's results. A bar chart on the wall shows this, and it does show the numbers from 1993—for comparison.
- Choose people for what they can become.
- Use your time to improve the organization.
- If a decision doesn't feel right, don't do it.

Globetrotter games begin with an exhibition of some very good basketball. Jackson wants to be sure that people know that the players are very good at basketball. Then, add to that the showmanship, the tricks, and the comedy. In addition, the Globetrotters continue to travel around the country offering "Basketball Camps" to help young people develop. Of course, these camps also get exposure for the Globetrotters Organization.

In 1993, annual attendance at games was 300,000; in 2001, it was 2 million. In 1993, the organization lost about $1 million. In 2001, the profit was about $6 million.

SOURCES: **http://www.harlemglobetrotters. com**, Web site, July 12, 2002; Mannie Jackson, "Bringing a Dying Brand Back to Life," *Harvard Business Review*, May 2001, 53–61; "Learning from a Globetrotter," *St. Louis Post-Dispatch*, July 13, 2002, L13.

SUMMARY

1. Leadership is broadly defined as a social influence process that inspires people to pursue goals that benefit the organization.

2. There are three primary leader-centered approaches to leadership. The earliest approach was the trait focus, which is based on the assumption that some people are born with certain physical characteristics, aspects of personality, and attitudes. The second approach is the behavior focus, which examines what effective leaders do rather than what effective leaders are. The power focus is the ability to marshal human, informational, or material resources to get something done.

3. Leaders have two primary types of power—position and personal. From their position in an organization, they have legitimate, coercive, reward, and information power. Personal power is derived from the interpersonal relationship between leaders and their followers, including expert and referent power.

4. Self-leadership is a paradigm founded on creating an organization of leaders who are ready to lead themselves.

5. Leadership substitutes are variables such as individual, task, and organizational characteristics that tend to outweigh the leader's ability to influence subordinates.

6. According to the situational leadership model, effective leader behavior depends on the match between leader behavior and subordinate readiness. The four leader behaviors are telling, selling, participating, and delegating.

7. Empowerment is the delegation of power or authority by those higher in the organizational structure to those at lower levels of the organization or the sharing of power with them. It includes holding people accountable for their decisions. Successful empowerment means that everyone understands his or her role in the organization and has the proper training, motivation, and guidance to make good decisions.

8. Transformational leadership refers to leadership that influences employees to achieve more than was originally expected or thought possible.

9. Leaders of the future will have to be innovative and creative, practice continuous learning, have a personal vision, be in charge of their own careers, motivate from within, plan, communicate, and seek harmonious relationships with stakeholders. They must have competence and character and work to improve the community inside and outside of the organization.

REVIEW QUESTIONS

1. (*Learning Objective 1*) Define leadership. How important is good leadership to an organization?

2. (*Learning Objective 2*) Explain the trait focus to leadership. Is this focus successful in identifying people who will be effective leaders?

3. (*Learning Objective 3*) Explain the base of legitimate power of a leader.

4. (*Learning Objective 4*) Explain what is meant by self-leadership and why is it important to organizations.

5. (*Learning Objective 5*) Identify four substitutes for leadership. Explain how each does substitute for leadership.

6. (*Learning Objective 6*) Explain what readiness is in the situational leadership model.

7. (*Learning Objective 7*) Explain how empowerment can help improve the effectiveness of an organization.

8. (*Learning Objective 8*) What does a leader do to be considered transformational?

9. (*Learning Objective 9*) Explain how women and men might differ as leaders.

DISCUSSION QUESTIONS

Improving Critical Thinking

1. Under what conditions would an organization want to promote self-leadership?

2. Select a popular television show and examine how power is used by the main characters. What types of power do they use most often? Least often? Provide examples. How does

the use of certain types of power affect the interactions between the main character and others?

3. Select two successful and well-known leaders. Compare the traits and characteristics of these two individuals and discuss how similar or different they are. To what degree to you think their traits led to success?

Enhancing Communication Skills

4. Read the discussion on reinforcement theory in Chapter 15. After you have done that, write a short report in which you explain the similarities between reinforcement theory and the situational leadership model.

5. Interview two women leaders and examine the types of experiences and opportunities they have had as they have progressed to higher ranks in their organizations. Are any of their experiences common? Does either leader think that the issues women face in organizations today have changed in the past 10 years? Write your interviews as a short report.

6. Give examples of situations in which you used your power to influence your peers, your family members, and your professor. Provide specific examples either as an oral presentation or in writing, as directed by your instructor.

Building Teamwork

7. Have each team member complete the survey in the Experiential Exercise 13.1. If you are working as part of a permanent team, complete a survey about one other team member. Follow the scoring instructions. Team members should each discuss the two behaviors with the lowest scores and then brainstorm about how practice and experience can be gained. This is a way in which each team member is acting supportively.

8. Select any leadership approach discussed in the chapter and analyze your own leadership style. When are you most effective? Ineffective? In a small group, exchange your ideas with others with whom you have worked. Discuss how your leadership style might work well with the style of another person or might conflict.

THINKING CRITICALLY: DEBATE THE ISSUE

Leadership Skills for the 21st Century

Divide into small teams as directed by your instructor. Teams will select one of the following statements and provide evidence from current literature to gain support for their position.

1. The changing business and global environment in the 21st century will demand successful leaders of the future to have different skills and characteristics than the leader of the past. Explain what those differences are and why they will be needed.

2. Regardless of the changing business and global environment in the 21st century, leaders of the future will need to continue following the successful practices of leaders of the past.

EXPERIENTIAL EXERCISE 13.1

What's Your Leadership Potential?

Read the following statements and give yourself a score using the scale of 1 (rarely), 2 (sometimes) or 3 (almost always). Then ask a coworker or team member to rate your potential and compare results.

As a leader, I:

____ **1.** Communicate effectively.

____ **2.** Set priorities and action plans.

____ **3.** Learn and improve procedures.

____ **4.** Accept accountability for the situation.

____ **5.** Analyze problems and make sound decisions.

____ **6.** Adapt to changing conditions, influences, and environments.

____ **7.** Accept risk and take on difficult assignments.

____ **8.** Inspire excellence and commitment in others.

____ **9.** Stand up when under pressure.

____ **10.** Learn from mistakes but don't take them personally.

____ **11.** Exhibit strong social and interpersonal skills.

____ **12.** Demonstrate a high tolerance for stress and pressure.

____ **Total**

Scoring

Total your points for questions 1 through 12. Your score can range from 12 to 36. Compare your score and the score received from the person you asked to provide feedback. How consistent are the scores? Discuss the importance of the consistency of these scores if the other person was your subordinate.

Score Interpretation

Scores below 18 indicate that you have not had experience or opportunities to learn effective leadership. Scores between 19 and 30 show that you are making progress toward developing potential leader effectiveness. If you scored above 30, congratulations on demonstrating high leadership potential. Continue learning and practicing your leader behavior.

CAPTURING THE POWER OF INFORMATION TECHNOLOGY

1. Go to one of the online bookstores such as Amazon.com (**http://www.amazon.com**) and search for books about leadership published in the last 12 months. Select 8 to 10 books and read the abstract or book summary for each one. Are there common themes? Do you think the themes are fads, or do they appear to be relevant to good leadership?

2. What do you think of the leadership style of Jeff Bezos, the CEO of Amazon.com? Does the leader of a dot-com company have to have different skills than the leader of other companies?

ETHICS: TAKE A STAND

Here are two recent examples of executive compensation and severance packages:

1. Gerald Hsu sold the software company, Avant, in June of 2002 and, as part of the deal, resigned as CEO and retired with an extra $30.6 million payment. Previously, he had pleaded no contest to conspiring to take trade secrets from a competitor and was fined. Avant paid the fine, Hsu's legal bill, and tax bill. This added up to another $5.3 million.

2. Dennis Kozlowski was forced to resign as CEO of Tyco Corporation and is under federal indictment. Some of the financial benefits that Kozlowski enjoyed: an $18 million apartment in New York City, a $13 million "relocation" loan, artwork painted by Monet and others, and engaging in certain practices so that he could avoid paying taxes on the artwork valued at several million dollars. The Board of Directors knew about some of these things but not all.

SOURCES: A. Lashinsky, "[What's] Hot: [What's] Not," *Fortune*, July 22, 2002, 29; J. Kahn, "Getting Paid in Planes, Perks, and Automobiles," *Fortune*, July 22, 2002, 36–38.

For Discussion

1. Is it ethical for the Board of Directors to approve payment of a manager's fine or legal bills if he or she is convicted of a felony?

2. Is it ethical for the Board of Directors to approve large amounts of money as bonuses or severance packages for retiring CEOs? How might these large payments and large salaries be related to the true value of the company? That is, might a CEO actually be worth that much?

3. How do these large severance packages, bonuses, and salaries affect the stockholders?

VIDEO CASE

Leading in a Dynamic Environment: The Buffalo Zoo

Founded in 1875, the Buffalo Zoo (located in Buffalo, New York) is the third oldest zoo in the United States. During its early years, the Buffalo Zoo was one of the best zoos. Dedicated to conservation, education, and recreation, the Buffalo Zoo plays an essential role in a variety of local, regional, and global conservation efforts. However, the outdated buildings and displays resulted in a dramatic decline in the number of annual visitors to the Buffalo Zoo.[1] Threatened with losing their national accreditation, zoo administrators announced a highly controversial plan to move the zoo from Delaware Park. Although the ill-fated plan was backed by Buffalo's mayor and major newspaper, the community strongly opposed the plan.

After more than two years, the community gained the necessary political support to reject the zoo's plan to change locations. The zoo president resigned when his plan failed, leaving the zoo with no direction, inadequate funding, and poor community relations.

After a national search for a zoo president and CEO, the board of directors hired Dr. Donna Fernandes, a newly minted MBA from Boston's Simmons Graduate School of Management.[2] She also has a master's and Ph.D. in ecology, evolution, and animal behavior from Princeton University and undergraduate degrees from Phillips Academy and Brown University (having graduated summa cum laude). Not only is she academically qualified, she has extensive zoological experience, including serving as Curator of Animals and Education at Brooklyn's Prospect Park Wildlife Center and Vice President of Operations at Zoo New England in Boston. As quoted in *The Buffalo News* (May 26, 2002), the chair of the zoo's board and executive vice president of M&T Bank recalled, "The first time we met Donna, we saw a subtleness that was understated, a real depth and background in the zoo world, and a way of sort of charming you that we thought would really work well in this area." During her interview, the 43-year-old told the board her vision of the Buffalo Zoo to regain its world class status would need to be a "shared dream" for them to accomplish it in 10–25 years.[3]

When the board offered Donna the job, they warned her of the resistance she'd face from the surrounding community, influential community members, board members who had their own visions of the zoo's future, and the employees who were antimanagement. Her predecessors had alienated employees and others due to their autocratic styles, using more negative feedback than positive. In addition, many of the employees and, especially, the senior staff had been with the zoo for 20 or more years and their morale was low. They had experienced many failed "master plans," including the recent hotly contested plan.

In her first few years, Donna gained board and community support, and her employees shared her vision, enthusiastically carrying out her initiatives. The zoo's director of development appreciates the collegial respect Donna has for her employees. While Donna's predecessors were rarely seen outside their office, she walks the zoo grounds daily interacting with employees and zoo visitors. She empowers her employees to make decisions and supports their efforts. Donna's employees report they feel like they're working *with* her rather than *for* her.

Donna attributes her leadership style to the mentoring she received during her four years at the New York City Wildlife Conservation Society that involved her in all aspects of zoo operations. She appreciated how her previous supervisor listened to her ideas and let her make decisions. Donna believes people give their best when allowed to make decisions and given timely feedback. Although she rarely overturns her employees' decisions, Donna likes to be informed of decisions to be sure things are consistent with the zoo's goals.

Recently, the Buffalo Zoo had their most successful summer in the past five years. Donna's business knowledge and abilities to inspire her staff, board, and community have steered the Buffalo Zoo toward a bright future. Current zoo programs focus on improving a better understanding of the natural world and how animals relate to each other, to their environment, and to humankind. However, raising the $60–$80 million and renovating the zoo will present continuing challenges over the next 15 years. Its new Vanishing Animals exhibit cost $2.4 million. Eventually, the zoo will rebuild every exhibit, one at a time in order to keep the zoo open for visitors.[4]

For Discussion

1. Explain how Donna illustrates the traits of successful leaders. What additional characteristics and achievements may contribute to her success as president and CEO?

2. Explain what leader behaviors Donna exhibits. How do these differ from those of her predecessor?

3. Describe various types of power Donna illustrates. Are these powers necessary for a leader to be effective?

4. Explain whether Donna appears to be a transformational leader. Would you like to work with her?

http://www.buffalozoo.org

Notes:

[1] Press release: Governor Pataki Announces $350,000 for Buffalo Zoo, May 2001, http://www.state.ny.us/governor/press/year01/may22_3_01.htm.

[2] News Library The Natural, Published on May 26, 2002, Author: Jane Kwiatkowski—News Staff Reporter © The Buffalo News Inc.

[3] Christina Abt, "Donna Fernandes, Director, Buffalo Zoologial Society," EVE Magazine, http://www.simmons.edu/gsm/alumnae/EVE.pdf.

[4] News Library What's New at the Buffalo Zoo? Published on October 16, 2001, Author: Caitlin Bell—NeXt Correspondent © The Buffalo News Inc.

CASE

Steve Ballmer at Microsoft

What do you think it would be like to replace Bill Gates as CEO of Microsoft? As the old saying goes, "Those are very large shoes to fill." Steve Ballmer doesn't seem to be too concerned.

In a memo sent to 50,000 employees on June 6, 2002, Ballmer listed the new mission statement of Microsoft: "To enable people and businesses throughout the world to realize their full potential." Then he wrote about making the company a great company that would last a long time—making it even more successful than it has ever been. He wants Microsoft to be truly great as a business and as a major positive contributor to a better society. Some of the goals and tasks he believes will achieve that level:

- Think now about what will be required to manage the business in the future.
- Push authority down in the organization and hold people accountable.
- Concentrate on coordinating the parts of the organization that have to work together—that is, coordinate business strategy and technological development of new products.
- Build trust that consumers have in Microsoft by improving the quality of products and services.
- Be honest with and respectful of competitors.

To support these goals and tasks, Ballmer has begun meetings and reviews with managers. This includes brainstorming sessions to improve operations, helping managers with accounting and financial tools to make better decisions, incorporating the corporate values into the performance reviews, employees ranking their supervisors, and many other similar things.

Then there is the video of Ballmer leading a pep rally at a company meeting. His actions were so lively that they earned him the nickname "Monkey Boy." Of course that may be upstaged by the picture of him jumping into "Lake Bill," a lake on the Redmond Headquarters Campus, in the winter wearing only a swim trunks—in front of thousands of employees. He jumped into the lake on a dare from a manager.

SOURCES: J. Green, S. Hamm, and J. Kerstetter, "Ballmer's Microsoft: How CEO Steve Ballmer Is Remaking the Company that Bill Gates Built," *BusinessWeek*, June 17, 2002, 66–74; B. Schlender, "All You Need is Love, $50 Billion, and Killer Software Code-Named Longhorn," *Fortune*, July 8, 2002, 56–68.

For Discussion

1. Identify Ballmer's actions and behaviors that demonstrate a task orientation; a relations orientation.

2. What types of power are demonstrated, or suggested, in the behaviors indicated above? Give examples.

3. Identify evidence of personalized power orientation; socialized power orientation.

4. Is there any evidence of delegating and empowerment?

5. Does Ballmer demonstrate the 3Cs Model of Leadership?

CHAP

EXPLORING INDIVIDUAL DIFFERENCES AND
TEAM DYNAMICS

LEADERSHIP

COMPETENCE

CHARACTER

COMMUNITY

TER 14

CHAPTER OVERVIEW

The leading organizations in the 21st century will be those whose culture allows them to move faster and react better to diverse customers, markets, and employees. They will be challenged to produce higher-quality products and services, be globally oriented, and involve everyone in a focused effort to serve ever more demanding customers. To eliminate the barriers that separate functions within them, organizations must move toward a culture that helps people understand how to work together at both the individual and the group level.

This chapter provides the foundations to understand individual behaviors. First, we examine some of the ways individuals differ in attitudes, personalities, perceptions, and abilities. We look at these factors with regard to how they affect performance. Since management effectiveness depends upon the ability of different individuals to pull together and focus on a common goal, we turn our attention to understanding the impact of groups of individuals and relevant team issues. We explore the different types of groups, the inputs for designing effective groups, how groups develop, and the processes that influence groups to be effective. Finally, we take a look at how managers can work to create and support successful teams.

LEARNING OBJECTIVES

When you have finished studying this chapter, you should be able to:

1. Discuss why it is important for managers to understand individual differences.
2. Define personality and briefly explain personality characteristics considered significant in the workplace.
3. Explain what is measured by both the Myers-Briggs Type Indicator and the "Big Five."
4. Explain the importance of matching personality characteristics to jobs and careers.
5. Discuss the importance of perception and perceptual errors.
6. Discuss the relationship between job satisfaction and performance.
7. Comment on the various types of team member roles.
8. Identify the development phases of groups.
9. Explain how cohesiveness can impact a team.
10. Clarify the primary elements of successful teams.

Facing The Challenge

Teamwork at United Technologies

Michael Rager, the Global Supply and Implementation Manager for United Technologies Corporation (UTC), had to save money in order to increase profits. UTC has branches throughout the world, and each branch was using its own transportation companies. The branches were paying very different rates and were receiving widely different levels of service. Rager decided that transportation throughout the world could be centralized, or at least coordinated, in order to achieve more consistent service and lower rates that would help increase profits.

To analyze the entire transportation situation, Rager set up three regional teams—one for North America, one for Asia, and one for Europe. Each team was made up of warehouse and operations people from branches in the region. They had different functional backgrounds as well as perspectives unique to their own part of the world. Al Emmons joined these teams and provided some guidance.

As Emmons said, ". . . some sparks flew in the early days." Everyone saw things quite differently. The different backgrounds and goals created many disagreements. Some branches wanted to keep their preferred transportation companies even if they were charging higher prices than others. Some branch people said that the better service was worth the higher price.

Meetings continued. Would UTC be able to achieve cost savings by coordinating transportation costs? Would the teams find a solution or continue to argue?

SOURCE: B. Milligan, "Team Approach Cuts Transportation Costs for Untied Technologies," *Purchasing*, October 7, 1999, 68.

INTRODUCTION

"We're all in this together." That probably should be the overall attitude of everyone in the same organization. After all, the organization would be much more successful if everyone in that organization was focused on the same mission and strategy. Another way to say this: "We're all on the same team." With this overall concept of teamwork as the foundation, we now turn our attention to a bit more narrow view of teams.

Procter & Gamble (P&G) is generally considered an important U.S. pioneer in applying teams to its operations. It began work with teams in the early 1960s, although these efforts were not publicized and virtually escaped media attention. P&G envisioned the team approach as a significant competitive advantage, and through the 1980s, it attempted to deflect attention away from its efforts. The company thought of its knowledge about the team organization as a trade secret and required consultants and employees to sign nondisclosure agreements.[1]

Other prominent companies have been active with teams as well: Gaines, Metzler, Kriner & Company; Cummins Engine; Digital Equipment; Ford; Motorola; Tektronix; Boeing; AT&T; Texas Instruments; and Xerox, to name just a few. In manufacturing, we have had extensive experience with self-managed teams, which started in the 1960s. Today they are a proven system, needing only a fine-tuning in specific sites.[2]

The use of teams in the service sector has been an exciting area of application. Service teams are well past the experimentation phase, although we still have much to learn about them. Teams in government are a rapidly changing area of application. Until recently, government agencies have shown little interest in empowered teams. Now, however, driven by downsizing, teams have become a normal organizational structure.

Teams are made up of individuals. Therefore, before we direct our attention to teams, we will examine individual differences and key aspects of personalities, attitudes, and abilities.

APPRECIATING INDIVIDUAL DIFFERENCES

Individual behavior is determined to a great extent by internal elements such as attitudes, personality, perceptions, and abilities. People respond differently to the same situation because of their unique combination of these elements, called individual differences. It is a continual challenge for managers to recognize, understand, and learn to appreciate the importance of individual differences in their employees because individual differences affect the work environment and the performance of the organization overall. In the following sections we examine some of the elements influencing individual behavior.

PERSONALITY CHARACTERISTICS

Personality is an enduring, organized, and distinctive pattern of behavior that describes an individual's adaptation to a situation.[3] It is used here to represent the overall profile or combination of traits that characterize the unique nature of a person. In short, personality characteristics help us to tell people apart and anticipate their behaviors.

Personality characteristics suggest tendencies to behave in certain ways and account for consistency in various situations. They can partly explain why learning certain new behaviors may be harder for some people than for others. A number of personality characteristics or traits have been convincingly linked to work behavior and performance. Organizational researchers have tended to focus on personality traits that are considered important in the workplace.

SELF-ESTEEM   **Self-esteem** indicates the extent to which people believe they are capable, significant, and worthwhile.[4] In short, a person's self-esteem is a judgment of worthiness that is expressed in the attitudes the individual holds toward himself or herself. A person's assessment of worthiness is affected somewhat by situations, successes or failures, the opinions of others, and thus the roles that one assumes.[5] Nevertheless, the assessments that a person makes are stable enough to be widely regarded as a basic characteristic or dimension of personality that, if positive, can enhance performance, increase the likelihood of success, and fuel motivation.

Self-esteem affects behavior in organizations and other social settings in several important ways. For example, self-esteem is related to initial vocational choice. Individuals with high self-esteem take more risks in job selection, may be more attracted to high-status occupations, and are more likely to choose nontraditional jobs than individuals with low self-esteem.[6] Individuals with low self-esteem set lower goals for themselves than individuals with high self-esteem and tend to be more easily influenced by the opinions of others in organizational settings.[7]

LOCUS OF CONTROL   **Locus of control** is a personality characteristic that describes the extent to which individuals believe that they can control the environment and external events affecting them.[8] What is your locus of control? Before reading further, take a few minutes to complete the questionnaire in the "Now Apply It" box. This will give you some insight into this aspect of your personality and help you determine whether you have an internal or external locus of control. Please keep in mind that this is not a judgment but simply a way for you to learn more about your own possible managerial style.

Individuals who have an **internal locus of control**, or internals (a low score on the scale), believe that many of the events in their lives are primarily the result of their own behavior and actions. They feel a sense of control over their lives and tend to attribute both their successes and their failures to their own efforts. As a

LEARNING OBJECTIVE 1

Discuss why it is important for managers to understand individual differences.

LEARNING OBJECTIVE 2

Define personality and briefly explain personality characteristics considered significant in the workplace.

Personality
An enduring pattern of an individual's behavior.

Self-esteem
The extent to which people believe they are capable, significant, successful, and worthwhile.

Locus of control
A personality characteristic that describes the extent to which individuals believe that they can control what happens to them.

Internal locus of control
A belief that one is in control of what happens to him or her.

Now Apply It

Measuring Your Locus of Control

For each of the following 10 questions, indicate the extent to which you agree or disagree using the following scale:

| Strongly Disagree 1 | Slightly Disagree 2 | Disagree 3 | Neither Agree Nor Disagree 4 | Agree 5 | Slightly Agree 6 | Strongly Agree 7 |

_____ 1. When I get what I want, it's usually because I worked hard for it.
_____ 2. When I make plans, I am almost certain to make them work.
_____ 3. On an exam or in competition, I like to know how well I do relative to everyone else.
_____ 4. I can learn almost anything if I set my mind to it.
_____ 5. My major accomplishments are entirely due to my hard work and ability.
_____ 6. I prefer games involving some luck over games requiring pure skill.
_____ 7. I usually don't set goals because I have a hard time following through on them.
_____ 8. Competition discourages excellence.
_____ 9. Often people get ahead just by being lucky.
_____10. It's pointless to keep working on something that's too difficult for me.

Scoring: For questions 1 through 5, reverse the scale so that 1 = 7, 2 = 6, 3 = 5, 5 = 3, 6 = 2, 7 = 1. Add the point values, and enter the results in Part 1 below. Now add the point values for questions 6 through 10, and enter the result in Part 2 below. Sum both subtotals and enter your total score.

Part 1 _____

Part 2 _____

Total _____

Scores can range from a low of 10 to a high of 70. The lower your score on this questionnaire, the more you tend to believe that you are generally responsible for what happens to you; the higher the score, the more you tend to believe forces are beyond your control. More specifically, a score of 10 to 30 indicates an internal locus of control: You tend to believe you can control the events and happenings in your life. A score of 50 to 70 indicates an external locus of control: You tend to believe that forces beyond your control, such as other people, fate, or chance, are responsible for what happens to you. Scores of 31 to 49 can be interpreted based on which end of the continuum you fall. The higher your score, the more you tend to demonstrate an external locus of control; the lower your score, the more internal locus of control behaviors you demonstrate.

External locus of control
A belief that what happens is determined by outside forces such as other people, fate, or luck.

result of such an approach, individuals with an internal locus of control, tend to be more proactive and take more risks.[9] In contrast, individuals with an **external locus of control**, or externals (a high score on the scale), believe that much of what happens to them is controlled and determined by outside external forces such as other people, fate, or luck. Such individuals do not generally perceive that they have control over their lives. As a result, they have been found to be more reactive to events and less able to rebound from stressful situations. Externals tend to rely on others' judgments and conform to authority more readily than internals.

The many differences between an internal and an external locus of control can help explain some aspects of individual behavior in organizational settings. For example, since internals believe they control their own behavior, they are more active politically and socially and are more active in seeking information about their situations than externals. Internals are more likely to try to influence or persuade others, are less likely to be influenced by others, and may be more achievement oriented than externals. For all these reasons, internals may be more highly motivated and set higher goals than externals. Refer to Table 14.1 for further details and differences between internals and externals. Remember, the table shows the extreme behavior. Most individuals have characteristics of both internal and external locus of control.

Table 14.1 | Internal versus External Locus of Control

	INTERNAL LOCUS OF CONTROL	EXTERNAL LOCUS OF CONTROL
Independence	More independent and proactive; less susceptible to the influence of others.	More dependent and reactive; susceptible to influence of others.
Use of Information	Good at utilizing information; active politically and socially.	Fewer attempts to acquire information; more satisfied than internals with amount of information they have.
Performance	Perform better than externals on learning and problem-solving tasks when performance leads to valued rewards; assumes personal responsibility for good and poor performance.	Perform better than internals on structured tasks when rewards are clearly proved; less likely than internals to assume responsibility for good or poor performance.
Satisfaction	Stronger job satisfaction-to-performance relationship than externals.	Less satisfied than internals; more alienated.
Motivation	Exhibit greater work motivation; expect that working hard will lead to good performance; feel more control over performance and time commitment than externals; establish difficult goals.	Feel that forces outside of their control influence performance efforts.
Risk	Engage in more risk than externals.	Show less self-control and more caution.

An internal locus of control is an important personality characteristic of entrepreneurs, since these individuals are convinced that they play a role in determining their success or failure and tend to feel that they have control of their fate through their own efforts. As you read about many new high-tech entrepreneurs—such as Jeff Bezos (Amazon.com), Ted Waitt (Gateway Computers), Steven Jobs (Apple Computer; NeXt Computers; Pixar Software), Michael Dell (Dell Computers)—you will be able to identify many of the traits of individuals with an internal locus of control that we have discussed. Traits include social activeness, establishing high goals, achievement orientation, high motivation, risk orientation, and being likely to influence others.

TYPE A AND TYPE B PERSONALITIES The concept of Type A or Type B personality has received considerable attention as a factor having significant implications for work and nonwork behaviors and reactions to stress.[10] **Type A personality** is characterized by a sense of commitment, high standards and goals, a devotion to work, and a sense of time urgency. Type A people tend to be competitive in work and social situations and measure results against others. They often do several things at once and tend to show diffused anger, intolerance for delays, and aggressiveness.

In contrast, the **Type B personality** is characteristically easygoing and less competitive in daily events. Type B individuals appear to be more relaxed and patient

Type A personality
A personality characteristic characterized by such things as a sense of urgency, impatience, and high drive.

Type B personality
A personality characterized as easygoing and less competitive in daily events.

and work at a more constant pace without the sense of time urgency. They are more likely to have a balanced, relaxed approach to life, listen more carefully, and communicate more precisely. Type B people may not be taken seriously because of their relaxed demeanor; their lack of concern for detail may lead to errors generally not perceived as critical. Without being driven by time constraints, the Type B personality may put off tasks or procrastinate. Type B individuals are not necessarily more or less successful than Type A people, but they are less likely to experience stress.

Keep in mind that many of the behaviors can be positive or negative depending on the situation. For example, recently Xerox had some difficulties with some of its self-managed work teams. The teams were dysfunctional. Nothing was happening, and members seemed to be relaxed and comfortable in their roles. An advisor to Xerox found that teams that were just forming needed a few Type A personalities who would take the leadership role, set high performance standards, push for details, and feel a sense of commitment. Once the team was launched and into its work process, the need for Type A personalities was likely to be replaced by the need for Type B personalities.[11]

Resiliency
The ability to absorb high levels of disruptive change.

RESILIENCE   **Resiliency** is the ability to absorb high levels of disruptive change while displaying minimal dysfunctional behavior. Since it is no longer sufficient to merely cope with the stress of uncertainty, employees must have the ability to move beyond mere survival and actually prosper in environments that are becoming increasingly more complex and unpredictable.[12]

A recent study by Motorola Corporation found that individuals with high levels of resiliency reported high levels of coworker cohesion, supervisor support, job involvement, and responsibility. In addition, the high-resiliency individuals reported greater social support and lower levels of perceived stress and engaged in more problem-focused coping than the individuals with low resiliency.[13]

Not all individuals have high resiliency; however, resiliency can be increased through training. One of the important outcomes of the Motorola study was that the company transformed the research findings into a training program, "Transforming Stress into Resilience." At Questar, an integrated energy resource company in Salt Lake City, personal resiliency training has been linked to lower turnover and higher productivity when employees face disruption in their lives.[14]

Self-monitoring
The degree to which one is capable of adjusting successfully to the situation.

SELF-MONITORING   **Self-monitoring (SM)** identifies the degree to which individuals are capable of reading and using cues from their environment to determine their behavior. Individuals who score high on the SM scale are able to read environmental and social cues about what is considered appropriate behavior and adjust accordingly. For people high on the SM scale, behavior is likely to be the result of perception of the environment and is, therefore, likely to adapt to the situation. People who score low on the SM scale tend to base their behaviors on internal things and are likely to appear consistent across different situations.[15]

People high on the SM scale tend to emerge as leaders more frequently and learn managerial skills more easily than do people who are low on the SM scale. Also, high SM managers are better able to cope with cross-cultural situations, since they adapt their behavior more to the situation.[16] As with almost everything, being high or low on the SM scale has advantages and disadvantages. While someone who is high SM is flexible, in some situations, he or she might be seen as not stable. In contrast, someone who is low on the SM scale is quite consistent. That may be proper in some situations but not in others.

Authoritarianism
The degree to which one prefers power and status differences between people.

AUTHORITARIANISM   **Authoritarianism** refers to the degree to which one prefers power and status differences between people. One who is high in authoritarianism would show respect for titles, formal authority, status, and rank. He or she would insist on following the formal chain of command. Doing so would provide order in knowing who is in charge.[17]

The degree to which managers believe in authoritarianism will influence how they use their power and how they expect subordinates to behave in response. If managers and subordinates have widely different beliefs about authoritarianism, there could be difficulty in their interactions.

MYERS-BRIGGS TYPE INDICATOR

One of the most widely used instruments to assess personality is the Myers-Briggs Type Indicator, or MBTI. The MBTI is a series of questions that ask people to indicate their preferred way of acting, thinking, or feeling in different situations. Responses to the questions assess where one tends to be on a continuum for each of the following four dimensions:[18]

1. Introversion/Extroversion (**I or E**). This dimension represents the source of one's energy. Introverts draw energy from inside, from themselves. They tend to enjoy being alone and prefer ideas, thoughts, and concepts. Extroverts draw energy from interacting with other people. Consequently, they tend to have a wide social network. In the United States extroverts outnumber introverts—70 percent to 30 percent. The U.S. culture tends to encourage extroversion.[19]

The I/E dimension, like the following three, is measured on a continuum. Therefore, one could score toward one end or the other, or somewhere in-between. A score in the center of the continuum would mean that the person has some characteristics of both introversion and extroversion.

2. Sensing/Intuitive (**S or N**). The S/N dimension describes how people prefer to gather data. Sensing (S) people prefer concrete, real, factual, and structured data. They think in a careful manner, rely upon facts, and are not comfortable with abstract data and theory. On the other hand, intuitive (N) people prefer the overall view, theories, and new things and become bored with details and facts. Intuitive people solve problems easily and are spontaneous in doing so, although they may make errors because they neglect details and facts.

3. Feeling/Thinking (**F or T**). F/T represents how people prefer to make judgments. People who are described as feeling tend to be interested in people and feelings rather than in analysis and logic. They tend to make judgments about people and things based on empathy and harmony rather than on achieving goals that are impersonal. Thinking people rely on analysis, evidence, and logic rather than on feelings and personal values. They may seem unemotional and uninterested in people.

4. Perceiving/Judging (**P or J**). This dimension represents decision-making styles. Perceiving people tend to see all sides of a situation and welcome new perspectives and new information before deciding. Consequently, they might be indecisive and put off decisions to a point of becoming frustrated. Perceivers tend to be flexible and "roll with life." Even after deciding, they might look back at decisions and wonder if another decision might have been better. People who are considered judging are decisive and sure of themselves. They set goals and stay with them. Judging people want to get things done and move on to the next thing. Sometimes, a judging person might leave an unfinished task if it takes too long and move on to the next one.

With these four dimensions, each with two extremes, 16 possible combinations of personality types exist—ISFP, INTJ, ENTJ, to name a few. Table 14.2 summarizes possible strengths and weaknesses of the two extremes of each of the four dimensions.

The MBTI is used to help understand one's personality type and thereby to predict behavior.[20] It can be used to help select and place people in situations that

LEARNING OBJECTIVE 3

Explain what is measured by both the Myers-Briggs Type Indicator and the "Big 5."

I or E

A personality dimension measuring the degree to which a person is introverted or extroverted.

S or N

A personality dimension measuring whether one is sensing or intuitive.

F or T

A personality dimension referring to whether one is feeling or thinking in making judgments.

P or J

A personality dimension representing the degree to which one is perceiving or judging in making decisions.

Table 14.2 | Possible Strengths and Weaknesses of MBTI Personality Types

POSSIBLE STRENGTHS		POSSIBLE WEAKNESSES
	Introvert (I)	
Independent, works alone		Avoids others, secretive
Diligent, reflective		Misunderstood by others
Careful		Dislikes being interrupted
Works with ideas		Loses opportunities to act
	Extrovert (E)	
Open, interacts with others		Less independence
Is well understood		Needs change, variety
Understands the external		Impulsive, impatient
Acts decisively		Doesn't work without people
	Senser (S)	
Good with detail		Loses sight of the overall
Practical		Frustrated with the complicated
Patient		Mistrusts intuition
Systematic		Doesn't see the new, caught in detail
	Intuitor (N)	
Sees overall possibilities		Inattentive to detail
Imagines		Impatient with tedious
Works with complicated		Jumps to conclusions, leaps of logic
Solves novel problems		Not practical
	Feeler (F)	
Considers needs of others		Not objective, is uncritical
Demonstrates feelings		Not guided by logic
Conciliatory		Less organized
Persuades, arouses		Justice based on feelings
	Thinker (T)	
Logical, analytical		Feelings not important
Objective, organized		Not interested in conciliation
Is just		Shows less mercy
Stands firm		Misunderstands values of others
	Perceiver (P)	
Sees all sides of issues		Indecisive, does not plan
Compromises, flexible		Does not control circumstances
Open to change		Easily distracted
Nonjudgmental, based on data		Does not finish things
	Judger (J)	
Decides, plans		Unyielding, inflexible
Makes quick decisions		Judgmental
Finishes things		Controlled by task or plan
Has order, control		Decides with insufficient data

SOURCES: R. McCrae and T. Costa, Jr., "Reinterpreting the Myers-Briggs Type Indicator from the Perspective of the Five Factor Model of Personality," *Journal of Personality*, March 1989, 17–40; N. Quenk, Essentials of Myers-Briggs Type Indicator Assessment, (New York: Wiley, 2000).

are more suited to their style of behavior. For example, someone who is highly introverted probably would not be a good salesperson who must interact with large numbers of people. If a manager is a judger and the subordinate is a perceiver, at the minimum, each would have to learn to work with the other. Other options include assigning only judging types to work with judging managers. That might help the people interact well. However, it might also cause a situation where decisions are made too quickly, without proper analysis. Overall, the MBTI should be used to help understand where a person is "coming from" so that interactions between people can be based on a better understanding.

THE "BIG FIVE" PERSONALITY TRAITS

A recent model of personality characteristics suggests that all personality characteristics can be reduced to five basic factors. It is called the Five-Factor Model, or more commonly, the **Big Five**. These five factors are extroversion, agreeableness, conscientiousness, emotional stability, and openness to experience.[21]

1. *Extroversion:* the degree to which one is assertive, gregarious, and sociable rather than quiet, reserved, and timid.
2. *Agreeableness:* the degree to which one is agreeable, warm, and cooperative as compared to disagreeable, cold, and uncooperative.
3. *Conscientiousness:* the degree that a person is organized, dependable, and responsible. The contrast is unorganized, unreliable, and irresponsible.
4. *Emotional stability:* the degree to which a person is calm, self-confident, and secure as compared to anxious, tense, insecure, and depressed.
5. *Openness to experience:* the degree to which a person is creative, curious, and intellectual rather than very practical with narrow interests.

Overall, the Big Five is a fairly valid predictor of performance on the job. Extroversion predicts success in occupations that involve social contact, such as salespeople and managers.[22] Other research has found that people who are extroverted tend to have more promotions and higher salaries and are more satisfied with their careers than people who are less extroverted.[23] Conscientiousness is a valid predictor of high performance across essentially all occupations.[24] For more specific occupations, certain combinations of factors predict performance. People with high emotional stability, agreeableness, and openness to experience tend to perform better in customer service jobs. As mentioned above, managers tend to do well if they are high on extroversion. Emotional stability is also associated with performance of a manager.[25] People who are more introverted and conscientious have lower absence rates.[26] Finally, people with high conscientiousness tend to rate peers on a tougher scale than do people with high agreeableness.[27]

Big Five
A model measuring personality traits which include extroversion, agreeableness, conscientiousness, emotional stability, and openness to experience.

MATCHING PERSONALITIES WITH JOBS

Many "interest inventories" attempt to help a person identify careers and jobs that he or she might be interested in. The most promising seems to be what is now called the RIASEC Vocational Interest Typology. This typology identifies six personality types in terms of the kind of activities, and therefore jobs and careers, that one would prefer.[28] They are:

1. *Realistic.* Preference for physical activities that require strength, skill, and coordination.
2. *Investigative.* Preference for activities that require thinking, understanding, and organizing.
3. *Artistic.* A preference for activities that call for creative expression and are ambiguous and nonsystematic.
4. *Social.* Preference for activities that involve other people.
5. *Enterprising.* Preference for activities that allow verbal skills that can be used to influence others and gain power.

LEARNING OBJECTIVE 4
Explain the importance of matching personality characteristics to jobs and careers.

6. *Conventional.* A preference for activities that are nonambiguous and include rules and order.

This typology is based on the reasoning that if an individual's personality matches his or her job or career, then he or she will be less likely to leave. The typology has been found to be useful in that it helps individuals select a job in which they will be more satisfied. Related, it helps career counselors better suggest personality/job matches.[29]

The RIASEC Typology also uses "hexagonal calculus." (See Figure 14.1.) That means that the two personality types that are directly across from each other are the most opposite. For example, a Realistic personality is most opposite from a Social, and an Investigative is most opposite from an Enterprising. It also means that a personality has some overlap with the two on either side. Realistic has some overlap with Investigative and with Conventional.

What does this hexagonal calculus mean? A Realistic type of personality would be most dissatisfied in a job or career that included activities that a Social personality would like, and vice versa. However, a Realistic personality, while not totally satisfied, would be "OK" in an Investigative setting or in a Conventional setting. Of course, the same application applies to all other relationships among personality types and job settings.[30]

PERCEPTION

Perception
The way people experience, process, define, and interpret the world around them.

Perception refers to the way people experience, process, define, and interpret the world around them. It can be considered an information screen or filter that influences the way in which individuals communicate and become aware of sensations and stimuli that exist around them. Acting as a filter, perception means that individuals might see only certain elements in a particular situation, and not the entire situation.

Perceptions are influenced by a variety of factors, including an individual's experiences, needs, personality, and education. As a result, a person's perceptions are not necessarily accurate. However, they are unique and help to explain why two individuals may look at the same situation or message and perceive it differently. For example, managers in the same organization but different departments, such as operations, marketing, and finance, will perceive the weekly sales data dif-

Figure 14.1 | RIASEC Vocational Interest Typology

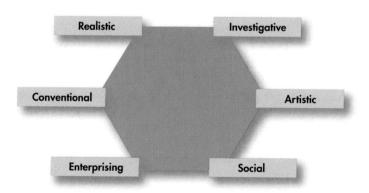

SOURCE: Based on J. Holland, *Making Vocational Choices: A Theory of Vocational Personalities and Work Environments* (Englewood Cliffs, NJ: Prentice Hall, 1985).

ferently. An individual's cultural background also may influence his or her perception and interpretation of certain company messages or symbols.

PERCEPTUAL PROCESS   The perceptual process is complex and involves selection, organization, and interpretation of environmental stimuli. First, we select or pay attention to some information and ignore other information, often without consciously realizing that we are doing so. For example, a hungry person is likely to focus on the food pictured in an advertisement for fine china, whereas a person who is not hungry may focus on the color and design of the china.

After selecting, we organize the information into a pattern and interpret it. How we interpret what we perceive also varies considerably. Depending on the circumstances and our state of mind, we may interpret a wave of the hand as a friendly gesture or a threat. Read the following sentence out loud:

A bird in the
the hand is worth two in the bush.

Did you see "the" repeated? Spatial arrangement may have caused you to not see the repetition.

The perceptual process is filled with possibilities for errors in judgment or misunderstandings. While these perceptual errors or biases allow us to make quick judgments and provide data for making predictions, they can also result in significant mistakes that can be costly to individuals and organizations. We will explore the following common errors or distortions in perception that have particular applications in managerial situations: (1) stereotyping, (2) the halo-and-horn effect, and (3) selective perception.

STEREOTYPING   **Stereotyping** is generalization, or the tendency to assign attributes to a person solely on the basis of a category or group to which that person belongs rather than on individual characteristics. In many ways, stereotypes lead to misunderstandings because they are inaccurate or biased. We readily expect someone identified as a professor, carpenter, police officer, poet, or surgeon to have certain attributes, even if we have not met the individual. Even identifying an employee by such broad categories as older, female, or Native American can lead to errors and misperceptions. Stereotyping may lead the perceiver to dwell on certain characteristics expected of all persons in the assigned category and to fail to recognize the characteristics that distinguish the person as an individual.

When we face new situations, stereotypes provide guidelines to help classify people. Unfortunately, stereotyping based on false premises may lead to a distorted view of reality because it assumes that all people of one gender, race, or age, for example, have similar characteristics, which simply isn't true. Stereotypes based on such factors as gender, age, ethnicity, religion, or sexual preference can, and unfortunately still do, bias perceptions of employees in some organizations.[31] A recent study even found gender bias in the college classroom and demonstrated that male professors were perceived to be more effective than females even though their performance ratings were identical.[32]

Some organizations, such as the Denny's Restaurant chain, which we discussed in Chapter 11 on page 347, have been forced by court orders and multimillion-dollar discrimination case settlements to institute training to demonstrate how stereotyping can lead to discrimination against both employees and customers and to teach employees to manage a diverse workforce. However, for the majority of organizations, training and mentoring programs have been used voluntarily to reduce stereotyping and help employees adjust to increasing workplace diversity.

HALO-AND-HORN EFFECT   The **halo-and-horn effect** refers to a process in which we evaluate and form an overall impression of an individual based solely on

© DOUG MENUEZ/GETTYIMAGES/PHOTODISC

Stereotyping often leads to a distorted view of reality because it assumes that all people in a particular category, such as professors, have the same attributes.

Stereotyping
Tendency to assign attributes to someone based on the group to which that person belongs.

Halo-and-horn effect
Judging a person all positive (halo) or all negative (horn) based on one thing.

a specific trait or dimension, such as enthusiasm, gender, appearance, or intelligence. If we view the observed trait as positive, we tend to apply a halo (positive) effect to other traits and to the entire person. If we think of the observed trait as negative, we apply a horn (negative) effect. Consider, for example, the student who scores a near-perfect grade on the first exam in a course and creates a favorable impression on the professor. The professor may then assume that the student is tops in all of his or her classes, efficient, bright, and loyal. Keep in mind that when evaluations are made on the basis of traits that aren't linked, halo-and-horn effects result. Of course, many traits are, in fact, related; therefore, not all judgments based on the halo-and-horn effect are necessarily perceptual errors.

Selective perception

Tendency to see or hear only what we want to see or hear.

SELECTIVE PERCEPTION   **Selective perception** is the tendency to screen out information with which we aren't comfortable or don't want to be bothered. We have all been accused of listening only to what we want to hear or "tuning out" what we don't wish to hear. Both are examples of selective perception.

A classic study of how selective perception influences managers involved executives in a manufacturing company.[33] When asked to identify the key problem in a comprehensive business strategy case, all executives in the study selected a problem consistent with their own functional area work assignments. For example, most marketing executives viewed the key problem area as sales; production people tended to see it as a production problem; and human resource people perceived it as a personnel issue. These differing viewpoints demonstrate how errors can occur and affect the way executives approach problems.

In organizations, employees often make this perceptual error. Marketing employees pay close attention to marketing problems and issues, research and development (R&D) engineers pay close attention to product technology or R&D funding, and accountants focus on issues specifically related to accounting. These employees selectively eliminate information that deals with other areas of the organization and focus only on information that is directly relevant to their own needs.

LEARNING OBJECTIVE 5

Discuss the importance of perception and perceptual errors.

REDUCING PERCEPTUAL ERRORS   Since perception is such an important process and plays a major role in determining our behavior, managers must recognize the common perceptual errors. Managers who fall prey to perceptual errors, such as stereotyping, lose sight of individual differences among people. The quality of their decisions can suffer, and the performance of capable people can also suffer. Simple knowledge of perceptual errors, such as stereotyping, halo-and-horn errors, and selective perception, is the first step in avoiding such mistakes.

ATTITUDES

Attitudes

The beliefs, feelings, and behavioral tendencies held by a person.

Attitudes are relatively lasting beliefs, feelings, and behavioral tendencies held by a person about specific objects, events, groups, issues, or people. Attitudes result from a person's background, personality, and life experiences. While these attitudes may not necessarily be factual or completely consistent with objective reality, managers still must be aware of those that have an impact on the organization, such as how satisfied individuals are with their jobs, how committed they are to the organization's values and goals, and how willing they are to expend considerable effort for the organization.[34]

Cognitive dissonance

An inconsistency among a person's attitudes or between an attitude and a behavior.

People tend to want consistency among their attitudes and between their attitudes and behaviors. If differences exist, people tend to want to reconcile those differences. This is known as the theory of **cognitive dissonance**, an inconsistency among attitudes or between an attitude and a behavior.[35] For example, if a person just purchased a product that might not clearly fit his or her attitude, the person probably feels some stress or tension and would try to justify the product to fit the attitude. That is one reason why so much advertising is actually aimed at the person who just purchased a product—to help him or her feel comfortable with the product. Possibly, in this situation, attitude may have changed a bit. On the other hand, if the person continues to feel very stressed about the new product, chances are the product will be discarded.

Marketers might actually try to create cognitive dissonance as a way to get attention for a product. Consider the example of milk. It tends to not have a glamorous image. That is why a long-running campaign featured celebrities with a "milk-moustache"—to place unglamorous milk in a setting that is very glamorous. The campaign was successful in selling more milk.

What is the significance of cognitive dissonance for a manager? Leon Festinger, the originator of the theory, suggested that three things affect what a person did if he or she experienced cognitive dissonance—the importance of the factors creating the dissonance, the influence that the person has over these factors, and the rewards associated with the dissonance.[36] If the factors that create the dissonance are low in importance, then the stress related to the dissonance will be low and the person probably will not do anything. If the factors are important, then the person will experience high stress and will want to correct the dissonance. Here is where the degree of influence that the person has comes into play. If the stress is high and the person cannot change the factors, he or she may leave the situation in order to get rid of the dissonance. Finally, rewards come into play. One example: Say that an employee believes that doing something in the job is not ethical. However, the manager insists that the employee do it because the managers sees nothing wrong with it. If the stress is very high, the employee might, as a last resort, leave the job or rationalize doing the unethical act by saying "Well, I need a job so I'll do it." The manager could directly influence this situation also by offering a reward. If the reward is important to the employee, then the employ can justify doing the task—"Well, I really need the promotion, so I guess this isn't so bad. Besides, doing it will make the company more successful and provide jobs for more people . . . ."

The most commonly studied work attitude is job satisfaction. **Job satisfaction** is the degree to which individuals feel positively or negatively about their jobs. It is an emotional response to tasks, leadership, peer relationships, and organizational politics, as well as other physical and social conditions of the workplace.[37] Job satisfaction can lead to a variety of positive and negative outcomes, from both an individual and an organizational perspective. It influences how employees feel about themselves, their work, and their organizations and can affect how they contribute to achieving their own goals and the organization's goals.[38]

The best-known scale that measures job satisfaction is the Job Descriptive Index (JDI). The JDI evaluates five specific characteristics of a person's job:[39]

1. The work itself—responsibility, interest, and growth.
2. Pay—adequacy of pay and perceived equity.
3. Relations with coworkers—social harmony and respect.
4. Quality of supervision—technical help and social support.
5. Promotional opportunities—chances for further advancement.

Certainly, an employee can be satisfied with some aspects of a job and at the same time be dissatisfied with others. A scale such as the JDI helps managers pinpoint sources of dissatisfaction so they can take appropriate action.

RELATIONSHIP BETWEEN SATISFACTION AND PERFORMANCE

Of particular interest to managers is the relationship between job satisfaction and performance at work. Over the years, some research has shown that job satisfaction causes job performance, while other studies have indicated that job performance causes job satisfaction. Yet other research shows no relationship between

Job satisfaction
The degree to which individuals feel positively or negatively about their jobs.

LEARNING OBJECTIVE 6

Discuss the relationship between job satisfaction and performance.

job satisfaction and performance. Contingency variables help slightly in finding relationships. The relationship might be stronger when the employee is not controlled or constrained by other things. For example, when a job is machine-paced, that influences performance more than does job satisfaction. Also, the relationship is a bit stronger for higher-level jobs.[40] The current viewpoint is that managers should not assume a simple cause-and-effect relationship between job satisfaction and job performance, because the relationship between the two in any particular situation will depend on a complex set of personal and situational variables. An employee's job performance depends on a large number of factors, such as ability, the quality of equipment and materials used, the competence of supervision, the working environment, peer relationships, and so on.

ABILITY

Ability
Capacity to perform various tasks needed; may be classified as mental, mechanical, or psychomotor.

Ability is defined as an existing capacity to perform various tasks needed in a given situation. Abilities are classified as mental, mechanical, and psychomotor. Mental or intellectual ability is important for problem solving because it involves the capacity to transform information, generate alternatives, memorize, and consider implications. Mechanical ability refers to the capacity to comprehend relationships between objects and to perceive how parts fit together. Psychomotor ability includes such things as manual dexterity, eye-hand coordination, and manipulative ability. In the organizational setting, ability and effort are key determinants of employee behavior and performance.

The key point is that not only do employee abilities vary substantially, but different tasks require different abilities and call for different personality characteristics. Such recognition is crucial to understanding and predicting work behaviors. This becomes even more evident when we begin to think about putting individuals together in teams. Up to this point in the chapter, we have focused on individual behavior. We now turn our attention to examining the power of individuals when they work together. The social environment of the workplace provides opportunities for individuals to interact and create working relationships that often lead to efficiency and effectiveness.

We know that individuals act differently in groups than when they are alone. In the next part of the chapter we explore groups since in most organizations teamwork has become a fact of life. Your first reaction may be to view teams either as a significant threat or as a wonderful opportunity for your own career. Regardless of your reaction, teams appear to be here to stay, and they can represent powerful organizational models.

Before we can understand how managers can create and maintain successful, high-performance teams, we need to know more about the very basic aspects of their functioning. This includes the definition of a team, the inputs for designing effective work teams, and the processes that lead to team success.

KEY INPUTS FOR DESIGNING EFFECTIVE TEAMS

The question of what a group or team is represents a good starting point toward a greater understanding of team and group dynamics. Organizations use numerous labels for the many types of teams. Perhaps the most basic distinction in labels surrounds the difference between a group and a team. A group is normally defined as two or more individuals who interact with one another.[41] A team is a group of interdependent individuals with shared commitments to accomplish a common purpose or goal. This suggests that a team is more than a group.[42] Our definition

Leaders In Action

Keith Alper: Leader of Team Leaders

Keith Alper is executive producer and CEO of Creative Producers Group, a corporate communications company (http://www.getcreative.com). Creative Producers Group assists client corporations to improve communications inside of their organizations as well as communication between them and various constituent groups. Clients include companies such as Abbott Labs, American Airlines, and Ernst & Young.

Projects for clients are accomplished with teams. The teams need to be quick; many times, the projects need to be completed in less than a week! The teams are put together and are effective immediately. How is this accomplished? Alper lists the requirements:

1. A team needs a leader. The leader must set direction, coach, and give direction.

2. The leader selects the team members based on personality, skill, and special needs of the project.
3. The leader must clearly specify roles, responsibilities, tasks, and items to be measured and monitored.
4. Trust must exist among all members of the team.
5. The "go to" person must be identified. This is the person who has the information or knows where to get it.

All of these things by themselves probably wouldn't make for successful teams, however. Above all else, every member of the company must understand the culture. The culture expects everyone to be excellent and to perform at their best all the time. To accomplish this expectation, everyone is trained about performance excellence, and new employ-

ees are "doubled-up" with a mentor on the teams.

In addition, feedback is provided to help everyone learn the culture and to measure performance against the culture of excellence. External clients are asked to complete a survey about the service. Internal clients complete a more thorough survey covering the team and individual team members.

That's how Creative Producers Group make teamwork successful. In addition, as Alper says, "It's not a good team without a leader."

SOURCES: Keith Alper, Interview, May 10, 2002; **http://www.getcreative.com**, Web site, May 8, 2002.

recognizes that success depends on the interdependent relationship and collective efforts of various team members, and that members are likely to have mutual influence and significant impact on one another as they work together.[43] While this distinction between a team and a group makes sense, determining the point at which a group becomes a team is impossible. In recent years, the word *team* has become popular in the business community, often replacing the word *group*. For our purposes in this chapter, we use the terms *group* and *team* somewhat interchangeably.

Simply placing individuals together and telling them to work together does not in and of itself promote productivity or success. Team effectiveness does not magically appear when a group is formed. Members must consciously work to build and maintain the effectiveness of their team in order to first achieve success and then maintain it.

The critical requirements of an effective team are shown in Figure 14.2. First, the team members must have an interdependent relationship; they are dependent on each other to accomplish the tasks. Second, interdependence dictates that members must interact through conversation or work activities. Third, a team is characterized by mutual influence among members, rather than having all the power held by a minority. Fourth, the team must have a clearly understood goal or common purpose that evokes high levels of commitment from all members. For a team to exist, both members and observers must be able to distinguish clearly those people who are included in the team from those who are part of the larger social system but are not included in the team.

Team members must consciously work to build and maintain the effectiveness of their team to be productive and successful.

© JACOBS STOCK PHOTOGRAPHY/GETTYIMAGES/PHOTODISC

Figure 14.2 | Critical Requirements of Effective Teams

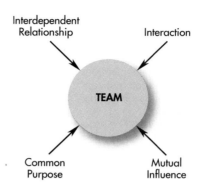

GROUP CATEGORIES

Groups come in many forms, shapes, and sizes. Most managers belong to many different groups at the same time—some at work and some in the community. In the performance of organizational work, two basic categories of teams exist—formal and informal. Both categories can influence the work performed either positively or negatively.

Formal groups
Groups that are deliberately created by managers.

FORMAL GROUPS   **Formal groups** are deliberately created by the organization's managers to accomplish goals and serve the needs of the organization. The major purpose of formal groups is to perform specific tasks and achieve specific objectives defined by the organization. The most common type of formal work group consists of individuals cooperating under the direction of a leader. Examples of formal groups are departments, divisions, task forces, project groups, quality circles, committees, and boards of directors. Boeing formed special quality-improvement teams when it was first testing the new 777 airplane. These are considered to be formal groups and will be maintained throughout production of the plane.

Informal groups
Groups that are not formed or planned by the organization's managers.

INFORMAL GROUPS   **Informal groups** are not formed or planned by the organization's managers. Rather, they are self-created and evolve out of the formal organization for a variety of reasons, such as proximity, common interests, or needs of individuals. It would be difficult to design an organization that prohibits informal working relationships from developing.

Because human beings receive reassurance from interacting with others and being part of a group, informal groups can meet a range of individual needs. Perhaps the major reason informal groups evolve is to fulfill individuals' needs for affiliation and friendship, social interaction, communication, power, safety, and status. For example, individuals who regularly eat lunch, carpool, or go to a football game together are members of an informal group that fulfills some of these needs. While some informal groups may complement the organization's formal groups, at times they can also work against the organization's goals. A number of factors affect the ways groups operate.

In the next section we examine the inputs for designing teams that lead to effectiveness. These include membership composition, size, and goals. Figure 14.3 illustrates the inputs.

Figure 14.3 | Inputs to Designing Effective Teams

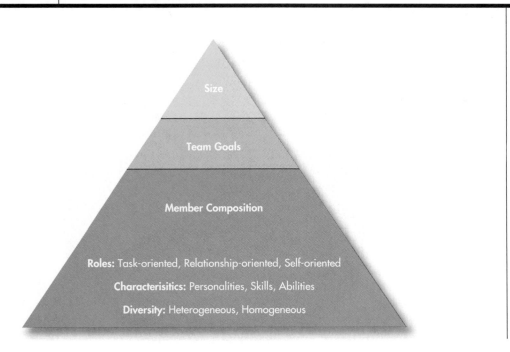

MEMBERSHIP COMPOSITION

A critical design feature of teams concerns the individuals who comprise the teams. Team composition is the mixture of individual inputs and skills included in a team. One way to understand team member input is to examine the roles of the team members.

LEARNING OBJECTIVE 7
Comment on the various types of team member roles.

ROLES A role is a set of behaviors that is characteristic of a person in a specific situation. People develop their roles and behaviors based on their own expectations, the team's expectations, and the organization's expectations—related to job description, goals that were set, and so on. As employees internalize the expectations of these three sources, they develop their roles.

People often have multiple roles within the same group.[44] For example, a professor may have the roles of teacher, researcher, writer, consultant, advisor, and committee member. Our roles also extend outside the workplace. The professor may also be a family member, belong to professional and civic organizations, and have social friends, all of whom may have very different expectations about the behaviors that are appropriate.

When operating in a work group, individuals typically fulfill several roles. Member roles fit into three categories, and each has associated behaviors: (1) task-oriented roles, (2) relationship-oriented roles, and (3) self-oriented roles.[45] As Figure 14.4 shows, each of these categories includes a variety of role behaviors.

Behaviors directly related to establishing and accomplishing the goals of the group or achieving the desired outcomes are **task-oriented roles**. They include seeking and providing information, initiating actions and procedures, building on ideas, giving and seeking information, testing consensus, giving opinions, summarizing progress, and energizing the quantity and quality of output.

Task-oriented roles
Behaviors that are directly related to establishing and accomplishing the goals of the group or achieving the desired outcomes.

Figure 14.4 | Group Roles and Associated Behaviors

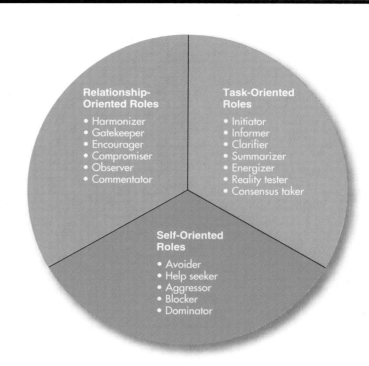

Relationship-oriented roles
Behaviors that cultivate the well-being, continuity, and development of the group.

Self-oriented role
When a personal need or goal of an individual occurs without regard for the group's problems.

Relationship-oriented roles include behaviors that cultivate the well-being, continuity, and development of the group. They focus on the operation of the group and the maintenance of good relationships and help the group survive, regulate, grow, and strengthen itself. They help foster group unity, positive interpersonal relationships among group members, and the development of the members' ability to work together effectively. These behaviors include encouraging, harmonizing, checking performance, setting standards, and relieving tension.

When some personal need or goal of an individual occurs without regard for the group's problems, the behavior is referred to as a **self-oriented role**. Such roles often have a negative influence on a group's effectiveness.[46] Examples of such behaviors include dominating the discussions, emphasizing personal issues, interrupting others, distracting the group from its work, and wasting the group's time.

Effective teams discover how to integrate relationship- and task-oriented roles. For example, Team EcoInternet, an adventure racing team, has been consistently recognized for being exceptionally effective. It focuses on shared decision making, member optimism and concentration, rotation of leadership to the strongest, and admission of weakness, if necessary.[47]

MEMBER CHARACTERISTICS   Certain member characteristics are needed to support effective working relationships, including the right combination of abilities, job-related knowledge and skills, and specific personality traits. Diversity in terms of age, race, gender, ethnicity, and functional areas certainly can help a team by providing rich input. Take, for example, the skill of handling conflict. Since some degree of conflict is beneficial for a team, members do not avoid or totally eliminate it. Instead, they encourage conflict that is constructive and discourage conflict that is destructive. Of course, this works only if the team is functioning well.

Effective communication skills are required for team members to engage in informal conversation and active and objective listening. Also, team members must develop appropriate communication networks. (Refer to Chapter 12.)

DIVERSITY Team composition can be homogeneous (similar) or heterogeneous (diverse). A team is considered similar or **homogeneous** when it is composed of individuals having group-related characteristics, backgrounds, interests, values, and attitudes that are alike. When the individuals are dissimilar with respect to these characteristics, the group is diverse and is referred to as **heterogeneous**. Rapidly growing global interdependence and the increasing emphasis on teamwork result in groups with quite diverse composition. This is no longer the exception; it is the rule. For example, teams at Intel typically work across great distances, geographic borders, and cultural boundaries. It is not unusual for people from six or seven different national cultures to work together to complete a project.[48]

Homogeneous
A group having many similarities.

Heterogeneous
A group with many differences among its members.

Does a similar or a diverse composition lead to a more effective team? Managers face this difficult question every time they assemble a group of individuals for a task. A manager needs to understand the purpose of the team and the nature of the task to determine whether the team is better served by a homogeneous or a heterogeneous composition.

For tasks that are standard and routine, a homogeneous team functions more quickly. Membership homogeneity contributes to member satisfaction, creates less conflict and less turnover, and increases the chances for harmonious working relationships among members. If a team is too homogeneous, however, it may exert excessive pressure on its members to conform to the team's rules and may lack the controversy and perspectives essential to high-quality decision making and creativity.[49]

For tasks that are nonroutine and require diverse skills, opinions, and behaviors, a heterogeneous group yields better results. A diverse membership can bring a variety of skills and viewpoints to bear on problems and thus facilitate task accomplishment. The more diverse the membership, however, the more skilled the manager or team leader will have to be in facilitating a successful experience.[50]

© GETTYIMAGES/DIGITAL VISION

Global interdependence and the increasing emphasis on teamwork result in heterogeneous groups of diverse composition.

As organizations become increasingly diverse in terms of gender, race, ethnicity, and age, this diversity brings potential benefits such as better decision making, greater creativity and innovation, and more successful marketing to different types of customers. However, increased cultural differences within a workforce can also make it harder to develop cohesive work teams and may result in higher turnover, interpersonal conflict, and communication breakdowns.[51]

Managers must be aware of these issues as they work to create high-performance teams. They need to be trained to capitalize on the benefits of diversity while minimizing the potential costs. Additionally, managers will need to work to integrate minority group members both formally and informally, strive to eliminate prejudice and discrimination, reduce alienation, and build organizational identity among minority group members. The organization that achieves these conditions will create an environment in which all members can contribute to their maximum potential and in which the value of diversity can be fully realized.[52]

SIZE

Effective task groups can be different sizes. Many people suggest a range from two members to about sixteen. It is difficult to pinpoint an ideal size because the appropriate size depends on the group's purpose.[53] Size affects how individuals interact with each other as well as the overall performance of the group. In groups of fewer than five members, more personal discussion and more complete participation will occur. As a team grows beyond several members, it becomes more difficult for all members to participate effectively. Communication and coordination among members become more difficult, and the team tends to split into subgroups. As a result, the interactions become more centralized, with a few individuals taking more active roles relative to the rest; disagreements may occur more easily; and satisfaction may decline unless team members put a good deal of effort into relationship-oriented roles.

As group size increases, more potential human resources are available to perform the work and accomplish needed tasks. While this can boost performance, the expanded size tends to increase turnover and absenteeism, as well as provide opportunities for free riding. **Free riding** describes a tendency of one or more team members to expend decreasing amounts of effort because their contributions are less visible.[54] They are willing to let others carry the workload.[55]

Free riding directly challenges the logic that the productivity of the group as a whole should at least equal the sum of the productivity of each individual in the group. In other words, group size and individual performance may be inversely related. Most students are acquainted with the concept of free riding, largely as a result of negative experiences they have encountered in working on group projects.[56]

Free riding
A tendency for a group member to not contribute to the group's efforts but to share in the rewards.

TEAM GOALS

Another critical element for designing effective teams is team goals. Goals provide a clear, engaging sense of direction and specify what is going to be accomplished.

At The Forefront

Best Practice: Creating Learning Teams

Remember the top five most important skills that recruiters are looking for in job applicants that we talked about at the beginning of Chapter 12 on page 371? Teamwork is in the top five. However, not any old team will do. An effective team must be put together and managed well. A *Harvard Business Review* survey reports that the best practices in accomplishing that is to create a learning team.

A learning team has three requirements; The team must be designed for learning; the team leader must present the situation in a way that motivates team members; and the leader must behave in such a way that members feel safe, which, in turn, promotes communication and creativity. A good example of putting these requirements into practice is Seagate Technology, a disk-drive company that is one of the oldest and is doing very well.

Seagate people believe that expertise has to be shared so that the team can be successful. In order to accomplish this, team members are encouraged to question things that don't look right so that the final de-

cision and actions of the team and, therefore, the entire company are successful. If a person doesn't question something or hides a problem, it can become a major issue later—perhaps after the customer has the defective product. The culture of the organization stresses that "The only way the team can do well is if everyone helps the person who's having the hardest time." To underscore all of this, performance of each team member is based on the results of the entire team.

Seagate teams learn to share information and to communicate in order to be successful in finding products and services in the very challenging computer components industry. They learn to look ahead and predict what products and services will be demanded. Team members and team leaders reward sharing of information and asking questions. Team members feel safe in doing this.

Team leaders assemble the right mix of people on teams so that opportunities and problems can be identified and addressed overall, rather than just one small piece at a

time. An example of this is putting people from production, marketing, and the other areas on teams so that all are motivated to identify what customers want and to create and deliver it better and faster than competitors can.

The teams continue to be open to changes outside and inside of the company. They share information. Trust is high. Rewards go to team accomplishments. Teams keep learning to improve in order to keep ahead of the fierce challenges in the personal computer industry. As the *Harvard Business Review* survey found, successful teams behave this way. This appears to be a trend in learning how to manage teams to make them more successful.

SOURCES: G. Anders, "The Innovator's Solution," *Fast Company*, June 2002, 138; N. Schullery and M. Gibson, "Working in Groups: Identification and Treatments of Students' Perceived Weaknesses," *Business Communication Quarterly*, June 2001, 64, 9–30; A. Edmondson, R. Bohmer, and G. Pisano, "Speeding Up Team Learning," *Harvard Business Review*, October 2001, 125–32.

For example, we read in "Facing The Challenge" on page 426 that United Technologies Corporation (UTC) had an overall goal of reducing the costs of transportation while maintaining a certain level of service from its transportation companies. These goals united the team members in finding common transportation companies that would serve their purposes while achieving the overall corporation's goals. When members share goals, they work harder and longer on the tasks required for high performance.[57]

PROCESSES FOR TEAM EFFECTIVENESS

Numerous intragroup processes can affect how a team functions. In this next section, we look at the developmental stages through which most teams pass. An understanding of the developmental stages will provide insight into how interactions and intrateam processes change over time and influence the team. Refer to Figure 14.5 as you examine the different stages of team progress. While no two teams develop in exactly the same way, Figure 14.5 illustrates the evolution processes.

Figure 14.5 | Stages of Team Development

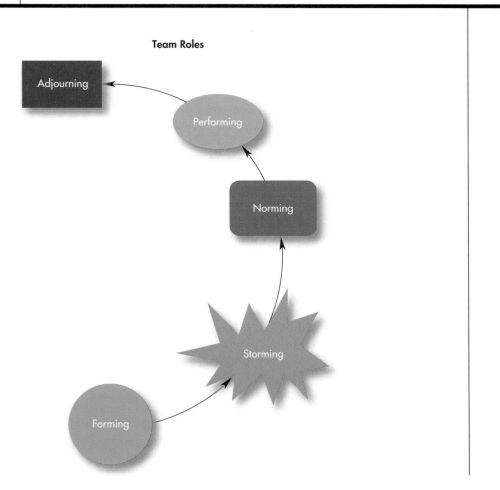

TEAM DEVELOPMENT

LEARNING OBJECTIVE 8

Identify the development phases of groups.

The team development process is dynamic. Although most groups are in a continuous state of change and rarely reach complete stability, team development does follow a general pattern. Teams appear to go through a five-stage developmental sequence: forming, storming, norming, performing, and adjourning.[58]

The types of behaviors observed in groups differ from stage to stage. The length of time spent in each stage can also vary greatly, with each stage lasting until its paramount issues are resolved. The group then moves on. The stages are not clearly delineated, and some overlap exists between them. In other words, the process of development is ongoing and complex. New groups may progress through these stages, but if the group's membership changes, the group may regress to an earlier stage, at least temporarily.

Forming

First stage of group development.

FORMING   In the **forming** stage, individuals come together and begin to think of themselves as members of a team. This forming stage is marked by apprehension, seeking basic information, defining goals, developing procedures for performing the task, and making a preliminary evaluation of how the team might interact to accomplish goals. A great deal of uncertainty often emerges at this point, as team members begin to test the extent to which their input will be valued.

Teams in the forming stage often require some time for members to get acquainted with each other before attempting to proceed with their task responsibilities. It is a time for members to become acquainted, understand leadership and member roles, and learn what is expected of them.[59] The behaviors most common for individuals in the forming stage of team development include dependency, keeping feelings to themselves, acting more secure than they actually feel, experiencing confusion and uncertainty about what is expected, being polite, showing hesitancy about how to proceed, and sizing up the personal benefits and personal costs of being involved in the team. If a leader is designated, members are likely to wait for that individual to make decisions.

Storming

Group development stage that occurs as team members begin to experience conflict with one another.

STORMING   Usually the emergence of conflict between members indicates the end of the forming stage and the beginning of the storming stage. The **storming** stage occurs as team members begin to experience conflict with one another. Being part of a team means that individuals may need to sacrifice many of their personal desires.

Arguments about roles and procedures surface, and the pleasant social interactions of the forming stage cease. Team members often experience negative emotions and become uncomfortable interacting with one another. Attempts to resolve differences of opinion about key issues, who is to be responsible for what, and the task-related direction of the leader are areas of conflict. Competition for the leadership role and conflict over goals are dominant themes at this stage. Some members may withdraw or try to isolate themselves from the emotional tension that is generated. Teams with members from diverse backgrounds or cultures may experience greater conflict than more homogenous teams.

At this stage it is important not to suppress or withdraw from the conflict. Suppressing conflict will likely create bitterness and resentment, which will last long after members attempt to express their differences and emotions. Withdrawal can cause the team to fail more quickly.

LEARNING OBJECTIVE 9

Explain how cohesiveness can impact a team.

Norming

The stage of group development where norms are established.

NORMING   Most teams make it through the storming stage, but the **norming** stage is a junction point.[60] If issues have not been resolved, the team will erupt into serious conflict and run the risk of failure. If mechanisms develop for handling conflict, the team will progress smoothly into the norming stage. The norming stage of development is a stage in which the team members come together and a real sense of cohesion and belonging begins to emerge. Team members feel good about each other and identify with the team. They share feelings, give and receive feedback, and begin to share a sense of success. The most important outcome of this stage of development is an increase in cohesiveness.

Have you ever been a member of a team whose members seemed to get along and work well with one another, were highly motivated, and worked in a coordinated way? When a team behaves in this way, it is considered to be cohesive. **Cohesiveness** is a strong sense of connectedness between team members that causes them to work together to attain an objective.[61] Think of cohesiveness as the strength of the members' desire to remain in the group, their commitment to it, and their ability to function as a unit. A team whose members have a strong desire to remain in the group and personally accept its goals would be considered highly cohesive.

The degree of cohesiveness is an important dimension influencing group effectiveness. Cohesiveness can influence communication and the job satisfaction of group members. For example, members of cohesive groups tend to communicate more frequently, are likely to feel more satisfied with their jobs, are more committed to working through issues, think more favorably of team members, and experience less conflict than members of groups that are not cohesive.[62]

Cohesiveness among members may be a positive organizational force when it helps unite a team behind organizational goals. For example, when team members are committed, they know each other's strengths and weaknesses, they bring problems to the surface, and they work hard at being a team.[63] Unfortunately, a highly cohesive team can be a problem to an organization if the team's goals are in conflict with the organization's goals. For example, if a team is not committed to the organization, its goals might include how much work the team can avoid or how many problems the team can cause for the manager. A highly cohesive team could cause considerable trouble in these situations.

Also, highly cohesive teams may become dysfunctional if they lead team members to groupthink. As we learned in Chapter 6, **groupthink** is an agreement-at-any-cost mentality that results in ineffective group decision making. Groupthink leads to ineffective group decisions when high cohesiveness coexists with significant conformity with the group and overrides the realistic appraisal of alternative courses of action.[64] But groupthink does not have to occur.

The other option for the cohesive team in the norming stage is the development of strong bonds between team members, thereby influencing them to work harder to achieve the collective goals. Effectiveness can be particularly high if teams vigilantly check the quality of their decisions and strive to help team members retain their individuality and to develop the potential for exchanging all kinds of information relevant to a task.[65]

What is the cohesiveness behavior of a team you are currently working with? Turn to Experiential Exercise 14.2 on page 452 and complete the short exercise to use as a team-building technique before reading about norms.

The norming stage is also important because it is during this phase that team norms develop. **Norms** are unwritten, informal rules and shared beliefs that regulate the appropriate behavior expectations of team members. Norms differ from organizational rules in that they are unwritten and members must accept them and behave in ways consistent with them before they can be said to exist.[66]

Norms cannot be imposed on a group; rather, they develop out of the interaction among members. For example, a typical work group may have norms that define how people dress, the upper and lower limits on acceptable productivity, the information that can be told to the boss, and the matters that need to remain secret. If a group member does not follow the norms, the other members will try to enforce compliance through acceptance and friendship or through such means as ridicule, ostracism, sabotage, and verbal abuse.

Work groups establish a variety of norms that may not always align with the formal standards set by the organization. Group norms can be positive, helping the

Cohesiveness
The degree to which group members want to stay together.

Groupthink
An agreement-at-any-cost mentality that results in ineffective group decision making.

Norms
Unwritten, informal rules and shared beliefs that regulate the appropriate behavior expectations of team members.

group meet its objective(s), or they can be negative, hindering the group's effectiveness. Once norms are established, they are very difficult to change. Thus, the early stages of development are critical to set high standards and reward positive norms.

Although we know that disagreement among group members is beneficial for productive and critical thinking, it is often discouraged by group norms. Once a group reaches the norming stage of development, dissenters from group norm behavior are often pressured into conforming to new standards. Managers need to understand the norms of the groups they manage and then work toward maintaining and developing positive norms while eliminating negative norms.

Performing

Group development stage that occurs when the team is fully functional; marked by interpersonal relations and high levels of interdependence.

PERFORMING   The **performing** stage, when the team is fully functional, is marked by interpersonal relationships and high levels of interdependence. It is also the most difficult stage to achieve. The team is oriented to maintaining good relations and to getting its task accomplished. Team members can now work well with everyone on the team, communication is constant, decisions are made with full agreement, and members understand the roles they need to perform for the team to be highly effective.[67]

At the performing stage, the team has learned to solve complex problems and implement the solutions. Members are committed to the task and willing to experiment to solve problems. Cohesiveness has progressed to the point of collaboration. Confidence reaches a high level for the few teams that achieve this stage. Unfortunately, even if a team reaches this stage, it still faces the difficult job of maintaining this level of success.

Adjourning

Group development stage that involves the termination of task behaviors and disengagement from relationship-oriented behaviors.

ADJOURNING   The **adjourning** stage involves the termination of task behaviors and disengagement from relationship-oriented behaviors. Some groups, such as a project team created to investigate and report on a specific program within a limited time frame, have a well-defined point of adjournment. Other groups, such as an executive committee, may go on indefinitely. Adjourning for this type of group is more subtle and takes place when one or more key members leave the organization.

Let's compare the first four team developmental stages with the experience of the United Technologies Corporation (See "Facing The Challenge" and "Meeting The Challenge" on pages 426 and 449). The formation stage, of course, is the establishment of the teams. Immediately, the members had disagreements based upon their view of the entire situation and their perspectives. Thus, we see signs of the storming stage clearly as team members argued about their needs and their preferred transportation companies. The norming stage, when members feel a sense of belonging to and identify with the team, began to emerge, as team members began to see that not only did they have the same overall goal, but they really had the same basic needs. The team goal became more important than individual branch goals. At the same time, the goals of each branch could be achieved by focusing upon the overall goals. Finally, the performing stage began as the teams identified transportation companies that they all could use. This led to securing transportation that provided the service that both UTC and its customers wanted and saved money for UTC.

LEARNING OBJECTIVE 10

Clarify the primary elements of successful teams.

IMPLICATIONS FOR LEADERS

Research indicates that the primary elements of successful teams are that they have specific, well-defined goals, develop interdependent and collaborative relationships, share leadership, provide feedback, recognize and reward performance, and celebrate victories.[68] Is there a secret to creating this type of team? No. As a manager you must create the environment for the development and nurturing of successful teams. Start by focusing on the following:[69]

- *Trust.* Team members must learn to trust. Trust leads to flexibility and information flow.
- *Involvement.* Every team member's participation counts; individuals are dependent and interdependent on a team regardless of where they fit into the hierarchy.
- *Emphasis on strengths.* Team members must look for ways that their strengths and weaknesses complement each other.
- *Instillment of accountability.* Team members must take personal responsibility for completing tasks and supporting each other.
- *Creation of precise goals.* Members need clearly defined, precise goals and specific deadlines.

The more a manager understands about his or her personality and the personalities of coworkers, the more successful the manager can be in guiding a team and in supervising individuals. It does begin with oneself. The manager must understand himself or herself first. For one thing, the personality of the manager influences how he or she sees and interprets characteristics of all of the other people in the organization. This is essentially saying that the manager must have competence and character, two Cs of the 3Cs Model of Leadership. This third C is seen in building community by developing a successful team, as discussed above.

Meeting The Challenge

Teamwork at United Technologies

Emmons guided each of the three teams in studying the transportation needs of each branch and the entire situation related to transportation companies in each area. He also helped the teams identify the level of service needed from the transportation companies and set standards that the companies had to meet. The goal of reducing the costs of transportation was also kept in mind.

As the teams discussed the situation, they often learned that they did have very common situations and problems. This was quite different from before when many of the people believed that each branch or region had quite different problems and needs. The team members did learn from each other and benefited from the different functional and regional views.

The teams learned that they could identify and agree upon certain transportation companies that would serve their needs. They even worked out an eight-step sourcing process to help their customers determine the best way to ship to them. Also, the teams worked with chosen transportation companies to guarantee the level of service needed by everyone. Everyone is satisfied—UTC, its customers, and the chosen transportation companies.

The three regional teams continue to meet monthly. They review common goals, customer satisfaction, and more opportunities for savings.

SOURCE: B. Milligan, "Team Approach Cuts Transportation Costs for Untied Technologies," *Purchasing*, October 7, 1999, 68.

SUMMARY

1. Individual differences are determined to a great extent by several internal elements such as personality, perceptions, attitudes, and abilities. People respond differently to the same situation because of the unique combination of these elements.

2. Personality is an enduring, organized, and distinctive pattern of behavior that describes an individual's adaptation to a situation. It is a combination of traits that characterizes the unique nature of a person. Many personality traits in-

fluence work behavior and performance, including self-esteem, locus of control, Type A or Type B personality, resiliency, self-monitoring, degree of authoritarianism, and personality traits measured by the Myers-Briggs Type Indicator and the "Big Five." The RIASEC Vocational Interest Typology is a successful tool to assist with matching an individual's personality with jobs and careers.

3. Perception is the way people experience, process, define, and interpret the world around them that influences the

way in which they communicate and become aware of sensations and stimuli. Perceptions are influenced by a variety of factors, including an individual's experiences, needs, personality, and education. Perceptual biases, such as stereotyping, halo-and-horn effects, and selective perception, cause managers to make errors that can be costly to the organization and to individuals.

4. To reduce perceptual errors, managers must make a conscious effort to attend to relevant information, actively seek evidence of whether or not their perceptions are accurate, compare their perceptions with those of others, and look for objective measures in relation to their own perceptions.

5. The relationship between job satisfaction and job performance is complex, because the two variables are affected by a number of personal and situational variables. An employee's job performance depends on a large number of factors, such as ability, the quality of equipment and materials used, the competence of supervision, the working environment, and peer relationships.

6. A group is normally defined as two or more individuals who interact with one another. A team is a group of interdependent individuals with shared commitments to accomplish a common purpose or goal. They can be classified as formal or informal.

7. A role is a set of behaviors that is a characteristic of a person in a specific situation. When operating in a work group, individuals typically fulfill several roles, including task-oriented, relationship-oriented, and self-oriented roles. Behaviors related to establishing and accomplishing the goals of the group or achieving the desired outcomes are task-orientated roles; behaviors that cultivate the well-being, continuity, and development of the group are relationship-oriented roles; behaviors that fulfill personal needs or goals of an individual without regard for the group are self-oriented roles.

8. The team development process is dynamic, and teams pass through stages that follow a general pattern. Teams appear to go through a five-stage developmental sequence: forming, storming, norming, performing, and adjourning.

9. Cohesiveness is a strong sense of connectedness between team members that causes them to work together to attain an objective. It can influence communication and the job satisfaction of group members and help unite a team behind organizational goals. Highly cohesive teams may become dysfunctional if they lead team members to groupthink or if the team's goals are in conflict with those of the organization.

10. The primary elements of successful teams are specific, well-defined goals, development of interdependent and collaborative relationships, shared leadership, feedback, recognition and reward of performance, and celebration of victories.

REVIEW QUESTIONS

1. *(Learning Objective 1)* Explain why managers need to learn to recognize and understand individual differences. What are the key factors that underlie individual differences?

2. *(Learning Objective 2)* Define personality.

3. *(Learning Objective 2)* Discuss the personality characteristics of resilience.

4. *(Learning Objective 2)* What are some of the positive and negative aspects of Type A and Type B personality characteristics?

5. *(Learning Objective 3)* What are the four personality dimensions measured by the MBTI?

6. *(Learning Objective 4)* Why is it important for an individual's personality to match his or her job requirements?

7. *(Learning Objective 5)* What is stereotyping? How is it both helpful and harmful?

8. *(Learning Objective 6)* Why is it important for managers to understand the relationship between job satisfaction and performance?

9. *(Learning Objective 7)* Describe the different roles team members can have on a team.

10. *(Learning Objective 8)* What are the five primary development stages of teams?

11. *(Learning Objective 9)* Explain how cohesiveness can impact a team.

12. *(Learning Objective 9)* What role do norms play in a team's performance?

13. *(Learning Objective 10)* What are the primary elements that make successful teams?

DISCUSSION QUESTIONS

Improving Critical Thinking

1. What types of careers are most appropriate for individuals with internal locus of control; high self-esteem; low extroversion; and preference for "realistic"?

2. Describe an effective and an ineffective team of which you have been a member. What role(s) did you play? How cohesive was the team? What could you have done to make the team more effective?

3. Consider the development process of a team of which you have been a member. How long did the team take to pass through the different stages of development? Did the team seem to proceed through all of the stages of development? Why or why not?

4. Discuss a stereotypical group to which you belong. What people or things belong to the group? Give an example of a member of the group who does not fit the stereotype.

Enhancing Communication Skills

5. Interview several managers about ways in which they handle the job satisfaction of their employees. Write up your interview results or present them to the class as directed by your professor.

6. Explain the ways managers can learn to reduce the perceptual errors that occur in the workplace. Prepare a presentation for a small group or the class that includes specific examples.

Building Teamwork

7. Write a brief description of a junior in college majoring in business. How would this description compare to students who attend a university different from yours? Compare your perceptions with others in a small group.

8. List different types of norms you have experienced working in formal work teams while engaged in class projects. Form a small group and develop a combined list. Do you find any norms common to most members? Highlight these. Discuss the norms that lead to positive work performance.

9. Find an article in a current business magazine that describes how an organization is using teams. Form a small group and share your findings. Select the article that best represents an unusual use of a team and share it with the class.

THINKING CRITICALLY: DEBATE THE ISSUE

Type A or Type B?

Form teams as directed by your instructor to debate whether the personality type, A or B, of managers and employees should be matched. That is, should a Type A manager have all Type A subordinates? Should a Type B manager have all Type B subordinates?

One team will present the position that the managers and subordinates should all be of the same personality type—the advantages of this. The second team will present the disadvantages of matching. After both sides present their positions, discuss whether or not there might be a better alternative to either extreme.

EXPERIENTIAL EXERCISE 14.1

Cohesive Behavior

How cohesive is your team? Identify a team of which you are a member. Respond to the following questions to see how cohesive the team is.

Use a scale from 1 (almost never) to 9 (almost always) to respond honestly to each statement. Place the number (1 through 9) in the space to the left of the statement number.

Almost Never								Almost Always
1	2	3	4	5	6	7	8	9

_____ **1.** We make sure that everyone enjoys being a member of the team.

_____ **2.** We discuss ideas, feelings, and reactions to what is currently taking place in the team.

_____ **3.** We express acceptance and support when other members disclose their ideas, feelings, and reactions to what is currently taking place in the team.

_____ **4.** We make all members feel valued and appreciated.

_____ **5.** We include other members in team activities.

_____ **6.** I'm influenced by other team members.

_____ **7.** We take risks in expressing new ideas and feelings.

_____ **8.** We express liking, affection, and concern for each other.

_____ **9.** We encourage team norms that support individuality and personal expression.

You can complete this exercise either alone or as part of a team-building experience with your team. By completing the exercise alone, you have your perception of your team's cohesiveness. If team members complete it alone and have different beliefs about how cohesive the team is, it would offer an opportunity to strengthen cohesion.

Scoring: Total all your responses to get an individual cohesiveness behavior score. Scores can range from a low of 9 to a high of 81. Scores of 9 to 27 indicate low cohesive behavior. Scores of 28 to 62 indicate a middle ground of cohesive behavior. Scores from 63 to 72 indicate that your behavior is very positive in establishing an effective team. Scores above 72 are generally considered high. However, keep in mind if you did this individually that these are your perceptions of your own behavior. It is important to talk with other members of the team to see if they share your view.

All nine statements identify important factors for team cohesiveness. Your team may also examine each of the nine statements and determine whether any are exceptionally high or low. Discuss your answers. These statements provide you with a picture of your own team cohesive behavior and can be used to focus upon several ways of increasing team cohesiveness.

Statement 1 describes a general attempt to keep cohesiveness high.

Statements 2 and 3 pertain to the expression of ideas and feelings and support for others' expressing ideas and feelings; such personal participation is essential for cohesiveness and for the development of trust.

Statements 4 and 8 also focus upon support for, and liking of, other team members.

Statement 5 refers to the inclusion of other members, and Statement 6 concerns one's willingness to be influenced by other members.

Statements 7 and 9 center on the acceptance of individuality within the team.

EXPERIENTIAL EXERCISE 14.2

How Resilient Are You?

Rate how much each of the following 14 statements applies to you. Circle the number using the following scale:

Almost Never	Infrequently	Sometimes	Frequently	Almost Always
1	2	3	4	5

1 2 3 4 5   Curious, ask questions, want to know how things work, experiment.
1 2 3 4 5   Constantly learn from your experience and the experiences of others.
1 2 3 4 5   Need and expect to have things work well for yourself and others; care for yourself.
1 2 3 4 5   Play with new developments, find the humor, laugh at self, chuckle.
1 2 3 4 5   Adapt quickly to change; highly flexible.
1 2 3 4 5   Anticipate problems and avoid difficulties.
1 2 3 4 5   Develop better self-esteem and self-confidence every year. Develop a conscious self-concept of a professional.
1 2 3 4 5   Feel comfortable with paradoxical qualities.
1 2 3 4 5   Listen well. Read others, including difficult people, with empathy.
1 2 3 4 5   Think up creative solutions to challenges; invent ways to solve problems. Trust intuition and hunches.
1 2 3 4 5   Manage the emotional side of recovery. Grieve, honor, and let go of the past.
1 2 3 4 5   Expect tough situations to work out well and keep on going. Help others bring stability to times of uncertainty and turmoil.
1 2 3 4 5   Find the gift in accidents and bad experiences.
1 2 3 4 5   Convert misfortune into good fortune.

Scoring: Sum the numbers circled for a total score. If you scored 60–70, you're highly resilient; 50–59, better than most; 40–49, adequate; 30–39, struggling; under 30, seek help! *Note:* To improve your resilience, practice more of the behaviors listed in the 14 statements above.

SOURCE: Adapted from A. Seibert, *The Survivor Personality* (Berkeley, Calif.: Berkeley Publishing Group, 1996), 38–40.

CAPTURING THE POWER OF INFORMATION TECHNOLOGY

1. Use the Internet to search for recent articles on Altrec.com. Assess the progress of the company. Who are its competitors?

2. Use the Internet to find personality measure instruments that you can take online, such as measures of self-esteem, resiliency, and others. Share your search results with others in class and exchange URL site addresses.

3. The public sector is only recently beginning to use teams for organizational decision making. Search the Internet for articles that discuss where these have been tried and whether they have been successful or unsuccessful.

ETHICS: TAKE A STAND

Stephanie is one of four members of a team that was working on a class project. The project required the team to write a report for a Principles of Management Class. One of Stephanie's tasks was to coordinate the parts that were written by the other team members. She was doing this at 10 P.M.; the paper was due at 11 A.M. the next morning.

Stephanie thought that much of Kevin's part sounded familiar. She checked one of the articles upon which the report was based and found that about 40 percent of Kevin's work was essentially "word-for-word" copy of the article. Worse, there were no footnotes. Stephanie believes that this is clearly unacceptable plagiarism and is not only unethical, but illegal.

Stephanie immediately told the other members of the team about what she had found. The other two members were good friends with Kevin and didn't see a problem. They said that Kevin frequently did this. Besides, there wasn't any time to do anything about this, and he had never been caught. If one overlooked this plagiarism, the report looked pretty good. All three team members believed it could earn at least a B+, maybe an A. However, if the professor caught this, it might be grounds for at least a failing grade for the paper, a failing grade for the entire group, or even possible expulsion from the university.

For Discussion

1. What would you do if you were Stephanie? Why?

2. What are Stephanie's options?

3. What are the primary norms in the group?

4. Would you want to work with Kevin given that you know that he frequently does this? Why or why not?

5. Is plagiarism acceptable if you don't get caught? What does your answer to this question suggest about your attitudes?

VIDEO CASE

Exploring Individual Differences and Team Dynamics: Cannondale I: Teamwork

Cannondale began in 1971 by introducing the cycling industry's first bicycle trailer. The company soon added cycle apparel and accessory lines. Cannondale grew quickly, earning a strong reputation for innovation and quality. That reputation proved invaluable when Cannondale introduced its first bicycle in 1983. It shocked the bike industry by offering an aluminum bicycle that was lighter and more flex-resistant than the steel models that dominated the industry. Cannondale's reputation encouraged dealers and customers to purchase the bike, resulting in some competitors quickly following their lead to use aluminum.

Today, Cannondale is the leading manufacturer of aluminum bicycles, selling more than 80 models in 60 countries. Its vision is to be the best cycling and off-road motorsports company in the world. Cannondale's focus is people—employees, customers, retailers, and vendors—working together to accomplish their mission. Its corporate values include:

- Devising flexible manufacturing processes in order to quickly produce innovative, quality products.
- Distributing products through only the best specialty retailers worldwide.
- Remaining lean, competitive, and entrepreneurial.
- Backing products with excellent customer service.
- Promoting from within whenever possible and striving to do what is "just and right."

Cannondale's corporate values also include pursuing continuous improvement, as demonstrated by its bicycle research and development (R&D) teams. These teams focus on making lighter, stronger, faster, and more comfortable bicycles. To further enhance its reputation as an innovation leader, another set of teams (Cannondale-sponsored bicycle racing teams) provides significant feedback regarding product design, performance, and durability.

The bicycle R&D team has been revising its Jekyll bicycle model. It has been evaluating various prototypes of the Jekyll for about four months. Each team member is an expert in a specialty area and relies on the other team members to address or coordinate their speciality areas. R&D Project Manager John Horn leads a team of nine bicycle project engineers. He oversees how the projects are integrated into other Cannondale departments including Sales and Product Development. He also establishes timelines for engineering and prototyping. Director of Product Management Steve Metz is responsible for the "big picture vision." He prioritizes the product goals, decides how the Jekyll can best meet customer needs, chooses the Jekyll components, and follows the bike to the ultimate end user. Lead Design Engineer Ron Litke designed the original Jekyll, so he was involved in the Jekyll frame revisions. Ron Litke oversees all aspects of designing the frame—everything from the initial concept to final production. He spends a lot of time communicating with relevant groups (e.g., marketing, manufacturing, testing, vendors) before, during, and after designing the frame. Such discussions have provided insight Ron Litke would not have otherwise had.

It can be fun to be part of a team. However, successful teams also need some adversarial relationships. Although they sell high-end bikes, Steve has to remind the engineers to keep their designs within budget so the product will be affordable. Disagreements also can occur between people who are friends during and after working hours. Usually they are able to resolve differences by openly discussing them. When two engineers can't agree, they typically go to the R&D project manager for resolution or mediation. If they still can't agree, they'll involve others who might offer insight. Steve has found that people will come to an agreement for the greater good of the project.

Cannondale's teams don't have many formal meetings because the company's founder and president, Joe Montgomery, encourages impromptu conversations. The open layout of the office, with low cubicle walls, allows employees to easily ask a quick question of each other. It is common for employees to group around someone's desk or in the hallway. This way, anyone can join in or leave the discussion when appropriate. The teams also meet outdoors around different bicycle parts to brainstorm the actualities of redesigning the bike.

Building an effective team is as complex as putting together a top-of-the-line mountain bike. Over the years, Cannondale's informal approach to teams has been very effective in improving the design, manufacturing, and marketing of its high-end lightweight bicycles. Cannodale's team approach has led to its being recognized as the bicycle industry's leading innovator. It has won numerous design awards by organizations, including *Bicycling* magazine, *Business Week*, and *VeloNews* magazine.

For Discussion

1. What characteristics appear to support the effective working relationships in the Cannondale team?

2. Explain how the Cannondale team's informal approach affects the development phases of "groups."

3. Explain whether the Cannondale team appears highly cohesive. How does its informal approach to teams affect its cohesiveness?

4. Illustrate the "primary elements of successful teams" exhibited by the Cannondale team. How do these elements compare to the "critical requirements of effective teams" described early in the chapter?

http://www.cannondale.com

CASE

Building a Team at Altrec

Entering the world of e-commerce is an adventure and a challenge for any new start-up company. Most e-commerce companies never gain profitability and many went out of existence during 2001. Altrec.com made it.

For Altrec.com, an Internet-only specialty retailer of outdoor and travel gear, the greatest challenge was to advance the learning process at a much quicker rate than would be found in an ordinary organization because its marketplace was so competitive. To build a company that would last, the 10-member senior management team had been selected carefully. Co-founder and CEO Mike Morford knew that each was a leader who would bring his or her own unique differences and talents. Nevertheless, he needed to fuse the senior management team and bring together their divergent personalities, abilities, and skill sets.

With speed so essential in today's fast-paced business world, Morford believed that he had to get the team to be effective immediately. Instead of sitting in a conference room at Altrec's Bellevue, Washington, headquarters, Morford challenged the senior management team to join forces and take a ride down the Salmon River, one of the most rapids-filled waterways in the lower 48 states. The 75-mile rafting experience demanded adapting to the changing environment of continuous movement and tough challenges—much like the start-up of a new business in e-commerce. Although the trip was normally a five-day adventure, the team had only four days to accomplish the task. The goal was to have the team members experience authentic team building that would be the foundation for building a successful organization.

Before attempting the river, the team had to create goals and confirm a shared vision for the expedition. Day one involved building a sense of trust: Who would come through and who wouldn't once the river pressured them? Was consensus needed on all decisions, or could trust be developed, enabling a few to make decisions when needed? Was there time for consensus on every decision? Beginning on day two, team members rotated the role of captain, and each had to make decisions and direct the team to prove that he or she had the ability to lead. At the end of day two, tension started to emerge as honest feedback was withheld.

Conflict was encountered on day three when Morford refused to follow the designated leader's routing decision and the team argued the issue of who leads and who follows. Not unexpected at this point in the team's development, the debate was about delegating versus consensus building and the willingness to trust each other completely. On the positive side, the team members were no longer holding back. Ultimately, the resolution was left to the day's leader. Everyone followed through because the team had to keep moving.

The Altrec team had faced many challenges in its journey on the Salmon River rapids. Most important for co-founder and CEO Mike Morford, the team had learned how to work together and become a cohesive unit. The sudden changes of the trip forced the group to be productive quickly and learn that team members needed to trust each other in decision making.

The company continues to move extraordinarily fast in the e-commerce world and is successful, but none of these endeavors would have succeeded without the lessons learned on the river. After experiencing the river adventure, Altrec's managers agreed that the greatest gain was learning how their individual differences could be strengths. This led to a high level of trust between units and meant that decision making followed regular patterns. A decision-making flow chart was just one component of a series of Altrec.com norms and values drafted on the river. Today that document, including guidelines for communication, respect, and leadership, is part of Altrec.com's culture and a piece of required reading for all veteran and rookie employees.

SOURCES: J. Cook, "Altrec.com Puts Outdoor Gear Online," *Journal Business Reporter*, March 15, 1999; N. Kim, "Rivals Gear Up to Play Outdoors With REI.com," *Puget Sound Business Journal*, March 22, 1999, 44–46; H. Jung, "Web Retailer Challenges Giant REI," *Seattle Times*, August 31, 1999, B19; T. Balf, "Extreme Off," *Fast Company*, November 1999, 384–98; A. Layne, "What Did Happen on the Salmon River?" *Fast Company*, January 2000.

For Discussion

1. Did the Altrec team go through the normal stages of group development? If you believe that it did, categorize the events into the "right" stage. If you believe that it did not, explain why.

2. The Altrec managers believed that the individual differences could be strengths for the team. Explain how that is possible.

3. Under what circumstances would individual differences probably lead to weaknesses for the team?

CHAP

MOTIVATING ORGANIZATIONAL MEMBERS

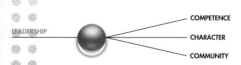

LEADERSHIP

COMPETENCE

CHARACTER

COMMUNITY

TER15

CHAPTER OVERVIEW

An organization's energy comes from the motivation of its employees. Although their abilities play a crucial role in determining their work performance, so does their motivation. Managers must ensure that employees are motivated to perform their tasks to the best of their abilities. Through motivation, managers are better able to create a working environment that is conducive to good effort and where employees are inspired to work to accomplish the organization's goals.

In this chapter, we discuss motivation as the force that energizes and gives direction to behavior. The topic of motivation has been the subject of numerous studies and debates since the early 1900s, and many approaches have emerged that are applicable for the contemporary manager. We examine the main approaches to motivating employees, including motivation through need satisfaction, motivation through complex processes, participative management in the organization, and the use of money as a motivator. We will consider motivation from an international perspective to better appreciate how diversity can affect motivation of employees in the global arena.

LEARNING OBJECTIVES

When you have finished studying this chapter, you should be able to:

1. Explain the basic motivation process.
2. Describe the different approaches to motivation.
3. Discuss needs-based approaches to employee motivation.
4. Explain the process approaches to employee motivation.
5. Outline how goal setting is used as a tool for motivating individuals.
6. Explain how reinforcement theory can be used to increase and decrease behavior in an organizational setting.
7. Address the application of participative management in contemporary organizations.
8. Clarify the use of money as a motivator.
9. Explain how to reward team performance.
10. Account for the importance of motivation from an international perspective.

Facing The Challenge

Nucor Steel Corporation

Kenneth Iverson took over Nucor Steel Corporation, a failing steel company, with the goal of rebuilding it, except the steel industry in the United States was in very poor condition. Many producers of steel products were failing, and the rest were barely breaking even. One of the biggest reasons for this was that producers of both steel products and the steel itself, steel refineries, couldn't compete against the lower costs of many companies in Japan. In addition, it seemed that Japanese steel companies, with the help of their government or at least with the approval, were selling steel in the U.S. markets at below cost.

About the only way to compete was to totally remake the company.

So, Iverson got very creative—and risky. He had to keep per unit costs extremely low. Blast furnaces, needed to handle the steel ore, were quite expensive. Mr. Iverson purchased smaller electric furnaces from suppliers in Europe. While they wouldn't handle the steel ore, they would work on scrap steel. Electric furnaces were a new technology in the United States at the time, and steel companies did not normally use scrap steel as the main raw material. It was risky, but Iverson had to keep per-unit costs down or the company would have no chance of succeeding.

Another main cost, salary and wages, had to be kept low also. Rather than use existing buildings in industrial, large city areas, Iverson

moved to a very rural area and started from scratch. He believed that the work ethic was better in rural areas and that people in those areas were against unionization. Essentially all other steel producers had unionized labor, and this appeared to be one cause of higher wages.

The strategy was in place. The plans for building the physical facilities were in place. The people were hired. Will all this work?

SOURCES: J. Michlitsch, *Video Guide to Accompany Strategic Management: Competitiveness and Globalization* by M. Hitt, R. Ireland, and R. Hoskisson, (St. Paul, MN: West Publishing Company, 1997); J. Collins, "Turning Goals Into Results: The Power of Catalytic Mechanisms," *Harvard Business Review,* July/August 1999, 71–82.

INTRODUCTION

Steven Kerr published a classic article some time ago entitled "On the Folly of Rewarding A While Hoping for B."[1] In the article, he argued that many organizations and managers want one thing but reward other things instead. Why do they do this? Reasons mentioned include:

- Managers have not clearly identified what is necessary for good performance—the behaviors, tasks, goals, and strategy that are needed.
- Managers have not determined how to measure successful performance.
- Employees do not see clear links between their performance and achievement of the goals.
- Employees may not have the right abilities to carry out the job.
- Employees want rewards different from what their supervisors think they want.
- Employees have different levels of motivation to do the job.

We have already discussed some of these reasons in previous chapters. Establishing strategy, plans, and goals; selecting the right employees; and determining the tasks necessary in each job have all been discussed before and are directly related to the performance of people that we discuss in this chapter. Other things discussed previously, at the minimum, indirectly relate to performance. Helping people understand what is expected in their jobs is also accomplished with good communication and leadership. Measuring successful performance has been mentioned in Chapter 10 and will be discussed in more detail in Chapter 16. We will focus on understanding the motivation of people in their jobs in this chapter so that we, as managers, can understand how to motivate and reward the behaviors that we really want—the behaviors that will make the people and the organization successful.

BASIC MOTIVATION PROCESS

LEARNING OBJECTIVE 1

Explain the basic motivation process.

Motivation

That which causes a person to expend effort to behave in a certain way.

Motivation is generally defined as the forces acting upon or within a person that cause that person to expend effort to behave in a specific, goal-directed manner.[2] It is a psychological process that gives purpose and direction to behavior.

Figure 15.1 | The Relationship between Motivation and Performance

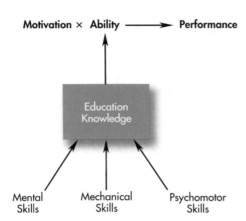

How does motivation occur? How is it related to performance? Since the early work of the scientific management and human relations theorists, management scholars have developed a number of different models that help us understand what motivates people at work.[3] Although the process of motivation is complex, organizations are primarily concerned with the relationship between motivation and performance. This is shown in Figure 15.1 and expressed in the formula $M \times A = P$, where P refers to performance, M refers to motivation, and A refers to ability. Recall from Chapter 14 that ability is an existing capacity to perform various tasks needed in a given situation and that abilities may include mental, mechanical, and psychomotor skills.

Consider, for example, that you are motivated and have a goal to become a financial analyst. Motivation alone is not enough. You also must have the ability to perform the job. You are in school to gain the required knowledge and skills through education. Let's look again at our formula:

$$
\begin{array}{lll}
\text{Motivation} & \times \text{Ability} & = \text{Performance} \\
\text{(Goal and desire)} & \times \text{(Education, knowledge)} & = \text{Financial analyst}
\end{array}
$$

The approaches to motivation that we present in this chapter are general approaches to the *what* and *how* of behavior. But we should remember that motivation is only one of many explanations of human behavior. Although some people view motivation as a personal trait—that is, some have it and others don't—this is not true. Certainly, individuals differ in their motivational drive, but motivation is the result of the interaction between the individual and the situation. Consequently, the level of motivation varies both between individuals and within individuals at different times.

MOTIVATIONAL APPROACHES

We will discuss motivation by using two broad approaches—need and process models. **Needs-based models** emphasize specific human needs, or the factors within a person that energize, direct, and stop behavior. **Process models** take a more dynamic view of motivation. They focus on understanding the thought or cognitive processes that take place within the individual's mind that influence behavior. We begin our discussion with needs-based approaches.

LEARNING OBJECTIVE 2

Describe the different approaches to motivation.

Needs-based models
Models of motivation that focus on a person's needs as motivators.

Process models
Models of motivation that focus on understanding the thought process in influencing motivation.

NEEDS-BASED APPROACHES OF EMPLOYEE MOTIVATION

LEARNING OBJECTIVE 3
Discuss needs-based approaches to employee motivation.

Many factors are believed to influence a person's desire to perform work or behave in a certain way. Approaches based on needs explain motivation primarily as a phenomenon that occurs intrinsically, or within an individual. Here we look at three widely recognized models: the hierarchy of needs (Maslow), the two-factor model (Herzberg), and the acquired-needs model.

MASLOW'S HIERARCHY OF NEEDS

Hierarchy of needs
Motivation model stating that a person has five fundamental needs.

According to the **hierarchy of needs**, a person has five fundamental needs: physiological, security, affiliation, esteem, and self-actualization.[4] Figure 15.2 shows these five needs arranged in a hierarchy, separated into higher and lower levels. Physiological and security needs are lower-order needs, which are generally satisfied externally, and affiliation, esteem, and self-actualization are higher-order needs, which are satisfied internally.

Physiological needs
Needs such as food, water, air, and shelter; at the bottom of the hierarchy of needs.

PHYSIOLOGICAL NEEDS   At the lowest level of the hierarchy are physiological needs. Food, water, air, and shelter are all **physiological needs**. People concentrate on satisfying these needs before turning to higher-order needs. Managers must understand that to the extent employees are motivated by physiological needs, their concerns do not center on the work they are doing. They will accept any job

Figure 15.2 | Maslow's Hierarchy of Needs

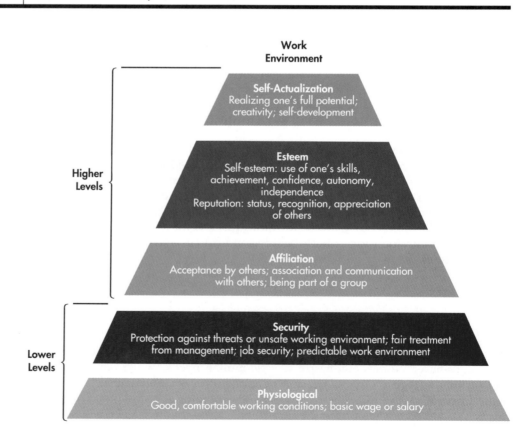

that serves to meet their needs. Managers who focus on physiological needs in trying to motivate subordinates assume that people work mainly for money and are primarily concerned with comfort, avoidance of fatigue, and their rate of pay.

SECURITY NEEDS   Next in the hierarchy are **security needs**, which reflect the desire to have a safe physical and emotional environment. Job security, grievance procedures, health insurance, and retirement plans are used to satisfy employees' security needs. Like physiological needs, unsatisfied security needs cause people to be preoccupied with satisfying them. People who are motivated primarily by security needs value their jobs mainly as a defense against the loss of basic need satisfaction. Managers who feel that security needs are most important will often emphasize rules, job security, and fringe benefits.

AFFILIATION NEEDS   **Affiliation needs** include the desire for friendship, love, and a feeling of belonging. After physiological and security needs have been satisfied, affiliation needs become more important as a motivator. When affiliation needs are primary sources of motivation, individuals value their work as an opportunity for finding and establishing friendly interpersonal relationships.

ESTEEM NEEDS   **Esteem needs** are met by personal feelings of achievement and self-worth and by recognition, respect, and prestige from others. People with esteem needs want others to accept them and to perceive them as competent and able. Managers who focus on esteem needs try to foster employees' pride in their work and use public rewards and recognition for services to motivate them.

SELF-ACTUALIZATION NEEDS   Finally, at the top of the hierarchy are self-actualization needs. Self-fulfillment and the opportunity to achieve one's potential are considered **self-actualization needs**. People who strive for self-actualization accept themselves and use their abilities to the fullest and most creative extent. Managers who emphasize self-actualization may involve employees in designing jobs or make special assignments that capitalize on employees' unique skills. Many entrepreneurs who break away from jobs in large corporations to start their own business may be looking for a way to satisfy their self-actualization needs.

The hierarchy provides a convenient framework for managers. It suggests that individuals have various needs and that they try to satisfy those needs using a priority system or hierarchy. Some research indicates that higher-order needs increase in importance over lower-order needs as individuals move up the organizational hierarchy. Other studies have reported that needs vary according to a person's career stage, organization size, and even geographical location. One of the major criticisms of the hierarchy model, however, is that no consistent evidence exists that the satisfaction of a need at one level will decrease its importance and increase the importance of the next-higher needs.

TWO-FACTOR MODEL

The two-factor model provides another way to examine employee needs. In the **two-factor model**, Herzberg examined the relationship between job satisfaction and productivity within a group of professional accountants and engineers. He found that the factors leading to job satisfaction were separate and distinct from those leading to job dissatisfaction—hence, the term *two-factor model.*[5]

The two-factor model is shown in Figure 15.3. At the top are the sources of work satisfaction, termed *motivator factors.* The sources of dissatisfaction, or hygiene factors, are shown at the bottom.

Security needs
The desire to have a safe physical and emotional environment.

Affiliation needs
The desire for friendship, love, and a feeling of belonging.

Esteem needs
Needs for personal feelings of achievement and self-worth.

Self-actualization needs
Needs for self-fulfillment and the opportunity to achieve one's potential; at the top of the hierarchy.

Two-factor model
The model of motivation that includes motivator factors and hygiene factors.

In examining the relationship between job satisfaction and productivity with a group of engineers, Herzberg found that factors leading to job satisfaction were separate and distinct from those leading to job dissatisfaction.

© GETTYIMAGES/EYE WIRE

Figure 15.3 | Herzberg's Two-Factor Theory

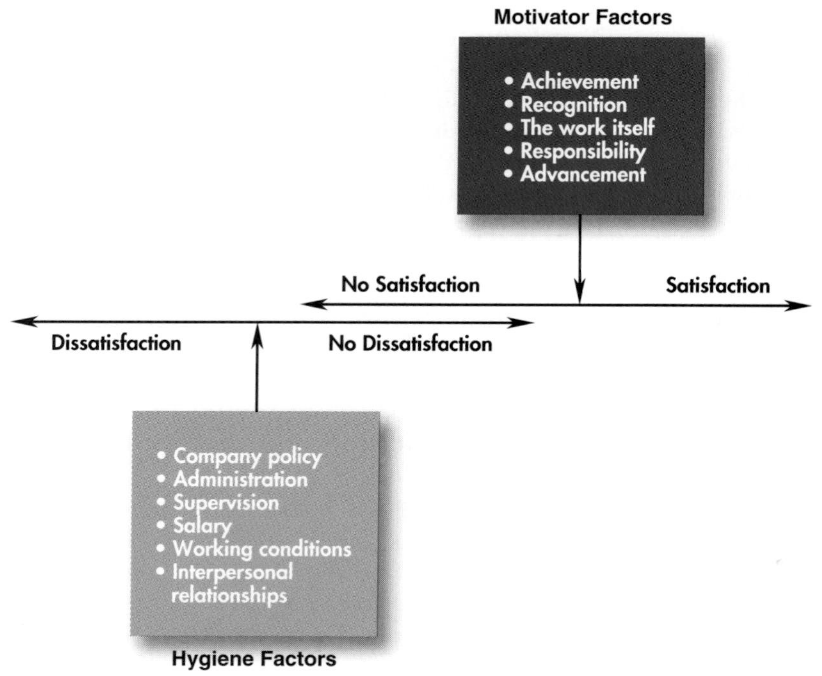

Motivator Factors

- Achievement
- Recognition
- The work itself
- Responsibility
- Advancement

No Satisfaction   Satisfaction

Dissatisfaction   No Dissatisfaction

- Company policy
- Administration
- Supervision
- Salary
- Working conditions
- Interpersonal relationships

Hygiene Factors

Motivator factors
Factors related to job content.

Hygiene factors
Factors associated with the job context or environment in which the job is performed.

MOTIVATOR FACTORS **Motivator factors** are related to job content, or what people actually do in their work, and are associated with an individual's positive feelings about the job. Based on the two-factor model, motivator factors include the work itself, recognition, advancement, a sense of achievement, and responsibilities.

HYGIENE FACTORS **Hygiene factors** are associated with the job context, or the environment in which the job is performed. Company policy and administration, technical supervision, salary, working conditions, and interpersonal relationships are examples of hygiene factors. These factors are associated with an individual's negative feelings about the job, but they do not contribute to motivation.

Studies on what managers value in their work support the two-factor model conclusion that factors such as achievement, recognition, and challenging work are valued more than factors such as pay or security. For example, at GE/Durham, feedback from employees showed they believed the most important characteristics of their jobs were that they were involved in work that was meaningful and provided a sense of accomplishment. Additionally, more than 75 percent of the respondents rated challenging work, participation in team decision making, and recognition for their accomplishments as important or very important.[6]

However, just because many people rate motivators above hygiene factors is no guarantee that the motivators will actually increase work motivation for all employees. These findings may not be applicable to the entire population, especially as the workforce becomes more diverse. Nevertheless, the two-factor model carries some clear messages for managers. The first step in motivation is to eliminate dissatisfaction, so managers are advised to make sure that pay, working conditions, company policies, and so forth are appropriate and reasonable. Then they can address motivation itself. According to the two-factor model, managers should strive to provide opportunities for growth, achievement, and responsibility—all things that the model predicts will enhance employee motivation, or as Herzberg calls it, satisfaction.

This brings us to two cautions about the model. One is the discussion/debate about the relationships between satisfaction, or job satisfaction, and performance. (See Chapter 14 for information about that.) The second caution is that the model says that pay is basically not a motivator. (See the discussion about pay as a motivator later in this chapter on page 475.)

ACQUIRED-NEEDS MODEL

A third needs-based approach to motivation is the acquired-needs model, which is rooted in culture. That is, needs are acquired or learned from the life experiences in the culture or country in which we live. The acquired-needs model focuses on three particularly important needs in the work environment: achievement, affiliation, and power.[7] The model proposes that when a need is strong, it will motivate the person to engage in behaviors to satisfy that need.

NEED FOR ACHIEVEMENT   The **need for achievement** is represented by the drive to excel, accomplish challenging tasks, and achieve a standard of excellence. The amount of achievement motivation people have depends on their childhood, their personal and occupational experiences, and the type of organization for which they work.[8] Managers who want to motivate high achievers need to ensure that such individuals have challenging but obtainable goals that allow relatively immediate feedback about their progress.

High achievers often pursue a professional career in sales and are successful in entrepreneurial activities such as running their own business, managing a self-contained unit within a large organization, or holding positions in which success depends largely on individual achievement.[9] Studies show that although almost all people feel they have an "achievement motive," probably only 10 percent of the U.S. population can be classified as having a high need for achievement.

A high need to achieve does not necessarily lead to being a good manager, especially in large organizations. Individuals with a high need for achievement like to set their own goals and favor tasks that provide immediate feedback. They prefer to accept personal responsibility for success or failure rather than leave the outcome to chance or the actions of others. In contrast, the needs for institutional power and for affiliation are closely related to management success.

NEED FOR POWER   Research has also focused on the desire and need for power to influence and control one's environment as a particularly important motivator in organizations. This **need for power** may involve either personal power or institutional power. Individuals with a high need for personal power want to dominate others for the sake of demonstrating their ability to influence and control. In contrast, individuals with a high need for institutional power want to solve problems and further organizational goals.[10]

NEED FOR AFFILIATION   Finally, the **need for affiliation** is the desire for friendly and close interpersonal relationships. Individuals with a high need for affiliation are likely to gravitate toward professions that involve high levels of interaction with others, such as teaching, counseling, and sales.

Although not all individuals have the appropriate needs profile to be managers, the acquired-needs model of motivation argues that employees can be trained to stimulate their achievement needs. If an organizational position requires a high achiever, management can select a person with a high need for achievement or develop its own candidate through training.

Need for achievement
The drive to excel, to accomplish, and to achieve a standard of excellence.

Need for power
The need to influence and control one's environment; may involve either personal power or institutional power.

Need for affiliation
The desire for friendly and close interpersonal relationships.

In summary, needs-based approaches to motivation provide managers with an understanding of the underlying needs that motivate people to behave in certain ways. However, these models do not explain why people choose a particular behavior to accomplish task-related goals. As useful as they are, needs-based models still emphasize the "what" aspect of motivation by describing what motivates individuals, but do not provide information on thought processes or the "how" aspect of motivation. We examine a more complex view of motivation in the next section.

PROCESS APPROACHES TO EMPLOYEE MOTIVATION

LEARNING OBJECTIVE 4

Explain the process approaches to employee motivation.

Managers must have a more complete perspective on the complexities of employee motivation. They must understand why different people have different needs and goals, why individuals' needs change, and how employees change to try to satisfy needs in different ways. Not all employees want the same things from their jobs. Understanding these aspects of motivation has become especially relevant as organizations deal with the diverse managerial issues associated with an increasingly global environment. Some models for understanding these complex processes are the expectancy model, the equity model, goal setting, and behavior modification (also known as reinforcement theory).

EXPECTANCY MODEL

Expectancy model

A motivation model suggesting that work motivation is determined by the individual's perceptions of the relationship between effort and performance, performance and rewards, and the desirability of the rewards.

The **expectancy model** suggests that motivation to expend effort to do something is determined by three basic individual perceptions: (1) the perception that effort will lead to performance, (2) the perception that rewards are attached to performance, and (3) the perception that the outcomes or rewards are valuable to the individual.[11] Simply put, given choices, individuals choose the option that promises to give them the greatest reward. When you have three choices, you'll choose the one that provides you with the result you value the most and has the highest probability of getting the result. The model applies to the career you select, the car you buy, the task you start the day with, the vacation site you choose, and so on. However, when individuals make choices, they must be reasonably sure that the reward they are looking for is attainable without undue risk or effort.

To help you understand the expectancy model, the next paragraphs briefly define the key terms of the model and discuss how they operate. Figure 15.4 shows how these terms are related.

Expectancy

The belief that a particular level of effort will be followed by a particular level of performance.

EXPECTANCY **Expectancy** is the belief that a particular level of effort will be followed by a particular level of performance. This is best understood in terms of the effort-performance linkage, or the individual's perception of the probability that a given level of effort will lead to a certain level of performance.

Instrumentality

The individual's perception that a specific level of achieved task performance will lead to outcomes or rewards.

INSTRUMENTALITY **Instrumentality** is the individual's perception that a specific level of achieved task performance will lead to various work outcomes. This is the performance-reward linkage, or the degree to which the individual believes that performing at a particular level will lead to the attainment of a desired outcome.

Valence

The value of the reward to the individual.

VALENCE **Valence** represents the value or importance of the outcomes to the individual.

Overall, the model says that a person will be motivated to expend effort based on his or her perceptions of the degree to which the effort will lead to performance, the degree to which rewards are tied to performance, and the value of the

Figure 15.4 | Expectancy Theory

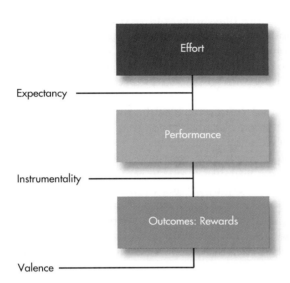

rewards. For motivation to be high, employees must value the outcomes that are available from high effort and good performance. Conversely, if employees do not place a high value on the outcomes and believe that there is not a strong link between effort and performance, and performance and rewards, motivation will be low.

Managers can influence expectancies by selecting individuals with the proper abilities, training them to use these abilities, supporting them by providing the needed resources, and identifying desired task goals.[12] Instrumentalities can be influenced by making sure that rewards are tied to good performance and by helping employees see that they are. In addition, managers must try to determine the outcomes that each employee values.

One of the problems with the expectancy model is that it is quite complex. Still, the logic of the model is clear, and the steps are useful for clarifying how managers can motivate people. Managers should first find out which rewards under their control have the highest valences for their employees. For example, the best reward for one productive employee may be an office with large windows overlooking a scenic view of mountains or water. Other employees may value interesting work, challenge, advancement opportunities, and the chance to contribute. Managers should then link these rewards to the performance they desire. If any expectancies are low, managers might provide coaching, leadership, and training to raise them.[13]

EQUITY MODEL

Equity, or fairness in the workplace, has been found to be a major factor in determining employee motivation.[14] For example, before each sports season opens, it is common to read about a baseball, basketball, or football star who is negotiating a higher contract. This in turn will trigger perceptions of inequity among teammates, many of whom called for renegotiation of their own contracts.

Although equity in the workplace is less visible than it is in the sports arena, feelings of unfairness were among the most frequently reported sources of job dissatisfaction found by research involving the two-factor model. For example, assume that you just received a 10 percent raise. Will this raise lead to higher performance, lower performance, or no change in your performance? Are you satisfied with this increase? What if you discovered that colleagues in your work group received 15 percent raises? How does that affect your performance now?

The **equity model** focuses on an individual's feelings about how fairly he or she is treated in comparison with others.[15] The model says that people have a perception of the ratio of their inputs compared to their own outcomes in a situation. They also have a perception of the ratio of everyone else's inputs to outcomes. Then each person compares his or her own ratio to that of everyone else. Figure 15.5 illustrates the basic components of the model. Given the social nature of human beings, it should come as no surprise that we compare our contributions and rewards to those of others.

In the workplace, employees contribute things such as their education, experience, expertise, time, and effort, and in return they get pay, security, and recognition. According to the equity model, we prefer a situation of balance or equity that exists when we perceive that the ratio of our inputs and outcomes is equal to the ratio of inputs and outcomes of one or more comparison persons. If people experience inequity, they are generally motivated to change something.

The equity model suggests that maintaining our self-esteem is an important priority. To reduce a perceived inequity, a person may take one of the following actions:

Equity model
A motivation model focusing on an individual's feelings about how fairly he or she is treated in comparison with others.

Figure 15.5 | Equity Theory

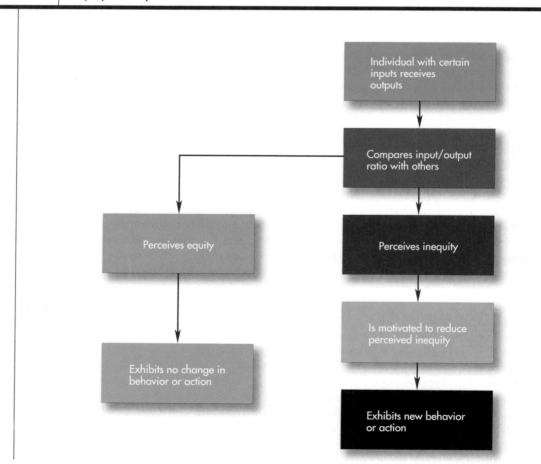

1. Change work inputs either upward or downward to what might be an equitable level. For example, people who believe that they are under rewarded might reduce the quality of their performance, work shorter hours, or be absent frequently (output).
2. Change outcomes to restore equity. For example, many union organizers try to attract nonmembers by pledging to improve working conditions, hours, and pay without an increase in employee effort (input).
3. Psychologically distort comparisons. For example, a person might rationalize or distort how hard she or he works or attempt to increase the importance of the job to the organization.
4. Change the comparison person she or he is using to another person.
5. Leave the situation. For example, quit the job, request a transfer to another department, or shift to a new reference group to reduce the source of the inequity. This type of action will probably be taken only in cases of high inequity when other alternatives are not feasible.

People often respond differently to the same situations, and therefore their reactions to inequity will vary. Some people are more willing to accept being underrewarded than others. If the perceived inequity results in a change in motivation, the inequity may also alter effort and performance. You can probably think of instances in school when you worked harder than others on a paper, yet received a lower grade. Although working hard doesn't necessarily imply that you wrote a high-quality paper, your sense of equity was probably violated.

Perception is an important aspect of the equity model. Feelings of inequity are determined solely by the individual's interpretation of the situation. Thus, it would be inaccurate to assume that all employees in a work unit will view their annual pay raise as fair. Rewards that are received with feelings of equity can foster job satisfaction and performance; rewards received with feelings of inequity can damage key work results. This conveys several clear messages to managers. First, people should be rewarded according to their contributions. Second, managers should make every effort possible to ensure that employees feel equitably treated. Finally, it is imperative for a manager to be aware that feelings of inequity are almost bound to arise. When they do, the manager should be patient and either correct the problem, if it is real, or help people recognize that things are not as inequitable as they seem.[16]

Employee feelings of inequity in rewards can damage key work results and cause employees to become frustrated.

© KEITH BROFSKY/GETTYIMAGES/PHOTODISC

GOAL SETTING

Goal setting as a motivation model is a process of increasing efficiency and effectiveness by specifying the desired outcomes toward which individuals, groups, departments, and organizations should work.[17] Goal setting can be a powerful tool to motivate employees.[18] Goals provide a clear, engaging sense of direction and specify what is going to be accomplished. They represent the future outcomes (results) to achieve. You may have a set goal, such as "I am planning to graduate with a 3.7 grade point average by the end of the summer semester."

Goals serve three purposes: (1) to guide and direct behavior toward overall organizational goals and strategies,[19] (2) to provide challenges and standards against which the individual can be assessed, and (3) to define what is important and provide a framework for planning.

For goal setting to be successful and lead to higher performance levels, goals must meet five requirements. An easy way to remember this is to use the acronym SMART, where S stands for specific, M represents measurable, A means achievable or realistic, R represents results oriented, and T means time related. For example, a department manager establishes a goal to increase profitability by 10 percent by the end of the year, as compared to profitability at the end of last year. Clear goals

LEARNING OBJECTIVE 5

Outline how goal setting is used as a tool for motivating individuals.

Goal setting
Using goals to motivate individual performance.

throughout the organization and jobs that encourage personal growth or personal goals have been very important to the success of John Bachmann, in his management of Edward Jones and Company, an investment brokerage company.[20] Research shows that people are more committed to their organizations when they are rewarded for achieving their job goals and when they perceive that the organization helps them achieve their personal goals.[21]

Although it is not always necessary to have employees participate in the goal-setting process, participation is probably preferable to managers assigning goals especially if they anticipate the employee will resist accepting more difficult challenges. Managers must also provide feedback to employees about their performance. A current study found that performance-review feedback followed by goal setting favorably influenced employee work satisfaction and organizational commitment to a greater extent than performance-review feedback alone.[22]

To use goal setting effectively as a motivational tool for employees, managers need to (1) meet regularly with subordinates, (2) work with subordinates to set goals jointly, (3) set goals that are specific and "appropriately" challenging, and (4) provide feedback about performance. When subordinates accept the goal-setting process, they are more likely to be committed and work hard to accomplish goals. The evidence thus far suggests that goal setting will become an increasingly important part of the motivational process in the future. Although it is limited, some research has suggested that employees achieve high levels of job satisfaction when they perceive that the probability of attaining goals at work is high. (Notice the link between this and the expectancy model.) Also, they are more satisfied when they perceive more positive than negative goals in their work environment.[23]

REINFORCEMENT THEORY

Reinforcement theory is based on the idea that people learn to repeat behaviors that are positively rewarded (reinforced positively) and avoid behaviors that are punished (not reinforced, or reinforced to avoid). Therefore, managers can influence employee performance by reinforcing behavior they see as supporting organizational goals. The application of reinforcement theory is frequently called behavior modification because it involves changing one's own behavior or the behavior of someone else.

The tools of behavior modification are four basic reinforcement strategies in which either a pleasant or an unpleasant event is applied or withdrawn following a person's behavior. These four reinforcers are illustrated in Figure 15.6. To increase desired behavior, positive reinforcement or avoidance is used; to decrease undesirable behavior, extinction or punishment is used.

POSITIVE REINFORCEMENT **Positive reinforcement** is the administration of positive and rewarding consequences or events following a desired behavior. This tends to increase the likelihood that the person will repeat the behavior in similar settings. For example, a manager praises the marketing representative's high monthly sales performance; a student gets a good grade; a professor receives high teaching evaluations.

NEGATIVE REINFORCEMENT **Negative reinforcement**, also called **avoidance learning** strengthens desired behavior by allowing escape from an undesirable consequence. For example, you avoid the penalties if you file your taxes by April 15.

EXTINCTION **Extinction** is the withdrawal of the positive reward or reinforcing consequences for an undesirable behavior. It weakens behavior as behavior that is no longer reinforced is less likely to occur in the future. For example, if an em-

LEARNING OBJECTIVE 6

Explain how reinforcement theory can be used to increase and decrease behavior in an organizational setting.

Reinforcement theory
A motivational theory that suggests that a person will learn to continue behaviors that are positively rewarded and discontinue behaviors that are ignored or punished.

Positive reinforcement
The administration of positive and rewarding consequences or events following a desired behavior.

Negative reinforcement or avoidance learning
Strengthening desired behavior by allowing escape from an undesirable consequence.

Extinction
The withdrawal of the positive reward or reinforcing consequences for an undesirable behavior.

Figure 15.6 | Four Types of Reinforcers

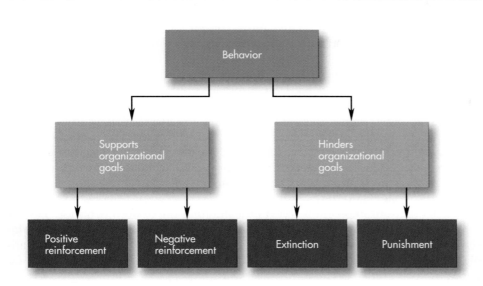

ployee who is not meeting sales quotas fails to receive bonus checks, he or she will begin to realize that the behavior is not producing desired outcomes. The undesirable behavior will gradually disappear.

PUNISHMENT Administering a negative consequence following undesirable behavior is called **punishment**. This tends to reduce the likelihood that the behavior will be repeated in similar settings. For example, a manager docks an employee's pay for being rude to a customer, being late, or loafing on the job.

Which type of reinforcer is most appropriate to use? As suggested by considerable research and some popular books such as *The One Minute Manager*, positive reinforcement probably is best.[24] As Table 15.1 shows, punishment may cause unwanted consequences. The manager who positively reinforces desirable behaviors among employees achieves performance improvements without generating the fear, suspicion, and revenge that may be associated with using punishment.

When an employee's behavior is supportive of the organizational goals, a manager should use either positive reinforcers or avoidance to increase this desirable behavior. Managers must not allow excellent performance to be ignored or taken for granted. When employee behaviors do not support organizational objectives, a

Punishment
Administering negative consequences following undesirable behavior.

Table 15.1 | Using Punishment

POSSIBLE NEGATIVE CONSEQUENCES	REASONS TO USE PUNISHMENT
May create negative stress	Temporarily stops or lessens damaging behavior
Attention may not be focused on desired behavior	Quick and easy to use
May lead to negative side effects (fear, suspicion, revenge)	
May cause emotional harm	

manager should use extinction or punishment (only as a last resort) since this behavior is considered to be undesirable.

Studies have shown that consistent rewards for organizationally desirable behavior result in positive performance in the long term. In contrast, punishment as a primary motivational tool contributes little to high motivation because employees learn to avoid the punisher rather than learning appropriate behaviors. Managers need to observe and manage the consequences of work-related behaviors carefully because individuals have different perceptions of what is a reward and what is punishment depending on their values and needs. As the workforce becomes increasingly diverse, this issue will present greater challenges to managers.

SCHEDULES OF REINFORCEMENT   To use behavior modification effectively, managers need to apply reinforcers properly. **Schedules of reinforcement** specify the basis for and timing of reinforcement. The basis for reinforcement includes interval and ratio. Interval means that reinforcement is based on time. Ratio means that reinforcement is based on exhibiting the desired behavior. Timing of reinforcement includes fixed or variable. Fixed reinforcement means that the reinforcement is administered at each interval or for each desired behavior. Variable reinforcement means that the reinforcer is given at essentially a random time or random occurrence of the desired behavior.

A **fixed-interval schedule** rewards employees at specified time intervals, assuming that the desired behavior has continued at an appropriate level. An example is the Friday paycheck many employees receive.

When a reinforcer is provided after a fixed number of occurrences of the desired behavior, it is called a **fixed-ratio schedule**. For example, Nordstrom department store wanted to increase charge card purchases during the holiday season. The store offered a reward to sales clerks for each purchase over $100 that customers made on their Nordstrom credit card during a three-week period. Most piece-rate pay systems are considered fixed-ratio schedules.

With a **variable-interval schedule**, reinforcement is administered at random or varying times that cannot be predicted by the employee. For example, a division manager might visit a territory five times a month to comment on employee performance, varying the days and times each month.

A **variable-ratio schedule** provides a reinforcer after a varying or random number of occurrences of the desired behavior rather than after variable time periods. For example, slot machine payoff patterns, which provide rewards after a varying number of pulls on the lever, use a variable-ratio schedule. While people anticipate that the machine will pay a jackpot after a certain number of plays, the exact number of plays is variable.

Reinforcers based on time are not very powerful in getting people to engage in and learn behaviors that are desired overall. Instead, they tend to influence people to engage in a certain behavior at a certain time. Behavior-based reinforcers are intended to teach a person to engage in behaviors that are desirable, for example behaviors that contribute to achieving a goal of good performance.

Let's look a bit deeper at reinforcers based on desired behavior. Fixed ratio is effective during the initial learning process, but it becomes tedious and loses its value on an ongoing basis. For example, a manager might praise an employee every time he or she performs a task correctly. That would help the person learn faster. However, once the person begins to learn the task or behavior, the constant reward seems silly. Furthermore, the desired behavior tends to stop almost immediately unless the reinforcement is continued.

As an alternative, a variable-ratio reinforcement can be used. In this case, the desired behavior is rewarded intermittently rather than each time it occurs. With a variable ratio schedule, a desired behavior can be rewarded more often as encouragement during the initial learning process and less often when the behavior

Schedules of reinforcement
The basis for, and timing of, reinforcement.

Fixed-interval schedule
Giving reinforcers at specified time intervals.

Fixed-ratio schedule
Reinforcers given after a fixed number of occurrences of the desired behavior.

Variable-interval schedule
Reinforcement administered at varying times that cannot be predicted by the employee.

Variable-ratio schedule
Reinforcers given after varying or random number of occurrences of the desired behavior.

Table 15.2 | Comparing Schedules of Reinforcement

SCHEDULE	FORM OF REINFORCEMENT	INFLUENCES ON BEHAVIOR WHEN APPLIED	EFFECTS ON BEHAVIOR WHEN WITHDRAWN	EXAMPLE
Fixed interval	Reward given on fixed time basis	Leads to average and irregular performance	Rapid extinction of behavior	Weekly or monthly paycheck
Fixed ratio	Reward tied to specific number of responses	Quickly leads to high and stable performance	Moderately fast extinction of behavior	Piece-rate system
Variable interval	Reward given at varying times	Leads to moderately high and stable performance	Slower extinction of behavior	Performance appraisals and rewards given at random times each month
Variable ratio	Reward given at variable amounts of output, or desired behavior	Leads to very high performance	Very slow extinction of behavior	Bonus given for the dollar value of sales made, with random levels of sales needed in order to get the bonus

has been learned. The variable-ratio schedule of reinforcement tends to be the most powerful in terms of getting a person to continue a desired behavior. Consider how difficult it is to walk away from a slot machine. "If it has paid out, I'll keep playing because it's likely to again. . . . If it hasn't paid out, then it will any minute now—because it's due, and it might be big! . . ." The four major types of reinforcement schedules are compared in Table 15.2.

USING BEHAVIOR MODIFICATION The application of reinforcement theory concepts is called behavior modification, especially when it is consciously or formally applied. The reason is that the intent of applying the concepts is to change or modify one's own or someone else's behavior.

Essentially, we all use the concepts in reinforcement theory constantly. We all perceive a response from other people for every behavior that we demonstrate. Based on our perception of the response, we tend to learn to repeat a behavior, avoid it, or stop doing it. Even if we are not aware of it, we may be influencing someone else's behavior by whether or not another person perceives a reward or punishment for a certain behavior. This is especially important for managers to keep in mind because their behavior tends to set examples for the behavior of others in the organization. Hopefully, managers reward behavior of employees that is desirable for the organization—high performance—and ignore (extinction) behavior that is not, or even punish it, if appropriate. Do you think that managers are aware that their leadership example may reward behaviors that are not good for the organization?

Some organizations have attempted to implement the concepts of reinforcement theory through formal behavior modification programs. Its use has had some notable successes. Emery Air Freight, Target Corporation, formerly Dayton Hudson, Starbucks, Nordstrom, Boeing, Michigan Bell (a subsidiary of Ameritech), and Weyerhaeuser are all using varied forms of behavior modification.

Dayton's Department Store, now Marshall Field's, *is using varied forms of behavior modification to implement the concepts of reinforcement theory.*

© AP/WIDE WORLD PHOTOS

Leaders In Action

Sallie Krawcheck Rewards, and Gets, Accurate Analysis

In the past few years, many investment and brokerage companies got into trouble, certainly ethical trouble, if not legal trouble, because of the way they rewarded their stock analysts. Most brokerage companies offer a variety of investments including stocks, mutual funds, insurance, investment banking, and others. The investment banking and rewards to analysts caused the trouble.

Investment banking means that the brokerage company's job is to "underwrite" or sell the initial offering of stock of a particular (target) company. Investment companies, such as Merrill Lynch, Morgan Stanley, and many others, paid large bonuses to analysts based on the sale of stock of the target company —the one they were analyzing. Apparently many analysts lost their objectivity when they were analyzing those companies. They issued "buy" conclusions in many situations, but

they said privately the company was a poor investment. When investors bought the stock, the analysts received their bonuses.

Sallie Krawcheck, the CEO and Chair of the Board of Sanford C. Bernstein, will not let that happen at her investment company. She leads a company that is highly respected for thorough and very accurate analysis of companies. Bernstein has 5,000 institutional investor clients who rely heavily on the research/analysis reports that Bernstein analysts prepare each month. Analysis, or research as it is called on Wall Street, is all that Bernstein does.

Many people believe that Krawcheck should add other products to the company, especially underwriting. Krawcheck says it will never happen. She insists that research analysts must be objective and that objectivity is challenged when analysts

recommend stock and when their level of pay rests directly on the number of shares that sell. Therefore, Krawcheck will keep Bernstein a research-only company and will reward analysts based on the quality of their research—how accurate they are in predicting how good an investment stock in other companies is.

Of course, Sallie Krawcheck was herself judged to be the best analyst in the "brokers and asset managers" category of investments in 1998. She was an analyst at Sanford C. Bernstein before being selected to be CEO and Chair of the Board in June 2001.

SOURCES: "Brokers & Asset Managers," *Institutional Investor*, 32, October 1998, 120–121; K. K., "The Straight Shooter," *Money*, 30, October 2001, 86–87; D. Rynecki, "The Bernstein Way," *Fortune*, June 10, 2002, 85–86.

CRITICISMS OF BEHAVIOR MODIFICATION   Critics of behavior modification charge that it is essentially bribery and that workers are already paid for performance. Because it disregards people's attitudes and beliefs, behavior modification has been called misleading and manipulative. One critic has noted that little difference exists between behavior modification and some key elements of scientific management presented more than 60 years ago by Taylor, particularly when money is involved. Is it a motivational technique for manipulating people? Does it decrease an employee's freedom? If so, is such action on the part of managers unethical? There are no easy answers to these questions.

CONTEMPORARY MOTIVATIONAL APPROACHES

LEARNING OBJECTIVE 7

Address the application of participative management in contemporary organizations.

Contemporary issues involving motivation offer challenges to today's managers. We will look at two of these issues: participative management and money as a means of motivating employees.

The use of participative management, an umbrella term that encompasses various activities in which subordinates share a significant degree of decision-making power with their immediate supervisors, involves any process whereby power, knowledge, information, and rewards are moved downward in the organization.[25] It is often difficult to determine exactly why participative management is successful because many changes are occurring simultaneously in several areas, including human resources, work structure, technology, training, and reward systems.

As a result of social and political developments over the past couple of decades, people today expect greater participation in choosing directions for their lives in general and their lives at work more specifically.[26] Participative management draws on and is linked to a number of motivational approaches. For example, employee involvement can motivate workers by providing more opportunities for growth, responsibility, and commitment in the work itself. Similarly, the process of making and implementing a decision and then seeing the results can help satisfy an employee's need for responsibility, recognition, growth, self-esteem, and achievement.

Participative management programs represent a shift away from traditional management styles and ways of doing business.[27] For participative management to work, however, an organization must change. As we discussed in Chapter 11, the culture of an organization has to be in harmony with and accept this new way of conducting business. It is often extremely difficult for managers to give up authority and for employees to translate that surrender of power by higher-ups into lasting improvements in quality and productivity. When organizations increase the amount of control and discretion workers have over their jobs, they are **empowering employees** and may improve the motivation of both employees and management.[28]

Do employee participation and involvement really work to motivate individuals? U.S. executives have indicated optimism toward employee involvement and participative management.[29] Participative management programs have been viewed as having positive influences on corporate quality, productivity, and customer service. For example, Corning Glass eliminated one management level at its corporate computer center, substituting a team advisor for three shift supervisors. Corning also produced $150,000 in annual savings and increased the quality of service. Perceptions of autonomy and responsibility among workers increased because they felt they experienced more meaningful and productive work. At its DuPont, Washington, desktop computer assembly operation, Intel successfully developed an employee participation system with operators working in two shifts of three teams. These teams are involved in everything, including training, selection, scheduling production, scheduling overtime, and rejecting products not up to quality standards.[30]

Participative management is one way that an organization can establish a supportive environment. One of the many ways in which the workforce is changing is that employees are less accepting of top-down control and expect growth, fulfillment, and dignity from their work.[31]

MONEY AS A MOTIVATOR

The issue of whether or not money motivates is particularly relevant to many managers. As a medium of exchange, money should motivate to the degree that people perceive it as a means to acquire other things they want. Money may also have symbolic meaning, be a measure of achievement, bring recognition, or satisfy some other need.

Research does show that money is a motivator when a "significant amount of money" is clearly tied to a desired behavior. Also, money has to be desired by the person engaging in the behavior, the employee. However, overall, money tends to not be associated with productive behavior and may even motivate unwanted behavior. In situations where money does not motivate productive behavior, the reasons usually are (1) proper (productive) behavior has not been defined, (2) there are poor measures or no measures of productive behavior, and (3) the amount of money is too small to make a difference.[32] These same reasons explain why profit-sharing or gain-sharing programs frequently do not motivate individual performance.

Money may not be motivational when employees believe that a certain amount is an entitlement. Even a raise based on productive behavior, when added to the

Empowering employees
Increasing the amount of control and discretion workers have over their jobs.

LEARNING OBJECTIVE **8**
Clarify the use of money as a motivator.

base salary for the next period of time, may be seen as an entitlement and, therefore, cease to be motivational. Money may motivate behavior that is not productive for an organization when people perceive that it is tied to the unwanted behavior. This, or course, may be due to differing perceptions and to poorly defined desired behavior.

EMPLOYEE OWNERSHIP AS A MOTIVATOR

It seems logical that if a person owned part of a company, that he or she would be more highly motivated to contribute to make the company more successful, more profitable. The person's stock in the company would therefore be worth more. As with money, the research shows that using ownership, including stock options, works to motivate productive behavior only when productive behavior and goals have been defined, good performance can be measured, and the awards of stock or stock options are tied directly to performance.[33]

In general, managers must consider that to motivate, money must be important to the employee and must be perceived as a direct reward for performance. The same principles hold true for nonmonetary rewards, and there are many nonmonetary rewards. See Table 15.3 for some examples.

REWARDING TEAM PERFORMANCE

LEARNING OBJECTIVE 9

Explain how to reward team performance.

Many managers use teams for various tasks. However, they tend to have trouble in getting the team members to work as a true team. One of the most important reasons for that is they reward individual performance.[34] So how do you reward team performance? First, a significant part of the reward given to team members must be based on total team performance. That will motivate the team to work together,

---

Table 15.3 | Reward Employees without Spending Money

1. Create flexible schedules. Once a worker shows that she or he is a consistent contributor, relax some of the supervisory structure. Let stellar employees use their own judgment about when they take breaks, how long lunchtime should be, and so on.

2. Provide advancement opportunities. Career advancement for employees, even outside your department, is a valuable way to motivate. Obviously, it would be better to keep good workers in your own department. But, if there are no opportunities for them there, actively seek out promotional possibilities in other departments. You'll lose some good workers this way, but that will be offset by the image of goodwill you project. Your employees will realize that you care about them.

3. Award plum assignments. When possible, find special assignments for exceptional workers—assignments that offer them a welcome change of pace. Sitting on a special task force, for example, or working on a new-project launch.

4. Praise in public. The human being has not yet been born who doesn't relish public praise. Remember, though, to reserve this powerful weapon for exceptional performance. Otherwise, you risk weakening its potential power.

5. Give feedback. More employees want to know how they are doing so they can learn more and improve.

6. Share your feelings—but only if you are sincere. "I really am proud of your contribution. . . ." Be specific. Try a handwritten thank-you note.

7. Use fun, simple, creative, and symbolic rewards. They are remembered longer.

SOURCE: Adapted from G. Fuller, *The Supervisor's Big Book of Lists* (Upper Saddle River, N.J.: Prentice Hall, 1994); B. Nelson, "The Ironies of Motivation," *Strategy & Leadership*, January/February 1999, 26–31.

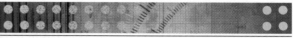

At The Forefront

Successful Senior Executives Under 40

Companies that have senior managers who are under 40 years of age are more successful than companies that have older senior managers! That is the finding of a survey conducted by the American Management Association (AMA). What are the reasons?

The AMA survey found that younger managers, so called Generation X, or Gen-X managers, first, tend to believe that nonmonetary rewards, especially forms of recognition are very important, and second, that the Gen-X managers are much more likely to give people a choice of rewards—because different people value different things. This is especially true as the workforce becomes more diverse.

Related is the trend of decreasing loyalty that organizations show to their employees and a related lower loyalty that employees have for the organizations. Rather than long-term loyal relationships that were common in the past, the employment relationship now is temporary where employees ". . . try to maximize their rewards while adding to their skills and capabilities."

Combining the two issues above results in more employees demanding that their managers recognize good work and reward the individuals achieving it. A manager at Bank-Boston did it right: The manager asked subordinates to jot down on an index card what rewards they preferred. One financial analyst wrote "time off, lunch with my manager, and Starbucks Coffee." After successfully finishing a job, she found a personal thank-you note

from her manager attached to a coupon for Starbucks Coffee on her desk. Handwritten thank-you notes from Jack Welch, the very successful and famous former CEO of General Electric, also were very valued by his subordinates.

[Younger] managers who tune into what different people value; less loyal employees who want nonmonetary rewards as well as monetary rewards and credit for good performance—is this the future of successful motivation?

SOURCES: J. Casison, "Young and in Charge," *Incentive*, 173, December 1999, 7; E. Lawler, III, "Pay Strategy: New Thinking for the New Millennium," *Compensation & Benefits Review*, 32, 1, 2000, 13–32; B. Nelson, "The Ironies of Motivation," *Strategy & Leadership*, January/February 1999, 26–31.

for the same goal.[35] (Review the "At The Forefront" box in the previous chapter on page 444.) Second, individual rewards probably should be given. However, individuals should be rewarded for contributing to the team success, effort, and functioning and not for individual performance itself.[36]

INTERNATIONAL PERSPECTIVES

Just as no one thing motivates everyone in the United States, the differences in what motivates individuals become greater as we go to other countries. Here are just a few examples.

The United States is an achievement-oriented society that has historically encouraged and honored individual accomplishment and the attainment of material prosperity. Individualism, independence, self-confidence, and speaking out against injustice and threats are important elements of the U.S. character. Japanese motivations and values are quite different, with obvious implications for management practices.[37] The Japanese place greater emphasis on socially oriented qualities. Their society is arranged in a rigid hierarchy, and all members are expected to maintain loyalty and obedience to authority. Dependency and security are part of the Japanese upbringing, whereas autonomy and early independence are typically American. In their corporate life, the Japanese show great dependency and are highly conforming and obedient. Japanese managers recognize that these characteristics can inhibit creativity and innovation and are consequently encouraging programs in their schools that will develop the creativity and ingenuity they envy in Americans.[38]

The cross-cultural research on achievement has been relatively consistent across cultures, stimulated by the realization that managers in multinational corporations must be sensitive to the underlying values and needs of their diverse employees.[39]

LEARNING OBJECTIVE 10

Account for the importance of motivation from an international perspective.

For example, managers in New Zealand appear to follow an achievement pattern developed in the United States. In general, managers in Anglo countries, such as the United States, Canada, and Great Britain, tend to have a high need for achievement as well as a high need to produce and a strong willingness to accept risk. In contrast, managers in countries such as Chile and Portugal tend to have a lower need for achievement. Keep in mind, however, that the word achievement itself is difficult to translate into other languages, and this influences any cross-cultural research findings.

The implications for managerial style, practices, and motivational planning for a U.S.-based company that is operating branches in other countries are apparent. Managers must take the social character, values, and cultural practices of each country into consideration. A well-managed, diverse workforce is instrumental for a firm's competitive advantage. In order to develop or maintain such an advantage, managers need to consider a broad definition of motivation when determining compensation packages, responsibilities, rules and procedures, organizational structure, control systems, job design, and management techniques.

IMPLICATIONS FOR LEADERS

Here are important conclusions that we can draw from the study of motivation:

- Find out what motivates each person: Every motivational theory and model, with the possible exception of the two-factor theory, directly or indirectly says that each person has different needs and wants so the same thing will not motivate everyone.

  In a classic study first conducted in the 1940s and repeated in the 1980s and the 1990s, Lawrence Lindahl asked managers to list, in order of importance, what they thought were most important to their employees. These lists were compared to those in which employees ranked what was important to them. Managers said that their employees wanted good wages, job security, and promotion opportunities more than anything else. The employees ranked recognition for a good job as number one; their managers ranked it eighth. Number two in importance to employees was "feeling in on things." Managers ranked it tenth, or last, in the 1–10 scale. Number three in importance to employees was "empathic managers"![40] This seems to be a cruel irony, since empathic managers would tune into what their subordinates wanted for rewards.

- Tie rewards to the behavior that you want: Managers have to clearly tie rewards that people want to the performance/behavior that is productive for the organization. That, of course, requires a clear mission, strategy, and goals so that what is "good" behavior or performance can be clearly seen.

- Help the people see what the right behavior and performance is: Select, train, teach, guide, encourage, and coach people so they can achieve the goals. Hold them accountable for results. Here is one place where the manager can set a positive example by his or her own behavior.

As a manager, you probably can't make your employees be motivated. You can, however, create an environment that lends itself to greater motivation. We conclude this chapter with a prescription for greater motivation that involves building value into people's work and increasing their expectation that they can be successful in attaining the rewards they want:

1. *Tell people what you expect them to do.* On a regular, periodic basis, tell employees what your goals are as well as your standards of performance. People need goals. No human activity exists without them. Don't assume that they know what you want. Tell them as specifically as possible.

2. *Make the work valuable.* When you can, assign people to the kinds of work they like and can do well—work that they regard as valuable to them. Give them work that enables them to achieve their personal goals, such as growth, advancement, self-esteem, professional recognition, status, and the like.

3. *Make the work doable.* Increase employees' confidence that they can do what you expect by training, coaching, mentoring, listening, scheduling, providing resources, and so on.

4. *Give feedback.* Provide employees feedback on how well they are doing. Positive feedback tells them what they need to continue doing; give criticism in ways that help them correct mistakes and truly learn from the mistakes.

5. *Reward successful performance.* When employees have done what you asked them to do, reward them with both monetary and nonmonetary recognition.

The 3Cs Model of Leadership applies directly to motivation. In order to be a successful leader, a manager must have the competence to understand the many issues related to motivation that are summarized above. Also, the manager's character directly influences motivation of subordinates by building trusting relationships. Finally, by influencing people to be motivated to achieve team goals, department goals, and ultimately, the organization's goals and overall mission, a true community is formed.

In this chapter we have examined motivation as a key management tool that organizations can use to energize employees. An organization can help create a

---

Now Apply It

What Is Your Motivation Related to Goals?

For each of the following three questions, place a check mark by all the responses that apply to you. Check the responses based on your usual and regular behavior. Ask two classmates to do the same. When you are all finished, discuss your responses and why you answered them as you did. The purpose of this is to develop awareness of your motivational behavior, especially as it relates to goals.

1. When I am a member of a group that does not seem to have clear awareness of its goals and how to achieve them, I usually
___ ask the group to stop and discuss its goals until all members clearly understand them and what actions the group needs to take to accomplish them.
___ feel disgusted and refuse to attend meetings.
___ state what I consider the goals to be and comment on how the present actions of the group relate to achieving them.

___ ask the designated leader, if there is one, to stop messing around and tell the group what it is supposed to do.

2. When I am a member of a group that has clear understanding of its goals but seems to have little commitment to accomplishing them, I usually
___ try to shame other group members into being more motivated.
___ blame the designated leader for being incompetent.
___ ask the group members to look at how meaningful, relevant, and acceptable the goals are to them.
___ try to change the group's goals in order to make them more relevant to members' needs and motives.
___ point out the sacrifices some members have made in the past toward goal accomplishment and hope that all members become more committed.

3. When I am a member of a group that has conflicting opin-

ions on what its goals should be, or that has members with conflicting needs and motives, I usually
___ figure out how much cooperative and competitive behavior exists in the group and give the group feedback in an attempt to increase cooperativeness.
___ start a group discussion on the personal goals, needs, and motives of each member in order to determine the extent to which there are competing goals among them.
___ declare one member of the group to be the winner and ask all others to work toward accomplishing that person's goals.
___ ask the group to determine how the members' actions can become more coordinated.
___ form a secret coalition with several other group members so that our goals will become dominant in the group.

motivating atmosphere by making the work environment pleasant and conducive to productive output. The organization that achieves these conditions will create a culture in which all members can contribute to their maximum potential and in which the value of diversity can be fully realized. Many companies are attempting to improve working conditions for employees based on the premise that a motivated workforce can reduce absenteeism, increase productivity, encourage labor-management harmony, and lead to a better product or service.

Meeting The Challenge

Nucor Steel Corporation

Along with all the other innovative and risky things that Kenneth Iverson did to build Nucor Steel, he uses a unique compensation plan based on the need to make all of the employees very efficient. Iverson began to build a culture based on very high productivity. He said that he wants to hire five people to do the work of ten (in other steel mills) and give them the pay of eight.

While beginning pay is up to 33 percent less than the industry average, employees can earn from 80 percent to 200 percent of base pay if their team of 20 to 40 people meets the productivity goals. Team productivity is posted every day. If a person is five minutes late for work, he or she loses the bonus for the

day; 30 minutes late costs the person the bonus for the week. If equipment breaks down, no adjustment for the reduced productivity for the team is made. Of course, the company does provide good equipment, but it needs to be maintained by the team. It is common for employees to be at work a half hour to an hour before starting time so that they can get everything ready. During downturns in demand for the company's products, productivity will have to go down because of reduced demand. Bonuses go down accordingly.

What about the managers? The same rules apply. For a plant manager, his or her team is the entire plant. For a corporate officer, the team is the entire corporation.

No discretionary bonuses are given. The rules are clear. If a person's team reaches the goal and he or she is not late for work, the bonus is earned.

How has the company done? It is one of the most efficient and profitable steel companies in the world. Nucor workers are the highest paid in the steel industry.

SOURCES: J. Michlitsch, *Video Guide to Accompany Strategic Management: Competitiveness and Globalization* by M. Hitt, R. Ireland, and R. Hoskisson, (St. Paul, MN: West Publishing Company, 1997); J. Collins, "Turning Goals Into Results: The Power of Catalytic Mechanisms," *Harvard Business Review,* July/August 1999, 71–82.

SUMMARY

1. Motivation is generally defined as the forces and expenditure of effort acting on or within a person that cause that person to behave in a specific, goal-directed manner. It is a psychological process that gives behavior purpose and direction.

2. Managers can draw upon several different approaches to motivation. Needs-based approaches emphasize specific human needs or the factors within a person that energize, direct, and stop behavior. They explain motivation as a phenomenon primarily occurring intrinsically, or within an individual. Process approaches take a more dynamic view of motivation. These models focus on understanding how the individual's thought or cognitive processes act to affect behavior.

3. Three needs-based models were examined. The hierarchy of needs explains that a person has five fundamental needs: physiological, security, affiliation, esteem, and self-actualization. Physiological and security needs are lower-order needs, which

are generally satisfied externally, and affiliation, esteem, and self-actualization are higher-order needs, which are satisfied internally. The two-factor model examines the relationship between job satisfaction and productivity. The sources of work satisfaction are motivator factors. The sources of dissatisfaction are hygiene factors. The acquired-needs model focuses on three particularly important or relevant needs in the work environment: achievement, affiliation, and power. The model proposes that when a need is strong, it will motivate the person to engage in behaviors to satisfy that need.

4. Four process approaches were examined. The expectancy model suggests that work motivation is determined by an individual's perceptions about the relationship between effort and performance, the relationship between performance and outcomes and the desirability of the outcomes or rewards. Individuals choose the option that promises to give them the greatest reward and that is most valued. The equity model focuses on individuals' feelings about how fairly they are treated

in comparison with others. It assumes that individuals evaluate their interpersonal relationships just as they evaluate any exchange process and compare their situations with those of others to determine the equity of their own situation. Goal setting is a process of increasing efficiency and effectiveness by specifying the desired outcomes. Reinforcement theory explains how a person learns to repeat a certain behavior or to stop the behavior based upon the consequences of that behavior. If the behavior is positively reinforced, the person will learn to repeat it. If the behavior is ignored or punished, the person will learn to stop it.

5. As a motivational tool, goal setting helps employees by serving three purposes: to guide and direct behavior toward supportive organizational goals, to provide challenges and standards against which the individual can be assessed, and to define what is important and provide a framework for planning. Goals must be specific, measurable, achievable, realistic, and timely.

6. The tools of reinforcement theory are four basic reinforcement strategies. To increase desired behavior, positive reinforcement or negative reinforcement, also known as avoidance, can be used. A positive reinforcement is the administration of positive and rewarding consequences or events following a desired behavior. Negative reinforcement, or avoidance, strengthens desired behavior by allowing escape from undesirable consequences. To decrease undesirable behavior, extinction or punishment is used. Extinction is the withdrawal of the positive reward or reinforcing consequences for an undesirable behavior. It weakens behavior because behavior that is no longer reinforced is less likely to occur in the future. Administering negative consequences following undesirable behavior is called punishment. This tends to reduce the likelihood that the behavior will be repeated in similar settings.

7. Participative management is an umbrella term that encompasses various activities in which subordinates share a significant degree of decision-making power with their immediate superiors. It involves any process whereby power, knowledge, information, and rewards are moved downward in the organization. Participative management motivates workers by providing more opportunities for growth, responsibility, and commitment in the work itself. In addition, the process of making and implementing a decision and then seeing the results can help satisfy an employee's need for responsibility, recognition, growth, self-esteem, and achievement.

8. Money is a motivator to the degree that people perceive it as a means to acquire other things they want. It may have symbolic meaning, be a measure of achievement, bring recognition, or satisfy a need. To motivate with money, it must be important to the employee and must be perceived as a reward for performance. The same ideas apply to employee ownership because the ownership is related to monetary outcomes.

9. In order to get true teamwork, a significant part of the reward to individual team members must be based on overall team results. The rest of an individual's reward should be based upon his or her contribution to the team's success or functioning.

10. In the international arena, managers must take the social character, values, and cultural practices of each country into consideration when applying motivation concepts. People of other cultures perceive work differently. Reward systems need to be designed carefully to ensure that the rewards are truly motivational in the local cultural framework.

REVIEW QUESTIONS

1. (*Learning Objective 1*) Define motivation.

2. (*Learning Objective 1*) Explain how motivation is related to performance by describing the model $M \times A = P$.

3. (*Learning Objective 2*) How are needs-based models different from process models of motivation?

4. (*Learning Objective 3*) Clarify hygiene and motivator factors in the two-factor model of motivation. How is satisfaction involved in the model?

5. (*Learning Objective 3*) Discuss the acquired-needs model of motivation and the three needs that are the basis for understanding the model.

6. (*Learning Objective 4*) Explain the primary differences between the expectancy model and the equity model of motivation.

7. (*Learning Objective 4*) If people experience inequity, what are they generally motivated to change?

8. (*Learning Objective 5*) Describe how goal setting can help employees become motivated.

9. (*Learning Objective 5*) For goal setting to be successful, what are the requirements that goals must have?

10. (*Learning Objective 6*) As a manager, you decide you need to decrease a behavior of an employee. What type of reinforcer will be appropriate to use and why?

11. (*Learning Objective 7*) Select and discuss some of the reasons why participative management is successful in organizations.

12. (*Learning Objective 8*) Explain when and why money might not be a good motivator of work performance.

13. (*Learning Objective 9*) Explain how to reward individual team members so they will contribute to a successful team.

14. (*Learning Objective 10*) Discuss why managers need to be aware of international perspectives when trying to motivate employees from different cultures?

DISCUSSION QUESTIONS

Improving Critical Thinking

1. Explain what a manager could do if one of his or her subordinates perceives a low relationship between effort and performance in a job.

2. Think about the best job you have ever had. What motivation approach was used in the organization or by your manager?

3. Explain why the variable-ratio schedule of reinforcement is more effective than the other schedules in motivating behavior.

4. What occupations or professions are people with a high need for affiliation likely to choose? a high need for achievement? a high need for power?

Enhancing Communication Skills

5. Think about the worst job you have ever had. What motivation approach was used in the organization? Prepare a short presentation that describes this job, citing specific examples of motivation approaches. Make suggestions for possible changes.

6. Research the acquired-needs model in more depth. Write a short paper in which you explain how one acquires the various needs.

Building Teamwork

7. In a team of four, discuss how to reward individual team members in order to achieve a successful team.

8. In a small group, identify a local health club or diet center that uses reinforcement theory/behavior modification as one of its tools. Ask for an interview with the manager and discuss the use of the reinforcers and the schedules of reinforcement. Be prepared to present your findings.

THINKING CRITICALLY: DEBATE THE ISSUE

Motivating Others

Form two teams as directed by your instructor to debate the role of money as a motivator. One team will take the position that money is the most important motivator of all people. The other team will take the position that nonmonetary rewards are the most important motivator.

EXPERIENTIAL EXERCISE 15.1

What Motivates You in This Class?

1. Make a list of your goals in completing your college or university degree.

2. Now make a list of your goals in this class.

3. Are the goals in these two lists coordinated with your overall career and life goals?

4. What motivates you to achieve the goals that you listed for this class? Be specific. How does the instructor of this class influence the things that motivate you in this class? How about this book, other readings, assignments, or other items?

5. Repeat step four for the goals that you listed for your college or university degree and for your career and life goals.

CAPTURING THE POWER OF INFORMATION TECHNOLOGY

1. In Chapter 11, you went to the Web sites for several organizations in order to assess the cultures of those organizations. Go back to those Web sites or select others and look at them now from the point of view of motivation. Make some notes about what you think are the main things that you think the organizations are using to motivate their employees.

   Ask someone else in your class to do the same. Then compare notes.

2. Go to Web sites of companies that offer products and services for sale. Do those Web sites motivate you to want to buy the product or service? If so, what is it? Is there something about the Web sites that influences you to not purchase the product or service?

ETHICS: TAKE A STAND

Some organizations use the concepts of reinforcement theory in formal behavior modification programs as a solution to control healthcare costs and keep employees healthy. They provide employees with financial incentives if they meet certain "wellness" criteria, such as not smoking, maintaining normal weight, and following a healthy lifestyle. The rewards or incentives used are typically either a lower premium contribution required from employees or higher benefits. For example, Baker Hughes, Inc., a Texas drilling and tool company, estimates it has saved $2 million annually by charging nonsmoking employees $100 less a year for health insurance than smokers. Adolph Coors Company claims it has saved $3 million a year by offering its employees incentives to meet weight, smoking, blood pressure, cholesterol, and other health criteria. Other companies adopting the strategy of rewarding healthy lifestyles include U-Haul, Control Data, and Southern California Edison.

SOURCE: G. Koretz, "Economic Trends," *BusinessWeek*, April 29, 1991, 22.

For Discussion

1. Is it ethical for a company to get involved in health matters of its employees?

2. Does a person's physical or emotional condition affect performance on the job?

3. Is it fair to charge a person who smokes or someone who is overweight more for his or her healthcare premiums?

4. Is using reinforcement theory concepts appropriate to get someone to change his or her personal behavior?

VIDEO CASE

Motivating Organizational Members: Buffalo Zoological Gardens

Dr. Donna Fernandes has taken on the challenge of a lifetime: to turn around a declining zoo with demoralized employees, many of whom have been with the Buffalo Zoological Gardens 20 years or more. The Zoo's mission is to provide the general public with an educationally, culturally, and recreationally significant community resource that advances the science of zoology and encourages conservation and environmental awareness. The Buffalo Zoo, located in Buffalo, New York, is the third oldest zoo in the United States, housing more than 320 different species of plants and about 1,000 diverse mammals, birds, reptiles, amphibians, and fish.

Donna's responsibilities include overseeing everyday operations, monitoring new construction, fund raising, and addressing employee issues. Her most challenging activities involve reinvigorating the dedicated employees. Not only were the zoo employees demoralized from years of unfulfilled promises to renovate the zoo's outdated facilities, they were anti-management, due to earlier nonsupportive, autocratic, Theory X-oriented zoo presidents.[1] Although she is the first female president and CEO of The Buffalo Zoo, Donna's employees appear to respond to her more supportive and Theory Y-oriented leadership style. One way she creates a more supportive environment is by taking daily walks around the zoo grounds and interacting with her employees and zoo visitors. Her extensive zoo background also helps the more than 150 employees accept her vision, since they now are being led by someone who knows the zoo business. They have risen to her expectations, accepting additional responsibilities and accountability for zoo activities.

As noted above, Donna is improving her employees' confidence in management and creating a more supportive and collegial culture at the zoo. Her education and extensive zoological experience showed her how zoo work is specialized, isolated, tedious, and frustratingly difficult.[2] She has introduced programs to help motivate and integrate her employees such as having her keepers cross-train each other. This has validated each person's special skill, provided valuable experience in training, increased employees' self-esteem, and helped them get along with their coworkers. Typically, keepers are introverts, choosing careers that limit interaction with other people. Her keepers have become more open and willing to be team players because they share common experiences and skills. Because she also is an introvert, her dog (an Australian Shepherd bought three days after the September 11, 2001, terrorist attacks on New York and the United States) shares her office, which helps break the ice with employees who may feel intimidated when talking with the zoo president. Donna's energetic dog, Liberty, must be helping because her employees brag about how Liberty likes them.[3]

Donna also encourages her employees to suggest ways to raise money. When an employee comes up with a creative way to make money, the zoo splits the proceeds with the employee (50-50) and he or she gets to spend 50 percent on what they want in their work areas or for professional development. The elephant trainer came up with the highly successful idea to sell art that's designed by all the zoo animals called "Art Gone Wild." The idea is totally keeper-driven. All the keepers and their animal charges participate, from peacocks to pachyderms, gorillas to geckos, and bears to binturongs. The event has been so successful that the keepers have decided to make "Art Gone Wild" an annual fund raiser.

Dedicated to conservation, education, and recreation, the Buffalo Zoo plays an essential role in a variety of local, regional, and global conservation efforts. Seventy-five percent of the zoo's 383,000-plus visitors return three or four times a year; so, it's important for Donna and her employees to continue to improve and expand the zoo experience. In general, even Donna's long-term employees now believe there is more support for what they feel is important. Among other things, Donna has increased their job variety by involving them in research, training, or education programs.

Donna's top management position also fulfills her goal of being a zoo director even though it means she and her husband of five plus years must continue their "commuter marriage"—living and working in different states (New York vs. western Massachusetts). Although he flies to Buffalo every other weekend, he is thinking of starting a future business venture in Buffalo so they can spend more time together.[4]

For Discussion

1. Given the strong community support for the zoo and her other duties, why might Donna place such importance on improving the motivational aspects at the zoo?

2. Use the principles of expectancy theory to explain why Donna's employees are motivated to suggest ways to raise funds. Explain how and why money can motivate in this situation.

3. Using the principles of behavior modification, explain how Donna is encouraging collegial behaviors and active involvement by her employees in the zoo's activities.

4. Explain how Donna is applying participative management. Why has it been so effective?

http://www.buffalozoo.org

Notes:

[1]News Library The Natural Published on May 26, 2002, Author: Jane Kwiatkowski—News Staff Reporter © The Buffalo News Inc.

[2]Christina Abt, "Donna Fernandes, Director, Buffalo Zoologial Society," *EVE Magazine*, http://www.simmons.edu/gsm/alumnae/EVE.pdf.

[3]News Library The Natural Published on May 26, 2002, Author: Jane Kwiatkowski—News Staff Reporter © The Buffalo News Inc.

[4]Christina Abt, "Donna Fernandes, Director, Buffalo Zoologial Society," *EVE Magazine*, http://www.simmons.edu/gsm/alumnae/EVE.pdf.

CASE

How's My [Teenager] Driving?

You have seen the bumper stickers on trucks and some cars, mostly commercial vehicles, that ask "How's my driving?" and then give a phone number to call. Here is the next step.

Carol Wood, a mother from Montana, has started a program called "Safe Teen Drivers." For $29.95 per year, her organization will issue a bumper sticker that says "How's my teen driving?" and it includes an ID number and a toll-free phone number to call. Parents can put the bumper sticker on the car that their teenager drives, and anyone can call the phone number to report both compliments and complaints. Calls to the toll-free number are passed on to the parent within 24 hours. They are not reported to law enforcement officials, and the driver's name is never given out. Parents can buy extra bumper stickers with the same ID number for only $1.50 each per year. That way, all of the family's cars can be covered.

SOURCE: Associated Press, "Keeping an Eye on Young Drivers," *Edwardsville (IL) Intelligencer: Weekender Flashback*, Saturday, June 15, 2002, 3.

For Discussion

1. Use reinforcement theory to explain how a teenage driver's behavior might be influenced by this bumper sticker. What are the reinforcers, and what are the schedules of reinforcement?

2. Explain how a teenage driver's behavior might be affected from the perspective of expectancy theory.

3. From the perspective of a parent, establish a plan to use goal setting as a motivator to help the teenager improve his or her driving.

PART ^{5}

CONTROL CHALLENGES IN THE 21ST CENTURY

CHAPTER 16

ORGANIZATIONAL CONTROL IN A
COMPLEX BUSINESS ENVIRONMENT

CHAPTER 17

PRODUCTIVITY AND QUALITY
IN OPERATIONS

CHAPTER 18

INFORMATION TECHNOLOGY
AND CONTROL

CHAP

ORGANIZATIONAL CONTROL IN A COMPLEX BUSINESS ENVIRONMENT

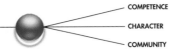

COMPETENCE

CHARACTER

COMMUNITY

TER 16

CHAPTER OVERVIEW

Control is the last of the four major management functions to be covered in this text. It is a critically important managerial function because it helps to ensure that all of our planning, organizing, and leading have gone as we intended. In today's rapidly changing and highly competitive global business environment, organizations can experience a rapid reversal of fortunes if they fail to control all aspects of their operations adequately. Individual and group behaviors and all organizational performance must be in line with the strategic focus of the organization. When economic, technological, political, societal, global, or competitive forces change, control systems must be capable of adjusting behaviors and performance to make them compatible with these shifts. The essence of the control process requires that business leaders determine performance standards, measure actual performance, compare actual performance with standards, and take corrective action when necessary.

In this chapter we begin by examining the steps in the control process. After this, we discuss several control system design considerations, criteria for effective control, and keys to selecting the proper amount of control. Because the control process can be implemented at almost any stage in an organization's operations, we examine the three basic organizational control focal points. In addition, we explore two opposing philosophies of control and raise some thought-provoking ethical issues in the control of employee behavior.

LEARNING OBJECTIVES

When you have finished studying this chapter, you should be able to:

1. Define and discuss the importance of organizational control.
2. Identify the sequence of steps to be undertaken in a thorough control system.
3. Identify the factors that are important considerations in the design of a control system.
4. Describe the various criteria of effective control.
5. Identify the factors that help determine the proper amount of control.
6. Define preventive control, concurrent control, and corrective control.
7. Describe the difference between the philosophies of bureaucratic control and organic control.
8. Describe some of the more important techniques and methods for establishing financial control.
9. Discuss some of the ethical issues related to the control of employee behavior.

Facing The Challenge

KARLEE Company's Quest to Break Away from the Pack

KARLEE Company, Inc., located in Garland, Texas, is a contract manufacturer of precision sheet metal and machined components. The company began as a one-person, garage-based machine shop in 1974 and incorporated in 1977. By 1979 KARLEE had a 3,000 square foot facility, 13 employees, and annual sales of $1 million. For many years the norm in this type of business has been single-customer machining or sheet metal fabrication shops. Almost all of KARLEE's eleven local competitors are small companies that typically perform a single process and derive 50 to 60 per-

cent of their business from one or two customers. Such a model was not the vision of Jo Ann Brumit, CEO and chair of this certified woman-owned company. She wanted to see KARLEE propelled into global markets, becoming a world-class, full-service manufacturing services company.

KARLEE made the strategic decision to break with tradition and diversify its customer base. A fundamental part of that strategy was to develop and maintain long-term partnerships with a few primary customers who are global leaders in their own markets. This would pose

some new challenges, for to maintain preferred supplier status with those customers, KARLEE would need to institute many changes. One of the changes that would be necessary related to KARLEE's control systems. It would be necessary for the company to develop control mechanisms that would enable the company to meet customer requirements for delivery, quality, and cost.

SOURCE: "KARLEE 2000 Application Summary," *Malcolm Baldrige National Quality Award,* **http://www.nist.gov**; "KARLEE Company, Inc.," *Baldrige Award Recipient Profile,* **http://www.nist.gov/public_affairs/baldrige00/Karlee.htm**.

INTRODUCTION

LEARNING OBJECTIVE 1

Define and discuss the importance of organizational control.

The KARLEE Company faced some significant challenges as it sought to break away from the mold that existed in its industry. If KARLEE was going to be successful in its quest to establish long-term partnerships with primary customers, the company would need to meet customer requirements for delivery, quality, and cost. This would require KARLEE to be very attentive to the process of control.

Control is the last of the four major management functions that we have been discussing. By its very nature, control is concerned with making sure that all of our planning, organizing, and leading have gone as we anticipated. Control is a critical function within any organization, for negative or even disastrous consequences can be associated with not meeting the established standards of performance. For example, poor inventory control can result in lost business because of a product shortage. Poor quality control may result in angry customers, lost business, and the necessity to provide customers with replacement products. Poor cost control can lead to negative profitability and perhaps even bankruptcy. The list of potential control problems is almost limitless. These problems all point to the fact that improving operational effectiveness and quality is virtually impossible without stringent control mechanisms.

Furthermore, in a world where quality often means the difference between success and failure, organizations simply cannot tolerate substandard product or service outputs. Organizations must develop and maintain control mechanisms capable of identifying and responding to deviations in organizational performance.

While the need for control is evident in all organizations, multinational organizations have particularly challenging and unique control needs. Maintaining internal control of units located in markets and regions around the globe can be far more problematic than maintaining control over a set of domestic operating units. Thus, control mechanisms must often be specifically designed to meet the challenges of global management.

In this chapter we examine several aspects of the control process. We begin by describing the basic steps in the control process and then build upon these basics.

A PROCESS OF CONTROL FOR DIVERSE AND MULTINATIONAL ORGANIZATIONS

Organizational control is defined as the systematic process through which leaders regulate organizational activities to make them consistent with the expectations established in plans and to help them achieve all predetermined standards of performance.[1] This definition implies that leaders must establish performance standards and develop mechanisms for gathering performance information in order to assess the degree to which standards are being met. Control, then, is a systematic set of four steps that must be undertaken: (1) setting standards of performance, (2) measuring actual performance, (3) comparing actual performance with standards, and (4) responding to deviations.[2] Figure 16.1 illustrates this sequence of steps. Let's now examine each of these steps in greater detail.

SETTING STANDARDS OF PERFORMANCE

The control process should begin with the establishment of standards of performance against which organizational activities can be compared. Standards of performance begin to evolve only after the organization has developed its overall

LEARNING OBJECTIVE 2

Identify the sequence of steps to be undertaken in a thorough control system.

Organizational control
A process through which leaders regulate organizational activities to make them consistent with the expectations established in plans and to help them achieve all predetermined standards of performance.

Figure 16.1 | Steps in the Control Process

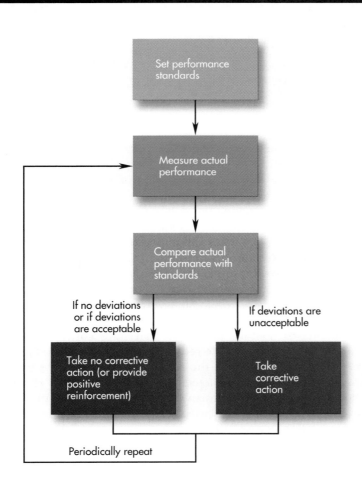

Leaders In Action

Culinary Concepts/Chef Creations

Culinary Concepts/Chef Creations, a company that outsources for upscale casual restaurant chains, is the latest venture in a long career for Manuel "Manny" Garcia. Garcia, one of Central Florida's best-known restaurateurs, comes from a family of restaurateurs. As a child in the 1950s, he washed dishes in his family's restaurant in the Cuban section of Tampa and learned about marketing from his grandfather, who took young Manny along to mom-and-pop hotels to drum up customers. From his father, he learned the importance of setting high-quality standards for ingredients and rigidly adhering to those standards. While his father and grandfather were self-educated, this third-generation restaurateur attended Cornell University, where he earned a bachelor's degree in hospitality management.

In 1969 Garcia ventured into the fast-food business when he, his father, and friends bought two Burger King outlets in Orlando. They used $10,000 of their own money and obtained a loan of slightly more than $300,000. Manny was able to turn those struggling restaurants

around and by 1996 managed to acquire more than 60 outlets from Orlando to Georgia. His Burger King units averaged sales more than 60 percent higher than other Burger King restaurants. Garcia gained a reputation for such high sales through his independent style and adherence to his self-imposed quality standards. His restaurants handed out candy to customers and served real butter. Burger King executives became tired of receiving complaints about the differences between various Burger Kings in different locations. They finally made it clear that Manny was not to continue his independent style and that he must adhere to the same quality standards as all other outlets. Unhappy about lowering his standards and realizing that Burger King was at the top of the fast food burger business, Garcia decided to sell. He received $55.6 million in the sale of most of his Burger King restaurants.

Burger King was not the only restaurant venture for Garcia during this time. He also owned two of Orlando's top downtown restaurants

and six California-style casual eateries in the area. In all of these ventures Garcia stayed true to his philosophy of setting high standards for ingredients and then strictly adhering to those standards. Garcia is currently involved in another new trend—outsourcing food for upscale, casual dining restaurants. As a supplier to several area restaurants, his food production commissary, Culinary Concepts/Chef Creations, has seen revenue grow to $8 million in four years. The success of this venture is due largely to Garcia's commitment to high standards with ingredients, although he shares the credit with his Pebbles chef, Tony Pace. These days Garcia is not yet ready to retire. Culinary Concepts runs two restaurants in Orlando and is trying to secure a new location for another. Garcia, who wants to share what he has learned with future generations is beginning to record his thoughts on paper.

SOURCE: http://orlando.bizjournals.com, January 2003; J. Jackson, "Manny Garcia Builds Future on His Past," Central Florida Business, July 29, 2002, 14–18.

strategic plan and leaders have defined goals for organizational departments. This was the case with the KARLEE Company. "Meeting The Challenge" on page 515 describes how teams of executives and front-line workers collaborated to set standards given the company's new strategic focus.

In some instances performance standards are generated from within an organization. Consider for the moment restaurateur Manny Garcia, described in "Leaders In Action" above. It was his self-imposed standards for quality that enabled his 67 Burger King Restaurants to routinely outperform the average Burger King Restaurant. Sometimes, however, the impetus for specific performance standards may originate with some outside source. For example, the Food and Drug Administration sets standards on allowable levels of certain chemicals or contaminants in food and beverage products, and food processing organizations must adhere to these standards. Failure to comply can have costly consequences, as evidenced by the mid-2002 nationwide recall of ConAgra processed ground beef.[3] External forces were also at work in the KARLEE Company. EPA guidelines for hazardous wastes and emissions impacted the amount and types of organic compounds and coolants used by the company in the manufacturing process. In a further effort to comply with EPA standards, KARLEE began to transition from wet to powder paint to eliminate volatile organic compounds (VOC) from its paint processes.

In other cases the desires and needs of the customer may dictate the standards set by both manufacturers and the providers of services. In fact, in today's environment, the emphasis on quality and customer satisfaction is increasing the influence that customers have on organizational standards of performance.

The organizational activities to be controlled may involve individual behavior, group behavior, production output, service delivery, and so forth. Whenever possible, the standards should be set in a manner that allows them to be compared with actual performance. Consider the professor who wishes to communicate to students the standards of classroom performance for his management class. Simply stating that "students should be prepared for class" is vague and provides little guidance to the students. However, if the syllabus says that "students should have read the assigned material prior to each class and should be prepared to discuss the issues when called upon in class," much more clarity is provided.

These brief examples hardly illustrate the wide diversity of performance standards that might be established. Standards of performance can be set for virtually any activity or behavior within an organization. For example, it is not unusual to find organizations that set standards for employee dress or grooming. For many years IBM required the men in its male-dominated supervisory positions to wear white dress shirts. The Walt Disney Company maintains strict standards for employee dress, grooming, jewelry, cosmetics, and even artificial hair coloring. As today's workforce becomes more diverse, setting and enforcing standards of individual behavior and performance can sometimes be more difficult. We have seen repeatedly throughout this book that the workplace is no longer composed of homogeneous individuals. Ethnic, racial, and gender differences often lead to different sets of individual values and expectations.

Furthermore, multinational organizations with operations in several countries often find it difficult, if not impossible, to maintain the same standards in all countries. It is difficult to establish organizationwide standards for subsidiaries that function within diverse sociocultural, technological, political-legal, and economic environments. For example, a multinational organization's facilities may have very different productivity targets in light of the different work attitudes in various countries. Similarly, plants in different nations may employ technologies with various levels of sophistication suitable to the education and skill levels of the local workforce; consequently, the plants may experience significant variation in productivity rates. Clearly, such circumstances can impede the development of organizationwide performance standards.

MEASURING ACTUAL PERFORMANCE

In some cases measuring actual performance can be relatively simple, but in others it can be quite complex. We have to decide such things as (1) what to measure (that is, a single item or multiple items such as sales, costs, profits, rejects, or orders), (2) when to measure, and (3) how frequently to measure. As we noted earlier, standards should be stated as clearly as possible so they can be compared with performance. Doing this is quite simple when the performance criteria are quantitative in nature and can be measured objectively. Sometimes, however, performance criteria are more qualitative in nature and do not easily lend themselves to absolute units of measure. Instead, they require a subjective assessment to determine whether or not the standard is being met. For example, even though a management student has read the assigned material and discussed the issues when called upon in class, the professor's assessment of the student's performance can be quite subjective when the issues do not have a single correct interpretation.

Suppose that the Chicago Cutlery Company states that its knives "must be honed to a high degree of sharpness, and the wooden handles must be polished to a bright luster." This is also a qualitative performance measure as determining whether a particular knife was sharp enough or bright enough would not be easy.

But regardless of whether the stated performance measure is quantitative or qualitative in nature, actual performance must be recorded for subsequent comparison with the performance standard.

COMPARING ACTUAL PERFORMANCE WITH STANDARDS

The first two steps of the control process provide managers with the information that allows them to make comparisons between actual performance and standards. The KARLEE Company steering committee planned carefully for this function. To ensure standardization throughout the company, the committee maintains a matrix that includes information on goals and objectives, data measures and targets, and a data review schedule. When viewing any control situation, if the actual performance is identical to the standard, then no deviation has occurred. Rarely, however, is there absolutely no deviation between actual and planned performance. Fortunately, in most real-world situations, actual performance does not always have to be identical to the standard.

Typically, the performance standard has a stated acceptable deviation. For example, suppose leaders in the Motorola Corporation set an average productivity standard of 50 cellular telephones per worker per hour, with an acceptable deviation of plus or minus 5 telephones per worker per hour. The acceptable deviations would define the control limits for this process. If productivity is between 45 and 55 cellular telephones per worker per hour, then the process is said to be "in control," meaning that no corrective action is necessary. Measurements outside this range indicate an "out-of-control" situation that requires corrective action.

Continuing with the Motorola example, an actual productivity of 47 telephones per worker per hour suggests that no corrective action is required. Suppose, on the other hand, that productivity is 58 telephones per worker per hour. Now the deviation from the standard is outside of the "in control" range, and the subsequent steps in the control process should attempt to correct it. One might initially think that this deviation (with its extra output) would be considered desirable and that no attempts would be made to correct it. But this deviation could lead to problems if the company has no market for the excess output or no room to store it. It is also possible that the extra production is using resources that were to be used elsewhere. This Motorola example provides an illustration in which unacceptable deviations can occur on either side of the standard. This need not always be the case. In "At The Forefront" we see how the Federal Aviation Administration (FAA) instituted control efforts to reduce an aircraft phenomenon known as "controlled flight into terrain." Here we see that the FAA determined that aircraft must maintain a minimum clearance standard of 500 feet above an obstacle. In this case actual clearances of more than 500 feet would be acceptable. However, any deviation in the other direction has the potential to be catastrophic and should immediately sound an alarm.

For a more personal example, suppose that you have established a performance standard of at least 85 for your scores on the midterm and final exams to help you achieve your goal of receiving a grade of B in your management course. If your midterm exam score is only 75, you would have an undesirable deviation. However, any score above 85 would prove to have an acceptable deviation from your established standard.

RESPONDING TO DEVIATIONS

After comparing actual performance with standards, we can choose to either (1) take no corrective action or (2) take corrective action. If the deviation was acceptable or if there was no deviation, then the response should be to take no cor-

At The Forefront

Federal Aviation Administration Updates Its Control Systems

One of the most troubling problems associated with flying is a phenomenon referred to by aviation experts as "controlled flight into terrain." It occurs when a fully functional plane with a capable crew simply flies into the ground. This usually happens during the night or in bad weather, and when it does happen, the crew is typically unaware of the location or impending danger. To combat this problem the Federal Aviation Administration (FAA) began to install Minimum Safe-Altitude Warning systems around airports as early as 1977. These systems are designed by dividing a large area around an airport into a grid of thousands of two-square-mile zones, extending out in a radius of 50 or more miles from the airport. The highest obstacle in each zone (land or structure) is entered into a database. When a plane descends to within 500 feet of the highest obstacle in any zone, the system is supposed to sound a warning in the control tower and the pilot is to be alerted. These systems can also project the descent path of an aircraft, and they are designed to issue an alarm even when a plane is merely projected to fly below a safe altitude.

Minimum Safe-Altitude Warning systems are built into 193 air traffic control facilities around the country. They monitor the airspace around almost every U.S. airport that has scheduled commercial traffic. But in the mid to late 1990s, several fatal controlled flights into terrain occurred, and in each case the critical radar-based warning system failed to let the pilots know their planes were flying too low. After Korean Airlines Flight 801 crashed into a hillside on the island of Guam in 1997, the FAA assembled a team of top computer programmers and technicians to investigate the warning systems around the nation. Those investigations revealed that the systems around the nation had problems, some minor and some potentially disastrous. The systems had failed to operate properly in many air traffic control centers across the country, including some controlling the approach paths to the nation's busiest airports. Some systems were programmed with incorrect altitudes for hills and obstructions. Some were programmed with incorrect compass headings. Such problems often caused alarms to be sounded when planes were not in danger, which in turn often prompted either improper reprogramming of the systems or simply disabling or muffling nuisance alarms. An extreme example of this contributed to the Guam crash. While the grid of two-square-mile zones was to extend out a radius of 55 miles from the airport, reprogramming effectively shut down the warning system within 54 miles of the airport. All that existed was a one-mile-wide ring of protection between 54 and 55 miles from the airport. That was the only place the low altitude alert functioned, and it was nothing more than a narrow band over open ocean, far from the hills that presented a danger to planes.

The FAA team's investigations ultimately found significant problems with the way the warning systems were programmed at some of the nation's largest airports. In addition, the team found that repairs were needed at nearly half of the 130 smaller airports that had the system. Because of their diligent efforts, and with the help of computer tools that became available in the late 1990s, the FAA has strengthened the supervision over the Minimum Safe-Altitude Warning systems, eliminated the problems, improved the air traffic control system, and made this nation's airspace a safer place for its 600 million annual airline passengers.

SOURCE: A. Levin, "Without Warning," *USA Today*, October 18, 1999, A1ff.

rective action, since the performance or behavior is acceptable in light of the standards. If, however, the deviation was unacceptable, then the response should be to take corrective action. Corrective action usually requires making a change in some behavior, activity, or aspect of the organization to bring performance into line with the standards. Even when no corrective action is necessary, it is often useful to provide positive feedback (and in some cases even rewards) to the responsible individuals so that they are motivated to continue performing to the standards. The KARLEE Company delegated this function to frontline workers who were given ownership of work tasks and were empowered to make measurements, compare performance with standards, and take corrective action when necessary.

Return to the earlier example in which you set a standard of 85 for your midterm and final exam scores. If your midterm exam score is only 75, the undesirable deviation requires a response on your part. You might attempt to compensate by preparing more thoroughly for the final exam. (Or you might decide to drop the course and try again another semester!) If your score on the midterm exam is 90, you do not need to take corrective action in preparing for the final exam (unless, of course, you decide to raise your goal to a course grade of A and reestablish your performance standard for the final exam to achieve this goal).

When exercising control in business organizations, a variety of types of changes are possible, depending upon the particular situation. Changes in materials, equipment, process, or staffing might be made. In some cases the corrective action might even involve changing the original performance standards. For example, an organization whose standards are rarely met might determine that the standards were set unrealistically high, making them too difficult to achieve consistently. Regardless of whether or not corrective action is taken, the control process does not end here. Even if performance standards are currently being achieved, there is no guarantee that this will be true in the future. Consequently, the measurement and comparison steps must be repeated periodically.

Developing and implementing creative and constructive responses to undesirable deviations can be exceptionally difficult for multinational organizations. Because the organization's leaders might have less understanding of each individual unit when units are scattered around the globe, developing solutions requires a substantial amount of information gathering. Furthermore, the development of solutions that are acceptable to both subsidiary and headquarters leaders may require active participation by key personnel at each level. Consequently, it may take longer to determine and implement the necessary corrective action, and that action may come at the expense of significant managerial time and energy.

Up to this point, we have seen that the basic process of control involves a few very fundamental steps: (1) establishing standards of performance, (2) measuring actual performance, (3) comparing actual performance with standards, and (4) responding to deviations when necessary. However, knowing the four steps in the control process is not enough to ensure that an effective control system will be developed. As we will see in the next sections, several other issues must be considered.

DESIGNING QUALITY AND EFFECTIVENESS INTO THE CONTROL SYSTEM

LEARNING OBJECTIVE 3

Identify the factors that are important considerations in the design of a control system.

Designing an effective control system can be far more complex than simply performing the four steps in the control process. Several other important factors must be considered as well. Once the control system has been designed and implemented, several criteria are available to help determine how effective it will be. Additionally, it is necessary to select the amount of control to be used and the point in the organization where the control effort will be focused. These issues must be considered as each step in the control process unfolds, as Figure 16.2 illustrates. We begin our treatment of control system design issues by examining several important design factors.

DESIGN FACTORS AFFECTING CONTROL SYSTEM QUALITY

When designing a control system, four important factors must be considered: (1) the amount of variety in the control system, (2) the ability to anticipate problems, (3) the sensitivity of the measuring device, and (4) the composition of the feedback reports. Let's examine each of these factors more thoroughly.

AMOUNT OF VARIETY IN THE CONTROL SYSTEM   One important design consideration is the amount of variety in the control system. Variety refers to the number of activities, processes, or items that are measured and controlled. Systems become more complex as the number of system elements and number of possible interactions among them increase. More uncertainty exists in complex systems because more things can go wrong with them. In other words, more variety leads

Figure 16.2 | Control System Design Issues

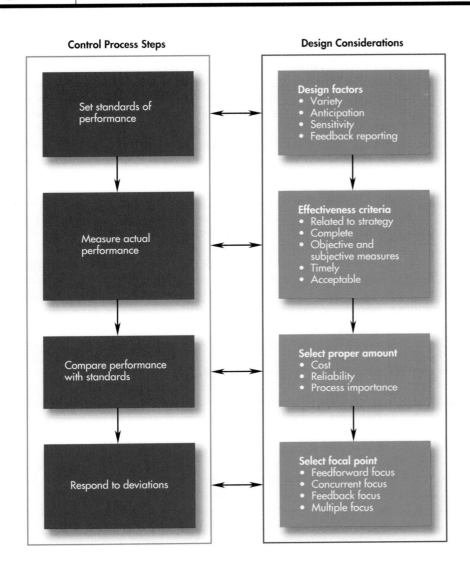

to less predictability. To maintain adequate control in any system, the control system must contain as much variety as the system being controlled. This is known as the **law of requisite variety**.[4] Although a simple control system might seem attractive, the law of requisite variety suggests that simple control systems may not have sufficient variety to cope with the complex systems they are trying to control.[5]

Consider the plight of General Motors or any other automobile manufacturer. Because so many materials and parts go into the complex finished product and those components have so many sources, the system's elements and their interactions contain considerable variety. Consequently, extensive control systems are needed at all stages in the manufacturing process to ensure that the finished automobiles meet the performance standards.

Requisite variety can be achieved by either (1) increasing the amount of variety in the control system or (2) reducing the amount of variety in the system being controlled. Increased variety in the control system can be achieved by increasing the number of performance standards and the number of items controlled. In the case of General Motors, top-level leaders will set a performance

Law of requisite variety
Control systems must have enough variety to cope with the variety in the systems they are trying to control.

In manufacturing, extensive controls are needed at all stages to ensure that the finished product meets industry standards.

standard for finished product quality. To ensure that this standard is achieved, lower-level managers and supervisors will employ additional performance standards to provide raw material input control, production scrap control, labor control, quality control, and similar other control systems. If the lower-level managers and supervisors are successful in achieving these standards, it is likely that the top-level standard for product quality will also be achieved.

Let's look back for a moment at the FAA Minimum Safe-Altitude Warning systems described in "At The Forefront" on page 495 to see how requisite variety might be achieved. Once a control radius is established around an airport, that area is divided into zones, and the highest obstacle in each zone must be identified. If the airport is located in an area with widely varying terrain elevations and many tall structures, more "zonal obstacle elevation" data would be necessary than for an airport located in level terrain with few tall structures.

ABILITY TO ANTICIPATE PROBLEMS   A second consideration in designing a control system is its ability to anticipate problems. When the control process is instituted, several distinct events occur when performance fails to meet the established standards. First, the undesirable deviation from standards is observed. Then, the situation is reported to the person or persons responsible for taking corrective action. Next, corrective action is instituted, and eventually, performance should return to an acceptable value. Inevitably, time lags occur between observation, reporting, instituting, and return. During these time lags, the performance may continue to be unacceptable. Figure 16.3 illustrates this sequence of events.

The damage caused by unacceptable performance during these time lags can be reduced by building the ability to anticipate problems into the control system. If unacceptable deviation can be anticipated before it occurs, corrective action can be instituted in a more timely fashion, and the negative consequences of the deviation can be reduced. This is precisely the situation with the FAA Minimum Safe-Altitude Warning systems. Not only are they designed to sound an alarm when the 500 foot clearance standard is not being observed, but they also can project a plane's descent path and alert the pilot and control tower when it appears that the plane is on course to violate the 500 foot rule.

To further illustrate the ability to anticipate problems, consider how Weyerhaeuser Company manages its timber reserves. It is a fact of nature that forest fires sometimes occur. If standard performance is defined as a fire-free forest, then a forest fire represents an undesirable deviation that needs corrective action. Weyerhaeuser can anticipate that fires are more likely to occur during prolonged dry

Figure 16.3 | Time Lags in Control

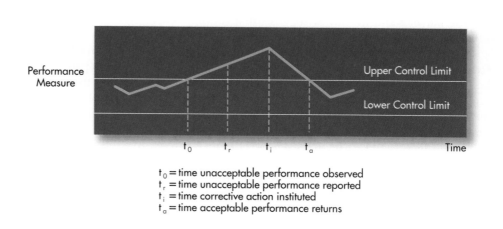

t_0 = time unacceptable performance observed
t_r = time unacceptable performance reported
t_i = time corrective action instituted
t_a = time acceptable performance returns

periods. By staffing watch towers, using spotter aircraft and reconnaissance satellites, and keeping fire-fighting equipment in a state of readiness during these periods, the company increases its anticipatory capability, enabling it to respond more quickly to the undesirable situation.

SENSITIVITY OF THE MEASURING DEVICE   A third consideration in control system design is the sensitivity of the measuring device. Sensitivity refers to the precision with which the measurement can be made. Care must be taken to use the appropriate measuring device for the system under consideration. For example, TEAC America Inc., which manufactures computer components and other electronic equipment, might need a high-precision micrometer to measure the diameter of the spindles used in its computer disk drive. However, it would be highly unnecessary for the Georgia-Pacific lumber company to use such a measuring device to check the thickness of two-by-four wall studs. A simple tape measure will suffice in this situation, for tolerances need to be expressed only in fractions of inches, not microns. It is critical that consistent units of measurement be used if proper control is to be attained in any process. Failure to do this resulted in the destruction of NASA's $125 million Mars Climate Orbiter. While flight computers on the ground performed calculations based on pounds of thrust per second, the spacecraft's computer used metric system units called newtons. A check to make sure the units were compatible was never done, and the orbiter burned up in the Mars atmosphere.[6]

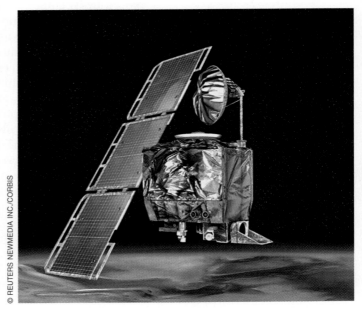

© REUTERS NEWMEDIA INC./CORBIS

Failure to use consistent units of measurement for control caused the Mars Climate Orbiter to burn up in the Mars atmosphere.

COMPOSITION OF FEEDBACK REPORTS   A final consideration in control system design involves the composition of feedback reports. As the control process measures performance and compares it with standards, much information and data are generated. Reports to leaders and managers will be based upon these data. But what data should be included in the reports? A simple answer, and one that users of such reports will view favorably, is "Don't tell me what is right with the system; tell me what is wrong." **Variance reporting** fulfills this desire by highlighting only those items that fail to meet the established standards. Focusing on the elements that are not meeting the standards provides the capability for **management by exception**. In this approach, management targets the trouble areas. If the system is operating acceptably, no information needs to come to the manager's attention. This is the model used by the FAA in its Minimum Safe-Altitude Warning systems. Alarms in the cockpit and control tower and a low-altitude warning flashing next to the plane's blip on the air traffic controller's radar screen all represent exception feedback reports.

Now that we have examined the factors that are important in the design of a control system, let's look at several criteria that measure the system's effectiveness.

Variance reporting
Highlighting only those things that fail to meet the established standards.

Management by exception
Focusing on the elements that are not meeting the standards.

CRITERIA FOR EFFECTIVE CONTROL

To be effective in detecting and correcting unacceptable performance, a control system must satisfy several criteria. The system must (1) be related to organizational strategy, (2) utilize all steps in the control process, (3) be composed of objective and subjective measures, (4) be timely in feedback reporting, and (5) be acceptable to a diverse workforce.[7] The next sections examine these criteria more closely.

LEARNING OBJECTIVE 4
Describe the various criteria of effective control.

IS RELATED TO ORGANIZATIONAL STRATEGY   In designing a control system, one must make sure that it measures what is important now and what will be important in the future, not what was important in the past. As an organization's strategic focus shifts over time, the measures and standards of performance that are important to the organization must also shift. When the control system is linked to organizational strategy, it recognizes strategic shifts and is flexible enough to measure what is important as indicated by the firm's strategy. This was an issue as the KARLEE Company shifted its strategic focus. The new control systems employed by its empowered workers were linked to meeting customer requirements for delivery, quality, and cost.

This issue also has implications for the standards of behavior and performance that are set for individuals and groups within the organization. As the workforce becomes more racially, ethnically, and gender diverse, organizations will often have to adjust their expectations of workers and performance standards in response to the differing attitudes, abilities, and cultural biases of their employees.

Multinational corporations often find it useful to maintain a centralized, integrated system of controls consistent with the strategic orientation of the organization. If the network of organizational units is to benefit from the organization's global orientation, there must be sufficient coordination and control of the units to ensure that such benefits are achieved. General Motors maintains a number of units that are interdependent through each of the sequential steps in the manufacturing process (for example, GM's Brazilian subsidiary supplies its U.S. subsidiary with engines); therefore, GM must have control systems that ensure that production processes are not disrupted.[8]

UTILIZES ALL STEPS IN THE CONTROL PROCESS   To be effective, a control system must employ all of the steps in the control process. Standards of performance must be set, measurements of actual performance taken, comparisons of standards with actual performance made, and when necessary, corrective action taken. Omitting any of these steps will detract from the system's effectiveness.

To return to our more personal example of your quest for a grade of B in your management course, suppose you never bothered to check your posted grade on the midterm exam. In that case, your control system would be incomplete. Without knowing your midterm exam score, you could not compare your actual performance with your standard. Consequently, you would not know whether there was an undesirable deviation and whether you should study harder for the final exam.

IS COMPOSED OF OBJECTIVE AND SUBJECTIVE MEASURES   It is unlikely that a control system will lend itself to the use of a single performance measure. More often than not, a number of performance measures are needed. As we discussed earlier, some of these performance measures may be objective and easily quantified, while others may be qualitative and more subjective. For example, management may have set specific targets for productivity. This performance goal has a precise formula for measurement, as we will see in the next chapter. Suppose that in that same situation, management has also expressed a desire to achieve high levels of worker satisfaction. Such a qualitative criterion is more difficult, if not impossible, to measure accurately. Situations like this often require leaders to blend quantitative (objective) and qualitative (subjective) performance measures in their control systems.

INCORPORATES TIMELINESS IN FEEDBACK REPORTING   Timeliness is the degree to which the control system provides information when it is needed. The key issue here is not how fast the feedback information is provided, but whether it is provided quickly enough to permit a response to an unacceptable deviation. For example, consider the air traffic controller at Chicago's O'Hare Airport who observes on the radar screen that an aircraft is descending too close to an obstacle. Feedback information on the position of the aircraft is needed very quickly if a tragedy is to be averted. Here timeliness would be measured in seconds. Now consider the manager of a Christmas tree farm who monitors the annual growth rate of the trees. If the amount of growth falls below standards in a particular year, an application of fertilizer might be called for as a corrective action. In this case, timeliness might be measured in weeks or even months.

Return again to the personal example of your grade. Suppose that the midterm exam was administered in the eighth week of the semester and the results were not posted until the tenth week. This feedback would not be timely if the deadline for dropping the course was in the ninth week of the semester.

IS ACCEPTABLE TO A DIVERSE WORK FORCE To be effective, organizational controls must be accepted by employees. The control system should motivate workers to recognize standards and act to achieve them. If the control system discourages employees, they are likely to ignore the standards, and undesirable deviations are likely to follow. The more committed employees are to the control system, the more successful the system will be.[9] In the increasingly diverse workplaces of today's organizations, one of the challenges to leaders is to develop control systems and establish standards that are acceptable and understandable to all workers. This presented a challenge to the KARLEE Company, whose workforce was 46.7 percent Hispanic, 34.3 percent Caucasian, 11.8 percent African American, and 7.2 percent Asian. More than 20 percent of this workforce spoke minimal English. To meet this challenge and promote good communication, KARLEE produced critical internal publications in English, Spanish, and Vietnamese. In addition, interpreters were provided at team meetings when needed.

To further illustrate acceptability, consider your situation as a student in a management course. Suppose that your professor has no problem assigning course grades of B or lower, but says that a grade of A can be achieved only by students who read a new chapter and five related journal articles every day and submit a 20-page, typewritten synopsis of these readings each day. Would you be discouraged from attempting to earn a grade of A? Most, if not all, students probably would be discouraged and would resign themselves to a grade of no higher than a B for the course.

Up to this point, we have seen several factors that are essential to the design of an effective control system. To assist managers in developing effective control systems, "Now Apply It" on page 502 presents a checklist that can be used to make sure that all important factors and characteristics have been included in the design of any control system.

Now that the control system has been established, it is necessary to determine how much control should be used. The amount of control needed depends upon several factors, as we will see in the next section.

SELECTING THE PROPER AMOUNT OF CONTROL

In almost any task, reasonable limits exist on the amount of energy that should be expended. This is also true in the area of control. In theory, the amount of control that a manager exercises over some aspect of the organization can vary from a minimum of zero control to a maximum of infinite control. It is possible for management to go too far and overcontrol some aspect of the organization, or not go far enough and thereby undercontrol. The result in either case is a suboptimal control system and suboptimal performance, which will decrease the overall effectiveness and efficiency of the organization.

Choosing the proper amount of control is critical to organizations that strive for quality in everything they do. Deciding how much control is enough is not a simple matter, however. Several factors can be used to help determine the proper

LEARNING OBJECTIVE 5

Identify the factors that help determine the proper amount of control.

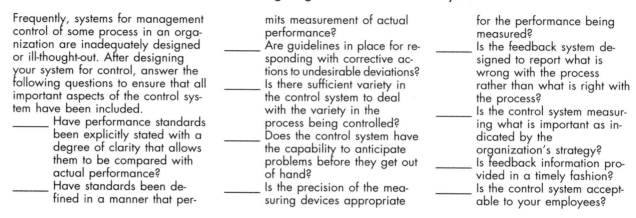

Checklist for Designing Effective Control Systems

Frequently, systems for management control of some process in an organization are inadequately designed or ill-thought-out. After designing your system for control, answer the following questions to ensure that all important aspects of the control system have been included.

_____ Have performance standards been explicitly stated with a degree of clarity that allows them to be compared with actual performance?

_____ Have standards been defined in a manner that permits measurement of actual performance?

_____ Are guidelines in place for responding with corrective actions to undesirable deviations?

_____ Is there sufficient variety in the control system to deal with the variety in the process being controlled?

_____ Does the control system have the capability to anticipate problems before they get out of hand?

_____ Is the precision of the measuring devices appropriate for the performance being measured?

_____ Is the feedback system designed to report what is wrong with the process rather than what is right with the process?

_____ Is the control system measuring what is important as indicated by the organization's strategy?

_____ Is feedback information provided in a timely fashion?

_____ Is the control system acceptable to your employees?

---

amount of control. These factors, which vary in their degree of objectivity, include the costs and benefits of a control system, the reliability of the item or process being controlled, and the importance of the thing or process being controlled.[10]

COSTS IN CONTROL SYSTEMS   Two basic categories of costs need to be considered in control systems: (1) the costs associated with the information needed to perform the control process, and (2) the costs associated with undesirable deviations from standards. These costs behave differently as the amount of control effort varies.[11]

Control systems rely on information. As the amount of control effort increases, information feedback is needed in greater amounts and with greater frequency. This information does not come without a cost. Time, effort, resources, and money must be expended to gather and assimilate information. Consequently, as the level of control effort increases, the information costs of the control system also increase.

As the level of control effort increases, undesirable deviations from performance standards will decrease. As a consequence, the costs associated with undesirable performance will also decrease. Reductions in the costs due to undesirable performance represent the benefits of control systems. Examples of these costs include costs to correct the problem that is causing the undesirable deviations; material scrap costs and rework costs when defective parts are detected in the manufacturing process; product warranty, repair, and replacement costs when defective output reaches the consumer; and worker compensation costs when workers are injured due to behaviors or actions that do not conform to standards. When these relationships are displayed in a graphical format, as in Figure 16.4, they reveal that, from an economic standpoint, there is an ideal amount of control to be exercised. This optimal amount of control corresponds to the minimum total cost.

To help clarify the relationships in Figure 16.4, let's again consider the situation that Motorola faces in manufacturing a cellular telephone. Management can increase the level of control by increasing the number of parts, components, and finished products that are inspected and tested. Additionally, more sophisticated testing and measuring devices might be obtained. These actions will increase the costs of obtaining the information needed in the control process as well as reduce the likelihood that defective units will be produced. When fewer defective units are produced, scrap, rework, product repair, product warranty, and product replace-

Figure 16.4 | Cost Trade-Offs in a Control System

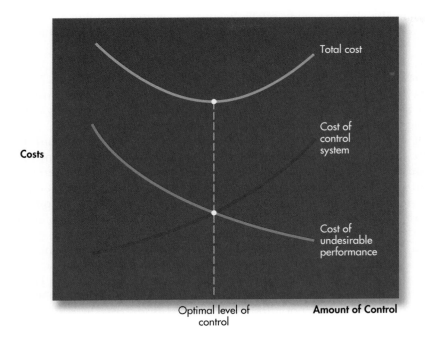

ment costs all decline. When the opposing costs are combined, the total cost is U-shaped, and its lowest point indicates the optimal level of control.

From a practical standpoint, this optimal value is not always easy to identify. When performance improvements are many and varied, quantifying the precise costs and benefits of the control system may be difficult. This is particularly true in situations like the FAA's Minimum Safe-Altitude Warning systems or in the monitoring of parts being manufactured for space shuttles. Undesirable deviations can result in catastrophic failures and corresponding loss of human life in both of these situations. In such cases, the value of the control system might be assessed by simply examining the number of areas of improvement and the level of improvement in each area.

RELIABILITY OF THE SYSTEM Reliability refers to the probability that the object or process being controlled will consistently behave in an acceptable manner. The basic premise is that the more reliable the process, the less control is needed. Here is a situation that is familiar to most of us. It seems that physicians are notorious for having poor handwriting, resulting in prescriptions that are difficult to decipher. This often leads to extra work on the part of the pharmacist (checkup calls to physicians) and sometimes incorrect medications being dispensed. These problems can be eliminated thanks to the Allscript Corporation, which developed a wireless, handheld electronic prescription pad. When a physician enters a prescription, the system can check for interactions with any other drugs the patient may be taking and also check for patient drug allergies. With a few clicks the prescription can be e-mailed to the patient's drug store. This new technology improves the process, reduces the controls necessary, and virtually eliminates the problems associated with unintelligibly written prescriptions.[12]

Process reliability is often difficult to assess because it is affected by the operating characteristics of the physical equipment and by the experience and attitudes of the workers. Equipment reliability can often be measured objectively; human operators present a bit more uncertainty. Although reliability can be expected to increase with worker experience, there is no way to accurately predict when a worker will have a "bad day." And of course, at times extraneous conditions (such as bad weather in the case of airline pilots) might impact the reliability of the workers. Business leaders must often make subjective judgments on the human aspect of reliability to aid in determining the proper amount of control.

IMPORTANCE OF THE PROCESS BEING CONTROLLED   Common sense suggests that the more important the object or process being controlled, the greater the amount of control that should be exercised. The difficulty here lies in selecting a measure for importance. Frequently, cost or value is used as a substitute for importance. The more valuable the item, the more important it is and, therefore, the more control it deserves. In the area of inventory control, a relatively small percentage of a company's inventory items (perhaps 20 percent) often account for a large percentage of the total inventory value (perhaps 80 percent). Although the percentages may vary, this "20/80 rule," as it has become known, would suggest that an "important few" items deserve close inventory control. The others (the "trivial many") require considerably less control.[13]

You should not automatically assume that importance can always be measured by cost or value. At first glance it might seem that extensive control systems are not needed to monitor quality in the manufacture of an inexpensive bolt. However, if that bolt is used to secure a window washer to the outside of a high-rise building, it has assumed a high level of importance despite its low cost. In a similar vein, recall the disaster that struck the space shuttle *Challenger*. Although the O-rings in the shuttle booster rockets were relatively inexpensive items, we are all painfully aware of the importance of the role they played in this highly complex spacecraft.

Now that the question of how much control is needed has been addressed, let's examine where in the transformation process control should be used. The place where control is applied is called the focal point for control.

SELECTING THE FOCAL POINT FOR CONTROL

LEARNING OBJECTIVE 6

Define preventive control, concurrent control, and corrective control.

Before managers design and implement a control system, they must decide where the control effort will be focused. Virtually all organizations maintain a structure in which inputs are subjected to a transformation process that converts them into usable and marketable outputs. Despite this similarity, inputs, transformations, and outputs can vary considerably among organizations.

Although Chapter 17 provides a much more extensive examination of the operations aspects of the input transformation process, we do need to note here that inputs can include such items as raw materials, supplies, people, capital, land, buildings, equipment, utilities, and information. Outputs of the transformation process will be either physical products or services. The list of transformation processes is lengthy and varied. Table 16.1 provides descriptions and examples of these processes.

Control can focus on the inputs, the transformation process, or the outputs of the operating system. The three different focal points yield three different types of control: (1) preventive control, (2) concurrent control, and (3) corrective control.[14] These control focal points are illustrated in Figure 16.5. The next sections examine them in greater detail.

Preventive (feedforward) control
Focuses on detecting undesirable material, financial, or human resources that serve as inputs to the transformation process.

PREVENTIVE CONTROL   When control focuses on the material, financial, or human resources that serve as inputs to the transformation process, it is referred to as **preventive (feedforward) control**. This type of control is sometimes called feedforward control because it is designed to ensure that the quality of inputs is high enough to prevent problems in the transformation process. For example, think

Table 16.1 | Descriptions and Examples of Operations Transformation Processes

TRANSFORMATION	DESCRIPTION	EXAMPLES
Physical or chemical	Cutting, bending, joining, or chemically altering raw materials to make a product	Manufacturing company, chemical processor, oil refinery
Locational	Provide transportation function	Airlines, trucking companies, package delivery service, U.S. Postal Service
Storage	Hold and then release a commodity or item	Warehouses and banks
Exchange	Transfer possession and ownership of a commodity or item	Wholesale and retail organizations
Physiological	Improve the physical or mental well-being of sick and injured people	Hospitals, healthcare clinics
Informational	Transmit information to customers	Radio and television news departments, computer information services
Entertainment	Impart an attitudinal change to their customers	Motion picture industry, programming departments of television networks
Educational	Impart knowledge to customers	Schools, universities

about the preventive controls that might take place prior to the manufacture of blue jeans. A primary input for manufacturers such as Levi Strauss is denim fabric. Long bolts of this material will have patterns overlaid and cut prior to the sewing operations. Before the patterns are laid out on the fabric, a system of preventive control could be used to inspect the denim fabric for knots, runs, tears, color variations, and other imperfections. If the fabric contains many imperfections, there could well be excessive levels of imperfections in the finished blue jeans. In such a case, the corrective action suggested by the preventive control

Figure 16.5 | Control Focal Points

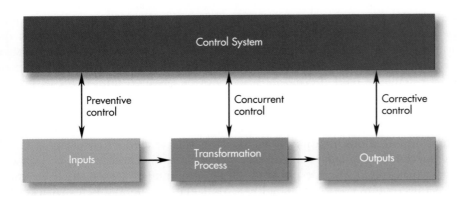

system might be to reject the entire bolt of fabric rather than trying to cut around the imperfections.

CONCURRENT CONTROL   When control focuses on the transformation phase, it is referred to as **concurrent control**. This form of control is designed to monitor ongoing activities to ensure that the transformation process is functioning properly and achieving the desired results. To illustrate, consider again the manufacture of blue jeans by Levi Strauss. Sewing-machine operators must continuously monitor their process to ensure that seams are being sewn straight and threads are interlocking appropriately. If these standards are not being met, corrective actions such as changing needles, adjusting thread tension, lubricating machines, and so forth may need to be taken.

Concurrent control
Focuses on the transformation process to ensure that it is functioning properly.

CORRECTIVE CONTROL   When control focuses on the output phase of Figure 16.5, it is referred to as **corrective (feedback) control**. This type of control is sometimes referred to as feedback control because it is intended to discover undesirable output and implement corrective action. We can illustrate this focal point by again considering the manufacture of blue jeans. After the jeans have been assembled, a final inspection is normally performed. Individuals responsible for assessing the quality of the jeans compare the finished product with established standards of performance. If an undesirable amount of deviation from the standards is identified, then corrective action must be prescribed. For example, if the design stitching on the back pockets is misaligned, corrective action would be needed at the pocket-stitching operation to correct this problem.

Corrective (feedback) control
Focuses on discovering undesirable output and implementing corrective action.

MULTIPLE FOCAL POINTS   Very few organizations rely on a single point of focus for their control process. Instead, most organizations use several control systems focused on various phases of the transformation process.[15] This way, leaders are better able to control resource inputs, ongoing transformation activities, and final outputs simultaneously. This approach gives the manager the capability to determine (1) whether current output is in accordance with standards, and (2) whether any impending problems are looming on the horizon. The FAA's Minimum Safe-Altitude Warning systems have both of these capabilities. Current positions are monitored to ensure proper obstacle clearance, and flight path projections also provide an alert to any impending problems.

The McDonald's restaurant chain provides a familiar example of a company that uses control mechanisms that are focused on inputs, transformation processes, and outputs. In its attempts to maintain consistency in its french fried potatoes, McDonald's utilizes preventive control with a stringent set of standards for purchased raw potatoes. It utilizes concurrent control by monitoring the oil temperature and frying time used in the cooking process and the amount of salt used in seasoning the french fries. Finally, it utilizes corrective control when the output (cooked french fries) is examined. If examination reveals improper color or excess oiliness, the cooking oil, the temperature of the cooking oil, the cooking time, or perhaps some combination of all three may need to be changed to attain the desired results. Multiple focal points are important here, for if only the finished product were monitored, potential problems caused by a bad batch of raw potatoes or a defective fryer thermostat would not be revealed until defective french fries were produced.

In addition to focusing on inputs, transformations, or outputs, control systems are also implemented in all functional specialty areas of the organization. Today's business organizations incorporate many highly interrelated and overlapping functional specialties. Management, marketing, finance, and accounting activities all play a critical role in the success of the organization, and as such, each has many aspects that require control mechanisms. Management theorist Peter Drucker has

McDonald's uses preventive control for purchasing raw potatoes and concurrent control to monitor oil temperature, frying time, and amount of salt to season the fries.

© MARK PETERSON/CORBIS SABA

identified eight areas in which performance objectives should be set and results measured. These areas—marketing, financial resources, productivity, physical resources, human organization, profit requirements, social responsibility, and innovation—extend through all of the interrelated functional specialties of the business.[16]

CONTROL PHILOSOPHIES FOR LEADERS

Instituting a control system requires that leaders do more than simply select the appropriate focal points. It is also necessary to make a choice between two philosophical control styles: bureaucratic control and organic control (often referred to as clan control).

BUREAUCRATIC CONTROL

Bureaucratic control involves the use of rules, procedures, policies, hierarchy of authority, written documents, reward systems, and other formal mechanisms to influence behavior, assess performance, and correct unacceptable deviations from standards.[17] This type of control is typical of the bureaucratic style of management introduced in Chapter 2. In this method of control, standard operating procedures and policies prescribe acceptable employee behavior and standards for employee performance. A rigid hierarchy of authority extends from the top down through the organization. Formal authority for the control process lies at the supervisor level, and lower-level employees are not expected to participate in the control process. Bureaucratic control relies on highly formalized mechanisms for selecting and training workers, and it emphasizes the use of monetary rewards for controlling employee performance. Formal quantitative tools such as budgets or financial reports and ratios are frequently used to monitor and evaluate performance in bureaucratic control systems.

As we discussed in Chapter 2, the bureaucratic style often has a negative connotation due to its very formal structure and perceived lack of flexibility. However, this method of control should not be viewed as a mechanism to restrain, force, coerce, or manipulate workers. Instead, it should be viewed as an effective, although rigid, mechanism to ensure that performance standards are met.

ORGANIC CONTROL

Organic control, often called **clan control**, is quite different from bureaucratic control. It relies upon social values, traditions, shared beliefs, flexible authority, looser job descriptions, and trust to assess performance and correct unacceptable deviations. The philosophy behind organic control is that employees are to be trusted and that they are willing to perform correctly without extensive rules and supervision. With its empowered workers and team concept, the KARLEE Company relies heavily on this control philosophy. This type of control is particularly appropriate when there is a strong organizational culture and the values are shared by all employees. When cohesive peer groups exist, less top-down bureaucratic control is necessary because employees are likely to pressure coworkers into adhering to group norms. When employees exercise self-discipline and self-control and believe in doing a fair day's work for their pay, managers can take advantage of this self-discipline and use fewer bureaucratic control methods.

Such cohesiveness and self-discipline are characteristic of self-managed teams (SMTs), as you will recall from earlier chapters.[18] Organic control is an appropriate style to use in conjunction with SMTs. Although organic control is less rigid

LEARNING OBJECTIVE 7
Describe the difference between the philosophies of bureaucratic control and organic control.

Bureaucratic control
Use of formal mechanisms to influence behavior, assess performance, and correct unacceptable deviations from standards.

Organic (clan) control
Reliance upon social values, traditions, shared beliefs, flexible authority, and trust to assess performance and correct unacceptable deviations.

Table 16.2 | Bureaucratic and Organic Methods of Control

	BUREAUCRATIC	**ORGANIC**
Purpose	Employee compliance	Employee commitment
Technique	Rigid rules and policies, strict hierarchy, formalized selection and training	Corporate culture, individual self-discipline, cohesive peer groups, selection and socialization
Performance expectation	Clearly defined standards of individual performance	Emphasizes group or system performance
Organizational structure	Tall structure, top-down controls Rules and procedures for coordination and control Authority resides in position	Flat structure, mutual influence Shared values, goals, and traditions for coordination and control Authority resides with knowledge and expertise
Rewards	Based upon individual employee achievements	Based upon group achievements and equity across employees
Participation	Formalized and narrow	Informal and broad

SOURCE: Adapted and reprinted by permission of *Harvard Business Review*. An exhibit from "From Control to Commitment in the Workplace" by R. E. Walton, March/April 1985, 76–85. Copyright © 1985 by the President and Fellows of Harvard College; All rights reserved.

than bureaucratic control, it would be a mistake to assume that it is a better method. Both the bureaucratic and organic approaches can be useful for organizational control, and most organizations use some aspects of both in their control mechanisms. Table 16.2 provides a brief comparison of the bureaucratic and organic methods of control.

Before deciding which of these two control styles to use in a particular situation, leaders must first evaluate several factors of their organization. The next sections describe the factors that help determine an appropriate choice of control style.

SELECTING A CONTROL STYLE IN TODAY'S DIVERSE AND MULTINATIONAL ORGANIZATIONS

The bureaucratic and organic approaches present two distinctly opposite control philosophies. Top-level leaders are often faced with a dilemma in choosing a style for their organization. This decision can be made more easily if leaders first evaluate these four factors: (1) individual management style, (2) organizational culture, (3) employee professionalism, and (4) performance measures.[19]

Individual management style refers to whether the manager has a task-oriented or a relationship-oriented leadership style. These concepts were described in Chapter 12, where we discussed behavioral approaches to understanding leadership. If a leader uses more relationship-oriented behaviors when interacting with subordinates, then an organic control style would tend to be more compatible with his or her leadership style. Examples of relationship-oriented behaviors include extending a high degree of trust, friendship, and respect to subordinates. In contrast, if a leader displays more task-oriented behaviors when interacting with subordinates, then a bureaucratic control style would tend to be more compatible with his or her leadership style. Task-oriented behavior occurs when the leader assumes the responsibility for planning, directing, providing job information, and maintaining standards of performance for subordinates. The key is that the control style needs to be consistent with the manager's leadership style.

The second factor that determines a control style is organizational culture. If the organizational culture encourages employees to participate in decision making and rewards them for this participation and loyalty, then an organic control style is more appropriate. If the culture of the organization favors decision making at the top and avoids employee participation, then a bureaucratic control style will be the better choice.

Employee professionalism can also influence the control style an organization uses. Employees who are highly educated, highly trained, and professional are more likely to want to participate in decision making and are more likely to accept the high standards of behavior displayed in the group's norms. These employees will be good candidates for an organic control style. Employees who lack experience, training, or the desire to participate would be better candidates for a bureaucratic control style.

Finally, performance measures influence the choice of control style. If performance can be quantified and explicitly measured, then a bureaucratic control style will work well. However, if task performance is difficult to measure or quantify, then an organic control style will be more appropriate.

You should recognize from the preceding discussion that achieving quality in the control process requires a good fit between the situation and the control system. Care must be taken to accurately assess management style, organizational culture, employee professionalism, and types of performance measures before selecting a philosophical approach to control. The choice of a control style is contingent upon all of these situational factors.

The selection of a control style for a multinational organization presents some unique challenges. Although most multinational organizations develop control systems that are a blend of bureaucratic and organic control, the high level of standardization in many multinational organizations permits a heavier use of bureaucratic control, since company manuals and specific rules, procedures, and policies may be applicable across certain subgroups of operating units. For example, because General Motors maintains a number of subsidiaries around the globe that manufacture the same types of engines, it has the potential to use bureaucratic controls in these units. Nevertheless, organic control mechanisms may also play an important part in the control process for multinational organizations, for it is critical that each organizational subunit understand the role it plays in the network of subsidiaries. Strong shared values and philosophies help to ensure that behaviors and output at the subsidiary level are compatible with organizationwide initiatives.[20]

IMPACT OF INFORMATION TECHNOLOGY ON ORGANIZATIONAL CONTROL

Advances and developments in information technology have had a profound and positive effect on organizational control. The very essence of control is deeply rooted in information. Just look at how the topics have progressed in this chapter. One of the basic steps in the control process involves gathering information on actual performance and then comparing it with preestablished standards of performance. Furthermore, the final step in the control process requires that feedback be provided, which is nothing more than the dissemination of information. As the chapter has unfolded we have seen that it is critical to gather information and also to disseminate feedback information in a timely fashion. We live in an age when advances in information processing hardware and software occur at almost dizzying speed. All of these technological advances and improvements serve to get critical control information to leaders in a more timely fashion, allow leaders to make the proper control responses more quickly, and finally disseminate the information on those decisions more quickly so that the negative consequences associated with out-of-control situations can be minimized.

There is an important footnote to the notion that technology can have a positive impact on control. When technology does not operate as it should, the impact on the control systems can be equally strong, but in the wrong direction. This was evident for Hershey Foods Corporation, the nation's largest candy maker. A few years ago, trouble with the company's new $112 million computer system for orders and deliveries fouled up distribution for the biggest candy-buying holiday of the year—Halloween. Distribution difficulties caused Hershey to lose as much as $100 million in sales during the quarter spanning that holiday.[21]

MECHANISMS FOR FINANCIAL CONTROL

One of the most important areas in which control must be exercised is in the finances of an organization. At times financial performance may not be meeting standards, or it may fall short of expectations. If such situations go undetected and corrective actions are not taken, the company's survival might be at stake. We will only briefly examine some of the more important techniques and methods for establishing financial control. More thorough coverage of these topics is left to your accounting and finance classes.

FINANCIAL STATEMENTS

Two financial statements provide much of the information needed to calculate ratios that are used to assess an organization's financial health. These statements are the balance sheet and the income statement.

BALANCE SHEET   The **balance sheet** provides a picture of an organization's financial position at a given point in time. It usually shows the financial status at the end of a fiscal year or a calendar year, although the time interval can certainly be shorter (for example, at the end of each quarter). The balance sheet summarizes three types of information: assets, liabilities, and owner's equity.

Assets are the things of value that the company owns; they are usually divided into current assets and fixed assets. **Current assets** are those items that can be converted into cash in a short time period; they include such items as accounts receivable, inventory, and of course, cash. **Fixed assets** are longer term in nature and include such things as buildings, land, and equipment.

Liabilities include the firm's debts and obligations. They can be divided into current liabilities and long-term liabilities. **Current liabilities** are the debts that must be paid in the near future; they include such obligations as accounts payable and not-yet-paid salaries earned by workers. **Long-term liabilities** are the debts payable over a long time span and include such obligations as payments on bonds and bank loans and mortgages for buildings and land.

Owner's equity is the difference between the assets and liabilities. It represents the company's net worth and consists of common stock and retained earnings. Table 16.3 shows an example of a balance sheet. Note that the totals on both sides of the balance sheet are equal; this must always be the case.

INCOME STATEMENT   The **income statement** summarizes the organization's financial performance over a given time interval, typically one year. It shows the revenues that have come into the organization, the expenses that have been incurred, and the bottom-line profit or loss realized by the firm for the given time interval. For this reason, the income statement is often called a **profit-and-loss statement**. Table 16.4 shows the general structure of an income statement.

Table 16.3 | Balance Sheet

CESTARO MANUFACTURING COMPANY
BALANCE SHEET
DECEMBER 31, 2003

ASSETS			LIABILITIES AND OWNERS' EQUITY		
Current assets:			Current liabilities:		
Cash	$ 30,000		Accounts payable	$ 20,000	
Accounts receivable	50,000		Accrued expenses	10,000	
Inventory	200,000		Income tax payable	40,000	
Total current assets		$280,000	Total current liabilities		$ 70,000
Fixed assets:			Long-term liabilities		
Land	$150,000		Mortgages	$300,000	
Buildings & equipment	400,000		Bonds	100,000	
Total fixed assets		550,000	Total long-term liabilities		400,000
			Owner's equity:		
			Common stock	$300,000	
			Retained earnings	60,000	
			Total owner's equity		360,000
Total assets		$830,000	Total liabilities and owner's equity		$830,000

FINANCIAL RATIOS

Several financial ratios can be used to interpret company performance. Each ratio is simply a comparison of a few pieces of financial data. These ratios can be used to compare a company's current performance with its past performance, or they can be used to compare the company's performance with the performance of other

Table 16.4 | Income Statement

CESTARO MANUFACTURING COMPANY
INCOME STATEMENT
DECEMBER 31, 2003

Gross sales	$2,400,000	
Less sales returns	100,000	
Net sales		$2,300,000
Less expenses and cost of goods sold:		
Cost of goods sold	$1,600,000	
Depreciation	50,000	
Sales expense	150,000	
Administrative expense	80,000	1,880,000
Operating profit		$ 420,000
Other income		10,000
Gross income		$ 430,000
Less interest expense		40,000
Taxable income		$ 390,000
Less taxes		160,000
Net income		$ 230,000

companies in the same industry. The KARLEE Company made extensive use of many of the financial ratios described below in its quest to maintain customer satisfaction and industry leadership.

Liquidity ratios
Indicators of the firm's ability to meet its short-term debts and obligations.

LIQUIDITY RATIOS   **Liquidity ratios** indicate the firm's ability to meet its short-term debts and obligations. The most commonly used liquidity ratio is the current ratio, which is determined by dividing current assets by current liabilities. The current ratio for the Cestaro Manufacturing Company, as illustrated in Tables 16.3 and 16.4, is 280,000/70,000, or 4. This ratio indicates that Cestaro has four dollars of liquid assets for each dollar of short-term debt. Another liquidity ratio is the quick ratio, which is calculated by dividing current assets less inventory by the current liabilities. This ratio assesses how well a firm can expect to meet short-term obligations without having to dispose of inventories. For the Cestaro Company, the quick ratio is (280,000 − 200,000)/70,000, or 1.14.

Profitability ratios
Indicators of the relative effectiveness, or profitability, of the organization.

PROFITABILITY RATIOS   **Profitability ratios** indicate the relative effectiveness of the organization. One important profitability ratio is the profit margin on sales, which is calculated as net income divided by sales. For the Cestaro Company, this ratio is 230,000/2,300,000, or 0.1 (10 percent). Another profitability measure is return on total assets (ROA), which is calculated by dividing the net income by total assets. For Cestaro, this ratio is 230,000/830,000, or 0.28 (28 percent). ROA is a valuable yardstick for potential investors, for its tells them how effective management is in using its assets to earn additional profits.

Debt ratios
Indicators of the firm's ability to handle long-term debt.

DEBT RATIOS   **Debt ratios** indicate the firm's ability to handle long-term debt. The most common debt ratio is calculated by dividing total liabilities by total assets. The debt ratio for Cestaro is 470,000/830,000, or 0.57 (57 percent). This indicates that the firm has 57 cents in debt for each dollar of assets. The lower the debt ratio, the better the financial health of the organization.

Activity ratios
Indicators of performance with respect to key activities defined by management.

ACTIVITY RATIOS   **Activity ratios** measure performance with respect to key activities defined by management. For example, the total cost of goods sold divided by the average daily inventory indicates how efficiently the firm is forecasting sales and ordering merchandise. When total sales are divided by average inventory, an inventory turnover ratio is calculated. This ratio indicates the number of times inventory is turned over to meet the total sales. A low figure means that inventory sits too long and money is wasted.[22]

These and other similar ratios should be used to gain insights into a company's financial relationships and to identify areas that are out of control so that corrective action can be taken. When a ratio is out of line with either past company performance or the performance of comparable companies within the industry, managers must probe through the numbers carefully to determine the cause of the problem and devise a solution. Many of the numbers on the balance sheet and income statement are interrelated, and making a change to improve one ratio may have an undesirable impact on another. Therefore, managers must be very familiar with company operations in order to arrive at a proper remedy when using financial controls.

ETHICAL ISSUES IN THE CONTROL OF A DIVERSE WORKFORCE

LEARNING OBJECTIVE 9

Discuss some of the ethical issues related to the control of employee behavior.

Organizations are increasingly employing controversial mechanisms to control the behavior of individuals and groups within the organization. Sometimes these control mechanisms are known to the individuals, and sometimes the individuals are totally oblivious to their existence. Considerable controversy exists over the ethics of using such control methods as drug testing, undercover surveillance, and computer monitoring. The next sections briefly review the debates over these practices.

DRUG TESTING

It has been estimated that the use of illegal drugs is costing U.S. organizations close to $100 billion per year.[23] Drug abuse results in increases in defective output, absenteeism, workplace accidents, healthcare costs, and insurance claims. To combat the costs associated with these drug-related problems, organizations have increasingly turned to drug testing. One type of drug testing is preemployment testing.[24] As the name suggests, organizations that use this approach require job applicants to submit to a drug detection test. In "Ethics: Take a Stand," at the end of this chapter on page 518, you will see how the Home Depot Corporation uses drug testing on job applicants.

Another type of drug testing focuses on testing current employees. Organizations that test existing employees can follow any of three policies. Random testing subjects employees to unannounced and unscheduled examinations. Testing can also be based upon probable cause. If an employee exhibits suspicious or erratic behavior, or if drug paraphernalia are found in an employee's locker, there may be probable cause for testing. Finally, testing may be prescribed after an accident. Since it is conceivable that impaired motor skills may be the cause of the accident, this is a reasonable time for a drug test. The Motorola Corporation began screening all employees for illegal drug use in 1990. Motorola estimates that lost productivity and absenteeism costs could be reduced by $190 million annually if drug addicts were removed from the workplace.[25]

The ethical issue posed by drug testing hinges on whether it constitutes an invasion of privacy. Do individuals have the right to do as they please with regard to drugs while on their own time, or do organizations have the right to test for drugs in an effort to reduce medical costs, lost-productivity costs, absenteeism costs, and accidents in the workplace?[26] This ethical issue has even spilled out of the workplace and onto the home front. Because of the large number of drug-related crimes in and around its South Florida Congress Park housing project, Atlanta-based developer Trammel Crow Residential is now requiring prospective residents to pass drug tests to gain entry. Furthermore, current residents must do the same before their leases are renewed.[27] There are no easy answers to the ethical questions raised by drug testing. The debate over drug testing continues and will undoubtedly continue for quite some time.

UNDERCOVER SURVEILLANCE

Organizations are constantly subjected to a variety of illegal activities that add to operating costs and decrease profit. Therefore, they are constantly looking for ways to control such activities. These activities include theft (such as pilferage, shoplifting, embezzlement and burglary), fraud (such as credit card fraud, check fraud, and insurance fraud), and malicious destruction of property (such as vandalism, arson, and most recently, the threat of terrorism).[28] Organizations often resort to a variety of surveillance techniques in order to control these illicit activities. Surveillance may be conducted by undercover internal security staffs, external security firms, or electronic devices. For example, General Electric uses tiny cameras hidden behind walls and ceilings to watch employees suspected of crimes, Du Pont uses hidden cameras to monitor its loading docks, and Las Vegas casinos use ceiling-mounted cameras to observe activities on the gaming floors.[29]

Few would find fault when surveillance attempts to detect illegal activities being performed by individuals who are not part of the organization. However, undercover surveillance becomes a delicate issue when an organization's own employees are the subject of the scrutiny.[30] Again, the issue of invasion of privacy often surfaces in such instances, as does the concern that management has a low regard for and little trust in its own employees.

COMPUTER MONITORING

In many businesses, employees spend much of their time working at computer terminals and other electronic devices. Among these employees are data processors, word processors, airline reservations clerks, insurance claims workers, telemarketers, communications network personnel, and workers in many other occupations. Technology has evolved to the point where the work of these employees can be monitored electronically without their knowledge through the computers with which they interface.[31]

Although it is a form of undercover surveillance, computer monitoring is concerned with measuring employee performance rather than detecting illegal activities. This form of surveillance raises serious questions as to whether it violates a worker's right to privacy.[32] Many would question the appropriateness of the organization's "electronically peeking over the workers' shoulders" to monitor their actions. They might argue that it is more appropriate to judge the net output of employees' efforts periodically (daily, weekly, or monthly) rather than to constantly monitor their every action or decision.[33] There are no easy answers to the ethical questions raised by these control methods.

IMPLICATIONS FOR LEADERS

Throughout this book, we have been continually stressing that the successful organizations in the new millennium will be those that achieve quality in all aspects of their operations. Successful leaders in these organizations will be those who can ensure that once plans have been set into place, all activities will be directed toward successfully carrying out those plans. The most effective device leaders have for assessing the success of organizational activities is a basic control system. In a sense, control systems help leaders to chart a course, or set a direction, when standards of behavior or performance are established. Control systems also help to tell them whether they are on course by providing a way to monitor performance. Leaders monitor behavior or performance by measuring what has been done and comparing it to what should have been done. Finally, when organizations stray off course, control systems help to guide them back onto the right path by forcing leaders to consider corrective actions to remove undesirable deviations from standards.

In addition to staying on the course they have charted, effective leaders of tomorrow must ensure that the course charted is the proper course. The 3Cs leadership model can help in this regard. Competency in their understanding of the control process will enable them to stay true to the course charted, while strength of character and commitment to community will ensure that the choices they make lead them down the proper path.

Successful business leaders of the future will be those who:

- Develop a control system for each important product, service, process, or activity within the organization.
- Incorporate sufficient variety, sensitivity, anticipation capability, and feedback into the control system.
- Gauge the control system's effectiveness by considering its relationship to corporate strategy, its completeness, the degree to which it incorporates objective and subjective performance measures, its timeliness, and its acceptability to individuals within the organization.
- Determine the appropriate points within the organization where control systems should be focused.

- Understand the intricacies of the financial data contained in the organization's financial statements, and can use various financial control techniques to assess the organization's financial health.
- Adopt a philosophy of control that is consistent with the management style, organizational culture, employee professionalism, and performance measures present within the organization.

The checklist shown earlier in "Now Apply It" on page 502 can be helpful in determining whether or not a control system has been designed effectively.

In short, the concepts of control presented in this chapter provide us with a mechanism for determining whether our plans and actions have turned out as we had expected or hoped they would. If they haven't, we will be alerted to that fact, allowing us to take the appropriate corrective action to keep matters on their proper course. By remaining on course, we stand a better chance of being successful in our organizational activities.

Meeting The Challenge

KARLEE Company Breaks from the Pack

The KARLEE Company has made great strides in its quest to break away from the traditional "single customer" model so prevalent in its industry and in the process has enjoyed phenomenal growth. By the year 2000 sales had approached $80 million, the workforce had grown to 550, and the facility had grown to 210,000 square feet. The company has expanded its customer base to include customers in the telecommunications, semi-conductor, and medical equipment industries. The company has also made significant strides in its quest to be seen in world markets. Although almost all of KARLEE customers are located in Texas, its manufactured components can be found worldwide, as KARLEE's customers are global leaders in their respective markets. KARLEE has also been successful in its quest to enter into long-term partnerships with customers. Four major customers with long-term contractual arrangements account for about 80 percent of sales. Total long-term partnership relationships with customers comprise 95 percent of the company's sales.

To get to this level KARLEE focused heavily on meeting customer requirements for delivery, quality, and cost. This required the company to institute many changes. Among the significant ones was the increased focus on the control process in many areas extending from the development of product prototypes, through scheduling and product fabrication, product assembly, and on to final product delivery. KARLEE implemented a team culture, forming operational, administrative, and support teams. It is through these teams of executives and frontline workers that targets are set for such diverse measures as scheduling lead times, quote response time, scrap and rework costs, customer returns, on-time delivery performance, assorted financial ratios, and customer satisfaction. In general, targets are set in a collaborative process as teams examine past experience, current capabilities, and available resources. This process is augmented, when possible, with benchmarking efforts to examine comparative information based on similar processes or markets. Each department and manufacturing cell team participates in establishing targets and measures. Each goal must have defined methods for measurement.

To assist in the measuring process, KARLEE's information system provides feedback on a wide variety of factors, such as shop floor and job management, purchasing, sales, inventory, and financial data, to name a few. A key to the success of its control efforts lies in the KARLEE environment of empowerment. Team members are empowered to take ownership of and are held accountable for the processes within their work area. Each team is empowered to change their recommended targets and request additional measures if they believe it will help them achieve higher performance. Team members plan and execute their own improvement activities to meet those targets. Teams are empowered to schedule work, manage inventory, and design the layout of their work areas. Perhaps most importantly, any team member can stop production if the process is not performing to process specifications.

The success of the changes at KARLEE has been dramatic. During the last five years of the 20th century, sales volume tripled while sales were increasing at an average annual rate of more than 25 percent. Customer satisfaction improved by nearly a third to an all time high. At the same time assembly lead times were trimmed from weeks to days (and in some instances a few hours!). These successes were instrumental in the company winning the Texas Quality Award in 1999 and being named Texas Business of the Year in 2000. The crowning glory came when KARLEE Company, Inc., was selected as a 2000 award recipient, manufacturing category, for the prestigious Malcolm Baldrige National Quality Award.

SOURCE: "KARLEE 2000 Application Summary," *Malcolm Baldrige National Quality Award*, **http://www.nist.gov**; "KARLEE Company, Inc.," *Baldrige Award Recipient Profile*, **http://www.nist.gov/public_affairs/baldrige00/Karlee.htm**.

SUMMARY

1. Organizational control is the systematic process through which business leaders regulate organizational activities to make them consistent with the expectations established in plans, targets, and standards of performance. Control is an extremely important managerial function because it ensures that all of the planning, organizing, and leading has gone as we hoped it would. If things have not gone as planned, this situation can result in a variety of negative consequences to the organization.

2. An organized system for control requires that (1) standards of performance be established, (2) actual performance be measured, (3) comparisons be made between standards and actual performance, and (4) corrective action be taken when unacceptable deviations of the actual performance from the standards occur.

3. When designing a control system, one should consider the amount of variety to include in the system, its ability to anticipate problems before they occur, the amount of sensitivity needed in the measuring instruments, and the type of data and information to be included in the feedback report.

4. To be effective, the control system should be related to the organizational strategy, incorporate all the steps in the control process, blend both objective and subjective performance measures, provide timely feedback, and be accepted by members of the organization.

5. To determine the proper amount of control that should be exercised in a given situation, several factors must be ex-

amined. The costs and benefits of the control effort must be assessed. The amount of control can also be affected by the reliability of the system being controlled or the importance of the item being controlled.

6. Preventive (feedforward) control systems focus on the inputs to the transformation process. Concurrent control systems focus on the ongoing activities of the transformation process. Corrective (feedback) control systems focus on the outputs of the transformation process.

7. Bureaucratic control is a more rigid philosophy of control that relies on prescribed rules and policies, a hierarchy of authority, written documents, and other formal mechanisms to influence behavior, assess performance, and correct unacceptable deviations from standards. Organic control is a more flexible philosophy that relies on social values, traditions, flexible authority, and trust to assess performance and correct unacceptable deviations.

8. Several financial control devices are available to assess an organization's financial health. The balance sheet and income statement are two important financial statements. In addition, several financial ratios can be used to interpret company performance.

9. It is becoming more common for organizations to test their employees for drug use, conduct undercover surveillance of their employees, and engage in computer monitoring. Such control procedures raise ethical questions of invasion of privacy and lack of confidence and trust in the employees.

REVIEW QUESTIONS

1. *(Learning Objective 1)* Why is control such a critical managerial function?

2. *(Learning Objective 2)* Discuss each of the four steps that should be taken in a systematic process of control.

3. *(Learning Objective 3)* Discuss the important factors that should be considered when designing a control system.

4. *(Learning Objective 4)* Discuss the various criteria that must be satisfied if a control system is to be effective.

5. *(Learning Objective 5)* Describe the factors that should be considered when trying to determine the proper amount of control to be exercised.

6. *(Learning Objective 6)* Describe the difference between preventive, concurrent, and corrective control.

7. *(Learning Objective 7)* Explain the difference between a bureaucratic control philosophy and an organic control philosophy.

8. *(Learning Objective 8)* Describe the differences between a balance sheet and an income statement.

9. *(Learning Objective 9)* Discuss some of the organizational control practices that raise ethical dilemmas.

DISCUSSION QUESTIONS

Improving Critical Thinking

1. Through your personal observations, identify a situation in which the use of technology seems to be enhancing the control effort and one in which the use of technology seems to be detracting from the control effort. Discuss the reasons you feel each situation is either enhanced or detracted from by the use of technology.

2. Recall some situations that you have encountered in which electronic or undercover surveillance was being performed. Discuss how you felt about those practices.

Enhancing Communication Skills

3. Think about your approach to this course and your quest for a particular grade. Then design a system with which you could control this activity. Be specific in describing the activity, how you would perform each of the steps in the control process, and the potential corrective actions you could take if your performance was not up to your standards. To enhance your written communication skills, write a short essay (one to two pages) in which you describe the design of this control system.

4. The chapter cited two brief examples (air traffic controller and tree farm manager) in which the response times for control feedback were quite different. Identify several situations with varying response-time requirements. Try to come up with examples having response times in seconds, minutes, hours, days, and months. To enhance your oral communication skills, prepare a short (10–15 minutes)

presentation for the class in which you describe your examples of each of these categories of response time.

Building Teamwork

5. Identify two situations that you have observed in which you think the sensitivity of the measuring device is inappropriate. One of those situations should have a device that is too sensitive and the other a device that is not sensitive enough. Thoroughly describe what is being measured and the device that is being used to measure it. Indicate why you feel that the sensitivity of the devices is inappropriate. To refine your teamwork skills, meet with a small group of students who have been given this same assignment. Compare and discuss your selections, and then reach a consensus on the two best choices (one overly sensitive device and one insufficiently sensitive device). Select a spokesperson to present your choices to the rest of the class.

6. Try to identify two situations in which the costs would suggest very different levels of control. In one situation, the cost trade-offs should suggest that high levels of control are warranted, and in the other they should suggest that low levels of control are appropriate. To refine your teamwork skills, meet with a small group of students who have been given this same assignment. Compare and discuss your selections, and then reach a consensus on the two best choices (one requiring low levels of control and one requiring high levels of control). Sketch the cost trade-off graphs for each situation. Then select a spokesperson to present your team's choices and graphs to the rest of the class.

THINKING CRITICALLY: DEBATE THE ISSUE

Pros and Cons of Undercover Surveillance

Form teams of four to five students as directed by your instructor. Half of the teams should prepare to argue the positive aspects of organizations using undercover surveillance to monitor

their employees. The other half of the teams should prepare to argue the negative impacts of this issue. Two teams will be selected by the instructor to present their findings to the class in a debate format.

EXPERIENTIAL EXERCISE 16.1

Assessing Timeliness of Control Systems

Purpose: To gain a greater awareness of the importance of timely feedback in control systems.

Procedure: Make a list of all the offices, departments, and officials that you have interacted with and received feedback from at your university. Then construct a table using the following column headings:

In the first column (Encounter), list all of the areas of interaction. In the second column (Actual Response Time), indi-

cate the amount of time that elapsed before you received the feedback that you desired. In the third column (Ideal Response Time), list what you feel would have been an appropriate amount of time in which to receive the feedback. Finally, in the fourth column (Problems and Difficulties), note any problems or difficulties that you encountered because you did not receive the feedback in what you considered to be a timely fashion.

EXPERIENTIAL EXERCISE 16.2

Detecting Devices to Control Human Behavior

Purpose: To gain a greater awareness of the extent to which various devices are used to control individual behavior.
Procedure: Visit a shopping mall in your vicinity. Browse through several departments in a large department store and also visit several of the small specialty shops in the mall. See how many devices you can discover for controlling individual behavior. Compare and contrast the types of devices being used in the large department stores with those in small specialty stores. What factors seem to influence the use or nonuse of such devices?

CAPTURING THE POWER OF INFORMATION TECHNOLOGY

1. In an effort to control its workforce, the Walt Disney Company has instituted several standards for personal grooming. Use whatever search vehicle is most convenient (Internet, e-mail, fax, newspaper/magazine advertisements, classified job advertisements, and the like) to gather information on these standards. Then use a word-processing package to prepare a one-page synopsis of these standards.

2. Use whatever search vehicle is most convenient (Internet, e-mail, fax, newspaper/magazine advertisements, and the like) to gather information on the technical capabilities of Motorola's most advanced cellular telephone and the ser-

vices it can provide. Then use presentation software to display your findings to your classmates.

3. Use the Internet to gather information on commercial airline crashes that occurred due to controlled flight into terrain. Organize this information in a spreadsheet that can be sorted on such parameters as date of occurrence, country of occurrence, severity (number of deaths), and any other parameters you find that might seem relevant. Compare the thoroughness of your spreadsheet data with that of your classmates.

ETHICS: TAKE A STAND

As this chapter mentioned, the use of illegal drugs is costing U.S. organizations close to $100 billion per year. Home Depot Corporation, a large chain of stores that specializes in the sale of home construction, home repair, home decorating, and household and gardening items, has a very strict policy on drugs. Anyone who approaches the front entrance of a Home Depot store is greeted by a sign in the window proclaiming: "We test all applicants for illegal drug use. If you use drugs, don't bother to apply!"

For Discussion

1. Discuss the ethical issues associated with this control mechanism for individual behavior.

2. Do you feel that preemployment, or even postemployment, drug screening constitutes ethical behavior on the organization's part, or is it an invasion of personal privacy?

VIDEO CASE

Organizational Control in a Complex Business Environment: Cannondale

Cannondale was founded in 1971 by Joseph Montgomery who remains president, CEO, and Chair of the Board of Directors. In 1983, the company introduced the first Cannondale bicycle—an aluminum-frame model unique in the industry. Today, Cannondale sells more than 80 bicycle models and earns more than $156 million in worldwide net sales. In addition to quality high-end bicycles, Cannondale has developed a highly acclaimed motocross motorcycle, an all-terrain vehicle, as well as a variety of accessory lines for pedal and motor powered sports.

Widely regarded as one of the bike industry's leading innovators, Cannondale and its bicycles have won numerous design awards including the "Publisher's Award for Innovation" from *Bicycling* magazine, "Technological Development of the Year Award" from *VeloNews* magazine, ""Best of What's New" award from *Popular Science*, "Best New Products of the Year Award" from *BusinessWeek*, "Design Recognition Award" from *ID* magazine, "Computer-Aided Design Award" from *Design News* magazine, and a "Design and Engineering Award" from *Popular Mechanics*. In order to produce award-winning products, Cannondale utilizes vigorous testing programs to ensure both the product design and the final product meet standards that usually exceed those recommended by ISO, the Consumer Product Safety Commission, and French and British engineering and product standards.

Cannondale nourishes a corporate culture in which production quality and product quality are designed and built *into* the final product rather than having quality inspected at the final product stage. An advantage that Cannondale enjoys over many of its competitors is that its manufacturing facilities are in Pennsylvania, versus offshore in countries subject to different political and cultural systems. Further, Cannondale's design and corporate offices are a short 45-minute flight to Connecticut. This close proximity enhances communications between designers, engineers, marketing personnel, and production managers and personnel. Routinely, designers travel to the factories to work with manufacturing and iron out any problems, find better ways to do things, or make design improvements. Clear and timely communication among departments allows Cannondale to react immediately to marketplace feedback as well as to design changes or production problems. Its standardized computer software further enhances communications among all of its offices and production facilities in the United States and worldwide—everyone speaks the same language.

Managers in the production facilities consider their management structure to be very flat. They explain that this allows them more flexibility and decision-making latitude. Plant Manager Rick Hinson sees his job as eliminating obstacles so his supervisors and employees can do their jobs better. Workers are expected to take care of quality and quality inspection in their respective areas. When workers weld a bike, they are expected to inspect the welds done by previous welders as well as their own work. If a problem is discovered, feedback regarding the problem is given to the responsible party. This way it won't happen again. Furthermore, production workers are empowered to pull the bike in question from the production process and send it for rework. If rework is not feasible, they send the bike to the scrap pile. Some areas rely on more traditional quality control processes, such as the paint department where quality control inspectors look for bubbles in the decals and on the painted bike frame.

Testing plays an integral part in Cannondale's quality program. New designs and vendor-supplied parts are tested before being sent to the production floor. This ensures that the part or frame meets or exceeds Cannondale's standards and expectations for consumer use. Testing is also used as an ongoing quality control tool. At random intervals, testers take bikes from the production line and "destruct test" them to ensure that the materials and work are the best possible quality. These tests are also used to review the work of production personnel. Because unsatisfactory welds produce inferior bike frames, a weld that tests poorly can be used to show the welder what was done incorrectly. Successive test failures may be noted in performance appraisals and may affect subsequent wage increases.

Cannondale has found that its decentralized control system coupled with a culture empowering employees to strive for perfection results in products that meet or exceed the highest industry standards. Quality products, continuous innovation, and effective communication ensure that Cannondale will continue to provide consumers with the best products.

For Discussion

1. Illustrate the factors that are important considerations in the design of Cannondale's control system.

2. Describe how Cannondale utilizes the various characteristics of effective control.

3. Explain how Cannondale uses preventive control, concurrent control, and corrective control. Explain how your examples relate to the steps in the control process.

4. Explain whether Cannondale applies the philosophy of bureaucratic control or organic control. Why might that chosen philosophy be more effective at Cannondale than the other philosophy?

http://www.cannondale.com

CASE

Motorola's Control of Quality

Motorola, Inc., headquartered in Schaumburg, Illinois, is an engineering-oriented company whose principal product lines are communications systems and semiconductors. With over 50 facilities worldwide and more than 100,000 employees, Motorola is recognized as one of the leading manufacturers of electronic equipment, systems, and components in the global marketplace. Its products are highly regarded for their quality and reliability. However, this was not always the reputation of Motorola.

Although Motorola commanded a large share of the electronics market, its share had been dwindling as customers increasingly complained about delivery time, product quality and reliability, and many other areas of dissatisfaction. These problems led then-chairman Robert Galvin to throw down the gauntlet. In this increasingly competitive, global industry, relatively high quality was not good enough. Galvin realized that Motorola needed control mechanisms that could ensure worker performance and production output were close to perfect. Contributing to the problems faced by Motorola was the fact that each division had its own performance measures. These dissimilar systems made it virtually impossible for top management to assess and compare performance across the corporation, much less work toward common objectives. Galvin began by creating a common culture and a common language. A single measure for quality, total defects per unit of work, was chosen. The company launched a crusade to implement a wide range of control techniques to improve quality, reliability, and cycle time.

Management set a goal to gradually improve quality to the point where defects would be fewer than four per million (its renowned "Six Sigma" level). Sampling inspection was to be used as a temporary means of control until permanent corrective actions could be implemented. Control processes were to be applied to cycle times, with the ultimate goal of a 90 percent reduction in the time to bring a product to market. Frontline employees were assigned the task of tracking defects, charting problems, and solving problems in cross-functional teams. To train its workers, the company established Motorola University, which provides one of the most comprehensive and effective corporate training programs in the world. Each Motorola employee receives a minimum of 40 hours training per year. To better control the quality of its inputs, a certification program was instituted for Motorola suppliers, each of whom must adhere to the Motorola standards.

To illustrate how successful these moves were, consider Motorola's highly successful MicroTac cellular telephone. By effectively controlling the design and developmental time, Motorola was able to bring it to market two years ahead of the competition and was able to sell over $1 billion worth of the 10.7-ounce pocket-sized telephone before there was a comparable competitor. In addition, the product even won two of the highest Japanese awards for quality. Motorola was well on its way toward achieving its "Six Sigma" goal of only 3.4 defects per million.

For Discussion

1. What benefits was Motorola likely to achieve by instituting a common performance measure across all divisions of the organization?

2. Describe the control philosophy adopted by Motorola when it assigned frontline workers the task of tracking defects and solving problems.

3. What evidence do you find that Motorola made use of feedforward controls as the company tried to improve the quality of its outputs?

CHAP

PRODUCTIVITY AND QUALITY IN OPERATIONS

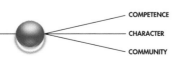

LEADERSHIP

COMPETENCE

CHARACTER

COMMUNITY

TER 17

CHAPTER OVERVIEW

All business organizations engage in operations that transform inputs into outputs. Regardless of whether their organization manufactures a product or provides a service, business leaders have one fundamental concern—that is, to provide the customers what they want, when they want it. As simple as this concept sounds, leaders must make many decisions prior to delivering the product or service. To achieve quality in operations, they must (1) understand the nature of the various decisions they will face and (2) understand the various tools, techniques, and approaches that can help them to make these decisions. How business leaders should approach these decisions depends to a large extent upon whether their organization is predominantly product or service oriented and upon the structural characteristics of the operating system.

In this chapter we first examine the differences between manufacturing and service organizations and review the basic system configurations that these organizations may exhibit. We then briefly examine some of the more important managerial decision areas for the long-term design of these systems, as well as some of the important decisions for their short-term operation and control. Since productivity and quality have a major impact upon the efficiency and effectiveness of operations decisions, ways to measure and improve them are examined. We also discuss the roles that productivity and quality play in achieving excellence in operations. The chapter concludes with an examination of some contributions of the most prominent contemporary quality philosophers.

LEARNING OBJECTIVES

When you have finished studying this chapter, you should be able to:

1. Identify the major differences between manufacturing and service organizations.
2. Describe the volume/variety continuum for identifying different operating system configurations and identify the different types of manufacturing and service organizations that might exist, as well as their locations on the volume/variety continuum.
3. Identify the two broad categories of decision-making areas within operating systems, and describe some of the important decisions in each category.
4. Define the concept of productivity, and identify the three approaches to improving productivity.
5. Provide definitions of quality from both a consumer perspective and a producer perspective.
6. Identify factors that can be used to assess the quality of products and services.
7. Describe the four categories of quality-related costs.
8. Identify the various areas of concentration and commitment for a program of total quality management.
9. Describe the major contributions of the most prominent contemporary quality philosophers.

Facing The Challenge

Operational Changes Needed at Clarke American Checks, Inc.

Clarke American Checks, Inc., is a major supplier of personalized checks, checking-account and bill-paying accessories, financial forms, and a growing portfolio of services to more than 4,000 financial institutions and their customers. Headquartered in San Antonio, Texas, since its founding in 1874, Clarke American employs about 3,300 people at 25 sites in 15 states. The company competes in an industry that has undergone massive consolidation in recent years. It is an industry where a small number of major competitors struggle to be responsive to changing customer needs and demands and, at the same time, provide quality and security in the products they deliver.

With the proliferation of credit card and debit card transactions in today's society, some might question the future of check writing and the long-term viability of check printing companies. Key findings of the Federal Reserve and Depository Institution on payment research should put such questions to rest. Data in the year 2002 reveal that for every 15 billion credit card transactions in the

United States, there are 50 billion transactions via check. Through the use of checks, $48 trillion travels through the monetary system, while only $7 trillion travels through all other electronic payment methods combined. Checks represent more than 62 percent of all non-cash transactions. During the last 20 years, check usage has risen by 55 percent. According to Dr. William Freund, Chief Economist Emeritus of the New York Stock Exchange, "The check is America's favorite way to pay. The check will remain an extremely popular, safe, and reliable form of payment in the years to come."

Clarke American emerged from the industry consolidation as one of the largest check printers in the United States. The company produces more than 11 billion personal and business checks a year for more than 4,500 banks, credit unions, and other financial services companies nationwide. Financial services companies also rely on Clarke American to deliver direct marketing, customer services, e-commerce solutions, treasury management doc-

uments, letterchecks, and other financial accessories. The challenges to the company were many. These documents had to be produced to customers' unique specifications, and it had to be done in a timely manner (custom printing orders are often accompanied by a request for next day delivery), and with complete accuracy (no errors in addresses or account numbers). Documents had to be designed with a level of security that would provide protection against photocopying, scanning, and other forms of counterfeiting. Furthermore, quality levels needed to be high so that magnetic ink character recognition (MICR) systems would be able to electronically read the information printed on the documents. In short, the production challenges facing Clarke American required solutions quite a bit more extensive than the simple printing presses that were used in the early days.

SOURCE: "Malcolm Baldrige National Quality Award, 2001 Award Recipient, Manufacturing Category, Clarke American Checks Inc.," **http://www.nist.gov; http://www.clarkeamerican.com.**

INTRODUCTION

Clarke American Checks faced some serious challenges in an industry that was seeing a dwindling number of players, but intense competition among those few who remained. The needs and demands of customers were changing. Financial institutions and their customers wanted faster service, a greater voice in the customization of their documents, greater levels of fraud protection with those documents, complete accuracy of the information contained on the documents, and security of information submitted to Clarke American, to name a few. Clarke American would have to implement changes in its operating system and make use of the latest technological innovations if the company had any hopes of responding to these customer demands.

In this chapter we will focus on issues of productivity and quality in operations. Recall that in Chapter 16 we presented a simple model for operations. It described a process in which inputs are subjected to a transformation process that converts them into the product or service outputs of the organization. We will see that operations management has a strong decision-making orientation and contains several design and operating decision areas. How managers should approach these decisions depends upon the structural characteristics of their own operating systems and whether their organizations are predominantly engaged in manufacturing products or providing services. Let's begin by examining those structural characteristics so we can see how manufacturing and service organizations differ.

WHAT IS OPERATIONS MANAGEMENT?

Operations management is concerned with the design, planning, and control of the factors that enable us to provide the product or service outputs of the organization. Decision making is central to operations management. Operations managers must make decisions to ensure that the firm's product or service output happens (1) in the amount demanded, (2) at the right time, (3) with the chosen quality level, and (4) in a manner that is compatible with the organization's goals.

The first three aspects of the operations manager's function are fairly straightforward: provide what the customers want, when they want it, and with a quality level that is acceptable to them. The fourth aspect can be a bit trickier. As we saw in Chapter 4, organizations often have multiple goals, and some may be in conflict with one another. When this happens, operations management decisions cannot satisfy all organizational goals simultaneously. Consider, for example, the dilemma you would face if you were in charge of operations in a steel mill. Suppose that two of your organization's many goals were to (1) maximize bottom-line profits and (2) reduce the amount of pollutants that the mill discharges into the atmosphere. Installing scrubbers in the mill's smokestacks would reduce pollution, but the expense of these scrubbers would detract from your organization's bottom-line profits. Likewise, consider the dilemma faced by the home-delivery pizza industry in recent years. A reasonable goal might be to deliver pizzas to the customers in as short a time as possible. Another reasonable goal might be to promote public safety in the delivery of the pizzas. These two goals are at odds with one another. Speedier delivery of the pizzas can result in dangerous driving practices on the part of delivery personnel. In fact, it was a dilemma like this that caused the major pizza delivery companies like Pizza Hut, Domino's, Papa John's, and many others to eliminate such traditional time guarantees as "30-minute delivery or the pizza is free."

The decisions faced by operations managers can be conveniently separated into two broad categories. The first set of decisions relates to the design of the operating system. After the system has been designed and built, operations managers must then make the operating and control decisions necessary to keep the system running smoothly and efficiently. Managers can draw on many tools, techniques, and models to help them make these decisions. For many operations decisions, the proper decision-making tools depend upon whether the system is a manufacturing or service system. We will see later in the chapter that the manufacturing-versus-service distinction also influences how quality and productivity are measured. Decision-making tool selection also depends upon the structural characteristics of the operating system. Consequently, before we explore the important operations management decision areas, we first examine the differences between manufacturing and service organizations and the structural differences among various manufacturing and service organizations.

MANUFACTURING VERSUS SERVICE OPERATING SYSTEMS

Although manufacturing and service organizations both display the same input-to-output transformation process, a fundamental output characteristic distinguishes manufacturing organizations from most service organizations. The output of manufacturing will always be a physical product—something that can be touched, measured, weighed, or otherwise examined. For example, IBM makes computers, General Motors makes automobiles, RCA makes audio and video equipment, and Nike makes athletic apparel.

Outputs of service organizations often lack physical properties. For example, H&R Block processes income tax returns, hospitals treat sick and injured people, and your college professors deliver lectures and convey knowledge to you. Some-

LEARNING OBJECTIVE 1

Identify the major differences between manufacturing and service organizations.

times, however, the outputs of service organizations do possess physical properties. When you order a hamburger at a fast-food restaurant, your selection certainly has physical properties associated with it. Does this make the fast-food restaurant a manufacturing organization? Not really. The physical characteristic of outputs is not the only feature that distinguishes manufacturing from service organizations. As we take a closer look at other differences, continue to think about fast-food restaurants. You should have a definite opinion as to whether they are manufacturing or service organizations by the time we get to the end of the discussion.

Several of the differences between manufacturing and service stem from the physical nature of the output. Manufacturing can stockpile inventories of finished products in advance of customer demand.[1] Service organizations usually cannot. For example, a barbershop cannot stockpile a supply of haircuts prior to the Saturday morning peak demand period, and H&R Block cannot stockpile an inventory of completed income tax returns prior to April's peak demand. Even when a physical product is made, stockpiling in advance of demand can sometimes be impractical. This is certainly true in the case of fast-food restaurants, as will be discussed in more detail shortly. Service capacity is often described as being time perishable.[2] This means that if a service organization has excess capacity that goes unused, that service capability has been lost forever. On the other hand, a manufacturing organization with excess capacity can use the surplus capacity to produce additional product for later consumption.

Another difference is that production and consumption usually occur simultaneously (or within a short time of one another) in service organizations. In addition, the customer is normally a participant in the service process.[3] For example, you must show up at the barbershop or beauty salon to receive a haircut, and it will be performed while you sit in the barber's or hairdresser's chair. These two characteristics also demonstrate another difference between manufacturing and service—the system location considerations. Service systems, such as barbershops, restaurants, income tax preparation firms, and hospitals, need to be located close to their customers, while manufacturing systems would not consider this to be of prime importance.[4] Most adult Americans own an automobile, but few live within walking distance or an easy drive to an automobile manufacturing plant. However, most would like to have reasonable access to an automobile repair shop, because none of us would want to take our automobile back to Detroit (or Japan!) for repair service.

A final difference between manufacturing and service relates to the measurement of quality and productivity. The quality of a product is usually much easier to assess than the quality of a service.[5] Physical products are designed to meet various specifications that involve physical traits such as weight, dimensions, color, durability, and so forth. After manufacture, precise objective measurements of these characteristics can be made to determine the degree to which the product meets the quality standards. For example, once manufactured, a Dell computer or a Hewlett-Packard printer can be put through a variety of tests to ensure that they operate exactly as they were designed. Such precision is usually more difficult when assessing the quality of a service output. In many instances only subjective assessments can be made of the quality of the service output. Precise standards usually do not exist to determine how good the haircut is, how accurately the income tax return was prepared, or how tasty the hamburger was. Productivity, which gauges the relationship between inputs and outputs, is also easier to assess in manufacturing situations, where the physical nature of the inputs and outputs allows them to be precisely measured.[6] "Now Apply It" that follows presents a checklist for determining whether an organization is predominantly a manufacturing organization or a service organization. Apply the checklist to any of the U.S. Big Three automakers (General Motors, DaimlerChrysler, and Ford). Into which category— manufacturing or service—do they fall?

Now Apply It

Checklist for Manufacturing/Service Classification

To determine whether a business firm is a manufacturing organization or a service organization, answer the following questions with a zero (0) for no and a one (1) for yes.

1. Does the firm provide a tangible, physical output?
2. Can the output be stored in inventory for future use or consumption?
3. Can the output be transported to distant locations?

4. Can excess capacity be used when there is no immediate demand?
5. Can the output be produced well in advance of its consumption?
6. Can the system operate without having the consumer of the output as an active participant?
7. Is it reasonable to have the system located a great distance from the consumer of the output?
8. Is productivity relatively easy to measure?

9. Is quality relatively easy to assess?

Total the value of your responses. The closer the total is to 9, the more inclined we would be to classify the system as a manufacturing organization. The closer the total is to 0, the more inclined we would be to classify the system as a service organization.

Now let's think again about fast-food restaurants and the checklist in "Now Apply It." The service capacity of a restaurant is usually time perishable. Excess capacity early in the day will go unused; it cannot be used to satisfy the needs of the lunch or dinner crowd. Using that early-morning excess capacity to stockpile inventory in advance of the meal hour rush is of limited practicality. Hamburgers cannot be cooked early in the day and then stored until the rush hours. In these situations, production and consumption must occur almost simultaneously, and the customer is an active participant in the process. The vast multitude of locations also points to a service orientation. One centralized McDonald's restaurant will not suffice. There must be plenty of outlets scattered about so that they are near the customers in order to facilitate direct interaction between the customer and the service system. Thus, when all the tests are applied, a service classification proves to be more appropriate for fast-food restaurants.

Let's now turn our attention to an examination of the structural differences that can exist among manufacturing and service organizations.

STRUCTURAL DIFFERENCES AMONG OPERATING SYSTEMS

Individual operating systems can be categorized along a volume/variety continuum, as illustrated in Figure 17.1. Companies can differ in the variety of outputs produced, as well as in the volume of each item that is provided. As you move toward the left extreme of low variety and high volume, you encounter systems that provide very few different types of output but deliver a large quantity of each. Toward the right extreme of high variety and low volume, you encounter systems that provide a very wide variety of different types of output but deliver a small number of each. The endpoints of this line represent two extremes in both manufacturing and service organizations. Let's take a closer look at these configurations, first in manufacturing organizations and then in service organizations.

TYPES OF MANUFACTURING SYSTEMS The left portion of the continuum represents systems that have a specific purpose.[7] The extreme left reflects companies that make only one product but produce it in large quantities. In such a system, operations can be standardized. When the product being made takes the form of discrete, individual units, the system is called a **repetitive**, **assembly-line**, or **mass-production system**. For example, a company that makes only yellow #2

LEARNING OBJECTIVE 2

Describe the volume/variety continuum for identifying different operating system configurations and identify the different types of manufacturing and service organizations that might exist, as well as their locations on the volume/variety continuum.

Repetitive, assembly-line, or mass-production system
Produces a high volume of discrete items.

Figure 17.1 | Classification Scheme for Different Operating Systems

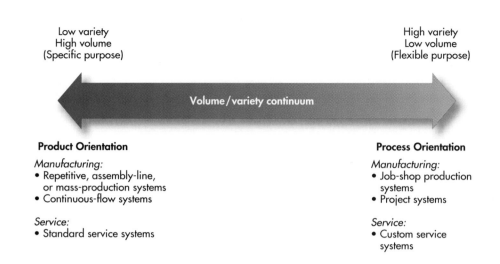

Low variety
High volume
(Specific purpose)

High variety
Low volume
(Flexible purpose)

Volume/variety continuum

Product Orientation

Manufacturing:
- Repetitive, assembly-line, or mass-production systems
- Continuous-flow systems

Service:
- Standard service systems

Process Orientation

Manufacturing:
- Job-shop production systems
- Project systems

Service:
- Custom service systems

Continuous-flow production system
Produces a high volume of a continuous product or nondiscrete item.

Fender Musical Instrument Corporation provides almost limitless options for its guitars and is an example of custom manufacturing at its finest.

© KURT STIER/CORBIS

pencils with an eraser would be at the left end of the continuum. When a product is made in a continuous stream, and not in discrete units, the system is called a **continuous-flow production system**. Examples here would include an Exxon-Mobil oil refinery, a Coors brewery, or perhaps a USX steel mill that produces long, continuous rolls of sheet steel. You may recall from Chapter 2 that Joan Woodward identified these two types of production systems as mass-production technology and continuous-process technology when she proposed that managerial style would be affected by the organization's technology. In that context she also identified a third type of technology that she called small batch technology and which is described next.

At the right end of the continuum are systems that have a flexible purpose. The extreme right reflects companies that make many different types of items but produce only one of each. This would be a custom manufacturing situation. In such a system, operations cannot be standardized; instead, they must be flexible enough to accommodate the wide variety of items that will be manufactured. When the items to be made require small to moderate amounts of resources and time (hours or days), the system is referred to as a **job-shop production system**. The term *unit production* is often used to signify systems that manufacture only a single unit of a particular item. A sign shop that custom-fabricates neon advertising signs for small businesses would be an example of a company near the right extreme of this continuum. Another example of a facility near the right extreme of the continuum is found in the custom shop of the Fender Musical Instruments Corporation. Most professional and amateur musicians are well aware of Fender's renowned, off-the-rack Stratocaster and Telecaster guitars. However, fewer are aware that the Fender custom shop can handle requests for Stratocasters and Telecasters that are tailored to a customer's ego and budget. Here they will fashion you a guitar body from any exotic wood or metal requested. Furthermore, if you are so inclined, they will inlay your signature (or any design of your liking) across the frets in gems, jewels, abalone, or whatever material suits your fancy. The options are almost limitless to Fender's master craftspeople. However, you will have to wait about a year, and depending upon your specifications, you may have to pay as much as $50,000 for your guitar.[8] This is custom manufacturing at its finest!

Sometimes flexible-purpose systems produce items that consume massive amounts of resources and require large amounts of time to complete (months or years). Such a system is referred to as a **project production system**. Examples here would include construction companies that develop shopping centers, build roads and bridges, and so forth.[9]

Although the endpoints have been neatly defined for the continuum of Figure 17.1, it is unusual to find an organization that lies at either extreme. While pencil manufacturer Dixon Ticonderoga is noted for its yellow #2 pencils with erasers, this company makes more than just that one product. It turns out pencils in a variety of colors with different types of lead. In addition, it also makes a variety of pens and marking pencils. All of these different writing instruments are produced in very large quantities. Consequently, Dixon Ticonderoga exhibits mass-production characteristics because it lies close to the left extreme of the volume/variety continuum. Although Clarke American processes orders that are different for each customer (check style, color, imprinting, and other items), the company does not print a single document for each order. For example, your order for replenishment checks would probably request that several hundred be printed. Hence, even though Clarke American would not lie at the right extreme of the continuum, the company would still exhibit the basic characteristics of the job-shop system.

TYPES OF SERVICE SYSTEMS   The continuum of Figure 17.1 also applies to different types of service systems. The left extreme reflects organizations that provide standard services, while the right extreme reflects organizations that provide custom services. Consider, for example, a college dormitory cafeteria line. It has all of the characteristics of an assembly line as each customer moving through the line is serviced in exactly the same manner at each serving station. In contrast, a walk-in emergency clinic might exhibit all the characteristics of a custom job shop since most patients are likely to have different types of injuries and illnesses and, consequently, will require different services.

As in the case of manufacturing, service organizations can easily lie somewhere between the extremes. The cafeteria line might have á la carte selections, in which case some customers might receive slightly different service. Likewise, the emergency clinic might have a few patients with broken arms whose service requirements are virtually identical. The wound will be cleaned and dressed, X-rays taken, and a cast applied for each of them.[10]

Whether an organization is a manufacturing or a service entity, and wherever it fits on the volume/variety continuum, its operations managers will have to make decisions. The next section examines the many decisions that must be made for both the design and operation of manufacturing and service organizations.

OPERATIONS MANAGEMENT DECISION AREAS

To operate any business organization, a number of decisions must be made. Based upon the time frame involved, these decisions can be conveniently categorized as long-term system design decisions or as short-term operating and control decisions.[11] It is not our intention to present a thorough description of each of the operations management decision areas. That level of detail is best left to separate operations management courses with their specialized textbooks. Instead, we provide a brief, introductory overview of some of the more important operations management decision areas.

LONG-TERM SYSTEM DESIGN DECISIONS   Long-term system design decisions require substantial investments of time, energy, money, and resources. As the name implies, they commit the decision maker to a particular system configu-

Job-shop production system
Produces small quantities of a wide variety of specialized items.

Project production system
Produces large-scale, unique items.

LEARNING OBJECTIVE 3

Identify the two broad categories of decision-making areas within operating systems, and describe some of the important decisions in each category.

ration (that is, an arrangement of buildings and equipment) that will exist for many years, if not the entire life of the organization. Once these decisions are made and implemented, changing them would be costly. Although a thorough treatment of these various decisions would require several chapters, the following brief overview will provide a basic understanding.

Choice of a Product or Service Prior to the development and start-up of any business, a fundamental decision must be made about what product or service will be provided. This decision is linked directly to the corporate strategy because it answers the question "What business are we in?" The choice of product or service will ultimately dictate what inputs will be necessary and what type of transformation will be performed. To make a viable product/service selection decision, considerable interaction with the marketing function will be needed. This interaction will help the decision maker accurately assess the wants and needs of the marketplace as well as the strength of the competition so that the product or service selected has a reasonable chance of success. Clarke American provides a good example of the long-term nature of this design decision. Clarke American made the decision in 1874 that it would be in the financial documents printing business. More than 125 years later the company is still in that business.

Product or Service Design From a manufacturing standpoint, the development of a product involves a sequence of steps, as illustrated in Figure 17.2.[12] These steps might also be applied in certain service situations that involve physical output. The sequence of design steps requires (1) development of a concept, (2) development of a preliminary design or prototype, (3) development of "make versus buy" choices, and (4) selection of production methods, equipment, and suppliers.

Although each step in the design process is usually carried out by a different unit of the organization, design quality is facilitated when all participants from mar-

Figure 17.2 | Steps in Product Design

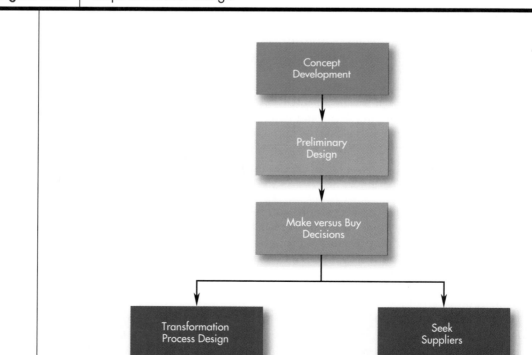

keting, engineering, production, purchasing, and any other relevant areas work together as a design team. The instant feedback and enhanced interactions within the team help to achieve more rapid product development. The design process can also be facilitated by such recent high-tech developments as computer-aided design (CAD), computer-aided engineering (CAE), and computer-aided manufacturing (CAM). By using virtual prototypes on computers to design and test cars, the U.S. Big Three automakers have made marked progress in reducing the time required to develop new vehicles, which will save them billions of dollars in costs.[13]

System Capacity   Another decision to be made involves the capacity of the system.[14] This decision will determine the level of product or service output that the system will be able to provide. It is here that the firm will make its major investment decisions. The number of facilities to be built, the size of each facility, their individual capabilities, and the amount and type of equipment to be purchased must all be determined. In order to make high-quality decisions in this area, the decision maker must forecast the market demand for the product or service to be offered and assess the competition so that the organization's market share potential can be estimated. Next, the amount of labor and equipment needed to meet these market share projections must be calculated. Marketing will play a key role here, because accurate projections of market demand and competition will help to establish the size of the system being developed. As a company's business grows, it may become necessary to revise that capacity decision (that is, capacity expansion). With an annual growth rate much higher than the industry average, Clarke American found it necessary to open a new facility in mid-2002, increasing its workforce by almost 20 percent.[15]

Process Selection   The selection of a framework for the transformation process will depend upon how the firm is likely to be categorized. Recall our classification scheme that categorized manufacturing and service organizations along a volume/variety continuum. An organization's self-assessment of the volume, variety, and type of product or service output likely to be generated will help to indicate the type of process to be selected. In a manufacturing setting, answers to these questions will indicate the types of material flows that can be expected through the system. This, in turn, will determine the process configuration to be selected—that is, whether the organization will be configured as a continuous-flow, repetitive, job-shop, or project system. In a service setting, the self-assessment of volume, variety, and type of service will determine whether the system process will provide custom or standard services. Once the decision makers select the process configuration, the firm can obtain machinery and equipment compatible with that process. We will see later in "Meeting The Challenge" on page 550 that process and equipment selection was one of the areas of focus for Clarke American. Its conversion to digital printing with high-quality magnetic ink character recognition (MICR) enabled the company to provide faster service, more customized products, reduced cycle time, reduced waste, and improved quality.

Facility Location   The facility location decision involves the selection of a geographic site on which to establish the organization's operations. This decision is extremely important because once the physical structure has been built, its high cost usually dictates that the location decision will remain in effect for a considerable amount of time. Manufacturing and service organizations emphasize very different factors in making this decision. Consider what would be important to a hospital, a gasoline service station, a fast-food restaurant, an automobile manufacturing plant, a cement-processing plant, and a ballpoint pen manufacturing plant. Some factors might be common to all, while other factors might be important for only certain types of systems. Survey data show that manufacturing location decisions are dominated by five factors: (1) favorable labor climate, (2) proximity to markets, (3) quality of life, (4) proximity to suppliers and resources, and (5) proximity to the parent company's facilities.[16] Table 17.1 describes these factors further. Earlier we noted that Clarke American expanded its capacity by opening a new facility. Since this new facility was to supplement the operations of the San Antonio center, this location decision was based solely on proximity to this existing company facility.

In service organizations, proximity to customers is often the primary location factor to be considered. Since customers must usually interact directly with service organizations, convenient locations are crucial. Barbershops, dry cleaners, supermarkets, gasoline service stations, and restaurants would do very little business if they were situated in remote, inaccessible areas. Traffic volume, residential population density, competition, and income levels all play an important part in the location decision for service organizations.

The location criteria mentioned here should not be interpreted as an exhaustive list. The Russell Stover Candy Company recently incorporated a somewhat unusual factor in its location decision. Although it had committed to building a plant in Corsicana, Texas, that decision was put on hold when plans were announced for an animal parts processing plant in the same town. Russell Stover officials feared that odors from the animal rendering facility would contaminate its sweets. The candy company gave the go-ahead with its construction plans only after the animal rendering plant was paid by town officials to locate elsewhere.[17]

Facility Layout The primary objective of the facility layout decision is to arrange the work areas and equipment so that inputs progress through the transformation process in as orderly a fashion as possible. This will result in a smooth flow of materials or customers through the system. The precise configuration for a given system will depend on where the system fits into the volume/variety continuum. Systems at the flexible-purpose extreme, which must be able to handle a wide variety of product or customer-service demands, will use a **process layout**. Conversely, systems at the specific-purpose extreme, in which all products or services are essentially the same, will use a **product layout**.

Lying between these extremes are a variety of systems that need layouts combining aspects of each of the extreme cases. These systems would incorporate a **hybrid layout**. Finally, a system that produces extremely large or bulky items may use a

Process layout
A configuration flexible enough to accommodate a wide diversity of products or customers.

Product layout
A configuration set for a specific purpose, with all product or service demands essentially identical.

Hybrid layout
A configuration containing some degree of flexibility, lying between the extremes of process and product layouts.

Table 17.1   Major Factors in Manufacturing Location Decisions

1. *Favorable labor climate.* Management's assessment of the labor climate would be based on such parameters as union activity, wage rates, available labor skill levels, required labor training, worker attitudes, and worker productivity.

2. *Proximity to markets.* Consideration would be given to both the actual distance to the markets and the modes of transportation available to deliver the products.

3. *Quality of life.* Attention would be paid to the quality and availability of schools, housing, shopping, recreation facilities, and other lifestyle indicators that reflect the quality of life.

4. *Proximity to suppliers and resources.* When companies rely on bulky or heavy raw materials and supplies, this factor is of prime concern. Distance and transportation modes would influence this factor.

5. *Proximity to the parent company's facilities.* This factor is important for companies with multiplant configurations. When parts and materials must be transferred between operating facilities, frequent interactions, communication, and coordination will be necessary. Additionally, the time and cost of material transfers must be minimized. All of this can be facilitated by geographical proximity between the facilities.

fixed-position layout, in which the item remains stationary while workers and equipment move to the item to provide processing. Just how important is the layout decision? Consider these examples. Recently, Toys R Us embarked on a massive project to revamp the layout of its stores by removing the maze of parallel aisles in an effort to rekindle customer interest.[18] Similar revolutionary changes are being tested in Albertsons and Food Lion grocery stores, where aisles have been replaced with clusters of grocery departments and service centers to spark consumer interest. In addition, Subway Restaurants has begun a makeover of the layout and décor of its units to add a Tuscany flair.[19]

Some of these long-term system design decisions present unique managerial challenges to multinational organizations. For example, before selecting and designing a product or service, the sociocultural and economic environments of the global markets in which the organization will operate must be assessed. In addition, it would be unwise to select international locations for operating units of the organization without first considering the political-legal climate, economic conditions, state of technological development, and cultural values of the workforce in the potential locations. Success will come more easily to multinational organizations that thoroughly research all of these parameters in their long-term system design decisions.

Fixed-position layout
A configuration used for large or bulky items that remain stationary in the manufacturing process.

© AP/WIDE WORLD PHOTOS

In an effort to rekindle customer interest, Toys R Us has reconfigured its stores into a more open layout with boutiques featuring merchandise targeted to specific age groups.

SHORT-TERM OPERATING AND CONTROL DECISIONS After the long-term system design decisions have been made and the system is operational, it is time to begin making the short-term operating and control decisions. These decisions are made frequently (daily, weekly, or perhaps monthly), can be readily changed, and in many cases are directly involved with the scheduling of work activities. In today's organizations, managers face new challenges as they schedule, lead, and control labor in the increasingly diverse workforce. Ethnic, racial, and gender differences often lead to different individual values and expectations. Hence, standards of individual behavior, performance, and productivity are sometimes more difficult to set and enforce.

Aggregate Planning Before initiating any detailed day-to-day or week-to-week scheduling activities in a manufacturing firm, management must first make a series of decisions designed to set the overall level of operations for a planning horizon that generally spans the upcoming year. At this point management uses demand forecasts to make rough production, labor-scheduling, and inventory decisions that will set the tone for the overall level of operations during the year. The goal is to ensure that customer demand can be satisfied, the firm's resources won't be overtaxed, and the relevant costs will be held to a minimum. These decisions constitute what is known as **aggregate planning**. This set of planning decisions represents the link between the more general business planning activities and the more specific master plans for short-range operation and control aspects of the firm.

In aggregate planning, management formulates a plan that involves such factors as production scheduling, workforce level adjusting, inventory scheduling, production subcontracting, and employment scheduling so that enough product or service will be available to satisfy customer demands.[20] By their very nature, aggregate plans are rather rough. They are usually stated in terms of product families rather than individual products. Their monthly or quarterly time periods are incapable of directing the day-to-day scheduling of operations. The main purpose of aggregate plans is to provide broad production scheduling, inventory scheduling, and human resource scheduling guidelines within which more detailed scheduling decisions eventually will be made.

Aggregate planning
Link between the more general business planning activities and the more specific master planning activities.

Master Production Scheduling Although the rough schedule provided by aggregate planning will be useful for projecting the overall levels of production and labor requirements over an intermediate planning horizon, it will not contain enough detail and information for scheduling the various production activities. Another schedule is needed that not only contains detailed information about individual product identities but also divides the planning horizon into finer increments of time. Such a schedule, which is known as the master production schedule, will be used to drive all of the ensuing production scheduling activities within the system.

Master production schedule
A detailed statement of projected production quantities for each item in each time period.

The **master production schedule** is a detailed statement of projected production quantities for each item in each time period.[21] Time periods are typically weekly intervals. The master production schedule is often thought of as an anticipated build schedule for finished products. A major constraint in the development of the master production schedule is that the total number of units scheduled for production must be compatible with the aggregate plan. Since the master production schedule is simply a more detailed breakdown of the aggregate plan, the sum of the parts (the master production schedule units) must equal the whole (the aggregate plan).

Inventory Management   One of the most studied of the short-term decisions deals with the control of inventories. Items in inventory may exist in any of four forms: (1) raw materials, (2) work-in-process, (3) finished goods, and (4) supplies. Raw materials are the basic inputs that have not yet been subjected to any processing transactions. Work-in-process represents semifinished items that are in various stages of completion. Finished goods are items that have had all processing transactions performed and are ready for delivery to the customer. Supplies represent purchased items that facilitate the completion of some production or service activity.[22] Two fundamental decisions must be made with respect to the replenishment of any item maintained in inventory: (1) how many should be ordered and (2) when they should be ordered. These decisions are referred to as lot-sizing and lot-timing decisions. The objective of inventory management is to make those decisions in a manner that minimizes the total of inventory-related costs.

Many models have been developed to aid in making lot-sizing and lot-timing decisions under varying conditions. The earliest and perhaps best-known of these models is the classic economic order quantity (EOQ) model. Table 17.2 provides a brief overview of the specifics of this model.

Material requirements planning (MRP)
Methodology that uses the production schedule for the finished products to derive demand and production schedules for component items that make up the final products.

Material Requirements Planning   Excellence in inventory control requires that lot-sizing and lot-timing decisions be made correctly for all items used to construct a product. EOQ models of the type described are quite capable of making the proper sizing and timing decisions for finished products. Unfortunately, they do a poor job of controlling the various raw materials, parts, and components that are assembled into those finished products. **Material requirements planning (MRP)** is a methodology that derives component demands from finished product manufacturing schedules and then uses this information to make the timing and sizing decisions for these lower-level items.

The basic approach of MRP requires that lot-sizing and lot-timing decisions be made first for the finished product so that sufficient finished product will be available to support the master production schedule. These timing and sizing decisions for the finished product will determine the needs for the various components that combine directly into the finished product (that is, the components that are one level of production removed from the finished product). The timing and sizing decisions can then be made for these components so that sufficient amounts will be available to support the planned production of the finished product. Once this has been done, attention is focused on the next lower level of manufacture. By continually linking the successive levels of manufacture, lot-sizing and lot-timing decisions for all raw materials, parts, and components used in making the finished product will be coordinated to ensure that the master production schedule will be met.[23] Since most multistage manufacturing systems have products that consist of

Table 17.2 | Economic Order Quantity Model

- Relevant costs: Annual ordering cost and annual carrying cost
- Symbols used: D = annual demand or usage
  S = cost per order (setup cost or purchase order cost)
  H = carrying cost per unit per year
  Q = order size (which is to be determined)

MODEL STRUCTURE

The total annual carrying cost is the average inventory level multiplied by the cost to carry a unit in inventory for a year. In symbolic form, the average inventory level is $Q/2$; therefore,

  Total annual carrying cost = $(Q/2)(H)$

The total annual ordering cost is equal to the number of orders placed during the year times the cost per order. In symbolic form, the number of orders placed per year is D/Q; therefore,

  Total annual ordering cost = $(D/Q)(S)$

Combining these two costs yields a total cost of

  $$TC = (Q/2)(H) + (D/Q)(S)$$

DETERMINATION OF EOQ

Take the derivative of TC with respect to Q and set equal to zero, then solve for Q:

  $$H/2 - DS/Q^2 = 0$$

An algebraic rearrangement of terms yields the following:

  $$Q^2 = 2DS/H$$

and

  $$Q = \sqrt{2DS/H} \quad \text{(Also called the EOQ)}$$

This is called the EOQ since this is the most economic order quantity.

hundreds or even thousands of individual raw materials, parts, components, subassemblies, and assemblies spanning dozens of levels of manufacture, a computerized system is necessary to perform the massive data-handling and manipulation chores of the MRP process.

Just-in-Time Inventory Management   A phenomenon that has strong implications in the area of inventory control is a philosophy known as just-in-time (JIT) inventory management. This concept initially received considerable attention and refinement within the Japanese industrial community, and it is now quickly spreading worldwide. Despite its concern with inventory, JIT is more than just a technique for dealing with inventory. **Just-in-time (JIT) inventory management** is an overall manufacturing philosophy that advocates eliminating waste, solving problems, and striving for continual improvement in operations.[24]

JIT attempts to reduce inventory because inventory can be costly and can hide problems. For example, problems such as machine breakdowns, high levels of defective output, and worker absenteeism may not cause noticeable disruptions to flow when high levels of inventory exist to "ride over" those problems. JIT attempts to reduce inventory by scheduling smaller but more frequent shipments from internal and external suppliers. Because the ultimate goal is the almost total elimination of inventory, JIT systems are often referred to as zero-inventory systems or

Just-in-time (JIT) inventory management
A philosophy that advocates eliminating waste, solving problems, and striving for continual improvement in operations.

At The Forefront

From Just-in-Case to Just-in-Time at State Industries

State Industries Inc., based in Ashland, Tennessee, is the world's leading manufacturer of water heaters, producing more than two million units each year. Until recently the company's manufacturing control system was home-grown and somewhat primitive. Inventories of fabricated parts were not being tracked very well. According to Lee Spann, Manufacturing Planning and Control Manager, "Because we could not see the shop floor and did not have good communication between departments, we were never sure where each job stood, how much inventory we had, or why our scrap was so high. We had no formal methods for planning work schedules or prioritizing trouble or rush orders." As a result, manufacturing supervisors often spent up to five hours per day trying to determine the status of materials and work-in-process (WIP). This was extremely unproductive use of their time, which would have been much better spent with their attention focused on scheduling and synchronizing the work flow. State had been under constant pressure from customers to

provide lower prices and faster order turnaround time. This was becoming increasingly difficult as production costs rose due to increased labor, energy, and raw material expense. On top of that, the company's antiquated scheduling system wasn't helping matters. WIP part quantities and locations were not visible or controlled. State often had too much of some items and not enough of what was really needed to satisfy short-term demand. Line shortages, rework, scrap, and machine downtime were inflating labor hours per unit produced.

State set an objective to embark on a quest to maximize production output and customer service while substantially reducing manufacturing cost. Spann recognized that State needed to "reengineer the way we work." He identified two goals that would assist in achieving the company's newly stated objective: (1) reduce inventory and (2) reduce the order-to-delivery cycle time. To help meet its objective State implemented dynamic production scheduling software that enabled the company to schedule work orders, coordinate

support functions, manage shop floor execution, and communicate work status and problems. By using this system, orders with material shortages could now be identified so that work would not be started on them if all the needed materials were not available. The system also provided detailed analysis of queue times, setup times, run times, and problem times. With this information, State could identify the best opportunities for cycle time reductions. Raw materials could now be synchronized to production schedules, which could be synchronized to customer demand. With the new scheduling approach the company has seen a 40 percent reduction in order-to-delivery cycle time, and raw materials and WIP inventory reductions on the order of 50 percent. According to Spann, State has changed its mindset from "just-in-case" to one of "just-in-time," and has "regained control of the shop floor."

SOURCE: "From Just-In-Case to Just-In-Time," *APICS-The Performance Advantage*, June 2001, 59.

stockless production systems.[25] Successful JIT requires close cooperation between the supplier and user of a commodity. The benefits of tighter coordination and synchronization of operations afforded by the JIT philosophy are evident in "At the Forefront." Here we see how the world's largest manufacturer of water heaters was able to reduce inventories and reduce delivery cycle times by better controlling the flow of materials through its production facility.

Because little inventory exists in a JIT system, there can be little tolerance for problems because these will inevitably disrupt flow and perhaps stop system output. This happened to General Motors when a 17-day labor strike occurred at two of its brake suppliers. GM was forced to close 22 of its 29 car and truck plants in North America until the labor problem was resolved.[26] This is why JIT is regarded as a broader philosophy of problem solving, waste elimination, and continual improvement. In addition to the zero-inventory ideal, JIT also seeks to attain zero defects (perfect quality), zero breakdowns, zero disruptions, and in general, zero problems. In such systems, workers play an important role in attaining these goals. Not only are workers responsible for their own manufacturing efforts, they are also responsible for such things as quality control, equipment maintenance, housekeeping duties in the work area, and general problem solving in the workplace.[27]

Supply Chain Management　One of the most important areas of focus in recent years has been in the area of **supply chain management,** or **SCM.** A supply chain is de-

Supply chain management (SCM) Management and control of the sequence of suppliers, warehouses, operations, and retail outlets for an organization.

fined as a sequence of suppliers, warehouses, operations, and retail outlets. Supply chain management is a philosophy that describes how organizations should manage their various supply chains to achieve a strategic advantage. SCM seeks to synchronize a firm's functions with those of its suppliers to match the flow of materials, services, and information with customer demand. This requires the development of an internal supply chain that links purchasing, production control, and distribution. Then suppliers and customers must be linked to this internal supply chain, forming an overall integrated supply chain.[28]

Today most organizations face challenges and opportunities brought about by our continuously shrinking world and our global marketplace. Multinational organizations with operating units in different countries may have to set different productivity goals to accommodate differences in work attitudes across national boundaries. In addition, the level of technological development may differ among nations, resulting in significant differences in attainable productivity rates. Political factors may also affect the way the organization can operate in foreign countries.

Even organizations that view themselves as purely domestic are not untouched by aspects of the global marketplace. As we saw in our brief treatment of supply chain management, raw material inputs, purchased parts, and supplies needed in their transformation processes often originate in foreign countries. In these instances, purchasing agreements must cut across national boundaries. Consequently, these so-called domestic companies must be sensitive to the sociocultural, political-legal, technological, and economic environments of the supplying countries.

In addition to global challenges and opportunities, many businesses face challenges and opportunities spawned by ever-increasing sophistication in technology and information-processing capabilities. Even traditional bookstores and music stores will see changes in the way they conduct business. Maintaining inventories may not be as important as in the past if the technologies described next take off. Sprout, Inc., has an arrangement with Borders Books that would allow them to deliver books on demand to customers. The bookstores would be able to download digital versions of books from Sprout, then digitally print, assemble, and bind using a normal paperback binding process. The entire process would be completed in 15 minutes.[29] In a similar vein, Sony Music Entertainment revealed plans to make more than 4,000 albums from its catalog available on demand. Digitally recorded music can be sent directly to stores via a high-speed computer network. A compact disc, complete with liner notes and artwork, would be made while the customer waits.[30]

Thus far, we have seen that operations managers face a wide variety of decisions. To improve the quality of their operations, managers must make these decisions in a way that supports the goals of the organization. We have already noted that organizations can have a variety of goals. When this is the case, managers can move toward achieving excellence in operations by focusing on productivity and quality.

THE ROLE OF PRODUCTIVITY AND QUALITY IN OPERATIONS

Organizational goals can be many and varied. In firms operating on a for-profit basis, bottom-line profit will always have a high priority, while not-for-profit organizations will be more inclined to view service and customer satisfaction as the prime goals. However, any of these firms might also strive to achieve other goals such as market share, improved satisfaction and welfare of its workforce, heightened social and environmental responsibility, and so forth. Operations managers rarely find it easy to relate their decisions directly to these system goals. Fortunately, there are two measures of operations efficiency and effectiveness that indirectly relate to these system goals. In the next section, we will see that productivity is a measure of operations efficiency and quality is a measure of operations effectiveness. Every decision that an operations manager makes—whether a long-term design decision or a short-term operating and control decision—has an impact on productivity and quality. Let's turn our attention to the fundamentals of productivity and examine the ways in which productivity can be improved.

FUNDAMENTALS OF PRODUCTIVITY

LEARNING OBJECTIVE 4

Define the concept of productivity, and identify the three approaches to improving productivity.

Productivity
A measure of the efficiency with which a firm transforms inputs into goods and services.

In Chapter 16 we saw a diagram that showed how all operating systems engage in the transformation of inputs into outputs. **Productivity** is a measure of the efficiency with which a firm performs that transformation process. In the broadest sense, productivity can be defined as the ratio of system outputs to system inputs, or

$$\text{Productivity} = \text{Output/Input}.$$

Measuring productivity is often easier said than done, for outputs can be quite varied and inputs quite diverse. Table 17.3 shows some of the various inputs and outputs for a few manufacturing and nonmanufacturing examples.

Interest in productivity has increased in the United States during recent years, in large part because of the alarming decline in international competitiveness suffered by many U.S. companies. In the last four decades of the 20th century, the United States had one of the lowest annual productivity increases of any of the industrialized nations. Its average annual increase of 3 percent was less than half that of Japan.[31] A lower level of productivity can result because less output is being produced from a given level of input or because more input is needed to achieve a given level of output. In either case, the cost incurred to produce a unit of the good or service will be higher, as will the purchase cost for the customers. This leads to a decline in sales volume, which results in decreased revenues. With less operating revenue, business and industry are likely to lower employment levels, which leads to idle capacity. This is likely to reduce productivity even further, resulting in a snowball effect. Fortunately, in recent years most U.S. industries have recognized this phenomenon. Many firms are attempting to break this vicious cycle by instituting productivity improvement programs.

Table 17.3 | Examples of Inputs and Outputs for Productivity Measurement

OUTPUT	INPUT
Number of refrigerators manufactured	Direct labor hours, raw materials, machinery, supervisory hours, capital
Number of patients treated	Doctor hours, nurse hours, lab technician hours, hospital beds, medical equipment, medicine and drugs, surgical supplies
Number of income tax returns prepared	Staff accounting hours, desktop computers, printers, calculators, typewriters, supplies

IMPROVING PRODUCTIVITY   Any increase in the numerator or decrease in the denominator of the productivity equation will result in a productivity increase. Simply stated, to increase productivity, all that is needed is an increase in output, a decrease in input, or a combination of both. Such changes can be achieved in several ways. We can categorize the productivity-enhancing tactics as being related to technology, people, or design.[32]

Productivity Improvement through Technology   Productivity can be improved through the use of new technology. If, for example, old office equipment and computers are replaced with newer, faster versions, the number of tax returns prepared per labor hour might be expected to increase. Likewise, in the case of manufacturing, if faster equipment replaces slower equipment, more units might be produced per labor hour. Clarke American was able to achieve a significant productivity improvement when the company developed digital printing capability. The productivity improvement was a direct result of the faster processing time, reduced errors, and reduced waste that resulted from the digital printing technology.

Another technological approach to improving productivity is to substitute capital for labor. For example, certain operations that are performed manually may be done by a machine or robot. If the machine has a lower hourly operating cost, higher output rate, and greater precision than a human operator, then the substitution should be considered as a possible means to improve productivity.

Productivity Improvement through People   One of the most important inputs to the productivity equation is the human resource element. We have seen repeatedly throughout this book that the workforce is becoming increasingly more racially, ethnically, and gender diverse. These groups of individuals all have unique sets of values, expectations, motivations, and skills. Their interaction often has a synergistic effect on the work team, enabling the team to achieve results that exceed previous norms.

Effective management of people can often result in significant increases in output without an appreciable increase in the labor cost. This feat can be accomplished through the use of employee compensation programs and employee teams. Many companies have found that compensation can encourage higher productivity. For example, the practice of paying employees bonuses based upon productivity and company profitability has become more popular in recent years.

The most common form of employee team in current practice is the quality circle, which is described more fully later in this chapter. Various companies have given their employee teams different names, but they all have the general objective of increasing employee satisfaction and productivity by providing them with more autonomy and a greater degree of involvement in the decision-making and problem-solving process. Clarke American made use of work teams, improvement teams, and cross-functional teams to achieve the improvements described in "Meeting The Challenge" on page 550.

Productivity Improvement through Design   Several system design issues were described earlier in this chapter. These design decisions can have a direct bearing on productivity. If a product is designed in a way that makes it easier to produce, less time will be spent producing the item, fewer defective units will be produced, and less scrap will result. These improvements will ultimately lead to an increase in productivity. The Ford Motor Company used design simplification to its advantage when it redesigned an instrument panel to contain 6 parts instead of the 22 parts contained in an earlier model. This simplified design led to productivity enhancements.

Process design can also have a significant impact on productivity. If the process has been designed poorly, material flow may be restricted by bottlenecks. Inappropriate placement of work areas and tools can lead to inefficient material flows through the system. These inefficiencies will ultimately lead to greater production time per unit and reduced productivity. Not only did Ford take advantage of simplified product design, as we just described, the company also streamlined many production processes, which resulted in improved productivity.[33]

As we discussed in Chapter 8, job design is the third design area that can impact productivity. If a worker's assigned job has been defined so narrowly that there is no job fulfillment, boredom and a lack of interest are likely to result. In such a situation, the quality of work can be expected to suffer. The resulting defects, scrap, and rework will diminish the level of productivity. To avoid these problems associated with excessive job specialization, many companies adopt philosophies of job enrichment, job enlargement, and job rotation.

As we continue through this chapter, we will encounter more and more evidence suggesting that productivity and quality are intertwined. Improvements in quality are likely to result in improved productivity. Later in this chapter, we will see more specifically how this occurs when we examine the five-step chain reaction of the late W. Edwards Deming, one of the world's foremost authorities on quality. But first, let's examine the fundamentals of quality.

FUNDAMENTALS OF QUALITY

LEARNING OBJECTIVE 5

Provide definitions of quality from both a consumer perspective and a producer perspective.

People sometimes have an inaccurate perception about quality. Too often they assume that quality implies a high degree of luxury or expense. Grandeur, luxuriousness, shininess, and expense are not the prime determinants of quality, however. The following two perspectives provide more accurate definitions of quality. From a consumer perspective, quality can be defined as the degree to which the product or service meets the expectations of the customer. From a producer perspective, quality can be defined as the degree to which the product or service conforms to design specifications. The more effective the organization is in meeting customer expectations and design specifications, the higher the implied quality level of its output.[34]

The Mercedes Benz and Honda Accord are two automobiles with very different prices and quite different features and accessories. However, this does not automatically mean that the more expensive and more elaborate Mercedes has a higher level of quality than the Honda. As the consumer perspective indicates, the test of quality is based upon user expectations. Each automobile has as its function the conveyance of passengers in a particular style, and those styles are different by design.

A similar observation could be made for service organizations. Ritz-Carlton Hotels and Holiday Inns both provide overnight lodging for guests. Ritz-Carlton Hotels feature larger, more elaborately decorated rooms with more amenities than Holiday Inns provide. However, one fact remains common to both. Each provides overnight sleeping and bathing accommodations for travelers. Ultimately, it is the individual guest who must determine the level of quality associated with these accommodations.

Once an organization selects the product or service it will provide, design decisions are made that ultimately shape the product or service design characteristics. If the completed product or service output meets those design characteristics, the output will be viewed as high quality from the production perspective. If this output fails to meet customer expectations, however, then the initial design was probably inadequate, for the customer is not likely to purchase it regardless of the quality level that production perceives. Businesses are increasingly adopting this consumer perspective on quality. For example, if an Eckerd Photolab fails to have a customer's film developed by its promised date, there is no charge to the customer. Southtrust Bank of Orlando will pay customers $1 if they have to wait more

Leaders In Action

Conway's BBQ Launches New Venture

Southerners do love their barbecue, and that is no more evident than in Central Florida. One locally owned restaurant with a growing reputation and growing customer base is Conway's BBQ. Started in 1995 with a single Orlando outlet, Conway's tripled its number of restaurants in a few short years. In addition to its sit-down and carryout restaurant business, Conway's has cashed in on the lucrative catering business; its catering service accounts for about 60 percent of the company's business. The concept is not new. Big cookers, typically pulled by a truck, have been a mainstay at catered backyard parties for years. But for Conway's, the geography of Central Florida often proved to be an impediment to this kind of catering. Look at a map of Central Florida and you will see terrain that is dotted with hundreds of lakes and waterways. Drive the streets and you will find many of the homes on these bodies of water lie in gated communities. As Douglas Colson, co-owner of Conway's BBQ, noted, "We had a hard time getting our big cookers into people's back yards." Problems encountered included getting clearance to enter gated communities, negotiating tight turns and narrow passageways into back yards, and tearing up landscaping.

Colson had a creative idea for a remedy—a custom-made "cooker boat," in effect, a floating mobile cooker. When he revealed his idea, many people thought he was crazy. But Colson found a tour-boat builder willing to work with him. The result—a 30-foot modified tri-hull pontoon-type boat with a 90 horsepower Mercury outboard motor and four gas-fired cookers. The floating mobile cooker is simply towed to a boat ramp and then launched. Complete with a computerized Global Positioning System (GPS), it can be operated on any navigable waterway. The boat will cruise right up to the boat dock or backyard to cater the private party. Diners will board the boat via a ramp, get their food, and then return to shore to eat. With all four cookers cranked up, it can turn out enough barbecued chicken and ribs for parties of 1,500 or more. In order to satisfy health regulations, the boat has been equipped to store hot and cold foods safely and has additional storage for all the accessories needed for a successful BBQ. The competition has already stood up and taken notice. Insiders fully expect to see competitors "launching" similar ventures in the near future.

SOURCES: **www.conwaysbbq.com**; J. Jackson, "Conway's BBQ Floats New Catering Idea," *Central Florida Business*, June 10, 2002, 6.

than one minute for service, $5 if they are not treated courteously, and $10 if a mistake is made on a customer's bank statement. Time Warner will provide free cable TV installation if their installation technician does not arrive at the appointed time. This list could go on and on. Think about the service encounters that you have had. Do you know any companies that make similar provisions in their attempts to deliver quality service? In "Leaders In Action" we can see how cleverness and ingenuity helped Conway's BBQ redesign a segment of its business to provide better service to its customers.

Although the terms *quality control, quality assurance,* and *total quality management* (or *total quality control*) are often used interchangeably, these concepts are not identical. **Quality control (QC)** has the narrowest focus; it refers to the actual measurement and assessment of output to determine whether the specifications are being met. The responsibility for taking corrective actions when standards are not being met is also in the domain of quality control. Statistical procedures are useful in quality control. **Quality assurance (QA)** concerns itself with any activity that influences the maintenance of quality at the desired level. It refers to the entire system of policies, procedures, and guidelines that the organization has established to achieve and maintain quality. Quality assurance extends from the design of products and processes to the quality assessment of the system outputs. **Total quality management (TQM)** has an even broader focus than quality assurance, for its goal is to manage the entire organization in a manner that allows it to excel in the delivery of a product or service that meets customer needs. Before we look at TQM in more detail, it will be helpful to examine the factors for assessing quality.

Quality control (QC)
Focuses on the actual measurement of output to see whether specifications have been met.

Quality assurance (QA)
Focuses on any activity that influences the maintenance of quality at the desired level.

Total quality management (TQM)
A systematic approach for enhancing products, services, processes, and operational quality control.

LEARNING OBJECTIVE 6

Identify factors that can be used to assess the quality of products and services.

FACTORS FOR ASSESSING QUALITY   A customer might evaluate many aspects of a product or service to determine whether it meets expectations. These aspects differ slightly for products and services.

Product Factors   When evaluating the quality of a product, a customer will probably first notice aesthetic characteristics, which are usually perceived by sensory re-

actions. The customer will observe how the product looks, sounds, feels, smells, or tastes. A product's features are also likely to be judged early. If you were about to purchase an automobile, for example, you might look for such features as a stereo system, air bags, and power seats. Performance is another aspect that helps determine whether the product meets the customer's needs and expectations. If you do a lot of highway driving, acceleration and passing power are probably important to you, so you would check these performance characteristics before making your purchase decision. Another important aspect of quality is reliability, which refers to the likelihood that the product will continue to perform satisfactorily through its guarantee period. You might ascertain this through product warranty information or by referring to a consumer magazine such as *Consumer Reports*.

This customer is evaluating how the product looks and feels to determine whether it meets her needs.

The serviceability aspect of a product's quality refers to the difficulty, time, and expense of getting repairs. In the case of your automobile purchase, you might assess this by considering the location and business hours of the dealer's automobile service center. The durability aspect refers to the length of time the product is likely to last. Both the manufacturer and independent consumer agencies might be a source of data here. Conformance reflects the degree to which the product meets the specifications set by the designers. For example, you will undoubtedly check to be sure that the automobile possesses all the accessories that the advertising suggests it will have. A final aspect is perceived quality, which has been described as an overall feeling of confidence based upon observations of the potential purchase, the reputation of the company, and any past experiences with purchases of this type.[35]

Service Factors   The product quality factors just described can be relevant to a service encounter if some physical commodity is delivered to the customer. For example, when you dine at a restaurant, the meal can be judged according to most of those characteristics. Unfortunately, service quality is sometimes more difficult to assess with quantitative measures. Suppose you visit a dentist for emergency treatment of a broken tooth. In this case you would use other attributes to measure your satisfaction with service quality. Responsiveness reflects the willingness and speed with which the service personnel (that is, the dentist, nurse, and receptionist) attend to you. Reliability is a measure of the dependability and accuracy of the service performed. Assurance refers to the feeling of trust and confidence you have in the service personnel. Empathy reflects the degree of attention and caring that the service personnel provide to you. Finally, tangibles are an assessment of such factors as the appearance of the service personnel, cleanliness of the equipment and physical system, and comfort of the surroundings.[36]

You should not get the mistaken impression that the list of product factors is applicable only to manufacturing situations and the list of service factors only to service encounters. Depending on the type of product or service being judged, items from either list might be applicable. These lists of product and service factors must be viewed as neither exclusive nor exhaustive.

LEARNING OBJECTIVE 7

Describe the four categories of quality-related costs.

COST OF QUALITY   Any costs that a company incurs because it has produced less than perfect quality output, or costs that it incurs to prevent less than perfect quality output, are referred to as the cost of quality. The cost of quality can be organized into the following four major categories:[37]

Prevention Costs Prior to the production of the product or the delivery of the service, several activities can be performed in an attempt to prevent defective output from occurring. These activities include designing products, processes, and jobs for quality; reviewing designs; educating and training workers in quality concepts; and working with suppliers. The costs of these activities are the prevention costs.

Appraisal Costs Appraisal costs are incurred to assess the quality of the product that has been manufactured or the service that has been provided. They include the costs of testing equipment and instruments, the costs of maintaining that equipment, and the labor costs associated with performing the inspections.

Internal-Failure Costs Defective output that is detected before it leaves the system will either be scrapped (discarded) or reworked (repaired). If it is scrapped, the company incurs the cost of all materials and labor that went into the production of that output. If it is reworked, a cost is incurred for the material and labor that went into the defective portion that was replaced or repaired. In addition, more material and labor costs are incurred for the rework activities. These costs all contribute to the internal-failure costs.

External-Failure Costs Defective output that is not detected before being delivered to the customer incurs external-failure costs. This category consists of the costs associated with customer complaints, returns, warranty claims, product recalls, and product liability suits.

The current popular view holds that prevention costs do not have to be increased substantially to reduce the number of defective units. Furthermore, this view suggests that as prevention costs increase, appraisal costs will decrease, since less testing and inspection will be necessary due to inherently lower numbers of defective units. Meanwhile, failure costs will also decrease with the reduced number of defective units.[38] Figure 17.3 displays these cost relationships and suggests that the most cost-effective way of doing business is close to, if not at, the zero-defect level.

Prevention costs
The costs associated with any activities that are performed in an attempt to prevent defective output from occurring.

Appraisal costs
The costs associated with any activities that are performed in an attempt to assess the quality of the product that has been manufactured or the service that has been provided.

Internal-failure costs
The costs associated with the repair or disposition of defective output that is detected prior to delivery to the customer.

External-failure costs
The costs resulting from defective output that is not detected prior to delivery to the customer.

Figure 17.3 | Quality Costs

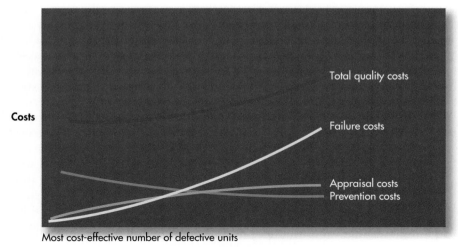

Although these concepts of quality-related costs may seem to apply only to the physical products of manufacturing systems, service organizations can also benefit from paying attention to quality-related costs. Providing poor-quality service will lead to failure costs, just as with poor-quality products. However, in the case of service organizations, external-failure costs tend to be much greater than internal-failure costs. This is a result of the customer's direct involvement in the service transaction. There is usually little opportunity to check the quality of the service before the service encounter with the customer. Defective service is generally not detected until the service act has transpired. At that point failure costs are by definition in the external category.

TOTAL QUALITY MANAGEMENT AS A TOOL FOR GLOBAL COMPETITIVENESS

LEARNING OBJECTIVE 8

Identify the various areas of concentration and commitment for a program of total quality management.

Emphasis on quality is a key to achieving excellence in operations in today's global economy. This emphasis on quality is crucial for two reasons: (1) customers are becoming increasingly conscious of quality in their choice of products and services, and (2) increased quality leads to increased productivity and its associated benefits. It is no secret that in recent years U.S. manufacturers have struggled with the loss of market share to foreign competitors in the global marketplace. These losses have been attributed to the notion (in some cases real and in some cases perceived) that the foreign competitors have been able to supply products of higher quality and at a lower price. People who are trying to get the most from their disposable income have understandably been attracted to these products. These shifts to foreign manufacturers are evidence that consumers do consider the product factors discussed earlier prior to making purchase decisions. Any manufacturer who hopes to reverse this declining market share can begin to do so by focusing on the quality aspects of the product. A program of total quality management is one of the most effective ways to enhance an organization's competitive position. Clarke American made a commitment to distinguish itself from its competitors by focusing on providing quality products and the highest level of customer service in the industry. Its First-In-Service (FIS) program ensured that associates at all levels of the organization understood and practiced its quality principles. This commitment was instrumental in Clarke American being named "Best of the Best" by the Master Printers of America (MPA) for 2001.[39]

External customer

User of an item who is not a part of the organization that supplies the item.

CUSTOMER-DRIVEN STANDARDS   Since one definition of quality centers on meeting customer expectations, the external customer should play a central role in establishing product or service standards. An **external customer** is a user who is not part of the organization that supplies the product or service. The external customer can be the ultimate consumer (that is, end user), or it can be some intermediary encountered as the product or service works its way toward the end user. Marketing will be instrumental in assessing the wants and needs of external customers. These wants and needs can then be conveyed to design engineers, who will make the product and service design decisions. Process design decisions will then follow. Ultimately, the product or service will be easier to sell if customers recognize that the product or service has been designed to satisfy their needs.

Internal customer

User of an item who is a member of, or employee of, the organization that supplies the item.

In some cases a customer may be an **internal customer**, which is a user who is part of the organization that supplies the product or service. For example, the internal customer might be the next worker or next department in the production process. Internal customers also have quality requirements that must be considered in the product or service design stage. In essence, everybody in the organization is a supplier to some customer, and these supplier-customer links represent a major area of concern in total quality management.

MANAGEMENT AND LABOR COMMITMENT Recall from Chapter 11 the concepts of organizational culture and organizational change. If total quality management is to pervade all levels of an organization successfully, management must develop an organizational culture in which all workers are committed to the philosophy. This requires a strong commitment from top-level management, where the values to be shared by the organization originate. If all parts of the organization are to coordinate toward a common goal, then this goal must be embraced at the top. Top-level management must not only communicate this goal, but also demonstrate a commitment to the goal through its actions, policies, and decisions. Management must back up slogans and catchy phrases with a willingness to institute changes, a receptiveness to employee suggestions, and recognition and reward for improvements. Clarke American embraced this philosophy when the company organized a Key Leadership Team (KLT) consisting of top executives, general managers of business divisions, and vice presidents. The function of the KLT was to establish, communicate, and deploy values, direction, and performance expectations. KLT members were expected to be role models who demonstrated commitment and passion for performance excellence. The company also instituted a S.T.A.R (Suggestions, Teams, Actions, Results) program that empowered workers to exercise individual initiative and innovation through its suggestion component. In 2001 employees received an average bonus of $5,000 per person for improvement suggestions made. You will see more detail on these programs and their results in "Meeting The Challenge."[40]

ORGANIZATION AND COORDINATION OF EFFORTS We have already seen that total quality management will result in a wide variety of diverse personnel interactions. Marketing serves as an intermediary between external customers and design engineers, who in turn interact with production personnel. In order to improve their operations, companies will often compare their own products, services, or processes against those of industry leaders. This process, called **benchmarking**, is a useful aid in understanding how outstanding companies do things so that their excellence in operations can be replicated. The internal supplier-customer links lead to many interactions among production personnel. Purchasing must interact with external suppliers. Since more and more organizations are buying and selling in international markets, many of these firms are striving to conform to a set of standards called ISO 9000. Devised by the International Organization for Standardization, ISO 9000 is a set of standards governing documentation of a quality program within a company. Upon becoming certified, companies are listed in a directory so that potential customers can see who has been certified. If total quality management is to be successful, communication links must be established between all of these internal and external entities to achieve proper coordination. Clarke American relied on emerging technology to establish such links. Its ServicePlus system allowed for electronic linkage between production facilities, partners, and customers. In addition, its InTouch printing and database interface allows financial institutions to communicate with customers.[41] As we saw in Chapter 9, such coordination efforts lead to a teamwork philosophy among all participants in the organization. A fundamental principle of total quality management is that all participants should be focused on making continuous improvements, or what the Japanese refer to as **kaizen**.

EMPLOYEE PARTICIPATION A central theme of the total quality management approach is that all employees should be brought into the decision-making and problem-solving process. After all, those who are doing the work are closest to the action and will probably have valuable opinions about methods for quality improvement. This is an outgrowth of what we learned in Chapter 6 about participative decision making and the advantages it can bring to an organization. By

Benchmarking
The process of comparing one's own products, services, or processes against those of industry leaders for the purpose of improvement.

Kaizen
Japanese term referring to the total quality management principle of continuous improvement.

providing the workers with an opportunity to express their opinions, worker morale and motivation are enhanced. Workers develop more of a sense of responsibility and connection to their jobs. Worker participation is further enhanced by the use of teams. In "Meeting The Challenge" on page 550 you will see detail on how Clarke American's use of work teams and improvement teams contributed heavily to improvements in quality, productivity, and bottom-line profitability. Two of the more popular types of teams are quality circles and special-purpose teams.

Quality circle
A work team that meets regularly to identify, analyze, and solve problems related to its work area.

Quality Circles   A **quality circle** is a small group of supervisors and employees from the same work area.[42] Most quality circles have between 6 and 12 members, and membership is voluntary. Quality circles meet on a regular basis (usually weekly) to identify, analyze, and solve production and quality problems related to the work done in their part of the company. Many benefits accrue from quality circles. When workers are allowed to help shape their work, they usually take more pride and interest in it. Furthermore, quality circles have the potential to uncover and solve many problems or suggest ways to achieve improvements in operations. Even though some of these improvements may be minor, collectively they can result in substantial cost savings, quality improvements, and productivity increases in the organization.

Special-purpose team
A temporary team formed to solve a special or nonrecurring problem.

Special-Purpose Teams   On occasion, a **special-purpose team** may have to be formed to solve a special or nonrecurring problem.[43] Unlike quality circles, special-purpose teams are likely to draw their members from many departments or work areas and bring together people from different functional specialties. For example, if some characteristic of a product no longer conforms to customer needs, marketing personnel will need to be on the team to explain the wants and needs of the customers. Design engineers would be needed to help translate those needs into new product design specifications. Production personnel would also be needed to determine whether and how the redesigned product can be manufactured. Special-purpose teams also differ from quality circles in longevity. Quality circles are standing teams that continue in existence over time. Special-purpose teams are *ad hoc* groups that disband after the problem has been resolved.

PROMINENT QUALITY MANAGEMENT PHILOSOPHERS

LEARNING OBJECTIVE 9

Describe the major contributions of the most prominent contemporary quality philosophers.

Many of today's business organizations are placing more and more emphasis on quality because they are aware of how much it has helped their competition. It is safe to say that, in general, U.S. business organizations were a step behind many of their foreign competitors. Those competitors were able to get a head start in quality by taking the advice of some of the noted quality philosophers and consultants long before U.S. organizations did.

Perhaps the most prominent quality philosopher was W. Edwards Deming, an American who was considered the father of quality control in Japan. Deming emphasized the importance of improving quality through his five-step chain reaction, which proposes that, when quality is improved, (1) costs decrease because of less rework, fewer mistakes, fewer delays, and better use of time and materials; (2) productivity improves; (3) market share increases with better quality and prices; (4) the company increases profitability and stays in business; and (5) the number of jobs increases.[44] Deming devised a 14-point plan to summarize his philosophy on quality improvement. Table 17.4 lists Deming's 14 points.

Joseph Juran is another of the pioneers in quality management. Juran's experiences revealed that over 80 percent of quality defects are caused by factors controllable by management. This led Juran to develop a trilogy of quality planning, control, and improvement.[45] Quality planning involves linking product and service design with process design to achieve the quality characteristics desired. Quality control involves comparing products or services to standards and then correcting

Table 17.4 | Deming's 14 Points

1. Create constancy of purpose for improvement of product and service, and communicate this aim to all employees.
2. Learn and adopt the new philosophy throughout all levels within the organization.
3. Understand that inspection only measures problems but does not correct them; quality comes from improving processes.
4. Reduce the number of suppliers, and do not award business on the basis of price tag alone.
5. Constantly improve processes, products, and services while reducing waste.
6. Institute modern aids to training on the job.
7. Improve supervision.
8. Drive out fear of expressing ideas and reporting problems.
9. Break down barriers between departments and get people working toward the goals of the organization as a team.
10. Eliminate slogans, exhortations, and targets for the workforce.
11. Eliminate numerical quotas for production; concentrate on quality, not quantity.
12. Remove barriers that rob people of pride of workmanship.
13. Institute a program of education and self-improvement for everyone.
14. Put everyone in the organization to work to accomplish the transformation.

SOURCE: Deming, W. Edwards, "Out of the Crisis," (Cambridge, MA: Massachusetts Institute of Technology, Center for Advanced Engineering Study, 1986).

undesirable deviations. (This part of the trilogy relates directly to what we learned about control in Chapter 16.) The final part of the trilogy involves getting into the habit of making significant improvements every year. An area with chronic quality problems is selected and analyzed, and an alternative is selected and implemented.

Other notable names in the area of quality are Armand Feigenbaum, Kaoru Ishikawa, and Phillip Crosby. Feigenbaum is credited with introducing the concept of total quality control and developing the quality cost categories described earlier in this chapter.[46] Ishikawa is credited with introducing quality-control circles, and he also developed the fishbone diagram (or cause-and-effect diagram), which helps to identify the causes of quality problems.[47] Crosby introduced the philosophy that "quality is free."[48] In his opinion, the most cost-effective level of defects is zero defects. Crosby contends that with no defects, rework costs are saved, scrap is eliminated, labor and machine time costs are reduced, and product failure costs are eliminated. Crosby believes that these cost reductions far outweigh the costs incurred in creating an environment that promotes the achievement of high quality. Crosby's philosophy is very much like the old adage "An ounce of prevention is worth a pound of cure."

NASA's experience with the Hubble Space Telescope dramatically illustrates this point. This $1.5 billion orbiting laboratory was launched for the purpose of viewing outer space. Not long after the launch, astronomers discovered that the telescope's view of the stars was somewhat blurred due to the incorrect grinding and polishing of its primary mirror. A relatively simple test costing a few hundred thousand dollars could have detected this flaw. As it turned out, repairs didn't come this easily or cheaply to NASA. To correct this defect and make a variety of other repairs, the space shuttle *Endeavour* embarked upon an 11-day mission. The repairs required five separate space walks by astronauts spaced over five days. The mission cost $750 million—$250 million for replacement parts and $500 million for the shuttle flight.[49]

We first learned in Chapter 1 of the increasing level of diversity in the work place, and we continued to see the implications of such diversity throughout this book. NASA provides one of the most visible examples of increasing diversity in the workforce. Astronaut crews on shuttle missions have become more diverse in race, nationality, and gender over the years. Kathy Thornton was one of the four astronauts who spent more than 35 space-walking hours repairing the ailing Hubble Telescope.[50] In late 1996 astronaut Shannon Lucid completed more than six months aboard space station *Mir*, eclipsing the space endurance record for women and, in the process, spending more time in space than any American astronaut before her.[51] And in mid-1999 Eileen Collins became the first woman to serve as commander of a space shuttle flight when she took the helm of *Columbia* on its five-day mission to deliver the Chandra X-ray Observatory into earth orbit.[52]

IMPACT OF INFORMATION TECHNOLOGY ON PRODUCTIVITY AND QUALITY

Advances and developments in information technology have had a profound and positive effect on productivity in operations. A quick reflection on the productivity formula (output divided by input) suggests that anything that enables one to achieve more output with the same amount of input, or the same amount of output with less input, will improve an organization's productivity. In the past few decades there have been many advances in information-processing capabilities that have positively influenced productivity. Computer-aided design and computer-aided manufacturing allow firms to link and manipulate information electronically, facilitating coordination of the design and manufacturing functions. Efficient designs and efficient manufacturing processes lead to less waste, smoother manufacturing, and a correspondingly higher level of productivity. On an even broader basis, information can be linked across all business functions within an organization by means of computer-integrated manufacturing (CIM). By linking the business functions with the engineering functions, companies are better able to respond to changes in the marketplace with new products or new designs of existing products. In the course of this chapter we have seen several examples of how Clarke American was able to use information technology to do such things as link its facilities with customers, provide better system-wide communication, and provide higher quality products more quickly to its customers.

Advances in information-processing capabilities have also allowed companies to gravitate toward being lean production systems (LPS). These systems combine an understanding of quality with a desire to eliminate all kinds of waste. The just-in-time, material requirements planning, and supply chain management systems described earlier in this chapter are compatible with this waste-elimination philosophy as they strive to have the right parts available in the right quantities and at the right time. The use of information technology to boost productivity is not restricted to manufacturing organizations. Ryder Systems, Inc., a seemingly low-tech trucking company, is actually on the cutting edge when it comes to using information technology to improve productivity and become more competitive. Its Fast Track Maintenance Service uses a computer chip to record information from electronic sensors on a truck's engine while the truck is being driven. When routine maintenance is due, or when a problem occurs, that information can be downloaded, resulting in greatly reduced downtime for maintenance or repair.[53]

It should not go unnoticed in this discussion that the technological advances that enhance productivity will also have a positive effect on quality. With more efficient and effective design tools, products and services that satisfy customer needs should result. With more efficient and effective production and delivery systems, there is a greater likelihood that the delivered goods or services will meet their design specifications and at the same time satisfy the wants and needs of the customers. Once again, witness the competitive advantages achieved by Clarke American, as described in "Meeting The Challenge" on the following page.

In this chapter we have seen that operations management has a strong decision-making orientation in both manufacturing and service organizations. We have also learned that the concepts of productivity and quality are extremely important for assessing the efficiency and effectiveness of operations decisions. Let's conclude the chapter by considering the implications of these concepts for tomorrow's leaders.

IMPLICATIONS FOR LEADERS

Excellence in operations can be achieved only if business leaders strive to achieve perfection in all of the decision-making areas related to operations. Particular attention should be paid to long-term system design decisions. Because of the difficulty in reversing decisions in this area, leaders may get only one chance at them. If a poor decision is made, operations may have to suffer the negative consequences for quite some time. Once the design decisions are behind them, leaders must shift their attention to short-term operating and control decisions. These decisions will continue to recur throughout the life of the organization, so leaders should strive for continual improvement in this decision-making focus.

If leaders are to make high-quality design and operating decisions, they will have to become thoroughly familiar with the nature of the specific decision issues in these broad areas, and at the same time must equip themselves with the tools and techniques that can aid in the making those decisions. This embodies the competence component of the 3Cs leadership model. However, as we saw earlier in Chapter 7, good decision making requires more than just competence; it also encompasses the remaining elements of the 3Cs leadership model. Good decision making requires that the decision maker possess strong character, infused with honesty, integrity, and driven by ethical behavior. It also requires a recognition that the impact of the decisions made may extend to the community and not be confined to the boundaries of the organization. In short, tomorrow's business leaders must:

- Be prepared to make the tough decisions that commit to a long-term design for the operating system.
- Strive for perfection in making recurring short-term operating and control decisions.
- Focus on achieving continual improvement as these operating and control decisions are made repeatedly throughout the life of the organization.
- Be aware of the importance of productivity to organizational success, and understand the ways in which productivity can be improved.
- Recognize the links between productivity and quality.
- Focus on improving the quality of the product or service provided.

The quality-productivity link is best illustrated by Deming's five-step chain reaction, which states that improved quality leads to lower labor and material costs, which lead to an improvement in productivity, which results in higher-quality and lower-cost items (and an associated increase in market share), which lead to increased profitability and an increase in the number of jobs. Emphasis on quality will enable tomorrow's business leaders to reap the benefits of this quality-productivity chain reaction.

Meeting The Challenge

Clarke American Responds with Operational Changes

In the early 1990s an excess manufacturing capacity in the check printing industry triggered aggressive price competition. It was at that point that Clarke American decided it was not going to enter that battle. Instead, the company elected to distinguish itself through service. Company leaders made a commitment to the firm's "First in Service" (FIS) approach to business excellence. FIS is the driving force behind the Clarke American continuous improvement initiatives, aligning the company's goals and actions with the goals of its partners and the customers of these financial institutions. The Key Leadership Team (KLT), consisting of top-level associates, demonstrated a commitment and passion for excellence that served as a role model for the rest of the organization.

Clarke American organized associates into work teams and improvement teams to seek short-term improvements and to guide the running of the business. Cross-functional project teams were also formed to seek long-term improvements and "changing the business" initiatives. Realizing that empowered and accomplishment-oriented associates are its greatest competitive advantage, Clarke American created its S.T.A.R. (Suggestions, Teams, Actions, Results) incentive program to foster individual initiative and innovation. Through S.T.A.R., associates are encouraged to contribute improvement ideas. In 2001 more than 20,000 process improvement ideas saved the company an estimated $10 million. As a result, financial rewards flowed back to the associates, who averaged nearly $5,000 in bonus and profit sharing payouts in 2001.

In addition to these changes in organization culture, Clarke American also invested substantially in new technology to improve performance and better satisfy its customers. The company developed a digital printing capability that enables it to provide faster and more customized products and services. Additional innovations from Clarke American include:

- MyStyle, a program that allows customers to order one-of-a-kind checks featuring photos of family, friends, pets, hobbies, special interests, among others.
- AddressNet, an error reduction and fraud protection program that ensures that addresses are printed correctly and destined for a verified, valid U.S. address. AddressNet will verify an address and can automatically change the ZIP code that goes with the address, add a missing suffix to the street address, and add the directional to the street name. The system can also detect streets that do not exist in a particular ZIP code, and house or building numbers that do not exist on a particular street.
- Check Reorder Express, an online check-reordering program that allows customers to easily change from their previous check design.
- ServiceLine Plus, a program that allows customers to send orders from anywhere, at any time, and through any channel, 24 hours per day and 7 days per week.
- InTouch, which is a printing and database interface that enables financial institutions to communicate directly with their customers.
- Enhanced Security Level (ESL) and Void Pantograph (VP) technologies to help deter and detect check alterations and counterfeiting. By taking advantage of advances in safety paper, check designs, invisible ink, and foil technologies, Clarke American has designed checks that protect against counterfeiting. If a check is photocopied or scanned, the word "VOID" will dramatically appear across the face of the copy.
- Late Day Rush Service, a program that allows customers to order checks by 4:00 P.M. Pacific Standard Time Monday through Friday, and receive delivery by the end of the next business day.
- Information Security, for which Clark American has earned its Internet environment security certification from TruSecure Corporation, the worldwide leader in security assurances for Internet connected companies.

This impressive list of innovations is by no means exhaustive, but it does illustrate the lengths Clarke American went to improve service to its customers.

The changes instituted by Clarke American certainly paid off. The company has been able to provide faster service, more customized products, reduced production cycle time, reduced errors, reduced waste, and improved quality. It is enjoying an unprecedented 96 percent satisfaction rate from customers, by far the highest in the industry. Partner loyalty increased some 33 percent in the first 18 months of the 21st century. Annual revenue growth, which was a little over 4 percent in the mid-1990s, increased to 16 percent in 2000. This far outshines the industry average of 1 percent per year. Many accolades have followed these stunning improvement figures. Clarke American was named San Antonio's "Organization of the Year" in 1999. The company was the single recipient of the prestigious Texas Award for Performance Excellence for the year 2001. The company also received the 2001 Best Workplace in America Award from the Master Printers of America. However, the crowning moment came in March 2002 when Clarke American was presented the Malcolm Baldrige National Quality Award for 2001 by President George W. Bush.

SOURCE: "Malcolm Baldrige National Quality Award, 2001 Award Recipient, Manufacturing Category, Clarke American Checks Inc.," **http://www.nist.gov; http://www.clarkeamerican.com**.

SUMMARY

1. Manufacturing organizations produce a physical product that can be stored in inventory and transported to different locations. Productivity and quality of this physical output are usually easy to measure. Service organizations differ in that their capacity is time perishable, customers are typically active participants in the service process, and their locations must be close to the customers.

2. Operating systems can lie anywhere along a volume/variety continuum that extends from high volume and low variety on one extreme to low volume and high variety on the other extreme. Manufacturing organizations can be classified as repetitive manufacturing systems or continuous-flow systems at the high-volume/low-variety extreme and job-shop systems or project systems at the low-volume/high-variety extreme. Service organizations can be classified as standard service systems at the high-volume/low-variety extreme and custom service systems at the low-volume/high-variety extreme.

3. Most operations management decisions can be classified as either long-term system design decisions or short-term operating and control decisions. Important long-term system design decisions include choice of a product or service, product or service design, system capacity, process selection, facility location, and facility layout. Important short-term operating and control decisions include aggregate planning, master production scheduling, inventory management, material requirements planning, just-in-time inventory management, and supply chain management.

4. Productivity is a measure of the efficiency with which an organization converts inputs to outputs. It is measured as a ratio of system outputs to system inputs. Productivity can be improved through technology, people, or design.

5. From a consumer perspective, quality can be defined as the degree to which the product or service meets the expectations of the customer. From a producer perspective, quality can be defined as the degree to which the product or service conforms to design specifications.

6. When evaluating the quality of a physical product, consumers often base their judgments on their sensory perceptions of the product (its look, sound, feel, smell, or taste), its features, performance, reliability, serviceability, durability, and conformance to specifications. In the case of service encounters, consumers' assessments of quality might also include consideration of their feeling of trust and confidence in the service personnel, the responsiveness and empathy provided by the service personnel, the dependability and accuracy of the service performance, and various tangible factors associated with the service environment.

7. There are four categories of quality-related costs. Prevention costs are incurred to prevent defective output from occurring. Appraisal costs are incurred to assess the quality of the output. Internal-failure costs are associated with defective units that are detected before they reach the customers. External-failure costs are associated with defective units that are not detected before they reach the customers.

8. To achieve a successful total quality management program, concentration, commitment, and improvement should be focused on meeting customer expectations, attaining commitment to the philosophy and participation from every individual within the organization, and achieving coordination among all departments and functional specialties within the organization.

9. W. Edwards Deming proposed a five-step chain reaction in which excellence in quality eventually leads to improved productivity, increased market share, increased profitability, and more jobs. Joseph Juran developed a trilogy of quality planning, control, and improvement. Armand Feigenbaum is credited with originating the concept of total quality control, Kaoru Ishikawa introduced the idea of quality circles, and Phillip Crosby developed the philosophy that quality is free.

REVIEW QUESTIONS

1. (*Learning Objective 1*) Discuss the differences between manufacturing and service organizations.

2. (*Learning Objective 2*) Discuss the volume/variety continuum for categorizing operating systems and provide examples of both manufacturing and service organizations for each of the major categories.

3. (*Learning Objective 3*) Identify the two major categories for classifying the decisions faced by the operations function and list the decision that operations managers face in each of these categories.

4. (*Learning Objective 4*) List and briefly describe the three categories of tactics that might be used to enhance productivity.

5. (*Learning Objective 5*) Provide a definition of quality from a consumer perspective and a definition from a producer perspective.

6. (*Learning Objective 6*) List the different aspects of a product that might be judged in an attempt to assess its quality, and list the different aspects of a service that might be judged in an attempt to assess its quality.

7. (*Learning Objective 7*) Briefly describe the four categories of quality costs, and provide an example of each.

8. *(Learning Objective 8)* Briefly describe the areas of concentration and commitment for a program of total quality management.

9. *(Learning Objective 9)* Describe the major contributions of several prominent quality philosophers.

DISCUSSION QUESTIONS

Improving Critical Thinking

1. JIT advocates a holistic view of workers that takes advantage of all their skills, knowledge, and experiences and gives them added duties and responsibilities. Discuss these added duties and responsibilities, and compare this view with the traditional manufacturing view of workers. How do you feel these enhanced responsibilities might affect worker motivation and dedication to the job?

2. It has often been said that poor quality and poor productivity will detract from a company's competitiveness. Discuss the chain of events that you think would lead from poor quality and poor productivity to the eventual loss of competitiveness.

Enhancing Communication Skills

3. Imagine the way material would flow through a custom machine shop that fabricates metal parts for customers. Then imagine the way patients would flow through a walk-in emergency clinic. Discuss the similarities between the flows in these two systems. To enhance your oral communication skills, prepare a short (10–15-minute) presentation for the class in which you describe the flow similarities in these two systems.

4. Consider the aggregate planning problem in which the demand for a product or service is seasonal. List as many strategies as you can that could be used to cope with the fluctuating demand pattern. Try to identify strategies that you might use from an operations standpoint, and also try to envision strategies that you might use from a marketing standpoint (in an attempt to induce changes in the demand pattern). Finally, indicate which of your strategies might not be viable in a service organization. To enhance your written communication skills, prepare a short (one- to two-page) essay in which you describe the strategies in each category and explain which strategies probably aren't appropriate for service organizations.

Building Teamwork

5. The Crosby "quality is free" philosophy suggests that the only acceptable level of behavior is zero defects. Try to think of examples that might contradict this philosophy. That is, identify situations where the cost of totally eliminating defects might be higher than the failure cost incurred with a moderate level of defects. To refine your teamwork skills, meet with a small group of students who have been given the same assignment. Compare and discuss your selections, and then reach a consensus on the two best choices. Select a spokesperson to present your choices to the rest of the class.

6. Meet with a small group of students as directed by your instructor. To refine your teamwork skills, this group will operate as a quality circle. Discuss with one another some of the problems you have encountered in conjunction with your college education. These problems can cover any aspect of your education and may relate to interactions with administration, faculty, or support services (for example, the library, the computer center, and the like). Reach a consensus on the most important or urgent problem, then conduct a brainstorming session to develop potential solutions to this problem. Select a spokesperson to present your problem and potential solutions to the rest of the class.

THINKING CRITICALLY: DEBATE THE ISSUE

Is Zero Defects the Most Cost-Effective Way?

Form teams of four or five students as directed by your instructor. Research the topic of quality costs and how they behave as one strives for higher levels of quality (that is, higher levels of conformance to standards or lower levels of defective output). You will find that one theory holds that total quality costs will continually decrease and be at their lowest at a zero-defects level. (This is the current popular theory described in this chapter.) Another theory, however, holds that total quality costs will initially decrease, but then begin to increase as defective output is further reduced. (This is the classical theory on quality costs.) Prepare to provide arguments in support of both of these theories. When it is time to debate this issue in front of the class, your instructor will tell you which position to take.

EXPERIENTIAL EXERCISE 17.1

Manufacturing Versus Service Organizations

Purpose: To gain a better understanding of the characteristics of manufacturing and service organizations.

Procedure: Visit a local strip mall and a local industrial park in your town. Focus on five businesses in each location. Use the checklist in "Now Apply It" on page 527 to classify each of these five businesses as either a manufacturing or a service organization.

EXPERIENTIAL EXERCISE 17.2

Assessing Quality

Purpose: To gain a better understanding of the aspects of a product and a service that might be used to assess its quality.

Procedure: Think of a product and a service that you recently purchased that did not totally meet your expectations. First, list the various factors for rating a product's quality, then give your product a rating from 1 to 10 (1 is the lowest rating, 10 the highest) for each of the factors. Jot down reasons for each of the ratings that you assigned to the product. Finally, calculate an overall average rating for the product to see where it falls on your 1 to 10 scale. Perform similar ratings and calculations for the service you chose.

CAPTURING THE POWER OF INFORMATION TECHNOLOGY

1. Using whatever search vehicle proves most fruitful (Internet, fax, telephone, and so on), gather information on menu items offered, sales, market share, and number of outlets for each of the major competitors in the pizza industry. Then, using presentation software, prepare for your classmates a slide show presentation that compares the information gathered for each of the companies.

2. Use the Internet to research any major U.S. manufacturing company. Gather information on product variety offered and nature of the manufacturing process. Using the information gathered in conjunction with presentation software, develop a classification diagram similar to Figure 17.1 that places your selected company in its proper position on the diagram. Present your findings and interpretations to your classmates for their comments.

3. Use whatever search vehicle proves most fruitful (Internet, fax, telephone, and so on) to gather information on female U.S. astronauts, missions flown, duration of missions, nature of missions, vehicles flown, and so on. Organize this information into an electronic spreadsheet that allows the data to be sorted on any of the information items collected. Compare your list with the lists of your classmates to determine who performed the most thorough search.

ETHICS: TAKE A STAND

When the demand for a product or service is seasonal, aggregate planning suggests several strategies for coping with the seasonal variations. One strategy calls for adjusting the size of the workforce by hiring and firing workers as demand fluctuates. This approach is often referred to as a chase strategy, since the organization is constantly varying its capacity to "chase" the contour of the fluctuating demand. The agricultural industry's need for people to harvest crops is highly seasonal. The industry typically follows a chase approach, hiring and firing migrant workers as the need arises.

For Discussion

1. Discuss the social and ethical implications of such a strategy. What alternative strategy or strategies might you suggest for such a situation?

2. Discuss the economic implications of your suggested strategies to agricultural firms and to you personally.

VIDEO CASE

Productivity and Quality in Operations: PING Golf Clubs

John Solheim makes putters that sing ("ping"). John is the president, CEO, and Chair of Karsten Manufacturing, a company started by his father, Karsten Solheim, in 1959 to design and manufacture PING golf clubs. For seven years, Karsten and his son designed and made PING golf clubs in their family garage at night after Karsten came home from his "day job": a mechanical design engineer working for General Electric. Today, the Karsten Manufacturing staff consists of about 900 employees working in 35 buildings on 30 acres in Phoenix, Arizona. The PING brand is an industry leader of custom-fit high-end golf clubs.

As an engineer, Karsten was involved in developing the first aircraft tricycle landing gear, the Fireball jet fighter, television rabbit ears antenna, and sophisticated radar and guidance systems. Karsten also was a frustrated golfer who believed he could apply the laws of physics and engineering to make better golf clubs that would improve his game. Karsten started custom fitting golf clubs in 1960 when he helped PGA Tour professionals (pros) improve their games by adjusting their clubs to fit their swings. Using each pro's favorite golf club as a starting point, he calibrated the angles of every iron to give each pro a perfectly matched set. Today all PING golf clubs are custom-fit to a player's specific stance and swing. PING claims it does not cost more or take longer to own custom-fit, custom-built PING clubs. After being fitted, a set of custom-fitted PING clubs can be made and shipped to the customer within one week of the fitting.

Although PING is confident they have the best golf clubs, they sometimes feel out of touch with their customers. So, PING regularly brings their custom-fitting professionals to their U.S. factory to train them about PING products, manufacturing processes, and club fitting procedures. Jay Richie, who teaches the PING fitting process to golf professionals, believes having the right components (with the right shaft, right loft, and right lie) is extremely important for every player, beginner or professional.

From the first heel-toe balanced putter to today's state-of-the-art custom fit club sets, PING employees strive to improve their products and services. PING is the only U.S. golf company certified by the International Organization for Standardization (ISO) a worldwide standard for quality assurance and environmental systems. Companies seeking certification voluntarily undergo a stringent audit of their entire quality and environmental systems—from product design to placement of an order. PING's ISO-9001-2000 designation relates to Quality Management Systems and ensures that PING continually improves its products and processes. To date, PING holds over 400 patents worldwide including such golf standards as heel-toe weighting, the first perimeter weighted iron, heat treating of clubs, variable club face thickness, and engraved serial numbers. Their ISO-14001 verifies PING's commitment to Environmental Management Systems.

To make sure all PING clubs meet the company's critical tolerances, PING stainless steel club heads are produced in their own foundry in Arizona. Each club head goes through several steps in preparation to be mated with a shaft and grip. Technicians align the grip by hand. This requires well-trained eyes and hands to position the grip perfectly. Each club has its own specifications and any deviations from the specifications are remedied. Every employee is empowered to be quality inspector and reject a club at any time. Clubs are color coded and engraved with the customer's personal serial number.

PING clubs are inscribed with the customer's unique serial numbers for several reasons. As a "product plus service" feature, the numbers match the clubs to one individual and can be used for warranty or identification purposes. If a club is lost or damaged, the customer can contact PING. The serial number enables PING to make an exact replacement using the customer's original specifications. This service can be used for discontinued models no longer offered by other club makers.

Everyone at PING has a passion for precision and quality. PING's vision is to strive to be number one in irons, putters, and metal woods—not necessarily in volume, but in high-performance, high-quality products. Obviously, they have to make a profit, but their business exists to build a better product. Karsten Solheim would tell his son, "If you build a better product, the dollars will take of themselves." John says, "If dollars are all you're chasing, you're not there. It's the wrong goal."

For Discussion:

1. Describe how PING addresses the two broad categories of decision-making areas within operating systems.
2. How does PING illustrate the three approaches to improving productivity?
3. Describe the factors PING uses to assess the quality of products and services.
4. Explain how PING illustrates Deming's 14 points. Are these points still relevant today? Explain.

http://www.pinggolf.com

CASE

Inventory Decision Making at ArtSource

ArtSource is a moderately sized New England wholesale distributor that specializes in providing picture framing supplies to approximately 50 small custom picture framing shops within its district. Hundreds of different frame molding styles and colors are carried along with a wide variety of mat boards, framing glass, and assorted framing hardware. ArtSource orders some of its stock items from national distributors and some directly from the manufacturers. ArtSource can then quickly ship items stocked in its warehouse directly to its local customers to fill their orders. One of the items that ArtSource warehouse manager Fred Fox was curious about was the nonreflective, nonglare glass used in custom picture framing. ArtSource orders this glass directly from the manufacturer in 4 ft. by 4 ft. square sheets. These sheets are then sold to the local picture framing shops, which cut the glass to the sizes required by each custom framing job. Fox had observed that there were times when ArtSource seemed to have a considerable amount of this item in stock, and he was concerned about the cost of storing this item. Fox decided to speak with ArtSource's main purchasing agent, Ruth Borman, to determine what the company policy was regarding the stocking of this item.

Borman sat down with Fox and gave him the details on this item. She noted that history seemed to indicate that demand for sheets of nonglare glass from frame shops was very uniform. Demand seemed to average 40 sheets for each day that ArtSource was open. Borman's figures also revealed that it cost Art-Source about $8 each time the company placed a replenishment order from the glass manufacturer. Furthermore, due to warehouse space costs and breakage costs, holding a sheet of this glass in inventory for a year would cost ArtSource roughly $4. When pressed by Fox about ArtSource's glass replenishment policy, Borman indicated that the company periodically reorders 1,000 sheets of glass from the manufacturer. Her justification was that 1,000 was a nice round number, and with ArtSource's 5-day-per-week and 50-week-per-year operation (they are closed for vacation 2 weeks of the year), this policy resulted in replenishment orders being placed about every 5 weeks, which in her words was, "Almost like clockwork." "Now I understand," said Fox as he left the meeting. However, all the way back to the warehouse he couldn't get over the nagging feeling that something wasn't right here. He felt that the glass stocks sometimes just looked too large.

For Discussion

1. What is the total annual inventory cost (ordering plus holding cost) that Art-Source is experiencing with the existing order policy for nonglare glass?

2. Using EOQ logic, what would you suggest as an appropriate order quantity for this item?

3. How much annual inventory cost savings could ArtSource expect to realize if the company changed its glass-ordering policy to the quantity you suggest in the prior question?

CHAP

INFORMATION TECHNOLOGY AND CONTROL

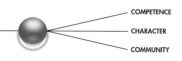

COMPETENCE

LEADERSHIP CHARACTER

COMMUNITY

TER 18

CHAPTER OVERVIEW

Consider all of the information that is available to assist organizational decision makers. Good information is necessary for good decision making. Information provides knowledge about past and current conditions in the organization and, if used carefully, can provide insights into possible future conditions. Ultimately, information provides a means of understanding the organization and its activities, and a means for making decisions on how to control the organizational system. The process of acquiring, processing, maintaining, and distributing this information increasingly involves information systems and information technology.

This chapter introduces the basic concepts of information as well as the information systems and technology that can be used to collect and distribute the information. We first examine information systems from an organizational perspective by focusing on worldwide changes that have altered the environment of business and have made it more reliant on information technology. We complete this organizational perspective by examining the basic intent and purpose of the different information systems that support workers at the different levels within an organization's hierarchy. We then shift our viewpoint to a technical perspective. Here we provide an introductory overview of the various components or building blocks of information systems. Some important points are made here on the distinction between data and information. This discussion also outlines the characteristics of good information. The technical overview next provides a description of the process used to develop high-quality information systems and an overview of some of the new information technologies. We conclude the chapter with a look at the impact of technology on the organization and some of the limitations of computer-based information systems.

LEARNING OBJECTIVES

When you have finished studying this chapter, you should be able to:

1. Discuss the recent changes that have altered the environment of business and made it more reliant on information technology.
2. Describe the four levels of decision specialties and their functions within an organization's hierarchy.
3. Describe the general types of information systems that would support decision makers at the different levels within an organization's hierarchy.
4. Describe the various components in an information system.
5. Explain the differences between data and information, and discuss the characteristics of useful information.
6. Illustrate the steps in the development of an information system.
7. Describe a variety of types of technology that is changing the way we work.
8. Discuss the impact of information technology on the organization.
9. Explain the limitations of information technology.

Facing The Challenge

What Kind of Information Systems Are Needed to Run the Olympic Winter Games?

How much information technology is needed for an organization whose visible efforts will span 17 days and then seemingly cease to exist? Not much, you think? Well, when that organization is the Salt Lake Olympic Committee (SLOC) preparing to stage the 2002 Olympic Winter Games, you'd better think again. Salt Lake City was no newcomer to Olympic bids. Its history of activity dates back to 1966, with four international campaigns. But the dream came true on June 16, 1995, when Salt Lake City was selected to host the 2002 Olympic Winter Games. Along with that dream came the nightmare of planning. Consider for a moment the sheer magnitude of the numbers. In February 2002 some 3,500 athletes from 80 nations would be assembling in Utah to compete in 70 medal events staged at 10 Olympic venues scattered around the Salt Lake City area. Approximately 9,000 members of the broadcast and print media would be on hand to cover the games. Over 18,000 paid or volunteer workers would be overseeing activities at the different

venues. And don't overlook the spectators—tens of thousands of them shuttling between events and venues. In the words of the SLOC, "the challenges of this project were formidable."

Many subprojects were identified as being critical to the success of the venture. Consider the following few (there are many more) to get a better sense of the magnitude of this undertaking. Systems would be needed for the timing and scoring of events; diffusing information to the press and broadcasters; delivering venue results; and dealing with athlete accreditation, transportation, accommodations, arrivals and departures, medical encounters, qualifications, and protocol. A local telecommunications network would need to be put into place, as would long distance services, PBX systems, and mobile telephone systems. Computer and audio/video equipment would have to be assembled; an Internet Web site would have to be developed for what was projected to be 10 million unique Web site visitors generating 750 million page views. The list of needed systems

goes on and on. And, oh by the way, the very nature of the event dictates that all this would be put into place in an area where weather conditions would be less than ideal—the mountain range where the alpine events were to be held sometimes received up to 500 inches of snow in a season. How about one more big constraint to make matters even more difficult—all these systems would need to be totally integrated. The total budget for this 17-day show? A staggering $1.33 billion!

SOURCES: "Information Technology—Project Overview and Update," *Salt Lake Organizing Committee for the Olympic Winter Games of 2002 Project Overview and Update*, October 2001; "Salt Lake Organization Draws High Marks," *International Olympic Committee Press Release*, March 7, 2001; "The International Olympic Committee Recognises Internet Organisations," *International Olympic Committee Press Release*, December 27, 2000; "IOC and SEMA Group Sign Olympic Technology Agreement for 2002 and Beyond," *International Olympic Committee Press Release*, March 13, 2000; "Dr. Philippe Verveer, Ph.D., to Join The International Olympic Committee as Technology Direction," *International Olympic Committee Press Release*, June 13, 1999.

INTRODUCTION

When the euphoria subsided after the announcement that Salt Lake City had been selected to host the 2002 Winter Olympics, the Salt Lake Olympic Committee (SLOC) faced a huge challenge not apparent to most observers. Certainly everyone recognized that the SLOC was faced with major projects in the construction of the venues for athletic competition, the construction of housing to accommodate athletes and visitors, and the construction of a transportation infrastructure to move people between venues (after all, the venues were scattered among Salt Lake City and five neighboring towns within a one-hour drive). However, what was not readily apparent to most observers was the challenge of developing information systems to make the Olympics work. The SLOC recognized early that it would take a coordinated effort among many information technology partners to ensure that the Olympics ran smoothly. Event results had to be recorded, tabulated, and disseminated quickly. Athletes and spectators had to be transported smoothly between venues. Communications networks needed to be established. The list goes on and on. Fortunately, the SLOC was prepared for this challenge. We shall see throughout this chapter and in "Meeting The Challenge" on page 586 that the SLOC took this challenge head on with its coordinated partner approach.

The dizzying rate at which new technologies are evolving and existing technologies are expanding is having a dramatic impact on organizations and society. The interaction between people and computers is growing rapidly. At the organizational level, an ever-increasing number of activities are relying on these human/machine interactions. On a personal level, an ever-increasing number of activities in our daily lives are also relying on such interactions. Although once relegated exclusively to such recurring activities as payroll processing and inventory monitoring, computerized information systems within organizations are now routinely applied to complex managerial decisions such as the evaluation of mergers and acquisitions. Business executives almost universally recognize that information technology (IT) is vital to their companies' success. The fundamental purpose of information technology is to monitor, process, and disseminate information to assist in managing, controlling, and making decisions for the organization. Although information technology in the world of business is barely 40 years old, it holds great promise for improving and even changing the way we manage and run our organizations.

ORGANIZATIONAL FOUNDATIONS OF INFORMATION SYSTEMS

If one were asked to characterize the current time in which we live and work, the response likely would be that we live in the "Information Age." Today, more than ever, businesses are using information to gain an advantage over their competitors. The fundamental principles (which we saw in detail in Chapter 17) are quite simple. Businesses and organizations must service their customers. To provide high levels of service to customers, businesses and organizations must provide the customers what they want, when they want it, and where they want it. The marketing discipline often refers to these requirements as the customers' form, time, and location requirements. Organizations that can satisfy these requirements efficiently and cost effectively stand to gain a coveted competitive advantage. Having knowledge of the customer form, time, and place requirements will enhance the organization's ability to meet those requirements. That knowledge comes from having information. Gaining knowledge through information is the role of information technology in today's information-based businesses. Information technology can help provide the right people with the right information so that the best decisions possible can be made regarding the servicing of customers.

> LEARNING OBJECTIVE 1
>
> Discuss the recent changes that have altered the environment of business and made it more reliant on information technology.

As this chapter unfolds, we will see that several types of information systems are prevalent in today's organizations. Computer applications that were once confined to simple transaction processing and monitoring are moving toward more sophisticated systems for analyzing problems and implementing solutions. As we transition into the 21st century, an increasing trend is emerging toward providing managers with information systems that can assist them directly in their most important task: making decisions.[1] Before examining some of the different types of information systems available to management, let's first look at some of the recently occurring powerful, worldwide changes that have altered the face of business and made organizations much more reliant on information systems.

THE CHANGING BUSINESS ENVIRONMENT

The world has seen several changes in the recent years that have altered the environment of business. In the last few decades of the 20th century, we saw the emergence and strengthening of the global economy, the transformation of many industrial economies to knowledge-based and information-based service economies, profound changes in the hierarchical structure of many organizations, and the emergence of technology-driven innovations like the virtual workplace, telecommuting, and electronic commerce. In one way or another, each of these phenomena is impacted by or reliant upon information technology.

INCREASING GLOBALIZATION   Look around you. It would be difficult to find an item within reach that can be classified as totally domestic. The pages in the book you are reading may well be printed on paper that originated in Canada. The pencil you use to jot down notes may have been manufactured in China using wood that was harvested in South America. A rapidly growing percentage of the businesses in the advanced industrial economies rely more and more on imports and exports. Globalization is a reality that will continue to shape tomorrow's business. Globalization is a result of such factors as improved worldwide transportation and telecommunications, deregulation, the emergence of transnational firms (firms that produce and sell products and services in countries all over the world), and the organization of trade blocs (such as the World Trade Organization, the European Union, and the North American Free Trade Agreement).

Information is crucial to firms that operate on a global basis. Organizations whose operations extend to the far reaches of the globe face the challenges of communicating with distributors and suppliers (often on a 24-hour basis due to time differences) while at the same time servicing local and international reporting needs. Information systems can provide the communication and analytic power needed to meet these challenges, enabling organizations to become effective and competitive participants in these international markets.

SHIFTING ECONOMIES   In recent years we have seen the relocation of many manufacturing industries to low-wage countries. At the same time the economies of the United States, Germany, Japan, and other major industrial powers have shifted in the direction of knowledge-based and information-based service economies. In these types of economies knowledge and information are key ingredients in the creation of wealth.

At the beginning of the 20th century more than 70 percent of the United States workforce was engaged in farming or were blue-collar workers employed in manufacturing. Less than 20 percent of U.S. workers were white-collar employees in offices. The number of white-collar workers did not exceed farm workers, service workers, and blue-collar workers until the mid 1970s, when it grew to about 40 percent of the workforce. As we entered the 21st century most people in the United States did not work on farms or in factories. Instead, most were involved in jobs that worked with, distributed, or created new knowledge and information. These jobs are found in such areas as banking, healthcare, education, sales, computer programming, insurance firms, and law firms. As the new millennium began, the number of white-collar workers employed in knowledge and information work accounted for almost 60 percent of the U.S. workforce and generated nearly 60 percent of the gross domestic product.[2]

We have seen the emergence of new kinds of knowledge-intense and information-intense organizations whose sole purpose is to produce, process, and distribute information. Even those industries that are engaged in the manufacture of traditional products have seen an intensification of knowledge utilization. Consider for the moment the automobile industry where design and production now rely heavily on knowledge-intensive information technology. This industry has seen an increase in the number of computer specialists, engineers, designers, and computer-controlled robots, and a concurrent reduction in the number of blue-collar production workers. Information and the technology that delivers it have become strategic assets for many firms. Information systems are needed to streamline the flow of information and knowledge in these organizations. When such systems are present, management will be better equipped to properly utilize the firm's knowledge and information resources.

FLATTENING OF ORGANIZATIONS   We saw in Chapter 1 that the traditional business organization is often viewed as a pyramid, narrow at the top and wide at the bottom. Between these extremes lies a hierarchical arrangement of workers and supervisors, each with different skills and responsibilities. Many large, bureaucratic organizations with this structure have proven to be inefficient, slow to change, and less competitive in recent years. Consequently, a trend has emerged toward reducing the number of employees and the number of levels in many organizational hierarchies. We've all heard of the phenomenon: corporate downsizing (often euphemistically referred to as "rightsizing"). In Chapter 1 we learned that the new organizational model could be lean and flexible. Since flatter organizations have fewer levels of management, lower-level employees tend to have greater decision-making authority.

These organizational-structural changes rely heavily on information technology. Information systems have been able to put more and better information into the hands of the workers so they can make decisions that had previously been made by managers. A flexible arrangement of teams and individuals working in task groups is often used to achieve coordination among employees as they work toward satisfying customer needs. A networked information system accessible to all the workers helps to facilitate this coordination.

EMERGING TECHNOLOGY-DRIVEN INNOVATIONS In the restructured organization described above, information technology innovations can result in teams and work groups that are no longer bound by departmental barriers. We have seen the emergence of a concept called the **virtual workplace**. Computerized information systems allow workers to be linked to other people and the information they need at any time and from any place. There are no walls and no boundaries.[3] Communication can also be established by voice mail, fax, e-mail, and videoconferencing. In essence, people can work together or individually on their work-related tasks without "coming in to the office." The concept is called **telecommuting** and will be discussed in more depth later in this chapter.[4] In many cases the success of the virtual workplace and telecommuting depends on the organization's ability to do business electronically. **Electronic commerce** (which will be examined in more detail later in the chapter) is the process of buying and selling goods and services electronically with computerized business transactions. Manual and paper-based procedures are replaced with electronic transmissions over information networks. The need for face-to-face interactions between the participants can be eliminated.[5] These and many other technology-driven innovations are changing the face of business today. More attention will be paid to these technical innovations later in this chapter.

Computerized information systems enable workers to telecommute or do their daily work at home.

TYPES OF INFORMATION SYSTEMS It would simplify our understanding of this topic if there were a single information system within organizations. Unfortunately, this is not the case. Most organizations develop a wide array of computerized information systems and attempt to maintain some level of integration among them. Despite the wide array of information systems, the basic structure of all of them is quite similar. An **information system** is a set of interrelated components that collects (or retrieves), processes, stores, and distributes information to support the activities of an organization. The simple structure (which will be expanded upon later in Figure 18.4) is that inputs are subjected to a transformation process that converts them into outputs. It is this basic transformation process that produces the information organizations need for making decisions, controlling operations, analyzing problems, and creating new products or services. At the input point, raw data are collected from within the organization or from its external environment. At the processing point the raw input is converted into a more meaningful form. This processing may entail classifying, arranging, or performing calculations on the input. At the output point the converted information

Virtual workplace
A workplace with no walls and no boundaries; workers can work anytime, anywhere by linking to other people and information through technology.

Telecommuting
The practice of working at a remote site by using a computer linked to a central office or other employment location.

Electronic commerce (e-commerce)
The process of buying and selling goods and services electronically with computerized business transactions.

Information system
A set of interrelated components that collects (or retrieves), processes, stores, and distributes information to support the activities of an organization.

is transferred to the people who will use it or to the organizational activities for which it is needed.

No single system can satisfy all the information needs of an organization. In its preparation for the 2002 Olympic Winter Games, the SLOC information technology team recognized this as it oversaw the development of more than a dozen major information systems. Different system architectures are often needed in an organization because there are different specialties and interests at the various levels within that organization. Figure 18.1 illustrates the typical pyramid structure of decision specialties within an organization.[6] In this pyramid structure we see an operational level at the base, comprised of operational managers who must monitor and control the day-to-day operations of the organization. **Operational-level information systems** support operational managers by keeping track of the basic activities and transactions of the organization, such as the flow of materials, sales, receipts, and payroll activities. Above the operational level is the knowledge level, comprised of knowledge workers and data workers. Generally speaking, knowledge workers create new information and knowledge. They normally hold university degrees and are typically members of a recognized profession, such as scientists, engineers, doctors, and lawyers. Data workers usually have less formal education, may lack college degrees, and generally process rather than create information. Data workers consist primarily of secretaries, filing clerks, accountants, and other workers whose job it is to manipulate and disseminate information. **Knowledge-level information systems** help knowledge workers to discover, organize, and integrate new knowledge into the business or help data workers to control the flow of paperwork and information.

Directly above the knowledge level lies the management level, which is comprised of middle managers who are responsible for monitoring and controlling the activities of the business and also responsible for making many routine and nonroutine decisions. **Management-level information systems** assist in the administrative activities of middle managers and aid in decision making and the monitoring

Figure 18.1 | Decision Specialties within Organizational Hierarchy

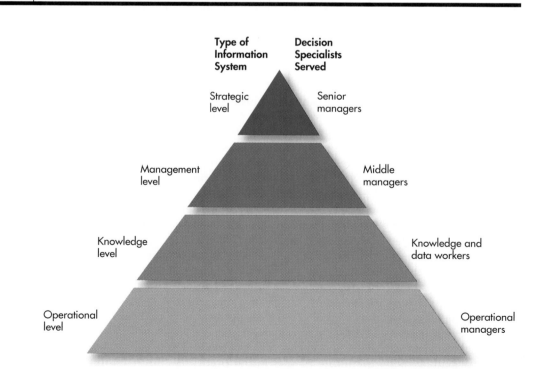

and controlling of operations. Finally, at the top of the pyramid lies the strategic level, which is comprised of senior level managers. **Strategic-level information systems** aid senior management as they address strategic issues and long-term decision making.

OPERATIONAL-LEVEL INFORMATION SYSTEMS **Transaction processing systems (TPS)** are the information systems that support workers at the operational level of the organization. They record daily business transactions and generally perform the routine, clerical record-keeping activities of the organization. These activities can be quite varied; therefore, most organizations will have several types of TPS. Table 18.1 displays the different categories of transaction processing systems. We see from this table that a TPS can be classified as sales/marketing systems, manufacturing/production systems, finance/accounting systems, human resource systems, or industry specific systems. An example in the manufacturing/production category would be an inventory TPS, which will record all additions to and withdrawals from inventory so an accurate inventory count can be retrieved at any time. An example in the finance/accounting category would be a payroll TPS, which will record time clock information and couple that with employee pay rates to generate paychecks, withholding statements, and any other payroll reports of interest to management and government agencies. At the 2002 Winter Olympic Games, the Timing and Scoring System represented an industry-specific type of TPS. Here raw data on athletes' times and scores were recorded and assembled for further processing.

KNOWLEDGE-LEVEL INFORMATION SYSTEMS **Knowledge management systems (KMS)** and **office automation systems (OAS)** are the information systems that support workers at the knowledge level of the organization. Knowledge management systems help knowledge workers create, organize, and make available important business knowledge wherever and whenever it is needed in an organization. This includes processes, procedures, patents, reference works, formulas, best practices, forecasts, and fixes.[7] Office automation systems are information technology applications designed to increase the productivity of data workers. Systems for office automation are typically computer-based information systems that assist the organization in the processing, storage, collection, and transmission of electronic documents and messages among individuals, work groups, and organizations. For example, office automation systems might handle and manage documents via word processing, desktop publishing, digital document imaging, and digital filing, while communication might be handled via electronic mail, voice mail, and videoconferencing. The SLOC clerical staff used many such applications in the Information Diffusion Systems that provided updates to broadcasters and media representatives at the 2002 Olympic Winter Games. SLOC's Document Processing Equipment and Services System also made ample use of these applications, as did the Local Telecommunications Network System. Figure 18.2 shows the full range of components in office automation systems. Many of these systems are important

Strategic-level information systems Information systems that aid senior management as they address strategic issues and long-term decision making.

Transaction processing systems (TPS) Information systems that support workers at the operational level of the organization by recording daily business transactions and performing the routine, clerical record-keeping activities of the organization.

LEARNING OBJECTIVE 3

Describe the general types of information systems that would support decision makers at the different levels within an organization's hierarchy.

Knowledge management systems (KMS) Information systems that support workers at the knowledge level of the organization by helping to create, organize, and make available important business knowledge wherever and whenever it is needed in an organization.

Office automation systems (OAS) Information technology applications designed to increase the productivity of data workers by assisting in the processing, storage, collection, and transmission of electronic documents and messages among individuals, work groups, and organizations.

Table 18.1 | Categories of Transaction Processing Systems

TYPES OF TPS

- Sales/Marketing Systems
- Manufacturing/Production Systems
- Finance/Accounting Systems
- Human Resource Systems
- Industry Specific Systems

Figure 18.2 | Components of Office Automation Systems

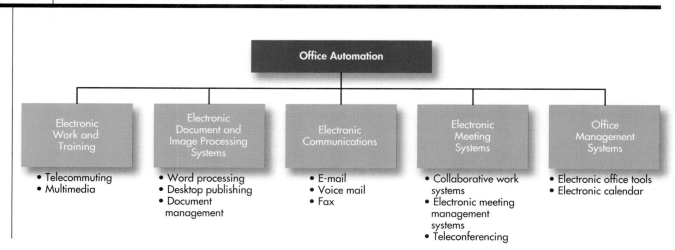

on their own merits, but when combined, they create an overall environment that supports all document and message processing.[8]

MANAGEMENT-LEVEL INFORMATION SYSTEMS   **Management information systems (MIS)** and **decision support systems (DSS)** are the information systems that support middle managers at the management level of the organization. Management information systems provide managers with periodic reports that summarize the organization's performance. MISs are designed primarily to summarize what has occurred and point people toward the existence of problems or opportunities. These systems are generally not flexible and have little analytical capability. Furthermore, MIS reports rarely tell someone why a problem exists or offer solutions. In many MISs, information is available on demand to facilitate monitoring exception conditions and to monitor moment-by-moment activities if desired. However, unanticipated reporting requirements and unusual operating conditions are not typically well supported by the systematic, structured nature of a traditional MIS.

Decision support systems are designed to help decision makers formulate high-quality decisions about *ad hoc*, semi-structured problems—situations in which procedures can be only partially specified in advance. Because the situations occur infrequently, the organization does not have routine procedures for dealing with them. This lack of routine means there are limited rules to guide decision behavior; therefore, outcomes are less predictable or obvious. DSSs have more analytical power than other systems and are built with a variety of models to analyze and condense data into a form, which can be used by decision makers. A DSS allows users to combine their own insights and judgment with the analytical models and information from the database to examine alternative approaches and solutions to the situation. In particular, "what if" analysis can be performed using the DSS. In other words, the decision maker can assess a variety of decision choices by modeling the expected outcomes of those decisions with the information that is currently available.

In the months leading up to the staging of the 2002 Olympic Winter Games, simulation DSS systems allowed the SLOC to examine "what if" situations by simulating a variety of bus transportation scenarios. Using this approach, they could determine optimal bus schedules in advance of the onslaught of competitors, media representatives, volunteer helpers, and spectators. On a grander scale, they simulated actual game time competitions and conditions in the final months of 2001 to see the entire system in action.

Management information systems (MIS)
Information systems that support middle managers at the management level of the organization by providing them with periodic reports that summarize the organization's performance.

Decision support systems (DSS)
Information systems that support middle managers at the management level of the organization by assisting them in the formulation of high-quality decisions about *ad hoc,* semi-structured problems.

Table 18.2 | Characteristics and Capabilities of Executive Support Systems

- Is tailored to individual user
- Allows user to filter, expand, compress, and track critical information
- Provides an up-to-date status report
- Gives access to broad range of internal and external information and data
- Is user-friendly and easily learned
- Supports electronic communications
- Provides a variety of data-analysis tools
- Often includes tools for personal productivity

STRATEGIC-LEVEL INFORMATION SYSTEMS **Executive support systems (ESS)** are the information systems that support senior managers at the strategic level of the organization. An ESS is a highly interactive MIS combined with decision support systems for helping senior managers identify and address problems and opportunities from a strategic perspective. ESSs are not designed to solve specific problems; instead, they provide a generalized computing and telecommunications capacity that can be applied to a changing array of unstructured decisions and problems. For example, ESSs can assist in answering such strategic questions as: What business should we be in? What acquisitions might help protect us from cyclical business swings? How can we raise cash for acquisitions? What are our competitors doing?[9] Table 18.2 summarizes many of the characteristics and capabilities of an ESS.[10]

Executive support systems (ESS) Information systems that support senior managers at the strategic level of the organization by helping them identify and address problems and opportunities from a strategic perspective.

INTEGRATION OF SYSTEMS

Figure 18.3 illustrates ways different types of information systems in an organization might relate to one another. Logic would suggest value in upward transfer of information between the systems at the different levels within an organization. In

Figure 18.3 | Interrelationships between Organizational Information Systems

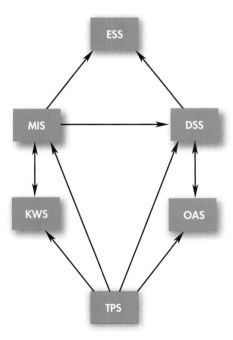

addition, there are a few places where there may be some utility in having information flow to lower level systems or horizontally between systems at the same level, as Figure 18.3 shows. A difficult question facing any organization is "How much can and should these systems be integrated?" Unfortunately, the standard answer is that "there is no one right level of integration and centralization."[11] It would certainly be advantageous to have some level of integration so that information can flow among the different parts of the organization. Examine "Leaders In Action" below and you will see how new leadership changed the focus at Hughes Supply to one of integration, centralization, and streamlining of operations. This focus resulted in a dramatic turnaround for a company that had just experienced its first quarterly loss in a decade.

Enterprise resource planning (ERP)
A management system that integrates all facets of the organization's business so that they can be more closely coordinated by sharing information.

Many organizations are now trying to use information technology for **enterprise resource planning (ERP)**. ERP is a management system that integrates all facets of the organization's business so that they can be more closely coordinated by sharing information.[12] However, integrating many different systems is very time consuming, extremely costly, and technologically difficult. Each organization must balance its needs for integrating systems against the costs and difficulties of mounting a large-scale systems integration effort. In the case of the 2002 Olympic Winter Games, the SLOC's mandate was to have all their systems totally integrated.

Leaders In Action

Hughes Supply Streamlines Operations

Hughes Supply, Inc., was founded in Orlando, Florida, in 1928. It is one of the largest publicly traded companies based in Central Florida. Hughes sells over 240,000 products to more than 75,000 customers. It has over 400 branches and 6 central distribution centers in the United States and Mexico. In 2001, sales totaled $3.3 billion. During the 1990s, Hughes diversified by acquiring over 90 companies across the country. However, in the 4th quarter of 2000 the company suffered a $9.1 million loss—its first quarterly loss in a decade. With a slowing economy, Hughes Chairman and Chief Executive Officer David Hughes decided it was time to focus on streamlining the organization and generating operating efficiencies. Hughes hired Tom Morgan as president to take on the challenge of streamlining the organization. With a strong background in distribution and technology and having been a chief executive for an information management and storage company and an office products company, Morgan was well-qualified to accept this challenge.

Morgan quickly realized that the information systems currently in place were less than ideal. Through its acquisitions, the company found itself dealing with about 30 different independent information systems that didn't communicate well with each other. Once the company's information systems were integrated, the company could then analyze its customers so it could focus on the most profitable ones. Morgan also recognized that the company could leverage its buying power if it reduced the number of vendors and made greater use of electronic data interchange. In addition, fewer vendors and consolidated shipments would significantly reduce freight costs. Morgan planned to trim the number of Hughes vendors from 13,600 to about 8,000. Further streamlining was accomplished by consolidating the number of business lines from six to three—plumbing and electrical; industrial pipes, valves, and fittings; and water and sewer-building materials. These are but a few of the immediate changes implemented by Morgan.

The addition of Tom Morgan and the changes he implemented have brought praise from analysts. In spite of the sluggish economy, which is a tough environment for a construction and industrial product supplier, Hughes has avoided any red ink since the streamlining and has seen profits rise in each quarter of 2001. Financial analysts agree that Hughes should be strongly positioned to benefit as the economy rebounds. The company's stock price reflects the analysts' optimism. At the end of 2000 (just prior to the hiring of Morgan), Hughes' stock was trading in the teens. At the end of 2001, it was trading in the upper twenties, quite an accomplishment given the hit that all stocks took after the September 11 terrorist attacks. As the company continues to rework itself into a more centralized, integrated corporation, CEO David Hughes insists that it will not lose sight of the customer. The focus of Hughes supply is to become the distributor of choice by offering custom-engineered solutions, technical advice, and delivery of products to customers when they need them.

SOURCE: **http://www.hughessupply.com**, January 2003; J. Snyder, "Hughes Supply Cuts the Fat," *Central Florida Business*, December 3, 2001, 16–17.

This was a costly venture, but the SLOC information technology budget of more than $300 million was prepared to support that level of integration.

TECHNICAL FOUNDATIONS OF INFORMATION SYSTEMS

The fundamental idea behind information systems is that they provide a systematic approach for collecting, manipulating, maintaining, and distributing information throughout an organization. Despite the common misconception, an information system does not require a computer. Systems of managing information existed long before computers. Even with the rapid increase in computers in recent years, many organizations still maintain systems for managing information that are not computerized. Nevertheless, computer systems and other advances in information technology are providing organizations and their workers with virtually unlimited opportunities to collect, explore, and manage information. These are opportunities that were not available a short time ago.

INFORMATION SYSTEM COMPONENTS

A general system consists of five basic components: inputs, the processing or transformation area, outputs, procedures for providing feedback to the system, and a means of controlling the system. As Figure 18.4 shows, a computer-based information system closely resembles the traditional general system model except that

LEARNING OBJECTIVE 4

Describe the various components in an information system.

Figure 18.4 | General Information System

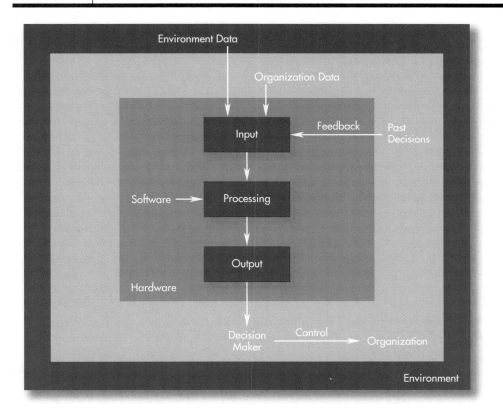

the former also includes hardware, software, and a database. The next few sections provide a summary glimpse of each of those components of a computer-based information system.

INPUT   The input portion of a computer-based information system consists of any type of computer input device that can provide data to the system. For example, the scanner cash registers in stores, often called point-of-sale terminals, provide input to the information system. We see these devices every day in grocery stores and department stores. Although not visible to most of us, similar technology is also used by the United States Postal Service, and with good reason. While one person can manually sort only about 500 pieces of mail per hour, a scanning machine can sort 30,000 to 40,000 pieces in the same amount of time.[13] Sensors and monitoring equipment in a manufacturing or production facility can provide input as can the timing devices used at the Olympic Winter Games. Input can also come via telephone lines, satellite transmission, and archival data stored on computer disks and tapes. Input data can also be directly entered into the system by a user at a terminal or microcomputer through a bar code reader and now even through pen-based computer systems that recognize handwriting.

PROCESSING   The processing component of an information system—what we typically think of as the "brains" of the computer—is called the central processing unit (CPU). When we think of a computer, we usually mean the CPU. This is the portion of the system where the raw data are manipulated and transformed into meaningful and useful information that can then be distributed to the relevant decision makers.

OUTPUT   The output portion of the system distributes the information that is the result of processing. Output can take a variety of forms, including paper print-outs, electronic data stored on computer disks, CDs, or magnetic tape, electronic transmissions through telephone systems or via satellite, displays on computer monitors, and sounds or synthetic voices made available through speakers for audio use. Output can even be made available through the control and manipulation of computer-controlled machinery.

In the general systems model, the output process provides information to the decision makers, who can then manage and control the larger organizational system. Feedback occurs when the decision makers interpret the information to determine what should occur next. The decisions that result from the interpretation and use of the information are a means of controlling the system.

HARDWARE   The physical components of the information system—the computer, terminals, monitors, printers, and so on—are the hardware. The storage devices, such as hard disks, floppy disks, CDs, zip disks, and magnetic tapes, are also hardware components. A wide variety of hardware components are available, and they can be combined as needed to meet organizational information-processing needs. A variety of hardware components were critical to the success of the SLOC information systems, and their numbers were prodigious. Among the computer hardware items needed to support the 2002 Olympic Winter Games were 5,700 workstations and laptop computers, 1,150 printers, and 550 computer servers.

SOFTWARE   The software portion of an information system consists of the various types of programs that are used to tell the hardware how to function. Software controls how the data are processed. Examples of software include word-processing, spreadsheet, and accounting packages; other business applications; and even the computer games we commonly play. Ultimately, software governs how the information is stored and distributed.

DATABASE   A **database** is the archived data and information that the organization uses. A database typically contains a vast amount of related information on company operations, financial records, employee data, customers, and so on. In the past, much of this information was maintained in separate files, which were often paper based. As a result, the data were often inconsistent and hard to locate and retrieve. Even early, computerized systems often maintained data in separate files, leading to similar problems. These problems can be overcome with modern database management systems.

A **database management system (DBMS)** is the software that allows an organization to store data, manage them efficiently, and provide access to the stored data. When an application program needs a particular type of data, the DBMS acts as an interface between the program and the physical data files. The DBMS finds and retrieves the necessary item from the database and then delivers it to the application program. For example, a program that generates payroll for hourly workers would have the DBMS retrieve each worker's wage rate from the database and that information would be used to prepare paychecks. An extensive database was in place at the Olympic Winter Games to enable systems to compare competition results with results from prior Olympic and World Championship competitions, thereby generating Olympic and world record information for broadcasters and media representatives.

INFORMATION VERSUS DATA

Several times we have used the terms *data* and *information* in our discussions up to this point. Often these words are used interchangeably. In the organizational context, however, a significant difference in meaning may exist. **Data** are the raw facts or details that represent some type of transaction or activity within an organization. For example, the sale of items at a grocery store or the sale of an automobile creates a great deal of data representing that event. Data, therefore, are the objective measurements of the characteristics of the objects or transactions that are occurring in an organization. In relation to the Olympic Winter Games described in "Facing The Challenge," you and I might view the elapsed time for a single run of a bobsled team as a piece of raw data.

Information is the result of the process of transforming data into a meaningful and useful form for a specific purpose. In other words, data go through a process whereby meaning is added, thus yielding information. In data processing, the data are aggregated and organized, manipulated through analysis, and placed in a proper context for evaluation and use by the end user. In a grocery store, the price and inventory amount for a particular product are examples of raw data. As sales occur, the inventory changes. The changes in inventory for this product, as well as the broader inventory changes that occur for all items available in the store, are examples of information. Each individual transaction is not that important in isolation; once combined, however, the transaction and sales figures provide useful information. Continuing with the Olympics example, when a bobsled team has finished all its runs, the individual times can be accumulated into a total time, which can be compared to the total times of all other teams. When these totals are sorted, we have information about medal winners.

Other aspects of the data/information relationship also add complexity to organizational decision making and control. Information for one person may be data to another. For example, as customers make their purchases at the grocery store, the store's inventory is altered. If the store has automated cash registers, it can update the inventory immediately. If the store does not have automated registers, the inventory will have to be updated and reconciled manually at the end of the day. The transaction data, generated by and representing details of customer purchases, are important to the store manager. From these raw data, the

Database
The archived data and information used by an organization.

Database management system (DBMS)
Software that allows an organization to store data, manage them efficiently, and provide access to stored data.

© AP/WIDE WORLD PHOTOS

The timing data when compared to other bobsled teams put the team of Brian Shimer, Mike Kohn, Doug Sharp, and Dan Steele in second place at the 2001 Winter Olympics.

LEARNING OBJECTIVE 5

Explain the differences between data and information, and discuss the characteristics of useful information.

Data
The raw facts or details that represent some type of transaction or activity within an organization.

Information
Data that have been processed or transformed into a meaningful and useful form.

manager derives information on the store's sales, the success or failure of specific specials, and inventories that need to be restocked as well as other such operations details. The regional manager for this chain of stores, however, is not as interested in the details of specific transactions. Instead, the regional manager is concerned with broader issues of how the stores as a whole are doing. Is one store in the region performing better than another? Do different specials or different store layouts generate better sales? Because the regional manager is interested in several stores as a unit, rather than in one store or individual customers, the information needs are different. In summary, information for the store managers is data for the regional manager.

In a similar vein, as a viewer of the Olympic Winter Games, your bobsledding interest might be limited to knowing which team had the lowest cumulative time for all runs. One team's individual time on one of its runs might not hold particular interest to you—it is merely a piece of raw data that will eventually contribute to the team's total (the piece of information of interest to you). However, to members of that bobsled team, this individual run time could represent a valuable piece of information that influences their actions and preparations for a subsequent run (for example, strive for a longer, more vigorous push off at start; crouch lower for improved aerodynamics; achieve better team balance in sled to avoid wall touches; among others).

CHARACTERISTICS OF USEFUL INFORMATION

When data are processed into information, the information must be in a form that is useful to decision makers and management. Useful information has several fundamental characteristics. First, its quality must be very high. Second, it must be available to decision makers in a timely fashion. Finally, the information must be complete and relevant. As we examine those characteristics in more detail, refer to Figure 18.5 for an illustration of the relationship among these three primary characteristics of information.

QUALITY   Quality is, perhaps, the single most important characteristic of information. Without high quality, the information is of little use. Quality consists of several attributes. One of these is accuracy. If the details do not accurately reflect current conditions, then any decision made using the information may be adversely affected. Clarity is another attribute of high-quality information. The meaning and

Figure 18.5 | Characteristics of Useful Information

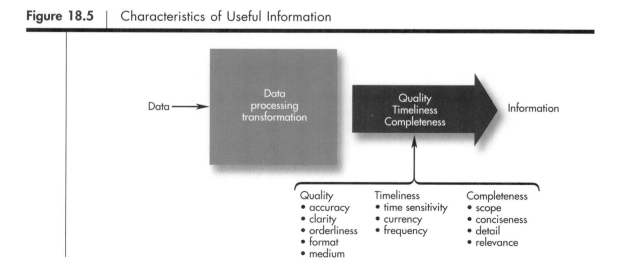

intent of the information must be clear to the decision maker. Orderliness and format are two more attributes of high-quality information. If information is presented in an orderly arrangement and in a format that assists the decision maker, the decision-making process will be facilitated. Finally, the medium through which the information is communicated is important. For example, providing the decision maker with a massive computer printout would be an inappropriate medium if a short e-mail transmission summarizing exceptions from standards conveyed all the information needed by the decision maker. Consider the time results for the competitors in the Olympic downhill skiing competition. Judges, broadcasters, competitors, and spectators would all like to have precise time measurements, sorted from fastest to slowest, so that the winners can be quickly identified.

TIMELINESS Most organizational decision making requires timely information, for many of these decisions must be made on a frequent basis. Timely information has several ingredients. One of them is time sensitivity, which refers to the information being provided when it is needed—not too late and, by the same token, not too early. This way the decision maker has the information when it is needed to support making a decision. A second key ingredient of timely information is currency. Information should be up to date when it is provided to the decision maker. A final characteristic of timely information is frequency. Information should be provided as often as needed. For example, reports should be generated and provided to the decision maker on a regular reporting schedule, such as daily, weekly, monthly, or quarterly.

Timely feedback of information is critical to most organizations. Consider how it is handled in the package-delivery industry where timely feedback of information on package location is critical to successful monitoring of parcels. Companies such as United Parcel Service and FedEx assign a bar-coded identifier the moment a parcel is picked up from the sender. The bar code is scanned at every change in its transport. Since this scanned information is communicated to a central computer, an up-to-date record of the status and location of each package is constantly maintained.[14] In the case of the Olympic Winter Games, information needs to be provided immediately upon the completion of each performance in a particular competitive event.

COMPLETENESS If information is to contribute to making good decisions, it must be complete. It would be impossible to determine the winner of a speed skating event if all competitors' times were not reported. Information completeness consists of several primary attributes. The scope of the information must be sufficient to allow the decision maker to make an accurate assessment of the situation and to arrive at a suitable decision. Where appropriate, decision makers should have access not only to current information, but also to past history and to future plans for the organization. Conciseness and detail are two additional attributes of completeness. Information should be presented to the decision maker in as concise a form as possible, but there should be sufficient detail to provide the decision maker with enough depth and breadth for the current situation. Too much detail, however, can overwhelm the decision maker, causing information overload, distracting from the decision, or making it virtually impossible to focus on the important information. A final attribute of complete information is relevance. Only information that is relevant to the decision at hand needs to be provided. Once again, too much information may do more harm than good.

To illustrate these concepts, consider this example. Imagine the job of air traffic controllers who must manage a number of aircraft flying through a designated airspace. The relevant information consists of aircraft identification, speed, direction, planned flight path, weather, other aircraft in the area, and so on. Clearly, high-quality, timely, and complete information is necessary if the controllers are to guide all the aircraft into and out of airports and airspace safely. The air traffic controllers do not need information on the number of passengers in each plane or how many passengers ordered special dietary meals. While such information is vital to others in the airline transportation network, it is irrelevant to the air traffic controllers.

STEPS IN THE DEVELOPMENT OF HIGH-QUALITY INFORMATION SYSTEMS

Most information systems are developed through a systematic process in which system design specialists and programmers collaborate with the end users. **End users** are all the people who will use and interact with the information system, particularly the decision makers in the organization. This process, depicted in Figure 18.6, is often called systems analysis and design.

INVESTIGATION   The initial phase in the development of an information system is systems investigation. During this phase, the organization determines whether a problem or opportunity exists that an information system can address. In addition, it performs a feasibility study to determine whether a new information system is attainable. Once an organization ascertains that an information system is both appropriate and feasible, it develops a plan for managing the project and obtaining management approval. Determining that an information system was appropriate was a "no brainer" for the SLOC. For example, without information systems event results could not be quickly determined and disseminated to the world; events could not be smoothly scheduled and coordinated; and spectators, judges, media, event workers, and competitors could not be moved around efficiently. This list could go on and on.

SYSTEMS ANALYSIS   Once the plan has been devised and management's approval has been obtained, the second phase, called systems analysis, begins. The

Figure 18.6 | Steps in the Design of Information Systems

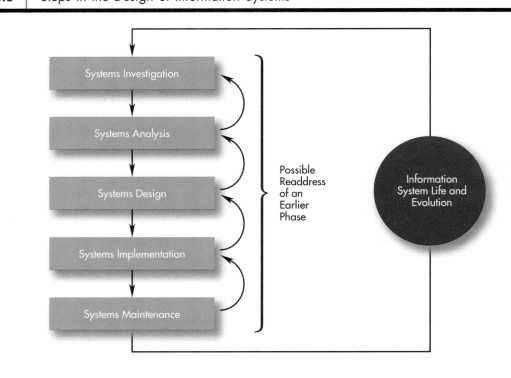

purpose of this phase is to develop the functional requirements for the information system. In other words, this phase concentrates on what needs to be done to provide the desired information. This phase begins with an examination and analysis of the current systems in use, an assessment of the organizational environment, and a detailed assessment of the information needs of the end users. The organizational environment consists of both internal factors, such as the organization's structure, people, and activities, and external factors, such as industry considerations and the competition.

After studying these components, the system designers develop a set of functional requirements, or a detailed description of the necessary functional performance capabilities of the information system. These requirements focus on the type of information that decision makers need; the response times the users will need; and the format, frequency, and volume of information that should be produced and distributed. The SLOC information technology team recognized in this phase of the process that there was a multitude of functional requirements, which resulted in the 16 subprojects identified in "Meeting The Challenge" on page 588. Each of these subprojects was responsible for bringing forward specific systems, infrastructure, and services for the 2002 Olympic Winter Games.

SYSTEMS DESIGN Phase three is the system design phase. This is the first phase in which the system's technological capabilities are addressed. The designers identify the hardware, software, people, and data resources that will be needed and describe the information products that will be produced to satisfy the functional requirements specified in the previous phase. More specifically, the user interface, or the point of interaction between the people and the information, is designed. The data, their attributes and structures, and the relationships among the various data elements are created. These data will ultimately become the input for the database. Finally, the software system—the various computer programs and procedures—is designed.

SYSTEMS IMPLEMENTATION Once the analysis and design phases have been completed, systems implementation can begin. The outcome of this phase will be an operational system. The hardware and software that will be incorporated into the new information system are developed or acquired. As the system is put together, extensive testing is necessary to ensure that the system will meet all specified requirements. Any problems can be corrected more easily at this phase than at any later phase. The SLOC information technology team performed extensive testing to ensure that the systems and venues would be ready for the 2002 Games. Beginning in 2001, assorted national and multinational championship events were staged at the different Olympic venues to test the systems under live conditions. A series of simulations was also conducted to test the systems, as noted in "Meeting The Challenge." Such testing was particularly critical to ensure that the systems were ready by February 17, 2002, the starting date of the Games. Unlike some commercial systems projects that can delay implementation when problems arise, the SLOC could not push back their deployment date, and they could not "work out the bugs" during the early weeks of implementation. The systems, equipment, and applications had to work correctly on the first day of competition, and they needed to continue working correctly throughout the Games.

Documentation of the new system, or the relationships among the various pieces of hardware and software, should also be emphasized. The information system may not work perfectly, and the individuals who designed and developed it will not always be around to maintain it. Therefore, detailed and accurate descriptions of what was done, why it was done, and how it all works together are needed to assist in managing and maintaining the system.

Once the testing is completed, the system is ready for use, and the organization can switch from its old procedures to the new information system. This transition process may require operating both the new and the old system for a time in parallel. Operating the systems in parallel gives people time to learn and become comfortable with the new system and an opportunity to identify and correct most system bugs. Many of us will soon experience (or have already experienced) this phenomenon of operating systems in parallel if we live in areas whose telephone systems are converting to 10-digit dialing for local calls. When this occurs, customers are given the option of using either the traditional 7-digit or the new 10-digit method for several months. In a similar vein, people in the 11 European nations that merged their currencies to create a common currency had a few months during which they could use either their national currency or the new euro after it became available on January 1, 2002.[15] Another method of transition involves bringing the new system into operation on a trial basis, one location at a time. This method is often referred to as "using a pilot system." A final, and more abrupt, alternative is the immediate cutover, whereby the old system is halted and the new system is started with no overlap in operations. The FBI recently performed an immediate cutover when it converted to a digital fingerprint recognition system.[16] Of course, in the case of the 2002 Olympic Winter Games, there was no "old" system so the only option was to simply implement the new system for the control of the Games. All these transition methods have positive and negative aspects. The organization should carefully assess the benefits and potential costs before selecting an approach.[17]

SYSTEMS MAINTENANCE　The final phase in the development of an information system is systems maintenance. Like an automobile, a house, or any piece of machinery, an information system will need to be maintained to keep it in top shape and to ensure that it will not encounter problems that could have been prevented. New hardware may be added to the system to address new needs or to replace older equipment. Software updates—new versions with added capabilities—are commonly available. In spite of extensive testing, most systems will contain errors or bugs, some of them quite major. In addition, as the users work with the information system, they will discover additional things that need to be added, better ways of doing some things, and possibly areas that can be removed from the system. While maintenance issues such as these are important for the information systems of most organizations, they were not particularly relevant to the SLOC systems. In less than a month after the start of the Games, the bulk of the systems would cease to be used.

One final aspect of any new information system is user training. The success of an information system depends on more than just thorough analysis, design, and implementation. Success is also, and perhaps ultimately, dependent upon the people who will use the system on a daily basis to assist in making decisions. To facilitate their use of the system, the users need to be trained in what the system can and cannot do and in how to accomplish the needed tasks. Training may be for simple tasks such as data entry or for very complex monitoring and operations of critical machinery within the organization. In larger organizations, the training role is commonly fulfilled by an information center.[18] The 600 permanent members of the SLOC IT team would see its ranks swell to almost 3,000 technology staff members during the conduct of the Olympic Winter Games. All these new staff members had to be thoroughly trained on the systems before the Games began. As cultural diversity increases in the workplace, the training process can become more difficult due to language barriers and communication problems. This was certainly an issue to contend with in the 2002 Olympic Winter Games where the IT developmental staff of 600 IT specialists represented 23 different nations; the more than 2,000 additional Games' staff would also display a similar international flavor. In addition, as with any type of change, the process can be slower and more tedious when cultural backgrounds cause resistance to change.

ATTRIBUTES OF SUCCESSFUL INFORMATION SYSTEMS

If the steps in the development of an information system have been successful, the resulting system will possess two important attributes. These attributes relate to the system's feasibility and the system's ability to meet the needs and expectations of its users.

FEASIBILITY An assessment of the information system's feasibility focuses on evaluating alternative systems that will best meet the needs of the organization and its workers. Feasibility has several dimensions.[19] **Organizational feasibility** examines how well the proposed system supports the strategic objectives of the organization as a whole. Systems that do not directly contribute to the short-range and long-range goals of the organization should be rejected. **Economic feasibility** focuses on whether the expected benefits will be able to cover the anticipated costs. A system whose benefits do not match or exceed the costs will not be approved unless mandated by other considerations, such as government regulations.

Technical feasibility addresses the hardware and software capabilities of the proposed system. Is the system, as proposed, capable of reliably providing the needed information to the appropriate people? Can the decision makers get the right kinds and amounts of data to support the desired decision making? And will the information be available when needed? The last type of feasibility is **operational feasibility**, which focuses on the willingness and ability of all concerned parties to operate, use, and support the information system as it is proposed and implemented. If any one of the relevant constituencies, such as management, employees, customers, or suppliers, does not support or use the system, it is doomed to failure. For example, if the system is too difficult for the employees to use successfully, they will reject it and use other approaches to do their work. Others who depend on the employees' use of the system for information will be unable to get what they need, leading to a further loss of opportunity.

ABILITY TO MEET NEEDS OF DIVERSE USERS A second attribute of successful system design is that the system should ultimately meet the needs and expectations of its users. Many reasons explain why an information system might fail to meet the needs and expectations of its users, and they can all doom the system to failure. The investigation, analysis, and design process is time consuming and can be very costly. Time and cost often put pressure on designers to take shortcuts that may lead to an inferior or flawed system that does not meet users' needs. Failure to meet the users' needs can also occur because users have difficulty describing their information needs adequately. This problem is exacerbated when, as is often the case, the systems specialists have little or no previous experience with the types of problems currently under consideration. Therefore, if care is not taken, the resulting system may not live up to the expectations of the users. In addition, as the users become more familiar with the system, their demands and expectations may increase.[20] Fortunately, such problems did not befall the development of the information systems for the 2002 Olympic Winter Games. The SLOC IT team started early and cut no corners (its more than $300 million IT budget allowed that luxury!). Furthermore, the SLOC chose the Sema Group as its major IT partner. Sema is one of the world's leading information technology and business services companies with extensive experience and proven skills in event manage-

Organizational feasibility
Refers to how well the proposed information system supports the strategic objectives of the organization.

Economic feasibility
Focuses on whether the expected benefits of an information system will be able to cover the anticipated costs.

Technical feasibility
Refers to the capability of the hardware and software of the proposed information system to provide the decision makers in the organization with the needed information.

Operational feasibility
Refers to the willingness and ability of all concerned parties to operate and support the information system as it is proposed and implemented.

A successful system is well-designed, easy to use, and meets the needs and expectations of its users.

© GETTYIMAGES/EYE WIRE

Now Apply It

Checklist for Successful Information System Design

Frequently, management information systems fail to do the job they were supposed to do because they were inadequately designed or poorly thought out. Before, during, and after the design of the information system, system designers should see whether they could provide a positive response to the questions on the following checklist:

_____ Is the information provided to the decision maker accurate and clear?

_____ Is the information provided to the decision maker current?

_____ Is the information provided to the decision maker in a timely fashion?

_____ Is the information provided to the decision maker frequently enough?

_____ Is the information provided to the decision maker complete?

_____ Have all of the steps in the information system development process been completely performed?

_____ Does the information system support the strategic objectives of the organization?

_____ Do the benefits of the information system outweigh the costs?

_____ Are the hardware and software capable of providing the needed information to the appropriate people?

_____ Does the information system meet the users' needs and expectations?

ment, having provided successful technology systems to prior Olympic games, World Cup Soccer, and other major sporting events.[21]

Another potential problem is that the users may resist the new system. This situation is especially common when workers are afraid that the new information technology may make some currently existing jobs unnecessary. Resistance is also more likely when the people who must work with the information systems are excluded from participating in its design and development. Not only does this lead to an incomplete analysis and design process, but it can also generate resentment toward the new system.[22] These potential pitfalls and problems underscore the importance of thoroughness in the analysis and design steps in the development of the information system. Since information systems frequently fail to do the job they were supposed to do, system designers can benefit from using the checklist in "Now Apply It" to improve their chances of achieving a successful information system design.

THE NEW TECHNOLOGIES

LEARNING OBJECTIVE 7

Describe a variety of types of technology that is changing the way we work.

In addition to the six organizational-level specific types of information systems described early in this chapter, organizations may take advantage of several other types of information technology. Many of these are used at all levels of the organization to assist in communication, information transmission, and decision making. An interesting phenomenon has accompanied the rapid advancements and new developments in information technology. An unprecedented number of entrepreneurial ventures by engineers, scientists, and technical experts is being spawned. We all know of the entrepreneurial success of Microsoft chairman Bill Gates, "The World's Richest Person," but there are many other success stories that aren't quite this prominent. Many engineers, scientists, and technical experts have been concocting their own schemes to grab that elusive brass ring. Consider John Pelka, a former Harris Corp. engineer, who co-founded Quali-Tool, a successful computer hardware manufacturer, or Don Schmaltz, former NASA engineer, and Peter Atwal, former Siemens engineer, who co-founded ISR Global Telecom, Inc. With a little help from a marketing consultant, they successfully launched their new telecommunications software package.[23]

Before you get the mistaken impression that such success stories are limited to the technical experts and computer "geeks" of the world, consider the story of Tricia Grady. This shrewd Tampa, Florida, homemaker realized that there is potential buyer for almost everything. She also understood that the local garage sales, flea markets, and estate sales were exposing their merchandise to a rather limited pool of potential customers. Grady started frequenting these events and began purchasing items that she thought might hold interest and appeal to someone beyond the local neighborhood. She then began placing those items on the eBay auction site, in effect putting the items up for sale to the entire world. Success was instantaneous, and in some cases staggering. Percent returns on some items were in the quadruple-digit range.[24] On almost a daily basis we learn of more success stories like these through the news media.

TELECOMMUNICATIONS AND NETWORKING

Telecommunications is the transmission of information in any form from one location to another using electronic or optical means. This definition applies to all types of telecommunications, including the ordinary telephone call. Generally, however, the term implies that computer systems and the people who use them can communicate from almost any location.

The global integration of organizations is rapidly increasing the need for international phone calls and information transmission. For example, the number of international calls made annually to or from the United States has increased almost tenfold during the past decade.[25] These numbers do not include the data and information that are transmitted through private communication systems.

The more advanced ideas in telecommunications typically concern the connection of multiple computer systems and multiple users in what is usually called a network. A **local-area network (LAN)** connects information systems and users within a small area, such as a building, an office, or a manufacturing plant. The computer network on a college campus is usually a LAN or may contain several LANs.[26] The notion of a local area network is even beginning to filter down to the level of the home. Several corporations are selling or preparing to sell home networking systems. Among the early entrants into this area are Bell Atlantic, IBM, Lucent Technologies, and Motorola. Compaq was among the first computer companies to announce that it would sell computers equipped with home networking cards. While the first home networking applications will connect PCs and printers, eventually video surveillance cameras, heating and air conditioning systems, and other electrical devices within the home might be connected. Some experts even envision the day when a home network will keep an inventory of a refrigerator's contents and automatically order more items as necessary.[27]

One of the IT projects associated with the 2002 Olympic Winter Games was the establishment of a telecommunications network to carry voice, data, video, and audio traffic between all venues and offices during the Games. Qwest, one of the SLOC IT partners, developed a fiber optic-based local area network to accomplish this. Additional Olympic telecommunications capabilities were provided in the form of a long distance system, a mobile telephone and pager system, and a broadband communications system by IT partners Qwest and AT&T. Some of the accompanying hardware for these systems included 32,000 fiber miles of optical fiber cable, 14,200 desktop telephones, 10,000 mobile telephones, and 7,000 two-way radios.

A network that stretches over a wide geographic area, such as a city, a region, a country, and even the world, is typically called a **wide-area network (WAN)**. For example, Wal-Mart, Sears, and Eckerd Drugs, as well as many other companies, can easily communicate with their stores through a WAN. Network arrangements are becoming increasingly common in organizations that need to transmit and receive day-to-day information on business operations from their employees, customers, suppliers, and other organizations. In addition, each day more and more of us are adapting to that widest of WANs, the Internet's World Wide Web. Almost daily we

Telecommunications
The transmission of information in any form from one location to another using electronic or optical means.

Local-area network (LAN)
An information system that connects users in a small area, such as a building, an office, or a manufacturing plant.

Wide-area network (WAN)
An information system that extends over a broad geographic area, such as cities, regions, countries, or the world.

seem to see new software that has been developed to facilitate the blending of desktop computing with the multimedia technology of the World Wide Web. This new technology will make it easier to find information, whether it is on the computer's hard drive or on the Internet. Furthermore, each piece of material created on a personal computer—whether an e-mail message, a memo to the boss, or any other type of document—could easily be embellished with images, audio, and video.[28]

A warning should accompany the rapid proliferation of information available on the Internet. There is no guarantee that the information to be found will always be accurate. With the explosion of electronic commerce (which will be discussed shortly), the distinction between objective information and advertising has become clouded. For example, most of us know of Dr. C. Everett Koop, who became one of America's most authoritative, recognizable, and trusted public figures during the eight years he served as the U.S. Surgeon General. After leaving that position, Dr. Koop became the subject of intense criticism from medical ethicists who complained that his health information Web site (http://www.drkoop.com) had frequently blurred the line between its objective information and its advertising or promotional content.[29] The caveat here is "Let the user of the information beware!"

Some profound sociological implications should be considered as the World Wide Web gets more and more refined and as we see more and more people using the Web for their own entertainment and enlightenment or to conduct business. The Internet might change the way we live and work as a society. Because the Internet will allow some people to work almost anywhere, workers may move away from major cities and spread to rural areas. Furthermore, if these workers are parents, they will be able to monitor their children's activities and well-being at daycare centers. Many childcare facilities have already begun installing monitoring cameras whose images are accessible via the Internet to parents possessing the proper password. Even the concept of communities may change, as geographically dispersed people gather and interact online.

Many activities are now possible due to the ease of access and relatively low cost of telecommunications. **Electronic data interchange (EDI)** is the electronic transmission of transaction data using telecommunications. These data can include sales invoices, purchase orders, shipping notices, and so on. EDI provides an almost immediate transmission of the data and allows for a significant savings in printing, mailing, and labor costs as well as in time. In addition, since the orders and information are transferred electronically, fewer people have to handle the data, thereby reducing the chances for data-entry and mishandling errors. Some companies have reported decreases of 25 to 50 percent in the amount of time it takes to receive and fill customer orders since adopting EDI. RCA has estimated that the cost to fill an order will drop from $50 to around $4 due to labor-saving use of EDI. General Motors has required all of its suppliers to use EDI, leading to estimated savings of about $200 per automobile produced. Likewise, the U.S. Department of Defense is moving toward a similar requirement for its suppliers.[30] Ford Motor Company used telecommunications to transmit information to various units around the world when it designed the new version of the classic Mustang and prepared it for production.[31] The Campbell Soup Company has put EDI to good use in coordinating orders placed by its customers. Implementing some of these new advances resulted in multimillion-dollar annual savings to Campbell, and in some cases a 50 percent increase in profit for some of its retail customers.[32] In "At The Forefront" we can see how the Pfizer Pharmaceutical Company moved to the forefront in the pharmaceutical industry when it comes to getting new drugs to the market. Pfizer took advantage of the EDI and Web technologies in the development of its Electronic Submission Navigator (ESUB), which has allowed Pfizer to cut in half the amount of time needed to gain FDA approval for its newly developed drugs.

Electronic data interchange (EDI)
Electronic transmission of transaction data using telecommunications.

At The Forefront

IT Prevents Pfizer and the FDA from Drowning in a Sea of Paper

In the United States, the process of getting a new drug approved by the Food and Drug Administration (FDA) has always been a long and arduous journey. Pharmaceutical companies must first conduct broad, expensive trials. After this development phase, the pharmaceutical companies must then submit the paperwork to support their claims. Typically, researchers and support staff assembled the results of their clinical trials into a master document called a *new drug application* (NDA), which was then sent to the FDA to start the approval process. The paperwork for a single drug was often more than one million pages. That's enough paper to fill an entire tractor-trailer! Portions of the NDA report would then be distributed by the FDA to reviewers, who would provide their analyses. Individual reviewers often worked with 20,000-page sections of an NDA, which could amount to a stack of paper five to six feet tall! Cross-referencing was a major challenge. If a reviewer needed to check something on a page outside of his or her sec-

tion, the FDA had to send runners to the library warehouse to locate the needed information from the master version of the NDA. This process resulted in a typical 18–24 month time to complete the review and bring the drug to market. Such a time frame was no longer acceptable, given a recent congressional mandate that the FDA shorten its review process to 12 months without compromising safety.

In the mid-1990s staff members of Pfizer Pharmaceuticals recognized that the Web was beginning to take off and decided that the time might be right to experiment with it. At that time Pfizer researchers were developing Trovan, a new antibiotic drug, which would prove to be the largest anti-infective submission ever received by the FDA. Pfizer's staff used computer-aided NDAs to build sections of the document electronically. Pfizer's IT team began developing what would eventually be called ESUB, for Electronic Submission Navigator. This system allows for the electronic submission of documents to the FDA, a vast improve-

ment over the former paper-based method of submitting documentation. Pfizer's system cost $3.2 million to develop, but it netted the company at least $142 million in revenues through the start of 2000 because of shorter times to get new drugs to the market.

The benefits of ESUB extend beyond return on investment. By working collaboratively with its business partners, Pfizer's IT team constructed a system that provides a global view of the status of a trial or application process, enhances Pfizer's competitive advantage by linking drug researchers around the world, enables Pfizer to penetrate world markets more quickly by filing concurrent submissions in different countries, and gives the company the ability to deliver five new drugs every 12 months—the fastest rate in the industry. Perhaps the most important benefit of ESUB is that it can offer new, safe, effective drugs to patients more quickly.

SOURCE: M. Blodgett, "Prescription Strength," *CIO Magazine,* February 1, 2000, 94–98.

EDI is not just for giant manufacturers and government, however. For example, InterDesign, of Solon, Ohio, makes plastic clocks, refrigerator magnets, soap dishes, and the like. Under pressure from a large retailer, the company adopted EDI. Now over half of the orders to InterDesign arrive via modems connected to its computer system instead of by mail or through a phone call. Virtually all order-entry and shipping errors have been eliminated. Now employees who used to staff phones taking orders spend their time collecting valuable information the company couldn't afford to collect before. Sales are tracked by product, color, customer, region, and so on.[33] According to some predictions, early in this new millennium as many as one-half of all business documents will be transmitted by EDI.

The banking and retail industries are moving increasingly toward an environment of **electronic funds transfer (EFT)**, where all financial transactions are done electronically. Many of us already depend on EFT for our banking and financial transactions. The automatic teller machine is one example of EFT. Being able to pay bills over the phone is another example. Furthermore, many of the point-of-sale terminals in retail stores depend on EFT as checks are approved and debit or credit cards are swiped.

Many organizations around the world are discovering that they can benefit from telecommunications. In its quest to help small and medium-sized businesses in developing countries become involved in world trade, the United Nations has established a global electronic trading network. It is the U.N.'s hope that the network will stimulate growth in international trade by helping those target businesses locate information that would help them enter global markets.[34]

Electronic funds transfer (EFT)
Electronic manipulation of financial transactions.

Telecommuting, another facet of telecommunications described earlier in this chapter on page 563, is a relatively new way to work. When workers telecommute, they operate from a remote location, such as a branch office or their home, and communicate with the office via telecommunications. Many jobs do not require an individual to be at the main office all of the time. In fact, some people find that working from a remote site, such as their home, provides some big benefits.

American Express Travel Services has been experimenting with telecommuting for some of its employees. These jobs are oriented around providing customer service and information by telephone. Many employees located in the Houston area had a 60- to 90-minute commute to and from work each day. By telecommuting from home, the workers found they had more time to spend with their families and were not stressed by the chore of driving in heavy traffic or bad weather. American Express has also seen some significant benefits. Thus far, workers have been able to handle 26 percent more calls with no reduction in the quality of service. In addition, the rent that would normally have been spent for office space for these employees could be saved. In New York, American Express estimates that it can save about $4,400 annually for every travel counselor who telecommutes. In addition, with advances in technology, managers can still monitor the employees' work performance in responding to customer phone calls.[35]

In an effort to help reduce pollution caused by automobiles, California became one of the first states to recognize the benefits of telecommuting when it instituted legislation that encouraged businesses to allow workers to telecommute.[36] In the last decade of the 20th century, an earthquake near Los Angeles did so much damage to the interstate highway system in the area that commuting times were significantly lengthened, sometimes by as much as two or three hours each way.[37] Telecommuting offers a way for companies to alleviate this type of difficulty. More recently, the events of the 9/11 attack on America have caused a dramatic surge in the interest in telecommuting. Concerns that the workplace could be a target of anthrax-tainted mail or another terrorist attack has many workers staying away and using technology to get the job done.[38]

Electronic mail (e-mail)
A computer-based system that allows individuals to exchange and store messages through computerized text-processing and communication networks.

Another advance that has grown out of telecommunications is **electronic mail (e-mail)** networks and bulletin board systems. E-mail systems, which are often a part of office automation systems (discussed later), are changing the way we work and communicate. You can think of e-mail as being like the postal system except that the messages and information are transmitted electronically through computer networks instead of being sent through the mail. Many Internet access companies offer e-mail services. Among the largest and most recognizable of these are America Online, Microsoft's MSN, AT&T Corporation's WorldNet, and EarthLink. Communication speeds are very fast. Whenever the people receiving messages are ready, they can read their mail.

ELECTRONIC COMMERCE

In recent years Internet technology has served as a catalyst for change in the ways organizations are conducting business. Thousands of organizations can be linked together into a single network via the Internet. Through such a linkage, prospective buyers and sellers can exchange information, products, services, and payments. In effect, they are acting as an electronic marketplace. Since the Internet knows no national boundaries and pays attention to no clock, this electronic marketplace is indeed global in scope, and it is open 24 hours per day. This linkage forms the basis for electronic commerce (e-commerce), which was described earlier on page 563 as the process of buying and selling goods and services electronically by means of computerized business transactions. The Internet has emerged as the dominant technology for conducting e-commerce. On almost a daily basis we read in the newspaper of some new organization that will sell its product or service online.

Computers, books, cars, stereos, appliances, tools, airline tickets, flowers, and count-less other items can be obtained in this fashion.[39] A study conducted by the Cen-ter for Research on Electronic Commerce showed that, near the end of the 20th century, the impact of the Internet on the U.S. economy exceeded $300 billion in revenue and accounted for more than 1.2 million jobs. That same study revealed that e-commerce alone generated nearly $102 billion in revenue.[40] Of that activity, direct retail sales to consumers generated revenues of $18 billion in 1999, and that figure is projected to surge to $108 billion in 2003.[41]

E-commerce has several advantages. By using electronic ordering rather than the traditional manual and paper-based procedures, ordering, delivery, and pay-ment can be accelerated. Often companies can achieve higher profits and at the same time charge lower prices due to the removal of intermediate steps in the dis-tribution and sales process. That is the approach used by such companies as the Dell Computer Corporation and Gateway Computers. Companies can face risks associated with offering their products online. Traditional retail outlets for their products often view such a process as taking away some of their business. This feel-ing caused Dell rivals IBM, Compaq, and Hewlett-Packard to initially move tenta-tively in this arena in fear of alienating the wholesalers and retailers who have helped make them among the world's top computer makers.[42] Such potential alienation of wholesalers and retailers is evidenced in a letter Home Depot re-cently sent to its suppliers warning them to consider the consequences of selling online. The letter stated that "We, too, have the right to be selective in regard to vendors we select, and we trust that you can understand that a company may be hesitant to do business with its competitors."[43] Such a feeling has caused many manufacturers to think twice before offending retailers that sell their products or quickly reverse their decision, as was the case with Gibson Musical Instruments of Nashville. When the company decided to offer its guitars through the Internet at a 10 percent discount, Gibson dealers were irate. Fearing that this new practice would jeopardize relations with its dealers, Gibson discontinued its Web sales of guitars within a month and changed its Web strategy. The company put its parts catalog on the Web, and now uses the Web only for the sale of strings, accessories, and repair parts.[44]

Another hot area that has evolved recently in electronic commerce is the on-line auction forum. Using e-mail and other interactive features of the Internet, people can make online bids for any number of items that someone else wants to sell. The system receives bids for items entered on the Internet, evaluates the bids, and notifies the highest bidder. One of the most visible success stories in this area is that of eBay. The company was founded in 1995 to sell Pez dispensers, but it has quickly evolved well beyond that under the leadership of CEO Meg Whitman, who has risen to the status of the world's richest female CEO, with a net worth well over $1 billion. In mid-1999 eBay could boast of more than 2 million items for auction daily, with 3.8 million registered members and a $2.4 million annual profit. It is one of the top 10 businesses on the Internet, with a daily flurry of deals for Beanie Babies, Star Wars toys, antiques, collectibles, and a wide variety of other items.[45]

As business transactions are made via the Internet, remuneration is typically made by means of an electronic payment. Such technologies as electronic funds transfer, credit cards, smart cards, debit cards, and new Internet-based payment sys-tems can be used to pay for products and services. Security of electronic communi-cations is a major control issue for companies that engage in electronic commerce. All information being transmitted between buyers and sellers must be kept confi-dential and secure as it is being transmitted electronically. This includes informa-tion related to the details of the order as well as information related to the mechanism for payment. Most organizations rely on sophisticated encryption procedures to pro-tect sensitive information as it is transmitted over networks. **Encryption** refers to the

Encryption
The coding and scrambling of sensitive information transmitted over networks to make it unintelligible to unauthorized viewers.

coding and scrambling of information to make it unintelligible to unauthorized viewers. Encryption is especially useful to protect transmission of payment data, such as credit card information. Several methods of encryption exist, each with its own proprietary methodology. These encryption methodologies will continue to change and new ones will evolve as businesses strive to keep confidential e-commerce information out of sight of those not authorized to see it.

ARTIFICIAL INTELLIGENCE

Artificial intelligence (AI)
Process in which computers and computer systems behave intelligently.

Artificial intelligence (AI) has the goal of developing computers and computer systems that can behave intelligently. Work in this area is derived from research in a variety of disciplines, including computer science, psychology, linguistics, mathematics, and engineering. Probably the most widely known application of artificial intelligence is in computer programs that play chess, some at or near the level of a grand master. But artificial intelligence applications go well beyond this. Two primary areas of research that have had some success in recent years are expert systems and robotics.

Expert system
A computer-based system that contains and can use knowledge about a specific, relatively narrow, complex application.

EXPERT SYSTEMS   An **expert system** is a knowledge-based information system. In other words, it is a computer-based system that contains and can use knowledge about a specific, relatively narrow, complex application. The knowledge the expert system contains and the way it is programmed to use this knowledge allow it to behave as an expert consultant to end users.

Fundamentally, an expert system is a type of software in which expert knowledge has been programmed to assist decision makers in a complex decision environment. The knowledge in an expert system has been painstakingly acquired from one or more experts in the knowledge domain of interest. Knowledge engineers, the expert system specialists, take this knowledge and carefully construct a knowledge base and the software that can use it. Users can then tap into this knowledge through the expert system and use it to provide expertise in difficult decision situations. Texas Instruments has developed an expert system called IEFCARES (Information Engineering Facility Customer Response Expert System) to assist in providing service and support for their CASE product called IEF. Like many other credit companies, both ITT Commercial Finance Corporation and American Express have expert systems to assist in managing and monitoring credit requests and approvals. Expert systems are also commonly used for tasks such as loan portfolio analysis, diagnostic troubleshooting, design and layout configuration, and process monitoring and control.[46]

Robotics
The technology of building and using machines with humanlike characteristics, such as dexterity, movement, vision, and strength.

ROBOTICS   The technology of building and using machines with humanlike characteristics, such as dexterity, movement, vision, and strength, is called **robotics**. A robot contains computer intelligence and uses research knowledge from AI, engineering, and physiology. Robots are often called "steel-collar" workers because they are frequently used to perform manufacturing tasks that were previously done by blue-collar workers. When used in this fashion, they are programmed to perform specific, repetitive tasks in exactly the same way with each repetition. These automated machines offer significant benefits. They can be programmed to do very complex tasks that require a variety of movements and strength over and over again with precision. Robots don't have some of the weaknesses of human workers, such as illness, fatigue, and absenteeism. In addition, robots can be valuable in hazardous work areas and with tasks that are dangerous for humans. For example, robots have been developed that can distance humans from dangerous situations, like assisting police bomb-squads in the removal of hazardous materials or aiding in the dismantling of damaged nuclear power plants. They can also be valuable in going where humans simply cannot go. Japanese electronics companies have developed micro-machines smaller than a coin. They are capable of crawling into the tiniest gaps around bundles of pipes, performing inspections, and even making repairs at electric and nuclear power plants while the plants keep running.[47] NASA continues to be a leader in the use of robotics with its unmanned space explorers that attempt to map foreign worlds. The latest of these ventures is the Galileo space probe, which was continuing to map Jupiter and its moon Callisto in early 2002.[48] NASA has funded the Robotics Engineering Consortium, which is devoted to turning robotic ideas into practical machines. Some of its successful developments thus far include an excavator for Caterpillar, an off-road vehicle for Boeing, and a forklift system for Ford. New Holland North America provides an illustration of just how sophisticated these robots can be. Its computer-driven harvester uses the satellite-based global positioning system (GPS), wheel sensors, and a video camera to "see" a crop line so it can harvest a field without a driver or a remote operator.[49]

IMPACT OF INFORMATION TECHNOLOGY ON DYNAMIC ORGANIZATIONS

An organization is a sociotechnical system that consists of people and their tasks, as well as the organization's culture, structure, and environment. All of these things are affected by and will affect technology. Information technology will have a profound impact on management efficiency, social relationships, and organizational structure.

LEARNING OBJECTIVE 8

Discuss the impact of information technology on the organization.

Information systems must produce useful and relevant information for management. Many of the areas that have been computerized have not yet resulted in the desired or expected gains. In part, this is because many organizations have used these new systems simply to replace traditional business practices instead of reassessing and redesigning the organization and the decision-making process to take advantage of the new technology's capabilities. Viewed another way, the primary or first-order effect of initial investments in information technology was simply to improve efficiency. Organizations still have a lot of room for improving the design and management of their information systems. Furthermore, we are discovering that the second-order effects, which are unintended and impossible to predict, are often more interesting and provide greater opportunities than the first-order effects.[50] These unintended and unanticipated effects lead to a second area of impact.

If only isolated individuals used information systems, the systems would have minimal impact on the social relationships among people. Currently, however, the very essence of the use of information technology within organizations is to enhance communication between people. Therefore, whenever information systems are used in this manner, they have a social component and potential social effects.

For example, what are the new technologies doing to power relationships within the organization? Does the technology change the dimensions and directions of determining priorities? If the use of the technology has negative consequences, who is accountable for the results? Furthermore, the expanding use of and dependence on information technology have created an interesting paradox. Information technology, like globalization, can extend an organization, making it less personal and less social. However, the effect of the technology often rewards intimacy.[51] These social implications suggest other, broader effects of information technology.

In the early years of computer-based information systems, the technology was so limited that it was difficult to computerize even one division of the organization. As a result, data-processing services tended to be decentralized. During the

1960s and 1970s, computer systems became much more powerful, and large systems were often able to handle many of the computing needs for the whole organization. This led to greater centralization of control over computer resources. The advent of the microcomputer in the late 1970s and the 1980s led to increased demands for computing access and power, creating a great deal of confusion and conflict within organizations as they struggled to manage the rapid proliferation of varieties of hardware and software.

Neither centralization nor decentralization alone is the appropriate response. Instead, organizations should examine their specific computing needs and try to align their information technology to those needs. Some aspects of information processing in an organization may require greater centralization of computing resources, while others may lend themselves to greater decentralization.

Many note that information technology can help managers control the interdependencies of their organizations. In particular, as the competitive environment has become more complex, so have the information needs of the decision makers. Information technology can help managers respond to this competitive environment. For example, unlike the situation during the Industrial Revolution, when the goal was to separate tasks and then make them simple and routine, current trends in information technology and data communications are to flatten the organization; fuse departments; create cross-functional teams; and increase and improve communications among employees, suppliers, and customers.[52] The structure of the organization can then be adjusted to take advantage of the varying needs. Despite its great promise, information technology also has limitations. We turn to them in the next section.

LIMITATIONS OF COMPUTER-BASED INFORMATION SYSTEMS

LEARNING OBJECTIVE 9

Explain the limitations of information technology.

As we have seen, although investments in computer-based information systems have been substantial, the improvements that can be traced directly to the investment in technology have in some instances been minimal. Several factors may explain this low return on investments in technology.

First, the technology has been changing so rapidly in the last 10 years that organizations have had difficulty keeping up. In 1981 IBM produced its first microcomputer, marking for many the beginning of the rapid proliferation of computers in organizations and homes. Apple introduced its Macintosh system in 1984 as an easier-to-use alternative to the DOS (disk operating system) environment of IBM and IBM-compatible machines. In 1986 the Intel 386 microchip became the norm for microcomputer systems. Five years later the Intel 486 was released, and a few years later the Pentium microchip began to show up in microcomputers. The Pentium II chip soon replaced the Pentium and thus became the standard for processing speed. Then, by 1999 the Pentium III had surfaced, establishing a new standard for speed.[53] The new millennium saw that speed eclipsed by the Pentium 4. When it was introduced in 2000, it boasted a speed 50 percent greater than the Pentium III.[54] By the time you read this, advances could be well beyond this new standard. Where will this dizzying escalation end? Looming on the distant horizon, but still in the research stage, are quantum computers. Instead of the traditional architecture of transistors mounted on microprocessor chips, these computers will do calculations using the spin of atoms. It is estimated that such a computer would be able to perform calculations one billion times faster than a Pentium 4 and search the entire Internet in the blink of an eye![55] All of these advances in technology have increased computing speed at a very low cost; they have also allowed larger and more sophisticated programs to be developed and have enabled almost all users to do types of computing that could be performed only on mainframe computers just a few years ago. As computers have become more powerful, so have software programs. However, this vast array of new hardware and software systems has made it difficult for organizations to maintain consistency throughout the organization. Furthermore, many people are reluctant to change their way of working to take full advantage of the capabilities of the technology.

IMPLICATIONS FOR LEADERS

Most organizations are only now coming to realize that the ways they incorporate technology into the workplace have a significant impact on their success or failure. A recent survey asked senior information system executives to name the 10 issues that are most important for the management and organizational use of information technology as we move into the 21st century. Their responses are listed in Table 18.3.

We have seen in this chapter that there are several different types of computerized information systems, serving several different types of decision specialists at different levels of the organization. Despite this diversity, there is one common element to all these information systems: they support decision making within the organization. In this context, the 3Cs leadership model will promote good decision making, as was seen in earlier chapters that focused on the decision-making process and decision-making tools. Leaders must be competent in their understanding of the information systems that can provide support to their decision-making efforts.

Table 18.3 | 21st Century Issues in the Use of Information Technology

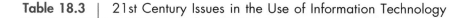

1. Information architecture—creating a high-level map of the information requirements of the organization.
2. Data resources—data are now viewed as the important factor of production.
3. Strategic planning—considered one of the most important issues, it involves the close alignment of technology with business plans.
4. Human resources—recognition of the limited number of information systems professionals available to develop and maintain increasingly technical and complex organizational computing environments.
5. Organizational learning—learning how to make appropriate use of information technology.
6. Technology infrastructure—a new issue for this survey, it involves building an infrastructure that will support current operations while remaining flexible enough to adapt to changing technology and evolving organizational needs.
7. Information system organization alignment—effectiveness of support for organizational activities and operations without constraining either the technology or the organization.
8. Competitive advantage—technology is no longer the sole arbiter of competitive advantage, but is becoming the necessary, but not sufficient condition. Competitive advantage comes from the proper role of information technology in streamlining internal business processes, forging electronic links with suppliers and customers, and shaping the organization's design.
9. Software development—developing new tools and techniques to facilitate the rapid and error-free development of needed software systems.
10. Telecommunications system planning—can be used to reduce structural, time, and spatial limits on organizational relationships.

SOURCE: F. Niederman, J.C. Brancheau, and J.C. Wetherbe, "Information Systems Management Issues for the 1990s," *MIS Quarterly*, December 1991, 475–500.

Meeting The Challenge

Building the Information Systems Needed to Run the Olympic Winter Games

The delivery of all hardware, software, telecommunications, and technology services for the Olympic Games was a monumental undertaking. SLOC's budget for the information technology project exceeded $300 million. To complete the 2002 technology solution, The International Olympic Committee (IOC) and SLOC assembled a consortium of leading companies to design, develop, and operate the technology required for the games. SLOC and its partners created one unified project team dedicated to the successful delivery of the 2002 information technology solution. In the months leading up to the big event, the size of the technology staff gradually increased to its maximum size of 2,900 members at the start of the Games. The IT team had a strong international flavor; 23 countries were represented on the team.

The SLOC IT project was broken down into several subprojects, some of which were briefly described in "Facing The Challenge." Each of these subprojects was responsible for delivering specific systems, infrastructure, and services for the Games. The specific subprojects were Timing and Scoring Systems; On-Venue Results; Information Diffusion Systems; Telecommunications Network; PBX systems; Long Distance Service; Radio Systems and Frequency Planning; Television, VCRs, Camcorders and Audio/Visual Products; Document Processing Equipment and Services; Internet; Games Management Systems; Hardware Deployment and Support; Systems Management; and Systems

Integration. SLOC and its IT partners first focused on designing the systems for these subprojects and then focused on the systems integration. In the course of developing the systems, SLOC and its partners deployed the largest telecommunications network in Utah.

The SLOC IT project had several unique dynamics. While most commercial systems projects can delay implementation when problems or issues arise, Olympic organizing committees cannot push back their deployment dates. They also don't have the luxury of working through the bugs during the first weeks that new systems are live. The equipment and applications deployed for the games must work correctly on the first day of competition. As a result, development processes and testing procedures were well planned out and thoroughly tested. In June 2000 the main technology partner, SchlumbergerSema (a.k.a. the Sema Group), began simulating events at all venues, generating timing and scoring data to test the networks. Another technology partner, The PROMODEL Corporation, engaged in a variety of simulations. For example, interactive transit simulations tested a variety of scenarios involving different numbers of buses, numbers of spectators, travel distance from park and ride lots, weather conditions, and security checks. The results revealed the optimal number of buses and bus schedules to reduce spectator waiting.

Beginning in 2001 various national and multinational championship events were staged at the

different venues to further test the systems under live conditions. In September 2001 a comprehensive exercise was conducted to test SLOC's on-venue results systems, press agency data feeds, and printed results applications. Application changes resulting from these tests were fully incorporated into the systems by November 15, 2001, at which time all Games software were frozen. By October 2001 Qwest (another IT partner) had completed the fiber infrastructure (32,000 fiber miles of optical fiber cable!). All PCs, servers, and laptops, as well as all TVs and audio/video hardware had been deployed to venues and staging areas. By late October 2001 everything had been put into place, and all that remained was a series of comprehensive exercises to simulate Games-time competitions and conditions. At that point SLOC was fully prepared to host the most watched Olympic Winter Games in history.

SOURCES: "Information Technology—Project Overview and Update," *Salt Lake Organizing Committee for the Olympic Winter Games of 2002 Project Overview and Update*, October 2001; "Salt Lake Organization Draws High Marks," *International Olympic Committee Press Release*, March 7, 2001; "The International Olympic Committee Recognises Internet Organisations," *International Olympic Committee Press Release*, December 27, 2000; "IOC and SEMA Group Sign Olympic Technology Agreement for 2002 and Beyond," *International Olympic Committee Press Release*, March 13, 2000; "Dr. Philippe Verveer, Ph.D., to Join The International Olympic Committee as Technology Direction," *International Olympic Committee Press Release*, June 13, 1999.

And as we have seen before, good decision making requires more than just competence; it also encompasses the remaining elements of the 3Cs leadership model. Good decision making requires that the decision maker possess strong character, infused with honesty, integrity, and driven by ethical behavior. It also requires a recognition that the impact of the decisions made may extend to the community and not be confined to the boundaries of the organization.

Successful leaders of the future will be those who:

- Understand the importance of quality information that is obtained in a timely fashion.
- Employ information systems capable of providing quality information that is both timely and complete.

- Are able to use that information to their advantage in the organizational decision-making process.
- Are well versed in the latest technological innovations for information gathering, processing, and disseminating.
- Are aware of the impact of information technology on management efficiency, organizational social relationships, and organizational structure.
- Are aware of the limitations of computer-based information systems.

As we have seen throughout this chapter, the ultimate success or failure of information technology is not always immediately clear. Technology is not the solution for all organization problems, and technology will not, in and of itself, provide relief from poor organizational practices. The benefits that can be gained from technology are many, but the ultimate benefits from technology are the vast amounts of information that can be processed and distributed more easily. Management success—and, on a larger scale, organizational success—is still based primarily on the skills and insightful decisions of the leaders. Still, it is up to the organization and its decision makers to take advantage of and properly use the information that becomes available.

SUMMARY

1. In recent years the world has seen the strengthening of the global economy, the transformation of many industrial economies to knowledge-based and information-based service economies, changes in the hierarchical structure of many organizations, and the emergence of many technology-driven innovations. These forces have altered the environment of business and made it more reliant on information technology.

2. Many organizations possess a hierarchical structure with a strategic level at the top, comprised of senior-level managers who address strategic issues and long-term decision making. Directly below this lies a management level, comprised of middle managers who monitor and control the organization's operations. Immediately below this lies a knowledge level, comprised of knowledge workers and data workers who create new information and knowledge or process the organization's information. Finally, at the bottom of the structure lies an operational level, which is comprised of operational managers who keep track of the basic activities and transactions of the organization.

3. Strategic-level information systems consist of executive support systems (ESS) and enterprise resource planning (ERP) systems. Management-level information systems consist of management information systems (MIS) and decision support systems (DSS). Knowledge-level information systems consist of knowledge management systems (KMS) and office automation systems (OAS). Operational-level information systems consist of transaction processing systems (TPS).

4. In general, the components of an information system consist of hardware, software, and data. The hardware consists of the input, processing, output, storage, and data-transmission devices. The software consists of the various programs, which are the instructions that tell the hardware components what to do and how to do it. Data, which are often stored and maintained in a database, are the objective measures of an organization's activities.

5. Data are the raw facts, details, or objective measures that represent some type of transaction or activity within an organization. Data processing is the process in which the data are aggregated and organized, manipulated through analysis, and placed in a proper context for evaluation and use by the end user. Information is the result of the process of transforming data into a meaningful form for a specific purpose. To facilitate good decision making, the people making decisions must have useful information. Useful information has three primary characteristics: (1) The quality of the information produced and distributed to decision makers must be very high; (2) the information must be available in a timely fashion; and (3) the information must be complete in its scope.

6. The development of an information system is a systematic process of examining and analyzing the current activities needed to maintain organizational operations. The systems design process involves several steps: (1) investigation, (2) systems analysis, (3) systems design, (4) systems implementation, and (5) systems maintenance. The systems development life cycle (SDLC) is a common model for how information systems evolve over time within an organization.

7. Various types of information technology are changing the way we work. Telecommunications and networking are especially important. Electronic data interchange (EDI) and electronic funds transfer (EFT) are allowing organizations

to establish and maintain business relationships without direct person-to-person contact. Among the most rapidly growing technology-based processes emerging is electronic commerce (e-commerce), which is the process of buying and selling goods and services electronically with computerized business transactions. Telecommuting is allowing more workers to conduct business activities at home or on the road with the customer. Applications of artificial intelligence, such as expert systems and robotics, are enabling technology to do tasks that were previously done by workers. Office automation is creating a technology-supported office environment to assist in the management and processing of office work and information.

8. Information technology will have an impact on management efficiency, social relationships, and the structure within an organization. Efficiency will improve only when the organization and the decision-making process are reassessed and redesigned to take advantage of the capabilities of the technology. When information systems are used to enhance communication between people in the organization, there is a social impact. Finally, as more aspects of an organization become integrated into the information system, more centralization of control over computer resources may occur.

9. Among the limitations of information technology are (1) the difficulty in keeping up with technological advances, (2) the potentially high cost and time involved in changing technologies, and (3) the failure of many people to take advantage of the technology because of their reluctance to change the way they work.

REVIEW QUESTIONS

1. *(Learning Objective 1)* Briefly describe the recent changes that have altered the environment of business and made it more reliant on information technology?

2. *(Learning Objective 2)* List the four levels of decision specialists within an organization's hierarchy and identify the major function of each.

3. *(Learning Objective 3)* Describe the types of information systems available to support decision makers at the different levels of an organization's hierarchy.

4. *(Learning Objective 4)* Briefly describe the various components in an information system.

5. *(Learning Objective 5)* Describe how data and information differ, and identify the characteristics of useful information.

6. *(Learning Objective 6)* List and describe the steps in the development of an information system.

7. *(Learning Objective 7)* Describe some of the information technologies-related advances that are changing the way we work.

8. *(Learning Objective 8)* Identify and discuss the various effects information technology can have on an organization.

9. *(Learning Objective 9)* What are some of the limitations of information technology? Briefly discuss the causes and outcomes of each type of limitation.

DISCUSSION QUESTIONS

Improving Critical Thinking

1. Assume that the health center at your school wishes to install an information system. Identify the major tasks necessary for each phase of a systems design process for the health center. What difficulties in design and development might you expect to encounter in each phase?

2. Explain the concept of expert systems. If it is possible to capture the knowledge of an expert and place it in an expert system, one can argue that there is no longer a need for an expert. Furthermore, if the data are in a database, the knowledge of the expert becomes permanent. It can be transferred to different settings and even reproduced through copying processes. Can an expert system produce more consistent, reproducible results than the human expert on whom it is based? Why or why not? Is it desirable to seek this result? Explain.

3. What can you do to ensure that you will have the technical knowledge and skills related to information technology necessary to compete effectively in the job market?

Enhancing Communication Skills

4. Examine the library at your school. What major types of activities must the library support as part of its mission? Which of these activities could be computerized? Can these various activities be integrated into one larger information system? Explain. Identify additional library functions that could be computerized. To enhance your oral communication skills, prepare a short (10- to 15-minute) presentation of your answer for the class.

5. What news stories dealing with electronic commerce have appeared in the news lately? What impact do you think this technology will have on organizations and management? To

enhance your written communication skills, write a short (one- to two-page) essay in which you discuss these impacts.

Building Teamwork

6. What do you think the office or organization of the future will be like? What technology do you think the office of the future will use? To refine your teamwork skills, meet with a small group of students who have been given this same assignment. Compare your visions of the office of the future, then reach a consensus about how this office will look. Select a spokesperson to present your team's vision to the rest of the class.

7. Identify several types of data that might be collected in a full-service bank. Think about how the information that can be derived from the data would differ for each hierarchical level in the bank. In other words, how might the various levels in the organization make different uses of the same basic data? To refine your teamwork skills, meet with a small group of students who have been given this same assignment. Compare your lists, and then, by consensus, consolidate your lists into a single list of the best four types of data. Select a spokesperson to present your team's findings to the rest of the class.

THINKING CRITICALLY: DEBATE THE ISSUE

Electronic Commerce—Opportunity for Business or Threat to Retail Workers?

Form teams of four or five students as directed by your instructor. Research the topic of electronic commerce. Identify aspects of its use that might be viewed as benefits for the businesses that use it to deliver products and services, and to consumers who purchase those products and services. Also identify aspects that might be viewed as threats to the livelihoods of retail workers. When it is time to debate this issue in front of the class, your instructor will tell your team which position (opportunity or threat) you will be assigned.

EXPERIENTIAL EXERCISE 18.1

What Technology Do You Need?

The purpose of this exercise is to explore the variety of options available to support you as a traveling businessperson.

Step 1. Assume you are a sales representative for a college textbook publishing company. A significant portion of your job is to travel to meet with faculty who might potentially adopt some of your titles. You travel more than 100,000 miles a year, with trips ranging from one day to two weeks for important contacts. Since your office is on the road as much as it is at headquarters, you need to be able to accomplish your job while traveling.

Step 2. Your task is to identify your hardware and software needs. Then investigate your options as if you were really going to purchase the required equipment. Remember that system compatibility and reliability are important. In addition, remember that you will be carrying this equipment with you along with your luggage.

Therefore, weight is also an important factor. You may also be using this equipment to assist you in presentations to potential clients and current customers. Therefore, a high-quality system display is also a factor to consider.

Step 3. Discuss your conclusion with others in your class.

For Discussion

1. What kind of trade-offs did you find yourself making in order to make your final selection of hardware and software? What hardware and software did you select?

2. What assumptions did you make about your job in the initial stages of working on this situation? What additional information would have been useful?

3. What maximum weight and cost limits, if any, did you use?

4. How did your decisions differ from those of others?

EXPERIENTIAL EXERCISE 18.2

Learning About E-Mail

If you have not done so before this time, see if you can acquire an account on your school's computer. Once this has been accomplished, learn about and try to use the e-mail system. With

several of your classmates, explore the benefits, limitations, and difficulties of working via e-mail.

Step 1. Acquire a computer account and learn how to use the e-mail facility.

Step 2. Conduct a discussion/debate with several of your classmates using the e-mail facilities. As the discussion progresses, be aware of the problems of using e-mail to communicate about and coordinate activities. Keep a list of your comments and observations.

Step 3. Discuss how e-mail can enhance and limit organizational communication. Develop a list of suggestions for an organization that is attempting to use e-mail to improve organizational effectiveness.

For Discussion

1. How difficult was it to become comfortable with e-mail?

2. How effective was e-mail in supporting your discussion? What were the benefits? What were the limiting factors?

CAPTURING THE POWER OF INFORMATION TECHNOLOGY

1. Use whatever search vehicle is most convenient (Internet, e-mail, fax, newspaper/magazine advertisements, and so on) to gather information on the technical specifications of the top-of-the-line notebook microcomputer models offered by Dell, Compaq, Hewlett-Packard, and IBM. Prepare a spreadsheet that displays the information on the technical specifications for each model. Arrange that information in an orderly fashion so that potential computer shoppers could easily make model comparisons. Print a one-page spreadsheet comparison table and distribute it to your classmates for their review.

2. Use the Internet to research the Olympic Games (you can focus on Winter Games or Summer Games, either the most recent staged Games, or the upcoming Games). Gather as much information as you can about the magnitude of this project (that is, search for the numbers, such as how much

hardware, software, and infrastructure is needed to move data, information, people, among others), and then organize that data into a spreadsheet. Compare your spreadsheet list with the lists of your classmates to determine who performed the most thorough search.

3. During a five-day school week, note each incident where you observe or encounter a device that might be construed to be a robot. These can be any machines or devices that are doing something, making something, or providing some service that a person might otherwise do. Organize your observations into meaningful categories and subcategories (for example, you might start with manufacturing, service, and government). Then use presentation software to display your findings to your classmates. Be prepared to defend your reasons for characterizing each device as a robot.

ETHICS: TAKE A STAND

What kind of privacy rights do workers have? The rapid proliferation of information technology within many organizations is putting this question to the test. Many organizations use electronic mail (e-mail) to communicate rapidly and easily among offices, suppliers, customers, and remote sites. Most of the computer systems that support e-mail automatically create archives of all messages that are sent. These archives are accessible to anyone with the administrative right to view the files or the technical skill to break into the system. Many organizations reserve the right to monitor the e-mail transmissions of their employees, telling new employees up front that the organization will be monitoring the employee's e-mail messages.

The privacy issues go well beyond monitoring e-mail messages. Employee activities can also be monitored and recorded by computer monitoring technology. For example, technology can allow a manager, even one who is miles away, to monitor employees' phone calls, read their e-mail messages, and even count the number of keystrokes an employee types in an hour or a day. The employee's activities provide a profile from which managers or the automated system can draw inferences about employee performance and effectiveness. The Internet presents additional privacy

issues. Management can use new Web-monitoring tools to observe what employees are doing on the Internet. This software can track down what Web sites users visit, the files they download, and even the categories of information they search.

Additional privacy issues revolve around electronically stored information concerning citizens, employees, customers, clients, and suppliers. One issue is what the company or agency that owns that information can do with it. For example, California recently joined a growing number of states that sell confidential information about their residents to banks, lenders, and car dealers.[56] Public outcry over privacy issues like this have caused many organizations to reconsider their positions. For example, the Bank of America has decided to stop sharing information about its customers with outside marketing companies.[57]

The Computer Professionals for Social Responsibility (CPSR) suggest that all companies should have a policy on privacy and should inform their employees and customers of the policy. The American Civil Liberties Union opposes companies' reading an employee's electronic communications. Unfortunately, the laws dealing with these issues at both the federal and state levels are confusing, inconsistent, and badly out of date. Alan Westin, professor of public law and government at Columbia University, suggests: "The new office calls for us to redefine the reasonable expectations of privacy—what's fair and just to do."[58]

For Discussion

1. Should organizations have the right to view an employee's e-mail messages without the employee's permission? Explain.

2. When might it be appropriate for an organization to examine an employee's e-mail messages without first receiving the employee's permission?

3. Justify the use of technology to monitor employee activities and productivity. What are the problems that can occur with this type of monitoring?

VIDEO CASE

Cannondale III: IT

When Cannondale started building bike trailers in 1971, they didn't have or know they needed computers to keep track of assembly processes or order-entry systems. Even after they became an industry leader manufacturing high-end quality lightweight bicycles, their Information Technology (IT) system was a home-grown conglomeration of independent personal computers (PCs). Separate machines had different software creating communication problems between departments and facilities. Problems in tracking their inventories and manufacturing resulted in long lead times between creating a new product and bringing it to market. In addition, there was no e-mail system.

To resolve these problems, Cannondale's vice president of IT, Mike Dower, spent considerable time and money researching and making improvements. Their new materials requirement planning (MRP) system helped get their daily processes under control and helped solve many of their inventory problems. It also helped them create new manufacturing and design processes. Installing the new Windows NT network (with an e-mail system) improved internal and external communications vital to an organization that lives by the creed, "Communication is everything and information is power."

Based in Connecticut, Cannondale manufactures virtually all of its products in Bedford, Pennsylvania, and operates subsidiaries in Holland, Japan, and Australia. Companies expect global distances to create coordination problems due to differences in time zones, language, etc. For example, a 12-hour time difference between the United States and Japan can create frustration in both countries. However, Cannondale also was having problems obtaining dealer sales and field data from U.S. sales representatives due to incompatible systems. The disparate systems used by Cannondale subsidiaries and individuals prevented them from effectively addressing marketplace changes. Today this has been remedied. Everyone at Cannondale uses compatible information and the same software programs on the same computer system.

The bicycle industry is seasonal and very dynamic. IT improvements have enabled Cannondale to change from a "made to stock" to a "made to order" company. They've changed from manufacturing large batches of hundreds of bicycles to small batches of ten bicycles. This allows them to quickly make design or production changes if they learn a product is not selling well at one or more dealers. Cannondale has made their IT systems to work closely with their dealers so they both profit.

As time goes on, Cannondale's IT system becomes more integrated with the various aspects of operations including design, manufacturing, sales, and delivery. Dower has placed the highest priority on using technology to help sales and manufacturing stay competitive. Previous sales and manufacturing transactions were manually recorded and difficult for the Purchasing people to use in ordering the right number and types of parts and materials. They were typically working with information that was two to five days old. Their more efficient IT system has shortened this process to four to five hours and could easily be modified if more up-to-date field data were to indicate changes are needed.

Because they design and manufacture bicycles in the United States, Cannondale has complete control over the product design and the time it takes to get a new product to market. The sophisticated CAD-CAM design software is used by both design and manufacturing personnel. Since everyone works on the same computer system, factory personnel, through their computers, can access design blueprints created elsewhere in Cannondale. Then, they can design production tooling from those prints.

Computers have become a more important part of people's work and personal lives. Cannondale seeks to computerize most, if not all, of their factory processes. For example, all Cannondale's bikes are cut by lasers linked by the same computer program. When a design or model change is necessary, relevant information can be downloaded directly to the lasers so they immediately can switch to the new cuts. Furthermore, bar code scanning readers are used on the factory floor. The computer connection allows data to be captured or transmitted to the next operation that is dependent on that data. Previously, it might have taken Cannondale months to bring a new or revised product to market. Now, they're able to bring a better product to market faster.

By its very nature, technology is dynamic and constantly changing. Staying aware of what's available requires an ongoing effort of reviewing new computer hardware and software and determining how to benefit from that technology. Cannondale is committed to the continued use of technology in all phases of their operation.

For Discussion

1. Explain recent changes in Cannondale's external environment making them more reliant on IT.

2. Explain the differences between Cannondale-related data and information. How do you think they decide what data and/or information they needed?

3. Illustrate the steps in the development of Cannondale's information systems.

4. Explain the impact Cannondale's use of IT has had on the company and their dealers.

http://www.cannondale.com

CASE

Safe Haven House

When Bill Nelson, director of Safe Haven House (an inner-city homeless shelter), recently had a problem on his hands, his first instinct was to call his old high school buddy, Jack Sheldon. Jack was now a professor of Information Systems at an urban university in the same town. When Bill's call was received by Jack's telephone answering device, Bill's message was short and to the point. "HEEEEELLLP!!!!" When Jack got the message, he returned Bill's call to determine what the problem was. "Jack," Bill said, "I am overwhelmed down here. The citizens and businesses in our community have always been very generous. Every day we have 10 to 20 people stop by to drop off donations of clothing, bedding, food, and other necessities of life. I gladly accept all of these donations, for everything can be put to good use. Unfortunately, I have not been able to get a handle on what we have. I've got storerooms and closets all over the shelter that are bursting with donated items. However, if someone came in with a request for a specific item, I would be hard pressed to know with certainty whether such an item was in the shelter. Even if I did recall having it, I would have no idea where it was located." Jack was eager to help his old friend but explained that he was about to leave town for an academic conference and then would be taking a sabbatical leave at another university. It would be six months before he could commit some time to help his old friend. Jack did have an idea. He suggested that he might stop by in the next day or so with two of his best Information Management students and have them examine the situation. Jack felt that they could possibly lend a hand and perhaps could pick up some extra credit along the way if they could make a meaningful project out of their encounter.

At 10:00 A.M. on the following Friday, Bill welcomed Jack and two of his students, Brandon Spilling and Dena Brister. Both were seniors, and both were interested in getting some real-world project experience. Bill gave the three of them a quick tour of the facility. The structure had once served as an inner-city convent, so it was quite spacious. All were impressed by the amenities. The two large gender-segregated dormitory-type rooms could each accommodate up to 40 people. In addition to these there were 15 individual rooms, each of which could accommodate a small family. The shelter had plenty of storage rooms, all with shelves from the floor to the ceiling. The kitchen area had pantry storage and even a large walk-in cooler. After the tour the four of them sat down and chatted for 30 minutes or so about the situation. It was during this discussion that Bill described how he had no way of keeping track of the donations that were coming into the shelter and those that were going out. Furthermore, no one on his small staff of five volunteers had the skills or the time to try to put some system into place to help with the situation. They had all they could do to receive donations and stuff them in some storage area, or they were too busy searching for requested items to give to needy people who wandered through or trying to pull together a meal for them. By 11:00 A.M., Jack, Brandon, and Dena had to leave. Brandon and Dena had to get back to the university to attend a class, and Jack had an airplane to catch.

After the meeting, on the drive back to the university Brandon and Dena talked excitedly about the prospect of helping with Bill's problem. Both felt that they had skills they could lend to this situation. They agreed that they would offer their assistance. That afternoon they called Bill and offered to develop a mechanism whereby Bill could keep track of what items were coming into the shelter and what items were being distributed. They also felt that they might be able to provide him with a simple database system that would allow him and the staff to know at all times just what items they had on hand. Finally, they thought they might bring a little organization to stockpiles of donated items. Bill was thrilled. His immediate reaction was, "When can you start?"

For Discussion

1. What general type of information system would Brandon and Dena most likely be considering for this situation, and for what level of the organization would it be intended?

2. What would represent the data input to a system that Brandon and Dena might build, and how would that system change the data into useful information?

3. If Brandon and Dena develop some sort of system that puts information into the hands of Director Bill Nelson, what do you feel would be a useful format for that information?

4. Suggest some ideas as to how Brandon and Dena might bring some organization to the stockpiles of donated items.

GLOSSARY

Ability An existing capacity to perform various tasks needed in a given situation; may be classified as mental, mechanical, or psychomotor.

Accountability Employees must justify their decisions and actions with regard to the task they have been assigned.

Acquired-needs model A model focusing on three particularly important or relevant needs in the work environment: achievement, affiliation, and power.

Activity ratios Indicators of performance with respect to key activities defined by management.

Adaptive organization An organization that eliminates bureaucracy that limits employee creativity and brings the decision makers of the organization closer to the customer.

Adjourning stage Group development stage that involves the termination of task behaviors and disengagement from relationship-oriented behaviors.

Administrative management Perspective on management that focuses on managers and the functions they perform.

Affiliation needs The desire for friendship, love, and a feeling of belonging.

Affirmative action Emphasizing the recruiting, hiring, and promoting of members of minority groups and other protected classes if such individuals are underrepresented in the organization.

Aggregate planning Link between the more general business planning activities and the more specific master planning activities.

Alternative courses of action Strategies that might be implemented in a decision-making situation.

Application form A form used to gather information about a job applicant.

Appraisal costs The costs associated with any activities that are performed in an attempt to assess the quality of the product that has been manufactured or the service that has been provided.

Artifacts Cultural routines that form the substance of public functions and events staged by the organization.

Artificial intelligence (AI) Process in which computers and computer systems behave intelligently.

Assessment center A type of situation of a more complex or higher-level managerial job used to predict a job applicant's performance.

Assets The things of value that an individual or organization owns.

Attitudes The beliefs, feelings, and behavioral tendencies held by a person about specific objects, events, groups, issues, or people.

Authoritarianism The degree to which one prefers power and status differences between people.

Authority The formal right of an employee to marshal resources and make decisions necessary to fulfill work responsibilities.

Autonomy The degree to which job holders have freedom, independence, and decision-making authority.

Avoidance learning Strengthening the desired behavior by allowing the escape from an undesirable consequence.

Balanced Scorecard A planning system that aligns the goals of individual employees with the strategic goals of the organization.

Balance sheet Summary of an organization's financial position at a given point in time, showing assets, liabilities, and owner's equity.

Base pay Wages and salaries received for performing a job.

BCG matrix Business portfolio matrix that uses market growth rate and relative market share as the indicators of the firm's strategic position.

Behavior focus The study of the behaviors that make leaders successful.

Behavioral decision model A descriptive framework for understanding that a person's cognitive ability to process information is limited.

Benchmarking The process of comparing one's own products, services, or processes against those of industry leaders for the purpose of improvement.

Benefits Indirect compensation given to employees as a reward for organizational membership.

Big Five A model measuring personality traits which include extroversion, agreeableness, conscientiousness, emotional stability, and openness to experience.

Bona fide occupational qualification A qualification of a job that is legal to use even if it tends to rule out members of employee classes protected by Title VII.

Boundary-spanning roles Lateral relationships that help to integrate and coordinate the activities of the organization (that is, liaisons, committees, task forces, integrating positions, and cross-functional work teams).

Bounded rationality Recognizes that people are limited by such organizational constraints as time, information, resources, and their own mental capacities.

Brainstorming A technique used to enhance creativity that encourages group members to generate as many novel ideas as possible on a given topic without evaluating them.

Breakeven analysis A graphic display of the relationship between volume of output, revenue, and costs.

Budgets Single-use plans that specify how financial resources should be allocated.

Bureaucratic control Use of formal mechanisms to influence behavior, assess performance, and correct unacceptable deviations from standards.

Bureaucratic management Perspective on management that focuses on the overall organizational system.

Business ethics The application of general ethics to business behavior.

Business portfolio matrix A two-dimensional grid that compares the strategic positions of each of the organization's businesses.

Business process reengineering Radically changing the organizational processes for delivering products and services.

Business strategy Defines how each business unit in the firm's corporate portfolio will operate in its market arena.

Cash cows Businesses that fall into the low market growth/high market share cell of a BCG matrix.

Central tendency Judging all employees as average, even though their performance varies.

Chain of command The line of authority and responsibility that flows throughout the organization.

Changing The process that focuses on learning new required behaviors.

Channel The carrier of the message or the means by which the message is sent.

Charismatic authority Subordinates voluntarily comply with a leader because of his or her special personal qualities or abilities.

Closed systems Systems that do not interact with the environment.

Code of ethics The general value system, principles, and specific rules that a company follows.

Coercive power The power to discipline, punish, and withhold rewards.

Cognitive dissonance An inconsistency among a person's attitudes or between an attitude and a behavior.

Cohesiveness A strong sense of connectedness between team members that causes them to work together to attain an objective.

Communication The process through which managers coordinate, lead, and influence subordinates; a process in which one person or group evokes a shared or common meaning to another person or group.

Communication feedback The process of verifying messages and the receiver's attempts to ensure that the message he or she decoded is what the sender really meant to convey.

Compensation Wages paid directly for time worked, incentives for better performance, and indirect benefits that employees receive as part of their employment relationship with the organization.

Competitive advantage Any aspect of an organization that distinguishes it from its competitors strategically.

Computer-aided software engineering (CASE) Tools that allow system developers to create prototype screens and report generators rapidly and easily.

Conceptual skills The ability to analyze complex situations and respond effectively to the challenges faced by the organization.

Concurrent control Focuses on the transformation process to ensure that it is functioning properly.

Constraints Algebraic statements, in equation form, that reflect any restrictions on the decision maker's flexibility in making decision choices.

Contingency perspective A view that proposes that there is no one best approach to management for all situations.

Contingency planning Development of two or more plans based on different strategic operating conditions.

Continuous-flow production system Produces a high volume of a continuous product or nondiscrete item.

Contrast error The tendency to rate employees relative to each other rather than to performance standards.

Controlling Monitoring the performance of the organization, identifying deviations between planned and actual results, and taking corrective action when necessary.

Controls The mechanisms used to monitor the organization's performance relative to its goals and plans.

Corporate social responsibility The interaction between business and the social environment in which it exists.

Corporate strategy Decisions and actions that define the portfolio of business units that an organization maintains.

Corrective (feedback) control Focuses on discovering undesirable output and implementing corrective action.

Cost leadership strategy A strategy for competing on the basis of price.

Current assets Items that can be converted into cash in a short time period.

Current liabilities Debts that must be paid in the near future.

Customer capital The value of established relationships with customers and suppliers.

Customer divisional structure A structure in which the tasks of the organization are grouped according to customer segments.

Data Raw facts or details that represent some type of transaction or activity within an organization.

Database The archived data and information used by an organization.

Database management system (DBMS) Software that allows an organization to store data, manage them efficiently, and provide access to stored data.

Debt ratios Indicators of the firm's ability to handle long-term debt.

Decision making The process through which managers identify and resolve problems and capitalize on opportunities.

Decision support system (DSS) Computer-based information system that uses imbedded analytical models to assist decision makers in analyzing and solving semistructured problems.

Decision tree A branching diagram that illustrates the alternatives and states of nature for a decision situation.

Decision variables The factors that the decision maker can manipulate.

Decisional roles The manager's responsibility for processing information and reaching conclusions.

Decoding The translation of received messages into interpreted meanings.

Delegating style The leader provides the subordinates with few task or relations behaviors.

Delegation The process of transferring the responsibility for a specific activity or task to another member of the organization and empowering that individual to accomplish the task effectively.

Delphi technique Uses experts to make predictions and forecasts about future events without meeting face to face.

Demand forecasting Determining the number of employees that the organization will need in the future as well as the knowledge, skills, and abilities these employees must possess.

Devil's advocacy An individual or subgroup is appointed to critique a proposed course of action and identify problems to consider before the decision is final.

Dialectical inquiry Approaches a decision from two opposite points and structures a debate between conflicting views.

Differentiation strategy A strategy for competing by offering products or services that are differentiated from those of competitors.

Diversity The heterogeneity of the work force in terms of gender, race, nationality, and ethnicity.

Divisional structure Members of the organization are grouped on the basis of common products, geographic markets, or customers served.

Dogs Businesses that fall into the low market growth/low market share cell of a BCG matrix.

Downward communication Messages sent from individuals at higher levels of the organization to those at lower levels.

Driving force The push for change of the status quo.

Dynamic network A network structure that makes extensive use of outsourcing through alliances with outside organizations.

Economic feasibility Focuses on whether the expected benefits of an information system will be able to cover the anticipated costs.

Effectiveness Pursuing the appropriate goals—doing the right things.

Efficiency Using the fewest inputs to generate a given output—doing things right.

Electronic commerce (e-commerce) The process of buying and selling goods and services electronically with computerized business transactions.

Electronic data interchange (EDI) Electronic transmission of transaction data using telecommunications.

Electronic funds transfer (EFT) Electronic manipulation of financial transactions.

Electronic mail (e-mail) A computer-based system that allows individuals to exchange and store messages through computerized text-processing and communication networks.

Employee-centered work redesign An approach whereby employees design their work roles to benefit the organization and satisfy their individual goals.

Employee fairness Expectations that individuals on a given job are paid fairly relative to coworkers on the same job.

Employment test Any instrument or device used to assess the qualification of a job applicant.

Empowering employees Increasing the amount of control and discretion workers have over their jobs.

Empowerment The interaction of the leader giving away or sharing power with those who use it to become involved and committed to independent, high-quality performance.

Encoding The process that translates the sender's ideas into a systematic set of symbols or a language expressing the communicator's purpose.

Encryption The coding and scrambling of sensitive information transmitted over networks to make it unintelligible to unauthorized viewers.

End users Those who will use and interact with the information system.

Enterprise resource planning (ERP) A management system that integrates all facets of the organization's business so that they can be more closely coordinated by sharing information.

Entropy The tendency for systems to decay over time.

Equity model A motivation model focusing on an individual's feelings about how fairly he or she is treated in comparison with others.

Escalation of commitment The tendency to increase commitment to a previously selected course of action beyond the level that would be expected if the manager followed an effective decision-making process.

Esteem needs Needs for personal feelings of achievement and self-worth and for recognition, respect, and prestige from others.

Ethical behavior Behavior that is morally accepted as good or right as opposed to bad or wrong.

Ethical dilemma A situation in which a person must decide whether or not to do something that, although benefiting oneself or the organization, may be considered unethical and perhaps illegal.

Ethics The established customs, morals, and fundamental human relationships that exist throughout the world.

Ethnocentrism The tendency to consider one's own culture and its values as being superior to others.

Executive support systems (ESS) The information systems that support senior managers at the strategic level of the organization by helping them identify and address problems and opportunities from a strategic perspective.

Expectancy The belief that a particular level of effort will be followed by a particular level of performance.

Expectancy model A motivation model suggesting that work motivation is determined by the individual's perception of the relationship between effort and performance and the desirability of various work outcomes associated with different performance levels.

Expected monetary value (EMV) The sum of each expected value for an alternative.

Expected value The product of a payoff and its probability of occurrence.

Expert power The power to influence another person because of expert knowledge and competence.

Expert system A computer-based system that contains and can use knowledge about a specific, relatively narrow, complex application.

External customer User of an item who is not a part of the organization that supplies the item.

External failure costs The costs resulting from defective output that is not detected prior to delivery to the customer.

External fairness Pay in one organization is fair relative to the pay for the same job in other organizations.

External forces Forces that are fundamentally beyond the control of management.

External locus of control A personality characteristic of people who believe that much of what happens to them is controlled and determined by outside external forces such as other powerful people, fate, or luck.

Extinction The withdrawal of the positive reward or reinforcing consequences for an undesirable behavior.

F or T A personality dimension referring to whether one is feeling or thinking in making judgments.

Feedback Information about the status and performance of a given effort or system.

Feedback controls Controls that compare the actual performance of the organization to its planned performance.

Feedforward controls Controls designed to identify changes in the external environment or the internal operations of the organization that may affect its ability to fulfill its mission and achieve its strategic goals.

Fixed assets Assets that are long-term in nature and cannot be converted quickly into cash.

Fixed-interval schedule Rewards employees at specified time intervals, assuming that the desired behavior has continued at an appropriate level.

Fixed-ratio schedule When a reinforcer is provided after a fixed number of occurrences of the desired behavior.

Focus strategy A strategy for competing by targeting a specific and narrow segment of the market.

Force-field analysis A systematic process for examining the pressures that are likely to support or resist a proposed change.

Formal groups Groups that are deliberately created by the organization's managers to accomplish goals and serve the needs of the organization.

Forming stage Group development stage marked by apprehension, seeking basic information, defining goals, developing procedures for performing the task, and making a preliminary evaluation of how the team might interact to accomplish goals.

Free riding A tendency whereby one or more team members expend decreasing amounts of effort because their contributions are less visible.

Functional managers Managers who are responsible for managing a work unit that is grouped based on the function served.

Functional strategy Specifies the production, research and development, financial, human resource management, and marketing activities necessary to implement the organization's corporate and business strategies.

Functional structure Members of the organization are grouped according to the function they perform within the organization.

GE matrix A business portfolio matrix that uses industry attractiveness and business strength as the indicators of the firm's strategic position.

General environment Those environmental forces that are beyond a firm's influence and over which it has no control.

General managers Managers who are responsible for managing several different departments that are responsible for different tasks.

Generic strategies The fundamental way in which an organization competes in the marketplace.

Geographic divisional structure A structure in which the activities of the organization are grouped according to the geographic markets served.

Goal setting A process of increasing efficiency and effectiveness by specifying the desired outcomes toward which individuals, groups, departments, and organizations should work.

Goals Provide a clear, engaging sense of direction and specify what is going to be accomplished.

Grand strategy A comprehensive, general approach for achieving the strategic goals of an organization.

Grapevine An informal method of transmitting information depicted as the wandering of messages throughout the organization.

Groupthink An agreement-at-any-cost mentality that results in ineffective group decision making.

Halo-and-horn effect A process in which we evaluate and form an overall impression of an individual based solely on a specific trait or dimension, such as enthusiasm, gender, appearance, or intelligence.

Halo effect Rating an employee high or low on all items because of one characteristic.

Hawthorne effect Phenomenon whereby individual or group performance is influenced by human behavior factors.

Heterogeneous When the individuals in a group are diverse and have dissimilar characteristics, backgrounds, interests, values, and attitudes.

Hierarchy of needs Motivation model stating that a person has five fundamental needs: physiological, security, affiliation, esteem, and self-actualization.

Homogeneous When a team is composed of individuals having group-related characteristics, backgrounds, interests, values, and attitudes that are alike.

Horizontal communication The flow of information that occurs both within and between departments.

Hostile environment harassment Harrassment produced by workplace conduct and/or setting that is considered to make an abusive working environment.

Human capital The cumulative skills and knowledge of the organization.

Human rights approach A situation in which decisions are made in light of the moral entitlements of human beings.

Human skills The ability to work effectively with others.

Hybrid layout A configuration containing some degree of flexibility, lying between the extremes of process and product layouts.

Hygiene factors Factors associated with the job context or environment in which the job is performed.

Hyperchange A condition of rapid, dramatic, complex, and unpredictable changes that has a significant effect on the ways in which organizations are managed.

I or E A personality dimension measuring the degree to which a person is introverted or extroverted.

Incentives Bonuses, commissions, sometimes stock options directly tied to performance or extraordinary performance.

Income statement (profit-and-loss statement) A summary of an organization's financial performance over a given time interval, showing revenues, expenses, and bottom-line profit or loss.

Informal groups Groups that are not formed or planned by the organization's managers.

Information The result of the process of transforming data into meaningful facts useful for a specific purpose.

Information overload Occurs when the amount of information we can process is exceeded.

Information power Control over information.

Informational roles The manager's responsibility for gathering and disseminating information to the stakeholders of the organization.

Information system A set of interrelated components that collects (or retrieves), processes, stores, and distributes information to support the activities of an organization.

Inputs Such diverse items as materials, workers, capital, land, equipment, customers, and information used in creating products and services.

Institutionalizing or **refreezing** The act of applying the new approaches and behaviors.

Instrumental values Standards of conduct or methods for attaining an end.

Instrumentality The individual's perception that a specific level of achieved task performance will lead to various work outcomes.

Integrating mechanisms Methods for managing the flow of information, resources, and tasks within the organization.

Intellectual capital The sum and synergy of an organization's knowledge, experience, relationships, processes, discoveries, innovations, market presence, and community influence.

Interdependence The degree to which work groups are interrelated.

Internal customer User of an item who is a member of, or employee of, the organization that supplies the item.

Internal failure costs The costs associated with the repair or disposition of defective output that is detected prior to delivery to the customer.

Internal fairness Pay for the job within the organization is fair relative to the pay of higher- and lower-level jobs in the same organization.

Internal forces Forces that are generally within the control of management.

Internal locus of control A personality characteristic of people who believe that many of the events in their lives are primarily the result of their own behavior and actions.

Internal network A network structure that relies on internally developed units to provide services to a core organizational unit.

Internet The vast interconnected electronic equipment that stores massive amounts of data that can be accessed with computers and related electronic equipment.

Interpersonal roles The manager's responsibility for managing relationships with organizational members and other constituents.

Interviews Relatively formal, in-depth conversations used to assess a candidate's readiness for a job and to provide information to the candidate.

Intuition An unconscious analysis based on past experience.

Jargon Pretentious terminology or language specific to a particular profession or group.

Job analysis Studying a job to understand what knowledge, skills, abilities, and attitudes are required for successful performance.

Job depth The degree of control given to a job holder to perform the job.

Job description Details of the responsibilities and tasks associated with a given position.

Job design The set of tasks and activities that are grouped together to define a particular job.

Job enlargement Programs designed to broaden job scope.

Job enrichment Programs designed to increase job depth.

Job rotation Assigning individuals to a variety of job positions.

Job satisfaction The degree to which individuals feel positively or negatively about their jobs.

Job scope The number of different activities required in a job and the frequency with which each activity is performed.

Job-shop production system Produces small quantities of a wide variety of specialized items.

Job specifications A list of the knowledge, skills, abilities, and other employee characteristics needed to perform the job.

Just-in-time (JIT) inventory management A philosophy that advocates eliminating waste, solving problems, and striving for continual improvement in operations.

Justice approach A situation in which decisions are based on an equitable, fair, and impartial distribution of benefits and costs among individuals and groups.

Kaizen Japanese term referring to the total quality management principle of continuous improvement.

Knowledge-level information systems Information systems that help knowledge workers to discover, organize, and integrate new knowledge into the business, or help data workers to control the flow of paperwork and information.

Knowledge management systems (KMS) The information systems that support workers at the knowledge level of the organization by helping to create, organize, and make available important business knowledge wherever and whenever it is needed in an organization.

Labor-management relations The formal process through which labor unions represent employees in negotiating with management.

Language, metaphors, and symbols The way that organizational members typically express themselves and communicate with each other.

Law of requisite variety Control systems must have enough variety to cope with the variety in the systems they are trying to control.

Leadership A responsibility and a process that is an observable, understandable, learnable set of skills and practices available to everyone, anywhere in the organization.

Leadership substitutes Variables such as individual, task, and organizational characteristics.

Leading Motivating and directing the members of the organization so that they contribute to the achievement of the goals of the organization.

Legitimate power Power that stems from formal authority.

Leniency error Evaluating someone in a group higher than the person should be rated or when the rater is unjustifiably easy in evaluating performance.

Liabilities The firm's debts and obligations.

Line personnel Those organizational members who are directly involved in delivering the products and services of the organization.

Linear programming A powerful quantitative tool that can help managers solve resource allocations problems.

Liquidity ratios Indicators of the firm's ability to meet its short-term debts and obligations.

Local-area network (LAN) An information system that connects users in a small area, such as a building, an office, or a manufacturing plant.

Locus of control A personality characteristic that describes the extent to which individuals believe that they can control the environment and external events affecting them.

Locus of decision making The degree to which decision making is centralized versus decentralized.

Long-term liabilities Debts payable over a long time span.

Management The process of administering and coordinating resources effectively and efficiently in an effort to achieve the goals of the organization.

Management by exception Focusing on the elements that are not meeting the standards.

Management by objectives (MBO) A method for developing individualized plans that guide the activities of individual members of an organization.

Management information system (MIS) The information systems that support middle managers at the management level of the organization by providing them with periodic reports that summarize the organization's performance.

Management-level information systems Information systems that assist in the administrative activities of middle managers and aid in decision making and the monitoring and controlling of operations.

Managers Organizational members who are responsible for planning, organizing, leading, and controlling the activities of the organization so that its goals can be achieved.

Master production schedule A detailed statement of projected production quantities for each item in each time period.

Material requirements planning (MRP) Methodology that uses the production schedule for the finished products to derive demand and production schedules for component items that make up the final products.

Matrix structure A structure in which the tasks of the organization are grouped along two organizing dimensions simultaneously (such as product/geographic market, product/function).

Mechanistic systems Highly centralized organizations in which decision-making authority rests with top-level management.

Messages The tangible forms of coded symbols that are intended to give a particular meaning to the information or data.

Moral agent A business's obligation to act honorably and to reflect and enforce values that are consistent with those of society.

Motivation The forces and expenditure of effort acting on or within a person that cause that person to behave in a specific, goal-directed manner.

Motivator factors Factors related to job content, or what people actually do in their work; associated with an individual's positive feelings about the job.

Need-based models Models of motivation that emphasize specific human needs or the factors within a person that energize, direct, and stop behavior.

Need for achievement The drive to excel, accomplish challenging tasks, and achieve a standard of excellence.

Need for affiliation The desire for friendly and close interpersonal relationships.

Need for power The need to influence and control one's environment; may involve either personal power or institutional power.

Negative reinforcement *See* avoidance learning.

Network structure A contemporary organizational structure that is founded on a set of alliances with other organizations that serve a wide variety of functions.

Neutralizer A condition that counteracts leader behavior and/or prevents the leader from having an effect on a follower or a specific situation.

Noise Any internal or external interference with or distraction from the intended message.

Nominal group technique (NGT) A structured process designed to stimulate creative group decision making where agreement is lacking or where the members have incomplete knowledge concerning the nature of the problem.

Nonprogrammed decision Decisions made in response to situations that are unique, unstructured, or poorly defined.

Nonverbal communication All messages that are nonlanguage responses.

Norming stage Group development stage in which the team members come together and a real sense of cohesion and belonging begins to emerge.

Norms Unwritten, informal rules and shared beliefs that regulate the appropriate behavior expectations of team members.

Objective function A symbolic, quantitative representation of the primary goal that the decision maker is seeking to optimize.

Objectives The desired results to be attained.

Office automation systems (OAS) Information technology applications designed to increase the productivity of data workers by assisting in the processing, storage, collection, and transmission of electronic documents and messages among individuals, work groups, and organizations.

Open systems Systems that must interact with the external environment to survive.

Operational feasibility Refers to the willingness and ability of all concerned parties to operate and support the information system as it is proposed and implemented.

Operational planning The process of determining the day-to-day activities that are necessary to achieve the long-term goals of the organization.

Operational plans An outline of the tactical activities necessary to support and implement the strategic plans of the organization.

Operational level information systems Information systems that support operational managers by keeping track of the basic activities and transactions of the organization.

Opportunity A situation that has the potential to provide additional beneficial outcomes.

Oral communication All forms of spoken information; by far the most preferred type of communication used by managers.

Organic (clan) control Reliance upon social values, traditions, shared beliefs, flexible authority, and trust to assess performance and correct unacceptable deviations.

Organic systems Decentralized organizations that push decision making to the lowest levels of the organization in an effort to respond more effectively to environmental change.

Organization A group of individuals who work together toward common goals.

Organization structure The primary reporting relationships that exist within an organization.

Organizational change Any alteration of activities in an organization.

Organizational control A process through which managers regulate organizational activities to make them consistent with expectations and help them achieve predetermined standards of performance.

Organizational culture The shared, emotionally charged beliefs, values, and norms that bind people together and help them make sense of the systems within an organization.

Organizational design The way in which the activities of an organization are arranged and coordinated so that its mission can be fulfilled and its goals achieved.

Organizational feasibility Refers to how well the proposed information system supports the strategic objectives of the organization.

Organizational mission The reasons for which the organization exists; it provides strategic direction for the members of the organization.

Organizational structure The primary reporting relationships that exist within an organization.

Organizing The process of determining the tasks to be done, who will do them, and how those tasks will be managed and coordinated.

Outputs The physical commodity, or intangible service or information, that is desired by the customers or users of the system.

Owner's equity The portion of a business that is owned by the shareholders. The difference between the assets of an organization and its liabilities.

P or J A personality dimension representing the degree to which one is perceiving or judging in making decisions.

Participating style The leader shares ideas and maintains two-way communication to encourage and support the skills the subordinates have developed.

Payoff table A matrix that organizes the alternative courses of action, states of nature, and payoffs for a decision situation.

Payoffs The outcomes of decision situations.

Perception The way people experience, process, define, and interpret the world around them.

Performance appraisal Any method used to assess a person's performance on a job.

Performing stage Group development stage that occurs when the team is fully functional; marked by interpersonal relations and high levels of interdependence.

Personal power Power derived from the interpersonal relationship between a leader and his or her followers. It includes both expert and referent power.

Personality An enduring, organized, and a distinctive pattern of behavior that describes an individual's adaptation to a situation.

Personality test Assessment of personality characteristics of a job applicant.

Personalized power orientation Associated with a strong need for esteem and status; power is often used impulsively.

PERT (Program Evaluation and Review Technique) A network approach for scheduling project activities.

Physiological needs Needs such as food, water, air, and shelter; at the bottom of the hierarchy of needs.

Plan A blueprint for action that prescribes the activities necessary for the organization to realize its goals.

Planning Setting goals and defining the actions necessary to achieve those goals.

Policies General guidelines for decision making within the organization.

Pooled interdependence Occurs when organizational units have a common resource but no interrelationship with one another.

Position power Includes legitimate power, coercive power, reward power, and information power.

Positive reinforcement The administration of positive and rewarding consequences or event following a desired behavior.

Power The ability to marshal human, informational, or material resources to get something done; the ability to get results.

Prevention costs The costs associated with any activities that are performed in an attempt to prevent defective output from occurring.

Preventive (feedforward) control Focuses on detecting undesirable material, financial, or human resources that serve as inputs to the transformation process.

Problem A situation in which some aspect of organizational performance is less than desirable.

Procedures Instructions on how to complete recurring tasks.

Process layout A configuration flexible enough to accommodate a wide diversity of products or customers.

Process models Models that focus on understanding the thought or cognitive processes that take place within the individual's mind and act to affect behavior.

Product divisional structure A structure in which the activities of the organization are grouped according to specific products or product lines.

Product layout A configuration set for a specific purpose, with all product or service demands essentially identical.

Productivity A measure of the efficiency with which a firm transforms inputs into outputs, calculated as output divided by input.

Profitability ratios Indicators of the relative effectiveness, or profitability, of the organization.

Programmed decision Decisions made in response to situations that are routine or recurring.

Programs Single-use plans that govern a comprehensive set of activities designed to accomplish a particular set of goals.

Project production system Produces large-scale, unique items.

Projects Single-use plans that direct the efforts of individuals or work groups toward the achievement of a specific goal.

Punishment Administering negative consequences following undesirable behavior.

Quality assurance (QA) Focuses on any activity that influences the maintenance of quality at the desired level.

Quality circle A work team that meets regularly to identify, analyze, and solve problems related to its work area.

Quality control (QC) Focuses on the actual measurement of output to see whether specifications have been met.

Question marks Businesses that fall into the high market growth/low market share cell of a BCG matrix.

Quid pro quo harassment Sexual harassment requiring sexual favors in exchange for positive job treatment.

Rational-legal authority Subordinates comply with a leader because of a set of impersonal rules and regulations that apply to all employees.

Readiness The extent to which a subordinate possesses the ability and willingness to complete a specific task.

Realistic job preview An accurate description of a job and/or company.

Recency error Evaluation on the employee's most recent performance rather than all of it.

Reciprocal interdependence Occurs when information, resources, and tasks must be passed back and forth between work groups.

Recruitment Finding and attracting qualified job candidates.

Referent power The ability to influence others based on personal liking,

charisma, and reputation. It is manifested through imitation or emulation.

Refreezing The act of applying the new approaches and behaviors.

Reinforcement theory A motivational theory that suggests that a person will learn to continue behaviors that are positively rewarded and discontinue behaviors that are ignored or punished.

Relations orientation A behavior that shows empathy for concerns and feelings, being supportive of needs, showing trust, demonstrating appreciation, establishing trusting relationships, and allowing subordinates to participate in decision making.

Relationship-oriented roles Behaviors that cultivate the well-being, continuity, and development of the group.

Reliability An employment tool measures the same thing each time it is used.

Repetitive, assembly-line, or **mass-production system** Produces a high volume of discrete items.

Resiliency The ability to absorb high levels of disruptive change while displaying minimal dysfunctional behavior.

Responsibility An obligation on the part of an employee to complete assigned activities.

Restraining force The force to keep the status quo.

Results-oriented approaches to performance appraisal Use of objective performance criteria.

Résumé Information prepared by a job applicant usually stating career goal, qualifications, and some related information.

Reward power Power derived from control over tangible benefits such as a promotion, a better job, better work schedule, a larger operating budget, an increased expense account, and formal recognition of accomplishments.

Rites, rituals, and ceremonies Relatively dramatic, planned recurring activities used at special times to influence the behavior and understanding of organizational members.

Robotics Use of machines with human-like characteristics, such as dexterity, movement, vision, and strength.

Rules Detailed and specific regulations for action.

S or N A personality dimension measuring whether one is sensing or intuitive.

Satisficing The search and acceptance of something that is satisfactory rather than perfect or optimal.

Scalar principle A clear line of authority must run throughout the organization.

Schedules of reinforcement Specify the basis for and timing of reinforcement.

Scientific management Perspective on management that focuses on the productivity of the individual worker.

Security needs The desire to have a safe physical and emotional environment.

Selective perception The tendency to screen out information with which we are not comfortable or do not want to be bothered.

Self-actualization needs Needs for self-fulfillment and the opportunity to achieve one's potential; at the top of the hierarchy.

Self-esteem The extent to which people believe they are capable, significant, successful, and worthwhile.

Self-leadership Sometimes referred to as followership; a paradigm founded on creating an organization of leaders who are ready to lead themselves.

Self-managed teams (SMTs) Groups of employees who design their jobs and work responsibilities to achieve the self-determined goals and objectives of the team.

Self-monitoring The degree to which one is capable of adjusting successfully to the situation.

Self-oriented role When a personal need or goal of an individual occurs without regard for the group's problems.

Selling style The leader explains decisions and provides opportunities for clarification.

Sender The person who initiates the communication process by encoding his or her meaning and sending the message through a channel.

Sequential interdependence Occurs when organizational units must coordinate the flow of information, resources, and tasks from one unit to another.

Severity error Being unjustifiably harsh in evaluating employee performance.

Single-use plans Plans that address specific organizational situations that typically do not recur.

Situational leadership model Examines the interaction between leadership behavior, the situation, and the follower's readiness.

Skill variety The degree to which a job challenges the job holder to use various skills and abilities.

Social context The setting in which the communication takes place.

Social contract An implied set of rights and obligations that are inherent in social policy and assumed by business.

Socialized power orientation The use of power for the benefit of others to make subordinates feel strong and responsible.

Span of control The number of employees reporting to a particular manager.

Special-purpose team A temporary team formed to solve a special or nonrecurring problem.

Spontaneous channels of communication Casual, opportunistic, and informal communication paths that arise from the social relationships that evolve in the organization.

Stable environments Environments that experience little change.

Stable network A network structure that utilizes external alliances selectively as a mechanism for gaining strategic flexibility.

Staff personnel Those organizational members who are not directly involved in delivering the products and services of the organization, but provide support for line personnel.

Stakeholders People who are affected by or can affect the activities of the firm.

Standing plans Plans that deal with organizational issues and problems that recur frequently.

Stars Businesses that fall into the high market growth/high market share cell of a BCG matrix.

States of nature Conditions over which the decision maker has little or no control.

Stereotyping Generalization, or the tendency to assign attributes to someone, not on individual characteristics, but solely on the basis of a category or group to which that person belongs.

Stories and sagas Narratives based on true events that are distorted to incorporate fictional embellishment. They graphically and quickly communicate emotionally charged beliefs to newcomers.

Storming stage Group development stage that occurs as team members begin to experience conflict with one another.

Strategic analysis An assessment of the internal and external conditions of the firm.

Strategic control The methods by which the performance of the organization is monitored.

Strategic decision-making matrix A two-dimensional grid used to select the best strategic alternative in light of multiple organizational objectives.

Strategic goals The results that an organization seeks to achieve in the long term.

Strategic plan A plan that identifies the markets in which an organization competes, as well as the ways in which it competes in those markets.

Strategic planning The process by which an organization makes decisions and takes actions to enhance its long-term performance.

Strategic-level information systems Information systems that aid senior management as they address strategic issues and long-term decision making.

Strategy formulation The establishment of an organizational vision, goals, and corporate- and business-level strategies.

Strategy implementation The actions required to ensure that the corporate- and business-level strategy of the organization is put into place.

Structural capital The accumulated knowledge and know-how of the organization represented by its patents, trademarks and copyrights, proprietary databases, and systems.

Supply chain management (SCM) Management and control of the sequence of suppliers, warehouses, operations, and retail outlets for an organization.

Supply forecasting Determining what human resources will be available both inside and outside the organization.

Synergy A phenomenon whereby an organization can accomplish more when its subsystems work together than it can accomplish when they work independently.

Systems analysis An approach to problem solving that attacks complex systems by breaking them down into their constituent elements.

Task environment Those environmental forces that are within the firm's operating environment and over which the firm has some degree of control.

Task identity The degree to which a job requires the completion of an identifiable piece of work.

Task orientation Setting performance goals, planning and scheduling work, coordinating activities, giving directions, setting standards, providing resources, and supervising worker performance.

Task-oriented roles Behaviors that are directly related to establishing and accomplishing the goals of the group or achieving the desired outcomes.

Task significance The degree to which a job contributes to the overall efforts of the organization.

Technical feasibility Refers to the capability of the hardware and software of the proposed information system to provide the decision makers in the organization with the needed information.

Technical skills The ability to utilize tools, techniques, and procedures that are specific to a particular field.

Technological communication A broad category of communication components that are rapidly influencing how managers communicate.

Telecommunications The transmission of information in any form from one location to another using electronic or optical means.

Telecommuting The practice of working at a remote site by using a computer linked to a central office or other employment location.

Telework Another word for telecommuting.

Telling style The leader provides specific instructions and closely supervises performance.

Terminal values Goals an individual will ultimately strive to achieve.

Theory X Managers perceive that subordinates have an inherent dislike of work and will avoid it if possible.

Theory Y Managers perceive that subordinates enjoy work and will gain satisfaction from their jobs.

Theory Z Advocates that managers place trust in the employees and make them feel like an integral part of the organization.

360-degree feedback Feedback from the supervisor, subordinates, coworkers, and self-appraisal.

Total quality management (TQM) A systematic approach for enhancing products, services, processes, and operational quality control.

Traditional authority Subordinates comply with a leader because of custom or tradition.

Training A planned effort to assist employees in learning job-related behaviors that will improve their performance.

Trait focus The assumption that some people are endowed with certain physical characteristics (e.g., height, appearance), aspects of personality (e.g., self-esteem, dominance, emotional stability), and aptitudes (e.g., general intelligence, verbal fluency, creativity) that make them successful leaders.

Transaction processing systems (TPS) The information systems that support workers at the operational level of the organization by recording daily business transactions and performing the routine, clerical record-keeping activities of the organization.

Transformation process The mechanism by which inputs are converted to outputs.

Transformational leadership The interaction process of the leader's behavior and attitudes with the attitudes and behavior of followers.

Turbulent environments Environments that are characterized by rapid and significant change.

Two-factor model A motivation model detailing the factors leading to job satisfaction and job dissatisfaction.

Type A personality Characterized by a sense of being in a hurry, impatient with delays, a devotion to work, and a sense of time urgency.

Type B personality A person who is characteristically easygoing and less competitive in daily events.

Unfreezing A process that involves developing an initial awareness of the need for change and the forces supporting and resisting change.

Unity of command A principle that each employee in the organization is accountable to one, and only one, supervisor.

Upward communication Messages sent up the line from subordinates to bosses.

Utility approach A situation in which decisions are based on an evaluation of the overall amount of good that will result.

Valence The value or importance that the individual attaches to various work outcomes.

Validity An employment tool must show that it predicts actual job performance.

Values Relatively permanent and deeply held preferences upon which individuals form attitudes and personal choices.

Variable-interval schedule When reinforcement is administered at random or varying times that cannot be predicted by the employee.

Variable-ratio schedule When reinforcement is provided after a varying, or random, number of occurrences of the desired behavior rather than after variable time periods.

Variance reporting Highlighting only those things that fail to meet the established standards.

Vertical communication The flow of information both up and down the chain of command.

Video conferencing An umbrella term referring to technologies that use live video to unite widely dispersed company operations.

Vigilance The concern for and attention to the process of making a decision that occurs when the decision maker considers seven critical procedures.

Virtual workplace A workplace with no walls and no boundaries; workers can work anytime, anywhere by linking to other people and information through technology.

Vision statement Description of what the organization aspires to be in the long term.

Whistleblower Someone who exposes organizational misconduct or wrongdoing to the public.

Wide-area network (WAN) An information system that extends over a broad geographic area, such as cities, regions, countries, or the world.

Work sample A small part of an actual job completed by an applicant to predict performance on the job.

Written communication Letters, memos, policy manuals, reports, forms, and other documents used to share information in an organization.

ENDNOTES

CHAPTER 1

1. J. Kotter, "What Leaders Really Do?" *Harvard Business Review*, December 2001, 85–97.

2. M.P. Follett, "Dynamic Administration," in *Dynamic Administration: The Collected Papers of Mary Parker Follett*, eds. H. Metcalf and L.F. Urwick (New York: Harper & Row, 1942).

3. P.F. Drucker, *The Effective Executive* (New York: Harper & Row, 1967).

4. See, for example, C.P. Hales, "What Do Managers Do? A Critical Review of the Evidence," *Journal of Management Studies*, 23, 1986, 88–113; C.M. Pavett and A.W. Lau, "Managerial Work: The Influence of Hierarchical Level and Functional Specialty," *Academy of Management Journal*, 26, 1983, 170–77; H. Willmott, "Images and Ideals of Managerial Work: A Critical Examination of Conceptual and Empirical Accounts," *Journal of Management Studies*, 21, 1984, 349–68; H. Willmott, "Studying Managerial Work: A Critique and a Proposal," *Journal of Management Studies*, 24, 1987, 249–70.

5. A.I. Kraut, P.R. Pedigo, D.D. McKenna, and M.D. Dunnette, "The Role of the Manager: What's Really Important in Different Management Jobs," *Academy of Management Executive*, 3, 1989, 286–93.

6. C.M. Pavett and A.W. Lau, "Managerial Work."

7. H. Mintzberg, "The Manager's Job: Folklore and Fact," *Harvard Business Review*, September–October 1974, 91.

8. H. Mintzberg, "The Manager's Job: Folklore and Fact," *Harvard Business Review*, July–August 1974, 49–61.

9. Ibid.

10. R.L. Katz, "Skills of an Effective Administrator," *Harvard Business Review*, September–October 1974, 91.

11. R.L. Katz, "Skills of an Effective Administrator," 92.

12. G. Land, *Grow or Die: The Unifying Principle of Transformation* (New York: Random House, 1973).

13. "Q&A: What Is the State of the New Economy," *Fast Company*, September 2001, 101–104.

14. M. Veverka, "Plugged In: New Economy? What New Economy?" *Barron's*, October 22, 2001, 47–51.

15. W. Kiechel III, "How We Will Work in the Year 2000," *Fortune*, May 17, 1993, 38–52.

16. J. Huey, "IS Impossible," *Fortune*, September 23, 1991, 135–40.

17. I.T. Siegel, "Catching the Ninth Wave: Information, Technology and Strategic Change," *Planning Review*, 23,
September–October 1995, 21–23; *Globalization, Technology, and Competition*, eds. S.P. Bradley, J.A. Hausman, and R.L. Nolan (Boston, Mass.: Harvard Business School Press, 1993).

18. See, for example, A.B. Shani and J.A. Sena, "Information Technology and the Integration of Change: Sociotechnical System Approach," *Journal of Applied Behavior Science*, 30, 2, June 1994, 227–47; P.W. Yetton, K.D. Johnston, and J.F. Craig, "Computer-Aided Architects: A Case Study of IT and Strategic Change," *Sloan Management Review*, Summer 1994, 57–67; E.K. Clemons, "Information Technology and the Boundary of the Firm: Who Wins, Who Loses, Who Has to Change," in *Globalization, Technology, and Competition*, eds. S.P. Bradley, J.A. Hausman, and R.L. Nolan, (Boston, Mass.: Harvard Business School Press, 1993), 219–42.

19. Price Waterhouse World Technology Centre, *Technology Forecast: 1996* (Menlo Park, Calif.: 1996), 645.

20. B. Su, "The U.S. Economy to 2010," *Monthly Labor Review*, November 2001, 3–19.

21. S. Bernhut, "Leading the Revolution: Gary Hamel," *Ivey Business Journal*, July–August 2001.

22. T. Coltman, T. Devinney, A. Latukefu, and D. Midgley, "E-Business: Revolution, Evolution, or Hype?" *California Management Review*, Fall 2001, 57–76.

23. B. Tedeschi, "GE Has a Bright Idea," *Smart Business*, June 2001, 86–91.

24. For examples of innovative information technology strategies in government and education, see "100 Innovators in Government and Education," *PC Week*, 16, 11, March 15, 1999, 67–68.

25. Price Waterhouse World Technology Centre, *Technology Forecast: 1996* (Menlo Park, Calif.: 1996), 645.

26. E. Brown, "9 Ways to Win on the Web," *Fortune*, 139, 10, May 24, 1999.

27. See for example, J. Doherty, "Same Old Story," *Barron's*, December 10, 2001, 13–16; J. Cooper and K. Madigan, "The Second Half Should Be Healthier," *Business Week*, August 13, 2001, 25–27; and J. Byrne, "A Highflier's Legacy: Low Comedy," *Business Week*, January 14, 2002, 16–19.

28. T. Groenfeldt, "Who's in the Driver's Seat?" *Journal of Business Strategy*, 18, 1, January–February 1997, 36–42; and K. Bruce, "Can You Align IT with Business Strategy?" *Strategy and Leadership*, 26, 5, November–December 1998, 16–22.

29. P. Haapaniemi and W. Hill, "Not Just for the Big Guys," *Chief Executive*, 137, September 1998, 62–72.

30. For an excellent discussion of the challenges of global competitiveness and leadership, see S. Zahra, "Competitiveness and Global Leadership in the 21st Century," *The Academy of Management Executive*, 12, 4, November 1998, 10–12; S. Zahra, "The Changing Rules of Global Competitiveness in the 21st Century," *The Academy of Management Executive*, 13, 1, February 1999; and R.D. Ireland and M.A. Hitt, "Achieving and Maintaining Strategic Competitiveness in the 21st Century: The Role of Strategic Leadership," *The Academy of Management Executive*, 13, 1, February 1999, 43–57.

31. J.W. Slocum Jr. and D. Lei, "Global Strategic Alliances: Payoffs and Pitfalls," *Organizational Dynamics*, 19, 3, 1991, 44–61.

32. L. Tansey, "Taking Ethics Abroad," *Across the Board*, 33, 6, June 1996, 56–58.

33. J. Franch and K. Kashani, "Rise of the Cross-National Manager," *The Financial Times*, March 13, 1998, FTS8.

34. For examples of six successful entrepreneurs, see M. Barrier, "Entrepreneurs Who Excel," *Nation's Business*, August 1996, 18–28.

35. H. Rosenberg, "This Generation Is All Business," *Business Week*, March 1, 1999, ENT4.

36. M. Ballon, "MIT Springboard Sends Internet Company Aloft," *Inc.*, 20, 18, December 1998, 23–25.

37. J. Mined, "A Gray Wave of Entrepreneurs," *The Futurist*, 33, 6, June 1, 1999, 10.

38. J.T. Chin, "The Internet Offers Entrepreneurial Opportunities," *Health Data Management*, June 1999.

39. I. Kunii, "Japan's High-Tech Hope," *Business Week*, May 31, 1999, 58.

40. T. Stewart, "Knowledge, the Appreciating Commodity," *Fortune*, 138, 7, October 12, 1998, 199–200.

41. W. Miller, "Building the Ultimate Resource," *Management Review*, 88, 1, January 1999, 42–45.

42. T. Stewart, *Intellectual Capital: The New Wealth of Organizations* (New York: Doubleday, 1998).

43. M. Martiny, "Knowledge Management at HP Consulting," *Organizational Dynamics*, 27, 2, Autumn 1998, 71–77.

44. W. Mark Fruin, *Knowledge Works: Managing Intellectual Capital at Toshiba* (New York: Oxford Press, 1997).

45. C.R. Celis, "Fruit of the Loom," *Inc.*, 20, 13, September 15, 1998, 27–28.

46. S. Tapsell, "Making Money from Brainpower: The New Wealth of Nations," *Management*, 45, 6, July 1998, 36–43.

47. "Face Value: A Viking with a Compass," *The Economist*, 346, 8071, June 6, 1998, 64.

48. T.A. Stewart, "The Search for the Organization of Tomorrow," *Fortune*, May 18, 1992, 92–98.

49. J.A. Byrne, "Requiem for Yesterday's CEO: Old-Style Execs Who Can't Adapt Are Losing Their Hold," *Business Week*, February 15, 1993, 32–33.

50. R. Charan and G. Colvin, "Why CEOs Fail," *Fortune*, 139, 12, June 1999, 68–78.

51. This leadership model was created by the faculty at the McColl School of Business and has been further developed by Karen Geiger, Director of Leadership Initiatives at the McColl School.

52. R. Brown, "Casting Off the Command and Control Yoke," *Works Management*, 51, 8, August 1998, 18–21.

53. See, for example, S.J. Wall and Sr. R. Wall, "The Evolution (Not the Death) of Strategy," *Organizational Dynamics*, 24, 2, Autumn 1995, 6–19.

54. S. Parker, T. Wall, J. Cordery, "Future Work Design Research and Practice: Towards an Elaborated Model of Work Design," *Journal of Occupational and Organizational Psychology*, November 2001, 413–425; D. Barry, "Managing the Bossless Team: Lessons in Distributed Leadership," *Organizational Dynamics*, Winter 1992, 31–47.

55. M. Moravec, O.J. Johannessen, and T.A. Hjelmas, "The Well-Managed SMT," *Management Review*, 87, 6, June 1998, 56–68.

56. B. Kirkman and D. Shapiro, "The Impact of Cultural Values on Job Satisfaction and Organizational Commitment in Self-Managing Work Teams: The Mediating Role of Employee Resistance," *Academy of Management Journal*, June 2001, 557–569.

57. L. McDermott, B. Waite, and N. Brawley, "Putting Together a World-Class Team," *Training and Development*, 53, 1, January 1999, 46–51.

58. "See You Online," *Fortune*, Winter 1999, 190.

59. J. Lipnack and J. Stamps, "Virtual Teams," *Executive Excellence*, 16, 5, May 1999, 14–15; and "Virtual Teams: The New Way to Work," *Strategy & Leadership*, 27, 1, January–February 1999, 14–19.

60. See for example, R. Yandrick, "A Team Effort," *HR Magazine*, June 2001, 136–141; and M. Finley, "All for One, But None for All?" *Across the Board*, January–February 2002, 45–51.

61. W.B. Johnstone, "Global Work Force 2000: The New World Labor Market," *Harvard Business Review*, March–April 1991, 115–29.

62. N.J. Perry, "More Women Are Executive VPs," *Fortune*, July 12, 1993, 16.

63. G. Hickman and A. Creighton-Zollar, "Diverse Self-

Directed Work Teams: Developing Strategic Initiatives for 21st Century Organizations," *Personnel Management*, 27, 2, Summer 1998, 187–200.

64. J. Crockett, "Diversity: Winning Competitive Advantage Through a Diverse Workforce," *HR Focus*, 76, 5, May 1999, 9–10; and J. Crockett, "Diversity as a Business Strategy," *Management Review*, 88, 5, May 1999, 62–63.

65. G. Flynn, "White Males See Diversity's Other Side," *Workforce*, 78, 2, February 1999, 53–55.

66. M. Wheeler, "Global Diversity: A Culture-Change Perspective," *Diversity*, 7, 2, Winter 1999, 31–34.

67. R. Miles, H. Coleman Jr., and W.E.D. Creed, "Keys to Success in Corporate Redesign," *California Management Review*, 37, 3, Spring 1995, 128–45.

68. N. Nohria and J.D. Berkley, "An Action Perspective: The Crux of the New Management," *California Management Review*, Summer 1994, 70–92.

69. R.E. Miles and C.C. Snow, "Organizations: New Concepts for New Forms," *California Management Review*, 28, 1986, 62–73.

70. H.H. Hinterhuber and B.M. Levin, "Strategic Networks—The Organization of the Future," *Long Range Planning*, 27, 3, 1994, 43–53; S. Tully, "The Modular Corporation," *Fortune*, February 8, 1993, A, 106–14; John Byrne, "The Virtual Corporation," *Business Week*, February 8, 1993, 98–103; R.E. Miles and C.C. Snow, "Organizations: New Concepts for New Forms," 62–71.

71. T. Kemp, "Partnerships R Us—Toysrus.com Is Building a Sustainable E-Retail Business by Drawing on the Strengths of Its Two Giant Business Partners," *Internetweek*, October 15, 2001, 14–21.

72. P. Christie and R. Levary, "Virtual Corporations: Recipe for Success," *Industrial Management*, 40, 4, July–August 1998, 7–12.

73. See for example, R. Dye, "The World of Work in 2010," *CMA Management*, December 2001/January 2002, 38–41.

74. "Knowledge Management Could Create Virtual Organizations," *Management Accounting*, 77, 4, April 1999, 4.

75. T.W. Malone, M.S.S. Morton, and R.R. Halperin, "Organizing for the 21st Century," *Strategy & Leadership*, July/August 1996, 7–10.

76. E. Thornton, "Japan's Struggle to Be Creative."

77. B. Keys and T. Case, "How to Become an Influential Manager," *Academy of Management Executive*, 4, 1990, 38–49.

78. B. Dumaine, "The New Non-Manager Managers," *Fortune*, February 22, 1993, 80–84.

79. See, for example, K.C. Green and D.T. Seymour, *Who's Going to Run General Motors?* (Princeton, N.J.: Peterson's Guides, 1991).

80. L.R. Dorsky, "Producing Managers Right the First Time," *Quality Progress*, February 1992, 37–41.

81. T. Peters, *Thriving on Chaos: Handbook for a Management Revolution* (New York: Random House, 1988).

82. W. Kiechel III, "Facing Up to Denial," *Fortune*, October 18, 1993, 163–66.

83. J. Fierman, "Beating the Midlife Career Crisis," *Fortune*, September 6, 1993, 163–166.

CHAPTER 2

1. S. Maxwell, "Prepare for Floyd: Storm Already Dwarfs Andrew," *The Orlando Sentinel*, September 13, 1999, A1ff; J. Jackson and M. Bell, "Prepare Yourselves: Floyd's Fury Will Pound Cape Canaveral," *The Orlando Sentinel*, September 14, 1999, A1ff; J. Kennedy and J. Jackson, "Floyd Focuses Fury on Carolina Coast," *The Orlando Sentinel*, September 16, 1999, A1ff; and J. Jackson, "Storm Douses Northeast," *The Orlando Sentinel*, September 17, 1999, A1ff.

2. J. Ball and J. White, "GM Offers to Enhance Job Security," *The Wall Street Journal*, September 7, 1999, A3ff.

3. J.A. Conger, "Leadership: The Art of Empowering Others," *Academy of Management Executive*, 3, 1989, 17–24.

4. J.A. Conway, "Harley Back in Gear," *Forbes*, April 20, 1987, 8.

5. "Nike, Inc. Increases Pay for Workers in Indonesia," *The Orlando Sentinel*, March 24, 1999, B5.

6. L.J. Krajewski and L.P. Ritzman, *Operations Management: Strategy and Analysis*, 5th ed. (Reading, Mass.: Addison-Wesley, 1999).

7. "UPS: The World's Leader in Package Delivery," *UPS Press Release*.

8. "Neglect Internet? Compaq Brass Did," *The Orlando Sentinel*, April 20, 1999, B5.

9. J.R. Evans, D.R. Anderson, D.J. Sweeney, and T.A. Williams, *Applied Production and Operations Management*, 3d ed. (St. Paul, Minn.: West Publishing, 1990), 423–28.

10. J. Evans and W. Lindsay, *Production/Operations Management: A Focus on Quality* (St. Paul, Minn.: West Publishing, 1993).

11. B. Brocka and M.S. Brocka, *Quality Management* (Homewood, Ill.: Business One Irwin, 1992), 18.

12. D. Wren, *Evolution of Management Thought*, 2d ed. (New York: Wiley, 1979).

13. F.W. Taylor, *Scientific Management* (New York: Harper & Row, 1911).

14. C. Wrege and A.G. Peroni, "Taylor's Pig-Tale: A Historical Analysis of Frederick W. Taylor's Pig-Iron Experiments," *Academy of Management Journal*, 17, March 1974, 6–27.

15. C. Wrege and A.M. Stotka, "Cooke Creates a Classic: The Story behind F.W. Taylor's Principles of Scientific Management," *Academy of Management Review*, 3, October 1978, 736–49.

16. M. Himmelberg, "Perks Other Than Money Keep Workers Happy," *The Orlando Sentinel*, May 9, 1999, H1ff.

17. D. Wren, *Evolution of Management Thought*.

18. F.B. Gilbreth, *Principles of Scientific Management* (New York: Van Nostrand, 1911).

19. M.K. Starr, *Operations Management: A Systems Approach* (Danvers, Mass.: Boyd & Fraser, 1996), 375.

20. H. Fayol, *Industrial and General Administration* (New York: Sir Isaac Pitman and Sons, 1930).

21. C. George Jr., *The History of Management Thought* (Englewood Cliffs, N.J.: Prentice-Hall, 1968).

22. J.F. Mee, "Pioneers of Management," *Advanced Management—Office Executive*, October 1962, 26–29.

23. M. Weber, *General Economic History*, trans. F. H. Knight (London: Allen & Unwin, 1927).

24. D. Wren, *Evolution of Management Thought*.

25. M. Weber, *The Theory of Social and Economic Organizations*, ed. and trans. A.M. Henderson and T. Parsons (New York: Free Press, 1947).

26. Ibid.

27. "Shareholders of Compaq Fume at Meeting," *The Orlando Sentinel*, April 23, 1999, B6.

28. D. Ignatius, "The Egyptian Bureaucracy Galls Both the Public and Foreign Investors," *The Wall Street Journal*, March 24, 1983.

29. M.P. Follett, *Creative Experience* (London: Longmans, Green, 1934).

30. M.P. Follett, "Dynamic Administration," in *Dynamic Administration: The Collected Papers of Mary Parker Follett*, ed. H. Metcalf and L.F. Urwick (New York: Harper & Row, 1942).

31. H.M. Parson, "What Happened at Hawthorne?" *Science*, 183, 1974, 922–32.

32. J.A. Sonnenfeld, "Shedding Light on the Hawthorne Studies," *Journal of Occupational Behavior*, 6, 1985, 111–30.

33. F. Kast and J. Rosenzweig, *Organization and Management: A Systems and Contingency Approach* (New York: McGraw-Hill, 1979).

34. D. McGregor, *The Human Side of Enterprise* (New York: McGraw-Hill, 1960), 33–58.

35. Ibid.

36. R.A. Baron and P.B. Paulus, *Understanding Human Relations: A Practical Guide to People at Work* (Needham Heights, Mass.: Allyn & Bacon, 1991), 312–13.

37. C. Barnard, *The Functions of the Executive* (Cambridge, Mass.: Harvard University Press, 1938).

38. B. Render and R.M. Stair Jr., *Introduction to Quantitative Models for Management* (Englewood Cliffs, N.J.: Prentice-Hall, 1996).

39. L. Austin and J. Burns, *Management Science* (New York: Macmillan, 1985).

40. T. Cook and R. Russell, *Introduction to Management Science* (Englewood Cliffs, N.J.: Prentice-Hall, 1985), 6–20.

41. K. Boulding, "General Systems Theory—The Skeleton of Science," *Management Science*, 2, April 1956, 197–208.

42. L.J. Krajewski and L.P. Ritzman, *Operations Management*, 3–4.

43. Kast and Rosenzweig, *Organization and Management*, 102.

44. F. Luthans, "The Contingency Theory of Management: A Path out of the Jungle," *Business Horizons*, 16, June 1973, 62–72.

45. J. Woodward, *Industrial Organizations: Theory and Practice*, 2d ed. (London: Oxford University Press, 1980).

46. Ibid.

47. F. Kast and J. Rosenzweig, *Contingency Views of Organizations and Management* (Chicago: Science Research Associates, 1973).

48. F. Robert, "As UPS Tries to Deliver More to Its Customers, Labor Problem Grows," *The Wall Street Journal*, May 23, 1994.

49. "More Businesses Hispanic-Owned, Government Says," *The Orlando Sentinel*, July 12, 1996, B1.

50. M.A. Vonderembse and G.P. White, *Operations Management: Concepts, Methods and Strategies*, 3d ed. (Minneapolis: West Publishing Company, 1996), 638–651.

51. E. Eldridge, "Thieves Hog Wild over Motorcycles," *USA Today*, July 19, 1996, B1.

52. M.K. Starr, *Operations Management*, 144.

53. J. Healey, "Global Competition Fells Japan Tradition," *USA Today*, October 27, 1999, 1B; J. Schmit, "Placard: Will Work For Pride," *USA Today*, November 12, 1999, 1B; and J. Schmit and P. Hadfield, "Japan's Students Uneasy About Jobs," *USA Today*, April 1, 1999, 5B.

54. W. Ouchi, *Theory Z: How American Business Can Meet the Japanese Challenge* (Reading, Mass.: Addison-Wesley, 1981), 60.

CHAPTER 3

1. See for example, J. Nasi, S. Nasi, N. Phillips, and S. Zyglidooulos, "The Evolution of Corporate Social Responsiveness," *Business and Society*, 36, 3, September 1997, 296–321.

2. A.B. Carroll, *Business & Society: Ethics and Stakeholder Management* (Cincinnati: South-Western, 1989).

3. *Ibid.*, 60.

4. See, for example, B. Harvey, ed., *European Perspectives on Business Ethics* (New York: Prentice-Hall, 1994); G. McDonald and P. Pak, "It's All Fair in Love, War, and Business: Cognitive Philosophies in Ethical Decision Making," *Journal of Business Ethics*, 15, 1996, 973–96.

5. M.L. Pava, "The Talmudic Concept of 'Beyond the Letter of the Law': Relevance to Business Social Responsibilities," *Journal of Business Ethics*, 15, 1996, 941–50.

6. T.R. Mitchell and W.G. Scott, "America's Problems and Needed Reforms: Confronting the Ethic of Personal Advantage," *Academy of Management Executive*, 4, 1990, 23–33.

7. H.R. Bowen, *Social Responsibilities of the Businessman* (New York: Harper & Row, 1953), 6.

8. Most of this discussion comes from S.L. Wartick and P.L. Cochran, "The Evolution of the Corporate Social Performance Model," *Academy of Management Review*, 10, 1985, 758–69.

9. A.B. Carroll, *Business & Society*, 60.

10. H. Geneen, "Baloney!" *Across the Board*, 34, 8, September 1997, 24–28.

11. C. Grant, "Friedman Fallacies," *Journal of Business Ethics*, 10, 1991, 907–14.

12. "A CEO Forum: What Corporate Social Responsibility Means to Me," *Business and Society Review*, Spring 1992.

13. L.E. Preston and J.E. Post, "Private Management and Public Policy," *California Management Review*, 23, 1991, 57.

14. B. Daviss, "Profits from Principle," *The Futurist*, 33, 3, March 1999, 28–33.

15. D.R. Dalton and R.A. Cosier, "The Four Faces of Social Responsibility," *Business Horizons*, May/June 1982, 19–27.

16. R. Reich, "The New Meaning of Corporate Social Responsibility," *California Management Review*, 20, 2, Winter 1998, 8–17.

17. A.B. Carroll, *Business & Society*, 60.

18. S.W. Gellerman, "Why 'Good' Managers Make Bad Ethical Choices," *Harvard Business Review*, July/August 1986, 85–90.

19. L. Alexander and W.F. Matthews, "The Ten Commandments of Corporate Social Responsibility," *Business and Society Review*, 50, 1984, 62–66.

20. S. Vyakarnam, "Social Responsibility: What Leading Companies Do," *Long Range Planning*, 25, 1992, 59–67.

21. L. Alexander and W.F. Matthews, "The Ten Commandments of Corporate Social Responsibility."

22. For example see K. Paul, L. Zalka, M. Downes, S. Perry, and S. Friday, "U.S. Consumer Sensitivity to Corporate Social Performance," *Business and Society*, 36, 4, December 1997, 408–18.

23. J. Bird, "Champions of the Cause," *Marketing*, June 18, 1998, 25–28.

24. L. Alberthal, "Corporate Policy on Community Outreach and Philanthropy," *Executive Speeches*, 13, 5, April/May 1999, 1–5.

25. R. Herman and J. Gioia, "Making Work Meaningful: Secrets of the Future-focused Corporation," *The Futurist*, 32, 9, December 1998, 24–26; and C. Neal, "A Conscious Change in the Workplace," *The Journal for Quality and Participation*, 22, 2, March/April 1999, 27–30.

26. L. Reynolds, "A New Social Agenda for the New Age," *Management Review*, January 1993, 39–41.

27. R.M. Kanter, "From Spare Change to Real Change," *Harvard Business Review*, 77, 3, May/June 1999, 122–32.

28. L. Alexander and W.F. Matthews, "The Ten Commandments of Corporate Social Responsibility."

29. R.N. Sanyal and J.S. Neves, "The Valdez Principles: Implications for Corporate Social Responsibility," *Journal of Business Ethics*, 10, 1991, 883–90.

30. W. Miller, "Citizenship: A Competitive Asset," *Industry Week*, 247, 15, August 1998, 104–8.

31. See, for example, J. DesJardins, "Corporate Environmental Responsibility," 17, 8, *Journal of Business Ethics*, June 1998, 825–38.

32. T.R. Mitchell and W.G. Scott, "America's Problems and Needed Reforms: Confronting the Ethic of Personal Advantage," *Academy of Management Executive*, 4, 1990, 23–33.

33. M. Lewis, *Liar's Poker: Rising Through the Wreckage on Wall Street* (New York: Norton, 1989); and M. Mayer, *Nightmare on Wall Street: Salomon Brothers and the Corruption of the Marketplace* (New York: Simon & Schuster, 1993).

34. "Wall Street Rules," *The Wall Street Journal*, August 11, 1999; and R. Buckman, "Scrutiny of Day-Trading Puts

All-Tech in the Spotlight," *The Wall Street Journal*, August 12, 1999.

35. D. Stipp, "I Stole to Get Even: Yet Another Charity Scam," *Fortune*, October 30, 1995, 24.

36. S.J. Harrington, "What Corporate America Is Teaching about Ethics," *Academy of Management Executive*, 5, 1991, 21–29.

37. For an interesting discussion, see D.M. Messick, "Why Ethics Is Not the Only Thing That Matters," *Business Ethics Quarterly*, 6, 2, April 1996, 223–26; M. Velasquez, "Why Ethics Matter: A Defense of Ethics in Business Organization," *Business Ethics Quarterly*, 6, 2, 201–22.

38. R. Berenbeim, "One Company, One Market, One Code, One World," *Vital Speeches of the Day*, 65, 22, September 1999, 696–98.

39. See for example, T. Donalson and T. Dunfee, "When Ethics Travel: The Promise and Peril of Global Business Ethics," *California Management Review*, 411, 4, Summer 1999, 45–63; and J. Beyer and D. Nino, "Ethics and Cultures in International Business," *Journal of Management Inquiry*, 8, 3, September 1999, 287–97.

40. R. Berenbeim, "Global Corporate Ethics Practices," *The Conference Board Research Report*, 121243-99-RR, 1999.

41. M. Rokeach, *The Nature of Human Values* (New York: Free Press, 1973).

42. G.F. Cavanaugh, *American Business Values in Transition* (Upper Saddle River, N.J.: Prentice Hall, 1980).

43. See for example, "Leadership and Business Ethics: Does It Matter? Implications for Management," *Journal of Business Ethics*, 20, 4, July 1999, 327–35.

44. For an example of leaders influencing the values of an organization, see P. Berman, "Throwing Away the Book," *Forbes*, 162, 10, November 1998, 174–81.

45. For a discussion of value-based culture, see P. Pruzan, "From Control to Value-Based Management and Accountability," *Journal of Business Ethics*, 17, 13, October 1998, 1379–94.

46. L. Schatzberg, "Ethics in Information Management," *Business and Society*, 37, 2, June 1998, 237–42.

47. S. Henderson, and C. Snyder, "Personal Information Privacy: Implications for MIS Managers," *Information and Management*, 36, 4, October 1999, 213–20.

48. "New Technology Strains Ethics," *USA Today*, 127, June 1999, 4.

49. See, for example, K. Lock, S. Conger and E. Oz, "Ownership, Privacy and Monitoring in the Workplace: A Debate on Technology and Ethics," *Journal of Business Ethics*, 17, 6, April 1998, 653–63; and W. Cordeiro, "Suggested Management Responses to Ethical Issues Raised by Technological Change," *Journal of Business Ethics*, 16, 12, September 1997, 1393–1400.

50. K. Andrews, "Ethics in Practice," *Harvard Business Review*, September/October 1989, 99–104.

51. See, for example, N. Dornenburg, "Is Ethics a Liability in Turbulent Competitive Environments?" *Business Ethics Quarterly*, 6, 2, April 1996, 233–39.

52. See B. Schwab, "Do Good Ethics Always Make for Good Business?" *Strategic Management Journal*, 17, 6, 499–500; and L.T. Hosmer, "Response to 'Do Good Ethics Always Make for Good Business?'" *Strategic Management Journal*, 17, 1996, 501.

53. L.T. Hosmer, *The Ethics of Management* (Homewood, Ill.: Irwin, 1987).

54. R. Perloff, "Self-Interest and Personal Responsibility Redux," *American Psychologist*, 42, 1987, 3–11.

55. M. Velasquez, D. Moberg, and G. Cavanagh, "Organizational Statesmanship and Dirty Politics: Ethical Guidelines for the Organizational Politician," *Organizational Dynamics*, Autumn 1993, 65–80.

56. B. Hager, "What's Behind Business' Sudden Fervor for Ethics," *Business Week*, September 23, 1991, 65.

57. D. Morf, M. Schumacer, and S. Vitel, "A Survey of Ethics Officers in Large Organizations," *Journal of Business Ethics*, 20, 3, July 1999, 265–71.

58. L.K. Trevino and K.A. Nelson, *Managing Business Ethics: Straight Talk about How to Do It Right* (New York: Wiley, 1995), 299.

59. D. Fritzsche and H. Becker, "Linking Management Behavior to Ethical Philosophy—An Empirical Investigation," *Academy of Management Journal*, 27, 1984, 166–75.

60. S.J. Harrington, "What Corporate America Is Teaching about Ethics."

61. C. Wiley, "The ABC's of Business Ethics: Definitions, Philosophies and Implementation," *Industrial Management*, 37, 1, January/February 1995, 22–27.

62. S. Modic, "Corporate Ethics: From Commandments to Commitment," *Industry Week*, December 1987, 33–36.

63. See R. Gilmartin, "Innovation, Ethics and Core Values: Keys to Global Success," *Vital Speeches of the Day*, 65, 7, January 15, 1999, 209–13; and R. Berenbeim, "Global Corporate Ethics Practices," *The Conference Board Research Report*, 121243-99-RR, 1999.

64. J. Huey, "Finding New Heroes for a New Era," *Fortune*, January 25, 1993, 62–69.

65. R. Berenbeim, "Global Corporate Ethics Practices," *The Conference Board Research Report*, 121243-99-RR, 1999.

66. Center for Business Ethics at Bentley College, "Are Corporations Institutionalizing Ethics?" *Journal of Business Ethics*, 5, 1986, 86–91.

67. B. Hager, "What's Behind Business' Sudden Fervor for Ethics."

68. A.L. Otten, "Ethics on the Job: Companies Alert Employees to Potential Dilemmas," *The Wall Street Journal*, July 14, 1986, 17.

69. M.P. Miceli and J.P. Near, "Whistleblowing: Reaping the Benefits," *Academy of Management Executive*, 8, 3, 1994, 65–72.

70. L. Driscoll, "A Better Way to Handle Whistle-Blowers: Let Them Speak," *Business Week*, July 27, 1992, 36.

71. For a discussion of whistleblowing, see P. Jubb, "Whistleblowing: A Restrictive Definition and Interpretation," *Journal of Business Ethics*, 21, 1, August 1999, 77–94; and G. King III, "The Implications of an Organization's Structure on Whistleblowing," 20, 4, July 1999, 315–26.

72. L. Driscoll, "A Better Way to Handle Whistle-Blowers: Let Them Speak," *Business Week*, July 27, 1992, 36.

73. Ibid.

74. J. Huey, "Finding New Heroes for a New Era."

75. S. Esrock and G. Leichty, "Social Responsibility and Corporate Web Pages: Self-presentation or Agenda-setting," *Public Relations Review*, 24, 3, Fall 1998, 305–19.

CHAPTER 4

1. A.P. DeGeus, "Planning As Learning," *Harvard Business Review*, March/April 1988, 70–74.

2. P.F. Drucker, *Managing for Results* (New York: Harper & Row, 1964); Drucker, *The Effective Executive* (New York: Harper & Row, 1967).

3. C. Perrow, "The Analysis of Goals in Complex Organizations," *American Sociological Review*, 26, 1961, 854.

4. J. Foster, "General Maliase at General Mills," *Business Week*, July 1, 2002, 68–70.

5. D. Aaker and E. Joachimsthaler, "The Lure of Global Branding," *Harvard Business Review*, 77, 6, November/December 1999, 137–144.

6. G. Anders, "AOL's True Believers," *Fast Company*, July 2002, 96–104.

7. E.E. Lawler III, "Total Quality Management and Employee Involvement: Are They Compatible?" *Academy of Management Executive*, 9, 1, 1995, 34–38.

8. D. Hastings, "Lincoln Electric's Harsh Lessons from International Expansion," *Harvard Business Review*, 77, 3, May/June 1999, 162–178.

9. R. Michaels, "Planning: An Effective Management Tool or Corporate Pastime?" *Journal of Marketing Management*, Spring 1986, 259.

10. "How Planning Can Destroy Value," *Harvard Business Review*, 77, 2, March/April 1999, 42–43.

11. W. Chan Kim and R. Mauborgne, "Charting Your Company's Future," *Harvard Business Review*, June 2002, 77–84.

12. "How Planning Can Destroy Value," *Harvard Business Review*, 77, 2, March/April 1999, 42–43.

13. G. Imperato, "Harley Shifts Gears," *Fast Company*, June 1997, 104–110.

14. W.H. Brickner and D.M. Cope, *The Planning Process* (Boston: Winthrop Publishers, 1977), 52–56.

15. R. Evered, "So What Is Strategy?" *Long Range Planning*, 16, 1983, 57–72.

16. M. Leontiades, "The Confusing Words of Business Policy," *Academy of Management Review*, 7, 1982, 45–48.

17. A. Ginsberg, "Operationalizing Organizational Strategy: Toward an Integrative Framework," *Academy of Management Review*, 9, 3, 1984, 548–557.

18. C.C. Snow and L.G. Hrebiniak, "Strategy, Distinctive Competence and Organizational Performance," *Administrative Science Quarterly*, 25, 1980, 317–336.

19. "H-P Chief Executive Wants Firm at Center of E-Services World," *The Wall Street Journal*, Eastern Edition, December 1, 1999, B6; and Q. Hardy, "The Cult of Carly," *Forbes*, December 13, 1999.

20. J. Mitchell, "Computer Hardware Industry," http://www.hoovers.com/industry/snapshot, Hoover's Company, Inc.

21. See, for example, I. Sager, "Compaq's Long Road Back," *BusinessWeek Online*, January 10, 2000; D. Fisher, "Desktop Battle Plan," *Forbes*, January 10, 2000; P. Burrows, "Can Apple Take Its Game to the Next Level?" *BusinessWeek Online*, December 20, 1999; M. Krantz, "Jobs' Golden Apple," *Time*, August 2, 1999; B. Schlender, "Steve Jobs' Apple Gets Way Cooler," *Fortune*, January 24, 2000.

22. S.S. Thune and R.J. House, "Where Long-Range Planning Pays Off," *Business Horizons*, 14, 1970, 81–87; L.C. Rhyne, "The Relationship of Strategic Planning to Financial Performance," *Strategic Management Journal*, 5, 1986, 423–436; Z.A. Malik and D.W. Karger, "Does Long-Range Planning Improve Company Performance?" *Management Review*, 64, 1975, 27–31; R. Rumelt, *Strategy, Structure, and Economic Performance* (Boston: Graduate School of Business Administration, Harvard University, 1974).

23. A.D. Chandler, *Strategy and Structure: Chapters in the History of the American Industrial Enterprise* (Cambridge, Mass.: MIT Press, 1962).

24. M. Gunther, "Turnaround Time for CBS," *Fortune*, August 19, 1996, 65–70.

25. See, for example, H. Jessell and S. McClellan, "The Viacom Vision," *Broadcasting & Cable*, November 15, 1999, 28–37; T. Hoffman, "Internet Challenges Top CBS Viacom List," *Computerworld*, September 13, 1999, 1+; R. Siklos and R. Grover, "CBS," *Business Week* (Industrial/Technology Edition), April 5, 1999, 74+.

26. Hoover Company Profiles, July 2002.

27. S.C. Wheelwright, "Strategy, Management, and Strategic Planning Approaches," *Interfaces*, 14, 1984, 19–33.

28. M. Porter, "From Competitive Advantage to Corporate Strategy," *Harvard Business Review*, May/June 1987, 43–59.

29. H. Ansoff, "Critique of Henry Mintzberg's "The Design School: Reconsidering the Basic Premises of Strategic Management," *Strategic Management Journal*, February 1991, 449–461.

30. T. Spaeth, "The Name Game," *Across the Board*, March/April 2002, 27–31.

31. Philip Morris, 1999 Annual Report.

32. R.A. Burgelman and A.S. Grove, "Strategic Dissonance," *California Management Review*, 38, 2, 1996, 8–28.

33. D.Q. Mills and G.B. Friesen, "Emerging Business Realities," *Journal of Management Consulting*, 10, 4, November 1999, 39–45.

34. A. Campbell, "Tailored, Not Benchmarked: A Fresh Look at Corporate Planning," *Harvard Business Review*, March/April 1999, 41–50.

35. J. Crockett, "Diversity: Winning Competitive Advantage Through a Diverse Workforce," *HR Focus*, 76, 5, May 1999, 9–10; and L. Wah, "Diversity at Allstate: A Competitive Weapon," *Management Review*, 88, 7, July/August 1999, 24–30.

36. P. Drucker, *The Practice of Management* (New York: Harper, 1954).

37. K. Davis and J. Newstrom, *Human Behavior at Work in Organizational Behavior* (New York: McGraw-Hill, 1989), 209.

38. J.L. Mendelson, "Goal Setting: An Important Management Tool," in *Executive Skills: A Management by Objectives Approach* (Dubuque, Iowa: Brown, 1980).

39. *Ibid.*

40. J. Gordon, *Management and Organizational Behavior* (Boston: Allyn & Bacon, 1990), 129–132.

41. W.B. Werther and W. Heinz, "Refining MBO through Negotiations," in *Executive Skills: A Management by Objectives Approach* (Dubuque, Iowa: Brown, 1980).

42. J.N. Kondrasuk, "Studies in MBO Effectiveness," *Academy of Management Review*, 6, 1981, 419–430.

43. G. Hofstede, "Motivation, Leadership, and Organization: Do American Theories Apply Abroad?" *Organizational Dynamics*, Summer 1980, 55.

44. A.S. Smith and A.P. Houser, *Personnel Management* (Reading, Mass.: Addison-Wesley, 1986).

45. J.S. Kaplan and D.P. Norton, *The Strategy-Focused Organization: How Balanced Scorecard Companies Thrive in the New Business Environment* (Boston: Harvard Business School Press, 2000).

46. D.D. McConkey, "Planning for Uncertainty," *Business Horizons*, January/February 1987, 40–43.

47. C. Farkas and P. DeBacker, *Maximum Leadership.*

48. See, for example, D. Briody et al., "Confident Yet Cautious, Industries Await Y2K," *Infoworld*, December 27, 1999, 8–10.

49. P. Wonacott, "Hong Kong's Y2K Plans Could Depend on Beijing—Mainland Glitches May Halt Supplies and Hurt Business," *The Wall Street Journal*, Eastern Edition, December 23, 1999, A13.

50. J. Friedland, "Mexico's Y2K Preparedness Looks Solid—Corporations, Government Seem to Be Way Ahead of Other Latin Nations," *The Wall Street Journal*, Eastern Edition, November 15, 1999, A32.

51. S. Brown, "Building America's Anti-Terror Machine," *Fortune*, July 22, 2002, 99–100.

52. I. Wylie, "There Is No Alternative Too . . .," *Fast Company*, July 2002, 106–111.

53. L.V. Gerstner, "Can Strategic Planning Pay Off?" in *Perspectives on Strategic Marketing Management* (Boston: Allyn & Bacon, 1980).

54. "Strategic Planning Is Back," *Business Week*, August 25, 1996, 25–30.

55. J. Rosenzweig, F. Kast, and T.R. Mitchell, *The Frank and Ernest Manager* (Los Altos, Calif.: Crisp Publications, 1991).

56. See, for example, J.P. Fernandez and M. Barr, *The Diversity Advantage: How American Business Can Outperform Japanese and European Companies in the Global Marketplace* (New York: Lexington Books, 1993); M.D. Gentile, ed., *Differences That Work: Organizational Excellence through Diversity* (Boston: Harvard Business School Press, 1994).

57. See, for example, E. DeBono, *Six Thinking Hats* (Boston: Little, Brown, 1985); K. Albrecht, *Brain Power: Learn to Improve Your Thinking Skills* (Upper Saddle River, N.J.: Prentice-Hall, 1990).

58. J. Martin, "Business Planning: The Gap between Theory and Practice," *Long Range Planning*, 1979, 48.

CHAPTER 5

1. H. Mintzberg, *The Rise and Fall of Strategic Planning* (New York: Free Press, 1994).

2. J. Champy, "The CEO's Plate for 00," *Computerworld*, January 3, 2000, 89.

3. M. Piturro, "Mindshift," *Management Review*, 88, 5, May 1999, 46–51.

4. G. Hamel, "Bringing Silicon Valley Inside," *Harvard Business Review*, September/October 1999, 70–84.

5. J.A. Byrne, "Strategic Planning: It's Back," *Business Week*, August 26, 1996, 46–53.

6. R. Evered, "So What Is Strategy?" *Long Range Planning*, 16, 1983, 57–72; A. Ginsberg, "Operationalizing Organizational Strategy: Toward an Integrative Framework," *Academy of Management Review*, 9, 1984, 548–57.

7. M. Leontiades, "The Confusing Words of Business Policy," *Academy of Management Review*, 7, 1982, 45–48.

8. See, for example, T. Peters, "The Circle of Innovation: You Can't Shrink Your Way to Greatness," (New York: Random House, 1999).

9. M. Thankur and L.M.R. Calingo, "Strategic Thinking Is Hip, But Does It Make a Difference?" *Business Horizons*, September/October 1992, 47–54.

10. For example, see J.A. Pearce, E.B. Freeman, and R.B. Robinson, "The Tenuous Link between Formal Strategic Planning and Financial Performance," *Academy of Management Review*, 12, 1987, 658–75; S. Schoeffler, R.D. Buzzell, and D.F. Heany, "Impact of Strategic Planning on Profit Performance," *Harvard Business Review*, March/April 1974, 137–45; and D.M. Herold, "Long-Range Planning and Organizational Performance: A Cross-Valuation Study," *Academy of Management Journal*, March 1972, 91–102.

11. J.A. Pearce II and W.A. Randolph, "Improving Strategy Formulation Pedagogies by Recognizing Behavioral Aspects," *Exchange*, December 1980, 7–10.

12. H.H. Hinterhuber and W. Popp, "Are You a Strategist or Just a Manager?" *Harvard Business Review*, January/February 1992, 105–14.

13. H. Mintzberg, "Crafting Strategy," *Harvard Business Review*, July/August 1987, 66–75.

14. R. Evered, "So What Is Strategy?" *Long Range Planning*, 16, 1983, 57–72.

15. S.R. Baldwin and M. McConnell, "Strategic Planning: Process and Plan Go Hand in Hand," *Management Solution*, June 1988, 29–37.

16. *Ibid.*

17. M. Goold and J. Quinn, "The Paradox of Strategic Control," *Strategic Management Journal*, 11, 1990, 43–57.

18. H. Mintzberg, "Crafting Strategy."

19. P.J.H. Schoemaker, "How to Link Strategic Vision to Core Capabilities," *Sloan Management Review*, Fall 1992, 67–81.

20. S.F. Stershirc, "Mission Statements Can Be a Field of Dreams," *Marketing News*, February 1, 1993, 7ff.

21. J.A. Pearce and F. David, "Corporate Mission Statements: The Bottom Line," *Academy of Management Executive*, 1, 1987, 109–16.

22. D.L. Calfee, "Get Your Mission Statement Working," *Management Review*, January 1993, 54–57.

23. B. Bartkus, M. Glassman, and R. Bruce McAffe, "Mission Statements: Are They Smoke and Mirrors?" *Business Horizons*, November 2000, 23–36.

24. See, for example, A. H. Van de Ven, "Medtronic's Chairman William George on How Mission-driven Companies Create Long-term Shareholder Value," *Academy of Management Executive*, November 2001, 39–48.

25. "Mission Possible," *Business Week*, August 16, 1999. 12.

26. R. Tedlow, "What the Titans Can Teach Us," *Harvard Business Review*, December 2001, 70–78.

27. C.C. Snow and L.G. Hrebiniak, "Strategy, Distinctive Competence, and Organizational Performance," *Administrative Science Quarterly*, 25, June 1980, 317–37.

28. J. Montanari, C. Morgan, and J. Bracker, *Strategic Management: A Choice Approach* (Chicago: Dryden Press, 1990), 81–85.

29. R. Mirabile, "The New Workplace," *The Human Resources Professional*, November/December 1999, 19–22.

30. J.P. Pfeffer, *Competitive Advantage through People: Unleashing the Power of the Work Force* (Boston: Harvard Business School Press, 1994).

31. P. Capelli, "A Market-Driven Approach to Retaining Talent," *Harvard Business Review*, January/February 2000, 103–11.

32. J.P. Fernandez and M. Barr, *The Diversity Advantage: How American Business Can Outperform Japanese and European Companies in the Global Marketplace* (New York: Lexington Books, 1993).

33. M.D. Gentile, ed., *Differences That Work: Organizational Excellence through Diversity* (Boston: Harvard Business School Press, 1994).

34. T. Wheelen and D.J. Hunger, *Strategic Management* (Reading, Mass.: Addison-Wesley, 1990), 100.

35. P. Bray, "Dentsply Extracts Market Share," *NASDAQ*, June 2002, 50–54.

36. See, for example, M. Maddocks, "Let's Hear It for Decrepitude," *New York Times*, August 27, 1999, 23.

37. L. Grant, "Stirring It Up at Campbell," *Fortune*, May 13, 1996, 80–86.

38. M. Gunther, "Turnaround Time for CBS," *Fortune*, August 19, 1996, 65–70.

39. "Why Moonves Didn't Lose Letterman," *Business Week*, March 25, 2002, 62.

40. "Home Center Industry Tailors Itself to Consumers," *Chain Store Age*, August 1999, A26–A28.

41. E. Fisher, "Levi's Panting for Youth Sales," *Insight on the News*, December 28, 1998, 40.

42. "Ground Wars," *Business Week*, May 21, 2001, 64; and "Out of the Box at UPS," *Business Week*, January 10, 2000, 76.

43. "2020 Strategic Technologies," *Signal*, February 2000, 8.

44. "Electronic Capabilities Prompting Changing Trends in Cardiovascular Monitoring," *Health Industry Today*, February 2000, 8.

45. G. Anders, "AOL's True Believers," *Fast Company*, July 2002, 96–105.

46. J. Dao, "Bradley Challenges Nation to Eliminate Child Poverty," *New York Times*, October 22, 1999, 22; and K. Seelye, "Embracing Clinton at Arm's Length, Gore Formally Begins Run for the President," *New York Times*, June 17, 1999, 26.

47. J. Carney, J. Dickerson, and M. Duffy, "Inside the Mind of the CEO President: Bush may be an M.B.A. and a former CEO, but his experiences haven't taught him to warm to Wall Street. Here's how the President does his figures," *Time*, August 5, 2002; and "The Good News in All That Bad News: The painful cleansing taking place could usher in a stronger, healthier market," *Business Week*, July 29, 2002, 20+.

48. *Ibid.*, 24.

49. R.A. D'Aveni, "Coping with Hypercompetition: Utilizing the New 7S's Framework," *Academy of Management Executive*, 9, 3, 1995, 45–60.

50. M.A. Hitt, B.B. Tyler, C. Hardee, and D. Park, "Understanding Strategic Intent in the Global Marketplace," *Academy of Management Executive*, 9, 2, 1995, 12–19.

51. S.A. Zahra and S.S. Chaples, "Blind Spots in Competitive Analysis," *Academy of Management Executive*, 7, 2, 1993, 7–28.

52. L. Grant, "Why Warren Buffett's Betting Big on American Express," *Fortune*, October 30, 1995, 70–84.

53. See, for example, M. McNamee, "Don't Leave Home Without a Freebie," *Business Week*, November 8, 1999, 150–52;

R. Buckman, "American Express Plans to Overhaul, Relaunch Online-Brokerage Operation," *The Wall Street Journal*, October 6, 1999, C7; and "AmEx Gets the Blues, But Smiles," *Credit Card Management*, 12, 7, October 1999, 10–12.

54. Anders, "The View From the Top: The Past, Present and Future of the Internet Economy, As Seen By Amazon.com's Jeff Bezos," *The Wall Street Journal*, July 12, 1999, R52.

55. "Labor Shortage Unlikely to Cause Soaring Wages in First Half of 2000," *HR Focus*, March 2000, 8.

56. M. Conlin, "The Big Squeeze on Workers," *Business Week*, May 13, 2002, 96.

57. See, for example, N. Wingfield, "E-Commerce (A Special Report)—The Industries—Reading the Riot Act: Amazon.com Isn't Bad, Says an Independent Bookseller; It's Just Dangerous," *The Wall Street Journal*, July 12, 1999, R46.

58. J. Barney, "Looking Inside for Competitive Advantage," *Academy of Management Executive*, 9, 4, 1995, 49–61.

59. L. Hays, "The Vision Thing Gets Another Look From IBM's Chief—Summer Statement Haunts Gerstner, Who Stresses Strategy in Annual Report," *The Wall Street Journal*, March 15, 1994, B6.

60. S. Ante, " What's Bugging Big Blue: Investors fear that Corporate America's woes will cast a shadow on IBM's services business," *Business Week*, July 22, 2002, 61+.

61. R.B. Robinson, "Planned Patterns of Strategic Behavior and Their Relationship to Business-Unit Performance," *Strategic Management Journal*, 9, 1988, 43–60.

62. J.A. Pearce, K. Robbins, and R. Robinson, "The Impact of Grand Strategy and Planning Formality on Financial Performance," *Strategic Management Journal*, 8, 1987, 125–34.

63. R.B. Robinson, "Planned Patterns of Strategic Behavior."

64. C. Dawson and D. Brady, "Land of the Rising Glue Gun: Is Japan's love affair with Martha Stewart a passing fancy?" *Business Week*, June 17, 2002, 24+.

65. "The Clouds Keep Getting Thicker," *Business Week*, November 26, 2001, 46+.

66. "The Fortunes—And Misfortunes—Of War," *Business Week*, January 14, 2002.

67. Adapted from M. Porter, *Competitive Advantage: Creating and Sustaining Superior Performance* (New York: Free Press, 1985).

68. P. Wright, "Strategic Options of Least-Cost, Differentiation, and Niche," *Readings in Strategic Management*, March/April 1986, 21–26.

69. M. Corboy and D. O'Corrbui, "The Seven Deadly Sins of Strategy," *Management Accounting*, 77, 10, November 1999, 29–30.

70. L.A. Huston, "Using Total Quality to Put Strategic Intent into Motion," *Conference Executive Summary*, September/October 1992, 21–23.

71. A. Ginsberg, "Operationalizing Organizational Strategy."

72. For example, see R. Hayes and S. Wheelwright, *Restoring Our Competitive Edge: Competing through Manufacturing* (New York: John Wiley and Sons, 1984).

73. A.D. Chandler, *Strategy and Structure: Chapters in the History of the American Industrial Enterprise* (Cambridge, Mass.: MIT Press, 1962).

74. R. Rumelt, *Strategy, Structure, and Economic Performance* (Boston: Graduate School of Business Administration, Harvard University, 1974).

75. A. Chandler, *Strategy and Structure.*

76. For example, see C. Bartlett, "How Multinational Organizations Evolve," *Journal of Business Strategy*, 3, Summer 1982, 20–32; R. Drazin and P. Howard, "Strategy Implementation: A Technique for Organizational Design," *Columbia Journal of World Business*, 19, Summer 1984, 40–54; J.R. Galbraith and R.K. Kazanjian, *Strategy Implementation: Structure Systems and Process* (St. Paul, Minn.: West Publishing, 1978).

77. For example, see D. Miller, "Configurations of Strategy and Structure: Towards a Synthesis," *Strategic Management Journal*, 7, 1986, 233–49; D. Miller, "Strategy Making and Structure: Analysis and Implications for Performance," *Academy of Management Journal*, 30, 1987, 7–32; and D. Miller, "Relating Porter's Business Strategies to Environment and Structure: Analysis and Performance Implications," *Academy of Management Journal*, 31, 1988, 280–308.

78. J.S. Ott, *The Organizational Culture Perspective* (Monterey, Calif.: Brooks/Cole, 1989).

79. T.J. Peters and R.H. Waterman, *In Search of Excellence: Lessons from America's Best-Run Companies* (New York: Harper & Row, 1982).

80. 3M, *1995 Annual Report*; and "Master of Innovation," *Business Week*, April 1990, 58–63.

81. See, for example, D.S. Elenkov, "Can American Management Concepts Work in Russia? A Cross-Cultural Comparative Study," *California Management Review*, 40, 4, Summer 1998, 133–56.

82. A.K. Gupta and B. Govindarajan, "Business Unit Strategy, Management Characteristics, and Business Unit Effectiveness at Strategy Implementation," *Academy of Management Journal*, 27, March 1984, 25–41.

83. See, for example, J. Garten, *The Mind of the C.E.O*, (New York Basic Book/Perseus Publishing, 2001).

84. F. Westley and H. Mintzberg, "Visionary Leadership and Strategic Management," *Strategic Management Journal*, 10, special issue, 1989, 17.

85. "Leading Ferociously," *Harvard Business Review*, May 2002, 22–24.

86. P. Lorange and D. Murphy, "Considerations Implementing Strategic Control," *Journal of Business Strategy*, 4, Spring 1984, 27–35.

87. J. Eckhouse, "In Search of the Customer-Centric Enterprise," *Informationweek*, December 6, 1999, 209–10.

88. M. Goold and J. Quinn, "The Paradox of Strategic Controls," *Strategic Management Journal*, 11, 1990, 43–57.

89. D. Roth Warner, E. Schonfeld, and M. Gunther, "10 Companies That Get It," *Fortune*, November 8, 1999, 115–117.

CHAPTER 6

1. H. Mintzberg, "The Manager's Job: Folklore and Fact," *Harvard Business Review*, March/April 1990, 163–76.

2. P. Fandt, *Management Skills: Practice and Experiences* (St. Paul, Minn.: West Publishing, 1994).

3. R. Burnette, "BP Connects With the Future," *The Orlando Sentinel*, January 19, 2002, B1ff.

4. C. O'Reilly, "Variations in Decision Makers' Use of Information Sources," *Academy of Management Journal*, 25, 1982, 756–71; C. O'Reilly, "The Use of Information in Organizational Decision Making: A Model and Some Propositions," in B. Staw and L. Cummings, eds., *Research in Organizational Behavior*, Vol. 5 (Greenwich, Conn.: JAI Press, 1983), 103–39.

5. Abigail Goldman, "Mattell Updates Aging Barbie," *The Orlando Sentinel*, February 10, 2002, H1ff.

6. "Coke's Brand-Loyalty Lesson," *Fortune*, August 5, 1985, 44–46.

7. D. Vaughan, "Autonomy, Interdependence, and Social Control: NASA and the Space Shuttle *Challenger*," *Administrative Science Quarterly*, 35, 1990, 225–57.

8. D. Jones and E. Neuborne, "Fate, Fortune Ride on Flow of Critical Data," *USA Today*, July 2, 1996, B1–2.

9. D. Vaughan, 225–57.

10. D. Snachez, "Burger King Sees How New Menu Stacks Up," *The Orlando Sentinel*, December 8, 2001, B1ff.

11. K. Eisenhardt, "Making Fast Strategic Decisions in High-Velocity Environments," *Academy of Management Journal*, 32, 1989, 543–76.

12. M.A. Verespej, "Gutsy Decisions of 1994: Gerstner Looked before Leaping," *Industry Week*, January 23, 1995, 36.

13. "Long Distance: Innovative MCI Unit Finds Culture Shock in Colorado Springs," *The Wall Street Journal*, June 25, 1996.

14. S.W. Floyd and B. Wooldridge, "Managing the Strategic Consensus: The Foundation of Effective Implementation," *Academy of Management Executive*, 6, 1992, 27–39.

15. A. Adler, "Saturn Recalls All Cars Made before April '93 for Fire Risk," *The Columbia SC State*, August 11, 1993, A1; B. Meier, "Engine Fires Prompt G.M. to Issue Recall of 80% of Saturns," *New York Times*, August 11, 1993, A1; O. Suris, "Recall by Saturn Could Tarnish Its Reputation," *The Wall Street Journal*, August 11, 1993, A3; and R. Truett, "Calls Swamp Saturn Dealers Since Recall," *Orlando Sentinel*, August 11, 1993, A1.

16. H. Mintzberg, 163–76.

17. "General Motors Cranks Up Its Virtual Auto Showroom," *The Orlando Sentinel*, March 11, 1999, B5; "GM to Roll Out Benchmark Internet Shopping Service Nationwide," *General Motors Press Release*, September 28, 1998; and "General Motors Launches World's Largest Virtual Showroom," *General Motors Press Release*, March 10, 1999.

18. J.G. March, "Decision Making Perspective," in A.H. Van de Ven and W.S. Joyce, eds., *Perspectives on Organization Design and Behavior* (New York: Wiley, 1981).

19. N.J. Adler, *International Dimensions of Organizational Behavior*, 2d ed. (Boston: PWS-Kent Publishing, 1991); and P. Sethi, N. Maniki, and C. Swanson, *The False Promise of the Japanese Miracle* (Marshfield, Mass.: Pitman, 1984).

20. F.N. Brady, *Ethical Managing: Rules and Results* (New York: Macmillan, 1990).

21. Adapted from S.W. Gellerman, "Why 'Good' Managers Make Bad Ethical Choices," *Harvard Business Review*, July/August 1986, 85–90; and K.H. Blanchard and N.V. Peale, *The Power of Ethical Management* (Homewood, Ill.: Irwin, 1987).

22. H.A. Simon, *Model of Man* (New York: John Wiley, 1957).

23. O. Behling and N.L. Eckel, "Making Sense out of Intuition," *Academy of Management Executive*, 5, 1991, 46–54.

24. R. Rowen, *The Intuitive Manager* (Boston: Little, Brown, 1986).

25. Robert Johnson, "Universal Orlando's New Thrill Seeker," *Central Florida Business*, April 15, 2002, 14–15; and Robert Johnson, "Universal Orlando Thinks Big," *The Orlando Sentinel*, March 16, 2002, A1ff.

26. O. Behling and N.L. Eckel, 46–54.

27. J. Schmit, "PC Maker Realizes a Dream," *USA Today*, July 17, 1996, B4.

28. C.R. Schwenk, "Information, Cognitive Biases, and Commitment to a Course of Action," *Academy of Management Review*, 11, 1986, 298–310.

29. M.H. Bazerman, *Judgment in Managerial Decision Making* (New York: John Wiley, 1986).

30. "Honda Pulls Plug on Electric Vehicles," *The Orlando Sentinel*, April 30, 1999, B5.

31. I. Janis and L. Mann, *Decision Making: A Psychological Analysis of Conflict, Choice, and Commitment* (New York: Free Press, 1977).

32. D. Ciampa, *Total Quality* (Reading, Mass.: Addison-Wesley, 1992).

33. V.H. Vroom and P.W. Yetton, *Leadership and Decision Making* (Pittsburgh, Penn.: University of Pittsburgh, 1973).

34. V.H. Vroom and A.G. Jago, *The New Leadership: Managing Participation in Organizations* (Upper Saddle River, N.J.: Prentice Hall, 1988).

35. V.H. Vroom, "A New Look at Managerial Decision Making," *Organizational Dynamics*, Spring 1973, 69–70.

36. Vroom and Jago, *The New Leadership: Managing Participation in Organizations*.

37. R.A. Cooke and J.A. Kernagan, "Estimating the Difference between Group versus Individual Performance on Problem-Solving Tasks," *Group and Organization Studies*, 12, 1987, 319–42.

38. W.L. Ury, J.M. Brett, and S.B. Goldberg, *Getting Disputes Resolved* (San Francisco: Jossey-Bass, 1989).

39. I.L. Janis, *Victims of Groupthink* (Boston: Houghton Mifflin, 1972).

40. L.R. Beach, *Making the Right Decision: Organizational Culture, Vision, and Planning* (Upper Saddle River, N.J.: Prentice Hall, 1993).

41. R. Whyte, "Groupthink Reconsidered," *Academy of Management Journal*, 14, 1989, 40–55.

42. Adapted from C.R. Schwenk and R.A. Cosier, "Effect of the Expert, Devil's Advocate, and Dialectic Inquiry Methods on Prediction Performance," *Organizational Behavior and Human Performance*, 1, 1980, 409–24.

43. L.R. Beach, *Making the Right Decision: Organizational Culture, Vision, and Planning*.

44. D.M. Schweiger, W.R. Sandberg, and J.W. Ragan, "Group Approaches for Improving Strategic Decision Making: Analysis of Dialectical Inquiry, Devil's Advocacy, and Consensus," *Academy of Management Journal*, 29, 1986, 51–71.

45. A.F. Osborn, *Applied Imagination*, rev. ed. (New York: Scribner, 1957).

46. Ibid.

47. B. Schlender, "How Bill Gates Keeps the Magic Going," *Fortune*, June 18, 1990, 82–89.

48. A. Delbecq, A. Van de Ven, and D. Gustafson, "Guidelines for Conducting NGT Meetings," in *Group Techniques for Program Planning* (Glenview, Ill.: Scott Foresman, 1975).

49. R. DeStephen and R. Hirokawa, "Small Group Consensus: Stability of Group Support of the Decision, Task Process, and Group Relationships," *Small Group Behavior*, 19, 1988, 227–39.

50. D.M. Hegedus and R.V. Rasmussen, "Task Effectiveness and Interaction Process of a Modified Nominal Group Technique in Solving an Evaluation Problem," *Journal of Management*, 12, 1986, 545–60.

51. R. Cosier and C. Schwenk, "Agreement and Thinking Alike: Ingredients for Poor Decisions," *Academy of Management Executive*, 4, 1990, 69–74.

52. C.R. Schwenk and R.A. Cosier, "Effect of the Expert, Devil's Advocate, and Dialectic Inquiry Methods on Prediction Performance."

53. Ibid.

54. L.R. Beach, *Making the Right Decision: Organizational Culture, Vision, and Planning*.

55. Developed from D.C. Couper and S.H. Lobitz, *Quality Policing: The Madison Experience* (Washington, D.C.: Police Executive Research Forum, 1991); and R.B. Denhardt, *The Pursuit of Significance* (Belmont, Calif.: Wadsworth, 1992).

56. "Mattel Leads Hunt for Safer Plastics," *The Orlando Sentinel*, December 9, 1999, B5.

CHAPTER 7

1. M.J. Hicks, *Problem Solving in Business and Management* (London: Chapman & Hall, 1991).

2. "Pepsi Puts Freshness Dates on Diet Soda Bottles, Cans," *The Orlando Sentinel*, March 31, 1994, B5.

3. D. Tommelleo, "Town Turns Out for 'Vanilla Day'," *The Orlando Sentinel*, May 9, 2002, C3.

4. S. Borenstein, "Not Just for the Taste of It: Colas Use Space for Ads," *The Orlando Sentinel*, May 1, 1996, A1ff.

5. "Cereal Wars," *USA Today*, June 27, 1996, B1.

6. C. Sheehan, "Bayer Cranks Up Cipro Output," *The Orlando Sentinel*, October 17, 2001, B1ff.

7. J. Schmeltzer, "Airport Security Draws Giants," *The Orlando Sentinel*, April 4, 2002, C2; "Lockheed Martin Team Awarded Homeland Security Contract to Plan, Coordinate Heightened Airport Security Measures," *Lockheed Martin Press Release*, April 25, 2002.

8. "Lucrative Idea Gels for Firefighters," *The Raleigh News and Observer*, April 27, 1999, 2A.

9. C. Deutsch, "The Handwriting on the Post-It Note," *The New York Times*, July 6, 1999, C1ff; S. Tully, "Why Go for Stretch Targets," *Fortune*, November 14, 1994, 148–150; "The Mass Production of Ideas, and Other Impossibilities," *The Economist*, March 18, 1995, 72.

10. J. Jackson, "Rockin' Back to Its Roots," *The Orlando Sentinel*, February 21, 2002, C1ff.

11. H.A. Simon, *The New Science of Management* (Upper Saddle River, N.J.: Prentice Hall, 1977), 47.

12. Z. Espinosa, "The Comeback Rig—Schwinn Bounces Back with a Hot New Suspension Bike," *Mountain Bike*, February 1995, 50–52.

13. J.M. Kopf, J.G. Krevze, and H.H. Beam, "Using a Strategic Planning Matrix to Improve a Firm's Competitive Position," *Journal of Accountancy*, 175, July 1993, 97–101.

14. F.R. David, "The Strategic Planning Matrix—A Quantitative Approach," *Long Range Planning*, 19, October 1986, 102.

15. F.R. David, *Strategic Management*, 4th ed. (New York: Macmillan, 1993), 234.

16. A.A. Thompson, Jr., and A.J. Strickland, III, *Strategic Management: Concepts and Cases* (Homewood, Ill.: Irwin, 1992), 193.

17. J.A. Pearce, III, and R.B. Robinson, Jr., *Strategic Management: Formulation, Implementation, and Control*, 4th ed. (Homewood, Ill.: Irwin, 1991), 263.

18. F.R. David, *Strategic Management*, 225–27.

19. Adapted from F.R. David, *Strategic Management*, 251–52.

20. P. Haspeslagh, "Portfolio Planning: Uses and Limitations," *Harvard Business Review*, 60, January/February 1982, 58–73.

21. D.F. Abell and J.S. Hammond, *Strategic Market Planning: Problems & Analytical Approaches* (Upper Saddle River, N.J.: Prentice Hall, 1979).

22. P. Kotler, *Marketing Management: Analysis, Planning, and Control*, 6th ed. (Upper Saddle River, N.J.: Prentice Hall, 1988).

23. A.A. Thompson, Jr., and A.J. Strickland, III, *Strategic Management*.

24. S.C. Certo and J.P. Peter, *Strategic Management: Concepts and Applications*, 2nd ed. (New York: McGraw-Hill, 1991), 107–10.

25. J.A. Pearce III and R.B. Robinson, Jr., *Strategic Management*, 267–72.

26. C.W. Hofer and D. Schendel, *Strategy Formulation: Analytical Concepts* (St. Paul, Minn.: West Publishing, 1978), 33.

27. M. Adams, "Limo Company Reinvents Itself to Survive, Thrive," *USA Today*, April 9, 2002, 2E.

28. T.M. Cook and R.A. Russell, *Introduction to Management Science*, 3d ed. (Upper Saddle River, N.J.: Prentice Hall, 1985), 399–402.

29. D.W. Miller and M.K. Starr, *The Structure of Human Decisions* (Upper Saddle River, N.J.: Prentice Hall, 1967), 106.

30. B. Render and R.M. Stair, Jr., *Introduction to Management Science* (Boston: Allyn & Bacon, 1992), 598.

31. E.F. Harrison, *The Managerial Decision-Making Process* (Boston: Houghton Mifflin, 1975), 151–58.

32. B. Render and R.M. Stair, Jr., *Introduction to Management Science*, 598.

33. D. Samson, *Managerial Decision Analysis* (Homewood, Ill.: Irwin, 1988), 148–51.

34. B. Render and R.M. Stair, Jr., *Introduction to Management Science*, 600.

35. D. Samson, *Managerial Decision Analysis*, 23–32.

36. "Decision Tree Analysis in the United States Postal Service," *Interfaces*, March/April 1987, 35–41.

37. T.M. Cook and R.A. Russell, *Introduction to Management Science*, 402–4.

38. J. Sengupta, *Decision Models in Stochastic Programming: Operational Methods of Decision Making under Uncertainty* (New York: North Holland, 1982).

39. R. Johnson, "Disney Zeros in on Resort Pools," *Central Florida Business*, December 24, 2001, 8.

40. "Burger King to Hire More Former Welfare Recipients," *The Orlando Sentinel*, February 27, 1999, C10.

41. "GM to Equip Cars with Sensors to Open Trunks," *The Orlando Sentinel*, June 8, 1999, A3.

42. "Colt Exiting Handgun Business," *The Orlando Sentinel*, October 11, 1999, A3.

43. R. Roy, "Expressway Not a Dead End for Homeless—Program Will Give Them Jobs," *The Orlando Sentinel*, April 21, 1993, 1ff.

44. "Boss Divides $128 Million Among 550 Loyal Workers," *The Jacksonville Times-Union*, September 12, 1999, A14.

45. L.J. Krajewski and L.P. Ritzman, *Operations Management: Strategy and Analysis*, 3rd ed. (Reading, Mass.: Addison-Wesley, 1993), 45.

46. *Ibid.*, 44–46.

47. B. Render and R.M. Stair, Jr., *Introduction to Management Science*, Ch. 2.

48. *Ibid.*, Chaps. 2, 4, 6.

49. *Ibid.*, Chap. 9.

50. *Ibid.*

CHAPTER 8

1. J.R. Hackman, G.R. Oldham, R. Janson, and K. Purdy, "A New Strategy for Job Enrichment," *California Management Review*, 17, Summer 1975, 57–71.

2. *Ibid.*, 58.

3. N. Dodd and D. Ganster, "The Interactive Effects of Variety, Autonomy, and Feedback on Attitudes and Performance," *Journal of Organizational Behavior*, 17, 1996, 329–47.

4. "Learning Without Limits," *Fast Company*, July/August 1999, 461.

5. C. Sittenfeld, "Letter Perfect," *Fast Company*, April 2002, 50.

6. See, for example, T.J. Galpin, *The Human Side of Change* (San Francisco: Jossey-Bass, 1996).

7. R. Hodgetts, F. Luthans, and J. Slocum, Jr., "Strategy and HRM Initiatives for the '00s Environment: Redefining Roles and Boundaries, Linking Competencies and Resources," *Organizational Dynamics*, 28, 2, Autumn 1999, 7–21.

8. A. Markels, "The Wisdom of Chairman Ko," *Fast Company*, November 1999, 258–76.

9. See, for example, J.W. Dean, Jr., and S.A. Snell, "Integrated Manufacturing and Job Design: Moderating Effects of Organizational Inertia," *Academy of Management Journal*, 34, 1991, 776–804; G. Johns, J.L. Xie, and F. Yongqing, "Mediating and Moderating Effects in Job Design," *Journal of Management*, 18, 1992, 657–76.

10. See, for example, S. Papmarcos and L. Sama, "Managing Diversity: Individual Differences in Work-Related Values, Gender, and the Job Characteristics-Job Involvement Linkage," *International Journal of Management*, 15, 4, December 1998, 431–41.

11. C. Sittenfeld, "Powered by the People," *Fast Company*, 26, July/August 1999, 178–189.

12. P. Cappelli, "A Market Driven Approach to Retaining Talent," *Harvard Business Review*, January 2000, 103.

13. J.B. Cunningham and T. Eberle, "A Guide to Job Enrichment and Redesign," *Personnel*, 67, February 1990, 56–61.

14. R. Zemke, C. Raines, and B. Filipczak, *Generations at Work: Managing the Clash of Veterans, Boomers, Xers, and Nexters in Your Workplace* (New York: American Management Association, March 2000).

15. R. Lieber, "Information Is Everything," *Fast Company*, November 1999, 246–54.

16. "Flexibility Is No Key to Stability," *Business Week*, March 5, 2001, 30.

17. M.A. Campion, L. Cheraskin, and M.J. Stevens, "Career-Related Antecedents and Outcomes of Job Rotation," *Academy of Management Journal*, 37, 6, 1994, 1518–42; S. Stites-Doe, "The New Story about Job Rotation," *Academy of Management Executive*, 10, 6, 86–87.

18. L. Thach, "14 Ways to Groom Executives," *Training*, 35, 8, August 1998, 52–55; and W.C. Byham, "Grooming Leaders," *Executive Excellence*, 16, 6, June 1999, 181.

19. S. Harryson, "How Canon and Sony Drive Product Innovation through Networking and Application-Focused R&D," *The Journal of Product Innovation Management*, 14, 4, July 1997, 288–95.

20. L. Burke, "Developing High-Potential Employees in the New Business Reality," *Business Horizons*, 40, 2, March/April 1997, 18–24.

21. See, for example, I. Mitroff, R.O. Mason, and C.M. Pearson, "Radical Surgery: What Will Tomorrow's Organizations Look Like?" *Academy of Management Executive*, 8, 1994, 11–21; S. Caudron, "Integrated Workplace Paradox," *Personnel Journal*, August 1996, 75, 8, 68–71.

22. T. Butler and J. Waldroop, "Job Sculpting: The Art of Retaining Your Best People," *Harvard Business Review*, 77, 5, September/October 1999, 144–52,

23. M. Hammer, *Beyond Reengineering* (New York: Harper-Collins, 1996), 50.

24. J. Oberle, "Quality Gurus: The Men and Their Message," *Training*, January 1990, 47–52.

25. R.M. Tomasko, "Intelligent Resizing: View from the Bottom Up (Part II)," *Management Review*, June 1993, 18–23.

26. "Working Better by Design," *USBanker*, 108, 5, May 1998.

27. S. Gibbons, "Business Experts Ponder the Past, Present and Future," *The Journal of Quality and Participation*, 22, 6, November/December 1999, 18–23.

28. A. Harrington, "The Big Ideas," *Fortune*, 140, 10, November 22, 1999, 152–54.

29. M. Hammer and S. Stanton, "How Process Enterprises Really Work," *Harvard Business Review*, 77, 6, November/December 1999, 108–18.

30. S.L. Perlman, "Employees Redesign Their Jobs," *Personnel Journal*, 67, November 1990, 37–40.

31. See, for example, J.A. Neal and C.L. Tromley, "From Incremental Change to Retrofit: Creating High-Performance Work Systems," *Academy of Management Executive*, 9, 1995, 42–54.

32. See, for example, S. Shellenbarger, "Three Myths That Make Managers Push Staff to the Edge of Burnout," *The Wall Street Journal*, March 17, 1999, B1; and S. Caudron, "Job Stress Is in Job Design," *Workforce*, 77, 9, September 1998, 21–23.

33. S. Shellenbargar, "Are Saner Workloads the Unexpected Key to More Productivity?" *The Wall Street Journal*, Eastern Edition, March 10, 1999, B1.

34. "C. Farren, "A Smart Team Makes the Difference," *The Human Resource Professional*, 12, 1, January/February 1999, 12–16; and A. Gregory, "Solving the Teambuilding Jigsaw," *Works Management*, 52, 1, January 1999, 56–59.

35. S. Bishop, "Cross-functional Project Teams in Functionally Aligned Organizations," *Project Management Journal*, 30, 3, September 1999, 61.

36. See, for example, M.A. Campion and A.C. Higgs, "Design Work Teams to Increase Productivity and Satisfaction," *HR Magazine*, October 1995, 101–07.

37. M. Belbin, *Management Teams—Why They Succeed or Fail* (Boston: Butterworth-Heinemann, 1996).

38. J. Katzenbach and J. Santamaria, "Firing Up the Front Line," *Harvard Business Review*, 77, 3, May/June 1999, 107–17.

39. See, for example, M.A. Campion, G.J. Medsker, and A.C. Higgs, "Relations between Work Group Characteristics and Effectiveness: Implications for Designing Effective Work Groups," *Personnel Psychology*, 46, 1993, 823–45; M.A. Campion, E. Papper, and G.J. Medsker, "Relations between Work Team Characteristics and Effectiveness: A Replication and Extension," *Personnel Psychology*, 49, 1996, 429–52.

40. M. Moravec, O. Johannessen, and T. Hjelmas, "The Well-Managed SMT," *Management Review*, 87, 6, June 1998, 56–58.

41. C. Christensen and M. Overdorf, "Meeting the Challenge of Disruptive Change," *Harvard Business Review*, March 2000, 66.

42. For more information on action learning, see M. Marquardt and R. Revans, *Action Learning in Action: Transforming Problems and People for World-Class Organizational Learning* (Palo Alto, Calif.: Davies-Black Publishing, 1999); and D. Dotlich and J. Noel, *Action Learning: How the World's Top Companies Are Re-Creating Their Leaders and Themselves* (San Francisco: Jossey-Bass Business and Management Series, 1998).

43. D. Mankin, S. Cohen, and T. Bikson, "Teams and Technology: Tensions in Participatory Design," *Organizational Dynamics*, 26, 1, Summer 1997, 63–76.

44. A. Stern, "Where the Action Is," *Across the Board*, 34, 8, September 1997, 43–47.

45. C. Solomon, "Building Teams Across Borders," *Workforce*, 3, 6, November 1998, 12–17; and S. Odenwald, "Global Work Teams," *Training and Development*, 50, 2, February 1996, 54–58.

46. See J. Lipnack and J. Stamps, "Virtual Teams," *Executive Excellence*, 16, 5, May 1999, 14–15; J. Lipnack and J. Stamps, "Virtual Teams: The New Way to Work," *Strategy and Leadership*, 27, 1, January/February 1999; and "See You Online," *Fortune*, Winter 1999, 190.

47. B. Palmer, "Hasbro's New Action Figure," *Fortune*, 139, 12, June 21, 1999, 189–92.

48. S. Wetlaufer, "Organizing for Empowerment: An Interview with AES's Roger Sant and Dennis Bakke," *Harvard Business Review*, 77, 1, January/February 1999, 110–23.

49. B. Brown, "Ten Trends for the New Year," *Nursing Management*, 29, 12, December 1998, 33–36.

50. H. Mintzberg, *The Structuring of Organization* (Upper Saddle River, N.J.: Prentice Hall, 1979), 136.

51. S. Wetlaufer, "Organizing for Empowerment: An Interview with AES' Roger Sant and Dennis Bakke."

52. R. Maruca, "Fighting the Urge to Fight Fires," *Harvard Business Review*, 77, 6, November/December 1999, 30–32.

53. S.C. Bushardt, D.L. Duhon, and A.R. Fowler Jr., "Management Delegation Myths and the Paradox of Task Assignment," *Business Horizons*, March/April 1991, 34, 37–43.

54. M.E. Douglas, "How to Delegate Safely," *Training and Development Journal*, February 1987, 8.

55. M. Schrage, "I Know What You Mean and I Can't Do Anything About It," *Fortune*, April 2, 2001, 186.

56. "Chris Galvin on the Record," *Business Week*, July 16, 2001, 76.

57. C.O. Longnecker, "The Delegation Dilemma," *Supervision*, 52, February 1991, 3–5.

58. See P. Senge, "Learning Leaders," *Executive Excellence*, 16, 11, November 1999, 12–13.

59. D. Vinton, "Delegation for Employee Development," *Training and Development Journal*, January 1987, 65–67.

60. P. Adler, "Building Better Bureaucracies," *Academy of Management Executive*, 13, 4, November 1999, 36–49.

61. J. Rau, "Two Stages of Decision Making," *Management Review*, 88, 11, December 1999, 101.

62. *Ibid.*

63. M. Yate, "Delegation: The Key to Empowerment," *Training and Development Journal*, April 1991, 23–24.

64. A. Balsamo, "The Power of Empowerment," *Management Review*, 88, 10, November 1999, 111.

65. J.H. Carter, "Minimizing the Risks from Delegation," *Supervisory Management*, February 1992, 1–2.

66. S. Gracie, "Delegate Don't Abdicate," *Management Today*, March 1999, 92–94.

67. R. Rohrer, "Does the Buck Ever Really Stop?" *Supervision*, 60, 4, April 1999, 11–12.

68. M. Douglas, "How to Delegate Safely."

69. M. Yate, "Delegation: The Key to Empowerment."

70. D. Vinton, "Delegation for Employee Development."

71. R. Wilkinson, "Think before You Open Your Mouth!" *Supervision*, 52, May 1991, 17–19.

72. M. Townsend, "Let the Employees Carry the Ball," *Personnel Journal*, 69, October 1990, 30–31.

73. M.E. Haynes, "Delegation: There's More to It than Letting Someone Else Do It," *Supervisory Management*, 25, January 1980, 9–15.

74. T.R. Horton, "Delegation and Team Building: No Solo Acts Please," *Management Review*, September 1992, 58–61.

75. J. Lawrie, "Turning around Attitudes about Delegation," reprinted by permission of publisher from *Supervisory Management*, December 1990, American Management Association, New York. All rights reserved.

CHAPTER 9

1. See, for example, D. Quinn Mills and G. Bruce Fieson, "Emerging Business Realities," *Journal of Management Consulting*, 10, 4, November 1999, 39–45.

2. See, for example, R.K. Kazanjian and R. Drazine, "Implementing Internal Diversification: Contingency Factors for Organization Design Choices," *Academy of Management Review*, 12, 2, 1987, 342–54; D. Miller, "The Genesis of Configuration," *Academy of Management Review*, 12, 4, 1987, 686–701; L.M. Kikulis, T. Slack, and C.R. Hinings, "Sector-Specific Patterns of Organizational Design Change," *Journal of Management Studies*, 32, January 1995, 67–100; M. Burke and K. Tulett, "Impact of Information Needs on Organizational Design," *Journal of the American Society for Information Science*, 50, 4, April 1999, 380–81; A. Barua and A. Whinston, "Decision Support for Managing Organizational Design Dynamics," *Decision Support Systems*, 22, 1, January 1998, 45–58.

3. For example, see C. Claycomb, C. Droge, and R. Germain, "The Effect of Just-in-Time with Customers on Organizational Design and Performance," *International Journal of Logistics Management*, 10, 1, 1999, 37–58.

4. J. Clancy and P. Cappelli, "Is Loyalty Really Dead?" *Across the Board*, 36, 6, June 1999, 14–19; and B. Carroll, "Self-

Managed Knowledge Teams Simplify High-Tech Manufacturing," *National Productivity Review*, 18, 2, Spring 1999, 35–39.

5. M. Goold and A. Campbell, "Do You Have a Well-Designed Organization?" *Harvard Business Review*, March 2002, 117–24.

6. R. Fournier, "Methods of Management," *InformationWeek*, 712, December 1998, 1A–10A.

7. B. Travic, "Information Aspects of New Organizational Designs: Exploring the Non-Traditional Organization," *Journal of the American Society for Information Science*, 49, 13, November 1998, 1224–44.

8. N. Nohria and J.D. Berkley, "An Action Perspective: The Crux of the New Management," *California Management Review*, Summer 1994, 70–92.

9. M. Youngblood, "Leadership at the Edge of Chaos: From Control to Creativity," *Strategy & Leadership*, 25, 5, September/October 1997, 8–14.

10. D. Miller, "Relating Porter's Business Strategies to Environment and Structure: Analysis and Performance Implications," *Academy of Management Journal*, 31, 1988, 280–308; D. Miller, C. Droge, and J.M. Toulouse, "Strategic Process and Content as Mediator between Organizational Context and Structure," *Academy of Management Journal*, 31, 1988, 544–69.

11. J. Menezes, "Companies Urged to Reexamine ERP Models," *Computer Dealer News*, 15, 25, June 25, 1999, 16.

12. B. Bahree, "Shell Shifts Top Division Management as It Moves toward Wide Restructuring," *The Wall Street Journal*, December 11, 1998, A13.

13. See Clariant's Web site, http://www.clariant.com.

14. PepsiCo, *1999 Annual Report*.

15. "Illinois Central Deal Spurs Reorganization by Canadian National," *The Wall Street Journal*, April 15, 1999, A4.

16. R. Sookdeo, "The New Global Consumer," *Fortune*, Autumn/Winter 1993, 68–77.

17. P.S. Lewis and P.M. Fandt, "The Strategy-Structure Fit in Multinational Corporations: A Revised Model," *International Journal of Management*, June 1990, 137–46.

18. Kellogg Company, *2001 Annual Report*.

19. "HM Creates International Division," *Publishers Weekly*, 246, 2, January 11, 1999, 12.

20. S. Johnston, "Microsoft Reorganizes," *InformationWeek*, 728, April 5, 1999, 30.

21. See Cisco Systems' Web site, http://www.cisco.com.

22. M. Davis and P.R. Lawrence, *Matrix* (Reading, Mass: Addison-Wesley, 1977), 3.

23. J.R. Galbraith, "Matrix Organization Designs: How to Combine Functional and Project Forms," *Business Horizons*, February 1971, 29–40.

24. E.W. Larson and D.H. Gobeli, "Matrix Management: Contradictions and Insights," *California Management Review*, Summer 1987, 126–38.

25. W. Bernasco, P. Weerd-Nederhof, H. Tillema, and H. Boer, "Balanced Matrix Structure and New Product Development Process at Texas Instruments' Material and Controls Division," *R&D Management*, 29, 2, April 1999, 121–31.

26. B. Dyer, A. Gupa, and D. Wilemon, "What First-to-Market Companies Do Differently," *Research Technology Management*, 42, 2, March/April 1999, 15–21.

27. For example, see J. Galbraith, *Competing with Flexible Lateral Organizations* (Reading, Mass.: Addison Wesley, 1994); E. Lawler, *From the Ground Up: Six Principles for Creating the New Logic Corporation* (San Francisco: Jossey-Bass, 1996); J. Galbraith, E. Lawler and Associates, *Organizing for the Future: The New Logic for Managing Complex Organizations*, (San Francisco: Jossey-Bass, 1996); D. Nadler and M. Tushman, *Competing by Design*, (New York: Oxford Press, 1997); and D. Nadler, M. Gerstein, and R. Shaw and Associates, *Organizational Architecture* (San Francisco: Jossey-Bass, 1992).

28. R.E. Miles and C.C. Snow, "Organizations: New Concepts for New Forms," *California Management Review*, 28, Spring 1986, 62–71.

29. S. Tully, "The Modular Corporation," *Fortune*, February 8, 1993, 106–14.

30. J.A. Byrne, "The Virtual Corporation," *Business Week*, February 8, 1993, 98–103.

31. R.E. Miles and C.C. Snow, "Organizations: New Concepts for New Forms."

32. E. Lawler III, "Rethinking Organization Size," *Organizational Dynamics*, 26, 2, Autumn 1997, 24–35.

33. C.C. Snow, R.E. Miles, and H.J. Coleman Jr., "Managing 21st Century Network Organizations," *Organizational Dynamics*, 10, February 1992, 5–20.

34. *Ibid.*

35. *Ibid.*

36. *Ibid.*

37. E. Lawler, "Rethinking Organization Size."

38. B. Low and K. Huat, "Managing Business Relationships and Positions in Industrial Networks," *Industrial Marketing Management*, 26, 2, March 1997, 189–202.

39. F.V. Guterl, "Goodbye, Old Matrix," *Business Month*, February 1989, 32–38.

40. J.B. Bush and A.L. Frohman, "Communication in a 'Network' Organization," *Organizational Dynamics*, 20, 2, 1991, 23–36.

41. C. Ching, C.W. Holsapple, and A.B. Whinston, "Toward IT Support for Coordination in Network Organizations," *Information & Management*, 30, 1996, 179–99.

42. J. Sampler and J. Short, "Strategy in Dynamic Information-Intensive Environments," *Journal of Management Studies*, 35, 4, July 1998, 429–36.

43. H.H. Hinterhuber and B.M. Levin, "Strategic Networks—The Organization of the Future," *Long Range Planning*, 27, 3, 1994, 43–53.

44. R.E. Miles and C.C. Snow, "Managing 21st Century Network Organizations."

45. See, for example, J.L. Chency, "Interdependence and Co-ordination in Organizations: A Role-System Analysis," *Academy of Management Journal*, 26, 1983, 156–62; J.K. Ito and R.B. Peterson, "Effects of Task Difficulty and Interunit Interdependence on Information Processing Systems," *Academy of Management Journal*, 4, 1986, 139–49; J.E. McCann and D.L. Ferry, "An Approach for Assessing and Managing Inter-Unit Interdependence," *Academy of Management Review*, 4, 1979, 113–20.

46. J.D. Thompson, *Organizations in Action* (New York: McGraw-Hill, 1967).

47. J.R. Galbraith, "Organizational Design: An Information Processing View," *Interfaces*, 4, May 1974, 3.

48. E. Lawler, "Rethinking Organization Size."

49. P.W. Yetton, K.D. Johnston, and J.F. Craig, "Computer-Aided Architects: A Case Study of IT and Strategic Change," *Sloan Management Review*, 35, 4, 1994, 57–68.

50. T.W. Malone, M.S.S. Morton, and R.R. Halperin, "Organizing for the 21st Century," *Strategy & Leadership*, July/August 1996, 7–10.

51. P.G. Keen, "Redesigning the Organization through Information Technology," *Planning Review*, May/June 1991, 4–9; A.B. Shani and J.A. Sena, "Information Technology and the Integration of Change: Sociotechnical System Approach," *Journal of Applied Behavioral Science*, 30, 2, June 1994, 247–70.

52. R. Leifer and P.K. Mills, "An Information Processing Approach for Deciding upon Control Strategies and Reducing Control Loss in Emerging Organizations," *Journal of Management*, 22, 1, 1996, 113–37.

53. S.P. Bradley, J.A. Hausman, and R.L. Nolan, eds., *Globalization, Technology, and Competition* (Boston, Mass.: Harvard Business School Press, 1993).

54. For example, see R. Jenson and R. Johnson, "The Enterprise Resource Planning System as a Strategic Solution," *Information Strategy*, 15, 4, Summer 1999, 28–33.

55. "S. Cliffe, "Knowledge Management: The Well-Connected Business," *Harvard Business Review*, 76, 4, July/August 1998, 17–21.

56. W.J. Altier, "Task Forces: An Effective Management Tool," *Management Review*, February 1987, 52–57.

57. D. Sobek II, J. Liker, and A. Ward, "Another Look at How Toyota Integrates Product Development," *Harvard Business Review*, 76, 4, July/August 1998, 36–49.

58. A. Townsend, S. DeMarie, and A. Hendrickson, "Virtual Teams: Technology and the Workplace of the Future," *The Academy of Management Executive*, 12, 3, August 1998, 17–29.

59. "Sharing Knowledge Through BP's Virtual Team Network," *Harvard Business Review*, 75, 5, September/October 1997, 152–53.

60. See, for example, B. Milligan, "Despite Attempts to Break Them, Functional Silos Live On," *Purchasing*, 127, 7, November 1999, 24–46.

61. G. Garnier, "Context and Decision Making Autonomy in Foreign Affiliates of U.S. Multinational Corporations," *Academy of Management Journal*, 25, 1982, 893–908.

62. T. Peters, "Letting Go of Controls," *Across the Board*, June 1991, 15–18.

63. B. Fulford, "Jack Welch Lite," *Forbes*, 163, 12, June 14, 1999, 64–68.

64. See, for example, B.R. Schlender, "Yet Another Strategy for Apple," *Fortune*, 122, 10, 1990, 81; and J. Sculley, *Odyssey: Pepsi to Apple—A Journey of Adventure Ideas for the Future* (New York: Harper & Row, 1987); S. Beale, "Apple Reorganizes Again," *Macworld*, 14, 4, April 1997, 32; "Apple Unifies Global Structure to Focus on Key Product Lines," *Computer Dealer News*, 13, 7, March 24, 1997, 42; L. Gomes, "Apple Reorganizes Itself, but Move Gets Cool Reaction," *The Wall Street Journal*, February 5, 1997, B2., S. Berglas, "What You Can Learn From Steve Jobs," *Inc.*, 21, 14, October 1999, 29–32; and E. Moltzen, "The 1999 Top 25 Executives: The Comeback Kids," *Computer Reseller News*, 869, November 15, 1999, 165.

65. "Can Anyone Fix the United Way?" *Fortune*, November 27, 2000, 170+; and "A Better Way to Make a Difference?" March 18, 2002, 66.

66. P. Kafta, "Diversify and Conquer," *Forbes*, May 12, 2002, 102.

67. C. Claycomb, C. Droge, and R. Germain, "The Effect of Just-in-Time with Customers on Organizational Design and Performance," *International Journal of Logistics Management*, 10, 1, 1999, 37–58.

68. T. Burns and G. Stalker, *The Management of Innovation* (London: Tavistock, 1961), 119–22.

69. See, for example, R. Quinn and G. Spreitzer, "The Road to Empowerment: Seven Questions Every Leader Should Consider," *Organizational Dynamics*, 26, 2, Autumn 1997, 37–49; G. Stewart and K. Carson, "Moving Beyond the Mechanistic Model: An Alternative Approach to Staffing for Contemporary Organizations," *Human Resource Management Review*, 7, 2, Summer 1997, 157–84; B. Durrance, "The Evolutionary Vision of Dee Hock: From Chaos to Chaords," *Training and Development*, 51, 4, April 1997, 24–31; S. Kalagnanam, and M. Lindsay, "The Use of Organic Models of Control in JIT Firms: Generalizing Woodward's Findings to Modern Manufacturing Practices," *Accounting, Organizations and Society*, 24, 1, January 1999, 1–30.

70. See, for example, M. Overholt, "Flexible Organizations: Using Organizational Design as a Competitive Advantage," *Human Resource Planning*, 20, 1, 1997, 22–32; "Organizational Design in the 21st Century," *The Journal of Business Strategy*, 19, 3, May/June 1998, 33–35; J. Byrne, "The Horizontal Corporation," *Business Week*, December 20, 1993, 76–81; and B. Pasterneck and A. Viscio, *The Centerless Corporation: A New Model for Transforming Your Organization for Growth and Prosperity* (New York: Simon & Shuster, 1998).

71. B. Dumain, "The Bureaucracy Busters," *Fortune*, June 17, 1991, 36–50; and "Becton Dickinson Facelift Unveils New Direction, New Logo for BD," *Health Industry Today*, 62, 10, October 1999, 1–12.

CHAPTER 10

1. J. Collins, "Turning Goals into Results: The Power of Catalytic Mechanisms," *Harvard Business Review*, July/August 1999, 77.

2. P. Wright, B. Dunford, and S. Snell, "Human Resources and the Resource-Based View of the Firm," *Journal of Management* 27, 2001, 701–21.

3. K. Rogg, D. Schmidt, C. Shull, and N. Schmitt, "Human Resource Practices, Organizational Climate, and Customer Satisfaction," *Journal of Management* 27, 2001, 431–49.

4. Covey Leadership Center, Inc., *QII Firefighters* (video) (Provo, Utah: Covey Leadership Center, Inc. 1995).

5. L. Bassi, S. Cheney, and E. Lewis, "Trends in Workplace Learning: Supply and Demand in Intersting Times," *Training and Development*, November, 1998, 51–69.

6. V. Scarpello and J. Ledvinka, *Personnel/Human Resource Management: Environments and Functions* (Boston: PWS-Kent, 1994).

7. L. Dyer, "Human Resource Planning," in K. Rowland and G. Ferris, eds., *Personnel Management* (Boston: Allyn & Bacon, 1992), 52–78.

8. R. Mathis and J. Jackson, *Personnel/Human Resource Management*, 7th ed. (St. Paul: West Publishing, 1994), 210.

9. "Business Facts," *The Tacoma News Tribune*, October 22, 1999, B29.

10. J. Clausing, "Bills Reopen Debate Over Visa Limit," *New York Times*, August 31, 1999, A6; P. Van Slambrouck, "Controversy Surrounds Demand for Imported High-Tech Labor," *Christian Science Monitor*, August 30, 1999, 21; and C. Lockhead, "Tech Firms' Plea for Work Visas Draws Criticism," *San Francisco Chronicle*, August 8, 1999, A3.

11. T. Peters, "Connoisseur of Talent."

12. P. Carbonara, "Hire for Attitude, Train for Skill," *Fast Company*, August 1996.

13. G. David, "You Just Hired Him: Should You Have Known Better?" *Fortune*, October 29, 2001, 205–06.

14. *Ibid.*

15. T. Peters and R. Waterman, Jr. *In Search of Excellence: Lessons from America's Best-Run Companies* (New York: Harper & Row, 1982).

16. I. Robertson and R. Kandola, "Work Sample Tests: Validity, Adverse Impact, and Applicant Reaction," *Journal of Occupational Psychology*, 55, 1982, 171–83.

17. G. Thornton, *Assessment Centers in Human Resource Management* (Reading, MA: Addison-Wesley, 1992).

18. C. Daniels, "Does This Man Need a Shrink?" *Fortune*, February 5, 2001, 205–07.

19. J. James, *Thinking in the Future Tense*.

20. R. Schatz, "Showtime at Athene," *BusinessWeek*, March 5, 2001.

21. R. Arveny and J. Campion, "The Employment Interview: A Summary and Review of Recent Research," *Personnel Psychology*, Summer, 1982, 281–322; M. Harris, "Reconsidering the Employment Interview: A Review of Recent Literature and Suggestions for Future Research," *Personnel Psychology*, Winter 1989, 691–726.

22. Daniels, p. 206.

23. B. Pappas, "Accentuate the Negative," *Forbes*, December 28, 1998, 47; J. Wanous, *Recruitment, Selection, Orientation, and Socialization of the Newcomers*, 2nd ed. (Reading, MA: Addison-Wesley, 1992).

24. T. Stewart, "Mystified by Training? Here are Some Clues," *Fortune*, April 2, 2001, 184.

25. E. Lawler, S. Mohrman, and G. Ledford, *Employee Involvement and Total Quality Management* (San Francisco: Jossey-Bass, 1992).

26. R. Mathis and J. Jackson, *Personnel/Human Resource Management*.

27. M. Syers, "Breakthrough in Orientation Models," *Harvard Business Review*, July/August 1996, 110–17.

28. Bureau of National Affairs, *Planning the Training Program: Personnel Management* (Washington, D.C.: BNA Books, 1975.

29. Steward, p. 184.

30. W. Casio, *Managing Human Resources*, 2nd ed. (New York: McGraw-Hill, 1989).

31. G. Latham and K. Wexley, *Increasing Productivity Through Performance Appraisal* (Reading, MA: Addison-Wesley, 1981), 61–64.

32. G. Huet-Cox, T. Nielsen, and E. Sundstrom, "Get the Most from 360-Degree Feedback: Put It on the Internet," *HR Magazine*, May 1999, 92–103; D. Waldman, I. Atwater, and D. Antonioni, "Has 360-Degree Feedback Gone Amok?" *Academy of Management Executive*, May 1998, 86–94.

33. C. Hartlove, "Pave the Way to Bigger Pay," *Fast Company*, June, 1997, 176; L. Bassi, S. Cheney, and E. Lewis, "Trends in Workplace Learning: Supply and Demand in Interesting Times," *Training and Development*, November 1998, 51–69.

34. G. Imperato, "How to Give Good Feedback," *Fast Company*, September 1998, 147–56.

35. "Compensation: Potent Hiring Tool?" *Industry Week*, September 6, 1999, 12.

36. For a more detailed discussion of benefits, see R. Mathis and J. Jackson, *Personnel/Human Resource Management*, 413–39.

37. D. Kunde, "Businesses Offering Backup Child Care," *The Dallas Morning News*, August 19, 1999, D2.

38. J. Morris, *Employee Benefits* (Washington, D.C.: Chamber of Commerce of the United States, 1986).

39. G. Milkovich and J. Newman, *Compensation* (Homewood, Ill: BPI/Irwin, 1990).

40. T. Leap and M. Crino, *Personnel/Human Resource Management* (New York: Macmillan, 1993).

41. L. Joel, III, *Every Employee's Guide to the Law* (New York: Pantheon Books, 1994).

42. For case examples, see the *U.S. Equal Employment Opportunity Commission Docket of ADA Litigation* at http://www.eeoc.gov/docs/ada98.txt.

43. Further information is available at http://www.ilr.cornell.edu/library/e_archive/GlassCeiling.

44. H. O'Neill, "California Undoing Affirmative Action," *Los Angeles Times*, November 17, 1996.

45. A. Morrison and M. Von Glinow, "Women and Minorities in Management," *American Psychologist*, 45, 1990, 200–08.

46. E. Robinson, "The Trickle-Up Effect," *Fortune*, July 19, 1999, 64.

47. S. Webber and L. Donahue, "Impact of Highly and Less Job-Related Diversity on Work Group Cohesion and Performance: A Meta-Analysis," *Journal of Management*, 27, 2001, 141–62.

48. G. Powell, "Sexual Harassment: Confronting the Issue of Definition," *Business Horizons*, July/August 1983, 24–28.

49. T. Bland and S. Stalcup, "Managing Harassment," *Human Resource Management*, 40, 1, Spring 2001, 51–61.

50. *Meritor Savings Bank v. Vinson*, 477 U.S. 57 (1986); EEOC, *Policy Guidance on Sexual Harassment*, March 1990.

51. *Robinson v. Jacksonville Shipyards*, USDC MFLA, No. 86–927–J–1 2 (1991); *Ellison v. Brady*, 54 FEP Case 1346 (1991).

52. Bland and Stalcup, 2001.

53. K. Weisul, "The PX Is Going PC," *BusinessWeek*, April 8, 2002, 10.

54. R. Walton and R. McKersie, *A Behavioral Theory of Labor Negotiations: An Analysis of a Social Interaction System* (New York: McGraw-Hill, 1965).

55. *Ibid.*

56. A. Bernstein, "Busting Unions Can Backfire on the Bottom Line," *Business Week*, March 18, 1991, 108.

57. M. Mendenhall, E. Dunbar, and G. Oddou, "Expatriate Selection, Training and Career-Pathing: A Review and Critique," *Human Resource Management*, 26, Fall 1987, 340.

58. C. Lee, "Cross-Cultural Training: Don't Leave Home Without It," *Training*, March 1993, 20–25.

59. P. Platt, *French or Foe?* (Polly Platt, 2000).

CHAPTER 11

1. M. France and W. Zellner, "Enron's Fish Story," *BusinessWeek*, February 25, 2002, 39–40.

2. F. Rice, "Denny's Changes Its Spots," *Fortune*, May 13, 1996, 133–42.

3. P. Vaccaro, "Time Management @ the Speed of Thought," Presentation at a meeting of the Institute of Management Consultants, April 19, 2002, St. Louis, MO.

4. M. Adams, "Making a Merger Work," *HR Magazine*, March 2002, 52–56; S. Ante and I. Sager, "Palmisano: From Backup Band to Front Man," *BusinessWeek*, February 11, 2002, 72; J. Boyett and D. Snyder, "Twenty-First Century

Workplace Trends," *On the Horizon*, March/April 1998, 1–8.

5. J. Kouzes and B. Posner, *Leadership Challenges*, 2nd ed. (San Francisco: Jossey-Bass, 1995).

6. H. Trice and J. Beyer, *The Cultures of Work Organizations* (Upper Saddle River, N.J.: Prentice Hall, 1993).

7. "IBM and the Birth of Corporate Culture," *Workforce*, January 2002, 150; Ante and Sager, 2002, 72.

8. C. Flash, "Amazon Maintaining Its Tight-Lipped Style as It Moves to Town," *The* [Tacoma, WA] *News Tribune*, October 19, 1999, D7; "Personalization Features Set Amazon.com Apart," *Computerworld*, October, 18, 1999, 40–42.

9. E. Cabrera and J. Bonache, "An Expert Human Resource System for Aligning Organizational Culture and Strategy," *Human Resource Planning*, March 1999, 51–63.

10. L. Beach, *Making the Right Decision: Organizational Culture, Vision, and Planning*, (Upper Saddle River, N.J.: Prentice Hall, 1993).

11. E. Cabera and J. Bonache, 1999.

12. D. Rosseau, "Assessing Organizational Culture: The Case for Multiple Methods," in B. Schneider, ed., *Organization Climate and Culture* (San Francisco: Jossey-Bass, 1990).

13. H. Trice and J. Beyer, "Studying Organizational Cultures Through Rites and Rituals," *Academy of Management Review*, 1984, 9, 653–69.

14. C. Bernick, "When Your Culture Needs a Makeover," *Harvard Business Review*, June 2001, 53–60; M. Ash, *Mary Kay on People Management* (New York: Warner Books, 1984).

15. R. Kilmann, M. Saxon, and R. Serpa, "Issues in Understanding and Changing Culture," *California Management Review*, 1986, 28, 87–94; E. Schein, *Organizational Culture and Leadership* (San Francisco: Jossey-Bass, 1985), 223–43.

16. B. Kaye and J. Jacobson, "True Tails and Tall Tales: The Power of Organizational Storytelling," *Training and Development*, March 1999, 45–50.

17. K. Friedberg, "Changing and Creating Organizational Cultures," in H. Trice and J. Beyer, eds., *The Cultures of Work Organizations* (Upper Saddle River, N.J.: Prentice Hall, 1993), 418.

18. K. Rogg, D. Schmidt, C. Shull, and N. Schmitt, "Human Resource Practices, Organizational Climate, and Customer Satisfaction," *Journal of Management*, 2001, 27, 431–49.

19. N. Tichy, "No Ordinary Boot Camp," *Harvard Business Review*, April 2001, 63–70.

20. D. Welch and G. Khermouch, "Can GM Save an Icon?" *BusinessWeek*, April 8, 2002, 60–67.

21. L. Lavelle, "What Campbell's New Chief Needs to Do Now," *BusinessWeek*, June 25, 2001, 60.

22. B. Munch, "Changing Culture of Fact Time," *Harvard Business Review*, November 2001, 125–31.

23. R. Levering and M. Moskowitz, "The 100 Best Companies to Work For," *Fortune*, January 10, 2000, 83–110.

24. C. Bernick, "When Your Culture Needs a Makeover," *Harvard Business Review*, June 2001, 53–60.

25. J. James, *Thinking in the Future Tense* (New York: Simon & Schuster, 1997).

26. N. Hoffman and R. Klepper, "Assimilating New Technologies: The Role of Organizational Culture," *Information Systems Management*, Summer 2000, 36–42.

27. J. Folan, "A Winning Culture Beats the Competition," *Communication World*, August/September 1998, 50–58.

28. R. Kegan and L. Lahey, "The Real Reason People Won't Change," *Harvard Business Review*, November 2001, 85–92.

29. T. Peters and R. Waterman, *In Search of Excellence: Lessons from America's Best Run Companies* (New York: Harper-Collins, 1982).

30. B. Nelson, "Creating an Energized Workplace," in F. Hesselbein and P. Cohen, eds., *Leader to Leader* (San Francisco: Jossey-Bass, 1999), 265–74.

31. C. Carson, K. Eckart, C. Flash, and G. Fysh, "It's Going the Way It Was Programmed," *The* [Tacoma, WA] *News Tribune*, September 8, 1996, d1.

32. J. James, 1997.

33. *Ibid.*

34. S. Alsop, "e or Be Eaten: Large Corporations Are Trying to Get Hip to e-Business," *Fortune*, November 8, 1999, 86–87; E. Brown, "Big Business Meets the e-World: Sears? Whirlpool? Now Even They Want to Create e-Businesses," *Fortune*, November 8, 1999, 88–98.

35. M. Arndt, "3M: A Lab for Growth?" *BusinessWeek*, January 21, 1002, 50–51; L. Lavelle, 2001; R. Kanter, *The Change Masters* (New York: Simon & Schuster, 1983).

36. K. Lewis, *Field Theory in Social Science* (New York: Harper & Row, 1951).

37. J. Kotter, "Leading Change: Why Transformation Efforts Fail," *Harvard Business Review*, March/April 1995, 59–67.

38. Q. Huy, "Time, Temporal Capability, and Planned Change," *Academy of Management Review*, 2001, 26, 4, 601–23.

39. J. Kotter and L. Schlesinger, "Choosing Strategies for Change," *Harvard Business Review*, March/April 1979, 109–12.

40. Summaized from *Work USA Survey*, (Washington, D.C.: The Wyatt Company, 1996).

41. C. Argyris, *Knowledge for Action: A Guide to Overcoming Barriers to Organizational Change* (San Francisco: Jossey-Bass, 1993).

42. Alsop, 1999.

43. J. Austin, "A Method for Facilitating Controversial Social Change in Organizations—Branch Rickey and the Brooklyn Dodgers," *Journal of Applied Behavioral Science*, 33, 1, 1997, 101–18.

44. K. Blanchard, *Executive Excellence*, (Provo, Utah: Excellence Publishing, 1999).

45. P. Drucker, *Managing for the Future: The 1990s and Beyond* (New York: Plume Books, 1993).

46. Kotter, 1995.

CHAPTER 12

1. J. Moody and B. Stewart, "Showing the Skilled Business Graduate: Expanding the Tool Kit," *Business Communication Quarterly*, March 2002, 65, 1, 21–36.

2. L. Pophal, "10 Steps to Better Communication," *Communication World*, December 2001/January 2002, 16–19; "New Year's Resolution: Improve Employee Communications," *Supervision*, January 1990, 26.

3. "CEO Communication Never More Critical to Corporate Prosperity," *Business, Media and Academic Leaders Analyze Growing Impact of Chief Executive Image*, New York, Stanton Crenshaw Forum, November 12, 2001.

4. A. Smidts, A. Pruyn, and B. Cees, "The Impact of Employee Communication and Perceived External Prestige on Organizational Identification," *Academy of Management Journal*, 2001, 49, 5, 1051–62.

5. T. Petzinger, *The New Pioneers: The Men and Women Who Are Transforming the Workplace and Marketplace*, (New York: Random House, 1999).

6. L. Landes, "Real-life, Real-time Communication," *Communication World*, December 2001/January 2002, 19, 20–23; L. Penley, E. Alexander, I. Jernigan, and C. Henwood, "Communication Abilities of Managers: The Relationship of Performance," *Journal of Management*, 1991, 17, 57–76.

7. J. Conger, "Inspiring Others: The Language of Leadership," *Academy of Management Executive*, 1991, 5, 1, 310–45.

8. For a thorough discussion, see M. Munter, *Guide to Managerial Communication*, 3rd. ed. (Upper Saddle River, N.J.: Prentice Hall, 1992).

9. K. Roberts, *Communication in Organizations* (Chicago: Science Research Associates, 1984).

10. *Advancing Women in Business—The Catalyst Guide—The Best Practices from the Corporate Leaders* (San Francisco: Jossey-Bass, 1998).

11. R. Lengel and R. Daft, "The Selection of Communication Media as an Executive Skill," *Academy of Management Executive*, 1988, 2, 225–32.

12. "The Technocrats," *Inc.*, February 1999, 55.

13. M. Hammer and J. Champy, *Reengineering the Corporation: A Manifesto for Business Revolution* (New York: Harper Business, 1993).

14. L. Willis, "Presentations in Everyday Life: Strategies for Effective Speaking," *Business Communication Quarterly*, March 2002, 111–14.

15. P. Fandt, *Management Skills: Practice and Experience* (St. Paul, Minnesota: West, 1994).

16. J. Collins, "Aligning Action and Values," in F. Hesselbein and P. Cohen, eds., *Leader to Leader* (San Francisco: Jossey-Bass, 1999); K. Blanchard, "Translating Body Talk," *Success*, April 1986, 10.

17. S. Divita, "Conflict Can Be Managed," *Marketing News*, January 6, 1997, 31, 18.

18. H. Sims and C. Manz, *Company of Heroes* (New York: John Wiley, 1996).

19. E. Schein, *The Corporate Culture Survival Guide: Sense and Nonsense about Culture Change* (San Francisco: Jossey-Bass, 1999); P. Morrow and J. McElroy, "Interior Office Design and Visitor Response: A Constructive Replication," *Journal of Applied Psychology*, 1981, 66, 646–50.

20. E. Brown, "Big Business Meets the e-World," *Fortune*, November 8, 1999, 88–98.

21. R. Hof and S. Hamm, "How E-Biz Rose, Fell, and Will Rise Anew," *Business Week*, May 13, 2002, 64–72; S. Levy, "How the Bust Saved Silicon Valley," *Newsweek*, March 25, 2002, 42–50.

22. M. Strum, "Telework, Telecommuting, Virtual Officing. . .: Redefining the 9–5 Routine," *Afp Exchange*, May/June 2001, 36–41.

23. *Ibid.* Also see C. Dickerson, "E.T., Phone Home," *InfoWorld*, March 25, 2002, 60; E. Prewitt, "Flextime and Telecommuting," *CIO*, April 15, 2002, 130.

24. D. Young, "The Relationship Between Electronic and Fact-to-Face Communication and Its Implication for Alternative Workplace Strategies," *Facilities*, May 1995, 20–27.

25. "The Technocrats," *Inc.*, February 1999, 55.

26. J. Zygmont, "Face to Face," *Sky Magazine*, February 1998, 10.

27. L. Landes, "Real-life, Real-time Communication," *Communication World*, December 2001/January 2002, 20–23.

28. N. Zaidman, "Cultural Codes and Language Strategies in Business Communication," *Management Communication Quarterly*, February 2001, 408–41.

29. M. Kets de Vries and E. Florent-Treacy, *The New Global Leaders: Richard Branson, Percy Barnevik, David Simon and the Remaking of International Business* (San Francisco: Jossey-Bass, 1999); N. Zaidman, "Cultural Codes and Language Strategies in Business Communication," *Management Communication Quarterly*, February 2001, 408–41.

30. S. Cady, P. Fandt, and D. Fernandez, "Investigating Cultural Differences in Personal Success: Implications for Designing Effective Reward Systems," *Journal of Value-Based Management*, 1993, 6, 65–80.

31. E. Schein, *The Corporate Culture Survival Guide: Sense and Nonsense about Culture Change* (San Francisco: Jossey-Bass, 1999).

32. G. Bonvillian and W. Nowlin, "Cultural Awareness: An Essential Element in Doing Business Abroad," *Business Horizons*, November 1994, 44–50; A very interesting discussion of these issues related to France can be found in P. Platt, *French or Foe?* 2nd. ed. (Lillington, NC: Polly Platt).

33. A. Farnham, "Trust Gap," *Fortune*, December 4, 1989, 70.

34. S. Covey, *The 7 Habits of Highly Effective People* (New York: Simon & Schuster, 1989).

35. R. Levering and M. Moskowitz, "The 100 Best Companies to Work For," *Fortune*, January 10, 2000, 83–110.

36. D. Welch, "The Car Guy Takes Charge at General Motors," *BusinessWeek*, November 21, 2001, 49.

37. M. Cooper, D. Friedman, and J. Koenig, "Empire of the Sun," *U.S. News & World Report*, May 28, 1990, 44–51.

38. E. Schonfeld, M. Gunther, D. Roth, and M Warner, "Ten Companies That Get It," *Fortune*, November 8, 1999, 115–119.

39. D. Allen and R. Griffeth, "A Vertical and Lateral Information Processing: The Effects of Gender, Employee Classification Level, and Media Richness on Communication and Work Outcomes," *Human Relations*, 1997, 50, 1239–60; K. Ashcraft, "Empowering 'Professional' Relationships," *Management Communication Quarterly*, 2000, 13, 347–93.

40. D. Borisoff, "Gender Issues and Listening," in D. Borisoff and M. Purdy, eds., *Listening in Everyday Life: A Personal and Professional Approach* (Lanham, MD: University Press of America, 1992).

41. "Seven Things We Do That Keep Us From Getting Ahead," *Women as Managers*, 1998, 98, 1, 4; J. Pearson and E. Aries, *Gender and Communication* (Dubuque, IA: William C. Brown, 1991).

42. S. Kirmeyer and T. Lin, "Social Support: Its Relationship to Observed Communication with Peers and Superiors," *Academy of Management Journal*, 1987, 30, 138–51.

43. C. Sittenfeld, "Power by the People," *Fast Company*, July/August 1999, 178.

44. G. Cancelada, "New Strategy Puts Workers Operating Like Owners," *St. Louis Post-Dispatch*, May 2, 2002, C1.

45. M. Montoya-Weiss, A. Massey, and M. Song, "Getting It Together: Temporal Coordination and Conflict Management in Global Virtual Teams," *Academy of Management Journal*, 2001, 44, 6, 1251–62.

46. "Getting the Message on Internal Communication," *Facilities*, September 1996, 14, 9, 15–16; J. Glauser, "Upward Information Flows in Organizations: Review and Conceptual Analysis," *Human Relations*, 1984, 37, 113–43; M. Montoya et al., 2001.

47. P. Roberts, "Live! From Your Office! It's . . .," *Fast Company*, October 1999, 151–62.

48. E. Walton, "How Efficient Is the Grapevine?" *Personnel*, 1961, 28, 45–48.

49. L. Landes, "Real-life, Real-time Communication," *Communication World*, December 2001/January 2002, 19, 1, 21.

50. D. Morand, "Language and Power: An Empirical Analysis of Linguistic Strategies Used in Superior-Subordinate Communication," *Journal of Organizational Behavior*, 2000, 21, 235–49; F. Luthans, R. Hodgetts, and S. Rosenkrantz, *Real Managers and Workplace Basics* (New York: Ballinger Publishing, 1988); L. Penley, E. Alexander, I. Jernigan, and C. Henwood, "Communication Abilities of Managers: The Relationship of Performance," *Journal of Management*, 1991, 17, 57–76.

51. S. Brutus and L. Kelly-Radford, "Receptivity to Feedback," *Leadership in Action*, 18, 5 (Greensboro, NC: Center for Creative Leadership, 1998).

52. I. McGill and L. Beatty, *Action Learning: A Guide for Professional, Management, and Educational Development* (London: Kogan, 1995); J. Sonnenfeld, "Director's Comments," *The Leadership Newsletter*, Fall 1996, 2.

53. S. Covey, 1989.

54. *Ibid.*

55. C. Rogers, "Barriers and Gateways to Communication," *Harvard Business Review*, November/December 1991, 69, 105–11.

56. E. Hall, "The Silent Language in Overseas Business," *Harvard Business Review*, May/June 1960, 58–64.

57. W. Kiechel, "Learn How to Listen," *Fortune*, August 17, 1987, 107–08; also see S. Covey, 1989.

58. Adapted from M. Munter, *Guide to Managerial Communication*, 3rd ed. (Upper Saddle River, NJ: Prentice Hall, 1992), xii.

CHAPTER 13

1. J. Schiro, "Leadership: Past, Present, and Future," *Futurics*, 1999, 23, 67–70; J. Byrne, "Restoring Trust in Corporate America: Business Must Lead the Way to Real Reform," *BusinessWeek*, June 24, 2002, 30–35; J. Nocera, "System Failure: Corporate America Has Lost its Way," *Fortune*, July 24, 2002, 62–74.

2. G. Yukl, *Leadership in Organizations*, 4th ed. (Upper Saddle River, NJ: Prentice Hall, 1998).

3. J. Kouzes and B. Posner, *The Leadership Challenge: How to Get Extraordinary Things Done With Ordinary People*, 2nd ed. (San Francisco: Jossey-Bass, 1995).

4. J. Kotter, *The Leadership Factor* (New York: The Free Press, 1987).

5. C. Hickman, *Mind of a Manager, Soul of a Leader* (New York: John Wiley, 1990); E. Zimmerman, "What's Under the Hood? The Mechanics of Leadership Versus Management," *Supervision*, August 2001, 10–12.

6. Summarized in G. Yukl, 1998.

7. J. Kouzes and B. Posner, 1995.

8. M. Leibovich, "Reich Rises Above Height Issue in Run for Governor," *St. Louis Post-Dispatch*, Sunday, March 17, 2002, A19.

9. N. Tichy and S. Sherman, *Control Your Destiny or Someone Else Will* (New York: Doubleday, 1993); S. Flax, "The Toughest Bosses in America," *Fortune*, August 6, 1984, 90–107.

10. D. Brady, "The Education of Jeff Immelt: The Jack Welch Era Is History," *BusinessWeek*, April 29, 2002, 80–87.

11. Task orientation may also be referred to as initiating structure, concern for production, job-centered, or authoritarian. Relationship orientation may also be referred to as democratic, people-centered, employee-centered, and consideration. For a review of earlier research findings, see S. Kirkpatrick and E. Locke, "Leadership: Do Traits Matter?" *Academy of Management Executive*, 1991, 5, 48–59; R. Stogdill, *Handbook of Leadership* (New York: The Free Press, 1974); R. Stogdill and A. Coons, *Leader Behavior: Its Description and Measurement* (Columbus, OH: Ohio State University Bureau of Business Research, 1957); R. Tannenbaum and W. Schmidt, "How to Choose a Leadership Pattern," *Harvard Business Review*, March/April, 1958, 95–101; R. Blake and J. Mouton, "How to Choose a Leadership Style," *Training and Development Journal*, February 1986, 39–46.

12. An excellent discussion is found in P. Drucker, *Managing for the Future: The 1990s and Beyond* ((New York: Plume Books, 1993); and T. Petzinger, *The New Pioneers: The Men and Women Who Are Transforming the Workplace and Marketplace* (New York: Simon & Schuster, 1999).

13. J. French and B. Raven, "The Bases of Social Power," in D. Cartwright, ed., *Studies of Social Power* (Ann Arbor, MI: Institute for Social Research, 1959).

14. N. Austen, "Saying Thank You," *Incentive*, September 1999, 173; F. Robert, "Carly Fiorina Is Turning into a Force to be Reckoned With," *Computer Reseller News*, September 18, 2000, 126; R. Karlgaard, "Vote Carly," *Forbes*, February 18, 2002, 169, 37.

15. C. Sittenfeld, "Leader on the Edge," *FastCompany*, October 1999, 212–26.

16. S. Hays, "Our Future Requires Collaborative Leadership," *Workforce*, December 1999, 30–34.

17. M. Marchetti, "A Sales Pro Tries to Energize HP," *Sales and Marketing Management*, September 1999, 15.

18. This term is used by H. Sims and C. Manz, *Company of Heroes* (New York: John Wiley & Sons, 1996). There are other perspectives that are developed around self-leadership. See for example, H. Sims and P. Lorenzi, *The New Leadership Paradigm: Social Learning and Cognition in Organizations* (Newbury Park, CA: Sage, 1992); Kouzes and Posner, 1995.

19. I. Chaleff, *The Courageous Follower: Standing Up To and For Our Leaders* (San Francisco: Berrett-Koehler Publishers, 1995).

20. J. Schiro, "Leadership: Past, Present, and Future," *Futurics*, 1999, 23, 67–70.

21. C. Lee, "Followership: The Essence of Leadership," *Training*, January 1991, 27–35; M. Abramson and J. Scanlon, "The Five Dimensions of Leadership," *Government Executive*, July 1991, 20–25.

22. D. Roth, "How to Cut Pay, Lay off 8,000 People, and Still Have Workers Who Love You," *Fortune*, February 4, 2002, 64–68.

23. D. Whitford, "A Human Place to Work," *Fortune*, January 8, 2001, 108–15.

24. F. Shipper and C. Manz, "W. L. Gore & Associates, Inc., In 1998," in A. Thompson and A. Strickland, eds. *Strategic Management: Concepts and Cases*, 11th ed. (Boston: Irwin McGraw-Hill, 1999), C491–C513.

25. C. Lee, 1991; M. Abramson and J. Scanlon, 1991.

26. S. Kerr and J. Jermier, "Substitutes for Leadership: Their Meaning and Measurement," *Organizational Behavior and Human Performance*, 1978, 375–403; P. Podsakoff, B. Niehoff, S. MacKenzie, and M. Williams, "Do Substitutes for Leadership Really Substitute for Leadership? An Empirical Examination of Kerr and Jermier's Situational Leadership Model," *Organizational Behavior and Human Decision Processes*, February 1993, 1–44.

27. See, for example, A. Zaleznik, "The Leadership Gap," *Academy of Management Executive*, 1990, 4, 7–22; C. Manz and H. Sims, "Leading Workers to Lead Themselves: The External Leadership of Self-Managing Work Teams," *Administrative Science Quarterly*, March 1987, 106–29; H. Sims and C. Manz, *Company of Heros*.

28. P. Hersey and K. Blanchard, *Management of Organizational Behavior: Utilizing Human Resources*, 5th. ed. (Upper Saddle River, NJ: Prentice Hall, 1988).

29. *Ibid.*

30. T. Kayser, *Building Team Power: How to Unleash the Collaborative Genius of Work Teams* (Burr Ridge, IL: Irwin, 1994).

31. S. Wall, *The New Strategists: Creating Leaders at All Levels* (New York: The Free Press, 1995); R. Ford and M. Fottler, "Empowerment: A Matter of Degree," *Academy of Management Executive*, 1995, 9, 21–30.

32. D. Olshfski and R. Cunningham, "The Empowerment Construct in Manager-Executive Relationships," *Administration & Society*, 1998, 30, 357–73.

33. S. Kerr, "GE's Collective Genius," in F. Hesselbein and P. Cohen, eds. *Leader to Leader* (San Francisco: Jossey-Bass, 1999), 227–36.

34. B. Bass, "From Transactional to Transformational Leadership: Learning to Share the Vision," *Organizational Dynamics*, 1990, 18, 19–31; B. Avolio and B. Bass, "Individual Consideration Viewed at Multiple Levels of Analysis: A Multi-Level Framework for Examining the Diffusion of Transformational Leadership," *Leadership Quarterly*, 1995, 6, 199–218.

35. J. Sparks and J. Schenk, "Explaining the Effects of Transformational Leadership: An Investigation of the Effects of Higher-Order Motives in Multilevel Marketing Organizations," *Journal of Organizational Behavior*, 2001, 22, 849–69.

36. A. Zalenzik, 1990; C. Lee, 1991; M. Abramson and J. Scanlon, 1991; J. Kouzes and B. Posner, 1995; R. Pillai, "Crisis and the Emergence of Charismatic Leadership in Groups: An Experimental Investigation," *Journal of Applied Social Psychology*, 1996, 26, 543–62.

37. J. Sosik and L. Megerian, "Understanding Leader Emotional Intelligence and Performance: The Role of Self-Other Agreement on Transformational Leadership Perceptions," *Group & Organization Management*, 1999, 24, 367–90. See also, J. Seltzer and B. Bass, "Transformational Leadership: Beyond Initiation and Consideration," *Journal of Management*, December 1990, 693–703.

38. See also S. Covey, *Principle-Centered Leadership* (New York: Simon & Schuster, 1992).

39. See L. Hanson, "What Boards Can Do About America's Corporate Leadership Crisis," *Directorship*, April 2002, 13–16, for a good discussion about how important it is for a leader to set a good example.

40. P. Sellers, "These Women Rule," *Fortune*, October 25, 1999, 94–107.

41. "The Grande Dame of Nonprofits," *Incentive*, January 1993, 30; S. Blank, "Managing for a Mission in Girl Scouting," *Management Review*, 1993, 76, 56; J. Muehrcke, "A Conversation with Frances Hesselbein," *Nonprofit World*, 1999, 15, 36–39.

42. E. Fagenson-Eland and P. Kidder, "A Conversation With Rear Admiral Louise Wilmot: Taking the Lead and Leading the Way," *Organizational Dynamics*, Winter 2000, 28, 80–92; "Margaret C. Whitman," *BusinessWeek*, January 8, 2001, 68.

43. J. Rosener, "Ways Women Lead," *Harvard Business Review*, November/December 1990, 119–25.

44. G. Powell, "One More Time: Do Female and Male Managers Differ?" *Academy of Management Executive*, August 1990, 3, 68–75; R. Sharpe, "The Waiting Game: Women Make Strides, But Men Stay Firmly in Top Company Jobs," *The Wall Street Journal*, March 29, 1994, B2.

45. J. Tingley, *Genderflex: Men & Women Speaking Each Other's Language at Work* (New York: American Mangement Association, 1994); D. Tannen, "The Power to Talk: Who Gets Heard and Why," *Harvard Business Review*, September/October 1995, 138–48; K. Parry, "Women Behaving as Leaders," *Management*, June 2000, 47, 24–26.

46. R. Thaler-Carter, "Whither Global Leaders?" *HR Magazine*, May 2000, 82–87; E. Rasmusson, "Becoming a Multicultural Manager," *Sales & Marketing Management*, June 2000, 152, 140.

47. Adapted from J. Schiro, 1999; and L. Ludewig, "The Ten Commandments of Leadership," *NASPA Journal*, Spring 1988, 297.

CHAPTER 14

1. H. Sims and C. Manz, *Company of Heroes: Unleashing the Power of Self-Leadership* (New York: John Wiley & Sons, 1996); H. Sims and P. Lorenzi, *The New Leadership Paradigm* (Newbury Park, CA: Sage Press, 1992).

2. H. Sims and C. Manz, 1996.

3. E. Robinson, *Why Aren't You More Like Me?* (Dubuque, IA: Kendall/Hunt, 1991).

4. *Ibid.*

5. M. Mitchell and P. Fandt, "Examining the Relationship between Role-Defining Characteristics and Self-Esteem of College Students," *College Student Journal*, 33, 1995, 99–120.

6. A. Korman, "Self-Esteem Variable in Vocational Choice," *Journal of Applied Psychology*, 50, 1966, 479–86; A. Korman, "Relevance of Personal Need Satisfaction for Overall Satisfaction as a Function of Self-Esteem," *Journal of Applied Psychology*, 51, 1967, 533–38.

7. G. Mitchell and P. Fandt, "Confident Role Models for Tomorrow's Classrooms: The Self-Esteem of Education Majors," *Education*, 113, 1993, 556–62.

8. J. Rotter, "Generalized Expectancies for Internal versus External Control of Reinforcement," *Psychological Monographs*, 80, 1966, 1–28.

9. C. Anderson, D. Hellriegel, and J. Slocum, "Managerial Response to Environmentally Induced Stress," *Academy of Management Journal*, 20, 2, 1977, 260–72.

10. Based on M. Jamal, "Type A Behavior and Job Performance: Some Suggestive Findings," *Journal of Human Stress*, Summer 1985, 60–68.

11. M. Fischetti, "Team Doctors, Report to ER," *Fast Company*, February 1998, 170–72.

12. J. Horne and J. Orr, "Assessing Behaviors That Create Resilient Organizations," *Employment Relations Today*, Winder, 1998, 290–329; T. Schwartz, "Making Waves: Training for Stress and Recovery," *Fast Company*, October 1999, 347.

13. S. Aitken and J. Morgan, "How Motorola Promotes Good Health," *The Journal for Quality and Participation*, January/February 1999, 54–57.

14. M. Guttman, "Resilience," *USA Weekend*, March 7, 1999, 4–5.

15. M. Snyder and S. Gangestad, "On the Nature of Self-Monitoring: Matters of Assessment, Matters of Validity," *Journal of Personality and Social Psychology*, 51, 1986, 123–39.

16. M. Kilduff and D. Day, "Do Chameleons Get Ahead? The Effects of Self-Monitoring on Managerial Careers," *Academy of Management Journal*, 37, 1994, 1047–60; A. Church, "Managerial Self-Awareness in High-Performing Individuals in Organizations," *Journal of Applied Psychology*, 82, 1997, 281–92.

17. T. Adorno, E. Frenkel-Brunswick, D. Levinson, and R. Sanford, *The Authoritarian Personality* (New York: Harper & Row, 1950).

18. I. Briggs-Myers, *Introduction to Type* (Palo Alto, CA: Consulting Psychologists Press, 1980).

19. O. Kroeger and J. Thuesen, *Type Talk* (New York: Delacorte Press, 1988).

20. W. Gardner and M. Martinko, "Using the Myers-Briggs Type Indicator to Study Managers: A Literature Review and Research Agenda," *Journal of Management*, 22, 1, 1996, 45–83.

21. J. Digman, "Personality Structure: Emergence of a Five-Factor Model," *Annual Review of Psychology*, 41, 1990, 417–40.

22. M. Barrick and M. Mount, "The Big Five Personality Dimensions and Job Performance: A Meta-Analysis," *Personnel Psychology*, 44, 1991, 1–26.

23. S. Seibert and M. Kraimer, "The Five-Factor Model of Personality and Career Success," *Journal of Vocational Behavior*, 2001, 58, 1–21.

24. L. Hough, N. Eaton, M. Dunnette, J. Kamp, and R. McCloy, "Criterion-Related Validities of Personality Constructs and the Effect of Response Distortion on Those Validities," *Journal of Applied Psychology*, 75, 1990, 581–95; Barrick and Mount, 1991; J. Salgado, "The Five-Factor Model of Personality and Job Performance in the European Community," *Journal of Applied Psychology*, 82, 1997, 30–43; F. De Fruyt, Filip, I. Mervielde, and Ivan, "Riasec Types and Big Five Traits as Predictors of Employment Status and Nature of Employment," *Personnel Psychology*, Autumn, 52, 1999, 701–28.

25. G. Hurtz and J. Donovan, "Personality and Job Performance: The Big Five Revisited," *Journal of Applied Psychology*, 2000, 85, 869–79.

26. T. Judge, J. Martocchio, and C. Thoresen, "Five-Factor Model of Personality and Employee Absence," *Journal of Applied Psychology*, 1997, 82, 745–55.

27. Seibert and Kraimer, 2001.

28. J. Holland, *Making Vocational Choices: A Theory of Vocational Personalities and Work Environments*, (Englewood Cliffs, NJ: Prentice Hall, 1985; J. Holland, *Making Vocational Choices: A Theory of Vocational Personalities and Environments*, (Odessa, FL: Psychological Assessment Resources, 1997).

29. De Fruyt et al., 1999.

30. Holland, 1997; De Fruyt et al., 1999.

31. "Throwing Stones at the Glass Ceiling," *BusinessWeek*, August 19, 1991, 19.

32. P. Fandt and G. Stevens, "Evaluation Bias in the Business Classroom: Evidence Related to the Effects of Previous Experiences," *Journal of Psychology*, 125, 1991, 469–77.

33. D. Dearborn and H. Simon, "Selection Perception: A Note on the Departmental Identification of Executives," *Sociometry*, 21, 1958, 140–44.

34. L. Porter, R. Steers, R. Mowday, and P. Boulian, "Organizational Commitment, Job Satisfaction, and Turnover Among Psychiatric Technicians," *Journal of Applied Psychology*, 5, 1974, 603.

35. L. Festinger, *A Theory of Cognitive Dissonance*, (Stanford, CA: Stanford University Press, 1957).

36. *Ibid.*

37. P. Smith, L. Kendall, and C. Hulin, *The Measurement of Satisfaction in Work and Retirement* (Chicago: Rand McNally, 1969).

38. L. Roberson, "Prediction of Job Satisfaction from Characteristics of Personal Work Goals," *Journal of Organizational Behavior*, 11, 1990, 29–41.

39. Smith and Kendall, 1969.

40. M. Petty, G. McGee, and J. Cavender, "A Meta-Analysis of the Relationship Between Individual Job Satisfaction and Individual Performance," *Academy of Management Review*, October 1984, 712–21.

41. M. Shaw, *Group Dynamics: The Psychology of Small Group Behavior* (New York: McGraw-Hill, 1981), 1.

42. Further differences are discussed in J. Katzenback and D. Smith, "The Discipline of Teams," *Harvard Business Review*, 71, 1993, 111–20.

43. G. Steward, C. Manz, and H. Sims, *Team Work and Group Dynamics* (New York: John Wiley & Sons, 1999); D. Johnson and R. Johnson, *Cooperation and Competition: Theory and Researach* (Edina, MN: Interaction Book Co., 1989); S. Wheelan, *Creating Effective Teams: A Guide for Members and Leaders* (Thousand Oaks, CA: Sage Publications, 1999).

44. D. Johnson and P. Johnson, *Joining Together: Group Theory and Group Skills* (Boston: Allyn & Bacon, 1994), 18–21.

45. T. Quick, *Successful Team Building* (New York: AMACOM, 1992).

46. Based on K. Benne and P. Sheats, "Functional Roles of Group Members," *Journal of Social Issues*, 4, 1948, 42–47.

47. C. Dahle, "Xtreme Teams," *Fast Company*, November 1999, 310–16.

48. C. Solomon, "Global Teams: The Ultimate Collaboration," *Personnel Journal*, September 1998, 49–58; for a broader discussion, see N. Zaidman, "Cultural Codes and Language Strategies in Business Communication," *Management Communication Quarterly*, 14, 3, 2001, 408–41.

49. S. Jackson, "Team Composition in Organizational Settings: Issues in Managing and Increasingly Diverse Work Force," in *Group Process and Productivity*, S. Worchell, W. Wood, and J. Simpson, eds. (Newbury Park, CA: Sage Publications, 1992), 138–73; D. Hambrick, T. Cho, and M. Jen, "The Influence of Top Management Team Heterogeneity on Firms' Competitive Moves," *Administrative Science Quarterly*, 41, 1996, 650–84.

50. G. Stewart and M. Barrick, "Designing Effective Work Teams: Task Interdependence, Team Self-Leadership, and Task Routineness," paper presented at the Annual Meeting of the Academy of Management, Boston, MA, August 1997.

51. H. Park, P. Lewis, and P. Fandt, "Ethnocentrism and Group Cohesiveness in International Joint Ventures," in *Multinational Strategic Alliances*, R. Culpan, ed. (Binghamton, NY: International Business Press, 1993).

52. T. Cox, "The Multicultural Organization," *Academy of Management Executive*, 5, 1991, 34–47.

53. B. Berelson and G. Steiner, *Human Behaviors: An Inventory of Scientific Findings* (New York: Harcourt, Brace & World, 1964), 356–60.

54. N. Kerr and S. Bruun, "The Dispensability of Member Effort and Group Motivation Losses: Free-Rider Effects," *Journal of Personality and Social Psychology*, 44, 1983, 78–94.

55. For more information, see D. Johnson and P. Johnson, *Joining Together*, 1994, 248–52.

56. B. Latane, K. Williams, and S. Harkins, "Many Hands Make Light the Work: The Causes and Consequences of Social Loafing," *Journal of Personality and Social Psychology*, 1978, 37, 822–32; E. Weldon and G. Gargano, "Cognitive Effort in Additive Task Groups: The Effects of Shared Responsibility on the Quality of Multiattribute Judgments," *Organizational Behavior and Human Decision Processes*, 36, 1985, 348–61.

57. A. O'Leary-Kelly, J. Martocchio, and D. Frink, "A Review of the Influence of Group Goals on Group Performance," *Academy of Management Review*, 37, 1994, 128–301.

58. B. Tuckman and M. Jensen, "Stages of Small Group Development Revisited," *Group and Organization Studies*, 2, 1977, 419–27; P. Buhler, "Group Membership," *Supervision*, May 1994, 8–10.

59. J. O'Brian, "Making New Hires Members of the Team," *Supervisory Management*, May 1992, 4; D. Johnson and F. Johnson, 1994.

60. S. Wheelan, 1999.

61. For a thorough discussion of cohesiveness, see P. Murdrack, "Defining Group Cohesiveness: A Legacy of Confusion?" *Small Group Behavior*, 20, 1989, 37–49.

62. N. Evans and P. Jarvis, "Group Cohesion: A Review and Reevaluation," *Small Group Behavior*, 11, 1980, 359–70.

63. T. Kayser, *Building Team Power: How to Unleash the Collaborative Genius of Work Teams* (Burr Ridge, IL: Irwin, 1994); T. Quick, 1992; S. Cohen, "A Monkey on the Back, A Lump in the Throat," *Inside Sports*, 4, 1992, 20.

64. I. Janis, *Victims of Groupthink*, 2nd ed. (Boston: Houghton Mifflin, 1982).

65. G. Whyte, "Groupthink Reconsidered," *Academy of Management Review*, 14, 1989, 40–55.

66. K. Bettenhausen and J. Murnighan, "The Development of an Intragroup Norm and the Effects of Interpersonal and

Structural Changes," *Administrative Science Quarterly*, 36, 1990, 20–35.

67. S. Wheelan, 1999.

68. M. McIntyre, *The Management Team Handbook: Five Key Strategies for Maximizing Group Performance* (San Francisco: Jossey-Bass, 1998); A. Edmondson, R. Bohmer, and G. Pisano, "Best Practice: Speeding Up Team Learning," *Harvard Business Review*, October 2001, 125–32; J. Shaw, M. Duffy, and E. Stark, "Team Reward Attitude: Construct Development and Initial Validation," *Journal of Organizational Behavior*, 22, 2001, 903–17.

69. J. Kouzes and Posner, *The Leadership Challenge: How to Keep Getting Extraordinary Things Done in Organizations* (San Francisco: Jossey-Bass, 1995); for an example of this in practice, see A. Arkin, "Award Finalist: Vesuvius Scotland," *People Management*, 5, November 11, 1999, 57–59.

CHAPTER 15

1. S. Kerr, "On the Folly of Rewarding A While Hoping for B," *Academy of Management Executive*, 9, 1, February 1995, 7–14.

2. R. Steers and L. Porter, eds., *Motivation and Work Behavior*, 3rd ed. (New York: McGraw-Hill, 1983).

3. For a comprehensive model, see H. Klein, "An Integrated Control Theory Model of Work Motivation," *Academy of Management Review*, 14, 1989, 150–72.

4. A. Maslow, "A Theory of Human Motivation," *Psychological Review*, 50, 1943, 270–396; M. Wahba and L. Bridwell, "Maslow Reconsidered: A Review of Research and the Need Hierarchy," *Organizational Behavior and Human Performance*, 16, 1976, 212–40.

5. F. Herzberg, "One More Time: How Do You Motivate Employees?" *Harvard Business Review*, January/February 1968, 53–68.

6. C. Fishman, "Engines of Democracy," *Fast Company*, October 1999, 180–202.

7. D. McClelland, *The Achieving Society* (New York: Van Nostrand Reinhold, 1961).

8. D. McClelland, *Human Motivation* (Glenview, Ill.: Scott, Foresman, 1985).

9. D. Miron and D. McClelland, "The Impact of Achievement Motivation Training on Small Businesses," *California Management Review*, Summer 1979, 13–28.

10. D. McClelland and H. Burnham, "Power Is the Great Motivator," *Harvard Business Review*, 54, March/April 1976, 100–10.

11. V. Vroom, *Work and Motivation* (New York: John Wiley & Sons, 1964).

12. *Creating and Motivating a Superior, Loyal Staff* (New York: National Institute of Business Management, 1992).

13. R. Griffin, "Effects of Work Redesign on Employee Perceptions, Attitudes, and Behaviors: A Long-Term Investigation," *Academy of Management Journal*, 34, 1991, 425–35.

14. S. Adams, "Toward an Understanding of Inequity," *Journal of Abnormal and Social Psychology*, 67, 1963, 422–36.

15. *Ibid.*; S. Adams, "Inequity in Social Exchange," in *Advances in Experimental Social Psychology*, Vol. 2, L. Berkowitz, ed. (New York: Academic Press, 1965), 267–300.

16. J. Hatfield and E. Miles, "A New Perspective on Equity Theory: The Equity Sensitivity Construct," *Academy of Management Review*, 12, 1987, 222–34; E. Miles, J. Hatfield, and R. Huseman, "The Equity Sensitivity Construct: Potential Implications for Work Performance," *Journal of Management*, 15, 1989, 581–88.

17. Goal-setting theory is well summarized in E. Locke and G. Latham, *Goal Setting: A Motivational Technique That Works!* (Upper Saddle River, NJ: Prentice Hall, 1984).

18. For a detailed review, see E. Locke, K. Shaw, L. Saari, and G. Latham, "Goal Setting and Task Performance, 1969–1980," *Psychological Bulletin*, 90, 1981, 125–52.

19. C. Fay and M. Thompson, "Contextual Determinants of Reward Systems' Success: An Exploratory Study," *Human Resource Management*, 40, 3, Fall 2001, 213–26.

20. C. Markides, "Strategy as Making Choices: A Discussion with John Bachmann, Managing Partner of Edward Jones," *European Management Journal*, 17, June 1999, 275–81; J. Byrne, "Main Street Trumps Wall Street," *BusinessWeek*, June 10, 2002, 134–38.

21. G. Maier and J. Brunstein, "The Role of Personal Work Goals in Newcomers' Job Satisfaction and Organization Commitment: A Longitudinal Analysis," *Journal of Applied Psychology*, 86, 2001, 1034–42.

22. A. Tziner and G. Latham, "The Effects of Appraisal Instrument, Feedback, and Goal-Setting on Worker Satisfaction and Commitment," *Journal of Organizational Behavior*, 10, 1989, 145–53; G. Maier and J. Brunstein, 2001.

23. L. Robertson, "Prediction of Job Satisfaction from Characteristics of Personal Work Goals," *Journal of Organizational Behavior*, 11, 1990, 29–41.

24. K. Blanchard and J. Johnson, *The One Minute Manager* (New York: Morrow, 1982).

25. G. Pinchot, "Creating Organizations with Many Leaders," in *The Leader of the Future*, F. Hesselbein, M. Goldsmith, and R. Beckhard, eds. (San Francisco: Jossey-Bass Publishers, 1996).

26. J. Miller, *The Corporate Coach* (New York: St. Martin's Press, 1994).

27. T. Kayser, *Building Team Power: How to Unleash the Collaborative Genius of Work Teams* (Burr Ridge, Ill.: Irwin, 1994); H. Sims and C. Manz, *Company of Heroes: Unleashing the Power of Self-Leadership* (New York: John Wiley & Sons, 1996).

28. J. Hirsch, "Now Hotel Clerks Provide More Than Keys," *The Wall Street Journal*, March 5, 1993, B1.

29. C. Manz and H. Sims, *Business Without Bosses: How Self-Managing Teams Are Building High Performing Companies* (New York: John Wiley & Sons, 1995); M. Hammer and J. Champy, *Reengineering the Corporation: A Manifesto for Business Revolution* (New York: HarperBusiness, 1994).

30. C. Carson, K. Eckart, C. Flash, G. Fysh, M. Maharry, and J. Szymariski, "It's Going the Way It Was Programmed," *Tacoma News Tribune*, September 8, 1996, D1.

31. B. Nelson, "The Ironies of Motivation," *Strategy & Leadership*, January/February 1999, 26–31.

32. E. Lawler, III, "Pay Strategy: New Thinking for the New Millennium," *Compensation & Benefits Review*, 32, 1, 2000, 7–12; M. Lockwood, "Performance-Based Reward Systems," *Executive Excellence*, 19, February 2002, 9–10; P. Zingheim and J. Schuster, "Pay It Forward," *People Management*, 8, February 7, 2002, 3–6.

33. E. Lawler, "Pay Can Be a Change Agent," *Compensation & Benefits Management*, 16, 3, Summer 2000, 23–26.

34. L. McClurg, "Team Rewards: How Far Have We Come?" *Human Resource Management*, 40, Spring 2001, 73–86.

35. G. Anders, "The Innovator's Solution," *Fast Company*, June 2002, 132–37.

36. J. McAdams, "The Essential Role of Rewarding Teams and Teamwork," *Compensation & Benefits Management*, 16, Autumn 2000, 15–28.

37. A. Howard, K. Shudo, and M. Umeshima, "Motivation and Values among Japanese and American Managers," *Personnel Psychology*, 36, 1983, 883–98.

38. J. Spence, "Achievement American Style: The Rewards and Costs of Individualism," *American Psychologist*, 40, 1985, 1285–94; N. Zaidman, "Cultural Codes and Language Strategies in Business Communication," *Management Communication Quarterly*, February 2001, 408–41.

39. S. Cady, P. Fandt, and D. Fernandez, "Investigating Cultural Differences in Personal Success: Implications for Designing Effective Reward Systems," *Journal of Value Based Management*, 6, 1993, 65–80; N. Adler, *International Dimensions of Organizational Behavior* (Boston: Kent, 1986); M. Dolecheck, "Cross-Cultural Analysis of Business Ethics: Hong Kong and American Business Personnel," *Journal of Managerial Issues*, 4, 1992, 288–303.

40. B. Nelson, 1999.

CHAPTER 16

1. K. A. Merchant, *Control in Business Organizations* (Marshfield, Mass.: Pitman, 1985).

2. T. Lowe and J. L. Machin, *New Perspectives on Management Control* (New York: Macmillan, 1987).

3. D. Paletta, "E. Coli Outbreak Has Stores Asking Consumers to Return Beef," *The Orlando Sentinel*, July 26, 2002, B1ff.

4. W. R. Ashby, *Introduction to Cybernetics* (New York: Wiley, 1963).

5. S. Beer, *Cybernetics and Management* (New York: Wiley, 1959), 44.

6. M. Cabbage, "Faulty Math Botched Mars Probe," *The Orlando Sentinel*, November 11, 1999, A4.

7. M. Goold and J. Quinn, "The Paradox of Strategic Controls," *Strategic Management Journal*, January 1990, 43–57.

8. D. Cray, "Control and Coordination in Multinational Corporations," *Journal of International Business Studies*, Fall 1984, 85–98.

9. P. Lorange and D. Murphy, "Considerations in Implementing Strategic Control," *Journal of Business Strategy*, 4, Spring 1984, 27–35.

10. P. P. Schoderbek, R. A. Cosier, and J. C. Aplin, *Management* (San Diego: Harcourt Brace Jovanovich, 1991).

11. J. R. Evans and W. M. Lindsay, *The Management and Control of Quality* (St. Paul, Minn.: West Publishing, 1993).

12. "Doctors Get an Rx for Messy Handwriting-Digital Prescriptions," *The Orlando Sentinel*, November 13, 1999, A8.

13. L. Krajewski and L. Ritzman, *Operations Management: Strategy and Analysis*, 5th ed. (Reading, Mass.: Addison-Wesley, 1999), 552.

14. W. H. Newman, *Construction Control* (Upper Saddle River, N.J.: Prentice Hall, 1975).

15. P. Lorange, M. F. S. Morton, and G. Sumantra, *Strategic Control* (St. Paul, Minn.: West Publishing, 1986).

16. P. F. Drucker, *Management: Tasks, Responsibilities, Practices* (New York: Harper & Row, 1973), 100.

17. W. G. Ouchi, "Markets, Bureaucracies, and Clans," *Administrative Science Quarterly*, 25, 1980, 128–41.

18. H. P. Sims Jr. and C. C. Manz, *SuperLeadership: Leading Others to Lead Themselves* (New York: Simon & Schuster, 1989).

19. C. Cortland and D. A. Nadler, "Fit Control Systems to Your Managerial Style," *Harvard Business Review*, January/February 1976, 65–72.

20. B. R. Baliga and A. M. Jaeger, "Multinational Corporations: Control Systems and Delegation Issues," *Journal of International Business Studies*, Fall 1984, 25–40.

21. "Computer Troubles Cast Wicked Spell on Hershey," *The Orlando Sentinel*, October 30, 1999, C1ff.

22. E. Brigham, *Financial Management: Theory and Practice*, 4th ed. (Chicago: Dryden Press, 1985).

23. F. J. Tasco and A. J. Gajda, "Substance Abuse in the Workplace," *Compensation and Benefits Management*, Winter 1990, 140–44.

24. T. Shoulberg, "Drug-Free Workplace Can Save on Premiums," *Central Florida Business Report*, November 29, 1999, 25; M. A. McDaniel, "Does Pre-Employment Drug Use Predict On-the-Job Suitability?" *Personnel Psychology*, Winter 1988, 717–30.

25. T. W. Ferguson, "Motorola Aims High, So Motorolans Won't Be Getting High," *The Wall Street Journal*, June 26, 1990, A19.

26. R. L. Campbell and R. E. Langford, *Substance Abuse in the Workplace* (Boca Raton, FL: Lewis Publisher, 1995).

27. "Housing Complex Requires Drug Tests for Tenants," *The Orlando Sentinel*, July 28, 1996, B3.

28. "Preventing Crime on the Job," *Nation's Business*, July 1990, 36–37.

29. J. Rothfeder, M. Galen, and L. Driscoll, "Is Your Boss Spying on You?" *BusinessWeek*, January 15, 1990, 74–75.

30. N. H. Snyder and K. E. Blair, "Dealing with Employee Theft," *Business Horizons*, May/June 1989, 27–34.

31. B. Dumaine, "Corporate Spies Snoop to Conquer," *Fortune*, November 7, 1988, 68–76.

32. M. McDonald, "They've Got Your Number," *Dallas Morning News*, April 7, 1991, F1.

33. H. J. Chalykoff and T. A. Kochan, "Computer-Aided Monitoring: Its Influence on Employee Job Satisfaction and Turnover," *Personnel Psychology*, Winter 1989, 807–34.

CHAPTER 17

1. L.J. Krajewski and L.P. Ritzman, *Operations Management: Strategy and Analysis*, 5th ed. (Reading, Mass.: Addison-Wesley, 1999).

2. J.R. Evans, *Applied Production and Operations Management*, 5th ed. (St. Paul, Minn.: West Publishing, 1997).

3. R.B. Chase and N.J. Acquilano, *Production and Operations Management: A Life Cycle Approach*, 8th ed. (Homewood, Ill.: Irwin, 1997).

4. L.J. Krajewski and L.P. Ritzman, *Operations Management: Strategy and Analysis*.

5. M.A. Vonderembse and G.P. White, *Operations Management: Concepts, Methods, and Strategies*, 3rd ed. (St. Paul, Minn.: West Publishing, 1996).

6. L.J. Krajewski and L.P. Ritzman, *Operations Management: Strategy and Analysis*.

7. M.A. Vonderembse and G.P. White, *Operations Management: Concepts, Methods, and Strategies*.

8. B. Spitz, "And on the Lead Guitar," *Sky*, August 1996, 55–60.

9. R.J. Schonberger and E.M. Knod Jr., *Operations Management: Improving Customer Service*, 6th ed. (Homewood, Ill.: Irwin, 1996)

10. R.B. Chase and N.J. Acquilano, *Production and Operations Management: A Life Cycle Approach*.

11. L.J. Krajewski and L.P. Ritzman, *Operations Management: Strategy and Analysis*.

12. M.A. Vonderembse and G.P. White, *Operations and Management: Concepts, Methods, and Strategies*.

13. R. Blumenstein, "Big Three Pare Design Time for New Autos," *The Wall Street Journal*, August 9, 1996, A3; M. Maynard, "GM Heads Down Road to Quick Development Time," *USA Today*, August 9, 1996, B2.

14. M.A. Vonderembse and G.P. White, *Operations and Management: Concepts, Methods, and Strategies*.

15. "Clarke American Expands Call Center Network," *Clarke American Press Release*, May 1, 2002.

16. R.W. Schmenner, *Making Business Decisions* (Upper Saddle River, N.J.: Prentice Hall, 1982).

17. "Plant's Plan Causes a Stink in Small Town," *The Orlando Sentinel*, June 27, 1996, B5; "Candy Plant to Be Built in Corsicana," *Dallas Morning News*, August 14, 1996, D12.

18. B. Kuhn, "Toys R Us Plays Around with Image," *The Orlando Sentinel*, July 13, 1996, C1ff.

19. J. Jackson, "Subway to Redecorate With a Tuscany Flair," *Central Florida Business*, May 27, 2002, 4; C. Boyd, "Pretty Stores May Bag More Profits," *The Orlando Sentinel*, July 28, 1999, B1ff; C. Boyd, "Grocery Stores Are Reinventing Themselves," *The Orlando Sentinel*, June 13, 1999, H1ff.

20. L.J. Krajewski and L. P. Ritzman, *Operations Management: Strategy and Analysis*.

21. J. Heizer and B. Render, *Operations Management*, 5th ed. (Upper Saddle River, N.J.: Prentice Hall, 1999).

22. J.R. Evans, *Applied Production and Operations Management*.

23. L.J. Krajewski and L.P. Ritzman, *Operations Management: Strategy and Analysis.*

24. N. Gaither, *Production and Operations Management*, 7th ed. (Belmont, Calif.: Wadsworth Publishing, 1996).

25. M.A. Vonderembse and G.P. White, *Operations Management: Concepts, Methods, and Strategies.*

26. T. Minaham, "Did GM Strike Prove That JIT Doesn't Work?" *Purchasing*, 120, 7, May 9, 1996.

27. J.R. Evans, *Applied Production and Operations Management.*

28. L.J. Krajewski and L.P. Ritzman, *Operations Management: Strategy and Analysis.*

29. "Borders, Partner Will Provide Paperbacks Printed on Demand," *The Orlando Sentinel*, June 2, 1999, p. B5.

30. "You Know That Album You Can Never Find? Sony Has a Solution," *The Orlando Sentinel*, June 11, 1999, p. B5.

31. M.A. Vonderembse and G.P. White, *Operations Management: Concepts, Methods, and Strategies.*

32. J.R. Evans, *Applied Production and Operations Management.*

33. N. Templin, "Team Spirit: A Decisive Response to Crisis Brought Ford Enhanced Productivity," *The Wall Street Journal*, December 15, 1992, A1; A. Taylor III, "Ford's $6 Billion Baby," *Fortune*, June 28, 1993, 76–81.

34. L.J. Krajewski and L.P. Ritzman, *Operations Management: Strategy and Analysis.*

35. J.R. Evans and W.M. Lindsay, *The Management and Control of Quality*, 4th ed. (Cincinnati, OH: South-Western College Publishing, 1999).

36. *Ibid.*

37. J.R. Evans, *Applied Production and Operations Management.*

38. M.A. Vonderembse and G.P. White, *Operations Management: Concepts, Methods, and Strategies.*

39. "Clarke American MICR Express Division Named 2001 Best Workplace in America by Master Printers of America," *Clarke American Press Release*, February 2002.

40. "Malcolm Baldrige National Quality Award, 2001 Award Recipient, Manufacturing Category," http://www.nist.gov.

41. "Clarke American's Call Centers Deliver 24-Hour Customer Service Solutions,"*Clarke American Press Release*, July, 2001; http://www.clarkeamerican.com.

42. J.R. Evans, *Applied Production and Operations Management.*

43. L.J. Krajewski and L.P. Ritzman, *Operations Management: Strategy and Analysis.*

44. W.E. Deming, "Improvement of Quality and Productivity through Action by Management," *National Productivity Review*, Winter 1981–1982, 12–22.

45. J.M. Juran and F. Gryna Jr., *Quality Planning and Analysis*, 2nd ed. (New York: McGraw-Hill, 1980).

46. A.V. Feigenbaum, *Total Quality Control*, 3rd ed. (New York: McGraw-Hill, 1983).

47. K. Ishikawa, *Guide to Quality Control* (Tokyo: Asian Productivity Organization, 1972).

48. P.B. Crosby, *Quality Is Free* (New York: McGraw-Hill, 1979).

49. S. Date, "No Gazing Off into Space on This Trip," *The Orlando Sentinel*, December 4, 1993, A1ff.

50. S. Date, "Endeavour Opens Some Eyes as Hubble Mission Ends at KSC," *The Orlando Sentinel*, December 13, 1993, A1ff.

51. "Shannon Lucid Leaves Mir, Boards Atlantis for Trip Back," *The Orlando Sentinel*, September 20, 1996, A14.

52. M. Cabbage, "Shuttle Finally Roars to Life," *The Orlando Sentinel*, July 23, 1999, pp. A1ff.

53. R. Henkoff, "Delivering the Goods," *Fortune*, November 28, 1994, 64–78; I. Sager, "The Great Equalizer," *Business Week, Special Issue on the Information Revolution*, 1994, 100–07.

CHAPTER 18

1. E. Turban and J.E. Aronson, *Decision Support Systems and Intelligent Systems* (Upper Saddle River, NJ: Prentice Hall, 2001), 8.

2. K.D. Laudon and J.P. Laudon, *Management Information Systems: Organization and Technology in the Networked Enterprise*, 6th ed. (Upper Saddle River, N.J.: Prentice Hall, 2000), 5–6.

3. S. Haag, M. Cummings, and J. Dawkins, *Management Information Systems for the Information Age*, 2nd ed. (Boston: Irwin McGraw-Hill, 2000), 13–14.

4. S. Haag, M. Cummings, and J. Dawkins, *Management Information Systems for the Information Age*, 14.

5. S. Haag, M. Cummings, and J. Dawkins, *Management Information Systems for the Information Age*, 14–17.

6. K.D. Laudon and J.P. Laudon, *Management Information Systems: Organization and Technology in the Networked Enterprise*, 37–38.

7. J.A. O'Brien, *Introduction to Information Systems*, 9th ed. (Boston: Irwin McGraw-Hill, 2000), 360–61.

8. J.A. O'Brien *Introduction to Information Systems*, 279–80.

9. J.F. Rockart and M.E. Treacy, "The CEO Goes On-line," *Harvard Business Review*, January/February 1982.

10. J. Rockart and D. DeLong, *Executive Support Systems: The Emergence of Top Management Computer Use* (Homewood, IL: Dow Jones-Irwin, 1988).

11. K.D. Laudon and J.P. Laudon, *Management Information Systems: Organization and Technology in the Networked Enterprise*, 48.

12. T. Davenport, "Living with ERP," *CIO Magazine*, December 19, 1998; D. Slater, "The Hidden Costs of Enterprise Software," *CIO Magazine*, January 15, 1998.

13. "Dynacorp Takes High-Tech to Mail-Carrying Business," *Central Penn Business Journal*, April 4, 1994.

14. "When Is Package Tracking Really Tracking?" *UPS Public Relations*, February 9, 1999; J. Moad, "Can High Performance Be Cloned? Should It Be?" *Datamation*, March 1, 1995; L.M. Grossman, "Federal Express, UPS Face Off on Computers," *The Wall Street Journal*, September 17, 1993, B1ff.

15. E. Hale, "The Euro Becomes Legal Tender," *USA Today On-line*, December 31, 2001; E. Hale, "Euro Queries and Answers," *USA Today On-line*, December 16, 2001; E. Hale, "Europeans Make Change to Euro," *USA Today On-line*, December 16, 2001; T. Kamm, "Emergence of Euro Embodies Challenge and Hope for Europe," *The Wall Street Journal*, January 4, 1999.

16. G. Fields, "FBI Digitizes Fingerprint System Today," *USA Today*, August 10, 1999, 1Aff.

17. E.W. Martin, D. DeHayes, J. Hoffer, and W. Perkins, *Managing Information Technology: What Managers Need to Know* (New York: Wiley-Interscience, 1971).

18. D. Amoroso and P. Cheney, "Testing a Causal Model for End User Applications Effectiveness," *Journal of Management Information Systems*, Summer 1991; K. Christoff, *Managing the Information Center* (Glenview, IL: Scott Foresman/Little, Brown, 1990).

19. J.A. O'Brien, *Management Information Systems: A Managerial End User Perspective*, 2nd ed. (Homewood, IL: Irwin, 1993).

20. R.R. Panko, *End User Computing: Management, Applications, and Technology* (New York: Wiley, 1988).

21. "IOC and Sema Group Sign Olympic Technology Agreement for 2002 and Beyond," *International Olympic Committee Press Release*, March 13, 2000.

22. L. Fried, "A Blueprint for Change," *Computerworld*, December 2, 1991, 91–93.

23. R. Burnett, "More 'Geeks' Braving Business World," *The Orlando Sentinel*, September 1, 1996, H1ff; "Gates Gets 26% Raise," *The Orlando Sentinel*, September 28, 1996, C1.

24. Personal interview with Tricia Grady.

25. "Welcome to the Revolution," *Fortune*, December 13, 1993, 66–78.

26. W. Stallings and R. Van Slyke, *Business Data Communications*, 2nd ed. (New York: Macmillan, 1994).

27. "Get Set to Network with Your Refrigerator," *USA Today*, February 3, 1999, 3B.

28. "Microsoft to Blend Desktop Computing, Global Networking," *The Orlando Sentinel*, July 22, 1996, B5.

29. "Koop Slammed for Corporate Link in Latex-Glove Flap," *The Orlando Sentinel*, October 30, 1999, C10; "Former Surgeon General Attacked for Web Site," *The Orlando Sentinel*, September 5, 1999, A7.

30. "The Strategic Value of EDI," *I/S Analyzer*, August 1989.

31. S. Sherman, "How to Bolster the Bottom Line," in "Information Technology Special Report," *Fortune*, Autumn 1993, 15–28.

32. "Invoice? What's an Invoice?" *Business Week*, June 10, 1996, 110–12.

33. "Welcome to the Revolution," *Fortune*, December 13, 1993, 66–78.

34. L. Radosevich, "United Nations Launches Worldwide Network," *Computerworld*, October 24, 1994, 64.

35. "Information Technology Special Report," *Fortune*, Autumn 1993, 15.

36. "The Race to Rewire," *Fortune*, April 19, 1993, 42–61.

37. "Quake Tosses L.A. Around: Buildings, Roads Fall in Tremblers Onslaught, *"The Orlando Sentinel*, January 18, 1994, A1ff.

38. S. Armour, "Worried Workers Turn to Telecommuting," *USA Today On-line*, October 17, 2001.

39. J. Jackson, "Flower, Fruit Companies Smell Success on Web," *Central Florida Business Report*, June 7, 1999, 18–19; E. Eldrige, "GM Pursues .Com Goals," *USA Today*, August 11, 1999, 6B; D. Levy, Superstores Seek Online Customers, *USA Today*, March 16, 1999, 3B; "Sears Puts Appliances Online," *The Orlando Sentinel*, May 13, 1999, B1; "Home Depot Targets Internet," *The Orlando Sentinel*, March 2, 1999, B1.

40. "E-Commerce Helps Boost U.S. Economy," *The Orlando Sentinel*, June 11, 1999, 3B.

41. S. Nathan, "Defining the Seller in On-Line Market," *USA Today*, August 26, 1999, 3B.

42. "Dell Clicks with Buyers by Deleting Middlemen," *The Orlando Sentinel*, June 22, 1999, B1ff.

43. S. Nathan, "Defining the Seller in On-Line Market," *USA Today*, August 26, 1999, 3B.

44. C. Wilder, "E-Commerce—Old Line Moves On-line," *Information* Week, January 11, 1999; S. Kalin, "Conflict Resolution," *CIO Magazine*, February 1, 1998.

45. "Ebay CEO Ventures a Bid—Wins Big," *The Orlando Sentinel*, June 6, 1999, H8.

46. E. Turban and J.E. Aronson, *Decision Support Systems and Intelligent Systems*.

47. "Ant-Sized Robots Designed to Fix, Inspect Plants," *The Orlando Sentinel*, June 22, 1999, B1.

48. "Probe Checks Out Callisto," *The Orlando Sentinel*, May 26, 2001, A25; "Galileo Mission Extended," *The Orlando Sentinel*, March 18, 2001, A17.

49. "Center Devoted to Robotic Revolution," *The Orlando Sentinel*, August 21, 1996, B1ff.

50. "Welcome to the Revolution," *Fortune*, December 13, 1993, 66–78.

51. D. Schuler, "Social Computing," *Communications of the ACM*, Special Issue, January 1994, 28–29.

52. "Welcome to the Revolution," *Fortune*, December 13, 1993, 66–78.

53. "Fast Processor," *USA Today*, February 24, 1999, 1B; "Pentium III Breaks Speed Record," *The Orlando Sentinel*, February 24, 1999, B7; "Faster Than a Speeding Pentium: Latest Is Here," *The Orlando Sentinel*, May 18, 1999, B5.

54. "Intel Rolls Out Pentium 4," *USA Today On-line*, November 20, 2000; "Intel Unveils Pentium 4 Chip," *USA Today On-line*, June 28, 2000.

55. K. Maney, "Beyond the PC: Atomic QC," *USA Today*, July 14, 1999, 1Bff.

56. "Another State Opts to Sell Income Data," *The Orlando Sentinel*, June 4, 1999, B5.

57. "Privacy Rules Are Set by Bank of America," *The Orlando Sentinel*, June 12, 1999, C10.

58. "Another State Opts to Sell Income Data," *The Orlando Sentinel*, June 4, 1999, B5.

NAME INDEX

A

Adamson, Jim, 347, 350
Allemang, Arnold, 128
Allen, Charles, 128
Alper, Keith, 439
Aramony, William, 92
Ash, Mary Kay, 55, 415
Atwal, Peter, 576

B

Bachmann, John, 470
Bakke, Dennis, 263, 265
Ballmer, Steve, 422
Balsamo, Anthony, 268
Barnard, Chester, 58, 59
Bartlett, John, 212
Baum, Herb, 263
Beastie Boys, 250
Beaudrault, Peter, 213
Beene, Betty, 302
Bennett, John G. Jr., 92
Bernick, Carol Lavin, 354, 409
Beyster, Robert, 266, 267, 268
Bezos, Jeff, 158, 350, 352, 429
Birnbaum, Joel, 17
Black, Albert C. Jr., 37
Black, Gwyneith, 37
Blank, Arthur M., 116
Bleustein, Jeffrey, 66
Bowen, H. R., 81
Bradley, Bill, 157
Branch, Michelle, 119
Brown, Dick, 282, 306
Brown, John, 302
Brumit, Jo Ann, 490
Burns, Tom, 302, 309
Bush, George W., 157, 550

C

Calufetti, Larry, 72
Carnegie, Andrew, 152
Casey, Jim, 44
Castellano, James G., 353
Chambers, John, 289
Chandler, Alfred, 167
Chavez, Cesar, 55
Clinton, President, 134
Collins, Eileen, 548
Collins, Jim, 315
Colson, Douglas, 541
Cosinni, Meg, 277
Covey, Stephen, 160, 383, 390
Crosby, Phillip, 547

D

Damigella, Ann, 210
Davis, M., 289
Dell, Michael, 292, 293, 429
Deming, W. Edwards, 65, 540, 546, 549
Denhardt, Robert, 201
Deutch, Donny, 337
Disney, Walt, 350
Dower, Mike, 591
Drucker, Peter, 161, 355, 506

E

Edvinsson, Leif, 23
Emmons, Al, 426, 449
Eskew, Michael, 56

F

Fayol, Henri, 51, 52
Feigenbaum, Armand, 65, 547
Fernandes, Dr. Donna, 421, 483
Festinger, Leon, 437
Fiorina, Carly, 406, 407, 415
Firestone, Harvey, 111
Follett, Mary Parker, 5, 56
Ford, Henry, 67, 111, 152
Franklin, Burke, 72, 311
Friedman, Milton, 82

G

Gallagher, Brian, 302
Galvin, Christopher, 266
Galvin, Robert, 521
Gandhi, Mahatma, 55
Garcia, Manuel "Manny," 492
Gates, Bill, 20, 55, 169, 422, 576
Gault, Bob, 191, 192
Geneen, Harold, 82
Gerstner, Lou, 160, 187
Gilbreth, Frank and Lillian, 51
Gilmartin, Raymond, 304
Goings, E. V. "Rick," 234
Goldin, Daniel, 169
Gore, Al, 157
Gradolf, Ted, 44, 68
Grady, Tricia, 577
Graham, Billy, 55
Griggs, Robert, 388
Grobar, George, 206

H

Haagan-Smit, Dr., 86
Hammer, Michael, 257
Hartley, Chuck, 277
Henderson, William, 148, 173
Herzberg, 462, 464, 465
Hesselbein, Francis, 415

Hewlett, Bill, 93
Hinson, Rick, 519
Holliday, Charles Jr., 171, 172
Horn, John, 454
Hughes, David, 566

I

Ishikawa, Kaoru, 547
Iverson, Kenneth, 460, 480

J

Jackson, Mannie, 402, 414, 417
Jago, A. G., 194, 196
Janis, Irving, 198, 200
Jenkins, Kevin, 405
Jewel, 119
Jobs, Steven, 429
Johnson, General Robert Wood, 93
Jung, Andrea, 415
Juran, Joseph, 65, 546

K

Katz, Johathan, 375
Kay, Alan, 17
Kelleher, Herb, 4, 13, 14, 134, 324, 350, 352, 405
Kelley, David, 389
Kellner, Jamie, 13
Kerr, Steven, 460
Kersher, Kim, 207
King, Martin Luther Jr., 55
King, Roland, 352
King, Rollin, 4, 14
Knight, Chuck, 128
Koop, Dr. C. Everett, 578
Koskinen, John, 134
Kotter, John, 5
Krawcheck, Sallie, 415, 474
Kux, Barbara, 121

L

La Porte, Todd, 305
Landes, Les, 389
Laube, Sheldon, 93
Law, Andy, 246, 247
Lawrence, P. R., 289
LeBlanc, Rene, 240
Lee, Joseph, 348
Lenhard, John, 221, 222
Lewin, Kurt, 357
Liana, Joe, 56
Lindahl, Lawrence, 478
Lipes, Edward, 302
Litke, Ron, 454
Lucid, Shannon, 548

Lutz, Robert, 383
Lyons, Jim, 387

M

Machado, Rodolfo, 238, 275
Mann, Darlene, 93
Marcus, Bernard, 116
Martin, David, 238
Martinez (Sears CEO), 359
Mary Kay, *see* Ash
Maslow, 462
Mayo, Elton, 57
McColl, Hugh, 25
McGregor, Douglas, 57
Metz, Steve, 454
Meyers, Mitch, 391, 392, 415
Miles, John, 155
Mintzberg, Henry, 8, 14
Montgomery, Joseph, 454, 518
Morford, Mike, 455–456
Morgan, Tom, 566

M

Nader, Ralph, 86
Nardelli, Bob, 116, 138
Nickles, Liz, 337

O

Ouchi, William, 67

P

Pace, Tony, 492
Packard, David, 93
Palmisano, Samuel, 160, 349
Paterno, Joe, 95
Pearl Jam, 250
Pelka, John, 576
Perot, Ross, 282
Perry, William, 186
Pesapane, Teri and Joel, 74
Peters, T. J., 168
Peters, Tom, 30
Peterson, Shirley, 99

Porter, Michael, 164
Post, Emily, 326

Q

Questrom, Allen, 338

R

Rager, Michael, 426
Reed, Colin, 201
Reich, Robert, 404
Richie, Jay, 554
Robert, Elizabeth, 143
Rockefeller, John D., 20
Roddick, Anita, 89, 356
Roscitt, Richard, 13
Rose, Michael, 201
Russo, Patricia, 13
Ryan, Jim, 405

S

Salisbury, James, 206
Sanger, Stephen, 117
Sant, Roger, 263, 265
Saperstein, Abe, 402
Schmaltz, Don, 576
Sendenberg, Ivan, 334
Shoyama, Etushiko, 301
Silvetti, Jorge, 238, 275
Simon, Herbert, 212
Sloan, Alfred, 93
Smith, Adam, 252
Smith, Fred, 148, 173, 193
Solheim, John, 554
Solheim, Karsten, 554
Sortini, John, 142
Spade, Kate, 326
Spann, Lee, 563
Spears, Britney, 407
Springsteen, Bruce, 250
Stalker, Gene, 302, 309
Stanton, John, 319, 405
Stewart, Thomas, 22
Swan, Robert, 406

Swartz, Jeffrey, 109
Swartz, Nathan, 109
Swartz, Sidney, 109
Szygenda, Ralph, 127, 135

T

Taylor, 474
Taylor, Frederick Winslow, 49, 50, 74
Thomas, Beth, 250
Thomas, Dave, 55
Thompson, Bob, 227
Thornton, Kathy, 548
Thorwegen, Jack, 392
Tupper, Earl, 210
Turner, Paul, 19

U

Urda, Christopher M., 102

V

van den Oord, Bob, 396
Vroom, V. H., 194, 196

W

Waitt, Ted, 429
Walton, Sam, 152
Waterman, R. H., 168
Watson, Thomas, 93, 349
Weber, Max, 53
Welch, Jack, 116, 405, 477
Whitman, Margaret, 415, 581
Wieand, Paul, 78, 79, 105
Williams, Frank, 92
Williams, Serina, 407
Williams, Venus, 407
Wilmot, Louise, 415
Wood, Carol, 485
Woods, Tiger, 407
Woodward, Joan, 62, 528

Y

Yetton, P. W., 194
Young, Michael, 89
Yusem, Mike, 238

COMPANY INDEX

2002 Winter Olympic Games, 558–577, 586

3Com, 262

3M Corporation, 26, 88, 168, 188, 212, 260

A

A&W, 165

Abbott Labs, 439

AccuData America, 320

ADC Telecommunications, 13

Adelphia, 157

Advanced Micro Devices, 319

AES, 263, 265

Agilent, 409

Alamo Rent A Car, 163

Albersons, 533

Alberto-Culver North America, 354, 409

AlliedSignal, 257

Allscript Corporation, 503

Allstate Insurance, 27, 130

Altrec, 455–456

Altria Group Inc., 125

Amazon.com, 18, 28, 148, 158, 350, 352, 416, 429

America Online, 580

American Airlines, 37, 159, 230, 439

American Eagle, 157

American Express, 158, 380, 582

American Express Travel Services, 580

American Greetings, 256

American Institute of Certified Public Accountants (AICPA), 353

American Management Association (AMA), 477

American Messenger Company, 44

American Parkinson Disease Association, 92

American Society for Quality Control, 268

Ameritech, 473

Amoco, 261

ANC Rental, 163

Anheuser-Busch (AB), 126, 392

AOL Time Warner, Inc., 119, 201

Apple Computer, 124, 158, 302, 312, 380, 429, 584

Aramark, 261

Archway Cookies, 72

Arthur Andersen, 157

Asea Brown Boveri, 291

AT&T Corporation's WorldNet, 580

AT&T, 13, 26, 58, 66, 133, 250, 426, 577

Athene, 349

Avon, 334, 415

B

Bahama Breeze Restaurant, 217, 218

Balance Bar, 126

Bank of America, 25, 61, 250, 259

Bank-Boston, 477

Barnes & Noble, 159

Barneys New York, 338

Barricade International, 212

Bausch and Lomb, 200

Baxter International, Inc., 100

Bayer Corporation, 212

Becton Dickinson & Co., 87, 304, 322

Bell Atlantic, 89, 334, 356, 577

Benetton, 291, 293, 294

Bentley College, 98

Bic, 164

Bindco Corporation, 311

BizRate.com, 142

BMW, 165, 293, 323

Boca Burger, Inc., 126

Body Shop, 89, 356

Boeing Corporation, 28, 102, 163, 212, 353, 426, 440, 473, 583

Borders Books, 159, 537

Boston Consulting Group (BCG), 165, 215, 216

Boston Public Library, 238, 275

BP Amoco Norge, 260

BP Connect, 185

BP Products North America, 184, 185, 300

Brandeis University, 404

Bristol Technology, 320, 349

British Petroleum, 185

Brooklyn's Prospect Park Wildlife Center, 421

Brown University, 421

Bucks County Bank, 78

Buffalo Zoological Gardens, 420, 483

Bureau of Labor Statistics, 159

Burger King Restaurants, 186, 227, 492

Bus Erin, 366

C

Cadillac, 66

Campbell's Soup Company, 155, 354, 578

Canadian Airlines International Ltd., 405

Canadian National Railway Company, 287, 288

Canadian Tire Corporation, 405

Cannondale, 453–454, 518–520, 591

Canon, 169, 256

Caterpillar, 250, 583

Catherines, 123

CBS Entertainment, 124, 155

Center for Advanced Emotional Intelligence (AEI), 105

Center for Business Ethics, 98

Center for Counterterrorism Technology and Analysis, 268

Center for Research on Electronic Commerce, 581

CenterBeam Inc., 93

Cestaro Manufacturing Company, 511, 512

Chaparral Steel, 250

Charles Schwab, 16, 148

Charleswood Company, 212

Charming Shoppes, Inc., 123, 129

Chase Bank of Texas, 331

Chase Manhattan, 334

Chevron, 255

Chicago Cutlery Company, 493

Chili's, 10

China Coast Restaurant, 218, 221

Chiquita, 177

CIGNA, 133

Cinnebar Inc., 375

Cisco Systems, 19, 148, 283, 289, 303

Civil Aeronautics Board, 159

Clariant, 287

Clarke American Checks, Inc., 524

Clarke American, 529, 530, 531, 532, 539, 544, 545, 548, 549, 550

Coca-Cola Company, 157, 166, 185, 205, 211, 368

Colt Manufacturing Company, 227

Compaq, 26, 47, 54, 124, 577, 581

Computer Sciences Corporation, 171

Con Edison, 275

ConAgra, 492

Conference Board, 103

Consolidated Diesel, 254, 387

Consumer Product Safety Commission, 519

Conway's BBQ, 541

Coors Brewery, 528

Cornell University, 492

Corning Glass, 66, 256, 475

Country Music Television (CMT), 182, 201

Creative Producers Group, 439

Cross, 165

Culinary Concepts/Chef Creations, 492

Cummins Engine Company, 336, 426

D

DaimlerChrysler, 250, 260, 283, 336, 526

Dana, 297

Darden Foods, 348

Darden Restaurants, 217, 221, 363
Dayton Hudson, 473
Dayton's Department Store, 473
Dell Computer Corporation, 19, 47, 124, 148, 158, 292, 293, 303, 349, 429, 526, 581
Deloitte Touche, 259, 261
Delta Air Lines, 61
Denny's Restaurants, 347, 350, 354, 356, 435
Dentsply, 155
Department of Defense, 133
Deutch, Inc., 337
Digital Equipment Company (DEC), 262, 291, 426
Dillards, 316
Disney World, 192, 384
Disney-ABC, 124
Dixon Ticonderoga, 529
Dole, 177
Dow Chemical Company, 127, 128
Dow Corning, 84
Drkoop.com Inc., 22
Duke Power, 258
Dun & Bradstreet, 142
DuPont, 171, 172, 380, 475, 513
Duracell, 212
Dyke College, 78

E

EarthLink, 580
EarthShell, 171
Eastman Kodak, 13, 66, 88, 256, 283
Eaton, 297
eBay, 206–207, 415, 581
E-Business Solutions, 291
Eckerd Drugs, 577
Eckert Photolab, 540
EDS, 289, 306
Edward Jones and Company, 470
Electronic Data Systems (EDS), 282
Eli Lilly, 123, 260
Emerson Electric, 127, 128
Emery Air Freight, 473
Enron, 25, 80, 347
Enterprise Rent-A-Car, 349
Environmental Protection Agency, 84, 380, 492
Ericsson, 37
Ernst & Young, 38, 439
ESRI, 134
European Union, 560
ExecuStaff, 311
ExxonMobil, 26, 63, 83, 250, 528

F

Fabiano Foods, 205
Fannie Mae, 342–343
FBI, 574

Federal Aviation Administration (FAA), 185, 494, 495, 498, 499, 503, 506
Federal Express (FedEx), 66, 148, 149, 153, 156, 168, 173, 193, 268, 354, 355, 571
Federal Housing Administration (FHA), 342
Federated Department Stores, 338
Federated, 316
Fender Musical Instruments Corporation, 528
Fiesta Mart, 165
Firestone, 111
Fleet Financial Services, 257
Food and Drug Administration (FDA), 84, 123, 492, 578, 579
Food Lion, 164, 533
Ford Motor Company, 18, 19, 26, 111, 336, 353, 426, 526, 539, 540, 578, 583
Foundation for New Era Philanthropy, 92
Fox, 124
Fresh Fields, 165
Frito-Lay Company, 287, 407

G

Gaines, 426
Gap, 157
Gateway Computers, 429, 581
Gaylord Digital, 201
Gaylord Entertainment Company, 182, 186, 201
Gaylord Palms, 202
GE Plastics, 88
GE/Durham, 464
General Dynamics, 100, 101
General Electric (GE), 18, 116, 159, 163, 165, 168, 218, 250, 254, 348, 353, 405, 477, 513, 554
General Foods, 125, 126
General Mills, 87, 117, 118, 120, 212, 261, 348
General Motors (GM) 19, 22, 27, 46, 55, 93, 120, 121, 127, 129, 130, 135, 156, 189, 227, 260, 282, 292, 293, 353, 354, 383, 497, 500, 509, 525, 526, 536, 578
Georgia-Pacific, 499
Gibson Musical Instruments, 581
Gillette, 153
Global Network Services, 291
Global Outsourcing, 291
Goodrich, 163
Goretex, 409
Granada, 127, 128
Grand Ole Opry, 182, 201
Growing Green, Inc., 74
GTE, 66, 257
Gulf Power, 88

H

H & R Block, 525, 526
Hampton Inns, 164
Hanes, 372, 393
Hard Rock Café, 212, 213
Hard Rock Café International, 213
Harlem Globetrotters, 402, 417
Harley-Davidson Motor Company, 46, 65, 121, 122, 283, 354
Harrah's Entertainment Inc., 201
Harris Corp., 576
Harvard University, 238, 275, 415
Hasbro, 263
Hatch Show Print, 250
Hershey Foods Corporation, 101, 510
Hewlett-Packard Corporation, 192
Hewlett-Packard Laboratories, 389
Hewlett-Packard, 17, 22, 93, 94, 95, 100, 123, 124, 158, 259, 297, 312, 383, 406, 407, 409, 415, 416, 526, 581
Hitachi, 301
Holiday Inns, 540
Home Depot Corporation, 45, 116, 138, 156, 389, 513, 581
Home Shopping Network, 234
Honda, 48, 88, 90, 193, 540
Honeywell, 402
Houghton Mifflin, 288
Hughes Supply, Inc., 566

I

IBM Corporation, 187
IBM, 22, 27, 66, 89, 93, 119, 156, 158, 159, 160, 258, 260, 286, 294, 301, 303, 334, 348, 349, 380, 407, 415, 493, 525, 577, 581, 584
IDEO Product Development, 389
IDeutch, 337
Independence Bancorp, 78, 79, 105
Intel Corporation, 26, 283, 300, 327, 356, 443
InterDesign, 579
International Communication Research, 94
International Olympic Committee (IOC), 586
International Organization for Standardization, 545
International Survey Research, 259
Islands of Adventure, 192
ISR Global Telecom, Inc., 576
ITT, 82
ITT Commercial Finance Corporation, 582

J

J. Paul Getty Villa and Museum, 238, 275
Jaguar, 111
JCPenney, 157, 315, 316, 338

JIAN Corporation, 72, 311
Johns Manville, 86
Johnson & Johnson, 24, 25, 93

K

Kaiser Aluminum, 88
KARLEE Company, 490, 495, 500, 501, 507, 512, 515
Karsten Manufacturing, 554
Kellogg, 118, 212, 288
Kmart, 46
Kodak, *see* Eastman Kodak
Kohl's, 316
Korean Airlines, 495
Kraft, Inc., 125, 126
Kraft Foods, 87, 126
Kraft General Foods, 88
Kriner & Company, 426
Kroger Company, 234
Kropf Fruit Company, 176–177

L

Land Rover, 111
Lane Bryant, 123, 129
Le Meridien Hotels and Resorts Ltd., 396
Levi Strauss, 156, 260, 351, 505, 506
Lightsource.com, 182
Limited, 250
Lincoln Electric, 120, 409
Lockheed Martin Corporation, 101, 212, 328
Lowes, 156
Lucent Technologies, 13, 334, 407, 577

M

Machado & Silvetti Associates, Inc., 238, 275
Major League Baseball, 230
Manville Corporation, 86
Marriott International, 89, 354
Marshall Field's, 473
Martha Stewart Omnimedia Inc., 163
Mary Kay Cosmetics, 55, 87, 351, 415
Master Printers of America (MPA), 544
MasterCard, 158
Mattel, 185
May, 316
Maytag, 165
Mazda, 111
McColl School of Business, 250
McDonald's, 87, 157, 186, 210, 506, 527
MCI, 187, 188
Medtronic, 260, 409
Mercedes Benz, 540
Mercedes-Benz Credit Corp., 261
Merck & Company, 88, 100, 259
Merrill Lynch, 407, 474
Metzler, 426
Michigan Bell, 473

Michigan State University, 36
Micron Electronics, 256
Microsoft, 6, 20, 22, 23, 169, 283, 289, 300, 303, 324, 348, 416
Microsoft's MSN, 580
Midvale Steel Company, 49, 50
Miller Brewing, 125, 126
Mobil Oil, 119, 262
Monsanto, 88, 250
Morgan Stanley, 474
Motorola Corporation, 494
Motorola, Inc., 26, 28, 47, 66, 101, 266, 293, 325, 426, 430, 502, 513, 520–521, 577
Musicforce.com, 182

N

Nabisco Foods, 256
NASA, 169, 198, 499, 547, 576, 583
Nashville Network (TNN), 182, 201
National Car Rental, 163
National Coalition of Free Men, 35
National Organization for Men Against Sexism, 35
National Organization for Men, 35
NCR, 26
Neiman Marcus, 338
Nestle, 84
Nestle S.A., 121
Netscape, 312
New Holland North America, 583
New Jersey Bell, 58
New York City Wildlife Conservation Society, 421
New York Stock Exchange, 524
NeXt Computers, 429
Next Door Food Store, 205–206
NextCard, 19
Nike, Inc., 28, 46, 157, 293, 294, 525
Nikko Hotels, 396
Nokia, 47
Nordstrom, 356, 472, 473
North American Culinary Institute, 240
Northrop Grumman Corporation, 99, 212
Norwich Union, 87
Notre Dame University, 275
Nucor Steel Corporation, 460, 480
NUMMI (New United Motors Manufacturing, Inc.), 260

O

O'Hare Airport, 500
Occupational Safety and Health Administration (OSHA), 46
Olive Garden Restaurant, 217, 218, 363, 348
Onset Ventures, 93
On-Target Supplies and Logistics, 37
Opryland Hotel, 182, 202

Orlando/Orange County Expressway Authority, 227
Owens Corning Fiberglas, 230

P

Papa John's, 525
Penn State University, 95
Pennsylvania Power & Light Company, 88
PepsiCo, Inc., 287
Pepsi Cola Company, 18, 157, 205, 211, 287
Peter Drucker Foundation, 415
Peter Pan Bus Lines, 366
Pez, 581
Pfizer Pharmaceutical Company, 578, 579
Philip Morris, 125, 126
Phillips Academy, 421
Physicians' Online Inc., 22
Pillsbury, 117, 118, 120
Ping Golf Clubs, 554
Pitney Bowes, 18, 19, 101
Pixar Software, 429
Pizza Hut, 6, 525
Post, 212
PricewaterhouseCoopers World Technology Centre, 19
Princeton University, 238, 275, 421
Procter & Gamble, 19, 168, 186, 426
PROMODEL Corporation, 586

Q

Quaker Oats Company, 212, 368
Quali-Tool, 576
Queens University of Charlotte, 250
Questar, 430
Qwest, 577, 586

R

Rand Corporation, 200
Raytheon, 37, 212
RCA, 525, 578
Red Lobster Restaurant, 217, 218, 348
Reebok, 28, 157, 293
Rice University, 238, 275
Ritz-Carlton Hotels, 66, 540
Robotics Engineering Consortium, 583
Roche, 25
Rokeach, 92
Rolls Royce, 26
Ronald McDonald Houses, 87
Royal Dutch/Shell, 134, 135, 286
Rubbermaid, 88, 283
Rubin, Brown, Gornstein & Co., LLP (RBG), 353
Ruby Tuesday's, 351
Running Room, 319, 352
Russell Stover Candy Company, 532
Ryder Systems, 548

S

Salt Lake Olympic Committee (SLOC), 558, 562, 563, 564, 567, 572, 573, 574, 575, 577, 586
Sanford C. Bernstein, 415, 474
SAP, 148
SAP Americas, 130
Sara Lee Corporation, 87, 100
Saturn Motor Company, 188, 211, 221
SchlumbergerSema (Sema Group), 586
School for Social Entrepreneurs, 89
Schwinn Bicycle Company, 213
Scientific Applications International Corporation (SAIC), 266, 268
Sea World Orlando, 192
Sea World San Diego, 192
Seagate Technology, 444
Sears, 22, 157, 158, 283, 357, 359, 577
Seiko, 165
Shell, 100
Siemens, 576
Simmons Graduate School of Management, 421
Singer Corporation, 102
Skandia, 23
Smokey Bones BBQ Sports Bar, 217, 218
Snapple, 368
Society for Human Resource Management, 322
Society of Professional Journalists, 99
Solectron, 250
Sony, 163, 256
Sony Music Entertainment, 537
South Florida Congress Park, 513
Southtrust Bank of Orlando, 540
Southwest Airlines, 4, 13, 14, 22, 23, 32–33, 134, 148, 153, 324, 336, 348, 349, 350, 352, 354, 405
Sovereign, 105
St. John Ambulance of the United Kingdom, 87
St. Luke's Communications, 246, 247, 271
Star Electronics, 277
Starbucks Coffee, 148, 283, 352, 473, 477
State Industries Inc., 536
Sterling Services, 222
Stryker Corporation, 302
Subway Restaurants, 533
Sun Microsystems, 19, 28, 312
Sunshine Cleaning Systems, 72
Systems and Technology, 291

T

TAC Worldwide, 268
Target Corporation, 234, 316, 473
TEAC America Inc., 499
Team EcoInternet, 442
Tektronix, 426
Temple University, 105
Tenet Healthcare, 103
Texas Instruments, 37, 66, 258, 291, 348, 426
Timberland Company, 109–110
Time Warner, 541
Timex, 164
Toshiba, 22
Toyota, 22, 48, 260, 299, 349
Toys "R" Us, 28, 36, 533
Trammel Crow Residential, 513
Triarc Beverages, 368
Trilogy, 353
Trinity Products, 388
Tropicana Products, 287
TRW, 212
Tupperware, 210, 227, 234
Tupperware Express, 210
Tupperware Home Parties, 210
Turner Broadcasting System (TBS), 13
Tyson Foods, 153

U

U.S. Department of Defense, 578
U.S. Navy, 305, 415
U.S. Postal Service, 55, 148, 149, 153, 156, 168, 173, 212, 226, 384, 568
UCLA, 36
U-Haul, 61
Ulster Bus, 366
UNICEF, 92
Union Carbide, 84, 257
Unisys, 291, 303
United Auto Workers (UAW), 46, 111
United Nations, 98, 579
United Nations Children's Fund, 87
United Parcel Service (UPS), 44, 47, 54, 56, 61, 65, 68, 133, 156, 254, 255, 571
United Technologies Corporation (UTC), 426, 445, 448, 449
United Way, 92, 302
Universal Orlando, 191
Universal Studios Hollywood, 192
Universal Studios Japan, 192
Universal Studios Orlando, 192
University of California, 305
University of South Carolina, 36

US West, 27, 256, 265
USX Steel, 528
Utah Museum of Fine Arts, 275

V

ValuJet, 185
Vermont Teddy Bear Company, 142
Viacom, 124
Virtual Loom, 22
Visa, 119, 158
Volkswagen, 119
Volvo, 120, 165

W

W. L. Gore & Associates, 409
Wal-Mart, 6, 16, 19, 20, 22, 28, 46, 316, 334, 577
Walt Disney Company, 206, 227, 493, 350
Walt Disney World, 202
Warner Music Group, 119
WB Network, 13
WebMD, 22
Wendy's, 55
Western Electric Company, 57
Westinghouse, 66
Weyerhaeuser, 357, 473
Whirlpool, 357
White Castle, 165
Wild Horse Saloon, 182
Wild Horse Saloon (Orlando), 201
Work USA, 358
World Cup Soccer, 576
World Entertainment, 201
World Trade Organization, 98, 560
Worldcom, 157
WSM-AM radio, 182, 201
Wyndham Hotels and Resorts, 37

X

Xerox Corporation, 17, 66, 88, 125, 200, 268, 300, 325, 332, 380, 426, 430
Xerox Palo Alto Research Center (PARC), 389

Y

Yahoo!, 18, 19, 142

Z

Zany Brainy, 36
Zipatoni Agency, 392, 415
Zoo New England, 421

SUBJECT INDEX

360-degree feedback, defined, 328

A

Ability, defined, 438
Ability to
  anticipate problems, 498
  meet needs of diverse users, 575
Accommodation, 87
Accountability, defined, 266
Acquired-needs model, 465
Activity ratios, defined, 512
Adaptive organization, defined, 304
Adjourning, defined, 448
Administrative management, 53
  defined, 51
Advanced listening skills, 390
Affiliation needs, defined, 463
Affirmative action, 333
Age Discrimination in Employment Act
  of 1967, 332
Aggregate planning, defined, 533
Aligning culture to maximize technol-
  ogy, 354
Alternative courses of action, defined,
  222
Alternatives,
  evaluating, 187
  generating, 186
Application form, defined, 322
Appraisal costs, defined, 543
Artificial intelligence, defined, 582
Assembly-line system, 527
Assessment centers, defined, 323
Assets, defined, 510
Assigning responsibility, 265
Attitudes, defined, 436
Authoritarianism defined, 430
Authority, defined, 266
Authority types, Weber's, 55
Automated storage and retrieval system
  (AS/RS), 47
Autonomy, defined, 249
Avoidance learning, defined, 470
Avoiding extremes (Toyota example),
  299

B

Balance sheet, 511
  defined, 510
Balanced scorecard (BSC),
  defined, 133
  measuring performance with, 133
Barriers to
  effective communication, 382
  effective planning, 136
  planning, overcoming, 137

Base pay, defined, 330
Bay of Pigs invasion, 198
BCG approach, 217–218, 220
BCG matrix, 216–217
  defined, 215
Behavior focus, defined, 404
Behavior modification,
  using, 473
  criticisms of, 474
Behavioral approaches, motivation, satis-
  faction, and productivity, 254
Behavioral decision model, defined, 191
Behavioral perspective, 55
Benchmarking, defined, 545
Benefits,
  defined, 330
  examples of, 330
Big five,
  defined, 433
  personality traits, 433
Bona fide occupational qualification, de-
  fined, 333
Bottom-up vs. top-down planning, 122
Boundary-spanning roles, defined, 298
Bounded rationality, defined, 191
Brainstorming, defined, 199
Breakeven analysis, defined, 228, 229
Budgets, defined, 130
Bureaucratic and organic methods of
  control, 508
Bureaucratic control, defined, 507
Bureaucratic hierarchical power struc-
  ture, 54
Bureaucratic management, defined, 53
Business environment, changing, 559
Business ethics,
  defined, 94
  fostering improved, 98
understanding, 91
Business portfolio matrix, defined, 215
Business process reengineering,
  defined, 257
  illustrated, 258
Business strategy, defined, 125

C

CAD, 531
CAE, 531
CAM, 531
Capital,
  customer (defined), 22
  human (defined), 22
  importance of intellectual, 21
  intellectual (defined), 22
  structural (defined), 22
Cash cows, defined, 216

Categories, group, 440
Central tendency, defined, 329
Centralized vs. decentralized decision
  making, 301
Chain of command, defined, 262
Change agent, 337
Changing environments, organizational
  design for, 304
Channel, defined, 375
Channels of communication, sponta-
  neous, 388
Character, 414
  defined, 7, 24
Charismatic authority, defined, 54
Checklist for designing effective control
  systems, 502
Civil Rights Act of 1964, 332
Civil Rights Act of 1991, 332
Civil Rights Restoration Act of 1988, 332
Clan control, defined, 507
Classical perspective of management, 48
  subfields of, 50
Closed systems, defined, 61
Code of ethics, defined, 99
Coercive power, defined, 406
Cognitive dissonance, defined, 436
Cohesiveness, defined, 447
Collaborative work relationships, from
  hierarchy to, 25
Communicating and sharing information, 360
Communicating within diverse organizations, introduction to, 372
Communication,
  barriers to effective, 382
  categories of interpersonal, 376
  defined, 373
  downward, 386
  horizontal, 388
  nonverbal, 377
  oral, 376
  spontaneous channels of, 388
  technological, 379
  upward, 387
  vertical, 386
  written, 377
Communication barriers, sources of,
  382
Communication channels, 385
  formal, 385
  spontaneous, 388
Communication competency challenges,
  389
Communication complexity, 372
Communication feedback, defined,
  376

Communication flows, formal, 386
Communication process, components
    of, 374
Community, 414
    defined, 7, 25
Comparing actual performance with
    standards, 494
Competence, 414
    defined, 24
Competencies of tomorrow's managers
    and leaders, 29
Competent, defined, 7
Competition, 157
Competitive advantage, 124
    and strategy formulation, 159
Completeness, 571
Complexity through integration, manag-
    ing, 294
Composed of objective and subjective
    measures, 500
Composition of feedback reports, 499
Computer monitoring, 514
Computer-aided design (CAD), 47
Computer-aided manufacturing (CAM),
    47
Computer-based information systems,
    limitations of, 584
Computer-integrated manufacturing
    (CIM), 47
Computerized numerically controlled
    machines (CNCM), 47
Conceptual skills,
    and managerial activities, 15
    defined, 14
Concurrent control, defined, 506
Constraints, defined, 230
Contemporary manager, 28
Contemporary motivational approaches,
    474
Contemporary organization,
    designing the, 281
    introduction to planning, 115
Contingency perspective,
    blending components into a, 64
    defined, 62
Contingency planning,
    and changing environments, 134
    defined, 134
Continuous-flow production system, de-
    fined, 528
Contrast error, defined, 329
Control,
    bureaucratic and organic methods
        of, 508
    concurrent, 506
    corrective, 506
    criteria for effective, 499
    organizational, 509
    preventive, 504
    selecting the focal point for, 504

selecting the proper amount of, 501
    time lags in, 498
Control decisions, short-term operating
    and, 533
Control focal points, 505
Control for diverse and multinational
    organizations, 491
Control of a diverse workforce, ethical
    issues in, 512
Control philosophies for leaders, 507
Control process,
    steps in the, 491
    utilizes all steps in, 500
Control style, selecting a, 508
Control system,
    amount of variety in, 496
    checklist for designing effective,
        502
    cost in, 502
    cost trade-offs in a, 503
    design issues, 497
    designing quality and effectiveness
        into, 496
    more effective, 120
Control system quality, design factors af-
    fecting, 496
Controlling, defined, 7
Controls, defined, 117
Coordination, better, 118
Coordination of efforts, 545
Core job dimensions, 248, 249
Core values of HP, 95
Corporate social responsibility, defined,
    80
Corporate strategic planning, 124, 125
Corporate strategy, defined, 124, 125
Corrective (feedback) control, defined,
    506
Corrective control, 506
Cost in control systems, 502
Cost leadership strategy, defined, 164
Cost trade-offs in a control system, 503
Credibility, trust and, 383
Criteria for effective control, 499
Criticisms of behavior modification,
    474
Cross-cultural diversity, 382
Culture,
    aligning to maximize technology,
        354
    on the organization, impact of, 352
    through organizational artifacts, ex-
        amining, 350
Current assets, defined, 510
Current liabilities, defined, 510
Customer capital, defined, 22
Customer divisional structure, defined,
    289
Customer profiles, 158
Customer-driven standards, 544

D

Data, defined, 569
Database, defined, 569
Database management system (DBMS),
    defined, 569
Debt ratios, defined, 512
Decision,
    nonprogrammed, 213
    programmed, 212
Decision making,
    advantages of group, 196, 197
    centralized vs. decentralized, 301
    defined, 182
    delay in, 120
    disadvantages of group, 197
    ethical and social implications in,
        227
    focus on, 301
    group considerations in, 194
    involving employees, 137
    models of, 189
    operational, 221
    participative, 194
    techniques for quality in group, 199
    techniques to enhance quality, 223
    under certainty, 224
    under risk, 224
    under uncertainty, 226
Decision model, rational-economic, 189
Decision situations,
    classification of, 212
    managerial, 211
Decision specialties within organiza-
    tional hierarchy, 562
Decision styles, 195
Decision support systems (DSS), de-
    fined, 564
Decision tree,
    defined, 225
    illustrated, 226
    Vroom and Jago, 196
Decision variables, 230
Decisional roles, defined, 9
Decision-making aids, quantitative, 228
Decision-making process,
    applying structure to the, 222
    information technology and, 189
    seven steps, 184
    steps in, 182
Decision-making skills, assessing, 183
Decision-making tools
    and techniques, introduction to, 210
    information technology and, 233
    strategic, 214
Decisions,
    high-quality, 193
    reaching, 187
    sources of organizational and entre-
        preneurial, 211
    types of defective, 198

Decoding, defined, 376
Defective decisions resulting from groupthink, 198
Defense, 86
Delay in decision making, 120
Delegate, reasons for failing to, 269
Delegate effectively, learning to, 269
Delegating style, defined, 411
Delegation,
    benefits of, 267
    defined, 265
    degree of, 270
    process of, 265
Delegation triangle, 267
Delphi technique, defined, 200
Demand forecasting, defined, 318
Demands on the manager's time, 136
Deming's 14 points, 547
Descriptions and examples of operations transformation processes, 505
Design decisions, long-term system, 529
Design factors affecting control system quality, 496
Designing effective control systems, checklist for, 502
Designing effective teams, key inputs for, 438
Designing quality and effectiveness into the control system, 496
Deviations, responding to, 494
Devil's advocacy, defined, 200
Dialectical inquiry, defined, 200
Differentiation strategy, defined, 165
Direct compensation, 330
Diverse organizations, control style for, 508
Diverse users, ability to meet needs of, 575
Diverse work force, is acceptable to, 501
Diverse workforce, ethical issues in the control of, 512
Diversity, 443
    as future issue, 65
    cross-cultural, 382
    defined, 27
    impact of social context, 374
    in the workplace, 27
Diversity of view, tolerating, 137
Divisional structure,
    defined, 286
    and focus, 286
Dogs, defined, 216
Downward communication, defined, 386
Driving and restraining forces, 359
Driving forces, defined, 358
Drug testing, 325, 513
Dynamic network, defined, 293
Dynamic organizations, impact of information technology on, 583

E

Economic
    environment, 154
    feasibility, defined, 575
    influences, 45
    order quantity model, 535
responsibility, 82
Economies, shifting, 560
Effective goals, criteria for, 162
Effective teams,
    critical requirements of, 440
    designing, 441
Effectiveness,
    defined, 5
    designing into the control system, 496
Efficiency,
    defined, 5
    focus on, 252
Electronic commerce (e-commerce), 580
    defined, 561
Electronic data interchange (EDI), defined, 578
Electronic funds transfer (EFT), defined, 579
Electronic mail (e-mail), defined, 380, 580
Employee
awareness of ethics, developing, 99
    fairness, defined, 331
    motivation, process approaches to, 466
    ownership, 268
        as a motivator, 476
    participation, 545
    rewards, without spending money, 476
Employee-centered work redesign, defined, 258
Employees involved in decision making, 137
Employment laws, major, 332
Employment test, defined, 322
Empowering employees, defined, 475
Empowering others to act on the vision, 360
Empowerment,
    benefits of, 267
    defined, 412
Encoding, defined, 375
Encryption, defined, 581
End users, defined, 572
Enterprise resource planning (ERP), defined, 566
Entrepreneurial
    decisions, sources of, 211
    firms, increasing predominance of, 20
Entropy, defined, 62

Environmental
    factors, management thought, 45
    stability, impact of, 303
    trends, 17
Environments, organizational design for changing, 304
Equal Employment Opportunity Commission (EEOC), 333
Equitable reward systems, designing, 331
Equity model, 467
    defined, 468
Equity theory, 468
Escalation of commitment, defined, 192–193
Esteem needs, defined, 463
Ethical and social implications in decision making, 227
Ethical behavior, defined, 91
Ethical dilemma,
    defined, 96, 190
    managerial guidelines for, 96
Ethical issues in the control of a diverse workforce, 512
Ethics,
    business, 91, 98
    codes of, 99
    defined, 91
    developing employee awareness of, 99
    foundations of, 92
    introduction to, 78
Ethics codes, subjects addressed by, 101
Ethics in the workplace, 104
Ethics policy, guide for developing, 102
Ethics training programs, 101
Ethnocentrism, defined, 382
European Union, 560
Evaluating alternatives, 187
Evaluation, 188, 361
Evolution of job design theory, 252
Evolving managerial skills, 31
Executive support system (ESS),
    characteristics and capabilities, 565
    defined, 565
Expectancy, defined, 466
Expectancy model, defined, 466
Expectancy theory, 467
Expected monetary value (EMV),
    calculation of, 225
    defined, 225
Expected value,
    defined, 225
    matrix, 225
Expert power, defined, 407
Expert system, defined, 582
External
    customer, defined, 544
    environmental analysis, conducting, 153
    fairness, defined, 331

forces, defined, 358
locus of control, defined, 428
External-failure costs, defined, 543
Extinction, defined, 470

F

F or T, defined, 431
Facility
layout, 532
location, 531
Factors, other, 385
Failing to delegate, reasons for, 269
False Claims Act, 102
Family and Medical Leave Act of 1993 (FMLA), 333
Fayol's General Principles of Management, 52
Feasibility, 575
Feedback, 376
defined, 61, 250
controls, defined, 170
report, composition of, 499
reporting, incorporates timeliness in, 500
skills, developing, 390
Feedforward controls, defined, 170
Feeling/thinking, defined, 431
Financial control, mechanisms for, 510
Fixed assets, defined, 510
Fixed-interval schedule, defined, 472
Fixed-position layout, defined, 533
Fixed-ratio schedule, defined, 472
Flat vs. tall structure, 264
Flattening of organizations, 560
Flexibility, and network structures, 291
Flexible manufacturing systems (FMS), 47
Focal point(s),
control, 505
for control, selecting, 504
multiple, 506
Focus, provided by divisional structures, 286
Focus strategy, defined, 165
Follower-centered approaches, 408
Force-field analysis, defined, 357
Foreign Corrupt Practices Act, 98
Formal groups, defined, 440
Forming, defined, 446
Forward thinking, focus on, 119
Fostering improved business ethics, 98
Foundations of ethics, 92
Four faces of social responsibility, 84–85
Free riding, defined, 444
Functional managers, defined, 10
Functional strategy,
defined, 126
examples of, 126, 167
formulating, 166
Functional structure, defined, 285

G

GE matrix, 218, 220, 221
defined, 218
Gender differences, 384
General environment, 154
defined, 153
sample issues in the, 155
General information system, 567
General managers, defined, 10
Generating alternatives, 186
Generic strategy,
defined, 164
matrix, 164
Geographic divisional structure,
defined, 287
example, 288
Global competitiveness, total quality management as a tool, 544
Global environment,
and organizational stakeholders, 79
strategic planning in a, 146
Global external environment, dimensions of the, 154
Global impact of social context, 374
Global influences, 47
Globalization,
as future issue, 65
increasing, 560
of the marketplace, 19
Goal setting, defined, 469
Goals, defined, 117
Grand strategy, 162
defined, 162
Granting authority, 266
Grapevine, defined, 389
Group categories, 440
Group considerations in decision making, 194
Group decision making,
advantages of, 196, 197
disadvantages of, 197
techniques for quality, 199
Group roles and associated behaviors, 442
Group size, 195
Groupthink,
characteristics of, 198
defined, 197, 447
Growth strategies, 163

H

Halo effect, defined, 329
Halo-and-horn effect, defined, 435
Hardware, 568
Hawthorne effect, defined, 57
Herzberg's two-factor theory, 464
Heterogeneous, defined, 443
Hierarchy
of needs, defined, 462
to collaborative work relationships, 25

High-quality decisions, 193
Homogeneous, defined, 443
Horizontal communications, defined, 388
Hostile environment harassment, defined, 334
Human capital, defined, 22
Human resource management, legal environment of, 331
Human rights approach, defined, 97
Human skills,
and managerial activities, 15
defined, 13
Hybrid layout, defined, 532
Hygiene factors, defined, 464
Hyperchange, defined, 15

I

I or E, defined, 431
Implementation strategies, choosing, 187
Importance of the process being controlled, 504
Incentives, defined, 330
Income statement, 511
defined, 510
Indirect compensation, 330
Individual differences
and team dynamics, introduction to, 426
appreciating, 427
Individual plans, 131
Industry attractiveness and business strength computations, illustration of, 220
Industry attractiveness/business strength matrix, 218–219
Informal groups, defined, 440
Information,
communicating and sharing, 360
defined, 569
Information overload, defined, 383
Information power, defined, 406
Information system(s),
attributes of successful, 575
components, 567
defined, 561
design checklist, 576
limitations of computer-based, 584
operational-level, 563
organizational foundations of, 559
steps in the development of high-quality, 572
technical foundations of, 567
types of, 561
Information technology,
advances in, 17
and control, introduction to, 558
and decision-making process, 189
and decision-making tools, 233

and management style, 63
and strategic planning, 171
impact on dynamic organizations, 583
impact on planning, 135
impact on productivity and quality, 548
issues in the use of, 585
on organizational control, impact of, 509
Information understanding and loss, 387
Information vs. data, 569
Informational roles, defined, 9
Input, 568
    defined, 61
Instant messaging, 381
Institutionalizing new approaches, 361
Instrumental values, defined, 93
Instrumentality, defined, 466
Integrating mechanisms, 297
    and coordination needs, matching, 300
    defined, 296
Integration, managing complexity through, 294
Integration needs, interdependence and, 295
Integration of systems, 565
Intellectual capital,
    defined, 22
    importance of, 21
Interactive approaches, 411
Interdependence
    and integration needs, 295
    defined, 295
    levels of work group, 295
    reciprocal, 296
    sequential, 296
Internal analysis, conducting, 152
Internal customer, defined, 544
Internal factors, 153
Internal fairness, defined, 331
Internal forces, defined, 358
Internal locus of control, defined, 427
Internal network, defined, 292
Internal-failure costs, defined, 543
International perspectives, 477
Internet, defined, 380
Interpersonal
    communication, categories of, 376
    roles, defined, 8
Interview,
    defined, 324
    questions that can discriminate, 325
Introversion/extroversion, defined, 431
Intuition, defined, 191
Inventory management, 534
    just-in-time, 535
Investigation, 572

J
Jargon, defined, 384
JIT system, 536
Job analysis, defined, 316
Job assessment and redesign, 251
Job depth, defined, 255
Job description,
    defined, 248, 318
    illustration, 248
Job design, 247
    defined, 248
Job design theory evolution, 252
Job dimensions, 248
Job enlargement, defined, 254
Job enrichment, defined, 255
Job rotation, defined, 255
Job satisfaction, defined, 437
Job scope, defined, 254
Job specialization, advantages and disadvantages, 253
Job specification, defined, 318
Jobs, matching personalities with, 433
Job-shop production system, defined, 528
Justice approach, defined, 97
Just-in-time inventory management, defined, 535

K
Kaizen, defined, 545
Knowledge management systems (KMS), defined, 563
Knowledge-level information systems, defined, 562

L
Labor commitment, 545
Labor-management relations, defined, 335
Language characteristics, 384
Language, metaphors, and symbols, defined, 351
Law of requisite variety, defined, 497
Laws, major employment, 332
Leader approaches, three categories of, 403
Leader-centered approaches, 403
Leaders,
    competencies of tomorrow's, 29
    control philosophies for, 507
    of the future, 415
Leaders, women as, 414
Leadership,
    defined, 402
    dimensions of transformational, 413
    introduction to, 402
    model of, 23
    new model of, 414
    transformational, 413
Leadership model, situational, 411–412

Leadership substitutes, defined, 410
Leading in a dynamic environment, 400
Leading, defined, 7
Legal environment of strategic human resource management, 331
Legitimate power, defined, 406
Leniency error, defined, 329
Levels of management, 10, 11
Levels of work group interdependence, 295
Liabilities, defined, 510
Line and staff responsibilities, 265
Line personnel, defined, 265
Linear programming,
    defined, 230
    illustration, 231
Linking mechanism, planning as a, 117
Liquidity ratios, defined, 512
Listening skills, advanced, 390
Local-area network (LAN), defined, 577
Locus of control,
    defined, 427
    external, 428
    internal, 427
    internal vs. external, 429
    measuring your, 427
Locus of decision making, defined, 301
Long-term liabilities, defined, 510
Long-term systems design decisions, 529

M
Major employment laws, 332
Management,
    and labor commitment, 545
    classical perspective on, 50
    defined, 5
    Fayol's principles, 52
    introduction to, 4
    levels of, 10, 11
    organizational context of, 6
    process of, 6
    skills needed at different levels, 12
    why we study it, 5
Management by exception, defined, 499
Management by objectives (MBO),
    advantages and disadvantages, 132
    cycle, 131
    defined, 131
Management decision areas, operations, 529
Management information systems (MIS), defined, 564
Management perspectives, chronological development of, 49
Management style, information technology and, 63
Management thought,
    environmental factors, 45
    evolution of, 42

introduction to, 44
schools of, 48
Management time, 120
Management-level information systems, 564
defined, 562
Manager(s),
competencies of tomorrow's, 29
contemporary, 28
defined, 7
functional (defined), 10
general (defined), 10
new profile, 29
scope and levels of, 10
what we know about them, 7
why they communicate, 381
Manager's time, demands on, 136
Managerial
activities and technical, human, and conceptual skills, 15
decision making, introduction to, 182
decision situations, 211
guidelines for ethical dilemmas, 96
planning, 116
roles, 8
Mintzberg's, 8
skills, evolving, 31
Managing complexity through integration, 294
Managing in the 21ˢᵗ century, 15
Manufacturing
location decisions, major factors in, 532
systems, types of, 527
vs. service operating systems, 525
Manufacturing/service classification, checklist for, 527
Marketplace, globalization of, 19
Maslow's Hierarchy of Needs, 462
Mass-production system, 527
Master production schedule, 533
defined, 534
Matching personalities with jobs, 433
Materials requirements planning (MRP), defined, 534
Matrix structure,
defined, 289
dual focus, 289
MBTI personality types, possible strengths and weaknesses, 432
MBTI, see also Myers-Briggs Type Indicator
Measuring actual performance, 493
Measuring device, sensitivity of the, 499
Mechanistic approach, focus on efficiency, 252
Mechanistic systems, defined, 302
Member characteristics, 442
Membership composition, 441

Message, defined, 375
Methods of control, bureaucratic and organic, 508
Minimum safe-altitude warning systems, 495
Mintzberg's managerial roles, 8
Model of leadership, 3Cs, 479
Model, a new organizational, 27
Money as a motivator, 475
Monitoring, 188
computer, 514
Moral agent, defined, 81
Motivating organizational members, 458
Motivation, 51
and performance, relationship between, 461
and relationship to goals, 479
defined, 460
employee, 466
focus on, 254
introduction to, 460
Motivation process, basic, 460
Motivational approaches, 461
contemporary, 474
Motivator,
employee ownership as a, 476
factors defined, 464
money as a, 475
Multinational
matrix structure, example, 290
Multinational organizations,
and human resources management, 336
control style for, 508
Multiple focal points, 506
Myers-Briggs Type Indicator, 431
personality types, possible strengths and weaknesses, 432

N

National Labor Relations Board (NLRB), 335
Need for
achievement, defined, 465
affiliation, defined, 465
power, defined, 465
Needs, hierarchy of, 462–463
Needs-based models, defined, 461
Negative reinforcement, defined, 470
Network structure,
defined, 291
example, 292
key to flexibility, 291
Networking, 577
Neutralizer, defined, 410
Noise, defined, 376
Nominal group technique (NGT), defined, 199
Nonprogrammed decision, defined, 213
Nonverbal communication, 377

Norming, defined, 446
Norms, defined, 447
North American Free Trade Agreement, 560

O

Objective and subjective measures, composed of, 500
Objective function, defined, 230
Objectives,
defined, 186
identifying, 186
Occupational qualification, bona fide, 333
Office automation systems (OAS), defined, 563
Office automations systems, components of, 564
Open systems, defined, 61
Operating and control decisions, short-term, 533
Operating environments, ambiguous and uncertain, 136
Operating systems,
classification scheme for different, 528
manufacturing vs. service, 525
structural differences among, 527
Operational decision making, 221
Operational efficiency, enhancing, 285
Operational feasibility, defined, 575
Operational planning, 124
defined, 127
Operational plans, defined, 127
Operational-level information systems, 563
defined, 562
Operations, role of productivity and quality in, 537
Operations management
decision areas, 529
defined, 525
Operations transformation processes, descriptions and examples, 505
Opportunities, identifying, 184
Opportunity, defined, 211
Oral communication, defined, 376
Oral presentations, guidelines for, 377
Organic control, defined, 507
Organic systems, defined, 302
Organization,
adaptive, 304
and coordination of efforts, 545
casting the vision for, 160
defined, 6
impact of culture on the, 352
mission of, 152
Organizational artifacts, examining culture through, 350
Organizational change, 23

challenge of, 356
defined, 356
managing, 357
Organizational context of management, 6
Organizational control,
    defined, 491
    impact of information technology on, 509
    in a complex business environment, 490
    introduction to, 490
Organizational culture,
    change, and development, introduction to, 348
    changing, 355
    components of, 350, 351
    defined, 168, 349
    foundations of, 349
Organizational decisions, sources of, 211
Organizational design,
    approaches, comparison of, 305
    components of, 283
    contingency perspective, 282
    defined, 282
    dimensions of, 284
    for changing environments, 304
    introduction to, 282
Organizational feasibility, defined, 575
Organizational foundations of information systems, 559
Organizational information systems, interrelationships between, 565
Organizational mission, defined, 152
Organizational model, new, 27
Organizational relationships, 262
Organizational strategy, is related to, 500
Organizational structure,
    advantages and disadvantages of traditional, 286
    assessing, 294
    defined, 167, 284
    traditional, 286
Organizations,
    control for diverse and multinational, 491
    diverse and multinational, 508
    flattening of, 560
Organizing for quality, productivity, and job satisfaction, introduction to, 246
Organizing,
    defined, 6, 246
    process of, 247
Output, 568
    defined, 61
Owner's equity, defined, 510

P

P or J, defined, 431
Paid-time-off (PTO) programs, 260

Participating style, defined, 411
Participation, employee, 545
Participative decision making, 194
Participative models, 194
Participatory approach, 257
Participatory work environment, 119
Payoff(s), 223
Payoff table, 223
    sample illustration, 224
    structure of, 223
Perceiving/judging, defined, 431
Perception,
    defined, 434
    selective, 436
Perceptual errors, reducing, 436
Perceptual process, 435
Perform, pressures to, 94
Performance,
    measuring actual, 493
    setting standards of, 491
Performance and motivation, relationship between, 461
Performance and satisfaction, relationship between, 437
Performance appraisal,
    defined, 327
    problems with, 329
Performance rating, 328
Performance with standards, comparing, 494
Performing, defined, 448
Personal power, defined, 407
Personalities with jobs, matching, 433
Personalities, type A and type B, 429
Personality,
    characteristics, 427
    defined, 427
    tests, defined, 324
    traits, big five, 433
Personalized power orientation, defined, 408
Perspectives, international, 477
PERT (Program Evaluation and Review Technique),
    analysis illustration, 232
    defined, 230
Physical exams, 325
Physiological needs, defined, 462
Plan, defined, 117
Planned change, steps for, 357–358
Planning,
    as a linking mechanism, 117
    barriers to effective, 136
    beginnings, 122
    benefits of, 118
    business strategic, 125
    corporate strategic, 124
    costs of, 120
    defined, 6, 117
    functional strategic, 126

impact of information technology on, 135
    managerial, 116
    operational, 127
    overcoming the barriers to, 137
    process, facilitating the, 136
    reasons for, 117
    strategic vs. operational, 124
    top-down vs. bottom-up, 122
Policies, defined, 129
Political influences, 46
Political-legal environment, 156
Pooled interdependence, defined, 295
Portfolios, evaluation of, 215
Position power, defined, 406
Positive reinforcement, defined, 470
Power, defined, 406
Power orientation,
    personalized, 408
    socialized, 408
Power structure, bureaucratic hierarchical, 54
Premises of the social responsibility debate, 80
Pressures to perform, 94
Prevention costs, defined, 543
Preventive (feedforward) control, defined, 504
Principles of management, Fayol's, 52
Proaction, 87
Proactive social responsiveness, examples of, 88
Problem(s),
    ability to anticipate, 498
    defined, 211
    diagnosing, 184
    with performance appraisal, 329
Procedures, defined, 129
Process
    approaches to employee motivation, 466
    being controlled, importance of the, 504
    for team effectiveness, 445
    layout, defined, 532
    models, defined, 461
    of management, 6
    selection, 531
Processing, 568
Product design, steps in, 530
Product divisional structure,
    defined, 286
    example, 287
Product factors, 542
Product layout, defined, 532
Product or service design, 530
Product or service, choice of, 530
Production technology examples, 63
Productivity,
    defined, 538

focus on, 254
fundamentals of, 538
improving, 539
Productivity and quality,
  impact of information technology on, 548
  in operations, introduction to, 524
  in operations, role of, 537
Productivity measurement, inputs and outputs, 538
Professional development plan, developing, 118
Profile, the new manager, 29
Profitability ratios, defined, 512
Profit-and-loss statement, defined, 510
Programmed decision, defined, 212
Programs, defined, 130
Project production system, defined, 529
Projects, defined, 130
Public responsibility, 82
Punishment, 471

Q
Quality, 570
  achieving through communications, 373
  and effectiveness, and strategy control, 170
  as future issue, 65
  control system, 496
  cost of, 542
  designing into the control system, 496
  factors for assessing, 542
  focus on, 257
  fundamentals of, 540
  in operations, role of, 537
Quality assurance (QA), defined, 541
Quality circles, defined, 546
Quality control (QC), defined, 541
Quality management philosophers, 546
Quantitative
  decision-making aids, 228
  perspective, 59
Question marks, 216
Quid pro quo harassment, defined, 334

R
Rational-economic decision model, 189
Rational-legal authority, defined, 54
Reaction, 86
Readiness, defined, 411
Realistic job preview, defined, 325
Receiver, 376
Recency error, defined, 329
Reciprocal interdependence, defined, 296
Recruitment,
  defined, 319
  internal vs. external, 320

Reengineering, business process, 257, 258
Referent power, defined, 407
Refreezing, defined, 361
Reinforcement, schedules of, 472
Reinforcement theory, defined, 470
Reinforcers, four types of, 471
Relations orientation, defined, 404
Relationship-oriented roles, defined, 442
Reliability,
  defined, 322
  of the system, 503
Repetitive, assembly-line, or mass-production system, defined, 527
Requisite variety, law of, 497
Resiliency, defined, 430
Resistance to change, 136
Resource availability, 158
Responding to deviations, 494
Responsibility,
  defined, 265
  scope of, 10
Restraining forces, defined, 358
Resume, defined, 322
Retrenchment strategies, 163
Reward, 329
Reward power, defined, 406
Reward systems, designing equitable, 331
Rewarding team performance, 476
RIASEC Vocational Interest Typology, 433–434
Rites, rituals, and ceremonies, defined, 350
Robotics, defined, 582
Roles, 441
  group, 442
Rules, defined, 129

S
S or N, defined, 431
Satisfaction, focus on, 254
Satisfaction and performance, relationship between, 437
Satisficing, defined, 192
Scalar principle, defined, 265
Schedules of reinforcement,
  comparing, 473
  defined, 472
Scientific management, defined, 49
Scope and levels of managers, 10
Scope of responsibility, 10
Security needs, defined, 463
Selecting
  a control style in today's diverse and multinational organizations, 508
  the focal point for control, 504
  the proper amount of control, 501
Selection methods, job candidates, 321
Selective perception, defined, 436

Self-actualization needs, defined, 463
Self-esteem, defined, 427
Self-leadership, essential strategies for, 408
Self-leadership focus, 408
Self-managed team (SMT), defined, 26, 259
Self-monitoring (SM), defined, 430
Self-oriented role, defined, 442
Selling style, defined, 411
Sender, defined, 375
Sensing/intuitive, defined, 431
Sensitivity of the measuring device, 499
Sequential interdependence, defined, 296
Service factors, 542
Service systems, types of, 529
Service vs. manufacturing operating systems, 525
Severity error, defined, 329
Sexual harassment, 334
  EEOC guidelines for preventing, 335
Shifting economies, 560
Short-term operating and control decisions, 533
Single-use plans, defined, 130
Situational leadership model, 412
  defined, 411
Size of groups, 443
Skill variety, defined, 248
Skills,
  and managerial activities, 15
  conceptual (defined), 14
  human (defined), 13
  needed at different levels of management, 12
  technical (defined), 12
SMART (and goal setting), 469
Social context, defined, 81, 374
Social implications in decision making, 227
Social influences, 45
Social innovation, defined, 89
Social responsibility, 80
  and ethics, 77
  four faces of, 84–85
  in the new millennium, 88
  introduction to, 78
  three perspectives of, 81
Social responsibility debate, premises of, 80
Social responsibility strategies, 85, 86
Social responsiveness, 83
  examples of proactive, 88
Socialized power orientation, 408
Sociocultural environment, 155
Software, 568
Space shuttle *Challenger*, 198
Span of control, defined, 263
Special-purpose team, defined, 546

Spontaneous channels of communication, defined, 388
Spontaneous communication channels, 388
Stability strategies, 162
Stable environments, defined, 303
Stable network, defined, 292
Staff personnel, defined, 265
Stakeholders,
    defined, 79
    organizational, 79
Standards, comparing performance with, 494
Standards of performance, setting, 491
Standing plans, defined, 128
Stars, defined, 216
States of nature, defined, 222
Stereotyping, defined, 435
Stories and sagas, defined, 352
Storming, defined, 446
Strategic alternatives, identifying, 162
Strategic analysis,
    components of, 151
    defined, 150
    in a global environment, 151
    process of, 150
Strategic control, defined, 150
Strategic decision-making
    matrix, defined, 214
    tools, 214
Strategic goals,
    defined, 160
    setting, 160
Strategic human resource management (SHRM),
    and multinational organizations, 336
    defined, 315
    process, 317
    introduction to, 316
Strategic plan, defined, 124, 149
Strategic planning,
    as a process, 150
    benefits of, 149
    defined, 124, 149
    importance of, 149
    information technology and, 171
    introduction to, 148
    levels of, 124, 125
    in a global environment, 146
    process, customizing, 127
Strategic thinking, encouraging, 137
Strategic vs. operational planning, 124
Strategic-level information systems, 565
    defined, 563
Strategies, choosing implementation, 187
Strategy,
    evaluating and choosing, 165
    institutionalizing, 166
Strategy alliances, 169

Strategy control, quality and effectiveness, 170
Strategy formulation,
    and competitive advantage, 159
    defined, 150
Strategy implementation, 166
    defined, 150
Strategy selection, 214
Structural capital, defined, 22
Structural differences among operating systems, 527
Subjective and objective measures, composed, of, 500
Supervision, 51
Supply chain management (SCM), 536, 537
Supply forecasting, defined, 318
Synergy, defined, 61
System, reliability of the, 503
System capacity, 531
Systems analysis, 572
    defined, 60
Systems design, 573
Systems implementation, 573
Systems maintenance, 574
Systems perspective, 60
Systems, basic structure of, 61

T

Taft-Hartley Act of 1947, 335
Tall vs. flat structure, 264
Targets for change, 356
Task environment, 157
    defined, 154
Task identity, defined, 249
Task orientation, defined, 404
Task performance, 49
Task significance, defined, 249
Task-oriented roles, defined, 441
Team development, 446
    stages of, 445
Team dynamics, introduction to, 426
Team effectiveness, processes for, 445
Team goals, 444
Team performance, rewarding, 476
Teams,
    and work groups, differences between, 261
    creating learning, 444
    designing effective, 438, 441
    effective, 440
Technical feasibility, defined, 575
Technical foundations of information systems, 567
Technical skills,
    and managerial activities, 15
    defined, 12
Technological
    communication, defined, 379

environment, 156
    influences, 47
Technologies, new, 576
Technology,
    aligning culture to maximize, 354
    impact of social context, 374
Technology-driven innovations, 561
Telecommunications, defined, 577
Telecommuting, defined, 379, 561
Telework, defined, 379
Telling style, defined, 411
Terminal values, defined, 93
Theory X, defined, 57
Theory X and Y assumption comparison, 58
Theory Y, defined, 58
Theory Z, defined, 67
Time lags in control, 498
Timeliness, 571
    in feedback reporting, incorporates, 500
Tomorrow's managers and leaders, competencies of, 29
Top-down vs. bottom-up planning, 122
Total quality management (TQM),
    as a tool for global competitiveness, 544
    defined, 541
Traditional authority, defined, 53
Training,
    defined, 326
    types of, 326
Trait focus, defined, 403
Transaction processing systems (TPS),
    categories of, 563
    defined, 563
Transformation process, defined, 61
Transformational leadership,
    defined, 413
    primary dimensions of, 413
Trust and credibility, 383
Turbulent environments, defined, 303
Two factor model, defined, 463
Type A personality, defined, 429
Type B personality, defined, 429

U

U.S. Bill of Rights, 97
Undercover surveillance, 513
Understanding business ethics, 91
Unfreezing, defined, 358
United Nations Declaration of Human Rights, 97
Unity of command, defined, 262
Upward communication, defined, 387
Useful information, characteristics of, 570
Using behavior modification, 473
Utility approach, defined, 96

V

Valence, defined, 466
Validity, defined, 322
Values,
    core (example), 95
    defined, 92
    instrumental, 93
    terminal, 93
Variable-interval schedule, defined, 472
Variable-ratio schedule, defined, 472
Variance reporting, defined, 499
Variety in the control system, 496
Vertical communication, defined, 386
Video conferencing, defined, 380
Vigilance, defined, 193
Virtual workplace, defined, 561

Vision statement,
    defined, 160
    developing, 161
Vision,
    creating a, 358
    empowering others to act on the, 360

W

Wagner Act of 1935, 335
Watergate cover-up, 198
Weber's authority types, 55
Whistleblower,
    defined, 102
    model of a policy, 103
Wide-area network (WAN), defined, 577
Women as leaders, 414
Work
    environment, participatory, 119

force, is acceptable to a diverse, 501
group interdependence, levels of, 295
groups and teams, differences between, 261
redesign, employee-centered, 258
relationships, hierarchy to collaborative, 25
samples, defined, 323
Workforce,
    control of a diverse, 512
    diversity, 334
    increasing diversity in, 27
Workplace, redefining the modern, 337
World Trade Organization, 560
Written communication, defined, 377